TENTH EDITION

PSYCHOLOGY
Themes and Variations

Wayne Weiten
University of Nevada, Las Vegas

CENGAGE
Learning·

Australia · Brazil · Mexico · Singapore · United Kingdom · United States

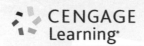

Psychology: Themes and Variations,
Tenth Edition
Wayne Weiten

Product Director: Jon-David Hague

Product Manager: Clayton Austin

Content Developer: Michelle Newhart

Product Assistant: Kimiya Hojjat

Marketing Manager: Andrew Ginsberg

Content Project Manager: Michelle Clark

Art Director: Vernon Boes

Manufacturing Planner: Karen Hunt

Production Service: Joan Keyes, Dovetail
   Publishing Services

Photo and Text Researcher: Lumina Datamatics

Copy Editor: Jude Berman

Illustrator: Graphic World, Inc.

Text and Cover Designer: Liz Harasymczuk

Cover Images: Blue door on green background
   © digifuture/123RF, Yellow and orange
   peaked door © sowari/123RF, Magenta
   doors with cross windows © Sergey
   Novikov/123RF, Lime green doors
   © edomor/Fotolia.com, Bright orange
   doors © nuttakit/Shutterstock.com, Blue
   door with mail slot © iolab/Shutterstock
   .com, Rustic red door © LesPalenik/
   Shutterstock.com, Vintage blue doors
   with pattern © Chamille White/
   Shutterstock.com

Compositor: Graphic World, Inc.

For product information and technology assistance, contact us at
Cengage Learning Customer & Sales Support, 1-800-354-9706.

For permission to use material from this text or product,
submit all requests online at **www.cengage.com/permissions.**
Further permissions questions can be e-mailed to
permissionrequest@cengage.com.

Library of Congress Control Number: 2015943643

Student Edition: ISBN: 978-1-305-49820-4
Loose-leaf Edition: ISBN: 978-1-305-63055-0

Cengage Learning
20 Channel Center Street
Boston, MA 02210
USA

Cengage Learning is a leading provider of customized learning solutions
with employees residing in nearly 40 different countries and sales in more
than 125 countries around the world. Find your local representative at
www.cengage.com.

Cengage Learning products are represented in Canada by Nelson
Education, Ltd.

To learn more about Cengage Learning Solutions, visit **www.cengage.com**.
Purchase any of our products at your local college store or at our preferred
online store **www.cengagebrain.com**.

Printed in the United States of America

Print Number: 10   Print Year: 2018

Beth and T. J., this one is for you

ABOUT THE AUTHOR

Wayne Weiten is a graduate of Bradley University and received his Ph.D. in social psychology from the University of Illinois, Chicago in 1981. He has taught at the College of DuPage and Santa Clara University, and currently teaches at the University of Nevada, Las Vegas. He has received distinguished teaching awards from Division Two of the American Psychological Association (APA) and from the College of DuPage. He is a Fellow of Divisions 1, 2, and 8 of the American Psychological Association and a Fellow of the Midwestern Psychological Association. In 1991, he helped chair the APA National Conference on Enhancing the Quality of Undergraduate Education in Psychology. He is a former President of the Society for the Teaching of Psychology and the Rocky Mountain Psychological Association. In 2006, one of the five national teaching awards given annually by the Society for the Teaching of Psychology was named in his honor. Weiten has conducted research on a wide range of topics, including educational measurement, jury decision making, attribution theory, pressure as a form of stress, and the technology of textbooks. He is also the co-author of *Psychology Applied to Modern Life: Adjustment in the 21st Century* (with Dana S. Dunn and Elizabeth Yost Hammer, Cengage, 2015, 11th ed.). Weiten has created an educational CD-ROM titled *PsykTrek: A Multimedia Introduction to Psychology,* and he recently co-authored a chapter on the Introductory Psychology course for *The Oxford Handbook of Psychology Education* (Weiten & Houska, 2015).

TO THE INSTRUCTOR

If I had to sum up in a single sentence what I hope will distinguish this text, the sentence would be this: I have set out to create a *paradox* instead of a *compromise*.

Let me elaborate. An introductory psychology text must satisfy two disparate audiences: professors and students. Because of the tension between the divergent needs and preferences of these audiences, textbook authors usually indicate that they have attempted to strike a compromise between being theoretical versus practical, comprehensive versus comprehensible, research oriented versus applied, rigorous versus accessible, and so forth. However, I believe that many of these dichotomies are false. As Kurt Lewin once remarked, "What could be more practical than a good theory?" Similarly, is rigorous really the opposite of accessible? Not in my dictionary. I maintain that many of the antagonistic goals that we strive for in our textbooks only *seem* incompatible and that we may not need to make compromises as often as we assume.

In my estimation, a good introductory textbook is a paradox in that it integrates characteristics and goals that appear contradictory. With this in mind, I have endeavored to write a text that is paradoxical in three ways. First, in surveying psychology's broad range of content, I have tried to show that our interests are characterized by diversity *and* unity. Second, I have emphasized both research *and* application and how they work in harmony. Finally, I have aspired to write a book that is challenging to think about *and* easy to learn from. Let's take a closer look at these goals.

Goals

1. *To show both the unity and the diversity of psychology's subject matter.* Students entering an introductory psychology course are often unaware of the immense diversity of subjects studied by psychologists. I find this diversity to be part of psychology's charm, and throughout the book I highlight the enormous range of questions and issues addressed by psychology. Of course, our diversity proves disconcerting for some students, who see little continuity between such disparate areas of research as neuroscience, motivation, cognition, and abnormal behavior. Indeed, in this era of specialization, even some psychologists express concern about the fragmentation of the field.

However, I believe that there is considerable overlap among the subfields of psychology and that we should emphasize their common core by accenting the connections and similarities among them. Consequently, I portray psychology as an integrated whole rather than as a mosaic of loosely related parts. A principal goal of this text, then, is to highlight the unity in psychology's intellectual heritage (the themes), as well as the diversity of psychology's interests and uses (the variations).

2. *To illuminate the process of research and its intimate link to application.* For me, a research-oriented book is not one that bulges with summaries of many studies but one that enhances students' appreciation of the logic and excitement of empirical inquiry. I want students to appreciate the strengths of the empirical approach and to see scientific psychology as a creative effort to solve intriguing behavioral puzzles. For this reason, the text emphasizes not only *what* we know (and don't know) but *how* we attempt to find out. It examines methods in some detail and encourages students to adopt the skeptical attitude of a scientist and to think critically about claims regarding behavior.

Learning the virtues of research should not mean that students cannot also satisfy their desire for concrete, personally useful information about the challenges of everyday life. Most researchers believe that psychology has a great deal to offer those outside the field and that psychologists should share the practical implications of their work. In this text, practical insights are carefully qualified and closely tied to data, so that students can see the interdependence of research and application. I find that students come to appreciate the science of psychology more when they see that worthwhile practical applications are derived from careful research and sound theory.

3. *To make the text challenging to think about and easy to learn from.* Perhaps most of all, I have sought to create a book of ideas rather than a compendium of studies. I consistently emphasize concepts and theories over facts, and I focus on major issues and tough questions that cut across the subfields of psychology (for example, the extent to which behavior is governed by nature, nurture, and their interaction), as opposed to parochial debates (such as the merits of averaging versus adding in impression formation). Challenging students to think also means urging them to confront the complexity and ambiguity of our knowledge. Thus, the text doesn't skirt gray areas, unresolved questions, and theoretical controversies. Instead, readers are encouraged to contemplate open-ended questions, to examine their assumptions about behavior, and to apply psychological concepts to their own lives. My goal is not simply to describe psychology but to stimulate students' intellectual growth.

However, students can grapple with "the big issues and tough questions" only if they first master the basic concepts and principles of psychology—ideally, with as little struggle as possible. In my writing, I never let myself forget that a textbook is a tool for teaching. Accordingly, I have taken great care to ensure that the book's content, organization, writing, illustrations, and pedagogical aids work in harmony to facilitate instruction and learning.

Admittedly, these goals are ambitious. If you're skeptical, you have every right to be. Let me explain how I have tried to realize the objectives I have outlined.

Special Features

This text has a variety of unusual features, each contributing in its own way to the book's paradoxical nature. These special features include unifying themes, Personal Application sections, Critical Thinking Application sections, a didactic illustration program, an integrated running glossary, Concept Checks, Key Learning Goals, and Practice Tests.

Unifying Themes

Chapter 1 introduces seven key ideas that serve as unifying themes throughout the text. The themes serve several purposes. First, they provide threads of continuity across chapters that help students see the connections among various areas of research in psychology. Second, as the themes evolve over the course of the book, they provide a forum for a relatively sophisticated discussion of enduring issues in psychology thus helping to make this a "book of ideas." Third, the themes focus a spotlight on a number of basic insights about psychology and its subject matter that should leave lasting impressions on your students. In selecting the themes, the question I asked myself (and other professors) was, "What do I really want students to remember five years from now?" The resulting themes are grouped into two sets.

THEMES RELATED TO PSYCHOLOGY AS A FIELD OF STUDY

Theme 1: Psychology is empirical. This theme is used to enhance the student's appreciation of psychology's scientific nature and to demonstrate the advantages of empiricism over uncritical common sense and speculation. I also use this theme to encourage the reader to adopt a scientist's skeptical attitude and to engage in more critical thinking about information of all kinds.

Theme 2: Psychology is theoretically diverse. Students are often confused by psychology's theoretical pluralism and view it as a weakness. I don't downplay or apologize for our field's theoretical diversity because I honestly believe that it is one of our greatest strengths. Throughout the book, I provide concrete examples of how clashing theories have stimulated productive research, how converging on a question from several perspectives can yield increased understanding, and how competing theories are sometimes reconciled in the end.

Theme 3: Psychology evolves in a sociohistorical context. This theme emphasizes that psychology is embedded in the ebb and flow of everyday life. The text shows how the spirit of the times has often shaped psychology's evolution and how progress in psychology leaves its mark on our society.

THEMES RELATED TO PSYCHOLOGY'S SUBJECT MATTER

Theme 4: Behavior is determined by multiple causes. Throughout the book, I emphasize, and repeatedly illustrate, that behavioral processes are complex and that multifactorial causation is the rule. This theme is used to discourage simplistic, single-cause thinking and to encourage more critical reasoning.

Theme 5: People's behavior is shaped by their cultural heritage. This theme is intended to enhance students' appreciation of how cultural factors moderate psychological processes and how the viewpoint of one's own culture can distort one's interpretation of the behavior of people from other cultures. The discussions that elaborate on this theme do not simply celebrate diversity. They strike a careful balance: accurately reflecting the research in this area while highlighting both cultural variations and similarities in behavior.

Theme 6: Heredity and environment jointly influence behavior. Repeatedly discussing this theme permits me to explore the nature-versus-nurture issue in all its complexity. Over a series of chapters, students gradually learn how biology shapes behavior, how experience shapes behavior, and how scientists estimate the relative importance of each. Along the way, students will gain an in-depth appreciation of what we mean when we say that heredity and environment interact.

Theme 7: Our experience of the world is highly subjective. All of us tend to forget the extent to which we view the world through our own personal lens. This theme is used to explain the principles that underlie the subjectivity of human experience, to clarify its implications, and to repeatedly remind readers that their view of the world is not the only legitimate view.

After introducing all seven themes in Chapter 1, I discuss different sets of themes in each chapter as they are relevant to the subject matter. The connections between a chapter's content and the unifying themes are highlighted in a standard section near the end of the chapter, in which I reflect on the "lessons to be learned" from the chapter. The discussions of the unifying themes are largely confined to these sections, titled "Reflecting on the Chapter's Themes." I have not tried to make every chapter illustrate a certain number of themes. Rather, the themes were allowed to emerge naturally, and I found that two to five surfaced in any given chapter. The chart on page viii shows which themes are highlighted in each chapter. Color-coded icons at the beginning of each chapter and in each "Reflecting on the Chapter's Themes" section indicate the specific themes featured in each chapter.

Personal Applications

To reinforce the pragmatic implications of theory and research stressed throughout the text, each chapter includes a Personal Application section that highlights the practical side of psychology. Each Personal Application devotes two to three *pages* of text (rather than the usual box) to a single issue that should be of special interest to many of your students. Although most of the Personal Application sections have a "how to" character, they continue to review studies and summarize data in much the same way as the main body of each chapter. Thus, they portray research and application not as incompatible polarities but as two sides of the same coin. Many of the Personal Applications—such as those on finding and reading journal articles, understanding art and illusion, and improving stress management—provide topical coverage unusual for an introductory text.

Critical Thinking Applications

A great deal of unusual coverage can also be found in the Critical Thinking Applications that follow the Personal Applications. These applications are based on the assumption

Unifying Themes Highlighted in Each Chapter

Chapter	THEME						
	1 Empiricism	2 Theoretical Diversity	3 Sociohistorical Context	4 Multifactorial Causation	5 Cultural Heritage	6 Heredity & Environment	7 Subjectivity of Experience
1. The Evolution of Psychology	●	●	●	●	●	●	●
2. The Research Enterprise in Psychology	●						●
3. The Biological Bases of Behavior	●			●		●	
4. Sensation and Perception		●			●		●
5. Variations in Consciousness		●	●	●	●		●
6. Learning			●			●	
7. Human Memory		●		●			●
8. Cognition and Intelligence	●		●		●	●	●
9. Motivation and Emotion		●	●	●	●	●	
10. Human Development Across the Life Span		●	●	●	●	●	
11. Personality		●	●		●		
12. Social Behavior	●			●	●		●
13. Stress, Coping, and Health				●			●
14. Psychological Disorders			●	●	●	●	
15. Treatment of Psychological Disorders		●			●		

that critical thinking skills can be taught. They do not simply review research controversies, as is typically the case in other introductory texts. Instead, they introduce and model a host of critical thinking skills, such as looking for contradictory evidence or alternative explanations; recognizing anecdotal evidence, circular reasoning, hindsight bias, reification, weak analogies, and false dichotomies; evaluating arguments systematically; and working with cumulative and conjunctive probabilities.

The specific skills discussed in the Critical Thinking Applications are listed in the accompanying table (see page ix), where they are organized into five categories using a taxonomy developed by Halpern (1994). In each chapter, some of these skills are applied to topics and issues related to the chapter's content. For instance, in the chapter that covers drug abuse (Chapter 5), the concept of alcoholism is used to highlight the immense power of definitions and to illustrate how circular reasoning can seem so seductive. Skills that are particularly important may surface in more than one chapter, so students see them applied in a variety of contexts. For example, in Chapter 7 students learn how hindsight bias can contaminate memory, and in Chapter 11 they see how hindsight can distort analyses of personality. Repeated practice across chapters should help students spontaneously recognize the relevance of specific critical thinking skills when they encounter certain types of information.

Taxonomy of Skills Covered in the Critical Thinking Applications

Verbal Reasoning and Argument Analysis Skills	
Understanding the way definitions shape how people think about issues	Chapter 5
Identifying the source of definitions	Chapter 5
Avoiding the nominal fallacy in working with definitions and labels	Chapter 5
Understanding the elements of an argument	Chapter 9
Recognizing and avoiding common fallacies, such as irrelevant reasons, circular reasoning, slippery slope reasoning, weak analogies, and false dichotomies	Chapters 9 and 10
Evaluating arguments systematically	Chapter 9
Understanding how Pavlovian conditioning can be used to manipulate emotions	Chapter 6
Developing the ability to detect conditioning procedures used in the media	Chapter 6
Recognizing social influence strategies	Chapter 12
Judging the credibility of an information source	Chapter 12
Skills in Thinking as Hypothesis Testing	
Looking for alternative explanations for findings and events	Chapters 1 and 10
Looking for contradictory evidence	Chapters 1 and 3
Recognizing the limitations of anecdotal evidence	Chapters 2 and 15
Understanding the need to seek disconfirming evidence	Chapter 7
Understanding the limitations of correlational evidence	Chapters 10 and 13
Understanding the limitations of statistical significance	Chapter 13
Recognizing situations in which placebo effects might occur	Chapter 15
Skills in Working with Likelihood and Uncertainty	
Utilizing base rates in making predictions and evaluating probabilities	Chapter 13
Understanding cumulative probabilities	Chapter 14
Understanding conjunctive probabilities	Chapter 14
Understanding the limitations of the representativeness heuristic	Chapters 8 and 14
Understanding the limitations of the availability heuristic	Chapters 8 and 14
Recognizing situations in which regression toward the mean may occur	Chapter 15
Understanding the limits of extrapolation	Chapter 3
Decision-Making and Problem-Solving Skills	
Recognizing framing effects	Chapter 8
Understanding loss aversion	Chapter 8
Using evidence-based decision making	Chapter 2
Recognizing the bias in hindsight analysis	Chapters 7 and 11
Seeking information to reduce uncertainty	Chapter 13
Making risk-benefit assessments	Chapter 13
Generating and evaluating alternative courses of action	Chapter 13
Recognizing overconfidence in human cognition	Chapter 7
Understanding the limitations and fallibility of human memory	Chapter 7
Understanding how contrast effects can influence judgments and decisions	Chapter 4
Recognizing when extreme comparitors are being used	Chapter 4

Reality Checks

Each chapter includes three or four Reality Checks, which address common misconceptions related to psychology and provide direct refutations of the misinformation. These Reality Checks are sprinkled throughout the chapters, appearing adjacent to the relevant material. Examples of misconceptions that are dispelled include the myth that B. F. Skinner raised his daughter in a Skinner box, which led to her becoming severely disturbed (Chapter 1); the notion that people use only 10% of their brains (Chapter 3); the assumption that people who are color blind see the world in black and white (Chapter 4); and the idea that it is dangerous to awaken someone who is sleepwalking (Chapter 5).

Most of the misconceptions covered in these Reality Checks were addressed in previous editions, but not with direct refutations. In other words, accurate information was provided on the issues, but usually without explicitly stating the misconception and providing a rebuttal. Why the change in strategy? The impetus was a fascinating article in *Teaching of Psychology* by Patricia Kowalski and Annette Taylor (2009). This article summarized evidence that students typically come into introductory psychology with a variety of misconceptions and that, for the most part, they tend to leave the course with their misconceptions intact. To see if this problem could be ameliorated, they tested the impact of direct refutations on students' misconceptions in the introductory course. Their data suggested that explicit repudiations of erroneous ideas reduce students' misconceptions more effectively than the simple provision of correct information. With that evidence in mind, I decided to craft this feature that explicitly confronts and disputes common fallacies that range from oversimplified to profoundly inaccurate. Because the Reality Checks mostly supplement the normal coverage in the text, I chose to keep them concise. For the most part, they can be found in the margins of the pages.

A Didactic Illustration Program

When I first outlined my plans for this text, I indicated that I wanted every aspect of the illustration program to have a genuine didactic purpose and that I wanted to be deeply involved in its development. In retrospect, I had no idea what I was getting myself into, but it has been a rewarding learning experience. In any event, I have been intimately involved in planning every detail of the illustration program. I have endeavored to create a program of figures, diagrams, photos, and tables that work hand in hand with the prose to strengthen and clarify the main points in the text.

The most obvious results of our didactic approach to illustration are the Illustrated Overviews that combine tabular information, photos, diagrams, and sketches to provide exciting overviews of key ideas in the areas of methods, sensation and perception, learning, personality theory, psychopathology, and psychotherapy. But I hope you will also notice the subtleties of the illustration program. For instance, diagrams of important concepts (conditioning, synaptic transmission, EEGs, experimental design, and so forth) are often repeated in several chapters (with variations) to highlight connections among research areas and to enhance students' mastery of key ideas. Numerous easy-to-understand graphs of research results underscore psychology's foundation in research, and photos and diagrams often bolster each other (for example, see the treatment of classical conditioning in Chapter 6). Color is used carefully as an organizational device, and visual schematics help simplify hard-to-visualize concepts (see, for instance, the figure explaining reaction range for intelligence in Chapter 8). All of these efforts have gone toward the service of one master: the desire to make this an inviting book that is easy to learn from.

Integrated Running Glossary

An introductory text should place great emphasis on acquainting students with psychology's technical language—not for the sake of jargon, but because a great many of our key terms are also our cornerstone concepts (for example, *independent variable, reliability,* and *cognitive dissonance*). This text handles terminology with a running glossary embedded in the prose itself. The terms are set off in **blue boldface italics**, and the definitions follow in **blue, boldface roman type**. This approach retains the two advantages of a conventional running glossary: vocabulary items are made salient, and their definitions are readily accessible. However, it does so without interrupting the flow of discourse, while eliminating redundancy between text matter and marginal entries.

Concept Checks

To help students assess their mastery of important ideas, Concept Checks are sprinkled throughout the book. In keeping with my goal of making this a book of ideas, the Concept Checks challenge students to apply ideas instead of testing rote memory. For example, in Chapter 6 the reader is asked to analyze realistic examples of conditioning and identify conditioned stimuli and responses, reinforcers, and schedules of reinforcement. Many of the Concept Checks require the reader to put together ideas introduced in different sections of the chapter. For instance, in Chapter 4 students are asked to identify parallels between vision and hearing. Some of the Concept Checks are quite challenging, but students find them engaging, and they report that the answers (available in Appendix A in the back of the book) are often illuminating.

Key Learning Goals

To help students organize, assimilate, and remember important ideas, each major section of every chapter begins with a succinct set of Key Learning Goals. The Key Learning Goals are found adjacent to the level-one headings that begin each major section. The Key Learning Goals are thought-provoking learning objectives that should help students focus on the key issues in each section.

Practice Tests

In addition to the answers to the Concept Checks, Appendix A at the back of the book includes a Practice Test for each chapter in the text. These twelve-item multiple-choice Practice Tests should give students realistic assessments of their mastery of specific chapters and valuable practice taking the type of test that many of them will face in the classroom (if the instructor uses the Test Bank). This feature grew out of some research that I conducted on students' use of textbook pedagogical devices (see Weiten, Guadagno, & Beck, 1996). This research indicated that students pay scant attention to some standard pedagogical devices. When I grilled my students to gain a better understanding of this finding, it quickly became apparent that students are very pragmatic about pedagogy. Essentially, their refrain was "We want study aids that will help us pass the next test." With this mandate in mind, I devised the Practice Tests. They should be useful, as I took most of the items from Test Banks for previous editions.

In addition to the special features just described, the text includes a variety of more conventional, tried-and-true features. The back of the book contains a standard *alphabetical glossary*. Opening *outlines* preview each chapter, I make frequent use of *italics for emphasis,* and I depend on *frequent headings* to maximize organizational clarity. The preface for students describes these pedagogical devices in more detail.

Content

The text is divided into 15 chapters that follow a traditional ordering. The chapters are not grouped into sections or parts, primarily because such groupings can limit your options if you want to reorganize the order of topics. The chapters are written in a way that facilitates organizational flexibility, as I always assumed that some chapters might be omitted or presented in a different order.

The topical coverage in the text is relatively conventional, but there are some subtle departures from the norm. For instance, Chapter 1 presents a relatively "meaty" discussion of the evolution of ideas in psychology. This coverage of history lays the foundation for many of the crucial ideas emphasized in subsequent chapters. The historical perspective is also my way of reaching out to the students who find that psychology isn't what they expected it to be. If we want students to contemplate the mysteries of behavior, we must begin by clearing up the biggest mysteries of them all: "Where did these rats, statistics, synapses, and genes come from; what could they possibly have in common; and why doesn't this course bear any resemblance to what I anticipated?" I use history as a vehicle to explain how psychology evolved into its modern form and why misconceptions about its nature are so common.

I also devote an entire chapter (Chapter 2) to the scientific enterprise—not just the mechanics of research methods but also the logic behind them. I believe that an appreciation of the nature of empirical evidence can contribute greatly to improving students' critical thinking skills. Ten years from now, many of the "facts" reported in this book will have changed, but an understanding of the methods of science will remain invaluable. An introductory psychology course, by itself, isn't going to make a student think like a scientist, but I can't think of a better place to start the process.

Changes in the Tenth Edition

A good textbook must evolve with the field of inquiry it covers, as well as new directions in higher education. Although the professors and students who used the first nine editions of this book did not clamor for alterations, there are some changes. First and foremost, this book represents a blended version of the full-length and briefer versions that preceded it. The last decade has seen a pronounced trend toward greater brevity in textbooks in psychology (Weiten & Houska, 2015), as well as many other fields. This trend is not limited to undergraduate texts, as I have also witnessed it in the medical textbooks that I often consult on topics such as neuroscience, sleep, pediatrics, and psychiatry. This new emphasis on brevity made the retention of separate versions of different length unnecessary. Hence, in writing the tenth edition of this book, I used the previous briefer version as the starting point. However, in many places I was able to further condense the coverage from the briefer version, allowing me to import a variety of topics that formerly appeared only in the full-length version. So, the result is something more than just the next edition of the briefer version. Rather, it is a fusion of the two previous versions, although its length (in words) is very close to recent editions of the briefer version.

You will also find a variety of other changes in this edition. The graphic design of the text has been refreshed and improved in a variety of ways. We have strived for a cleaner, less cluttered look. In the line art, we have increased the use of color-coded text, and wherever possible, we have replaced drawings of humans with actual photos that are integrated into our graphics and diagrams. And we have worked to increase the pedagogical value of the photos by pairing each one with an explanatory caption and eliminating photos that were largely decorative. We have also refreshed the treatments of the level-one headings and the Concept Checks. At the end of each chapter, we have replaced the Reviews of Key Learning Goals—which were conventional, narrative summaries—with more conceptual and concise Concept Charts. The Chapter Concept Charts are color-coded, hierarchically organized overviews that create "snapshots" of the chapters that allow students to quickly see the relationships between ideas and sections.

Of course, the book has been thoroughly updated to reflect recent advances in the field. One of the exciting things about psychology is that it is not a stagnant discipline. It continues to move forward at what seems a faster and faster pace. This progress has necessitated a host of specific content changes that you'll find sprinkled throughout the chapters. Also reflecting this progress, more than 1200 of the reference citations in the book are new to this edition. Following is a partial list of specific changes in each chapter. These changes are presented in relation to the ninth edition of the briefer version, so the list includes various topics imported from the ninth edition of the full-length version.

Chapter 1: The Evolution of Psychology
- Updated discussion of pathological gambling in the chapter-opening vignette
- Expanded discussion of William James's contributions
- Expanded coverage of the contributions of humanistic psychology
- New discussion of the role of newly invented computers in the cognitive revolution
- New data on how many students embrace flawed models of how they learn and remember
- New discussion of how students overestimate their ability to multitask while studying
- Revised discussion of the value of text highlighting in the coverage of study skills
- New research on how surfing the Internet in class undermines academic performance
- Coverage of gender differences in spatial skills in the Critical Thinking Application includes new analysis attributing such differences to males' higher testosterone levels
- Coverage of gender differences in spatial skills in the Critical Thinking Application features new study that failed to find gender disparities on a naturalistic wayfinding task

Chapter 2: The Research Enterprise in Psychology
- New example of steps in a scientific investigation using an interesting study of how the color red leads men to view women as more attractive and sexually desirable
- Added discussion of how manipulating two or more variables in an experiment can permit the detection of interactions between variables
- New example of naturalistic observation focuses on how larger plate sizes lead to increased eating at real-world buffets
- Another new example of naturalistic observation profiles a study of how depression affects everyday social behavior
- New example of case-study research evaluating anxiety and depressive disorders as risk factors for dementia
- New discussion of how clinicians sometimes publish individual case histories to share insights regarding effective treatment
- New example of survey research focusing on trends in tobacco use among American high school students
- Another new example of survey research describes a Danish study on age trends in the experience of hangovers after binge drinking
- New discussion of how placebo effects amplify the effects of genuine drugs
- New coverage of proposed method for evaluating the ethical acceptability of animal studies

Chapter 3: The Biological Bases of Behavior
- New information on axons' patterns of myelinization
- New data on the number of neurons versus glial cells in the human brain
- Updated coverage of glial cells' role in nervous system signaling
- New coverage of how glial cells may contribute to various diseases
- New estimate of the number of neurons in the human brain
- New study of how LSAT preparation results in changes in brain structure
- New research on brain plasticity finds structural changes in the brains of taxi drivers who master the layout of London
- New brain-imaging studies of hemispheric lateralization, including findings that highlight the extensive and dynamic nature of interhemispheric communication
- New study suggests that exceptional connectivity between the right and left hemispheres may have contributed to Albert Einstein's brilliance
- New studies relating oxytocin to relationship fidelity in men, and fathers' engagement with their infant children
- New data on oxytocin and personality, and susceptibility to deception
- New coverage of genetic mapping
- New discussion of "missing heritability" in molecular genetics research
- New data debunking the notion that people are left-brained or right-brained
- New findings on how musical training may change the architecture of the brain and provide cognitive benefits late in life

Chapter 4: Sensation and Perception

- New information on how dilation of the pupils is an indicator of interest in something
- Revised estimate of the number of rods and cones in the retina
- New discussion of whether face-detector cells are devoted exclusively to facial recognition
- New discussion of individual differences in facial recognition ability
- Added coverage of how people have a tendency to see what they want to see
- New research on inattentional blindness
- Section on visual illusions now includes discussion of the Ames room
- New coverage of auditory localization
- New coverage of the perception of flavor and the role of smell in this process
- New data on the number of odors humans can distinguish
- Added discussion of how humans perform poorly in odor identification tasks
- New discussion of the prevalence and cost of chronic pain in America
- New research demonstrating the role of endorphins in pain relief
- New discussion of sensory integration of stimulus inputs
- Streamlined Application on art and illusion

Chapter 5: Variations in Consciousness

- New coverage of the typical contents of conscious experience
- New data on the extent to which our minds wander from the task at hand
- Coverage of sleep stages follows revised guidelines of the American Academy of Sleep Medicine scoring system
- New data on gender and age-related changes in sleep architecture
- New data on the degree to which drowsy driving increases accident risk
- New findings on how sleep enhances complicated decision making and problem solving
- New research on the link between sleep duration and academic performance
- New data on how insomnia is related to increases in a remarkable diversity of health problems
- Startling new findings on how the use of sleep medication is associated with elevated mortality
- New graphic depicting the vicious circle of dependence on sleeping pills
- Coverage of narcolepsy includes discussion of how it is caused by dysregulation of REM sleep due to loss of orexin neurons in the hypothalamus
- New data on the prevalence of sleep apnea and its mortality risk and effects on cognitive functioning
- New findings on the prevalence of somnambulism
- New graphic showing sleep stages where sleepwalking and REM behavior disorder occur
- Expanded discussion of the risk for injuries among sleepwalkers
- Updated description of Cartwright's problem-solving/mood-regulation view of dreaming
- New findings on how meditation is associated with decreases in anxiety and negative emotions and increases in empathy and well-being
- New discussion of how meditation is used as an adjunct in treatment of depression, anxiety disorders, and chronic pain
- New discussion of the reformulation of OxyContin to make it less susceptible to abuse
- New discussion of binge drinking among college students and associated problems
- New data relating binge drinking to impaired neural functioning in the adolescent brain
- New findings on the extent to which excessive drinking is related to elevated mortality
- New graphic on stimulant drugs and neurotransmitter activity
- New discussion of marijuana use in relation to attention, learning, and memory
- New research on the extent to which marijuana intoxication impairs driving
- Expanded discussion of the importance of sound sleep hygiene in facilitating quality sleep
- New discussion of the use of melatonin and alcohol for their sedative properties
- New data supporting the assertion that everyone dreams even if they do not remember their dreams
- New data on individual differences in the likelihood of dream recall
- New data on the prevalence of alcohol-related deaths due to accidents and other acute incidents
- New data on alcohol and chronic diseases

Chapter 6: Learning
- New coverage of studies of evaluative conditioning
- New discussion of theoretical issues related to evaluative conditioning
- New discussion of how the renewal effect in classical conditioning makes it difficult to extinguish troublesome phobias
- Expanded discussion of stimulus generalization, with added graphic
- New coverage of how panic disorder may be due to overly broad stimulus generalization
- New coverage of the renewal effect in operant conditioning and the context-dependent nature of operant extinction
- Added coverage of "roborats" trained through shaping and the use of remote-controlled discriminative stimuli
- New discussion of how corporal punishment remains commonplace in spite of evidence on its negative effects
- New naturalistic observation study of physical punishment in the home, which shows that it is routinely used in anger, not used as a last resort, not limited to major offenses, and not very effective
- Added graphic on possible causality underlying the correlation between reliance on physical punishment and increased aggressiveness in children
- Added coverage of Tolman's classic work on latent learning and cognitive maps
- New findings on how exposure to media violence distorts subjects' perceptions of aggressive acts in everyday life
- New discussion of whether the effects of media violence on aggression are weak effects
- New coverage of the benefits that can be derived from playing video games

Chapter 7: Human Memory
- New coverage of research suggesting that the people who multitask the most tend to be the least adept at it
- New data on mind-wandering in relation to working memory capacity
- New evidence of flashbulb memories for positive events
- Added coverage of how knowledge is represented in memory
- Added coverage of semantic networks in memory storage
- New data on the portion of people who believe that memory operates like pulling up a mental videotape
- New research shows that the misinformation effect can distort basic factual knowledge as well as personal memories
- New example of how forgetting is functional in making room for new memories
- New coverage of theory that asserts that decay does occur in long-term memory
- New large-sample study documenting the creation of false memories for fabricated political events
- New research on the process of reconsolidation
- New theory that neurogenesis may contribute to forgetting
- Expanded description of episodic versus semantic memory
- Expanded description of the distinction between retrospective and prospective memory
- New discussion of how prospective memory failures can have disastrous effects in the workplace
- New findings on test-enhanced learning
- Expanded discussion of the eyewitness post-identification feedback effect
- New data on how often faulty eyewitness testimony contributes to wrongful convictions

Chapter 8: Cognition and Intelligence
- New section on theories of language acquisition, with new graphic
- New research suggesting that the human brain is wired for learning language
- New section on bilingualism and the pace of language development
- New section on how bilingualism affects cognitive processes
- New coverage of the linguistic relativity hypothesis
- New coverage of how language affects the perception of colors
- New research on the cause of functional fixedness and how it can be overcome
- Expanded discussion of why mental sets occur and how they are not necessarily bad

- New discussion of the concept of insight and whether insights emerge suddenly or incrementally
- New mention of how changing the representation of problems contributes to insight and creativity
- New research on factors influencing the likelihood of choice overload
- New brain-imaging research on the deliberation-without-attention effect
- Expanded discussion of complexities in dual-process theories
- New graphic on laypersons' conceptions of intelligence
- Expanded discussion of issues with heritability estimates
- New molecular genetics research that estimates the heritability of intelligence in an entirely new way
- New discussion of the failure to find specific genes that govern intelligence
- Expanded discussion of how socioeconomic disadvantage contributes to cultural disparities in IQ scores
- Expanded description of Sternberg's theory of successful intelligence
- New research on how living abroad enhances creativity
- New Critical Thinking Application on pitfalls in reasoning about decisions
- New coverage of framing effects, with a graphic

Chapter 9: Motivation and Emotion
- New research on how the quantity of food served affects the amount eaten
- New discussion of stress-induced eating
- New coverage of the prevalence and health consequences of obesity
- New coverage of evolutionary explanations of rising obesity
- New coverage of the causes of obesity
- Two new graphics on the genetics and medical consequences of obesity
- New material on gender disparities in the use of pornography, self-stimulation, and extramarital sex
- New research on gender differences in interest in casual sex
- New data on how gender disparities in mating preferences may be shaped by culture
- Updated data on the prevalence of homosexuality
- New discussion of how the belief that the vast majority of people are either straight or gay is a misleading oversimplification
- Updated data on genetic factors and sexual orientation
- New material on the ramifications of high need for achievement in the world of work
- New discussion of how people experience mixed emotions
- Expanded explanation of why our affective forecasting is often inaccurate
- New graphic depicting the results of a study on affective forecasting
- New research and theory on the role of the amygdala in the regulation of fear
- New graphic provides overview of the facial-feedback hypothesis
- New evidence favoring the facial-feedback hypothesis from a study of Botox and depression
- New critique of the notion that facial expressions of emotions transcend culture
- New discussion of how subjective well-being is predictive of important life outcomes
- New research on materialism and subjective well-being
- New research on how spending on experiences rather than material goods, and on others rather than oneself, are associated with greater happiness
- New discussion of religiosity and happiness
- Revised discussion of marital status and happiness emphasizing the importance of relationship satisfaction

Chapter 10: Human Development Across the Life Span
- Updated data on the age of viability
- New graphic on highlights of fetal development
- New findings on the effects of maternal stress on prenatal development
- New research on how children learn to walk
- New coverage of how physical growth in early childhood occurs in sudden bursts of growth
- New coverage of the effects of day care on attachment
- New findings on how parental responsiveness influences variations in the pace of language development

- New discussion of the importance of vocabulary growth
- Streamlined coverage of cognitive development
- New coverage of disparities in Vygotsky's and Piaget's theories of cognitive development
- New discussion of the importance of private speech in Vygotsky's theory
- New research on infants' apparently innate understanding of what is edible
- Added graphic on relations between age and stages of moral reasoning
- New discussion of Haidt's view that moral reasoning is often used to rationalize moral intuitions
- New research relating adolescent risk-taking to the brain's early-maturing reward system overpowering the late-maturing prefrontal cortex
- New research linking identity confusion to maladaptive behavioral outcomes
- Added graphic on emerging adulthood as a stage marked by feeling between adolescence and adulthood
- Revised overview of research on the stability of personality in adulthood
- New discussion of the influence of optimism in adjusting to new roles in marriage
- New data and graphic on how the division of housework between husbands and wives has changed over the years
- New findings on whether relationship satisfaction declines after the transition to parenthood
- New data and graphic on how the prevalence of chronic diseases climbs with age
- New discussion of psychological factors that have protective value in diminishing the deleterious effects of aging on physical health
- New findings suggesting that the erosion of cognitive speed may begin in people's mid-twenties
- New discussion of attitudes about death and dying
- New coverage of the work of Kübler-Ross on reactions to bereavement
- New discussion of cultural variations in dealing with bereavement
- New coverage of various patterns of grieving
- Revised coverage of gender differences in relational/verbal aggression

Chapter 11: Personality
- New coverage of how factor analysis is used in personality research
- New data on correlates of agreeableness and openness to experience
- New coverage of repressive coping style in discussion of psychoanalytic theory
- New findings relating reaction formation to homophobia
- New discussion of defense mechanisms and mental health
- New research relating reduced reliance on defense mechanisms to progress in therapy
- New graphic depicting Jung's concept of the collective unconscious
- New discussion of Adler's concept of overcompensation
- New discussion of Adler's emphasis on social context and birth order
- Expanded critique of Freudian theory
- New graphic on the operant view of personality development
- New research on the correlates of self-efficacy
- New research supporting a key tenet of Maslow's hierarchy of needs
- New graphic summarizing twin studies of the Big Five personality traits
- New discussion of genetic mapping in relation to specific personality traits
- New research testing evolutionary analyses of the origins of individual differences in extraversion
- New research relating narcissism to empathy and consumer preferences
- New research showing that narcissism is more prevalent in upper social classes
- New research on narcissism and entrepreneurial activity
- New research showing the upside and downside of narcissism as it relates to leadership
- New coverage of the distinction between grandiose narcissism and vulnerable narcissism
- Revised assessment of the cross-cultural universality of the five-factor model
- New data on the inaccuracy of perceptions of national character
- New discussion of the public exposure of the Rorschach inkblots on the Internet
- New discussion of how hindsight bias leads to single-cause thinking and overconfidence in analyzing decisions that went awry

Chapter 12: Social Behavior

- Expanded coverage of the attractiveness stereotype and its relation to perceptions of personality and job success
- New discussion of the consequences of the attractiveness stereotype for unattractive individuals
- New coverage of how people draw inferences about others based on instant reactions to their faces
- New data on perceptions of competence based on facial features and political success
- New discussion of how Weiner's model of attribution can shed light on people's explanations for poverty
- New discussion of how liberals and conservatives make different attributions for poverty
- New data on Protestantism and the fundamental attribution error
- Expanded discussion of the matching hypothesis
- Updated coverage regarding trends in the erosion of passionate love
- New findings on attachment anxiety and problems in intimate relationships
- New discussion of the assumption that arranged marriages are less successful than those based on romantic love
- New coverage of how Facebook usage relates to loneliness and other aspects of well-being
- New discussion of how online matching sites have changed the landscape of dating and mating
- New research showing a lower percentage of marital breakups in relationships formed online as opposed to offline
- New discussion of why women's waist-to-hip ratio is an aspect of physical attractiveness that transcends culture
- New research examining whether evolutionary hypotheses regarding gender differences in mating preferences hold up in speed-dating situations
- New evolutionary research on how menstrual cycles influence women's mating preferences and strategies
- New evolutionary research on how men use conspicuous consumption to signal wealth and success to potential mating partners
- New discussion of how men tend to overestimate women's sexual interest, whereas women tend to underestimate men's sexual interest
- New research linking implicit attitudes to real-world behavior
- New discussion of the tendency for people to see others as more conforming than themselves
- New coverage of normative versus informational influence as factors contributing to conformity
- New discussion of the factors that promoted high levels of obedience in Milgram's classic study
- New coverage of whether Milgram's study reflects blind obedience and whether it can really explain the Holocaust
- New critique of the Stanford Prison Simulation
- New research on group polarization and groupthink
- New discussion of how racially based stereotypes can lead people to see a weapon that is not really there
- New coverage of how modern prejudice often involves unintentional, inconspicuous microaggressions
- New discussion of how negative stereotypes can be used to justify discrimination
- New analysis suggesting that ingroup favoritism fosters more discrimination than outgroup hostility

Chapter 13: Stress, Coping, and Health

- New findings on physical and mental health problems in the aftermath of natural disasters
- New research on hassles as a form of stress and mortality
- New data linking emotional reactivity to stress to mood disorders ten years later
- New research on stress, materialism, and compulsive shopping
- Expanded coverage of the subtypes and symptoms of Internet addiction
- New coverage of the prevalence of Internet addiction and its association with other psychological symptoms
- New discussion of how healthful coping responses may or may not be effective

- New research on how outbursts of anger temporarily increase one's risk for a heart attack
- New findings on the association between social isolation and health
- New research on the surprising benefits of weak social ties
- New findings suggesting that the link between optimism and health transcends culture
- Expanded discussion of why conscientiousness promotes health and longevity
- New discussion of the relationship between social class and health
- New research on how one's stress mindset affects one's response to stress
- New evidence linking moderate levels of adversity to future resilience
- New data linking exercise to reduced vulnerability to Alzheimer's disease
- New data linking humor to health

Chapter 14: Psychological Disorders
- Expanded discussion of how the stigma of mental illness is a source of stress and an impediment to treatment
- New discussion of the exponential growth of the DSM system and its tendency to medicalize everyday problems
- New discussion of how people with generalized anxiety disorder hope their worry will prepare them for the worst and its association with physical health problems
- Agoraphobia covered as an independent disorder rather than a complication of panic disorder
- Added explanation of why multiple personality disorder was renamed dissociative identity disorder
- Revised explanation of sociocognitive views of dissociative identity disorder
- New clarification that not all individuals with bipolar illness experience episodes of depression
- Revised data on the prevalence and course of depression
- New data relating severity of depression and sense of hopelessness to suicidality
- New table on suicide prevention
- New coverage of hormonal factors in the etiology of depression
- Added discussion of excessive reassurance seeking as social factor in depression
- New coverage of stormy social relations as a source of stress generation in the etiology of depression
- New discussion of how stress becomes progressively less of a factor as people go through more recurrences of episodes of depression
- New discussion of how and why schizophrenia subtypes were discarded in DSM-5
- New tabular overview of positive and negative symptoms in schizophrenia
- New coverage of brain overgrowth as etiological factor in autism spectrum disorder
- New section on personality disorders, including a table describing all ten DSM-5 personality disorder diagnoses
- New coverage of antisocial personality disorder, narcissistic personality disorder, and borderline personality disorder
- New discussion of the etiology of personality disorders
- Coverage of eating disorders condensed and moved into the main body of the chapter
- Revised data on the prevalence of various eating disorders
- New mention of peer influence and history of child abuse as etiological factors in eating disorders
- New research on the importance of early life stress in increasing the risk for a wide variety of adult-onset disorders many years later
- New research on genetic and neurobiological overlap among depression, bipolar disorder, schizophrenia, and autism
- New Personal Application on legal issues related to psychological disorders
- New discussion of the insanity defense and misconceptions about its use
- New coverage of involuntary commitment and problems in predicting dangerousness

Chapter 15: Treatment of Psychological Disorders
- New findings on the importance of empathy and unconditional positive regard to therapeutic climate
- New graphic on improvement in therapy over time

- New coverage of common factors as an explanation for the beneficial effects of therapy
- New empirical effort to partition the variance in therapeutic outcomes to quantify the influence of common factors
- New data on prescription trends for antianxiety, antipsychotic, antidepressant, and mood-stabilizing drugs
- New discussion of long-acting, injectable antipsychotic medications
- Revised coverage of the side effects of SSRI antidepressants
- New data on antidepressants, suicide, and the FDA warnings
- New coverage of how the medicalization of psychological disorders has undermined the provision of psychotherapy
- New data on the availability and use of ECT
- New findings on relapse rates after ECT treatment
- New research on ECT and autobiographical memory loss
- New research on the effect of ethnic matching between therapist and client
- New discussion of the need to expand the delivery of clinical services to reduce the number of people who go untreated
- New discussion of how therapy can be delivered via videoconferencing and telephone
- New coverage of computerized treatments delivered via the Internet
- New data on psychiatric readmission rates
- New discussion of how the homeless mentally ill are often incarcerated, meaning that the revolving door problem refers not only to psychiatric facilities, but also to jails and prisons
- New discussion of a recent *JAMA* opinion piece arguing for a rollback of deinstitutionalization policies

MindTap™

MindTap for *Psychology: Themes and Variations* creates a unique learning path that fosters increased comprehension and efficiency. It engages students and empowers them to produce their best work—consistently. In MindTap, course material is seamlessly integrated with videos, activities, apps, and more.

In MindTap, instructors can:

- control the content. Instructors select what students see and when they see it.
- create a unique learning path. In MindTap, your textbook is enhanced with multimedia and activities to encourage and motivate learning and retention, moving students up the learning taxonomy. Materials can be used as-is or be modified to match an instructor's syllabus exactly.
- integrate their own content. Instructors can modify the MindTap Reader using their own documents or by pulling from sources like RSS feeds, YouTube videos, websites, Google docs, and more.
- follow student progress. Powerful analytics and reports provide a snapshot of class progress, the time students spend logging into the course, and completion to help instructors assess levels of engagement and identify problem areas.

Other Supplementary Materials

The teaching/learning package that has been developed to supplement *Psychology: Themes and Variations* includes many other useful tools for instructors. The development of all supplements for this text have been carefully coordinated so that they are mutually supportive.

Instructor's Resource Manual (by Randolph A. Smith)

The *Instructor's Resource Manual* (IRM) was developed under the guidance of Randolph Smith, the former editor of the journal *Teaching of Psychology*. It contains a wealth of detailed suggestions for lecture topics, class demonstrations, exercises, discussion questions, and suggested readings organized around the content of each chapter in the text. Instructors will appreciate how this array of materials facilitates efforts to teach the introductory course.

Test Bank (by Jeff Holmes)

A large, diversified, and carefully constructed *Test Bank* accompanies this text. The questions are closely tied and tagged to each chapter's Key Learning Goals. The items are categorized using a simplified Bloom's taxonomy as (a) understand, (b) apply, and (c) think critically. Data on item difficulty are included for many questions. These tags can be used to sort and filter to help instructors find the questions they need. For this edition, Jeff Holmes of Ithaca College carefully scrutinized every item for quality before he even began the update to accommodate the revised content of the text. To keep item quality high, we decided to keep the items per chapter at a manageable number. It is quicker, easier, and more efficient to select test questions from a reasonable number of items than to sift through hundreds and hundreds of items, which inevitably include superficial variations on the same questions.

Online PowerPoint® Lecture Slide Decks

These are designed to facilitate an instructor's use of PowerPoint in lectures. Slides are provided for each chapter; they contain main concepts with figures, graphics, and tables to visually illustrate main points from the text. The Notes section of the slide provides guidelines and text references to support lecture preparation. Slides have been designed to be easily modifiable so instructors are able to customize them with their own materials.

ACKNOWLEDGMENTS

Creating an introductory psychology text is a complicated challenge, and a small army of people have contributed to the evolution of this book. Foremost among them are the psychology editors I have worked with—Claire Verduin, C. Deborah Laughton, Phil Curson, Eileen Murphy, Edith Beard Brady, Michele Sordi, Jon-David Hague, Tim Matray, and Clay Austin—and the developmental editor for the first edition of this book, John Bergez. They have helped me immeasurably, and each has become a treasured friend along the way. I am especially indebted to Claire, who educated me in the intricacies of textbook publishing, and to John, who has left an enduring imprint on my writing.

The challenge of meeting a difficult schedule in producing this book was undertaken by a talented team of people coordinated by Joan Keyes, who did a superb job of pulling it all together. Credit for coordination of the text design goes to Vernon Boes, who was very creative in building on the previous design. Jude Berman did an outstanding job in copyediting the manuscript. Over the years, Fred Harwin and Carol Zuber-Mallison have made stellar contributions to the artwork.

A number of psychologists deserve thanks for the contributions they made to this book. I am grateful to Diane Halpern for her work on the Critical Thinking Applications; to Susan Koger and Britain Scott for crafting a compelling online appendix on sustainability; to Rick Stalling and Ron Wasden for their work on previous editions of the *Study Guide*; to Jeff Holmes for his revision of the *Test Bank*; to Randy Smith for his work on the *Instructor's Resource Manual*; to Harry Upshaw, Larry Wrightsman, Shari Diamond, Rick Stalling, and Claire Etaugh for their help and guidance over the years; and to the chapter consultants listed on page xxiii and the reviewers listed on pages xxiv-xxvi, who provided insightful and constructive critiques of various portions of the manuscript.

Many other people have also contributed to this project, and I am grateful to all of them for their efforts. Bill Roberts, Tom Dorsaneo, Nancy Sjoberg, John Odam, Fiorella Ljunggren, Jim Brace-Thompson, Susan Badger, Sean Wakely, Eve Howard, Linda Rill, Margaret Parks, Kim Russell, Lauren Keyes, Jennie Redwitz, Pat Waldo, Kristin Makarewycz, Liz Rhoden, and Trina Tom helped with varied aspects of previous editions. At Cengage, Michelle Clark, Kimiya Hojjat, and especially Shelli Newhart made valuable contributions to the current edition. At the College of DuPage, where I taught until 1991, all of my colleagues in psychology provided support and information at one time or another, but I am especially indebted to Barb Lemme, Alan Lanning, Pat Puccio, and Don Green. I also want to thank my former colleagues at Santa Clara University (especially Tracey Kahan, Tom Plante, and Jerry Burger) and my current colleagues at UNLV, who have been fertile sources of new ideas. And I am indebted to the many graduate students who I have worked with at UNLV, and to Gabriel Allred and Vince Rozalski, who helped complete the new reference entries.

My greatest debt is to my wife, Beth Traylor, who has been a steady source of emotional sustenance while enduring the rigors of her medical career, and to my son T. J., for making dad laugh all the time.

Wayne Weiten

CHAPTER CONSULTANTS

Chapter 1
David Baker
University of Akron
Charles L. Brewer
Furman University
C. James Goodwin
Wheeling Jesuit University
E. R. Hilgard
Stanford University
David Hothersall
Ohio State University
Michael G. Livingston
St. John's University

Chapter 2
Larry Christensen
Texas A & M University
Francis Durso
University of Oklahoma
Donald H. McBurney
University of Pittsburgh
Wendy Schweigert
Bradley University

Chapter 3
Nelson Freedman
Queen's University at Kingston
Michael W. Levine
University of Illinois, Chicago
Corinne L. McNamara
Kennesaw State University
James M. Murphy
Indiana University–Purdue University at Indianapolis
Paul Wellman
Texas A & M University

Chapter 4
Stephen Blessing
University of Tampa
Nelson Freedman
Queen's University at Kingston
Kevin Jordan
San Jose State University
Michael W. Levine
University of Illinois, Chicago
John Pittenger
University of Arkansas, Little Rock

Chrislyn E. Randell
Metropolitan State College of Denver
Lawrence Ward
University of British Columbia

Chapter 5
Frank Etscorn
New Mexico Institute of Mining and Technology
Tracey L. Kahan
Santa Clara University
Charles F. Levinthal
Hofstra University
Wilse Webb
University of Florida

Chapter 6
A. Charles Catania
University of Maryland
Michael Domjan
University of Texas, Austin
William C. Gordon
University of New Mexico
Russell A. Powell
Grant MacEwan College
Barry Schwartz
Swarthmore College
Deborah L. Stote
University of Texas, Austin

Chapter 7
Tracey L. Kahan
Santa Clara University
Ian Neath
Purdue University
Tom Pusateri
Loras College
Stephen K. Reed
San Diego State University
Patricia Tenpenny
Loyola University, Chicago

Chapter 8
John Best
Eastern Illinois University
David Carroll
University of Wisconsin, Superior
Charles Davidshofer
Colorado State University

Shalynn Ford
Teikyo Marycrest University
Richard J. Haier
University of California, Irvine
Tom Pusateri
Loras College
Stephen K. Reed
San Diego State University
Timothy Rogers
University of Calgary
Dennis Saccuzzo
San Diego State University

Chapter 9
Robert Franken
University of Calgary
Russell G. Geen
University of Missouri
Douglas Mook
University of Virginia
D. Louis Wood
University of Arkansas, Little Rock

Chapter 10
Ruth L. Ault
Davidson College
John C. Cavanaugh
University of Delaware
Claire Etaugh
Bradley University
Doug Friedrich
University of West Florida
Barbara Hansen Lemme
College of DuPage

Chapter 11
Susan Cloninger
Russel Sage College
Caroline Collins
University of Victoria
Howard S. Friedman
University of California, Riverside
Christopher F. Monte
Manhattunville College
Ken Olson
Fort Hays State University

Chapter 12
Jerry M. Burger
Santa Clara University
Donelson R. Forsyth
Virginia Commonwealth University
Stephen L. Franzoi
Marquette University
Cheryl Kaiser
Michigan State University

Chapter 13
Robin M. DiMatteo
University of California, Riverside
Jess Feist
McNeese State University
Regan A. R. Gurung
University of Wisconsin, Green Bay
Chris Kleinke
University of Alaska, Anchorage

Chapter 14
David A. F. Haaga
American University
Richard Halgin
University of Massachusetts, Amherst
Chris L. Kleinke
University of Alaska, Anchorage
Elliot A. Weiner
Pacific University

Chapter 15
Gerald Corey
California State University, Fullerton
Herbert Goldenberg
California State University, Los Angeles
Jane S. Halonen
Alverno College
Thomas G. Plante
Santa Clara University

REVIEWERS

Lyn Y. Abramson
University of Wisconsin

Bill Adler
Collin County Community College

James R. M. Alexander
University of Tasmania

Gordon A. Allen
Miami University of Ohio

Randy Allen
Trocaire College

Elise L. Amel
University of St. Thomas

Elizabeth S. Athens
Kennesaw State University

Ruth L. Ault
Davidson College

Jeff D. Baker
Southeastern Louisiana University

Bart Bare
Caldwell Community College

Mark Basham
Regis University

Gina J. Bates
Southern Arkansas University

Scott C. Bates
Utah State University

Marcelle Bartolo
Abela Southern New Hampshire University

Derryl K. Beale
Cerritos Community College

Holly Beard
Midlands Technical College

Ashleah Bectal
U.S. Military Academy

Robert P. Beitz
Pima County Community College

Daniel R. Bellack
Trident Technical College

Mitchell Berman
University of Southern Mississippi

Chris A. Bjornsen
Longwood University

Stephen Blessing
University of Tampa

Charles B. Blose
MacMurray College

Frederick Bonato
Saint Peter's College

Robert Bornstein
Miami University

Bette L. Bottoms
University of Illinois, Chicago

Lyn Boulter
Catawba College

Amy Badura Brack
Creighton University

Edward Brady
Belleville Area College

Nicole Bragg
Mount Hood Community College

Allen Branum
South Dakota State University

Robert G. Bringle
Indiana University–Purdue University Indianapolis

Michael Brislawn
Bellevue Community College

David R. Brodbeck
Sir Wilfred Grenfall College, Memorial University of Newfoundland

Paula Brown-Weinstock
Fulton-Montgomery Community College

Dan W. Brunworth
Kishwaukee College

David M. Buss
University of Texas, Austin

James Butler
James Madison University

Kate Byerwalter
Grand Rapids Community College

Mary M. Cail
University of Virginia

James F. Calhoun
University of Georgia

William Calhoun
University of Tennessee

Cheryl Camenzuli
Hofstra University

Cari B. Cannon
Santiago Canyon College

Elaine Cassel
Lord Fairfax Community College

Heather Chabot
New England College

Monica Chakravertti
Mary Washington College

Janet L. Chapman
U.S. Military Academy

Kevin Chun
University of San Francisco

Jennifer Clark
University of North Carolina

Michael Clayton
Youngstown State University

Elizabeth Coccia
Austin Community College

Francis B. Colavita
University of Pittsburgh

Thomas B. Collins
Mankato State University

Luis Cordon
Eastern Connecticut State University

Stan Coren
University of British Columbia

Verne C. Cox
University of Texas at Arlington

Kenneth Cramer
University of Windsor

Dianne Crisp
Kwantlen University College

Christopher Cronin
Saint Leo University

Norman Culbertson
Yakima Valley College

Robert DaPrato
Solano Community College

Betty M. Davenport
Campbell University

Stephen F. Davis
Emporia State University

Peggy A. DeCooke
Purchase College SUNY

Kenneth Deffenbacher
University of Nebraska

Kathy Denton
Douglas College

Marcus Dickson
Wayne State University

Deanna L. Dodson
Lebanon Valley College

Delores Doench
Southwestern Community College

Roger Dominowski
University of Illinois, Chicago

Joan Doolittle
Anne Arundel Community College

Dale V. Doty
Monroe Community College

Robert J. Douglas
University of Washington

Kimberley Duff
Cerritos College

Jim Duffy
Sir Wilfred Grenfall College, Memorial University of Newfoundland

David Eckerman
University of North Carolina

James Eison
Southeast Missouri State University

Kenneth Elliott
University of Maine, Augusta

Pamela G. Ely
St. Andrews Presbyterian College

M. Jeffrey Farrar
University of Florida

Meredyth Fellows
West Chester University

Donald Fields
University of New Brunswick

Alison Finstad
University of North Dakota

Thomas P. Fitzpatrick
Rockland Community College

Bob Fletcher
Truckee Meadows Community College

Karen E. Ford
Mesa State College

Donelson R. Forsyth
Virginia Commonwealth University

Leslie D. Frazier
Florida International University

Christina Frederick
Southern Utah University

Barry Fritz
Quinnipiac College

William J. Froming
University of Florida

Mary Ellen Fromuth
Middle Tennessee State University

Dean E. Frost
Portland State University

Nancy Frye
Long Island University

Ronald Gage-Mosher
Imperial Valley College

Judy Gentry
Columbus State Community College

Cassandra Germain
Campbell University

Linda Gibbons
Westark College

Amber Gilewski
Burlington County College

Doba Goodman
York University

Jeffrey D. Green
Soka University

Richard Griggs
University of Florida

Arthur Gutman
Florida Institute of Technology

Robert Guttentag
University of North Carolina, Greensboro

Cheryl Hale
Jefferson College

Jane Halonen
James Madison University

Kevin B. Handey
Germanna Community College

Roger Harnish
Rochester Institute of Technology

Philip L. Hartley
Chaffey College

Brad M. Hastings
Mount Aloysius College

Glenn R. Hawkes
Virginia Commonwealth University

Myra D. Heinrich
Mesa State College

Paul Herrle
College of Southern Nevada

George Hertl
Northwest Mississippi Community College

Patricia Hinton
Cumberland College

Lyllian B. Hix
Houston Community College

Mark A. Hopper
Loras College

John P. Hostetler
Albion College

Jeremy Ashton Houska
Nevada State University

Stephen Hoyer
Pittsburgh State University

Allen I. Huffcutt
Bradley University

Bruce Hunsberger
Wilfrid Laurier University

Mir Rabiul Islam
Charles Sturt University Mississippi

Heide Island
University of Montana

Nancy Jackson
Johnson & Wales University

Robert A. Johnston
College of William and Mary

Robert Kaleta
University of Wisconsin, Milwaukee

Cindy Kamilar
Pikes Peak Community College

Margaret Karolyi
University of Akron

Jagdeep Kaur-Bala
University of Oregon

Sheila Kennison
Oklahoma State University

Alan R. King
University of North Dakota

Melvyn B. King
State University of New York, Cortland

James Knight
Humboldt State University

Mike Knight
Central State University

Ronald Kopcho
Mercer Community College

Mark Krause
University of Portland

Barry J. Krikstone
Saint Michael's College

Jerry N. Lackey
Stephen F. Austin State University

Robin L. Lashley
Kent State University, Tuscarawas

Peter Leppman
University of Guelph

Charles F. Levinthal
Hofstra University

Gary Levy
University of Wyoming

Wolfgang Linden
University of British Columbia

John Lindsay
Georgia College & State University

Evan Loehle-Conger
Madison Area Technical College

Laura Madson
New Mexico State University

Kathleen Malley-Morrison
Boston University

Diane Martichuski
University of Colorado, Boulder

Donald McBurney
University of Pittsburgh

Kathleen McCormick
Ocean County College

David G. McDonald
University of Missouri

Deborah R. McDonald
New Mexico State University

Siobhan McEnaney-Hayes
Chestnut Hill College

Ronald K. McLaughlin
Juniata College

Marisa McLeod
Santa Fe Community College

Sean P. Meegan
University of Utah

Steven E. Meier
University of Idaho

Sheryll Mennicke
University of Minnesota

Mitchell Metzger
Pennsylvania State University, Shenango

Le'Ann Milinder
New England College

Antoinette R. Miller
Clayton State University

Richard Miller
Western Kentucky University

Jack J. Mino
Holyoke Community College

Joel Morogovsky
Brookdale Community College

Mary Morris
Northern Territory University

Dirk W. Mosig
University of Nebraska at Kearney

Dan Mossler
Hampden-Sydney College

Darwin Muir
Queen's University at Kingston

David R. Murphy
Waubonsee Community College

Eric S. Murphy
University of Alaska, Anchorage

James M. Murphy
Indiana University–Purdue University Indianapolis

Michael Murphy
Henderson State University

Carnot E. Nelson
University of South Florida

John Nezlek
College of William and Mary

Bonnie J. Nichols
Mississippi County Community College

Bonnie Nicholson
University of Southern Mississippi

Rachel Nitzberg
University of California, Davis

Susan Nolan
Seton Hall University

David L. Novak
Lansing Community College

Caroline Olko
Nassau Community College

Richard Page
Wright State University

Joseph J. Palladino
University of Southern Indiana

John N. Park
Mankato State University

Phil Pegg
Western Kentucky University

Gayle Pitman
Sacramento City College

Bobby J. Poe
Belleville Area College

Edward I. Pollack
West Chester University of Pennsylvania

Gary Poole
Simon Fraser University

Michael Poulin
State University of New York, Buffalo

Russell Powell
Grant MacEwan College

Tracy Powell
Western Oregon University

Maureen K. Powers
Vanderbilt University

Rose Preciado
Mount San Antonio College

Janet Proctor
Purdue University

Frank. J. Provenzano
Greenville Technical College

Rebecca L. Rahschulte
Ivy Tech Community College

Bryan Raudenbush
Wheeling Jesuit University

Robin Raygor
Anoka-Ramsey Community College

Celia Reaves
Monroe Community College

Sean Reilley
Morehead State University

Gary T. Reker
Trent University

Daniel W. Richards
Houston Community College

Elizabeth A. Rider
Elizabethtown College

Alysia Ritter
Murray State University

Vicki Ritts
St. Louis Community College, Meramec

James Rodgers
Hawkeye Community College

Jayne Rose
Augustana College

Kenneth M. Rosenberg
State University of New York, Oswego

Lori Rosenthal
Lasell College

Patricia Ross
Laurentian University

Eileen Roth
Glendale Community College

Ana Ruiz
Alvernia College

Angela Sadowski
Chaffey College

Sabato D. Sagaria
Capital University

Roger Sambrook
University of Colorado, Colorado Springs

H. R. Schiffman
Rutgers University

Heide Sedwick
Mount Aloysius College

George Shardlow
City College of San Francisco

Fred Shima
California State University Dominguez Hills

Susan A. Shodahl
San Bernardino Valley College

Randolph A. Smith
Ouachita Baptist University

Steven M. Smith
Texas A & M University

Thomas Smith
Vincennes University

Rita Smith-Wade-El
Millersville University of Pennsylvania

Susan Snycerski
San Jose State University

James L. Spencer
West Virginia State College

Steven St. John
Rollins College

Paul Stager
York University

Jutta M. Street
Campbell University

Marjorie Taylor
University of Oregon

Frank R. Terrant, Jr.
Appalachian State University

Tim Tomczak
Genesee Community College

Iva Trottier
Concordia College

Travis Tubre
University of Southern

Jim Turcott
Kalamazoo Valley Community College

Donald Tyrrell
Franklin and Marshall College

Mary Ann Valentino
Reedley College

Robin Valeri
St. Bonaventure University

Frank J. Vattano
Colorado State University

Doris C. Vaughn
Alabama State University

Wayne Viney
Colorado State University

Paul Vonnahme
New Mexico State University

Shelly Watkins
Modesto Junior College

Julia Watson
Lakeland Community College

Will Wattendorf
Adirondack Community College

Paul Wellman
Texas A & M University

Keith D. White
University of Florida

Randall D. Wight
Ouachita Baptist University

Carol Winters-Smith
Bay Path College

Daniel E. Wivagg
Baylor University

D. Louis Wood
University of Arkansas, Little Rock

John W. Wright
Washington State University

Cecilia Yoder
Oklahoma City Community College

Dawn Young
Bossier Parish Community College

Brief Contents

CHAPTER 1

THE EVOLUTION OF PSYCHOLOGY 1

CHAPTER 2

THE RESEARCH ENTERPRISE IN PSYCHOLOGY 30

CHAPTER 3

THE BIOLOGICAL BASES OF BEHAVIOR 64

CHAPTER 4

SENSATION AND PERCEPTION 106

CHAPTER 5

VARIATIONS IN CONSCIOUSNESS 146

CHAPTER 6

LEARNING   182

CHAPTER 7

HUMAN MEMORY 222

CHAPTER 8

COGNITION AND INTELLIGENCE 260

CHAPTER 9

MOTIVATION AND EMOTION 302

CHAPTER 10

HUMAN DEVELOPMENT ACROSS THE LIFE SPAN 338

CHAPTER 11

PERSONALITY 378

CHAPTER 12

SOCIAL BEHAVIOR 418

CHAPTER 13

STRESS, COPING, AND HEALTH   456

CHAPTER 14

PSYCHOLOGICAL DISORDERS 490

CHAPTER 15

TREATMENT OF PSYCHOLOGICAL DISORDERS 532

TO THE STUDENT

Welcome to your introductory psychology textbook. In most college courses, students spend more time with their textbooks than with their professors, so it helps if students like their textbooks. Making textbooks likable, however, is a tricky proposition. By its very nature, a textbook must introduce students to many complicated concepts, ideas, and theories. If it doesn't, it isn't much of a textbook, and instructors won't choose to use it. Nevertheless, in writing this book I've tried to make it as likable as possible without compromising the academic content that your instructor demands. I've especially tried to keep in mind your need for a clear, well-organized presentation that makes the important material stand out and yet is interesting to read. Above all else, I hope you find this book's content challenging to think about and easy to learn from.

Before you plunge into your first chapter, let me introduce you to the book's key features. Becoming familiar with how the book works will help you to get more out of it.

Key Features

You're about to embark on a journey into a new domain of ideas. Your text includes some important features that are intended to highlight certain aspects of psychology's landscape.

Unifying Themes

To help you make sense of a complex and diverse field of study, I introduce seven themes in Chapter 1 that reappear in a number of variations as we move from chapter to chapter. These unifying themes are meant to provoke thought about important issues and to highlight the connections between chapters. They are discussed at the end of each chapter in a section called "Reflecting on the Chapter's Themes." Icons for the specific themes covered in a chapter appear in these sections (as well as at the beginning of the chapters) to help make the book's thematic structure more prominent.

Personal Applications

Toward the end of each chapter, you'll find a Personal Application section that shows how psychology is relevant to everyday life. Some of these sections provide concrete, practical advice that could be helpful to you in your educational endeavors, such as those on improving academic performance, improving everyday memory, and achieving self-control. So, you may want to jump ahead and read some of these Personal Applications early.

Critical Thinking Applications

Each Personal Application is followed by a two-page Critical Thinking Application that teaches and models basic critical thinking skills. I think you will find that these sections are refreshing and interesting. Like the Personal Applications, they are part of the text's basic content and should be read unless you are told otherwise by your instructor. Although the "facts" of psychology will gradually change after you take this course (thanks to scientific progress), the critical thinking skills modeled in these sections should prove valuable for many years to come.

Reality Checks

Students typically come into the introductory psychology course with a variety of misconceptions. To foster a more accurate picture of psychology, each chapter includes three or four Reality Checks, which address common misconceptions related to psychology and provide direct refutations of the misinformation. These Reality Checks are sprinkled throughout the chapters, appearing adjacent to the relevant material. Examples of popular misconceptions that are dispelled include the myth that B. F. Skinner raised his daughter in a Skinner box, which led to her becoming severely disturbed (Chapter 1); the notion that people use only 10% of their brains (Chapter 3); the assumption that people who are color blind see the world in black and white (Chapter 4); and the idea that it is dangerous to awaken someone who is sleepwalking (Chapter 5). This text feature is based on recent research suggesting that explicit repudiations of erroneous ideas reduce students' misconceptions more effectively than the simple provision of correct information (Kowalski & Taylor, 2009). For the most part, the Reality Checks can be found in the margins of the pages, but they are a critical component of the text's educational material.

Learning Aids

This text contains a great deal of information. A number of learning aids have been incorporated into the book to help you digest it all.

An *outline* at the beginning of each chapter provides you with an overview of the topics covered in that chapter. Think of the outlines as road maps, and bear in mind that it's easier to reach a destination if you know where you're going.

Headings serve as road signs in your journey through each chapter. Four levels of headings are used to make it easy to see the organization of each chapter.

Key Learning Goals, found at the beginning of major sections, can help you focus on the important issues in the material you are about to read.

Chapter Concept Charts, found at the end of the chapters, are detailed summaries of each chapter's key ideas. They provide color-coded, hierarchically organized overviews that create "snapshots" of the chapters that allow you to quickly see the relationships between ideas and sections. It's wise to read over these review materials to make sure you've digested the information in the chapter.

Italics (without boldface) are used liberally throughout the text to emphasize crucial points.

Key terms are identified with ***italicized blue boldface*** type to alert you that these are important vocabulary items that are part of psychology's technical language.

An *integrated running glossary* provides an on-the-spot definition of each key term as it's introduced in the text. These formal definitions are printed in **blue boldface** type. Becoming familiar with psychology's terminology is an essential part of learning about the field. The integrated running glossary should make this learning process easier.

Concept Checks are sprinkled throughout the chapters to let you test your mastery of important ideas. Generally, they ask you to integrate or organize a number of key ideas, or to apply ideas to real-world situations. Although they're meant to be engaging and fun, they do check conceptual *understanding,* and some are challenging. But if you get stuck, don't worry; the answers (and explanations, where they're needed) are in the back of the book in Appendix A.

Illustrations in the text are important elements in your complete learning package. Some illustrations provide enlightening diagrams of complicated concepts; others furnish examples that help flesh out ideas or provide concise overviews of research results. Careful attention to the tables and figures in the book will help you understand the material discussed in the text.

A twelve-item *Practice Test* is provided for each chapter that should give you a realistic assessment of your mastery of that chapter and valuable practice in taking multiple-choice tests. These Practice Tests are found in Appendix A.

An *alphabetical glossary* is provided in the back of the book. Most key terms are formally defined in the integrated running glossary only when they are first introduced. So if you run into a technical term a second time and can't remember its meaning, it may be easier to look it up in the alphabetical glossary.

MindTap™ for Psychology: Themes and Variations

Psychology: Themes and Variations is also available as a digital course in MindTap. In its digital version, the book is integrated into a unique learning path of activities that foster increased comprehension and efficiency. It empowers you with tools developed to help you do your best work—consistently. In MindTap, course material is seamlessly integrated with videos, activities, apps, and more.

- MindTap delivers real-world relevance with activities and assignments designed to help you build critical thinking and analytical skills that can be applied to other courses and to your professional lives.
- MindTap serves as a single destination for all course materials, so you stay organized and efficient, and have the necessary tools to master the content.
- MindTap shows you where you stand at all times—both individually and compared to the highest performers in the class. This information helps to motivate and empower performance.

A Few Footnotes

Psychology textbooks customarily identify the studies, theoretical treatises, books, and articles that information comes from. These *citations* occur (1) when names are followed by a date in parentheses, as in "Smith (2014) found that . . ." or (2) when names and dates are provided together within parentheses, as in "In one study (Burke, Martinez, & Jones, 2008), the researchers attempted to. . . ." All of the cited publications are listed by author in the alphabetized *References* section in the back of the book. The citations and references are a necessary part of a book's scholarly and scientific foundation. Practically speaking, however, you'll probably want to glide right over them as you read. You definitely don't need to memorize the names and dates.

A Final Word

I'm pleased to be a part of your first journey into the world of psychology, and I sincerely hope that you'll find the book as thought provoking and as easy to learn from as I've tried to make it. If you have any comments or advice on the book, please write to me in care of the publisher (Cengage Learning, 500 Terry A. Francois Boulevard, Second Floor, San Francisco, CA 94158). You can be sure I'll pay careful attention to your feedback. Finally, let me wish you good luck. I hope you enjoy your course and learn a great deal.

Wayne Weiten

CHAPTER 1

THE EVOLUTION OF PSYCHOLOGY

Themes in this Chapter

Empiricism

Theoretical Diversity

Sociohistorical Context

Multifactorial Causation

Cultural Heritage

Heredity & Environment

Subjectivity of Experience

André Schulze/Moment Open/Getty Images

W hat is psychology? Why is it worth your time to study? Let me approach these questions by sharing a couple of stories with you.

In 2005, Greg Hogan, a college sophomore, briefly achieved national notoriety when he was arrested for a crime. Greg wasn't anybody's idea of a likely criminal. He was the son of a Baptist minister and the president of his class. He played cello in the university orchestra. He even worked part-time in the chaplain's office. So it shocked everybody who knew Greg when police arrested him at his fraternity house for bank robbery.

It seems that Greg had faked having a gun and made away with over $2800 from a local bank. His reason? Over a period of months he had lost $5000 playing poker on the Internet. His lawyer said Greg's gambling habit had become "an addiction" (Dissell, 2005; McLoughlin & Paquet, 2005).

Greg eventually entered a clinic for treatment of his gambling problem. In a way, he was lucky—at least he got help. Moshe Pergament, a 19-year-old community college student in Long Island, New York, wasn't so fortunate. Moshe was shot to death after brandishing a gun at a police officer. The gun turned out to be plastic. On the front seat of his car was a note that began, "Officer, it was a plan. I'm sorry to get you involved. I just needed to die." Moshe had just lost $6000 betting on the World Series. His death was what people in law enforcement call "suicide by cop" (Lindsay & Lester, 2004).

These stories are at the extreme edge of a trend that concerns many public officials and mental health professionals: The popularity of gambling —from lotteries to sports betting to online poker—is booming, especially among the young (D. F. Jacobs, 2004). College students seem to be leading the way. To some observers, gambling on college campuses has become an "epidemic." Student bookies on some campuses make tens of thousands of dollars a year taking sports bets from other students. Television shows such as *The World Series of Poker* are marketed squarely at college-student audiences. Poker sites on the web invite students to win their tuition by gambling online.

For most people, gambling is a relatively harmless—if sometimes expensive—pastime. However, estimates suggest that 5%–6% of teens and young adults develop serious problems with gambling—roughly double the rate observed for older adults (D. F. Jacobs, 2004; Moore et al., 2013; Sassen, Kraus, & Bühringer, 2011). The enormous growth of pathological gambling among young people raises a number of questions. Is gambling dangerous? Can it really be addictive? What is an

© Air Images/Shutterstock.com

The perplexing problem of pathological gambling, which has increased dramatically among college students in recent years, raises a variety of complicated questions. As you will see throughout this text, psychologists investigate an endless variety of interesting questions.

addiction, anyway? If pathological gamblers abuse drugs or commit crimes, is gambling the cause of their troubles, or is it a symptom of a deeper problem? Perhaps most critically of all, why do some people become pathological gamblers while the great majority do not? Every day millions of people in the United States play the lottery, bet on sports, or visit casinos without apparent harm. Yet others can't seem to stop gambling until they have lost everything—their savings, their jobs, their homes, and their self-respect. Why? What causes such perplexing, self-destructive behavior?

Psychology is about questions like these. More generally, psychology is about understanding *all* the things we do. All of us wonder sometimes about the reasons underlying people's behavior—why it's hard to diet, why we procrastinate about studying, why we fall in love with one person rather than another. We wonder why some people are outgoing while others are shy. We wonder why we sometimes do things that we know will bring us pain and anguish, whether it's clinging to a destructive relationship or losing our tuition money in a game of Texas Hold 'Em. The study of psychology is about all these things, and infinitely more.

Many of psychology's questions have implications for people's everyday lives. For me, this is one of the field's major attractions—*psychology is practical.* Consider the case of gambling. Pathological gamblers suffer all kinds of misery, yet they can't seem to stop. Listen to the anguish of a gambler named Steve: "Over the past two years I have lost literally thousands. . . . I have attempted to give up time after time after time, but failed every time. . . . I have debts around my neck which are destroying mine and my family's life. . . . I just want a massive light to be turned on with a message saying, 'This way to your old life, Steve'" (SJB, 2006).

What is the best way to help someone like Steve? Should he join a group like Gamblers Anonymous? Would counseling work? Are there drugs that can help? By probing the whys and hows of human behavior, psychology can help us find answers to pressing questions like these, as well as better understand issues that affect each of us every day. You will see the practical side of psychology throughout this book, especially in the Personal Applications at the ends of chapters. These Applications focus on everyday problems, such as coping more effectively with stress, improving self-control, and dealing with sleep difficulties.

Beyond its practical value, psychology is worth studying because it provides a powerful *way of thinking.* All of us make judgments every day about why people do the things they do. For example, we might think that pathological gamblers are weak willed, or irrational, or just too dumb to understand that the odds are stacked against them. Or we might believe they are in the grip of an addiction that simply overpowers them. How do we decide which of these judgments—if any—are right?

Psychologists are committed to investigating questions about human behavior in a scientific way. This means that they seek to formulate precise questions about behavior and then test possible answers through systematic observation. This commitment to testing ideas means that psychology provides a means of building knowledge that is relatively accurate and dependable. It also provides a basis for assessing the assertions we hear every day about behavior, from friends and family, as well as in the popular media. Although most people probably don't think about it much, psychology is in the news all the time—in newspapers and magazines, on TV and radio, and on the Internet. Unfortunately, this coverage is often distorted or grossly oversimplified, so that misinformation is commonplace. Thus, many "truisms" about behavior come to be widely believed, when they really are misconceptions or myths. A small sampling of some popular myths related to psychology is shown in **Table 1.1**. This list of common misconceptions comes from an excellent book titled *50 Great Myths of Popular Psychology* (Lilienfeld et al., 2010). In the pages to come we'll touch upon a host of misconceptions about psychology and provide more accurate, science-based information on these matters. For example, in Chapter 3 you will learn that the idea that people only use 10% of their brains is utter nonsense. Research suggests that the best way to dispel students' misconceptions is to confront these beliefs head-on and provide a direct refutation (Kowalski & Taylor, 2009). Hence, throughout this book you will find a feature called Reality Checks that will highlight common fallacies and counter them with more accurate, realistic information. The Reality Check features will be found adjacent to relevant material, supplementing the normal text by explicitly attacking naïve, fallacious beliefs.

In the case of gambling, for example, researchers have designed careful studies to probe the relationship of gambling problems to any number of possible influences, such as the link between college students' drinking and their gambling (Hodgins & Racicot, 2013) and the impact of belonging to a

TABLE 1.1 Popular Myths Related to Psychology

Myth	Relevant Chapter
Most people use only 10% of their brain power.	Chapter 3
Playing Mozart's music to infants boosts their intelligence.	Chapter 3
Hypnosis is a unique "trance" state that differs in kind from wakefulness.	Chapter 5
Hypnosis is useful for retrieving memories of forgotten events.	Chapter 7
The polygraph ("lie detector") test is an accurate means of detecting dishonesty.	Chapter 9
Opposites attract: We are most romantically attracted to people who differ from us.	Chapter 12
People with schizophrenia have multiple personalities.	Chapter 14
A large portion of criminals successfully use the insanity defense.	Chapter 14

SOURCE: Based on Lilienfeld, S.O., Lynn, S. J., Ruscio ,J., & Beyerstein, B. L. (2010). *50 great myths of popular psychology: Shattering widespread misconceptions about human behavior.* Malden, MA: Wiley-Blackwell.

college fraternity (Rockey et al., 2005). They have probed deeply into problem gamblers' minds, looking for distortions in their thinking (Goodie & Fortune, 2013). They have used state-of-the-art brain-imaging techniques to look for abnormalities in the brains of pathological gamblers (Tschernegg et al., 2013). They have even looked at whether some people are predisposed by their genes to develop problems with gambling (Slutske et al., 2013).

If there is one clear conclusion that emerges from these studies, it is that there is no simple answer to the mystery of pathological gambling. Instead, a full explanation of gambling problems will likely involve many influences that interact in complex ways (Derevensky & Gupta, 2004; Petry, 2005). As you'll see throughout this course, the same is true of most aspects of behavior. In my opinion, this is yet another reason to study psychology: It teaches us a healthy respect for the *complexity* of behavior. In a world that could use more understanding—and compassion—this can be an invaluable lesson.

As you go through this course, I hope you'll come to share my enthusiasm for psychology as a fascinating and immensely practical field of study. Let's begin our exploration by seeing how psychology has evolved from early speculations about behavior to a modern science. By looking at this evolution, you'll better understand psychology as it is today, a sprawling, multifaceted science and profession. We'll conclude our introduction with a look at seven unifying themes that will serve as connecting threads in the chapters to come. The chapter's Personal Application reviews research that provides insights into how to be an effective student. Finally, the Critical Thinking Application discusses how critical thinking skills can be enhanced.

1.1 PSYCHOLOGY'S EARLY HISTORY

1.1

Key Learning Goals

- Summarize Wundt's contributions to psychology, and describe the chief tenets of structuralism and functionalism.
- Articulate Freud's principal ideas and why they inspired controversy.
- Trace the development of behaviorism, and assess Watson's impact on the evolution of psychology.
- Summarize Skinner's key insights, and explain the emergence of humanism and its underlying philosophy.

Psychology's story is one of people groping toward a better understanding of themselves. As the discipline has evolved, its focus, methods, and explanatory models have changed. Let's look at how psychology has developed from philosophical speculations about the mind into a modern research-based science.

The term *psychology* comes from two Greek words, *psyche,* meaning the soul, and *logos,* referring to the study of a subject. These two Greek roots were first put together to define a topic of study in the 16th century, when *psyche* was used to refer to the soul, spirit, or mind, as distinguished from the body (Boring, 1966). Not until the early 18th century did the term *psychology* gain more than rare usage among scholars. By that time it had acquired its literal meaning, "the study of the mind."

Of course, people have always wondered about the mysteries of the mind. In that sense, psychology is as old as the human race. But it was only about 140 years ago that psychology emerged as a scientific discipline.

A New Science Is Born

Psychology's intellectual parents were the disciplines of *philosophy* and *physiology.* By the 1870s a small number of scholars in both fields were actively exploring questions about the mind. How are bodily sensations turned into a mental awareness of the outside world? Are our perceptions of the world accurate reflections of reality? How do mind and body interact? The philosophers and physiologists who were interested in the mind viewed such questions as fascinating issues *within* their respective fields. It was a German professor, Wilhelm Wundt (1832–1920), who eventually changed this view. Wundt mounted a campaign to make psychology an independent discipline rather than a stepchild of philosophy or physiology (Fuchs & Evans, 2013).

In 1879 Wundt succeeded in establishing the first formal laboratory for research in psychology at the University of Leipzig. In recognition of this landmark event, historians have christened 1879 as psychology's "date of birth." Soon after, in 1881, Wundt established the first journal devoted to publishing research on psychology. All in all, Wundt's campaign was so successful that today he is widely characterized as the founder of psychology (Benjamin, 2014).

FIGURE 1.1

Early research laboratories in North America. This map highlights the location and year of founding for the first 23 psychological research labs established in North American colleges and universities. Many of these labs were founded by the students of Wilhelm Wundt. (Based on Benjamin, 2000).

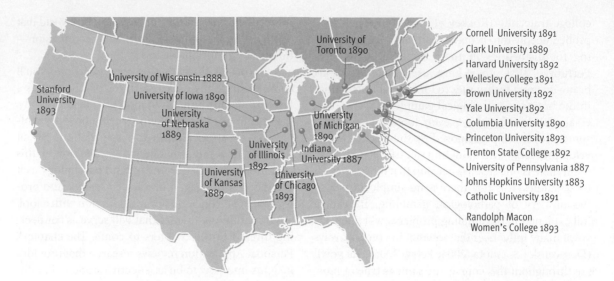

University of Toronto 1890

University of Wisconsin 1888

University of Iowa 1890

Stanford University 1893

University of Nebraska 1889

University of Michigan 1890

University of Illinois 1892

Indiana University 1887

University of Kansas 1889

University of Chicago 1893

University of Chicago 1893

Cornell University 1891
Clark University 1889
Harvard University 1892
Wellesley College 1891
Brown University 1892
Yale University 1892
Columbia University 1890
Princeton University 1893
Trenton State College 1892
University of Pennsylvania 1887
Johns Hopkins University 1883
Catholic University 1891

Randolph Macon Women's College 1893

Wundt's conception of psychology dominated the field for two decades and was influential for several more. Borrowing from his training in physiology, Wundt (1874) declared that the new psychology should be a science modeled after fields such as physics and chemistry. What was the subject matter of the new science? According to Wundt, it was *consciousness*—the awareness of immediate experience. *Thus, psychology became the scientific study of conscious experience.* This orientation kept psychology focused squarely on the mind. But it demanded that the methods used to investigate the mind be as scientific as those of chemists or physicists.

Many outstanding scholars came to Leipzig to study under Wundt and then fanned out around the world, establishing laboratories that formed the basis for the new science of psychology. The growth of this new field was particularly rapid in North America, where some 23 new psychological research labs sprang up between 1883 and 1893 at the universities shown in **Figure 1.1** (Benjamin, 2014). Although psychology was born in Germany, it blossomed into adolescence in North America.

The Battle of the "Schools" Begins: Structuralism Versus Functionalism

Competing schools of thought exist in most scientific disciplines. Sometimes the disagreements among these schools are sharp. Such diversity in thought is natural and often stimulates enlightening debate. In psychology, the first two major schools of thought, *structuralism* and *functionalism,* were entangled in the first great intellectual battles in the field (Wertheimer, 2012).

Structuralism emerged through the leadership of Edward Titchener, an Englishman who emigrated to the United States in 1892. After training in Wundt's lab, he taught for decades at Cornell University. *Structuralism* **was based on the notion that the task of psychology is to analyze consciousness into its basic elements and investigate how these elements are related.** Just as physicists were studying how matter is made up of basic particles, the structuralists wanted to identify the fundamental components of conscious experience, such as sensations, feelings, and images.

Although the structuralists explored many questions, most of their work concerned sensation and perception in vision, hearing, and touch. To examine the contents of consciousness, the structuralists depended on the method of **introspection, or the careful, systematic self-observation of one's own conscious experience.** As practiced by the structuralists, introspection required training to make the *subject*—the person being studied—more objective and more aware. Once trained, participants were typically exposed to auditory tones and visual stimuli, and then they were asked to analyze and describe the quality, intensity, and clarity of what they experienced.

The functionalists were heavily influenced by William James (1842–1910), a brilliant American scholar, who took a different view of psychology's task. **Functionalism was based on the belief that psychology should investigate the function or purpose of consciousness, rather than its structure.** James argued that the structuralists' approach missed the real nature of conscious experience. Consciousness, he argued, consists of a continuous *flow* of thoughts. In analyzing consciousness into its "elements," the structuralists were looking at static points in that flow. James wanted to understand the flow itself, which he called the *stream of consciousness*. Today, people take this metaphorical description of mental life for granted, but at the time it was a revolutionary insight. James went on to make many important contributions to psychology, including a theory of emotion that remains influential today (Laird & Lacasse, 2014; see Chapter 9). His landmark book, *Principles of Psychology* (1890), became standard reading for generations of psychologists. It is perhaps the most influential text in the history of psychology (Weiten & Wight, 1992).

Whereas structuralists naturally gravitated to the lab, the functionalists were more interested in how people adapt their behavior to the demands of the real world around them. Instead of focusing on sensation and perception, the functionalists began to investigate mental testing, patterns of development in children, the effectiveness of educational practices, and behavioral differences between the sexes. These new topics may have played a role in attracting the first women into the field of psychology (see **Figure 1.2**).

Mary Whiton Calkins (1863–1930)	Margaret Floy Washburn (1871–1939)	Leta Stetter Hollingworth (1886–1939)

Mary Calkins, who studied under William James, founded one of the first dozen psychology laboratories in America at Wellesley College in 1891, invented a widely used technique for studying memory, and became the first woman to serve as president of the American Psychological Association in 1905. Ironically, however, she never received her Ph.D. in psychology. Because she was a woman, Harvard University only reluctantly allowed her to take graduate classes as a "guest student." When she completed the requirements for her Ph.D., Harvard would only offer her a doctorate from its undergraduate sister school, Radcliffe. Calkins felt that this decision perpetuated unequal treatment of the sexes, so she refused the Radcliffe degree.	Margaret Washburn was the first woman to receive a Ph.D. in psychology. She wrote an influential book, *The Animal Mind* (1908), which served as an impetus to the subsequent emergence of behaviorism and was standard reading for several generations of psychologists. In 1921 she became the second woman to serve as president of the American Psychological Association. Washburn studied under James McKeen Cattell at Columbia University, but like Mary Calkins, she was only permitted to take graduate classes unofficially, as a "hearer." Hence, she transferred to Cornell University, which was more hospitable toward women, and completed her doctorate in 1894. Like Calkins, Washburn spent most of her career at a college for women (Vassar).	Leta Hollingworth did pioneering work on adolescent development, mental retardation, and gifted children. Indeed, she was the first person to use the term *gifted* to refer to youngsters who scored exceptionally high on intelligence tests. Hollingworth (1914, 1916) also played a major role in debunking popular theories of her era that purported to explain why women were "inferior" to men. For instance, she conducted a study refuting the myth that phases of the menstrual cycle are reliably associated with performance decrements in women. Her careful collection of objective data on gender differences forced other scientists to subject popular, untested beliefs about the sexes to skeptical, empirical inquiry.

FIGURE 1.2

Women pioneers in the history of psychology. Women have long made major contributions to the development of psychology (Milar, 2000; Russo & Denmark, 1987), and today roughly half of all psychologists are female. As in other fields, however, women have often been overlooked in histories of psychology (Furumoto & Scarborough, 1986). The three psychologists profiled here demonstrate that women have been making significant contributions to psychology almost from its beginning—despite formidable barriers to pursuing their academic careers.

SOURCE: Photos courtesy of the Archives of the History of American Psychology, The Center for the History of Psychology, University of Akron.

The impassioned advocates of structuralism and functionalism saw themselves as fighting for high stakes: the definition and future direction of the new science of psychology. Their war of ideas continued energetically for many years. Who won? Most historians give the edge to functionalism. Both schools of thought gradually faded away. But the practical orientation of functionalism fostered the development of two important descendants—behaviorism and applied psychology (Green, 2009). We will discuss both momentarily.

Freud Brings the Unconscious into the Picture

Sigmund Freud (1856–1939) was an Austrian physician whose theories made him one of the most influential—and controversial—intellectual figures of the twentieth century. Freud's (1900, 1933) approach to psychology grew out of his efforts to treat mental disorders. In his medical practice, Freud treated people troubled by psychological problems such as irrational fears, obsessions, and anxieties with an innovative procedure he called *psychoanalysis* (described in detail in Chapter 15). Decades of experience probing into his patients' lives provided much of the inspiration for Freud's theory.

His work with patients persuaded Freud of the existence of what he called the *unconscious*. According to Freud, **the *unconscious* contains thoughts, memories, and desires that are well below the surface of conscious awareness but that nonetheless exert great influence on behavior.** Freud based his concept of the unconscious on a variety of observations. For instance, he noticed that seemingly meaningless slips of the tongue (such as "I decided to take a summer school *curse*") often appeared to reveal a person's true feelings. He also noted that his patients' dreams often seemed to express important feelings that they were unaware of. Knitting these and other observations together, Freud eventually concluded that psychological disturbances are largely caused by personal conflicts existing at an unconscious level. More generally, his ***psychoanalytic theory* attempts to explain personality, motivation, and mental disorders by focusing on unconscious determinants of behavior.**

© Orange Line Media/Shutterstock.com

CONCEPT CHECK 1.1

Understanding the Implications of Major Theories: Wundt, James, and Freud

Check your understanding of the implications of some of the major theories reviewed in this chapter by indicating who is likely to have made each of the statements quoted below. Choose from the following theorists: (a) Wilhelm Wundt, (b) William James, and (c) Sigmund Freud. You'll find the answers in Appendix A in the back of the book.

_____ 1. "He that has eyes to see and ears to hear may convince himself that no mortal can keep a secret. If the lips are silent, he chatters with his finger-tips; betrayal oozes out of him at every pore. And thus the task of making conscious the most hidden recesses of the mind is one which it is quite possible to accomplish."

_____ 2. "The book which I present to the public is an attempt to mark out a new domain of science. . . . The new discipline rests upon anatomical and physiological foundations. . . . The experimental treatment of psychological problems must be pronounced from every point of view to be in its first beginnings."

_____ 3. "Consciousness, then, does not appear to itself chopped up in bits. Such words as 'chain' or 'train' do not describe it fitly. . . . It is nothing jointed; it flows. A 'river' or 'stream' are the metaphors by which it is most naturally described."

Freud's concept of the unconscious was not entirely new, but he put it on the map for the general population and elaborated on it like never before (Lothane, 2006). It is important to emphasize that the concept of the unconscious was a major departure from the prevailing belief that people are fully aware of the forces affecting their behavior. In arguing that behavior is governed by unconscious forces, Freud made the disconcerting suggestion that people are not masters of their own minds. Other aspects of Freud's theory also stirred up debate. For instance, he proposed that behavior is greatly influenced by how people cope with their sexual urges. At a time when people were far less comfortable discussing sexual issues than they are today, even scientists were offended and scandalized by Freud's emphasis on sex. Small wonder, then, that Freud was soon engulfed in controversy.

In spite of its controversial nature, Freud's theory gradually won acceptance, attracting prominent followers such as Carl Jung and Alfred Adler. Important public recognition from psychology came in 1909, when G. Stanley Hall invited Freud to give a series of lectures at Clark University in Massachusetts. By the 1920s psychoanalytic theory was widely known around the world. Although psychoanalytic theory continued to generate heated debate, it survived to become an influential theoretical perspective (Luborsky, O'Reilly-Landry, & Arlow, 2011). Today, many psychoanalytic concepts have filtered into the mainstream of psychology (Eagle, 2013; Westen, Gabbard, & Ortigo, 2008).

Watson Alters Psychology's Course as Behaviorism Makes Its Debut

In the early 1900s, another major school of thought appeared that dramatically altered the course of psychology. Founded by John B. Watson (1878–1958), *behaviorism* is a theoretical orientation based on the premise that scientific psychology should study only observable behavior. It is important to understand what a radical change this definition represents. Watson (1913, 1919) was proposing that psychologists *abandon the study of consciousness altogether* and focus exclusively on behaviors they could observe directly. In essence, he was redefining what scientific psychology should be about.

Why did Watson argue for such a fundamental shift in direction? Because to him, the power of the scientific method rested on the idea of *verifiability*. In principle, scientific claims can always be verified (or disproved) by anyone who is able and willing to make the required observations. However, this power depends on studying things that can be observed objectively. Otherwise, the advantage of using the scientific approach— replacing vague speculation and personal opinion with reliable, exact knowledge—is lost. In Watson's view, mental processes are not a proper subject for scientific study because they are ultimately private events. After all, no one can see or touch another's thoughts. Consequently, if psychology was to be a science, it would have to give up consciousness as its subject matter and become instead the *science of behavior*.

Behavior refers to any overt (observable) response or activity by an organism. Watson asserted that psychologists could study anything that people do or say— shopping, playing chess, eating, complimenting a friend. However, according to Watson they could *not* study scientifically the thoughts, wishes, and feelings that might accompany these behaviors.

Watson's radical reorientation of psychology did not end with his redefinition of its subject matter. He also took an extreme position on one of psychology's oldest and most fundamental questions: the issue of *nature versus nurture*. This age-old debate is concerned with whether behavior is determined mainly by genetic inheritance ("nature") or by environment and experience ("nurture"). To oversimplify, the question is this: Is a great concert pianist or a master criminal born, or made?

Watson argued that each is made, not born. He discounted the importance of heredity. He maintained that behavior is governed entirely by the environment. Indeed, he boldly claimed:

Give me a dozen healthy infants, well-formed, and my own special world to bring them up in and I'll guarantee to take any one at random and train him to become any type of specialist I might select—doctor, lawyer, artist, merchant-chief, and yes, even beggar-man and thief, regardless of his talents, penchants, tendencies, abilities, vocations and race of his ancestors. I am going beyond my facts and I admit it, but so have the advocates of the contrary and they have been doing it for many thousands of years. (1924, p. 82)

For obvious reasons, Watson's tongue-in-cheek challenge was never put to a test. Although this widely cited quote overstated and oversimplified Watson's views on the nature-nurture issue (Todd & Morris, 1992), his writings contributed to the environmental slant that became associated with behaviorism (Horowitz, 1992).

Behaviorism's approach also contributed to the rise of animal research in psychology. Although a modest amount of animal research was conducted prior to the advent of behaviorism (Fuchs & Evans, 2013), when the behaviorists deleted consciousness from their scope of concern, psychologists no longer needed to study human subjects who could report on their mental processes. Many psychologists thought that animals would make better research subjects anyway. One key reason was that experimental research is often more productive if experimenters can exert considerable *control* over their subjects. Obviously, a researcher can exert much more control over a laboratory rat or pigeon than over a human subject. Thus, the discipline that had begun its life a few decades earlier as the study of the mind gradually found itself heavily involved in the study of simple responses made by lab animals.

The gradual emergence of behaviorism contributed to the rise of animal research in psychology. From the 1930s through the 1950s the behavior of the humble laboratory rat was the focus of thousands upon thousands of studies. Animal research remains very important in contemporary psychology.

Although Watson's views shaped the evolution of psychology for many decades, he ended up watching the field's progress from the sidelines. Because of a heavily publicized divorce scandal in 1920, Watson was forced to resign from Johns Hopkins University (Buckley, 1994). Bitterly disappointed, he left academia at the age of 42, never to return. Psychology's loss proved to be the business world's gain, as Watson went on to become an innovative, successful advertising executive (Brewer, 1991; King, Woody, & Viney, 2013). The advertising industry was just emerging as a national force in the 1920s, and Watson quickly became one of its most prominent practitioners. He pioneered fear appeals, testimonials, selling the "prestige" of products, and the promotion of style over substance, all of which remain basic principles in modern marketing (Buckley, 1982). Moreover, "through an enormous output of books, magazine articles, and radio broadcasts he was able to establish himself as the public spokesman for the profession of psychology and an expert on subjects ranging from childrearing to economics. In effect, Watson became the first 'pop' psychologist" (Buckley, 1982, p. 217). So, ironically, Watson became the public face of the discipline that had banished him from its mainstream.

Skinner Questions Free Will as Behaviorism Flourishes

The advocates of behaviorism and psychoanalysis tangled frequently during the 1920s, 1930s, and 1940s. As psychoanalytic thought slowly gained a foothold within psychology, many psychologists softened their stance on the acceptability of studying internal mental events. However, this movement toward the consideration of internal states was dramatically reversed in the 1950s by a Harvard psychologist named B. F. Skinner (1904–1990).

Skinner did not deny the existence of internal mental events. However, he insisted that they could not be studied scientifically. Moreover, he maintained, there was no need to study them. According to Skinner, if the stimulus of food is followed by the response of eating, we can fully describe what is happening without making any guesses about whether the animal is experiencing hunger. Like Watson, Skinner also emphasized how environmental factors mold behavior.

The fundamental principle of behavior documented by Skinner is deceptively simple: *Organisms tend to repeat responses that lead to positive outcomes, and they tend not to repeat responses that lead to neutral or negative outcomes.* Despite its simplicity, this principle turns out to be quite powerful. Working with laboratory rats and pigeons in a small chamber called a Skinner box (see Chapter 6), Skinner showed that he could exert remarkable control over the behavior of animals by manipulating the outcomes of their responses. He was even able to train animals to perform unnatural behaviors. For example, he once trained some pigeons to play a respectable version of table tennis. They pecked a ball back and forth on a ping-pong table. Skinner's followers eventually showed that the principles uncovered in their animal research could be applied to complex human behaviors as well. Behavioral principles are now widely used in factories, schools, prisons, mental hospitals, and a variety of other settings.

Skinner's ideas had repercussions that went far beyond the debate among psychologists about what they should study. Skinner spelled out the full implications of his findings in his book *Beyond Freedom and Dignity* (1971). There he asserted that all behavior is fully governed by external stimuli. In other words, your behavior is determined in predictable ways by lawful principles, just as the flight of an arrow is governed by the laws of physics. Thus, if you believe that your actions are the result of conscious decisions, you're wrong. According to Skinner, we are all controlled by our environment, not by ourselves. In short, Skinner arrived at the conclusion that *free will is an illusion.*

As you can readily imagine, such a disconcerting view of human nature was not universally acclaimed. Like Freud, Skinner was the target of harsh criticism. Much of this criticism stemmed from misinterpretations of his ideas reported in the popular press (Rutherford, 2000). For example, his analysis of free will was often misconstrued as an attack on the concept of a free society—which it was not. Somehow, a myth also emerged that Skinner raised his daughter in a version of a Skinner box and that this experience led her to be severely disturbed later in life. Despite the misinformation and controversy, however, behaviorism flourished as the dominant school of thought in psychology during the 1950s and 1960s (Gilgen, 1982).

The Humanists Revolt

By the 1950s behaviorism and psychoanalytic theory had become the most influential schools of thought in psychology. However, many psychologists found these theoretical orientations unappealing. The principal charge hurled at both schools was that they were "dehumanizing." Psychoanalytic theory was attacked for its belief that behavior is dominated by primitive, sexual urges. Behaviorism was condemned for its preoccupation with the study of simple animal behavior. Both theories were criticized because they suggested that people are not masters of their own destinies. Above all, many people argued, both schools of thought failed to recognize the unique qualities of *human* behavior.

Beginning in the 1950s, the diverse opposition to behaviorism and psychoanalytic theory blended into a loose alliance that eventually became a new school of thought called "humanism" (Bühler & Allen, 1972). In psychology, **humanism is a theoretical orientation that emphasizes the unique qualities of humans, especially their freedom and their potential for personal growth.** Some of the key differences between the

▶ **REALITY CHECK**

Misconception

B. F. Skinner raised his daughter, Deborah, in a Skinner box, contributing to her becoming severely disturbed later in life, which led to her suicide.

Reality

Skinner did design an innovative crib called a "baby tender" for Deborah, which was featured in *Ladies' Home Journal* (Skinner, 1945; see the photo below). But it was not analogous to a Skinner box, was not used for experiments, and apparently was quite comfortable. Deborah grew up normally, was very close to her father (Buzan, 2004). She has not suffered from psychological problems as an adult, and is alive and well, working as an artist.

Bettmann/Corbis

humanistic, psychoanalytic, and behavioral viewpoints are summarized in **Figure 1.3**. It compares six contemporary theoretical perspectives in psychology.

Humanists take an *optimistic* view of human nature. They maintain that people are not pawns of either their animal heritage or environmental circumstances. Furthermore, these theorists say, because humans are fundamentally different from other animals, research on animals has little relevance to the understanding of human behavior. The most

Perspective and Its Influential Period	Principal Contributors	Subject Matter	Basic Premise
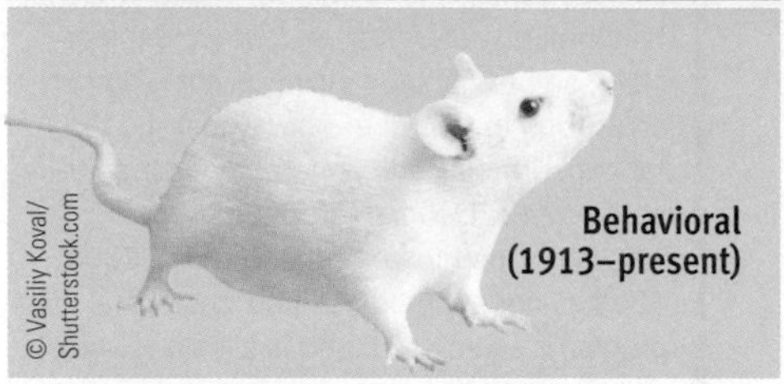 **Behavioral** (1913–present)	John B. Watson Ivan Pavlov B. F. Skinner	Effects of environment on the overt behavior of humans and animals	Only observable events (stimulus-response relations) can be studied scientifically.
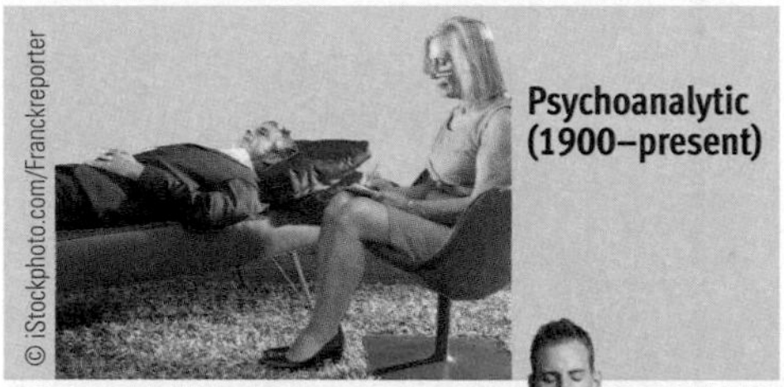 **Psychoanalytic** (1900–present)	Sigmund Freud Carl Jung Alfred Adler	Unconscious determinants of behavior	Unconscious motives and experiences in early childhood govern personality and mental disorders.
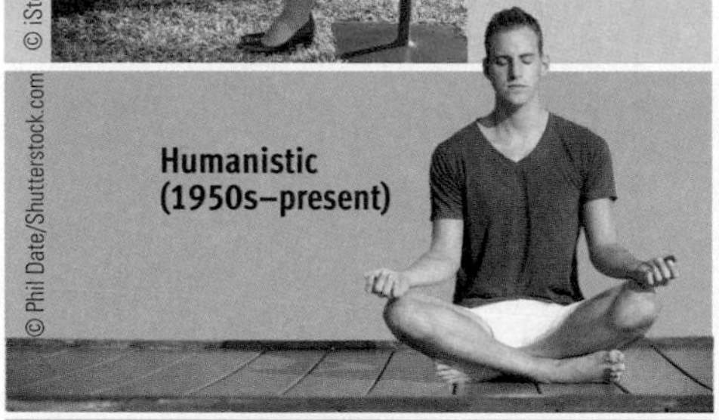 **Humanistic** (1950s–present)	Carl Rogers Abraham Maslow	Unique aspects of human experience	Humans are free, rational beings with the potential for personal growth, and they are fundamentally different from animals.
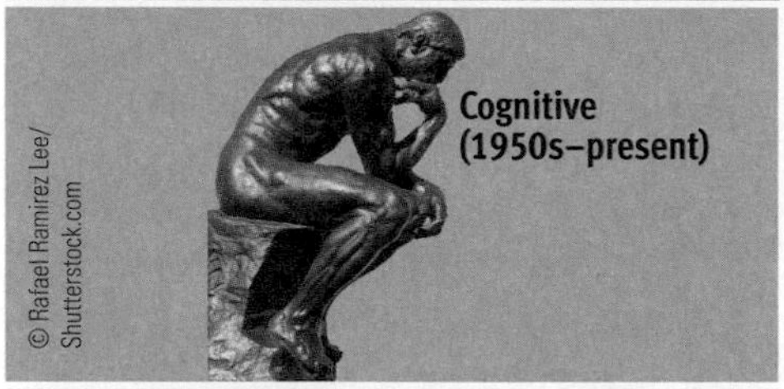 **Cognitive** (1950s–present)	Jean Piaget Noam Chomsky Herbert Simon	Thoughts; mental processes	Human behavior cannot be fully understood without examining how people acquire, store, and process information.
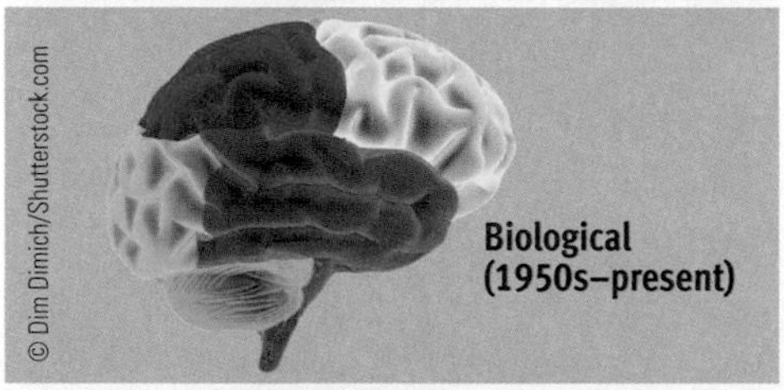 **Biological** (1950s–present)	James Olds Roger Sperry David Hubel Torsten Wiesel	Physiological, genetic, and neural bases of behavior in humans and animals	An organism's functioning can be explained in terms of the brain structures and biochemical processes that underlie behavior.
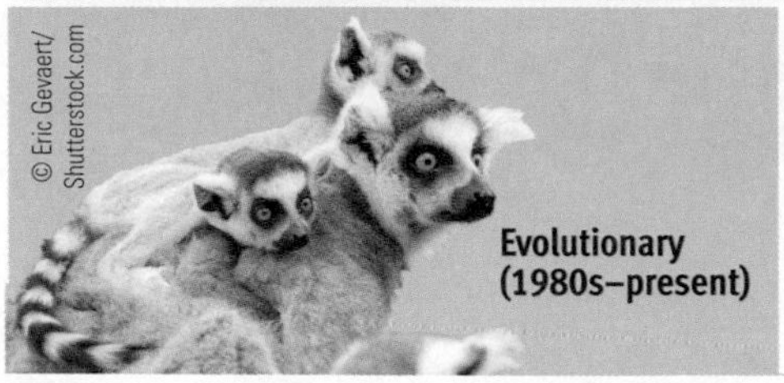 **Evolutionary** (1980s–present)	David Buss Martin Daly Margo Wilson Leda Cosmides John Tooby	Evolutionary bases of behavior in humans and animals	Behavior patterns have evolved to solve adaptive problems; natural selection favors behaviors that enhance reproductive success.

FIGURE 1.3

Contemporary theoretical perspectives in psychology. The theoretical approaches outlined in this chart remain influential in modern psychology. As you can see, each theoretical perspective has its own take on what psychology should study.

prominent architects of the humanistic movement have been Carl Rogers (1902–1987) and Abraham Maslow (1908–1970). Rogers (1951) argued that human behavior is governed primarily by each individual's sense of self, or "self-concept"—which animals presumably lack. Both he and Maslow (1954) maintained that to fully understand people's behavior, psychologists must take into account the human drive toward personal growth. They asserted that people have a basic need to continue to evolve as human beings and to fulfill their potentials. To date, the humanists' greatest contribution to psychology has probably been their innovative treatments for psychological problems and disorders (Schneider & Längle, 2012). They have pioneered many influential approaches to psychotherapy, including client-centered therapy, Gestalt therapy, and existential therapy.

CONCEPT CHECK 1.2

Understanding the Implications of Major Theories: Watson, Skinner, and Rogers

Check your understanding of the implications of some of the major theories reviewed in this chapter by indicating who is likely to have made each of the statements quoted below. Choose from the following: (a) John B. Watson, (b) B. F. Skinner, and (c) Carl Rogers. You'll find the answers in Appendix A at the back of the book.

_____ 1. "In the traditional view, a person is free. . . . He can therefore be held responsible for what he does and justly punished if he offends. That view, together with its associated practices, must be reexamined when a scientific analysis reveals unsuspected controlling relations between behavior and environment."

_____ 2. "I do not have a Pollyanna view of human nature. . . . Yet one of the most refreshing and invigorating parts of my experience is to work with [my clients] and to discover the strongly positive directional tendencies which exist in them, as in all of us, at the deepest levels."

_____ 3. "Our conclusion is that we have no real evidence of the inheritance of traits. I would feel perfectly confident in the ultimately favorable outcome of careful upbringing of a healthy, well-formed baby born of a long line of crooks, murderers and thieves, and prostitutes."

1.2 PSYCHOLOGY'S MODERN HISTORY

The principal storyline of psychology's early history was its gradual maturation into a research-based science. The seminal work of Wundt, James, Watson, Pavlov, Skinner, and a host of other pioneers served to establish psychology as a respected scientific discipline in the halls of academia. As you will learn momentarily, the principal storyline of psychology's modern history has been its remarkable growth into a multifaceted scientific and professional enterprise. In more recent decades psychology's story has been marked by expanding boundaries and broader interests.

Psychology Comes of Age as a Profession

As you know, psychology is not all pure science. It has a highly practical side. Many psychologists provide a variety of professional services to the public. The first applied arm of psychology to achieve any prominence was *clinical psychology*. As practiced

---

1.2

Key Learning Goals

- Discuss how historical events contributed to the emergence of psychology as a profession.
- Describe two trends emerging in the 1950s–1960s that represented a return to psychology's intellectual roots.
- Explain why Western psychology has shown an increased interest in cultural variables in recent decades.
- Discuss the emergence and basic ideas of evolutionary psychology and positive psychology.

today, *clinical psychology* **is the branch of psychology concerned with the diagnosis and treatment of psychological problems and disorders.** In the early days, however, the emphasis was almost exclusively on psychological testing and adjustment problems in schoolchildren, and clinicians were a small minority in a field devoted primarily to research (Goldenberg, 1983).

That picture changed with dramatic swiftness during and after World War II, in the 1940s and 1950s (Cautin, Freedheim, & DeLeon, 2013). Because of the war many academic psychologists were pressed into service as clinicians. They were needed to screen military recruits and to treat soldiers suffering from trauma. Many of these psychologists (often to their surprise) found the clinical work to be challenging and rewarding, and a substantial portion continued to do clinical work after the war. More significantly, some 40,000 American veterans, many with severe psychological scars, returned to seek post-war treatment in Veterans Administration (VA) hospitals. With the demand for clinicians far greater than the supply, the VA stepped in to finance many new training programs in clinical psychology (Routh, 2013). Within a few years, about half of the new Ph.D.'s in psychology were specializing in clinical psychology.

Since the 1950s, the professionalization of psychology has spread into additional areas of psychology. Today the broad umbrella of applied psychology covers a variety of professional specialties, including school psychology, industrial/organizational psychology, and counseling psychology (Benjamin & Baker, 2004).

Psychology Returns to Its Roots: Renewed Interest in Cognition and Physiology

While applied psychology has blossomed in recent years, scientific research has continued to progress. Ironically, two of the latest trends in research hark back more than a century to psychology's beginning, when psychologists were primarily interested in consciousness and physiology. Today psychologists are showing renewed interest in consciousness (now called "cognition") and the biological bases of behavior.

Cognition **refers to the mental processes involved in acquiring knowledge.** In other words, cognition involves thinking or conscious experience. For many decades, the dominance of behaviorism discouraged investigation of "unobservable" mental processes, and most psychologists showed little interest in cognition (Mandler, 2002). During the 1950s and 1960s, however, research on cognition slowly began to emerge (Miller, 2003). The new interest in cognition was inspired in part by the information-processing capabilities of newly invented computers. In 1954, Herbert Simon, who would go on to win the 1981 Nobel Prize in economics, was one of the first to draw attention to the parallels between computer and human cognition (Leahey, 2013). Soon, major advances were reported in the study of memory, decision making, and problem solving.

Cognitive theorists argue that psychology must include the study of internal mental events to fully understand human behavior (Gardner, 1985; Neisser, 1967). Advocates of the *cognitive perspective* point out that our mental processes surely influence how we behave. Consequently, focusing exclusively on overt behavior yields an incomplete picture of why we behave as we do. Equally important, psychologists investigating decision making, reasoning, and problem solving have shown that methods *can* be devised to study cognitive processes scientifically. Although the methods are different from those used in psychology's early days, recent research on the inner workings of the mind has put the *psyche* back in contemporary psychology. In fact, many observers maintain that the cognitive approach has become the dominant perspective in contemporary psychology. Some interesting data support this assertion, as can be seen in **Figure 1.4**. It plots estimates of the research productivity of four theoretical perspectives since 1950. As you can see, since 1975 the cognitive perspective has generated more published articles than any other perspective (Spear, 2007).

The 1950s and 1960s also saw many discoveries that highlighted the interrelations among mind, body, and behavior (Clark et al., 2013). For example, researchers demonstrated that electrical stimulation of the brain could evoke emotional responses such as pleasure and rage in animals (Olds, 1956). Other work, which eventually earned a Nobel Prize for Roger Sperry (in 1981), showed that the right and left halves of the brain are specialized to handle different types of mental tasks (Gazzaniga, Bogen, & Sperry, 1965). These and many other findings stimulated an increase in research on the biological bases of behavior. Advocates of the *biological perspective* maintain that much of human and animal behavior can be explained in terms of the brain structures and biochemical processes that allow organisms to behave. As you can see in **Figure 1.4**, the prominence of the neuroscience perspective has grown steadily since the 1950s (Spear, 2007). As you know, in the 19th century the young science of psychology had a heavy physiological emphasis. Thus, the renewed interest in the biological bases of behavior represents another return to psychology's heritage.

The cognitive and biological perspectives have become important theoretical orientations in modern psychology. They are increasingly influential viewpoints regarding what psychology should study and how. The cognitive and biological perspectives are compared to other contemporary theoretical perspectives in **Figure 1.3**.

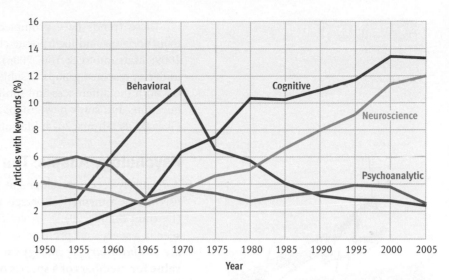

FIGURE 1.4

The relative prominence of four major schools of thought in psychology. To estimate the relative productivity and influence of various theoretical orientations in recent decades, Joseph Spear (2007) conducted a keyword search of the psychological research literature to estimate the percentage of articles relevant to each school of thought. Obviously, this is just one of many ways one might gauge the prominence of various theoretical orientations. Nonetheless, the data are thought provoking. His findings suggest that the cognitive perspective surpassed the behavioral perspective in its influence on research sometime around 1975 and that it has continued as the leading perspective since then. As you can see, his data also demonstrate that the neuroscience perspective has grown steadily in influence since the 1950s.

SOURCE: Adapted from Spear, J. H. (2007). Prominent schools or other active specialties? A fresh look at some trends in psychology. *Review of General Psychology, 11,* 363–380. Copyright © 2007 by the American Psychological Association. Reprinted by permission of the author.

Psychology Broadens Its Horizons: Increased Interest in Cultural Diversity

Throughout psychology's history, most researchers have worked under the assumption that they were seeking to identify general principles of behavior that would be applicable to all of humanity (Smith, Spillane, & Annus, 2006). In reality, however, psychology has largely been a Western (North American and European) enterprise with a rather provincial slant (Hall, 2014; Norenzayan & Heine, 2005). Traditionally, Western psychologists have paid scant attention to how well their theories and research might apply to non-Western cultures, to ethnic minorities in Western societies, or even to women as opposed to men.

However, in recent decades Western psychologists have begun to recognize that their neglect of cultural variables has diminished the value of their work. They are now devoting increased attention to culture as a determinant of behavior. What brought about this shift? The new interest in culture appears mainly attributable to two recent trends: (1) Advances in communication, travel, and international trade have "shrunk" the world and increased global interdependence, bringing more and more Americans and Europeans into contact with people from non-Western cultures; and (2) the ethnic makeup of the Western world has become an increasingly diverse multicultural mosaic (Brislin, 2000; Hermans & Kempen, 1998; Mays et al., 1996; Valsiner, 2012).

The increasingly multicultural makeup of many Western societies undoubtedly contributed to psychology's increased interest in how culture shapes behavior.

These trends have prompted more and more Western psychologists to broaden their horizons and incorporate cultural factors into their theories and research (Lonner, 2009; Matsumoto & Yoo, 2006). These psychologists are striving to study previously underrepresented groups of subjects to test the generality of earlier findings and to catalog both the differences and similarities among cultural groups. These efforts to ask new questions and study new groups promise to enrich the discipline of psychology (David, Okazaki, & Giroux, 2014; Matsumoto, 2003; Sue, 2003).

Psychology Adapts: The Emergence of Evolutionary Psychology

A relatively recent development in psychology has been the emergence of *evolutionary psychology,* a theoretical perspective that is likely to be influential in the years to come (Durrant & Ellis, 2013). Evolutionary psychologists assert that the patterns of behavior seen in a species are products of evolution in the same way that anatomical characteristics are. **Evolutionary psychology examines behavioral processes in terms of their adaptive value for members of a species over the course of many generations.** The basic premise of evolutionary psychology is that natural selection favors behaviors that enhance organisms' reproductive success—that is, passing on genes to the next generation. Thus, if a species is highly aggressive, evolutionary psychologists argue that it's because aggressiveness confers a survival or reproductive advantage for members of that species. Hence, genes that promote aggressiveness are more likely to be passed on to the next generation.

Evolutionary psychology began to emerge in the middle to late 1980s. A growing band of evolutionary psychologists (Buss, 1985, 1989; Cosmides & Tooby, 1989; Daly & Wilson, 1985) published widely cited studies on a broad range of topics. These topics included mating preferences, jealousy, aggression, sexual behavior, decision making, and development. By the mid-1990s, it became clear that psychology was witnessing the birth of its first major, new theoretical perspective since the cognitive revolution in the 1950s and 1960s.

Psychology Moves in a Positive Direction

Shortly after Martin Seligman was elected president of the American Psychological Association in 1997, he experienced a profound insight that he characterized as an "epiphany." This pivotal insight came from an unusual source—Seligman's 5-year-old daughter, Nikki. She scolded her overachieving, task-oriented father for being "grumpy" far too much of the time. Provoked by his daughter's criticism, Seligman suddenly realized that his approach to life *was* overly and unnecessarily negative. More important, he recognized that the same assessment could be made of the field of psychology—that, it too, was excessively and needlessly negative in its approach (Seligman, 2003). This revelation inspired Seligman to launch an influential new initiative within psychology that came to be known as the *positive psychology movement.*

Seligman went on to argue convincingly that the field of psychology had historically devoted too much attention to pathology, weakness, and damage, and ways to heal suffering. He acknowledged that this approach had yielded valuable insights and progress. But he argued that it also resulted in an unfortunate neglect of the forces that make life worth living. Seligman convened a series of informal meetings with influential psychologists and then more formal conferences to gradually outline the philosophy and goals of positive psychology. Emphasizing some of the same themes as humanism, positive psychology seeks to shift the field's focus away from negative experiences (Downey & Chang, 2014). Thus, **positive psychology uses theory and research to better understand the positive, adaptive, creative, and fulfilling aspects of human existence.**

The emerging field of positive psychology has three areas of interest (Seligman, 2003). The first is the study of *positive subjective experiences,* or positive emotions, such as happiness, love, gratitude, contentment, and hope. The second focus is on *positive individual traits*—that is, personal strengths and virtues. Theorists are working to identify, classify, and analyze the origins of such positive traits as courage, perseverance, nurturance, tolerance,

The praying mantis has an astonishing ability to blend in with its environment, along with remarkably acute hearing and vision that permit it to detect prey up to 60 feet away and powerful jaws that allow it to devour its prey. They are so deadly they will eat each other, which makes sex quite a challenge, but males have evolved a reflex module that allows them to copulate successfully while being eaten (even after decapitation)! These physical characteristics obviously represent adaptations that have been crafted by natural selection over the course of millions of generations. Evolutionary psychologists maintain that many patterns of behavior seen in various species are also adaptations that have been shaped by natural selection.

creativity, integrity, and kindness. The third area of interest is in *positive institutions and communities*. Here the focus is on how societies can foster civil discourse, strong families, healthful work environments, and supportive neighborhood communities.

Our review of psychology's past has shown how the field has evolved. We have seen psychology develop from philosophical speculation into a rigorous science committed to research. We have seen how a highly visible professional arm involved in mental health services emerged from this science. We have seen how psychology's focus on physiology is rooted in its 19th-century origins. We have seen how and why psychologists began conducting research on lower animals. We have seen how psychology has evolved from the study of mind and body to the study of behavior, and how the investigation of mind and body has been welcomed back into the mainstream of modern psychology. We have seen how different theoretical schools have defined the scope and mission of psychology in different ways. We have seen how psychology's interests have expanded and become increasingly diverse. Above all else, we have seen that psychology is a growing, evolving intellectual enterprise.

Psychology's history is already rich, but its story has barely begun. The century or so that has elapsed since Wilhelm Wundt put psychology on a scientific footing is only an eyeblink of time in human history. What has been discovered during those years, and what remains unknown, is the subject of the rest of this book.

1.3 PSYCHOLOGY TODAY: VIGOROUS AND DIVERSIFIED

1.3

Key Learning Goals

- Discuss the growth of psychology, and identify the most common work settings for contemporary psychologists.
- List and describe the major research areas and professional specialties in psychology.

We began this chapter with an informal description of what psychology is about. Now that you have a feel for how psychology has developed, you can better appreciate a definition that does justice to the field's modern diversity: *Psychology* **is the science that studies behavior and the physiological and cognitive processes that underlie behavior, and it is the profession that applies the accumulated knowledge of this science to practical problems.**

Contemporary psychology is a thriving science and profession. Its growth has been remarkable. One simple index of this growth is the dramatic rise in membership in the American Psychological Association (APA), a national organization devoted to the advancement of psychology. The APA was founded by G. Stanley Hall in 1892 with just 31 members (Wertheimer, 2012). Today, the APA has over 90,000 members. Moreover, as **Figure 1.5** shows, APA membership has increased ninefold since 1950. In the United States, psychology is the second most popular undergraduate major. The field accounts for nearly 10% of all doctoral degrees awarded in the sciences and humanities. Of course, psychology is an international enterprise. Today, over 2500 technical journals from all over the world

▷ REALITY CHECK

Misconception

Psychology is the study of the mind.

Reality

When the term was coined in the 16th century, *psychology* did refer to the study of the mind, but the term's original meaning is much too narrow today. Since the 19th century, scientific psychology has focused heavily on physiological processes, and the 20th century brought a new focus on overt behavior. Modern psychology encompasses the study of behavior and the mental and physiological processes that regulate behavior.

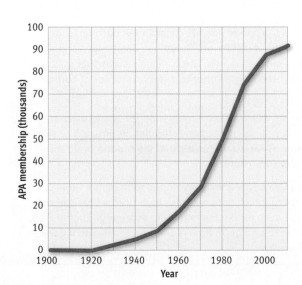

FIGURE 1.5

Membership in the American Psychological Association, 1900–2010. The steep rise in the number of psychologists in the APA since 1950 testifies to psychology's remarkable growth as a science and a profession. If graduate student members are also counted, the APA has over 150,000 members. (Adapted from data published by the American Psychological Association, by permission).

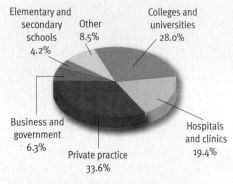

FIGURE 1.6

Employment of psychologists by setting.
The work settings in which psychologists are employed have become very diverse. Survey data on the primary employment setting of APA members indicate that one-third are in private practice (compared to 12% in 1976), while only 28% work in colleges and universities (compared to 47% in 1976). (Based on data published by the American Psychological Association).

publish research articles on psychology. Thus, by any standard of measurement—the number of people involved, the number of degrees granted, the number of studies conducted, the number of journals published—psychology is a healthy, growing field.

Psychology's vigorous presence in modern society is also demonstrated by the great variety of settings in which psychologists work. The distribution of psychologists employed in various categories of settings can be seen in **Figure 1.6**. They were once found almost exclusively in academia. However, today only about one-fourth of American psychologists work in colleges and universities. The remaining three-fourths work in hospitals, clinics, police departments, research institutes, government agencies, business and industry, schools, nursing homes, counseling centers, and private practice.

Clearly, contemporary psychology is a multifaceted field. This is especially apparent when we consider the many areas of specialization within psychology today. Let's look at the current areas of specialization in both the science and the profession of psychology.

Research Areas in Psychology

Most psychologists receive broad training that provides them with knowledge about many areas of psychology. However, they usually specialize when it comes to doing research. Such specialization is necessary because the subject matter of psychology has become so vast over the years. Today it is virtually impossible for anyone to stay abreast of the new research in all specialties. Specialization is also necessary because specific skills and training are required to do research in some areas.

The nine major research areas in modern psychology are (1) developmental psychology, (2) social psychology, (3) experimental psychology, (4) physiological psychology, (5) cognitive psychology, (6) personality, (7) psychometrics, (8) educational psychology, and (9) health psychology. **Figure 1.7** briefly describes each of these areas of inquiry.

CONCEPT CHECK 1.3

Understanding the Major Research Areas in Contemporary Psychology

Check your understanding of the various research areas in psychology reviewed in this chapter by indicating which type of psychologist would be most likely to perform each of the investigations described below. Choose from the following: (a) physiological psychology, (b) cognitive psychology, (c) developmental psychology, (d) psychometrics, and (e) personality. You'll find the answers in Appendix A at the back of the book.

_____ 1. Researchers interviewed the parents of 141 children (all born in 1956) every few months throughout childhood. Questions dealt with various aspects of the children's temperaments. The conclusion was that most children fall into one of three temperamental categories: "easy," "difficult," or "slow to warm up."

_____ 2. It was discovered that rats will work extremely hard (pressing a lever, for instance) to earn small amounts of electrical stimulation directed to specific areas of their brains. Research indicates that the human brain may also contain similar "pleasure centers."

_____ 3. The Sensation Seeking Scale (SSS) was developed to measure individual differences in the extent to which people prefer high or low levels of sensory stimulation. People such as skydivers tend to score high on the SSS, while someone whose idea of a good time is settling down with a good book would tend to score low.

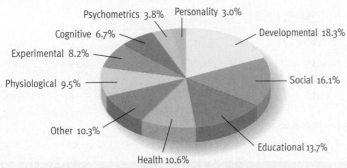

FIGURE 1.7

Major research areas in contemporary psychology. Most research psychologists specialize in one of the nine broad areas described here. The figures in the pie chart reflect the percentage of academic and research psychologists belonging to APA who identify each area as their primary interest. (Based on data published by the American Psychological Association).

Area	Focus of research
Developmental psychology	Looks at human development across the life span. Developmental psychology once focused primarily on child development, but today devotes a great deal of research to adolescence, adulthood, and old age.
Social psychology	Focuses on interpersonal behavior and the role of social forces in governing behavior. Typical topics include attitude formation, attitude change, prejudice, conformity, attraction, aggression, intimate relationships, and behavior in groups.
Educational psychology	Studies how people learn and the best ways to teach them. Examines curriculum design, teacher training, achievement testing, student motivation, classroom diversity, and other aspects of the educational process.
Health psychology	Focuses on how psychological factors relate to the promotion and maintenance of physical health and the causation, prevention, and treatment of illness.
Physiological psychology	Examines the influence of genetic factors on behavior and the role of the brain, nervous system, endocrine system, and bodily chemicals in the regulation of behavior.
Experimental psychology	Encompasses the traditional core of topics that psychology focused on heavily in its first half-century as a science: sensation, perception, learning, conditioning, motivation, and emotion. The name experimental psychology is somewhat misleading, as this is not the only area in which experiments are done. Psychologists working in all the areas listed here conduct experiments.
Cognitive psychology	Focuses on "higher" mental processes, such as memory, reasoning, information processing, language, problem solving, decision making, and creativity.
Psychometrics	Is concerned with the measurement of behavior and capacities, usually through the development of psychological tests. Psychometrics is involved with the design of tests to assess personality, intelligence, and a wide range of abilities. It is also concerned with the development of new techniques for statistical analysis.
Personality	Is interested in describing and understanding individuals' consistency in behavior, which represents their personality. This area of interest is also concerned with the factors that shape personality and with personality assessment.

Professional Specialties in Psychology

Applied psychology consists of four well-established areas of specialization. The four main professional specialties are (1) clinical psychology, (2) counseling psychology, (3) school psychology, and (4) industrial/organizational psychology. Descriptions of these specialties can be found in **Figure 1.8**. Clinical psychology is currently the most widely practiced professional specialty.

Some people are confused about the difference between clinical psychology and psychiatry. The confusion is understandable, as both clinical psychologists and psychiatrists are involved in analyzing and treating psychological disorders. Although some overlap exists between the two professions, the training and educational requirements

FIGURE 1.8

Principal professional specialties in contemporary psychology. Most psychologists who deliver professional services to the public specialize in one of the four areas described here. The figures in the pie chart reflect the percentage of APA members delivering professional services who identify each area as their chief specialty. (Based on data published by the American Psychological Association).

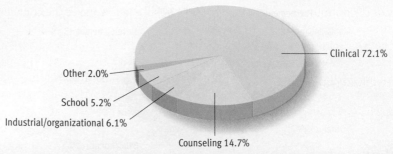

Clinical 72.1%

Other 2.0%

School 5.2%

Industrial/organizational 6.1%

Counseling 14.7%

Specialty	Focus of professional practice
Clinical psychology	Clinical psychologists are concerned with the evaluation, diagnosis, and treatment of individuals with psychological disorders, as well as treatment of less severe behavioral and emotional problems. Principal activities include interviewing clients, psychological testing, and providing group or individual psychotherapy.
Counseling psychology	Counseling psychology overlaps with clinical psychology in that specialists in both areas engage in similar activities—interviewing, testing, and providing therapy. However, counseling psychologists usually work with a somewhat different clientele, providing assistance to people struggling with everyday problems of moderate severity. Thus, they often specialize in family, marital, or career counseling.
Industrial and organizational psychology	Psychologists in this area perform a wide variety of tasks in the world of business and industry. These tasks include running human resources departments, working to improve staff morale and attitudes, striving to increase job satisfaction and productivity, examining organizational structures and procedures, and making recommendations for improvements.
School psychology	School psychologists strive to promote the cognitive, emotional, and social development of children in schools. They usually work in elementary or secondary schools, where they test and counsel children having difficulties in school and aid parents and teachers in solving school-related problems.

▶ REALITY CHECK

Misconception

Psychology and psychiatry are largely the same.

Reality

Psychiatry is a branch of medicine that has focused almost exclusively on the treatment of mental disorders. Psychology is an academic field that is vastly broader in scope, focusing on learning, perception, human development, memory, intelligence, and social behavior, although it does have a clinical arm concerned with mental disorders. Clinical psychologists and psychiatrists get very different kinds of training, earn different degrees, and tend to have different approaches to the treatment of mental illness (see Chapter 15).

for the two are quite different. Clinical psychologists go to graduate school to earn one of several doctoral degrees (Ph.D., Ed.D., or Psy.D.) in order to enjoy full status in their profession. Psychiatrists go to medical school for their postgraduate education, where they receive general training in medicine and earn an M.D. degree. They then specialize by completing residency training in psychiatry at a hospital. Clinical psychologists and psychiatrists also differ in the way they tend to approach the treatment of mental disorders, as we will see in Chapter 15. To summarize, ***psychiatry is a branch of medicine concerned with the diagnosis and treatment of psychological problems and disorders.*** In contrast, clinical psychology takes a nonmedical approach to such problems.

1.4

Key Learning Goals

- Understand the text's three unifying themes relating to psychology as a field of study.
- Understand the text's four unifying themes relating to psychology's subject matter.

1.4 SEVEN UNIFYING THEMES

The enormous breadth and diversity of psychology make it a challenging subject for the beginning student. In the pages ahead you will be introduced to many areas of research and a multitude of new ideas, concepts, and principles. Fortunately, not all ideas are created equal. Some are far more important than others. In this section, I will highlight seven fundamental themes that will reappear in a number of variations as we move from one area of psychology to another in this text. You have already met some of these key ideas in our review of psychology's past and present. Now we will isolate them and highlight their significance. In the remainder of the book these ideas serve as organizing themes to provide threads of continuity across chapters. They will also help you see the connections among the various areas of research in psychology.

In studying psychology, you are learning about both behavior and the scientific discipline that investigates it. Accordingly, our seven themes come in two sets. The first set consists of statements highlighting crucial aspects of psychology as a way of thinking and as a field of study. The second set consists of broad generalizations about psychology's subject matter: behavior and the cognitive and physiological processes that underlie it.

Themes Related to Psychology as a Field of Study

Looking at psychology as a field of study, we see three central ideas: (1) psychology is empirical, (2) psychology is theoretically diverse, and (3) psychology evolves in a sociohistorical context. Let's look at each of these ideas in more detail.

Theme 1: Psychology Is Empirical

Empiricism

Everyone tries to understand behavior. Most of us have developed our own personal answers to such questions as why some people are hard workers, why some are overweight, and why others stay in demeaning relationships. If all of us are amateur psychologists, what makes scientific psychology any different or better? The critical difference is that psychology is *empirical*.

What do we mean by empirical? *Empiricism* **is the premise that knowledge should be acquired through observation.** This premise is crucial to the scientific method that psychology embraced in the late 19th century. To say that psychology is empirical means that its conclusions are based on direct observation rather than on reasoning, speculation, traditional beliefs, or common sense. Psychologists are not content with having ideas that sound plausible. They conduct research to test their ideas. Is intelligence higher on the average in some social classes than in others? Are men more aggressive than women? Psychologists find a way to make direct, objective, and precise observations to answer such questions.

The empirical approach requires a certain attitude—a healthy brand of skepticism. Empiricism is a tough taskmaster. It demands data and documentation. Psychologists' commitment to empiricism means that they must learn to think critically about generalizations concerning behavior. If someone asserts that people tend to get depressed around Christmas, a psychologist is likely to ask, "How many people get depressed? In what population? In comparison to what baseline rate of depression? How is depression defined and measured?" Their skeptical attitude means that psychologists are trained to ask, "Where's the evidence? How do you know?" If psychology's empirical orientation rubs off on you (and I hope it does), you will be asking similar questions by the time you finish this book.

Theme 2: Psychology Is Theoretically Diverse

Theoretical Diversity

Although psychology is based on observation, a string of unrelated observations would not be terribly enlightening. Psychologists do not set out to collect isolated facts; they seek to explain and understand what they observe. To achieve these goals they must construct theories. **A** *theory* **is a system of interrelated ideas used to explain a set of observations.** In other words, a theory links apparently unrelated observations and tries to explain them. As an example, consider Sigmund Freud's observations about slips of the tongue, dreams, and psychological disturbances. On the surface, these observations appear unrelated. By devising the concept of the *unconscious,* Freud created a theory that links and explains these seemingly unrelated aspects of behavior.

Our review of psychology's past should have made one thing abundantly clear: Psychology is marked by theoretical diversity. Why do we have so many competing points of view? One reason is that no single theory can adequately explain everything that is known about behavior. Sometimes different theories focus on different aspects of behavior—that is, different collections of observations. Sometimes there is simply more than one way to look at something. Is the glass half empty or half full? Obviously, it is both. To take an example from another science, physicists wrestled for years with the nature of light. Is it a wave, or is it a particle? In the end, it proved useful to think of light sometimes as a wave and sometimes as a particle. Similarly, if a business executive lashes out at her employees with stinging criticism, is she releasing pent-up aggressive urges (a psychoanalytic view)? Is she making a habitual response to the stimulus of incompetent work (a behavioral view)? Or is she scheming to motivate her employees with "mind games" (a cognitive view)? In some cases, all three of these explanations might have some validity. In short, it is an oversimplification to expect that one view has to be right while all others are wrong. Life is rarely that simple.

Students are often troubled by psychology's many conflicting theories. They tend to view this diversity as a weakness. *However, contemporary psychologists increasingly recognize that theoretical diversity is a strength rather than a weakness.* As we proceed through this text, you will learn how clashing theories have often stimulated productive research. You will also see how approaching a problem from several theoretical perspectives can often provide a more complete understanding than could be achieved by any one perspective alone.

Sociohistorical
Context

Theme 3: Psychology Evolves in a Sociohistorical Context

Science is often seen as an "ivory tower" undertaking, isolated from the ebb and flow of everyday life. In reality, however, psychology and other sciences do not exist in a cultural vacuum. Dense interconnections exist between what happens in psychology and what happens in society at large (Altman, 1990; Danziger, 1990; Runyan, 2006). Trends, issues, and values in society influence psychology's evolution. Similarly, progress in psychology affects trends, issues, and values in society. To put it briefly, psychology develops in a *sociohistorical* (social and historical) context.

Psychology's past is filled with examples of how social trends have left their imprint on psychology. For example, Sigmund Freud's groundbreaking ideas emerged out of a specific sociohistorical context. Cultural values in Freud's era encouraged the suppression of sexuality. As a result, people tended to feel guilty about their sexual urges to a much greater extent than is common today. This situation clearly contributed to Freud's emphasis on unconscious sexual conflicts. As another example, consider how World War II sparked the rapid growth of psychology as a profession.

If we reverse our viewpoint, we can see that psychology has in turn left its mark on society. Consider, for instance, the pervasive role of mental testing in modern society. Your own career success may depend in part on how well you weave your way through a complex maze of intelligence and achievement tests made possible (to the regret of some) by research in psychology. As another example of psychology's impact on society, consider the influence that various theorists have had on parenting styles. Trends in childrearing practices have been shaped by the ideas of John B. Watson, Sigmund Freud, B. F. Skinner, and Carl Rogers—not to mention many more psychologists yet to be discussed. In short, society and psychology influence each other in complex ways. In the chapters to come, we will frequently have occasion to notice this dynamic relationship.

Themes Related to Psychology's Subject Matter

Looking at psychology's subject matter, we see four additional fundamental ideas: (4) behavior is determined by multiple causes, (5) behavior is shaped by cultural heritage, (6) heredity and environment jointly influence behavior; and (7) people's experience of the world is highly subjective.

Multifactorial
Causation

Theme 4: Behavior Is Determined by Multiple Causes

As psychology has matured, it has provided more and more information about the forces that govern behavior. This growing knowledge has led to a deeper appreciation of a simple but important fact: Behavior is exceedingly complex, and most aspects of behavior are determined by multiple causes.

Although the complexity of behavior may seem self-evident, people usually think in terms of single causes. Thus, they offer explanations such as "Andrea flunked out of school because she is lazy." Or they assert that "teenage pregnancies are increasing because of all the sex in the media." Single-cause explanations are sometimes accurate insofar as they go, but they are usually incomplete. In general, psychologists find that behavior is governed by a complex network of interacting factors. This idea is referred to as the *multifactorial causation of behavior.*

As a simple illustration, consider the multiple factors that might influence your performance in your introductory psychology course. Relevant personal factors might include your overall intelligence, your reading ability, your memory skills, your motivation, and your study skills. In addition, your grade could be affected by numerous situational factors, including whether you like your psychology professor, whether you like your assigned text, whether the class meets at a good time for you, whether your work schedule is light or heavy, and whether you're having any personal problems. As you proceed through this book, you will learn that complexity of causation is the rule rather than the exception. If we expect to understand behavior, we usually have to take into account multiple determinants.

Theme 5: Behavior Is Shaped by Cultural Heritage

Cultural Heritage

Among the multiple determinants of human behavior, cultural factors are particularly prominent. Just as psychology evolves in a sociohistorical context, so, too, do individuals. Our cultural backgrounds exert considerable influence over our behavior. As Markus and Hamedani (2007) put it, "The option of being *a*social or *a*cultural—that is, living as a neutral being who is not bound to particular practices and socioculturally structured ways of behaving— is not available. People eat, sleep, work, and relate to one another in culture-specific ways" (p. 5). What is *culture?* Theorists have argued about the exact details of how to define culture for over a century, and the precise boundaries of the concept remain a little fuzzy (Matsumoto & Yoo, 2006). Broadly speaking, **culture refers to the widely shared customs, beliefs, values, norms, institutions, and other products of a community that are transmitted socially across generations.** Culture is a broad construct, encompassing everything from a society's legal system to its assumptions about family roles, from its dietary habits to its political ideals, from its technology to its attitudes about time, from its modes of dress to its spiritual beliefs, and from its art and music to its unspoken rules about sexual liaisons.

Much of our cultural heritage is invisible (Brislin, 2000). Assumptions, ideals, attitudes, beliefs, and unspoken rules exist in people's minds and may not be readily apparent to outsiders. Moreover, because our cultural background is widely shared, we feel little need to discuss it with others, and we often take it for granted. For example, you probably don't spend much time thinking about the importance of living in rectangular rooms, trying to minimize body odor, limiting yourself to one spouse at a time, or using credit cards to obtain material goods and services. We often fail to appreciate its influence, but our cultural heritage has a pervasive impact on our thoughts, feelings, and behavior (Matsumoto & Juang, 2008; Triandis, 2007).

Although the influence of culture is everywhere, generalizations about cultural groups must always be tempered by the realization that great diversity exists within any society or ethnic group (Markus & Hamedani, 2007). Researchers may be able to pinpoint genuinely useful insights about Ethiopian, Korean American, or Ukrainian culture, for example, but it would be foolish to assume that all Ethiopians, Korean Americans, or Ukrainians exhibit identical behavior. It is also important

Cultural background has an enormous influence on people's behavior, shaping everything from modes of dress to sexual values and norms. Increased global interdependence brings more and more people into contact with cultures other than their own. This increased exposure to diverse cultures only serves to underscore the importance of cultural factors.

Universal Images Group Limited/Alamy

to realize that *both differences and similarities in behavior occur across cultures.* As we will see repeatedly, psychological processes are characterized by both cultural variance and invariance. Caveats aside, if we hope to achieve a sound understanding of human behavior, we need to consider cultural determinants.

Theme 6: Heredity and Environment Jointly Influence Behavior

Are we who we are—athletic or artistic, quick-tempered or calm, shy or outgoing, energetic or laid back—because of our genetic inheritance or because of our upbringing? This question about the importance of nature versus nurture, or heredity versus environment, has been asked in one form or another since ancient times. Historically, the nature versus nurture question was framed as an all-or-none proposition. In other words, theorists argued that personal traits and abilities are governed entirely by heredity or entirely by environment. John B. Watson, for instance, asserted that personality and ability depend almost exclusively on an individual's environment. In contrast, Sir Francis Galton, a pioneer in mental testing, maintained that personality and ability depend almost entirely on genetic inheritance.

Today, most psychologists agree that heredity and environment are both important. A century of research has shown that genetics and experience jointly influence individuals' intelligence, temperament, personality, and susceptibility to many psychological disorders (Manuck & McCaffery, 2014; Rutter, 2012). If we ask whether people are born or made, psychology's answer is "Both." This response does not mean that nature versus nurture is a dead issue. Lively debate about the *relative influence* of genetics and experience continues unabated. Furthermore, psychologists are actively seeking to understand the complex ways in which genetic inheritance and experience interact to mold behavior.

Theme 7: People's Experience of the World Is Subjective

Our experience of the world is highly subjective. Even elementary perception—for example, of sights and sounds—is not a passive process. We actively process incoming stimulation, selectively focusing on some aspects of that stimulation while ignoring others. Moreover, we impose organization on the stimuli that we pay attention to. These tendencies combine to make perception personalized and subjective.

The subjectivity of perception was demonstrated nicely in a study by Hastorf and Cantril (1954). They showed students at Princeton and Dartmouth universities a film of a hotly contested football game between the two rival schools. The students were told to watch for rules infractions. Both groups saw the same film, but the Princeton students "saw" the Dartmouth players engage in twice as many infractions as the Dartmouth students "saw," and vice versa. The investigators concluded that the game "actually was many different games and that each version of the events that transpired was just as 'real' to a particular person as other versions were to other people" (Hastorf & Cantril, 1954). This study showed how people sometimes see what they *want* to see. Other studies have demonstrated that people also tend to see what they *expect* to see (Kelley, 1950).

Human subjectivity is precisely what the scientific method is designed to counteract. In using the scientific approach, psychologists strive to make their observations as objective as possible. Left to their own subjective experience, people might still believe that the Earth is flat and that the Sun revolves around it. Thus, psychologists are committed to the scientific approach because they believe it is the most reliable route to accurate knowledge.

Now that you have been introduced to the text's organizing themes, let's turn to an example of how psychological research can be applied to the challenges of everyday life. In our first Personal Application, we'll focus on a subject that should be highly relevant to you: how to be a successful student. In the Critical Thinking Application that follows it, we discuss the nature and importance of critical thinking skills.

David McNew/Getty Images

Nature or nurture? As a young actress, Lindsay Lohan appeared to have a wonderful career ahead of her. But then it began unraveling, as she battled alcohol and drug problems, started exhibiting erratic behavior, and became embroiled in a host of legal problems. What might account for this deterioration? Heredity? Environment? Or some combination of the two? One could point to experience, as she came from a broken home that was apparently riddled with parental conflict. But one could also speculate about the role of genetics, as her father has had his own issues with alcohol, and he has indicated that his father was an alcoholic. It is often very difficult to tease apart the intertwined contributions of heredity and environment. In any event, the nature versus nurture question comes up endlessly in efforts to understand behavior.

1.5 PERSONAL APPLICATION
Improving Academic Performance

1.5

Key Learning Goals
- Discuss some strategies for promoting adequate study, improving reading comprehension, and getting more out of lectures.

Answer the following "true" or "false."

____ 1 If you have a professor who delivers chaotic, hard-to-follow lectures, there is little point in attending class.

____ 2 Cramming the night before an exam is an efficient method of study.

____ 3 In taking lecture notes, you should try to be a "human tape recorder" (that is, write down everything your professor says).

____ 4 You should never change your answers to multiple-choice questions, because your first hunch is your best hunch.

All of the above statements are false. If you answered them all correctly, you may have already acquired the kinds of skills and habits that facilitate academic success. If so, however, you are not typical. Today, many students enter college with poor study skills and habits, and it's not entirely their fault. Our educational system generally provides minimal instruction on good study techniques. Hence, it is not surprising that a recent review of research reported that a great many students embrace flawed models of how they learn and remember, waste precious time on activities that do not promote effective learning, and routinely misjudge their mastery of material (Bjork, Dunlosky, & Kornell, 2013). In this first Personal Application, I will try to remedy this situation to some extent by reviewing some insights that psychology offers on how to improve academic performance. We will discuss how to promote better study habits, how to enhance reading efforts, and how to get more out of lectures. You may also want to jump ahead and read the Personal Application for Chapter 7, which focuses on how to improve everyday memory.

Developing Sound Study Habits

People tend to assume that academic performance in college is largely determined by students' intelligence or general mental ability. This belief is supported by the fact that college admissions tests (the SAT and ACT), which basically assess general cognitive ability, predict college grades fairly well (Berry & Sackett, 2009; Kobrin et al., 2008). What is far less well known, however, is that measures of study skills, habits, and attitudes also predict college grades pretty well. In a large-scale review of 344 independent samples consisting of over 72,000 students, Crede and Kuncel (2008) reported that aggregate measures of study skills and habits predicted college grades almost as well as admissions tests, and that these factors accounted for variability in performance that the admissions tests could not account for. In other words, this massive review of evidence found that study habits are almost as influential as ability in determining college success. The practical meaning of this finding is that most students probably underestimate the importance of their study skills. And bear in mind that whereas most adults probably cannot increase their mental ability much, they can usually enhance their study habits considerably.

In any event, the first step toward effective study habits is to face up to the reality that studying usually involves hard work. You don't have to feel guilty if you don't look forward to studying. Most students don't. Once you accept the premise that studying doesn't come naturally, it should be apparent that you need to set up an organized program to promote adequate study. According to Siebert and Karr (2003), such a program should include the following considerations:

1. *Set up a schedule for studying.* If you wait until the urge to study strikes you, you may still be waiting when the exam rolls around. Thus, it is important to allocate definite times for studying. Review your various time obligations (work, chores, and so on) and figure out in advance when you can study. When allotting certain times to studying, keep in mind that you need to be wide awake and alert. Be realistic about how long you can study at one time before you wear down from fatigue. Allow time for study breaks—they can revive sagging concentration.

It's important to write down your study schedule. A written schedule serves as a reminder and increases your commitment to following it. You should begin by setting up a general schedule for the quarter or semester, like the one in **Figure 1.9**. Then, at the beginning of each week, plan the specific assignments that you intend to work on during each study session. This approach to scheduling should help you avoid cramming for exams at the last minute. Cramming is an ineffective study strategy for most students (Underwood, 1961; Wong, 2006; Zechmeister & Nyberg, 1982). It will strain your memorization capabilities, can tax your energy level, and may stoke the fires of test anxiety.

In planning your weekly schedule, try to avoid the tendency to put off working on major tasks such as term papers and reports. Time-management experts, such as Alan Lakein (1996), point out that many of us tend to tackle simple, routine tasks first, saving larger tasks for later when we supposedly will have more time. This common tendency leads many of us to repeatedly delay working on major assignments until it's too late to do a good job. You can avoid this trap by breaking major assignments down into smaller component tasks that can be scheduled individually.

2. *Find a place to study where you can concentrate.* Where you study is also important. The key is to find a place where distractions are likely to be minimal. Most people cannot study effectively while texting their friends, surfing the Internet,

Weekly Activity Schedule							
	Monday	Tuesday	Wednesday	Thursday	Friday	Saturday	Sunday
8 A.M.						Work	
9 A.M.	History	Study	History	Study	History		
10 A.M.	Psychology	French	Psychology	French	Psychology		
11 A.M.	Study	↓	Study	↓	Study		
Noon	Math	Study	Math	Study	Math	↓	Work
1 P.M.							
2 P.M.	Study	English	Study	English	Study		
3 P.M.	↓	↓	↓	↓	↓		↓
4 P.M.							
5 P.M.							
6 P.M.	Work	Study	Study	Work			Work
7 P.M.							
8 P.M.							
9 P.M.	↓	↓	↓				↓
10 P.M.	↓			↓			

FIGURE 1.9

One student's general activity schedule for a semester. Each week the student fills in the specific assignments to work on during each study period.

watching TV, or listening to others' conversation. Students routinely claim that they can multitask in these situations, but the research indicates that students tend to greatly overestimate their ability to multitask effectively (Chew, 2014; Ravizza, Hambrick, & Fenn, 2014).

3. *Reward your studying.* One reason it is so difficult to be motivated to study regularly is that the payoffs often lie in the distant future. The ultimate reward, a degree, may be years away. Even more short-term rewards, such as an A in the course, may be weeks or months away.

To combat this problem, it helps to give yourself immediate, tangible rewards for studying, such as a snack, TV show, or phone call to a friend. Thus, you should set realistic study goals for yourself and then reward yourself when you meet them. The systematic manipulation of rewards involves harnessing the principles of behavior modification described by B. F. Skinner and other behavioral psychologists. These principles are covered in the Chapter 6 Personal Application.

Improving Your Reading

Much of your study time is spent reading and absorbing information. The keys to improving reading comprehension are to preview reading assignments section by section, work hard to actively process the meaning of the information, strive to identify the key ideas of each paragraph, and carefully review these key ideas after each section. Modern textbooks often contain a variety of learning aids that you can use to improve your reading. If a book provides a chapter outline or learning objectives, don't ignore them. These *advance organizers* can encourage deeper processing and enhance your encoding of information (Marsh & Butler, 2013). In other words, they can help you recognize the important points in the chapter. *Graphic organizers* (such as the Concept Charts available at the end of each chapter) can also enhance understanding of text material (Nist & Holschuh, 2000). A lot of effort and thought go into formulating these and other textbook learning aids. It is wise to take advantage of them.

Another important issue related to textbook reading is whether and how to mark up one's reading assignments. Many students deceive themselves into thinking that they are studying by running a marker through a few sentences here and there in their text. If they do so without thoughtful selectivity, they are simply turning a textbook into a coloring book. This situation probably explains why a recent review of the evidence on highlighting reported that it appears to have limited value (Dunlosky et al., 2013). That said, the review also noted that the value of highlighting

People tend to assume that success in college depends on one's intelligence. Academic ability *is* important, but research indicates that sound study skills and habits are nearly as important.

probably depends on the skill with which it is executed. Consistent with this conclusion, other experts have asserted that highlighting textbook material *is* a useful strategy—*if* students are reasonably effective in focusing on the main ideas in the material and if they subsequently review what they have highlighted (Caverly, Orlando, & Mullen, 2000; Hayati & Shariatifar, 2009).

In theory, when executed effectively, highlighting should foster active reading, improve reading comprehension, and reduce the amount of material that one has to review later (Van Blerkom, 2012). The key to effective text marking is to identify (and highlight) only the main ideas, key supporting details, and technical terms (Daiek & Anter, 2004). Most textbooks are carefully crafted such that every paragraph has a purpose for being there. Try to find the sentence or two that best captures the purpose of each paragraph. Text marking is a delicate balancing act. If you highlight too little of the content, you are not identifying enough of the key ideas. But if you highlight too much of the content, you probably are not engaging in active reading and you are not going to succeed in making the important information stand out (Dunlosky et al., 2013). Overmarking appears to undermine the utility of highlighting more than undermarking.

Getting More out of Lectures

Although lectures are sometimes boring and tedious, it is a simple fact that poor class attendance is associated with poor grades. For example, in one study, Lindgren (1969) found that absences from class were much more common among "unsuccessful" students (grade average C− or below) than among "successful" students (grade average B or above). Even

when you have an instructor who delivers hard-to-follow lectures, it is still important to go to class. If nothing else, you can get a feel for how the instructor thinks, which can help you anticipate the content of exams and respond in the manner expected by your professor.

Fortunately, most lectures are reasonably coherent. Studies indicate that attentive note taking *is* associated with enhanced learning and performance in college classes (Marsh & Butler, 2013; Titsworth & Kiewra, 2004). However, research also shows that many students' lecture notes are surprisingly incomplete, with the average student often recording less than 40% of the crucial ideas in a lecture (Armbruster, 2000). Thus, the key to getting more out of lectures is to stay motivated, stay attentive, and expend the effort to make your notes as complete as possible. By the way, recent research has demonstrated that surfing the Internet while in class undermines learning and leads to lower performance on exams, regardless of one's academic ability (Ravizza et al., 2014). Another study found that students sitting nearby who could see a peer surfing the Internet in class also were distracted and earned lower grades (Sana, Weston, & Cepeda, 2013).

Books on study skills (Longman & Atkinson, 2005; McWhorter, 2007) offer a number of suggestions on how to take good-quality lecture notes, some of which are summarized here:

- Extracting information from lectures requires *active listening*. Focus full attention on the speaker. Try to anticipate what's coming and search for deeper meanings.
- When course material is especially complex, it is a good idea to prepare for the lecture by *reading ahead* on the scheduled subject in your text. Then you have less new information to digest.

- You are not supposed to be a human tape recorder. Insofar as possible, try to write down the lecturer's thoughts *in your own words*. Doing so forces you to organize the ideas in a way that makes sense to you.
- In taking notes, pay attention to clues about what is most important. These clues may range from subtle hints, such as an instructor repeating a point, to not-so-subtle hints, such as an instructor saying "You'll run into this again."
- In delivering their lectures most professors follow an organized outline, which they may or may not share with the class (on the blackboard or via a presentation tool, such as PowerPoint). Insofar as you can decipher the outline of a lecture, try to organize your notes accordingly. When you go back to review your notes later, they will make more sense and it should be easier to identify the most important ideas.
- *Asking questions* during lectures can be helpful. Doing so keeps you actively involved in the lecture and allows you to clarify points that you may have misunderstood. Many students are more bashful about asking questions than they should be. They don't realize that most professors welcome questions.

In summary, sound study skills and habits are crucial to academic success. Intelligence alone won't do the job (although it certainly helps). Good academic skills do not develop overnight. They are acquired gradually, so be patient with yourself. Fortunately, tasks such as reading textbooks, writing papers, and taking tests get easier with practice. Ultimately, I think you'll find that the rewards—knowledge, a sense of accomplishment, and progress toward a degree—are worth the effort.

1.6

Key Learning Goals
- Explain the nature of critical thinking, and evaluate evolutionary explanations for gender differences in spatial abilities.

1.6 CRITICAL THINKING APPLICATION
Developing Critical Thinking Skills: An Introduction

If you ask any group of professors, parents, employers, or politicians, "What is the most important outcome of an education?" the most popular answer is likely to be "the development of the ability to think critically." *Critical thinking* **is purposeful, reasoned, goal-directed thinking that involves solving problems, formulating inferences, working with probabilities, and making carefully thought-out decisions.** Critical thinking is the use of cognitive skills and strategies that increase the probability of a desirable outcome. Such outcomes would include good career choices, effective decisions in the workplace, wise investments, and so forth. In the long run, critical thinkers should have more desirable outcomes than people who are not skilled in critical thinking (Halpern, 1998, 2014). Here are some of the skills exhibited by critical thinkers:

- They understand and use the principles of scientific investigation. (How can the effectiveness of punishment as a disciplinary procedure be determined?)
- They apply the rules of formal and informal logic. (If most people disapprove of sex sites on the Internet, why are these sites so popular?)
- They think effectively in terms of probabilities. (What is the likelihood of being able to predict who will commit a violent crime?)
- They carefully evaluate the quality of information. (Can I trust the claims made by this politician?)
- They analyze arguments for the soundness of the conclusions. (Does the rise in drug use mean a stricter drug policy is needed?).

The topic of thinking has a long history in psychology. It dates back to Wilhelm Wundt in the 19th century. Modern cognitive psychologists have found that a useful model of critical thinking has at least two components: It consists of knowledge of the skills of critical thinking—the *cognitive component*—as well as the attitude or disposition of a critical thinker—the *emotional* or *affective component*. Both are needed for effective critical thinking.

The Skills and Attitudes of Critical Thinking

Instruction in critical thinking is based on two assumptions: (1) a set of skills or strategies exists that students can learn to recognize and apply in appropriate contexts, and (2) if the skills are applied appropriately, students will become more effective thinkers (Halpern, 2007). Critical thinking skills that would be useful in any context might include understanding how reasons and evidence support or refute conclusions; distinguishing among facts, opinions, and reasoned judgments; using principles of likelihood and uncertainty when thinking about probabilistic events; generating multiple solutions to problems and working systematically toward a desired goal; and understanding how causation is determined. This list provides some typical examples of what is meant by the term *critical thinking skills*. Because these skills are useful in a wide variety of contexts, they are sometimes called *transcontextual skills*.

It is of little use to know the skills of critical thinking if you are unwilling to exert the hard mental work to use them or if you have a sloppy or careless attitude toward thinking. A critical thinker is willing to plan, flexible in thinking, persistent, able to admit mistakes and make corrections, and mindful of the thinking process. The use of the word *critical* represents the notion of a critique or evaluation of thinking processes and outcomes. It is not meant to be negative (as in a "critical person") but rather is intended to convey that critical thinkers are vigilant about their thinking (Riggio & Halpern, 2006).

The Need to Teach Critical Thinking

Decades of research on instruction in critical thinking have shown that the skills and attitudes of critical thinking need to be deliberately and consciously taught, because they often do not develop by themselves with standard instruction in a content area (Nisbett, 1993). For this reason, each chapter in this text ends with a "Critical Thinking Application." The material presented in each of these Critical Thinking Applications relates to the chapter topics, but the focus is on how to think about a particular issue, line of research, or controversy. Because the emphasis is on the thinking process, you may be asked to consider conflicting interpretations of data, judge the credibility of information sources, or generate your own testable hypotheses. The specific critical thinking skills highlighted in each Application are summarized in a table so that they are easily identified. Some of the skills will show up in multiple chapters. The goal is to help you spontaneously select the appropriate critical thinking skills when you encounter new information. Repeated practice with selected skills across chapters should help you develop this ability.

An Example

As explained in the main body of the chapter, *evolutionary psychology* is emerging as an influential school of thought. To show you how critical thinking skills can be applied to psychological issues, let's examine the evolutionary explanation of gender differences in spatial talents and then use some critical thinking strategies to evaluate this explanation.

On the average, males tend to perform slightly better than females on most visual-spatial tasks, especially tasks involving mental rotation of images and navigation in space (Halpern, 2012; Clint et al., 2012; see **Figure 1.10**). Evolutionary theorists maintain that these gender differences

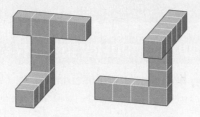

Can the set of blocks on the left be rotated to match the set at the right?

FIGURE 1.10

An example of a spatial task involving mental rotation.
Spatial reasoning tasks can be divided into a variety of sub-types. Studies indicate that males perform slightly better than females on most, but not all, spatial tasks. The tasks on which males are superior often involve mentally rotating objects, such as in the problem shown here, for which the answer is no.

SOURCE: From Kalat, J. W. (2013). *Biological psychology* (11 ed.). Belmont, CA: Cengage/Wadsworth. Reproduced by permission. www.cengage.com/permissions

originated in human evolution as a result of the sex-based division of labor in ancient hunting-and-gathering societies (Silverman, Choi, & Peters, 2007). According to this analysis, males' superiority in mental rotation and navigation developed because the chore of *hunting* was largely assigned to men over the course of human history. These skills would have facilitated success on hunting trips (by helping men to traverse long distances, aim projectiles at prey, and so forth) and thus would have been favored by natural selection. In contrast, women in ancient societies generally had responsibility for *gathering* food rather than hunting it. This was an efficient division of labor because women spent much of their adult lives pregnant, nursing, or caring for the young. Therefore, they could not travel long distances. Thus, Silverman and Eals (1992) hypothesized that females ought to be superior to males on spatial skills that would have facilitated gathering, such as memory for locations. This is exactly what they found in a series of four studies. Thus, evolutionary psychologists explain gender differences in spatial

ability—like other aspects of human behavior—in terms of how such abilities evolved to meet the adaptive pressures faced by our ancestors.

How can you critically evaluate these claims? If your first thought was that you need more information, good for you. You are already showing an aptitude for critical thinking. Some additional information about gender differences in cognitive abilities is presented in Chapter 10 of this text. You also need to develop the habit of asking good questions, such as, "Are there alternative explanations for these results? Are there contradictory data?" Let's briefly consider each of these questions.

Are there alternative explanations for gender differences in spatial skills? Well, there certainly are other potential explanations for males' superiority on most spatial tasks. For example, we could attribute this finding to the gender-typed activities that males are encouraged to engage in more than females, such as playing with building blocks, Lego sets, Lincoln Logs, and various types of construction sets, as well as a host of spatially oriented video games. These gender-typed activities appear to provide boys with more practice than girls on most types of spatial tasks (Voyer, Nolan, & Voyer, 2000), and experience with spatial activities appears to enhance spatial skills (Feng, Spence, & Pratt, 2007). Another possible explanation was recently proposed by Clint and colleagues (2012). They note that males' advantage in spatial navigation is seen in many animal species that do not exhibit the sex-based division of labor

for hunting and gathering seen in humans. Hence, they marshall evidence for a simpler explanation, arguing that males' spatial superiority is simply a side effect of males' higher testosterone levels across a variety of species. If we can explain gender differences in spatial abilities in terms of disparities in the everyday activities of males and females, or simple hormone levels, we may have no need to appeal to natural selection.

Are there data that run counter to the evolutionary explanation for modern gender differences in spatial skills? Again, the answer is yes. One recent study failed to find gender differences in spatial navigation in a natural, real-world environment, leading the researchers to question whether traditional laboratory measures of spatial abilities are accurate indicators of the wayfinding that would have been critical to hunting (Burke, Kandler, & Good, 2012). Other scholars who have studied hunting-and-gathering societies suggest that women often traveled long distances to gather food and that women were often involved in hunting (Adler, 1993). Moreover—think about it—men on long hunting trips obviously needed to develop a good memory for locations or they might never have returned home. So, there is room for some argument about exactly what kinds of adaptive pressures males and females faced in ancient hunting-and-gathering societies.

Thus, you can see how considering alternative explanations and contradictory evidence weakens the evolutionary explanation of gender differences in spatial abilities. The questions we raised about alternative explanations and contradictory data are two generic critical thinking questions that can be asked in a wide variety of contexts. The answers to these questions do *not* prove that evolutionary psychologists are wrong in their explanation of gender differences in visual-spatial skills. They do, however, *weaken* the evolutionary explanation. In thinking critically about psychological issues, you will see that it makes more sense to talk about the *relative strength* of an argument, as opposed to whether an argument is right or wrong, because we will be dealing with complex issues that rarely lend themselves to being correct or incorrect.

TABLE 1.2 **Critical Thinking Skills Discussed in This Application**

Skill	Description
Looking for alternative explanations for findings and events	In evaluating explanations, the critical thinker explores whether there are other explanations that could also account for the findings or events under scrutiny.
Looking for contradictory evidence	In evaluating the evidence presented on an issue, the critical thinker attempts to look for contradictory evidence that may have been left out of the debate.

PSYCHOLOGY'S EARLY HISTORY

A new science is born

- Philosophy and physiology are psychology's intellectual parents.
- Psychology's founder was Wilhelm Wundt, who set up the first research lab in 1879 in Germany.
- Wundt argued that psychology should be the scientific study of consciousness.

The battle of the schools begins

- Advocates of *structuralism* argued that psychology should use introspection to analyze consciousness into its basic elements.
- Advocates of *functionalism*, such as William James, argued that psychology should investigate the purposes (or functions) of consciousness.
- Functionalism had a more lasting impact on psychology because it fostered the emergence of behaviorism and applied psychology.

Freud focuses on unconscious forces

- Sigmund Freud's views were controversial but gradually became influential.
- *Psychoanalytic theory* emphasizes unconscious determinants of behavior and the importance of sexuality.
- According to Freud, the *unconscious* consists of thoughts that one is not aware of but that still influence one's behavior.

Behaviorism debuts

- *Behaviorism*, founded by John B. Watson, asserted that psychology should study only observable behavior.

- Behaviorism gradually took hold, and psychology became the scientific study of *behavior* (instead of *consciousness*).
- Behaviorists stressed the importance of environment over heredity, and pioneered animal research.

© Vasiliy Koval/Shutterstock.com

Behaviorism flourishes with the work of Skinner

- Boosted by the research of B. F. Skinner, behaviorism reached its peak of influence in the 1950s.
- Like Waston, Skinner emphasized animal rresearch, a strict focus on observable behavior, and the importance of the environment.
- Skinner generated controversy by arguing that free will is an illusion.

The humanists revolt

- Finding both behaviorism and psychoanalysis unappealing, advocates of *humanism*, such as Carl Rogers and Abraham Maslow, began to gain influence in the 1950s.
- Humanists emphasize the unique qualities of human behavior and the irrelevance of animal research.
- Humanists take an optimistic view of human nature, stressing humans' freedom and potential for growth.

© Phil Date/Shutterstock.com

PSYCHOLOGY'S MODERN HISTORY

Psychology becomes a profession

- Professional psychological services to the public were rare in first half of the 20th century.
- However, stimulated by the demands of World War II, *clinical psychology* grew rapidly as a profession, starting in the 1950s.
- Today, psychology includes many professional specialties, such as school psychology, industrial/organizational psychology, and counseling psychology.

Cognition and physiology resurface

- In its early days, psychology emphasized the study of consciousness and physiology, but these topics languished as behaviorism grew dominant.
- During the 1950s and 1960s, advances in research on mental and physiological processes led to renewed interest in cognition and the biological bases of behavior.

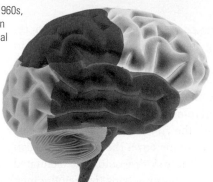

© Dim Dimich/Shutterstock.com

Interest in cultural factors grows

- In the 1980s, Western psychologists developed an increased interest in how culture influences behavior.
- This trend was stimulated by the increased cultural diversity in Western societies and by growing global interdependence.

Evolutionary psychology gains prominence

- In the 1990s, *evolutionary psychology* emerged as a major new theoretical perspective.
- Evolutionary psychology's premise is that behavior patterns in a species are the product of evolution, just like anatomical characteristics.
- Evolutionary psychologists argue that *natural selection* favors behaviors that enhance an organism's reproductive success.

© Eric Gevaert/Shutterstock.com

Psychology moves in a positive direction

- Arguing that psychology had historically focused too much on pathology and suffering, Martin Seligman launched the *positive psychology* movement in the late 1990s.
- Positive psychology uses theory and research to understand the adaptive, creative, and fulfilling aspects of human experience.

PSYCHOLOGY TODAY

Psychology is the science that studies behavior and the physiological and cognitive processes that underlie behavior, and it is the profession that applies this science to practical problems.

Professional specialties

- Clinical psychology
- Counseling psychology
- School psychology
- Industrial/organizational psychology

Research specialties

- Developmental psychology
- Social psychology
- Experimental psychology
- Physiological psychology
- Cognitive psychology
- Personality
- Psychometrics
- Educational psychology
- Health psychology

© iStockphoto.com/Franckreporter

APPLICATIONS

- To foster sound study habits, you should devise a written study schedule, find a place to study where you can concentrate, and use active reading techniques to select the most important ideas from the material you read.

- Good note taking depends on active listening techniques and recording ideas in your own words.

- Critical thinking is the use of cognitive skills and strategies that increase the probability of a desirable outcome.

KEY THEMES

Themes related to psychology as a field of study

Psychology is empirical—it is based on objective observations made through research.

Psychology is theoretically diverse—a variety of perspectives are needed to fully understand behavior.

Psychology evolves in a sociohistorical context—dense connections exist between what happens in psychology and what happens in society.

Themes related to psychology's subject matter

Behavior is determined by multiple causes—complex causation is the rule, and single-cause explanations are usually incomplete.

Behavior is shaped by cultural heritage—cultural factors exert influence over most aspects of behavior.

Heredity and environment jointly influence behavior—nature and nurture interactively shape most behavioral traits.

People's experience of the world is highly subjective—people tend to see what they expect to see and what they want to see.

CHAPTER 2

THE RESEARCH ENTERPRISE IN PSYCHOLOGY

Ann Cutting/The Image Bank/Getty Images

Themes in this Chapter

Empiricism   Subjectivity of Experience

30

- Does sleeping less than 7 hours a day reduce how long you will live?
- Do violent video games make people more aggressive?
- Can you make better decisions by not deliberating about them?
- Do men tend to overestimate women's interest in sexual liaisons?
- Do IQ scores predict how long people will live?

Questions, questions, questions—everyone has questions about behavior. Investigating these questions is what psychology is all about.

Some of these questions pop up in everyday life. Many a parent, for example, has wondered whether violent video games could have a harmful effect on their children's behavior. Other questions explored by psychologists might not occur to most people. For example, you may never have wondered what effects your sleeping habits or IQ could have on your life expectancy or whether women can judge men's testosterone levels. Of course, now that you've been exposed to these questions, you may be curious about the answers!

In the course of this book, you'll find out what psychologists have learned about the five questions asked above. Right now I want to call your attention to the most basic question of all—namely, how should we go about investigating questions like these? How do we find answers that are accurate and trustworthy?

As noted in Chapter 1, *psychology is empirical.* Psychologists are committed to addressing questions about behavior through formal, systematic observation. This commitment to the empirical method is what makes psychology a scientific endeavor. Many people may have beliefs about the effects of playing violent video games based on personal opinion, a feeling of aversion toward violence, a generally permissive attitude toward children's games, anecdotal reports from parents, or other sources. As scientists, however, psychologists withhold judgment on questions like these until they have objective evidence based on valid, reproducible studies.

In their scientific studies psychologists rely on a large toolkit of research methods because different kinds of questions call for different strategies of investigation. In this chapter, you'll learn about some of the principal methods used by psychologists in their research.

We'll begin our introduction to the research enterprise in psychology by examining the scientific approach to the study of behavior. From there we'll move to the specific research methods that psychologists use most frequently. Although scientific methods have stood the test of time, individual scientists are human and fallible. For this reason we'll conclude our discussion with a look at some common flaws in research. This section alone can make you a more skilled evaluator of claims that are said to be based on psychological studies. Then, in the Personal Application, you'll learn how to find and read journal articles that report on research. Finally, in the Critical Thinking Application, we'll examine the perils of a type of evidence people are exposed to all the time—anecdotal evidence.

2.1 LOOKING FOR LAWS: THE SCIENTIFIC APPROACH TO BEHAVIOR

Key Learning Goals

- Describe the goals of the scientific enterprise, and clarify the relationships among theory, hypotheses, and research.
- Identify the steps in a scientific investigation, and list the advantages of the scientific approach.

Whether the object of study is gravitational forces or people's behavior under stress, *the scientific approach assumes that events are governed by some lawful order.* As scientists, psychologists assume that behavior is governed by laws or principles, just as the movement of the Earth around the Sun is governed by the laws of gravity. The behavior of living creatures may not seem as lawful and predictable as the "behavior" of planets. However, the scientific enterprise is based on the belief that there are consistencies or laws that can be uncovered. Fortunately, the value of applying this fundamental assumption has been supported by the discovery of a great many such consistencies in behavior, some of which provide the subject matter for this text.

Goals of the Scientific Enterprise

Psychologists and other scientists share three sets of interrelated goals: measurement and description, understanding and prediction, and application and control.

1. *Measurement and description.* Science's commitment to observation requires that researchers figure out a way to measure the phenomenon under study. For example, a psychologist could not investigate whether men are more or less sociable than women without first developing some means of measuring sociability. Thus, the first goal of psychology is to develop measurement techniques that make it possible to describe behavior clearly and precisely.

2. *Understanding and prediction.* A higher-level goal of science is understanding. Scientists believe that they understand events when they can explain the reasons for their occurrence. To evaluate such understanding, scientists make and test predictions called hypotheses. **A *hypothesis* is a tentative statement about the relationship between two or more variables. *Variables* are any measurable conditions, events, characteristics, or behaviors that are controlled or observed in a study.** If we predicted that putting people under time pressure would lower the accuracy of their time perception, the variables in our study would be time pressure and accuracy of time perception.

3. *Application and control.* Ultimately, most scientists hope that the information they gather will be of some practical value in helping to solve everyday problems. Once people understand a phenomenon, they can often exert more control over it. Today, the profession of psychology attempts to apply research findings to practical problems in schools, businesses, factories, and mental hospitals. For example, a school psychologist might use findings about the causes of math anxiety to devise a program to help students control their math phobias.

How do theories help scientists achieve their goals? As noted in Chapter 1, psychologists do not set out to just collect isolated facts about relationships between variables. To build toward a better understanding of behavior, they construct theories. **A *theory* is a system of interrelated ideas used to explain a set of observations.** For example, using a handful of concepts, such as natural selection and reproductive fitness, evolutionary theory (Durrant & Ellis, 2013) purports to explain a diverse array of known facts about mating preferences, jealousy, aggression, sexual behavior, and so forth (see Chapter 1). Thus, by integrating apparently unrelated facts and principles into a coherent whole, theories permit psychologists to make the leap from the *description* of behavior to the *understanding* of behavior. Moreover, the enhanced understanding afforded by theories guides future research by generating new predictions and suggesting new lines of inquiry (Fiske, 2004; Higgins, 2004).

A scientific theory must be testable. The cornerstone of science is its commitment to putting ideas to an empirical test. Most theories are too complex to be tested all at once. For example, it would be impossible to devise a single study that could test all the many aspects of evolutionary theory. Rather, in a typical study, investigators test one or two specific hypotheses derived from a theory. If their findings support the hypotheses, confidence in the theory grows. If their findings fail to support the hypotheses, confidence in the theory diminishes. The theory may then be revised or discarded. Thus, theory construction is a gradual, iterative process that is always subject to revision.

Steps in a Scientific Investigation

Curiosity about a question provides the point of departure for any kind of investigation, scientific or otherwise. Scientific investigations, however, are *systematic*. They follow an orderly pattern, which is outlined in **Figure 2.1**. Let's look at how this standard series of steps was followed in a study of the effects that specific colors have on psychological functioning conducted by Andrew Elliot and Daniela Niesta (2008). They wanted to investigate whether the color red increases men's attraction to women.

Step 1: Formulate a Testable Hypothesis

The first step in a scientific investigation is to translate a theory or an intuitive idea into a testable hypothesis. Although there has long been an extensive popular literature on how colors affect behavior, this literature has mostly been based on speculation rather than sound empirical research. However, Andrew Elliot and Markus Maier (2012, 2014) have formulated a theory of how color might influence behavior. According to their theory, colors can have automatic, unconscious effects on behavior. The theory asserts that these effects are probably rooted in two basic sources. First, people learn associations based on certain colors being paired repeatedly with certain experiences. For instance, red ink is usually used to mark students' errors, and red lights and red signs are often used to warn of danger. Second, over the course of human evolution, certain colors may have had adaptive significance for survival or reproduction. For example, blood and fire, which often appear red, both can signal danger.

In their first study of the behavioral effects of color, Elliot et al. (2007) theorized that red is associated with the danger of failure in achievement settings. Consistent with their theory, they found that subjects exposed to a red cover on an IQ test scored significantly lower on the test than those exposed to green or white covers. Although red has negative effects in achievement contexts, the researchers believed that it may have positive effects in sexual contexts. They noted a host of ways in which the color red is associated with romance (red hearts on Valentine's day), lust (red-light districts), and sexual liaisons (the redness of aroused sexual organs). *Thus, they hypothesized that red clothing might lead men to view women as more sexually desirable.*

To be testable, scientific hypotheses must be formulated precisely, and the variables under study must be clearly defined. Researchers achieve these clear formulations by providing operational definitions of the relevant variables. **An *operational definition* describes the actions or operations that will be used to measure or control a variable.** Operational definitions—which may be quite different from dictionary definitions—establish precisely what is meant by each variable in the context of a study.

To illustrate, let's see how Elliot and Niesta (2008) operationalized their variables. The manipulations of the color of the clothing worn by a woman were executed by taking a photo of a moderately attractive young woman and then using Adobe Photoshop to alter the color of her blouse. Although this sounds simple, when they compared red to other colors such as blue and green, they had to make sure that the different blouses were equal in brightness and saturation, so that *only* the color was different. In the specific study that we will look at, they measured the men's attraction to the woman by asking the men to rate her overall attractiveness, her sexual desirability, and their interest in dating her on a scale from 1 to 9. The subjects were also asked how much money they would be willing to spend on a date with the woman.

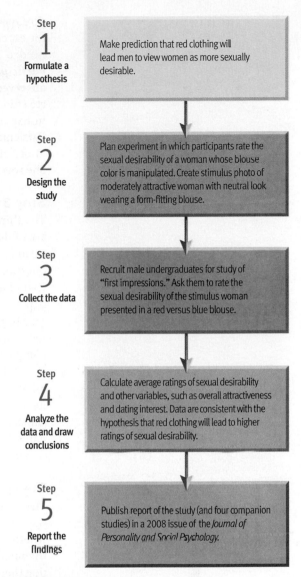

Step 1 — Formulate a hypothesis: Make prediction that red clothing will lead men to view women as more sexually desirable.

Step 2 — Design the study: Plan experiment in which participants rate the sexual desirability of a woman whose blouse color is manipulated. Create stimulus photo of moderately attractive woman with neutral look wearing a form-fitting blouse.

Step 3 — Collect the data: Recruit male undergraduates for study of "first impressions." Ask them to rate the sexual desirability of the stimulus woman presented in a red versus blue blouse.

Step 4 — Analyze the data and draw conclusions: Calculate average ratings of sexual desirability and other variables, such as overall attractiveness and dating interest. Data are consistent with the hypothesis that red clothing will lead to higher ratings of sexual desirability.

Step 5 — Report the findings: Publish report of the study (and four companion studies) in a 2008 issue of the *Journal of Personality and Social Psychology.*

FIGURE 2.1

Flowchart of steps in a scientific investigation. As illustrated in the study by Elliot and Niesta (2008), a scientific investigation consists of a sequence of carefully planned steps, beginning with the formulation of a testable hypothesis and ending with the publication of the study, if its results are worthy of examination by other researchers.

Step 2: Select the Research Method and Design the Study

The second step in a scientific investigation is to figure out how to put the hypothesis to an empirical test. The research method chosen depends to a large degree on the nature of the question under study. The various methods—experiments, case studies, surveys, naturalistic observation, and so forth—each have advantages and disadvantages. The researcher has to ponder the pros and cons, then select the strategy that appears to be the most appropriate and practical. In this case, Elliot and Niesta decided that their question called for an *experiment*, which involves manipulating one variable to see if it has an impact on another variable (we will describe the experimental method in more detail later in the chapter). Actually, they chose to conduct a series of five experiments to evaluate their hypothesis. We will mostly focus on Experiment 5 in their series.

Once researchers have chosen a general method, they must make detailed plans for executing their study. Thus, Elliot and Niesta had to decide how many people they needed to recruit for each experiment and where they would get their participants. *Participants, or subjects, are the persons or animals whose behavior is systematically observed in a study.* For their series of studies Elliot and Niesta chose to use undergraduate students. Their sample size in the series of studies ranged from 23 to 63. The sample in Experiment 5 consisted of 23 male undergraduates whose mean age was 19.77 years. Participation was restricted to heterosexuals who were not color-blind. The stimulus photo of the woman was a head and upper torso shot similar to that seen in yearbooks. She was shown in a form-fitting blouse with a neutral look.

Step 3: Collect the Data

The third step in the research enterprise is to collect the data. Researchers use a variety of *data collection techniques,* **which are procedures for making empirical observations and measurements.** Commonly used techniques include direct observation, questionnaires, interviews, psychological tests, physiological recordings, and examination of archival records (see **Table 2.1**). The data collection techniques used in a study depend largely on what is being investigated. For example, questionnaires are well suited for studying attitudes, psychological tests for studying personality, and physiological recordings for studying the biological bases of behavior. Depending on the nature and complexity of the study, data collection can often take months or even longer. In this case, the volunteer participants came to a lab where they were informed that the experiment concerned first impressions of the opposite sex. A manila folder was put on a desk in front of them. The folder contained the stimulus photo and the questionnaire. The subjects were instructed to look at the photo briefly and then respond to the questionnaire. Participants were randomly assigned to see the same woman in either a red blouse or a blue blouse.

Step 4: Analyze the Data and Draw Conclusions

The observations made in a study are usually converted into numbers, which constitute the raw data of the study. Researchers use *statistics* to analyze their data and to decide whether their hypotheses have been supported. Thus, statistics play an essential role in the scientific enterprise. Based on their statistical analyses, Elliot and Niesta concluded that their data supported their hypothesis. As predicted, the red blouse led to significantly higher attractiveness ratings than the blue blouse. The data for sexual desirability and dating interest are shown in **Figure 2.2**. As you can see, the red blouse produced higher ratings on both variables. Participants in the red condition also reported that they would be

TABLE 2.1 Key Data Collection Techniques in Psychology

Technique	Description
Direct observation	Observers are trained to watch and record behavior as objectively and precisely as possible. They may use some instrumentation, such as a stopwatch or video recorder.
Questionnaire	Subjects are administered a series of written questions designed to obtain information about attitudes, opinions, and specific aspects of their behavior.
Interview	A face-to-face dialogue is conducted to obtain information about specific aspects of a subject's behavior.
Psychological test	Participants are administered a standardized measure to obtain a sample of their behavior. Tests are usually used to assess mental abilities or personality traits.
Physiological recording	An instrument is used to monitor and record a specific physiological process in a subject. Examples include measures of blood pressure, heart rate, muscle tension, and brain activity.
Examination of archival records	The researcher analyzes existing institutional records (the archives), such as census, economic, medical, legal, educational, and business records.

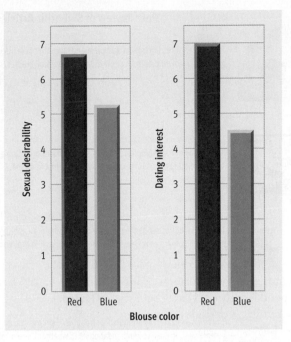

FIGURE 2.2

Color and sexual attraction. As you can see, in the study by Elliot and Niesta (2008), the color of the woman's blouse had a substantial impact on participants' attraction to her. When her blouse was red, males rated her as being more sexually desirable (left) and indicated that they had a greater interest in dating her (right).

SOURCE: Elliot, A. J., & Niesta, D. (2008). Romantic red: Red enhances men's attraction to women. *Journal of Personality and Social Psychology, 95,* 1150–1164. Figure 5b and 5d. Copyright © American Psychological Association.

willing to spend more money on a date with the woman than those in the blue condition. The findings of this experiment were consistent with the results of the other experiments in the series, leading the authors to conclude that the color red enhances men's attraction to women. Interestingly, the data from the studies also suggested that the men were unaware of how they were swayed by the color red.

Step 5: Report the Findings

The publication of research results is a fundamental aspect of the scientific enterprise (Roberts, Brown, & Smith-Boydston, 2003). Scientific progress can be achieved only if researchers share their findings with one another and with the general public. Therefore, the final step in a scientific investigation is to write up a concise summary of the study and its findings. Typically, researchers prepare a report that is delivered at a scientific meeting and submitted to a journal for publication. **A *journal* is a periodical that publishes technical and scholarly material, usually in a narrowly defined area of inquiry.** The series of studies by Elliot and Niesta (2008) was published in the *Journal of Personality and Social Psychology*.

The process of publishing scientific studies allows other experts to evaluate and critique new research findings. When articles are submitted to scientific journals, they go through a demanding *peer review process* that is summarized in **Figure 2.3**. Experts thoroughly scrutinize each submission. They carefully evaluate each study's methods, statistical analyses, and conclusions, as well as its contribution to knowledge and theory. The peer review process is so demanding that many top journals reject over 90% of submitted articles! The purpose of this process is to ensure that journals publish reliable findings based on high-quality research. The peer review process is a major strength of the scientific approach because it greatly reduces the likelihood of publishing erroneous findings.

Advantages of the Scientific Approach

Science is certainly not the only method that can be used to draw conclusions about behavior. We all use logic, casual observation, and good old-fashioned common sense. Because the scientific method requires painstaking effort, it seems reasonable to ask what advantages make it worth the trouble.

FIGURE 2.3

Peer Review of Scientific Articles

 Researcher or research team authors manuscript that describes the methods, findings, and implications of an empirical study or series of related studies.

 Manuscript is submitted to the editor of a professional journal (such as *Journal of Abnormal Psychology* or *Psychological Science*) that seems appropriate given the topic of the research. A manuscript can be submitted to only one journal at a time.

 The journal editor sends the manuscript to two to four experts in the relevant area of research who are asked to serve as reviewers. The reviewers provide their input anonymously and are not paid for their work.

 The reviewers carefully critique the strengths, weaknesses, and theoretical significance of the research and make a recommendation as to whether it is worthy of publication in that specific journal. If the research has merit, the reviewers usually offer numerous suggestions for improving the clarity of the manuscript.

 The editor reads the manuscript and expert reviews and decides whether the submission deserves publication. Most journals reject a substantial majority of submissions. The editorial decision, the reasoning behind it, and the expert reviews are sent to the author.

 If the manuscript is accepted, the author may incorporate suggestions for improvement from the reviews, make final revisions, and resubmit the article to the journal editor.

If the manuscript is rejected, the author may (a) abandon the publication effort, or (b) use reviewers' suggestions to make revisions and then submit the article to another journal.

 The article is published in a professional journal usually three to six months after final acceptance. Many articles are posted online soon after final revisions.

Following rejection, researchers sometimes give up on a line of research, but often they go back to the drawing board and attempt to design a better study.

Basically, the scientific approach offers two major advantages. The first is its clarity and precision. Common sense notions about behavior tend to be vague and ambiguous. Consider the old adage "Spare the rod and spoil the child." What exactly does this generalization about childrearing amount to? How severely should children be punished if parents are not to "spare the rod"? How do we assess whether a child qualifies as "spoiled"? A fundamental problem is that such statements have different meanings, depending on the person. In contrast, the scientific approach requires that people specify *exactly* what they are talking about when they formulate hypotheses. This clarity and precision enhance communication about important ideas.

The second and perhaps greatest advantage offered by the scientific approach is its relative intolerance of error. Scientists are trained to be skeptical. They subject their ideas to empirical tests. They also inspect one another's findings with a critical eye. They demand objective data and thorough documentation before they accept ideas. When the findings of two studies conflict, the scientist tries to figure out why, usually by conducting additional research. In contrast, common sense analyses involve little effort to verify ideas or detect errors.

All this is not to say that science has an exclusive copyright on truth. However, the scientific approach does tend to yield more accurate and dependable information than casual analyses and armchair speculation do. Knowledge of scientific data can thus provide a useful benchmark against which to judge claims and information from other kinds of sources.

Now that we have had an overview of how the scientific enterprise works, we can focus on how specific research methods are used. **Research methods consist of differing approaches to the observation, measurement, manipulation, and control of variables in empirical studies.** In other words, they are general strategies for conducting studies. No single research method is ideal for all purposes and situations. Much of the ingenuity in research involves selecting and tailoring the method to the question at hand. The next two sections of this chapter discuss the two basic types of methods used in psychology: *experimental research methods* and *descriptive/correlational research methods.*

2.2 LOOKING FOR CAUSES: EXPERIMENTAL RESEARCH

2.2

Key Learning Goals

- Describe the experimental method, independent and dependent variables, and experimental and control groups.
- Explain how experiments can vary in design, and evaluate the major advantages and disadvantages of the experimental method.

Does misery love company? This question intrigued social psychologist Stanley Schachter. When people feel anxious, he wondered, do they want to be left alone, or do they prefer to have others around? Schachter's review of relevant theories suggested that in times of anxiety people would want others around to help them sort out their feelings. Thus, his hypothesis was that increases in anxiety would cause increases in the desire to be with others, which psychologists call the *need for affiliation*. To test this hypothesis, Schachter (1959) designed a clever experiment.

The *experiment* **is a research method in which the investigator manipulates a variable under carefully controlled conditions and observes whether any changes occur in a second variable as a result.** The experiment is a relatively powerful procedure that allows researchers to detect cause-and-effect relationships. Psychologists depend on this method more than any other. To see how an experiment is designed, let's use Schachter's study as an example.

Independent and Dependent Variables

The purpose of an experiment is to find out whether changes in one variable (let's call it X) cause changes in another variable (let's call it Y). To put it more concisely, we want to find out *how X affects Y*. In this formulation, we refer to X as the *independent variable* and to Y as the *dependent variable.*

An *independent variable* **is a condition or event that an experimenter varies in order to see its impact on another variable.** The independent variable is the variable that the experimenter controls or manipulates. It is hypothesized to have some effect on the dependent variable. The experiment is conducted to verify this effect. **The** *dependent variable* **is the variable that is thought to be affected by manipulation of the independent variable.** In psychology studies, the dependent variable is usually a measurement of some aspect of the subjects' behavior. The independent variable is called *independent* because it is *free* to be varied by the experimenter. The dependent variable is called *dependent* because it is thought to *depend* (at least in part) on manipulations of the independent variable.

In Schachter's experiment, *the independent variable was the participants' anxiety level.* He manipulated anxiety level in a clever way. Subjects assembled in his lab were told by a "Dr. Zilstein" that they would be participating in a study on the physiological effects of electric shock. They were further informed that during the experiment they would receive a series of electric shocks from an intimidating-looking apparatus while their pulse and blood pressure were being monitored. Half of the participants were warned that the shocks would be very painful. They made up the *high-anxiety* group. The other half of the participants (the *low-anxiety* group) were told that the shocks would be mild and painless. In reality, there was no plan to shock anyone at any time. These orientation procedures were simply intended to evoke different levels of anxiety. After the orientation, the experimenter indicated that there would be a delay while he prepared the shock apparatus for use. The participants were asked whether they would prefer to wait alone or in the company of others. *The subjects' desire to be with others was the dependent variable.*

CONCEPT CHECK 2.1

Recognizing Independent and Dependent Variables

Check your understanding of the experimental method by identifying the independent variable (IV) and dependent variable (DV) in the following investigations. Note that one study has two IVs and another has two DVs. You'll find the answers in Appendix A in the back of the book.

1. A researcher is interested in how heart rate and blood pressure are affected by viewing a violent film sequence as opposed to a nonviolent film sequence.

   IV _____

   DV _____

2. An organizational psychologist develops a new training program to improve clerks' courtesy to customers in a large chain of retail stores. She conducts an experiment to see whether the training program leads to a reduction in the number of customer complaints.

   IV _____

   DV _____

3. A researcher wants to find out how stimulus complexity and stimulus contrast (light/dark variation) affect infants' attention to stimuli. He manipulates stimulus complexity and stimulus contrast and measures how long infants stare at various stimuli.

   IV _____

   DV _____

4. A social psychologist investigates the impact of group size on subjects' conformity in response to group pressure.

   IV _____

   DV _____

Experimental and Control Groups

In an experiment the investigator typically assembles two groups of subjects who are treated differently with regard to the independent variable. These two groups are referred to as the *experimental group* and the *control group.* **The *experimental group* consists of the subjects who receive some special treatment in regard to the independent variable. The *control group* consists of similar subjects who do not receive the special treatment given to the experimental group.**

In the Schachter study, those in the high-anxiety condition constituted the experimental group. They received a special treatment designed to create an unusually high level of anxiety. The participants in the low-anxiety condition constituted the control group. They were not exposed to the special anxiety-arousing procedure.

It is crucial that the experimental and control groups in a study be very similar, except for the different treatment that they receive in regard to the independent variable. This stipulation brings us to the logic that underlies the experimental method. If the two groups are alike in all respects *except for the variation created by the manipulation of the independent variable,* then any differences between the two groups on the dependent variable *must be due to the manipulation of the independent variable.* In this way researchers isolate the effect of the independent variable on the dependent variable. Schachter, for example, isolated the impact of anxiety on the need for affiliation. As predicted, he found that increased anxiety led to increased affiliation. As **Figure 2.4** indicates, the percentage of participants in the high-anxiety group who wanted to wait with others was roughly twice that of the low-anxiety group.

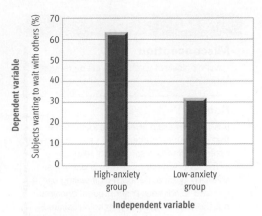

FIGURE 2.4

Results of Schachter's study of affiliation. The percentage of people wanting to wait with others was higher in the high-anxiety (experimental) group than in the low-anxiety (control) group, consistent with Schachter's hypothesis that anxiety would increase the desire for affiliation. The graphic portrayal of these results allows us to see at a glance the effects of the experimental manipulation on the dependent variable.

Extraneous Variables

As we have seen, the logic of the experimental method rests on the assumption that the experimental and control groups are alike except for their treatment in regard to the independent variable. Any other differences between the two groups can cloud the situation and make it difficult to draw conclusions about how the independent variable affects the dependent variable.

In practical terms, of course, it is impossible to ensure that two groups of subjects are exactly alike in *every* respect. The experimental and control groups have to be alike only on dimensions that are relevant to the dependent variable. Thus, Schachter did not need to worry about whether his two groups were similar in hair color, height, or interest in ballet. Obviously, these variables weren't likely to influence the dependent variable of affiliation behavior.

Instead, experimenters concentrate on making sure that the experimental and control groups are alike on a limited number of variables that could have a bearing on the results of the study. These variables are called extraneous, secondary, or nuisance variables. ***Extraneous variables* are any variables other than the independent variable that seem likely to influence the dependent variable in a specific study.**

In Schachter's study, one extraneous variable would have been the participants' tendency to be sociable. Why? Because subjects' sociability could affect their desire to be with others (the dependent variable). If the participants in one group had happened to be more sociable (on the average) than those in the other group, the variables of anxiety and sociability would have been confounded. **A *confounding of variables* occurs when two variables are linked in a way that makes it difficult to sort out their specific effects.** When an extraneous variable is confounded with an independent variable, a researcher cannot tell which is having what effect on the dependent variable.

Unanticipated confoundings of variables have wrecked innumerable experiments. That is why so much care, planning, and forethought must go into designing an experiment. A key quality that separates a talented experimenter from a mediocre one is the ability to foresee troublesome extraneous variables and control them to avoid confoundings.

Experimenters use a variety of safeguards to control for extraneous variables. For instance, subjects are usually assigned to the experimental and control groups randomly. **Random assignment of subjects occurs when all subjects have an equal chance of being assigned to any group or condition in the study.** When experimenters distribute subjects into groups through some random procedure, they can be reasonably confident that the groups will be similar in most ways.

To summarize the essentials of experimental design, **Figure 2.5** provides an overview of the elements in an experiment, using Schachter's study as an example.

Variations in Designing Experiments

We have discussed the experiment in only its simplest format, with just one independent variable and one dependent variable. Actually, many variations are possible in conducting experiments (Kirk, 2013). *Sometimes it is advantageous to use only one group of subjects who serve as their own control group.* The effects of the independent variable are evaluated by exposing this single group to two different conditions: an *experimental condition* and a *control condition*. For example, imagine that you wanted to study the effects of loud music on typing performance. You could have a group of participants work on a typing task while loud music was played (experimental condition) and in the absence of music (control condition). This approach would ensure that the participants in the experimental and control conditions would be alike on any extraneous variables involving their personal characteristics, such as motivation or typing skill (Davis & Bremner, 2006). After all, the same people would be studied in both conditions.

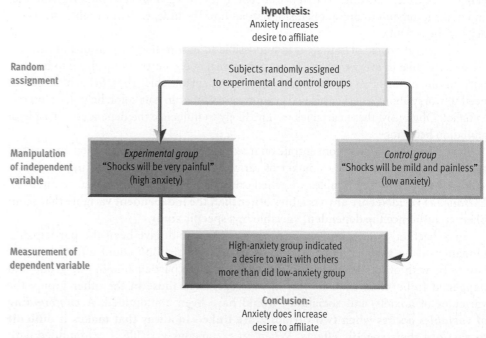

FIGURE 2.5

The basic elements of an experiment. As illustrated by the Schachter study, the logic of experimental design rests on treating the experimental and control groups exactly alike (to control for extraneous variables) except for the manipulation of the independent variable. In this way, the experimenter attempts to isolate the effects of the independent variable on the dependent variable.

It is also possible to manipulate more than one independent variable or measure more than one dependent variable in a single experiment. For example, in another study of typing performance, you could vary both room temperature and the presence of distracting music as independent variables (see **Figure 2.6**), while measuring two aspects of typing performance (speed and accuracy) as dependent variables. The main advantage of manipulating two or three independent variables is that this approach permits the experimenter to see whether two variables interact (Smith, 2014). An *interaction* means that the effect of one variable depends on the effect of another. For instance, if we found that distracting music impaired typing performance only when room temperature was high, we would be detecting an interaction.

Advantages and Disadvantages of Experimental Research

The experiment is a powerful research method. Its principal advantage is that it permits conclusions about cause-and-effect relationships between variables. Researchers are able to draw these conclusions about causation because the precise control allows them to isolate the relationship between the independent variable and the dependent variable, while neutralizing the effects of extraneous variables. No other research method can duplicate this strength of the experiment. This advantage is why psychologists usually prefer to use the experimental method whenever possible.

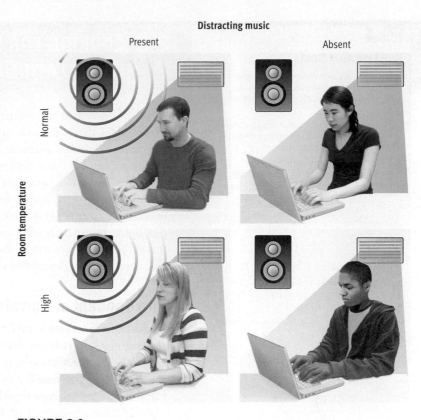

FIGURE 2.6

Manipulation of two independent variables in an experiment. As this example shows, when two independent variables are manipulated in a single experiment, the researcher has to compare four groups of subjects (or conditions) instead of the usual two. The main advantage of this procedure is that it allows an experimenter to see whether two variables interact.

For all its power, however, the experiment has limitations. One problem is that experiments are often artificial. Because experiments require great control over proceedings, researchers must often construct simple, contrived situations to test their hypotheses experimentally. For example, to investigate decision making in juries, psychologists have conducted many experiments in which participants read a brief summary of a trial and then record their individual "verdicts" of innocence or guilt. However, critics have pointed out that having a participant read a short case summary and make an individual decision is quite artificial in comparison to the complexities of real jury trials, which require group verdicts that are often the product of heated debates (Weiten & Diamond, 1979). When experiments are highly artificial, doubts arise about the applicability of findings to everyday behavior outside the experimental laboratory.

Another disadvantage is that the experimental method can't be used to explore some research questions. Psychologists are often interested in the effects of factors that cannot be manipulated as independent variables because of ethical concerns or practical realities. For instance, you might be interested in whether a nutritionally poor diet during pregnancy increases the likelihood of birth defects. This clearly is a significant issue. However, you obviously cannot select 100 pregnant women and assign 50 of them to a condition in which they consume an inadequate diet. The potential risk to the health of the women and their unborn children would make this research strategy unethical. To explore this question, you would have to use descriptive/correlational research methods, which we turn to next.

Key Learning Goals
- Distinguish between positive and negative correlations, and discuss correlation in relation to prediction and causation.
- Explain the role of naturalistic observation, case studies, and surveys in psychological research.
- Evaluate the major advantages and disadvantages of descriptive/correlational research.

2.3 LOOKING FOR LINKS: DESCRIPTIVE/ CORRELATIONAL RESEARCH

As we just noted, in some situations psychologists cannot exert experimental control over the variables they want to study. In such situations, investigators must rely on *descriptive/ correlational research methods.* What distinguishes these methods is that the researcher cannot manipulate the variables under study. This lack of control means that these methods cannot be used to demonstrate a cause-and-effect relationship between variables. *Descriptive/ correlational methods permit investigators to see only whether there is a link or association between the variables of interest.* Such an association is called a *correlation,* and the results of descriptive research are often summarized with a statistic called the *correlation coefficient.* In this section, we'll take a close look at the concept of correlation and then examine three specific approaches to descriptive research: naturalistic observation, case studies, and surveys.

The Concept of Correlation

In descriptive research, investigators often want to determine whether there is a correlation between two variables. **A correlation exists when two variables are related to each other.** A correlation may be either positive or negative, depending on the nature of the association between the variables measured. A *positive* correlation indicates that two variables covary (change together) in the *same* direction. This means that high scores on variable *X* are associated with high scores on variable *Y* and that low scores on variable *X* are associated with low scores on variable *Y*. For example, there is a positive correlation between high school grade point average (GPA) and subsequent college GPA. That is, people who do well in high school tend to do well in college. Likewise, those who perform poorly in high school tend to perform poorly in college (see **Figure 2.7**).

In contrast, a *negative* correlation indicates that two variables covary in the *opposite* direction. This means that people who score high on variable *X* tend to score low on variable *Y,* whereas those who score low on *X* tend to score high on *Y*. For example, in most college courses, there is a negative correlation between how frequently students are absent and how well they perform on exams. Students who have a high number of absences tend to get low exam scores, while students who have a low number of absences tend to earn higher exam scores (see **Figure 2.7**).

FIGURE 2.7

Positive and negative correlations. Notice that the terms *positive* and *negative* refer to the direction of the relationship between two variables, not to its strength. Variables are positively correlated if they tend to increase and decrease together and are negatively correlated if one tends to increase when the other decreases.

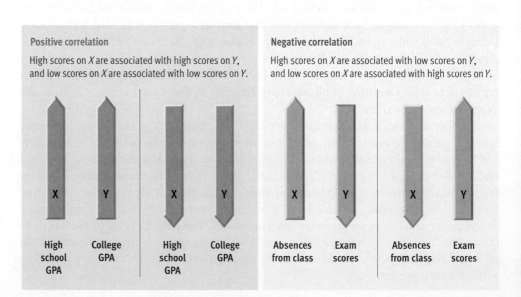

Positive correlation

High scores on *X* are associated with high scores on *Y*, and low scores on *X* are associated with low scores on *Y*.

High school GPA | College GPA | High school GPA | College GPA

Negative correlation

High scores on *X* are associated with low scores on *Y*, and low scores on *X* are associated with high scores on *Y*.

Absences from class | Exam scores | Absences from class | Exam scores

Strength of the Correlation

The strength of an association between two variables can be measured with a statistic called the correlation coefficient. **The *correlation coefficient* is a numerical index of the degree of relationship between two variables.** This coefficient can vary between 0 and +1.00 (if the correlation is positive) or between 0 and −1.00 (if the correlation is negative). A coefficient near zero indicates no relationship between the variables. That is, high or low scores on variable *X* show no consistent relationship to high or low scores on variable *Y*. A coefficient of +1.00 or −1.00 indicates a perfect, one-to-one correspondence between the two variables. Most correlations fall between these extremes.

The closer the correlation is to either −1.00 or +1.00, the stronger the relationship (see **Figure 2.8**). Thus, a correlation of .90 represents a stronger tendency for variables to be associated than a correlation of .40. Likewise, a correlation of −.75 represents a stronger relationship than a correlation of −.45. Keep in mind that the *strength* of a correlation depends only on the *size of the coefficient*. The positive or negative sign simply indicates the direction of the relationship. Therefore, a correlation of −.60 reflects a stronger relationship than a correlation of +.30.

Correlation and Prediction

You may recall that one of the key goals of scientific research is accurate *prediction*. A close link exists between the magnitude of a correlation and scientists' ability to make predictions. *As a correlation increases in strength (gets closer to either −1.00 or +1.00), the ability to predict one variable based on knowledge of the other variable increases.*

To illustrate, consider how college admissions tests (such as the SAT or ACT) are used to predict college performance. When students' admissions test scores and college GPA are correlated, researchers generally find moderate positive correlations in the .40s and .50s (Kobrin et al., 2008). Because of this relationship, college admissions committees can predict with modest accuracy how well prospective students will do in college. Admittedly, the predictive power of these admissions tests is far from perfect. But it's substantial enough to justify the use of the tests as one factor in making admissions decisions. However, if this correlation were much higher, say .90, admissions tests could predict with superb accuracy how students would perform. In contrast, if this correlation were much lower, say .20, the tests' prediction of college performance would be so poor that considering the test scores in admissions decisions would be unreasonable.

Correlation and Causation

Although a high correlation allows us to predict one variable on the basis of another, it does not tell us whether a cause-and-effect relationship exists between the two variables. The problem is that variables can be highly correlated even though they are not causally related.

When we find that variables *X* and *Y* are correlated, we can safely conclude only that *X* and *Y* are related in some way. We do not know whether *X* causes *Y* or *Y* causes *X*, or whether both are caused by a third variable. For example, survey studies have found a

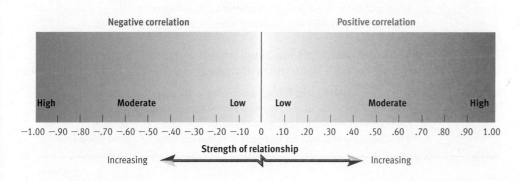

FIGURE 2.8

Interpreting correlation coefficients. The magnitude of a correlation coefficient indicates the strength of the relationship between two variables. The sign (plus or minus) indicates whether the correlation is positive or negative. The closer the coefficient comes to +1.00 or −1.00, the stronger the relationship between the variables.

FIGURE 2.9

Three possible causal relationships between correlated variables. If variables X and Y are correlated, does X cause Y, does Y cause X, or does some hidden third variable, Z, account for the changes in both X and Y? As the relationship between smoking and depression illustrates, a correlation alone does not provide the answer. We will encounter this problem of interpreting the meaning of correlations frequently in this text.

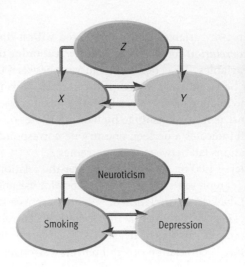

► REALITY CHECK

Misconception

A strong correlation between variables suggests that one of those variables causes the other.

Reality

The magnitude of a correlation is not a useful guide to the likelihood of causation. Two variables could be highly correlated but both could be caused by a third variable. In contrast, a relatively low correlation might reflect a genuine, but weak causal effect.

positive correlation between smoking and the risk of experiencing a major depressive disorder (Arnold et al., 2014; Liverant et al., 2014). It's clear that there is an association between smoking and depression, but it's hard to tell what's causing what. The investigators acknowledge that they don't know whether smoking makes people more vulnerable to depression or whether depression increases the tendency to smoke. Moreover, they note that they can't rule out the possibility that both are caused by a third variable (Z). Perhaps anxiety and neuroticism increase the likelihood of both taking up smoking and becoming depressed. The plausible causal relationships in this case are diagrammed in **Figure 2.9**. It illustrates the "third-variable problem" in interpreting correlations. This is a common problem in research. You'll see this type of diagram again when we discuss other correlations. Thus, it is important to remember that *correlation is not equivalent to causation.*

CONCEPT CHECK 2.2

Understanding Correlation

Check your understanding of correlation by interpreting the meaning of the correlation in item 1 and by guessing the direction (positive or negative) of the correlations in item 2. You'll find the answers in Appendix A.

1. Researchers have found a substantial positive correlation between youngsters' self-esteem and their academic achievement (measured by grades in school). Check any acceptable conclusions based on this correlation.
   _____ a. Low grades cause low self-esteem.
   _____ b. There is an association between self-esteem and academic achievement.
   _____ c. High self-esteem causes high academic achievement.
   _____ d. High ability causes both high self-esteem and high academic achievement.
   _____ e. Youngsters who score low in self-esteem tend to get low grades, and those who score high in self-esteem tend to get high grades.

2. Indicate whether you would expect the following correlations to be positive or negative.
   _____ a. The correlation between age and visual acuity (among adults)
   _____ b. The correlation between years of education and income
   _____ c. The correlation between shyness and the number of friends one has

Naturalistic Observation

Is eating behavior influenced by the size of the plates and bowls that people use? How do depressive disorders influence individuals' social behavior? These are just a couple examples of the kinds of questions that have been explored through naturalistic observation in recent studies. **In *naturalistic observation* a researcher engages in careful observation of behavior without intervening directly with the subjects.** This type of research is called *naturalistic* because behavior is allowed to unfold naturally (without interference) in its natural environment—that is, the setting in which it would normally occur. Of course, researchers have to make careful plans to ensure systematic, consistent observations (Heyman et al., 2014). Let's look at two examples.

One recent study investigated whether plate size influenced the amount of food consumed at all-you-can-eat buffets. Laboratory studies have shown that people eat more when they are served on larger plates. Wansink and van Ittersum (2013) wanted to determine whether similar findings would be observed in real buffet restaurants where patrons could choose between two plate sizes when they served themselves. At four buffets the eating behavior of 43 unsuspecting diners was monitored by carefully trained observers who estimated consumption and waste. Consistent with previous research, diners who chose the larger plate served themselves 52% more food than those who used the smaller plate. Those using the larger plates ended up consuming 41% more food and wasted 135% more than those using the smaller plates. These findings provide further support for the hypothesis that larger dinnerware leads to increased food consumption.

Another study (Baddeley, Pennebaker, & Beevers, 2013) examined social behavior in subjects diagnosed with major depressive disorder. Research has suggested that depression is associated with social isolation and a variety of social deficits, but the vast majority of the research has been based on self-report data rather than observation of depressed individuals in everyday life. The recent development of an innovative device called an electronically activated recorder (EAR) allowed the investigators to explore these social deficits in a more sensitive way. The EAR is an unobtrusive, portable audio recorder carried by participants that periodically records their conversations and other ambient sounds as they go about their normal daily activities (Mehl & Robbins, 2012). Using this clever device, the researchers were able to compare the real-life social behavior of 29 depressed participants against that of 28 healthy control subjects. Surprisingly, the two groups spent similar amounts of time talking, laughing, and being with another person. However, the depressed individuals spent less time in groups and spoke more of negative emotions, especially around romantic partners. Overall, the social deficits observed in the depressed participants were not as severe as previous research using other methods had suggested, leading the researchers to conclude that depression may affect the *quality* rather than the *quantity* of social interactions.

The major strength of naturalistic observation is that it allows researchers to study behavior under conditions that are less artificial than in experiments. Another plus is that engaging in naturalistic observation can be a good starting point when little is known about the behavior under study. And, unlike case studies and surveys, naturalistic observation can be used to study animal behavior. Many landmark studies of animal behavior, such as Jane Goodall's (1986, 1990) work on the social and family life of chimpanzees, have depended on naturalistic observation. More recent examples of naturalistic observation with animals include studies of communication in Australian sea lions (Pitcher, Harcourt, & Charrier, 2012), parental favoritism in Eastern bluebirds (Barrios-Miller & Siefferman, 2013), and tool use in capuchin monkeys and chimpanzees (la Cour et al., 2014).

A major problem with this method is that researchers often have trouble making their observations unobtrusively so they don't affect their participants' behavior. ***Reactivity***

Wansink and van Ittersum (2013) used naturalistic observation to replicate laboratory findings on how plate size affects the amount eaten. Consistent with laboratory research, they found that real-world diners at buffet restaurants consumed more food when given larger plates.

The method of naturalistic observation can be particularly useful in studying animals in their natural habitats. For example, Jane Goodall conducted groundbreaking research on the social lives of chimpanzees through years of painstaking naturalistic observation.

occurs when a subject's behavior is altered by the presence of an observer. Even animals may exhibit reactivity if observational efforts are readily apparent (Iredale, Nevill, & Lutz, 2010). Another disadvantage is that it often is difficult to translate naturalistic observations into numerical data that permit precise statistical analyses.

Case Studies

Are people who suffer from depression more likely to subsequently develop dementia than others? How about people who are diagnosed with anxiety disorders? To investigate these questions, a research team in the United Kingdom (Burton et al., 2013) conducted a large-scale study of risk factors for dementia. *Dementia* is an abnormal condition marked by multiple cognitive deficits that revolve around memory impairment. Dementia can be caused by a variety of diseases, but Alzheimer's disease accounts for about 70% of the cases (Albert, 2008). Previous research has suggested that depression is a risk factor for dementia, but little is known about the possible role of anxiety disorders, and even less about the joint effects of anxiety and depressive disorders.

The research team decided that their question called for a case study approach. **A case study is an in-depth investigation of an individual subject.** A variety of data collection techniques can be used in case studies. Typical techniques include interviewing the subjects, interviewing people who are close to the subjects, direct observation of the participants, examination of records, and psychological testing. In probing dementia risk factors, Burton et al. (2013) took advantage of an existing, large database of medical case histories compiled from 13 medical practices since 1998. They identified 400 new cases of dementia that were diagnosed during the 8-year period covered by the study. For each of these cases they identified three or four patients in the database who were similar in age and gender but did not suffer from dementia. These 1353 cases served as controls for comparison purposes. All of the case records were then examined carefully to screen for preexisting anxiety disorders or depressive disorders. As expected, the prevalence of preexisting depressive disorders was elevated in the dementia cases, which supported the notion that depression is a risk factor for dementia. However, the prevalence of preexisting anxiety disorders was also elevated in the dementia cases, suggesting that anxiety disorders are a previously overlooked risk factor for dementia. Indeed, the statistical analyses of their joint influence suggested that anxiety disorders were more strongly associated with risk for dementia than depressive disorders.

Clinical psychologists, who diagnose and treat psychological problems, routinely do case studies of their clients. When clinicians assemble a case study for diagnostic purposes, they generally are *not* conducting empirical research. Case study *research* typically involves investigators analyzing a collection of case studies to look for patterns that permit general conclusions. For example, one recent study (Arcelus et al., 2009) evaluated the efficacy of a treatment called *interpersonal psychotherapy* (IPT) for people suffering from bulimia (an eating disorder marked by out-of-control overeating followed by self-induced vomiting, fasting, and excessive exercise). Careful case assessments were made of 59 bulimic patients before, during, and after the 16-session course of IPT treatment. The results demonstrated that IPT can be an effective treatment for bulimic disorders. Although case study research typically involves looking for common threads in a series of cases, descriptions of individual case studies are sometimes published when they are particularly interesting or perhaps valuable to other clinicians. For example, Ale et al. (2014) describe their family-based behavioral treatment of a 9-year-old girl exhibiting compulsive hoarding. These kinds of publications allow clinicians to share insights about effective approaches to treatment.

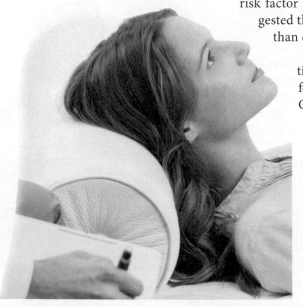

Case studies are used in both clinical work and research. When used in research, investigators look for threads of continuity across a series of case studies.

Alain Shroder/Getty Images

Case studies are particularly well suited for investigating certain phenomena, especially the roots of psychological disorders and the efficacy of selected therapeutic practices (Fishman, 2007). They can also provide compelling, real-life illustrations that bolster a hypothesis or theory. However, the main problem with case studies is that they are highly subjective. Information from several sources must be knit together in an impressionistic way. In this process, clinicians and researchers often focus selectively on information that fits with their expectations, which usually reflect their theoretical slant. Thus, it is relatively easy for investigators to see what they expect to see in case study research.

Surveys

Is the prevalence of smoking and other tobacco use declining among America's youth? Does the prevalence of hangovers increase or decrease as people grow older? These are two examples of practical questions explored in recent survey research. **In a *survey* researchers use questionnaires or interviews to gather information about specific aspects of participants' background, attitudes, beliefs, or behavior.** To investigate trends in tobacco use, Arrazola, Kuiper, and Dube (2014) administered detailed, anonymous questionnaires to over 77,000 high school students over a period of 12 years (2000 to 2012). The students were queried about their use of various tobacco products in the last 30 days. The percentage of students who reported any tobacco use declined from 33.6% in 2000 to 20.4% in 2012. And the percentage of students who only smoked cigarettes declined from 14.0% in 2000 to 4.7% in 2012. Although these are very encouraging trends, the authors emphasize that one-fifth of high school students still use tobacco and about half of those use multiple tobacco products, a pattern of use that is thought to be associated with greater addiction and negative health effects.

Relatively little research has been conducted on hangovers following episodes of binge drinking. Folk wisdom suggests that the prevalence of hangovers increases with advancing age, but there were no data on age trends in hangovers until a recent survey study conducted by a research team in Denmark (Tolstrup, Stephens, & Gronbaek, 2014). Questions on drinking habits and the experience of hangovers were included in a broad survey of health habits. Binge drinking was defined as the consumption of more than five drinks on a single occasion. The incidence of hangovers was assessed with a nine-point scale based on symptoms reported after binge drinking. Over 76,000 participants from 13 municipalities in Denmark responded to the survey. The study found clear age trends, as the incidence of hangovers after binge drinking declined steadily with increasing age, as you can see in **Figure 2.10**. Contrary to folk wisdom, the incidence of *severe* hangovers also declined as subjects grew older.

Surveys are often used to obtain information on aspects of behavior that are difficult to observe directly. Surveys also make it relatively easy to collect data on attitudes and opinions from large samples of participants. Survey methods are widely used in psychological research (Krosnick, Lavrakas, & Kim, 2014). However, potential participants' tendency to cooperate with surveys appears to have declined noticeably in recent decades (Tourangeau, 2004). The growing resentment of intrusive telemarketing and heightened concerns about privacy and identity theft seem to be the culprits underlying the reduced response rates for research surveys. The major weakness of surveys is that they depend on *self-report data*. As we'll discuss later, intentional deception, wishful thinking, memory lapses, and poorly worded questions can distort participants' verbal reports about their behavior (Krosnick, 1999).

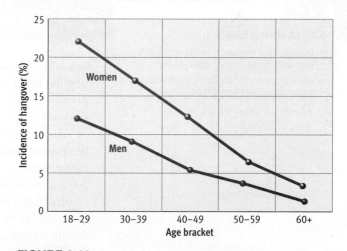

FIGURE 2.10

The incidence of hangovers in relation to age. The survey data collected by Tolstrup, Stephens, and Gronbaek (2014) show that older adults are less likely to experience a hangover after binge drinking than younger adults, even though older adults are thought to be more vulnerable to hangovers. The researchers speculate that older adults may tend to engage in less intense binge drinking, or that they may become more skilled at avoiding hangovers.

Advantages and Disadvantages of Descriptive/Correlational Research

Descriptive/correlational research methods have advantages and disadvantages, which are compared with the strengths and weaknesses of experimental research in the Illustrated Overview of research methods on pages 54–55. As a whole, the foremost advantage of correlational methods is that they give researchers a way to explore questions they could not examine with experimental procedures. For example, after-the-fact analyses would be the only ethical way to investigate the possible link between poor maternal nutrition and birth defects in humans. In a similar vein, if researchers hope to learn how urban versus rural upbringing relates to people's values, they have to depend on descriptive methods, since they can't control where subjects grow up. Thus, *descriptive research broadens the scope of phenomena that psychologists are able to study.*

Unfortunately, descriptive methods have one significant disadvantage: Investigators cannot control events to isolate cause and effect. *Consequently, descriptive/correlational research cannot demonstrate conclusively that correlated variables are causally related.* Consider for instance, the correlation between plate size and food consumption observed in the study by Wansink and van Ittersum (2013). The correlational data from this specific study do not permit us to conclude that larger plates *caused* people to consume more food. Other factors might play a role in this association. For example, it could be that hungrier people grabbed larger plates, and their increased eating could be caused by their greater hunger. To draw causal conclusions about the relationship between larger plates and increased eating would require experiments on this issue—which have been conducted, and which do suggest that there is a causal link between bigger plates and greater eating. You may be wondering: If we already had experimental data linking plate size to consumption, why conduct the naturalistic observation study? The value of the naturalistic observation study lies in its demonstration that laboratory findings generalize to the real world. As you can see, the various research methods each make different types of contributions to our understanding of behavior.

Key Learning Goals

- Understand the importance of replication and meta-analysis in research.
- Recognize common flaws in the design and execution of research.

2.4 LOOKING FOR FLAWS: EVALUATING RESEARCH

Scientific research is a more reliable source of information than casual observation or popular belief. However, it would be wrong to conclude that all published research is free of errors. Scientists are fallible human beings, and flawed studies do make their way into the body of scientific literature.

That is one of the reasons that scientists often try to replicate studies. **Replication is the repetition of a study to see whether the earlier results are duplicated.** The replication process helps science identify and purge inaccurate findings (Pashler & Harris, 2012; Simons, 2014). Of course, the replication process sometimes leads to contradictory results. You'll see some examples in later chapters. Inconsistent findings on a research question can be frustrating and confusing for students. However, some inconsistency in results is to be expected, given science's commitment to replication.

Fortunately, one of the strengths of the empirical approach is that scientists work to reconcile or explain conflicting results. In their efforts to make sense of inconsistent research results, psychologists are increasingly depending on a technique called *meta-analysis,* which came into vogue in the 1980s (Cooper, 2010; Johnson & Eagly, 2014). *Meta-analysis* **combines the statistical results of many studies of the same question, yielding an estimate of the size and consistency of a variable's effects.** For example, Gentile and colleagues (2009) combined the results of 115 studies of gender differences in specific aspects of self-esteem. Among other things, they found that males tend to have somewhat higher self-esteem related to physical appearance and athletic ability, females score higher in self-esteem related to moral-ethical attributes, and gender differences in academic self-esteem are negligible. Meta-analysis allows researchers to test the generalizability of findings and the strength of a variable's effects across people, places, times, and variations in procedure in a relatively precise and objective way (Schmidt, 2013; Valentine, 2012).

As you will see in upcoming chapters, scientific advances often emerge out of efforts to double-check perplexing findings or to explain contradictory research results. Thus, like all sources of information, scientific studies need to be examined with a critical eye. This section describes a number of common methodological problems that often spoil studies. Being aware of these pitfalls will make you more skilled in evaluating research.

Sampling Bias

Empirical research always involves making statistical inferences about a population based on a sample (Sturgis, 2006). **A *sample* is the collection of subjects selected for observation in an empirical study.** In contrast, **the *population* is the much larger collection of animals or people (from which the sample is drawn) that researchers want to generalize about.** For example, when political pollsters attempt to predict elections, all of the voters in a jurisdiction represent the population. The voters who are actually surveyed constitute the sample. If researchers were interested in the ability of 6-year-old children to form concepts, those 6-year-olds actually studied would be the sample, and all similar 6-year-old children (perhaps those in modern, Western cultures) would be the population.

The strategy of observing a limited sample in order to generalize about a much larger population rests on the assumption that the sample is reasonably *representative* of the population. A sample is representative if its composition (its demographic makeup in terms of age, sex, income, and so forth) is similar to the composition of the population (see **Figure 2.11**). *Sampling bias* **exists when a sample is not representative of the population from which it was drawn.** If a sample is not representative, generalizations about the population may be inaccurate. For instance, if a political pollster were to survey only people in posh shopping areas frequented by the wealthy, the pollster's generalizations about the voting public as a whole would be off the mark.

As we discussed in Chapter 1, American psychologists have historically tended to undersample ethnic minorities and people from non-Western cultures. In a recent analysis of this problem, Jeffrey Arnett (2008) reviewed the sample composition of studies published in six major APA-owned journals in recent years. He found that 68% of the samples came from the United States and another 27% from Europe or English-speaking countries, with only 5% coming from the remainder of the world. He asserts that the focus on American subjects is extremely disproportionate given that the United States accounts for less than 5% of the world's population. Moreover, Arnett notes that the vast majority of American samples were predominantly European American and that they depended much too heavily on white middle- and upper-class college students. He argues that this excessive reliance on American samples and college students is likely to distort findings in many research areas. In general, then, when you have concerns or doubts about the results of a study, the first thing to examine is the composition of the sample.

Researchers depend on surveys to investigate a wide range of issues. However, resentment of intrusive telemarketing and concerns about privacy have undermined individuals' willingness to participate in survey research.

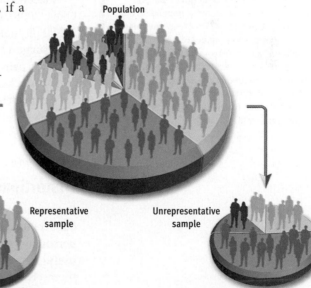

FIGURE 2.11

The relationship between the population and the sample. The process of drawing inferences about a population based on a sample works only if the sample is reasonably representative of the population. A sample is representative if its demographic makeup is similar to that of the population, as shown on the left. If some groups in the population are overrepresented or underrepresented in the sample, as shown on the right, inferences about the population may be skewed or inaccurate.

When lab subjects are given "alcoholic beverages" that do not really contain alcohol, many of them show signs of intoxication, illustrating the power of placebo effects.

Placebo Effects

A *placebo* is a substance that resembles a drug but has no actual pharmacological effect. In studies that assess the effectiveness of medications, placebos are given to some participants to control for the effects of a treacherous extraneous variable: subjects' expectations. Placebos are used because researchers know that participants' expectations can influence their feelings, reactions, and behavior (Benedetti, 2009). Thus, **placebo effects occur when participants' expectations lead them to experience some change even though they receive empty, fake, or ineffectual treatment.** In studies of new medications, inert placebos often produce surprisingly large beneficial effects (Agid et al., 2013). The power of people's expectations has also been demonstrated in studies in which hospitalized subjects are given genuine painkillers covertly (morphine is slipped into their IV without their knowledge). With expectations of pain relief not aroused (due to the hidden drug administration), analgesic medications are typically found to be much less effective than they are under normal circumstances (Benedetti, 2013). This finding suggests that the benefits of genuine drugs are amplified considerably by expectations.

In a similar vein, psychologists have found that participants' expectations can be powerful determinants of their perceptions and behavior when they are under the microscope in an empirical study (Boot et al., 2013). For example, placebo effects have been seen in lab experiments on the effects of alcohol. In these studies, some of the participants are led to believe that they are drinking alcoholic beverages when in reality the drinks only appear to contain alcohol. Many of the subjects show effects of intoxication even though they haven't really consumed any alcohol (Assefi & Garry, 2003). If you know someone who shows signs of intoxication as soon as he or she starts drinking, before alcohol intake can have taken effect physiologically, you have seen placebo effects in action.

Placebo effects are attributable to people's expectations (Colagiuri & Boakes, 2010; Oken, 2008). However, recent studies have demonstrated that mere expectations can have actual physiological effects. For example, studies of placebos given to subjects to reduce pain suggest that the placebos actually alter activity in brain circuits that are known to suppress pain (Benedetti, 2013; Wager, Scott, & Zubieta, 2007).

Researchers should guard against placebo effects whenever participants are likely to have expectations that a treatment will affect them in a certain way. The possible role of placebo effects can be assessed by including a fake version of the experimental treatment (a placebo condition) in a study.

▶ REALITY CHECK

Misconception

Placebo effects tend to be weak effects.

Reality

Not necessarily. In recent years scientists have developed new respect for the power of the placebo. The strength of placebo effects varies considerably, depending on the condition treated, the plausibility of the placebo, and a variety of other factors. However, a careful review of the evidence concluded that placebo effects are often powerful, frequently approaching the strength of the treatment effects to which they are compared (Wampold et al., 2005; Wampold, Imel, & Minami, 2007).

Distortions in Self-Report Data

Research psychologists often work with *self-report data,* made up of participants' verbal accounts of their behavior. This is the case whenever questionnaires, interviews, or personality inventories are used to measure variables. Self-report methods can be quite useful. They take advantage of the fact that people have a unique opportunity to observe themselves full-time (Baldwin, 2000). However, self-reports can be plagued by several kinds of distortion.

One of the most problematic of these distortions is the *social desirability bias,* which is a tendency to give socially approved answers to questions about oneself. Subjects who are influenced by this bias work overtime trying to create a favorable impression, especially when they are asked about sensitive issues (Tourangeau & Yan, 2007). For example, many survey respondents will report that they voted in an election or gave to a charity when in fact it is possible to determine that they did not (Granberg & Holmberg,

1991; Hadaway, Marler, & Chaves, 1993). Interestingly, people who answer questions in socially desirable ways take slightly longer to respond to the questions. This tendency suggests that they are carefully "editing" their responses (Holtgraves, 2004).

Other problems can also produce distortions in self-report data (Krosnick, 1999; Schuman & Kalton, 1985). Conducting consistent, sensitive, and effective interviews is always challenging (Madill, 2012). Respondents misunderstand questionnaire items surprisingly often. Even the order in which questions are asked can shape participants' responses (Rasinski, Lee, & Krishnamurty, 2012). Memory errors can also undermine the accuracy of verbal reports. Another source of distortion is that, in responding to certain kinds of scales, some people tend to agree with nearly all of the statements, while others tend to disagree with nearly everything (Krosnick & Fabrigar, 1998). An additional cause for concern is the *halo effect,* **which occurs when someone's overall evaluation of a person, object, or institution spills over to influence more specific ratings.** For example, a supervisor's global assessment of an employee's merit might sway specific ratings of the employee's dependability, initiative, communication, knowledge, and so forth. The crux of the problem is that a rater is unable to judge specific evaluative dimensions independently. Obviously, distortions like these can produce inaccurate results. Although researchers have devised ways to neutralize these problems, we should be especially cautious in drawing conclusions from self-report data (Schaeffer, 2000).

Experimenter Bias

As scientists, psychologists try to conduct their studies in an objective, unbiased way so that their own views will not influence the results. However, objectivity is a *goal* that scientists strive for, not an accomplished fact that can be taken for granted (MacCoun, 1998). In reality, most researchers have an emotional investment in the outcome of their research. Often they are testing hypotheses that they have developed themselves and that they would like to see supported by the data. It is understandable, then, that *experimenter bias* is a possible source of error in research.

Experimenter bias **occurs when a researcher's expectations or preferences about the outcome of a study influence the results obtained.** Experimenter bias can slip through to influence studies in many subtle ways. One problem is that researchers, like others, sometimes *see what they want to see.* For instance, when experimenters make apparently honest mistakes in recording subjects' responses, the mistakes tend to be heavily slanted in favor of supporting the hypothesis (O'Leary, Kent, & Kanowitz, 1975).

Research by Robert Rosenthal (1976) suggests that experimenter bias may lead researchers to unintentionally influence the behavior of their subjects. In one study, Rosenthal and Fode (1963) recruited undergraduate psychology students to serve as the "experimenters." The students were told that they would be collecting data for a study of how participants rated the success of people portrayed in photographs. In a pilot study, photos were selected that generated (on the average) neutral ratings on a scale extending from −10 (extreme failure) to +10 (extreme success). Rosenthal and Fode then manipulated the expectations of their experimenters by telling half of them that they would probably obtain average ratings of −5 and telling the other half to expect average ratings of +5. The experimenters were forbidden from conversing with their subjects except for reading some standardized instructions. Even though the photographs were exactly the same for both groups, the experimenters who *expected* positive ratings *obtained* significantly higher ratings than those who expected negative ones.

How could the experimenters have swayed the participants' ratings? According to Rosenthal, the experimenters unintentionally influenced their subjects by sending subtle nonverbal signals as the experiment progressed. Without realizing it, they sometimes smiled, nodded, or sent other positive cues when participants made ratings that were in line with their expectations. Thus, experimenter bias may influence both researchers' observations and their subjects' behavior (Rosenthal, 1994, 2002).

The problems associated with experimenter bias can be neutralized by using a double-blind procedure. **The *double-blind procedure* is a research strategy in which neither subjects nor experimenters know which subjects are in the experimental or control groups.** It's not particularly unusual for subjects to be "blind" about their treatment condition. However, the double-blind procedure keeps the experimenter in the dark as well. Of course, a member of the research team who isn't directly involved with subjects keeps track of who is in which group.

CONCEPT CHECK 2.3

Detecting Flaws in Research

Check your understanding of how to conduct sound research by looking for methodological flaws in the following studies. You'll find the answers in Appendix A.

Study 1. A researcher announces that he will be conducting an experiment to investigate the detrimental effects of sensory deprivation on perceptual-motor coordination. The first 40 students who sign up for the study are assigned to the experimental group, and the next 40 who sign up serve in the control group. The researcher supervises all aspects of the study's execution. Experimental subjects spend 2 hours in a sensory deprivation chamber, where sensory stimulation is minimal. Control subjects spend 2 hours in a waiting room that contains magazines and a TV. All subjects then perform ten 1-minute trials on a pursuit-rotor task that requires them to try to keep a stylus on a tiny rotating target. The dependent variable is their average score on the pursuit-rotor task.

Study 2. A researcher wants to know whether there is a relationship between age and racial prejudice. She designs a survey in which respondents are asked to rate their prejudice against six different ethnic groups. She distributes the survey to over 500 people of various ages who are approached at a shopping mall in a low-income, inner-city neighborhood.

Check the flaws that are apparent in each study.

Methodological flaw	Study 1	Study 2
Sampling bias	_____	_____
Placebo effects	_____	_____
Distortions in self-report	_____	_____
Confounding of variables	_____	_____
Experimenter bias	_____	_____

Key Learning Goals

- Discuss the controversies regarding deception in research and the use of animals in research.

2.5 LOOKING AT ETHICS: DO THE ENDS JUSTIFY THE MEANS?

Think back to Stanley Schachter's (1959) study on anxiety and affiliation. Imagine how you would have felt if you had been one of the participants in Schachter's high-anxiety group. You show up at a research lab, expecting to participate in a harmless experiment. The room you are sent to is full of unusual electronic equipment. An official-looking man in a lab coat announces that this equipment will be used to give you a series of painful electric shocks. His statement that the shocks will leave "no permanent tissue damage" is hardly reassuring. Surely, you think, there must be a mistake. All of a sudden, your venture into research has turned into a nightmare! Your stomach knots up in anxiety. The researcher explains that there will be a delay while he prepares his apparatus. He asks you to fill out a short questionnaire about whether you would prefer to wait alone or with others. Still reeling in dismay at the prospect of being shocked, you fill out the questionnaire. He takes it and then announces that you won't be shocked after all. It was all a hoax! Feelings of relief wash over you, but they're mixed with feelings of anger. You feel as though the experimenter has just made a fool out of you. You're embarrassed and resentful.

Should researchers be allowed to play with your feelings in this way? Should they be permitted to deceive participants in such a manner? Is this the cost that must be paid to advance scientific knowledge? As these questions indicate, the research enterprise sometimes presents scientists with difficult ethical dilemmas (Fried, 2012). *These dilemmas reflect concern about the possibility for inflicting harm on subjects.* In psychological research, the major ethical dilemmas center on the use of deception and the use of animals.

The Question of Deception

Elaborate deception, such as that seen in Schachter's study, has been fairly common in psychological research since the 1960s, especially in the area of social psychology (Epley & Huff, 1998; Korn, 1997). Over the years, psychologists have faked fights, thefts, muggings, faintings, epileptic seizures, rapes, and automobile breakdowns to explore a number of issues. Researchers have led subjects to believe that they (the subjects) were hurting others with electric shocks, had homosexual tendencies, and were overhearing negative comments about themselves. Why have psychologists used so much deception in their research? Quite simply, they are trying to deal with the methodological problems discussed earlier. They often misinform participants about the purpose of a study to reduce problems resulting from placebo effects, the unreliability of self-reports, and other factors that can undermine the scientific value and validity of research (Berghmans, 2007).

Critics argue against the use of deception on several grounds (Baumrind, 1985; Kelman, 1982; Ortmann & Hertwig, 1997). First, they assert that deception is only a nice word for lying, which they see as inherently immoral. Second, they argue that by deceiving unsuspecting participants, psychologists may undermine many individuals' trust in others. Third, they point out that many deceptive studies produce distress for participants who were not forewarned about that possibility. Specifically, participants may experience great stress during a study or be made to feel foolish when the true nature of a study is explained.

Those who defend the use of deception in research maintain that many important issues could not be investigated if experimenters were not permitted to mislead subjects (Bröder, 1998). They argue that most research deceptions involve "white lies" that are not likely to harm participants. A review of the relevant research by Larry Christensen (1988) suggests that deception studies are *not* harmful to participants. Indeed, most subjects who participate in experiments involving deception report that they enjoyed the experience and that they didn't mind being misled. Moreover, the empirical evidence does not support the notions that deceptive research undermines subjects' trust in others or their respect for psychology or scientific research (Kimmel, 1996; Sharpe, Adair, & Roese, 1992). Finally, researchers who defend deception argue that the benefits—advances in knowledge that often improve human welfare—are worth the costs.

The Question of Animal Research

Psychology's other major ethics controversy concerns the use of animals in research. Psychologists use animals as research subjects for several reasons. Sometimes they simply want to know more about the behavior of a specific type of animal. In other instances, they want to identify general laws of behavior that apply to both humans and animals. Finally, in some cases psychologists use animals because they can expose them to treatments that clearly would be unacceptable with human participants. For example, most of the research on the relationship between deficient maternal nutrition during pregnancy and the incidence of birth defects has been done with animals.

Illustrated Overview Key Research Methods in Psychology

RESEARCH METHOD	DESCRIPTION	EXAMPLE APPLIED TO RESEARCH ON AGGRESSION

EXPERIMENT

Manipulation of an independent variable under carefully controlled conditions to see whether any changes occur in a dependent variable.

Example: Schachter's (1959) study of whether increased anxiety leads to increased affiliation.

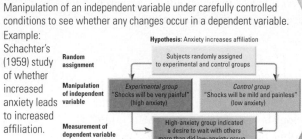

Hypothesis: Anxiety increases affiliation

Random assignment → Subjects randomly assigned to experimental and control groups

Manipulation of independent variable → Experimental group "Shocks will be very painful" (high anxiety) | Control group "Shocks will be mild and painless" (low anxiety)

Measurement of dependent variable → High-anxiety group indicated a desire to wait with others more than did low-anxiety group

Youngsters are randomly assigned to watch a violent or nonviolent film (manipulation of the independent variable), and some aspect of aggression (the dependent variable) is measured in a laboratory situation.

© T.M.0 Pictures/Alamy. (TV screen) © Aastock/Shutterstock.com

NATURALISTIC OBSERVATION

Careful, usually prolonged observation of behavior in its natural setting, without direct intervention.

Example: The Wansink and van Ittersum (2013) study examining the effect of plate size on amount eaten in buffet restaurants.

© Caroline von Tuempling/Getty Images

Youngsters' spontaneous acts of aggression during recreational activities on their playgound are recorded unobtrusively by a team of carefully trained observers.

Laurence Mouton/PhotoAlto Agency RF Collections/Getty Images

CASE STUDIES

© Alain Shroder/Getty Images

In-depth investigation of a single individual using direct interview, direct observation, review of records, interviews of those close to the person, and other data sources.

Example: The study by Burton et al. (2013), which looked at medical case records to determine whether a history of depressive or anxiety disorders increased the likelihood of developing dementia later in life.

Detailed case histories are worked up for youngsters referred to counseling because of excessive aggressive behavior in school. The children are interviewed, as are their parents and teachers.

© Monkey Business Images/Shutterstock.com

SURVEYS

Use of questionnaires or interviews to gather information about specific aspects of participants' behavior, attitudes, and beliefs.

Example: The study by Arrazola et al. (2014) in which over 77,000 high school students were surveyed about their use of tobacco products.

© Igor Kova chuk/Shutterstock.com

A large sample of youngsters are given a questionnaire describing hypothetical scenarios that might be expected to trigger aggressive behavior and are asked about how they think they would respond in the situations.

© David Grossman/Alamy

Precise control over variables can eliminate alternative explanations for findings.

Researchers are able to draw conclusions about cause-and-effect relationships between variables.

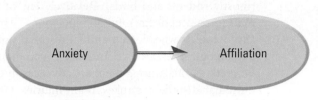

Confounding of variables must be avoided.

Contrived laboratory situations are often artificial, making it risky to generalize findings to the real world.

Ethical concerns and practical realities preclude experiments on many important questions.

Artificiality that can be a problem in laboratory studies is minimized.

It can be good place to start when little is known about the phenomena under study.

Unlike other descriptive/correlational methods, it can be used to study animal as well as human behavior.

DAVID GRAY/Reuters/Corbis

It can be difficult to remain unobtrusive; even animal behavior may be altered by the observation process.

Researchers are unable to draw causal conclusions.

Observational data are often difficult to quantify for statistical analyses.

Case studies are well suited for study of psychological disorders and therapeutic practices.

Individual cases can provide compelling illustrations to support or undermine a theory.

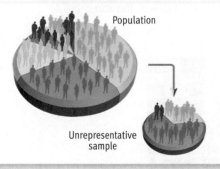

Population

Unrepresentative sample

Subjectivity makes it easy to see what one expects to see based on one's theoretical slant.

Researchers are unable to draw causal conclusions.

Clinical samples are often unrepresentative and suffer from sampling bias.

Data collection can be relatively easy, saving time and money.

Researchers can gather data on difficult-to-observe aspects of behavior.

Questionnaires are well suited for gathering data on attitudes, values, and beliefs from large samples.

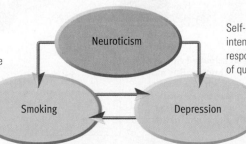

Self-report data are often unreliable, due to intentional deception, social desirability bias, response sets, memory lapses, and poor wording of questions.

Researchers are unable to draw causal conclusions.

It's this third reason for using animals that has generated most of the controversy. Some people maintain that it is wrong to subject animals to harm or pain for research purposes. Essentially, they argue that animals are entitled to the same rights as humans (J. Johnson, 2013; Ryder, 2006). They assert that researchers violate these rights by subjecting animals to unnecessary cruelty in many trivial studies (Bowd & Shapiro, 1993; Hollands, 1989). They also argue that most animal studies are a waste of time because the results may not even apply to humans (Millstone, 1989; Norton, 2005). Some of the more militant animal rights activists have broken into laboratories, destroyed scientists' equipment and research records, and stolen experimental animals.

In spite of the great furor, only 7%–8% of all psychological studies involve animals (mostly rodents and birds). Relatively few of these studies require subjecting the animals to painful or harmful manipulations (American Psychological Association, 1984). Psychologists who defend animal research point to the major advances attributable to psychological research on animals, which many people are unaware of (Baldwin, 1993; Bennett, 2012). Among them are advances in the treatment of mental disorders, neuromuscular disorders, strokes, brain injuries, visual defects, headaches, memory defects, high blood pressure, and problems with pain (Carroll & Overmier, 2001; Domjan & Purdy, 1995). In a defense of animal research, Neal Miller (1985), a prominent psychologist who has done pioneering work in several areas, noted the following:

> At least 20 million dogs and cats are abandoned each year in the United States; half of them are killed in pounds and shelters, and the rest are hit by cars or die of neglect. Less than 1/10,000 as many dogs and cats were used in psychological laboratories. . . . Is it worth sacrificing the lives of our children in order to stop experiments, most of which involve no pain, on a vastly smaller number of mice, rats, dogs, and cats? (p. 427)

As you can see, the manner in which animals can ethically be used for research is a highly charged controversy. Seeking a balanced solution to this issue, Bateson (2011) suggests that the ethical acceptability of specific animal studies should be judged by assessing the studies along three independent dimensions: (1) the extent of anticipated animal suffering, (2) the importance of the research problem addressed, and (3) the likelihood of beneficial discoveries. Psychologists are becoming increasingly sensitive to questions about animal research. Although they continue to use animals in research, strict regulations have been imposed that control nearly every detail of how laboratory animals must be treated (Akins & Panicker, 2012).

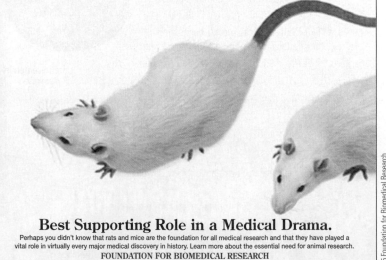

Best Supporting Role in a Medical Drama.
Perhaps you didn't know that rats and mice are the foundation for all medical research and that they have played a vital role in virtually every major medical discovery in history. Learn more about the essential need for animal research.
FOUNDATION FOR BIOMEDICAL RESEARCH
www.fbresearch.org

Many important scientific discoveries have been achieved through animal research, as the advertisement on the right notes. But many people remain vigorously opposed to animal research. The animal liberation activist shown above was covered in fake blood and strapped to a giant vivisection board as part of a protest against animal research in Melbourne, Australia. Clearly, the ethics of animal research is a highly charged controversy.

Ethical Principles in Research

The ethics issues that we have discussed in this section have led the APA to develop a set of ethical standards for researchers (American Psychological Association, 2002). Some of the most important guidelines for research with human participants include the following: (1) people's participation in research should always be voluntary and they should be allowed to withdraw from a study at any time; (2) participants should not be subjected to harmful or dangerous treatments; (3) if a study requires deception, participants should be debriefed (informed of the true nature and purpose of the research) as soon as possible; and (4) participants' right to privacy should never be compromised. Guidelines for research with animals include: (1) harmful or painful procedures cannot be justified unless the potential benefits of the research are substantial, and (2) research animals are entitled to decent living conditions.

2.6 REFLECTING ON THE CHAPTER'S THEMES

Key Learning Goals
- Identify the two unifying themes highlighted in this chapter.

Two of our seven unifying themes have emerged strongly in this chapter. First, the entire chapter is a testimonial to the idea that psychology is empirical. Second, the discussion of methodological flaws in research provides numerous examples of how people's experience of the world can be highly subjective. Let's examine each of these points in more detail.

As explained in Chapter 1, the empirical approach entails testing ideas, basing conclusions on systematic observation, and relying on a healthy brand of skepticism. All of those features of the empirical approach have been apparent in this chapter. As you have seen, psychologists test their ideas by formulating clear hypotheses that involve predictions about relationships between variables. They then use a variety of research methods to collect data, so they can see whether their predictions are supported. The data collection methods are designed to make researchers' observations systematic and precise. The entire venture is saturated with skepticism. In planning and executing their research, scientists are constantly on the lookout for methodological flaws. They publish their findings so that other experts can subject their methods and conclusions to critical scrutiny. Collectively, these procedures represent the essence of the empirical approach.

 Empiricism

 Subjectivity of Experience

The subjectivity of personal experience became apparent in the discussion of methodological problems, especially placebo effects and experimenter bias. When research participants report beneficial effects from a fake treatment (the placebo), it's because they expected to see these effects. The studies showing that many subjects start feeling intoxicated just because they think that they have consumed alcohol are striking demonstrations of the enormous power of people's expectations. Like everyone else, psychologists and other scientists are not immune to the effects of subjective experience. Although they are trained to be objective, even scientists may see what they expect to see or what they want to see. This is one reason that the empirical approach emphasizes precise measurement and a skeptical attitude. The highly subjective nature of experience is exactly what the empirical approach attempts to neutralize.

The publication of empirical studies allows us to apply our skepticism to the research enterprise. However, you cannot critically analyze studies unless you know where and how to find them. In the upcoming Personal Application, we will discuss where studies are published, how to find studies on specific topics, and how to read research reports. In the subsequent Critical Thinking Application, we'll analyze the shortcomings of anecdotal evidence, which should help you appreciate the value of empirical evidence.

2.7 PERSONAL APPLICATION
Finding and Reading Journal Articles

Answer the following "yes" or "no."

____ **1** I have read about scientific studies in newspapers and magazines and sometimes wondered, "How did they come to those conclusions?"

____ **2** When I go to the library, I often have difficulty figuring out how to find information based on research.

____ **3** I have tried to read scientific reports and found them to be too technical and difficult to understand.

If you responded "yes" to any of the above statements, you have struggled with the information explosion in the sciences. We live in a research-oriented society. The number of studies conducted in most sciences is growing at a dizzying pace.

This Personal Application is intended to help you cope with the information explosion in psychology. It assumes that there may come a time when you need to examine original psychological research. Perhaps it will be in your role as a student (working on a term paper, for instance), in another role (parent, teacher, nurse, administrator), or merely out of curiosity. In any case, this Application explains the nature of technical journals and discusses how to find and read articles in them.

The Nature of Technical Journals

As you will recall from earlier in the chapter, a *journal* is a periodical that publishes technical and scholarly material, usually in a narrowly defined area of inquiry. Journal articles represent the core of intellectual activity in any academic discipline. Although they are periodicals, you generally will not find technical journals at your local newsstand. Even public libraries carry relatively few professional

journals. Academic libraries and professors account for the vast majority of subscriptions to technical journals.

In psychology, most journal articles are reports that describe original empirical studies. These reports permit researchers to communicate their findings to the scientific community. Another common type of article is the review article. *Review articles* summarize and reconcile the findings of a large number of studies on a specific issue. Some psychology journals also publish comments or critiques of previously published research, book reviews, theoretical treatises, and descriptions of methodological innovations.

Finding Journal Articles

Reports of psychological research are commonly mentioned in newspapers and on the Internet. These summaries can be helpful to readers, but they often embrace the most sensational conclusions that might be drawn from the research. They also tend to include many oversimplifications and factual errors. Thus, if a study mentioned in the press is of interest to you, you may want to track down the original article to ensure that you get accurate information.

Most discussions of research in the popular press do not mention where you can locate the original technical article. However, there is a way to find out. A computerized database called PsycINFO makes it possible to locate journal articles by specific researchers or scholarly work on specific topics. This huge online database, which is updated constantly, contains brief summaries, or *abstracts*, of journal articles, books, and chapters in edited books, reporting, reviewing, or theorizing about psychological research. Over 2500 journals are checked regularly to select items for inclusion. The abstracts are concise—about 75 to 175 words. They briefly describe the hypotheses, methods, results, and conclusions of the studies.

Each abstract should allow you to determine whether an article is relevant to your interests. If it is, you should be able to find the article in your library (or to order it) because a complete bibliographic reference is provided. The PsycINFO database can be accessed online through most academic libraries or directly via the Internet.

Although news accounts of research rarely mention where a study was published, they often mention the name of the researcher. If you have this information, the easiest way to find a specific article is to search PsycINFO for materials published by that researcher. For example, let's say you read a magazine article about the study we discussed earlier in the chapter that found that men were more sexually attracted to women who wore the color red. Let's assume that the news report mentioned the name of Andrew Elliot as the lead author and indicated that the article was published in 2008. To track down the original article, you would search for journal articles published by Andrew Elliot in 2008. If you conducted this search, you

The various types of research studies conducted by psychologists are published in professional journals, such as those shown here.

would turn up a list of seven articles, and the relevant article, titled "Romantic red: Red enhances men's attraction to women" (Elliot & Niesta, 2008), would be obvious. **Figure 2.12** shows what you would see if you clicked to obtain the Abstract and Citation for this article. As you can see, the abstract shows that the original report was published in the November 2008 issue of the *Journal of Personality and Social Psychology*. Armed with this information, you could obtain the article easily.

You can also search PsycINFO for research literature on particular topics, such as achievement motivation, aggressive behavior, alcoholism, appetite disorders, or artistic ability. These computerized literature searches can be much more powerful, precise, and thorough than traditional, manual searches in a library. PsycINFO can sift through a few million articles in a matter of seconds to identify *all* the articles on a subject, such as alcoholism. Obviously, there is no way you can match this efficiency stumbling around in the stacks at your library. Moreover, the computer allows you to pair up topics to swiftly narrow your search to exactly those issues that

interest you. For example, if you were preparing a term paper on whether marijuana affects memory, you could quickly identify all the articles dealing with marijuana *and* memory, which would be invaluable.

Reading Journal Articles

Once you find the journal articles you want to examine, you need to know how to decipher them. You can process the information in such articles more efficiently if you understand how they are organized. Depending on your needs and purpose, you may want to simply skim through some of the sections. Journal articles follow a fairly standard organization, which includes the following sections and features.

Abstract

Most journals print a concise summary at the beginning of each article. This abstract allows readers scanning the journal to quickly decide whether articles are relevant to their interests.

Introduction

The introduction presents an overview of the problem studied in the research.

It mentions relevant theories and quickly reviews previous research that bears on the problem, usually citing shortcomings in previous research that necessitate the current study. This review of the state of knowledge on the topic usually progresses to a specific and precise statement regarding the hypotheses under investigation.

Method

The next section provides a thorough description of the research methods used in the study. Information is provided on the subjects used, the procedures followed, and the data collection techniques employed. This description is made detailed enough to permit another researcher to attempt to replicate the study.

Results

The data obtained in the study are reported in the results section. This section often creates problems for novice readers because it includes complex statistical analyses, figures, tables, and graphs. This section does not include any inferences based on the data, as such conclusions are supposed to follow in the next section. Instead, it simply contains a concise summary of the raw data and the statistical analyses.

Discussion

In the discussion section you will find the conclusions drawn by the author(s). In contrast to the results section, which is a straightforward summary of empirical observations, the discussion section allows for interpretation and evaluation of the data. Implications for theory and factual knowledge in the discipline are discussed. Conclusions are usually qualified carefully. Any limitations in the study may be acknowledged. This section may also include suggestions for future research on the issue.

References

At the end of each article is a list of bibliographic references for any studies cited. This list permits the reader to examine firsthand other relevant studies mentioned in the article. The references list is often a rich source of leads about other articles that are germane to the topic that you are looking into.

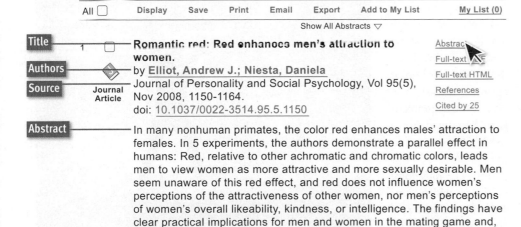

All ☐   Display   Save   Print   Email   Export   Add to My List   My List (0)

Show All Abstracts ▽

Title — 1 ☐ **Romantic red: Red enhances men's attraction to women.**

Authors — by **Elliot, Andrew J.; Niesta, Daniela**

Source — Journal Article — Journal of Personality and Social Psychology, Vol 95(5), Nov 2008, 1150-1164.
doi: 10.1037/0022-3514.95.5.1150

Abstract
Full-text PDF
Full-text HTML
References
Cited by 25

Abstract — In many nonhuman primates, the color red enhances males' attraction to females. In 5 experiments, the authors demonstrate a parallel effect in humans: Red, relative to other achromatic and chromatic colors, leads men to view women as more attractive and more sexually desirable. Men seem unaware of this red effect, and red does not influence women's perceptions of the attractiveness of other women, nor men's perceptions of women's overall likeability, kindness, or intelligence. The findings have clear practical implications for men and women in the mating game and, perhaps, for fashion consultants, product designers, and marketers. Furthermore, the findings document the value of extending research on signal coloration to humans and of considering color as something of a common language, both within and across species. (PsycINFO Database Record © 2010 APA, all rights reserved)

FIGURE 2.12

Example of a PsycINFO abstract. This information is what you would see if you clicked to see the abstract of the study by Elliot and Niesta (2008), which reported that the color red increases men's attraction to women. It is a typical abstract from the online PsycINFO database. Each abstract in PsycINFO provides a summary of a specific journal article, book, or chapter in an edited book, and complete bibliographical information.

2.8

Key Learning Goals
- Recognize anecdotal evidence, and understand why it is unreliable.

2.8 CRITICAL THINKING APPLICATION
The Perils of Anecdotal Evidence: "I Have a Friend Who..."

Here's a tough problem. Suppose you are the judge in a family law court. As you look over the cases that will come before you today, you see that one divorcing couple have managed to settle almost all of the important decisions with minimal conflict. They have worked out who gets the house, who gets the car and the dog, and who pays which bills. However, there is one crucial issue left: Each parent wants custody of the children. Because they could not reach an agreement on their own, the case is now in your court. You will need the wisdom of the legendary King Solomon for this decision. How can you determine what is in the best interests of the children?

Child custody decisions have major consequences for all of the parties involved. As you review the case records, you see that both parents are loving and competent. So, there are no obvious reasons for selecting one parent over the other as the primary caretaker. In considering various alternatives, you mull over the possibility of awarding *joint custody*. In this arrangement, children spend half their time with each parent instead of the more usual situation where one parent has primary custody and the other has visitation rights. Joint custody seems to have some obvious benefits. But you are not sure how well these arrangements actually work. Will the children feel more attached to both parents if the parents share custody equally? Or will the children feel hassled by always moving around, perhaps spending half the week at one parent's home and half at the other parent's home? Can parents who are already feuding over child custody issues make these complicated arrangements work? Or is joint custody just too disruptive to everyone's life? You really don't know the answer to any of these vexing questions.

One of the lawyers involved in the case knows that you are thinking about the possibility of joint custody. She also understands that you want more information about how well joint custody tends to work before you make a decision. To help you make up your mind, she tells you about a divorced couple who have had a joint custody arrangement for many years. She offers to have them appear in court to describe their experiences "firsthand." They and their children can answer any questions you might have about the pros and cons of joint custody. They should be in the best position to know how well joint custody works because they are living it. Sounds like a reasonable plan. What do you think?

I hope you said, "No, no, no!" What's wrong with asking someone who's been there how well joint custody works? The crux of the problem is that the evidence a single family brings to the question of joint custody is **anecdotal evidence, which consists of personal stories about specific incidents and experiences.** Anecdotal evidence can be seductive. For example, one study found that psychology majors' choices of future courses to enroll in were influenced more by a couple of students' brief anecdotes than by extensive statistics on many other students' ratings of the courses from the previous term (Borgida & Nisbett, 1977). The power of anecdotes was also apparent in a more recent study that explored how to persuade people to take a personal health risk (for hepatitis B infection) more seriously. The researchers found that

An abundance of anecdotal reports suggest that an association exists between the full moon and strange, erratic behavior. These reports often sound compelling, but as the text explains, anecdotal evidence is flawed in many ways. When researchers have examined the issue systematically, they have consistently found no association between lunar phases and the incidence of psychiatric emergencies, domestic violence, suicide, and so forth (Biermann et al., 2005; Chudler, 2007; Dowling, 2005; Kung & Mrazek, 2005; Lilienfeld & Arkowitz, 2009; McLay, Daylo, & Hammer, 2006).

© iStockphoto.com/Eerik

anecdotal accounts had more persuasive impact than sound factual and statistical evidence (de Wit, Das, & Vet, 2008). Anecdotes readily sway people because they are often concrete, vivid, and memorable. Many politicians are keenly aware of the power of anecdotes, and they frequently rely on a single vivid story rather than on solid data to sway voters' views. However, anecdotal evidence is fundamentally flawed (Ruscio, 2006; Stanovich, 2004).

Let's use some of the concepts introduced in the main body of the chapter to analyze the shortcomings of anecdotal evidence. First, in the language of research designs, the anecdotal experiences of one family resemble a single *case study*. The story they tell about their experiences with joint custody may be quite interesting, but their experiences—good or bad—cannot be used to generalize to other couples. Why not? Because they are only one family. They may be unusual in some way that affects how well they manage joint custody. To draw general conclusions based on the case study approach, you need a systematic series of case studies. Then you can look for threads of consistency. A single family is a sample size of one, which surely is not large enough to derive broad principles that would apply to other families.

Second, anecdotal evidence is similar to *self-report data,* which can be distorted for a variety of reasons, such as people's tendency to give socially approved information about themselves (the *social desirability bias*). When researchers use tests and surveys to gather self-report data, they can take steps to reduce or assess the impact of distortions in their data. But there are no comparable safeguards with anecdotal evidence. Thus, the family that appears in your courtroom may be eager to make a good impression and unknowingly slant their story accordingly.

Anecdotes are often inaccurate and riddled with embellishments. We will see in Chapter 7 that memories of personal experiences are far less accurate and reliable than widely assumed (Loftus, 2004; Schacter, 2001). And, although it would not be an issue in this case, in other situations *anecdotal evidence often consists of stories that people have heard about others' experiences.* Hearsay evidence is not accepted in courtrooms for good reason. As stories are passed on from one person to another, they often become increasingly distorted and inaccurate.

Can you think of any other reasons for being wary of anecdotal evidence? After reading the chapter, perhaps you thought about the possibility of *sampling bias.* Do you think that the lawyer will pick a couple at random from all those who have been awarded joint custody? It seems highly unlikely. If she wants you to award joint custody, she will find a couple for whom this arrangement has worked very well. However, if she wants you to award sole custody to her client, she will find a couple whose inability to make joint custody work had dire consequences for their children. One reason people love to work with anecdotal evidence is that it is so readily manipulated. They can usually find an anecdote or two to support their position, whether or not the anecdotes are representative of most people's experiences.

If the testimony of one family cannot be used in making this critical custody decision, what sort of evidence should you be looking for? One goal of effective critical thinking is to make decisions based on solid evidence. This process is called *evidence-based decision making.* In this case, you would need to consider the overall experiences of a large sample of families who have tried joint custody arrangements. In general, across many different families, did the children in joint custody develop well? Did the children or the parents experience an exceptionally high rate of emotional problems or other signs of stress? Did a higher percentage of families return to court at a later date to change their joint custody arrangements than did families with other types of custody arrangements? You can probably think of additional information that you would want to collect regarding the outcomes of various custody arrangements.

In examining research reports, many people recognize the need to evaluate the evidence by looking for the types of flaws described in the main body of the chapter (sampling bias, experimenter bias, and so forth). Curiously, though, many of the same people then fail to apply the same principles of good evidence to their personal decisions in everyday life. The tendency to rely on the anecdotal experiences of a small number of people is sometimes called the *"I have a friend who . . ." syndrome,* because no matter what the topic is, it seems that someone will provide a personal story about a friend as evidence for his or her particular point of view. In short, when you hear people support their assertions with personal stories, a little skepticism is in order.

TABLE 2.2 Critical Thinking Skills Discussed in This Application

Skill	Description
Recognizing the limitations of anecdotal evidence	The critical thinker is wary of anecdotal evidence, which consists of personal stories used to support one's assertions. Anecdotal evidence tends to be unrepresentative, inaccurate, and unreliable.
Using evidence-based decision making	The critical thinker understands the need to seek sound evidence to guide decisions in everyday life.

CHAPTER 2 CONCEPT CHART

THE SCIENTIFIC APPROACH

Goals

- Measurement and description
- Understanding and prediction
- Application and control

Steps in an investigation

1. Formulate a testable hypothesis.
2. Select the method and design the study.
3. Collect the data.
4. Analyze the data and draw conclusions.
5. Report the findings.

Advantages

- Clarity and precision yield better communication.
- Intolerance of error yields more reliable data.

EXPERIMENTAL RESEARCH

Elements

Independent variable (IV): Condition or event manipulated by the experimenter

Dependent variable (DV): Aspect of behavior thought to be affected by the independent variable

Experimental group: Participants, or subjects, who receive special treatment

Control group: Similar subjects who do not receive the treatment given to the experimental group

Extraneous variables: Factors besides the IV that might affect the DV; hence, they need to be controlled

Variations

- Can have one group of subjects serve as their own control group
- Can manipulate more than one independent variable in a study

Advantages and disadvantages

- Permits conclusions about cause-and-effect relationships
- Manipulations and control often make experiments artificial
- Practical realities and ethical concerns make it impossible to conduct experiments on many issues

Hypothesis:
Anxiety increases desire to affiliate

Subjects randomly assigned to experimental and control groups

Manipulation of independent variable

Experimental group
"Shocks will be very painful"
(high anxiety)

Control group
"Shocks will be mild and painless"
(low anxiety)

Measurement of dependent variable

High-anxiety group indicated a desire to wait with others more than did low-anxiety group

Conclusion:
Anxiety does increase desire to affiliate

DESCRIPTIVE/CORRELATIONAL RESEARCH

Correlation

Correlation exists when two variables are related to each other.

Types: *Positive* (variables covary in the same direction) or *negative* (variables covary in the opposite direction)

Correlation coefficient: Numerical index of degree of relationship between two variables

Strength: The closer the correlation to either -1.00 or +1.00, the stronger the relationship.

Prediction: The stronger the correlation, the better one can predict.

Causation: Correlation is not equivalent to causation.

Examples of specific correlational methods

Naturalistic observation: Careful, systematic observation, but no intervention with subjects

Case study: In-depth investigation of a single participant, typically involving data from many sources

Survey: Questionnaires and interviews are used to gather information about specific aspects of participants' behavior

Advantages and disadvantages

- Broadens the scope of the phenomena that psychologists can study (can explore issues that could not be examined with experimental methods)
- Cannot demonstrate that two variables are causally related

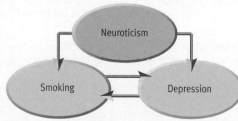

COMMON FLAWS IN RESEARCH

Sampling bias
Exists when a sample is not representative of the population

Placebo effects
Occur when participants' expectations lead them to experience some change, even though they receive empty or fake treatment

Distortions in self-report data
Result from problems, such as social desirability bias and halo effects, that happen when participants give verbal accounts of their behavior

Experimenter bias
Occurs when a researcher's expectations or preferences about the outcome of a study influence the results obtained

ETHICAL ISSUES

The question of deception

Q: Should researchers be permitted to mislead participants?

Yes
- Otherwise, important issues could not be investigated.
- Empirical evidence suggests that deception is not harmful to subjects.

No
- Deception is inherently immoral and may undermine participants' trust in others.
- Deceptive studies often create stress for subjects.

© 2005 Foundation for Biomedical Research

The question of animal research

Q: Should researchers be permitted to subject animals to harmful or painful procedures?

Yes
- Otherwise, important issues could not be investigated.
- Relatively little animal research involves pain or harm.

No
- Animals are entitled to the same rights as humans.
- Animal studies are often trivial or may not apply to humans.

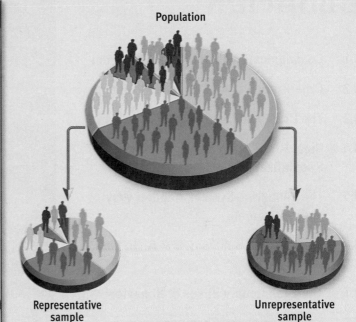

Population

Representative sample

Unrepresentative sample

APPLICATIONS

- Most original research in psychology is published in journal articles.
- PsycINFO is a computerized database that contains brief summaries of newly published journal articles, books, and chapters in edited books.
- Anecdotes tend to influence people because they are often concrete, vivid, and memorable.
- However, anecdotal evidence is based on the equivalent of a single case study; there are no safeguards to reduce distortions in self-report data; and many anecdotes are inaccurate, second-hand reports.

© Wayne Weiten

CHAPTER 3

THE BIOLOGICAL BASES OF BEHAVIOR

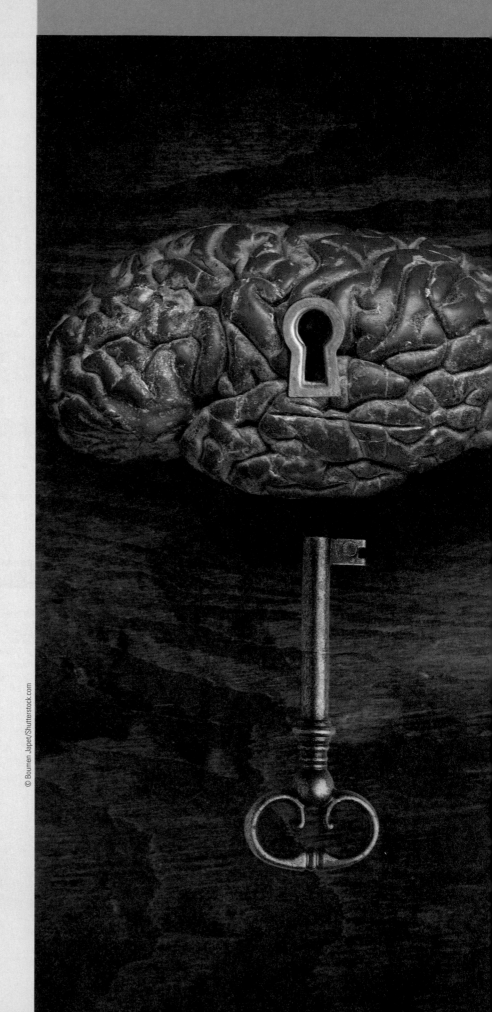

© Boumen Japet/Shutterstock.com

Themes in this Chapter

Heredity & Environment

Multifactorial Causation

Empiricism

An ordinary-looking, 30-year-old mother of three is walking down the street in a seedy neighborhood around 10:00 p.m. when she encounters a drugged-out man who presses a knife to her throat and threatens to kill her. Remarkably, the woman shows no signs of fear. Her heart rate doesn't quicken, her breathing doesn't change, she doesn't get nervous. Her completely calm, unruffled response to her attacker so unnerves *him* that he lets her go! Meet the woman who knows no fear.

The woman in this story, known by her initials, S.M., has attracted interest from scientists who are intrigued by her apparent inability to experience fear. In a recent study designed to investigate S.M.'s fearlessness, researchers exposed her to a variety of situations that would trigger fear in most people (Feinstein et al., 2011). For ethical reasons they chose fear-inducing stimuli that posed relatively little risk of actual harm. For example, they took her to an exotic pet store, where they exposed her to snakes and spiders. What was her reaction? Instead of being scared, S.M. was fascinated and repeatedly asked to touch large snakes and a tarantula that were not safe to handle. Next, the scientists took S.M. to a famous haunted house. While other patrons screamed in fright, S.M. giggled and poked one of the monsters in the head—again scaring *him*. Taking yet another tack, the researchers showed S.M. clips from well-known scary movies, such as *The Ring*. She found the clips entertaining, but she experienced no fear. Finally, the researchers used a variety of methods to determine whether S.M. experiences other emotions. Their results revealed that she exhibits all the other basic emotions—anger, sadness, disgust,

happiness, surprise—much like anyone else. Other tests demonstrated that S.M. scores normally on measures of intelligence, language, and memory.

Why is this woman absolutely fearless, yet she experiences other emotions? What could cause such a bizarre, exquisitely specific emotional deficit? It turns out that in childhood S.M. suffered an extremely rare disease that destroyed a small structure called the *amygdala*, which is located in both the right and left halves of her brain. Many studies, mostly with animals, have suggested that the amygdala is a crucial control center for the experience of fear. S.M.'s case provides compelling, new *human* evidence that the amygdala has a unique role in the regulation of fear. By the way, if you are thinking that being fearless sounds appealing, think again. The research on S.M. has shown that she is fundamentally lacking when it comes to detecting when she's in danger, which is why she has a long history of getting herself into perilous situations.

SM's unusual case provides a dramatic demonstration that behavioral functioning is ultimately controlled by the brain. The fact that S.M. feels all the other emotions except fear shows just how precise the biological bases of behavior can be. The human brain is so complex, no computer has ever come remotely close to duplicating it. Your nervous system contains as many cells busily integrating and relaying information as there are stars in our galaxy. Whether you are scratching your nose or composing an essay, the activity of those cells underlies what you do. It is little wonder, then, that many psychologists have dedicated themselves to exploring the biological bases of behavior.

3.1 COMMUNICATION IN THE NERVOUS SYSTEM

Key Learning Goals

- Identify the various parts of the neuron and the main functions of glial cells.
- Describe the neural impulse, and explain how neurons communicate at chemical synapses.
- Discuss some of the functions of acetylcholine, the monoamine neurotransmitters, GABA, and endorphins.

Imagine that you are watching a scary movie. As the tension mounts, your palms sweat and your heart beats faster. You begin shoveling popcorn into your mouth, carelessly spilling some in your lap. If someone were to ask you what you are doing at this moment, you would probably say, "Nothing—just watching the movie." Yet some highly complex processes are occurring without your thinking about them. A stimulus (the light from the screen) is striking your eye. Almost instantaneously, your brain is interpreting the light stimulus, and signals are flashing to other parts of your body, leading to a flurry of activity. Your sweat glands are releasing perspiration; your heartbeat is quickening; and muscular movements are enabling your hand to find the popcorn, and more or less successfully, lift it to your mouth.

Even in this simple example, you can see that behavior depends on rapid information processing. Information travels immediately from your eye to your brain, from your brain to the muscles of your arm and hand, and from your palms back to your brain. In essence, your nervous system is a complex communication network in which signals are constantly being received, integrated, and transmitted. The nervous system handles information, just as the circulatory system handles blood. In this section, we take a close look at communication in the nervous system.

Nervous Tissue: The Basic Hardware

Your nervous system is living tissue composed of cells. The cells in the nervous system fall into two major categories: *glia* and *neurons*. Let's look at neurons first.

Neurons

Neurons **are individual cells in the nervous system that receive, integrate, and transmit information.** They are the basic links that permit communication within the nervous system. The vast majority of them communicate only with other neurons. However, a small minority receive signals from outside the nervous system (from sensory organs) or carry messages from the nervous system to the muscles that move the body.

A highly simplified drawing of two "typical" neurons is shown in **Figure 3.1**. **The** *soma*, **or cell body, contains the cell nucleus and much of the chemical machinery common to most cells** (*soma* is Greek for "body"). The rest of the neuron is devoted exclusively to handling information. The neurons in **Figure 3.1** have a number of branched, feeler-like structures called *dendritic trees* (*dendrite* is a Greek word for "tree"). Each individual branch is a *dendrite*. **Dendrites are the parts of a neuron that are specialized to receive information.** Most neurons receive information from many other cells—sometimes thousands of others—and so have extensive dendritic trees.

From the many dendrites, information flows into the cell body, then travels away from the soma along the *axon* (from the Greek for "axle"). **The** *axon* **is a long, thin fiber that transmits signals away from the soma to other neurons or to muscles or glands.** Axons may be quite long (sometimes several feet), and they may branch off to communicate with a number of other cells.

In humans, many axons are wrapped in cells with a high concentration of a white, fatty substance called *myelin*. **The** *myelin sheath* **is insulating material that encases some axons.** Myelin wrapping functions to speed up the transmission of signals that move along axons (Zorumski, Isenberg, & Mennerick, 2009). By preventing axons from

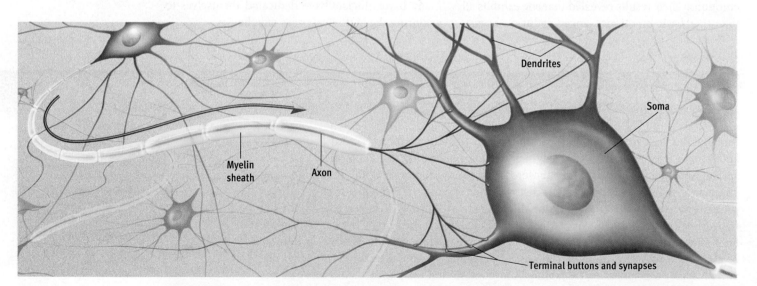

Dendrites

Soma

Myelin sheath

Axon

Terminal buttons and synapses

FIGURE 3.1

Structure of the neuron. Neurons are the communication links of the nervous system. This diagram highlights the key parts of a neuron, including specialized receptor areas (dendrites); the cell body (soma); the axon fiber along which impulses are transmitted; and the terminal buttons, which release chemical messengers that carry signals to other neurons. Neurons vary considerably in size and shape and are usually densely interconnected.

sprouting in new directions, myelin also stabilizes axon structure and patterns of connectivity in neural networks (Fields, 2014). If certain axons' myelin sheaths deteriorate, signals may not be transmitted effectively. The loss of muscle control seen with the disease *multiple sclerosis* is due to a degeneration of myelin sheaths (Joffe, 2009). That said, not all axons are myelinated, and among those that are, the myelin sheaths can be distributed in a variety of ways. In some axons, segments that have myelin sheaths may be interspersed with long segments that are unmyelinated (Tomassy et al., 2014).

The axon ends in a cluster of **terminal buttons, which are small knobs that secrete chemicals called *neurotransmitters*.** These chemicals serve as messengers that may activate neighboring neurons. The points at which neurons interconnect are called *synapses*. **A *synapse* is a junction where information is transmitted from one neuron to another** (*synapse* is from the Greek for "junction"). To summarize, information is received at the dendrites, is passed through the soma and along the axon, and is transmitted to the dendrites of other cells at meeting points called synapses.

Glia

***Glia* are cells found throughout the nervous system that provide various types of support for neurons.** Glia (literally "glue") tend to be much smaller than neurons. It was once thought that they outnumbered neurons by as much as 10 to 1, but recent research suggests that the human brain consists of roughly equal numbers of neurons and glial cells (Azevedo et al., 2009). Glial cells serve many functions. For example, they supply nourishment to neurons, help remove neurons' waste products, and provide insulation around many axons. The myelin sheaths that encase some axons are derived from special types of glial cells. Glia also play a complicated role in the development of the nervous system in the human embryo.

These functions, which have been known for many years, made glial cells the unsung heroes of the nervous system. Until recently, it was thought that the "glamorous" work in the nervous system—the transmission and integration of informational signals—was the exclusive province of the neurons. New research, however, suggests that glia may also send and receive chemical signals (Deitmer & Rose, 2010; Fields, 2011). Some types of glia can detect neural impulses and send signals to other glial cells, some of which can feed signals back to neurons. Surprised by this discovery, neuroscientists are now trying to figure out how this signaling system interfaces with the neural communication system. One view is that glia *modulate* the signaling of neurons, dampening or amplifying synaptic activity (Halassa & Haydon, 2010). Another view is that glial cells' primary role is to shield synapses from the "chatter" of surrounding neuronal activity, thus enhancing the signal-to-noise ratio in the nervous system (Nedergaard & Verkhratsky, 2012). These alternate viewpoints are not necessarily incompatible, and much remains to be learned.

Recent research suggesting that glial cells may play a role in a variety of major disorders underscores their importance. For example, some studies indicate that dysfunction in glial cells may contribute to the cognitive impairment seen in schizophrenic disorders (Mitterauer, 2011) and to some forms of depressive disorders (Jellinger, 2013). Another line of research has raised the possibility that a gradual deterioration of glial tissue might contribute to Alzheimer's disease (Olabarria et al., 2010). Glial cells have also been implicated as a key factor in the experience of chronic pain (Ji, Berta, & Nedergaard, 2013).

Although glia may contribute to information processing in the nervous system, the bulk of this crucial work is handled by the neurons. Thus, we need to examine the process of neural activity in more detail.

The Neural Impulse: Using Energy to Send Information

What happens when a neuron is stimulated? What is the nature of the signal—the *neural impulse*—that moves through the neuron? These were the questions that Alan Hodgkin and Andrew Huxley set out to answer in their groundbreaking experiments with axons removed

> **REALITY CHECK**

Misconception

Neurons are responsible for all the information processing in the nervous system.

Reality

Until recently, it *was* thought that the transmission and integration of informational signals was the exclusive role of the neurons. However, newer research has demonstrated that glial cells also play an important role in information processing.

from squid. Why did they choose to work with squid axons? Because squid have a pair of "giant" axons that are about a hundred times larger than those in humans (which still makes them only about as thick as a human hair). This large size permitted Hodgkin and Huxley to insert fine wires called *microelectrodes* into the axons. By using the microelectrodes to record the electrical activity in individual neurons, Hodgkin and Huxley were able to unravel the mystery of the neural impulse.

The Neuron at Rest: A Tiny Battery

Hodgkin and Huxley (1952) learned that the neural impulse is a complex electrochemical reaction. Both inside and outside the neuron are fluids containing electrically charged atoms and molecules called *ions*. Positively charged sodium and potassium ions and negatively charged chloride ions flow back and forth across the cell membrane, but they do not cross at the same rate. The difference in flow rates leads to a slightly higher concentration of negatively charged ions inside the cell. The resulting voltage means that the neuron at rest is a tiny battery, a store of potential energy. **The *resting potential* of a neuron is its stable, negative charge when the cell is inactive.** As shown in **Figure 3.2(a)**, this charge is about −70 millivolts, roughly one-twentieth of the voltage of a flashlight battery.

The Action Potential

As long as the voltage of a neuron remains constant, the cell is quiet, and no messages are being sent. When the neuron is stimulated, channels in its cell membrane open, briefly allowing positively charged sodium ions to rush in. For an instant, the neuron's charge is less negative, but then it gradually becomes positive, creating an action potential (McCormick, 2008). **An *action potential* is a very brief shift in a neuron's electrical charge that travels along an axon.** The firing of an action potential is reflected in the voltage spike shown in **Figure 3.2(b)**. Like a spark traveling along a trail of gunpowder, the voltage change races down the axon.

After the firing of an action potential, the channels in the cell membrane that opened to let in sodium close up. Some time is needed before they are ready to open again, and until that time, the neuron cannot fire. **The *absolute refractory period* is the minimum length of time after an action potential, during which another action potential cannot begin.** This "down time" isn't very long, only 1 or 2 milliseconds.

The All-or-None Law

The neural impulse is an all-or-none proposition, like firing a gun. You can't half-fire a gun. The same is true of the neuron's firing of action potentials. Either the neuron fires or it doesn't, and its action potentials are all the same size (Kandel, Barres, & Hudspeth, 2013). That is, weaker stimuli do not produce smaller action potentials and stronger stimuli do not evoke larger action potentials.

Even though the action potential is an all-or-nothing event, neurons *can* convey information about the strength of a stimulus. They do so by varying the *rate* at which they fire action potentials. In general, a stronger stimulus will cause a

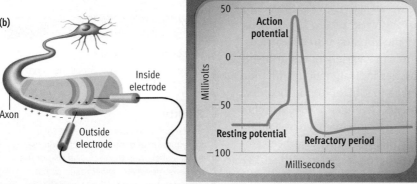

FIGURE 3.2

The neural impulse. The electrochemical properties of the neuron allow it to transmit signals. The electric charge of a neuron can be measured with a pair of electrodes connected to an oscilloscope, as Hodgkin and Huxley showed with a squid axon. Because of its exceptionally thick axons, the squid has frequently been used by scientists studying the neural impulse. **(a)** At rest, the neuron's voltage hovers around −70 millivolts. **(b)** When the axon is stimulated, there is a brief jump in a neuron's voltage, resulting in a spike on the oscilloscope recording of the neuron's electrical activity. This change in voltage, called an action potential, travels along the axon like a spark traveling along a trail of gunpowder.

cell to fire a more rapid volley of neural impulses than a weaker stimulus will. For example, a dim light might trigger 5 action potentials per second in a visual cell, whereas brighter lights might trigger 100 or 200 impulses per second (Burkhardt, 2010).

The Synapse: Where Neurons Meet

In the nervous system, the neural impulse functions as a signal. For that signal to have any meaning for the system as a whole, it must be transmitted from the neuron to other cells. As noted earlier, this transmission takes place at special junctions called *synapses,* which depend on *chemical* messengers.

Sending Signals: Chemicals as Couriers

A "typical" synapse is shown in **Figure 3.3**. The first thing that you should notice is that the two neurons don't actually touch. They are separated by the **synaptic cleft, a microscopic gap between the terminal button of one neuron and the cell membrane**

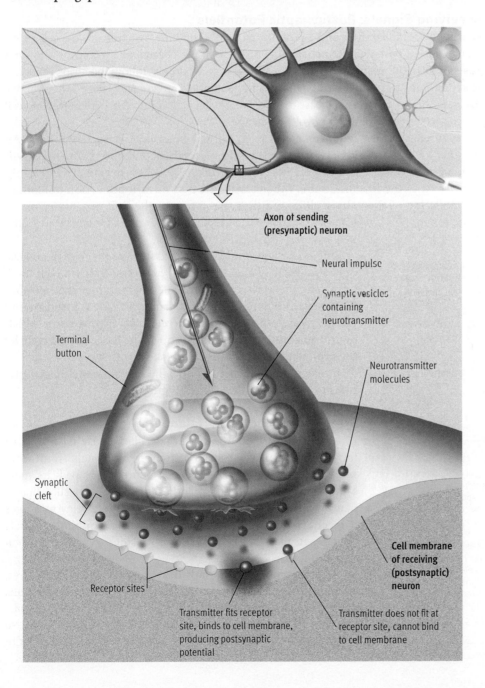

FIGURE 3.3

The synapse. When a neural impulse reaches an axon's terminal buttons, it triggers the release of chemical messengers called neurotransmitters. The neurotransmitter molecules diffuse across the synaptic cleft and bind to receptor sites on the postsynaptic neuron. A specific neurotransmitter can bind only to receptor sites that its molecular structure will fit into, much like a key must fit a lock.

Axon of sending (presynaptic) neuron

Neural impulse

Synaptic vesicles containing neurotransmitter

Terminal button

Neurotransmitter molecules

Synaptic cleft

Cell membrane of receiving (postsynaptic) neuron

Receptor sites

Transmitter fits receptor site, binds to cell membrane, producing postsynaptic potential

Transmitter does not fit at receptor site, cannot bind to cell membrane

of another neuron. Signals have to cross this gap to permit neurons to communicate. In this situation, the neuron that sends a signal across the gap is called the *presynaptic neuron,* and the neuron that receives the signal is called the *postsynaptic neuron.*

How do messages travel across the gaps between neurons? As mentioned earlier, the arrival of an action potential at an axon's terminal buttons triggers the release of **neurotransmitters—chemicals that transmit information from one neuron to another.** Within the buttons, most of these chemicals are stored in small sacs, called *synaptic vesicles.* The neurotransmitters are released when a vesicle fuses with the membrane of the presynaptic cell and its contents spill into the synaptic cleft (Schwarz, 2008). After their release, neurotransmitters diffuse across the synaptic cleft to the membrane of the receiving cell. There they may bind with special molecules in the postsynaptic cell membrane at various *receptor sites.* These sites are specifically "tuned" to recognize and respond to some neurotransmitters but not to others (Siegelbaum & Kandel, 2013).

Receiving Signals: Postsynaptic Potentials

When a neurotransmitter and a receptor molecule combine, reactions in the cell membrane cause a **postsynaptic potential (PSP), a voltage change at a receptor site on a postsynaptic cell membrane.** Postsynaptic potentials do *not* follow the all-or-none law as action potentials do. Instead, postsynaptic potentials are *graded.* That is, they vary in size, and they increase or decrease the *probability* of a neural impulse in the receiving cell in proportion to the amount of voltage change.

Two types of messages can be sent from cell to cell: excitatory and inhibitory. An *excitatory PSP* is a positive voltage shift that *increases* the likelihood that the postsynaptic neuron will fire action potentials. An *inhibitory PSP* is a negative voltage shift that *decreases* the likelihood that the postsynaptic neuron will fire action potentials. The direction of the voltage shift, and thus the nature of the PSP (excitatory or inhibitory), depends on which receptor sites are activated in the postsynaptic neuron (Kandel, 2000).

The excitatory or inhibitory effects produced at a synapse last only a fraction of a second. Then neurotransmitters drift away from receptor sites or are inactivated by enzymes that metabolize (convert) them into inactive forms. Most are reabsorbed into the presynaptic neuron through **reuptake, a process in which neurotransmitters are sponged up from the synaptic cleft by the presynaptic membrane.** Reuptake allows synapses to recycle their materials. Reuptake and the other key processes in synaptic transmission are summarized in **Figure 3.4.**

Integrating Signals: A Balancing Act

Most neurons are interlinked in complex, dense networks. In fact, a neuron may receive a symphony of signals from *thousands* of other neurons. That same neuron may pass its messages along to thousands of other neurons, as well. Thus, a neuron must do a great deal more than simply relay messages it receives. It must *integrate* excitatory and inhibitory signals arriving at many synapses before it "decides" whether to fire a neural impulse.

Most neurons are interlinked in complex chains, pathways, circuits, and networks. Our perceptions, thoughts, and actions depend on *patterns* of neural activity in elaborate, widely distributed neural networks (van den Heuvel & Sporns, 2013). These networks consist of interconnected neurons that frequently fire

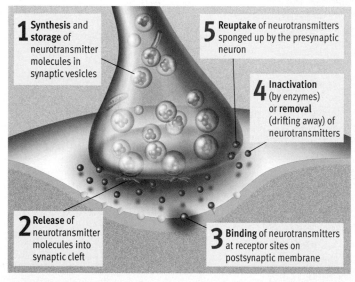

1 **Synthesis** and **storage** of neurotransmitter molecules in synaptic vesicles

2 **Release** of neurotransmitter molecules into synaptic cleft

3 **Binding** of neurotransmitters at receptor sites on postsynaptic membrane

4 **Inactivation** (by enzymes) or **removal** (drifting away) of neurotransmitters

5 **Reuptake** of neurotransmitters sponged up by the presynaptic neuron

FIGURE 3.4

Overview of synaptic transmission. The main processes in synaptic transmission are summarized here. The five key processes involved in communication at synapses are (1) synthesis and storage, (2) release, (3) binding, (4) inactivation or removal, and (5) reuptake of neurotransmitters. As you'll see in this chapter and the remainder of the book, the effects of many phenomena—such as pain, drug use, and some diseases—can be explained in terms of how they alter one or more of these processes (usually at synapses releasing a specific neurotransmitter).

either together or sequentially to perform certain functions. The links in these neural networks are fluid, as new synaptic connections may be made while some old synaptic connections wither away. Moreover, many aspects of behavior appear to depend on dynamic interactions between these complicated networks (Turk-Browne, 2013).

Ironically, the *elimination of old synapses* appears to play a larger role in the sculpting of neural networks than does the *creation of new synapses*. The nervous system normally forms more synapses than needed and then gradually eliminates the less-active synapses. For example, the number of synapses in the human visual cortex peaks at around age 1 and then declines (Huttenlocher, 1994). This elimination of old or less-active synapses is called *synaptic pruning*. It appears to be a key process in the formation of the neural networks that are crucial to communication in the nervous system (Sanes & Jessell, 2013).

Neurotransmitters and Behavior

As we have seen, the nervous system relies on chemical couriers to communicate information between neurons. These neurotransmitters are fundamental to behavior, playing a key role in everything from muscle movements to moods and mental health.

Specific neurotransmitters function at specific kinds of synapses. You may recall that transmitters deliver their messages by binding to receptor sites on the postsynaptic membrane. However, a transmitter cannot bind to just any site. The binding process operates much like a lock and key, as was shown in **Figure 3.3**. Just as a key has to fit a lock to work, a transmitter has to fit into a receptor site for binding to occur. Hence, specific transmitters can deliver signals at only certain locations on cell membranes.

Quite a number of chemical substances serve as neurotransmitters (Schwartz & Javitch, 2013). Why are there many different neurotransmitters, each of which works only at certain synapses? This variety and specificity reduces crosstalk between densely packed neurons, making the nervous system's communication more precise (Deutch & Roth, 2008). Let's look at some of the most interesting findings about how specific neurotransmitters regulate behavior, as summarized in **Table 3.1**.

TABLE 3.1 Common Neurotransmitters and Some of Their Relations to Behavior

Neurotransmitter	Characteristics and Relations to Behavior	Disorders Associated with Dysregulation
Acetylcholine (ACh)	Released by motor neurons controlling skeletal muscles Contributes to the regulation of attention, arousal, and memory Some ACh receptors stimulated by nicotine	Alzheimer's disease
Dopamine (DA)	Contributes to control of voluntary movement Cocaine and amphetamines elevate activity at DA synapses Dopamine circuits in medial forebrain bundle characterized as "reward pathway"	Parkinsonism Schizophrenic disorders Addictive disorders
Norepinephrine (NE)	Contributes to modulation of mood and arousal Cocaine and amphetamines elevate activity at NE synapses	Depressive disorders
Serotonin	Involved in regulation of sleep and wakefulness, eating, aggression Prozac and similar antidepressant drugs affect serotonin circuits	Depressive disorders Obsessive-compulsive disorders Eating disorders
GABA	Serves as widely distributed inhibitory transmitter, contributing to regulation of anxiety and sleep/arousal Valium and similar antianxiety drugs work at GABA synapses	Anxiety disorders
Endorphins	Resemble opiate drugs in structure and effects Play role in pain relief and response to stress Contribute to regulation of eating behavior	

Acetylcholine

The discovery that cells communicate by releasing chemicals was first made in connection with the transmitter *acetylcholine* (ACh). ACh has been found throughout the nervous system. It is the only transmitter between motor neurons and voluntary muscles. Every move you make—walking, talking, breathing—depends on ACh released to your muscles by motor neurons (Kandel & Siegelbaum, 2013). ACh also appears to contribute to attention, arousal, and memory. An inadequate supply of ACh in certain areas of the brain is associated with the memory losses seen in Alzheimer's disease (Mesulam, 2013). Although ACh depletion does *not* appear to be the crucial causal factor underlying Alzheimer's disease, the drug treatments currently available, which can produce slight improvements in cognitive functioning, work by amplifying ACh activity (Weiner, 2014).

Monoamines

The *monoamines* include three neurotransmitters: dopamine, norepinephrine, and serotonin. Neurons using these transmitters regulate many aspects of everyday behavior. Dopamine (DA), for example, is used by neurons that control voluntary movements. The degeneration of such neurons apparently causes *Parkinson's disease,* a neurological illness marked by tremors, muscular rigidity, and reduced control over voluntary movements (Marsh & Margolis, 2009).

Serotonin appears to be one of several neurotransmitters that contribute to the regulation of sleep and arousal (McGinty & Szymusiak, 2011). Considerable evidence also suggests that neural circuits using serotonin regulate aggressive behavior in animals, and some preliminary evidence relates serotonin activity to aggression in humans (Duke et al., 2013; Wallner & Machatschke, 2009).

Abnormal levels of monoamines in the brain have been related to the development of certain psychological disorders. For example, people who suffer from depression appear to have lowered levels of activation at norepinephrine (NE) and serotonin synapses. Although numerous other biochemical changes may also contribute to depression, abnormalities at NE and serotonin synapses appear to play a central role, as most antidepressant drugs exert their main effects at these synapses (Thase, 2009). Abnormalities in serotonin circuits have also been implicated as a factor in eating disorders, such as anorexia (Haleem, 2012), and in obsessive-compulsive disorders (Hollander & Simeon, 2008).

Cosmetic botox treatments temporarily reduce wrinkles by blocking ACh receptors at synapses between motor neurons and voluntary muscles (in the vicinity of the injection). This action basically paralyzes muscles to prevent wrinkles from forming. The cosmetic effects last only about 3–5 months, however, because the synapse adapts and new ACh receptors are gradually generated.

© Iuliia Gusakova/Shutterstock.com

In a similar fashion, the dopamine hypothesis asserts that abnormalities in activity at dopamine synapses play an important role in the development of *schizophrenia*. This severe mental illness is marked by irrational thought, hallucinations, poor contact with reality, and deterioration of routine adaptive behavior. Afflicting roughly 1% of the population, schizophrenia requires hospitalization more often than any other psychological disorder (see Chapter 14). Studies suggest, albeit with many caveats, that overactivity at DA synapses is the neurochemical basis for schizophrenia (Lau et al., 2013). Why? Primarily because the therapeutic drugs that tame schizophrenic symptoms are known to block some DA receptor sites and thus reduce dopamine activity (Stroup et al., 2014).

Temporary alterations at monoamine synapses also appear to account for the powerful effects of some widely abused drugs, including amphetamines and cocaine. These stimulant drugs seem to exert most of their effects by creating a storm of increased activity at dopamine and norepinephrine synapses (Paczynski & Gold, 2011). Some theorists believe that the rewarding effects of most abused drugs depend on increased activity in a particular dopamine pathway (Schmidt, Vassoler, & Pierce, 2011) (see Chapter 5). Furthermore, dysregulation in this dopamine pathway appears to be the chief factor underlying drug craving and addiction (Wise, 2013).

GABA

Another group of transmitters consists of *amino acids*. One of these, *gamma-aminobutyric acid* (GABA), is notable in that it seems to produce only *inhibitory* postsynaptic potentials. Some transmitters, such as ACh and NE, are versatile. They can produce either excitatory or inhibitory PSPs, depending on the synaptic receptors they bind to. However, GABA appears to have inhibitory effects at virtually all synapses where it is present. GABA receptors are widely distributed in the brain and may be present at 40% of all synapses. GABA appears to be responsible for much of the inhibition in the central nervous system. Studies suggest that GABA is involved in the regulation of anxiety in humans, and that disturbances in GABA circuits may contribute to some types of anxiety disorders (Long et al., 2013; Rosso et al., 2014). GABA circuits also appear to contribute to the modulation of sleep and arousal (Luppi, Clement, & Fort, 2013; Nguyen et al., 2013).

Endorphins

In 1970, after a horseback-riding accident, Candace Pert, a graduate student working with scientist Solomon Snyder, lay in a hospital bed receiving frequent shots of *morphine*, a painkilling drug derived from the opium plant. This experience left her with a driving curiosity about how morphine works. A few years later, she and Snyder rocked the scientific world by showing that *morphine exerts its effects by binding to specialized receptors in the brain* (Pert & Snyder, 1973).

This discovery raised a perplexing question: Why would the brain be equipped with receptors for morphine, a powerful, addictive opiate drug not normally found in the body? It occurred to Pert and others that the nervous system must have its own, endogenous (internally produced) morphine-like substances. Investigators dubbed these as-yet undiscovered substances *endorphins—internally produced chemicals that resemble opiates in structure and effects.* A search for the body's natural opiate ensued. Soon, a number of endogenous opioids were identified (Hughes et al., 1975). Subsequent studies revealed that endorphins and their receptors are widely distributed in the human body and that they clearly contribute to the modulation of pain (Millecamps et al., 2013), as we will discuss in Chapter 4. Subsequent research has suggested that the endogenous opioids also contribute to the regulation of eating behavior and the body's response to stress (Adam & Epel, 2007).

Muhammed Ali is a well-known victim of Parkinson's disease. Roughly one million Americans suffer from this disease, which is caused by a decline in the synthesis of the neurotransmitter dopamine. The reduction in dopamine synthesis occurs because of the deterioration of a structure located in the midbrain.

© Featureflash/Shutterstock.com

Long-distance runners sometimes report experiencing a "runner's high." Recent research suggests that the release of endorphins probably underlies this experience.

The discovery of endorphins has led to new theories and findings on the neurochemical bases of pain and pleasure. In addition to their painkilling effects, opiate drugs such as morphine and heroin produce highly pleasurable feelings of euphoria, which explains why heroin is so widely abused. Researchers suspect that the body's natural endorphins may also be capable of producing feelings of pleasure. This capacity might explain why joggers sometimes experience a "runner's high." The pain caused by a long run may trigger the release of endorphins, which neutralize some of the pain and create a feeling of exhilaration (Harte, Eifert, & Smith, 1995). The long-held suspicion that endorphins might underlie the "runner's high" experience was supported in a study that used brain-imaging technology to track endorphin release in the brain (Boecker et al., 2008). Ten joggers were administered brain scans just before and just after a 2-hour endurance run. As hypothesized, the post-run brain scans showed a surge in the production of endorphins in selected areas of the participants' brains.

In this section we have highlighted just a few of the more interesting connections between neurotransmitters and behavior. But biochemical processes in the nervous system are incredibly complex. Although scientists have learned a great deal about neurotransmitters and behavior, much still remains to be discovered.

3.2

Key Learning Goals

- Distinguish between the central nervous system and the peripheral nervous system.

3.2 ORGANIZATION OF THE NERVOUS SYSTEM

Clearly, communication in the nervous system is fundamental to behavior. So far we have looked at how individual cells communicate with one another. In this section, we examine the organization of the nervous system as a whole.

The most recent and carefully calibrated calculations suggest that there are roughly *86 billion* neurons in the human brain (Azevedo et al., 2009). Obviously, this is only an *estimate*. If you counted them nonstop at the rate of one per second, you'd be counting for more than 3000 years! And, remember, most neurons have synaptic connections to many other neurons, so there may be *100 trillion* synapses in a human brain!

The fact that neurons are so abundant as to be uncountable is probably why it is widely believed that "we only use 10% of our brains." This curious tidbit of folk wisdom is utter nonsense (McBurney, 1996). If

CONCEPT CHECK 3.1

Linking Brain Chemistry to Behavior

Check your understanding of relations between brain chemistry and behavior by indicating which neurotransmitters or other biological chemicals have been linked to the phenomena listed below. Choose your answers from the following list: (a) acetylcholine, (b) norepinephrine, (c) dopamine, (d) serotonin, (e) endorphins. Indicate your choice (by letter) in the spaces on the left. You'll find the answers in Appendix A.

_____ 1. A transmitter involved in the regulation of sleep, eating, and aggression

_____ 2. The two monoamines that have been linked to depression

_____ 3. Chemicals that resemble opiate drugs in structure and that are involved in pain relief

_____ 4. A neurotransmitter for which abnormal levels have been implicated in schizophrenia

_____ 5. The only neurotransmitter between motor neurons and voluntary muscles

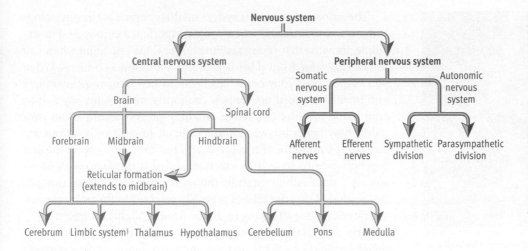

FIGURE 3.5
Organization of the human nervous system.
This overview of the human nervous system shows the relationships of its various parts and systems. The brain is traditionally divided into three regions: the hindbrain, the midbrain, and the forebrain. The reticular formation runs through both the midbrain and the hindbrain on its way up and down the brainstem. These and other parts of the brain are discussed in detail later in the chapter. The peripheral nervous system is made up of the somatic nervous system, which controls voluntary muscles and sensory receptors, and the autonomic nervous system, which controls the involuntary activities of smooth muscles, blood vessels, and glands.

90% of the human brain consists of unused "excess baggage," localized brain damage would not be a problem much of the time. In reality, damage in even very tiny areas of the brain usually has severe disruptive effects (Zillmer, Spiers, & Culbertson, 2008). Furthermore, brain-imaging research shows that even simple mental operations depend on activity spread across several or more areas in the brain. Even during sleep, the brain is highly active.

In any event, the multitudes of neurons in the nervous system have to work together to keep information flowing effectively. To see how the nervous system is organized to accomplish this task, we will divide it into parts. In many instances, the parts will be divided once again. **Figure 3.5** presents an organizational chart that shows the relationships between the major parts of the nervous system.

The Peripheral Nervous System

The first and most important division separates the *central nervous system* (the brain and spinal cord) from the *peripheral nervous system*. **The *peripheral nervous system* is made up of all those nerves that lie outside the brain and spinal cord.** *Nerves* **are bundles of neuron fibers (axons) that are routed together in the peripheral nervous system.** This portion of the nervous system is just what it sounds like: the part that extends to the periphery (the outside) of the body. The peripheral nervous system can be subdivided into the somatic nervous system and the autonomic nervous system.

The Somatic Nervous System

The somatic nervous system lets you feel the world and move around in it. **The *somatic nervous system* is made up of nerves that connect to voluntary skeletal muscles and to sensory receptors.** These nerves are the cables that carry information from receptors in the skin, muscles, and joints to the central nervous system and that carry commands from the central nervous system to the muscles. These functions require two kinds of nerve fibers. *Afferent nerve fibers* **are axons that carry information inward to the central nervous system from the periphery of the body.** *Efferent nerve fibers* **are axons that carry information outward from the central nervous system to the periphery of the body.** Each body nerve contains many axons of each type. Thus, somatic nerves are "two-way streets," with incoming (afferent) and outgoing (efferent) lanes.

The Autonomic Nervous System

The *autonomic nervous system (ANS)* **is made up of nerves that connect to the heart, blood vessels, smooth muscles, and glands.** As its name hints, the autonomic system is a separate (autonomous) system, although it is ultimately controlled by the central nervous system. The autonomic nervous system controls automatic, involuntary, visceral functions that people don't normally think about, such as heart rate, digestion, and perspiration (Powley, 2008).

> **▶ REALITY CHECK**
>
> **Misconception**
> People only use about 10% of their brains.
>
> **Reality**
> There is no way to quantify the percentage of the brain that is "in use" at any specific time or over longer spans of time. The 10% myth appeals to people because it suggests that they have a huge reservoir of untapped potential. Hucksters selling self-improvement programs often talk about the 10% myth because it makes their claims and promises seem more realistic ("Unleash your potential!").

The fight-or-flight response, which can occur in humans as well as animals, reflects physiological arousal mediated by the sympathetic division of the autonomic nervous system.

The autonomic nervous system mediates much of the physiological arousal that occurs when people experience emotions. For example, imagine that you're arriving home alone one night when you notice that your front door is ajar and a window is broken. When you suspect that your home has been broken into, your heart rate and breathing speed up. As you cautiously make your way inside, your blood pressure may surge, you may get goosebumps, and your palms may begin to sweat. These difficult-to-control reactions are aspects of autonomic arousal. Walter Cannon (1932), one of the first psychologists to study this reaction, called it the *fight-or-flight response*. After Cannon carefully monitored this response in animals, he concluded that organisms generally respond to threat by preparing physically for attacking (fight) or fleeing (flight) the enemy.

The autonomic nervous system can be subdivided into two branches: the sympathetic division and the parasympathetic division (see **Figure 3.6**). **The *sympathetic division* is the branch of the autonomic nervous system that mobilizes the body's resources for emergencies.** It creates the fight-or-flight response. Activation of the sympathetic division slows digestive processes and drains blood from the periphery, lessening bleeding in the case of an injury. Key sympathetic nerves send signals to the adrenal glands, triggering the release of hormones that ready the body for exertion. In contrast, **the *parasympathetic division* is the branch of the autonomic nervous system that generally conserves bodily resources.** It activates processes that allow the body to save and store energy.

FIGURE 3.6

The autonomic nervous system (ANS). The ANS is composed of the nerves that connect to the heart, blood vessels, smooth muscles, and glands. The ANS is divided into the sympathetic division, which mobilizes bodily resources in times of need, and the parasympathetic division, which conserves bodily resources. Some of the key functions controlled by each division of the ANS are summarized in the diagram.

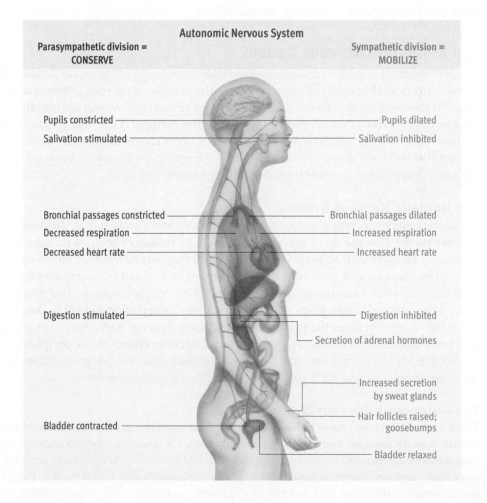

Autonomic Nervous System

Parasympathetic division = **CONSERVE**

Sympathetic division = **MOBILIZE**

Parasympathetic	Sympathetic
Pupils constricted	Pupils dilated
Salivation stimulated	Salivation inhibited
Bronchial passages constricted	Bronchial passages dilated
Decreased respiration	Increased respiration
Decreased heart rate	Increased heart rate
Digestion stimulated	Digestion inhibited
	Secretion of adrenal hormones
	Increased secretion by sweat glands
	Hair follicles raised; goosebumps
Bladder contracted	Bladder relaxed

For example, actions by parasympathetic nerves slow heart rate, reduce blood pressure, and promote digestion.

The Central Nervous System

The central nervous system is the portion of the nervous system that lies within the skull and spinal column. Thus, **the *central nervous system (CNS)* consists of the brain and the spinal cord.** The CNS is bathed in its own special nutritive "soup," called *cerebrospinal fluid* (CSF). This fluid nourishes the brain and provides a protective cushion for it. Although derived from the blood, the CSF is carefully filtered. To enter the CSF, substances in the blood have to cross the *blood-brain barrier*, a semipermeable membrane that stops some chemicals, including drugs, from leaving the bloodstream to enter the brain.

The Spinal Cord

The *spinal cord* connects the brain to the rest of the body through the peripheral nervous system. Although the spinal cord looks like a cable from which the somatic nerves branch, it is part of the central nervous system. The spinal cord runs from the base of the brain to just below the level of the waist. It houses bundles of axons that carry the brain's commands to peripheral nerves and that relay sensations from the periphery of the body to the brain. Many forms of paralysis result from spinal cord damage, a fact that underscores the critical role the spinal cord plays in transmitting signals from the brain to the neurons that, in turn, signal the body's muscles to move.

The Brain

The crowning glory of the central nervous system is, of course, the *brain*. Anatomically, the *brain* is the part of the central nervous system that fills the upper portion of the skull. Although it weighs only about 3 pounds and could be held in one hand, the brain contains billions of interacting cells that integrate information from inside and outside the body; coordinate the body's actions; and enable people to talk, think, remember, plan, create, and dream. Because of its central importance for behavior, the brain is the subject of the next two sections of this chapter.

3.3 THE BRAIN AND BEHAVIOR

Key Learning Goals

- Describe how lesioning, electrical stimulation, and various brain-imaging procedures are used to investigate brain function.
- Know the principal functions of key structures in the brain.
- Identify the four lobes in the cortex and their key functions, and summarize evidence of the brain's plasticity.

Scientists who want to find out how parts of the brain are related to behavior are faced with a formidable task because mapping brain *function* requires a working brain. These scientists use a variety of specialized techniques to investigate brain-behavior relations. We will briefly discuss some of the innovative methods that permit scientists to look inside the brain, and then outline the major findings of this research.

Looking Inside the Brain: Research Methods

Researchers sometimes observe what happens when specific brain structures in animals are purposely disabled. *Lesioning* **involves destroying a piece of the brain**. It is typically done by inserting an electrode into a brain structure and passing a high-frequency electric current through it to burn the tissue and disable the structure. Another valuable technique is *electrical stimulation of the brain (ESB)*, **which involves sending a weak electric current into a brain structure to stimulate (activate) it.** As with lesioning, the current is delivered through an implanted electrode, but a different type of current is used. This sort of electrical stimulation does not exactly duplicate normal electrical

FIGURE 3.7

CT technology. CT scans are used to examine aspects of brain structure. They provide computer-enhanced X-rays of horizontal slices of the brain.

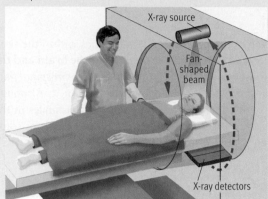

(a) An X-ray beam and X-ray detector rotate around the patient's head, taking multiple X rays of a horizontal slice of the patient's brain.

X-ray source

Fan-shaped beam

X-ray detectors

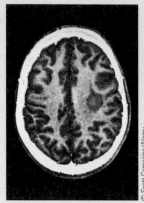

(b) A computer combines X rays to create an image of a horizontal slice of the brain. This scan shows a tumor (in blue) on the right.

© Scott Camazine/Alamy

iStockphoto.com/MachineHeadz

FIGURE 3.8

MRI scans. MRI scans can be used to produce remarkably high-resolution pictures of brain structure. A vertical view of a brain from the left side is shown here.

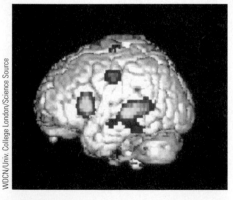

WDCN/Univ. College London/Science Source

FIGURE 3.9

PET scans. PET scans are used to map brain activity rather than brain structure. They provide color-coded maps that show areas of high activity in the brain over time. The PET scan shown here pinpointed areas of high activity (indicated by the red and yellow colors) when a research participant worked on the task of repeating words.

signals in the brain. However, it is usually a close enough approximation to activate the brain structures in which the electrodes are lodged (Desmurget et al., 2013). Obviously, these invasive procedures are largely limited to animal research, although ESB is occasionally used on humans in the context of brain surgery required for medical purposes.

Fortunately, in recent decades, the invention of new brain-imaging devices has led to dramatic advances in scientists' ability to look inside the human brain. The *CT (computerized tomography) scan* is a computer-enhanced X-ray of brain structure. Multiple X-rays are shot from many angles, and the computer combines the readings to create a vivid image of a horizontal slice of the brain (see **Figure 3.7**). The more recently developed *MRI (magnetic resonance imaging) scan* uses magnetic fields, radio waves, and computerized enhancement to map out brain structure. MRI scans provide much better images of brain structure than do CT scans (Wilde et al., 2014), producing three-dimensional pictures of the brain that have remarkably high resolution (see **Figure 3.8**). Using CT and MRI scans, researchers have found abnormalities in brain structure in people suffering from specific types of mental illness, especially schizophrenia (Shenton & Kubicki, 2009) (see Chapter 14).

In research on how brain and behavior are related, *PET (positron emission tomography) scans* have been especially valuable (Staley & Krystal, 2009). PET scans use radioactive markers to map chemical activity in the brain over time. Thus, a PET scan can provide a color-coded map indicating which areas of the brain become active when subjects clench their fist, sing, or contemplate the mysteries of the universe (see **Figure 3.9**). In efforts to pinpoint the brain areas that handle various types of mental tasks, neuroscientists are increasingly using *functional magnetic resonance imaging (fMRI),* which consists of several new variations on MRI technology that monitor blood flow and oxygen consumption in the brain to identify areas of high activity (Small & Heeger, 2013). This technology is exciting because, like PET scans, it can map actual *activity* in the brain over time, but with vastly greater precision (Wilde et al., 2014) For example, using fMRI scans, researchers have identified patterns of brain activity associated with specific creative thinking tasks (Abraham et al., 2014); the contemplation of complex decisions related to gambling (Hinvest et al., 2014); and reactions to pictures of alcoholic beverages (Dager et al., 2014).

Now that we have discussed a few approaches to brain research, let's look at what scientists have discovered about the functions of various parts of the brain. The brain is divided into three major regions: the hindbrain, the midbrain, and the forebrain. The principal structures found in each of these regions are listed in the organizational chart of the nervous system in **Figure 3.5**. You can see where these regions are located in the brain by looking at **Figure 3.10**. They can be found easily in relation to the *brainstem.*

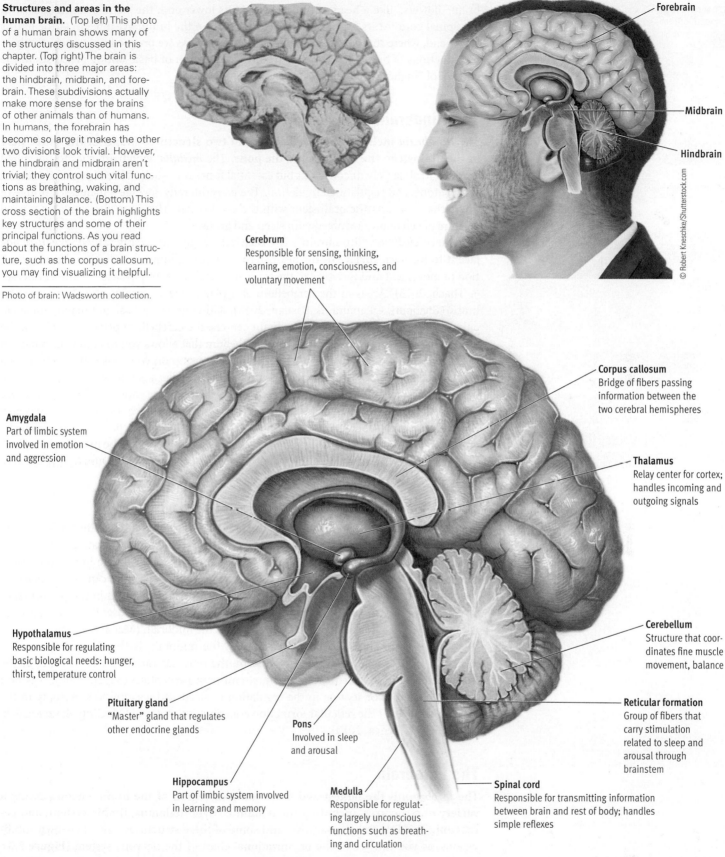

FIGURE 3.10

Structures and areas in the human brain. (Top left) This photo of a human brain shows many of the structures discussed in this chapter. (Top right) The brain is divided into three major areas: the hindbrain, midbrain, and forebrain. These subdivisions actually make more sense for the brains of other animals than of humans. In humans, the forebrain has become so large it makes the other two divisions look trivial. However, the hindbrain and midbrain aren't trivial; they control such vital functions as breathing, waking, and maintaining balance. (Bottom) This cross section of the brain highlights key structures and some of their principal functions. As you read about the functions of a brain structure, such as the corpus callosum, you may find visualizing it helpful.

Photo of brain: Wadsworth collection.

© Robert Kneschke/Shutterstock.com

Forebrain

Midbrain

Hindbrain

Cerebrum
Responsible for sensing, thinking, learning, emotion, consciousness, and voluntary movement

Amygdala
Part of limbic system involved in emotion and aggression

Corpus callosum
Bridge of fibers passing information between the two cerebral hemispheres

Thalamus
Relay center for cortex; handles incoming and outgoing signals

Hypothalamus
Responsible for regulating basic biological needs: hunger, thirst, temperature control

Cerebellum
Structure that coordinates fine muscle movement, balance

Pituitary gland
"Master" gland that regulates other endocrine glands

Pons
Involved in sleep and arousal

Reticular formation
Group of fibers that carry stimulation related to sleep and arousal through brainstem

Hippocampus
Part of limbic system involved in learning and memory

Medulla
Responsible for regulating largely unconscious functions such as breathing and circulation

Spinal cord
Responsible for transmitting information between brain and rest of body; handles simple reflexes

The brainstem looks like its name—it appears to be a stem from which the rest of the brain "flowers," like a head of cauliflower. At its lower end, the stem is contiguous with the spinal cord. At its higher end, it lies deep within the brain. We'll begin at the brain's lower end, where the spinal cord joins the brainstem. As we proceed upward, notice how the functions of brain structures go from the regulation of basic bodily processes to the control of "higher" mental processes.

The Hindbrain

The *hindbrain* includes the cerebellum and two structures found in the lower part of the brainstem: the medulla and the pons. The *medulla,* which attaches to the spinal cord, controls largely unconscious but essential functions, such as breathing, maintaining muscle tone, and regulating circulation. The *pons* (literally "bridge") includes a bridge of fibers that connects the brainstem with the cerebellum. The pons also contains several clusters of cell bodies involved with sleep and arousal.

The *cerebellum* ("little brain") is a relatively large and deeply folded structure adjacent to the back surface of the brainstem. The cerebellum is involved in the coordination of movement and is critical to the sense of equilibrium, or physical balance (Lisberger & Thach, 2013). Areas in the cerebellum also play a role in sensing the position of our limbs (Bhanpuri, Okamura, & Bastian, 2013). Although the actual commands for muscular movements come from higher brain centers, the cerebellum plays a key role in the execution of these commands. It is your cerebellum that allows you to hold your hand out to the side and then smoothly bring your finger to a stop on your nose. This exercise is a useful roadside test for drunk driving because the cerebellum is one of the structures first depressed by alcohol. Damage to the cerebellum disrupts fine motor skills, such as those involved in writing, typing, or playing a musical instrument. Recent research has revealed that the cerebellum contributes to the control of other kinds of functions, as well. Brain circuits running from the cerebellum to the prefrontal cortex appear to be involved in higher-order functions, including attention, planning, and visual perception (Dum & Strick, 2009).

The Midbrain

The *midbrain* is the segment of the brainstem that lies between the hindbrain and the forebrain. The midbrain contains an area that is concerned with integrating sensory processes, such as vision and hearing (Stein, Wallace, & Stanford, 2000). An important system of dopamine-releasing neurons that projects into various higher brain centers originates in the midbrain. Among other things, this dopamine system is involved in the performance of voluntary movements. The decline in dopamine synthesis that causes Parkinson's disease is caused by degeneration of a structure located in the midbrain (Marsh & Margolis, 2009).

Running through both the hindbrain and the midbrain is the *reticular formation.* Situated at the central core of the brainstem, the reticular formation contributes to the modulation of muscle reflexes, breathing, and pain perception (Saper, 2000). It is best known, however, for its role in the regulation of sleep and wakefulness. Activity in the ascending fibers of the reticular formation contributes to arousal (McGinty & Szymusiak, 2011; Jones & Benca, 2013).

The Forebrain

The *forebrain* is the largest and most complex region of the brain, encompassing a variety of structures, including the thalamus, hypothalamus, limbic system, and cerebrum. This list is not exhaustive, and some of these structures have their own subdivisions, as you can see in the organizational chart of the nervous system (**Figure 3.5**). The thalamus, hypothalamus, and limbic system form the core of the forebrain. All three structures are located near the top of the brainstem. Above them is the *cerebrum*—the seat of complex thought. The wrinkled surface of the cerebrum is the *cerebral cortex*—the outer layer of the brain, the part that looks like a cauliflower.

The Thalamus: A Relay Station

The *thalamus* **is a structure in the forebrain through which all sensory information (except smell) must pass to get to the cerebral cortex.** This way station is made up of a number of clusters of cell bodies, or *somas*. Each cluster is concerned with relaying sensory information to a particular part of the cortex. However, it would be a mistake to characterize the thalamus as nothing more than a passive way station. The thalamus also appears to play an active role in integrating information from various senses.

The Hypothalamus: A Regulator of Biological Needs

The *hypothalamus* **is a structure found near the base of the forebrain that is involved in the regulation of basic biological needs.** It lies beneath the thalamus (*hypo* means "under," making the hypothalamus the area under the thalamus). Although no larger than a kidney bean, the hypothalamus contains various clusters of cells that have many key functions. One such function is to control the autonomic nervous system (Horn & Swanson, 2013). The hypothalamus also plays a major role in the regulation of basic biological drives related to survival, including the so-called four F's: fighting, fleeing, feeding, and "mating."

The Limbic System: The Seat of Emotion

The *limbic system* **is a loosely connected network of structures located roughly along the border between the cerebral cortex and deeper subcortical areas** (hence the term *limbic*, which means "edge"). First described by Paul MacLean (1954), the limbic system is not a well-defined anatomical system with clear boundaries. Broadly speaking, it includes parts of the thalamus and hypothalamus, the *hippocampus,* the *amygdala,* and other nearby structures.

The *hippocampus* and adjacent structures clearly play a role in memory processes (Eichenbaum, 2013). Some theorists believe that the hippocampal region is responsible for the *consolidation* of memories for factual information and perhaps other types of memories (Albouy et al., 2013). Consolidation involves the conversion of information into a durable memory code.

Similarly, there is ample evidence linking the limbic system to the experience of emotion, but the exact mechanisms of control are not yet well understood. Evidence suggests that the *amygdala* may play a central role in the learning of fear responses and the processing of other basic emotional responses (LeDoux & Damasio, 2013; Phelps, 2006).

The limbic system also appears to contain emotion-tinged "pleasure centers." This intriguing possibility first surfaced, quite by chance, in brain stimulation research with rats. James Olds and Peter Milner (1954) accidentally discovered that a rat would press a lever repeatedly to send brief bursts of electrical stimulation to a specific spot in its brain where an electrode was implanted (see **Figure 3.11**). Much to their surprise, the rat kept coming back for more self-stimulation in this area. Subsequent studies showed that rats and

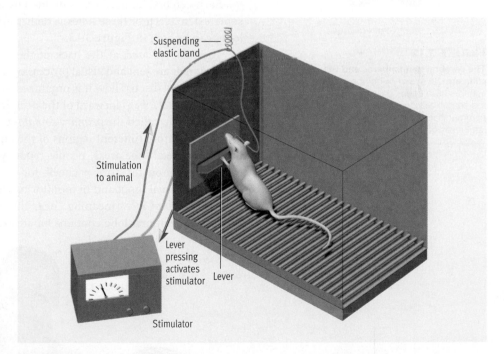

FIGURE 3.11

Electrical stimulation of the brain (ESB) in the rat. Olds and Milner (1954) were using an apparatus like that depicted here when they discovered self-stimulation centers, or "pleasure centers," in the brain of a rat. In this setup, the rat's lever pressing earns brief electrical stimulation that is sent to a specific spot in the rat's brain where an electrode has been implanted.

monkeys would press a lever *thousands of times* per hour to stimulate certain brain sites. Although the experimenters obviously couldn't ask the animals about it, they *inferred* that these self-stimulation sites produced some sort of pleasure.

Where are the pleasure centers located in the brain? Many of them have been found in the limbic system (Olds & Fobe, 1981). The heaviest concentration appears to be where the *medial forebrain bundle* (a bundle of axons) passes through the hypothalamus. The medial forebrain bundle is rich in dopamine-releasing neurons. The rewarding effects of ESB at self-stimulation sites may be largely mediated by the activation of these dopamine circuits (Koob, Everitt, & Robbins, 2008). The pleasurable effects of opiates and stimulant drugs (cocaine and amphetamines) may also depend on excitation of this dopamine system (Schmidt, Vassoler, & Pierce, 2011). Recent evidence suggests that the so-called pleasure centers in the brain may not be anatomical centers so much as neural circuits releasing dopamine.

The Cerebrum: The Seat of Complex Thought

The *cerebrum* is the largest and most complex part of the human brain. It includes the brain areas that are responsible for our most complex mental activities, including learning, remembering, thinking, and consciousness itself. **The *cerebral cortex* is the convoluted outer layer of the cerebrum.** The cortex is folded and bent, so that its large surface area—about 1.5 square feet—can be packed into the limited volume of the skull (Hubel & Wiesel, 1979).

The cerebrum is divided into two halves, called hemispheres. Hence, **the *cerebral hemispheres* are the right and left halves of the cerebrum** (see **Figure 3.12**). The hemispheres are separated in the center of the brain by the longitudinal fissure (a split or crevice) that runs from the front to the back. This fissure descends to a thick band of fibers called the *corpus callosum* (also shown in **Figure 3.12**). **The *corpus callosum* is the major structure that connects the two cerebral hemispheres.** We'll discuss the functional specialization of the cerebral hemispheres in the next section of this chapter.

Each cerebral hemisphere is divided by deep fissures into four parts called *lobes.* To some extent, each of these lobes is dedicated to specific purposes. The location of these lobes can be seen in **Figure 3.13**.

The *occipital lobe,* at the back of the head, includes the cortical area where most visual signals are sent and visual processing is begun. This area is called the *primary visual cortex.* We will discuss how it is organized in Chapter 4.

The *parietal lobe* is forward of the occipital lobe. It includes the area that registers the sense of touch, called the *primary somatosensory cortex.* Various sections of this area receive signals from different regions of the body. When electrical stimulation is delivered in these parietal lobe areas, people report physical sensations—as if someone actually touched them on the arm or cheek, for example. The parietal lobe is also involved in integrating visual input and in monitoring the body's position in space.

The *temporal lobe* (meaning "near the temples") lies below the parietal lobe. Near its top, the temporal lobe contains an area devoted to auditory processing, the *primary*

Corpus callosum

FIGURE 3.12

The cerebral hemispheres and the corpus callosum. In this drawing, the cerebral hemispheres have been "pulled apart" to reveal the corpus callosum. This band of fibers is the communication bridge between the right and left halves of the human brain.

What areas of the brain are activated in these people?

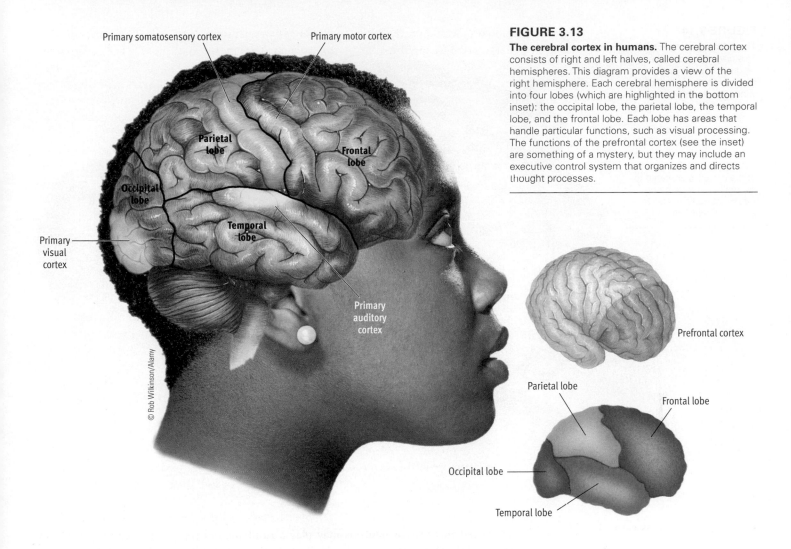

FIGURE 3.13

The cerebral cortex in humans. The cerebral cortex consists of right and left halves, called cerebral hemispheres. This diagram provides a view of the right hemisphere. Each cerebral hemisphere is divided into four lobes (which are highlighted in the bottom inset): the occipital lobe, the parietal lobe, the temporal lobe, and the frontal lobe. Each lobe has areas that handle particular functions, such as visual processing. The functions of the prefrontal cortex (see the inset) are something of a mystery, but they may include an executive control system that organizes and directs thought processes.

auditory cortex. As we will see momentarily, damage to an area in the temporal lobe on the left side of the brain can impair the ability to comprehend speech and language.

Continuing forward, we find the *frontal lobe,* the largest lobe in the human brain. It contains the principal areas that control the movement of muscles, the *primary motor cortex.* Electrical stimulation applied in these areas can cause actual muscle contractions. The amount of motor cortex allocated to the control of a body part depends not on the part's size but on the diversity and precision of its movements. Thus, more of the cortex is given to parts we have fine control over, such as the fingers, lips, and tongue. Less of the cortex is devoted to larger parts that make crude movements, such as the thighs and shoulders (see **Figure 3.14**).

An area just forward of the primary motor cortex is where "mirror neurons" were first discovered accidentally in the mid-1990s. An Italian research team (Gallese et al., 1996) was recording activity in individual neurons as monkeys reached for various objects. A member of the team happened to reach out and pick up one of the designated objects, and much to his amazement, the monkey's neuron fired just as it had when the monkey picked up the object itself. The researchers went on to find many such neurons in the frontal lobe, which they christened *mirror neurons*—**neurons that are activated by performing an action or by seeing another monkey or person perform the same action.** Research soon showed that humans also have mirror neuron circuits (Iacoboni & Dapretto, 2006; Rizzolatti & Craighero, 2004). Mirror neurons appear to provide a new model for understanding complex social cognition at a neural level. Research has

FIGURE 3.14

The primary motor cortex. This diagram shows the amount of motor cortex devoted to the control of various muscles and limbs. The anatomical features in the drawing are distorted because their size is proportional to the amount of cortex devoted to their control. As you can see, more of the cortex is allocated to controlling muscle groups that must make relatively precise movements.

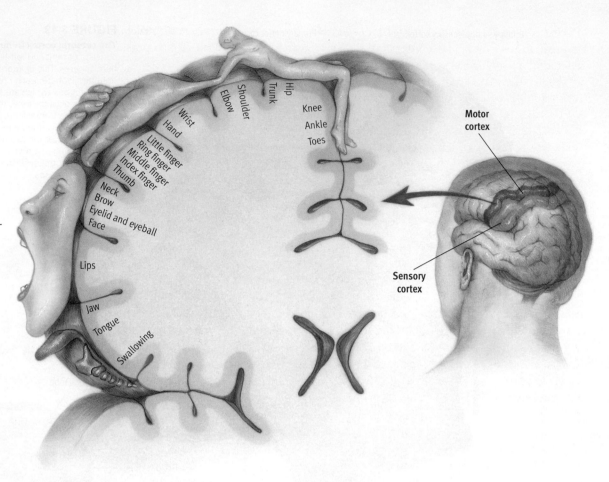

suggested that mirror neurons may play a fundamental role in the acquisition of new motor skills (Buccino & Riggio, 2006); the imitation of others, which is crucial to much of human development (Iacoboni, 2012); and the understanding of others' intentions and the ability to feel empathy for others (Baird, Scheffer, & Wilson, 2011). Thus, the accidental discovery of mirror neurons may have a dramatic impact on brain-behavior research in the years to come.

The portion of the frontal lobe to the front of the motor cortex, called the *prefrontal cortex* (see the inset in **Figure 3.13**), is something of a mystery. This area is disproportionately large in humans, accounting for about one-third of the cerebral cortex (Huey, Krueger, & Grafman, 2006). Its apparent contribution to certain types of decision making and key aspects of self-control (Gläscher et al., 2012) has led some theorists to suggest that the prefrontal cortex houses some sort of "executive control system," which is thought to organize and direct thought processes (Beer, Shimamura, & Knight, 2004). Much remains to be learned, however, as the prefrontal cortex constitutes a huge chunk of the brain, with many subareas whose specific functions are still being worked out (Miller & Wallis, 2008).

The Plasticity of the Brain

It was once believed that significant changes in the anatomy and organization of the brain were limited to early periods of development in both humans and animals. However, research has gradually demonstrated that the anatomical structure and functional organization of the brain are more flexible, or "plastic," than widely assumed (Pascual-Leone, 2009). This conclusion is based on several lines of research.

First, studies have shown that aspects of experience can sculpt features of brain structure. For example, neuroimaging studies have shown that subjects given 3 months to practice and master a juggling routine show structural changes in brain areas known to handle the processing of visual and motor tasks (Draganski et al., 2004). In a similar vein, a recent study found that 3 months of intense preparation for the Law School Admission Test produced structural changes in brain areas crucial to reasoning (Mackey, Whitaker, & Bunge, 2012). Another study focused on London taxi drivers, who are required to *master* the complex streets of London and pass extremely demanding exams on their layout to get a license (Woollett & Maguire, 2011). The researchers found structural changes in the hippocampal areas of trainees who passed their exams—changes that were not evident in the trainees who failed. *Second, research has shown that damage to incoming sensory pathways or the destruction of brain tissue can lead to neural reorganization.* For example, when scientists amputated the third finger in an owl monkey, the part of its cortex that formerly responded to the third finger gradually became responsive to the second and fourth fingers (Kaas, 2000). And in some blind people, areas in the occipital lobe that are normally dedicated to visual processing are "recruited" to help with verbal processing (Amedi et al., 2004).

Third, studies now indicate that the adult brain can generate new neurons (Gage, 2002). Until relatively recently, it was believed that **neurogenesis—the formation of new neurons**—did not occur in adult humans. It was thought that the brain formed all its neurons by infancy at the latest (Gross, 2000). However, new evidence suggests that adult humans and monkeys can form new neurons in the olfactory bulb and the hippocampus (DiCicco-Bloom & Falluel-Morel, 2009). Now that neuroscientists know where to look, neurogenesis has been found in the brains of all vertebrate species studied thus far (Kozorovitskiy & Gould, 2008). Neurogenesis taking place in the dentate gyrus of the hippocampus appears to be particularly important (Drew, Fusi, & Hen, 2013). The new neurons generated here migrate to areas in the cortex where they sprout axons and form new synapses with existing neurons, becoming fully integrated into the brain's communication networks. Neuroscientists are now scrambling to figure out the functional significance of neurogenesis. An accumulating body of evidence suggests that neurogenesis may play an important role in learning and memory (Koehl & Abrous, 2011; Benarroch, 2013) (see Chapter 7). Much remains to be learned about neurogenesis, but many theorists believe that it is a key factor in the brain's plasticity (Kohman & Rhodes, 2013).

In sum, research suggests that the brain is not "hard wired" the way a computer is. It appears that the neural wiring of the brain is flexible and constantly evolving. That said, this plasticity is not unlimited. Rehabilitation efforts with people who have suffered brain damage clearly demonstrate limits on the extent to which the brain can rewire itself (Zillmer et al., 2008). And the evidence suggests that the brain's plasticity declines with increasing age (Rains, 2002). Younger brains are more flexible than older brains. Still, the neural circuits of the brain show substantial plasticity, which certainly helps organisms adapt to their environments.

3.4 RIGHT BRAIN/LEFT BRAIN: CEREBRAL SPECIALIZATION

3.4

Key Learning Goals

- Explain how split-brain research changed our understanding of the brain's hemispheric organization.

- Describe research on cerebral specialization in normal subjects and what this research has revealed.

As noted in the previous section, the cerebrum—the seat of complex thought—is divided into two separate hemispheres (see **Figure 3.12**). Recent decades have seen an exciting flurry of research on the specialized abilities of the right and left cerebral hemispheres. Some theorists have gone so far as to suggest that people really have two brains in one!

Hints of this hemispheric specialization have been available for many years, from cases in which one side of a person's brain has been damaged. The left hemisphere was

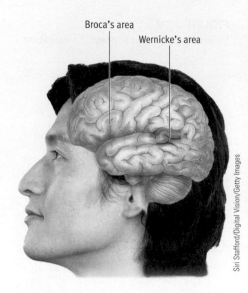

FIGURE 3.15

Language processing in the brain. This view of the left hemisphere highlights the location of two centers for language processing in the brain: Broca's area, which is involved in speech production, and Wernicke's area, which is involved in language comprehension.

Broca's area

Wernicke's area

Siri Stafford/Digital Vision/Getty Images

implicated in the control of language as early as 1861, by Paul Broca, a French surgeon. Broca was treating a patient who had been unable to speak for 30 years. After the patient died, Broca showed that the probable cause of his speech deficit was a small lesion on the left side of the frontal lobe. Since then, many similar cases have shown that this area of the brain—known as *Broca's area*—plays an important role in the production of speech (see **Figure 3.15**). Another major language center—*Wernicke's area*—was identified in the temporal lobe of the left hemisphere in 1874. Damage in Wernicke's area (also shown in **Figure 3.15**) usually leads to problems with the *comprehension* of language.

Evidence that the left hemisphere usually processes language led scientists to characterize it as the "dominant" hemisphere. Because thoughts are usually coded in terms of language, the left hemisphere was given the lion's share of credit for handling the "higher" mental processes, such as reasoning, remembering, planning, and problem solving. Meanwhile, the right hemisphere came to be viewed as the "nondominant," or "dumb," hemisphere, lacking any special functions or abilities.

This characterization of the left and right hemispheres as major and minor partners in the brain's work began to change in the 1960s. It all started with landmark research by Roger Sperry, Michael Gazzaniga, and their colleagues, who studied "split-brain" patients: individuals whose cerebral hemispheres had been surgically disconnected (Gazzaniga, 1970; Gazzaniga, Bogen, & Sperry, 1965; Levy, Trevarthen, & Sperry, 1972; Sperry, 1982). In 1981 Sperry received a Nobel Prize in physiology/medicine for this work.

Bisecting the Brain: Split-Brain Research

In *split-brain surgery*, the bundle of fibers that connects the cerebral hemispheres (the corpus callosum) is cut to reduce the severity of epileptic seizures. It is a radical procedure that is chosen only in exceptional cases that have not responded to other forms of treatment (Wolford, Miller, & Gazzaniga, 2004). But the surgery provides scientists with an unusual opportunity to study people who have had their brain literally split in two.

To appreciate the logic of split-brain research, you need to understand how sensory and motor information is routed to and from the two hemispheres. *Each hemisphere's primary connections are to the opposite side of the body.* Thus, the left hemisphere controls, and communicates with, the right hand, right arm, right leg, right eyebrow, and so on. In contrast, the right hemisphere controls, and communicates with, the left side of the body.

Vision and hearing are more complex. Both eyes deliver information to both hemispheres, but input is still separated. Stimuli in the right half of the visual field are registered by receptors on the left side of each eye, which send signals to the left hemisphere. Stimuli in the left half of the visual field are transmitted by both eyes to the right hemisphere (see **Figure 3.16**). Auditory inputs to each ear also go to both hemispheres. However, connections to the opposite hemisphere are stronger or more immediate. That is, sounds presented to the right ear are registered in the left hemisphere first, while sounds presented to the left ear are registered more quickly in the right hemisphere.

For the most part, people don't notice this asymmetric, "crisscrossed" organization because the two hemispheres are in close communication with each other. Information received by one hemisphere is readily shared with the other via the corpus callosum. However, when the two hemispheres are surgically disconnected, the functional specialization of the brain becomes apparent.

In their classic study of split-brain patients, Gazzaniga, Bogen, and Sperry (1965) presented visual stimuli, such as pictures, symbols, and words, in a single visual field (the left or the right), so that the stimuli would be sent to only one hemisphere. The stimuli were

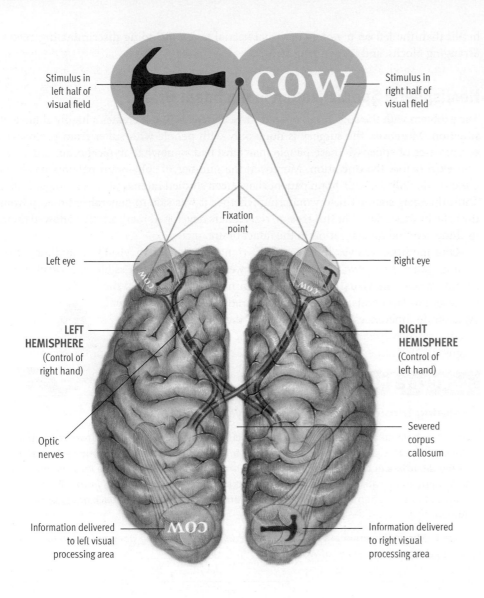

Stimulus in left half of visual field

Stimulus in right half of visual field

Fixation point

Left eye

Right eye

LEFT HEMISPHERE (Control of right hand)

RIGHT HEMISPHERE (Control of left hand)

Optic nerves

Severed corpus callosum

Information delivered to left visual processing area

Information delivered to right visual processing area

FIGURE 3.16

Visual input in the split brain. If a participant stares at a fixation point, the point divides the subject's visual field into right and left halves. Input from the right visual field (the word *cow* in this example) strikes the left side of each eye and is transmitted to the left hemisphere. Input from the left visual field strikes the right side of each eye and is transmitted to the right hemisphere. Normally, the hemispheres share the information from the two halves of the visual field, but in split-brain patients, the corpus callosum is severed, and the two hemispheres cannot communicate. Hence, the experimenter can present a visual stimulus to just one hemisphere at a time.

projected onto a screen in front of the subjects, who stared at a fixation point (a spot) in the center of the screen (see **Figure 3.17**). The images were flashed to the right or the left of the fixation point for only a split second. Thus, the subjects did not have a chance to move their eyes, and the stimuli were glimpsed in only one visual field.

When pictures were flashed in the right visual field and thus sent to the left hemisphere, the split-brain subjects were able to name and describe the objects depicted (such as a cup or spoon). However, the subjects were *not* able to name and describe the same objects when they were flashed in the left visual field and sent to the right hemisphere. These findings supported the notion that language is housed in the left hemisphere.

Although the split-brain subjects' right hemisphere was not able to speak up for itself, further tests revealed that it was processing the information presented. If subjects were given an opportunity to *point out a picture* of an object that had been flashed to the left visual field, they were able to do so. Furthermore, the right hemisphere (left hand) turned out to be *superior* to the left hemisphere (right hand) in assembling little puzzles and copying drawings, even though the subjects were right-handed. These findings provided the first compelling demonstration that the right hemisphere has its own special talents. Subsequent studies of additional split-brain patients showed the right hemisphere to be

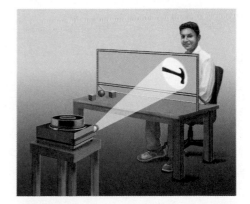

FIGURE 3.17

Experimental apparatus in split-brain research. On the left is a special slide projector that can present images very briefly, before the subject's eyes can move and thus change the visual field. Images are projected on one side of the screen to present stimuli to just one hemisphere. The portion of the apparatus beneath the screen is constructed to prevent participants from seeing objects that they may be asked to handle with their right or left hand, another procedure that can be used to send information to just one hemisphere.

better than the left on a variety of visual-spatial tasks, including discriminating colors, arranging blocks, and recognizing faces.

Hemispheric Specialization in the Intact Brain

The problem with the split-brain operation, of course, is that it creates a highly abnormal situation. Moreover, the surgery is done only with people who suffer from prolonged, severe cases of epilepsy. These people may have had somewhat atypical brain organization even before the operation. Moreover, the number of split-brain patients has been quite small; only ten split-brain patients have been studied intensively (Gazzaniga, 2008). Thus, theorists couldn't help wondering whether it was safe to generalize broadly from the split-brain studies. For this reason, researchers developed methods that allowed them to study cerebral specialization in the intact brain.

One method involves looking at left-right imbalances in visual or auditory processing, called *perceptual asymmetries*. As we have seen, it is possible to present visual stimuli to just one visual field at a time. In normal individuals, the input sent to one hemisphere is quickly shared with the other. However, subtle differences in the "abilities" of the two hemispheres

CONCEPT CHECK 3.2

Relating Disorders to the Nervous System

Imagine that you are working as a neuropsychologist at a clinic. You are involved in the diagnosis of the cases described below. You are asked to identify the probable cause(s) of the disorders in terms of nervous system malfunctions. Based on the information in this chapter, indicate the probable location of any brain damage or the probable disturbance of neurotransmitter activity. The answers can be found in the back of the book in Appendix A.

Case 1. Miriam is exhibiting language deficits. In particular, she does not seem to comprehend the meaning of words. _____

_____

_____

Case 2. Camille displays tremors and muscular rigidity and is diagnosed as having Parkinson's disease. _____

_____

_____

Case 3. Ricardo, a 28-year-old computer executive, has gradually seen his strength and motor coordination deteriorate badly. He is diagnosed as having multiple sclerosis. _____

_____

_____

Case 4. Wendy is highly irrational, has poor contact with reality, and reports hallucinations. She is given a diagnosis of schizophrenic disorder. _____

_____

_____

can be detected by precisely measuring how long it takes subjects to recognize different types of stimuli. For instance, when verbal stimuli are presented to the right visual field (and thus sent to the *left hemisphere* first), they are identified more quickly and more accurately than when they are presented to the left visual field (and sent to the right hemisphere first). The faster reactions in the left hemisphere presumably occur because it can recognize verbal stimuli on its own, while the right hemisphere has to take extra time to "consult" the left hemisphere. In contrast, the *right hemisphere* is faster than the left on *visual-spatial* tasks, such as locating a dot or recognizing a face (Bradshaw, 1989).

Researchers have used a variety of other approaches to explore hemispheric specialization in normal people. In recent years, they have depended heavily on brain-imaging studies that can reveal patterns of activation when participants work on specific types of cognitive tasks. For the most part, their findings have converged nicely with the results of the split-brain studies (Hervé et al., 2013). Overall, the data suggest that the two hemispheres *are* specialized, with each handling certain types of cognitive tasks better than the other (Corballis, 2003; Gazzaniga, 2005; Machado et al., 2013). *The left hemisphere is usually better on tasks involving verbal processing, such as language, speech, reading, and writing. The right hemisphere exhibits superiority on many tasks involving nonverbal processing, such as most spatial, musical, and visual recognition tasks (including the perception of emotions).*

Although brain-imaging research has provided additional support for the notion that areas in the right and left hemisphere are specialized to handle certain cognitive functions, this research has also provided evidence that the two sides of the brain are constantly collaborating. Newer brain-imaging methods that can map fluid communication networks in the brain reveal a great deal of highly dynamic interhemisperic communication and coordination (Doron, Bassett, & Gazzaniga, 2012). Interestingly, a recent study of Albert Einstein's brain suggests that the quality of this communication may be of vital importance (Men et al., 2013). Working with newly published photos of Einstein's brain (originally taken after his death in 1955) and an innovative method to quantify the nerve fibers in the corpus callosum, the research team concluded that Einstein's brilliance may have been partly due to an exceptional degree of connectivity between his right and left hemispheres.

The specialization of the right and left halves of the brain is a burgeoning area of research that has broad implications, which we will discuss further in the Personal Application. For now, however, let's leave the brain and turn our attention to the endocrine system.

3.5 THE ENDOCRINE SYSTEM: ANOTHER WAY TO COMMUNICATE

Key Learning Goals
- Identify the key elements of the endocrine system, and describe ways in which hormones regulate behavior.

The major way the brain communicates with the rest of the body is through the nervous system. However, the body has a second communication system that is also important to behavior. **The *endocrine system* consists of glands that secrete chemicals into the bloodstream that help control bodily functioning.** The messengers in this communication network are called hormones. ***Hormones* are the chemical substances released by the endocrine glands.** In a way, hormones are much like neurotransmitters in the nervous system, but they can't match the high speed of neural transmission and they tend to be less specific, as they often act on many target cells throughout the body. The major

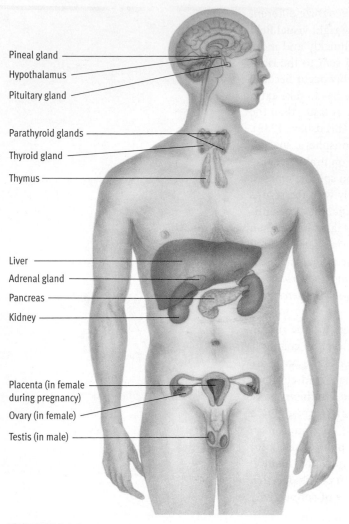

Pineal gland
Hypothalamus
Pituitary gland

Parathyroid glands
Thyroid gland

Thymus

Liver
Adrenal gland
Pancreas
Kidney

Placenta (in female during pregnancy)
Ovary (in female)
Testis (in male)

FIGURE 3.18

The endocrine system. This graphic depicts most of the major endocrine glands. The endocrine glands secrete hormones into the bloodstream. These hormones regulate a variety of physical functions and affect many aspects of behavior.

Research suggests that oxytocin, a hormone released by the pituitary gland, may help to foster empathy and trust in humans.

endocrine glands and their functions are shown in **Figure 3.18**. Hormone release tends to be *pulsatile*. That is, hormones tend to be released several times per day in brief bursts that last only a few minutes.

Much of the endocrine system is controlled by the nervous system through the *hypothalamus*. This structure at the base of the forebrain has intimate connections with the pea-sized *pituitary gland,* to which it is adjacent. **The *pituitary gland* releases a great variety of hormones that fan out within the body, stimulating actions in the other endocrine glands.** In this sense, the pituitary is the "master gland" of the endocrine system, although the hypothalamus is the real power behind the throne.

The intermeshing of the nervous system and the endocrine system can be seen in the fight-or-flight response described earlier. In times of stress, the hypothalamus sends signals along two pathways—through the autonomic nervous system and through the pituitary gland—to the adrenal glands (Clow, 2001). In response, the adrenal glands secrete hormones that radiate throughout the body, preparing it to cope with an emergency.

A topic of current research interest centers on the effects of *oxytocin*—**a hormone that is released by the pituitary gland and regulates reproductive behaviors.** Oxytocin has long been known to trigger contractions when a woman gives birth and to stimulate the mammary glands to release milk for breastfeeding, but newer research suggests that this hormone has far-reaching effects on complex social behavior (Carter, 2014). For example, an extensive body of research indicates that oxytocin fosters adult-adult pair bonding in many mammals (Lim & Young, 2006). Consistent with this finding, a recent study found that oxytocin may promote relationship fidelity in men (Scheele et al., 2012). After inhaling an oxytocin spray, males who were in committed relationships kept more distance between themselves and an attractive female than did those who inhaled the placebo spray.

Other research with humans suggests that oxytocin fosters feelings of extraversion, openness, and warmth, which promote social bonding between people (Cardoso, Ellenbogen, & Linnen, 2012). Studies have also found that oxytocin may enhance fathers' engagement with their infant children (Weisman, Zagoory-Sharon, & Feldman, 2014); increase empathy for others' suffering (Shamay-Tsoory et al., 2013); and promote the sharing of one's emotions (Lane et al., 2013).

Another line of research suggests that oxytocin fosters trust in humans. In one fascinating study, male students participated in an investment-bargaining simulation in which the "investors" could send a portion of their financial stake to a "trustee," which tripled the money, but then they had to *hope* that the trustee would send a decent portion of the investment back to them (Kosfeld et al., 2005). Investors who inhaled an oxytocin spray before the simulation were far more trusting and sent more money to the trustees than did control subjects. Other studies have also found a link between oxytocin and trusting behavior (Merolla et al., 2013). However, in some situations, this increased trust could backfire, as a recent study found that oxytocin decreased subjects' ability to detect deception by others (Israel, Hart, & Winter, 2013).

3.6 HEREDITY AND BEHAVIOR: IS IT ALL IN THE GENES?

3.6

Key Learning Goals

- Describe basic structures involved in genetic transmission, and discuss the nature of polygenic traits.

- Compare the special methods used to investigate the influence of heredity, and discuss how heredity and environment interact.

Most people realize that physical characteristics such as height, hair color, blood type, and eye color are largely shaped by heredity. But what about psychological characteristics, such as intelligence, moodiness, impulsiveness, and shyness? To what extent are people's behavioral qualities molded by their genes? As we saw in Chapter 1, questions about the relative importance of heredity versus environment are very old ones in psychology. The nature-versus-nurture debate will continue to surface in many of the upcoming chapters. To help you appreciate the complexities of this debate, we will outline some basic principles of genetics and describe the methods that investigators use to assess the effects of heredity.

Basic Principles of Genetics

Every cell in your body contains enduring messages from your mother and father. These messages are found on the *chromosomes* that lie within the nucleus of each cell. *Chromosomes* **are threadlike strands of DNA (deoxyribonucleic acid) molecules that carry genetic information** (see **Figure 3.19**). With the exception of sex cells (sperm and eggs), every cell in humans contains forty-six chromosomes. These chromosomes operate in twenty-three pairs, with one chromosome of each pair coming from each parent. Each chromosome, in turn, contains thousands of biochemical messengers called genes. *Genes* **are DNA segments that serve as the key functional units in hereditary transmission.**

If all offspring are formed by a union of the parents' sex cells, why aren't family members identical clones? The reason is that a single pair of parents can produce an extraordinary variety of combinations of chromosomes. Each parent's twenty-three chromosome pairs can be scrambled in over 8 million (2^{23}) different ways, yielding roughly 70 trillion possible configurations when sperm and egg unite. Thus, genetic transmission is a complicated process, and everything is a matter of probability. Except for identical twins, each person ends up with a unique genetic blueprint.

Although different combinations of genes explain why family members aren't all alike, the overlap among these combinations explains why family members do tend to resemble one another. Members of a family share more of the same genes than do non-members, and closer relatives share larger proportions of genes. For example, the genetic overlap for identical twins is 100%. Parents and their children, and full siblings including fraternal twins, share 50% of their genes. More-distant relatives share less genetic overlap, as outlined in **Figure 3.20**.

Like chromosomes, genes operate in pairs, with one gene of each pair coming from each parent. In the simplest scenario, a single pair of genes determines a trait. However, most human characteristics appear to be *polygenic traits,* **or characteristics that are influenced by more than one pair of genes.** For example, three to five gene pairs are thought to interactively determine skin color. Complex physical abilities, such as motor coordination, may be influenced by tangled interactions among a great many pairs of genes. Most psychological characteristics that appear to be affected by heredity seem to involve complex polygenic inheritance (Plomin, DeFries, et al., 2013).

Detecting Hereditary Influence: Research Methods

How do scientists disentangle the effects of genetics and experience to determine how heredity affects human behavior? Researchers have designed special types of studies to assess the impact of heredity. The three most important methods are family studies, twin studies, and adoption studies.

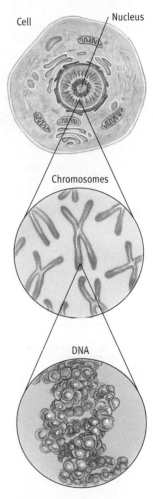

FIGURE 3.19

Genetic material. This series of enlargements shows the main components of genetic material. (Top) In the nucleus of every cell are chromosomes, which carry the information needed to construct new human beings. (Center) Chromosomes are threadlike strands of DNA that carry thousands of genes, the functional units of hereditary transmission. (Bottom) DNA is a spiraled double chain of molecules that can copy itself to reproduce.

FIGURE 3.20

Genetic relatedness. Research on the genetic bases of behavior takes advantage of the different degrees of genetic relatedness between various types of relatives. If heredity influences a trait, relatives who share more genes should be more similar with regard to that trait than are more distant relatives, who share fewer genes. Comparisons involving various degrees of biological relationships will come up frequently in later chapters.

Relationship	Degree of relatedness	Genetic overlap
Identical twins		100%
Fraternal twins Brother or sister Parent or child	First-degree relatives	50%
Grandparent or grandchild Uncle, aunt, nephew, or niece Half-bother or half-sister	Second-degree relatives	25%
First cousin	Third-degree relatives	12.5%
Second cousin	Fourth-degree relatives	6.25%
Unrelated		0%

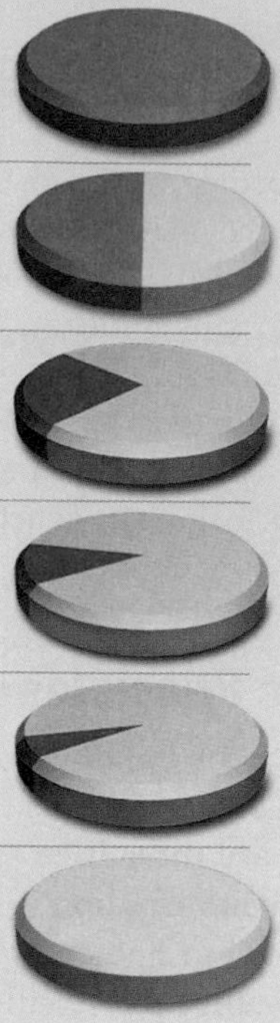

Family Studies

In *family studies*, **researchers assess hereditary influence by examining blood relatives to see how much they resemble one another on a specific trait.** If heredity affects the trait under scrutiny, researchers should find trait similarity among relatives. Furthermore, they should find more similarity among relatives who share more genes. For instance, siblings should exhibit more similarity than cousins.

Illustrative of this method are the numerous family studies conducted to assess the contribution of heredity to the development of schizophrenic disorders. These disorders strike approximately 1% of the population, yet 9% of the siblings of schizophrenic patients exhibit schizophrenia themselves (Gottesman, 1991). Thus, these first-degree relatives of schizophrenic patients show a risk for the disorder that is nine times higher than normal. This risk is greater than that observed for second-degree relatives, such as nieces and nephews (4%), which is greater than that found for third-degree relatives, such as first cousins (2%), and so on. This pattern of results supports the hypothesis that genetic inheritance influences the development of schizophrenic disorders (Kirov & Owen, 2009).

Family studies can indicate whether a trait runs in families. However, this correlation does not provide conclusive evidence that the trait is influenced by heredity. Why not? Because family members generally share not only genes but also similar environments. Furthermore, closer relatives are more likely to live together than distant relatives. Thus, genetic similarity and environmental similarity both tend to be greater for closer relatives. Either of these confounding variables could be responsible when greater trait similarity is found in closer relatives. Family studies can offer useful insights about the possible impact of heredity, but they cannot provide definitive evidence.

Twin Studies

Twin studies can yield better evidence about the possible role of genetic factors. **In *twin studies*, researchers assess hereditary influence by comparing the resemblance of identical twins and fraternal twins with respect to a trait.** The logic of twin studies

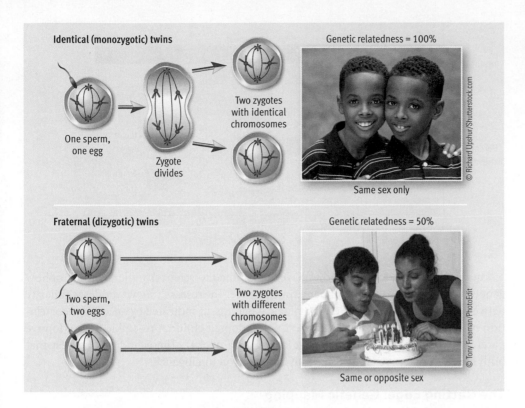

FIGURE 3.21

Identical versus fraternal twins. Identical (monozygotic) twins emerge from one zygote that splits, so their genetic relatedness is 100%. Fraternal (dizygotic) twins emerge from two separate zygotes, so their genetic relatedness is only 50%.

SOURCE: Adapted from Kalat, J. (1996). *Introduction to psychology.* Belmont, CA: Wadsworth. Reprinted by permission.

Inside the figure:

Identical (monozygotic) twins

One sperm, one egg → Zygote divides → Two zygotes with identical chromosomes

Genetic relatedness = 100%

Same sex only

Fraternal (dizygotic) twins

Two sperm, two eggs → Two zygotes with different chromosomes

Genetic relatedness = 50%

Same or opposite sex

hinges on the genetic relatedness of identical and fraternal twins (see **Figure 3.21**). *Identical (monozygotic) twins* emerge when a single fertilized egg splits for unknown reasons. Thus, they have exactly the same genetic blueprint; their genetic overlap is 100%. *Fraternal (dizygotic) twins* result when two separate eggs are fertilized simultaneously. Fraternal twins are no more alike in genetic makeup than any two siblings born to a pair of parents at different times. Their genetic overlap averages 50%.

Fraternal twins provide a useful comparison to identical twins because in both cases the twins usually grow up in the same home, at the same time, and are exposed to the same configuration of relatives, neighbors, peers, teachers, events, and so forth. Thus, both kinds of twins normally develop under equally similar environmental conditions. However, identical twins share more genetic kinship than fraternal twins. Consequently, if sets of identical twins tend to exhibit more similarity on a trait than sets of fraternal twins do, it is reasonable to infer that this greater similarity is probably due to heredity.

Twin studies have been conducted to assess the impact of heredity on a variety of traits. For example, researchers have found that identical twins tend to be more similar to each other than fraternal twins on measures of general intelligence and measures of specific personality traits, such as extraversion (see **Figure 3.22**) (Plomin, DeFries, et al., 2013). These results support the notion that these traits are influenced to some degree by genetic makeup.

Adoption Studies

Adoption studies **assess hereditary influence by examining the resemblance between adopted children and both their biological and their adoptive parents.** If adopted children resemble their biological parents on a trait, even though they were not raised by them, genetic factors probably influence that trait. In contrast, if adopted children resemble their adoptive parents, even though they inherited no genes from them, environmental factors probably influence the trait.

FIGURE 3.22

Twin studies of intelligence and personality.
Identical twins tend to be more similar than
fraternal twins (as reflected in higher correlations) with regard to intelligence and specific
personality traits, such as extraversion. These
findings suggest that intelligence and personality are influenced by heredity. (Data from Plomin
et al., 2001).

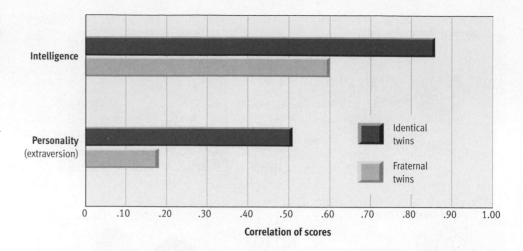

In recent years, adoption studies have contributed to science's understanding of how
genetics and the environment influence intelligence. The research shows modest similarity
between adopted children and their biological parents, as indicated by an average correlation of .24 (McGue et al., 1993). Interestingly, adopted children resemble their adoptive
parents just as much (also an average correlation of .24). These findings suggest that
both heredity and environment have an influence on intelligence.

The Cutting Edge: Genetic Mapping

Genetic mapping is the process of determining the location and chemical sequence of
specific genes on specific chromosomes. Gene maps, by themselves, do not reveal which
genes govern which traits. However, when the Human Genome Project completed
its compilation of a precise genetic map for humans in 2003, experts expected to see
a quantum leap in the ability of scientists to pinpoint links between specific genes
and specific traits and disorders. Many breakthrough findings *were* reported. For
example, medical researchers quickly identified the genes responsible for cystic fibrosis,
Huntington's chorea, and muscular dystrophy. However, the challenge of discovering the
specific genes responsible for *behavioral traits,* such as intelligence, extraversion, and musical ability, has proven far more daunting than anticipated (Manuck & McCaffery, 2014;
Plomin, 2013; Roofeh et al., 2013). This failure to identify the specific genes that account
for variations in behavioral traits is sometimes referred to as the *missing heritability
problem.*

Why has progress in this area of research been painstakingly slow? Thus far, the
major medical breakthroughs from genetic mapping have involved dichotomous traits
(you either do or do not have the trait, such as muscular dystrophy) governed by a single
gene pair. However, most behavioral traits do not involve a dichotomy, as everyone has
varying amounts of intelligence, extraversion, musical ability, and so forth. Moreover,
virtually all behavioral traits appear to be *polygenic,* which means they are shaped by
many genes rather than a single gene. These problems are not unique to psychological
traits. For example, efforts to pinpoint the genetic bases for variations in height, which
are known to be heavily influenced by heredity, have also been disappointing. Roughly
180 relevant genes have been identified, but collectively they only account for about 10%
of the variation in height (Lango et al., 2010). These data suggest that *thousands* of genes
may influence complex abilities and traits.

Hence, contrary to early expectations for genetic mapping techniques, it appears that
scientists are not likely to identify a handful of specific genes that control intelligence,
extraversion, musical talent, or other behavioral traits, including psychological disorders.
That reality does not mean that genetic mapping studies have no role to play in unraveling the hereditary bases of behavior. Scientists remain optimistic. The challenge will
be to identify collections of genes that each exert very modest influence over aspects of

behavior and to figure out how these genes interact with environmental factors (Manuck & McCaffery, 2014; Plomin, 2013).

The Interplay of Heredity and Environment

We began this section by asking, is it all in the genes? When it comes to behavioral traits, the answer clearly is no. What scientists find again and again is that heredity and experience *jointly* influence most aspects of behavior. Moreover, their effects are interactive—they play off each other (Asbury & Plomin, 2014; Rutter, 2012).

For example, consider what researchers have learned about the development of schizophrenic disorders. Although the evidence indicates that genetic factors influence the development of schizophrenia, it does not appear that anyone directly inherits the disorder itself. Rather, what people seem to inherit is a certain degree of *vulnerability* to the disorder (McDonald & Murphy, 2003). Whether this vulnerability is ever converted into an actual disorder depends on each person's experiences in life. Thus, as Danielle Dick and Richard Rose (2002) put it in a review of behavioral genetics research, "Genes confer dispositions, not destinies" (p. 73).

In recent years, research in the emerging field of *epigenetics* has only served to further demonstrate that genetic and environmental factors are inextricably intertwined. **Epigenetics is the study of heritable changes in gene expression that do not involve modifications to the DNA sequence.** It turns out that specific genes' effects can be dampened or silenced by chemical events at the cellular level, leading to alterations in traits, health, and behavior (Tsankova et al., 2007). Moreover, these chemical events can be stimulated by environmental events, such as poor nurturance when offspring are young, exposure to stress, or peculiarities in diet (Kofink et al., 2013). What has surprised scientists is that these *epigenetic marks* that influence gene expression can be passed on to successive generations (Bohacek et al., 2013). Theorists suspect that epigenetic changes may contribute to a variety of psychological disorders, including drug addiction, schizophrenia, and bipolar disorder (Dempster et al., 2011; Nestler, 2014). The finding that genes themselves are not exempt from environmental influence has a number of far-reaching implications. Among other things, it means that efforts to quantify the respective influences of heredity and environment—informative though they may be—are ultimately artificial.

© lenetstan/Shutterstock.com

CONCEPT CHECK 3.3

Recognizing Hereditary Influence

Check your understanding of the methods scientists use to explore hereditary influences on specific behavioral traits by filling in the blanks in the descriptive statements below. The answers can be found in the back of the book in Appendix A.

1. The findings from family studies indicate that heredity may influence a trait if _____ show more trait similarity than _____.

2. The findings from twin studies suggest that heredity influences a trait if _____ show more trait similarity than _____.

3. The findings from adoption studies suggest that heredity influences a trait if children adopted at a young age share more trait similarity with their _____ than their _____.

4. The findings from family studies, twin studies, and adoption studies suggest that heredity does not influence a trait when _____ is not related to _____.

Key Learning Goals

- Understand the key insights that represent the essence of Darwin's theory of evolution.
- Describe subsequent refinements to evolutionary theory, and give some examples of animal behavior that represent adaptations.

To round out our look at the biological bases of behavior, we need to discuss how evolutionary forces have shaped many aspects of human and animal behavior. As you may recall from Chapter 1, *evolutionary psychology* is a relatively new theoretical perspective in the field that analyzes behavioral processes in terms of their adaptive significance. In this section, we outline some basic principles of evolutionary theory and relate them to animal behavior. These ideas will create a foundation for forthcoming chapters, in which we'll see how these principles can enhance our understanding of many aspects of human behavior.

Darwin's Insights

Charles Darwin, the legendary British naturalist, was *not* the first person to describe the process of evolution. Well before Darwin's time, other biologists who had studied the Earth's fossil record noted that various species appeared to have undergone gradual changes over the course of a great many generations. What Darwin contributed in his landmark book, *The Origin of Species* (1859), was a creative, new explanation for *how and why* evolutionary changes unfold over time. He identified *natural selection* as the engine that fuels the process of evolution (Dewsbury, 2009).

The mystery that Darwin set out to solve was complicated. He wanted to explain how the characteristics of a species might change over generations and why these changes tended to be surprisingly adaptive. In other words, he wanted to shed light on why organisms tend to have characteristics that serve them well in the context of their environments. How did giraffes acquire their long necks that allow them to reach high into acacia trees to secure their main source of food? How did woodpeckers develop their sharp, chisel-shaped beaks that permit them to probe trees for insects so effectively? Darwin's explanation for the seemingly purposive nature of evolution centered on four main insights.

First, he noted that organisms vary in endless ways, such as size, speed, strength, aspects of appearance, visual abilities, hearing capacities, digestive processes, cell structure, and so forth. Second, he noted that some of these characteristics are heritable; that is, they are passed down from one generation to the next. Although genes and chromosomes had not yet been discovered, the concept of heredity was well established. Third, borrowing from the work of Thomas Malthus, he noted that organisms tend to produce offspring at a pace that outstrips the local availability of food supplies, living space, and other important resources. As a population increases and resources dwindle, the competition for precious resources intensifies. Thus, it occurred to Darwin—and this was his grand insight—that variations in hereditary traits might affect organisms' ability to obtain the resources necessary for survival and reproduction. Fourth, building on this insight, Darwin argued that if a specific heritable trait contributes to an organism's survival or reproductive success, organisms with that trait should produce more offspring than do those without the trait (or those with less of the trait), and the prevalence of that trait should gradually increase over generations—resulting in evolutionary change.

Although evolution is widely characterized as a matter of "survival of the fittest," Darwin recognized from the beginning that survival is important only insofar as it relates to reproductive success. Indeed, in evolutionary theory, ***fitness** refers to the reproductive success (number of descendants) of an individual organism relative to the average reproductive success in the population.* *Variations in reproductive success are what really fuels evolutionary change.* But survival is crucial because organisms typically need

© Michael Woodruff/Shutterstock.com

Among other things, Darwin wanted to explain why the physical traits of organisms are often curiously adaptive for their environment. For example, how did woodpeckers develop their remarkable beaks, which allow them to extract insects from trees?

to mature and thrive before they can reproduce. So, Darwin theorized that there ought to be two ways in which traits might contribute to evolution: by providing either a survival advantage or a reproductive advantage. For example, a turtle's shell has great protective value that provides a survival advantage. In contrast, a firefly's emission of light is a courtship overture that provides a reproductive advantage.

To summarize, the principle of **natural selection posits that heritable characteristics that provide a survival or reproductive advantage are more likely than alternative characteristics to be passed on to subsequent generations, and thus they come to be "selected" over time.** Please note, the process of natural selection works on *populations* rather than *individual organisms*. Evolution occurs when the gene pool in a population changes gradually as a result of selection pressures. Although there are occasional exceptions, this process tends to be extremely gradual—it generally takes thousands to millions of generations for one trait to be selected over another.

Darwin's theory had at least two important, far-reaching implications (Buss, 2009). First, it suggested that the awe-inspiring diversity of life is the result of an unplanned, natural process rather than divine creation. Second, it implied that humans are not unique and that they share a common ancestry with other species. Although these implications would prove highly controversial, Darwin's theory eventually gained considerable acceptance because it provided a compelling explanation for how the characteristics of various species gradually changed over many generations and for the functional, adaptive direction of these changes.

Later Refinements to Evolutionary Theory

Although Darwin's evolutionary theory quickly gained many supporters, it also remained controversial for decades. Eventually, advances in the understanding of heredity were sufficient to permit Theodore Dobzhansky (1937) to write a fairly comprehensive account of the evolutionary process in genetic terms. Dobzhansky's synthesis of Darwin's ideas and modern genetics was enormously influential. By the 1950s, the core tenets of evolutionary theory enjoyed widespread acceptance among scientists.

Contemporary models of evolution recognize that natural selection operates on the gene pool of a population. *Adaptations* are the key product of this process. **An *adaptation* is an inherited characteristic that increased in a population (through natural selection) because it helped solve a problem of survival or reproduction during the time it emerged.** Because of the slow, gradual nature of evolution, adaptations sometimes linger in a population even though they no longer provide a survival or reproductive advantage (Durrant & Ellis, 2013). For example, humans show a taste preference for fatty substances that was adaptive in an era of hunting and gathering, when dietary fat was a scarce source of important calories. However, in our modern world, where dietary fat is typically available in abundance, this taste preference leads many people to consume too much fat, resulting in obesity, heart disease, and other health problems. Thus, the preference for fatty foods has become a liability for human survival (although its impact on reproductive success is more difficult to gauge). As you will see, evolutionary psychologists have found that many aspects of human nature reflect the adaptive demands faced by our ancient ancestors rather than contemporary demands. Of course, as natural selection continues to work, these formerly adaptive traits should gradually be eliminated, but the process is extremely slow.

In evolutionary theory, fitness is a matter of reproductive success—the number of offspring produced by an organism.

Behaviors as Adaptive Traits

Scholarly analyses of evolution have focused primarily on the evolution of *physical characteristics* in the animal kingdom, but from the very beginning, Darwin recognized that natural selection was applicable to *behavioral traits,* as well (Durrant & Ellis, 2013). Modern evolutionary psychology is based on the well-documented assumption that a species' typical patterns of behavior often reflect evolutionary solutions to adaptive problems.

Consider, for instance, the eating behavior of rats, which show remarkable caution when they encounter new foods. Rats are versatile animals that are found in an enormous range of habitats and can live off quite a variety of foods, but this diet variety can present risks, as they need to be wary of consuming toxic substances. When rats encounter unfamiliar foods, they consume only small amounts and won't eat two new foods together. If the consumption of a new food is followed by illness, they avoid that food in the future (Logue, 1991). These precautions allow rats to learn what makes them sick, while reducing the likelihood of consuming a lethal amount of something poisonous. These patterns of eating behavior are highly adaptive solutions to the food selection problems faced by rats.

Let's look at some additional examples of how evolution has shaped organisms' behavior. Avoiding predators is a nearly universal problem for organisms. Because of natural selection, many species, such as the grasshopper shown in the adjacent photo, have developed physical characteristics that allow them to blend in with their environments, making detection by predators more difficult. Many organisms also engage in elaborate *behavioral maneuvers* to hide themselves. For example, the pictured grasshopper has dug itself a small trench in which to hide and has used its midlegs to pull pebbles over its back (Alcock, 1998). This clever hiding behavior is just as much a product of evolution as the grasshopper's remarkable camouflage.

Many behavioral adaptations are designed to improve organisms' chances of reproductive success. Consider, for instance, the wide variety of species in which females choose which male to mate with. In many such species, females demand material goods and services from males in return for copulation opportunities. For example, in one type of moth, males have to spend hours extracting sodium from mud puddles, which they then transfer to prospective mates, who use it to supply their larvae with an important nutritional element (Smedley & Eisner, 1996). In the black-tipped hangingfly, females insist on a gift of food before they mate. They reject suitors bringing unpalatable food and tie the length of subsequent copulation to the size of the gift (Thornhill, 1976).

Courtesy of John Alcock

The behavior that helps this grasshopper hide from predators is a product of evolution, just like the physical characteristics that help it blend in with its surroundings.

3.8 REFLECTING ON THE CHAPTER'S THEMES

Heredity & Environment

Multifactorial Causation

Empiricism

Three of our seven themes stood out in this chapter: (1) heredity and environment jointly influence behavior, (2) behavior is determined by multiple causes, and (3) psychology is empirical. Let's look at each of these points.

In Chapter 1, when it was first emphasized that heredity and environment jointly shape behavior, you may have been a little perplexed about how your genes could be responsible for your sarcastic wit or your interest in art. In fact, there are no genes for behavior per se. Experts do not expect to find genes for sarcasm or artistic interest, for example. Insofar as your hereditary endowment plays a role in your behavior, it does so *indirectly,* by molding the physiological machine that you work with. Thus, your genes influence your physiological makeup, which in turn influences your personality, temperament, intelligence, interests, and other traits. Bear in mind, however, that genetic factors do not operate in a vacuum. Genes exert their effects in an environmental context.

The impact of genetic makeup depends on environment, and the impact of environment depends on genetic makeup.

It was evident throughout the chapter that behavior is determined by multiple causes, but this theme was particularly apparent in the discussions of schizophrenia. At different points in the chapter, we saw that schizophrenia may be a function of (1) abnormalities in neurotransmitter activity (especially dopamine), (2) structural abnormalities in the brain identified with CT and MRI scans, and (3) genetic vulnerability to the illness. These findings do not contradict one another. Rather, they demonstrate that a complex array of biological factors are involved in the development of schizophrenia. In Chapter 14, we'll see that a host of environmental factors also play a role in the multifactorial causation of schizophrenia.

The empirical nature of psychology was apparent in the numerous discussions of the specialized research methods used to study the physiological bases of behavior. As you know, the empirical approach depends on precise observation. Throughout this chapter, you've seen how investigators have come up with innovative methods to observe and measure elusive phenomena, such as neural impulses, brain function, cerebral specialization, and the impact of heredity on behavior. The point is that empirical methods are the lifeblood of the scientific enterprise. When researchers figure out how to better observe something, their findings usually facilitate major advances in scientific knowledge. That is why the new brain-imaging techniques hold exciting promise for neuroscientists.

The importance of empiricism will also be apparent in the upcoming Personal Application and in the Critical Thinking Application that follows. In both applications, you'll see the importance of learning to distinguish between scientific findings and conjecture based on those findings.

3.9 PERSONAL APPLICATION
Evaluating the Concept of "Two Minds in One"

3.9

Key Learning Goals
• Describe and evaluate three popular beliefs regarding the specialization of the cerebral hemispheres.

Answer the following "true" or "false."
___ 1 Each half of the brain has its own special mode of thinking.
___ 2 Some people are left-brained while others are right-brained.
___ 3 The two hemispheres of the brain are specialized to handle different cognitive functions.

Do we have two minds in one that think differently? Do some of us depend on one side of the brain more than the other? Is the right side of the brain neglected? These questions are too complex to resolve with a simple "true" or "false," but in this Application, we'll take a closer look at the issues involved in these generalizations about cerebral specialization. You'll learn that some of these ideas are plausible, but in many cases the hype has outstripped the evidence.

Cerebral Specialization and Cognitive Processes

Using a variety of methods, scientists have compiled mountains of data on the specialized abilities of the right and left hemispheres. These findings have led to extensive theorizing about how the right and left brains might be related to cognitive processes. Some of the more intriguing ideas include the following:

1. *The two hemispheres are specialized to process different types of cognitive tasks* (Corballis, 1991). Research findings have been widely interpreted as showing that the left hemisphere handles verbal tasks, including language, speech, writing, math, and logic, while the right hemisphere handles nonverbal tasks, including spatial problems, music, art, fantasy, and creativity. These conclusions have attracted a great deal of public interest and media attention. For example, **Figure 3.23** shows a *Newsweek* artist's depiction of how the brain supposedly divides its work.

2. *The two hemispheres have different modes of thinking* (Davis & Dean, 2005). According to this notion, the documented differences between the hemispheres in dealing with verbal and nonverbal materials are due to more basic differences in how the hemispheres process information. This theory holds that the reason the left hemisphere handles verbal material well is that it is analytic, abstract, rational, logical, and linear. In contrast, the right hemisphere is thought to be better equipped to handle spatial and musical material because it is synthetic, concrete, nonrational, intuitive, and holistic.

HOW THE BRAIN DIVIDES ITS WORK

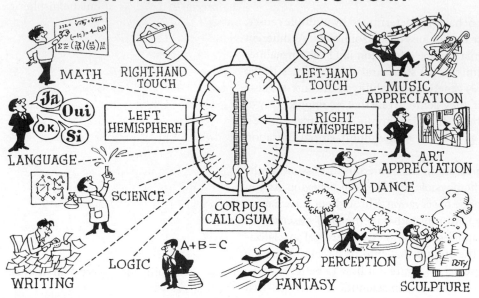

FIGURE 3.23

Popular conceptions of hemispheric specialization. As this *Newsweek* diagram illustrates, depictions of hemispheric specialization in the popular press have often been oversimplified.

SOURCE: Cartoon courtesy of Roy Doty.

3. *People vary in their reliance on one hemisphere as opposed to the other* (Pink, 2005). Allegedly, some people are "left-brained." Their greater dependence on their left hemisphere supposedly makes them analytic, rational, and logical. Other people are "right-brained." Their greater use of their right hemisphere supposedly makes them intuitive, holistic, and irrational. Being right-brained or left-brained is thought to explain many personal characteristics, such as whether an individual likes to read, is good with maps, or enjoys music. This notion of "brainedness" has even been used to explain occupational choice. Supposedly, right-brained people are more likely to become artists or musicians, while left-brained people are more likely to become writers or scientists.

Complexities and Qualifications

The ideas just outlined are intriguing and have clearly captured the imagination of the general public. However, the research on cerebral specialization is complex, and these ideas have to be qualified carefully. Let's examine each point.

1. There *is* ample evidence that the right and left hemispheres are specialized to handle different types of cognitive tasks, *but only to a degree* (Corballis, 2003; Hervé et al., 2013). Doreen Kimura (1973) compared the abilities of the right and left hemispheres to quickly recognize letters, words, faces, and melodies in a series of perceptual asymmetry studies. She found that the superiority of one hemisphere over the other on specific types of tasks was usually quite modest (see **Figure 3.24**). Most tasks probably engage both hemispheres, albeit to different degrees.

Furthermore, people differ in their patterns of cerebral specialization (Springer & Deutsch, 1998). Some people display little specialization; that is, their hemispheres seem to have equal abilities on various types of tasks. Others even reverse the usual specialization, so that verbal processing might be housed in the right hemisphere. These unusual patterns are especially common among left-handed people (Josse & Tzourio-Mazoyer, 2004). Accomplished musicians may be another exception to the rule. Two studies found that experienced musicians exhibit more bilateral cerebral organization than do comparable nonmusicians (Gibson, Folley, & Park, 2009; Patston et al., 2007). This bilaterality may develop because musicians often have to use both hands independently to play their instruments. If this explanation is accurate, it would provide another example of how experience can shape brain organization. In any

Does musical ability depend on being right-brained? The popular press has certainly suggested that this is the case, but as your text explains, there is no solid empirical evidence to support this assertion.

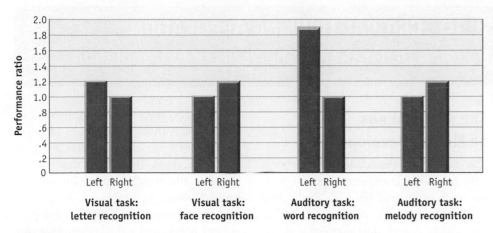

FIGURE 3.24

Relative superiority of one brain hemisphere over the other in studies of perceptual asymmetry. These performance ratios from a study by Doreen Kimura (1973) show the degree to which one hemisphere was "superior" to the other on each type of task in one study of normal participants. For example, the right hemisphere was 20% better than the left hemisphere in quickly recognizing melodic patterns (ratio 1.2 to 1). Most differences in the performance of the two hemispheres are quite small.

Unfortunately, the tentative, conjectural nature of these ideas about hemispheric specialization has gotten lost in the popular magazine descriptions of research on right and left brains (Coren, 1992). Commenting on this popularization, Hooper and Teresi (1986) note: "A widespread cult of the right brain ensued, and the duplex house that Sperry built grew into the Kmart of brain science. Today our hairdresser lectures us about the Two Hemispheres of the Brain" (p. 223). Cerebral specialization is an important and intriguing area of research. However, it is unrealistic to expect that the hemispheric divisions in the brain will provide a biological explanation for every dichotomy or polarity in modes of thinking.

event, it is clear that the functional specialization of the cerebral hemispheres is not set in concrete.

2. Little direct evidence has been found to support the notion that each hemisphere has its own mode of thinking, or cognitive style (Corballis, 2007). This notion is plausible, and there *is* some supportive evidence, but that evidence is inconsistent and more research is needed (Reuter-Lorenz & Miller, 1998). One key problem with this idea is that aspects of cognitive style have proven difficult to define and measure. For instance, there is debate about the meaning of analytic versus synthetic thinking, or linear versus holistic thinking.

3. The assertion that some people are left-brained while others are right-brained also appears more mythical than real. Recent brain-imaging research has not supported the idea that some people consistently display more activation of one hemisphere than the other (Nielsen et al., 2013). Contrary to popular belief, researchers do not have convincing data linking "brainedness" to musical ability, occupational choice, personality, or the like (Knecht et al., 2001).

In summary, the theories linking cerebral specialization to cognitive processes are highly speculative. There's nothing wrong with theoretical speculation.

> **REALITY CHECK**

Misconception

People are either left-brained or right-brained, and this disparity can predict their abilities and interests.

Reality

Pop psychology books with no scientific basis routinely discuss how being right-brained or left-brained ought to relate to personal talents and occupational choice. There is just one small problem. If you search the research literature, there are no studies that have linked brainedness to specific talents, and a recent brain-imaging study undermined the notion that people are right- or left-brained.

3.10

Key Learning Goals

• Explain how neuroscience research has been overextrapolated to educational issues.

3.10 CRITICAL THINKING APPLICATION
Building Better Brains: The Perils of Extrapolation

Summarizing the implications of certain widely discussed findings in brain research, science writer Ronald Kotulak (1996) concluded, "The first three years of a child's life are critically important to brain development" (pp. ix–x). Echoing this sentiment, the president of a U.S. educational commission asserted that "research in brain development suggests it is time to rethink many educational policies" (Bruer, 1999, p. 16). Based on research in the neurosciences (the various scientific disciplines that study the brain and the nervous system), many states in the 1990s launched expensive programs intended to foster better neural development in infants. For example, the governor of Georgia at the time, Zell Miller, sought state funding to distribute classical music tapes to the state's infants, saying, "No one doubts that listening to music, especially at a very early age, affects the spatial-temporal reasoning that underlies math, engineering, and chess" (Bruer, 1999, p. 62). Well-intentioned educational groups have argued for the creation of schools for infants on the grounds that the first 3 years of life are especially critical to brain development. This popular movement has yielded a host of books claiming to link neuroscience research to educational practices, such as *Brain-Based Early Learning Activities* (Darling-Kuria, 2010) and *Brain-Based Strategies to Reach Every Learner* (Connell, 2005).

What are these practical, new discoveries about the brain that will permit parents and educators to optimize infants' brain development? Well, we will discuss the pertinent research momentarily, but it is not as new or as practical as suggested in many quarters. Unfortunately, as we saw in our discussion of research on hemispheric specialization, the hype in the media has greatly outstripped the realities of what scientists have learned in the laboratory (Chance, 2001), providing an enlightening case study in the perils of overextrapolation.

The Key Findings on Neural Development

The education and childcare reformers who have used brain science as the basis for their campaigns have primarily cited two key findings: the discovery of critical periods in neural development and the demonstration that rats raised in "enriched environments" have more synapses than do rats raised in "impoverished environments." Let's look at each of these findings.

A *critical period* is a limited time span in the development of an organism when it is optimal for certain capacities to emerge because the organism is especially responsive to certain experiences. The groundbreaking research on critical periods in neural development was conducted by David Hubel and Torsten Wiesel (1963) in the 1960s. They showed that if an eye of a newborn kitten is sewn shut early in its development (typically the first 4–6 weeks), the kitten will become permanently blind in that eye, but if the eye is covered for the same amount of time at later ages (after 4 months), blindness does not result. Such studies show that certain types of visual input are necessary during a critical period of development or neural pathways between the eye and brain will not form properly. Basically, what happens is that the inactive synapses from the closed eye are displaced by the active synapses from the open eye. Critical periods have been found for other aspects of neural development and in other species, but a great deal remains to be learned. Based on this type of research, some educational and childcare reformers have argued that the first 3 years of life are a critical period for human neural development.

The pioneering work on environment and brain development was begun in the 1960s by Mark Rosenzweig and his colleagues (1961, 1962). They raised some rats in an impoverished environment, (housed individually in small, barren cages) and other rats in an enriched environment (housed in groups in larger cages, with a variety of objects available for exploration). They found that the rats raised in the enriched environment performed better on problem-solving tasks than the impoverished rats and had slightly heavier brains and a thicker cerebral cortex in some areas. Subsequent research by William Greenough demonstrated that enriched environments resulted in heavier and thicker cortical areas by virtue of producing denser dendritic branching, more synapses, and richer neural networks (Greenough, 1975; Greenough & Volkmar, 1973). More recently, scientists have learned that enriched environments also promote the newly discovered process of *neurogenesis* in the brain (Nithianantharajah & Hannan, 2006). Based on this type of research, some childcare reformers have argued that human infants need to be brought up in enriched environments during the critical period before age 3 to promote synapse formation and to enhance the development of their emerging neural circuits.

The findings on critical periods and the effects of enriched environments were genuine breakthroughs in neuroscience, but they certainly aren't *new* findings, as suggested by various political action groups. Moreover, one can raise many doubts about whether this research can serve as a meaningful guide for decisions about parenting practices, day-care programs, educational policies, and welfare reform (Goswami, 2006; Thompson & Nelson, 2001).

The Tendency to Overextrapolate

Extrapolation occurs when an effect is estimated by extending beyond some known values or conditions. Extrapolation is a normal process, but some extrapolations are conservative, plausible projections drawn from directly relevant data, whereas others are wild leaps of speculation based on loosely related data. The extrapolations made regarding the educational implications of critical periods and environmental effects on synapse formation are highly conjectural *overextrapolations*. The studies that highlighted the possible importance of early experience in animals all used extreme conditions to make their comparisons, such as depriving an animal of all visual input or raising it in stark isolation. The so-called enriched environments probably resemble normal conditions in the real world, whereas the standard laboratory environment may reflect extreme environmental deprivation (Gould, 2004). In light of the findings, it seems plausible to speculate that children probably need normal stimulation to experience normal brain development. However, great difficulty arises when these findings are extended to conclude that adding *more* stimulation to a normal environment will be beneficial to brain development.

The ease with which people fall into the trap of overextrapolating has been particularly apparent in recent recommendations that infants listen to classical music to enhance their brain development. These recommendations were derived from two studies that showed that college students' performance on spatial reasoning tasks was enhanced slightly for about 10–15 minutes after listening to a brief Mozart recording (Rauscher, Shaw, & Ky, 1993, 1995). This peculiar finding, dubbed the "Mozart effect," has proven difficult to replicate (Gray & Della Sala, 2007; Steele, 2003), but the pertinent point here is that at the time there was no research on how classical music affects *infants*, no research relating classical music to *brain development*, and no research on anyone showing *lasting effects*. Nonetheless, many people (including the governor of Georgia) were quick to extrapolate the shaky findings on the Mozart effect to infants' brain development.

Ironically, there is much better evidence linking *musical training* in childhood to enhanced cognitive performance. Studies have found a thought-provoking association between measures of intelligence and the extent of individuals' exposure to music lessons (Moreno et al., 2011; Schellenberg, 2006, 2011). Of course, if you think critically about this correlation, it might only mean that brighter youngsters are more likely to take music lessons. That caveat aside, recent studies have found that musical training is associated with structural changes in the brain (James et al., 2014; Rodrigues, Loureiro, & Caramelli, 2010). Moreover, evidence is accumulating that the cortical changes produced by musical training may slow age-related cognitive decline late in life (Hanna-Pladdy & MacKay, 2011; Oechslin et al., 2013).

As discussed in Chapter 1, thinking critically about issues often involves asking questions such as: What is missing from this debate? Is there any contradictory evidence? In this case, there is some contradictory evidence that is worthy of consideration. The basis for advocating infant educational programs is the belief that brain development is more rapid and malleable during the hypothesized critical period of birth to age 3 than at later ages. However, Greenough's work on synaptic formation and other lines of research suggest that the brain remains malleable throughout life (Thompson & Nelson, 2001). Thus, advocates for the aged could just as readily argue for new educational initiatives for the elderly to help them maximize their intellectual potential. Indeed, recent years have seen a surge of interest in designing cognitive training programs for older adults that might slow age-related cognitive decline (Bamidis et al., 2014; Rebok et al., 2014). Another problem is the implicit assumption that greater synaptic density is associated with greater intelligence. There is quite a bit of evidence that infant animals and humans begin life with an overabundance of synaptic connections and that learning involves selective *pruning* of inactive synapses, which gradually give way to heavily used neural pathways (Huttenlocher, 2002). Thus, in the realm of synapses, more may *not* be better.

In conclusion, there may be many valid reasons for increasing educational programs for infants, but research in neuroscience does not appear to provide a clear rationale for much in the way of specific infant care policies (Bruer, 2002). One problem in evaluating these proposals is that few people want to argue against high-quality child care or education. But modern societies need to allocate their limited resources to the programs that appear most likely to have beneficial effects, so even intuitively appealing ideas need to be subjected to critical scrutiny.

> **REALITY CHECK**

Misconception

Exposing infants and children to classical music can enhance their brain development and boost their intelligence.

Reality

If only it were that easy! The so-called Mozart effect has garnered a great deal of publicity, but the actual findings are utterly unimpressive. A meta-analysis of nearly 40 studies concluded that "there is little support for the Mozart effect" (Pietschnig, Voracek, & Formann, 2010). The typical dependent variable in these studies is a low-level spatial task (paper folding and cutting) that won't get anyone through college. When small, short-term positive effects are observed, they appear to be due to the fact that music can be arousing, not to any durable change in the architecture of the brain.

TABLE 3.2 Critical Thinking Skills Discussed in This Application

Skill	Description
Understanding the limits of extrapolation	The critical thinker appreciates that extrapolations are based on certain assumptions, vary in plausibility, and ultimately involve speculation.
Looking for contradictory evidence	In evaluating the evidence presented on an issue, the critical thinker attempts to look for contradictory evidence that may have been left out of the debate.

COMMUNICATION IN THE NERVOUS SYSTEM

Key parts of the neuron

Soma: Cell body

Dendrites: Branching structures that receive signals from other cells

Axon: Fiber that carries signals away from soma to other cells

Myelin sheath: Insulating material that encases some axons

Terminal buttons: Small knobs (at ends of axons) that release neurotransmitters at synapses

Glia

Glia are cells that provide support for neurons and contribute to signaling in the nervous system.

The neural impulse

Resting potential: Neuron's stable, negative charge when inactive

Action potential: Voltage spike that travels along an axon

Absolute regractory period: Brief time after an action potential, before another action potential can begin

All-or-none law: A neuron either fires or doesn't fire

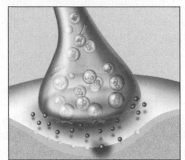

Synaptic transmission

Synthesis and storage of neurotransmitters in synaptic vesicles

↓

Release of neurotransmitters into synaptic cleft

↓

Binding of neurotransmitters at receptor sites leads to *excitatory* and *inhibitory* PSPs

↓

Inactivation or **removal** (drifting away) of neurotransmitters

Reuptake of neurotransmitters by presynaptic neuron

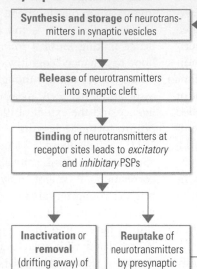

Neurotransmitters and behavior

Acetylcholine: Released by neurons that control skeletal muscles

Serotonin: Involved in the regulation of sleep and arousal, and aggression; abnormal levels linked to depression

Dopamine: Abnormal levels linked to schizophrenia; dopamine circuits activated by cocaine and amphetamines

Norepinephrine: Abnormal levels linked to depression; norepinephrine circuits can be activated by cocaine and amphetamines

GABA: Inhibitory transmitter that contributes to regulation of anxiety

Endorphins: Opiate-like chemicals involved in modulation of pain

ORGANIZATION OF THE NERVOUS SYSTEM

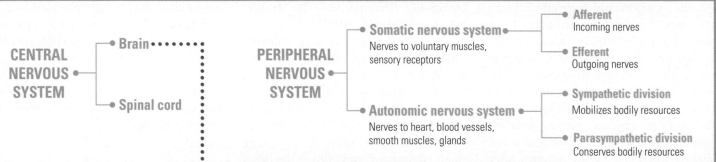

CENTRAL NERVOUS SYSTEM
- Brain
- Spinal cord

PERIPHERAL NERVOUS SYSTEM
- **Somatic nervous system**
  Nerves to voluntary muscles, sensory receptors
  - **Afferent** Incoming nerves
  - **Efferent** Outgoing nerves
- **Autonomic nervous system**
  Nerves to heart, blood vessels, smooth muscles, glands
  - **Sympathetic division** Mobilizes bodily resources
  - **Parasympathetic division** Conserves bodily resources

BRAIN AND BEHAVIOR

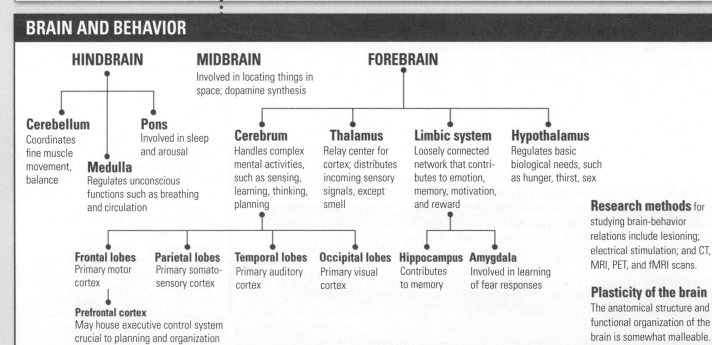

HINDBRAIN

MIDBRAIN
Involved in locating things in space; dopamine synthesis

FOREBRAIN

Cerebellum
Coordinates fine muscle movement, balance

Pons
Involved in sleep and arousal

Medulla
Regulates unconscious functions such as breathing and circulation

Cerebrum
Handles complex mental activities, such as sensing, learning, thinking, planning

Thalamus
Relay center for cortex; distributes incoming sensory signals, except smell

Limbic system
Loosely connected network that contributes to emotion, memory, motivation, and reward

Hypothalamus
Regulates basic biological needs, such as hunger, thirst, sex

Frontal lobes
Primary motor cortex

Parietal lobes
Primary somato-sensory cortex

Temporal lobes
Primary auditory cortex

Occipital lobes
Primary visual cortex

Hippocampus
Contributes to memory

Amygdala
Involved in learning of fear responses

Prefrontal cortex
May house executive control system crucial to planning and organization

Research methods for studying brain-behavior relations include lesioning; electrical stimulation; and CT, MRI, PET, and fMRI scans.

Plasticity of the brain
The anatomical structure and functional organization of the brain is somewhat malleable.

RIGHT BRAIN / LEFT BRAIN

Methods for study of lateralization

Split brain surgery: Bundle of fibers (corpus callosum) that connects two hemispheres is severed.

Perceptual asymmetries: Left-right imbalances in speed of processing are studied in normal subjects.

Left hemisphere

Usually handles verbal processing, including language, speech, reading, writing

Right hemisphere

Usually handles nonverbal processing, including spatial and musical processing, and visual recognition tasks

HEREDITY AND BEHAVIOR

Basic concepts

- *Chromosomes* are threadlike strands of DNA that carry information.
- *Genes* are DNA segments that are the key functional units in hereditary transmission.
- Closer relatives share greater genetic overlap.
- Most behavioral traits appear to involve *polygenic inheritance*.

Research methods

Family studies assess trait resemblance among blood relatives.

Twin studies compare trait resemblance of identical and fraternal twins.

Adoption studies compare adopted children to their adoptive parents and to their biological parents.

Genetic mapping facilitates efforts to link specific genes to specific traits.

Interactions

- Research indicates that most behavioral qualities are influenced jointly by heredity and environment, which play off of each other in complex interactions.
- New work in *epigenetics* has further demonstrated that genetic and environmental factors are deeply intertwined.

ENDOCRINE SYSTEM

- System consists of *glands* that secrete *hormones* into the bloodstream in a pulsatile fashion.
- Governed by the hypothalamus and pituitary gland, the endocrine system regulates our response to stress.
- Recent research suggests that the hormone *oxytocin* fosters bonding, and influences social behavior.

EVOLUTIONARY BASES OF BEHAVIOR

Darwin's insights

- Organisms vary in endless ways.
- Some traits are heritable.
- Variations in hereditary traits might affect organisms' survival and reproductive success.
- Heritable traits that provide a survival or reproductive advantage will become more prevalent over generations (natural selection will change the gene pool of the population).

© Michael Woodruff/Shutterstock.com

Key concepts

Fitness refers to the reproductive success of an organism relative to the population.

Adaptations are inherited characteristics sculpted through natural selection because they helped solve a problem of survival or reproduction when they emerged.

Behaviors as adaptive traits

- Species' typical patterns of behavior often reflect evolutionary solutions to adaptive problems.
- For example, behavioral strategies that help organisms avoid predators have obvious adaptive value.
- Many behavioral adaptations improve organisms' chances of reproductive success.

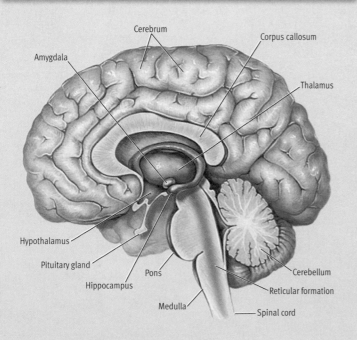

APPLICATIONS

- It is widely believed that the cerebral hemispheres are specialized to handle specific cognitive tasks, that people are right- or left-brained, and that each hemisphere has its own cognitive style.
- However, task specialization is a matter of degree, evidence does not support the idea that people are right- or left-brained, and the data on hemispheres' cognitive style are inconclusive.
- Efforts to use brain science to justify various education initiatives have shown that people often overextrapolate the implications of research findings.

CHAPTER 4

SENSATION AND PERCEPTION

Themes in this Chapter

Theoretical   Subjectivity   Cultural
Diversity   of Experience   Heritage

© Gabriele Maltinti/Shutterstock.com

Take a look at the photo in the margin on the right. What do you see? You probably answered, "a rose" or "a flower." But is that what you really see? No, this isn't a trick question. Let's examine the odd case of "Dr. P." It shows that there's more to seeing than meets the eye.

Dr. P was an intelligent and distinguished music professor who began to exhibit some worrisome behaviors that seemed to be related to his vision. Sometimes he failed to recognize familiar students by sight, though he knew them instantly by the sound of their voices. Sometimes he acted as if he saw faces in inanimate objects, cordially greeting fire hydrants and parking meters as if they were children. On one occasion, reaching for what he thought was his hat, he took hold of his wife's head and tried to put it on! Except for these kinds of visual mistakes, Dr. P was a normal, talented man.

Ultimately, Dr. P was referred to Oliver Sacks, a neurologist, for an examination. During one visit, Sacks handed Dr. P a fresh red rose to see whether he would recognize it. Dr. P took the rose as if he were being given a model of a geometric solid rather than a flower. "About six inches in length," Dr. P observed, "a convoluted red form with a linear green attachment."

"Yes," Sacks persisted, "and what do you think it is, Dr. P?"

"Not easy to say," the patient replied. "It lacks the simple symmetry of the Platonic solids . . ."

"Smell it," the neurologist suggested. Dr. P looked perplexed, as if being asked to smell symmetry, but he complied and brought the flower to his nose. Suddenly, his confusion cleared up. "Beautiful. An early rose. What a heavenly smell" (Sacks, 1987, pp. 13–14).

What accounted for Dr. P's strange inability to recognize faces and familiar objects by sight? There was nothing wrong with his eyes. He could readily spot a pin on the floor. If you're thinking that he *must* have had something wrong with his vision, look again at the photo of the rose. What you see *is* "a convoluted red form with a linear green attachment." It doesn't occur to you to describe it that way only because, without thinking about it, you instantly perceive that combination of form and color as a flower. This is precisely

what Dr. P was unable to do. He could see perfectly well, but he was losing the ability to assemble what he saw into a meaningful picture of the world. Technically, he suffered from a condition called *visual agnosia,* an inability to recognize objects through sight. As Sacks (1987) put it, "Visually, he was lost in a world of lifeless abstractions" (p. 15).

As Dr. P's case illustrates, without effective processing of sensory input, our familiar world can become a chaos of confusing sensations. To acknowledge the needs to both take in and process sensory information, psychologists distinguish between sensation and perception. *Sensation* **is the stimulation of sense organs.** *Perception* **is the selection, organization, and interpretation of sensory input.** Sensation involves the absorption of energy, such as light or sound waves, by sensory organs, such as the eyes and ears. Perception involves organizing and translating sensory input into something meaningful.

The distinction between sensation and perception stands out in Dr. P's case of visual agnosia. His eyes were doing their job of registering sensory input and transmitting signals to the brain. However, damage in his brain interfered with his ability to put these signals together into organized wholes. Thus, Dr. P's process of visual *sensation* was intact, but his process of visual *perception* was severely impaired.

We'll begin our discussion of sensation and perception with a long look at vision, then take a briefer look at the other senses. As we examine each of the sensory systems, we'll see repeatedly that people's experience of the world depends on both the physical stimuli they encounter (sensation) and their active processing of stimulus inputs (perception). The chapter's Personal Application explores how principles of visual perception come into play in art and illusion. The Critical Thinking Application discusses how perceptual contrasts can be manipulated in persuasive efforts.

Steve Cole/Photodisc Green/Getty Images

What do you see? Would it occur to you to describe it as a convoluted red form with a linear green attachment?

Key Learning Goals

- Identify the three properties of light, and describe the role of key eye structures in vision.
- Trace the routing of signals from the eye to the brain, and explain the brain's role in visual information processing.
- Distinguish two types of color mixing and compare the trichromatic and opponent process theories of color vision.

"Seeing is believing." Good students are "bright," and a good explanation is "illuminating." As these common expressions show, humans are visual animals. People rely heavily on their sense of sight, and they virtually equate it with knowing what is trustworthy (seeing is believing). Although it is taken for granted, you'll see (there it is again) that the human visual system is amazingly complex. Furthermore, as in all sensory domains, what people "sense" and what they "perceive" may be quite different.

The Stimulus: Light

For people to see, there must be light. *Light* is a form of electromagnetic radiation that travels as a wave, moving, naturally enough, at the speed of light. As **Figure 4.1(a)** shows, light waves vary in *amplitude* (height) and in *wavelength* (the distance between peaks). Amplitude affects mainly the perception of brightness, while wavelength affects mainly the perception of color. The lights humans normally see are mixtures of different wavelengths. Hence, light can also vary in its *purity* (how varied the mix is). Purity influences perception of the *saturation,* or richness, of colors. Saturation refers to the relative amount of whiteness in a color. As whiteness declines, saturation increases. Of course, most objects do not emit light, they reflect it (the sun, lamps, and fireflies being some exceptions).

What most people call light includes only the wavelengths that humans can see. But as **Figure 4.1(c)** shows, the visible spectrum is only a slim portion of the total range of wavelengths. Vision is a filter that permits people to sense only a fraction of the real

FIGURE 4.1

Light, the physical stimulus for vision. (a) Light waves vary in amplitude and wavelength. **(b)** Within the spectrum of visible light, amplitude (corresponding to physical intensity) affects mainly the experience of brightness. Wavelength affects mainly the experience of color, and purity is the key determinant of saturation. **(c)** If white light (such as sunlight) passes through a prism, the prism separates the light into its component wavelengths, creating a rainbow of colors. However, visible light is only the narrow band of wavelengths to which human eyes happen to be sensitive.

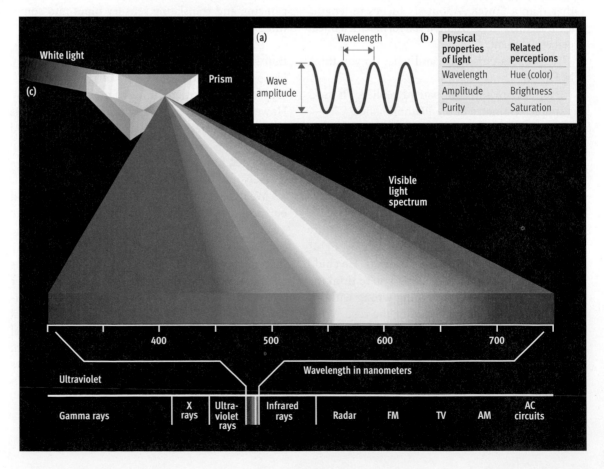

world. Other animals have different capabilities and so live in a quite different visual world. For example, many insects can see shorter wavelengths than humans can see, in the *ultraviolet* spectrum, whereas many fish and reptiles can see longer wavelengths, in the *infrared* spectrum.

Although the sense of sight depends on light waves, in order for people to see, incoming visual input must be converted into neural impulses that are sent to the brain. Let's investigate how this transformation is accomplished.

The Eye: A Living Optical Instrument

The structure of the eye is shown in **Figure 4.2**. Each eye is a living optical instrument that creates an image of the visual world on the light-sensitive retina that lines its inside back surface. Light enters the eye through a transparent "window" at the front, the *cornea*. The cornea and the crystalline *lens*, located behind it, form an upside down image of objects on the retina and adjust the focus of the image. It might seem disturbing that the image is upside down, but the arrangement works. It doesn't matter how the image sits on the retina, as long as the brain knows the rule for relating positions on the retina to the corresponding positions in the world.

The *lens* is a transparent eye structure that focuses the light rays falling on the retina. The lens is made up of relatively soft tissue, capable of adjustments that facilitate a process called accommodation. *Accommodation* occurs when the curvature of the lens adjusts to alter visual focus. When you focus on a close object, the lens of your eye gets fatter (rounder) in order to give you a clear image. When you focus on distant objects, the lens flattens out to give you a better image.

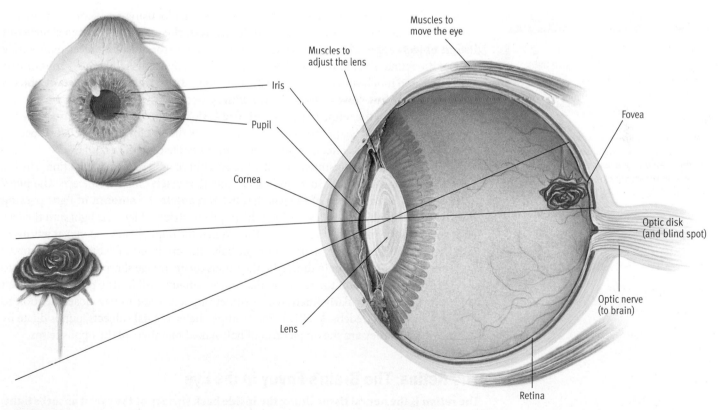

FIGURE 4.2

The human eye. Light passes through the cornea, pupil, and lens and falls on the light-sensitive surface of the retina, where images of objects are reflected upside down. The lens adjusts its curvature to focus the images falling on the retina. The pupil regulates the amount of light passing into the rear chamber of the eye.

FIGURE 4.3

Nearsightedness and farsightedness. The pictures on the right simulate how a scene might look to nearsighted and farsighted people. Nearsightedness occurs because light from distant objects focuses in front of the retina. Farsightedness results from the opposite situation—light from close objects focuses behind the retina.

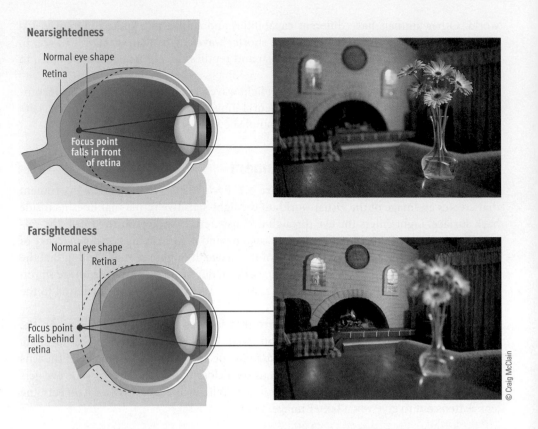

Nearsightedness
Normal eye shape
Retina
Focus point falls in front of retina

Farsightedness
Normal eye shape
Retina
Focus point falls behind retina

© Craig McClain

A number of common visual problems are caused by focusing problems or defects in the lens (Hall, 2011). For example, **in *nearsightedness*, close objects are seen clearly but distant objects appear blurry** because the focus of light from distant objects falls a little short of the retina (see **Figure 4.3**). This focusing problem occurs when the cornea or lens bends light too much or when the eyeball is too long. **In *farsightedness*, distant objects are seen clearly but close objects appear blurry** because the focus of light from close objects falls behind the retina (again, see **Figure 4.3**). This focusing problem typically occurs when the eyeball is too short. A *cataract* is a lens that is clouded. This defect occurs mainly in older persons, affecting three out of four people over the age of 65.

The eye also makes adjustments to alter the amount of light reaching the retina. The *iris* is the colored ring of muscle surrounding the *pupil*, or black center of the eye. **The *pupil* is the opening in the center of the iris that helps regulate the amount of light passing into the rear chamber of the eye.** When the pupil constricts, it lets less light into the eye, but it sharpens the image falling on the retina. When the pupil dilates (opens), it lets more light in, but the image is less sharp. In bright light, the pupils constrict to take advantage of the sharpened image. But in dim light, the pupils dilate. Image sharpness is sacrificed to allow more light to fall on the retina so that more remains visible. The pupils also widen when people are particularly interested in something and want to pay close attention to it (Laeng, Sirois, & Gredeback, 2012). For example, heterosexual subjects' pupils dilate by about 20% when they are shown pictures of half-naked members of the opposite sex.

The Retina: The Brain's Envoy in the Eye

The *retina* is the neural tissue lining the inside back surface of the eye; it absorbs light, processes images, and sends visual information to the brain. Much as the spinal cord is a complicated extension of the brain, the retina is the brain's envoy in the eye. About half as thick as a credit card, this thin sheet of neural tissue contains a complex network of specialized cells arranged in layers (Baker, 2013), as shown in **Figure 4.4**.

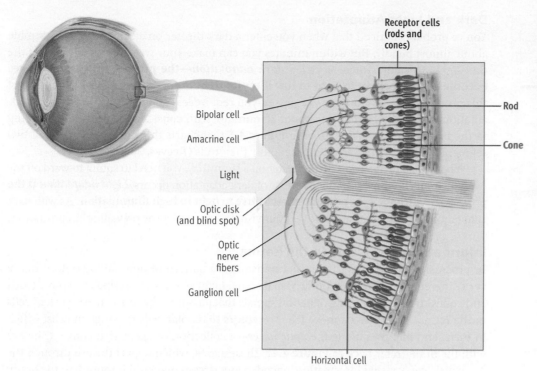

Receptor cells (rods and cones)

Bipolar cell

Amacrine cell

Light

Optic disk (and blind spot)

Optic nerve fibers

Ganglion cell

Horizontal cell

Rod

Cone

FIGURE 4.4

The retina. The close-up shows the several layers of cells in the retina. The cells closest to the back of the eye (the rods and cones) are the receptor cells that actually detect light. The intervening layers of cells receive signals from the rods and cones and form circuits that begin the process of analyzing incoming information before it is sent to the brain. These cells feed into many optic fibers, all of which head toward the "hole" in the retina where the optic nerve leaves the eye—the point known as the optic disk (which corresponds to the blind spot).

The axons that run from the retina to the brain converge at a single spot where they exit the eye. At that point, all the fibers dive through a hole in the retina called the *optic disk*. Since the optic disk is a *hole* in the retina, you cannot see the part of an image that falls on it. It is therefore known as the *blind spot*. Most people are not aware that they have a blind spot in each eye. Why? Because each eye compensates for the blind spot of the other and because the brain somehow "fills in" the missing part of the image.

Visual Receptors: Rods and Cones

The retina contains millions of receptor cells that are sensitive to light. Surprisingly, these receptors are located in the innermost layer of the retina (see **Figure 4.4**). Hence, light must pass through several layers of cells before it gets to the receptors that actually detect it. The retina contains two types of receptors: *rods* and *cones*. Their names are based on their shapes, as rods are elongated and cones are stubbier. Rods outnumber cones by a huge margin; humans have about 100 million rods, but only about 6 million cones (Meister & Tessier-Lavigne, 2013).

Cones **are specialized visual receptors that play a key role in daylight vision and color vision.** The cones handle most of people's daytime vision, because bright lights dazzle the rods. The special sensitivities of cones also allow them to play a major role in the perception of color. However, cones do not respond well to dim light, which is why you don't see color very well in low illumination. Nonetheless, cones provide better *visual acuity*—that is, sharpness and precise detail—than rods. Cones are concentrated most heavily in the center of the retina and quickly fall off in density toward its sides. **The** *fovea* **is a tiny spot in the center of the retina that contains only cones; visual acuity is greatest at this spot** (consult **Figure 4.2** again). When you want to see something in sharp focus, you usually move your eyes to center the object in the fovea.

Rods **are specialized visual receptors that play a key role in night vision and peripheral vision.** Rods handle night vision because they are up to 100 times more sensitive than cones to dim light (Kefalov, 2010). They handle the lion's share of peripheral vision because they greatly outnumber cones in the periphery (outer areas) of the retina. The density of the rods is greatest just outside the fovea and gradually decreases toward the periphery of the retina.

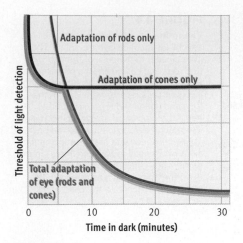

FIGURE 4.5

The process of dark adaptation. The declining thresholds over time indicate that your visual sensitivity is improving, as less and less light is required to see. Visual sensitivity improves markedly during the first 5 to 10 minutes after entering a dark room, as the eye's bright-light receptors (the cones) rapidly adapt to low light levels. However, the cones' adaptation, which is plotted in purple, soon reaches its limit, and further improvement comes from the rods' adaptation, which is plotted in red. The rods adapt more slowly than the cones, but they are capable of far greater visual sensitivity in low levels of light.

Dark and Light Adaptation

You've probably noticed that when you enter a dark theater on a bright day, you stumble about almost blindly. But within minutes you can make your way about quite well in the dim light. This adjustment is called *dark adaptation*—**the process in which the eyes become more sensitive to light in low illumination.** **Figure 4.5** maps out the course of this process. It shows how, as time passes, you require less and less light to see. Dark adaptation is virtually complete in about 30 minutes, with considerable progress occurring in the first 10 minutes. The curve in **Figure 4.5** that charts this progress consists of two segments because cones adapt more rapidly than rods (Reeves, 2010).

When you emerge from a dark theater on a sunny day, you need to squint to ward off the overwhelming brightness, and the reverse of dark adaptation occurs. *Light adaptation* **is the process in which the eyes become less sensitive to light in high illumination.** As with dark adaptation, light adaptation improves your visual acuity under the prevailing circumstances.

Information Processing in the Retina

In processing visual input, the retina transforms a pattern of light falling onto it into a very different representation of the visual scene. Light striking the retina's receptors (rods and cones) triggers the firing of neural signals that pass into the intricate network of cells in the retina. Thus, signals move from receptors to bipolar cells to ganglion cells, which in turn send impulses along the *optic nerve*—a collection of axons that connect the eye with the brain (refer back to **Figure 4.4**). These axons, which depart the eye through the optic disk, carry visual information, encoded as a stream of neural impulses, to the brain.

A great deal of complex information processing goes on in the retina itself before visual signals are sent to the brain. Ultimately, the information from over 100 million rods and cones converges to travel along "only" 1 million axons in the optic nerve. This means that the bipolar and ganglion cells in the intermediate layers of the retina integrate and compress signals from many receptors.

The collection of rod and cone receptors that funnel signals to a particular visual cell in the retina (or ultimately in the brain) make up that cell's *receptive field*. Thus, **the** *receptive field of a visual cell* **is the retinal area that, when stimulated, affects the firing of that cell.** Receptive fields in the retina come in a variety of shapes and sizes. Particularly common

CONCEPT CHECK 4.1

Understanding Sensory Processes in the Retina

Check your understanding of sensory receptors in the retina by completing the following exercises. Consult Appendix A for the answers.

The receptors for vision are rods and cones in the retina. These two types of receptors have many important differences, which are compared systematically in the chart below. Fill in the missing information to finish the chart.

Dimension	Rods	Cones
1. Physical shape	Elongated	
2. Number in the retina		6 million
3. Area of the retina in which they are dominant receptor	Periphery	
4. Critical to color vision		
5. Critical to peripheral vision		No
6. Sensitivity to dim light	Strong	
7. Speed of dark adaptation		Rapid

are circular fields with a center-surround arrangement (Levitt, 2010). In these receptive fields, light falling in the center has the opposite effect of light falling in the surrounding area. For example, the rate of firing of a visual cell might be *increased* by light in the center of its receptive field and *decreased* by light in the surrounding area.

Vision and the Brain

Light falls on the eye, but you see with your brain. Although the retina does a lot of information processing for a sensory organ, visual input is meaningless until it is processed in the brain.

Visual Pathways to the Brain

How does visual information get to the brain? Axons leaving the back of each eye form the optic nerves, which travel to the **optic chiasm, the point at which the axons from the inside half of each eye cross over and then project to the opposite half of the brain** (as we first discussed in Chapter 3). This arrangement ensures that signals from both eyes go to both hemispheres of the brain. Thus, as **Figure 4.6** shows, axons from the left half of each retina carry signals to the left side of the brain, and axons from the right half of each retina carry information to the right side of the brain.

FIGURE 4.6

Visual pathways through the brain. (a) Input from the right half of the visual field strikes the left side of each retina and is transmitted to the left hemisphere (shown in blue). Input from the left half of the visual field strikes the right side of each retina and is transmitted to the right hemisphere (shown in red). The nerve fibers from each eye meet at the optic chiasm, where fibers from the inside half of each retina cross over to the opposite side of the brain. After reaching the optic chiasm, the major visual pathway projects through the lateral geniculate nucleus (LGN) in the thalamus and onto the primary visual cortex (shown with solid lines). A second pathway detours through the superior colliculus and then projects through the thalamus and onto the primary visual cortex (shown with dotted lines). **(b)** This inset shows a side view of how the optic pathways project through the thalamus and onto the visual cortex in the back of the brain (the two pathways mapped out in diagram **(a)** are virtually indistinguishable from this angle).

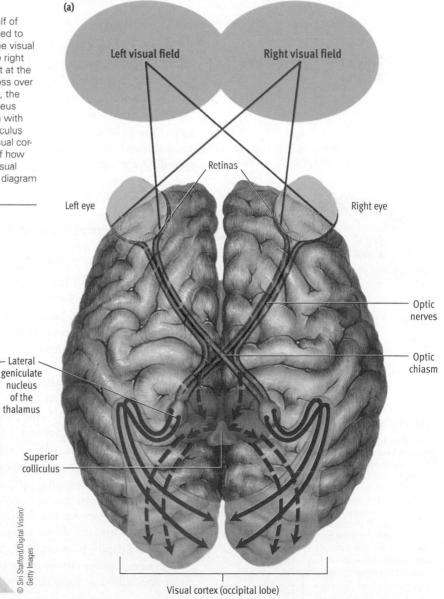

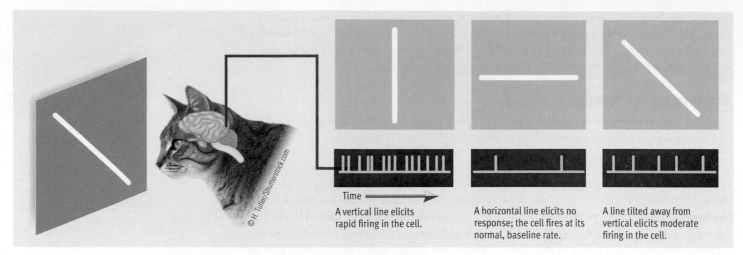

FIGURE 4.7

Hubel and Wiesel's procedure for studying the activity of neurons in the visual cortex. As the cat is shown various stimuli, a microelectrode records the firing of a neuron in the cat's visual cortex. The figure shows the electrical responses of a visual cell apparently "programmed" to respond to lines oriented vertically.

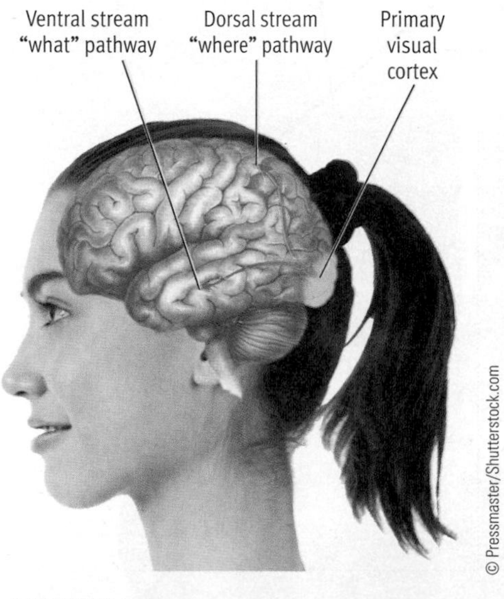

Time →

A vertical line elicits rapid firing in the cell.

A horizontal line elicits no response; the cell fires at its normal, baseline rate.

A line tilted away from vertical elicits moderate firing in the cell.

Ventral stream "what" pathway   Dorsal stream "where" pathway   Primary visual cortex

FIGURE 4.8

The *what* and *where* pathways from the primary visual cortex. Cortical processing of visual input is begun in the primary visual cortex. From there, signals are shuttled onward to a variety of other areas in the cortex along a number of pathways. Two prominent pathways are highlighted here. The dorsal stream, or *where pathway,* which processes information about motion and depth, moves on to areas of the parietal lobe. The ventral stream, or *what pathway,* which processes information about color and form, moves on to areas of the temporal lobe.

After reaching the optic chiasm, the optic nerve fibers split along two pathways. The main pathway projects into the thalamus, the brain's major relay station. Here, about 90% of the axons from the retinas synapse in the *lateral geniculate nucleus* (LGN) (Baker, 2013). Visual signals are processed in the LGN and then distributed to areas in the occipital lobe that make up the *primary visual cortex.* The second visual pathway leaving the optic chiasm branches off to an area in the midbrain (the *superior colliculus*) before traveling through the thalamus to the occipital lobe. However, the second pathway projects into different areas of the thalamus and the occipital lobe than the main visual pathway does. The principal function of the second pathway appears to be the coordination of visual input with other sensory input (Casanova et al., 2001).

Information Processing in the Visual Cortex

Visual input ultimately arrives in the primary visual cortex located in the occipital lobe. Research that won a Nobel Prize for David Hubel and Torsten Wiesel (1962, 1963) demonstrated that cells in the visual cortex respond to very specific types of stimuli. Some are sensitive to lines, some respond to edges, and some only react to more complicated stimuli. Some respond best to a line of the correct width, oriented at the correct angle, and located in the correct position in its receptive field (see **Figure 4.7**).

The key point of all this is that the cells in the visual cortex seem to be highly specialized. They have been characterized as ***feature detectors*, neurons that respond selectively to very specific features of more complex stimuli.** Ultimately, most visual stimuli could be represented by combinations of lines, such as those registered by these feature detectors. Some theorists believe that feature detectors are registering the basic building blocks of visual perception and that the brain somehow assembles the blocks into a coherent picture of complex stimuli (Maguire, Weisstein, & Klymenko, 1990).

After visual input is processed in the primary visual cortex, it is often routed to other cortical areas for additional processing. These signals travel through two streams that have sometimes been characterized as the *what* and *where pathways* (see **Figure 4.8**). The *ventral stream* processes the details of *what* objects are out there (the perception of form and color), while the *dorsal stream* processes *where* the objects are (the perception of motion and depth) (Connor et al., 2009).

As signals move farther along in the visual processing system, neurons become even more specialized or fussy about what turns them on, and the stimuli that activate them become more and more complex. For example, researchers have identified cells in the temporal lobe (along the *what* pathway) of monkeys and humans that are especially sensitive to pictures of faces (Kanwisher & Yovel, 2009). These neurons respond even to pictures that merely *suggest* the form of a face (Cox, Meyers, & Sinha, 2004).

The discovery of neurons that respond to facial stimuli raises an obvious question: Why does the cortex have face detectors? Theorists are far from sure, but one line of thinking is that the ability to quickly recognize faces—such as those of friends or foes—probably has had adaptive significance over the course of evolution (Sugita, 2009). Thus, natural selection *may* have wired the brains of some species to quickly respond to faces. Although this hypothesis seems plausible, a recent study raised questions about whether the face-detector areas in the brain are devoted *exclusively* to facial recognition (McGugin et al., 2012). The study found that people with expertise on automobiles have cells in these areas that are especially sensitive to images of cars. Another interesting finding in this area of research is that individuals vary in their ability to quickly and accurately recognize faces. Some people are very skilled at the task, whereas others are deficient (Rhodes, 2013).

Viewing the World in Color

So far, we've considered only how the visual system deals with light and dark. Let's journey now into the world of color. Color adds not only spectacle but information to perceptions of the world. The ability to identify objects against a complex background is enhanced by the addition of color (Tanaka, Weiskopf, & Williams, 2001). Thus, some theorists have suggested that color vision evolved in humans and monkeys because it improved their abilities to find food through foraging, to spot prey, and to quickly recognize predators (Spence et al., 2006). Although the purpose of color vision remains elusive, scientists have learned a great deal about the mechanisms underlying the perception of color.

The Stimulus for Color

As noted earlier, the lights people see are mixtures of different wavelengths. Perceived color is primarily a function of the dominant wavelength in these mixtures. Although wavelength wields the greatest influence, the perception of color depends on complex blends of all three properties of light.

People can perceive many different colors. Indeed, experts estimate that humans can discriminate between millions of colors (Webster, 2010), with females showing slightly better color discrimination than males (Abramov et al., 2012). Most of these diverse variations are the result of mixing a few basic colors. There are two kinds of color mixture: subtractive and additive. *Subtractive color mixing* **works by removing some wavelengths of light, leaving less light than was originally there.** You probably became familiar with subtractive mixing as a child when you mixed yellow and blue paints to make green. Paints yield subtractive mixing because pigments *absorb* most wavelengths, selectively reflecting back specific wavelengths that give rise to particular colors. Subtractive color mixing can also be demonstrated by stacking color filters. If you look through a sandwich of yellow and blue cellophane filters, they will block out certain wavelengths. The middle wavelengths that are left will look green.

Additive color mixing **works by superimposing lights, putting more light in the mixture than exists in any one light by itself.** If you shine red, green, and blue spotlights on a white surface, you'll have an additive mixture. As **Figure 4.9** shows, additive and subtractive mixtures of the same colors produce different results. Human processes of color perception parallel additive mixing much more closely than subtractive mixing, as you'll see in the following discussion of theories of color vision.

Trichromatic Theory of Color Vision

The trichromatic theory of color vision (*tri* for "three," *chroma* for "color") was first stated by Thomas Young and modified later by Hermann von Helmholtz (1852). The *trichromatic theory* **holds that the human eye has three types of receptors with differing**

FIGURE 4.9

Additive versus subtractive color mixing.
Lights mix additively because all the wavelengths contained in each light reach the eye. If red, blue, and green lights are projected onto a white screen, they produce the colors shown on the left, with white at the intersection of all three lights. If paints of the same three colors were combined in the same way, the subtractive mixture would produce the colors shown on the right, with black at the intersection of all three colors.

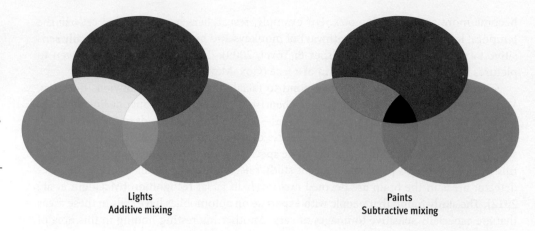

Lights
Additive mixing

Paints
Subtractive mixing

▶ REALITY CHECK

Misconception

People who are color-blind see the world in black and white.

Reality

The term color *blindness* is somewhat misleading, since only a tiny minority of those who are characterized as color-blind are monochromats, who see the world in black and white. The vast majority of color-blind people are dichromats, who cannot see certain colors. Panel (a) in the illustration shows what the most common type of dichromat would see if presented with the batch of paper flowers shown in Panel (b).

(a)

(b)

SOURCE: From Goldstein, E.B. (2007). *Sensation and perception* (7 ed). Belmont, CA: Wadsworth. Wadsworth is part of Cengage Learning, Inc. Reproduced by permission of Bruce Goldstein. www.cengage.com/permissions

sensitivities to different light wavelengths. Helmholtz believed that the eye contains specialized receptors sensitive to the wavelengths associated with red, green, and blue. According to this model, people can see all the colors of the rainbow because the eye does its own "color mixing" by varying the ratio of neural activity between these three types of receptors.

The impetus for the trichromatic theory was the demonstration that a light of any color can be matched by the additive mixture of three *primary colors*. (Any three colors that are appropriately spaced out in the visible spectrum can serve as primary colors, although red, green, and blue are usually used.) Does it sound implausible that three colors should be adequate for creating all other colors? If so, consider that this phenomenon is exactly what happens on your color TV screen or computer monitor (Stockman, 2010). Additive mixtures of red, green, and blue fool you into seeing all the colors of a natural scene.

Most of the known facts about color blindness also meshed well with trichromatic theory. **Color blindness encompasses a variety of deficiencies in the ability to distinguish among colors.** Color blindness occurs much more frequently in males than in females (Tait & Carroll, 2010). Most people who are color-blind are *dichromats*; that is, they make do with only two types of color receptors. There are three types of dichromats, and each type is insensitive to one of the primary colors: red, green, or blue, although the latter is rare (Reid & Usrey, 2008). The three deficiencies, then, support the notion that there are three sets of receptors for color vision, as proposed by trichromatic theory.

Opponent Process Theory of Color Vision

Although trichromatic theory explained some facets of color vision well, it ran aground in other areas. Consider complementary afterimages, for instance. **Complementary colors are pairs of colors that produce gray tones when mixed together.** The various pairs of complementary colors can be arranged in a *color circle*, such as the one in **Figure 4.10**. If you stare at a strong color and then look at a white background, you'll see an *afterimage—a visual image that persists after a stimulus is removed.* The color of the afterimage will be the *complement* of the color you originally stared at. Trichromatic theory cannot account for the appearance of complementary afterimages.

Here's another peculiarity to consider. If you ask people to describe colors but restrict them to using three names, they run into difficulty. For example, using only red, green, and blue, they simply don't feel comfortable describing yellow as "reddish green." However, if you let them have just one more name, they usually choose yellow. Then they can describe any color quite well (Gordon & Abramov, 2001). If colors are reduced to three channels, why are four color names required to describe the full range of possible colors?

In an effort to answer questions such as these, Ewald Hering proposed the *opponent process theory* of color vision in 1878. **The *opponent process theory* holds that color perception depends on receptors that make antagonistic responses to three pairs of colors.** The three pairs of opponent colors he hypothesized were red versus green, yellow versus blue, and black versus white. The antagonistic processes in this theory provide plausible explanations for complementary afterimages and the need for four names (red, green, blue, and yellow) to describe colors. Opponent process theory also explains some aspects of color blindness. For instance, it can explain why dichromats typically find it hard to distinguish either green from red or yellow from blue.

Reconciling Theories of Color Vision

Advocates of trichromatic theory and opponent process theory argued about the relative merits of the two models for almost a century. Most researchers assumed that one theory must be wrong and the other must be right. In recent decades; however, it has become clear that *it takes both theories to explain color vision.* Eventually a physiological basis for both theories was found. Research that earned George Wald a Nobel Prize demonstrated that *the eye has three types of cones*, with each type being most sensitive to a different band of wavelengths, as shown in **Figure 4.11** (Gegenfurtner, 2010). The three types of cones represent the three different color receptors predicted by trichromatic theory.

Researchers also discovered a biological basis for opponent processes. They found cells in the retina, the thalamus, and the visual cortex *that respond in opposite ways to red versus green and blue versus yellow* (Purves, 2009). For example, some ganglion cells in the retina are excited by green and inhibited by red. Other ganglion cells in the retina work in just the opposite way, as predicted by opponent process theory.

In summary, the perception of color appears to involve stages of information processing (Gegenfurtner, 2010). The receptors that do the first stage of processing (the cones) seem to follow the principles outlined in trichromatic theory. In later stages of processing, cells in the retina and the brain seem to follow the principles outlined in opponent process theory. As you can see, vigorous theoretical debate about color vision produced a solution that went beyond the contributions of either theory alone.

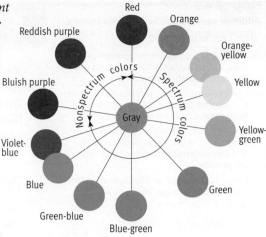

FIGURE 4.10

The color circle and complementary colors. Colors opposite each other on this color circle are complements, or opposites. Additively mixing complementary colors produces gray. Opponent process principles help explain this effect as well as the other peculiarities of complementary colors.

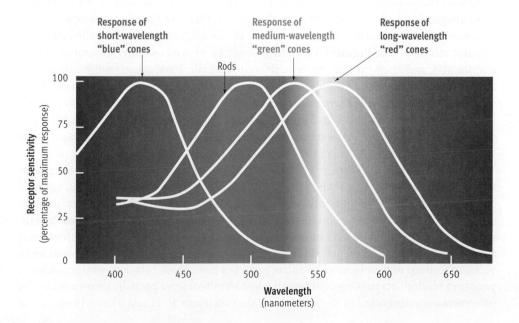

FIGURE 4.11

Three types of cones. Research has identified three types of cones that show varied sensitivity to different wavelengths of light. As the graph shows, these three types of cones correspond only roughly to the red, green, and blue receptors predicted by trichromatic theory, so it is more accurate to refer to them as cones sensitive to short, medium, and long wavelengths.

- Discuss the subjectivity of form perception, inattentional blindness, and the concept of feature analysis.
- Understand Gestalt principles of visual perception and the role of perceptual hypotheses in form perception.
- Identify the monocular and binocular cues used in depth perception, and discuss cultural variations in depth perception.
- Describe perceptual constancies, and discuss what visual illusions reveal about perception.

4.2 THE VISUAL SYSTEM: PERCEPTUAL PROCESSES

We have seen how sensory receptors in the eye transform light into neural impulses that are sent to the brain. We focus next on how the brain makes sense of it all: How does it convert streams of neural impulses into perceptions of chairs, doors, friends, automobiles, and buildings? In this section, we explore perceptual processes in vision, such as the perception of forms, objects, depth, and so forth.

Perceiving Forms, Patterns, and Objects

The drawing in **Figure 4.12** is a poster for a circus act involving a trained seal. What do you see?

No doubt you see a seal balancing a ball on its nose, and a trainer holding a fish and a whip. But suppose you had been told that the drawing is actually a poster for a costume ball. Would you have perceived it differently?

If you focus on the idea of a costume ball (stay with it a minute if you still see the seal and trainer), you will probably see a costumed man and woman in **Figure 4.12**. She's handing him a hat, and he has a sword in his right hand. This tricky little sketch was made ambiguous quite intentionally. It's a *reversible figure,* **a drawing that is compatible with two different interpretations that can shift back and forth.** Another classic reversible figure is shown in **Figure 4.13**. What do you see? A rabbit or a duck? It all depends on how you look at the drawing.

The key point is simply this: *The same visual input can result in radically different perceptions.* There is no one-to-one correspondence between sensory input and what you perceive. *This is a principal reason that people's experience of the world is subjective.* Perception involves much more than passively receiving signals from the outside world. It involves the *interpretation* of sensory input.

In this case, your interpretations result in two different "realities" because your *expectations* have been manipulated. Information given to you about the drawing has created **a** *perceptual set***—a readiness to perceive a stimulus in a particular way.** A perceptual set creates a certain slant in how you interpret sensory input.

Like expectations, motivational forces can foster perceptual sets, as demonstrated in a study using reversible figures as stimuli (Balcetis & Dunning, 2006). Participants were told that a computer would flash a *number* or a *letter* to indicate whether they were assigned to a pleasant or unpleasant experimental task (trying some orange juice or a nasty-looking health-food drink). Each of the subjects briefly saw the same ambiguous stimulus (see **Figure 4.14**), which could be viewed as either a number (13) or a letter (B), and then the computer appeared to crash. Participants were asked what they had seen before the computer crashed. Subjects hoping for a letter were much more likely to interpret the stimulus as a B, and those hoping for a number were much more likely to view the stimulus as the number 13. A variety of other studies have also demonstrated that, to some extent, we have a tendency to see what we want to see (Dunning & Balcetis, 2013).

Form perception also depends on the *selection* of sensory input; that is, what people focus their attention on. A visual scene may include many objects and forms. Some of these may capture viewers' attention, while others may not. This fact has been demonstrated in dramatic fashion in studies of *inattentional blindness,* **which involves the failure to see fully visible objects or events in a visual display because one's attention is focused elsewhere.** In one such study (Simons & Chabris, 1999), participants watched a video of a group of people in white shirts passing a basketball, laid over another video of people in black shirts passing a basketball (the two videos were partially transparent). The observers were instructed to focus on one of the two teams and press a key whenever that

FIGURE 4.12

A poster for a trained seal act. Or is it? The picture is an ambiguous figure, which can be interpreted as either of two scenes, as explained in the text.

FIGURE 4.13

Another ambiguous figure. What animal do you see here? As the text explains, two very different perceptions are possible. This ambiguous figure was devised around 1900 by Joseph Jastrow, a prominent psychologist at the turn of the 20th century (Block & Yuker, 1992).

team passed the ball. Thirty seconds into the task, a woman carrying an umbrella clearly walked through the scene for 4 seconds. You might guess that this bizarre development would be noticed by virtually all the observers, but 44% of the participants failed to see the woman. Moreover, when someone in a gorilla suit strolled through the same scene, even more subjects (73%) missed the unexpected event!

Additional studies using other types of stimulus materials have demonstrated that people routinely overlook obvious forms that are unexpected (Most et al., 2005). Inattentional blindness has been attributed to subjects having a perceptual set that leads them to focus most of their attention on a specific feature in a scene (such as the basketball passes), while neglecting other facets of the scene (Most et al., 2001). Inattentional blindness may account for many automobile accidents, as accident reports often include the statement "I looked right there, but never saw them" (Shermer, 2004). The idea that we see much less of the world than we think we do surprises many people, but there is an auditory parallel that people take for granted (Mack, 2003). Think of how often you have had someone clearly say something to you, but you did not hear a word of what was said because you were "not listening." Inattentional blindness is essentially the same thing in the visual domain.

An understanding of how people perceive forms, patterns, and objects also requires knowledge of how people *organize and interpret* visual input. Several influential approaches to this question emphasize *feature analysis*.

Feature Analysis: Assembling Forms

The information received by your eyes would do you little good if you couldn't recognize objects and forms—ranging from words on a page to the microwave in your kitchen and friends in the distance. According to some theories, perceptions of form and pattern entail *feature analysis* (Lindsay & Norman, 1977). **Feature analysis is the process of detecting specific elements in visual input and assembling them into a more complex form.** In other words, you start with the components of a form, such as lines, edges, and corners, and build them into perceptions of squares, triangles, stop signs, bicycles, ice cream cones, and telephones. An application of this model of form perception is diagrammed in **Figure 4.15**.

Feature analysis assumes that form perception involves **bottom-up processing, a progression from individual elements to the whole** (see **Figure 4.16**). The plausibility of this model was bolstered greatly when Hubel and Wiesel showed that cells in the visual cortex operate as highly specialized feature detectors. Indeed, their findings strongly suggested that at least some aspects of form perception involve feature analysis.

FIGURE 4.14

Ambiguous stimulus used by Balcetis and Dunning (2006). Participants saw brief presentations of this stimulus, which could be viewed as a letter (B) or as a number (13). The study demonstrated that motivational factors influence what people tend to see.

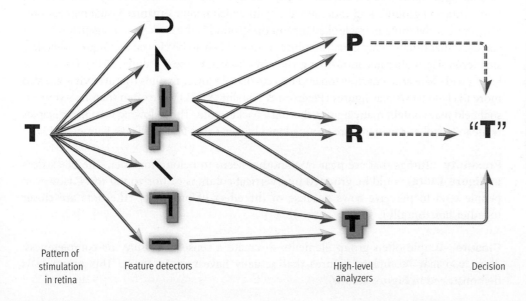

Pattern of stimulation in retina   Feature detectors   High-level analyzers   Decision

FIGURE 4.15

Feature analysis in form perception. One vigorously debated theory of form perception is that the brain has cells that respond to specific aspects or features of stimuli, such as lines and angles. Neurons functioning as higher-level analyzers then respond to input from these "feature detectors." The more input each analyzer receives, the more active it becomes. Finally, other neurons weigh signals from these analyzers and make a "decision" about the stimulus. In this way perception of a form is arrived at by assembling elements from the bottom up.

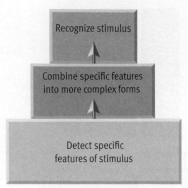

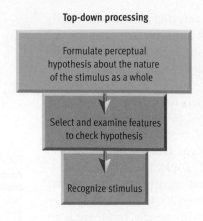

FIGURE 4.16

Bottom-up versus top-down processing. As explained in these diagrams, bottom-up processing progresses from individual elements to whole elements, whereas top-down processing progresses from the whole to the individual elements.

Can feature analysis provide a complete account of how people perceive forms? Clearly not. A crucial problem for the theory is that form perception often does not involve bottom-up processing. In fact, there is ample evidence that perceptions of form frequently involve ***top-down processing, a progression from the whole to the elements*** (Bar & Bubic, 2013) (see **Figure 4.16**). For example, there is evidence that people can perceive a word before its individual letters, a phenomenon that has to reflect top-down processing (Johnston & McClelland, 1974). If readers depended exclusively on bottom-up processing, they would have to analyze the features of letters in words to recognize them and then assemble the letters into words. This task would be time-consuming and would slow down reading speed to a snail's pace.

Looking at the Whole Picture: Gestalt Principles

Sometimes a whole, as we perceive it, may have qualities that don't exist in any of the parts. This insight—*that the whole can be greater than the sum of its parts*—became the basic assumption of *Gestalt psychology,* an influential school of thought that emerged out of Germany during the first half of the 20th century (*Gestalt* is a German word for "form" or "shape").

A simple example of this principle, which you have experienced countless times, is the *phi phenomenon,* first described by Max Wertheimer in 1912. **The *phi phenomenon* is the illusion of movement created by presenting visual stimuli in rapid succession.** You encounter examples of the phi phenomenon nearly every day. For example, movies and TV consist of separate still pictures projected rapidly one after the other. You *see* smooth motion, but in reality the "moving" objects merely take slightly different positions in successive frames. Viewed as a whole, a movie has a property (motion) that isn't evident in any of its parts (the individual frames).

The Gestalt psychologists formulated a series of principles that describe how the visual system organizes a scene into discrete forms (Schirillo, 2010). Let's explore some of these principles.

FIGURE 4.17

The principle of figure and ground. Whether you see two faces or a vase depends on which part of this drawing you see as figure and which as background. Although this reversible drawing allows you to switch back and forth between two ways of organizing your perception, you can't perceive the drawing both ways at once.

Figure and Ground Take a look at **Figure 4.17**. Do you see the figure as two silhouetted faces against a white background, or as a white vase against a black background? This reversible figure illustrates the Gestalt principle of *figure and ground.* Dividing visual displays into figure and ground is a fundamental way in which people organize visual perceptions. The figure is the thing being looked at, and the ground is the background against which it stands. Other things being equal, an object is more likely to be viewed as a figure when it is smaller in size, higher in contrast, or greater in symmetry (Tse & Palmer, 2013). Forms that have a wide base and a narrow top and objects that are lower in one's frame of view are also more likely to be seen as figures (Peterson & Kimchi, 2013). More often than not, your visual field may contain many figures sharing a background. The following Gestalt principles relate to how these elements are grouped into higher-order figures (Tse & Palmer, 2013).

Proximity Things that are near one another seem to belong together. The black dots in **Figure 4.18(a)** could be grouped into vertical columns or horizontal rows. However, people tend to perceive rows because of the effect of proximity (the dots are closer together horizontally).

Closure People often group elements to create a sense of *closure,* or completeness. Thus, you may "complete" figures that actually have gaps in them. This principle is demonstrated in **Figure 4.18(b)**.

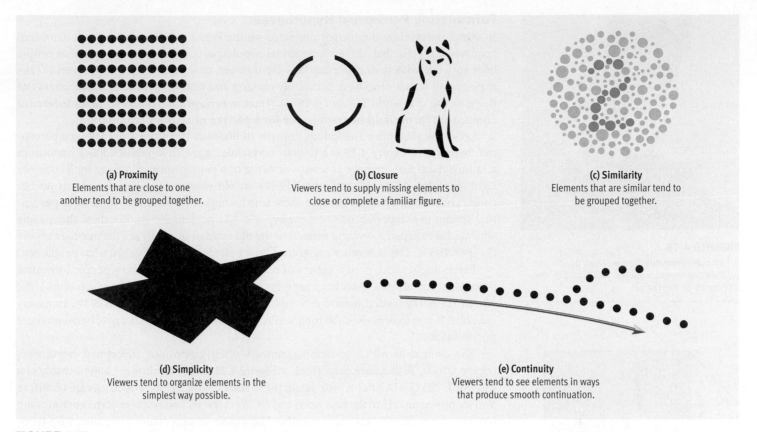

FIGURE 4.18

Gestalt principles of perceptual organization. Gestalt principles help explain some of the factors that influence form perception. **(a) Proximity:** These dots might well be organized in vertical columns rather than horizontal rows, but because of proximity (the dots are closer together horizontally), they tend to be perceived in rows. **(b) Closure:** Even though the figures are incomplete, you fill in the blanks and see a circle and a dog. **(c) Similarity:** Because of similarity of color, you see dots organized into the number 2 instead of a random array. If you did not group similar elements, you wouldn't see the number 2 here. **(d) Simplicity:** You could view this as a complicated 11-sided figure, but given the preference for simplicity, you are more likely to see it as an overlapping rectangle and triangle. **(e) Continuity:** You tend to group these dots in a way that produces a smooth path rather than an abrupt shift in direction.

Similarity   People also tend to group stimuli that are similar. This principle is apparent in **Figure 4.18(c)**, where elements of similar darkness are grouped into the number 2.

Simplicity   The Gestaltists' most general principle was the law of *Pragnanz,* which translates from German as "good form." The idea is that people tend to group elements that combine to form a good figure. This principle is somewhat vague in that it's often difficult to spell out what makes a figure "good." Some theorists maintain that goodness is largely a matter of simplicity, asserting that people tend to organize forms in the simplest way possible (see **Figure 4.18(d)**).

Continuity   The principle of continuity reflects people's tendency to follow in whatever direction they've been led. Thus, people tend to connect points that result in straight or gently curved lines that create "smooth" paths, as shown in **Figure 4.18(e)**.

Although Gestalt psychology is no longer an active theoretical orientation in modern psychology, its influence is still felt in the study of perception. The Gestalt psychologists raised many important questions that still occupy researchers, and they left a legacy of many useful insights about form perception that have stood the test of time (Sharps & Wertheimer, 2000).

FIGURE 4.19
A famous reversible figure. What do you see? Consult the text to learn the two possible interpretations of this figure.

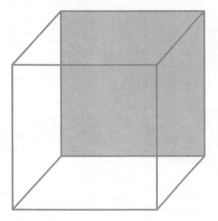

FIGURE 4.20
The Necker cube. The tinted surface of this reversible figure can become either the front or the back of the cube.

THE MAN

FIGURE 4.21
Context effects. The context in which a stimulus is seen can affect your perceptual hypotheses. The middle character in the word on the left is assumed to be an "H," whereas in the word on the right the same character is assumed to be an "A." In addition to showing the potential influence of context, this example shows the power of expectations and top-down processing.

Formulating Perceptual Hypotheses

In visual perception, the images projected on the retina are distorted, two-dimensional versions of their actual, three-dimensional counterparts. If the sensory input that people have to work with is so distorted, how do they get an accurate view of the world? One explanation is that people are constantly making and testing *hypotheses* about what's out there in the real world (Gregory, 1973). Thus, **a *perceptual hypothesis* is an inference about what form could be responsible for a pattern of sensory stimulation.**

Let's look at another ambiguous drawing to illustrate the process of making a perceptual hypothesis. **Figure 4.19** is a famous reversible figure, first published as a cartoon in a humor magazine. Perhaps you see a drawing of a young woman looking back over her right shoulder. Alternatively, you might see an old woman with her chin down on her chest. The ambiguity exists because there isn't enough information to force your perceptual system to accept only one of these hypotheses. Incidentally, studies show that people who are led to *expect* the young woman or the old woman generally see the one they expect (Leeper, 1935). This is another example of how perceptual sets influence what people see.

Psychologists have used a variety of reversible figures to study how people formulate perceptual hypotheses. Another example can be seen in **Figure 4.20**, which shows the *Necker cube.* The shaded surface can appear as either the front or the rear of the transparent cube. If you look at the cube for a while, your perception may alternate between these possibilities.

The *context* in which something appears often guides our perceptual hypotheses (Bravo, 2010). To illustrate, take a look at **Figure 4.21**. What do you see? You probably saw the words "THE MAN." But look again; the middle characters in both words are identical. You identified an "H" in the first word and an "A" in the second because of the surrounding letters, which shaped your expectations. The power of expectations explains why typographical errors like those in this sentence often pass unoberved (Lachman, 1996).

Perceiving Depth or Distance

More often than not, forms and figures are objects in space. Spatial considerations add a third dimension to visual perception. ***Depth perception* involves interpretation of visual cues that indicate how near or far away objects are.** To make judgments of distance, people rely on quite a variety of clues, which can be classified into two types: binocular cues and monocular cues (Proffitt & Caudek, 2013).

Binocular Cues

Because they are set apart, the eyes each have a slightly different view of the world. ***Binocular depth cues* are clues about distance based on the differing views of the two eyes.** The technology of 3D movies takes advantage of this fact. Two cameras are used to record slightly different images of the same scene. The special polarized glasses that viewers wear separate the images for each eye. The brain then supplies the "depth," and you perceive a three-dimensional scene.

The principal binocular depth cue is *retinal disparity,* **which refers to the fact that objects within 25 feet project images to slightly different locations on the right and left retinas, so the right and left eyes see slightly different views of the object.** The closer an object gets, the greater the disparity between the images seen by each eye. Thus, retinal disparity increases as objects come closer, providing information about distance.

Monocular Cues

***Monocular depth cues* are clues about distance based on the image in either eye alone.** There are two kinds of monocular cues to depth. One kind is the result of active use of the eye in viewing the world. For example, as an object comes closer, you may sense the accommodation (the change in the curvature of the lens) that must occur for the eye to adjust its focus.

Linear perspective Parallel lines that run away from the viewer seem to get closer together.

Texture gradient As distance increases, a texture gradually becomes denser and less distinct.

Interposition The shapes of near objects overlap or mask those of more distant ones.

Relative size If separate objects are expected to be of the same size, the larger ones are seen as closer.

Height in plane Near objects are low in the visual field; more distant ones are higher up.

Light and shadow Patterns of light and dark suggest shadows that can create an impression of three-dimensional forms.

FIGURE 4.22

Pictorial cues to depth. Six pictorial depth cues are explained and illustrated here. Although one cue stands out in each photo, in most visual scenes several pictorial cues are present. Try looking at the light-and-shadow picture upside down. The change in shadowing reverses what you see.

The other kind of monocular cues are *pictorial depth cues—cues about distance that can be given in a flat picture.* There are many pictorial cues to depth, which is why paintings and photographs can seem so realistic that you feel you can climb right into them. Six prominent pictorial depth cues are described and illustrated in **Figure 4.22**. The first of these, *linear perspective,* is a depth cue reflecting the fact that lines converge in the distance. Because details are too small to see when they are far away, *texture gradients* can also provide information about depth. If an object comes between you and another object, it must be closer to you, a cue called *interposition. Relative size* is a cue because closer objects appear larger. *Height in plane* reflects the fact that distant objects appear higher in a picture. Finally, the familiar effects of shadowing make *light* and *shadow* useful in judging distance.

Some cultural differences appear to exist in the ability to take advantage of pictorial depth cues in two-dimensional drawings. These differences were first investigated by Hudson (1960, 1967), who presented pictures such as the one in **Figure 4.23** to various cultural groups in South Africa. Hudson's approach was based on the assumption that subjects who indicate that the hunter is trying to spear the elephant instead of the antelope don't

FIGURE 4.23

Testing understanding of pictorial depth cues. In his cross-cultural research, Hudson (1960) asked subjects to indicate whether the hunter is trying to spear the antelope or the elephant. He found cultural disparities in subjects' ability to make effective use of the pictorial depth cues, which place the elephant in the distance and make it an unlikely target.

SOURCE: Adapted by permission from an illustration by Ilil Arbel in Deregowski, J. B. (1972, November). Pictorial perception and culture. *Scientific American, 227*(5), p. 83. Copyright © 1972 by Scientific American, Inc. All rights reserved.

understand the depth cues (interposition, relative size, height in plane) in the picture, which place the elephant in the distance. Hudson found that subjects from a rural South African tribe (the Bantu), who had little exposure at that time to pictures and photos, frequently misinterpreted the depth cues in his pictures. Similar difficulties with depth cues in pictures have been documented for other cultural groups who have little experience with two-dimensional representations of three-dimensional space (Berry et al., 1992; Phillips, 2011). Thus, the application of pictorial depth cues to pictures varies to some degree across cultures.

Perceptual Constancies in Vision

When a person approaches you from the distance, his or her image on your retinas gradually changes in size. Do you perceive that person as growing right before your eyes? Of course not. Your perceptual system constantly makes allowances for this variation in visual input. In doing so, it relies in part on perceptual constancies. **A *perceptual constancy* is a tendency to experience a stable perception in the face of continually changing sensory input.** Among other things, people tend to view objects as having a stable size, shape, brightness, hue (color), and location in space (Goldstein, 2010). Perceptual constancies such as these help impose some order on the surrounding world.

The Power of Misleading Cues: Visual Illusions

In general, perceptual constancies, depth cues, and principles of visual organization (such as the Gestalt laws) help people perceive the world accurately. Sometimes, however, perceptions are based on inappropriate assumptions, and *visual illusions* can result. **A *visual illusion* involves**

CONCEPT CHECK 4.2

Recognizing Pictorial Depth Cues

Figure 4.22 describes and illustrates six pictorial depth cues, most of which are apparent in the adjacent photo. Check your understanding of depth perception by trying to spot the depth cues in the picture. In the list below, check off the depth cues seen in the photo. The answers can be found in Appendix A.

_____ 1. Interposition

_____ 2. Height in plane

_____ 3. Texture gradient

_____ 4. Relative size

_____ 5. Light and shadow

_____ 6. Linear perspective

an apparently inexplicable discrepancy between the appearance of a visual stimulus and its physical reality.

One famous visual illusion is the *Müller-Lyer illusion,* shown in **Figure 4.24**. The two vertical lines in this figure are equally long, but they certainly don't look that way. Why not? Several mechanisms probably play a role (Day, 1965; Gregory, 1978). The figure on the left looks like the outside of a building, thrust toward the viewer, while the one on the right looks like an inside corner, thrust away (see **Figure 4.25**). The vertical line in the left figure therefore seems closer. If two lines cast equally long retinal images but one seems closer, the closer one is assumed to be shorter. Thus, the Müller-Lyer illusion may be due largely to a combination of size constancy processes and misperception of depth.

The geometric illusions shown in **Figure 4.26** also demonstrate that visual stimuli can be highly deceptive. The *Ponzo illusion,* shown in **Figure 4.26**, appears to result from the same factors as the Müller-Lyer illusion (Coren & Girgus, 1978). The upper and lower horizontal lines are the same length, but the upper one appears longer. This illusion probably occurs because the converging lines convey linear perspective, a key depth cue suggesting that the upper line lies farther in the distance. **Figure 4.27** is a drawing by Stanford University psychologist Roger Shepard (1990) that creates a similar, but more dramatic illusion. The second monster appears much larger than the first, even though they are really identical in size.

In the 1930s, Adelbert Ames designed a striking illusion that makes use of misperception of distance (Behrens, 2010). It's called, appropriately enough, the *Ames room.* It's a specially contrived room built with a trapezoidal rear wall and a sloping floor and ceiling. When viewed from the correct point, as in the diagram (see **Figure 4.28**), it looks like an ordinary rectangular room. But in reality, the left corner is much taller and much farther from the viewer than the right corner. Hence, bizarre illusions unfold in the Ames room. People standing in the right corner appear to be giants, while those standing in the left

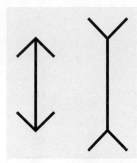

FIGURE 4.24

The Müller-Lyer illusion. Go ahead, measure them: The two vertical lines are of equal length.

FIGURE 4.25

Explaining the Müller-Lyer illusion. The figure on the left seems to be closer, since it looks like an outside corner, thrust toward you, whereas the figure on the right looks like an inside corner thrust away from you. Given retinal images of the same length, you assume that the "closer" line is shorter.

Ponzo   Poggendorff   Upside-down T

Zollner

FIGURE 4.26

Four geometric illusions. Ponzo: The horizontal lines are the same length. **Poggendorff:** The two diagonal segments lie on the same straight line. **Upside-down T:** The vertical and horizontal lines are the same length. **Zollner:** The long diagonals are all parallel (try covering up some of the short lines if you don't believe it).

FIGURE 4.27

A monster of an illusion. The principles underlying the Ponzo illusion also explain the striking illusion seen here, in which two identical monsters appear to be quite different in size.

SOURCE: Shepard, R. N. (1990). *Mind sights.* New York, NY: W. H. Freeman. Copyright © 1990 by Roger N. Shepard. Used by permission of Henry Holt & Co., LLC.

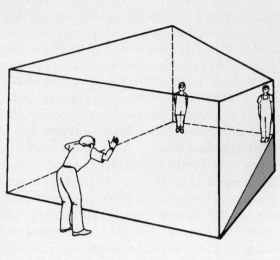

FIGURE 4.28

The Ames room. The diagram on the right shows the room as it is actually constructed. However, the viewer assumes that the room is rectangular, and the image cast on the retina is consistent with this hypothesis. Because of this reasonable perceptual hypothesis, the normal perceptual adjustments made to preserve size constancy lead to the illusions described in the text. For example, naïve viewers "conclude" that the boy on the right is much larger than the other, when in fact he is merely closer.

A puzzling perceptual illusion common in everyday life is the moon illusion: the moon looks larger when at the horizon than when overhead.

corner appear to be midgets. Even more disconcerting, a person who walks across the room from right to left appears to shrink before your eyes! The Ames room creates these misperceptions by toying with the perfectly reasonable assumption that the room is vertically and horizontally rectangular.

Yet another well-known visual illusion is the *moon illusion.* The full moon appears to be as much as 50% smaller when overhead than when looming on the horizon (Ross & Plug, 2002). As with many of the other illusions we have discussed, the moon illusion seems to result mainly from size constancy effects, coupled with the misperception of distance (Kaufman et al., 2007).

Cross-cultural studies have uncovered some interesting differences between cultural groups in their tendency to see certain illusions (Masuda, 2010; Phillips, 2011). For example, Segall, Campbell, and Herskovits (1966) found that people from Western cultures are more susceptible to the Müller-Lyer illusion than are people from some non-Western cultures. The most plausible explanation is that in the West, we live in a "carpentered world" dominated by straight lines, right angles, and rectangular rooms, buildings, and furniture. Thus, our experience prepares us to readily view the Müller-Lyer figures as inside and outside corners of buildings, inferences that help foster the illusion (Segall et al., 1990).

Like ambiguous figures, visual illusions demonstrate that human perceptions are not simple reflections of objective reality. Once again, we see that perception of the world is subjective. We will encounter this insight again as we examine other sensory systems, such as hearing, which we turn to next.

Unlike people in Western nations, the Zulus live in a culture where straight lines and right angles are scarce. Thus, they are not affected by such phenomena as the Müller-Lyer illusion nearly as much as are people raised in environments that abound with rectangular structures.

4.3 THE AUDITORY SYSTEM: HEARING

4.3

Key Learning Goals

- Identify the three properties of sound, and summarize information on human hearing capacities.
- Describe how sensory processing occurs in the ear, compare the place and frequency theories of pitch perception, and discuss factors in auditory localization.

Like vision, the auditory (hearing) system provides input about the world "out there," but not until incoming information is processed by the brain. An auditory stimulus—a screech of tires, someone laughing, the hum of the refrigerator—produces sensory input in the form of sound waves reaching the ears. The perceptual system must somehow transform this stimulation into the psychological experience of hearing. We'll begin our discussion of hearing by looking at the stimulus for auditory experience: sound.

The Stimulus: Sound

Sound waves are vibrations of molecules, which means that they must travel through some physical medium, such as air. They move at a fraction of the speed of light. Sound waves are usually generated by vibrating objects, such as a guitar string, a loudspeaker cone, or your vocal cords. However, they can also be generated by forcing air past a chamber (as in a pipe organ), or by suddenly releasing a burst of air (as when you clap).

Like light waves, sound waves are characterized by their *wavelength*, their *amplitude*, and their *purity* (see **Figure 4.29**). These physical properties affect mainly the perceived (psychological) qualities of *pitch, loudness,* and *timbre*, respectively. However, they interact in complex ways to produce perceptions of these sound qualities.

Human Hearing Capacities

Wavelengths of sound are described in terms of their *frequency,* which is measured in cycles per second, or *hertz* (Hz). For the most part, higher frequencies are perceived as having higher pitch. That is, if you strike the key for high C on a piano, it will produce higher-frequency sound waves than the key for low C. Although the perception of pitch depends mainly on frequency, the amplitude of the sound waves also influences it.

Just as the visible spectrum is only a portion of the total spectrum of light, so, too, what people can hear is only a portion of the available range of sounds. Humans

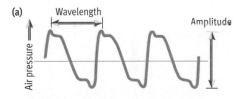

(a)

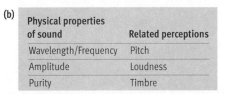

(b)

Physical properties of sound	Related perceptions
Wavelength/Frequency	Pitch
Amplitude	Loudness
Purity	Timbre

FIGURE 4.29

Sound, the physical stimulus for hearing.
(a) Like light, sound travels in waves—in this case, waves of air pressure. A smooth curve would represent a pure tone, such as that produced by a tuning fork. Most sounds, however, are complex. For example, the wave shown here is for middle C played on a piano. The sound wave for the same note played on a violin would have the same wavelength (or frequency) as this one, but the "wrinkles" in the wave would be different, corresponding to the differences in timbre between the two sounds. **(b)** The table shows the main relations between objective aspects of sound and subjective perceptions.

can hear sounds ranging in frequency from a low of 20 Hz up to a high of about 20,000 Hz. Sounds at either end of this range are harder to hear, and sensitivity to high-frequency tones declines as adults grow older (Yost, 2013). Other organisms have different capabilities. Low-frequency sounds under 10 Hz are audible to homing pigeons, for example. At the other extreme, bats and porpoises can hear frequencies well above 20,000 Hz.

In general, the greater the amplitude of sound waves, the louder the sound perceived. Whereas frequency is measured in hertz, amplitude is measured in *decibels* (dB). The relationship between decibels (which measure a physical property of sound) and loudness (a psychological quality) is complex. A rough rule of thumb is that perceived loudness doubles about every 6–10 decibels (Florentine & Heinz, 2010).

Very loud sounds can have negative effects on the quality of your hearing. Even brief exposure to sounds over 120 decibels can be painful and may cause damage to your auditory system. In recent years, there has been great concern about hearing loss in young people using personal listening devices who play their music too loudly (Punch, Elfenbein, & James, 2011). Portable music players can easily deliver over 100 decibels through headphones. One study found significant hearing impairment in 14% of the young people sampled (Peng, Tao, & Huang, 2007). Unfortunately, adolescents tend to not worry much about the risk of hearing loss (Vogel et al., 2008). However, it is a serious problem that is likely to lead to a great deal of preventable hearing loss given the increased popularity of portable music players (Muchnik et al., 2012).

People are also sensitive to variations in the purity of sounds. The purest sound is one that has only a single frequency of vibration, such as that produced by a tuning fork. Most everyday sounds are complex mixtures of many frequencies. The purity or complexity of a sound influences how *timbre* is perceived. To understand timbre, think of a note with precisely the same loudness and pitch played on a piano and then on a violin. The difference you perceive between the sounds is a difference in timbre.

Sensory Processing in the Ear

Like your eyes, your ears channel energy to the neural tissue that receives it. **Figure 4.30** shows that the human ear can be divided into three sections: the external ear, the middle ear, and the inner ear. Sound is conducted differently in each section. The external ear depends on the *vibration of air molecules*. The middle ear depends on the *vibration of movable bones*. And the inner ear depends on *waves in a fluid*, which are finally converted into a stream of neural signals sent to the brain (Kaas, O'Brien, & Hackett, 2013).

The *external ear* consists mainly of the *pinna,* a sound-collecting cone. When you cup your hand behind your ear to try to hear better, you are augmenting that cone. Sound waves collected by the pinna are funneled along the auditory canal toward the *eardrum,* a taut membrane that vibrates in response.

In the *middle ear,* the vibrations of the eardrum are transmitted inward by a mechanical chain made up of the three tiniest bones in your body (the hammer, anvil, and stirrup), known collectively as the *ossicles.* The ossicles form a three-stage lever system that converts relatively large movements with little force into smaller motions with greater force. The ossicles serve to amplify tiny changes in air pressure.

The *inner ear* consists largely of **the cochlea, a fluid-filled, coiled tunnel that contains the receptors for hearing.** The term *cochlea* comes from the Greek word for a spiral-shelled snail, which this chamber resembles (see **Figure 4.30**). The ear's neural tissue, which is functionally similar to the retina in the eye, lies within the cochlea on the basilar membrane. **The *basilar membrane,* which runs the length of the spiraled cochlea, holds the auditory receptors, called hair cells.** Waves in the fluid of the

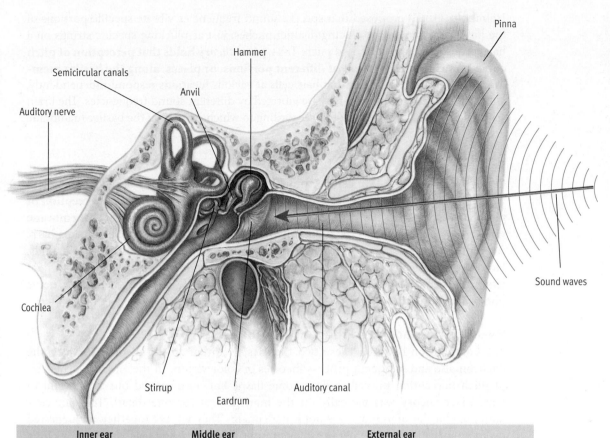

Pinna

Hammer

Semicircular canals

Anvil

Auditory nerve

Cochlea

Stirrup

Eardrum

Auditory canal

Sound waves

Inner ear　　**Middle ear**　　**External ear**

FIGURE 4.30

The human ear. Converting sound pressure to information processed by the nervous system involves a complex relay of stimuli. Waves of air pressure create vibrations in the eardrum, which in turn cause oscillations in the tiny bones in the inner ear (the hammer, anvil, and stirrup). As they are relayed from one bone to the next, the oscillations are magnified and then transformed into pressure waves moving through a liquid medium in the cochlea. These waves cause the basilar membrane to oscillate, stimulating the hair cells that are the actual auditory receptors (see **Figure 4.31**).

inner ear stimulate the hair cells. Like the rods and cones in the eye, the hair cells convert this physical stimulation into neural impulses that are sent to the brain (Hudspeth, 2013). These signals are routed through the thalamus to the auditory cortex, which is located mostly in the temporal lobes of the brain.

Auditory Perception: Theories of Hearing

Theories of hearing need to account for how sound waves are physiologically translated into perceptions of pitch, loudness, and timbre. To date, most of the theorizing about hearing has focused on the perception of pitch, which is reasonably well understood. Researchers' understanding of loudness and timbre perception is primitive by comparison. Consequently, we'll limit our coverage to theories of pitch perception.

Place Theory

There have been two influential theories of pitch perception: *place theory* and *frequency theory.* You'll be able to follow the development of these theories more easily if you can imagine the spiraled cochlea unraveled, so that the basilar membrane becomes a long, thin sheet, lined with about 25,000 individual hair cells (see **Figure 4.31**). Long ago, Hermann von

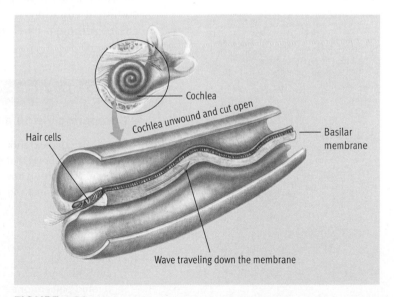

Cochlea

Cochlea unwound and cut open

Hair cells

Basilar membrane

Wave traveling down the membrane

FIGURE 4.31

The basilar membrane. This graphic shows how the cochlea might look if it were unwound and cut open to reveal the basilar membrane, which is covered with thousands of hair cells (the auditory receptors). Pressure waves in the fluid filling the cochlea cause oscillations to travel in waves down the basilar membrane, stimulating the hair cells to fire. Although the entire membrane vibrates, as predicted by frequency theory, the point along the membrane where the wave peaks depends on the frequency of the sound stimulus, as suggested by place theory.

Helmholtz (1863) proposed that specific sound frequencies vibrate specific portions of the basilar membrane, producing distinct pitches, just as plucking specific strings on a harp produces sounds of varied pitch. Thus, *place theory* **holds that perception of pitch corresponds to the vibration of different portions, or places, along the basilar membrane.** Place theory assumes that hair cells at various locations respond independently, and that different sets of hair cells are vibrated by different sound frequencies. The brain then detects the frequency of a tone according to which area along the basilar membrane is most active.

Frequency Theory

Other theorists in the 19th century proposed an alternative theory of pitch perception, called frequency theory (Rutherford, 1886). *Frequency theory* **holds that perception of pitch corresponds to the rate, or frequency, at which the entire basilar membrane vibrates.** This theory views the basilar membrane as more like a drumhead than a harp. According to frequency theory, the whole membrane vibrates in response to sounds. However, a particular sound frequency causes the basilar membrane to vibrate at a specific rate. The brain detects the frequency of a tone by the rate at which the auditory nerve fibers fire.

Reconciling Place and Frequency Theories

The competition between these two theories is similar to the dispute between the trichromatic and opponent process theories of color vision. In the end, both theories of pitch perception proved to have some flaws, but both turned out to be valid in part. Place theory was basically on the mark except for one detail. The hair cells along the basilar membrane are not independent. They vibrate together, as suggested by frequency theory. The pattern of vibration is a traveling wave that moves along the basilar membrane. Place theory is correct, however, in that the wave peaks at a particular place, depending on the frequency of the sound wave. In sum, the current thinking is that pitch perception depends on *both* place and frequency coding of vibrations along the basilar membrane (Moore, 2010, Yost, 2010). Although much remains to be learned, once again we find

CONCEPT CHECK 4.3

Comparing Vision and Hearing

Check your understanding of both vision and hearing by comparing key aspects of sensation and perception in these senses. The dimensions of comparison are listed in the first column. The second column lists the answers for the sense of vision. Fill in the answers for the sense of hearing in the third column. The answers can be found in Appendix A.

Dimension	Vision	Hearing
1. Stimulus	Light waves	_____
2. Elements of stimulus and related perceptions	Wavelength/hue Amplitude/brightness Purity/saturation	_____ _____ _____
3. Receptors	Rods and cones	_____
4. Location of receptors	Retina	_____
5. Main location of processing in brain	Occipital lobe, visual cortex	_____

© Christo/Shutterstock.com

that theories that were pitted against each other for decades are complementary rather than contradictory.

Auditory Localization: Perceiving Sources of Sound

You're driving down a street when suddenly you hear a siren wailing in the distance. As the wail grows louder, you glance around, cocking your ear to the sound. Where is it coming from? Behind you? In front of you? From one side? This example illustrates a common perceptual task called *auditory localization*—**locating the source of a sound in space.** The process of recognizing where a sound is coming from is analogous to recognizing depth or distance in vision. Both processes involve spatial aspects of sensory input. The fact that human ears are set *apart* contributes to auditory localization, just as the separation of the eyes contributes to depth perception.

Many features of sounds can contribute to auditory localization, but two cues are particularly important: the intensity (loudness) and the timing of sounds arriving at each ear (Yost, 2000). For example, a sound source to one side of the head produces a greater intensity at the ear nearer to the sound. This difference is due partly to the loss of sound intensity with extra distance. Another factor at work is the "shadow," or partial sound barrier, cast by the head itself (see **Figure 4.32**). The intensity difference between the two ears is greatest when the sound source is well to one side. The human perceptual system uses this difference as a clue in localizing sounds. Furthermore, because the path to the farther ear is longer, a sound takes longer to reach that ear. This fact means that sounds can be localized by comparing the timing of their arrival at each ear. Such comparison of the timing of sounds is remarkably sensitive. Evidence suggests that people depend primarily on timing differences to localize low-frequency sounds, and on intensity differences to localize high-frequency sounds (Yost, 2013).

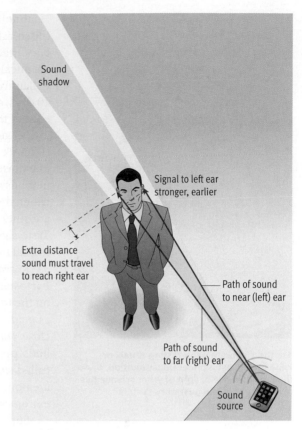

FIGURE 4.32

Cues in auditory localization. A sound coming from the left reaches the left ear sooner than the right. When the sound reaches the right ear, it is also less intense because it has traveled a greater distance and because it is in the sound shadow produced by the listener's head. These cues are used to localize the sources of sound in space.

4.4 THE OTHER SENSES: TASTE, SMELL, AND TOUCH

4.4

Key Learning Goals

- Describe the stimulus and receptors for taste, and review research on individual differences in taste sensitivity.
- Describe the stimulus and receptors for smell, and evaluate humans' olfactory capabilities.
- Describe the stimulus and receptors for touch, and explain what is known about pain perception.

Psychologists have devoted most of their attention to the visual and auditory systems. Although less is known about the senses of taste, smell, and touch, they also play a critical role in people's experience of the world. Let's start by taking a brief look at what psychologists have learned about the *gustatory system*—**the sensory system for taste.**

Taste: The Gustatory System

True wine lovers go through an elaborate series of steps when they are served a good bottle of wine. Typically, they begin by drinking a little water to cleanse their palate. Then they sniff the cork from the wine bottle, swirl a small amount of the wine around in a glass, and sniff the odor emerging from the glass. Finally, they take a sip of the wine, rolling it around in their mouth for a short time before swallowing it. At last they are ready to indicate their approval or disapproval. Is all this activity really a meaningful way to put the wine to a sensitive test? Or is it just a harmless ritual passed on through tradition? You'll find out in this section.

Are the elaborate wine-tasting rituals of wine lovers just a pretentious tradition, or do they make sense in light of what science has revealed about the gustatory system?

▶ **REALITY CHECK**

Misconception

Sensitivity to the four primary tastes varies greatly across the tongue, as depicted in the tongue map shown in the illustration.

Reality

For decades, it was reported that taste buds sensitive to the four primary tastes are distributed unevenly across the tongue in the manner shown here. However, these classic tongue maps were based on a misinterpretation of early research data. Although there are some small variations in sensitivity to specific tastes on the tongue, all four primary tastes can be detected wherever there are taste receptors.

The physical stimuli for the sense of taste are chemical substances that are soluble (dissolvable in water). The gustatory receptors are clusters of taste cells found in the *taste buds* that line the trenches around tiny bumps on the tongue. When these cells absorb chemicals dissolved in saliva, neural impulses are triggered that are routed through the thalamus to the cortex. Interestingly, taste cells have a short life. They last only about 10 days, and they are constantly being replaced (Cowart, 2005). New cells are born at the edge of the taste bud and migrate inward to die at the center.

It's generally agreed that there are four *primary tastes:* sweet, sour, bitter, and salty (Buck & Bargmann, 2013). However, scientists are increasingly recognizing a fifth primary taste called *umami,* which is a Japanese word for the *savory* taste of glutamate found in foods such as meats and cheeses (DuBois, 2010). Sensitivity to the primary tastes is distributed somewhat unevenly across the tongue. However, these variations in sensitivity are quite small and very complicated (Di Lorenzo & Youngentob, 2013) (see **Figure 4.33**). Taste signals are routed through the thalamus and sent on to the *insular cortex* in the frontal lobe, where the initial cortical processing takes place.

Research reveals that people vary considerably in their sensitivity to certain tastes. Bartoshuk (1993) noted that these differences depend in part on the density of taste buds on the tongue, which appears to be a matter of genetic inheritance. People characterized as *nontasters*—as determined by their insensitivity to PTC (phenythiocarbamide), or its close relative, PROP (propylthiouracil)—tend to have about one-fourth as many taste buds per square centimeter as do people at the other end of the spectrum, who are called *supertasters* (Miller & Reedy, 1990). In the United States, roughly 25% of people are nontasters, another 25% are supertasters, and the remaining 50% fall between these extremes and are characterized as *medium tasters* (Di Lorenzo & Youngentob, 2003).

Supertasters and nontasters respond similarly to many foods, but supertasters are more sensitive to certain sweet and bitter substances (Prescott, 2010). These differences in taste sensitivity influence people's eating habits in ways that can have repercussions for their physical health. For example, supertasters are less likely to be fond of sweets (Yeomans et al., 2007) and tend to consume fewer high-fat foods, both of which are likely to reduce their risk for cardiovascular disease (Duffy, Lucchina, & Bartoshuk, 2004). Supertasters also tend to react more negatively to alcohol and smoking, thereby reducing their likelihood of developing drinking problems or nicotine addiction (Snedecor et al., 2006). The only health disadvantage identified for supertasters thus far is that they respond more negatively to many vegetables, which seems to hold down their vegetable intake (Duffy et al., 2010). Overall, however, supertasters tend to have better health habits than nontasters, thanks to their strong reactions to certain tastes.

Women are more likely than men to be supertasters (Bartoshuk, Duffy, & Miller, 1994). Some psychologists speculate that the gender gap in this trait may have evolutionary significance. Over the course of evolution, women have generally been more involved than men in feeding children. Increased reactivity to sweet and bitter tastes would have been adaptive in that it would have made women more sensitive to the relatively scarce high-caloric foods (which often taste sweet) needed for survival and to the toxic substances (which often taste bitter) that hunters and gatherers needed to avoid.

When you eat, you are constantly mixing food and saliva and moving it about in your mouth, so the stimulus is constantly changing. However, if you place a flavored substance in a single spot on your tongue, the taste will fade until it vanishes (Krakauer & Dallenbach, 1937). This fading effect is an example of *sensory adaptation*—**a gradual decline in sensitivity to prolonged stimulation.** Sensory adaptation is not unique to taste. This phenomenon occurs in other senses, as well. In the taste system, sensory adaptation can leave aftereffects. For example, adaptation to a sour solution makes water taste sweet, whereas adaptation to a sweet solution makes water taste bitter.

So far, we've been discussing taste, but what we're really interested in is the *perception of flavor.* Flavor is a combination of taste, smell, and the tactile sensation of food in one's mouth. Odors make a surprisingly great contribution to the perception of flavor

FIGURE 4.33

The tongue and taste. Taste buds are clustered around tiny bumps on the tongue called papillae. There are three types of papillae, which are distributed as shown here. The taste buds found in each type of papilla show slightly different sensitivities to the four basic tastes, as mapped out in the graph at the top. Thus, sensitivity to the primary tastes varies across the tongue, but these variations are small and all four primary tastes can be detected wherever there are taste receptors. (Data adapted from Bartoshuk, 1993a)

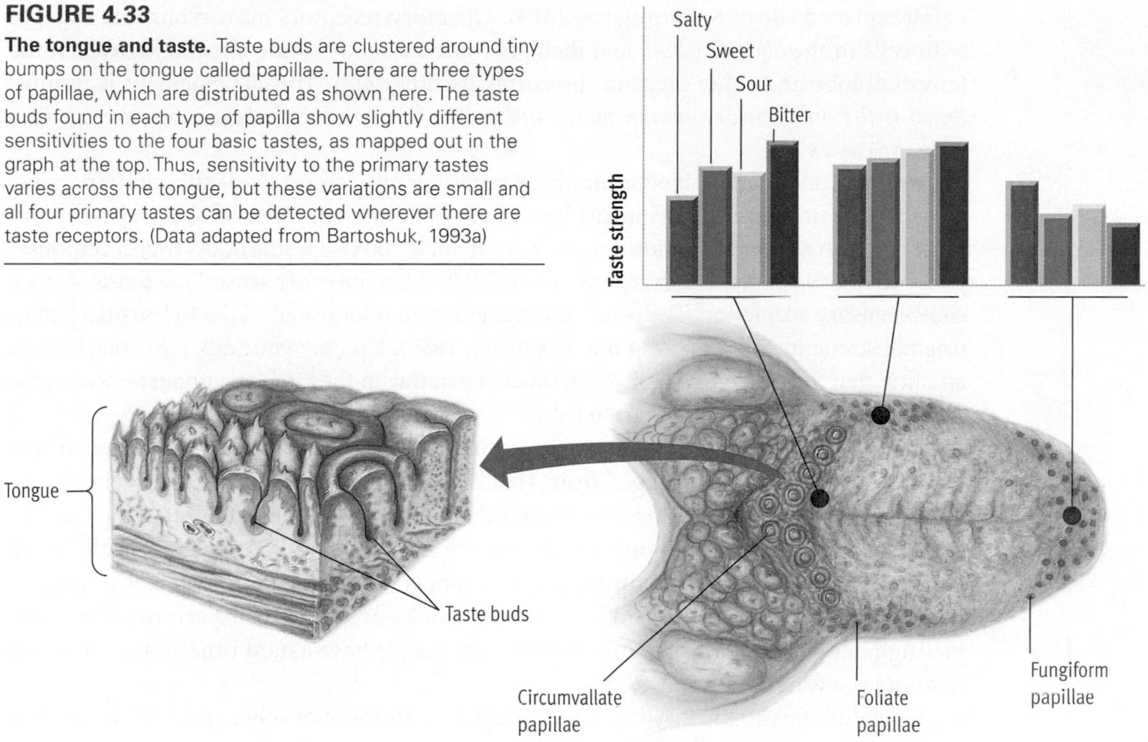

Salty
Sweet
Sour
Bitter

Taste strength

Tongue

Taste buds

Circumvallate papillae

Foliate papillae

Fungiform papillae

(Di Lorenzo & Youngentob, 2013). The ability to identify flavors declines noticeably when odor cues are absent. You might have noticed this interaction when you ate a favorite meal while enduring a severe head cold. The food probably tasted bland because your stuffy nose impaired your sense of smell.

Now that we've explored the dynamics of taste, we can return to our question about the value of the wine-tasting ritual. This elaborate ritual is indeed an authentic way to put wine to a sensitive test. The aftereffects associated with sensory adaptation make it wise to cleanse one's palate before tasting the wine. Sniffing the cork, and the wine in the glass, is important because odor is a major determinant of flavor. Swirling the wine in the glass helps release the wine's odor inside the glass. Rolling the wine around in your mouth is especially critical because it distributes the wine over the full range of taste cells. It also forces the wine's odor up into the nasal passages. Thus, each action in this age-old ritual makes a meaningful contribution to the tasting.

Smell: The Olfactory System

Humans are usually characterized as being relatively insensitive to smell. In this regard they are often compared unfavorably to dogs, which are renowned for their ability to track a faint odor over long distances. Are humans really inferior in the sensory domain of smell? Let's examine the facts.

The *olfactory system*, **the sensory system for smell,** resembles the sense of taste in many ways. The physical stimuli are chemical substances—volatile ones that can evaporate and be carried in the air. These chemical stimuli are dissolved in fluid—specifically, the mucus in the nose. The receptors for smell are *olfactory cilia,* hairlike structures located in the upper portion of the nasal passages (see **Figure 4.34**). They resemble taste cells in that they have a short life and are constantly

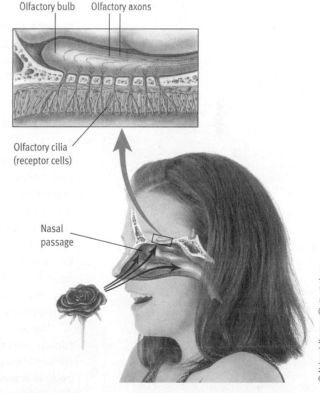

Olfactory bulb   Olfactory axons

Olfactory cilia (receptor cells)

Nasal passage

© Aleksandr Kurganov/Shutterstock.com

FIGURE 4.34

The olfactory system. Odor molecules travel through the nasal passages and stimulate olfactory cilia. An enlargement of these hairlike olfactory receptors is shown in the inset. The olfactory axons transmit neural impulses through the olfactory bulb to the brain.

being replaced (Buck & Bargmann, 2013). Olfactory receptors have axons that synapse with cells in the *olfactory bulb* and then are routed directly to the olfactory cortex in the temporal lobe and other areas in the cortex (Scott, 2008). This arrangement is unique. *Smell is the only sensory system that is not routed through the thalamus before it projects onto the cortex.*

Odors cannot be classified as neatly as tastes because efforts to identify primary odors have proven unsatisfactory. Humans have about 350 different types of olfactory receptors, most of which respond to a wide range of odors (Buck, 2004). Specific odors trigger responses in different *combinations* of receptors (Doty, 2010). Like the other senses, the sense of smell shows sensory adaptation. The perceived strength of an odor usually fades to less than half its original strength within about 4 minutes (Cain, 1988). Let's say you walk into your kitchen and find that the garbage has started to smell. If you stay in the kitchen without removing the garbage, the stench will soon start to fade.

Humans can distinguish a great many odors. Until very recently, estimates of the number of distinct odors ranged from 10,000 (Axel, 1995) to 100,000 (Firestein, 2001). However, a recent study using more sophisticated methods yielded a much higher estimate: humans can discriminate between more than 1 trillion odors (Bushdid et al., 2014). Although humans can distinguish a huge numbers of odors, when people are asked to identify the sources of specific odors (such as smoke or soap), their performance is surprisingly mediocre. For some unknown reason, people have a hard time attaching names to odors (Cowart & Rawson, 2001).

How do human olfactory capacities compare with those of other species? We do have notably fewer olfactory receptors than many other animals (Wolfe et al., 2006). However, recent studies have found that humans and monkeys, when compared with other mammals, have a better sense of smell than previously thought (Laska, Seibt, & Weber, 2000; Shepherd, 2004). For example, one innovative study (Porter et al., 2007) asked humans to get on their hands and knees to track the scent of chocolate oil that had been dribbled through a field. The subjects performed quite well, and their patterns of tracking mimicked those of dogs. Gordon Shepherd (2004) offers several possible explanations for our surprising olfactory capabilities, including the fact that "humans smell with bigger and better brains" (p. 0574).

Touch: Sensory Systems in the Skin

The physical stimuli for touch consist of mechanical, thermal, and chemical energy that comes into contact with the skin. These stimuli can produce perceptions of tactile stimulation (the pressure of touch against the skin), warmth, cold, and pain. The human skin is saturated with at least six types of sensory receptors. To some degree, these different types of receptors are specialized for different functions, such as the registration of pressure, heat, cold, and so forth. However, these distinctions are not as clear as researchers had originally thought.

If you've been to a mosquito-infested picnic lately, you'll appreciate the need to quickly know where tactile stimulation is coming from. The sense of touch is set up to meet this need for tactile localization with admirable efficiency. Cells in the nervous system that respond to touch are sensitive to specific patches of skin. These skin patches, which vary considerably in size, are the functional equivalents of *receptive fields* in vision.

The nerve fibers that carry incoming information about tactile stimulation are routed along two pathways that both run through the thalamus and onward to the *somatosensory cortex* in the brain's parietal lobes (Klatzky & Lederman, 2013). The entire body is sensitive to touch. However, in humans, the bulk of the somatosensory cortex is devoted to processing signals coming from the fingers, lips, and tongue.

As unpleasant as it is, pain is a marvelous warning system that is crucial to survival. However, chronic pain is a demoralizing affliction that affects roughly 100 million Americans (Gatchel et al., 2014) and has a profoundly negative impact on their quality of life (Jensen & Turk, 2014). Estimates suggest that chronic pain costs American society

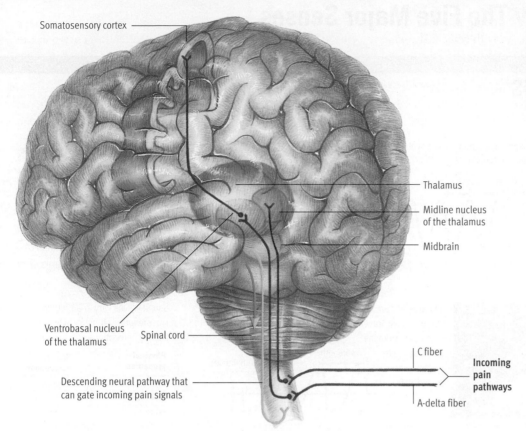

Somatosensory cortex

Thalamus

Midline nucleus
of the thalamus

Midbrain

Ventrobasal nucleus
of the thalamus

Spinal cord

C fiber

**Incoming
pain
pathways**

Descending neural pathway that
can gate incoming pain signals

A-delta fiber

FIGURE 4.35

Pathways for pain signals. Pain signals are sent inward from receptors to the brain along the two ascending pathways. The fast pathway, shown in red, and the slow pathway, shown in black, depend on different types of nerve fibers and are routed through different parts of the thalamus. The gate-control mechanism hypothesized by Melzack and Wall (1965) apparently depends on signals in a descending pathway (shown in green) that originates in an area of the midbrain.

around $600 billion a year, with roughly half this sum due to treatment expenses, and the other half due to reduced productivity (Gaskin & Richard, 2012).

The receptors for pain are mostly free nerve endings in the skin. Pain messages are transmitted to the brain via two pathways that pass through different areas in the thalamus (Cholewiak & Cholewiak, 2010) (see **Figure 4.35**). One is a *fast pathway* that registers localized pain and relays it to the cortex in a fraction of a second. This is the system that hits you with sharp pain when you first cut your finger. The second system uses a *slow pathway,* routed through the limbic system, that lags a second or two behind the fast system. This pathway (which also carries information about temperature) conveys the less localized, longer-lasting aching or burning pain that comes after the initial injury.

Pain perception is inherently subjective (Rollman, 2010). Some people with severe injuries report little pain, whereas other people with much more modest injuries report agonizing pain (Coderre, Mogil, & Bushnell, 2003). The perception of pain can be influenced greatly by beliefs, expectations, personality, mood, and other factors involving higher mental processes (Turk & Okifuji, 2003). The subjective nature of pain is illustrated by placebo effects. As we saw in Chapter 2, many people suffering from pain report relief when given a placebo, such as an inert "sugar pill" that is presented to them as if it were a painkilling drug (Benedetti, 2009).

As you can see, then, tissue damage that sends pain impulses on their way to the brain doesn't necessarily result in the experience of pain. Cognitive and emotional processes that unfold in higher brain centers can sometimes block pain signals coming from peripheral receptors.

How are incoming pain signals blocked? In an influential effort to answer this question, Ronald Melzack and Patrick Wall (1965) devised the gate-control theory of pain. *Gate-control theory holds that incoming pain sensations must pass through a "gate" in the spinal cord that can be closed, thus blocking ascending pain signals.* The gate in this model is not an anatomical structure but a pattern of neural activity that inhibits

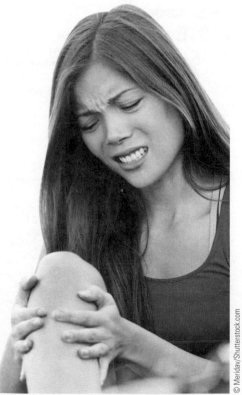

People tend to assume that the perception of pain is an automatic result of bodily injuries, but the process of pain perception is much more complex and subjective than widely appreciated.

Illustrated Overview **The Five Major Senses**

SENSE	STIMULUS	ELEMENT OF THE STIMULUS

SIGHT

The Visual System

Light is electromagnetic radiation that travels in waves. Humans can register only a slim portion of the total range of wavelengths, from 400 to 700 nanometers.

© John White Photos/Alamy

Light waves vary in *amplitude, wavelength,* and *purity,* which influence perceptions as shown below.

Physical properties	Related perceptions
Wavelength	Hue (color)
Amplitude	Brightness
Purity	Saturation

HEARING

The Auditory System

© Photodisc/Stockbyte/Getty Images

Sound waves are vibrations of molecules, which means that they must travel through some physical medium, such as air. Humans can hear wavelengths between 20 and 20,000 Hz.

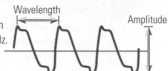

Sound waves vary in *amplitude, wavelength,* and *purity,* which influence perceptions as shown below.

Physical properties	Related perceptions
Amplitude	Loudness
Wavelength	Pitch
Purity	Timbre

TASTE

The Gustatory System

The stimuli for taste generally are chemical substances that are soluble (dissolvable in water). These stimuli are dissolved in the mouth's saliva.

© bikeriderlondon/Shutterstock.com

It is generally, but not universally, agreed that there are four primary tastes: *sweet, sour, bitter,* and *salty.*

SMELL

The Olfactory System

© JGI/Blend Images/Getty Images

The stimuli are volatile chemical substances that can evaporate and be carried in the air. These chemical stimuli are dissolved in the mucus of the nose.

Efforts to identify primary odors have proven unsatisfactory. If primary odors exist, there must be a great many of them.

TOUCH

The Tactile System

The stimuli are mechanical, thermal, and chemical energy that impinge on the skin.

© Image Source Plus/Alamy

Receptors in the skin can register *pressure, warmth, cold,* and *pain.*

NATURE AND LOCATION OF RECEPTORS

The *retina*, which is neural tissue lining the inside back surface of the eye, contains millions of receptor cells called *rods* and *cones*. Rods play a key role in night and peripheral vision; cones play a key role in daylight and color vision.

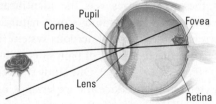

The receptors for hearing are tiny *hair cells* that line the *basilar membrane* that runs the length of the *cochlea*, a fluid-filled, coiled tunnel in the inner ear.

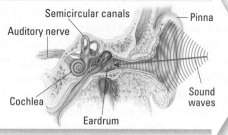

The gustatory receptors are clusters of *taste cells* found in the *taste buds* that line the trenches around tiny bumps in the tongue. Taste cells have a short lifespan (about 10 days) and are constantly being replaced.

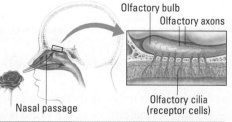

The receptors for smell are *olfactory cilia*, hairlike structures in the upper portion of the nasal passages. Like taste cells, they have a short lifespan (about 30–60 days) and are constantly being replaced.

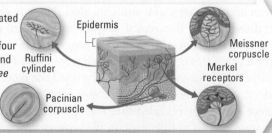

The human skin is saturated with at least six types of sensory receptors. The four types shown here respond to pressure, whereas *free nerve endings* in the skin respond to pain, warmth, and cold.

BRAIN PATHWAYS IN INITIAL PROCESSING

Neural impulses are routed through the *LGN* in the *thalamus* and then distributed to the *primary visual cortex* at the back of the *occipital lobe*.

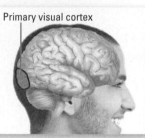

Neural impulses are routed through the *thalamus* and then sent to the *primary auditory cortex*, which is mostly located in the *temporal lobe*.

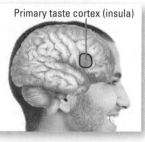

Neural impulses are routed through the *thalamus* and on to the *insular cortex* in the frontal lobe.

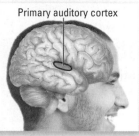

Neural impulses are routed through the *olfactory bulb* and then sent directly to the *olfactory cortex* in the *temporal lobe* and other cortical areas. Smell is the only sensory input not routed through the thalamus.

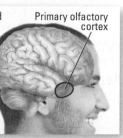

Neural impulses are routed through the *brainstem* and *thalamus* and on to the *somatosensory cortex* in the *parietal lobe*.

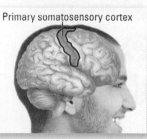

Head photo (all): © Robert Kneschke/Shutterstock.com

SENSATION AND PERCEPTION **137**

incoming pain signals. Melzack and Wall suggested that this imaginary gate can be closed by signals from peripheral receptors or by signals from the brain. They theorized that the latter mechanism can help explain how factors such as attention and expectations can shut off pain signals. As a whole, research suggests that the concept of a gating mechanism for pain has merit (Sufka & Price, 2002). However, relatively little support has been found for the neural circuitry originally hypothesized by Melzack and Wall. Other neural mechanisms, discovered after gate-control theory was proposed, appear to be responsible for blocking the perception of pain (Basbaum & Jessell, 2013).

One of these discoveries was the identification of endorphins. As discussed in Chapter 3, *endorphins* are the body's own natural morphine-like painkillers, which are widely distributed in the central nervous system (Millecamps et al., 2013). For example, placebo effects in the treatment of pain often (but not always) depend on the action of endorphins (Eippert et al., 2009). One study showed that endorphins play a key role when distractions temporarily reduce the experience of pain (Sprenger et al., 2012). In this study, the pain-relieving effects of a distraction were reduced by 40% when subjects were given a drug that temporarily blocks the activity of endorphins.

The other discovery involved the identification of a descending neural pathway that mediates the suppression of pain (Basbaum & Jessell, 2013). This pathway appears to originate in an area of the midbrain (see **Figure 4.35**). Neural activity in this pathway is probably initiated by endorphins. The circuits in this pathway inhibit the activity of neurons that would normally transmit incoming pain impulses to the brain.

Research also suggests that certain types of *glial cells* may contribute to the regulation of pain (Millecamps et al., 2013). At least two types of glia in the spinal cord appear to play an important role in the experience of *chronic pain* (Milligan & Watkins, 2009). The discovery that glia play a role in the human pain system may eventually open up new avenues for treating chronic pain.

One final point merits emphasis as we close our tour of the human sensory systems. Although we have discussed the various sensory domains separately, it's important to remember that all the senses send signals to the same brain, where the information is pooled. We have already encountered examples of sensory integration. For example, it is at work when the sight and smell of food influence taste. *Sensory integration is the norm in perceptual experience.* For instance, when you sit around a campfire, you *see* it blazing, you *hear* it crackling, you *smell* it burning, and you feel the *touch* of its warmth. If you cook something over it, you may even *taste* it. Thus, perception involves building a unified model of the world out of integrated input from all the senses.

4.5

4.5 REFLECTING ON THE CHAPTER'S THEMES

Key Learning Goals

• Identify the three unifying themes that were highlighted in this chapter.

 Theoretical Diversity

 Subjectivity of Experience

 Cultural Heritage

In this chapter, three of our unifying themes were highlighted: (1) psychology is theoretically diverse, (2) people's experience of the world is highly subjective, and (3) our behavior is shaped by our cultural heritage. Let's discuss the value of theoretical diversity first.

Contradictory theories about behavior can be disconcerting and frustrating for theorists, researchers, teachers, and students alike. Yet this chapter provided two dramatic demonstrations of how theoretical diversity can lead to progress in the long run. For decades, the trichromatic and opponent process theories of color vision and the place and frequency theories of pitch perception were viewed as fundamentally incompatible. These competing theories generated and guided the research that now provides a fairly solid understanding of how people perceive color and pitch. As you know, in each case, the evidence eventually revealed that the opposing theories were not really incompatible. Both were needed to fully explain the sensory processes that each sought to explain individually. If it hadn't been for these theoretical debates, our current understanding of color vision and pitch perception might be far more primitive.

This chapter should have also enhanced your appreciation of why human experience of the world is highly subjective. As ambiguous figures and visual illusions clearly show, there is no one-to-one correspondence between sensory input and perceived experience of the world. Perception is an active process in which people organize and interpret the information received by the senses. Thus, individuals' experience of the world is subjective because the process of perception is inherently subjective.

Finally, this chapter provided numerous examples of how cultural factors can shape behavior—in an area of research where one might expect to find little cultural influence. Most people are not surprised to learn that there are cultural differences in attitudes, values, social behavior, and development. But perception is widely viewed as a basic, universal process that should be invariant across cultures. In most respects it is, as the similarities among cultural groups in perception far outweigh the differences. Nonetheless, we saw cultural variations in depth perception and susceptibility to illusions. Thus, even a fundamental, heavily physiological process such as perception can be modified to some degree by one's cultural background.

The following Personal Application highlights the subjectivity of perception once again. It focuses on how painters have learned to use the principles of visual perception to achieve a variety of artistic goals.

4.6 PERSONAL APPLICATION
Appreciating Art and Illusion

4.6

Key Learning Goals
- Discuss how artists have used various principles of visual perception.

Answer the following multiple-choice question.

Artistic works such as paintings:

____ **(a)** render an accurate picture of reality.

____ **(b)** create an illusion of reality.

____ **(c)** provide an interpretation of reality.

____ **(d)** make us think about the nature of reality.

____ **(e)** do all of the above.

The answer to this question is (e), "all of the above." Historically, artists have had many and varied purposes, including each of those listed in the question (Goldstein, 2001). To realize their goals, artists have had to use a number of principles of perception—sometimes quite deliberately, and sometimes not. Here we'll use the example of painting to explore the role of perceptual principles in art and illusion.

The goal of most early painters was to produce a believable picture of reality. This goal immediately created a problem familiar to most of us who have attempted to draw realistic pictures: The real world is three-dimensional, but a canvas or a sheet of paper is flat. Paradoxically, then, painters who set out to re-create reality had to do so by creating an *illusion* of three-dimensional reality.

Prior to the Renaissance, these efforts to create a convincing illusion of reality were awkward by modern standards. Why? Because artists did not understand how to use depth cues. This fact is apparent in **Figure 4.36**, a religious scene painted around 1300. The painting clearly lacks a sense of depth. The people seem paper-thin. They have no real position in space.

Although earlier artists made *some* use of depth cues, Renaissance artists manipulated the full range

Scala/Art Resource, NY

FIGURE 4.36

Master of the Arrest of Christ (detail, central part) by S. Francesco, Assisi, Italy (circa 1300). Notice how the absence of depth cues makes the painting seem flat and unrealistic.

FIGURE 4.37
A painting by the Italian Renaissance artists Gentile and Giovanni Bellini (circa 1480). In this painting a number of depth cues—including linear perspective, relative size, height in plane, and interposition—enhance the illusion of three-dimensional reality.

of pictorial depth cues, especially linear perspective (Solso, 1994). **Figure 4.37** dramatizes the resulting transition in art. This scene, painted by Italian Renaissance artists Gentile and Giovanni Bellini, seems much more realistic and lifelike than the painting in **Figure 4.36** because it uses a number of pictorial depth cues. Notice how the buildings on the sides converge to make use of linear perspective. Additionally, distant objects are smaller than nearby ones, an application of relative size. This painting also uses height in relation to plane, as well as interposition. By taking advantage of pictorial depth cues, an artist can enhance a painting's illusion of reality.

In the centuries since the Renaissance, painters have adopted a number of

FIGURE 4.38
Georges Seurat's _Sunday Afternoon on the Island of La Grande Jatte_ (without artist's border) (1884–1886). Seurat used thousands of tiny dots of color and the principles of color mixing; the eye and brain combine the points into the colors the viewer actually sees.

SOURCE: Georges Seurat, French, 1859–1891, _Sunday Afternoon on the Island of La Grande Jatte_ oil on canvas, 1884–1886, 207.6 X 308 cm, Helen Birch Bartlett Memorial Collection, 1926.224, © 1990 The Art Institute of Chicago. All rights reserved.

viewpoints about the portrayal of reality. For instance, the French Impressionists of the 19th century did not want to re-create the photographic "reality" of a scene. They set out to interpret a viewer's fleeting perception or impression of reality. To accomplish this end, they worked with color in unprecedented ways.

Consider, for instance, the work of Georges Seurat, a French artist who used a technique called *pointillism*. Seurat carefully studied what scientists knew about the composition of color in the 1880s, then applied this knowledge in a calculated, laboratory-like manner. Indeed, critics in his era dubbed him the "little chemist." Seurat constructed his paintings out of tiny dots of pure, intense colors. He used additive color mixing, a departure from the norm in painting, which usually depends on subtractive mixing of pigments.

A famous result of Seurat's "scientific" approach to painting was *Sunday Afternoon on the Island of La Grande Jatte* (see **Figure 4.38**). As the work of Seurat illustrates, modernist painters were moving away from attempts to re-create the world as it is literally seen.

So too, were the Surrealists, who toyed with reality in a different way. Influenced by Sigmund Freud's writings on the unconscious, the Surrealists explored the world of dreams and fantasy. Specific elements in their paintings are often depicted realistically, but the strange combination of elements yields a disconcerting irrationality reminiscent of dreams. A prominent example of this style is Salvador Dali's *Mae West's Face which May be Used as a Surrealist Apartment,* shown in **Figure 4.39**. Notice that this is a reversible figure that can be seen as a face or a room.

Dali often used reversible figures to enhance the ambiguity of his surreal visions.

Perhaps no one has been more creative in manipulating perceptual ambiguity than M. C. Escher, a modern Dutch artist. Escher closely followed the work of the Gestalt psychologists, and he readily acknowledged his debt to psychology as a source of inspiration (Teuber, 1974). *Waterfall,* a 1961 lithograph by Escher, is a perplexing drawing that appears to defy the law of gravity (see **Figure 4.40**). The puzzling problem here is that a level channel of water terminates in a waterfall that "falls" into the same channel two levels "below." You have to look carefully to realize that this structure could not exist in the real world. Escher's goal, which he achieved admirably, was to challenge viewers to think long and hard about the remarkable process of perception.

FIGURE 4.39
Salvador Dali's *Mae West's Face which May be Used as a Surrealist Apartment* **(1934–1935).** This painting can be viewed as a room or as the face of the legendary actress.

FIGURE 4.40
Escher's lithograph *Waterfall* **(1961).** Escher's clever manipulation of depth cues deceives the brain into seeing water flow uphill.

4.7

Key Learning Goals
• Understand how contrast effects can be manipulated to influence or distort judgments.

4.7 CRITICAL THINKING APPLICATION
Recognizing Contrast Effects: It's All Relative

You're sitting at home one night when the phone rings. It's Simone, an acquaintance from school who needs help with a recreational program for youngsters that she runs for the local park district. She tries to persuade you to volunteer 4 hours of your time every Friday night throughout the school year to supervise the volleyball program. The thought of giving up your Friday nights and adding this sizable obligation to your already busy schedule makes you cringe with horror. You politely explain to Simone that you can't possibly afford to give up that much time and you won't be able to help her. She accepts your rebuff graciously, but the next night she calls again. This time she wants to know whether you would be willing to supervise volleyball every third Friday. You still feel like it's a big obligation that you really don't want to take on, but the new request seems much more reasonable than the original one. So, with a sigh of resignation, you agree to Simone's request.

What's wrong with this picture? Well, there's nothing wrong with volunteering your time for a good cause, but you just succumbed to a social influence strategy called the *door-in-the face technique*. The ***door-in-the-face technique* involves making a large request that is likely to** **be turned down as a way to increase the chances that people will agree to a smaller request later** (see **Figure 4.41**). The name for this strategy is derived from the expectation that the initial request will be quickly rejected (hence, the door is slammed in the salesperson's face). Although they may not be familiar with the strategy's name, many people use this manipulative tactic. For example, a husband who wants to coax his frugal wife into agreeing to buy a $30,000 sports car might begin by proposing that they purchase a $50,000 sports car. By the time the wife talks her husband out of the $50,000 car, the $30,000 price tag may look quite reasonable to her—which is what the husband wanted all along.

Research has demonstrated that the door-in-the-face technique is a highly effective persuasive strategy (Cialdini, 2007). One of the reasons it works so well is that it depends on a simple and pervasive perceptual principle: When it comes to perceptual experience, *everything is relative*. This relativity means that people are easily swayed by *contrast effects*. For example, lighting a match or a small candle in a dark room will produce a burst of light that seems quite bright, but if you light the same match or candle in a well-lit room, you may not even detect the additional illumination. The relativity of perception is apparent in the painting by Josef Albers shown in **Figure 4.42**. The two X's are exactly the same color, but the X in the top half looks yellow, whereas the X in the bottom half looks brown. These varied perceptions occur because of contrast effects: the two X's are contrasted against different background colors. Another example of how contrast effects can influence perception can be seen in **Figure 4.43**. The middle disk in each panel is exactly the same size, but the one in the top panel looks larger because it is surrounded by much smaller disks.

The same principles of relativity and contrast that operate when people make judgments about the intensity or color of visual stimuli also affect the way they make judgments in a wide variety of areas. For example, a 6'3" basketball player, who is really quite tall, can look downright small when surrounded by teammates who are all over 6'8". And a salary of $42,000 per year for your first full-time job may seem like a princely sum, until a close friend gets an offer of $75,000 a year. The assertion that everything is relative raises the issue of *relative to what*? **Comparators are people, objects, events, and other standards that are used as a baseline for comparison in making judgments.** It is fairly easy to manipulate many types of judgments by selecting *extreme* comparators that may be unrepresentative.

© Blaj Gabriel/Shutterstock.com

FIGURE 4.41
The door-in-the-face technique. The door-in-the-face technique is a frequently used compliance strategy in which you begin with a large request and work down to the smaller request you are really after. It depends in part on contrast effects.

FIGURE 4.42

Contrast effects in visual perception. This composition by Joseph Albers shows how one color can be perceived differently when contrasted against different backgrounds. The top X looks yellow and the bottom X looks brown, but they're really the same color.

SOURCE: Albers, Joseph. *Interaction of Color.* Copyright © 1963 and reprinted by permission of the publisher, Yale University Press.

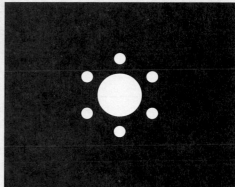

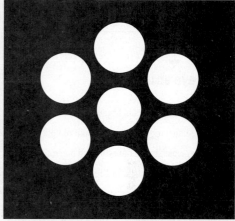

FIGURE 4.43

Contrast effects in size perception. The middle disk in the top panel looks larger than the middle disk in the bottom panel, but they really are exactly the same size. This illusion occurs because of contrast effects created by the surrounding disks.

The influence of extreme comparators was demonstrated in some interesting studies of judgments of physical attractiveness. In one study, undergraduate males were asked to rate the attractiveness of an average-looking female (who was described as a potential date for another male in the dorm) presented in a photo either just before or just after the participants watched a TV show dominated by strikingly beautiful women (Kenrick & Gutierres, 1980). The female was viewed as less attractive when the ratings were obtained just after the men had seen gorgeous women on TV, as opposed to when they hadn't. In other studies, both male and female participants have rated *themselves* as less attractive after being exposed to many pictures of extremely attractive models (Little & Mannion, 2006; Thornton & Maurice, 1999). Thus, contrast effects can influence important social judgments that are likely to affect how people feel about themselves and others.

Anyone who understands how easily judgments can be manipulated by a careful choice of comparators could influence your thinking. For example, a politician who is caught in some illegal or immoral act could sway public opinion by bringing to mind (perhaps subtly) the fact that many other politicians have committed acts that were much worse. When considered against a backdrop of more extreme comparators, the politician's transgression will probably seem less offensive. A defense attorney could use a similar strategy in an attempt to obtain a lighter sentence for a client by comparing the client's offense to much more serious crimes. And a realtor who wants to sell you an expensive house that will require huge mortgage payments will be quick to mention other homeowners who have taken on even larger mortgages.

In summary, critical thinking is facilitated by conscious awareness of the way comparators can influence and perhaps distort a wide range of judgments. In particular, it pays to be vigilant about the possibility that others may manipulate contrast effects in their persuasive efforts. One way to reduce the influence of contrast effects is to consciously consider comparators that are both worse and others that are better than the event you are judging, as a way of balancing the effects of the two extremes.

TABLE 4.1 Critical Thinking Skills Discussed in This Application

Skill	Description
Understanding how contrast effects can influence judgments and decisions	The critical thinker appreciates how striking contrasts can be manipulated to influence many types of judgments.
Recognizing when extreme comparators are being used	The critical thinker is on the lookout for extreme comparators that distort judgments.

THE VISUAL SYSTEM

Light waves

vary in		which affect perceptions of
Amplitude	▶	Brightness
Wavelength	▶	Color (hue)
Purity	▶	Satruation

Light is registered by receptors in the eye

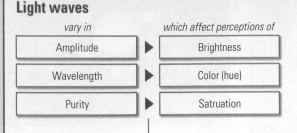
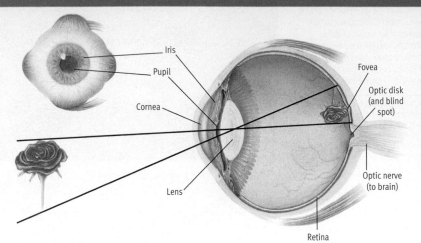

Iris
Pupil
Cornea
Lens
Fovea
Optic disk (and blind spot)
Optic nerve (to brain)
Retina

Key eye structures

include:

Lens, which focuses light rays falling on the retina

Pupil, which regulates the amount of light passing to the rear of the eye.

Retina, which is the neural tissue lining the inside back surface of the eye

Optic disk, which is a hole in the retina that corresponds to the blind spot

Fovea, which is a tiny spot in the center of the retina where visual acuity is greatest

In the retina

Visual receptors

consist of *rods* and *cones*, which are organized into *receptive fields*.

Rods play a key role in night and peripheral vision and greatly outnumber cones.

Cones play a key role in day and color vision and provide greater acuity than rods.

Receptive fields are collections of rods and cones that funnel signals to specific visual cells in the retina or the brain.

Visual signals are sent onward to the brain

Visual pathways and processing

Main visual pathway projects through the thalamus, where signals are processed and distributed to the occipital lobe

Second visual pathway handles coordination of visual input with other sensory input

Primary visual cortex in the *occipital lobe* handles initial processing of visual input

Feature detectors are neurons that respond selectively to specific features of complex stimuli

After processing in the primary visual cortex, visual input is routed to other cortical areas along the *where pathway* (dorsal stream) and the *what pathway* (ventral stream).

Color perception

Subtractive color mixing works by removing some wavelengths of light, leaving less light.

Additive color mixing works by putting more light in the mixture than any one light.

Trichromatic theory holds that the eye has three groups of receptors sensitive to wavelengths associated with red, green, and blue.

Opponent process theory holds that receptors make antagonistic responses to three pairs of colors.

Conclusion: The evidence suggests that both theories are necessary to explain color perception.

Form perception

- The same visual input can result in very different perceptions.
- Form perception is selective, as the phenomenon of *inattentional blindness* demonstrates.
- Some aspects of form perception depend on *feature analysis,* which involves detecting specific elements and assembling them into complex forms.
- *Gestalt principles*—such as *figure and ground, proximity, closure, similarity, simplicity,* and *continuity*—help explain how scenes are organized into discrete forms.
- Form perception often involves *perceptual hypotheses,* which are inferences about the forms that could be responsible for the stimuli sensed.

Depth perception

Binocular cues are clues about distance based on the differing views of the two eyes.

Retinal disparity, for example, refers to the fact that the right and left eyes see slightly different views of objects within 25 feet.

Monocular cues are clues about distance based on the image in either eye alone.

Pictorial cues are monocular cues that can be given in a flat picture, such as *linear perspective, texture gradients, relative size, height in plane, interposition,* and *light and shadow.*

Visual illusions

- *A visual illusion* is a discrepancy between the appearance of a visual stimulus and its physical reality.
- Illusions—such as the *Müller-Lyer illusion,* the *Ponzo illusion,* and the *moon illusion*—show that perceptual hypotheses can be wrong and that perception is not a simple reflection of objective reality.

THE AUDITORY SYSTEM

Sound waves

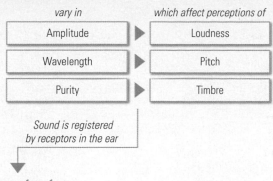

vary in		which affect perceptions of
Amplitude	▶	Loudness
Wavelength	▶	Pitch
Purity	▶	Timbre

Sound is registered by receptors in the ear

Key ear structures

include:

Pinna, which is the external ear's sound-collecting cone

Eardrum, which is a taut membrane (at the end of the auditory canal) that vibrates in response to sound waves

Ossicles, which are three tiny bones in the middle ear that convert the eardrum's vibrations

Cochlea, which is the fluid-filled, coiled tunnel that houses the inner ear's neural tissue

Basilar membrane, which holds the hair cells that serve as auditory receptors

Pitch perception

Place theory: Perception of pitch depends on the portion of the basilar membrane vibrated.

Frequency theory: Perception of pitch depends on the basilar membrane's rate of vibration.

Conclusion: Evidence suggests that both theories are needed to explain pitch perception.

Auditory localization

- *Auditory localization* consists of locating where a sound is coming from in space.
- Two key cues are differences in the *intensity* (loudness) and the *timing* of sounds arriving at each ear.

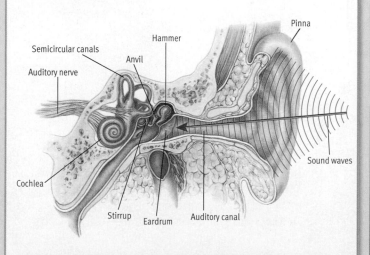

OTHER SENSES

Taste

- Taste cells absorb chemicals in saliva and trigger neural impulses routed through the thalamus.
- Taste buds are sensitive to four basic tastes: sweet, sour, bitter, and salty. Umami may be a fifth basic taste.
- Sensitivity to these tastes is distributed somewhat unevenly across the tongue, but the variations are small.
- Supertasters have more taste buds and are more sensitive than others to certain sweet and bitter substances.
- Roughly 25% of people are supertasters, another 25% are nontasters, and the remaining 50% fall in between.
- Women are more likely to be supertasters than are men.
- Nontasters tend to be more susceptible to the lure of sweets, high-fat foods, alcohol, and smoking, which means their consumption habits tend to be less healthy than those of supertasters.

Smell

- Olfactory cilia absorb chemicals in the nose and trigger neural impulses.
- Olfactory receptors have a short life and are constantly being replaced.
- Smell is the only sensory system that is not routed through the thalamus.
- Most olfactory receptors respond to more than one odor.
- Humans can distinguish a great many odors, perhaps over one trillion.
- When compared with other mammals, humans may have a better sense of smell than previously thought.

© bikeriderlondon/Shutterstock.com

Touch

- Sensory receptors in the skin respond to pressure, temperature, and pain.
- Pain signals travel along a *fast pathway* that registers localized pain and a *slow pathway* that carries less localized pain sensations.
- Cultural variations in the experience of pain show the subjective nature of pain perception.
- *Gate-control theory* holds that incoming pain signals can be blocked in the spinal cord.
- Endorphins and a descending neural pathway appear responsible for this suppression of pain.
- Recent studies indicate that glial cells contribute to the modulation of chronic pain.

APPLICATIONS

- Painters routinely use pictorial depth cues to make their scenes more lifelike.
- The Cubists applied feature analysis to canvas, the Surrealists toyed with reality, and Escher tried to stimulate thinking about perception.
- The study of perception highlights the relativity of experience, which can be manipulated through contrast effects.
- Critical thinking is enhanced by awareness of how extreme comparators can distort judgments.

CHAPTER 5

VARIATIONS IN CONSCIOUSNESS

Shaun R. George Fotografix/Moment/Getty Images

Themes in this Chapter

Sociohistorical Context   Subjectivity of Experience   Cultural Heritage   Multifactorial Causation

Theoretical Diversity

Nathaniel Kleitman and Eugene Aserinsky couldn't believe their eyes—or their subject's eyes, either. It was the spring of 1952, and Kleitman, a prominent sleep researcher, was investigating the slow, rolling eye movements displayed by subjects at the onset of sleep. Kleitman had begun to wonder whether these eye movements might show up during later phases of sleep. The trouble was that watching a participant's closed eyelids all night long was a surefire way to put the *researcher* to sleep. Cleverly, Kleitman and Aserinsky, a graduate student, came up with a better way to document eye movements. They hooked subjects up to an apparatus that was connected to electrodes pasted near the eyes. The electrodes picked up the small electrical signals generated by moving eyeballs. These signals moved a pen on a chart recorder, much like an electroencephalograph (EEG) traces brain waves. The result was an objective record of sleepers' eye movements that could be studied at any time (Dement, 1992).

One night, while one of their subjects was asleep, the researchers were surprised to see a tracing in the recording that suggested a different, much more rapid, eye movement. This result was so unexpected that they at first thought the recording device was on the blink. Only when they decided to walk in and personally observe sleeping subjects were they convinced that the eye movements were real. The subjects were deeply asleep, yet the bulges in their closed eyelids showed that their eyeballs were moving laterally back and forth in sharp jerks. The researchers wondered: What in the world was going on?

In retrospect, it's amazing that no one had discovered these rapid eye movements before. It turns out that periods of rapid eye movement are a routine part of sleep in humans and many animals. In fact, you can observe them for yourself in your pet dog or cat. The phenomenon had been there for everyone to see for eons, but anyone who noticed must not have attached any significance to it.

Kleitman and Aserinsky's discovery might have remained something of an oddity, but then they had a brainstorm. Could the rapid eye movements perhaps be related to dreaming? With the help of William Dement, a graduate student who was interested in dreams, they soon found the answer. When Dement woke up subjects during periods of rapid eye movement, about 80% reported that they had just been having a vivid dream. By contrast, only a small minority of participants awakened from other phases of sleep reported that they had been dreaming. Subsequently, EEG recordings showed that periods of rapid eye movement were also associated with marked changes in brain-wave patterns. What Kleitman and his graduate students had stumbled on was considerably more than an oddity. It was a window into the most private aspect of consciousness imaginable—the experience of dreaming (Gottesmann, 2009). As you will learn in this chapter, the discovery of rapid eye movement (REM) sleep blossomed into a number of fascinating insights about what goes on during sleep. This is just one example of how modern psychologists have tried to come to grips with the slippery topic of consciousness.

We'll begin our tour of variations in consciousness with a few general points about the nature of consciousness. After that, much of the chapter will be a "bedtime story," as we take a long look at sleep and dreaming. We'll continue our discussion of consciousness by examining hypnosis, meditation, and the effects of mind-altering drugs. The Personal Application addresses a number of practical questions about sleep and dreams. Finally, the Critical Thinking Application returns to the topic of drugs and looks at the concept of alcoholism to highlight the power of definitions.

5.1 ON THE NATURE OF CONSCIOUSNESS

Key Learning Goals

- Discuss the nature of consciousness and the relationship between consciousness and brain activity.

What is consciousness? **Consciousness is the awareness of internal and external stimuli.** Your consciousness includes (1) your awareness of external events ("The professor just asked me a hard question about medieval history"), (2) your awareness of your internal sensations ("My heart is racing and I'm starting to sweat"), (3) your awareness of your *self* as the unique being having these experiences ("Why me?"), and (4) your awareness of your thoughts about these experiences ("I'm going to make a fool of myself!"). In short, consciousness is personal awareness.

To explore the typical contents of conscious experience Heavey and Hurlburt (2008) had subjects carry a beeper and asked them to immediately record their inner experiences when they were beeped at random times. They found that five phenomena were particularly common: (1) envisioning images of things/events not actually present; (2) speaking words to oneself; (3) feeling emotions, such as joy, anger, or anxiety; (4) focusing on sensory aspects of one's environment; and (5) thinking specific thoughts without the thoughts being conveyed in words or images.

The contents of your consciousness are continually changing. Rarely does consciousness come to a standstill. It moves, it flows, it fluctuates, it wanders. For example, in one study, 2250 adults were contacted randomly during waking hours and asked whether their mind was wandering from their current activity (Killingsworth & Gilbert, 2010). Almost half (47%) of the times they were asked to report, the participants said their mind was wandering. Another study concluded that mind wandering was more likely when subjects were bored, anxious, tired, or stressed (Kane et al., 2007). Recognizing that consciousness fluctuates continuously, William James (1902) long ago named this flow the *stream of consciousness*. If you could tape-record your thoughts, you would find an endless flow of ideas that zigzag in all directions. As you will soon learn, even when you sleep, your consciousness moves through a series of transitions. Constant shifting and changing seem to be part of the essential nature of consciousness.

Variations in Levels of Awareness

While William James emphasized the stream of consciousness, Sigmund Freud (1900) wanted to examine what goes on beneath the surface of this stream. As explained in Chapter 1, Freud argued that people's feelings and behavior are influenced by *unconscious* needs, wishes, and conflicts that lie below the surface of conscious awareness. According to Freud, the stream of consciousness has depth. Conscious and unconscious processes are different *levels of awareness*. Thus, Freud was one of the first theorists to recognize that consciousness is not an all-or-none phenomenon.

Since Freud's time, research has shown that people continue to maintain some awareness during sleep and even when they are put under anesthesia for surgery. How do we know? Because some stimuli can still penetrate awareness. For example, people under surgical anesthesia occasionally hear comments made during their surgery, which they later repeat to their surprised surgeons (Kihlstrom & Cork, 2007). Research also indicates that while asleep, some people remain aware of external events to some degree (Dang-Vu et al., 2009). A good example is the new parent who can sleep through a loud thunderstorm or a buzzing alarm clock, but who immediately hears the muffled sound of the baby crying down the hall. The parent's selective sensitivity to sounds means that some mental processing must be going on even during sleep.

Consciousness and Brain Activity

Consciousness does not arise from any distinct structure in the brain, but rather is the result of activity in distributed networks of neural pathways (Singer, 2007). Scientists are increasingly using brain-imaging methods to explore the link between brain activity and consciousness. But historically, the most commonly used indicator of variations in consciousness has been the EEG, which records activity from broad swaths of the cortex. **The *electroencephalograph* (*EEG*) is a device that monitors the electrical activity of the brain over time by means of recording electrodes attached to the surface of the scalp.** Ultimately, the EEG summarizes the rhythm of cortical activity in the brain in terms of line tracings called *brain waves.* These tracings vary in *amplitude* (height) and *frequency* (cycles per second, abbreviated *cps*). You can see what brain waves look like if you glance ahead to **Figure 5.3**. Human brain-wave activity is usually divided into four principal bands, based on the frequency of the brain waves. These bands, named after letters in the Greek alphabet, are *beta* (13–24 cps), *alpha* (8–12 cps), *theta* (4–7 cps), and *delta* (under 4 cps).

TABLE 5.1 EEG Patterns Associated with States of Consciousness

EEG Pattern	Frequency (cps)	Typical States of Consciousness
Beta (β)	13–24	Normal waking thought, alert problem solving
Alpha (α)	8–12	Deep relaxation, blank mind, meditation
Theta (θ)	4–7	Light sleep
Delta (Δ)	less than 4	Deep sleep

Different patterns of EEG activity are associated with different states of consciousness, as is summarized in **Table 5.1**. For instance, when you are alertly engaged in problem solving, beta waves tend to dominate. When you are relaxed and resting, alpha waves increase. When you slip into deep, dreamless sleep, delta waves become more prevalent. Although these correlations are far from perfect, changes in brain activity are closely related to variations in consciousness. As is often the case with correlations, it is hard to say whether changes in brain-wave activity cause changes in consciousness or vice versa. Moreover, we cannot rule out the possibility that shifts in consciousness and brain-wave activity may *both* be caused by a *third* factor—perhaps signals coming from a subcortical area in the brain (see **Figure 5.1**). All that is known for sure is that variations in consciousness are associated with variations in brain activity.

5.2 BIOLOGICAL RHYTHMS AND SLEEP

Key Learning Goals

- Summarize what is known about human biological clocks and their relationship to sleep.
- Explain how getting out of sync with one's circadian rhythms can have effects on sleep.

Variations in consciousness are shaped in part by biological rhythms. Rhythms pervade the world around us. The daily alternation of light and darkness, the annual pattern of the seasons, and the phases of the moon all reflect this rhythmic quality of repeating cycles. Humans and many other animals display biological rhythms that are tied to these planetary rhythms (Kriegsfeld & Nelson, 2009). *Biological rhythms* **are periodic fluctuations in physiological functioning.** The existence of these rhythms means that organisms have internal "biological clocks" that somehow monitor the passage of time.

The Role of Circadian Rhythms

Circadian rhythms **are the 24-hour biological cycles found in humans and many other species.** In humans, circadian rhythms are particularly influential in the regulation of sleep (Moore, 2006). However, daily cycles also produce rhythmic variations in blood pressure, urine production, hormonal secretions, and other physical functions. These cycles also affect alertness, short-term memory, and other aspects of cognitive performance (Refinetti, 2006).

Research indicates that people generally fall asleep as their body temperature begins to drop and they awaken as it begins to ascend once again (Szymusiak, 2009). Investigators have concluded that circadian rhythms can leave individuals physiologically primed to fall asleep most easily at a particular time of day. This optimal time varies from person to person, depending on their schedules, but each individual may have an "ideal" time for going to bed. Retiring at this ideal bedtime may also promote better-quality sleep during the night (Akerstedt et al., 1997). People often characterize themselves as a "night person" or a "morning person." These preferences reflect individual variations in circadian rhythms (Minkel & Dinges, 2009).

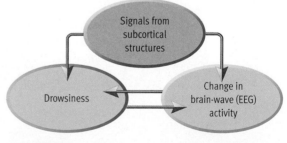

FIGURE 5.1

The correlation between mental states and cortical activity. As discussed in Chapter 2, correlations alone do not establish causation. For example, there are strong correlations between drowsiness and a particular pattern of cortical activity, as reflected by EEG brain waves. But does drowsiness cause a change in cortical activity, or do changes in cortical activity cause drowsiness? Or does some third variable—such as signals from the brainstem or other subcortical structures—account for the changes in both brain waves and drowsiness?

Researchers have a pretty good idea of how the day-night cycle resets human biological clocks. When exposed to light, some receptors in the retina send direct inputs to a small structure in the hypothalamus called the *suprachiasmatic nucleus* (SCN) (Saper, 2013). The SCN sends signals to the nearby *pineal gland,* whose secretion of the hormone *melatonin* plays a key role in adjusting biological clocks (Guardiola-Lemaitre & Quera-Salva, 2011).

Ignoring Circadian Rhythms

What happens when you ignore your biological clock and go to sleep at an unusual time? Typically, the quality of your sleep suffers. Getting out of sync with your circadian rhythms also causes *jet lag.* When you fly across several time zones, your biological clock keeps time as usual, even though official clock time changes. You then go to sleep at the "wrong" time and are likely to experience difficulty falling asleep and poor-quality sleep. This inferior sleep, which can continue to occur for several days, can make you feel fatigued, sluggish, and irritable during the daytime (Sletten & Arendt, 2012).

People differ in how quickly they can reset their biological clocks to compensate for jet lag, and the speed of readjustment depends on the direction traveled. Generally, it's easier to fly westward and lengthen your day than it is to fly eastward and shorten it (Sletten & Arendt, 2012). This east-west disparity in jet lag is sizable enough to have an impact on the performance of sports teams. Studies have found that teams flying westward perform significantly better than teams flying eastward in professional baseball (Recht, Lew, & Schwartz, 1995) (see **Figure 5.2**) and college football (Worthen & Wade, 1999). A rough rule of thumb for jet lag is that the readjustment process takes about a day for each time zone crossed when flying eastward and about two-thirds of a day per time zone when

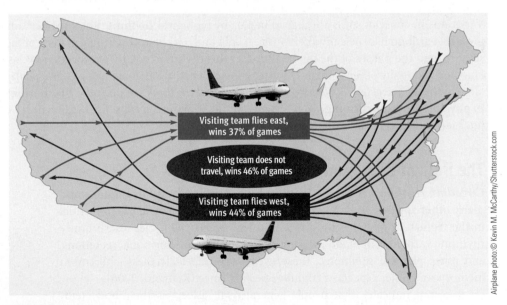

Airplane photo:© Kevin M. McCarthy/Shutterstock.com

FIGURE 5.2

Effects of direction traveled on the performance of professional baseball teams. To gain some insight into the determinants of jet lag, Recht, Lew, and Schwartz (1995) analyzed the performance of visiting teams in major league baseball over a 3-year period. In baseball, visiting teams usually play three or four games in each destination city, so there are plenty of games in which the visiting team has not traveled the day before. These games, which served as a baseline for comparison, were won by the visiting team 46% of the time. Consistent with the observation that flying west creates less jet lag than flying east, visiting teams who flew westward the day (or night) before performed only slightly worse, winning 44% of the time. In contrast, visiting teams who flew eastward the day before won only 37% of their games, presumably because flying east and shortening one's day creates greater jet lag.

SOURCE: Adapted from Kalat, J. W. (2001). *Biological psychology.* Belmont, CA: Wadsworth. Reprinted by permission.

flying westward (Monk, 2006). With advancing age, individuals take longer to realign their circadian rhythms (Bliwise, 2011).

The rotating and late-night work shifts endured by many nurses, firefighters, and industrial workers also play havoc with biological rhythms. Shift rotation tends to have far more detrimental effects than jet lag (Monk, 2000). People suffering from jet lag get their circadian rhythms realigned within a matter of days, but workers on night or in rotating shifts are constantly at odds with local time cues and normal rhythms. Studies show that such workers get less total sleep and poorer-quality sleep (Akerstedt & Kecklund, 2012). These work schedules can have a negative impact on employees' productivity at work, social relations, and mental health (Drake & Wright, 2011; Waage et al., 2009). Studies have also linked rotating shifts to a higher incidence of many physical diseases, including cancer, diabetes, ulcers, high blood pressure, and heart disease (Kriegsfeld & Nelson, 2009; Vyas et al., 2012).

The phenomenon of jet lag illustrates the importance of circadian rhythms. Getting out of sync with one's circadian rhythms can have very disruptive effects on one's sleep and daytime functioning.

Realigning Circadian Rhythms

As scientists have come to appreciate the importance of circadian rhythms, they have begun to look for new ways to help people realign their daily rhythms. One promising line of research has focused on giving people small doses of the hormone melatonin, which appears to regulate the human biological clock. The evidence from a number of studies suggests that melatonin *can* reduce the effects of jet lag by helping travelers resynchronize their biological clocks, but the results are inconsistent (Monk, 2006). One reason for the inconsistent findings is that when melatonin is used to combat jet lag, the timing of the dose is crucial. But, because calculating the optimal timing is rather complicated, it is easy to get it wrong (Arendt, 2009).

A strategy that can help shift workers involves carefully planning their rotation schedules to reduce the severity of their circadian disruption (Smith, Fogg, & Eastman, 2009). The negative effects of shift rotation can be reduced if workers move through progressively later starting times (instead of progressively earlier starting times) and if they have longer periods between shift changes. Although enlightened scheduling practices can help, the unfortunate reality is that most people find rotating shift work very difficult (Arendt, 2010).

5.3 THE SLEEP AND WAKING CYCLE

Although it is a familiar state of consciousness, sleep is widely misunderstood. Historically, people have thought of sleep as a single, uniform state of physical and mental inactivity, during which the brain is "shut down," when in reality, sleepers experience quite a bit of physical and mental activity throughout the night (Peigneux, Urbain, & Schmitz, 2012). Scientists have learned a great deal about sleep since the landmark discovery of REM sleep in the 1950s.

The advances in our understanding of sleep have been the result of hard work by researchers who have spent countless nighttime hours watching other people sleep. This work is done in sleep laboratories, where volunteer participants come to spend the night. Sleep labs have one or more "bedrooms" in which the subjects retire, usually after being hooked up to a variety of physiological recording devices. In addition to an EEG, these devices typically include an *electromyograph* (*EMG*), **which records muscular activity and tension; an *electrooculograph* (*EOG*), which records eye movements; and**

5.3
Key Learning Goals

- Describe the nightly sleep cycle, and explain how age and culture influence sleep.

- Describe evidence on the effects of sleep deprivation and the health ramifications of sleep loss.

- Identify the symptoms of insomnia, narcolepsy, sleep apnea, somnambulism, and REM sleep behavior disorder.

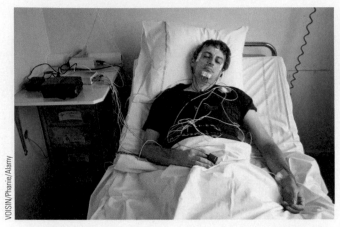

VOISIN/Phanie/Alamy

Researchers in a sleep laboratory can observe subjects while using elaborate equipment to record physiological changes during sleep. This kind of research has disclosed that sleep is a complex series of physical and mental states.

an *electrocardiograph* (*EKG*), which records the contractions of the heart (Keenan & Hirshkowitz, 2011). Other instruments monitor breathing, pulse rate, and body temperature. The researchers observe the sleeping subject through a window (or with a video camera) from an adjacent room, where they also monitor their elaborate physiological recording equipment. It takes most people a night to adapt to the strange bedroom and the recording devices, and to return to their normal mode of sleeping.

Cycling Through the Stages of Sleep

Not only does sleep occur in a context of daily rhythms, but subtler rhythms are evident within the experience of sleep itself. During sleep, people cycle through a series of five distinct stages. Let's take a look at what researchers have learned about the many types of changes that occur during these sleep stages (Carskadon & Dement, 2011; Peigneux et al., 2012).

Stages 1–3

Although it may only take a few minutes, the onset of sleep is gradual, with no obvious transition point between wakefulness and sleep. In laboratory studies, subjects are considered to have fallen asleep when their predominant EEG activity shifts from alpha waves to theta waves. The length of time it takes people to fall asleep varies considerably, but the *average* in a study of more than 35,000 people from ten countries was 25 minutes (Soldatos et al., 2005). This time period depends on quite an array of factors, including how long it has been since you have slept; where you are in your circadian cycle; the amount of noise or light in the sleep environment; and your age, desire to fall asleep, boredom level, recent caffeine or drug intake, and stress level, among other things. In any event, stage 1 is a brief transitional stage of light sleep that usually lasts only 10–12 minutes (Rama, Cho, & Kushida, 2006).

As you descend through stages 2 and 3 of the sleep cycle, your respiration rate, heart rate, muscle tension, and body temperature continue to decline. Stage 2 consists of light sleep and typically lasts about 10–25 minutes. Gradually, your brain waves become higher in amplitude and slower in frequency as you move into stage 3 (see **Figure 5.3**). This stage brings a deep form of sleep that is often referred to as *slow-wave sleep* because low-frequency delta waves become prominent in EEG recordings. Typically, you reach slow-wave sleep in less than an hour and stay there for roughly 20–40 minutes. Then the sleep cycle reverses itself, and you

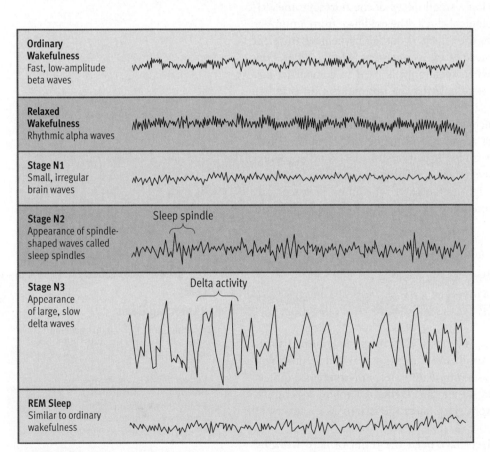

FIGURE 5.3

EEG patterns in sleep and wakefulness. Characteristic brain waves vary depending on one's state of consciousness. Generally, as people move from an awake state through deeper stages of sleep, their brain waves decrease in frequency (cycles per second) and increase in amplitude (height). However, brain waves during REM sleep resemble "wide awake" brain waves.

SOURCE: Adapted from Nevid, J. S. (2012). *Essentials of psychology: Concepts and applications*. Belmont, CA: Wadsworth. Reprinted by permission.

gradually move upward through the lighter stages of sleep. That's when things start to get interesting.

REM Sleep

When you reach what should be stage 1 once again, you usually go into the fourth stage of sleep. This is the stage that is most widely known as *REM sleep. REM* is the abbreviation for *rapid eye movements,* which are prominent during this stage. In a modern sleep lab, researchers use an electrooculograph to monitor these lateral movements, which occur beneath the sleeping person's closed eyelids.

As we discussed at the beginning of the chapter, the discovery of REM sleep was made accidentally in the 1950s (Dement, 2005). The REM stage tends to be a "deep" stage of sleep in the conventional sense that it is relatively hard to awaken a person from it (although arousal thresholds vary during REM). The REM stage is also marked by irregular breathing and pulse rate. Muscle tone is extremely relaxed—so much so that bodily movements are minimal, and the sleeper is virtually paralyzed. Although REM is a relatively deep sleep stage, EEG activity is dominated by high-frequency beta waves that resemble those observed when people are alert and awake (see **Figure 5.3** again).

This paradox is probably related to the association between REM sleep and dreaming. When researchers systematically awaken subjects from various stages of sleep to ask whether they were dreaming, dream reports are notably more likely during the REM stage (McCarley, 1994). Although decades of research have revealed that some dreaming occurs in the non-REM stages, dreaming is more frequent, vivid, memorable, emotional, dramatic, and rich in characters during REM sleep (Nielsen, 2011; Pace-Schott, 2011).

To summarize, **REM sleep is a deep stage of sleep marked by rapid eye movements, high-frequency brain waves, and dreaming.** It is such a special stage of sleep that the other three stages are often characterized as "non-REM sleep." **Non-REM sleep consists of sleep stages 1 through 3, which are marked by an absence of rapid eye movements, relatively little dreaming, and varied EEG activity.** The three non-REM stages are often referred to as N1, N2, and N3, as you can see in **Figure 5.4**.

Repeating the Cycle

During the course of a night, people usually repeat the sleep cycle about four times. As the night wears on, the cycle changes gradually. The first REM period is relatively short, lasting only a few minutes. Subsequent REM periods get progressively longer, peaking at around 40–60 minutes. Additionally, non-REM intervals tend to get shorter. These trends can be seen in **Figure 5.4**, which provides an overview of a typical night's sleep cycle. These trends mean that most slow-wave sleep (N3) occurs early in the sleep cycle, and that REM sleep tends to pile up in the second half of the sleep cycle. Summing across the entire cycle, young adults typically spend about 2%–5% of their sleep time in N1, 45–55% in N2, 15%–20% in slow-wave sleep (N3), and another 20%–25% in REM sleep (Carskadon & Dement, 2011).

What we have described thus far is the big picture—the typical structure of sleep averaged over many people. However, research by Tucker, Dinges, and Van Dongen (2007) showed that the "architecture" of sleep—how quickly one falls asleep, how long one sleeps, how one cycles through the various stages—varies from one person to the next more than sleep researchers previously realized. And these personal variations are pretty stable from one night to the next, meaning that each of us has a signature sleep pattern.

Age, Culture, and Sleep

Now that we have described the basic architecture of sleep, let's take a look at a couple of factors that contribute to variations in patterns of sleeping: age and culture.

REM sleep is not unique to humans. Nearly all mammals and birds exhibit REM sleep. The only known exceptions among warm-blooded vertebrates are dolphins and some whales (Morrison, 2003). Dolphins are particularly interesting because they sleep while swimming, resting one hemisphere of the brain while the other hemisphere remains alert.

FIGURE 5.4

An overview of the cycle of sleep. The white line charts how a typical healthy young adult moves through the various stages of sleep during the course of a night. This diagram also shows how dreams and rapid eye movements tend to coincide with REM sleep, whereas posture changes occur in between REM periods (because the body is nearly paralyzed during REM sleep). Notice how the person cycles into REM four times, as descents into non-REM sleep get shallower and REM periods get longer. Thus, slow-wave sleep is prominent early in the night, while REM sleep dominates the second half of a night's sleep. Although these patterns are typical, keep in mind that sleep patterns vary from one person to another and that they change with age.

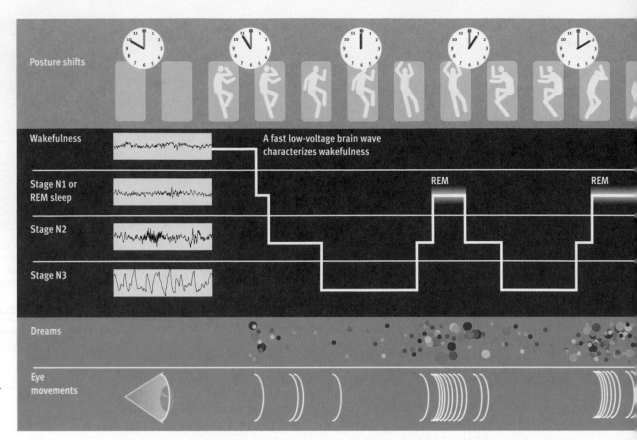

Age Trends

Age alters the sleep cycle. What we have described so far is the typical pattern for young to middle-aged adults. Children, however, display different patterns (Lee & Rosen, 2012). Newborns will sleep six to eight times in a 24-hour period, often exceeding a total of 16 hours of sleep (see **Figure 5.5**). Fortunately for parents, during the first several months, much of this sleep begins to get unified into one particularly long nighttime sleep period (Huber & Tononi, 2009). Interestingly, infants spend much more of their sleep time than adults do in the REM stage. In the first few months, REM accounts for about 50% of babies' sleep, as compared with 20% of adults' sleep. During the remainder of the first year, the REM portion of infants' sleep declines to roughly 30% (Ohayon et al., 2004). The REM portion of sleep continues to decrease gradually until it levels off at about 20% during adolescence (see **Figure 5.5**).

During adulthood, gradual, age-related changes in sleep continue (Bliwise, 2011). The proportion of REM sleep declines slightly in both genders. In males, the percentage of slow-wave sleep declines, and the time spent in stages N1 and N2 increases slightly. These shifts toward lighter sleep are not seen in women, which is perplexing given that elderly women report more insomnia than elderly men do. As **Figure 5.5** shows, the average amount of total sleep time also declines with advancing age.

Cultural Variations

Although age clearly affects the nature and structure of sleep itself, the psychological and physiological experience of sleep does not appear to vary much across cultures. For example, a cross-cultural survey of ten divergent countries (Soldatos et al., 2005) found relatively modest differences in the average amount of time that people sleep, and in the time that it takes for them to fall asleep. That said, a recent poll of people in the United States found some ethnic disparities in subjective estimates of individuals' sleep quality (National Sleep Foundation, 2010). In this poll, whites (20%) and African Americans

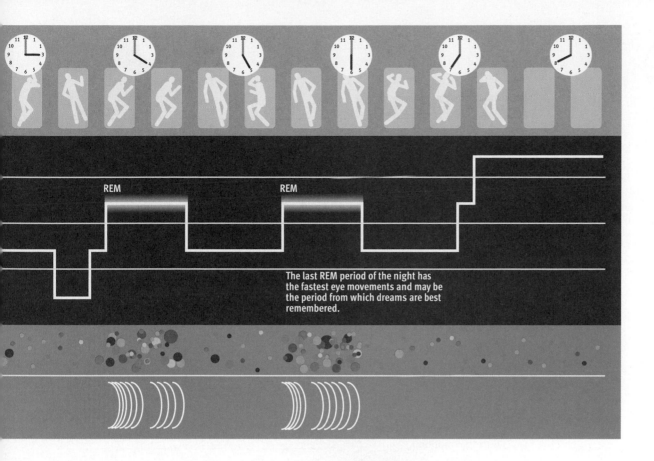

The last REM period of the night has the fastest eye movements and may be the period from which dreams are best remembered.

FIGURE 5.5

Changes in sleep patterns over the life span. Both the total amount of sleep per night and the portion of sleep that is REM sleep change with age. Sleep patterns change most dramatically during infancy, with total sleep time and amount of REM sleep declining sharply in the first 2 years of life. After a noticeable drop in the average amount of sleep in adolescence, sleep patterns remain relatively stable, although total sleep and slow-wave sleep continue to decline gradually with age.

SOURCE: Adapted from an updated revision of a figure in Roffwarg, H. P., Muzio, J. N., & Dement, W. C. (1966). Ontogenetic development of human sleep-dream cycle. *Science, 152,* 604–609. Copyright © 1966 by the American Association for the Advancement of Science. Adapted and revised by permission of the authors.

Comparing REM and NREM Sleep

A table here could have provided you with a systematic comparison of REM sleep and non-REM sleep, but that would have deprived you of the opportunity to check your understanding of these sleep phases by creating your own table. Try to fill in each of the blanks below with a word or phrase highlighting the differences between REM and non-REM sleep with regard to the various characteristics specified. As usual, you can find the answers in Appendix A.

Characteristic	REM sleep	Non-REM sleep
1. Type of EEG activity		
2. Eye movements		
3. Dreaming		
4. Depth (difficulty in awakening)		
5. Percentage of total sleep (in adults)		
6. Increases or decreases (as percentage of sleep) during childhood		
7. Timing in sleep cycle (dominates early or late)		

(18%) were more likely to report that they "rarely" or "never" enjoyed a good night's sleep than were either Hispanics (14%) or Asians (9%).

Napping practices also vary along cultural lines. In many societies, shops close and activities are curtailed in the afternoon to permit people to enjoy a 1- to 2-hour midday nap. These "siesta cultures" are found mostly in tropical regions of the world (Webb & Dinges, 1989). There, this practice is adaptive in that it allows people to avoid working during the hottest part of the day. As a rule, the siesta tradition is not found in cultures where it conflicts with the emphasis on productivity and the philosophy that "time is money."

Doing Without: Sleep Deprivation

Scientific research on sleep deprivation presents something of a paradox. On the one hand, some studies suggest that sleep deprivation is not as detrimental as most people subjectively feel it to be. On the other hand, evidence suggests that sleep deprivation may be a major social problem, undermining efficiency at work and contributing to countless accidents.

Research has mostly focused on *partial sleep deprivation,* or *sleep restriction,* which occurs when people make do with substantially less sleep than normal over a period of time. Many sleep experts believe that much of American society suffers from chronic sleep deprivation (Walsh, Dement, & Dinges, 2011). It appears that more and more people are trying to squeeze additional waking hours out of their days as they attempt to juggle conflicting work, family, household, and school responsibilities. The epidemic of sleep deprivation does not appear to be limited to America; a recent study showed that inadequate sleep is a global problem (Stranges et al., 2012).

How serious are the effects of partial sleep deprivation? The emerging consensus is that sleep restriction has far more negative effects than most people assume. Studies indicate that sleep restriction can impair individuals' attention, reaction time, motor coordination, and decision making and may also have negative effects on endocrine and immune system functioning (Banks & Dinges, 2011). Sleep deprivation has also been blamed for a large proportion of transportation accidents and mishaps in the workplace (Walsh et al., 2011). For example, research suggests that drowsy driving increases accident risk eightfold and is a contributing factor in about 20% of motor vehicle accidents (Philip, Sagaspe, & Taillard, 2011). Unfortunately, research shows that sleep-deprived individuals are not particularly good at predicting if and when they will fall asleep (Kaplan, Itoi, & Dement, 2007). Thus, tired drivers often fail to pull off the road when they should.

The unique quality of REM sleep led researchers to look into the effects of a special type of partial sleep deprivation—*selective deprivation*. In a number of laboratory studies, participants were awakened over a period of nights whenever they began to go into the REM stage. These subjects usually got a decent amount of sleep in non-REM stages, but they were selectively deprived of REM sleep.

Many traffic accidents occur because drivers get drowsy or fall asleep at the wheel. Although the effects of sleep deprivation seem innocuous, sleep loss can be deadly.

What are the effects of REM deprivation? The evidence indicates that it has little impact on daytime functioning and task performance, but it *does* have some interesting effects on subjects' patterns of sleeping (Bonnet, 2005). As the nights go by in REM deprivation studies, it becomes necessary to awaken the participants more and more often to deprive them of their REM sleep, because they spontaneously shift into REM more and more frequently. Whereas most subjects normally go into REM about four times a night, REM-deprived participants start slipping into REM every time the researchers turn around. Furthermore, when a REM-deprivation experiment comes to an end and participants are allowed to sleep without interruption, they experience a "rebound effect." That is, they spend extra time in REM periods for one to three nights to make up for their REM deprivation (Achermann & Borbely, 2011).

Similar results have been observed when subjects have been selectively deprived of slow-wave sleep (Achermann & Borbely, 2011). What do theorists make of these spontaneous pursuits of REM and slow-wave sleep? They conclude that people must have specific *needs* for REM and slow-wave sleep—and rather strong needs, at that.

Why do we need REM and slow-wave sleep? Some influential studies suggest that REM and slow-wave sleep contribute to firming up learning that takes place during the day—a process called *memory consolidation*. Efforts to explore this hypothesis have led to some interesting findings. For example, in one study, participants were given training on a perceptual-motor task and then retested 12 hours later. Those who slept during the 12-hour interval showed substantial *improvement* in performance that was not apparent in participants who did not sleep (Walker et al., 2002). A growing number of similar studies have shown that sleep seems to enhance subjects' memory of specific learning activities that occurred during the day (Nguyen, Tucker, et al., 2013; Payne et al., 2012; Stickgold & Walker, 2013). These studies have found sleep-enhanced recall on a wide range of very different types of memory tasks. The theoretical meaning of these findings is still being debated, but the most widely accepted explanations center on how time spent in specific stages of sleep may stabilize or solidify memories formed during the day (Stickgold & Wamsley, 2011). In addition, recent theorizing on the issue suggests that sleep may also contribute to assimilating new memories into existing networks of knowledge (Stickgold, 2013; Walker, 2012).

Further underscoring the importance of REM sleep, some studies even suggest that REM may promote creative insights related to previous learning (Stickgold & Walker, 2004). In one study, participants worked on a challenging task requiring creativity before and after an opportunity to take a nap or enjoy quiet rest (Cai et al., 2009). The naps were monitored physiologically, and subjects were divided into those who experienced

REM during their nap and those who did not. The REM-sleep group showed dramatic increases in creative performance after the nap that were not seen in the group without REM or the group that engaged in quiet rest.

Another study found that sleep improved performance on a complicated decision-making task that resembled casino gambling (Pace-Schott et al., 2012). The participants who played the game following sleep (rather than a day of waking activities) made more advantageous draws and showed a better understanding of the game. The researchers attributed the sleep-enhanced performance to subjects' opportunity to experience REM sleep. Yet another study found that sleep led to superior performance on difficult verbal insight problems (Sio, Monaghan, & Ormerod, 2013). These studies suggest that the beneficial effects of sleep may not be limited to enhancing memory; sleep may also improve learning and problem solving. Obviously, this conclusion has important implications for students who want to maximize their academic success. Consistent with this conclusion, studies have found modest correlations between sleep duration and measures of academic performance (Dewald et al., 2010). As you might guess, students who sleep less tend to get lower grades. Moreover, a recent study of high school students found that sacrificing sleep in order to fit in additional study can actually backfire, resulting in lower performance on tests, quizzes, and homework (Gillen-O'Neel, Huynh, & Fuligni, 2013).

Sleep Loss and Health

In recent years, researchers have begun to investigate the notion that sleep deprivation might have serious health consequences. Accumulating evidence suggests that sleep loss can affect physiological processes in ways that may undermine physical health. For example, sleep restriction appears to trigger hormonal changes that increase hunger (Shlisky et al., 2012). One study found that just one night of sleep deprivation increased the caloric value of food purchased the next morning by 9% (Chapman et al., 2013). Consistent with these findings, studies have found a link between short sleep duration and increased obesity, which is a risk factor for a variety of health problems (Knutson, 2012). Researchers have also found that sleep loss leads to impaired immune system functioning (Motivala & Irwin, 2007) and increased inflammatory responses (Patel et al., 2009), which are likely to heighten vulnerability to a variety of diseases. Thus, it is not surprising that studies have uncovered links between short sleep duration and an increased risk of diabetes, hypertension, and coronary disease (Grandner et al., 2012, 2014).

These findings have motivated researchers to explore the correlation between habitual sleep time and overall mortality. The results of this research have provided a bit of a surprise. As expected, people who consistently sleep less than 7 hours exhibit an elevated mortality risk, but so do those who routinely sleep *more* than 8 hours. In fact, mortality rates are especially high among those who sleep more than 10 hours (see **Figure 5.6**) (Grandner et al., 2010; Kakizaki et al., 2013). Researchers are now scrambling to figure out why long sleep duration is correlated with elevated mortality. It could be that prolonged sleep is a "marker" for other problems,

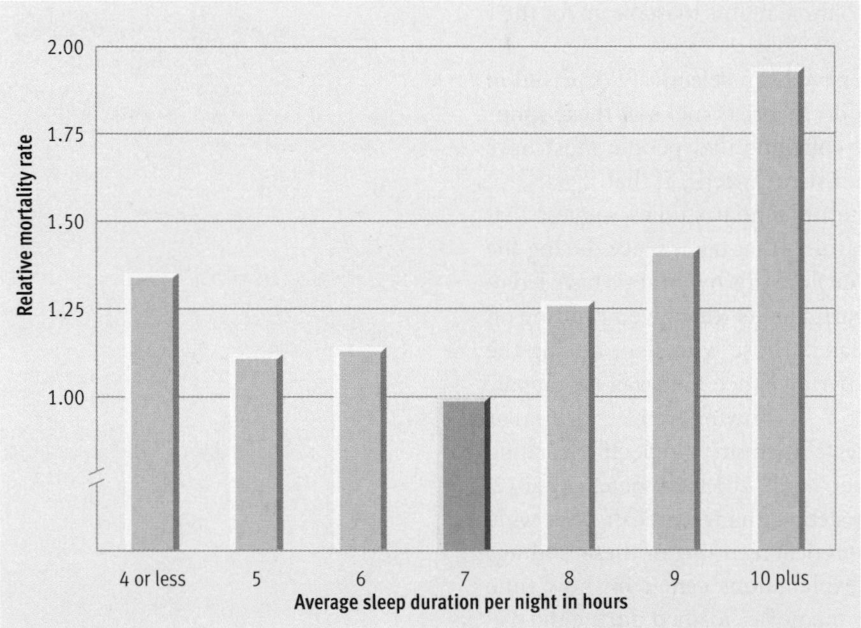

FIGURE 5.6

Mortality rates as a function of typical sleep duration. In a study of over 100,000 subjects followed for 10 years, Tamakoshi et al. (2004) estimated mortality rates in relation to typical sleep duration. The lowest mortality rate was found among those who slept 7 hours, so that figure was arbitrarily set to 1.00 and the mortality rates for other sleep lengths were calculated relative to that baseline. The rates shown here are averaged for males and females. As you can see, higher mortality rates are associated with both shorter sleep durations and longer sleep durations. Mortality rates were especially elevated among those who reported that they slept 10 or more hours per night. (Data from Tamakoshi et al., 2004).

such as depression or a sedentary lifestyle, that have negative effects on health (Patel et al., 2006). Bear in mind, also, that the studies linking typical sleep duration to mortality have depended on participants' *self-report estimates* of how long they normally sleep, and these subjective reports may be inaccurate (Bianchi et al., 2013). In any event, the relationship between sleep duration and health is an emerging area of research that will probably yield some interesting findings in the years to come.

Problems in the Night: Sleep Disorders

Not everyone is able to consistently enjoy the luxury of a good night's sleep. In this section, we briefly discuss what is known about a variety of sleep disorders.

Insomnia

Insomnia is the most common sleep disorder. **Insomnia refers to chronic problems in getting adequate sleep that result in daytime fatigue and impaired functioning.** It occurs in three basic patterns: (1) difficulty in falling asleep initially, (2) difficulty in remaining asleep, and (3) persistent early-morning awakening. Insomnia may sound like a minor problem to those who haven't struggled with it, but it can be a very unpleasant ailment. Moreover, insomnia is associated with reduced productivity; increased absenteeism at work; an elevated risk for accidents, anxiety, and depression; and notable increases in quite a variety of serious health problems, as shown in **Figure 5.7** (Kucharczyk, Morgan, & Hall, 2012; Sivertsen et al., 2014).

How common is insomnia? Nearly everyone suffers occasional sleep difficulties because of stress, disruptions of biological rhythms, or other temporary circumstances. Fortunately, these problems clear up spontaneously for most people. However, studies suggest that about 10% of adults suffer from chronic, serious problems with insomnia, and another 20%–30% report intermittent symptoms of insomnia (Morgan, 2012). The prevalence of insomnia increases with age and is about 50% more common in women than in men (Partinen & Hublin, 2011).

A large portion of people suffering from insomnia do not pursue professional treatment. Many of them probably depend on over-the-counter sleep aids, which have

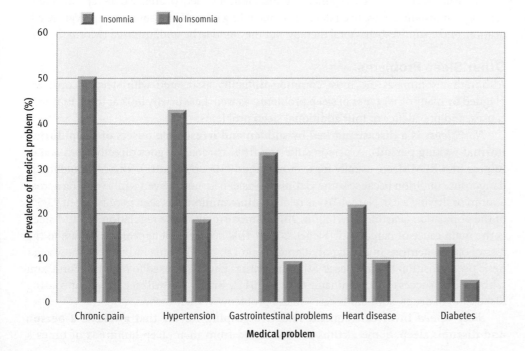

FIGURE 5.7

Insomnia and medical conditions. Insomnia is associated with quite a variety of medical problems. As you can see in this graph, people with insomnia (blue bars) are more likely to suffer from a number of serious medical conditions than people without insomnia (green bars). The causal relations underlying these findings are under investigation. (Based on data from Lichstein et al., 2011).

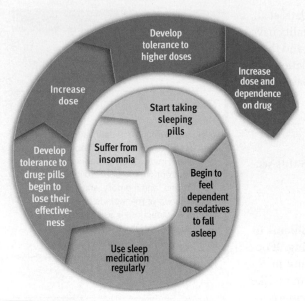

FIGURE 5.8

The vicious circle of dependence on sleeping pills. Because of the body's ability to develop tolerance to drugs, using sedatives routinely to "cure" insomnia can lead to a vicious circle of escalating dependency as larger and larger doses of the sedative are needed to produce the same effect.

questionable value (Mahowald & Schenck, 2005). The most common approach in the medical treatment of insomnia is the prescription of two classes of drugs: *benzodiazepine sedatives* (such as Dalmane, Halcion, and Restoril), which were originally developed to relieve anxiety, and newer *nonbenzodiazepine sedatives* (such as Ambien, Sonata, and Lunesta), which were designed primarily for sleep problems (Mendelson, 2011). Both types of sedative medications are fairly effective in helping people fall asleep more quickly, and they reduce nighttime awakenings and increase total sleep (Walsh & Roth, 2011).

Nonetheless, sedatives can be a problematic long-range solution for insomnia, for a number of reasons. It is possible to overdose on sleeping pills (especially in conjunction with alcohol use), and they have some potential for abuse. Sedatives also have carryover effects that can make people drowsy and sluggish the next day (Walsh & Roth, 2011). Moreover, with continued use, sedatives gradually become less effective, so people need to increase their dose, creating a vicious circle of escalating dependency (Lader, 2002) (see **Figure 5.8**). Another problem is that when people abruptly discontinue their sleep medication, they can experience unpleasant withdrawal symptoms (Lee-Chiong & Sateia, 2006). Fortunately, the newer nonbenzodiazepine sedatives have reduced (but not eliminated) some of the problems associated with earlier generations of sleeping pills (Mendelson, 2011).

The potential risks of sleep medications have been put in sharp focus by studies that report dramatic increases in mortality among those who use sleeping pills. One study of electronic medical records compared 10,529 patients who had received sedative prescriptions against 23,676 matched control cases from the same database (Kripke, Langer, & Kline, 2012). In just 2.5 years, 6.1% of the sedative users died, whereas the death rate among non-users was only 1.2%. Thus, sleep medications were associated with a fivefold increase in mortality in a relatively short time frame! Another study, using a database of more than 104,000 medical records, yielded similar results (Weich et al., 2014). Patients who were prescribed benzodiazepine sedatives exhibited an almost fourfold elevation in mortality over a period of 7.5 years. Although many physicians assert that the problems associated with sleeping pills have been exaggerated (Walsh & Roth, 2011), these surprising findings on mortality rates raise new questions about the safety of sleep medications.

There *are* alternatives to sleep medications. Quite a variety of effective therapeutic interventions for insomnia have been developed, including relaxation training, sleep hygiene education, and cognitive-behavioral therapy, but they tend to be underutilized (Morin, 2011).

Other Sleep Problems

Although insomnia is the most common difficulty associated with sleep, people are plagued by many other types of sleep problems, as well. Let's briefly look at the symptoms, causes, and prevalence of four additional sleep problems.

Narcolepsy **is a disease marked by sudden and irresistible onsets of sleep during normal waking periods.** A person suffering from narcolepsy goes directly from wakefulness into REM sleep, usually for a short period (10–20 minutes). This is a potentially dangerous condition because some victims fall asleep instantly, even while walking across a room or driving a car. Narcolepsy is relatively uncommon; it is seen in only about 0.05% of the population (Partinen & Hublin, 2011). Impairment in the regulation of REM sleep is the main cause of narcolepsy (Siegel, 2011). This impairment appears to be due to the loss of orexin neurons in the hypothalamus (Sakurai, 2013). Some individuals show a genetic predisposition to the disease. Stimulant drugs have been used to treat this condition with modest success (Guilleminault & Cao, 2011). But as you will see in our upcoming discussion of drugs, stimulants carry many problems of their own.

Sleep apnea **involves frequent, reflexive gasping for air that awakens a person and disrupts sleep.** Some victims are awakened from their sleep hundreds of times a night. Apnea occurs when a person literally stops breathing for a minimum of 10 seconds. This disorder, which is usually accompanied by loud snoring, is seen in about 8% of adults, and its prevalence is increasing (Cao, Guilleminault, & Kushida, 2011). A higher incidence is seen among males, older adults, postmenopausal women, obese people, and those with a genetic predisposition to the disease (Redline, 2011; Sanders & Givelber, 2006). As you might expect, sleep apnea can have a disruptive effect on sleep, leading to excessive daytime sleepiness. Sleep apnea is a more serious disorder than widely appreciated because it increases vulnerability to cardiovascular diseases and more than doubles one's overall mortality risk (Kendzerska et al., 2014; Lee, Lee, et al., 2013). Apnea is also associated with declines in attention, memory, and other aspects of cognitive functioning (Weaver

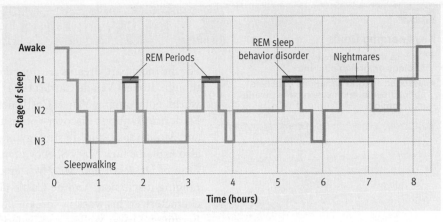

FIGURE 5.9

Sleep problems and the cycle of sleep. Different sleep problems tend to occur at different points in the sleep cycle. Whereas sleepwalking tends to occur during slow-wave sleep, disturbances due to REM-sleep behavior disorder obviously occur during REM periods. Routine nightmares are also associated with the heightened dream activity of REM sleep.

& George, 2011). Apnea may be treated with lifestyle modifications (weight loss, reduced alcohol intake, improved sleep hygiene); drug therapy; special masks and oral devices that improve airflow; and upper airway and craniofacial surgery (Phillips & Kryger, 2011).

Somnambulism, **or sleepwalking, occurs when a person arises and wanders about while remaining asleep.** About 15% of children exhibit sleepwalking (Cartwright, 2006). A survey of a representative sample of more than 19,000 adults in the United States found that 3.6% of adults reported a sleepwalking episode in the last year (Ohayon et al., 2012). A study of a hundred individuals who sought treatment for their somnambulism (and presumably had relatively severe cases) found that 23% had daily episodes of sleepwalking, and 43% had weekly episodes (Lopez et al., 2013). Sleepwalking tends to occur during the first 3 hours of sleep, when individuals are in slow-wave sleep (see **Figure 5.9**) (Zadra & Pilon, 2012). Episodes can last from a minute or 2 up to 30 minutes. Sleepwalkers may awaken during their journey, or they may return to bed without any recollection of their excursion. The causes of this unusual disorder are unknown, although it appears to have a genetic predisposition, and episodes are associated with prior sleep deprivation and increased stress (Lopez et al., 2013). Also, episodes may be more likely in people who use nonbenzodiazepine sedatives, especially Ambien (Gunn & Gunn, 2006). During sleepwalking episodes, some people engage in inappropriate aggressive or sexual behavior. Accidents and injuries are common during sleepwalking, including life-threatening incidents (Zadra & Pilon, 2012). A history of injuries is often what finally motivates people to seek treatment for their somnambulism. For example, the sleepwalkers who sought treatment in the Lopez et al. (2013) study included an individual who had jumped out a third-story window and another who had fallen down a flight of stairs.

REM sleep behavior disorder (RBD) **is marked by potentially troublesome dream enactments during REM periods.** People who exhibit this syndrome may talk, yell, gesture, flail about, or leap out of bed during their REM dreams. When questioned, many report they were being chased or attacked in their dreams. Their dream enactments can get surprisingly violent, and they often hurt themselves or their bed partners (Mahowald & Schenck, 2011). RBD occurs mostly in men, who typically begin experiencing this problem in their 50s or 60s. As noted earlier, people in REM sleep normally are virtually paralyzed, which prevents dream enactments. The cause of RBD appears to be deterioration in the brainstem structures that are normally responsible for immobilization during REM periods (Chen et al., 2013). A majority of people who suffer from RBD eventually go on to develop neurodegenerative disorders, especially Parkinson's disease (Mahowald & Schenck, 2011). The RBD symptoms may precede the emergence of Parkinson's disease by as much as 10 years.

▶ **REALITY CHECK**

Misconception

Sleepwalkers are acting out their dreams, and it is dangerous to awaken them.

Reality

Sleepwalking does not occur in conjunction with dreams. It is not rare for sleepwalkers to hurt themselves. Hence, it's best to awaken people (gently) from a sleepwalking episode. Awakening them is much safer than letting them wander about.

Key Learning Goals

- Discuss the importance of dreams and findings on dream content.
- Describe cultural variations in beliefs about dreams, and explain three theories of dreaming.

5.4 THE WORLD OF DREAMS

For the most part, dreams are not taken very seriously in Western societies. Paradoxically, though, Robert Van de Castle (1994) points out that dreams have sometimes changed the world. For example, Van de Castle describes how René Descartes's philosophy of dualism, Frederick Banting's discovery of insulin, Elias Howe's refinement of the sewing machine, and Mohandas Gandhi's strategy of nonviolent protest were all inspired by dreams. He also explains how Mary Shelley's *Frankenstein* and Robert Louis Stevenson's *The Strange Case of Dr. Jekyll and Mr. Hyde* emerged out of their dream experiences. In his wide-ranging discussion, Van de Castle also relates how the Surrealist painter Salvador Dali characterized his work as "dream photographs," and how legendary filmmakers Ingmar Bergman, Orson Welles, and Federico Fellini all drew on their dreams in making their films. Thus, Van de Castle concludes that "dreams have had a dramatic influence on almost every important aspect of our culture and history" (p. 10).

The Contents of Dreams

What do people dream about? Overall, dreams are not as exciting as advertised. Perhaps dreams are seen as exotic because people are more likely to remember their more bizarre nighttime dramas (De Koninck, 2000). After analyzing the contents of more than 10,000 dreams, Calvin Hall (1966) concluded that most dreams are relatively mundane. They tend to unfold in familiar settings with a cast of characters dominated by family, friends, and colleagues (Zadra & Domhoff, 2011). People *are* more tolerant of logical discrepancies and implausible scenarios in their dreams than in their waking thought (Kahn, 2007), although they generally move through coherent virtual worlds in their dreams. The one nearly universal element of dreams is a stable, coherent sense of self—people almost always experience dreams from a first-person perspective (Valli & Revonsuo, 2009).

Certain themes tend to be more common than others. **Figure 5.10** lists the most common dream themes reported by 1181 college students in one study of typical dream content (Nielsen et al., 2003). If you glance through this list, you will notice that people dream quite a bit about sex, aggression, and misfortune. As you can see, people often dream about negative and potentially traumatic events, including being killed. However, the notion that a traumatic dream could be fatal is nonsense. Hall (1966) was struck by how little people dream about public affairs and current events. Typically, dreams are self-centered; people dream mostly about themselves.

Though dreams seem to belong in a world of their own, what people dream about is affected by what is going on in their lives (Wamsley & Stickgold, 2009). If you're struggling with financial problems, worried about an upcoming exam, or sexually attracted to a classmate, these themes may very well show up in your dreams. Freud noticed long ago that the contents of waking life tend to spill into dreams. He labeled this spillover the *day residue*. Events that have emotional significance are especially likely to be incorporated into one's dreams (Malinowski & Horton, 2014).

On occasion, the contents of dreams can also be affected by external stimuli experienced while one is dreaming (De Koninck, 2000). For example, William Dement sprayed water on one hand of sleeping subjects while they were in the REM stage (Dement & Wolpert, 1958). Subjects who weren't awakened by the water were roused by the experimenter a short time later and asked what they had been dreaming about. Dement found that 42% of the participants had incorporated the water into their dreams. They said they had dreamed they were in rainfalls, floods, baths, swimming pools, and the like. Some people report that they occasionally experience the same phenomenon at home when the sound of their alarm clock fails to awaken them. The alarm is incorporated into their dream as a loud engine or a siren, for instance.

Rank	Dream content	Total prevalence
1	Chased or pursued, not physically injured	81.5%
2	Sexual experiences	76.5
3	Falling	73.8
4	School, teachers, studying	67.1
5	Arriving too late, e.g., missing a train	59.5
6	Being on the verge of falling	57.7
7	A person now alive as dead	54.1
8	Trying again and again to do something	53.5
9	Flying or soaring through the air	48.3
10	Vividly sensing . . . a presence in the room	48.3
11	Failing an examination	45.0
12	Physically attacked (beaten, stabbed, raped)	42.4
13	Being frozen with fright	40.7
14	A person now dead as alive	38.4
15	Being a child again	36.7
16	Being killed	34.5
17	Swimming	34.3
18	Insects or spiders	33.8
19	Being nude	32.6
20	Being inappropriately dressed	32.5
21	Discovering a new room at home	32.3
22	Losing control of a vehicle	32.0
23	Eating delicious foods	30.7
24	Being half awake and paralyzed in bed	27.2
25	Finding money	25.7

FIGURE 5.10

Common themes in dreams. Studies of dream content find that certain themes are particularly common. The data shown here are from a study of 1181 college students in Canada (Nielsen et al., 2003). This list shows the twenty-five dreams most frequently reported by the students. Total prevalence refers to the percentage of students reporting each dream.

SOURCE: Nielsen, T. A., Zadra, A. L., Simard, V., Saucier, S., Stenstrom, P., Smith, C., & Kuiken, D. (2003). The typical dreams of Canadian university students. *Dreaming, 13,* 211–235. Copyright © 2003 Association for the Study of Dreams. [from Table 1, p. 217]

Culture and Dreams

Striking cross-cultural variations occur in beliefs about the nature of dreams and the importance attributed to them (Lohmann, 2007). In modern Western society, we typically make a distinction between the "real" world we experience while awake and the "imaginary" world we experience while dreaming. Some people realize that events in the real world can affect their dreams, but few believe that events in their dreams hold any significance for their waking life. Although a small minority of individuals take their dreams seriously, dreams are largely written off in Western cultures as insignificant and meaningless (Tart, 1988).

In many non-Western cultures, however, dreams are viewed as important sources of information about oneself, the future, or the spiritual world (Kracke, 1991). Although no culture confuses dreams with waking reality, many view events in dreams as another type of reality that may be just as important as, or perhaps even more important than, events experienced while awake. In some instances, people are even held responsible for their dream actions. Among the New Guinea Arapesh, for example, an erotic dream about someone may be viewed as the equivalent of an adulterous act. In many cultures, dreams are seen as a window into the spiritual world, permitting communication with ancestors or supernatural beings (Bourguignon, 1972). People in some cultures believe that dreams provide information about the future—good or bad omens about upcoming battles, hunts, births, and so forth (Tedlock, 1992).

In regard to dream content, both similarities and differences occur across cultures in the types of dreams that people report (Domhoff, 2005b). Some basic dream themes appear to be nearly universal (falling, being pursued, having sex). However, the contents of dreams vary some from one culture to another because people in different societies deal with different worlds while awake.

Theories of Dreaming

Many theories have been proposed to explain the purposes of dreaming (see **Figure 5.11**). Sigmund Freud (1900), who analyzed clients' dreams in therapy, believed that the principal purpose of dreams is *wish fulfillment*. He thought that people fulfill unmet needs from waking hours through wishful thinking in dreams. For example, if you were feeling unconscious guilt about being rude to a friend, you might dream about the incident in a way that renders you blameless. Freud asserted that the wish-fulfilling quality of many dreams may not be obvious because the unconscious attempts to censor and disguise the true meaning of dreams. Freud's influential theory sounded plausible when it was proposed more than 100 years ago, but research has not provided much support for Freud's conception of dreaming (Fisher & Greenberg, 1996). Nonetheless, Freud's view remains popular among many people. One study found that a substantial majority of people from three very different cultures endorsed the Freudian notion that dreams contain hidden truths (Morewedge & Norton, 2009).

Other theorists, such as Rosalind Cartwright, have proposed that dreams provide an opportunity to work through everyday problems and emotional issues (Cartwright, 2011; Cartwright & Lamberg, 1992). According to her *problem-solving/mood-regulation view*, dreams allow people to reflect on recent emotional experiences and regulate their emotional tone. She asserts that dreaming contributes to improvements in mood when people awaken. Proponents of this view believe that dreams allow people to engage in creative thinking about problems because dreams are not restrained by logic or realism. Research showing that REM sleep can enhance learning has added new credibility to the problem-solving view of dreams (Cartwright, 2004).

J. Allan Hobson and colleagues argue that dreams are simply the by-product of bursts of activity emanating from subcortical areas in the brain. Their *activation-synthesis model* (Hobson & McCarley, 1977; McCarley, 1994) and its more recent revisions (Hobson,

FIGURE 5.11

Three theories of dreaming. Dreams can be explained in a variety of ways. Freud stressed the wish-fulfilling function of dreams. Cartwright emphasizes the problem-solving function of dreams. Hobson asserts that dreams are merely a by-product of periodic neural activation. All three theories are speculative and have their critics.

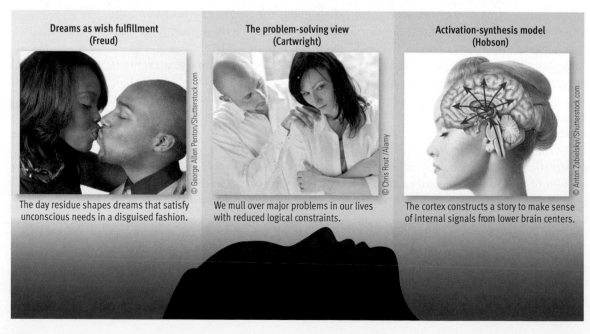

Dreams as wish fulfillment (Freud)
The day residue shapes dreams that satisfy unconscious needs in a disguised fashion.

The problem-solving view (Cartwright)
We mull over major problems in our lives with reduced logical constraints.

Activation-synthesis model (Hobson)
The cortex constructs a story to make sense of internal signals from lower brain centers.

2007) propose that dreams are *side effects* of the neural activation that produces the beta brain waves during REM sleep that are associated with wakefulness. According to this model, neurons firing periodically in lower brain centers (especially the pons) send random signals to the cortex (the seat of complex thought). The cortex supposedly synthesizes (constructs) a dream to make sense out of these signals. In contrast with the theories of Freud and Cartwright, this theory obviously downplays the role of emotional factors as determinants of dreams. Like other theories of dreams, the activation-synthesis model has its share of critics. They point out that the model has a hard time explaining the fact that dreaming occurs outside REM sleep, that damage to the pons does not eliminate dreaming, and that the contents of dreams are considerably more meaningful than the model would predict (Domhoff, 2005a).

5.5 Hypnosis: Altered Consciousness or Role Playing?

5.5
Key Learning Goals
- Discuss hypnotic susceptibility, and list some prominent effects of hypnosis.
- Compare the role-playing and altered-state theories of hypnosis.

Hypnosis has a long and checkered history. It all began with a flamboyant 18th-century Austrian by the name of Franz Anton Mesmer (Pintar, 2010). Working in Paris, Mesmer claimed to cure people of illnesses through an elaborate routine involving a "laying on of hands." Mesmer had some complicated theories about how he had harnessed "animal magnetism." However, we know today that he had simply stumbled onto the power of suggestion (Green, Laurence, & Lynn, 2014). Eventually, he was dismissed as a charlatan and run out of town by the local authorities. Although officially discredited, Mesmer inspired followers—practitioners of "mesmerism"—who continued to ply their trade. To this day, our language preserves the memory of Franz Mesmer: when we are under the spell of an event or a story, we are "mesmerized."

A Scottish physician, James Braid, became interested in the trancelike state that could be induced by the mesmerists. It was Braid who popularized the term *hypnotism* in 1843, borrowing it from the Greek word for sleep (Pintar, 2010). Braid thought that hypnotism could be used to produce anesthesia for surgeries. However, just as hypnosis was catching on as a general anesthetic, more powerful and reliable chemical anesthetics were discovered. Interest in hypnotism then dwindled.

Since then, hypnotism has led a curious dual existence. On the one hand, it has been the subject of numerous scientific studies. Furthermore, it has enjoyed considerable use as a clinical tool by physicians, dentists, and psychologists for more than a century and has empirically supported value in the treatment of a variety of psychological and physical ailments (Green et al., 2014). On the other hand, an assortment of entertainers and quacks have continued in the less respectable tradition of mesmerism, using hypnotism for parlor tricks and chicanery.

Hypnotic Induction and Phenomena

Hypnosis **is a systematic procedure that typically produces a heightened state of suggestibility.** It may also lead to passive relaxation, narrowed attention, and enhanced fantasy. If only in popular films, virtually everyone has seen a *hypnotic induction* enacted with a swinging pendulum. Actually, many techniques can be used (Gibbons & Lynn, 2010). Usually, the hypnotist suggests to the subject that he or she is relaxing. Repetitively, softly, subjects are told that they are getting tired, drowsy, or sleepy. Often, the hypnotist vividly describes bodily sensations that should be occurring. Subjects are told that their arms are going limp, that their feet are getting warm, that their eyelids are getting heavy. Gradually, most subjects succumb and become hypnotized.

People differ in how well they respond to hypnotic induction. About 10%–20% of people don't respond well at all. At the other end of the continuum, about 15% of people are exceptionally good hypnotic subjects (Barnier, Cox, & McConkey, 2014). Many interesting effects can be produced in people who are susceptible to hypnosis. Some of the more prominent hypnotic phenomena include:

1. *Anesthesia.* Drugs are more reliable, but hypnosis can be surprisingly effective in the treatment of both acute and chronic pain (Boly et al., 2007; Jensen & Patterson, 2014). Although the practice is not widespread, some physicians, dentists, and psychologists use hypnosis as a treatment for problems with pain, especially chronic pain.

2. *Sensory distortions and hallucinations.* Hypnotized subjects may be led to experience auditory or visual hallucinations (Spiegel, 2003b). They may hear sounds or see things that are not there, or fail to hear or see stimuli that are present (Spiegel et al., 1985). Subjects may also have their sensations distorted so that something sweet tastes sour or an unpleasant odor smells fragrant.

3. *Disinhibition.* Hypnosis can sometimes reduce inhibitions that would normally prevent subjects from acting in ways they would see as immoral or unacceptable. In experiments, hypnotized subjects have been induced to throw what they believed to be nitric acid into the face of a research assistant. Similarly, stage hypnotists are sometimes successful in getting people to disrobe in public. This disinhibition effect may occur simply because hypnotized people feel that they cannot be held responsible for actions taken while hypnotized.

4. *Posthypnotic suggestions and amnesia.* Suggestions made during hypnosis may influence a participant's later behavior (Cox & Bryant, 2008). The most common posthypnotic suggestion is the creation of posthypnotic amnesia. That is, subjects who are told that they will remember nothing that happened while they were hypnotized do indeed usually remember nothing.

Theories of Hypnosis

Although a number of theories have been developed to explain hypnosis, it is still not well understood. One popular view is that hypnotic effects occur because participants are put into a special, altered state of consciousness, called a *hypnotic trance* (Christiansen, 2005). Although hypnotized subjects may feel as though they are in an altered state, they do not seem to show reliable alterations in brain activity that are unique to hypnosis (Burgess, 2007; Lynn et al., 2007). The failure to find changes in brain activity that are consistently associated with hypnosis has led some theorists to conclude that hypnosis is a normal state of consciousness that is characterized by dramatic role playing.

Hypnosis as Role Playing

The role-playing view asserts that hypnosis produces a normal mental state in which suggestible people act out the role of a hypnotic subject and behave as they think hypnotized people are supposed to (Kirsch, 2000; Spanos, 1991). According to this notion, it is subjects' *role expectations* that produce hypnotic effects, rather than a special, trancelike state of consciousness.

Two lines of evidence support the role-playing view. First, many of the seemingly amazing effects of hypnosis have been duplicated by nonhypnotized subjects or have been shown to be exaggerated (Kirsch, Mazzoni, & Montgomery, 2007). This finding suggests that no special state of consciousness is required to explain hypnotic feats.

The second line of evidence involves demonstrations that hypnotized participants are often acting out a role. For example, Martin Orne (1951) regressed hypnotized subjects back to their sixth birthday and asked them to describe it. They responded with detailed descriptions that appeared to represent great feats of hypnosis-enhanced memory.

However, instead of accepting this information at face value, Orne compared it with information he had obtained from the participants' parents. It turned out that many of the subjects' memories were inaccurate and invented! Many other studies have also found that age-regressed subjects' recall of the distant past tends to be more fanciful than factual (Green, 1999). Thus, the role-playing explanation of hypnosis suggests that situational factors lead suggestible subjects to act out a certain role in a highly cooperative manner (Lynn, Kirsch, & Hallquist, 2008; Wagstaff et al., 2010).

Hypnosis as an Altered State of Consciousness

Despite the doubts raised by role-playing explanations, many prominent theorists still maintain that hypnotic effects are attributable to a special, altered state of consciousness (Naish, 2006; Spiegel, 2003a; Woody & Sadler, 2008). These theorists argue that it is doubtful that role playing can explain all hypnotic phenomena. For instance, they assert that even the most cooperative subjects are unlikely to endure surgery without a drug anesthetic just to please their physician and live up to their expected role. They also cite studies in which hypnotized participants have continued to display hypnotic responses when they thought they were alone and not being observed (Perugini et al., 1998). If hypnotized participants were merely acting, they would drop the act when alone.

The most influential explanation of hypnosis as an altered state of awareness has been offered by Ernest Hilgard (1986, 1992). According to Hilgard, hypnosis creates a *dissociation* in consciousness. **Dissociation is a splitting off of mental processes into two separate, simultaneous streams of awareness.** In other words, Hilgard theorizes that hypnosis splits consciousness into two streams: one stream is in communication with the hypnotist and the external world, while the other is a difficult-to-detect "hidden observer." Hilgard believes that many hypnotic effects are a product of this divided consciousness. For instance, he suggests that a hypnotized subject might appear unresponsive to pain because the pain isn't registered in the portion of consciousness that communicates with other people.

One appealing aspect of Hilgard's theory is that *divided consciousness* is a common, normal experience. For example, people will often drive a car a great distance, responding to traffic signals and other cars, with no recollection of having consciously done those specific actions. In such cases, consciousness is clearly divided between driving and the person's thoughts about other matters. Interestingly, this common experience has long been known as *highway hypnosis*. In summary, Hilgard presents hypnosis as a plausible variation in consciousness that has continuity with everyday experience.

A resolution to the debate about whether hypnosis involves an altered state of consciousness does not appear imminent. The issue continues to generate insightful research that enhances our understanding of hypnosis, but the results remain equivocal and open to varied interpretations (Accardi et al., 2013; Mazzoni et al., 2013).

▶ **REALITY CHECK**

Misconception

Under hypnosis, people can perform feats they could never perform otherwise.

Reality

Stage hypnotists make their living by getting people to do things that appear out of the ordinary. For example, much has been made of the fact that hypnotized subjects can be used as "human planks" (see the photo below). However, it turns out that nonhypnotized subjects can match this feat. Research suggests that all the phenomena produced in hypnosis can also be produced by suggestion without hypnosis.

imago stock&people/imago/PanoramiC/Newscom

5.6 MEDITATION: PURSUING HIGHER CONSCIOUSNESS

5.6

Key Learning Goals

- Explain the nature of meditation, and describe the two main styles of meditation.
- Assess the evidence of the long-term benefits of meditation.

Recent years have seen growing interest in the ancient discipline of meditation. *Meditation* **refers to a family of practices that train attention to heighten awareness and bring mental processes under greater voluntary control.** In North America, the most widely practiced approaches to meditation are those associated with yoga, Zen, and transcendental meditation (TM). All three are rooted in Eastern religions (Hinduism, Buddhism, and Taoism). However, meditation has been practiced throughout history as an element of all religious and spiritual traditions, including Judaism and Christianity (Walsh & Shapiro, 2006). Moreover, the practice of meditation can be largely divorced

Although there are many approaches to meditation, they all involve bringing one's cognitive processes under greater self-control. Research suggests that this mental self-discipline can yield a variety of benefits, especially when it comes to dealing with stress.

from religious beliefs. In fact, most Americans who meditate have only vague ideas regarding its religious significance. Of interest to psychology is the fact that meditation involves a deliberate effort to alter consciousness.

Approaches to meditation can be classified into two main styles that reflect how attention is directed: *focused attention* and *open monitoring* (Cahn & Polich, 2006; Manna et al., 2010). In focused attention approaches, attention is concentrated on a specific object, image, sound, or bodily sensation (such as breathing). The intent in narrowing attention is to clear the mind of its clutter. In open monitoring approaches, attention is directed to the contents of one's moment-to-moment experience in a nonjudgmental and nonreactive way. The intent in expanding attention is to become a detached observer of the flow of one's own sensations, thoughts, and feelings. Both approaches seek to achieve a "higher" form of consciousness than what people normally experience. The meditative disciplines that have received the most research attention are TM and mindfulness meditation. Mindfulness meditation is an open monitoring approach with roots in Zen Buddhism, whereas TM is primarily a focused attention approach with roots in Hinduism.

What are the findings on the long-term benefits of meditation? One intriguing finding is that alpha waves become more prominent in EEG recordings (Cahn & Polich, 2006), indicating that meditation is associated with relaxation. Consistent with this finding, research suggests that meditation may have some value in reducing the effects of stress. In particular, regular meditation is associated with lower levels of some "stress hormones" (Infante et al., 2001); enhanced immune response (Davidson et al., 2003a); and reduced inflammation (Rosenkranz et al., 2013). Studies also suggest that meditation can lead to decreases in anxiety and other negative emotions, and to increases in empathy for others and in general well-being (Sedlmeier et al., 2012). Meditation has shown some value as an adjunct in the treatment of depression, anxiety disorders, and chronic pain (Goyal et al., 2014; Marchand, 2013). In the physiological domain, research has suggested that meditation may promote improved cardiovascular health (Schneider et al., 2012) and enhance patterns of sleep (Pattanashetty et al., 2010). Finally, although more difficult to measure, some theorists assert that meditation can enhance human potential by improving concentration, heightening awareness, and building emotional resilience (Walsh & Shapiro, 2006). At first glance, these results are impressive, but critics wonder whether placebo effects, sampling bias, and other methodological problems may have exaggerated some of the reported benefits of meditation (Canter, 2003; Caspi & Burleson, 2005; Ireland, 2012).

That said, the quality of meditation research appears to be improving, and recent years have brought some eye-opening findings. For example, a number of experiments have demonstrated that meditation can increase the tolerance of pain, which could have important implications for the management of a variety of health problems (Grant et al., 2010; Zeidan et al., 2010). Grant and Rainville (2009) compared the pain sensitivity of thirteen experienced Zen meditators and thirteen comparable non-meditators. Carefully controlled pain was administered by applying a heating plate to participants' calves. The meditators were able to handle considerably more pain than were the non-meditators. Moreover, a follow-up study suggested that the meditators' greater pain tolerance was associated with increased thickness in brain regions that register pain (Grant et al., 2010). In other words, it appeared that meditation

CONCEPT CHECK 5.2

Relating EEG Activity to Variations in Consciousness

Early in the chapter, we emphasized the intimate relationship between brain activity and variations in consciousness. Check your understanding of this relationship by indicating the kind of EEG activity (alpha, beta, theta, or delta) that would probably be dominant in each of the following situations. The answers are in Appendix A.

_____ 1. You are playing a video game.

_____ 2. You are deep in meditation.

_____ 3. You have just fallen asleep.

_____ 4. You are in the midst of a pleasant dream.

_____ 5. You are a novice typist, practicing your typing.

experience had produced enduring alterations in brain structure that were responsible for meditators' increased pain tolerance. Other studies have found that meditation is associated with long-term changes in brain structure (Kang et al., 2013; Luders et al., 2013). Clearly, a great deal of additional research is needed, but these thought-provoking findings would seem to undermine the idea that meditation is nothing more than relaxation.

5.7 ALTERING CONSCIOUSNESS WITH DRUGS

5.7

Key Learning Goals

- Identify the major types of abused drugs and their main effects.
- Understand why drug effects vary, how drugs affect the brain, and drug dependence.
- Summarize evidence of the major health risks associated with drug abuse.

Like hypnosis and meditation, drugs are commonly used in deliberate efforts to alter consciousness. In this section, we focus on the use of drugs for nonmedical purposes, commonly referred to as "recreational drug use." Such drug use involves personal, moral, political, and legal issues that are not matters for science to resolve. However, the more knowledgeable you are about drugs, the more informed your decisions and opinions about them will be. Accordingly, this section describes the types of drugs that are most commonly used for recreational purposes and summarizes their effects on consciousness, behavior, and health.

Principal Abused Drugs and Their Effects

The drugs that people use recreationally are termed *psychoactive*. **Psychoactive drugs are chemical substances that modify mental, emotional, or behavioral functioning.** Not all psychoactive drugs produce effects that lead to recreational use. Generally, users prefer drugs that elevate their mood or produce other pleasurable alterations in consciousness. The principal types of recreational drugs are described in **Table 5.2**. The table

TABLE 5.2 Psychoactive Drugs: Medical Uses and Effects

Drugs	Principal Medical Uses	Desired Effects	Potential Short-Term Side Effects
Narcotics (opiates) Morphine Heroin Oxycodone	Pain relief	Euphoria, relaxation, anxiety reduction, pain relief	Lethargy, drowsiness, nausea, impaired coordination, impaired mental functioning, constipation
Sedatives Barbiturates (e.g., Seconal) Nonbarbiturates (e.g., Quaalude)	Sleeping pill, anticonvulsant	Euphoria, relaxation, anxiety reduction, reduced inhibitions	Lethargy, drowsiness, severely impaired coordination, impaired mental functioning, emotional swings, dejection
Stimulants Amphetamines Cocaine	Treatment of hyperactivity and narcolepsy, local anesthetic (cocaine only)	Elation, excitement, increased alertness, increased energy, reduced fatigue	Increased blood pressure and heart rate, increased talkativeness, restlessness, irritability, insomnia, reduced appetite, increased sweating and urination, anxiety, paranoia, increased aggressiveness, panic
Hallucinogens LSD Mescaline Psilocybin	None	Increased sensory awareness, euphoria, altered perceptions, hallucinations, insightful experiences	Dilated pupils, nausea, emotional swings, paranoia, jumbled thought processes, impaired judgment, anxiety, panic reaction
Cannabis Marijuana Hashish THC	Treatment of glaucoma and chemotherapy-induced nausea and vomiting; other uses under study	Mild euphoria, relaxation, altered perceptions, enhanced awareness	Elevated heart rate, bloodshot eyes, dry mouth, reduced short-term memory, sluggish motor coordination, sluggish mental functioning, anxiety
Alcohol	None	Mild euphoria, relaxation, anxiety reduction, reduced inhibitions	Severely impaired coordination, impaired mental functioning, increased urination, emotional swings, depression, quarrelsomeness, hangover

lists representative drugs in each of six categories. It also summarizes the drugs' medical uses, their effects on consciousness, and their common side effects (based on Levinthal, 2014; Ruiz & Strain, 2011). The six categories of psychoactive drugs that we will focus on are narcotics, sedatives, stimulants, hallucinogens, cannabis, and alcohol.

Narcotics, or *opiates,* **are drugs derived from opium that are capable of relieving pain.** The main drugs in this category are heroin and morphine, although less potent opiates—such as codeine, Demerol, and methadone—are also abused. The emerging problem in this category has been a relatively new drug called *oxycodone* (trade name OxyContin). Its time-release format was supposed to make it an effective analgesic with less potential for abuse than the other opiates. But people quickly learned that they could grind it up and snort or inject it for a powerful high. This trend has led to a new epidemic of serious drug abuse, especially in rural areas of the United States (Young & Havens, 2012). The drug was reformulated in 2010 to make it more difficult to manipulate, and abuse of OxyContin has declined considerably (Havens et al., 2014). In sufficient dosages, the drugs in this category can produce an overwhelming sense of euphoria or well-being. This euphoric effect has a relaxing, "Who cares?" quality that makes the high an attractive escape from reality.

Sedatives **are sleep-inducing drugs that tend to decrease central nervous system activation and behavioral activity.** Historically, the most widely abused sedatives have been the *barbiturates.* But in recent decades stricter controls have reduced their availability and people have turned to the *benzodiazepine* sedatives—which, fortunately, have notably less appeal as a drug of abuse. People abusing sedatives, or "downers," generally consume larger doses than are prescribed for medical purposes. The desired effect is a euphoria similar to that produced by drinking large amounts of alcohol. Feelings of tension or dejection are replaced by a relaxed, pleasant state of intoxication, accompanied by loosened inhibitions.

Stimulants **are drugs that tend to increase central nervous system activation and behavioral activity.** Stimulants range from mild, widely available drugs, such as caffeine and nicotine, to stronger, carefully regulated ones, such as cocaine and amphetamines. We will focus on cocaine and amphetamines. Cocaine is a natural substance that comes from the coca shrub. In contrast, amphetamines ("speed") are synthesized in a pharmaceutical laboratory. Cocaine and amphetamines have fairly similar effects, except that cocaine produces a briefer high. Stimulants produce a euphoria very different from that created by narcotics or sedatives. They produce a buoyant, elated, energetic, "I can conquer the world!" feeling, accompanied by increased alertness. In recent years, cocaine and amphetamines have become available in much more potent (and dangerous) forms than before. "Crack" consists of relatively pure chips of cocaine that are usually smoked. Amphetamines are increasingly sold as a crystalline powder—called "crank" or "crystal meth" (short for methamphetamine)—that may be snorted or injected intravenously.

Hallucinogens **are a diverse group of drugs that have powerful effects on mental and emotional functioning, marked most notably by distortions in sensory and perceptual experience.** The principal hallucinogens are LSD, mescaline, and psilocybin. These drugs have similar effects, although they vary in potency. Hallucinogens produce euphoria, increased sensory awareness, and a distorted sense of time. In some users, they lead to profound, dreamlike, "mystical" feelings that are difficult to describe. The latter effect is why they have been used in religious ceremonies for centuries in some cultures. Unfortunately, at the other end of the emotional spectrum, hallucinogens can also produce nightmarish feelings of anxiety and paranoia, commonly called a "bad trip."

Cannabis **is the hemp plant from which marijuana, hashish, and THC are derived.** Marijuana is a mixture of dried leaves, flowers, stems, and seeds taken from the plant, while hashish comes from the plant's resin. Smoking is the usual route of ingestion for both marijuana and hashish. THC, the active chemical ingredient in cannabis, can be synthesized for research purposes (for example, to give to animals, who can't very well smoke marijuana). When smoked, cannabis has an immediate impact that may last several hours. The desired effects of the drug are a mild, relaxed euphoria and enhanced sensory awareness.

Alcohol encompasses a variety of beverages containing ethyl alcohol, such as beers, wines, and distilled spirits. The concentration of ethyl alcohol varies from about 4% in most beers to 40% in 80-proof liquor—and occasionally more in higher-proof liquors. When people drink heavily, the central effect is a relaxed euphoria that temporarily boosts self-esteem, as problems seem to melt away and inhibitions diminish. Common side effects include impairments in mental and motor functioning, mood swings, and quarrelsomeness. Alcohol is the most widely used recreational drug in our society. Because alcohol is legal, many people use it casually without even thinking of it as a drug.

Excessive drinking is a particularly prevalent problem on college campuses. Researchers from the Harvard School of Public Health (Wechsler et al., 2002) surveyed nearly 11,000 undergraduates at 119 schools and found that 81% of the students drank. Moreover, 49% of the men and 41% of the women reported that they engage in binge drinking with the intention of getting drunk. A follow-up survey at eighteen of the original 119 colleges found that levels of binge drinking remained quite high (Nelson et al. 2009). With their inhibitions released, some drinkers become argumentative and prone to aggression. In the Harvard survey, 29% of the students who did *not* engage in binge drinking reported that they had been insulted or humiliated by a drunken student; 19% had experienced serious arguments; 9% had been pushed, hit, or assaulted; and 19.5% had been the target of unwanted sexual advances (Wechsler et al., 2002). Worse yet, alcohol appears to contribute to about 90% of student rapes and 95% of violent crimes on campus. Alcohol can also contribute to reckless sexual behavior. In the Harvard survey, 21% of students who drank reported that they had unplanned sex as a result of drinking, and 10% indicated that their drinking had led to unprotected sex. Yet another problem is that the brain is still maturing during adolescence, making it particularly vulnerable to the negative effects of alcohol. Thus, recent studies have found that binge drinking may impair neural functioning in the adolescent brain (Lisdahl et al., 2013; Lopez-Caneda et al., 2014).

Overindulging in alcohol is particularly common among college students and young people in general. Because it is legal, people often don't think of alcohol as a drug, but if you look at the health risks in **Table 5.3**, it is apparent that alcohol can have very damaging effects on one's health.

Factors Influencing Drug Effects

The drug effects summarized in **Table 5.2** are the *typical* ones. Drug effects can vary from person to person and even for the same person in different situations. The impact of any drug depends in part on the user's age, mood, motivation, personality, previous experience with the drug, body weight, and physiology. The dose and potency of a drug, the method of intake, and the setting in which a drug is taken are also likely to influence its effects (Leavitt, 1995). Our theme of *multifactorial causation* clearly applies to the effects of drugs.

So, too, does our theme emphasizing the *subjectivity of experience*. Expectations are potentially powerful factors that can influence the user's perceptions of a drug's effects. You may recall from the discussion of placebo effects in Chapter 2 that some people who are misled to *think* that they are drinking alcohol show signs of intoxication (Assefi & Garry, 2003). If people expect a drug to make them feel giddy, serene, or profound, their expectation may contribute to the feelings they experience.

A drug's effects can also change as the person's body develops a *tolerance* to the chemical. *Tolerance* **refers to a progressive decrease in a person's responsiveness to a drug as a result of continued use.** Tolerance usually leads people to consume larger and larger doses of a drug to attain the effects they desire. Most drugs produce tolerance, but some do so more rapidly than others. For example, tolerance to alcohol usually builds slowly, while tolerance to heroin increases much more quickly. **Table 5.3** indicates whether various categories of drugs tend to produce tolerance rapidly or gradually.

TABLE 5.3 Psychoactive Drugs: Tolerance, Dependence, and Health Risks

Drugs	Tolerance	Risk of Physical Dependence	Risk of Psychological Dependence	Health Risks
Narcotics (opiates)	Rapid	High	High	Infectious diseases, accidents, immune suppression, overdose
Sedatives	Rapid	High	High	Accidents, overdose
Stimulants	Rapid	Moderate	High	Sleep problems, malnutrition, nasal damage, hypertension, respiratory disease, stroke, liver disease, heart attack, overdose
Hallucinogens	Gradual	None	Very low	Accidents, acute panic
Cannabis	Gradual	None	Low to moderate	Accidents, lung cancer, respiratory disease, pulmonary disease, increased vulnerability to psychosis, cognitive deficits
Alcohol	Gradual	Moderate	Moderate	Accidents, liver disease, malnutrition, brain damage, neurological disorders, heart disease, stroke, hypertension, ulcers, cancer, birth defects, overdose

Mechanisms of Drug Action

Most drugs have effects that reverberate throughout the body. However, psychoactive drugs work mainly by altering neurotransmitter activity in the brain. As we discussed in Chapter 3, *neurotransmitters* are chemicals that transmit signals between neurons at junctions called *synapses*.

The actions of amphetamines illustrate how drugs have selective, multiple effects on neurotransmitter activity. Amphetamines exert their main effects on two neurotransmitter systems: norepinephrine (NE) and dopamine (DA). Amphetamines appear to have two key effects at DA and NE synapses (Koob & Le Moal, 2006). First, they increase the release of dopamine and norepinephrine by presynaptic neurons. Second, they interfere with the reuptake of DA and NE from synaptic clefts. These actions serve to increase the levels of dopamine and norepinephrine at the affected synapses. Cocaine shares some of these actions, which is why cocaine and amphetamines produce similar stimulant effects (see **Figure 5.12**).

FIGURE 5.12

Stimulant drugs and neurotransmitter activity. Like other psychoactive drugs, amphetamines and cocaine alter neurotransmitter activity at specific synapses. Amphetamines primarily increase the release of dopamine (DA) and norepinephrine (NE), and secondarily inhibit the reuptake of these neurotransmitters. Cocaine slows the reuptake process at DA, NE, and serotonin synapses. The psychological and behavioral effects of the drugs have largely been attributed to their impact on dopamine circuits.

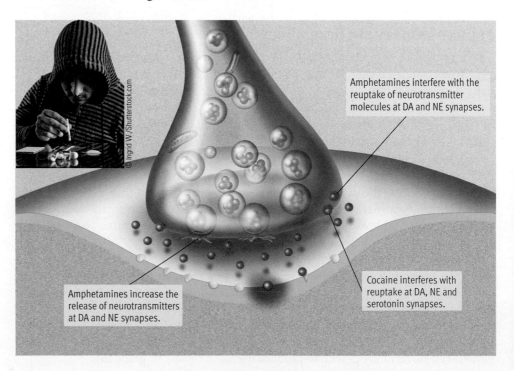

Amphetamines interfere with the reuptake of neurotransmitter molecules at DA and NE synapses.

Amphetamines increase the release of neurotransmitters at DA and NE synapses.

Cocaine interferes with reuptake at DA, NE and serotonin synapses.

Although specific drugs exert their initial effects in the brain on a wide variety of neurotransmitter systems, many theorists believe that virtually all abused drugs eventually increase activity in a particular neural pathway, called the *mesolimbic dopamine pathway* (Schmidt, Vassoler, & Pierce, 2011). This neural circuit—which runs from an area in the midbrain, through the *nucleus accumbens,* and on to the prefrontal cortex (see **Figure 5.13**)—has been described as a "reward pathway." Large and rapid increases in the release of dopamine along this pathway are thought to be the neural basis of the reinforcing effects of most abused drugs (Knapp & Kornetsky, 2009; Koob, 2012).

Drug Dependence

People can become either physically or psychologically dependent on a drug. Physical dependence is a common problem with narcotics, sedatives, and alcohol and is an occasional problem with stimulants. *Physical dependence* **exists when a person must continue to take a drug to avoid withdrawal illness.** The symptoms of withdrawal illness depend on the specific drug. Withdrawal from heroin, barbiturates, and alcohol can produce fever, chills, tremors, convulsions, vomiting, cramps, diarrhea, and severe aches and pains. Withdrawal from stimulants leads to a more subtle syndrome, marked by fatigue, apathy, irritability, depression, and disorientation.

Psychological dependence **exists when a person must continue to take a drug to satisfy intense mental and emotional craving.** Psychological dependence is more subtle than physical dependence, but the need it creates can be powerful. Cocaine, for instance, can produce an overwhelming psychological need for continued use. Psychological dependence is possible with all recreational drugs, although it seems rare for hallucinogens.

Both types of dependence are established gradually with repeated use of a drug. Drugs vary in their potential for creating either physical or psychological dependence. **Table 5.3** provides estimates of the risk of each kind of dependence for the six categories of recreational drugs covered in our discussion.

Drugs and Health

Recreational drug use can affect physical health in a variety of ways. The three principal risks are overdose, tissue damage (direct effects), and health-impairing behavior that results from drug abuse (indirect effects).

Overdose

Any drug can be fatal if a person takes enough of it, but some drugs are much more dangerous than others. Drugs that are CNS depressants—sedatives, narcotics, and alcohol—carry the greatest risk of overdose. It's important to remember that these drugs are synergistic with each other, so many overdoses involve lethal *combinations* of CNS depressants. What happens when a person overdoses on these drugs? The respiratory system usually grinds to a halt, producing coma, brain damage, and death within a brief period. Fatal overdoses with CNS stimulants usually involve a heart attack, stroke, or cortical seizure.

Direct Effects

In some cases, drugs cause tissue damage directly. For example, chronic snorting of cocaine can damage nasal membranes. Cocaine use can also foster cardiovascular disease, and crack smoking is associated with a number of respiratory problems (Paczynski & Gold, 2011). Long-term, excessive alcohol consumption is associated with

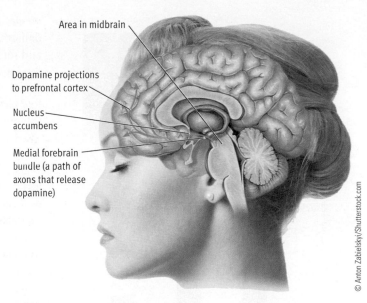

© Anton Zabielskyi/Shutterstock.com

Area in midbrain

Dopamine projections to prefrontal cortex

Nucleus accumbens

Medial forebrain bundle (a path of axons that release dopamine)

FIGURE 5.13

The "reward pathway" in the brain. The neural circuits shown here in blue make up the *mesolimbic dopamine pathway.* Axons in this pathway run from an area in the midbrain through the medial forebrain bundle to the *nucleus accumbens* and on to the prefrontal cortex. Recreational drugs affect a variety of neurotransmitter systems, but theorists believe that heightened dopamine activity in this pathway—especially the portion running from the midbrain to the nucleus accumbens—is responsible for the reinforcing effects of most abused drugs.

© Featureflash/Shutterstock.com

In 2011, after years of struggling with substance abuse, singer Amy Winehouse died from an accidental overdose of alcohol. Her tragic death illustrates the seductive risks of psychoactive drugs and the fact that alcohol by itself can be quite dangerous.

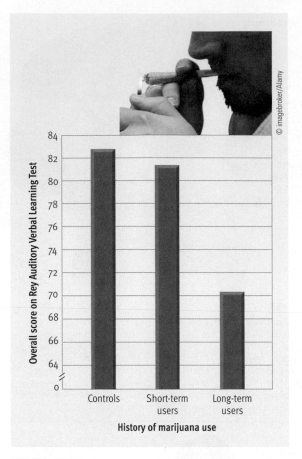

FIGURE 5.14

Chronic cannabis use and cognitive performance. Solowij and associates (2002) administered a battery of neuropsychological tests to fifty-one long-term cannabis users who had smoked marijuana regularly for an average of 24 years, fifty-one short-term cannabis users who had smoked marijuana regularly for an average of 10 years, and thirty-three control subjects who had little or no history of cannabis use. The cannabis users were required to abstain from smoking marijuana for a minimum of 12 hours prior to their testing. The study found evidence suggestive of subtle cognitive impairments among the long-term cannabis users on many of the tests. The graph depicts the results observed for overall performance on the Rey Auditory Verbal Learning Test, which measures several aspects of memory functioning.

an elevated risk for a wide range of serious health problems, including liver damage, ulcers, hypertension, stroke, heart disease, neurological disorders, and some types of cancer (Hernandez-Avila & Kranzler, 2011; Lee, McNeely, & Gourevitch, 2011). One recent study of alcohol-dependent individuals found a twofold increase in mortality among males, and more than a fourfold elevation in mortality among females (John et al., 2013). Another study (Stahre et al., 2014) estimated that one in ten deaths among working age (20–64) adults in the United States are attributable to excessive drinking!

The health risks of marijuana have generated considerable debate in recent years. Although many people have come to view marijuana as a relatively harmless drug, many experts assert that the risks of cannabis use have been underestimated (Volkow et al., 2014). The available evidence suggests that chronic marijuana use increases the risk of respiratory and pulmonary disease (Budney, Vandrey, & Fearer, 2011). Some studies have found a link between long-term marijuana use and the risk of lung cancer, although the data are surprisingly inconsistent (Aldington et al., 2008; Callaghan, Allebeck, & Sidorchuk, 2013). Finally, a rash of recent studies have reported an unexpected link between cannabis use and severe, psychotic disorders, including schizophrenia (Burns, 2013; Greiner et al., 2013). Obviously, the vast majority of marijuana users do not develop psychoses, but it appears that cannabis can trigger psychotic illness in individuals who have a genetic vulnerability to such disorders (Parakh & Basu, 2013). A number of studies have found an association between chronic, heavy marijuana use and measurable impairments in attention, learning, and memory that show up when users are not high (Hanson et al., 2010; Thames, Arbid, & Sayegh, 2014). The results of one such study (Solowij et al., 2002) are shown in **Figure 5.14**. However, these cognitive deficits may disappear after 3–4 weeks of marijuana abstinence (Schreiner & Dunn, 2012). Clearly, marijuana is not harmless, although some widely publicized dangers have been exaggerated by the popular press. For instance, contrary to popular reports, it appears that cannabis does *not* produce meaningful reductions in immune system responding (Hall & Degenhardt, 2009) or any significant effects on male smokers' fertility or sexual functioning (Grinspoon, Bakalar, & Russo, 2005).

CONCEPT CHECK 5.3

Recognizing the Unique Characteristics of Commonly Abused Drugs

From our discussion of the principal psychoactive drugs, it is clear that considerable overlap exists among the categories of drugs in terms of their medical uses, desired effects, and short-term side effects. Each type of drug, however, has at least one or two characteristics that make it different from the other types. Check your understanding of the unique characteristics of each type of drug by indicating which has the characteristics listed below. Choose from the following: (a) narcotics, (b) sedatives, (c) stimulants, (d) hallucinogens, (e) cannabis, and (f) alcohol. You'll find the answers in Appendix A.

_____ 1. Increases alertness and energy, reduces fatigue

_____ 2. No recognized medical use; may lead to insightful or "mystical" experiences

_____ 3. Used as a "sleeping pill" because it reduces CNS activity

_____ 4. Increases one's risk of a number of diseases, including liver disease and neurological disorders

_____ 5. Derived from opium; used for pain relief

_____ 6. Health risks include respiratory and pulmonary disease, and the development of psychotic disorders

Indirect Effects

The negative effects of drugs on physical health are often indirect results of the drugs' impact on behavior. For instance, people using stimulants often do not eat or sleep properly. Sedatives increase the risk of accidental injuries because they severely impair motor coordination. People who abuse downers often trip down stairs, fall off stools, and suffer other mishaps. Many drugs impair driving ability, increasing the risk of automobile accidents. Alcohol, for instance, may contribute to roughly 40% of all automobile deaths (Hingson & Sleet, 2006). Although cannabis impairs driving less than alcohol intoxication does, marijuana use within 3 hours of driving appears to roughly double one's risk of an accident (Asbridge, Hayden, & Cartwright, 2012). Intravenous drug users risk contracting infectious diseases that can be spread by unsterilized needles. For example, acquired immune deficiency syndrome (AIDS) has been transmitted at an alarming rate through the population of intravenous drug users (Epstein, Phillips, & Preston, 2011).

The major health risks of various recreational drugs are listed in the fifth column of **Table 5.3**. As you can see, alcohol appears to have the most diverse negative effects on physical health. The irony, of course, is that alcohol is the only recreational drug listed that has a long history of being legal.

5.8 REFLECTING ON THE CHAPTER'S THEMES

5.8
Key Learning Goals
- Identify the five unifying themes highlighted in this chapter.

This chapter highlighted five of our unifying themes. First, we saw how psychology evolves in a sociohistorical context. Research on consciousness dwindled to almost nothing after John B. Watson (1913, 1919) and others redefined psychology as the science of behavior. However, in the 1960s, people began to turn inward, showing a new interest in altering consciousness through drug use, meditation, hypnosis, and biofeedback. Psychologists responded to these social trends by beginning to study variations in consciousness in earnest. This shift shows how social forces can have an impact on psychology's evolution.

A second theme that surfaced in this chapter is the idea that people's experience of the world is highly subjective. We encountered this theme toward the end of the chapter when we discussed the subjective nature of drug effects, noting that the changes of consciousness produced by drugs depend significantly on personal expectations.

Third, we saw once again how culture molds some aspects of behavior. Although the basic physiological process of sleep appears largely the same from one society to another, culture influences certain aspects of sleep habits. And culture has a dramatic impact on whether people remember their dreams and how they interpret and feel about their dreams. If not for space constraints, we might also have discussed cross-cultural differences in patterns of recreational drug use, which vary considerably from one society to the next.

Fourth, we learned once again that behavior is governed by multifactorial causation. For example, we discussed how the effects of jet lag, sleep deprivation, and psychoactive drugs depend on a number of interacting factors.

Finally, the chapter illustrated psychology's theoretical diversity. We discussed conflicting theories about dreams, hypnosis, and meditation. For the most part, we did not see any of the opposing theories converging toward reconciliation, as we did in the previous chapter. However, it's important to emphasize that rival theories do not always merge neatly into tidy models of behavior. While it's always nice to resolve a theoretical debate, the debate itself can advance knowledge by stimulating and guiding empirical research.

Indeed, our upcoming Personal Application demonstrates that theoretical debates need not be resolved in order to advance knowledge. Many theoretical controversies and enduring mysteries remain in the study of sleep and dreams. Nonetheless, researchers have accumulated a great deal of practical information on these topics, which we'll discuss next.

 Sociohistorical Context

 Subjectivity of Experience

 Cultural Heritage

 Multifactorial Causation

 Theoretical Diversity

5.9

Key Learning Goals
- Summarize the evidence of various practical questions about sleep and dreams.

5.9 PERSONAL APPLICATION
Addressing Practical Questions about Sleep and Dreams

Indicate whether the following statements are "true" or "false."

_____ 1 Naps are rarely refreshing.

_____ 2 Some people never dream.

_____ 3 When people cannot recall their dreams, it's because they are trying to repress them.

These assertions were drawn from the Sleep and Dreams Information Questionnaire (Palladino & Carducci, 1984), which measures practical knowledge about sleep and dreams. Are they true or false? You'll see in this Application.

Common Questions About Sleep

How much sleep do people need? The average amount of daily sleep for adults is 7 hours (Dijk & Lazar, 2012). However, people differ considerably in how much they sleep, which suggests that sleep needs vary. As noted earlier, sleep experts believe that most people would function more effectively if they increased their amount of sleep (Banks & Dinges, 2011). Bear in mind, too, that research suggests that people who sleep 7–8 hours per night have the lowest mortality rates (Kakizaki et al., 2013).

Can short naps be refreshing? Some naps are beneficial and some are not. The effectiveness of napping varies from person to person. Also, the benefits of any specific nap depend on the time of day and the amount of sleep one has had recently. Naps tend to be more beneficial when they are rich in slow-wave sleep or REM sleep (Mednick & Drummond, 2009). Unfortunately, you're often just getting into these deeper stages of sleep when your nap time is up. Nonetheless, naps can enhance subsequent alertness and task performance, and reduce sleepiness (Ficca et al., 2010). Evidence also suggests that naps can improve learning and memory—even more so than loading up on caffeine (Mednick

et al., 2008). In conclusion, naps can be refreshing for many people, so the first statement opening this Application is false.

What is the significance of snoring? Snoring is a common phenomenon that is seen in roughly 40% of adults (Li & Hoffstein, 2011). Snoring occurs in men more than women, and is more common among people who are overweight (Partinen & Hublin, 2011). Many factors, including obesity, colds, allergies, smoking, and some drugs, can contribute to snoring, mainly by forcing people to breathe through their mouths while sleeping. Some people who snore loudly disrupt their own sleep as well as that of their bed partners. It can be difficult to prevent snoring in some people, whereas other people can reduce their snoring by losing weight, consuming less alcohol, or sleeping on their side instead of their back (Li & Hoffstein, 2011). Snoring may seem like a trivial problem, but it is associated with sleep apnea and cardiovascular disease, and has more medical significance than many people may realize (Endeshaw et al., 2013).

What can be done to avoid sleep problems? There are many ways to improve your chances of getting satisfactory sleep. Most of them involve developing sensible daytime habits that won't interfere with sleep (see Epstein & Mardon, 2007; Maas, 1998; Stevenson, 2014). For example, if you've been having trouble sleeping at night, it's a good idea to avoid daytime naps, so that you'll be tired when bedtime arrives. Some people find that daytime exercise helps them fall asleep more readily at bedtime (Flausino et al., 2012).

It's wise to minimize consumption of stimulants, such as caffeine and nicotine. Because coffee and cigarettes aren't prescription drugs, people don't appreciate how much the stimulants they contain can heighten physical arousal. Many foods (such as chocolate) and beverages (such as cola drinks) contain more caffeine than people realize. Also, bear in mind that

ill-advised eating habits can interfere with sleep. Try to avoid going to bed hungry, uncomfortably stuffed, or soon after eating foods that disagree with you.

It's also a good idea to try to establish a reasonably regular bedtime. This habit will allow you to take advantage of your circadian rhythm, so you'll be trying to fall asleep when your body is primed to cooperate. And do not underestimate the importance of sleeping in an environment that is conducive to sleep. This advice belabors what should be obvious, but many people fail to heed it. Make sure you have a good bed that is comfortable for you. Take steps to ensure that your bedroom is quiet enough and that the humidity and temperature are to your liking. Take steps to ensure that your bedroom is dark because even small amounts of light can undermine sleep quality. And do not sleep with your cell phone or other devices that are likely to awaken you.

What can be done about insomnia? First, don't panic if you run into a little trouble sleeping. An overreaction to sleep difficulties can begin a vicious circle of escalating problems. If you jump to the conclusion that you are becoming an insomniac, you may approach sleep with anxiety, which will only aggravate the problem. The harder you work at falling asleep, the less success you're likely to have. As noted earlier, temporary sleep problems are common and generally clear up on their own.

It's often a good idea to simply launch yourself into a pleasant daydream. This normal presleep process can take your mind off your difficulties. Whatever you think about, try to avoid ruminating about the current stresses and problems in your life. Research has shown that the tendency to ruminate is one of the key factors contributing to insomnia (Gehrman, Findley, & Perlis, 2012). Anything that relaxes you—whether it's music, meditation, prayer, a warm bath, or a systematic relaxation procedure—can aid you in falling asleep.

Many people fail to understand the extent to which caffeine consumption can have disruptive effects on sleep.

Evidence also suggests that melatonin can help you fall asleep without all the issues and risks associated with sleeping pills (Buysse, 2011). Many people consume alcohol near bedtime for its sedative effects. The evidence related to this strategy is a mixed bag (Ebrahim et al., 2013). On the one hand, alcohol does tend to help people fall asleep more quickly and stay asleep more effectively for the first half of the night. On the other hand, alcohol disrupts sleep in the second half of the night and decreases the time spent in REM sleep in a dose-related manner. Given the accumulating findings on the importance of REM sleep, alcohol's REM-suppressing effects are certainly cause for concern.

Common Questions About Dreams

Does everyone dream? Yes. Some people just don't *remember* their dreams. However, when these people are brought into a sleep lab and awakened from REM sleep, they report having been dreaming—much to their surprise (statement 2 at the start of this Application is false). In a recent study, seven participants who reported rarely recalling a dream were brought into a sleep lab and monitored with an extra sensitive EEG (Yu, 2014). The extra precise REM awakenings resulted in dream recall 94% of the time. Scientists have studied a small number of people who have sustained brain damage in the area of the *pons* that

has wiped out their REM sleep, but even these people report dreams (Klosch & Kraft, 2005).

Why don't some people remember their dreams? The evaporation of dreams appears to be quite normal. Most dreams are lost forever unless people wake up during or just after a dream. Even then, dream recall fades quickly (Nir & Tononi, 2010). One recent study (Eichenlaub et al, 2014) found that people who tend to remember their dreams tend to awaken more during the night than those who rarely recall dreams. Hobson's (1989) educated guess is that people probably forget 95%–99% of their dreams. This forgetting is natural and is not due to repression (statement 3 is also false). People who tend to not remember their dreams probably have a sleep pattern that puts too much time between their REM/dream periods and awakening.

Do dreams require interpretation? Yes, but interpretation may not be as difficult as generally assumed. People have long believed that dreams are symbolic and that it is necessary to interpret the symbols to understand the meaning of dreams. Freud, for instance, made a distinction between the *manifest content* and the *latent content* of a dream. **The *manifest content* consists of the plot of a dream at a surface level. The *latent content* refers to the hidden or disguised meaning of the events in the plot.** Thus, a Freudian therapist might equate such dream events as walking into a tunnel, mounting a horse, or riding a roller coaster with sexual intercourse. Freudian theorists assert that dream interpretation is a complicated task requiring considerable knowledge of symbolism.

However, many dream theorists argue that symbolism in dreams is less deceptive and mysterious than Freud thought (Faraday, 1974; Foulkes, 1985). Zadra and Domhoff (2011) note that modern dream research reveals that the content of most dreams is relatively realistic and transparent. Calvin Hall (1979) makes the point that dreams may require some interpretation simply because they are more visual than verbal; that is, pictures need to be translated into ideas. Unfortunately, there is no definitive way to judge the validity of different dream interpretations.

People typically get very upset when they have difficulty falling asleep. Unfortunately, this emotional distress tends to make it even harder for them to get to sleep.

5.10

Key Learning Goals
• Recognize the influence of definitions, and understand the nominal fallacy.

5.10 CRITICAL THINKING APPLICATION

Is Alcoholism a Disease? The Power of Definitions

Alcoholism is a major problem in most—perhaps all—societies. It destroys countless lives and tears families apart. With roughly 17 million problem drinkers in the United States (National Institute on Alcohol Abuse and Alcoholism, 2013), it seems likely that alcoholism has touched the lives of a majority of Americans.

In almost every discussion about alcoholism, someone will ask, "Is alcoholism a disease?" If alcoholism is a disease, it is a strange one because the alcoholic is the most direct cause of his or her own sickness. If alcoholism is *not* a disease, what else might it be? Over the course of history, alcoholism has been categorized under many labels—from a personal weakness to a crime, a sin, a mental disorder, and a physical illness (Meyer, 1996). Each of these definitions carries important personal, social, political, and economic implications.

Consider, for instance, the consequences of characterizing alcoholism as a disease. If that is the case, alcoholics should be treated like diabetics, heart patients, or victims of other physical illnesses. That is, they should be viewed with sympathy and should be given appropriate medical and therapeutic interventions to foster recovery from their illness. These treatments should be covered by medical insurance and delivered by health care professionals. Just as important, if alcoholism is defined as a disease, it should lose much of its stigma. After all, we don't blame people with diabetes or heart disease for their illnesses. Yes, alcoholics admittedly contribute to their own disease (by drinking too much), but so do many victims of diabetes and heart disease who eat all the wrong foods, fail to control their weight, and so forth (McLellan et al., 2000). And, as is the case with many physical illnesses, one can inherit a genetic vulnerability to alcoholism (Nguyen et al., 2011), so it is difficult to argue that alcoholism is caused solely by one's behavior.

Alternatively, if alcoholism is defined as a personal failure or a moral weakness, alcoholics are less likely to be viewed with sympathy and compassion. They might be admonished to quit drinking, put in prison, or punished in some other way. These responses to their alcoholism would be administered primarily by the legal system, rather than the health care system, because medical interventions are not designed to remedy moral failings. Obviously, the interventions that would be available would not be covered by health insurance, which would have enormous financial repercussions (for both health care providers and alcoholics).

The key point here is that definitions lie at the center of many complex debates. People tend to think of definitions as insignificant, arbitrary sets of words found buried in the obscurity of thick dictionaries compiled by ivory tower intellectuals. Much of this characterization may be accurate, but definitions are not insignificant. They are vested with enormous power to shape how people think about important issues. An endless array of issues boil down to matters of definition. For example, the next time you hear people arguing over whether a particular movie is pornographic, whether the death penalty is cruel and unusual punishment, or whether spanking is child abuse, you'll find it helps to focus the debate on clarifying the definitions of the crucial concepts.

The Power to Make Definitions

So, how can we resolve the debate about whether alcoholism is a disease? Scientists generally try to resolve their debates by conducting research. You may have noticed already that "we need more research on this issue" is a frequent refrain in this text. Is more research the answer in this case? For once, the answer is "no." There is no conclusive way to determine whether alcoholism is a disease. It is not as though there is a "right" answer to this question that we can discover through more and better research.

The question of whether alcoholism is a disease is a *matter of definition:* Does alcoholism fit the currently accepted definition of what constitutes a disease? If you consult medical texts or dictionaries, you will find that disease is typically defined as *an impairment in the normal functioning of an organism that alters its vital functions.* Given that alcoholism clearly impairs people's normal functioning and disrupts a variety of vital functions, it seems reasonable to characterize it as a disease. Moreover, like other diseases, it causes increased mortality due to acute incidents, such as automobile accidents (see **Figure 5.15**), and due to its contribution to various chronic diseases (see **Figure 5.16**). Thus, the disease model has been the dominant view of alcoholism in the United States since the middle of the 20th century (Meyer, 1996). This view has only been strengthened by recent evidence that addiction to alcohol (and other drugs) is the result of dysregulation in key neural circuits in the brain (Koob, 2012). Still, some critics express vigorous doubts about the wisdom of defining alcoholism as a disease (Peele, 1989, 2000; Satel & Lilienfeld, 2013). They raise a question that comes up frequently in arguments about definitions: Who should have the power to make the definition? In this case, the power lies in the hands of the medical community, which seems sensible, given that disease is a medical concept. But some critics argue that the medical community has a strong bias in favor of defining conditions as diseases because doing so creates new markets and fuels economic growth for the health industry (Nikelly, 1994). Framing alcoholism as a brain disease has also elevated the prestige of addiction research and helped well-intentioned researchers to coax more funding out of government agencies (Satel & Lilienfeld, 2013). Thus, debate about whether alcoholism is a disease seems likely to continue for the indefinite future.

To summarize, definitions generally do not emerge out of research. They are

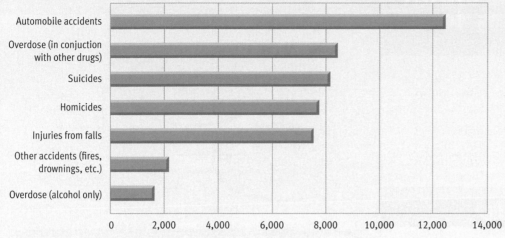

FIGURE 5.15

Alcohol and acute causes of death. This graph shows estimates of the average number of annual deaths from acute causes that are attributable to excessive drinking. The death toll for alcohol-related accidents, overdoses, suicides, and homicides is staggering. (Based on data from Stahre et al., 2014)

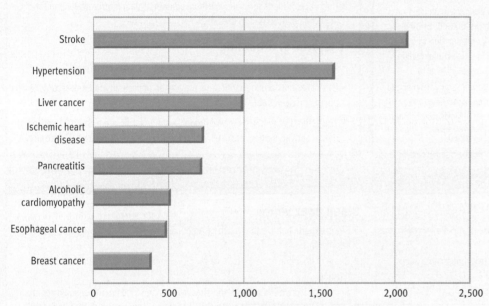

FIGURE 5.16

Alcohol and chronic diseases. Although the death toll for alcohol-induced chronic diseases is not as staggering as that attributed to acute causes, excessive drinking contributes to quite a variety of chronic diseases that lead to elevated mortality risk. (Based on data from Stahre et al., 2014)

TABLE 5.4 Critical Thinking Skills Discussed in This Application

Skill	Description
Understanding the way definitions shape how people think about issues	The critical thinker appreciates the enormous power of definitions and the need to clarify definitions in efforts to resolve disagreements.
Identifying the source of definitions	The critical thinker recognizes the need to determine who has the power to make specific definitions and to evaluate their credibility.
Avoiding the nominal fallacy in working with definitions and labels	The critical thinker understands that labels do not have explanatory value.

typically crafted by experts or authorities in a specific field who try to reach a consensus about how to best define a particular concept. Thus, in analyzing the validity of a definition, you need to look not only at the definition itself but at where it came from. Who decided what the definition should be? Does the source of the definition seem legitimate? Did the authorities who formulated the definition have any biases that should be considered?

Definitions, Labels, and Circular Reasoning

One additional point about definitions is worth discussing. Perhaps because definitions are imbued with so much power, people have an interesting tendency to incorrectly use them as *explanations* for the phenomena they describe. This logical error, which equates *naming* something with *explaining* it, is sometimes called the *nominal fallacy*. Names and labels that are used as explanations often sound quite reasonable at first. *But definitions do not really have any explanatory value; they simply specify what certain terms mean.* Consider an example. Let's say your friend, Frank, has a severe drinking problem. You are sitting around with some other friends discussing why Frank drinks so much. Rest assured, at least one of these friends will assert that "Frank drinks too much because he is an alcoholic." This is *circular reasoning*, which is just as useless as explaining that Frank is an alcoholic because he drinks too much.

The diagnostic labels that are used in the classification of mental disorders—labels such as schizophrenia and autism—also seem to invite this type of circular reasoning. For example, people often say things like "That person is delusional because she is schizophrenic" or "He is afraid of small, enclosed places because he is claustrophobic." These statements may sound plausible, but they are no more logical or insightful than saying "She is a redhead because she has red hair." The logical fallacy of mistaking a label for an explanation will get us as far in our understanding as a dog gets in chasing its own tail.

CONSCIOUSNESS

The nature of consciousness

- **Consciousness** is awareness of internal and external stimuli, including awareness of a self and your thoughts.

- Consciousness involves varied levels of awareness or alertness.

- Variations in consciousness are associated with variations in brain activity, as measured by an EEG.

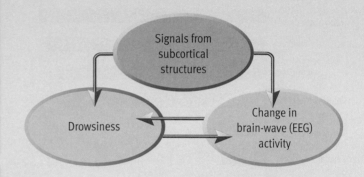

BIOLOGICAL RHYTHMS AND SLEEP

- **Biological rhythms** are periodic fluctuations in physiological functions tied to planetary rhythms.
- **Circadian rhythms** are 24-hour cycles that are influential in the regulation of sleep.
- Internal biological clocks are reset by exposure to light, which stimulates the SCN in the hypothalamus.

- The poor sleep associated with jet lag and rotating work shifts is due to being out of sync with circadian rhythms.
- Melatonin and well-planned rotation schedules can reduce the effects circadian rhythm disruption.

THE WORLD OF DREAMS

The nature of dreams
- Dreams are less exotic than widely assumed.

- Dreams can be affected by external stimuli and events in one's life.

- Cultural variations are seen in dream content, dream interpretation, and the importance attributed to dreams.

Theories of dreaming

- Freud asserted that the chief purpose of dreams is wish fulfillment.

- Other theorists argue that dreams provide an opportunity to think creatively about personal problems.

- The activation-synthesis model proposes that dreams are side effects of the neural activation that produces waking-like brain waves during REM sleep.

SLEEP

The architecture of sleep

- **Non-REM sleep** (stages 1–3) is marked by an absence of rapid eye movements, relatively little dreaming, and varied EEG activity.
- **REM sleep** is a deep stage of sleep marked by rapid eye movements, high-frequency brain waves, and dreaming.
- During the course of sleep, REM periods gradually get longer and non-REM periods get shorter and shallower.
- The architecture of sleep varies somewhat from one person to the next.

Age, culture, and sleep

- Time spent in REM sleep declines from 50% among newborns to about 20% among adults.
- Total sleep time declines with advancing age.
- Cultural variations in sleep patterns appear to be small.
- Napping practices vary along cultural lines, and siesta cultures are found in tropical regions.

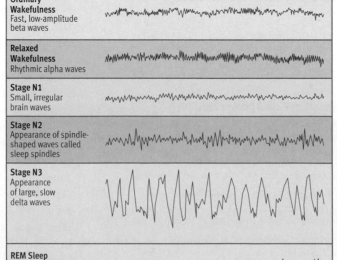

Sleep deprivation

- Sleep experts believe that much of American society suffers from chronic sleep deprivation.
- Sleep deprivation appears to have far more negative effects than most people assume.
- Selective deprivation of REM and slow-wave sleep leads to increased attempts to shift into these stages of sleep and increased time in these stages after sleep deprivation ends.
- REM and slow-wave sleep may help with memory consolidation.
- Short sleep duration is associated with a variety of health problems, but both short and long sleepers exhibit elevated mortality rates.

Sleep disorders

Insomnia: Chronic problems in getting adequate sleep

Narcolepsy: Marked by sudden, irresistible onsets of sleep during normal waking hours

Sleep apnea: Frequent reflexive gasping for air that disrupts sleep

Somnambulism (sleepwalking): Wandering around while remaining asleep

REM sleep behavior disorder (RBD): Potentially troublesome, even violent, dream enactments during REM periods

HYPNOSIS

Hypnotic induction and phenomena

- *Hypnosis* is a procedure that produces a heightened state of suggestibility.

- People vary in their susceptibility to hypnosis.

- Hypnosis can produce a variety of effects, including anesthesia, sensory distortions, disinhibition, and posthypnotic amnesia.

Theories of hypnosis

- According to some theorists, hypnosis produces a normal state of consciousness in which people act out the role of a hypnotized subject.

- The *role-playing view* is supported by evidence that hypnotic feats can be duplicated by non-hypnotized subjects and that hypnotic subjects are often acting out a role.

- According to Ernest Hilgard, hypnosis produces an altered state of awareness characterized by dissociation.

- The *altered-state view* is supported by evidence that divided consciousness is a common experience, as illustrated by highway hypnosis.

MEDITATION

© Dean Mitchell/Shutterstock.com

Types and effects

- Meditation refers to a family of practices that train attention to heighten awareness and bring mental processes under greater voluntary control.

  - Two main styles: *focused attention* and *open monitoring*.

  - Effective meditation leads to a beneficial physiological state that may be accompanied by changes in brain activity.

  - Meditation may produce alterations in brain structure.

ALTERING CONSCIOUSNESS WITH DRUGS

Principal abused drugs

Narcotics: Drugs derived from opium, such as heroin

Sedatives: Sleep-inducing drugs that decrease CNS activation, such as barbiturates

Stimulants: Drugs that increase CNS activation, such as cocaine and amphetamines

Hallucinogens: Drugs that produce sensory distortions and diverse mental and emotional effects, such as LSD and mescaline

Cannabis: Hemp plant from which marijuana, hashish, and THC are derived

Alcohol: Includes a variety of beverages that contain ethyl alcohol

Factors influencing drug effects

- Drug effects depend on users' age, mood, personality, weight, and expectations.

- Drug effects also depend on the potency of the drug, the method of administration, and the user's tolerance.

- *Tolerance* refers to a progressive decrease in a person's responsiveness to a drug as a result of continued use.

Mechanisms of drug action

- Psychoactive drugs exert their effects by selectively altering neurotransmitter activity.

- Increased activation in the *mesolimbic dopamine pathway* may be responsible for the reinforcing effects of many drugs.

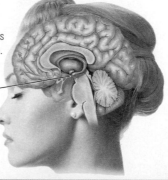

Mesolimbic dopamine pathway

© Anton Zabielskyi/Shutterstock.com

Risks associated with drug abuse

- *Physical dependence* exists when drug use must be continued to avoid withdrawal illness.

- *Psychological dependence* exists when drug use must be continued to satisfy craving for the drug.

- Many drugs, especially CNS depressants, can produce a lethal overdose.

- Many drugs cause deleterious health effects by producing direct tissue damage.

- The negative effects of drugs on physical health are often due to indirect behavioral effects.

APPLICATIONS

- Naps can prove helpful, but their effects vary; snoring has more medical significance than most people realize.

- Individuals troubled by insomnia should avoid panic, pursue relaxation, and try distracting themselves.

- Everyone dreams, but some people don't remember their dreams. Freud distinguished between the manifest and latent content of dreams.

- In evaluating the validity of a definition, one should look not only at the definition but also at where it came from.

© Photographee.eu/Shutterstock.com

CHAPTER 6

LEARNING

Vstock LLC/Tetra/Corbis

Themes in this Chapter

Heredity &   Sociohistorical
Environment   Context

Let's see if you can guess the answer to a riddle. What do the following scenarios have in common?

- In 1953 a Japanese researcher observed a young macaque (a type of monkey) on the island of Koshima washing a sweet potato in a stream before eating it. No one had ever seen a macaque do this before. Soon other members of the monkey's troop were showing the same behavior. Several generations later, macaques on Koshima still wash their potatoes before eating them (De Waal, 2001).

- In 2005, Wade Boggs was elected to baseball's Hall of Fame. Boggs was as renowned for his superstitions as he was for his great hitting. For 20 years Boggs ate chicken every day of the year. Before games he followed a strict set of rituals that included stepping on the bases in reverse order, running wind sprints at precisely 17 minutes past the hour, and tossing exactly three pebbles off the field. Every time he stepped up to hit during a game, he drew the Hebrew letter *chai* in the dirt with his bat. For Boggs, the slightest change in this routine was very upsetting (Gaddis, 1999; Vyse, 2000).

- Barn swallows in Minnesota have built nests inside a Home Depot warehouse, safe from the weather and from predators. So how do they get in and out to bring food to their babies when the doors are closed? They flutter around the motion sensors that operate the doors until they open!

What common thread runs through these diverse situations? What connects a superstitious ballplayer to potato washing monkeys and door-opening swallows?

The answer is *learning*. This may surprise you. When most people think of learning, they picture students reading textbooks or novices gaining proficiency in a skill, such as skiing or playing the guitar. To a psychologist, however, **learning** is any **relatively durable change in behavior or knowledge that is due to experience.** Macaques aren't born with the habit of washing their sweet potatoes, nor do swallows begin life knowing how to operate motion sensors. These behaviors are the product of experience; that is, they represent learning.

Learning is one of the most fundamental concepts in all of psychology. Learning shapes personal habits, such as nail-biting; personality traits, such as shyness; personal preferences, such as a distaste for formal clothes; and emotional responses, such as reactions to favorite songs. If all your learned responses could somehow be stripped away, little of your behavior would be left. You would not be able to talk, read a book, or cook yourself a hamburger. You would be about as complex and interesting as a turnip.

As the examples at the start of this chapter show, learning is not an exclusively human process. It is pervasive in the animal world, as well—a fact that won't amaze anyone who has ever owned a dog or seen a trained seal in action. Indeed, many of the most fascinating discoveries in the study of learning originated in studies of animals.

In this chapter, you will see how fruitful the research into learning has been and how wide ranging its applications are. We will focus most of our attention on a specific kind of learning: conditioning. **Conditioning** involves learning associations between events that occur in an organism's environment. In investigating conditioning, psychologists study learning at a fundamental level. This strategy has paid off with insights that have laid the foundation for the study of more complex forms of learning. In the Personal Application, you'll see how you can harness the principles of conditioning to improve your self-control. The Critical Thinking Application shows how conditioning procedures can be used to manipulate emotions.

6.1 CLASSICAL CONDITIONING

Do you go weak in the knees at the thought of standing on the roof of a tall building? Does your heart race when you imagine encountering a harmless garter snake? If so, you can understand, at least to some degree, what it's like to have a phobia. *Phobias* are irrational fears of specific objects or situations. Mild phobias are common. Over the years, students in my classes have described their phobic responses to a diverse array of stimuli, including bridges, elevators, tunnels, heights, dogs, cats, bugs, snakes, professors, doctors, strangers, thunderstorms, and germs. If you have a phobia, you may have wondered how you managed to acquire such a foolish fear. Chances are, it was through classical conditioning (Field & Purkis, 2012). **Classical conditioning** is a type of learning in which a stimulus acquires the capacity to evoke a response that was originally evoked by another stimulus. The process was first described in 1903 by Ivan Pavlov, and it was originally called *Pavlovian conditioning* in tribute to him. This learning process was characterized as "classical" conditioning decades later (starting in the 1940s) to distinguish it from other types of conditioning that attracted research interest around that time (Clark, 2004).

Pavlov's Demonstration: "Psychic Reflexes"

Pavlov was a prominent Russian physiologist who did Nobel Prize–winning research on digestion. He was studying the role of saliva in the digestive processes of dogs when he stumbled onto what he called "psychic reflexes" (Pavlov, 1906). Like many great discoveries, Pavlov's was partly accidental, although he had the insight to recognize its significance. His subjects were dogs restrained in harnesses in an experimental chamber (see **Figure 6.1**). Their saliva was collected by means of a surgically implanted tube in the salivary gland. Pavlov would present meat powder to a dog and then collect the resulting saliva. As his research progressed, he noticed that dogs accustomed to the procedure would start salivating *before* the meat powder was presented. For instance, they would salivate in response to a clicking sound made by the device that was used to present the meat powder.

Intrigued by this unexpected finding, Pavlov decided to investigate further. He paired the presentation of the meat powder with various stimuli that would stand out in the laboratory situation. For instance, he used a simple auditory stimulus: the presentation of a tone. After the tone and the meat powder had been presented together a number of times, the tone was presented alone. What happened? The dogs responded by salivating to the sound of the tone alone.

What was so significant about a dog salivating when a tone was sounded? The key is that the tone had started out as a *neutral* stimulus; that is, it did not originally produce

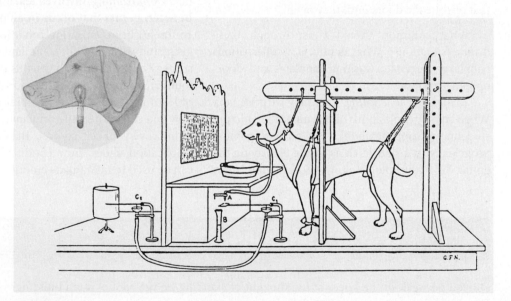

FIGURE 6.1

Classical conditioning apparatus. An experimental arrangement similar to the one depicted here (taken from Yerkes & Morgulis, 1909) has typically been used in demonstrations of classical conditioning, although Pavlov's original setup (see inset) was quite a bit simpler. The dog is restrained in a harness. A tone is used as the conditioned stimulus (CS), and the presentation of meat powder is used as the unconditioned stimulus (US). The tube inserted into the dog's salivary gland allows precise measurement of its salivation response. The pen and rotating drum of paper on the left are used to maintain a continuous record of salivary flow. **(Inset)** The less elaborate setup that Pavlov originally used to collect saliva on each trial is shown here (Goodwin, 1991).

the response of salivation. However, Pavlov managed to change that by pairing the tone with a stimulus (meat powder) that *did* produce the salivation response. Through this process, the tone acquired the capacity to trigger the response of salivation. What Pavlov had demonstrated was how stimulus-response associations—the basic building blocks of learning—are formed by events in an organism's environment. Based on this insight, he built a broad theory of learning that attempted to explain aspects of emotion, temperament, neuroses, and language.

Terminology and Procedures

There is a special vocabulary associated with classical conditioning. It might look intimidating, but it's really not all that mysterious. The bond Pavlov noted between the meat powder and salivation was a natural, unlearned association. It did not have to be created through conditioning. It is therefore called an *unconditioned* association. In unconditioned bonds, **the *unconditioned stimulus* (US) is a stimulus that evokes an unconditioned response without previous conditioning. The *unconditioned response* (UR) is an unlearned reaction to an unconditioned stimulus that occurs without previous conditioning.**

In contrast, the link between the tone and salivation was established through conditioning. It is therefore called a *conditioned* association. In conditioned bonds, **the *conditioned stimulus* (CS) is a previously neutral stimulus that has, through conditioning, acquired the capacity to evoke a conditioned response. The *conditioned response* (CR) is a learned reaction to a conditioned stimulus that occurs because of previous conditioning.**

In Pavlov's initial demonstration, the UR and CR were both salivation. When evoked by the US (meat powder), salivation was an unconditioned response. When evoked by the CS (the tone), salivation was a conditioned response. Although the unconditioned response and conditioned response sometimes consist of the same behavior, subtle differences usually exist between them, as conditioned responses often are weaker or less intense. And in some cases the UR and CR are quite different, albeit intimately related. For example, if an animal is given a brief shock as a US, the unconditioned response is *pain*, whereas the conditioned response is *fear* of imminent pain. In any event, the procedures involved in classical conditioning are outlined in **Figure 6.2**.

Pavlov's "psychic reflex" came to be called the *conditioned reflex*. Classically conditioned responses have traditionally been characterized as reflexes and are said to be *elicited* (**drawn forth**) because most of them are relatively automatic or involuntary. Finally, **a *trial* in classical conditioning consists of any presentation of a stimulus or pair of stimuli.** Psychologists are interested in how many trials are required to establish a particular conditioned bond. The number needed to form an association varies considerably. Although classical conditioning generally proceeds gradually, it can occur quite rapidly, sometimes in just one pairing of the conditioned stimulus and unconditioned stimulus.

Classical Conditioning in Everyday Life

In laboratory experiments on classical conditioning, researchers have generally worked with extremely simple responses. Besides salivation, commonly studied favorites include eyelid closure, knee jerks, and the flexing of various limbs. The study of such simple responses has proven both practical and productive. However, these responses do not even begin to convey the rich diversity of everyday behavior that is regulated by classical conditioning. Let's look at some examples of classical conditioning drawn from everyday life.

Conditioned Fear and Anxiety

Classical conditioning often plays a key role in shaping emotional responses, such as fear and anxiety. Phobias are a good example of such responses. Case studies of

FIGURE 6.2

The sequence of events in classical conditioning. (a) Moving downward, this series of three panels outlines the sequence of events in classical conditioning, using Pavlov's original demonstration as an example. **(b)** As we encounter other examples of classical conditioning throughout the book, you will see many diagrams, like the one in this panel, that provide snapshots of specific instances of classical conditioning.

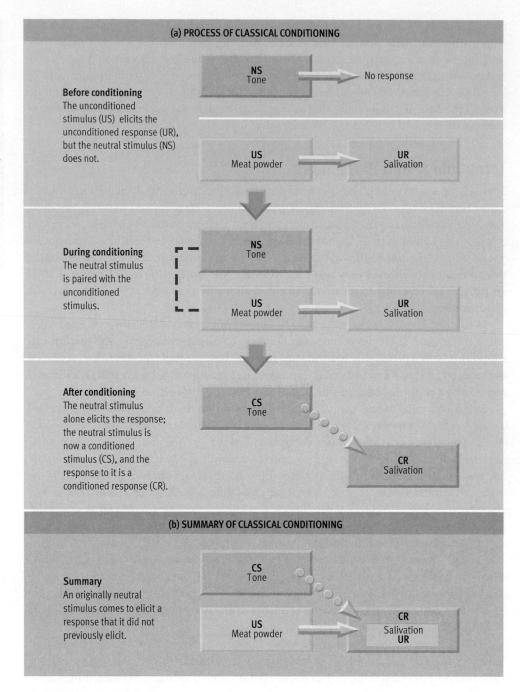

(a) PROCESS OF CLASSICAL CONDITIONING

Before conditioning
The unconditioned stimulus (US) elicits the unconditioned response (UR), but the neutral stimulus (NS) does not.

NS Tone → No response

US Meat powder → UR Salivation

During conditioning
The neutral stimulus is paired with the unconditioned stimulus.

NS Tone

US Meat powder → UR Salivation

After conditioning
The neutral stimulus alone elicits the response; the neutral stimulus is now a conditioned stimulus (CS), and the response to it is a conditioned response (CR).

CS Tone → CR Salivation

(b) SUMMARY OF CLASSICAL CONDITIONING

Summary
An originally neutral stimulus comes to elicit a response that it did not previously elicit.

CS Tone

US Meat powder → CR Salivation UR

---

patients suffering from phobias suggest that many irrational fears can be traced back to experiences that involve classical conditioning (Field & Purkis, 2012). It is easy to imagine how such conditioning can occur outside the laboratory. For example, a student of mine was troubled by a bridge phobia so severe that she couldn't drive on interstate highways because of all the bridges that had to be crossed. She was able to pinpoint the source of her phobia as something that had happened during her childhood. Whenever her family drove to visit her grandmother, they had to cross a rickety, old bridge in the countryside. Her father, in a misguided attempt at humor, made a major production out of these crossings. He would stop short of the bridge and carry on about the great danger. Obviously, he thought the bridge was safe or he wouldn't have driven across it. However, the naïve young girl was terrified by her father's scare tactics. Thus, the bridge became a conditioned stimulus eliciting great fear (see **Figure 6.3**). Unfortunately, the fear spilled over to all bridges, and 40 years later she was still carrying the burden of this phobia.

Everyday anxiety responses that are less severe than phobias may also be products of classical conditioning. For instance, if you cringe when you hear the sound of a dentist's drill, this response is the result of classical conditioning. In this case, the pain you have experienced from dental drilling is the US. This pain has been paired with the sound of the drill, which became a CS eliciting your cringing behavior.

That is *not* to say that traumatic experiences associated with stimuli *automatically* lead to conditioned fears or phobias. Whether fear conditioning takes place depends on a constellation of factors (Oehlberg & Mineka, 2011). Conditioned fears are less likely to develop when events seem escapable and controllable, and when people have a history of nontraumatic encounters in similar situations (for example, with dentists). People who are relatively low in anxiety probably acquire conditioned fears less readily than those who are highly anxious.

Other Conditioned Responses

Classical conditioning affects not only overt behaviors but *physiological processes,* as well. For example, studies have demonstrated that the functioning of the immune system can be influenced by conditioning (Szczytkowski & Lysle, 2011). For example, Ader and Cohen (1993) have shown that classical conditioning procedures can lead to *immune suppression*—a decrease in the production of antibodies. In a typical study, animals are injected with a drug (the US) that *chemically* causes immune suppression, while they are simultaneously given an unusual-tasting liquid to drink (the CS). Days later, after the chemically induced immune suppression has ended, some of the animals are reexposed to the CS by giving them the unusual-tasting solution. Measurements of antibody production indicate that animals exposed to the CS show a reduced immune response (see **Figure 6.4**).

Studies have also demonstrated that classical conditioning can influence *sexual arousal* (Domjan & Akins, 2011). For example, research has shown that quail can be conditioned to become sexually aroused by a neutral, nonsexual stimulus—such as a red light—that has been paired with opportunities to copulate (Domjan, 1994). Researchers have also conditioned quail to develop sexual fetishes for inanimate objects (Cetinkaya & Domjan, 2006). Classical conditioning may also underlie the development of sexual fetishes in humans. It seems likely that humans could be conditioned to be aroused by objects—such as shoes, boots, leather, and undergarments—that have been paired with sexual encounters.

Evaluative Conditioning of Attitudes

Pavlovian conditioning can also influence people's attitudes. In recent decades, researchers have shown great interest in a subtype of classical conditioning called *evaluative conditioning*. **Evaluative conditioning refers to changes in the liking of a stimulus that result from pairing that stimulus with other positive or negative stimuli.** In other words, evaluative conditioning involves the acquisition of likes and dislikes, or preferences, through classical conditioning (De Houwer, 2011). For example, a neutral stimulus might be paired with an unconditioned stimulus that triggers positive reactions so that the neutral stimulus becomes a conditioned stimulus that elicits similar positive reactions. For example, in one study, funny cartoons paired with two types of energy drinks increased participants' liking of the drinks (Strick et al., 2009) (see **Figure 6.5**). Another study showed that pairing pictures of high-calorie snacks with images of adverse health effects (obesity and cardiovascular disease) fostered more negative attitudes about the unhealthy snacks, and subsequently led subjects to choose fruit over highly caloric snacks (Hollands, Prestwich, & Marteau, 2011). Other studies have found that evaluative conditioning can be used to reduce prejudicial attitudes toward the homeless (Balas & Sweklej, 2013); foster

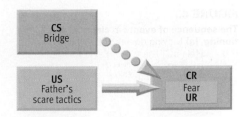

FIGURE 6.3

Classical conditioning of a fear response. Many emotional responses that would otherwise be puzzling can be explained by classical conditioning. In the case of one woman's bridge phobia, the fear originally elicited by her father's scare tactics became a conditioned response to the stimulus of bridges.

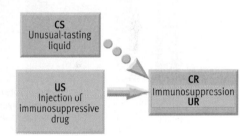

FIGURE 6.4

Classical conditioning of immune suppression. When a neutral stimulus is paired with a drug that chemically causes suppression of the immune response, it can become a CS that elicits immune suppression on its own. Thus, even the immune response can be influenced by classical conditioning.

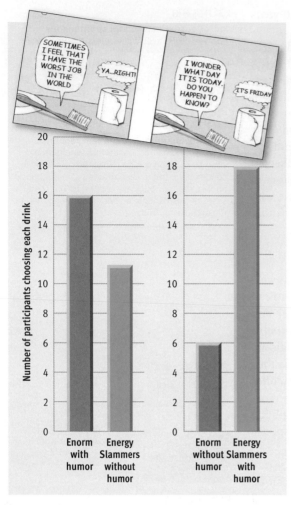

FIGURE 6.5

Evaluative conditioning with humor. In a study of evaluative conditioning, Strick et al. (2009) paired ten humorous or non-humorous cartoons with two energy drinks. The nonhumorous control cartoons were created by taking an amusing cartoon and changing the text so it was no longer funny (see example at top). Pairing the energy drinks with humor had a positive effect on participants' attitudes about the drinks. Moreover, these positive attitudes influenced subjects' actual behavior when they later had a chance to consume one of the drinks. When the drink Enorm had been paired with humor, participants tended to prefer it, and when the drink Energy Slammers had been paired with humor, it was chosen far more often.

SOURCE: Adapted from Strick, M., van Baaren, R. B., Holland, R. W., & van Knippenberg, A. (2009). Humor in advertisements enhances product liking by mere association. *Journal of Experimental Psychology: Applied, 15,* 35-45. Figures 1 and 4. Copyright © 2009 American Psychological Association.

more favorable attitudes about recycling (Geng et al., 2013); and to create more negative attitudes toward beer drinking (Houben, Schoenmakers, & Wiers, 2010).

In sum, studies of evaluative conditioning have consistently shown that the liking of a stimulus can be increased by pairing it with positive stimuli and decreased by pairing it with negative stimuli (Gast, Gawronski, & De Houwer, 2012; Hoffmann et al., 2010). Moreover, research suggests that attitudes altered via evaluative conditioning are especially durable (Walther, Weil, Dusing, 2011). Although there is much debate about the issue (Sweldens, Corneille, & Yzerbyt, 2014), it also appears that evaluative conditioning may sometimes occur without individuals being aware of the stimulus pairings (Hutter et al., 2012; Balas & Sweklej, 2012). These finding have obvious practical implications; for example, advertising campaigns routinely try to take advantage of classical conditioning (Schachtman, Walker, & Fowler, 2011) (see the Personal Application for this chapter).

Basic Processes in Classical Conditioning

Classical conditioning is often portrayed as a mechanical process that inevitably leads to a certain result. This view reflects the fact that most conditioned responses are reflexive and difficult to control. Pavlov's dogs would have been hard pressed to withhold their salivation. However, this vision of classical conditioning as an "irresistible force" is misleading because it fails to consider the many factors involved in classical conditioning. In this section, we'll look at basic processes in classical conditioning to expand on the rich complexity of this form of learning.

Acquisition

We have already discussed *acquisition* without attaching a formal name to the process. ***Acquisition* refers to the initial stage of learning a new response tendency.** Pavlov theorized that the acquisition of a conditioned response depends on *stimulus contiguity*. Stimuli are contiguous if they occur together in time and space.

Stimulus contiguity is important, but learning theorists now realize that contiguity alone doesn't automatically produce conditioning (Urcelay & Miller, 2014). People are bombarded daily by countless stimuli that could be perceived as being paired, yet only some of these pairings produce classical conditioning. If conditioning does not occur with all the stimuli present in a situation, what determines its occurrence? Evidence suggests that stimuli that are novel, larger, or especially intense have more potential to become CS's than routine stimuli, probably because they are more *salient;* that is, they are more likely to stand out among other stimuli (Miller & Grace, 2013).

Extinction

Fortunately, a newly formed stimulus-response bond does not necessarily last indefinitely. If it did, learning would be inflexible, and organisms would have difficulty adapting to new situations. Instead, the right circumstances produce ***extinction,* the gradual weakening and disappearance of a conditioned response tendency.**

What leads to extinction in classical conditioning? The consistent presentation of the conditioned stimulus *alone,* without the unconditioned stimulus. For example, when Pavlov consistently presented only the tone to a previously conditioned dog, the tone gradually lost its capacity to elicit the response of salivation. Such a sequence of events

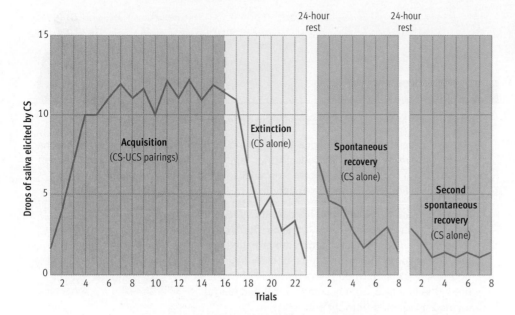

FIGURE 6.6

Acquisition, extinction, and spontaneous recovery. During acquisition, the strength of the dog's conditioned response (measured by the amount of salivation) increases rapidly and then levels off near its maximum. During extinction, the CR declines erratically until it's extinguished. After a "rest" period in which the dog is not exposed to the CS, a spontaneous recovery occurs, and the CS once again elicits a (weakened) CR. Repeated presentations of the CS alone reextinguish the CR, but after another "rest" interval, a weaker spontaneous recovery occurs.

is depicted in the left portion of **Figure 6.6**, which graphs the amount of salivation by a dog over a series of conditioning trials. Note how the salivation response declines during extinction.

For an example of extinction from outside the laboratory, let's assume that you cringe at the sound of a dentist's drill, which has been paired with pain in the past. You take a job as a dental assistant and you start hearing the drill (the CS) day in and day out without experiencing any pain (the US). Your cringing response will gradually diminish and extinguish altogether.

Spontaneous Recovery

Some conditioned responses can "reappear from the dead" after having been extinguished. Learning theorists use the term *spontaneous recovery* to describe such a resurrection from the graveyard of conditioned associations. ***Spontaneous recovery is the reappearance of an extinguished response after a period of nonexposure to the conditioned stimulus.***

Pavlov (1927) observed this phenomenon in some of his early studies. He fully extinguished a dog's CR of salivation to a tone and then returned the dog to its home cage for a "rest interval" (a period of nonexposure to the CS). On a subsequent day, when the dog was brought back to the experimental chamber for retesting, the tone was sounded and the salivation response reappeared. However, the recovered response was weak: there was less salivation than when the response had been at its peak strength. If Pavlov consistently presented the CS by itself again, the response reextinguished quickly. Interestingly, in some of the dogs, the response made still another spontaneous recovery (typically even weaker than the first) after they had spent another period in their cages (consult **Figure 6.6** once again).

Research has uncovered a related phenomenon called the ***renewal effect—if a response is extinguished in a different environment than it was acquired, the extinguished response will reappear if the animal is returned to the original environment where acquisition took place.*** This phenomenon, along with recent evidence on the neural bases of fear extinction, suggests that extinction somehow *suppresses* a conditioned response rather than *erasing* a learned association (Milad & Quirk, 2012). In other words, *extinction does not appear to lead to unlearning* (Bouton & Woods, 2009). The theoretical meaning of spontaneous recovery and the renewal effect is complex and the subject of some debate. However, their practical significance is quite simple: even if you manage to rid yourself of an unwanted conditioned response (such as cringing when you hear a dental drill), there is an excellent chance that it may make a surprise reappearance later. Unfortunately, this

CONCEPT CHECK 6.1

Identifying Elements in Classical Conditioning

Check your understanding of classical conditioning by trying to identify the unconditioned stimulus (US), unconditioned response (UR), conditioned stimulus (CS), and conditioned response (CR) in each of the examples below. Fill in the diagram accompanying each example. You'll find the answers in Appendix A.

1. Sam is 3 years old. One night, his parents build a roaring fire in the family room fireplace. The fire spits out a large ember that hits Sam in the arm, giving him a nasty burn that hurts a great deal for several hours. A week later, when Sam's parents light another fire in the fireplace, Sam becomes upset and fearful, crying and running from the room.

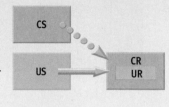

2. Melanie is driving to work on a rainy highway when she notices that the brake lights of all the cars just ahead of her have come on. She hits her brakes, but watches in horror as her car glides into a four-car pileup. She's badly shaken up in the accident. A month later, she's driving in the rain again and notices that she tenses up every time she sees brake lights come on ahead of her.

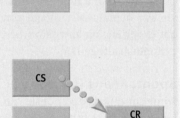

3. At the age of 24, Tyrone has recently developed an allergy to cats. When he's in the same room with a cat for more than 30 minutes, he starts wheezing. After a few such allergic reactions, he starts wheezing as soon as he sees a cat in a room.

insight also applies to behavior therapies that are used to extinguish troublesome phobias. Although patients are prone to relapse after these treatments, new research on extinction has yielded new techniques designed to reduce the likelihood of relapse (Laborda, McConnell, & Miller, 2011).

Stimulus Generalization

After conditioning has occurred, organisms often show a tendency to respond not only to the exact CS used but also to other, similar stimuli. For example, Pavlov's dogs might have salivated in response to a different tone, or you might cringe at the sound of a jeweler's as well as a dentist's drill. These are examples of stimulus generalization. **Stimulus generalization occurs when an organism that has learned a response to a specific stimulus responds in the same way to new stimuli that are similar to the original stimulus.** Generalization is adaptive given that organisms rarely encounter the exact same stimulus more than once (Miller & Grace, 2013). Stimulus generalization is also commonplace. We have already discussed a real-life example: the woman who acquired a bridge phobia during her childhood because her father scared her whenever they went over a particular old bridge. The original CS for her fear was that specific bridge, but her fear was ultimately *generalized* to all bridges.

John B. Watson, the founder of behaviorism (see Chapter 1), conducted an influential early study of generalization. Watson and a colleague, Rosalie Rayner, examined the

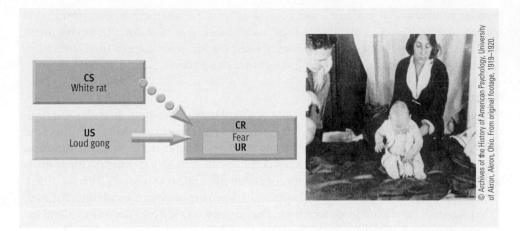

© Archives of the History of American Psychology, University of Akron, Akron, Ohio. From original footage, 1919–1920.

generalization of conditioned fear in an 11-month-old boy, known in the annals of psychology as "Little Albert." Like many babies, Albert was initially unafraid of a live white rat. Then Watson and Rayner (1920) paired the presentation of the rat with a loud, startling sound (made by striking a steel bar with a hammer). Albert *did* show fear in response to the loud noise. After seven pairings of the rat and the gong, the rat was established as a CS eliciting a fear response (see **Figure 6.7**). Five days later, Watson and Rayner exposed the youngster to other stimuli that resembled the rat in being white and furry. They found that Albert's fear response generalized to a variety of stimuli, including a rabbit, a dog, a fur coat, a Santa Claus mask, and Watson's hair.

Generalization depends on the similarity between the new stimulus and the original CS. The basic law governing generalization is this: *The more similar new stimuli are to the original CS, the greater the likelihood of generalization.* This principle can be quantified in graphs called *generalization gradients,* such as those shown in **Figure 6.8**. These generalization gradients map out how a dog conditioned to salivate to a tone of 1200 hertz might respond to other tones. As you can see, the strength of the generalization response declines as the similarity between the new stimuli and the original CS decreases.

The process of generalization can have important implications. For example, it appears to contribute to the development of *panic disorder*, which involves recurrent, overwhelming anxiety attacks that occur suddenly and unexpectedly (see Chapter 14). Research suggests that panic patients have a tendency to overgeneralize; that is, to have

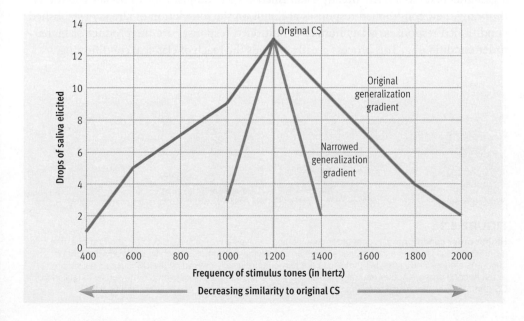

FIGURE 6.8

Generalization gradients. In a study of stimulus generalization, an organism is typically conditioned to respond to a specific CS, such as a 1200-hertz tone, and then is tested with similar stimuli, such as other tones between 400 and 2000 hertz. Graphs of the organisms responding are called *generalization gradients.* The graphs normally show, as depicted here, that generalization declines as the similarity between the original CS and the new stimuli decreases. When an organism gradually learns to *discriminate* between a CS and similar stimuli, the generalization gradient tends to narrow around the original CS (as shown in orange).

broader generalization gradients than control subjects do, when exposed to stimuli that trigger anxiety (Lissek et al., 2010). Thus, conditioned fear to a stimulus environment where panic occurs (say, a specific shopping mall) readily generalizes to similar stimulus situations (all shopping malls), fueling the growth of a patient's panic disorder.

Stimulus Discrimination

Stimulus discrimination is just the opposite of stimulus generalization. ***Stimulus discrimination* occurs when an organism that has learned a response to a specific stimulus does not respond in the same way to new stimuli that are similar to the original stimulus.** Like generalization, discrimination is adaptive in that an animal's survival may hinge on its being able to distinguish friend from foe, or edible from poisonous food (Thomas, 1992). Organisms can gradually learn to discriminate between the original CS and similar stimuli if they have adequate experience with both. For instance, let's say your dog runs around excitedly wagging his tail whenever he hears your car pull up in the driveway. Initially it will probably respond to *all* cars that pull into the driveway (stimulus generalization). However, if there is anything distinctive about the sound of your car, your dog may gradually respond with excitement only to your car and not to other cars (stimulus discrimination).

The development of stimulus discrimination usually requires that the original CS (your car) continues to be paired with the US (your arrival), while similar stimuli (the other cars) are not paired with the US. As with generalization, a basic law governs discrimination: *The less similar new stimuli are to the original CS, the greater the likelihood (and ease) of discrimination.* Conversely, if a new stimulus is quite similar to the original CS, discrimination will be relatively hard to learn.

Higher-Order Conditioning

Imagine that you were to conduct the following experiment. First, you condition a dog to salivate in response to the sound of a tone by pairing the tone with meat powder. Once the tone is firmly established as a CS, you pair the tone with a new stimulus—let's say a red light—for 15 trials. You then present the red light alone, without the tone. Will the dog salivate in response to the red light?

The answer is "yes." Even though the red light has never been paired with the meat powder, it will acquire the capacity to elicit salivation by virtue of being paired with the tone (see **Figure 6.9**). This is a demonstration of *higher-order conditioning,* **in which a conditioned stimulus functions as if it were an unconditioned stimulus.** Higher-order conditioning shows that classical conditioning does not depend on the presence of a genuine, natural US. An already established CS will do just fine. In higher-order conditioning, new conditioned responses are built on the foundation of already established conditioned responses. Many human conditioned responses are the product of higher-order conditioning. This process greatly extends the reach of classical conditioning.

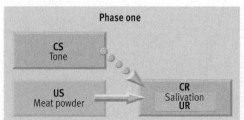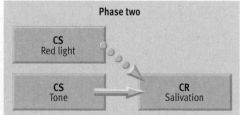

FIGURE 6.9

Higher-order conditioning. Higher-order conditioning involves a two-phase process. In the first phase, a neutral stimulus (such as a tone) is paired with an unconditioned stimulus (such as meat powder) until it becomes a conditioned stimulus that elicits the response originally evoked by the US (such as salivation). In the second phase, another neutral stimulus (such as a red light) is paired with the previously established CS (the tone), so that it also acquires the capacity to elicit the response originally evoked by the US.

6.2 OPERANT CONDITIONING

6.2

Key Learning Goals

- Explain Skinner's principle of reinforcement, and describe the terminology and procedures in operant research.
- Describe shaping, extinction, generalization, and discrimination in operant conditioning.
- Identify various types of schedules of reinforcement, and discuss their typical effects.
- Distinguish between positive and negative reinforcement and between escape learning and avoidance learning.
- Describe punishment, and assess issues related to punishment as a disciplinary procedure.

Even Pavlov recognized that classical conditioning is not the only form of conditioning. Classical conditioning best explains reflexive responding that is largely controlled by stimuli that *precede* the response. However, humans and other animals make a great many responses that don't fit this description. Consider the response that you are engaging in right now: studying. It is definitely not a reflex (life might be easier if it were). The stimuli that govern it (exams and grades) do not precede it. Instead, your studying is mainly influenced by stimulus events that *follow* the response—specifically, its *consequences*.

In the 1930s, this kind of learning was named *operant conditioning* by B. F. Skinner (1938, 1953, 1969). The term was derived from his belief that in this type of responding, an organism "operates" on the environment instead of simply reacting to stimuli. Thus, **operant conditioning is a form of learning in which voluntary responses come to be controlled by their consequences.** Learning theorists originally distinguished between classical and operant conditioning on the grounds that the former regulated reflexive, involuntary responses, whereas the latter governed voluntary responses. This distinction holds up much of the time, but it is not absolute because the two types of conditioning jointly and interactively govern some aspects of behavior (Schachtman & Reilly, 2011).

Skinner's Demonstration: It's All a Matter of Consequences

B. F. Skinner had great admiration for Pavlov's work and used it as the foundation for his own theory, even borrowing some of Pavlov's terminology (Dinsmoor, 2004). And, like Pavlov, Skinner (1953, 1984) conducted some deceptively simple research that became enormously influential. The fundamental principle of operant conditioning is uncommonly simple: *Skinner demonstrated that organisms tend to repeat those responses that are followed by favorable consequences.* This fundamental principle is embodied in Skinner's concept of reinforcement. *Reinforcement* **occurs when an event following a response increases an organism's tendency to make that response.** In other words, a response is strengthened because it leads to rewarding consequences.

The principle of reinforcement may be simple, but it is immensely powerful. Skinner and his followers have shown that much of people's everyday behavior is regulated by reinforcement. For example, you study hard because good grades are likely to follow as a result. You go to work because this behavior leads to receiving paychecks. Perhaps you work extra hard because promotions and raises tend to follow such behavior. You tell jokes, and your friends laugh—so you tell some more. The principle of reinforcement clearly governs complex aspects of human behavior. Paradoxically, though, this principle emerged out of Skinner's research on the behavior of rats and pigeons in exceptionally simple situations. Let's look at that research.

Terminology and Procedures

Like Pavlov, Skinner created a prototype experimental procedure that has been repeated (with variations) thousands of times. In this procedure, an animal, typically a rat or a pigeon, is placed in an *operant chamber* that has come to be better known as a "Skinner box." **A *Skinner box* is a small enclosure in which an animal can make a specific response that is systematically recorded while the consequences of the response are controlled.** In the boxes designed for rats, the main response made available is pressing a small lever mounted on one side wall (see **Figure 6.10**). In the boxes made for pigeons, the designated response is pecking a small disk mounted on a side wall.

© Vasiliy Koval/Shutterstock.com

Although operant conditioning can explain countless aspects of complex human behavior, much of the early research was conducted with laboratory rats.

FIGURE 6.10

Skinner box and cumulative recorder. (a) This diagram highlights some of the key features of an operant chamber, or Skinner box. In this apparatus designed for rats, the response under study is lever pressing. Food pellets, which serve as reinforcers, are delivered into the food cup on the right. The speaker and light permit manipulations of visual and auditory stimuli, and the electric grid gives the experimenter control over aversive consequences (shock) in the box. **(b)** A cumulative recorder connected to the box keeps a continuous record of responses and reinforcements. A small segment of a cumulative record is shown here. The entire process is automatic as the paper moves with the passage of time; each lever press moves the pen up a step, and each reinforcement is marked with a slash. **(c)** This photo shows the real thing—a rat being conditioned in a Skinner box.

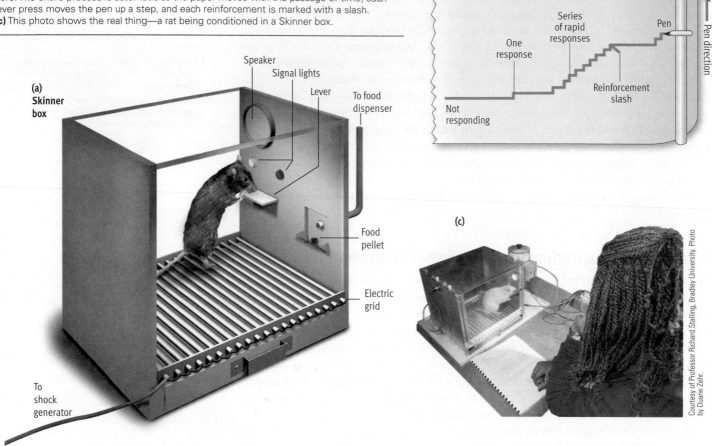

Operant responses, such as lever pressing and disk pecking, are said to be *emitted* rather than *elicited*. **To *emit* means to send forth.** This word was chosen because, as already noted, operant conditioning mainly governs *voluntary* responses instead of reflex responses.

The Skinner box permits the experimenter to control the reinforcement contingencies that are in effect for the animal. ***Reinforcement contingencies* are the circumstances or rules that determine whether responses lead to the presentation of reinforcers.** Typically, the experimenter manipulates whether positive consequences occur when the animal makes the designated response. The main positive consequence is usually delivery of a small bit of food into a cup mounted in the chamber. Because the animals are deprived of food for a while prior to the experimental session, their hunger virtually ensures that the food serves as a reinforcer.

The key dependent variable in most research on operant conditioning is the subjects' *response rate* over time. An animal's rate of lever pressing or disk pecking in the Skinner box is monitored continuously by a device known as a cumulative recorder (see **Figure 6.10**). **The *cumulative recorder* creates a graphic record of responding and reinforcement in a Skinner box as a function of time.** The recorder works by means of a roll of paper that moves at a steady rate underneath a movable pen. When there is no responding, the pen stays still and draws a straight horizontal line, reflecting the passage of time. Whenever the designated response occurs, however, the pen moves up a notch. The pen's movements produce a graphic summary of the animal's responding over time. The pen also makes slash marks to record the delivery of each reinforcer. The results of operant conditioning studies are usually portrayed in graphs. In these graphs, the horizontal axis is used to mark the passage of time, while the vertical axis is used to plot the accumulation of responses (consult the four graphs in **Figure 6.13** for examples). In interpreting these graphs, the key consideration is the *slope* of the line that represents the record of responding. *A rapid response rate produces a steep slope, whereas a slow response rate produces a shallow slope.*

Basic Processes in Operant Conditioning

Although the principle of reinforcement is strikingly simple, many other processes involved in operant conditioning make this form of learning just as complex as classical conditioning. In fact, some of the same processes are involved in both types of conditioning. In this section, we'll discuss how the processes of acquisition, extinction, generalization, and discrimination occur in operant conditioning.

Acquisition and Shaping

As in classical conditioning, *acquisition* in operant conditioning is the formation of a new response tendency. However, the procedures used to establish a tendency to emit a voluntary operant response are different from those used to create a reflexive conditioned response. Operant responses are typically established through a gradual process called *shaping—***the reinforcement of closer and closer approximations of a desired response.**

Shaping is necessary when an organism does not, on its own, emit the desired response. For example, when a rat is first placed in a Skinner box, it may not press the lever at all. In this case, an experimenter begins shaping by releasing food pellets whenever the rat moves toward the lever. As this response becomes more frequent, the experimenter starts requiring a closer approximation of the desired response, possibly releasing food only when the rat actually touches the lever. As reinforcement increases the rat's tendency to touch the lever, the rat will spontaneously press the lever on occasion, finally providing the experimenter with an opportunity to reinforce the designated response. These reinforcements gradually increase the rate of lever pressing.

Shaping molds many aspects of both human and animal behavior. For instance, it is the key to training animals to perform impressive tricks. When you go to a zoo, circus, or marine park and see bears riding bicycles, monkeys playing the piano, and whales leaping through hoops, you are witnessing the results of shaping. To demonstrate the power of shaping techniques, Skinner once trained some pigeons so that they appeared to play a crude version of ping-pong. They would run about at opposite ends of a tiny ping-pong table and peck the ball back and forth. Keller and Marian Breland, a couple of psychologists influenced by Skinner, applied shaping in their business of training animals for advertising and entertainment purposes. One of their better-known feats was shaping "Priscilla, the Fastidious Pig" to turn on a radio, eat at a kitchen table, put dirty clothes in a hamper, run a vacuum, and then "go shopping" with a shopping cart (see the photo on the next page). Of course, Priscilla picked the sponsor's product off the shelf in her shopping expedition (Breland & Breland, 1961).

Extinction

In operant conditioning, *extinction* refers to the gradual weakening and disappearance of a response tendency because the response is no longer followed by reinforcement. Extinction begins in operant conditioning whenever previously available reinforcement is stopped. In laboratory studies with rats, this situation usually occurs when the experimenter stops delivering food as reinforcement for lever pressing. When the extinction

Shaping—an operant technique in which an organism is rewarded for closer and closer approximations of the desired response—is used in teaching both animals and humans. It is the main means of training animals to perform unnatural tricks. Breland and Breland's (1961) famous subject "Priscilla, the Fastidious Pig" is shown in the photo above.

process is begun, a brief surge often occurs in the rat's responding, followed by a gradual decline in response rate until it approaches zero. The same effects are generally seen in the extinction of human behavior.

A key issue in operant conditioning is how much *resistance to extinction* an organism will display when reinforcement is halted. **Resistance to extinction occurs when an organism continues to make a response after delivery of the reinforcer for it has been terminated.** The greater the resistance to extinction, the longer the responding will continue. Thus, if a researcher stops giving reinforcement for lever pressing and the response tapers off slowly, the response shows high resistance to extinction. However, if the response tapers off quickly, it shows relatively little resistance to extinction.

Resistance to extinction may sound like a matter of purely theoretical interest, but it's actually quite practical. People often want to strengthen a response in such a way that it will be relatively resistant to extinction. For instance, most parents want to see their child's studying response survive even if the child hits a rocky stretch when studying doesn't lead to reinforcement (good grades). In a similar fashion, a casino wants to see patrons continue to gamble even if they encounter a lengthy losing streak.

Another complexity relating to extinction is that the *renewal effect* seen in classical conditioning is also seen in operant conditioning. Bouton and colleagues (2011) tested for a renewal effect by modifying two Skinner boxes to create very different contexts. The two chambers had different scents, different floors (even versus uneven), and different walls and ceilings (painted with dots versus stripes). They found that if acquisition of lever-pressing occurred in one context and subsequent extinction in another context, responding recovered when the rats were returned to the original context or placed in a new, neutral context. *In other words, it appears that the result of extinction is that organisms learn not to make a specific response in a specific context, as opposed to any and all contexts* (Bouton & Todd, 2014). The context-dependent nature of extinction may help explain why maladaptive responses that are successfully extinguished in behavior therapists' offices can reappear in other contexts.

Stimulus Control: Generalization and Discrimination

Operant responding is ultimately controlled by its consequences, as organisms learn response-outcome (R-O) associations (Colwill, 1993). However, stimuli that *precede* a response can also influence operant behavior. When a response is consistently followed by a reinforcer in the presence of a particular stimulus, that stimulus comes to serve as a "signal" indicating that the response is likely to lead to a reinforcer. Once an organism learns the signal, it tends to respond accordingly. For example, a pigeon's disk pecking may be reinforced only when a small light behind the disk is lit. When the light is out, pecking does not lead to the reward. Pigeons quickly learn to peck the disk only when it is lit. The light that signals the availability of reinforcement is called a discriminative stimulus. ***Discriminative stimuli* are cues that influence operant behavior by indicating the probable consequences (reinforcement or nonreinforcement) of a response.**

Discriminative stimuli play a key role in the regulation of operant behavior. For example, birds learn that hunting for worms is likely to be reinforced after a rain. Children learn to ask for sweets when their parents are in a good mood. Drivers learn to slow down when the highway is wet. The potential power of discriminative stimuli to govern behavior was demonstrated in dramatic fashion in a study by Talwar and associates (2002). They showed that it's possible to use operant procedures to train what *Time* magazine called "roborats"—radio-controlled rodents that can be precisely directed through complex environments, such as collapsed buildings (see **Figure 6.11**).

Reactions to a discriminative stimulus are governed by the processes of *stimulus generalization* and *stimulus discrimination,* just like reactions to a CS in classical conditioning. For instance, envision a cat that gets excited whenever it hears the sound of a can opener because that sound has become a discriminative stimulus signaling a good chance of its getting fed. If the cat also responded to the sound of a new kitchen appliance (say a blender), this response would represent *generalization*—responding to a new stimulus as if it were the original. *Discrimination* would occur if the cat learned to respond only to the can opener and not to the blender.

As you have learned in this section, the processes of acquisition, extinction, generalization, and discrimination in operant conditioning parallel these same processes in classical conditioning. **Table 6.1** compares these processes in the two kinds of conditioning.

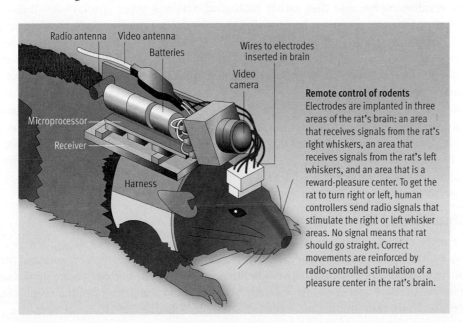

Radio antenna Video antenna
Batteries
Wires to electrodes inserted in brain
Video camera
Microprocessor
Receiver
Harness

Remote control of rodents
Electrodes are implanted in three areas of the rat's brain: an area that receives signals from the rat's right whiskers, an area that receives signals from the rat's left whiskers, and an area that is a reward-pleasure center. To get the rat to turn right or left, human controllers send radio signals that stimulate the right or left whisker areas. No signal means that rat should go straight. Correct movements are reinforced by radio-controlled stimulation of a pleasure center in the rat's brain.

FIGURE 6.11

Remote-controlled rodents: An example of operant conditioning in action. In a study that almost reads like science fiction, Sanjiv Talwar and colleagues (2002) used operant conditioning procedures to train radio-controlled "roborats" that could have a variety of valuable applications, such as searching for survivors in a collapsed building. As this graphic shows, radio signals can be used to direct the rat to go forward or turn right or left, while a video feed is sent back to a control center. The *reinforcer* in this setup is brief electrical stimulation of a pleasure center in the rat's brain (see Chapter 3), which can be delivered by remote control. The brief shocks sent to the right or left whiskers are *discriminative stimuli* that indicate which types of responses will be reinforced. The entire procedure depended on extensive *shaping*.

TABLE 6.1 Comparison of Basic Processes in Classical and Operant Conditioning

Process and Definition	Description in Classical Conditioning	Description in Operant Conditioning
Acquisition: The initial stage of learning	CS and US are paired, gradually resulting in CR.	Responding gradually increases because of reinforcement, possibly through shaping.
Extinction: The gradual weakening and disappearance of a conditioned response tendency	CS is presented alone until it no longer elicits CR.	Responding gradually slows and stops after reinforcement is terminated.
Stimulus generalization: An organism's responding to stimuli other than the original stimulus used in conditioning	CR is elicited by new stimulus that resembles original CS.	Responding increases in the presence of new stimulus that resembles original discriminative stimulus.
Stimulus discrimination: An organism's lack of response to stimuli that are similar to the original stimulus used in conditioning	CR is not elicited by new stimulus that resembles original CS	Responding does not increase in the presence of new stimulus that resembles original discriminative stimulus.

Reinforcement

Although it is convenient to equate reinforcement with reward and the experience of pleasure, strict behaviorists object to this practice. Why? Because the experience of pleasure is an unobservable event that takes place within an organism. As explained in Chapter 1, most behaviorists believe that scientific assertions must be limited to what can be observed.

In keeping with this orientation, Skinner said that reinforcement occurs whenever an outcome strengthens a response, as measured by an increase in the rate of responding. This definition avoids the issue of what the organism is feeling and focuses on observable events. Thus, the central process in reinforcement is the *strengthening of a response tendency.*

Reinforcement is therefore defined *after the fact,* in terms of its *effect* on behavior. Something that is clearly reinforcing for an organism at one time may not function as a reinforcer later (Catania, 1992). Food will reinforce lever pressing by a rat only if the rat is hungry. Similarly, something that serves as a reinforcer for one person may not function as a reinforcer for another person. For example, parental approval is a potent reinforcer for most children, but not all.

Operant theorists make a distinction between unlearned, or primary, reinforcers and conditioned, or secondary, reinforcers. **Primary reinforcers are events that are inherently reinforcing because they satisfy biological needs.** A given species has a limited number of primary reinforcers because these reinforcers are closely tied to physiological needs. In humans, primary reinforcers include food, water, warmth, sex, and perhaps affection expressed through hugging and close bodily contact. ***Secondary,* or *conditioned, reinforcers* are events that acquire reinforcing qualities by being associated with primary reinforcers.** The events that function as secondary reinforcers vary among members of a species because they depend on learning. Examples of common secondary reinforcers in humans include money, good grades, attention, flattery, praise, and applause. Most of the material things that people work hard to earn are secondary reinforcers. For example, many people learn to find that stylish clothes, sports cars, fine jewelry, elegant china, and state-of-the-art TVs can be reinforcing.

Schedules of Reinforcement

In operant conditioning, a favorable outcome is much more likely to strengthen a response if the outcome follows *immediately.* If a delay occurs between a response and the positive outcome, the response may not be strengthened. Furthermore, studies show that the longer the delay between the designated response and the delivery of the reinforcer, the more slowly conditioning proceeds (McDevitt & Williams, 2001).

Obviously, organisms make innumerable responses that do *not* lead to favorable consequences. It would be nice if people were reinforced every time they took an exam, watched a movie, hit a golf shot, asked for a date, or made a sales call. However, in the real world, most responses are reinforced only some of the time. How does this situation affect the potency of reinforcers? To find out, operant psychologists have devoted an enormous amount of attention to how *schedules of reinforcement* influence operant behavior (Ferster & Skinner, 1957; Skinner, 1938, 1953).

A *schedule of reinforcement* is a specific pattern of presentation of reinforcers over time. The simplest pattern is continuous reinforcement. ***Continuous reinforcement* occurs when every instance of a designated response is reinforced.** In the laboratory, experimenters often use continuous reinforcement to shape and establish a new response before moving on to more realistic schedules involving intermittent, or partial, reinforcement. ***Intermittent reinforcement* occurs when a designated response is reinforced only some of the time.**

Which do you suppose leads to longer-lasting effects: being reinforced every time you emit a response, or being reinforced only some of the time? Studies show that, given an equal number of reinforcements, *intermittent* reinforcement makes a response more resistant to extinction than continuous reinforcement does (Falls, 1998). This reality explains why behaviors that are reinforced only occasionally—such as temper tantrums in children—can be very durable and difficult to eliminate.

Reinforcement schedules come in many varieties, but four particular types of intermittent schedules have attracted the most interest (Miller & Grace, 2013). These schedules are described here, along with examples drawn from the laboratory and everyday life (see **Figure 6.12** for additional examples).

Ratio schedules require the organism to make the designated response a certain number of times to gain each reinforcer. **In a *fixed-ratio (FR) schedule,* the reinforcer is given after a fixed number of nonreinforced responses.** *Examples:* (1) A rat is reinforced for every tenth lever press. (2) A salesperson receives a bonus for every fourth gym membership sold. **In a *variable-ratio (VR) schedule,* the reinforcer is given after a variable number of nonreinforced responses.** The number of nonreinforced responses varies around a predetermined average. *Examples:* (1) A rat is reinforced for every tenth lever press on the average. The exact number of responses required for reinforcement varies from one time to the next. (2) A slot machine in a casino pays off once every six tries

REALITY CHECK

Misconception

The best way to ensure that a desired behavior will persist is to reward the behavior every time it occurs.

Reality

This statement certainly sounds logical, but research clearly shows that continuous reinforcement generates less resistance to extinction than does intermittent reinforcement. If you want a response to remain strong in the absence of reinforcement, you should reinforce the response intermittently so that the organism becomes accustomed to some degree of nonreinforcement.

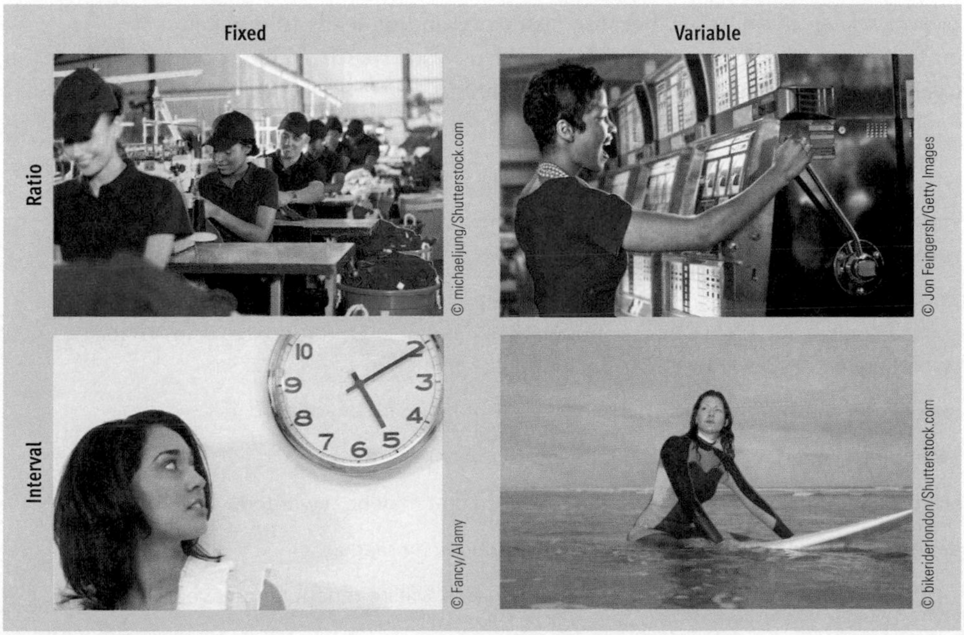

FIGURE 6.12

Reinforcement schedules in everyday life. Complex human behaviors are regulated by schedules of reinforcement. Piecework is reinforced on a fixed-ratio schedule. Playing slot machines is based on variable-ratio reinforcement. Watching the clock at work is rewarded on a fixed-interval basis (the arrival of quitting time is the reinforcer). Surfers waiting for a big wave are rewarded on a variable-interval basis.

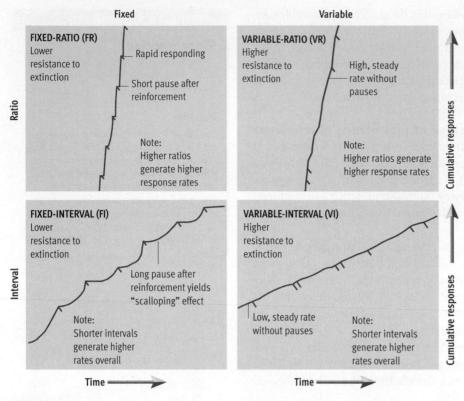

FIGURE 6.13

Schedules of reinforcement and patterns of response. In graphs of operant responding such as these, a steeper slope indicates a faster rate of response and the slash marks reflect the delivery of reinforcers. Each type of reinforcement schedule tends to generate a characteristic pattern of responding. In general, ratio schedules tend to produce more rapid responding than interval schedules (note the steep slopes of the FR and VR curves). In comparison with fixed schedules, variable schedules tend to yield steadier responding (note the smoother lines for the VR and VI schedules on the right).

on the average. The number of nonwinning responses between payoffs varies greatly from one time to the next.

Interval schedules require a time period to pass between the presentation of reinforcers. **In a *fixed-interval (FI) schedule*, the reinforcer is given for the first response that occurs after a fixed time interval has elapsed.** *Examples:* (1) A rat is reinforced for the first lever press after a 2-minute interval has elapsed and then must wait 2 minutes before being able to earn the next reinforcement. (2) You can get clean clothes out of your washing machine every 35 minutes. **In a *variable-interval (VI) schedule*, the reinforcer is given for the first response after a variable time interval has elapsed. The interval length varies around a predetermined average.** *Examples:* (1) A rat is reinforced for the first lever press after a 1-minute interval has elapsed, but the following intervals are 3 minutes, 2 minutes, 4 minutes, and so on—with an average length of 2 minutes. (2) A person repeatedly dials a busy phone number (getting through is the reinforcer).

Decades of research have yielded an enormous volume of data on how these schedules of reinforcement are related to patterns of responding (Williams, 1988; Zeiler, 1977). Some of the more prominent findings are summarized in **Figure 6.13**, which depicts typical response patterns generated by each schedule. For example, with fixed-interval schedules, a pause in responding usually occurs after each reinforcer is delivered, and then responding gradually increases to a rapid rate at the end of the interval. This pattern of behavior yields a "scalloped" response curve. In general, *ratio schedules tend to produce more rapid responding than interval schedules do.* Why? Because faster responding leads to quicker reinforcement when a ratio schedule is in effect. *Variable schedules tend to generate steadier response rates and greater resistance to extinction than their fixed counterparts do.*

CONCEPT CHECK 6.2

Recognizing Schedules of Reinforcement

Check your understanding of schedules of reinforcement in operant conditioning by indicating the type of schedule that would be in effect in each of the examples below. In the spaces on the left, fill in CR for continuous reinforcement, FR for fixed-ratio, VR for variable-ratio, FI for fixed-interval, and VI for variable-interval. The answers can be found in Appendix A.

_____ 1. Sarah is paid on a commission basis for selling computer systems. She gets a bonus for every third sale.

_____ 2. Juan's parents let him earn some pocket money by doing yard work *approximately* once a week.

_____ 3. Martha is fly-fishing. Think of each time that she casts her line as the response that may be rewarded.

_____ 4. Jamal, who is in the fourth grade, gets a gold star from his teacher for every book he reads.

_____ 5. Skip, a professional baseball player, signs an agreement that his salary increases will be renegotiated every 3rd year.

Most of the research on reinforcement schedules was conducted on rats and pigeons in Skinner boxes. However, psychologists have found that humans react to schedules of reinforcement in much the same way as lower animals (de Villiers, 1977; Perone, Galizio, & Baron, 1988). For example, when animals are placed on ratio schedules, shifting to a higher ratio (that is, requiring more responses per reinforcement) tends to generate faster responding. Managers who run factories that pay on a piecework basis (a fixed-ratio schedule) have seen the same reaction in humans. In a similar vein, most gambling is reinforced according to variable-ratio schedules, which tend to produce rapid, steady responding and great resistance to extinction—exactly what casino operators want.

Positive Versus Negative Reinforcement

According to Skinner, reinforcement can take two forms, which he called *positive reinforcement* and *negative reinforcement* (see **Figure 6.14**). **Positive reinforcement occurs when a response is strengthened because it is followed by the presentation of a rewarding stimulus.** Thus far, for purposes of simplicity, our examples have involved positive reinforcement. Good grades, tasty meals, paychecks, scholarships, promotions, nice clothes, nifty cars, attention, and flattery are all positive reinforcers.

In contrast, **negative reinforcement occurs when a response is strengthened because it is followed by the removal of an aversive (unpleasant) stimulus.** Don't let the word "negative" confuse you. Negative reinforcement is reinforcement. Like all reinforcement, it involves a favorable outcome that strengthens a response tendency. However, this strengthening takes place because a response leads to the removal of an aversive stimulus rather than the arrival of a pleasant stimulus (see **Figure 6.14**).

In laboratory studies, negative reinforcement is usually accomplished as follows: While a rat is in a Skinner box, a moderate electric shock is delivered to the animal through the floor of the box. When the rat presses the lever, the shock is turned off for

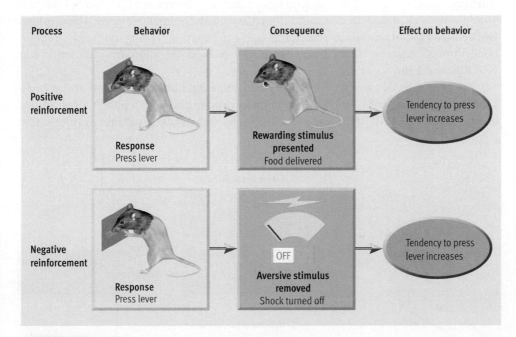

FIGURE 6.14

Positive reinforcement versus negative reinforcement. In positive reinforcement, a response leads to the presentation of a rewarding stimulus. In negative reinforcement, a response leads to the removal of an aversive stimulus. Both types of reinforcement involve favorable consequences and both have the same effect on behavior: the organism's tendency to emit the reinforced response is strengthened.

a period of time. Thus, lever pressing leads to removal of an aversive stimulus (shock). Although this sequence of events is different from those for positive reinforcement, it reliably strengthens the rat's lever pressing response.

Everyday human behavior is regulated extensively by negative reinforcement. Consider a handful of examples. You rush home in the winter to get out of the cold. You clean house to get rid of a mess. You give in to your child's begging to halt the whining. You give in to a roommate or spouse to bring an unpleasant argument to an end.

Negative reinforcement plays a key role in both escape learning and avoidance learning. **In *escape learning*, an organism acquires a response that decreases or ends some aversive stimulation.** Psychologists often study escape learning in the laboratory with dogs or rats that are conditioned in a *shuttle box*. The shuttle box has two compartments connected by a doorway, which can be opened and closed by the experimenter, as depicted in **Figure 6.15a**. In a typical study, an animal is placed in one compartment and the shock in the floor of that chamber is turned on, with the doorway open. The animal learns to escape the shock by running to the other compartment. This escape response leads to the removal of an aversive stimulus (shock), so it is strengthened through negative reinforcement. If you were to leave a party where you were getting picked on by peers, you would be engaging in an escape response.

Escape learning often leads to avoidance learning. **In *avoidance learning*, an organism acquires a response that prevents some aversive stimulation from occurring.** In shuttle box studies of avoidance learning, the experimenter simply gives the animal a signal that a shock is forthcoming. The typical signal is a light that goes on a few seconds prior to the shock. At first, the dog or rat runs only when shocked (escape learning). Gradually, however, the animal learns to run to the safe compartment as soon as the light comes on, showing avoidance learning. Similarly, if you were to quit going to parties because of your concern about being picked on by peers, you would be demonstrating avoidance learning.

Avoidance learning presents an interesting example of how classical conditioning and operant conditioning can work together to regulate behavior (Levis, 1989). In avoidance learning, the warning light that goes on before the shock becomes a CS (through classical conditioning) eliciting reflexive, conditioned fear in the animal. However, the response of fleeing to the other side of the box is operant behavior. This response is strengthened through *negative reinforcement* because it reduces the animal's conditioned fear (see **Figure 6.15b**).

The principles of avoidance learning shed some light on why phobias are so resistant to extinction (Levis, 1989). For example, suppose you have a phobia of elevators, so you always take the stairs instead. Taking the stairs is an avoidance response that

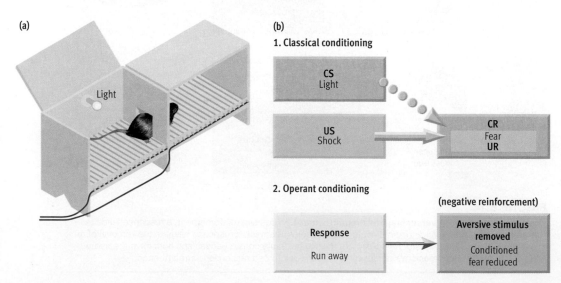

FIGURE 6.15

Escape and avoidance learning.
(a) Escape and avoidance learning are often studied with a shuttle box like that shown here. Warning signals, shock, and the animal's ability to flee from one compartment to another can be controlled by the experimenter. **(b)** Avoidance begins because classical conditioning creates a conditioned fear that is elicited by the warning signal (panel 1). Avoidance continues because it is maintained by operant conditioning (panel 2). Specifically, the avoidance response is strengthened through negative reinforcement because it leads to removal of the conditioned fear.

should lead to consistent negative reinforcement by relieving your conditioned fear—so your avoidance behavior is strengthened and continues. Moreover, your avoidance behavior prevents any opportunity to extinguish the phobic conditioned response because you're never exposed to the conditioned stimulus (in this case, riding in an elevator).

Punishment

Reinforcement is defined in terms of its consequences. It *strengthens* an organism's tendency to make a certain response. Are there also consequences that *weaken* an organism's tendency to make a particular response? Yes. In Skinner's model of operant behavior, such consequences are called *punishment*.

Punishment **occurs when an event following a response weakens the tendency to make that response.** In a Skinner box, the use of punishment is very simple. When a rat presses the lever or a pigeon pecks the disk, it receives a brief shock. This procedure usually leads to a rapid decline in the animal's response rate (Dinsmoor, 1998). Punishment typically involves presentation of an aversive stimulus (for instance, spanking a child). However, punishment can also involve the removal of a rewarding stimulus (for instance, taking away a child's TV-watching privileges).

The concept of punishment in operant conditioning is confusing to many students, on two counts. First, they often confuse it with negative reinforcement, which is entirely different. Negative reinforcement involves the *removal* of an aversive stimulus, thereby *strengthening* a response. Punishment, on the other hand, involves the *presentation* of an aversive stimulus, thereby *weakening* a response. Thus, punishment and negative reinforcement are *opposite procedures* that *yield opposite effects* on behavior (see **Figure 6.16**).

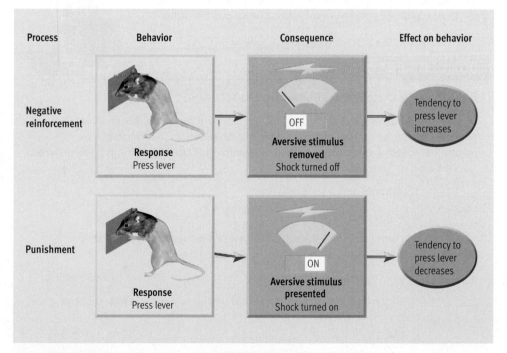

FIGURE 6.16

Comparison of negative reinforcement and punishment. Although punishment can occur when a response leads to the removal of a rewarding stimulus, it more typically involves the presentation of an aversive stimulus. Students often confuse punishment with negative reinforcement because they associate both with aversive stimuli. However, as this diagram shows, punishment and negative reinforcement represent opposite procedures that have opposite effects on behavior.

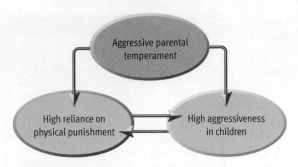

FIGURE 6.17

The correlation between physical punishment and aggressiveness. As we discussed before, a correlation does not establish causation. It seems plausible that extensive reliance on physical punishment causes children to be more aggressive, as many experts believe. However, it is also possible that highly aggressive children cause their parents to depend heavily on physical punishment. Or perhaps parents with an aggressive, hostile temperament pass on genetic tendencies for aggressiveness to their children, model aggressive behavior, and rely on heavy use of physical punishment.

The second source of confusion involves the tendency to equate punishment with *disciplinary procedures* used by parents, teachers, and other authority figures. In the operant model, punishment occurs any time undesirable consequences weaken a response tendency. Defined in this way, the concept of punishment goes far beyond things such as parents spanking children and teachers handing out detentions. For example, if you wear a new outfit and your schoolmates make fun of it, your behavior will have been punished and your tendency to emit this response (wear the same clothing) will probably decline. Similarly, if you go to a restaurant and have a horrible meal, your response will have been punished, and your tendency to go to that restaurant will probably decline.

Although punishment in operant conditioning encompasses far more than disciplinary acts, it *is* used frequently for disciplinary purposes. In light of this situation, it is worth looking at the research on punishment as a disciplinary measure. Controversy exists about the wisdom of using *physical* punishment. The main concern is that spanking and other forms of corporal punishment may produce many unintended and undesirable side effects. Studies generally find that corporal punishment is associated with elevated aggression, delinquency, and behavioral problems in youngsters (Gershoff, 2002) In the long term, physical punishment is also associated with slowed cognitive development, increases in criminal behavior, and a wide range of mental health problems (Durrant & Ensom, 2012; Straus, Douglas, & Medeiros, 2014). Some critics have pointed out that the evidence linking spanking to negative effects is correlational, and correlation is no assurance of causation (Kazdin & Benjet, 2003). Perhaps spanking causes children to be more aggressive, but it's also plausible that aggressive children cause their parents to rely more on physical punishment (see **Figure 6.17**).

Although this critique has merit, evidence on the negative effects of corporal punishment has continued to pile up

CONCEPT CHECK 6.3

Recognizing Outcomes in Operant Conditioning

Check your understanding of the various types of consequences that can occur in operant conditioning by indicating whether the examples below involve positive reinforcement (PR), negative reinforcement (NR), punishment (P), or extinction (E). The answers can be found in Appendix A.

_____ 1. Antonio gets a speeding ticket.

_____ 2. Diane's supervisor compliments her on her hard work.

_____ 3. Leon goes to the health club for a rare workout and pushes himself so hard that his entire body aches and he throws up.

_____ 4. Audrey lets her dog out so she won't have to listen to its whimpering.

_____ 5. Richard shoots up heroin to ward off tremors and chills associated with heroin withdrawal.

_____ 6. Sharma constantly complains about minor aches and pains to obtain sympathy from colleagues at work. Three co-workers who share an office with her decide to ignore her complaints instead of responding with sympathy.

(Gershoff et al., 2012; Smith, 2012). Many of the newer studies have statistically controlled for children's initial level of aggression and other confounding variables, which strengthens the case for a causal link between spanking and negative outcomes (Durrant & Ensom, 2012). In spite of all the evidence of its negative effects, physical punishment continues to be widely used by parents (Lee, Grogan-Kaylor, & Berger, 2014; MacKenzie et al., 2013). Ironically, research suggests that corporal punishment is not very effective in ensuring children's obedience (Gershoff, 2013). For example, one recent study (Holden, Williamson, & Holland, 2014) based on audio recordings of family interactions (as opposed to self-report data) found that when children were spanked, 73% of the time they misbehaved again within 10 minutes! This study also revealed that parents who use physical punishment do not use it as a last resort when other techniques have failed; that they mostly spank their children for mundane, trivial offenses; and that the parents are often angry when they administer spankings. These findings, which probably provide a more accurate snapshot of parental disciplinary practices than self-report data do, paint a rather ugly portrait of corporal punishment in the home. Although professional societies in psychology, psychiatry, pediatrics, nursing, and social work have issued statements urging parents to abandon physical punishment, declines in reliance on corporal punishment have been modest (Durrant & Ensom, 2012; Gershoff, 2013).

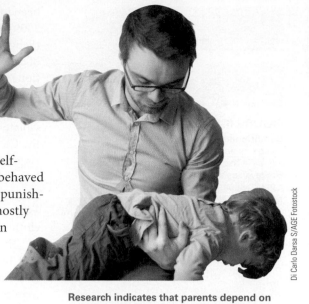

Di Carlo Darsa S/AGE Fotostock

Research indicates that parents depend on corporal punishment extensively. Although physical punishment is frequently administered to suppress aggressive behavior, in the long run it appears that it often fosters greater aggressiveness in children.

6.3 CHANGING DIRECTIONS IN THE STUDY OF CONDITIONING

6.3

Key Learning Goals

- Articulate the theoretical significance of conditioned taste aversion and preparedness.
- Understand the theoretical implications of research on latent learning, signal relations, and response-outcome relations.

As you learned in Chapter 1, science is constantly evolving and changing in response to new research and new thinking. Such change certainly has occurred in the study of conditioning. In this section, we will examine two major changes in thinking about conditioning that have emerged in recent decades. First, we'll consider the growing recognition that an organism's biological heritage can limit or channel conditioning. Second, we'll discuss the increased appreciation of the role of cognitive processes in conditioning.

Recognizing Biological Constraints on Conditioning

Learning theorists have traditionally assumed that the fundamental laws of conditioning have great generality—that they apply to a wide range of species. Although no one ever suggested that hamsters could learn physics, until the 1960s most psychologists assumed that associations could be conditioned between any stimulus an organism could register and any response it could make. However, findings in recent decades have demonstrated that there are limits to the generality of conditioning principles—limits imposed by an organism's biological heritage.

Conditioned Taste Aversion

A number of years ago, a prominent psychologist, Martin Seligman, dined out with his wife and enjoyed a steak with sauce béarnaise. About 6 hours afterward, he developed a wicked case of stomach flu and endured severe nausea. Subsequently when he ordered sauce béarnaise, he was chagrined to discover that its aroma alone nearly made him throw up. Seligman's experience is not unique. Many people develop aversions to food that has

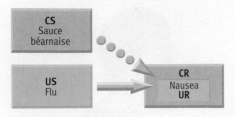

FIGURE 6.18

Conditioned taste aversion. Taste aversions can be established through classical conditioning, as in the "sauce béarnaise syndrome." However, as the text explains, taste aversions can be acquired in ways that *seem* to violate basic principles of classical conditioning.

been followed by nausea from illness, alcohol intoxication, or food poisoning (Rosenblum, 2009). However, Seligman was puzzled by what he called his "sauce béarnaise syndrome" (Seligman & Hager, 1972). On the one hand, it appeared to be the straightforward result of classical conditioning. A neutral stimulus (the sauce) had been paired with an unconditioned stimulus (the flu), which caused an unconditioned response (the nausea). Thus, the béarnaise sauce became a conditioned stimulus eliciting nausea (see **Figure 6.18**).

On the other hand, Seligman recognized that his aversion to béarnaise sauce seemed to violate certain basic principles of conditioning. First, the lengthy delay of 6 hours between the CS (the sauce) and the US (the flu) should have prevented conditioning from occurring. In laboratory studies, a delay of more than *30 seconds* between the CS and US makes it difficult to establish a conditioned response, yet this conditioning occurred in just one pairing. Second, why was it that *only* the béarnaise sauce became a CS eliciting nausea? Why not other stimuli that were present in the restaurant? Shouldn't plates, knives, tablecloths, or his wife, for example, also trigger Seligman's nausea?

The riddle of Seligman's sauce béarnaise syndrome was solved by John Garcia (1989) and his colleagues. They conducted a series of studies on *conditioned taste aversion* (Garcia, Clarke, & Hankins, 1973; Garcia & Rusiniak, 1980). In these studies, they manipulated the kinds of stimuli preceding the onset of nausea and other noxious experiences in rats, using radiation to artificially induce the nausea. They found that when taste cues were followed by nausea, rats quickly acquired conditioned taste aversions. However, when taste cues were followed by other types of noxious stimuli (such as shock), rats did *not* develop conditioned taste aversions. Furthermore, visual and auditory stimuli followed by nausea also failed to produce conditioned aversions. In short, Garcia and his co-workers found that it was almost

© lenetstan/Shutterstock.com

CONCEPT CHECK 6.4

Distinguishing Between Classical Conditioning and Operant Conditioning

Check your understanding of the usual differences between classical conditioning and operant conditioning by indicating the type of conditioning process involved in each of the following examples. In the space on the left, place a C if the example involves classical conditioning, an O if it involves operant conditioning, or a B if it involves both. The answers can be found in Appendix A.

_____ 1. Whenever Midori takes her dog out for a walk, she wears the same old blue windbreaker. Eventually, she notices that her dog becomes excited whenever she puts on this windbreaker.

_____ 2. The Wailing Creatures are a successful rock band with three hit albums to their credit. They begin their U.S. tour featuring many new, unreleased songs, all of which draw silence from their concert fans. The same fans cheer wildly when the Wailing Creatures play any of their old hits. Gradually, the band members reduce the number of new songs they play, and start playing more of the old standbys.

_____ 3. When Cindy and Mel first fell in love, they listened constantly to the Wailing Creatures' hit song "Transatlantic Obsession." Although several years have passed, whenever they hear this song, they experience a warm, romantic feeling.

_____ 4. For nearly 20 years, Ralph has worked as a machinist in the same factory. His new foreman is never satisfied with his work and criticizes him constantly. After a few weeks of heavy criticism, Ralph experiences anxiety whenever he arrives at work. He starts calling in sick more and more frequently to evade this anxiety.

impossible to create certain associations, whereas taste-nausea associations (and odor-nausea associations) were almost impossible to prevent.

What is the theoretical significance of this unique readiness to make connections between taste and nausea? Garcia argues that it is a by-product of the evolutionary history of mammals. Animals that consume poisonous foods and survive must learn not to repeat their mistakes. Natural selection will favor organisms that quickly learn what *not* to eat. Thus, evolution may have biologically programmed some organisms to learn certain types of associations more easily than other types.

Preparedness and Phobias

According to Martin Seligman (1971), evolution has also programmed organisms to acquire certain fears more readily than others because of a phenomenon called *preparedness*. **Preparedness involves species-specific predispositions to be conditioned in certain ways and not others.** Seligman believes that preparedness can explain why certain phobias are vastly more common than others. People tend to develop phobias to snakes, spiders, heights, and darkness relatively easily. However, even after having painful experiences with hammers, knives, hot stoves, and electrical outlets, people's phobic fears of these objects are rare. What characteristics do common phobic objects share? Most were once genuine threats to our ancient ancestors. Consequently, a fear response to such objects may have survival value for our species. According to Seligman, evolutionary forces gradually wired the human brain to acquire conditioned fears of these stimuli easily and rapidly. Laboratory simulations of phobic conditioning have provided considerable support for the concept of preparedness (Oehlberg & Mineka, 2011).

Recognizing Cognitive Processes in Conditioning

Pavlov, Skinner, and their followers traditionally viewed conditioning as a mechanical process in which stimulus-response associations are "stamped in" by experience. Learning theorists asserted that if creatures such as snails can be conditioned, conditioning can't depend on higher mental processes. This viewpoint did not go entirely unchallenged, but mainstream theories of conditioning did not allocate any role to cognitive processes. In recent decades, however, research findings have led theorists to shift toward more cognitive explanations of conditioning. Let's review some of this research.

People tend to develop phobias to snakes very easily, but to hot stoves rarely, even though the latter can be just as painful. Preparedness theory can explain this paradox.

Latent Learning and Cognitive Maps

The first major "renegade" to chip away at the conventional view of learning was Edward C. Tolman (1932, 1938), an American psychologist who was something of a gadfly for the behaviorist movement in the 1930s and 1940s. Tolman and his colleagues conducted a series of studies that posed some difficult questions for the prevailing views of conditioning. In one landmark study (Tolman & Honzik, 1930), three groups of food-deprived rats learned to run a complicated maze over a series of once-a-day trials (see **Figure 6.19a**). The rats in Group A received a food reward when they got to the end of the maze each day. Because of this reinforcement, their performance in running the maze (measured by how many "wrong turns" they made) gradually improved over the course of 17 days (see **Figure 6.19b**). The rats in Group B did not receive any food reward. Lacking reinforcement for getting to the goal box swiftly, this group made many "errors" and showed only modest improvement in performance. Group C was the critical group; they did not get any reward for their first ten trials in the maze, but they were rewarded from the eleventh trial onward. The rats in this group showed little improvement in performance over the first ten trials (just like Group B), but after finding food in the goal box on the eleventh trial, they showed sharp improvement on subsequent trials (see **Figure 6.19b**).

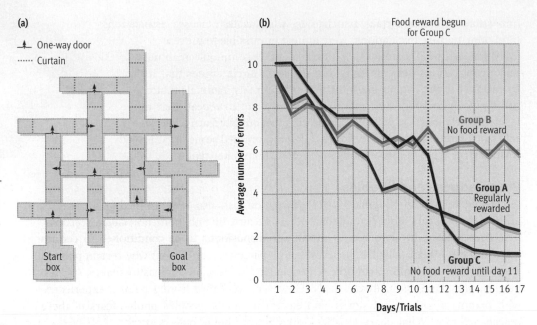

FIGURE 6.19

Latent learning. (a) In the study by Tolman and Honzik (1930), rats learned to run the complicated maze shown here. **(b)** The results obtained by Tolman and Honzik (1930) are summarized in this graph. The rats in Group C showed a sudden improvement in performance when a food reward was introduced on Trial 11. Tolman concluded that the rats in this group were learning about the maze all along, but that their learning remained "latent" until reinforcement was made available.

SOURCE: Adapted from Tolman, E. C., & Honzik, C. H. (1930). Introduction and removal of reward and maze performance in rats. *University of California Publications in Psychology, 4,* 257–275.

Tolman concluded that the rats in Group C had been learning about the maze all along, just as much as the rats in group A, but they had no motivation to demonstrate this learning until a reward was introduced. Tolman called this phenomenon **latent learning—learning that is not apparent from behavior when it first occurs.** *Why did these findings present a challenge for the prevailing view of learning?* First, they suggested that learning can take place in the absence of reinforcement—at a time when learned responses were thought to be stamped in by reinforcement. Second, they suggested that the rats who displayed latent learning had formed a *cognitive map* of the maze (a mental representation of the spatial layout) at a time when cognitive processes were thought to be irrelevant to understanding conditioning even in humans.

Tolman (1948) went on to conduct other studies that suggested that cognitive processes play a role in conditioning. But his ideas were ahead of their time and mostly attracted rebuttals and criticism from the influential learning theorists of his era (Hilgard, 1987). In the long run, however, Tolman's ideas prevailed, and models of conditioning were eventually forced to incorporate cognitive factors.

Signal Relations

One theorist who was especially influential in demonstrating the importance of cognitive factors in classical conditioning was Robert Rescorla (1978, 1980). Rescorla asserts that environmental stimuli serve as signals and that some stimuli are better, or more dependable, signals than others. A "good" signal is one that allows accurate prediction of the US. Hence, he has manipulated the *predictive value* of a conditioned stimulus by varying the proportion of trials in which the CS and US are paired. For example, in one study, a CS (tone) and US (shock) were paired 100% of the time for one group of rats and only 50% of the time for another group.

What did Rescorla find when he tested the two groups of rats for conditioned fear? He found that the CS elicited a much stronger fear response in the group that had been exposed to the more dependable signal. Many other studies of signal relations have also shown that the predictive value of a CS is an influential factor governing classical conditioning (Rescorla, 1978). These studies suggest that classical conditioning may involve information processing rather than reflexive responding.

Response-Outcome Relations and Reinforcement

Studies of response-outcome relations and reinforcement also highlight the role of cognitive processes in conditioning. Imagine that on the night before an important exam you study hard while repeatedly playing a Coldplay song. The next morning you earn an A on your exam. Does this result strengthen your tendency to play Coldplay's music before exams? Probably not. Chances are, you will recognize the logical relation between the response of studying hard and the reinforcement of a good grade, and only the response of studying will be strengthened (Killeen, 1981).

However, it's not out of the realm of possibility that you might develop a habit of playing Coldplay before big exams. Many years ago, B. F. Skinner argued that "superstitious behavior" could be established through *noncontingent reinforcement,* which occurs when a response is accidentally strengthened by a reinforcer that follows it, even though delivery of the reinforcer was not a result of the response. In a classic study, Skinner (1948) put eight pigeons in operant chambers that were set up to deliver reinforcement every 15 seconds, regardless of what responses the pigeons were making. In Skinner's judgment, six of the eight pigeons started displaying quirky, superstitious responses, such as head-bobbing or turning counter-clockwise. Skinner's theory that noncontingent reinforcement is the basis for superstitious behavior held sway for many years, but researchers eventually failed to replicate his findings (Staddon & Simmelhag, 1971).

That said, superstitious behavior is extremely common, and accidental reinforcements *may* sometimes contribute to these superstitions, along with various types of erroneous reasoning (Ono, 1987; Vyse, 1997). There are extensive anecdotal reports of athletes, such as Wade Boggs, exhibiting superstitious responses, such as wearing a special pair of socks, eating the same lunch, going through special rituals, and so on, to enhance their chances of success (Bleak & Frederick, 1998; Ciborowski, 1997). And these quirks are certainly not limited to athletes. For example, most people compulsively need to "knock on wood" after mentioning their good fortune in some area. One study (Risen & Gilovich, 2008) showed that many people subscribe to the belief that it is bad luck to "tempt fate." In one part of the study, participants read about a student named Jon who had applied to prestigious Stanford University for graduate school, and whose mother had sent him a Stanford T-shirt before he learned whether he had been accepted. The subjects believed that Jon's prospects of acceptance would be higher if he did not tempt fate by wearing the T-shirt before getting the results. Contemporary research on superstitious behavior tends to ascribe it to normal cognitive biases and errors that promote irrational reasoning (discussed in Chapter 8) rather than to the unpredictable vagaries of operant conditioning (Pronin et al., 2006; Wegner & Wheatley, 1999).

In any case, it is clear that reinforcement is *not* automatic when favorable consequences follow a response. People actively reason out the relations between responses and the outcomes that follow. When a response is followed by a desirable outcome, the response is more likely to be strengthened if the person thinks that the response *caused* the outcome. In sum, modern, reformulated models of conditioning view it as a matter of detecting the *contingencies* among environmental events (De Houwer, 2014; Schachtman & Reilly, 2011).

Surprisingly, research suggests that superstitions can enhance performance. One study found that using a "lucky ball" helped golfers sink more putts.

6.4 OBSERVATIONAL LEARNING

6.4

Key Learning Goals

- Explain the nature, importance, and basic processes of observational learning.
- Discuss Bandura's research on TV models and aggression, and modern research on the effects of media violence.

Can classical and operant conditioning account for all human learning? Absolutely not. Consider how people learn a fairly basic skill, such as driving a car. They do not hop naïvely into an automobile and start emitting random responses until one leads to favorable consequences. On the contrary, most people learning to drive know exactly where to place the key and how to get started. How are these responses acquired? Through *observation.* Most new drivers have years of experience observing others drive, and they put those observations to work. Learning through observation accounts for a great deal of learning in both animals and humans.

Observational learning occurs when an organism's responding is influenced by the observation of others, who are called *models*. This process has been investigated extensively by Albert Bandura (1977, 1986). He does not see observational learning as entirely separate from classical and operant conditioning. Instead, he asserts that it greatly extends the reach of these conditioning processes. Whereas previous conditioning theorists emphasized the organism's direct experience, Bandura has demonstrated that both classical and operant conditioning can take place vicariously through observational learning.

Basic Processes

Essentially, observational learning involves being conditioned indirectly by virtue of observing another's conditioning (see **Figure 6.20**). To illustrate, suppose you observe a friend behaving assertively with a car salesperson. You see your friend's assertive behavior reinforced by the exceptionally good buy she gets on the car. Your own tendency to behave assertively with salespeople might well be strengthened as a result. Notice that the reinforcement is experienced by your friend, not you. The good buy should strengthen your friend's tendency to bargain assertively, but your tendency to do so may also be strengthened indirectly.

Bandura identified four key processes that are crucial in observational learning. The first two—attention and retention—highlight the importance of cognition in this type of learning:

- *Attention.* To learn through observation, you must pay attention to another person's behavior and its consequences.
- *Retention.* You may not have occasion to use an observed response for weeks, months, or even years. Thus, you must store a mental representation of what you have witnessed in your memory.
- *Reproduction.* Enacting a modeled response depends on your ability to reproduce the response by converting your stored mental images into overt behavior.
- *Motivation.* Finally, you are unlikely to reproduce an observed response unless you are motivated to do so. Your motivation depends on whether you encounter a situation in which you believe the response is likely to pay off for you.

Observational Learning and the Media Violence Controversy

The power of observational learning has been at the center of a long-running controversy about the effects of media violence. Ever since television became popular in the 1950s, social critics have expressed concern about the amount of violence on TV. In the 1960s, Bandura and his colleagues conducted landmark research on the issue that remains widely cited and influential.

In one classic study, Bandura, Ross, and Ross (1963) showed how the observation of filmed models can influence the learning of aggressive behavior in children. They manipulated whether or not nursery-school children saw an aggressive model on film, and whether the aggressive model experienced positive or negative consequences. Soon after the manipulations, the children were taken to a room where their play was observed through a one-way mirror. Among the toys available in the room were two "Bobo dolls" that served as convenient targets for kicks, punches, and other aggressive responses. Children who had seen the aggressive model rewarded engaged in more aggression toward the toys than children in the other conditions did. This study was one of the earliest experimental demonstrations of a cause-and-effect relationship between exposure to TV depictions of aggression and increased aggressive behavior.

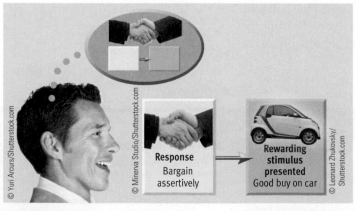

FIGURE 6.20

Observational learning. In observational learning, an observer attends to and stores a mental representation of a model's behavior (example: assertive bargaining) and its consequences (example: a good buy on a car). If the observer sees the modeled response lead to a favorable outcome, the observer's tendency to emit the modeled response will be strengthened.

Observational learning occurs in both humans and animals. For example, no one trained this dog to "pray" with its owner; the Chihuahua just picked up the response through observation. In a similar vein, children acquire a diverse array of responses from role models through observational learning.

Decades of research since Bandura's pioneering work have indicated that media violence fosters increased aggression (Bushman & Huesmann, 2012; Gentile & Bushman, 2012). The short-term effects of media violence have been investigated in hundreds of experimental studies, which consistently demonstrate that exposure to violent content in TV shows, movies, and video games increases the likelihood of physical aggression, verbal aggression, aggressive thoughts, and aggressive emotions in both children and adults (Anderson et al., 2010; Warburton, 2014).

A particular source of concern in recent research has been the finding that exposure to media violence appears to desensitize people to the effects of aggression in the real world (Krahe et al., 2011). Desensitization means that people show muted reactions to real violence. For example, one study showed that subjects who had played violent video games for a mere 20 minutes showed smaller physiological reactions to video recordings of real-life aggression (prison fights and such) than did those who played nonviolent games (Carnagey, Anderson, & Bushman, 2007). Another study found that playing violent video games changed participants' perceptions of aggression in everyday life, as they rated specific acts of aggressive behavior as being less aggressive than control subjects did (Greitemeyer, 2014).

Yet another study suggested that the "numbing" effect of media violence makes people less sensitive to the suffering of others and less likely to help others in need (Bushman & Anderson, 2009). In this study, participants who had just played a violent or nonviolent video game overheard a staged fight (just outside the door of the lab) in which one person was injured. The aggressive actor clearly had left the scene, so there was no perceived danger to the participants. Researchers monitored how long it took subjects to come out into the hall to offer help to the groaning victim. Participants who had just played a violent video game took much longer to help (average 73 seconds) than those who had just played a nonviolent game (16 seconds). Thus, it appears that media violence can desensitize individuals to acts of aggression.

The real-world and long-term effects of media violence have been investigated through correlational research. The findings of these studies show that the more violence children watch on TV, the more aggressive they tend to be at home and at school (Krahe, 2013). Of course, critics point out that this correlation could reflect a variety of causal relationships (Ferguson & Savage, 2012). Perhaps high aggressiveness

Illustrated Overview **Three Types of Learning**

TYPE OF LEARNING	PROCEDURE	RESULT

CLASSICAL CONDITIONING

Ivan Pavlov

A neutral stimulus (for example, a tone) is paired with an unconditioned stimulus (such as food) that elicits an unconditioned response (salivation).

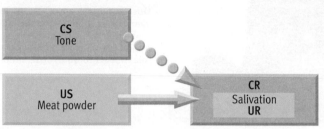

CS Tone

US Meat powder

CR Salivation **UR**

The neutral stimulus becomes a conditioned stimulus that elicits the conditioned response (for example, a tone triggers salivation).

OPERANT CONDITIONING

B.F. Skinner

In a stimulus situation, a response is followed by favorable consequences (reinforcement) or unfavorable consequences (punishment).

Response Press lever

Rewarding or aversive stimulus presented or removed Food delivery or shock

If reinforced, the response is strengthened (emitted more frequently); if punished, the response is weakened (emitted less frequently).

OBSERVATIONAL LEARNING

Albert Bandura

An observer attends to a model's behavior (for example, aggressive bargaining) and its consequences (for example, a good buy on a car).

© Yuri Arcurs/Shutterstock.com

© Minerva Studio/Shutterstock.com

Response Bargain assertively

Rewarding stimulus presented Good buy on car

© Leonard Zhukovsky/Shutterstock.com

The observer stores a mental representation of the modeled response; the observer's tendency to emit the response may be strengthened or weakened, depending on the consequences observed.

TYPICAL KINDS OF RESPONSES	EXAMPLES IN ANIMALS	EXAMPLES IN HUMANS
Mostly (but not always) involuntary reflexes and visceral responses	Dogs learn to salivate to the sound of a tone that has been paired with meat powder.	Little Albert learns to fear a white rat and other white, furry objects through classical conditioning.  Archives of the History of American Psychology, University of Akron From original footage, 1919–1920.
Mostly (but not always) voluntary, spontaneous responses	Trained animals perform remarkable feats because they have been reinforced for gradually learning closer and closer approximations of responses they do not normally emit.  Courtesy of Animal Behavior Enterprises, Inc.	Casino patrons tend to exhibit high, steady rates of gambling, as most games of chance involve complex variable-ratio schedules of reinforcement.  © Jon Feingers v/Getty Images
Mostly voluntary responses, often consisting of novel and complex sequences	A dog spontaneously learns to mimic a human ritual.  © AP Images/Itsuo Inouye	A young girl performs a response that she has acquired through observation.  © Szocs Jozsef/Shutterstock.com

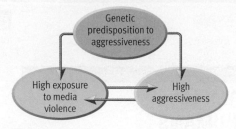

FIGURE 6.21

The correlation between exposure to media violence and aggression. The more violence children watch on TV, the more aggressive they tend to be, but this correlation could reflect a variety of underlying causal relationships. Although watching violent shows probably causes increased aggressiveness, it is also possible that aggressive children are drawn to violent shows. Or perhaps a third variable (such as a genetic predisposition to aggressiveness) leads to both a preference for violent shows and high aggressiveness.

in children causes an increased interest in media violence (see **Figure 6.21**). However, a growing number of studies have controlled for initial levels of subjects' aggressiveness and still found that a diet of media violence promotes increased aggression (Bushman & Huesmann, 2014).

Critics have also argued that the effects of media violence on aggression are relatively weak effects (Elson & Ferguson, 2014; Ferguson, 2013). This assertion is accurate, but exactly what one would expect. Like other aspects of complex human behavior, aggression is surely influenced by a host of factors, such as genetic predispositions, parental modeling, and peer influences. Exposure to media violence is just one actor on a crowded stage. That said, the researchers who are concerned about the effects of media violence worry that even weak effects may have far-reaching repercussions. They point out that TV shows, movies, and video games reach millions upon millions of people (Bushman & Anderson, 2001). Suppose that 25 million people watch an extremely violent movie. Even if only 1 in 1000 viewers become a little more prone to aggression, that is 25,000 people who are a bit more likely to wreak havoc in someone's life.

As an aside, it is worth noting that the research findings on the effects of video games are not all bad. Studies have found that a number of benefits can be derived from playing video games, including the much-maligned first-person shooter games that are extremely violent (Granic, Lobel, & Engels, 2014). The cognitive benefits of gaming include improvements in attention allocation, visual-spatial processing, and problem solving. Video games can also demonstrate the rewards of persistence in the face of setbacks. And the advent of games that unfold in virtual communities can have some payoffs in terms of enhancing social skills.

In any event, the heated debate about media violence shows that observational learning plays an important role in regulating behavior. It represents a third major type of learning that builds on the first two types (classical conditioning and operant conditioning). These three basic types of learning are summarized and compared in the Illustrated Overview on pages 212–213.

Heredity & Environment

Sociohistorical Context

6.5 REFLECTING ON THE CHAPTER'S THEMES

Two of our unifying themes stand out in this chapter: (1) nature and nurture interactively govern behavior, and (2) dense interconnections exist between psychology and events in the world at large. Let's examine each of these points in more detail.

In regard to nature versus nurture, research on learning has clearly and repeatedly demonstrated the enormous power of the environment and experience in shaping behavior. Indeed, many learning theorists once believed that *all* aspects of behavior could be explained in terms of environmental determinants. In recent decades, however, evidence on conditioned taste aversion and preparedness has shown that there are biological constraints on conditioning. Thus, even in explanations of learning—an area once dominated by nurture theories—we see again that heredity and environment jointly influence behavior.

The history of research on conditioning also shows how progress in psychology can seep into every corner of society. For example, Skinner's ideas on the power of positive reinforcement have influenced patterns of discipline in American society. Research on operant conditioning has also affected management styles in the business world, leading to an increased emphasis on positive reinforcement. The fact that the principles of conditioning are routinely applied in homes, businesses, child-care facilities, schools, and factories clearly shows that psychology is not an ivory tower endeavor.

In the upcoming Personal Application, you will see how you can apply the principles of conditioning to improve your self-control, as we discuss the technology of behavior modification.

6.6

Key Learning Goals
- Describe how to specify your target behavior and gather baseline data for a self-modification program.
- Discuss how to design and execute a self-modification program.

Answer the following "yes" or "no."

____ 1 Do you have a hard time passing up food, even when you're not hungry?

____ 2 Do you wish you studied more often?

____ 3 Would you like to cut down on your smoking or drinking?

____ 4 Do you experience difficulty in getting yourself to exercise regularly?

If you answered "yes" to any of these questions, you have struggled with the challenge of self-control. This Application discusses how you can use the principles and techniques of behavior modification to improve your self-control. **Behavior modification is a systematic approach to changing behavior through the application of the principles of conditioning.** Advocates of behavior modification assume that behavior is mainly a product of learning, conditioning, and environmental control. They further assume that *what is learned can be unlearned*. Thus, they set out to "recondition" people to produce more desirable and effective patterns of behavior.

The technology of behavior modification has been applied with great success in schools, businesses, hospitals, factories, childcare facilities, prisons, and mental health centers (Kazdin, 2001; Miltenberger, 2012). Moreover, behavior modification techniques have proven particularly valuable in efforts to improve self-control. Our discussion will borrow liberally from an excellent book on self-modification by David Watson and Roland Tharp (2014). We will discuss four steps in the process of self-modification, which are outlined in **Figure 6.22**.

Specifying Your Target Behavior

The first step in a self-modification program is to specify the target behavior(s) that you want to change. Behavior modification can only be applied to a clearly defined, overt response, yet many people have difficulty pinpointing the behavior they hope to alter. They tend to describe their problems in terms of unobservable personality *traits* rather than overt *behaviors*. For example, asked what behavior he would like to change, a man might say, "I'm too irritable." That statement may be true, but it is of little help in designing a self-modification program. To use a behavioral approach, vague statements about traits need to be translated into precise descriptions of specific target behaviors.

To identify target responses, you need to ponder past behavior and pay careful attention to behavior over the next week so you can list specific *examples* of responses that lead to the trait description. For instance, the man who regards himself as "too irritable" might identify two overly frequent responses, such as arguing with his wife and snapping at his children. These are specific behaviors for which he could design a self-modification program.

Gathering Baseline Data

The second step in behavior modification is to gather baseline data. You need to systematically observe your target behavior for a period of time (usually a week or two) before you work out the details of your program. In gathering your baseline data, you need to monitor three things.

First, you need to determine the initial response level of your target behavior. After all, you can't tell whether your program is working effectively unless you have a baseline for comparison. In most cases, you would simply keep track of how often the target response occurs in a certain time interval. Thus, you might count the daily frequency of snapping at your children, smoking cigarettes, or biting your fingernails. *It is crucial to gather accurate data.* You should keep permanent written records, and it is usually best to portray these records graphically (see **Figure 6.23**).

Second, you need to monitor the *antecedents* of your target behavior. Antecedents are events that typically precede the target response. Often these events play a major role in evoking this behavior. For example, if your target is overeating, you

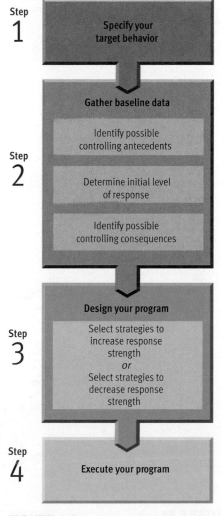

FIGURE 6.22

Steps in a self-modification program. This flowchart provides an overview of the four steps necessary to execute a self-modification program.

Smoking and drinking are among the many self-control issues that can be conquered using the principles of self-modification.

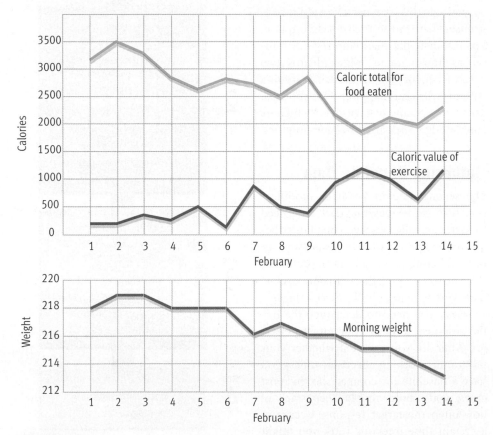

FIGURE 6.23

Example of recordkeeping in a self-modification program. Graphic records are ideal for tracking progress in behavior modification efforts. The records shown here illustrate what someone would be likely to track in a behavior modification program for weight loss.

might discover that the bulk of your overeating occurs late in the evening while you watch TV. If you can pinpoint this kind of antecedent-response connection, you may be able to design your program to circumvent or break the link.

Third, you need to monitor the typical consequences of your target behavior. Try to identify the reinforcers that are maintaining an undesirable target behavior or the unfavorable outcomes that are suppressing a desirable target behavior. Bear in mind that a response may not be reinforced every time because most behavior is maintained by intermittent reinforcement.

Designing Your Program

Once you have selected a target behavior and gathered adequate baseline data, it is time to plan your intervention program. Generally speaking, your program will be designed to either increase or decrease the frequency of a target response.

Increasing Response Strength

Efforts to increase the frequency of a target response depend largely on the use of positive reinforcement. In other words, you reward yourself for behaving properly. Although the basic strategy is quite simple, doing it skillfully involves a number of considerations, including selecting the right reinforcer and arranging contingencies.

Selecting a reinforcer. To use positive reinforcement, you need to find a reward that will be effective for you. Reinforcement is subjective. What is reinforcing for one person may not be reinforcing for another. To determine your personal reinforcers, you need to ask yourself questions such as: What do I like to do for fun? What makes me feel good? What would be a nice present? What would I hate to lose? (see **Figure 6.24**).

You don't have to come up with spectacular new reinforcers that you've never experienced before. *You can use reinforcers that you are already getting.* However, you have to restructure the contingencies so that you get them only if you behave appropriately. For example, if you normally buy two DVDs per week, you might make

Selecting a Reinforcer

1. What will be the rewards of achieving your goal?
2. What kind of praise do you like to receive, from yourself and others?
3. What kinds of things do you like to have?
4. What are your major interests?
5. What are your hobbies?
6. What people do you like to be with?
7. What do you like to do with those people?
8. What do you do for fun?
9. What do you do to relax?
10. What do you do to get away from it all?
11. What makes you feel good?
12. What would be a nice present to receive?
13. What kinds of things are important to you?
14. What would you buy if you had an extra $20? $50? $100?
15. On what do you spend your money each week?
16. What behaviors do you perform every day? (Don't overlook the obvious or commonplace.)
17. Are there any behaviors you usually perform instead of the target behavior?
18. What would you hate to lose?
19. Of the things you do every day, which would you hate to give up?
20. What are your favorite daydreams and fantasies?
21. What are the most relaxing scenes you can imagine?

FIGURE 6.24

Choosing a reinforcer for a self-modification program. Finding a good reinforcer to use in a behavior modification program can require a lot of thought. The questions listed here can help people identify their personal reinforcers.

SOURCE: Adapted from Watson, D. L., & Tharp, R. G. (1997). *Self-directed behavior: Self-modification for personal adjustment.* Belmont, CA: Wadsworth. Reprinted by permission.

these purchases contingent on studying a certain number of hours during the week.

Arranging the contingencies. Once you have chosen your reinforcer, you have to set up reinforcement contingencies. These contingencies will describe the exact behavioral goals that must be met and the reinforcement that may then be awarded. For example, in a program to increase exercise, you might make spending $50 on clothes (the reinforcer) contingent on having jogged fifteen miles during the week (the target behavior).

Try to set behavioral goals that are both challenging and realistic. You want your goals to be challenging so that they lead to improvement in your behavior. However, setting unrealistically high goals—a common mistake in self-modification—often leads to unnecessary discouragement.

Decreasing Response Strength

Let's turn now to the challenge of reducing the frequency of an undesirable response. You can go about this task in a number of ways. Your principal options include reinforcement, control of antecedents, and punishment.

Reinforcement. Reinforcers can be used in an indirect way to decrease the frequency of a response. This may sound paradoxical because you have learned that reinforcement strengthens a response. The trick lies in how you define the target behavior. For example, in the case of overeating, you might define your target behavior as eating more than 1600 calories a day (an excess response that you want to decrease) or eating less than 1600 calories a day (a deficit response that you want to increase). You can choose the latter definition and reinforce yourself whenever you eat less than 1600 calories in a day. Thus, you can reinforce yourself for not emitting a response, or for emitting it less, and thereby decrease a response through reinforcement.

Control of antecedents. A worthwhile strategy for decreasing the occurrence of an undesirable response can be to identify its antecedents and avoid exposure to them. This strategy is especially useful when you are trying to decrease the frequency of a consummatory response, such as smoking or eating. In the case of overeating, for instance, the easiest way to resist temptation is to avoid having to face it. Thus, you might stay away from favorite restaurants, minimize time spent in your kitchen, shop for groceries just after eating (when willpower is higher), and avoid purchasing favorite foods.

Punishment. The strategy of decreasing unwanted behavior by punishing yourself for that behavior is an obvious option that people tend to overuse. The biggest problem with punishment in a self-modification effort is that it is difficult to follow through and punish yourself. Nonetheless, there may be situations in which your manipulations of reinforcers need to be bolstered by the threat of punishment. If you're going to use punishment, keep two guidelines in mind. First, do not use punishment alone. Use it in conjunction with positive reinforcement. If you set up a program in which you can earn only negative consequences, you probably won't stick to it. Second, use a relatively mild punishment so that you will actually be able to administer it to yourself.

Executing Your Program

Once you have designed your program, the next step is to put it to work by enforcing the contingencies that you have carefully planned. During this period, you need to continue to accurately record the frequency of your target behavior so you can evaluate your progress. The success of your program depends on your not "cheating." The most common form of cheating is to reward yourself when you have not actually earned it. You can reduce the likelihood of cheating by having someone other than yourself dole out the reinforcers and punishments.

Generally, when you design your program, you should spell out the conditions under which you will bring it to an end. Doing so involves setting terminal goals, such as reaching a certain weight, studying with a certain regularity, or going without cigarettes for a certain length of time. Often, it is a good idea to phase out your program by planning a gradual reduction in the frequency or potency of your reinforcement for appropriate behavior.

6.7

Key Learning Goals
- Recognize how classical conditioning is used to manipulate emotions.

6.7 CRITICAL THINKING APPLICATION
Recognizing Contrast Effects: It's All Relative

With all due respect to the great Ivan Pavlov, when we focus on his demonstration that dogs can be trained to slobber in response to a tone, it is easy to lose sight of the importance of classical conditioning. At first glance, most people do not see a relationship between Pavlov's slobbering dogs and anything that they are even remotely interested in. However, in the main body of the chapter, we saw that classical conditioning actually contributes to the regulation of many important aspects of behavior, including fears, phobias, and other emotional reactions; immune function; and even sexual arousal. In this Application you will learn that classical conditioning is routinely used to manipulate emotions in persuasive efforts. If you watch TV, you have been subjected to Pavlovian techniques. An understanding of these techniques can help you recognize when your emotions are being manipulated by advertisers, politicians, or the media.

Manipulation efforts using Pavlovian conditioning generally involve *evaluative conditioning*. As noted earlier in the chapter, evaluative conditioning consists of efforts to transfer the liking attached to a US to a new CS. The key to this process is simply to manipulate the automatic, subconscious associations that people make in response to various stimuli. Let's look at how this manipulation is done in advertising, business negotiations, and the world of politics.

Classical Conditioning in Advertising

The art of manipulating people's associations has been perfected by the advertising industry, leading Till and Priluck (2000) to comment, "Conditioning of attitudes towards products and brands has become generally accepted and has developed into a unique research stream" (p. 57). Advertisers consistently endeavor to pair the products they are peddling with stimuli that seem likely to elicit positive emotional responses (Schachtman et al., 2011) (see **Figure 6.25**). An extensive variety of stimuli are used for this purpose. Products are paired with well-liked celebrity spokespersons; depictions of warm, loving families; beautiful pastoral scenery; cute, cuddly pets; enchanting, rosy-cheeked children; upbeat, pleasant music; and opulent surroundings that reek of wealth. Advertisers also like to pair their products with exciting events, such as the NBA Finals, and cherished symbols, such as flags and the Olympic rings insignia. But, above all else, advertisers like to link their products with sexual imagery and extremely attractive models—especially, glamorous, alluring women (Reichert, 2003; Reichert & Lambiase, 2003).

Advertisers mostly seek to associate their products with stimuli that evoke pleasurable feelings of a general sort, but in some cases they try to create more specific associations. For example, cigarette brands sold mainly to men are frequently paired with tough-looking men in rugged settings to create an association between the cigarettes and masculinity. In contrast, cigarette brands that are mainly marketed to women are paired with images that evoke feelings of femininity. In a similar vein, manufacturers of designer jeans typically seek to forge associations between their products and things that are young, urban, and hip. Advertisers marketing expensive automobiles or platinum credit cards pair their products with symbols of affluence, luxury, and privilege, such as mansions, butlers, and dazzling jewelry.

FIGURE 6.25

Classical conditioning in advertising. Many advertisers attempt to make their products serve as conditioned stimuli that elicit pleasant emotional responses by pairing their products with attractive or popular people or sexual imagery.

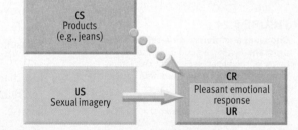

Classical Conditioning in Business Negotiations

In the world of business interactions, two standard practices are designed to get a company's customers to make an association between the company and pleasurable feelings. The first is to take customers out to dinner at fine restaurants. The provision of delicious food and fine wine in a luxurious environment is a powerful unconditioned stimulus that reliably elicits pleasant feelings that are likely to be associated with the host. The second practice is the strategy of entertaining customers at major events, such as concerts and football games. Over the last couple of decades, America's sports arenas have largely been rebuilt with vastly more "luxury skyboxes" to accommodate this business tactic. It reaches its zenith every year at the Super Bowl, where most of the seats go to the guests of Fortune 500 corporations. This practice pairs the host with both pleasant feelings and the excitement of a big event.

It is worth noting that these strategies take advantage of other processes besides classical conditioning. They also make use of the *reciprocity norm*—the social rule that one should pay back in kind what one receives from others (Cialdini, 2007). Thus, wining and dining clients creates a sense of obligation that they should reciprocate their hosts' generosity—presumably in their business dealings.

Classical Conditioning in the World of Politics

Like advertisers, candidates running for election need to influence the attitudes of many people quickly, subtly, and effectively—and they depend on evaluative conditioning to help them do so. For example, have you noticed how politicians show up at an endless variety of pleasant public events (such as the opening of a new mall) that often have nothing to do with their public service? When a sports team wins some sort of championship, local politicians are drawn like flies to the subsequent celebrations. They want to pair themselves with these positive events, so that they are associated with pleasant emotions.

Election campaign ads use the same techniques as commercial ads (except they don't rely much on sexual appeals). Candidates are paired with popular celebrities, wholesome families, pleasant music, and symbols of patriotism. Cognizant of the power of classical conditioning, politicians also exercise great care to ensure that they are not paired with people or events that might trigger negative feelings. For example, in the 2008 presidential election, it was reported that Republican candidate John McCain tried to minimize his public appearances with incumbent President George W. Bush because Bush's popularity ratings were extremely low.

The ultimate political perversion of the principles of classical conditioning probably occurred in Nazi Germany. The Nazis used many propaganda techniques to create prejudice toward Jews and members of other targeted groups (such as Gypsies). One such strategy was the repeated pairing of disgusting, repulsive images with stereotypical pictures of Jews. For example, the Nazis would show alternating pictures of rats or roaches crawling over filthy garbage and stereotypical Jewish faces, so that the two images would become associated in the minds of the viewers. Thus, the German population was conditioned to have negative emotional reactions to Jews and to associate them with vermin subject to extermination. The Nazis reasoned that if people would not hesitate to exterminate rats and roaches, then why not human beings associated with these vermin?

How effective are the efforts to manipulate people's emotions through classical conditioning? It's hard to say. In the real world, these strategies are always used in combination with other persuasive tactics, which creates multiple confounding factors that make it difficult to assess the impact of the Pavlovian techniques (Walther, Nagengast, & Trasselli, 2005). Laboratory research can eliminate these confounding factors, but surprisingly little research on these strategies has been published, and virtually all of it has dealt with advertising. The advertising studies suggest that classical conditioning can be effective and leave enduring imprints on consumers' attitudes (Schachtman et al., 2011; Walther & Grigoriadis, 2003). And research indicates that sexual appeals in advertising are attention-getting, likable, and persuasive (Reichert, Heckler, & Jackson, 2001). But a great deal of additional research is needed. Given the monumental sums that advertisers spend using these techniques, it seems reasonable to speculate that individual companies have data on their specific practices to demonstrate their efficacy, but these data are not made available to the public.

What can you do to reduce the extent to which your emotions are manipulated through Pavlovian procedures? Well, you could turn off your radio and TV, close up your magazines, stop your newspaper, disconnect your Internet, and withdraw into a media-shielded shell, but that hardly seems realistic for most people. Realistically, the best defense is to make a conscious effort to become more aware of the pervasive attempts to condition your emotions and attitudes. Some research on persuasion suggests that *to be forewarned is to be forearmed* (Pfau et al., 1990). In other words, if you know how media sources try to manipulate you, you should be more resistant to their strategies.

TABLE 6.2 Critical Thinking Skills Discussed in This Application

Skill	Description
Understanding how Pavlovian conditioning can be used to manipulate emotions	The critical thinker understands how stimuli can be paired together to create automatic associations that people may not be aware of.
Developing the ability to detect conditioning procedures used in the media	The critical thinker can recognize Pavlovian conditioning tactics in commercial and political advertisements.

CHAPTER 6 CONCEPT CHART

CLASSICAL CONDITIONING

Description

- *Classical conditioning* is a type of learning in which a stimulus acquires the capacity to evoke a response originally evoked by another stimulus.
- Classical conditioning was pioneered by Ivan Pavlov, who conditioned dogs to salivate when a tone was presented.
- Classical conditioning mainly regulates involuntary, reflexive responses.
- Examples include emotional responses (such as fears) and physiological responses (such as immunosuppression and sexual arousal).

Terminology and procedures

- Responses controlled through classical conditioning are said to be *elicited*.
- Classical conditioning begins with an *unconditioned stimulus (US)* that elicits an *unconditioned response (UR)*.
- Then a neutral stimulus is paired with the US until it becomes a *conditioned stimulus (CS)* that elicits a *conditioned response (CR)*.

Basic processes

- *Acquisition* occurs when a CS and US are paired, gradually resulting in a CR.

- *Extinction* occurs when a CS is repeatedly presented alone until it no longer elicits a CR.
- *Spontaneous recovery* is the reappearance of an extinguished response after a period of non-exposure to the CS.

- *Generalization* occurs when a CR is elicited by a new stimulus that resembles the original CS, as in Watson and Rayner's study of Little Albert.

- *Discrimination* occurs when a CR is not elicited by a new stimulus that resembles the original CS.

- *Higher-order conditioning* occurs when a CS functions as if it were a US.

OPERANT CONDITIONING

Description

- *Operant conditioning* is a type of learning in which responses come to be controlled by their consequences.
- Operant conditioning was pioneered by B.F. Skinner, who showed that rats and pigeons tend to repeat responses that are followed by favorable outcomes.
- Operant conditioning mainly regulates voluntary, spontaneous responses.
- Examples include studying, going to work, telling jokes, asking someone out, gambling.

Terminology and procedures

- *Reinforcement* occurs when an event following a response increases an organism's tendency to make that response.
- Responses controlled through operant conditioning are said to be *emitted*.
- Demonstrations of operant conditioning typically occur in a *Skinner box*, where an animal's reinforcement is controlled.
- The key dependent variable is the animal's *response rate*, as monitored by a *cumulative recorder*, with results portrayed in graphs.

Basic processes

- *Acquisition* occurs when a response gradually increases due to contingent reinforcement.
- Acquisition may involve *shaping*—the reinforcement of closer and closer approximations of the desired response.

- *Extinction* occurs when responding gradually slows and stops after reinforcement is terminated.

- *Generalization* occurs when responding increases in the presence of a stimulus that resembles the original discriminative stimulus.

- *Discrimination* occurs when responding does not increase in the presence of a stimulus that resembles the original discriminative stimulus.

- *Primary reinforcers* are inherently reinforcing, whereas *secondary reinforcers* develop through learning.

Acquisition is the formation of a conditioned response tendency.

Extinction is the gradual weakening of a conditioned response tendency.

Generalization occurs when an organism responds to new stimuli besides the original stimulus.

Discrimination occurs when an organism does not respond to other stimuli that resemble the original stimulus.

Schedules of reinforcement

- *Intermittent reinforcement* occurs when a response is reinforced only some of the time.

- In *ratio schedules*, the reinforcer is given after a fixed (FR) or variable (VR) number of nonreinforced responses.

- In *interval schedules*, the reinforcer is given for the first response that occurs after a fixed (FI) or variable (VI) time interval has elapsed.

- Ratio schedules (FR and VR) tend to yield higher response rates, whereas variable schedules (VR and VI) tend to yield more resistance to extinction.

Distinctions among operant outcomes

- *Positive reinforcement* occurs when a response is followed by the presentation of a rewarding stimulus.

- *Negative reinforcement* occurs when a response is followed by the removal of an aversive stimulus.

- Negative reinforcement plays a key role in *escape learning* and *avoidance learning*.

- *Punishment* occurs when an event following a response weakens the tendency to make that response.

- When used as a disciplinary procedure, physical punishment is associated with a variety of negative outcomes.

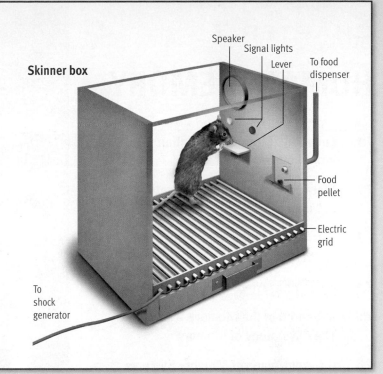

Skinner box

NEW DIRECTIONS IN THE STUDY OF CONDITIONING

Recognizing biological constraints on learning

- John Garcia found that it is almost impossible to create some associations, whereas conditioned taste aversions are readily acquired in spite of long CS-US delays, which he attributed to evolutionary influences.

- *Preparedness* appears to explain why people acquire phobias to ancient sources of threat much more readily than to modern sources of threat.

Recognizing cognitive processes in conditioning

- Tolman's studies suggested that learning can take place in the absence of reinforcement.

- Robert Rescorla showed that the predictive value of a CS influences the process of classical conditioning.

- When a response is followed by a desirable outcome, the response is more likely to be strengthened if it appears to have caused the favorable outcome.

- Noncontingent reinforcement, cognitive biases, and irrational reasoning appear to contribute to superstitious behavior.

- Modern theories hold that conditioning is a matter of detecting the contingencies that govern events.

© Don Farrall/Digital Vision/Getty Images

OBSERVATIONAL LEARNING

- *Observational learning* occurs when an organism's responding is influenced by the observation of others, called *models*.

- Observational learning was pioneered by Albert Bandura, who showed that conditioning does not have to be a product of direct experience.

- Both classical and operant conditioning can take place through observational learning.

- Observational learning depends on the processes of attention, retention, reproduction, and motivation.

- In research on the effects of media violence, both experimental and correlational studies suggest that violent media contribute to increased aggression among children and adults.

APPLICATIONS

- Behavior modification techniques can be used to increase self-control; if you are trying to increase the strength of a response, you'll depend on positive reinforcement.

- A number of strategies can be used to decrease the strength of a response, including reinforcement, control of antecedents, and punishment.

- Evaluative conditioning can be used to manipulate people's emotional responses, making it a very useful tool for advertisers.

CHAPTER 7

HUMAN MEMORY

Themes in this Chapter

Subjectivity of Experience

Theoretical Diversity

Multifactorial Causation

Brad Wenner/Moment/Getty Images

If you live in the United States, you've undoubtedly handled thousands of American pennies. Surely, then, you remember what a penny looks like—or do you? Take a look at **Figure 7.1**. Which drawing corresponds to a real penny?

Did you have a hard time selecting the real one? If so, you're not alone. Nickerson and Adams (1979) found that most people can't recognize the real penny in this collection of drawings. How can that be? Why do most of us have so poor a memory for an object we see every day?

Let's try another exercise. A definition of a word follows. It's not a particularly common word, but there's a good chance that you're familiar with it. Try to think of the word.

Definition: Favoritism shown or patronage granted by persons in high office to relatives or close friends.

If you can't think of the word, perhaps you can remember what letter of the alphabet it begins with or what it sounds like. If so, you're experiencing the *tip-of-the-tongue phenomenon,* in which forgotten information feels like it's just out of reach. In this case, the word you may be reaching for is *nepotism.* You've probably endured the tip-of-the-tongue phenomenon while taking exams. You blank out on a term that you're sure you know. You may feel as if you're on the verge of remembering the term, but you can't quite come up with it. Later, perhaps while you're driving home, the term suddenly comes to you. "Of course," you may say to yourself, "how could I forget that?" That's an interesting question. Clearly, the term was stored in your memory.

As these examples suggest, memory involves more than taking in information and storing it in

FIGURE 7.1

A simple memory test. Nickerson and Adams (1979) presented similar versions of an object most people have seen hundreds or thousands of times and asked, "Which one is correct?" Can you identify the real penny? (Adapted from Nickerson & Adams, 1979).

some mental compartment. In fact, psychologists probing the workings of memory have had to grapple with three enduring questions: (1) How does information get *into* memory? (2) How is information *maintained* in memory? (3) How is information *pulled back out* of memory? These three questions correspond to the three key processes involved in memory (see **Figure 7.2**): *encoding* (getting information in), *storage* (maintaining it), and *retrieval* (getting it out).

***Encoding* involves forming a memory code.** For example, when you form a memory code for a word, you might emphasize how it looks, how it sounds, or what it means. Encoding usually requires attention, which is why you may not be able to recall exactly what a penny looks like—most people don't pay much attention to the appearance of a penny. As you'll see throughout this chapter, memory is largely an active process. For the most part, you're unlikely to remember something unless you make

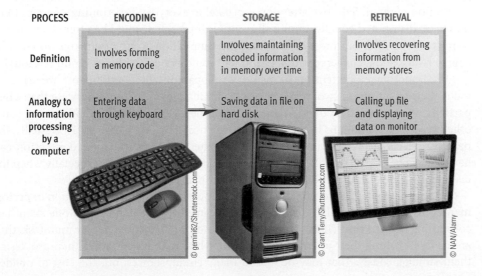

PROCESS	ENCODING	STORAGE	RETRIEVAL
Definition	Involves forming a memory code	Involves maintaining encoded information in memory over time	Involves recovering information from memory stores
Analogy to information processing by a computer	Entering data through keyboard	Saving data in file on hard disk	Calling up file and displaying data on monitor

FIGURE 7.2

Three key processes in memory. Memory depends on three sequential processes: encoding, storage, and retrieval. Some theorists have drawn an analogy between these processes and elements of information processing by computers, as depicted here. The analogies for encoding and retrieval work pretty well, but the storage analogy is somewhat misleading. When information is stored on a hard drive, it remains unchanged indefinitely, and you can retrieve an exact copy. As you will learn in this chapter, memory storage is a much more dynamic process. Memories change over time and are rough reconstructions rather than exact copies of past events.

a conscious effort to do so. *Storage* **involves maintaining encoded information in memory over time.** Psychologists have focused much of their memory research on trying to identify just what factors help or hinder memory storage. But, as the tip-of-the-tongue phenomenon shows, information storage isn't enough to guarantee that you'll remember something. You need to be able to get information out of storage. *Retrieval* **involves recovering information from memory stores.** Research issues concerned with retrieval include the study of how people search memory and why some retrieval strategies are more effective than others.

Most of this chapter is devoted to an examination of memory encoding, storage, and retrieval. These basic processes help explain the ultimate puzzle in the study of memory: why people forget. After our discussion of forgetting, we will take a brief look at the physiological bases of memory. Finally, we will discuss the controversy about whether there are separate memory systems for different types of information. The chapter's Personal Application provides some practical advice on how to improve your memory. The Critical Thinking Application discusses some reasons that memory is less reliable than people assume it to be.

Key Learning Goals

- Clarify the role of attention and depth of processing in memory.
- Explain how elaboration, visual imagery, and motivation to remember can enrich encoding.

7.1 ENCODING: GETTING INFORMATION INTO MEMORY

Have you ever been embarrassed because you couldn't remember someone's name? Perhaps you realized only 30 seconds after meeting someone that you had already "forgotten" his or her name. This familiar kind of forgetting frequently results from a failure to form a memory code for the name. When you're introduced to people, you're often busy sizing them up and thinking about what you're going to say. With your attention diverted, names go in one ear and out the other. You don't remember them because they are never encoded for storage.

This problem illustrates that encoding is an important process in memory. In this section, we discuss the role of attention in encoding, types of encoding, and ways to enrich the encoding process.

The Role of Attention

You generally need to pay attention to information if you intend to remember it (Lachter, Forster, & Ruthruff, 2004). For example, if you sit through a class lecture but pay little attention to it, you're unlikely to remember much of what the professor had to say. *Attention* **involves focusing awareness on a narrowed range of stimuli or events.** Psychologists routinely refer to "selective attention," but the words are really redundant. Attention *is* selection of input. Selective attention is critical to everyday functioning. If your attention were distributed equally among all stimulus inputs, life would be utter chaos. If you weren't able to filter out most of the potential stimulation around you, you wouldn't be able to read a book, converse with a friend, or even carry on a coherent train of thought.

The importance of attention to memory is apparent when participants are asked to focus their attention on two or more inputs simultaneously. Studies indicate that when participants are forced to divide their attention between memory encoding and some other task, large reductions in memory performance are seen (Craik, 2001). Actually, the negative effects of divided attention are not limited to memory. Divided attention can have a negative impact on the performance of quite a variety of tasks, especially when the tasks are complex or unfamiliar (Pashler, Johnston, & Ruthruff, 2001).

Although people tend to think that they can multitask with no deterioration in performance, research suggests that the human brain can effectively handle only one attention-consuming task at a time (Lien, Ruthruff, & Johnston, 2006). When people multitask, they are really switching their attention back and forth among tasks, rather than processing them simultaneously. That may be fine in many circumstances, but the cost of divided attention does have profound implications for the advisability of driving while conversing on a cell phone, for example. Carefully controlled research clearly demonstrates that cell phone conversations undermine people's driving performance, even when hands-free phones are used (Chen & Yan, 2013; Strayer, Drews, & Crouch, 2006).

One study shed light on why cell phone conversations are more distracting to drivers than conversations with passengers. The research showed that passengers adapt their conversation to the demands of the traffic and can provide assistance to the driver (Drews, Pasupathi, & Strayer, 2008). In other words, when passengers see that traffic is heavy or that the driving task has become complicated, they reduce the rate and complexity of their communication and try to help the driver navigate through the situation. As distracting as cell phone conversations are, research indicates that texting while driving is substantially more dangerous (Drews et al., 2009). There is some variability in how well people can juggle multiple tasks. Unfortunately, those who report that they engage in more multitasking tend to be those who are least able to juggle multiple tasks (Sanbonmatsu et al., 2013).

People think they can do several things simultaneously, but in reality they are switching their attention back and forth among various tasks.

Levels of Processing

Attention is critical to the encoding of memories. But not all attention is created equal. You can attend to things in different ways, focusing on different aspects of the stimulus input. According to some theorists, these qualitative differences in *how* people attend to information are the main factors influencing how much they remember. For example, Fergus Craik and Robert Lockhart (1972) argue that different rates of forgetting occur because some methods of encoding create more durable memory codes than others do.

Craik and Lockhart propose that incoming information can be processed at different levels. For instance, they maintain that in dealing with verbal information, people engage in three progressively deeper levels of processing: structural, phonemic, and semantic encoding (see **Figure 7.3**). *Structural encoding* is relatively shallow processing that emphasizes the physical structure of the stimulus. For example, if words are flashed on a

Level of processing	Type of encoding	Example of questions used to elicit appropriate encoding
Shallow processing	*Structural encoding:* emphasizes the physical structure of the stimulus	Is the word written in capital letters?
Intermediate processing	*Phonemic encoding:* emphasizes what a word sounds like	Does the word rhyme with weight?
Deep processing	*Semantic encoding:* emphasizes the meaning of verbal input	Would the word fit in the sentence: "He met a _____ on the street"?

Depth of processing

FIGURE 7.3

Levels-of-processing theory. According to Craik and Lockhart (1972), structural, phonemic, and semantic encoding—which can be elicited by questions such as those shown on the right—involve progressively deeper levels of processing.

screen, structural encoding registers such things as how the words are printed (capital, lowercase, and so on) or their length (how many letters). Further analysis may result in *phonemic encoding*, which emphasizes what a word sounds like. Phonemic encoding involves naming or saying (perhaps silently) the words. Finally, *semantic encoding* emphasizes the *meaning* of verbal input; it involves thinking about the objects and actions the words represent. **Levels-of-processing theory proposes that deeper levels of processing result in longer-lasting memory codes.**

In one experimental test of levels-of-processing theory, Craik and Tulving (1975) compared the durability of structural, phonemic, and semantic encoding. They directed subjects' attention to particular aspects of briefly presented stimulus words by asking them questions about various characteristics of the words (examples are in **Figure 7.3**). The questions were designed to engage the participants in different levels of processing. After responding to sixty words, the participants received an unexpected test of their memory for the words. As predicted, the subjects' recall was low after structural encoding, notably better after phonemic encoding, and highest after semantic encoding. The hypothesis that deeper processing leads to enhanced memory has been replicated in many studies (Craik, 2002; Lockhart & Craik, 1990). Levels-of-processing theory has been enormously influential; it has shown that memory involves more than just storage and has inspired a great deal of research on how processing considerations affect memory (Roediger, Gallo, & Geraci, 2002).

Enriching Encoding

Structural, phonemic, and semantic encoding are not the only processes involved in forming memory codes. Other dimensions that can enrich the encoding process and thereby improve memory include elaboration, visual imagery, and one's motivation to remember.

Elaboration

Semantic encoding can often be enhanced through a process called *elaboration—the linking of a stimulus to other information at the time of encoding.* For example, let's say you read that phobias are often caused by classical conditioning, and you apply this idea to your own fear of spiders by analyzing how you were conditioned. In doing so, you are engaging in elaboration. The additional connections created by elaboration usually help people remember information. Differences in elaboration can help explain why different approaches to semantic processing result in varied amounts of retention (Toyota & Kikuchi, 2004, 2005).

Visual Imagery

Imagery—the creation of visual images to represent the words to be remembered—can also be used to enrich encoding. Of course, some words are easier to create images for than others. If you were asked to remember the word *juggler*, you could readily form an image of someone juggling balls. However, if you were asked to remember the word *truth*, you would probably have more difficulty forming a suitable image. The difference is that *juggler* refers to a concrete object, whereas *truth* refers to an abstract concept. Allan Paivio (1986) points out that it is easier to form images of concrete objects than of abstract concepts. He believes that this ease of image formation affects memory. For example, in one study, he found that subjects given pairs of words to remember showed better recall for high-imagery than low-imagery pairings (see **Figure 7.4**), demonstrating that visual imagery enriches encoding (Paivio, Smythe, & Yuille, 1968). Similar results were observed in a subsequent study that controlled for additional confounding factors (Paivio, Khan, & Begg, 2000).

According to Paivio (1986, 2007), imagery facilitates memory because it provides a second kind of memory code, and two codes are better than one. His **dual-coding theory**

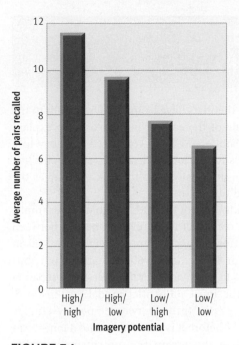

FIGURE 7.4

The effect of visual imagery on retention.
Paivio, Smythe, and Yuille (1968) asked subjects
to learn a list of sixteen pairs of words. They
manipulated whether the words were concrete,
high-imagery words or abstract, low-imagery
words. In terms of imagery potential, the list
contained four types of pairings: high-high
(*juggler-dress*), high-low (*letter-effort*), low-high
(*duty-hotel*), and low-low (*quality-necessity*). The
impact of imagery was quite evident. The best
recall was of high-high pairings, and the worst
recall was of low-low pairings.

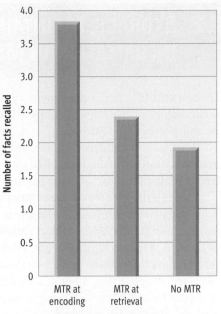

FIGURE 7.5

**The effect of motivation to remember (MTR)
on subsequent recall.** Participants' motivation
to remember was increased at the time of
encoding, at the time of retrieval, or not at all in
a control condition. Raising MTR at the time of
encoding increased recall, but raising MTR at
the time of retrieval did not.

SOURCE: Adapted from Kassam, K. S., Gilbert, D. T.,
Swencionis, J. K., & Wilson, T. D. (2009). Misconceptions of memory: The Scooter Libby effect. *Psychological Science, 20,* 551–552.

holds that memory is enhanced by forming both semantic and visual codes since
either can lead to recall. Although some aspects of his theory have been questioned, it's
clear that the use of mental imagery can enhance memory in many situations (McCauley,
Eskes, & Moscovitch, 1996). The value of visual imagery demonstrates once again that
encoding plays a critical role in memory.

Motivation to Remember

Another factor that appears to influence encoding effectiveness is one's motivation to
remember (MTR) at the time of encoding. When MTR is high at the time of encoding—
typically because the information is perceived to be important—people are more likely
to exert extra effort to attend to and organize information in ways that facilitate future
recall. In one investigation, participants were asked to memorize facts about six people
presented in photos (Kassam et al., 2009). Motivation to remember was manipulated, either at the time of encoding or at the time of retrieval, by offering participants a financial
bonus for every fact they recalled about a specific target person. The results showed that
increasing MTR at the time of encoding led to greater recall, whereas increasing MTR
at the time of retrieval had little effect (see **Figure 7.5**). Thus, encoding processes can
be enhanced by strong motivation. But encoding is only one of the three key processes
in memory. We turn next to the process of storage, which for many people is virtually
synonymous with memory.

Key Learning Goals

- Describe the sensory store in memory, and discuss the durability and capacity of short-term memory.
- Describe Baddeley's model of working memory, and discuss research on working memory capacity.
- Evaluate the permanence of long-term memory, and discuss how knowledge is represented in memory.

7.2 STORAGE: MAINTAINING INFORMATION IN MEMORY

In their efforts to understand memory storage, theorists have historically related it to the technologies of their age (Roediger, 1980). One of the earliest models used to explain memory storage was the wax tablet. Both Aristotle and Plato compared memory to a block of wax that differed in size and hardness for various individuals. Remembering, according to this analogy, was like stamping an impression into the wax. As long as the image remained in the wax, the memory would remain intact.

Modern theories reflect the technological advances of the 20th century. For example, many theories formulated at the dawn of the computer age drew an analogy between information storage by computers and information storage in human memory (Atkinson & Shiffrin, 1968, 1971; Broadbent, 1958; Waugh & Norman, 1965). The main contribution of these *information-processing theories* was to subdivide memory into three separate memory stores (Estes, 1999). According to the most influential model (Atkinson & Shiffrin, 1968, 1971), incoming information passes through two temporary storage buffers—the sensory store and short-term store—before it is transferred into a long-term store (see **Figure 7.6**). Like the wax tablet before it, the information-processing model of memory is a metaphor; the three memory stores are not viewed as anatomical structures in the brain, but rather as functionally distinct types of memory.

Sensory Memory

Sensory memory **preserves information in its original sensory form for a brief time, usually only a fraction of a second.** Sensory memory allows the sensation of a visual pattern, sound, or touch to linger for a brief moment after the sensory stimulation is over. In the case of vision, people really perceive an *afterimage* rather than the actual stimulus. You can demonstrate the existence of afterimages for yourself by rapidly moving a light in circles in the dark. If you move the light fast enough, you should see a complete circle even though the light source is only a single point (see the adjacent photo). The sensory memory preserves the sensory image long enough for you to perceive a continuous circle rather than separate points of light.

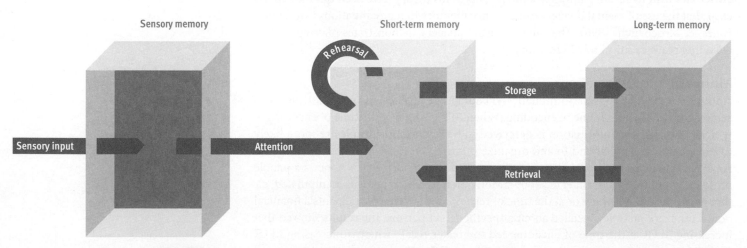

FIGURE 7.6

The Atkinson and Shiffrin model of memory storage. Atkinson and Shiffrin (1971) proposed that memory is made up of three information stores. *Sensory memory* can hold a large amount of information just long enough (a fraction of a second) for a small portion of it to be selected for longer storage. *Short-term memory* has a limited capacity, and unless aided by rehearsal, its storage duration is brief. *Long-term memory* can store an apparently unlimited amount of information for indeterminate periods.

The brief preservation of sensations in sensory memory gives you additional time to try to recognize stimuli. However, you'd better take advantage of sensory storage immediately because it doesn't last long. In a classic experiment, George Sperling (1960) demonstrated that the memory trace in the visual sensory store decays in about one-quarter of a second. There is some debate about whether stimulus persistence really involves *memory storage* (Nairne & Neath, 2013). Some theorists view it as an artifact of the perceptual processing of incoming stimuli that is attributable to excitatory feedback in specific neural circuits (Francis, 1999). In other words, stimulus persistence may be more like an echo than a memory.

Short-Term Memory

Short-term memory (STM) **is a limited-capacity store that can maintain unrehearsed information for up to about 20 seconds.** In contrast, information stored in long-term memory may last weeks, months, or years. Actually, you can maintain information in your short-term store for longer than 20 seconds. How? Primarily, by engaging in *rehearsal—***the process of repetitively verbalizing or thinking about information.** You surely have used the rehearsal process on many occasions. For instance, if you get a phone number from directory assistance, you might recite it over and over until you can dial the number. Rehearsal keeps recycling the information through your short-term memory. In theory, this recycling could go on indefinitely, but in reality something eventually distracts you and breaks the rehearsal loop.

Durability of Storage

Without rehearsal, information in short-term memory is lost in 10 to 20 seconds (Nairne, 2003). This rapid loss was demonstrated in a study by Peterson and Peterson (1959). They measured how long undergraduates could remember three consonants if they couldn't rehearse them. To prevent rehearsal, the Petersons required the students to count backward by threes from the time the consonants were presented until they saw a light that signaled the recall test (see **Figure 7.7**). Participants' recall accuracy was pretty dismal after only 15 seconds. Other approaches to the issue have suggested that the typical duration of short-term memory storage may even be shorter (Baddeley, 1986). Theorists originally believed that the loss of information from short-term memory was attributable purely to time-related *decay* of memory traces, but follow-up research showed that *interference* from competing material also contributes (Oberauer & Lewandowsky, 2014; Nairne & Neath, 2013).

Capacity of Storage

Short-term memory is also limited in the number of items it can hold. The small capacity of short-term memory was pointed out by George Miller (1956) in a famous paper called "The Magical Number Seven, Plus or Minus Two: Some Limits on Our Capacity for Processing Information." Miller noticed that people could recall only about seven items in tasks that required the use of short-term memory. When short-term memory is filled to capacity, the insertion of new information "bumps out" some of the information currently in short-term memory. The limited capacity of short-term memory constrains people's ability to perform tasks in which they need to mentally juggle various pieces of information (Baddeley & Hitch, 1974).

The capacity of short-term memory may even be less than widely assumed. Nelson Cowan (2005, 2010) cites evidence indicating that the capacity of short-term memory is 4 plus or minus 1. The consensus on the capacity of short-term memory seems to be moving toward this smaller estimate (Lustig et al., 2009). According to Cowan, the capacity of short-term memory has historically been overestimated because researchers have often failed to take steps to prevent covert rehearsal, or *chunking*, by participants. It has long been known that people can increase the capacity of their short-term memory by combining

Because the image of the sparkler persists briefly in sensory memory, when the sparkler is moved fast enough, the blending of after-images causes people to see a continuous stream of light instead of a succession of individual points.

► REALITY CHECK

Misconception

The capacity of short-term memory (STM) is 7 plus or minus 2.

Reality

Calling this assertion a misconception is a little harsh because this has been the conventional wisdom since the 1950s, and there is room for argument on the matter. However, in the last decade or so, researchers using more sophisticated methods have been chipping away at this maxim. The consensus among memory experts has shifted toward the belief that the capacity of short-term memory is 4 plus or minus 1.

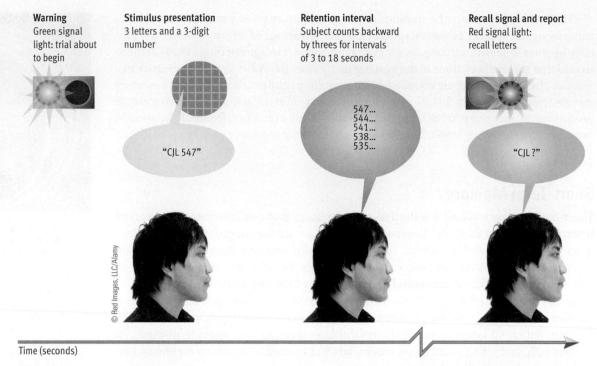

Warning
Green signal light: trial about to begin

Stimulus presentation
3 letters and a 3-digit number

"CJL 547"

Retention interval
Subject counts backward by threes for intervals of 3 to 18 seconds

547...
544...
541...
538...
535...

Recall signal and report
Red signal light: recall letters

"CJL ?"

Time (seconds)

FIGURE 7.7

Peterson and Peterson's (1959) study of short-term memory. After a warning light was flashed, the participants were given three consonants to remember. The researchers prevented rehearsal by giving the subjects a three-digit number at the same time and telling them to count backward by three from that number until given the signal to recall the letters. By varying the amount of time between stimulus presentation and recall, Peterson and Peterson (1959) were able to measure how quickly information was lost from short-term memory.

stimuli into larger, possibly higher-order units, called *chunks* (Simon, 1974). **A *chunk* is a group of familiar stimuli stored as a single unit.** You can demonstrate the effect of chunking by asking someone to recall a sequence of twelve letters grouped in the following way:

FB - INB - CC - IAIB - M

As you read the letters aloud, pause at the hyphens. Your subject will probably attempt to remember each letter separately because there are no obvious groups or chunks. But a string of twelve letters is too long for STM, so errors are likely. Now present the same string of letters to another person, but place the pauses in the following locations:

FBI - NBC - CIA - IBM

The letters now form four familiar chunks that should occupy only four slots in short-term memory, resulting in successful recall (Bower & Springston, 1970).

To successfully chunk the letters I B M, a subject must first recognize these letters as a familiar unit. This familiarity has to be stored somewhere in long-term memory. Thus, in this case, information was transferred from long-term into short-term memory. This type of transfer is not unusual. People routinely draw information out of their long-term memory banks to evaluate and understand information that they are working with in short-term memory.

Short-Term Memory as "Working Memory"

Research eventually suggested that short-term memory involves more than a simple rehearsal buffer, as originally believed. The findings prompted Alan Baddeley (1992, 2001, 2012) to propose a more complex model of short-term memory that characterizes it as *working memory*—**a modular system for temporary storage and manipulation of information.** Baddeley's model of working memory consists of four components (see **Figure 7.8**). The first component is the *phonological loop*, which represented all of short-term memory in earlier models. This component is at work when you use recitation to temporarily hold onto a phone number. Baddeley (2003) believes that the phonological loop evolved to foster the acquisition of language. The second component in working memory is a *visuospatial sketchpad* that permits people to temporarily hold and manipulate visual images. This component is at work when you try to mentally rearrange the furniture in your bedroom. The third component is the *central executive* system. It controls the deployment of attention, switching the focus of attention and dividing attention, as needed. The fourth component is the *episodic buffer,* a temporary, limited capacity store that allows the various components of working memory to integrate information and that serves as an interface between working memory and long-term memory.

The two key characteristics that originally defined short-term memory—small capacity and short storage duration—are still present in the concept of working memory. However, Baddeley's model accounts for evidence that short-term memory handles a greater variety of functions and depends on more complicated processes than previously thought.

Baddeley's model of working memory has generated an enormous volume of research. For example, research has shown that people vary in how well they can juggle information in their working memory while fending off distractions (Wiley & Jarosz, 2012). **Working memory capacity (WMC) refers to one's ability to hold and manipulate information in conscious attention.** Working memory capacity is a stable personal trait (Unsworth et al., 2005) that appears to be influenced to a considerable degree by heredity (Kremen et al., 2007). That said, working memory capacity can be temporarily reduced by situational factors, such as pressure to perform or rumination (Curci et al., 2013; Gimmig et al., 2006). Interestingly, people with greater working memory capacity tend to be especially flexible and effective in their allocation of working memory (Rummel & Boywitt, 2014). In other words, high-WMC individuals tend to let their mind wander from the task at hand more than low-WMC individuals when the attentional demands of the task are modest—presumably because they can afford to do so—but they also are better at staying focused when they need to do so.

Variations in working memory capacity correlate positively with measures of high-level cognitive abilities, such as reading comprehension, complex reasoning, and even intelligence (Logie, 2011; Unsworth et al., 2014). This finding has led some theorists to conclude that working memory capacity is critical to complex cognition (Lepine, Barrouillet, & Camos, 2005). Variations in working memory capacity also appear to influence musical ability because reading music while playing an instrument taxes WMC (Hambrick & Meinz, 2013). Some theorists argue that increases in working memory capacity tens of thousands of years ago were crucial to the evolution of complex cognitive processes and creativity in humans (Coolidge & Wynn, 2009). Their analyses are highly speculative, but they highlight the profound importance of working memory capacity (Balter, 2010).

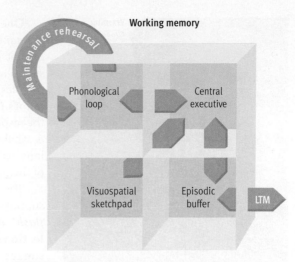

FIGURE 7.8

Short-term memory as working memory. This diagram depicts the revised model of the short-term store proposed by Alan Baddeley. According to Baddeley (2001), working memory includes four components: a phonological loop, a visuospatial sketchpad, a central executive system, and an episodic buffer.

Long-Term Memory

Long-term memory (LTM) **is an unlimited capacity store that can hold information over lengthy periods of time.** Unlike sensory and short-term memory, which decay rapidly, long-term memory can store information indefinitely. Long-term memories are durable. Some information may remain in long-term memory across an entire lifetime.

Flashbulb memories are vivid and detailed recollections of momentous events. For example, many people will long remember exactly where they were and how they felt when they learned about the terrorist attacks on the World Trade Center.

One point of view is that all information stored in long-term memory is stored there *permanently*. According to this view, forgetting occurs only because people sometimes cannot retrieve needed information. To draw an analogy, imagine that memories are stored in long-term memory like marbles in a barrel. According to this view, none of the marbles ever leak out. When you forget, you just aren't able to dig out the right marble, but it's there—somewhere. In a survey of the general public's views on memory, 48% of the respondents endorsed the idea that long-term memory storage is permanent (Simons & Chabris, 2011). An alternative point of view assumes that some memories stored in long-term memory do vanish forever. According to this view, the barrel is leaky and some of the marbles roll out, never to return.

The existence of *flashbulb memories* is one piece of evidence that has been cited to support the notion that long-term memory storage may be permanent. At first glance, **flashbulb memories, which are thought to be unusually vivid and detailed recollections of momentous events,** provide striking examples of seemingly permanent storage (Brown & Kulik, 1977). Many American adults, for instance, can remember exactly where they were, what they were doing, and how they felt when they learned of the 1997 death of Princess Diana, or the 2001 terrorist attacks that took place in New York and Washington, DC, on September 11, 2001. Although flashbulb memories have mostly been studied in relation to negative events, people also report flashbulb memories of positive events (Kraha & Boals, 2014). For example, Tinti and colleagues (2014) studied flashbulb memories in Italian citizens after Italy won the World Cup in 2006.

Does the evidence on flashbulb memories provide adequate support for the idea that long-term memory storage is permanent? No, research eventually showed that flashbulb memories are neither as accurate nor as special as once believed (Hirst et al., 2009; Schmolck, Buffalo, & Squire, 2000). Like other memories, they become less detailed and complete with time and are often inaccurate (Talarico & Rubin, 2009). Research suggests that it is not extraordinary accuracy or longevity that distinguish flashbulb memories. Rather, what makes them special is that people subjectively feel that these memories are exceptionally vivid, that they have exceptional confidence (albeit misplaced) in their memories' accuracy, and that more emotional intensity is attached to these recollections (Talarico & Rubin, 2003, 2007). So, perhaps flashbulb memories are "special," but not in the way originally envisioned.

Returning to the question at hand, the research findings on flashbulb memories clearly conflict with the hypothesis that memory storage is permanent. Although the possibility cannot be ruled out completely, there is still no convincing evidence that memories are stored away permanently and that forgetting is all a matter of retrieval failure (Payne & Blackwell, 1998; Schacter, 1996).

CONCEPT CHECK 7.1

Comparing the Memory Stores

Check your understanding of the three memory stores by filling in the blanks in the table below. The column on the left lists three features of the memory stores that can be compared. The answers can be found in Appendix A.

Feature	Sensory memory	Short-term memory	Long-term memory
1. Main encoding format	copy of input		largely semantic
2. Storage capacity	limited		
3. Storage duration		up to 20 seconds	

How Is Knowledge Represented in Memory?

Over the years, memory researchers have wrestled with another major question relating to memory storage: How is knowledge represented and organized in memory? Most theorists seem to agree that memories probably take a variety of forms, depending on the nature of the material. Most of the theorizing has focused on how factual knowledge can be represented in long-term memory.

Categories and Conceptual Hierarchies

People spontaneously organize information into categories for storage in memory. This fact was apparent in a study by Bousfield (1953), who asked subjects to memorize a list of sixty words. Although presented in a scrambled order, each of the words in the list fit into one of four categories: animals, men's names, vegetables, or professions. Bousfield showed that subjects recalling this list engage in *clustering*—the tendency to remember similar items in groups. The words were not presented in organized groups, yet participants tended to remember them in bunches that belonged in the same category. Thus, when applicable, factual information is routinely organized into simple categories.

Similarly, when possible, factual information can be organized into conceptual hierarchies. **A *conceptual hierarchy* is a multilevel classification system based on common properties among items.** A conceptual hierarchy that a person might construct for a tiny portion of the animal world can be found in **Figure 7.9**. According to Gordon Bower (1970), organizing information into a conceptual hierarchy can improve recall dramatically.

Schemas

Imagine that you've just visited Professor Smith's office, which is shown in the adjacent photo. Take a brief look at the photo and then cover it up. Now pretend you must describe Professor Smith's office to a friend. Write down what you saw (in the picture).

Compare your description with the picture. Chances are your description will include elements—books or filing cabinets, for instance—that were *not* in the office. This common phenomenon demonstrates how *schemas* can influence memory. **A *schema* is an organized cluster of knowledge about a particular object or event abstracted from previous experience with the object or event.** For example, college students have schemas for what professors' offices are like. When Brewer and Treyens (1981) tested the recall of thirty subjects who had briefly visited the office shown in the photo, most subjects recalled the desks and chairs. Few, though, recalled the wine bottle or the picnic basket, which aren't part of a typical office schema. Moreover, nine subjects falsely recalled that the office contained books.

These results and other studies (Tuckey & Brewer, 2003) suggest that *people are more likely to remember things that are consistent with their schemas than things that are not.* Although this principle seems applicable much of the time, the inverse is also true: *people sometimes exhibit better recall of things that violate their schema-based expectations* (Neuschatz et al., 2002). Information that really clashes with a schema may attract extra attention and deeper processing, and thus

Professor Smith's office is shown in this photo. Follow the instructions in the text to learn how Brewer and Treyens (1981) used it in a study of memory.

FIGURE 7.9

Conceptual hierarchies and long-term memory. Some types of information can be organized into a multilevel hierarchy of concepts like the one shown here. Bower and colleagues (1969) found that subjects remember more information when they organize it into a conceptual hierarchy.

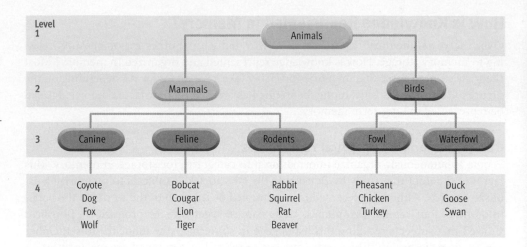

become more memorable. For instance, if you saw a slot machine in a professor's office, you would probably remember it. In either case, it's apparent that information stored in memory is often organized around schemas (Brewer, 2000).

Semantic Networks

Of course, not all information fits neatly into conceptual hierarchies or schemas. Much knowledge seems to be organized into less systematic frameworks, called *semantic networks* (Collins & Loftus, 1975). **A *semantic network* consists of nodes representing concepts, joined together by pathways that link related concepts.** A small semantic network is shown in **Figure 7.10**. The ovals are the nodes, and the words inside the ovals are the interlinked concepts. The lines connecting the nodes are the pathways. The length of each pathway represents the degree of association between two concepts. Shorter pathways imply stronger associations.

FIGURE 7.10

A semantic network. Much of the organization of long-term memory depends on networks of associations among concepts. In this highly simplified depiction of a fragment of a semantic network, the shorter the line linking any two concepts, the stronger the association between them. The coloration of the concept boxes represents activation of the concepts. This is how the network might look just after a person hears the word *apple*.

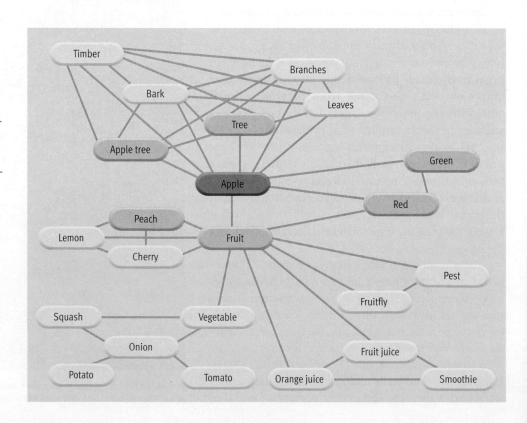

Semantic networks have proven useful in explaining why thinking about one word (such as *butter*) can make a closely related word (such as *bread*) easier to remember. According to Collins and Loftus (1975), when people think about a word, their thoughts naturally go to related words. They call this process *spreading activation* within a semantic network. They assume that activation spreads out along the pathways of the semantic network surrounding the word. They also theorize that the strength of this activation decreases as it travels outward, much as ripples decrease in size as they radiate outward from a rock tossed into a pond. Consider again the semantic network shown in **Figure 7.10**. If subjects see the word *fruit*, words that are closely linked to it (such as *peach*) should be easier to recall than words that have longer links (such as *orange juice*).

7.3 RETRIEVAL: GETTING INFORMATION OUT OF MEMORY

7.3

Key Learning Goals

- Explain the tip-of-the-tongue phenomenon, and understand how context cues can influence retrieval.
- Summarize research on the reconstructive nature of memory, and apply the concept of source monitoring to everyday memory errors.

Entering information into long-term memory is a worthy goal, but it is an insufficient one if you can't get the information back out again when you need it. Fortunately, recall often occurs without much effort. But occasionally a planned search of long-term memory is necessary. For instance, imagine that you were asked to recall the names of all fifty states in the United States. You would probably conduct your memory search systematically, recalling states in alphabetical order or by geographical location. Although this example is rather simple, retrieval is a complex process, as you'll see in this section.

Using Cues to Aid Retrieval

At the beginning of this chapter we discussed the ***tip-of-the-tongue phenomenon—the temporary inability to remember something you know, accompanied by a feeling that it's just out of reach.*** The tip-of-the-tongue phenomenon is a common experience that happens about once a week, although its occurrence increases with age (Salthouse & Mandell, 2013; Schwartz & Metcalfe, 2014). It clearly represents a failure in retrieval. However, the exact mechanisms underlying this failure are the subject of debate. A number of explanations have been proposed for this phenomenon (A. S. Brown, 2012a; Schwartz & Metcalfe, 2011).

Fortunately, memories can often be jogged with *retrieval cues*—stimuli that help gain access to memories, such as hints, related information, or partial recollections. This was apparent when Roger Brown and David McNeill (1966) studied the tip-of-the-tongue phenomenon. They gave participants definitions of obscure words and asked them to think of the words. Our example at the beginning of the chapter (the definition for *nepotism*) was taken from their study. Brown and McNeill found that subjects groping for obscure words were correct in guessing the first letter of the missing word 57% of the time. This figure far exceeds chance and shows that partial recollections are often headed in the right direction.

Reinstating the Context of an Event

Let's test your memory: What did you have for breakfast two days ago? If you can't immediately answer, you might begin by imagining yourself sitting at the breakfast table (or wherever you usually have breakfast). Trying to recall an event by putting yourself back in the context in which it occurred involves working with *context cues* to aid retrieval.

Context cues often facilitate the retrieval of information (Hanczakowski, Zawadzka, & Coote, 2014). Most people have experienced the effects of context cues on many occasions. For instance, when people return after a number of years to a place where they used to live, they are typically flooded with long-forgotten memories. Or consider how often you have gone from one room to another to get something (scissors, perhaps), only to discover that you can't remember what you were after. However, when you return to the first room (the original context), you suddenly recall what it was ("Of course, the scissors!"). These examples illustrate the potentially powerful effects of context cues on memory.

The value of reinstating the context of an event may account for how hypnosis *occasionally* stimulates eyewitness recall in legal investigations (Meyer, 1992). The hypnotist usually attempts to reinstate the context of the event by telling the witness to imagine being at the scene of the crime once again. Although it is widely believed by the general public that hypnosis can help people remember things that they would not normally recall (Simons & Chabris, 2011), extensive research has failed to demonstrate that hypnosis can reliably enhance retrieval (Mazzoni, Heap, & Scoboria, 2010). Quite to the contrary, research suggests that hypnosis often increases individuals' tendency to report *incorrect* information (Mazzoni, Laurence, & Heap, 2014).

Reconstructing Memories

A survey on people's notions about memory found that 63% believe that when you retrieve information from long-term memory, you're able to pull up a "mental videotape" that provides an exact replay of the past (Simons & Chabris, 2011). However, countless studies have demonstrated that this is a naïve and extremely inaccurate view of memory. In reality, all memories are *reconstructions* of the past that may be distorted and may include details that did not actually occur (Gallo & Wheeler, 2013; Schacter & Loftus, 2013).

Research by Elizabeth Loftus (1979, 1992, 2005) and others on the *misinformation effect* has shown that reconstructive distortions show up frequently in eyewitness testimony. **The *misinformation effect* occurs when participants' recall of an event they witnessed is altered by introducing misleading post-event information.** For example, in one study, Loftus and Palmer (1974) showed participants a videotape of an automobile accident. Participants were then "grilled" as if they were providing eyewitness testimony, and biasing information was introduced. Some subjects were asked, "How fast were the cars going when they *hit* each other?" Other subjects were asked, "How fast were the cars going when they *smashed into* each other?" A week later, participants' recall of the accident was tested. They were asked whether they remembered seeing any broken glass in the accident (there was none). Subjects who had earlier been asked about the cars *smashing into* each other were more likely to "recall" broken glass. Why would they add this detail to their reconstructions of the accident? Probably because broken glass is consistent with their schemas for cars *smashing* together (see **Figure 7.11**). The misinformation effect, which has been replicated in countless studies (Frenda, Nichols, & Loftus, 2011),

FIGURE 7.11

The misinformation effect. In an experiment by Loftus and Palmer (1974), participants who were asked leading questions in which cars were described as *hitting* or *smashing* each other were prone to recall the same accident differently 1 week later, demonstrating the reconstructive nature of memory.

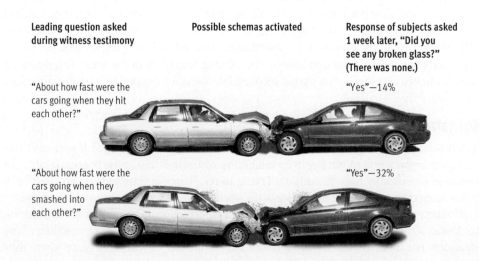

Leading question asked during witness testimony	Possible schemas activated	Response of subjects asked 1 week later, "Did you see any broken glass?" (There was none.)
"About how fast were the cars going when they hit each other?"		"Yes"—14%
"About how fast were the cars going when they smashed into each other?"		"Yes"—32%

is a remarkably reliable phenomenon that "challenged prevailing views about the validity of memory" (Zaragoza, Belli, & Payment, 2007, p. 37). Indeed, the effect is so difficult to escape that even subjects who have been forewarned can be swayed by post-event misinformation (Chrobak & Zaragoza, 2013).

Studies have demonstrated that the influence of misinformation is not limited to memories of events that one has personally experienced or witnessed; it can also distort one's knowledge of basic facts (Bottoms, Eslick, & Marsh, 2010). For example, most people know that the Pacific is the largest ocean on Earth and that Thomas Edison invented the light bulb. These are facts that most people have encountered repeatedly. They should be stable memories that ought to be resistant to change. But, consider what happened when Fazio and colleagues (2013) had participants read short fictional stories that contradicted these facts by casually mentioning that the Atlantic was the largest ocean and that Benjamin Franklin invented the light bulb. Although the participants had shown correct knowledge of these and other well-known facts 2 weeks earlier, when they took a test of general knowledge after reading misleading stories, about 20% got basic facts wrong—such as indicating that Franklin invented the light bulb—even though they were explicitly warned that the fictional stories might contain factual errors. Thus, in a portion of subjects, a single, brief exposure to misinformation disrupted basic factual knowledge. Sorry to say, these findings suggest that just reading about this study might distort your own future recall of these simple facts.

Other research on the reconstructive nature of memory has demonstrated that the simple act of retelling a story can introduce inaccuracies into memory (Marsh, 2007). When people retell a story, they may streamline it, embellish the facts, exaggerate their role, and so forth. In such retellings, people may be aware that they are being a little loose with the facts (Marsh & Tversky, 2004). However, what is interesting is that their intentional distortions can reshape their subsequent recollections of the same events. Somehow, the "real" story and the storyteller's "spin" on it begin to blend imperceptibly. So, even routine retellings of events can contribute to the malleability of memory.

Source Monitoring

The misinformation effect appears to be due, *in part,* to the unreliability of *source monitoring*—**the process of making inferences about the origins of memories.** Marcia Johnson and her colleagues (Johnson, 1996, 2006; Johnson et al., 2012) maintain that source monitoring is a crucial facet of memory retrieval that contributes to many of the mistakes that people make in reconstructing their experiences. According to Johnson, memories are not tagged with labels that specify their sources. Thus, when people pull up specific memory records, they have to make decisions *at the time of retrieval* about where the memories came from (example: "Did I read that in the *New York Times* or *Rolling Stone*?"). Much of the time, these decisions are so easy and automatic that people make them without being consciously aware of the source-monitoring process. In other instances, however, they may consciously struggle to pinpoint the source of a memory. **A *source-monitoring error* occurs when a memory derived from one source is misattributed to another source.** For example, you might attribute something that your roommate said to your psychology professor, or something you heard on *Dr. Phil* to your psychology textbook. Inaccurate memories that reflect source-monitoring errors can seem quite compelling. People often feel quite confident about the authenticity of their assertions even though the recollections really are inaccurate (Lampinen, Neuschatz, & Payne, 1999).

Source-monitoring errors appear to be commonplace and may shed light on many interesting memory phenomena. For instance, in studies of eyewitness suggestibility, some subjects have gone so far as to insist that they "remember" seeing something that was only verbally suggested to them. Most theories have a hard time explaining how people can have memories of events that they never actually saw or experienced. But this paradox doesn't seem all that perplexing when it is explained as a source-monitoring error (Lindsay et al., 2004).

> ▶ **REALITY CHECK**

Misconception

Memory is like a mental videotape that can provide faithful reproductions of past events.

Reality

Countless studies in recent decades have demonstrated that memories are incomplete, distorted, fuzzy reconstructions of past events. The adjectives that best describe memory are not *exact* or *accurate,* but *fragile, fallible,* and *malleable.*

7.4 FORGETTING: WHEN MEMORY LAPSES

Key Learning Goals

- Describe Ebbinghaus's forgetting curve and three measures of retention.
- Understand the potential causes of forgetting.
- Summarize evidence of the controversy regarding recovered memories of childhood sexual abuse.

Forgetting gets a "bad press" that it may not deserve. People tend to view forgetting as a failure, weakness, or deficiency in cognitive processing. Although forgetting important information *can* be frustrating, some memory theorists argue that forgetting is actually adaptive. How so? Imagine how cluttered your memory would be if you never forgot anything. According to some theorists (Schacter, 1999; Storm, 2011), people need to forget information that is no longer relevant, such as out-of-date phone numbers, discarded passwords, and lines that were memorized for a tenth-grade play. Forgetting can reduce competition among memories that can cause confusion. Laney (2013) offers a simple but compelling example. Imagine what would happen if all your many memories of parking your car at a nearby shopping mall were equally vivid? Good luck finding your car! It is highly functional if your memory of where you parked at a mall today is much stronger than your memory of where you parked at the same mall 5 days or 2 weeks ago.

Although forgetting may be adaptive in the long run, the fundamental question of memory research remains: Why do people forget information that they would like to remember? There isn't one simple answer to this question. Research has shown that forgetting can be caused by defects in encoding, storage, retrieval, or some combination of these processes.

How Quickly We Forget: Ebbinghaus's Forgetting Curve

The first person to conduct scientific studies of forgetting was Hermann Ebbinghaus. He published a series of insightful memory studies way back in 1885. Ebbinghaus studied only one subject—himself. To give himself lots of new material to memorize, he invented *nonsense syllables*—**consonant-vowel-consonant arrangements that do not correspond to words** (such as BAF, XOF, VIR, and MEQ). He wanted to work with meaningless materials that would be uncontaminated by his previous learning.

Ebbinghaus was a remarkably dedicated researcher. For instance, in one study, he went through more than 14,000 practice repetitions, as he tirelessly memorized 420 lists of nonsense syllables (Slamecka, 1985). He tested his memory of these lists after various time intervals. **Figure 7.12** shows what he found. This diagram, called a *forgetting curve,* **graphs retention and forgetting over time.** Ebbinghaus's forgetting curve shows a sharp

FIGURE 7.12

Ebbinghaus's forgetting curve for nonsense syllables. From his experiments on himself, Ebbinghaus (1885) concluded that forgetting is extremely rapid immediately after the original learning and then levels off. Although this generalization remains true, subsequent research has shown that forgetting curves for nonsense syllables are unusually steep.

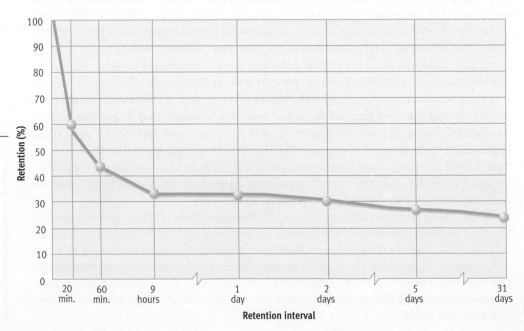

drop in retention during the first few hours after the nonsense syllables were memorized. He forgot more than 60% of the syllables in less than 9 hours! Thus, he concluded that most forgetting occurs very rapidly after learning something.

That's a depressing conclusion. What is the point of memorizing information if you're going to forget it all right away? Fortunately, subsequent research showed that Ebbinghaus's forgetting curve was unusually steep (Postman, 1985). Forgetting isn't usually as swift or as extensive as Ebbinghaus thought. One problem was that he was working with such meaningless material. When participants memorize more meaningful material, such as prose or poetry, forgetting curves aren't nearly as steep. Studies of how well people recall their high school classmates suggest that forgetting curves for autobiographical information are much shallower (Bahrick, 2000). Also, different methods of measuring forgetting yield varied estimates of how quickly people forget. This variation underscores the importance of the methods used to measure forgetting, the matter we turn to next.

Measures of Forgetting

To study forgetting empirically, psychologists need to be able to measure it precisely. Measures of forgetting inevitably measure retention, as well. ***Retention* refers to the proportion of material retained (remembered).** In studies of forgetting, the results may be reported in terms of the amount forgotten or the amount retained. In these studies, the *retention interval* is the length of time between the presentation of materials to be remembered and the measurement of forgetting. Psychologists use three methods to measure forgetting/retention: recall, recognition, and relearning.

Who is the current U.S. secretary of state? What movie won the Academy Award for best picture last year? These questions involve recall measures of retention. **A *recall measure* requires participants to reproduce information on their own without any cues.** If you were to take a recall test on a list of twenty-five words you had memorized, you would simply be told to write down on a blank sheet of paper as many of the words as you could remember.

In contrast, in a recognition test, you might be shown a list of 100 words and asked to choose the twenty-five words you had memorized. **A *recognition measure* of retention requires participants to select previously learned information from an array of options.** Subjects not only have cues to work with, they have the answers right in front of them. In educational testing, multiple-choice, true-false, and matching questions are recognition measures; essay questions and fill-in-the-blanks questions are recall measures.

If you're like most students, you probably prefer multiple-choice tests over essay tests. This preference is understandable because evidence shows that recognition measures tend to yield higher scores than do recall measures of memory for the same information (Lockhart, 2000). This tendency was demonstrated many years ago in a study by Luh (1922), who measured subjects' retention of nonsense syllables with both a recognition test and a recall test. He found that participants' performance on the recognition measure was far superior to their performance on the recall measure (see **Figure 7.13**). There are two ways of looking at this disparity between recall and recognition tests. One view is that recognition tests are especially *sensitive* measures of retention. The other view is that recognition tests are excessively easy measures of retention.

The third method of measuring forgetting is relearning. **A *relearning measure* of retention requires a participant to memorize information a second time to determine how much time or effort is saved by having learned it before.** To use this method, a researcher measures how much time (or how many practice trials) a person needs in order to memorize something. At a later date, the participant is asked to relearn the information. The researcher measures how much more quickly the material is memorized the second time.

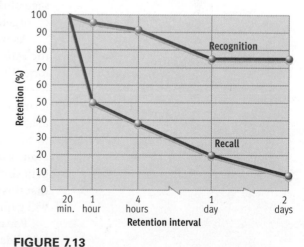

FIGURE 7.13

Recognition versus recall in the measurement of retention. Luh (1922) had participants memorize lists of nonsense syllables and then measured their retention with either a recognition test or a recall test at various intervals up to 2 days. As you can see, the forgetting curve for the recall test was quite steep, whereas the recognition test yielded much higher estimates of subjects' retention.

Participants' *savings scores* provide an estimate of their retention. For example, if it takes you 20 minutes to memorize a list the first time and only 5 minutes to memorize it a week later, you've saved 15 minutes. Your savings score of 75% (15/20 = 3/4 = 75%) suggests that you have retained 75% and forgotten the remaining 25% of the information. Relearning measures can detect retention that is overlooked by recognition tests (Crowder & Greene, 2000).

Why We Forget

Measuring forgetting is only the first step in the long journey toward explaining why forgetting occurs. In this section, we explore the possible causes of forgetting, looking at factors that may affect encoding, storage, and retrieval processes.

Ineffective Encoding

A great deal of forgetting may only *appear* to be forgetting. The information in question may never have been inserted into memory in the first place. Since you can't really forget something you never learned, this phenomenon is sometimes called *pseudoforgetting.* We opened the chapter with an example of pseudoforgetting. People usually assume that they know what a penny looks like. However, most people have actually failed to encode this information. Pseudoforgetting is usually attributable to *lack of attention.*

Even when memory codes are formed for new information, subsequent forgetting may be the result of ineffective or inappropriate encoding (Brown & Craik, 2000). The research on levels of processing shows that some approaches to encoding lead to more forgetting than others (Craik & Tulving, 1975). For example, if you're distracted while you read your textbooks, you may be doing little more than saying the words to yourself. This is an example of *phonemic encoding,* which is inferior to *semantic encoding* for retention of verbal material.

Decay

Instead of focusing on encoding, decay theory attributes forgetting to the impermanence of memory storage. **Decay theory proposes that forgetting occurs because memory traces fade with time.** The implicit assumption is that decay occurs in the physiological mechanisms responsible for memories. According to decay theory, the mere passage of time produces forgetting. This notion meshes nicely with common sense views of forgetting.

As we saw earlier, decay *does* appear to contribute to the loss of information from the sensory and short-term memory stores. However, the critical task for theories of forgetting is to explain the loss of information from long-term memory. Researchers have *not* been successful in providing clear demonstrations that decay causes long-term memory forgetting (Roediger, Weinstein, & Agarwal, 2010). Not all theorists have abandoned the concept of decay, however. Based on complicated evidence relating to the neurological and molecular bases of memory, Hardt, Nader, and Nadel (2013) argue that decay processes contribute to the selective removal of some memories. They believe that decay weakens the neurobiological substrate of selected memories, and that this process unfolds primarily during sleep. It remains to be seen if this new theory will gain traction.

For many decades, the key problem for decay theory has been researchers' inability to validate its cornerstone prediction that the principal cause and strongest correlate of forgetting should be the passage of time. In studies of long-term memory, researchers have repeatedly found that the passage of time is not nearly as influential as *what happens* during the time interval. Research has shown that forgetting depends not on the amount of time that has passed since learning, but on the amount, complexity, and type of information that subjects have had to absorb *during* that period of time. The negative impact of competing information on retention is called *interference,* which we turn to next.

Interference

Interference theory **proposes that people forget information because of competition from other material.** Although demonstrations of decay in long-term memory have remained elusive, hundreds of studies have shown that interference influences forgetting (Anderson & Neely, 1996; Bjork, 1992). In many of these studies, researchers have controlled interference by varying the similarity between the original material given to subjects (the test material) and the material studied in the intervening period. Interference is assumed to be greatest when intervening material is most similar to the test material. Decreasing the similarity should reduce interference and cause less forgetting. This is exactly what McGeoch and McDonald (1931) found in an influential study. They had participants memorize test material that consisted of a list of two-syllable adjectives. They varied the similarity of intervening learning by having subjects then memorize one of five lists. In order of decreasing similarity to the test material, these were synonyms of the test words, antonyms of the test words, unrelated adjectives, nonsense syllables, and numbers. Later, subjects' recall of the test material was measured. The results showed that as the similarity of the intervening material decreased, the amount of forgetting also decreased—because of reduced interference.

There are two kinds of interference: *retroactive* and *proactive* (Marsh & Roediger, 2013). *Retroactive interference* **occurs when new information impairs the retention of previously learned information.** Retroactive interference occurs between the original learning and the retest on that learning (see **Figure 7.14**). For example, the interference manipulated by McGeoch and McDonald (1931) was retroactive interference. In contrast, *proactive interference* **occurs when previously learned information interferes with the retention of new information.** Proactive interference is rooted in learning that comes before exposure to the test material. For example, when you get a new phone number, your old number (previous learning) may create proactive interference that hampers your recall of your new number. The evidence indicates that both types of interference can have powerful effects on how much you forget.

Retrieval Failure

People often remember things that they were unable to recall at an earlier time. This phenomenon may be obvious only during struggles with the tip-of-the-tongue phenomenon, but it happens frequently. In fact, a great deal of forgetting may be due to breakdowns in the process of retrieval.

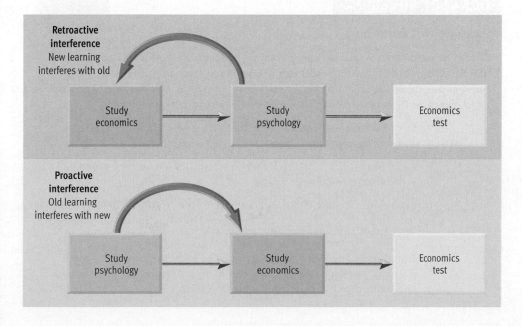

FIGURE 7.14

Retroactive and proactive interference. Retroactive interference occurs when learning produces a "backward" effect, reducing recall of previously learned material. Proactive interference occurs when learning produces a "forward" effect, reducing recall of subsequently learned material. For example, if you were to prepare for an economics test and then study psychology, the interference from the psychology study would be *retroactive* interference. However, if you studied psychology first and then economics, the interference from the psychology study would be *proactive* interference.

Why does an effort to retrieve something fail on one occasion and succeed on another? That's a tough question. One theory is that retrieval failures may be more likely when a mismatch exists between retrieval cues and the encoding of the information you're searching for. According to Tulving and Thomson (1973), a good retrieval cue is consistent with the original encoding of the information to be recalled. If the sound of a word—its phonemic quality—was emphasized during encoding, an effective retrieval cue should emphasize the sound of the word. If the meaning of the word was emphasized during encoding, semantic cues should be best. A general statement of the principle at work here was formulated by Tulving and Thomson (1973): **The *encoding specificity principle* states that the value of a retrieval cue depends on how well it corresponds to the memory code.** This principle provides one explanation for the inconsistent success of retrieval efforts.

Motivated Forgetting

Over a century ago, Sigmund Freud (1901) came up with an entirely different explanation for retrieval failures. As we noted in Chapter 1, Freud asserted that people often keep embarrassing, unpleasant, or painful memories buried in their unconscious. For example, a person who was deeply wounded by perceived slights at a childhood birthday party might suppress all recollection of that party. In his therapeutic work with patients, Freud recovered many such buried memories. He theorized that the memories were there all along, but their retrieval was blocked by unconscious avoidance tendencies.

The tendency to forget things one doesn't want to think about is called *motivated forgetting,* or to use Freud's terminology, *repression.* In Freudian theory, **repression refers to keeping distressing thoughts and feelings buried in the unconscious** (see Chapter 11). A number of experiments suggest that people don't remember anxiety-laden material as readily as emotionally neutral material, just as Freud proposed (Guenther, 1988; Reisner, 1998). Thus, when you forget unpleasant things—such as a dental appointment, a promise to help a friend move, or a term paper deadline—motivated forgetting may be at work.

The Repressed Memories Controversy

Although the concept of repression has been around for a century, interest in this phenomenon has surged in recent years, thanks to a spate of prominent reports involving the return of long-lost memories of sexual abuse

---

CONCEPT CHECK 7.2

Figuring Out Forgetting

Check your understanding of why people forget by identifying the probable causes of forgetting in each of the following scenarios. Choose from (a) motivated forgetting (repression), (b) decay, (c) ineffective encoding, (d) proactive interference, (e) retroactive interference, or (f) retrieval failure. You will find the answers in Appendix A.

_____ 1. Ellen can't recall the reasons for the Webster-Ashburton Treaty because she was daydreaming when it was discussed in history class.

_____ 2. Rufus hates his job at Taco Heaven and is always forgetting when he is scheduled to work.

_____ 3. Ray's new assistant in the shipping department is named Jason Timberlake. Ray keeps calling him Justin, mixing him up with the singer Justin Timberlake.

_____ 4. Tania studied history on Sunday morning and sociology on Sunday evening. It's Monday, and she's struggling with her history test because she keeps mixing up prominent historians with influential sociologists.

© Orange Line Media/Shutterstock.com

and other traumas during childhood. The media have been flooded with reports of adults accusing their parents, teachers, and neighbors of horrible child abuse decades earlier, based on previously repressed memories of these travesties. These parents, teachers, and neighbors have mostly denied the allegations. In an effort to make sense of the charges, some accused parents have argued that their children's recollections are false memories created inadvertently by well-intentioned therapists through the power of suggestion. What do psychologists and psychiatrists have to say about the recovery of repressed memories? They are sharply divided on the issue.

Support for Recovered Memories

Many psychologists and psychiatrists, especially clinicians involved in the treatment of psychological disorders, accept recovered memories of abuse at face value (Banyard & Williams, 1999; Briere & Conte, 1993; Legault & Laurence, 2007; Skinner, 2001; Terr, 1994). They assert that sexual abuse in childhood is far more widespread than most people realize. For example, one large-scale survey (MacMillan et al., 1997), using a random sample of 9953 residents of Ontario, Canada, found that 12.8% of the females and 4.3% of the males reported that they had been victims of sexual abuse during childhood. Supporters further assert that there is ample evidence that it is common for people to bury traumatic incidents in their unconscious (Brewin, 2012; DePrince et al., 2012). For instance, in a study of psychiatric patients hospitalized for posttraumatic or dissociative disorders (see Chapter 14), one-third of those who reported childhood sexual abuse said they had experienced complete amnesia for the abuse at some point in their lives (Chu et al., 1999). Furthermore, experimental studies suggest that people can suppress retrieval of unwanted memories in ways that may lead to forgetting of those memories (Anderson & Huddleston, 2012).

Skepticism of Recovered Memories

In contrast, many other psychologists, especially memory researchers, have expressed skepticism about the recent upsurge of recovered memories of abuse (Kihlstrom, 2004; Laney & Loftus, 2013; Loftus, 2003; McNally, 2012). The skeptics do *not* argue that people are lying about their previously repressed memories. Rather, they maintain that some suggestible people wrestling with emotional problems have been convinced by persuasive therapists that their emotional problems must be the result of abuse that occurred years before. Critics blame a small minority of therapists who presumably have good intentions but who operate under the questionable assumption that most or even all psychological problems are attributable to childhood sexual abuse (Loftus & Davis, 2006). Using hypnosis, dream interpretation, and leading questions, they supposedly prod and probe patients until they inadvertently create the memories of abuse that they are searching for (Thayer & Lynn, 2006).

Psychologists who doubt the authenticity of repressed memories support their analysis by pointing to discredited cases of recovered memories (Brown, Goldstein, & Bjorklund, 2000). For example, with the help of a church counselor, one woman recovered memories of how her minister father had repeatedly raped her, got her pregnant, and then aborted the pregnancy with a coat-hanger, but subsequent evidence revealed that the woman was still a virgin and that her father had had a vasectomy years before (Brainerd & Reyna, 2005). The skeptics also point to published case histories that clearly involved suggestive questioning and to cases in which patients have recanted recovered memories of sexual abuse after realizing that these memories were implanted by their therapists (Shobe & Schooler, 2001).

Those who question the accuracy of repressed memories also point to findings on the misinformation effect, research on source-monitoring errors, and other demonstrations of the relative ease of creating "memories" for events that never happened (Lindsay et al., 2004; Loftus & Cahill, 2007; Strange, Clifasefi, & Garry, 2007). For example, working with college students, Ira Hyman and his colleagues managed to implant recollections of

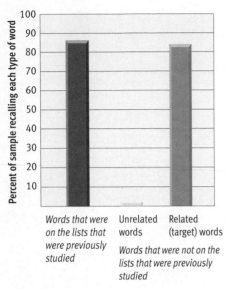

FIGURE 7.15

The prevalence of false memories observed by Roediger and McDermott (1995). The graph shown here summarizes the recognition test results in Study 1 conducted by Roediger and McDermott (1995). Participants correctly identified words that had been on the lists they had studied 86% of the time and only misidentified unrelated words that had not been on the lists 2% of the time, indicating that they were paying careful attention to the task. Nonetheless, they mistakenly reported that they "remembered" related target words that were not on the lists 84% of the time—a remarkably high prevalence of false memories.

fairly substantial events—such as spilling a punch bowl at a wedding, being in a grocery store when the fire sprinkler system went off, being hospitalized for an earache—in about 25% of their subjects, just by asking them to elaborate on events supposedly reported by their parents (Hyman & Kleinknecht, 1999). Other studies succeeded in implanting false memories of nearly drowning (Heaps & Nash, 2001), of being attacked by a vicious animal (Porter, Yuille, & Lehman, 1999), and of becoming ill after eating a certain food (Bernstein & Loftus, 2009). A recent study run through the Slate.com website, involving more than 5000 participants, used doctored photos in an attempt to create false memories of political events that actually never took place (Frenda et al., 2013). The results indicated that 47% of the subjects "remembered" seeing President Obama shake hands with the president of Iran at a United Nations conference, and 31% "remembered" seeing coverage of President Bush entertaining famed baseball pitcher Roger Clemens at his Texas ranch in the midst of the Hurricane Katrina crisis. Interestingly, subjects in these studies often felt very confident about their false memories, which frequently generated strong emotional reactions and richly detailed "recollections" (Laney & Loftus, 2013).

In a similar vein, building on much earlier work by James Deese (1959), Henry Roediger and Kathleen McDermott (1995, 2000) devised a simple laboratory paradigm that is remarkably reliable in producing memory illusions. In this procedure, now known as the *Deese-Roediger-McDermott (DRM) paradigm,* a series of lists of fifteen words is presented to participants, who are asked to recall the words immediately after each list is presented and are given a recognition measure of their retention at the end of the session. The trick is that each list consists of a set of words (such as *bed, rest, awake, tired*) that are strongly associated with another target word that is not on the list (in this case, *sleep*). When subjects *recall* the words on each list, they remember the nonpresented target word more than 50% of the time, and when they are given the final *recognition* test, they typically indicate that about 80% of the nonstudied target words were presented in the lists (see **Figure 7.15**).

The memory illusions created in this experiment may seem trivial in comparison with the vivid, detailed recollections of previously forgotten sexual abuse that have generated the repressed memories controversy. But these false memories can be reliably created in normal, healthy participants in a matter of minutes, with little effort and no pressure or misleading information. Thus, this line of research provides a dramatic demonstration of how easy it is to get people to remember that they saw something they really didn't see (McDermott, 2007).

Conclusions

So, what can we conclude about the recovered memories controversy? It seems pretty clear that therapists can unknowingly create false memories in their patients and that a significant portion of recovered memories of abuse are the product of suggestion (Follette & Davis, 2009; Loftus & Davis, 2006). But it also seems likely that some cases of recovered memories are authentic (Colangelo, 2009; Ost, 2013). It is difficult to estimate what proportion of recovered memories of abuse fall in each category. That said, some evidence suggests that memories of abuse recovered through therapy are more likely to be false memories than are those recovered spontaneously (McNally & Geraerts, 2009). People who report recovered memories of abuse seem to fall into two very different groups. Some gradually recover memories of abuse with the assistance of suggestive therapeutic techniques, whereas others suddenly and unexpectedly recover memories of abuse when they encounter a relevant retrieval cue (such as returning to the scene of the abuse). A study that sought to corroborate reports of abuse from both groups found a much higher corroboration rate among those who recovered their memories spontaneously (37%) as opposed to those who recovered their memories in therapy (0%) (Geraerts, 2012).

The recovered memories controversy continues to generate heated debate (Patihis et al., 2014). One upside is that the debate has inspired a tremendous amount of research that has greatly increased our understanding of just how fragile, fallible, malleable, and subjective human memory can be. Indeed, the implicit dichotomy underlying the repressed memories debate—that some memories are true, whereas others are false—is misleading and oversimplified. Research demonstrates that all human memories are imperfect reconstructions of the past that are subject to many types of distortion.

7.5 IN SEARCH OF THE MEMORY TRACE: THE PHYSIOLOGY OF MEMORY

For decades, neuroscientists have ventured forth in search of the anatomical and neural bases of memory. A great deal of progress has been made, but much remains to be learned. In this section we'll look at some of the more influential research.

The Anatomy of Memory

Cases of amnesia (extensive memory loss) resulting from head injury are a useful source of clues about the anatomical bases of memory. There are two basic types of amnesia: retrograde and anterograde (see **Figure 7.16**). In *retrograde amnesia, a person loses memories for events that occurred prior to the injury.* For example, a 25-year-old gymnast who sustains a head trauma might find 3 years, 7 years, or perhaps her entire lifetime erased. In *anterograde amnesia, a person loses memories for events that occur after the injury.* For instance, after her accident, the injured gymnast might suffer impaired ability to remember people she meets, where she has parked her car, and so on. The two types of amnesia are not mutually exclusive; many patients display both types.

Because victims' current memory functioning is impaired, cases of anterograde amnesia have been especially rich sources of information about the brain and memory. One well-known case, that of a man referred to as H.M., was followed from 1953 until his death in 2008 (Corkin, 1984, 2002; Scoville & Milner, 1957). H.M. had surgery to relieve debilitating epileptic seizures that occurred up to ten times a day. The surgery greatly reduced his seizures. Unfortunately, however, the surgery inadvertently wiped out most of his ability to form long-term memories. H.M.'s short-term memory remained fine, but he had no recollection of anything that had happened since 1953 (other than about the most recent 20 seconds of his life). He did not recognize the doctors treating him, he couldn't remember routes to and from places, and he didn't know his own age. H.M. was unable to remember what he ate a few minutes ago, let alone what he had done in the years since his surgery. At age 66, after he'd had gray hair for years, he could not remember whether he had gray hair when asked, even though he looked in the mirror every day. Although he could not form new long-term memories, H.M.'s intelligence remained intact. He could care for himself (around his own home), carry on complicated conversations, and solve crossword puzzles. This man's misfortune provided a golden opportunity for memory researchers.

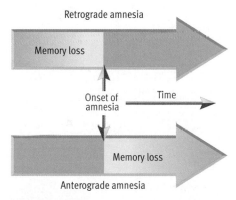

FIGURE 7.16

Retrograde versus anterograde amnesia. In retrograde amnesia, memory for events that occurred prior to the onset of amnesia is lost. In anterograde amnesia, memory for events that occur subsequent to the onset of amnesia suffers.

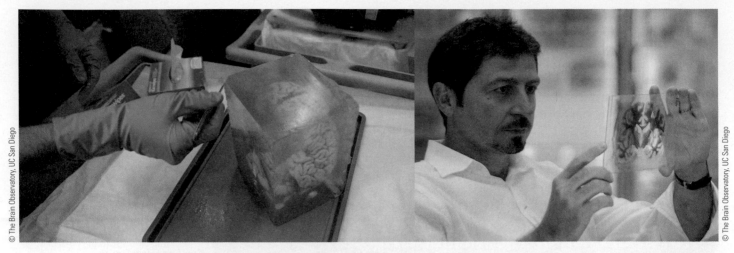

To protect his privacy, H.M. was identified only by his initials for over 50 years. After his death, it was revealed that his name was Henry Molaison. His death triggered a complex, multifaceted team effort, orchestrated by Suzanne Corkin of MIT, to preserve, image, and dissect the brain of the most important research subject in the history of neuroscience. His brain is shown in a mold of gelatin at left. The challenge of slicing Molaison's brain into razor-thin sections for preservation and digital imaging was allocated to Jacob Annese of UCSD, who spent years preparing for the delicate task. Annese is shown looking at a mounted slide of a brain slice on the right. The digital atlas of Molaison's brain will reveal the exact boundaries of his surgical lesions. This information will permit scientists to analyze the precise relations between his brain damage and 50 years of data on his memory performance.

In the decades after his surgery, over 100 researchers studied various aspects of H.M.'s memory performance, leading to several major discoveries about the nature of memory (Maugh, 2008). As one scientist put it in commenting on the case, "More was learned about memory by research with just one patient than was learned in the previous 100 years of research on memory" (Miller, 2009). More than 15 years prior to his death, Suzanne Corkin arranged for H.M.'s brain to be donated to Massachusetts General Hospital, where it was immediately subjected to extensive brain imaging after he passed away in 2008. His brain was subsequently moved to a lab at the University of California, San Diego, where one year after H.M.'s death, it was cut into 2401 extremely thin slices for further study by scientists all over the world (Becker, 2009; Carey, 2009). The painstaking, methodical 53-hour dissection was broadcast live over the Internet, where portions of the process were watched by over 400,000 people. The meticulous dissection eventually led to the creation of a three-dimensional microscopic model of H.M.'s brain that should foster additional research (Annese et al., 2014).

H.M.'s memory losses were originally attributed to the removal of his *hippocampus* (see **Figure 7.17**), although theorists now understand that other nearby structures that were removed also contributed to H.M.'s dramatic memory deficits (Delis & Lucas, 1996). Based on decades of additional research, scientists now believe that the entire *hippocampal region* and adjacent areas in the cortex are critical for many types of long-term memory (Zola & Squire, 2000). Many scientists now refer to this broader memory complex as the *medial temporal lobe memory system* (Shrager & Squire, 2009).

Do these findings mean that memories are stored in the hippocampal region and adjacent areas? Probably not. Most theorists believe that the medial temporal lobe memory system plays a key role in the *consolidation* of memories (Dudai, 2004). **Consolidation is a hypothetical process involving the gradual conversion of new, unstable memories into stable, durable memory codes stored in long-term memory.** According to this view, memories are consolidated in the hippocampal region and then stored in diverse

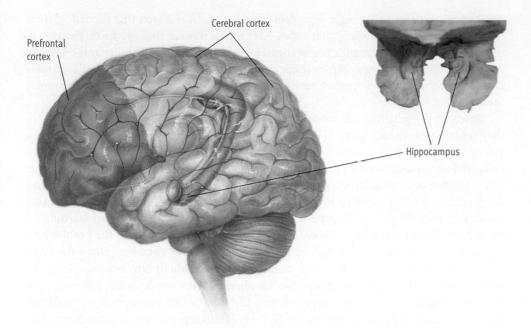

FIGURE 7.17

The hippocampus and memory. The hippocampus and adjacent areas in the brain are thought to play an especially central role in memory. The hippocampus appears to be responsible for the initial consolidation of memories, which are then stored in diverse and widely distributed areas of the cortex.

and widely distributed areas of the cortex (Shrager & Squire, 2009). This setup allows new memories to become independent of the hippocampal region and to gradually be integrated with other memories already stored in various areas of the cortex. Interestingly, research suggests that much of the consolidation process may unfold while people sleep (Born & Wilhelm, 2012).

Even after consolidation, however, memories may be subject to modification, primarily when they are reactivated. Studies suggest that when consolidated memories are retrieved, the reactivated memories are temporarily returned to an unstable state, from which they must be restabilized through a process called *reconsolidation* (Hardt, Einarsson, & Nader, 2010). During reconsolidation, depending on what happens, the memories may be weakened, strengthened, or updated to take into account more recent information (Schwabe, Nader, & Pruessner, 2014). This dynamic flexibility is thought to make long-term memory more adaptive than it would be if memories were etched in concrete, but it is important to note that the updating process can introduce distortions (St. Jacques & Schacter, 2013). Hence, even the neural architecture of long-term memory seems to be inherently reconstructive.

The Neural Circuitry of Memory

Richard F. Thompson (1992, 2005, 2013) and his colleagues have shown that specific memories may depend on *localized neural circuits* in the brain. In other words, memories may create unique, reusable pathways in the brain along which signals flow. Thompson has traced the pathway that accounts for a rabbit's memory of a conditioned eye blink response. Thompson theorizes that other memories probably create entirely different pathways in other areas of the brain.

Another line of research suggests that memory formation results in *alterations in synaptic transmission* at specific sites. Eric Kandel (2001) and his colleagues have studied conditioned reflexes in a simple organism—a sea slug. In research that earned a Nobel Prize for Kandel, they showed that reflex learning in the sea slug produces changes in the strength of specific synaptic connections by enhancing the availability and release of neurotransmitters at these synapses (Bailey & Kandel, 2009). Kandel believes that durable changes in synaptic transmission may be the neural building blocks of more complex memories, as well.

Research suggests that the process of *neurogenesis*—the formation of new neurons— may contribute to the sculpting of neural circuits that underlie memory (Koehl & Abrous, 2011). As we noted in Chapter 3, scientists have recently discovered that new brain cells are formed constantly in the *dentate gyrus* of the *hippocampus* (Drew, Fusi, & Hen, 2013; Leuner & Gould, 2010). Animal studies show that manipulations that suppress neurogenesis lead to memory impairments on many types of learning tasks, and that conditions that increase neurogenesis tend to be associated with enhanced learning on many tasks (Leuner, Gould, & Shors, 2006). Neurogenesis may provide the brain with a supply of neurons that vary in age, and these variations may somehow allow the brain to "timestamp" some memories. That said, the theorizing about how neurogenesis contributes to memory is highly speculative (Jessberger, Aimone, & Gage, 2009). In fact, some theorists believe that neurogenesis may also play a role in forgetting (Frankland, Köhler, & Josselyn, 2013). According to this line of thinking, neurogenesis leads to a continuous remodeling of hippocampal circuits that incrementally clears memories from the hippocampus.

In summary, a number of anatomical structures and neural circuits appear to play a role in memory. Does all this sound confusing? It should, because it is. The bottom line is that neuroscientists are still assembling the pieces of the puzzle that will explain the physiological basis of memory. Although they have identified many of the puzzle pieces, they're not sure how the pieces fit together. Their difficulty is probably due to the complex, multifaceted nature of memory. Looking for the physiological basis for memory is only slightly less daunting than looking for the physiological basis for thought itself.

7.6 DIFFERENT TYPES OF MEMORY SYSTEMS

Key Learning Goals

- Compare and contrast declarative and nondeclarative memory.
- Distinguish between episodic and semantic memory, and retrospective and prospective memory.

Some theorists believe that evidence on the physiology of memory is confusing because investigators are unwittingly probing into several distinct memory systems that may have different physiological bases. The various memory systems are distinguished primarily by the types of information they handle.

Declarative Versus Nondeclarative Memory

The most basic division of memory into distinct systems contrasts *declarative memory* with *nondeclarative*, or *procedural*, *memory* (Squire, 2004, 2009; see **Figure 7.18**). **The *declarative memory system* handles factual information.** It contains recollections of words, definitions, names, dates, faces, events, concepts, and ideas. **The *nondeclarative memory system* houses memory for actions, skills, conditioned responses, and emotional memories.** It contains procedural memories of how to execute such actions as riding a bike, typing, and tying one's shoes. To illustrate the distinction, if you know the rules of tennis (the number of games in a set, scoring, and such), this factual information is stored in declarative memory. If you remember how to hit a serve and swing through a backhand, these perceptual-motor skills are stored in nondeclarative memory.

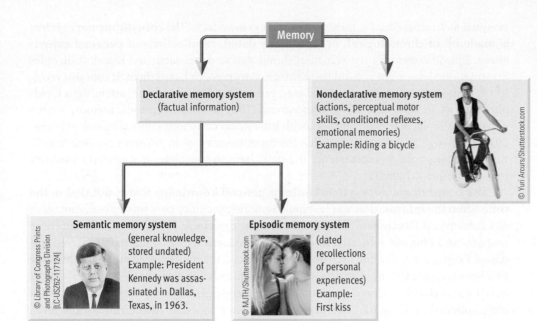

FIGURE 7.18
Theories of independent memory systems.
Theorists have distinguished between declarative memory, which handles facts and information, and nondeclarative memory, which handles motor skills, conditioned responses, and emotional memories. Declarative memory is further subdivided into semantic memory (general knowledge) and episodic memory (dated recollections of personal experiences). The extent to which nondeclarative memory can be usefully subdivided remains the subject of debate.

Support for the distinction between declarative and nondeclarative memory comes from evidence that the two systems seem to operate somewhat differently (Johnson, 2013b; Squire, Knowlton, & Musen, 1993). For example, the recall of factual information generally depends on conscious, effortful processes, whereas memory for conditioned reflexes is largely automatic, and memories for skills often require little effort and attention (Johnson, 2003). People execute perceptual-motor tasks—such as playing the piano or typing—with little conscious awareness of what they're doing. In fact, performance on such tasks sometimes deteriorates if people think too much about what they're doing. Another disparity is that the memory for skills—such as typing and bike riding—doesn't decline much over long retention intervals, whereas declarative memory is more vulnerable to forgetting.

The notion that declarative and procedural memories are separate is supported by certain patterns of memory loss seen in amnesiacs. In many cases, declarative memory is severely impaired, while procedural memory is left largely intact (Mulligan & Besken, 2013). For example, H.M., the victim of amnesia discussed earlier, was able to learn and remember new motor skills, even though he couldn't remember what he looked like as he aged. The sparing of procedural memory in H.M. provided crucial evidence for the distinction between declarative and nondeclarative memory. The finding also suggested that different brain structures may be involved in the two types of memory. Indeed, decades of research have led to progress toward identifying the neural bases for declarative versus nondeclarative memory (Eichenbaum, 2013).

Semantic Versus Episodic Memory

Endel Tulving (1993, 2002) has further subdivided declarative memory into semantic and episodic memory (see **Figure 7.18**). Both contain factual information. However, episodic memory contains

Memory for perceptual-motor skills, such as hitting a drive shot in golf, appears to be quite different than memory for factual information. Motor skills involve procedural memories that are part of the nondeclarative memory system.

personal facts, and semantic memory contains *general facts.* **The *episodic memory system* is made up of chronological, or temporally dated, recollections of personal experiences.** Episodic memory is a record of things you've done, seen, and heard. It includes information about *when* you did these things, saw them, or heard them. It contains recollections about being in a ninth-grade play, visiting the Grand Canyon, attending a Coldplay concert, or going to a movie last weekend. The encoding of episodic memories often occurs in a rapid, automatic fashion, with little or no conscious effort (Gallo & Wheeler, 2013). Tulving (2001) emphasizes that the function of episodic memory is "time travel"; that is, to allow one to reexperience the past. He also speculates that episodic memory may be unique to humans.

The *semantic memory system* contains general knowledge that is not tied to the time when the information was learned. Semantic memory contains information such as Christmas is December 25th, dogs have four legs, the U.S. Supreme Court has nine justices, and Phoenix is located in Arizona. Information like this is usually stored undated. People generally don't remember when or where they learned facts such as these (McNamara, 2013). The distinction between episodic and semantic memory can be better appreciated by drawing an analogy to books: episodic memory is like an autobiography, while semantic memory is like an encyclopedia. At the time of retrieval, episodic memories are associated with a sense of "remembering," whereas semantic memories are associated with a sense of "knowing" (Gallo & Wheeler, 2013). The memory deficits seen in some cases of amnesia suggest that episodic and semantic memory are separate systems. For instance, some amnesiacs forget most personal facts, while their recall of general facts is largely unaffected (Szpunar & McDermott, 2009). However, debate continues about whether episodic and semantic memory have distinct neural bases.

Prospective Versus Retrospective Memory

A 1984 paper with a clever title, "Remembering to Do Things: A Forgotten Topic" (Harris, 1984), introduced yet another distinction between types of memory: *prospective memory* versus *retrospective memory* (see **Figure 7.19**). This distinction does not refer to independent *memory systems,* but rather to fundamentally different types of *memory tasks.* **Retrospective memory involves remembering events from the past or previously learned information.** Retrospective memory is at work when you try to remember who won the Super Bowl last year or when you reminisce about your high

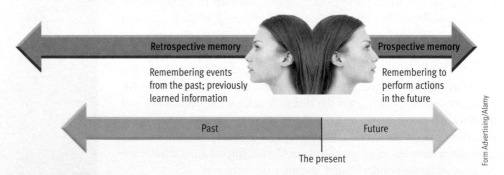

FIGURE 7.19

Retrospective versus prospective memory. Most memory research has explored the dynamics of *retrospective memory,* which focuses on recollections from the past. However, *prospective memory,* which requires people to remember to perform actions in the future, also plays an important role in everyday life.

school days. *Prospective memory* **involves remembering to perform actions in the future.** Examples of prospective memory tasks include remembering to bring your umbrella, to walk the dog, to call someone, or to grab the tickets for the big game. A key difference between retrospective and prospective memory is that in the latter no one prompts the individual to remember the intended action. Thus, one needs to *remember to remember*. However, experiments demonstrate that it is easy to *forget to remember,* especially when one is confronted by interruptions and distractions. Although our examples of prospective memory involve relatively trivial tasks, failures of prospective memory can potentially have serious consequences. Dismukes (2012) discusses what can happen when prospective memory goes awry in the workplace. For example, it appears that several airline disasters have been attributable to pilots forgetting to complete intended actions. In a similar vein, medical errors that lead to negative consequences for hospital patients often involve lapses in following through on intentions. Research indicates that sleep deprivation tends to increase prospective memory failures, which may contribute to major mistakes in aviation, medicine, and other work areas where safety is of paramount importance (Grundgeiger, Bayen, & Horn, 2014).

People vary considerably in their ability to successfully carry out prospective memory tasks. Individuals who appear deficient in prospective memory are often characterized as "absentminded." Research suggests that older adults are somewhat more vulnerable to problems with prospective memory than younger people are, although the findings are complicated and not entirely consistent (Niedźwieńska & Barzykowski, 2012).

© Christo/Shutterstock.com

CONCEPT CHECK 7.3

Recognizing Various Types of Memory

Check your understanding of the various types of memory discussed in this chapter by matching the definitions below with the following: (a) sensory memory, (b) short-term memory, (c) long-term memory, (d) declarative memory, (e) nondeclarative memory, (f) episodic memory, (g) semantic memory, (h) retrospective memory, and (i) prospective memory. The answers can be found in Appendix A.

_____ 1. Memory for factual information

_____ 2. An unlimited capacity store that can hold information over lengthy periods of time

_____ 3. The preservation of information in its original sensory form for a brief time, usually only a fraction of a second

_____ 4. Chronological, or temporally dated, recollections of personal experiences

_____ 5. The repository of memories for actions, skills, operations, and conditioned responses

_____ 6. General knowledge that is not tied to the time when the information was learned

_____ 7. Remembering to perform future actions

_____ 8. A limited-capacity store that can maintain unrehearsed information for about 20 seconds

7.7 REFLECTING ON THE CHAPTER'S THEMES

Key Learning Goals

• Identify the three unifying themes high-lighted in this chapter.

 Subjectivity of Experience

 Theoretical Diversity

 Multifactorial Causation

One of our integrative themes—the idea that people's experience of the world is subjective—stood head and shoulders above the rest in this chapter. Let's briefly review how the study of memory has illuminated this idea.

First, our discussion of attention as inherently selective should have shed light on why people's experience of the world is subjective. To a great degree, what you see in the world around you depends on where you focus your attention. This is one of the main reasons two people can be exposed to the "same" events and walk away with entirely different perceptions. Second, the reconstructive nature of memory should further explain people's tendency to view the world with a subjective slant. When you observe an event, you don't store an exact copy of the event in your memory. Instead, you store a rough, "bare bones" approximation of the event that may be reshaped as time goes by.

A second theme that was apparent in our discussion of memory was psychology's theoretical diversity. We saw illuminating theoretical debates about the nature of memory storage, the causes of forgetting, and the existence of multiple memory systems.

Finally, the multifaceted nature of memory demonstrated once again that behavior is governed by multiple causes. For instance, your memory of a specific event may be influenced by your attention to it, your level of processing, your elaboration, how you search your memory store, how you reconstruct the event, and so forth. Given the multifaceted nature of memory, it should come as no surprise that there are many ways to improve memory. We discuss a variety of strategies in the Personal Application section.

7.8 PERSONAL APPLICATION
Improving Everyday Memory

7.8

Key Learning Goals

• Discuss the importance of rehearsal, distributed practice, and interference in efforts to improve everyday memory.

• Discuss the value of deep processing, good organization, and mnemonic devices in efforts to improve everyday memory.

Answer the following "true" or "false."

___ 1 Memory strategies were recently invented by psychologists.

___ 2 Overlearning of information leads to poor retention.

___ 3 Outlining what you read is not likely to affect retention.

___ 4 Massing practice in one long study session is better than distributing practice across several shorter sessions.

***Mnemonic devices* are strategies for enhancing memory.** They have a long and honorable history. In fact, one of the mnemonic devices covered in this Application—the method of loci—was described in Greece as early as 86–82 B.C. (Yates, 1966). Actually, mnemonic devices were even more crucial in ancient times than they are today. In ancient Greece and Rome, for instance, paper and pencils—let alone iPads—were not readily available for people to jot down things they needed to remember, so they had to depend heavily on mnemonic devices.

Are mnemonic devices the key to improving one's everyday memory? No. They clearly can be helpful in some situations (Wilding & Valentine, 1996), but they are not a cure-all. They can be hard to use and hard to apply to many everyday situations. Most books and training programs designed to improve memory probably overemphasize mnemonic techniques (Searleman & Herrmann, 1994). Although less exotic strategies—such as increasing rehearsal, engaging in deeper processing, and organizing material—are more crucial to everyday memory, we will discuss some popular mnemonics as we proceed through this Application. Along the way, you'll learn that all our opening true-false statements are false.

Engage in Adequate Rehearsal

Practice makes perfect, or so you've heard. In reality, practice is not likely to guarantee perfection. However, it usually leads to improved retention. Studies show that retention improves with increased rehearsal. This improvement presumably occurs because rehearsal helps transfer information into long-term memory. Although the benefits of practice are well known, people have a curious tendency to overestimate their knowledge of a topic and how well they will perform on a subsequent memory test of this knowledge (Koriat & Bjork, 2005). That's one reason it's a good idea to informally test yourself on information that you think you have mastered before confronting a real test.

In addition to checking your mastery, research suggests that testing actually enhances retention, a phenomenon dubbed the *testing effect* or *test-enhanced learning* (Pyc, Agarwal, & Roediger, 2014). Studies have shown that taking a test on material increases performance on a subsequent test even more than studying or rereading for an equal amount of time does. The testing effect has been seen across a wide range of different types of content, and the benefits grow as the retention interval gets longer (Pyc et al., 2014). The favorable effects of testing are enhanced if participants are provided feedback on their test performance (Kornell & Metcalfe, 2014). Studies have demonstrated that the laboratory findings on test-enhanced learning replicate in real-world educational settings (McDermott et al., 2014). Moreover, the testing effect is not limited to rote learning; it can enhance in-depth meaningful learning, as well (Karpicke & Blunt, 2011). Better yet, research suggests that testing improves not just the retention of information, but also the *application* of that information in new contexts (S. K. Carpenter, 2012). Unfortunately, given the recent nature of this discovery, relatively few students are aware of the value of testing in retention (Karpicke, 2012).

Why is testing so beneficial? The key appears to be that testing forces students to engage in effortful retrieval of information (Roediger et al., 2010). Indeed, even *unsuccessful* retrieval efforts can enhance retention (Kornell, Hays, & Bjork, 2009). In any event, self-testing appears to be an excellent memory tool. This suggests that it would be prudent to take the Practice Tests in this text (see Appendix A) or additional tests available on the website for the book.

One other point related to rehearsal is also worth mentioning. If you are memorizing some type of list, be aware of the serial-position effect, which is often observed when subjects are tested on their memory of lists (Murdock, 2001). **The serial-position effect occurs when subjects show better recall for items at the beginning and end of a list than for items in the middle** (see **Figure 7.20**). The reasons for the serial-position effect are complex and need not concern us. However, its pragmatic implications are clear: if you need to memorize a list of, say, cranial nerves or past presidents, devote extra practice trials to items in the middle of the list and check your memorization of those items very carefully.

Schedule Distributed Practice and Minimize Interference

Let's assume that you need to study 9 hours for an exam. Should you "cram" all your studying into one 9-hour period (*massed practice*)? Or is it better to distribute your study among, say, three 3-hour periods on successive days (*distributed practice*)? The evidence indicates that retention tends to be greater after distributed practice than after massed practice (Carpenter, 2014; Kornell et al., 2010). Moreover, a review of more than 300 experiments (Cepeda et al., 2006) showed that the longer the retention interval between studying and testing, the bigger the advantage for distributed practice, as shown in **Figure 7.21**. The same review concluded that the longer the retention interval, the longer the optimal "break" between practice trials. When an upcoming test is more than 2 days away, the optimal interval between practice periods appears to be around 24 hours. The superiority of distributed practice over massed practice suggests that cramming is an ill-advised approach to studying for exams (Marsh & Butler, 2013).

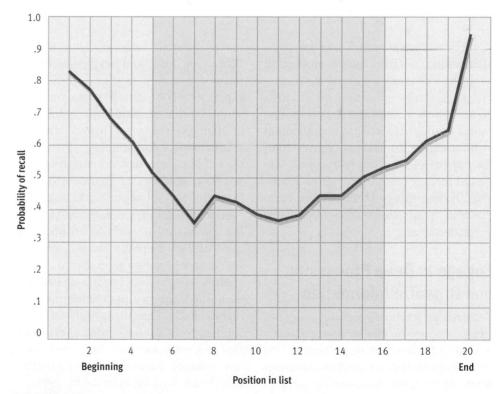

FIGURE 7.20

The serial-position effect. After learning a list of items to remember, people tend to recall more of the items from the beginning and end of the list than from the middle, producing the characteristic U-shaped curve shown here. This phenomenon is called the *serial-position effect*.

SOURCE: Adapted from Rundus, D. (1971). Analysis of rehearsal processes in free recall. *Journal of Experimental Psychology, 89,* 63–77. Copyright © 1971 by the American Psychological Association. Adapted by permission of the author.

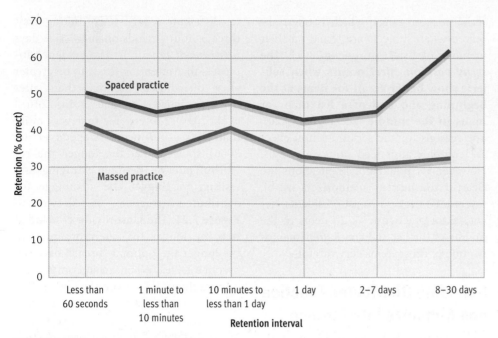

FIGURE 7.21

Effects of massed versus distributed practice on retention. In a review of more than 300 experiments on massed versus distributed practice, Cepeda et al. (2006) examined the importance of the retention interval. As you can see, spaced practice was superior to massed practice at all retention intervals, but the gap widened at longer intervals. These findings suggest that distributed practice is especially advantageous when you need or want to remember material over the long haul.

Because interference is a major cause of forgetting, you'll probably want to think about how you can minimize it. This issue is especially important for students because memorizing information for one course can interfere with the retention of information for another course. Thus, the day before an exam in a course, you should study for that course only—if possible. If demands in other courses make that plan impossible, you should study the test material last.

Engage in Deep Processing and Organize Information

Research on levels of processing suggests that how *often* you go over material is less critical than the *depth* of processing that you engage in. If you expect to remember what you read, you have to fully comprehend its meaning (Marsh & Butler, 2013). Many students could probably benefit if they spent less time on rote memorization and more on paying attention to and analyzing the meaning of their reading assignments. In particular, it is useful to make material *personally* meaningful. When you read your textbooks, try to relate information to your own life and experience. For example, when you read about classical conditioning, try to think of your own responses that are attributable to classical conditioning.

It is also important to understand that retention tends to be greater when information is well organized (Einstein & McDaniel, 2004). Gordon Bower (1970b) has shown that hierarchical organization is particularly helpful when it is applicable. Thus, it may be a good idea to *outline* reading assignments for school because outlining forces you to organize material hierarchically. Consistent with this reasoning, there is some empirical evidence that outlining material from textbooks can enhance retention of that material (McDaniel, Waddill, & Shakesby, 1996).

Enrich Encoding with Mnemonic Devices

Although it's often helpful to make information personally meaningful, it's not always easy to do so. For instance, when you study chemistry, you may have a hard time relating to polymers at a personal level. Thus, many mnemonic devices—such as acrostics, acronyms, and narrative methods—are designed to make abstract material more meaningful. Other mnemonic devices depend on visual imagery. As you may recall, Allan Paivio (1986, 2007) believes that visual images create a second memory code, and that two codes are better than one.

Acrostics and Acronyms

Acrostics are phrases (or poems) in which the first letter of each word (or line) functions as a cue to help you recall information to be remembered. For instance, you can remember the order of musical notes with the saying "Every Good Boy Does Fine." A slight variation on acrostics is the *acronym*—a word formed out of the first letters of a series of words. Students memorizing the order of colors in the light spectrum often store the name "Roy G. Biv" to remember red, orange, yellow, green, blue, indigo, and violet. Notice that this acronym takes advantage of the principle of chunking. Acrostics and acronyms that individuals create for themselves can be effective memory tools (Hermann, Raybeck, & Gruneberg, 2002).

Link Method

The *link method* involves forming a mental image of items to be remembered in a way that links them together. For instance, suppose that you need to remember some items to pick up at the drugstore: a news magazine, shaving cream, film, and pens. To remember these items, you might visualize a public figure on the magazine cover shaving with a pen while being photographed. The more bizarre you make your image, the more helpful it is likely to be (McDaniel & Einstein, 1986).

Method of Loci

The *method of loci* involves taking an imaginary walk along a familiar path where images of items to be remembered are associated with certain locations. The first step is to commit to memory a series of loci, or places, along a path.

FIGURE 7.22

The method of loci. In this example from Bower (1970a), a person about to go shopping pairs items to remember with familiar places (loci) arranged in a natural sequence: (1) hot dogs/driveway, (2) cat food/garage interior, (3) tomatoes/front door, (4) bananas/coat closet shelf, and (5) whiskey/kitchen sink. The shopper then uses imagery to associate the items on the shopping list with the loci, as shown in the drawing: (1) giant hot dog rolls down a driveway, (2) a cat noisily devours cat food in the garage, (3) ripe tomatoes are splattered on the front door, (4) bunches of bananas are hung from the closet shelf, and (5) the contents of a bottle of whiskey gurgle down the kitchen sink. As the last panel shows, the shopper recalls the items by mentally touring the loci associated with them.

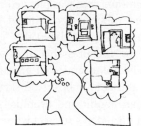

SOURCE: From Bower, G. H. (1970a). Analysis of a mnemonic device. *American Scientist, 58,* 496–499. Copyright © 1970 by Scientific Research Society. Reprinted by permission.

Usually these loci are specific locations in your home or neighborhood. Then envision each thing you want to remember in one of these locations. Try to form distinctive, vivid images. When you need to remember the items, imagine yourself walking along the path. The various loci on your path should serve as cues for the retrieval of the images that you formed (see **Figure 7.22**). Evidence suggests that the method of loci can be effective in increasing retention (Gross et al., 2014; Moè & De Beni, 2004). Moreover, this method ensures that items are remembered in their *correct order.*

7.9 CRITICAL THINKING APPLICATION
Understanding the Fallibility of Eyewitness Accounts

A number of decades ago, the Wilmington, Delaware, area was plagued by a series of armed robberies committed by a perpetrator who was dubbed the "gentleman bandit" by the press because he was an unusually polite and well-groomed thief. The local media published a sketch of the gentleman bandit and eventually an alert resident turned in a suspect who resembled the sketch. Much to everyone's surprise, the accused thief was a Catholic priest named Father Bernard Pagano—who vigorously denied the charges. Unfortunately for Father Pagano, his denials and alibis were unconvincing, and he was charged with the crimes. At the trial, *seven* eyewitnesses confidently identified Father Pagano as the gentleman bandit. The prosecution was well on its way to a conviction when there was a stunning turn of events: another man, Ronald Clouser, confessed to the police that he was the robber. The authorities dropped the charges against Father Pagano, and the relieved priest was able to return to his normal life (Rodgers, 1982).

This bizarre tale of mistaken identity—which sounds like it was lifted from a movie script—raises some interesting questions about memory. How could seven people "remember" seeing Father Pagnano commit armed robberies that he had nothing to do with? How could they mistake him for Ronald Clouser, when the two really didn't look very similar (see the adjacent photos)? How could the witnesses be so confident when they were so wrong? Perhaps you're thinking that this is just one case and it must be unrepresentative (which would be sound critical thinking). Well, yes, it is a rather extreme example of eyewitness fallibility, but researchers have compiled mountains of evidence that eyewitness testimony is not nearly as reliable or as accurate as widely assumed (Wells & Loftus, 2013). This finding is ironic in that people are most confident about their assertions when they can say "I saw it with

my own eyes." Television news shows like to use the title "Eyewitness News" to create the impression that they chronicle events with great clarity and accuracy. And our legal system accords special status to eyewitness testimony because it is considered much more dependable than hearsay or circumstantial evidence.

So, why are eyewitness accounts surprisingly inaccurate? Well, a variety of factors and processes contribute. Let's briefly review some of the relevant processes that were introduced in the main body of the chapter; then we'll focus on two common errors in thinking that also play a role.

Can you think of any memory phenomena described in the chapter that seem likely to undermine eyewitness accuracy? You could point to the fact that *memory is a reconstructive process,* and eyewitness recall is likely to be *distorted by schemas* that people have for various events. Another consideration is that *witnesses sometimes make source-monitoring errors* and get confused about where they saw a face. For example, one rape victim mixed up her assailant with a guest on a TV show that she was watching when she was attacked. Fortunately, the falsely accused suspect had an airtight alibi

because he could demonstrate that he was on live television when the rape occurred (Schacter, 1996). Perhaps the most pervasive factor is the misinformation effect (Davis & Loftus, 2007). *Witnesses' recall of events is routinely distorted by information introduced after the event* by police officers, attorneys, news reports, and so forth. In addition to these factors, eyewitness inaccuracy is fueled by *hindsight bias* and *overconfidence effects.*

The Contribution of Hindsight Bias

Hindsight bias **is the tendency to mold one's interpretation of the past to fit how events actually turned out.** When you know the outcome of an event, this knowledge slants your recall of how the event unfolded and what your thinking was at the time. With the luxury of hindsight, people have a curious tendency to say, "I knew it all along" when explaining events that objectively would have been difficult to foresee. The tendency to exhibit the hindsight bias is normal, pervasive, and surprisingly strong (Guilbault et al., 2004). With regard to eyewitnesses, their recollections can often be distorted

Although he doesn't look that much like the real "gentleman bandit," who is shown on the left, seven eyewitnesses identified Father Pagano (right) as the gentleman bandit, showing just how unreliable eyewitness accounts can be.

Although courts give special credence to eyewitness testimony, scientific evidence indicates that eyewitness accounts are less reliable than widely assumed.

by knowing that a particular person has been arrested and accused of the crime in question. For example, Wells and Bradfield (1998) had simulated eyewitnesses select a perpetrator from a photo lineup. The participants' confidence in their identifications tended to be quite modest, which made sense given that the actual perpetrator was not even in the lineup. But when some subjects were told, "Good, you identified the actual suspect," they became highly confident about their identifications, which obviously were incorrect. In the last 15 years, a host of studies have replicated this effect (Steblay, Wells, & Douglass, 2014). When the authorities confirm people's lineup identifications, this confirmation alters their recollection of the crime scene. Their recall of how good their view was and how much attention they paid to the event increases

dramatically, and their certainty about their identification grows, thanks to hindsight bias.

The Contribution of Overconfidence

Another flaw in thinking that contributes to inaccuracy in eyewitness accounts is people's tendency to be overconfident about the reliability of their memories. When tested for their memory of general information, people tend to overestimate their accuracy (Koriat & Bjork, 2005). In studies of eyewitness recall, participants also tend to be overconfident about their recollections. Although jurors tend to be more convinced by eyewitnesses who appear confident, the assumption that confidence is an excellent indicator of accuracy is clearly wrong (Roediger, Wixted, & DeSoto, 2012). Research shows that there is only a modest correlation between eyewitness confidence and eyewitness accuracy (Shaw, McClure, & Dykstra, 2007). Hence, many convictions of innocent people have been attributed to the impact of testimony from highly confident but mistaken eyewitnesses (Loftus, 2013). In recent decades, the advent of DNA testing has led to the exoneration of hundreds of individuals who were wrongfully convicted

of crimes. Faulty eyewitness testimony turned out to be a major factor in about three-quarters of those overturned convictions (Garrett, 2011).

Can you learn to make better judgments of the accuracy of your recall of everyday events? Yes, with effort you can get better at making accurate estimates of how likely you are to be correct in the recall of some fact or event. One reason that people tend to be overconfident is that if they can't think of any reasons they might be wrong, they assume they must be right. Thus, overconfidence is fueled by yet another common error in thinking: *the failure to seek disconfirming evidence.*

Thus, to make more accurate assessments of what you know and don't know, it helps to engage in a deliberate process of considering why you might be wrong. Here is an example. Based on your reading of Chapter 1, write down the schools of thought associated with the following major theorists: William James, John B. Watson, and Carl Rogers. After you provide your answers, rate your confidence that the information you just provided is correct. Now, write three reasons that your answers might be wrong and three reasons that they might be correct. Most people will balk at this exercise, arguing that they cannot think of any reasons they might be wrong, but after some resistance, they can come up with several. Such reasons might include "I was half asleep when I read that part of the chapter" or "I might be confusing Watson and James." After listing reasons you might be right and might be wrong, rate your confidence in your accuracy once again. Guess what? Most people are less confident after going through such an exercise than they were before (depending, of course, on the nature of the topic).

The new confidence ratings tend to be more realistic than the original ratings (Koriat, Lichtenstein, & Fischhoff, 1980). Thus, the process of considering reasons you might be wrong about something—a process that people rarely engage in—is a useful critical thinking skill that can reduce overconfidence effects.

TABLE 7.1 Critical Thinking Skills Discussed in This Application

Skill	Description
Understanding the limitations and fallibility of human memory	The critical thinker appreciates that memory is reconstructive and that even eyewitness accounts may be distorted or inaccurate.
Recognizing the bias in hindsight analysis	The critical thinker understands that knowing the outcome of events biases our recall and interpretation of the events.
Recognizing overconfidence in human cognition	The critical thinker understands that people are frequently overconfident about the accuracy of their projections for the future and their recollections of the past.
Understanding the need to seek disconfirming evidence	The critical thinker understands the value of thinking about how or why one might be wrong about something.

ENCODING

- *Attention*, which entails a selective focus on certain input, enhances encoding.
- *Divided attention* undermines encoding and can have a negative effect on the performance of other tasks.
- *Levels-of-processing theory* proposes that deeper levels of processing result in more durable memory codes.
- *Elaboration*, which involves linking a stimulus to other information, can enrich encoding.
- According to *dual-coding theory*, visual imagery may facilitate memory by providing two memory codes rather than just one.
- Increasing the motivation to remember at the time of encoding can enhance memory.

STORAGE

- Information-processing theories propose people have three memory stores: *sensory memory, short-term memory (STM)*, and *long-term memory (LTM)*.
- Atkinson and Shiffrin posited that incoming information passes through two temporary storage buffers before being placed into long-term memory.

RETRIEVAL

- Recall is often guided by partial information, as demonstrated by the *tip-of-the-tongue phenomenon*.
- Reinstating the context of an event can often enhance retrieval efforts.
- Memories are sketchy reconstructions of the past that may be distorted.
- The *misinformation effect* occurs when recall of an event is changed by misleading post-event information.
- Even the simple act of retelling a story can introduce inaccuracies into memory.
- *Source monitoring* is the process of making inferences about the origins of memories.

Sensory memory

© Jeff Lueders/Shutterstock.com

- *Sensory memory* preserves information in its original form for a very brief time.
- Memory traces in the sensory store appear to decay in about one-quarter of a second.
- Some theorists view stimulus persistence as more like an echo than a memory.

Short-term memory

- *Short-term memory (STM)* can maintain unrehearsed information for about 10–20 seconds.
- STM has a limited capacity that has long been believed to be about seven items plus or minus two.
- However, a more recent estimate that the capacity of STM is four items plus or minus one is becoming increasingly influential.
- Baddeley proposed a more complex model of STM called *working memory*.
- *Working memory capacity (WMC)* refers to one's ability to hold and manipulate information in conscious attention.

Long-term memory

- *Long-term memory (LTM)* is an unlimited capacity store that can hold information indefinitely.
- Flashbulb memories suggest that LTM storage may be permanent, but the data are not convincing.
- Research has shown that the flashbulb memories are not as durable or accurate as claimed.

© SETH MCALLISTER/AFP/Getty Images

Working memory

Maintenance rehearsal

Phonological loop

Central executive

Visuospatial sketchpad

Episodic buffer

LTM

Organization in LTM

- People spontaneously organize information into categories for storage in memory.
- A *conceptual hierarchy* is a multilevel classification system based on common properties among items.
- A *schema* is an organized cluster of knowledge about a particular object or event.
- A *semantic network* consists of nodes representing concepts, joined together by pathways that link related concepts.

FORGETTING

Measuring forgetting

- People view forgetting as a deficiency, but it can be adaptive by making it easier to remember important information.

- Ebbinghaus's work suggested that most forgetting occurs very rapidly but subsequent research indicated that his *forgetting curve* was exceptionally steep.

- Retention can be assessed with a *recall* measure, a *recognition* measure, or a *relearning* measure.

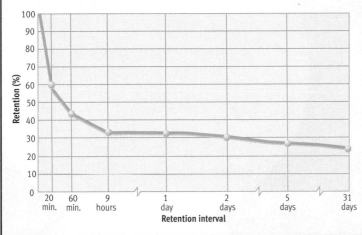

Why we forget

- A great deal of forgetting, including pseudoforgetting, is due to *ineffective encoding*.

- *Decay theory* proposes that memory traces fade with time, but decay in long-term memory has proven hard to demonstrate.

- *Interference theory* asserts that people forget information because of competition from other material, which has proven easy to demonstrate.

- Forgetting is often due to *retrieval failure*, which can include repression.

The repressed memories controversy

- Recent years have seen a surge of reports of recovered memories of previously forgotten sexual abuse in childhood.

- Many clinicians accept these recovered memories, arguing that it is common for people to bury traumatic memories in their unconscious.

- Many memory researchers are skeptical of recovered memories because they have demonstrated that it is easy to create inaccurate memories in laboratory studies.

- Although it is clear that some therapists have created false memories in their patients, it seems likely that some cases of recovered memories are authentic.

- Memories recovered spontaneously appear more likely to be authentic than memories recovered in therapy.

PHYSIOLOGY OF MEMORY

Anatomy of memory

- In *retrograde amnesia*, a person loses memory for events prior to the amnesia.

- In *anterograde amnesia*, a person shows memory deficits for events subsequent to the onset of the amnesia.

- Studies of amnesia and other research suggest that the hippocampus and broader medial temporal lobe system play a major role in memory.

- These areas may be crucial to the *consolidation* of memories.

Neural circuitry of memory

- Thompson's research suggests that memory traces may consist of *localized neural circuits*.

- According to Kandel, memory traces reflect alterations in neurotransmitter release at specific synapses.

- *Neurogenesis* may contribute to the sculpting of neural circuits for memory.

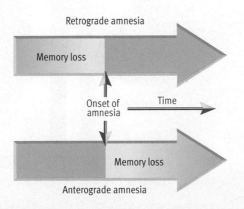

PROPOSED MEMORY SYSTEMS

Declarative memory

Handles recall of factual information, such as names, dates, events, and ideas.

Nondeclarative memory

Handles recall of actions, skills, and operations, such as riding a bike or typing.

Semantic versus episodic memory

- *Semantic memory system* contains general knowledge that is not temporally dated.

- *Episodic memory system* handles temporally dated recollections of personal experiences.

Prospective versus retrospective memory

- *Prospective memory* involves remembering to perform actions in the future.

- *Retrospective memory* involves remembering events from the past or previously learned information.

APPLICATIONS

- Increased rehearsal and testing yourself on material both enhance retention.
- In memorizing lists, be wary of the serial-position effect.
- Distributed practice tends to be more efficient than massed practice.
- Deeper processing of material and organizing material both tend to result in greater retention.
- Meaningfulness can be enhanced through the use of mnemonic devices.
- Eyewitness memory is not nearly as reliable or as accurate as widely believed.
- Hindsight bias is the tendency to reshape one's interpretation of the past to fit with known outcomes.

CHAPTER 8

COGNITION AND INTELLIGENCE

© Peshkova/Shutterstock.com

Themes in this Chapter

Empiricism

Cultural Heritage

Heredity & Environment

Sociohistorical Context

Subjectivity of Experience

"Mr. Watson—Mr. Sherlock Holmes," said Stamford, introducing us. *"How are you?"* he said, cordially, gripping my hand with a strength for which I should hardly have given him credit. *"You have been in Afghanistan, I perceive."*

"How on earth did you know that?" I asked, in astonishment. (From A Study in Scarlet by Arthur Conan Doyle)

If you've ever read any Sherlock Holmes stories, you know that the great detective constantly astonished his loyal companion, Dr. Watson, with his extraordinary deductions. Obviously, Holmes could not arrive at his conclusions without a chain of reasoning. Yet to him even an elaborate reasoning process was a simple, everyday act. Consider his feat of knowing at once, upon first meeting Watson, that the doctor had been in Afghanistan. When asked, Holmes explained his reasoning as follows:

"I knew you came from Afghanistan. From long habit the train of thought ran so swiftly through my mind that I arrived at the conclusion without being conscious of the intermediate steps. There were such steps, however. The train of reasoning ran: 'Here is a gentleman of a medical type, but with the air of a military man. Clearly an army doctor, then. He has just come from the tropics, for his face is dark, and that is not the natural tint of his skin, for his wrists are fair. He has undergone hardship and sickness, as his haggard face says clearly. His left arm has been injured. He holds it in a stiff and unnatural manner. Where in the tropics could an English army doctor have seen much hardship and got his arm wounded? Clearly in Afghanistan.' The whole train of thought did not occupy a second."

Admittedly, Sherlock Holmes's deductive feats are fictional. But even to read about them—let alone imagine them, as Sir Arthur Conan Doyle

did—is a remarkably complex mental act. Our everyday thought processes seem ordinary to us only because we take them for granted, just as Holmes saw nothing extraordinary in what to him was a simple deduction.

In reality, everyone is a Sherlock Holmes, continually performing magical feats of thought. Even elementary perception—for instance, watching a football game or a ballet—involves elaborate cognitive processes. People must sort through distorted, constantly shifting perceptual inputs and deduce what it is they are seeing out there in the real world. Imagine, then, the complexity of thought required to read a book, fix an automobile, or balance a checkbook.

Our topics in this chapter center on *thinking*. In the first half of the chapter, we will summarize research on cognition, or *how people think*, as we look at the subjects of language, problem solving, and decision making. In the second half of the chapter, we will focus on *how well people think*, as measured by tests of intelligence. Thus, the first half of the chapter examines the intricacies of thinking *processes* (cognition), whereas the second half focuses on variations among people in thinking *ability* (intelligence).

The topics of cognition and intelligence have very different histories. As we will discuss later, the first useful tests of general mental ability were created between 1904 and 1916, and intelligence testing flourished throughout the 20th century. In contrast, during the first half of the 20th century, the study of cognition was actively discouraged by the theoretical dominance of behaviorism. Herbert Simon, a pioneer of cognitive psychology, recalls that "you couldn't use a word like *mind* in a psychology journal—you'd get your mouth washed out with soap" (Holden, 1986). However, the 1950s and 1960s brought a "cognitive revolution" in psychology, as pioneering theorists developed creative new approaches to research on cognitive processes (Baars, 1986). Thus, it was only in the second half of the 20th century that the study of cognition grew into a robust area of research.

8.1 LANGUAGE: TURNING THOUGHTS INTO WORDS

8.1

Key Learning Goals

- Compare behavioral, nativist, and interactionist perspectives on language acquisition.
- Discuss the effects of bilingualism, and assess the status of the linguistic relativity hypothesis.

Language obviously plays a fundamental role in human behavior. If you were to ask people, "What characteristic most distinguishes humans from other living creatures?" a great many would reply, "Language." In this section, we discuss the processes that underlie children's learning of language, bilingualism, and whether language shapes thought.

Language Acquisition

Since the 1950s, there has been great debate about the key processes involved in language acquisition. As with arguments we have seen in other areas of psychology, this one centers on the *nature versus nurture* issue.

Behaviorist Theories

The behaviorist approach to language was first outlined by B. F. Skinner in his book *Verbal Behavior* (1957). He argued that children learn language the same way they learn everything else: through imitation, reinforcement, and other established principles of conditioning. According to Skinner, vocalizations that are not reinforced gradually decline in frequency. The remaining vocalizations are shaped with reinforcers until they're correct. Behaviorists assert that by controlling reinforcement, parents encourage their children to learn the correct meaning and pronunciation of words (Staats & Staats, 1963). For example, as children grow older, parents may insist on closer and closer approximations of the word *water* before supplying the requested drink. If children's imitations of adults' and older children's sentences are understood, parents are able to answer their questions or respond to their requests, thus reinforcing their verbal behavior.

Nativist Theories

Skinner's explanation of language acquisition soon inspired a critique and rival explanation from Noam Chomsky (1959, 1965). Chomsky pointed out that there are an infinite number of sentences in a language. It's therefore unreasonable to expect that children learn language by imitation. For example, in English, we add *ed* to the end of a verb to construct past tense. Children routinely overregularize this rule, producing incorrect verbs such as *goed, eated,* and *thinked.* Mistakes such as these are inconsistent with Skinner's emphasis on imitation because most adult speakers don't use ungrammatical words such as *goed.* Children can't imitate things they don't hear. According to Chomsky, children learn *the rules of language,* not specific verbal responses, as Skinner proposed.

An alternative theory favored by Chomsky (1975, 1986, 2006) is that humans have an inborn, or "native," propensity to develop language. *Nativist theory* proposes that humans are equipped with a ***language acquisition device (LAD)—an innate mechanism or process that facilitates the learning of language.*** According to this view, humans learn language for the same reason that birds learn to fly—because they're biologically equipped for it. The exact nature of the language acquisition device has not been spelled out in nativist theories. It presumably consists of brain structures and neural wiring that leave humans well prepared to discriminate among linguistic sounds, acquire rules of syntax, and so on.

Why does Chomsky believe that children have an innate capacity for learning language? One reason is that children seem to acquire language quickly and effortlessly. How could they develop so complex a skill in such a short time unless they had a built-in capacity for it? Another reason is that language development tends to unfold at roughly the same pace for most children, even though children obviously are reared in diverse home environments. This finding suggests that language development is determined by biological maturation more than personal experience.

Interactionist Theories

Like Skinner, Chomsky has his critics (Bohannon & Bonvillian, 2009). They ask: What exactly is a language acquisition device? What are the neural mechanisms involved? They argue that the language acquisition device concept is awfully vague. Other critics question whether the rapidity of early language development is as exceptional as nativists assume. They assert that it isn't fair to compare the rapid progress of toddlers, who are immersed in their native language, against the struggles of older students, who may devote only 10–15 hours per week to their foreign language course.

The problems apparent in Skinner's and Chomsky's explanations of language development have led some researchers to outline *interactionist theories* of language acquisition. These theories (Bates, 1999; MacWhinney, 2001, 2004) assert that biology and experience *both* make important contributions to the development of language. Like the nativists, interactionists believe that the human organism is biologically well equipped for learning language. They also agree that much of this learning involves the acquisition of rules. However, like the behaviorists, they believe that social exchanges with parents and others play a critical role in molding language skills (see **Figure 8.1**).

Recent years have brought research that supports the assertion of both the nativists and the interactionists that humans are biologically prepared to learn language readily. A groundbreaking study using brain-imaging technology found that the human brain reacts differently to artificial syllables that are good and bad word candidates (Berent et al., 2014). This disparity is even seen in infants (Gómez et al., 2014). The findings suggest that the human brain is hard wired to readily recognize the sound patterns that make up human languages.

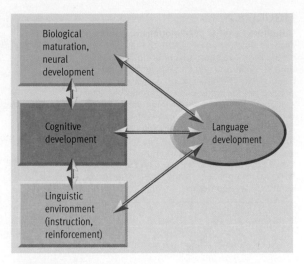

FIGURE 8.1

Interactionist theories of language acquisition. The interactionist view is that nature and nurture are both important to language acquisition. Maturation is thought to drive language development directly and to influence it indirectly by fostering cognitive development. Meanwhile, verbal exchanges with parents and others are also thought to play a critical role in molding language skills. The complex bidirectional relations depicted here shed some light on why there is room for extensive debate about the crucial factors in language acquisition.

Learning More than One Language: Bilingualism

Given the complexities involved in acquiring one language, you may be wondering about the ramifications of being asked to learn *two* languages. *Bilingualism* **is the acquisition of two languages that use different speech sounds, vocabulary, and grammatical rules.** Nearly half of the world's population grows up bilingual (Snow, 1998), but bilingualism has sparked considerable controversy in the United States. A number of laws and court rulings have reduced the availability of bilingual educational programs in many school systems (Wiese & Garcia, 2006). These laws are based on the assumption that bilingualism hampers language development and has a negative impact on students' educational progress. Let's take a look at the evidence.

Does Learning Two Languages in Childhood Slow Down Language Development?

If children are learning two languages simultaneously, does one language interfere with the other so that the acquisition of both is impeded? Some studies *have* found that bilingual children have smaller vocabularies in each of their languages than *monolingual* children have in their one language (Umbel et al., 1992). But when their two overlapping vocabularies are added, their total vocabulary is similar or slightly superior to that of children learning a single language (Oller & Pearson, 2002). Taken as a whole, the available evidence suggests that bilingual and monolingual children are largely similar in the course and rate of their language development (Costa & Sebastián-Gallés, 2014). There is little empirical support for the belief that bilingualism has serious negative effects on language development (Hoff, 2014).

Does Bilingualism Affect Cognitive Processes and Skills?

Studies have found that bilingualism is associated with both advantages and disadvantages. The chief disadvantage is that bilinguals appear to have a slight handicap in terms of raw language *processing speed* and *verbal fluency* (the ease with which people can think of words). Evidence suggests that when bilingual people are reading, listening, or speaking in a specific language, to some extent both their first language (L1) and their second language (L2) are simultaneously active (Gullifer, Kroll, & Dussias, 2013). In other words, there is no way to turn off L1 when using L2, or vice versa. This creates some cross-language interference that slows language processing (Michael & Gollan, 2005; Sandoval et al., 2010).

FIGURE 8.2

Cognitive benefits of bilingualism. A meta-analysis (Adesope et al., 2010) of research on the cognitive correlates of bilingualism uncovered some interesting benefits associated with bilingualism. The data shown here are mean *effect sizes* for five cognitive variables. An effect size is an estimate of the magnitude of one variable's effects on another. An effect size from .20 to .50 is considered meaningful but small, from .50 to .80 is characterized as moderate, and above .80 is regarded as large. Obviously, the effects sizes vary, but the data suggest that bilingualism enhances, rather than undermines, cognitive development.

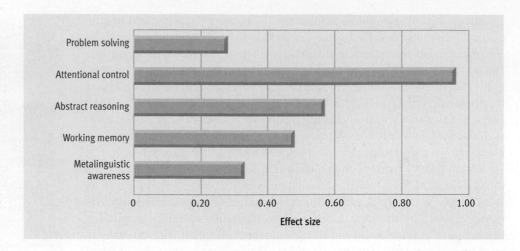

> **REALITY CHECK**

Misconception

Bilingualism undermines cognitive development.

Reality

It is widely believed that bilingualism interferes with cognitive development. But when researchers control for social class in their comparisons, they do not find cognitive deficits in bilingual youngsters. Moreover, research suggests that bilingualism may be associated with unexpected cognitive benefits.

In contrast with this relatively minor disadvantage, new research in this area suggests that bilingualism is associated with a variety of significant advantages. A meta-analysis of sixty-three studies found that bilingual individuals tend to score moderately higher than monolinguals on measures of attention control, working memory capacity, abstract reasoning, and certain types of problem solving (Adesope et al., 2010) (see **Figure 8.2**). How might bilingualism lead to these cognitive benefits? The current thinking focuses on the realization that L1 and L2 are simultaneously active in bilinguals. This competition forces bilinguals to learn to maximize their control over attention to resist intrusions and enhance the efficiency of their working memory. The resulting increases in attention control and working memory may promote enhanced reasoning and problem solving. Moreover, recent studies suggest that the cognitive benefits of bilingualism persist into adulthood and that they may even protect to some degree against age-related cognitive decline and dementia (Bialystok et al., 2014; Guzmán-Vélez & Tranel, 2015).

Culture, Language, and Thought

Does your training in English lead you to think about certain things differently than someone who was raised to speak Chinese or French? In other words, does a cultural group's language determine their thought? Or does thought determine language? Benjamin Lee Whorf (1956) has been the most prominent advocate of *linguistic relativity,* **the hypothesis that one's language determines the nature of one's thought.** Whorf speculated that different languages lead people to view the world differently. His classic example compared English and Eskimo views of snow. He asserted that the English language has just one word for snow, whereas the Eskimo language has many words that distinguish among falling snow, wet snow, and so on. Because of this language gap, Whorf argued that Eskimos perceive snow differently than English-speaking people do. However, Whorf's conclusion about these perceptual differences was based on casual observation rather than systematic cross-cultural comparisons of perceptual processes. Moreover, critics noted that advocates of the linguistic relativity hypothesis had carelessly overestimated the number of Eskimo words for snow, while ignoring the variety of English words that refer to snow, such as slush and blizzard (Martin, 1986; Pullum, 1991).

Whorf's hypothesis has been the subject of considerable research and continues to generate debate (Chiu, Leung, & Kwan, 2007; Gleitman & Papafragou, 2005). Many studies have focused on cross-cultural comparisons of how people perceive colors because substantial variations exist among cultures in how colors are categorized with names. For example, some languages have a single color name that includes both blue and green (Davies, 1998). If a language doesn't distinguish between blue and green, do people who speak that language think about colors differently than people in other cultures do?

Does the language you speak determine how you think? Yes, said Benjamin Lee Whorf, who argued that the Eskimo language, which has numerous words for snow, leads Eskimos to perceive snow differently than English speakers perceive it. Whorf's hypothesis has been the subject of spirited debate.

Early efforts to answer this question suggested that the color categories in a language have relatively little influence on how people perceive and think about colors (Berlin & Kay, 1969; Rosch, 1973). However, more recent studies have provided new evidence favoring the linguistic relativity hypothesis (Davidoff, 2001, 2004; Roberson et al., 2005). Studies of subjects who speak African languages that do not have a boundary between blue and green have found that language affects their color perception. They have more trouble making quick discriminations between blue and green colors than English-speaking subjects do (Ozgen, 2004). Additional studies have found that a culture's color categories shape subjects' similarity judgments and groupings of colors (Pilling & Davies, 2004; Roberson, Davies, & Davidoff, 2000). Other studies have found that language also has some impact on how people think about motion (Gennari et al., 2002); time (Boroditsky, 2001); and shapes (Roberson, Davidoff, & Shapiro, 2002).

So, what is the status of the linguistic relativity hypothesis? At present, the debate seems to center on whether the new data are sufficient to support the original, "strong" version of the hypothesis (that a given language makes certain ways of thinking obligatory or impossible) or a "weaker" version of the hypothesis (that a language makes certain ways of thinking easier or more difficult). The current thinking seems to favor the weaker version of the linguistic relativity hypothesis (Kreiner, 2011).

8.2 PROBLEM SOLVING: IN SEARCH OF SOLUTIONS

Look at the two problems below. Can you solve them?

In the Thompson family there are five brothers, and each brother has one sister. If you count Mrs. Thompson, how many females are there in the Thompson family?

Fifteen percent of the people in Topeka have unlisted telephone numbers. You select 200 names at random from the Topeka phone book. How many of these people can be expected to have unlisted phone numbers?

8.2

Key Learning Goals

- Identify four common barriers to effective problem solving.
- Review general problem-solving strategies and heuristics, and discuss cultural variations in cognitive style.

These problems, borrowed from Sternberg (1986, p. 214), are exceptionally simple, but many people fail to solve them. The answer to the first problem is two. The only females in the family are Mrs. Thompson and her one daughter, who is a sister to each of her brothers. The answer to the second problem is none. You won't find any people with unlisted phone numbers in the phone book.

Why do many people fail to solve these simple problems? You'll learn why in a moment, when we discuss barriers to effective problem solving. But first let's examine a scheme for classifying problems into a few basic types.

Types of Problems

Problem solving **refers to active efforts to discover what must be done to achieve a goal that is not readily attainable.** Obviously, if a goal is readily attainable, there isn't a problem. But in problem-solving situations, one must go beyond the given information to overcome obstacles and reach a goal. Jim Greeno (1978) has proposed that problems can be categorized into three basic classes:

1. *Problems of inducing structure.* The person must discover the relations among the parts of the problem. The *series completion problems* and the *analogy problems* in **Figure 8.3** are examples of problems of inducing structure.

2. *Problems of arrangement.* The person must arrange the parts in a way that satisfies some criterion. The parts can usually be arranged in many ways. However, only one or a few of the arrangements form a solution. The *string problem* and the *anagrams* in **Figure 8.3** fit in this category.

3. *Problems of transformation.* The person must carry out a sequence of transformations in order to reach a specific goal. The *hobbits and orcs problem* and the *water jar problem* in **Figure 8.3** are examples of transformation problems. Transformation problems can be challenging. Even though you know exactly what the goal is, it's often not obvious how the goal can be achieved.

Greeno's list is not an exhaustive scheme for classifying problems, but it provides a useful system for understanding some of the variety seen in everyday problems.

Barriers to Effective Problem Solving

On the basis of their studies of problem solving, psychologists have identified a number of barriers that frequently impede people's efforts to arrive at solutions. Common obstacles to effective problem solving include a focus on irrelevant information, functional fixedness, mental set, and imposition of unnecessary constraints.

Irrelevant Information

We began our discussion of problem solving with two simple problems that people routinely fail to solve. The catch is that these problems contain *irrelevant information* that leads people astray. In the first problem, the number of brothers is irrelevant in determining the number of females in the Thompson family. In the second problem, participants tend to focus on the figures of 15% and 200 names. But this numerical information is irrelevant because all the names came out of the phone book.

Sternberg (1986) points out that people often incorrectly assume that all the numerical information in a problem is necessary to solve it. They therefore try to figure out how to use this information before they even consider whether it's relevant. Focusing on irrelevant information can have adverse effects on reasoning and problem solving (Gaeth & Shanteau, 2000). Thus, effective problem solving requires that you attempt to figure out what information is relevant and what is irrelevant before proceeding.

A. Analogy
What word completes the analogy?
Merchant : Sell : : Customer : _____
Lawyer : Client : : Doctor : _____

B. String problem
Two strings hang from the ceiling but are too far apart to allow a person to hold one and walk to the other. On the table are a book of matches, a screwdriver, and a few pieces of cotton. How could the strings be tied together?

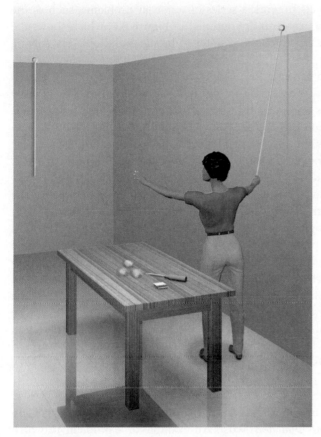

C. Hobbits and orcs problem
Three hobbits and three orcs arrive at a river bank, and they all wish to cross onto the other side. Fortunately, there is a boat, but unfortunately, the boat can hold only two creatures at one time. Also, there is another problem. Orcs are vicious creatures, and whenever there are more orcs than hobbits on one side of the river, the orcs will immediately attack the hobbits and eat them up. Consequently, you should be certain that you never leave more orcs than hobbits on either river bank. How should the problem be solved? It must be added that the orcs, though vicious, can be trusted to bring the boat back! (From Matlin, 1989, p. 319)

D. Water jar problem
Suppose that you have a 21-cup jar, a 127-cup jar, and a 3-cup jar. Drawing and discarding as much water as you like, you need to measure out exactly 100 cups of water. How can this be done?

E. Anagram
Rearrange the letters in each row to make an English word.
RWAET
KEROJ

F. Series completion
What number or letter completes each series?
1 2 8 3 4 6 5 6 _____
A B M C D M _____

FIGURE 8.3

Six standard problems used in studies of problem solving. Try solving the problems and identifying which class each belongs to before reading further. The problems can be classified as follows. The *analogy problems* and *series completion problems* are problems of inducing structure. The solutions for the analogy problems are *Buy* and *Patient.* The solutions for the series completion problems are *4* and *E*. The *string problem* and the *anagram problems* are problems of arrangement. To solve the string problem, attach the screwdriver to one string and set it swinging as a pendulum. Hold the other string and catch the swinging screwdriver. Then you need only untie the screwdriver and tie the strings together. The solutions for the anagram problems are *WATER* and *JOKER*. The *hobbits and orcs problem* and the *water jar problem* are problems of transformation. The solutions for these two problems are outlined in **Figures 8.4** and **8.5.**

Functional Fixedness

Another common barrier to successful problem solving is *functional fixedness*—**the tendency to perceive an item only in terms of its most common use.** Functional fixedness has been seen in the difficulties that people have with the string problem in **Figure 8.3** (Maier, 1931). Solving this problem requires finding a novel use for one of the objects: the screwdriver. Participants tend to think of the screwdriver in terms of its usual functions—turning screws and perhaps prying things open. They have a hard time viewing the screwdriver as a weight. Their rigid way of thinking about the screwdriver illustrates functional fixedness (Bassok & Novick, 2012). According to McCaffrey (2012),

FIGURE 8.4

Solution to the hobbits and orcs problem.
This problem is difficult because it is necessary to temporarily work "away" from the goal.

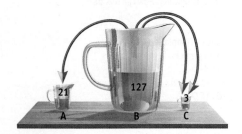

FIGURE 8.5

The method for solving the water jar problem. As explained in the text, the correct formula is B – A – 2C.

the root cause of functional fixedness is that people tend to overlook obscure, little-noticed features of problems. To combat functional fixedness he has devised a strategy that helps people to discern the obscure features of problems. This strategy involves successively decomposing problems into their constituent parts. In an initial study, he found that training in this strategy led to enhanced problem solving.

Mental Set

Rigid thinking is also at work when a mental set interferes with effective problem solving. **A *mental set* exists when people persist in using problem-solving strategies that have worked in the past.** The effects of mental set were seen in a classic study by Abraham Luchins (1942). He asked subjects to work a series of water jar problems, such as the one introduced earlier. Six such problems are outlined in **Figure 8.6**, which shows the capacities of the three jars and the amounts of water to be measured out. Try solving these problems.

Were you able to develop a formula for solving these problems? The first four all require the same strategy, which is described in **Figure 8.5**. You have to fill jar B, draw off the amount that jar A holds once, and draw off the amount that jar C holds twice. Thus, the formula for your solution is B – A – 2C. Although the fifth problem has an obvious and much simpler solution (A – C) (see **Figure 8.10**), Luchins found that most participants stuck with the more cumbersome strategy they had used in problems 1–4. Moreover, most subjects couldn't solve the sixth problem in the allotted time because they kept trying to use their proven strategy, which does not work for this problem. The participants' reliance on their "tried and true" strategy is an illustration of mental set in problem solving. The compelling power of mental sets has even been demonstrated in chess *experts* working on chess problems (Bilalić, McLeod, & Gobet, 2010). Data on the chess players' eye movements indicated that the first solution that comes to mind focuses attention on information consistent with that solution and directs attention away from alternative strategies. Mental sets are not necessarily bad. They reflect sensible learning from past experience. In many situations, if you have an adequate solution, it may be inefficient to expend additional time and effort to search for an even better one. But, mental sets may explain why having expertise in an area sometimes backfires and hampers problem-solving efforts (Leighton & Sternberg, 2003).

Unnecessary Constraints

Effective problem solving requires specifying all the constraints governing a problem *without assuming any constraints that don't exist*. An example of a problem in which people place an unnecessary constraint on the solution is shown in **Figure 8.7**. Without lifting your pencil from the paper, try to draw four straight lines that will cross through all nine dots. If you struggle with this one, don't feel bad. When a time limit of a few minutes is imposed on this problem, the typical solution rate is 0% (MacGregor, Ormerod, & Chronicle, 2001). The key factor that makes this a difficult problem is that most people will not draw lines outside the imaginary boundary that surrounds the dots (Bassok & Novick, 2012). Notice that this constraint is not part of the problem statement. It's imposed only by the problem solver. Correct solutions, two of which are shown in **Figure 8.11**, extend outside the imaginary boundary. To solve this problem, you need to literally "think outside the box." This popular slogan, spawned by the nine-dot problem, reflects the fact that people often make assumptions that impose unnecessary constraints on problem-solving efforts.

The nine-dot problem is a classic insight problem—meaning that when people succeed in solving it, they typically experience a burst of insight. **Insight occurs when people suddenly discover the correct solution to a problem after struggling with it for a while.** Although insight feels like a sudden "aha!" experience to problem solvers, some researchers have questioned whether insight solutions emerge full blown or are preceded by incremental movement toward a solution (van Steenburgh et al., 2012).

Approaches to Problem Solving

People use a variety of strategies in attempting to solve problems. In this section, we'll examine some general strategies.

Trial and Error and Heuristics

Trial and error is a common, albeit primitive, approach to solving problems. ***Trial and error involves trying possible solutions sequentially and discarding those that are in error until one works.*** Trial and error can be effective when there are relatively few possible solutions to be tried out. However, this method becomes impractical when the number of possible maneuvers is large. Consider, for instance, the problem shown in **Figure 8.8**. The challenge is to move just two matches to create a pattern containing four equal squares. Sure, you could use a trial-and-error approach in moving pairs of matches. But you'd better allocate plenty of time to this effort because there are over 60,000 possible rearrangements to check out (see **Figure 8.12** for the solution).

Because trial and error is inefficient, people often use shortcuts called *heuristics* in problem solving. **A *heuristic* is a guiding principle or "rule of thumb" used in solving problems or making decisions.** Heuristics are often useful, but they don't guarantee success. Helpful heuristics in problem solving include forming subgoals, searching for analogies, and changing the representation of the problem.

Forming Subgoals

It is often useful to tackle problems by formulating *subgoals,* intermediate steps toward a solution (Catrambone, 1998). When you reach a subgoal, you've solved part of the problem. Some problems have fairly obvious subgoals, and research has shown that people take advantage of them. For instance, in analogy problems, the first subgoal usually is to figure out the possible relations between the first two parts of the analogy.

The wisdom of formulating subgoals can be seen in the *tower of Hanoi problem,* depicted in **Figure 8.9**. The terminal goal for this problem is to move all three rings on peg A to peg C while abiding by two restrictions: only the top ring on a peg can be moved, and a ring must never be placed above a smaller ring. See whether you can solve the problem before continuing.

Dividing this problem into subgoals facilitates a solution (Kotovsky, Hayes, & Simon, 1985). If you think in terms of subgoals, your first task is to get ring 3 to the bottom of peg C. Breaking this task into sub-subgoals, subjects can figure out that they should move ring 1 to peg C, ring 2 to peg B, and ring 1 from peg C to peg B. These maneuvers allow you to place ring 3 at the bottom of peg C, thus meeting your first subgoal. Your next subgoal—getting ring 2 over to peg C—can be accomplished in just two steps: move ring 1 to peg A and ring 2 to peg C. It should then be obvious how to achieve your final subgoal—getting ring 1 over to peg C.

Searching for Analogies

Searching for analogies is another of the major heuristics for solving problems (Holyoak, 2012). We reason by analogy constantly, and these efforts to identify analogies make major contributions to effective thinking (Gentner & Smith, 2013). If you can spot an analogy between problems, you may be able to use the solution to a previous problem to solve a current one. Of course, using this strategy depends on recognizing the similarity between the two problems, which may itself be a challenging problem. Nonetheless, studies of real-world problem-solving efforts show that we depend on analogies far more than most people appreciate. For example, one study recorded design engineers during their product development meetings and found that they came up with an average of eleven analogies per hour of deliberation (Christensen & Schunn, 2007). Clearly, analogies can be a powerful tool in efforts to solve problems.

	Capacity of empty jars			Desired amount of water
Problem	A	B	C	
1	14	163	25	99
2	18	43	10	5
3	9	42	6	21
4	20	59	4	31
5	23	49	3	20
6	28	76	3	25

FIGURE 8.6

Additional water jar problems. Using jars A, B, and C, with the capacities indicated in each row, figure out how to measure out the desired amount of water specified on the far right. The solutions are shown in **Figure 8.10**. (Based on Luchins, 1942).

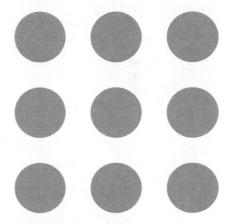

FIGURE 8.7

The nine-dot problem. Without lifting your pencil from the paper, draw no more than four lines that will cross through all nine dots. For possible solutions, see **Figure 8.11**.

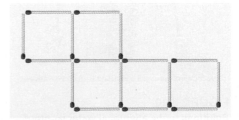

FIGURE 8.8

The matchstick problem. Move two matches to form four equal squares. You can find the solution in **Figure 8.12**.

SOURCE: Kendler, H. H. (1974). *Basic psychology.* Menlo Park, CA: Benjamin-Cummings. Copyright © 1974 The Benjamin-Cummings Publishing Co. Adapted by permission of Howard H. Kendler.

FIGURE 8.9

The tower of Hanoi problem. Your mission is to move the rings from peg A to peg C. You can move only the top ring on a peg and can't place a larger ring above a smaller one. The solution is explained in the text.

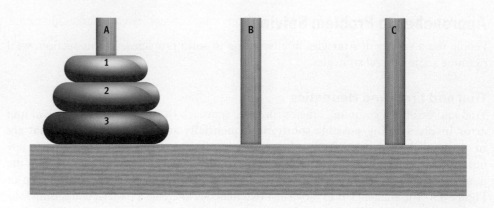

Changing the Representation of the Problem

Whether you solve a problem often hinges on how you envision it—your *representation of the problem*. Many problems can be represented in a variety of ways, such as verbally, mathematically, or spatially. You might represent a problem with a list, a table, an equation, a graph, a matrix of facts or numbers, a hierarchical tree diagram, or a sequential flowchart (Halpern, 2014). When you fail to make progress with your initial representation of a problem, changing your representation is often a good strategy (Bassok & Novick, 2012). As an illustration, see whether you can solve the *Buddhist monk problem*:

> At sunrise, a Buddhist monk sets out to climb a tall mountain. He follows a narrow path that winds around the mountain and up to a temple. He stops frequently to rest and climbs at varying speeds, arriving around sunset. After staying a few days, he begins his return journey. As before, he starts at sunrise, rests often, walks at varying speeds, and arrives around sunset. Prove that there must be a spot along the path that the monk will pass on both trips at precisely the same time of day.

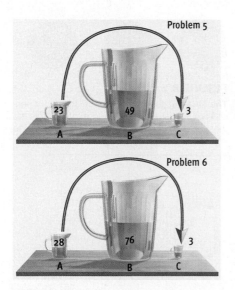

FIGURE 8.10

Solutions to the additional water jar problems. The solution for problems 1–4 is the same as the solution shown in **Figure 8.5** (B − A − 2C). This method will work for problem 5, but there also is a simpler solution (A − C), which is the only solution for problem 6. Many subjects exhibit a mental set on these problems because they fail to notice the simpler solution for problem 5.

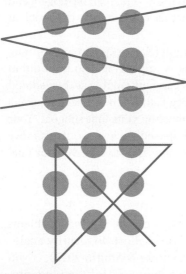

FIGURE 8.11

Two solutions to the nine-dot problem. The key to solving the problem is to recognize that nothing in the problem statement forbids going outside the imaginary boundary surrounding the dots.

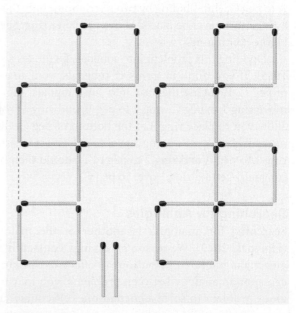

FIGURE 8.12

Solution to the matchstick problem. The key to solving this problem is to "open up" the figure, something many subjects are reluctant to do because they impose unnecessary constraints on the problem.

SOURCE: Kendler, H. H. (1974). *Basic psychology.* Menlo Park, CA: Benjamin-Cummings. Copyright © 1974 The Benjamin-Cummings Publishing Co. Adapted by permission of Howard H. Kendler.

Why should there be such a spot? The monk's walking speed varies. Shouldn't it all be a matter of coincidence if he reaches a spot at the same time each day? Moreover, if there is such a spot, how would you prove it? Participants who represent this problem in terms of verbal, mathematical, or spatial information struggle. Subjects who work with a graphic representation fare much better. The best way to represent the problem is to envision the monk (or two different monks) ascending and descending the mountain at the same time. The two monks must meet at some point. If you construct a graph (see **Figure 8.13**) you can vary the speed of the monks' descent in endless ways, but you can see that there's always a place where they meet. Research suggests that restructuring the representation of problems is often the key to solving insight problems. Restructuring of problems can also contribute to creativity (Cunningham & MacGregor, 2014).

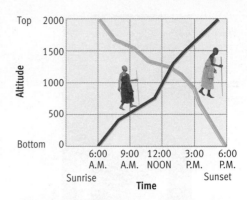

FIGURE 8.13

Solution to the Buddhist monk problem. If you represent this problem graphically and think in terms of two monks, it is readily apparent that the monk does pass a single spot at the same time each day.

Taking a Break: Incubation

When a problem is resistant to solution, there is much to be said for taking a break and not thinking about it for a while. After the break, you may find that you see the problem in a different light, and new solutions may spring to mind. Obviously, there is no guarantee that a break will facilitate problem solving. But breaks pay off often enough that researchers have given the phenomenon a name: *incubation*. **An *incubation effect* occurs when new solutions surface for a previously unsolved problem after a period of not consciously thinking about the problem.** Depending on the nature of the problem, incubation periods may be measured in minutes, hours, or days. The likelihood of an incubation effect depends on a number of task-related factors, but on the whole, incubation does tend to enhance problem solving (Dodds, Ward, & Smith, 2011). Some theorists believe that incubation effects occur because people continue to work on problems at an unconscious level after conscious effort has been suspended (Ellwood et al., 2009). However, other evidence suggests that a high level of mind wandering during the incubation break is associated with a greater likelihood of coming up with a new solution (Baird et al., 2012).

CONCEPT CHECK 8.1

Thinking About Problem Solving

Check your understanding of problem solving by answering some questions about the following problem. Begin by trying to solve the problem.

The Candle Problem

Using the objects shown—candles, a box of matches, string, and some tacks—figure out how you could mount a candle on a wall so it can be used as a light.

Work on the problem for a while, then turn to the next page to see the solution. After you've seen the solution, respond to the following questions. The answers are in Appendix A.

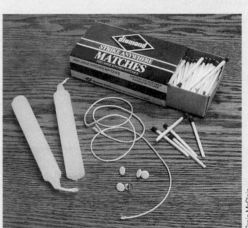

1. If it didn't occur to you that the matchbox could be converted from a container to a platform, this illustrates _____ _____.

2. While working on the problem, if you thought to yourself, "How can I create a platform attached to the wall?" you used the heuristic of _____ _____.

3. If it occurred to you suddenly that the matchbox could be used as a platform, this realization would be an example of _____.

4. If you had a hunch that there might be some similarity between this problem and the string problem in **Figure 8.3** (the similarity is the novel use of an object), your hunch would illustrate the heuristic of _____ ___ _____.

5. In terms of Greeno's three types of problems, the candle problem is a(n) _____ problem.

Culture, Cognitive Style, and Problem Solving

Do the varied experiences of people from different cultures lead to cross-cultural variations in problem solving? Yes, at least to some degree. Researchers have found cultural differences in the cognitive style people exhibit in solving problems (Cole & Packer, 2011).

Richard Nisbett and his colleagues (Nisbett et al., 2001; Nisbett & Miyamoto, 2005) argue that people from Eastern Asian cultures (such as China, Japan, and Korea) display a *holistic cognitive style* that focuses on context and relationships among elements, whereas people from Western cultures (America and Europe) exhibit an *analytic cognitive style* that focuses on objects and their properties rather than context. To put it simply, *Easterners see wholes where Westerners see parts.*

In one test of this hypothesis, Masuda and Nisbett (2001) presented computer-animated scenes of fish and other underwater objects to Japanese and American participants and asked them to report what they had seen. The initial comments of American subjects typically referred to the focal fish, whereas the initial comments of Japanese subjects usually referred to background elements (see **Figure 8.14**). Furthermore, the Japanese participants made about 70% more statements about context or background and about twice as many statements about relationships between elements in the scenes. Based on these and many other findings, Nisbett et al. (2001) conclude that cultural differences in cognitive style are substantial and that "literally different cognitive processes are often invoked by East Asians and Westerners dealing with the same problem" (p. 305). These disparities in cognitive style seem to be rooted in variations in cultures' social orientation (Varnum et al., 2010). They appear to grow out of Western cultures' emphasis on the individual and independence, as opposed to Eastern cultures' emphasis on the group and interdependence (see Chapters 11 and 12).

Problems are not the only kind of cognitive challenge that people grapple with on a regular basis. Life also seems to constantly demand decisions. As you might expect, cognitive psychologists have shown great interest in the process of decision making, which is our next subject.

The solution to the candle problem in Concept Check 8.1.

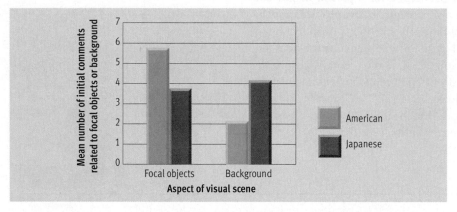

FIGURE 8.14

Cultural disparities in cognitive style. In one of the studies conducted by Masuda and Nisbett (2001), the participants were asked to describe computer-animated visual scenes. As you can see, the initial comments made by American subjects referred more to focal objects in the scenes, whereas the initial comments made by Japanese subjects referred more to background elements in the scenes. These findings are consistent with the hypothesis that Easterners see wholes (a holistic cognitive style) where Westerners see parts (an analytic cognitive style).

8.3 DECISION MAKING: CHOICES AND CHANCES

Key Learning Goals

- Articulate Simon's theory of bounded rationality, and discuss research on decisions about preferences.

- Understand the availability and representativeness heuristics, and how they contribute to the tendency to ignore base rates and the conjunction fallacy.

- Describe the nature of fast and frugal heuristics, and discuss dual-process theories of decision making.

Decisions, decisions. Life is full of them. You decided to read this book today. Earlier today you decided when to get up; whether to eat breakfast; and if so, what to eat. Usually you make routine decisions such as these with little effort. But on occasion you need to make important decisions that require more thought. Big decisions—such as selecting a car, a home, or a job—tend to be more difficult. The alternatives usually have a number of facets that need to be weighed. For instance, in choosing between several cars, you may want to compare their costs, roominess, fuel economy, handling, acceleration, stylishness, reliability, safety features, and warranties.

Decision making involves evaluating alternatives and making choices among them. Most people try to be systematic and rational in their decision making. However, the work that earned Herbert Simon the 1978 Nobel Prize in economics showed that people don't always live up to these goals. Before Simon's work, most traditional theories in economics assumed that people made rational choices to maximize their economic gains. Simon (1957) noted that people have a limited ability to process and evaluate information on numerous facets of possible alternatives. Thus, Simon's **theory of bounded rationality asserts that people tend to use simple strategies in decision making that focus on only a few facets of available options and often result in "irrational" decisions that are less than optimal.**

Spurred by Simon's analysis, psychologists have devoted several decades to the study of how cognitive biases distort people's decision making. Let's look at this research—and the criticism it has inspired.

Making Choices About Preferences

Many decisions involve choices about *preferences,* which can be made using a variety of strategies. Barry Schwartz (2004) argues that people in modern societies are overwhelmed by an overabundance of such choices about preferences. For example, Schwartz describes how a simple visit to a local supermarket can require a consumer to choose from 285 varieties of cookies, 61 suntan lotions, 150 lipsticks, and 175 salad dressings. Increased choice is most tangible in the realm of consumer goods. But Schwartz argues that it also extends into more significant domains of life. Today, people tend to have unprecedented opportunities to make choices about how they will be educated, how and where they will work, how their intimate relationships will unfold, and even how they will look. Although enormous freedom of choice sounds attractive, Schwartz argues that the overabundance of choices in modern life has unexpected costs. He suggests that people routinely make errors even when choosing among a handful of alternatives and that errors become much more likely when decisions become more complex. And he explains how *choice overload* increases the potential for rumination and post-decision regret.

Consistent with this analysis, quite a number of studies have suggested that when consumers have too many choices (for a specific product), they are more likely to leave a store empty-handed (Jessup et al., 2009; Park & Jang, 2013). Why? Studies show that when there are many choices available, people are more likely to struggle deciding which is the best option, and so defer their decision (White & Hoffrage, 2009). How many choices are too many? That depends on a host of factors, but it appears that people prefer more choices up to a point, and then further increases in options lead to decreased satisfaction with the situation (Reutskaja & Hogarth, 2009). That said, variations in how knowledgeable consumers feel about a specific product can influence the likelihood of choice overload. In one recent study, participants who subjectively felt knowledgeable about specific products were less likely to buy when given many options (showing choice overload), but those who did not feel very knowledgeable tended to welcome additional options when the extra choices helped them to educate themselves about the product (Hadar & Sood, 2014). Thus, the prediction of when choice overload will occur is a complicated matter.

Another line of research has looked at whether decisions about preferences work out better when people engage in conscious deliberation or go with intuitive, unconscious feelings based on minimal deliberation. Ap Dijksterhuis and colleagues (Dijksterhuis & Nordgren, 2006; Dijksterhuis & van Olden, 2006) argue that, given the limited capacity of conscious thought, deliberate decisions should be superior to intuitive decisions when choices are simple, but intuitive, unconscious decisions should be superior when choices are complex. In a test of this hypothesis, they had a sample of people indicate how many facets they would evaluate in deciding to purchase forty consumer products, such as shampoos, shoes, and cameras, yielding a *decision complexity* score for each product (Dijksterhuis et al., 2006). Subsequently, another group of participants picked a product they recently bought from this list, and were asked how much conscious thought they put into the decision and how satisfied they were with their choice. As predicted, conscious

People often have to decide between alternative products—such as TVs, cars, refrigerators, and so forth—that vary along a variety of dimensions. They often struggle with abundant choices and deliberate at length. However, as the text explains, extra deliberation does not necessarily lead to better decisions.

deliberation promoted greater satisfaction when decisions were simple. However, just the opposite occurred for complex decisions. Dijksterhuis calls this phenomenon the *deliberation-without-attention effect*—when people are faced with complex choices, they tend to make better decisions if they don't devote careful attention to the matter. Dijksterhuis believes that deliberations are taking place, but outside conscious awareness.

This assertion was bolstered by a recent replication of the deliberation-without-attention effect that incorporated neuroimaging (fMRI) of participants' brains while they engaged in conscious deliberation regarding a product choice and while they worked on a distractor task thought to promote unconscious deliberation about the choice (Creswell, Bursley, & Satpute, 2013). The study found that the same brain regions that were activated by conscious deliberation about the decision remained active during the period of unconscious deliberation.

Heuristics in Judging Probabilities

- What are your chances of passing your next psychology test if you study only 3 hours?
- How likely is a major downturn in the stock market during the upcoming year?
- What are the odds of your getting into graduate school in the field of your choice?

These questions ask you to make probability estimates. Such estimates are crucial in **risky decision making, which involves making choices under conditions of uncertainty.** Uncertainty exists when people don't know what will happen. Amos Tversky and Daniel Kahneman (1982; Kahneman & Tversky, 2000) conducted extensive research on the *heuristics,* or mental shortcuts, people use in grappling with probability estimates. This research earned Kahneman the Nobel Prize in economics in 2002 (unfortunately, his collaborator, Amos Tversky, died in 1996).

Availability is one such heuristic. **The *availability heuristic* involves basing the estimated probability of an event on the ease with which relevant instances come to mind.** For example, you may estimate the divorce rate by recalling the number of divorces among your friends' parents. Recalling specific instances of an event is a reasonable strategy to use in estimating the event's probability. However, if instances occur frequently but you have difficulty retrieving them from memory, your estimate will be biased. For instance, it's easier to think of words that begin with a certain letter than words that contain that letter at some other position. Thus, people should tend to respond that there are more words starting with the letter *K* than words having a *K* in the third position. To test this hypothesis, Tversky and Kahneman (1973) selected five consonants (*K, L, N, R, V*) that occur more frequently in the third position of a word than in the first. Subjects were asked whether each of the letters appears more often in the first or third position. Most of the subjects erroneously believed that all five letters were much more frequent in the first than in the third position, confirming the hypothesis.

Representativeness is another guide in estimating probabilities identified by Kahneman and Tversky (1982). **The *representativeness heuristic* involves basing the estimated probability of an event on how similar it is to the typical prototype of that event.** To illustrate, imagine that you flip a coin six times and keep track of how often the result is heads (H) or tails (T). Which of the following sequences is more likely?

1. T T T T T T
2. H T T H T H

People generally believe that the second sequence is more likely. After all, coin tossing is a random affair, and the second sequence looks much more representative of a random process than the first. In reality, the probability of each exact sequence is precisely the same ($1/2 \times 1/2 \times 1/2 \times 1/2 \times 1/2 \times 1/2 = 1/64$).

The influential work of Tversky and Kahneman (1974, 1982) spawned an enormous volume of research on risky decision making. This research showed that people deviate in predictable ways from optimal decision strategies—with surprising regularity (Griffin et al., 2012). For two examples, we'll look at how overdependence on the representativeness heuristic has been used to explain the tendency to ignore base rates and the conjunction fallacy.

The Tendency to Ignore Base Rates

Steve is very shy and withdrawn, invariably helpful, but with little interest in people or in the world of reality. A meek and tidy soul, he has a need for order and structure and a passion for detail. Do you think Steve is a salesperson or a librarian? (Adapted from Tversky & Kahneman, 1974, p. 1124)

Using the *representativeness heuristic*, participants tend to guess that Steve is a librarian because he resembles their prototype of a librarian (Tversky & Kahneman, 1982). In reality, this is not a very wise guess because *it ignores the base rates* of librarians and salespeople in the population. Virtually everyone knows that salespeople outnumber librarians by a wide margin (roughly 75 to 1 in the United States). This fact makes it much more likely that Steve is in sales. But in estimating probabilities, people often ignore information on base rates. People are particularly bad about applying base rates to themselves. For example, entrepreneurs starting new companies ignore the high failure rate for new businesses, and burglars underestimate the likelihood that they will end up in jail.

The Conjunction Fallacy

Let's look at another common mistake in decision-related reasoning. Imagine that you're going to meet a man who is an articulate, ambitious, power-hungry wheeler-dealer. Do you think it's more likely that he's a college teacher or a college teacher who's also a politician? People tend to guess that the man is a "college teacher who's a politician" because the description fits with the typical prototype of politicians. But stop and think for a moment. The broader category of college teachers completely includes the smaller subcategory of college teachers who are politicians

FIGURE 8.15

The conjunction fallacy. People routinely fall victim to the conjunction fallacy, but as this diagram makes obvious, the probability of being in a subcategory (college teachers who are politicians) cannot be higher than the probability of being in the broader category (college teachers). As this case illustrates, it often helps to represent a problem in a diagram.

COLLEGE PROFESSORS

COLLEGE PROFESSORS WHO ARE ALSO POLITICIANS

(see **Figure 8.15**). The probability of being in the subcategory cannot be higher than the probability of being in the broader category. It's a logical impossibility! Tversky and Kahneman (1983) call this error the *conjunction fallacy*. **The *conjunction fallacy* occurs when people estimate that the odds of two uncertain events happening together are greater than the odds of either event happening alone.** It has generally been attributed to the powerful influence of the representativeness heuristic.

CONCEPT CHECK 8.2

Recognizing Flaws in Decision Making

Check your understanding of heuristics and tendencies in decision making by trying to identify the quirks in reasoning apparent in the following examples. Write the letter for the cognitive phenomenon at work in the space on the left, choosing from the following: (a) the availability heuristic, (b) the representativeness heuristic, (c) the tendency to ignore base rates, and (d) the conjunction fallacy. You can find the answers in Appendix A.

_____ 1. Alex is an outstanding linebacker for his high school football team. He is well aware that only a small minority of high school stars earn college scholarships and that an even tinier fraction of college athletes go on to play professional ball. Nonetheless, he is confident he will be a star in the NFL someday.

_____ 2. Reggie is enjoying a delightful vacation at a plush beachfront hotel in Florida. But his friends cannot talk him into going into the ocean because he is extremely worried about the possibility of a shark attack. His friends say he is being silly, but he explains to them that over the years he has seen a great many news reports about shark attacks.

_____ 3. Maurice and Whitney are the proud parents of four girls, but they still yearn for a baby boy. In contemplating whether to try to have another child in the hopes of adding a boy to the family, they figure, "What the heck, the laws of probability are in our favor. The probability of having five girls in a row has to be pretty low. Let's go for it."

Evolutionary Analyses of Fast and Frugal Heuristics

A central conclusion of the last 30 years of research on decision making has been that human decision-making strategies are riddled with errors and biases that yield surprisingly irrational results (Griffin et al., 2012; LeBoeuf & Shafir, 2012). Theorists have concluded that human thinking is not as rational and effective as widely assumed. However, some evolutionary psychologists have argued that humans only *seem* irrational because cognitive psychologists have been asking the wrong questions and formulating problems in the wrong ways—ways that have nothing to do with the adaptive problems that the human mind has evolved to solve (Cosmides & Tooby, 1996). Expanding on this view, Gerd Gigerenzer asserts that humans' reasoning largely depends on "fast and frugal heuristics" that are quite a bit simpler than the complicated mental processes studied in traditional cognitive research (Gigerenzer, 2008; Katsikopoulos & Gigerenzer, 2013). According to Gigerenzer, organisms from toads to stockbrokers have to make fast decisions under demanding circumstances, with limited information. In most instances, organisms (including humans) do not have the time, resources, or cognitive capacities to gather all the relevant information, consider all the possible options, calculate all the probabilities and risks, and then make the statistically optimal decision. Instead, they use quick and dirty heuristics that are less than perfect but that work well enough most of the time to be adaptive in the real world.

Gigerenzer and his colleagues have shown that fast and frugal heuristics can be surprisingly effective. One heuristic that is often used in selecting between alternatives based on some quantitative dimension is the *recognition heuristic* (Pachur et al., 2012). It works as follows: if one of two alternatives is recognized and the other is not, assume that the recognized alternative has the higher value. Consider the following questions. Which city has more inhabitants: San Diego or San Antonio? Hamburg or Munich? In choosing between U.S. cities, American college students weighed a lifetime of facts useful for inferring population and made the correct choice 71% of the time. In choosing between German cities about which they knew very little, the same students depended on the recognition heuristic and chose correctly 73% of the time (Goldstein & Gigerenzer, 2002). Thus, the recognition heuristic allowed students to perform just as well with very limited knowledge as they did with extensive knowledge.

Gigerenzer and his colleagues studied a variety of other quick, one-reason decision-making strategies and showed that they can yield inferences that are just as accurate as much more elaborate strategies that carefully weigh many factors (Marewski, Gaissmaier, & Gigerenzer, 2010). And the researchers demonstrated that people actually use these fast and frugal heuristics in a diverse array of situations. Thus, the study of fast and frugal heuristics promises to be an intriguing new line of research in the study of human decision making.

How have traditional decision-making theorists responded to the challenge presented by Gigerenzer and other evolutionary theorists? They acknowledge that people often rely on fast and frugal heuristics, but they argue that this finding does not make decades of research on carefully reasoned approaches to decision making meaningless. Rather, they propose *dual-process theories* positing that people depend on two different modes, or systems, of thinking when making decisions (Evans & Stanovich, 2013; Gilovich & Griffin, 2010; Kahneman, 2011). One system consists of quick, simple, effortless, automatic judgments, like Gigerenzer's fast and frugal heuristics, which traditional theorists prefer to characterize as "intuitive thinking." The second system consists of slower, more elaborate, effortful, controlled judgments, like those studied in traditional decision research. According to this view, the second system monitors and corrects the intuitive system, as needed, and takes over when complicated or important decisions loom. Thus, traditional theorists maintain that fast and frugal heuristics and reasoned, rule-governed decision strategies exist side by side and that both need to be studied to fully understand decision making. Dual-process theories have generated a great deal of research, but this approach raises many complicated questions about how we decide which system to listen

► REALITY CHECK

Misconception

Effective decision making requires careful analysis of the alternatives and thoughtful deliberation.

Reality

Research on fast and frugal heuristics and the deliberation-without-attention effect demonstrate that good decision making does not necessarily *require* systematic, thorough deliberation. Although many decisions call for careful reflection, it appears that intuition has been underrated. Quick, simple, intuitive strategies can also yield good decisions. The challenge is to know when to go with intuition and when to rely on deliberation.

to, how the systems interact, and how they exchange information (Newell, 2013). Theorists have also expressed concern that the contrasts between the two systems have been described in vague, imprecise, and oversimplified ways (Evans, 2012).

Although sound decision making and effective problem solving obviously are key aspects of intelligence, there has been relatively little overlap between research on cognition and research on intelligence. As you have seen, cognitive research investigates how people use their intelligence; the focus is on *process*. In contrast, the study of intelligence has usually been approached from a testing perspective, which emphasizes measuring the *amount* of intelligence people have and figuring out why some have more than others. Let's look at how these measurements are made.

8.4

Key Learning Goals

- Summarize the contributions of Binet, Terman, and Wechsler to the evolution of intelligence testing.
- Explain the meaning of deviation IQ scores, and summarize evidence on the reliability and validity of IQ scores.
- Discuss how well IQ scores predict vocational success, and describe the use of IQ tests in non-Western cultures.

8.4 MEASURING INTELLIGENCE

We'll begin our discussion with a brief overview of the history of intelligence testing; then we will address some practical questions about how intelligence tests work.

A Brief History

Intelligence tests were invented a little over a hundred years ago. The key breakthrough came in 1904, when a commission on education in France asked Alfred Binet to devise a test to identify mentally subnormal children. The commission wanted to single out youngsters in need of special training. It also wanted to avoid complete reliance on teachers' evaluations, which might often be subjective and biased. In response to this need, Binet and a colleague, Theodore Simon, created the first useful test of general mental ability in 1905. Their scale was a success because it was inexpensive, easy to administer, objective, and capable of predicting children's performance in school fairly well (Siegler, 1992). Thanks to these qualities, its use spread across Europe and America.

The Binet-Simon scale expressed a child's score in terms of "mental level" or "mental age." A child's *mental age* **indicated that he or she displayed the mental ability typical of a child of that chronological (actual) age.** Thus, a child with a mental age of 6 performed like the average 6-year-old on the test. Binet realized that his scale was a somewhat crude initial effort at measuring mental ability. He revised it in 1908 and again in 1911. Unfortunately, his revising came to an abrupt end with his death in 1911. However, other psychologists continued to build on Binet's work.

In America, Lewis Terman and his colleagues at Stanford University soon went to work on a major expansion and revision of Binet's test. Their work led to the 1916 publication of the Stanford-Binet Intelligence Scale (Terman, 1916). This revision was quite loyal to Binet's original conceptions. However, it incorporated a new scoring scheme based on William Stern's "intelligence quotient" (Weiner, 2013b). **An *intelligence quotient (IQ)* is a child's mental age divided by chronological age, multiplied by 100.** IQ scores originally involved actual quotients, calculated as follows:

$$IQ = \frac{\text{Mental age}}{\text{Chronological age}} \times 100$$

The IQ ratio placed all children (regardless of age) on the same scale, which was centered at 100 if their mental age corresponded to their chronological age (see **Table 8.1** for examples of IQ calculations).

Terman's technical and theoretical contributions to psychological testing were modest. Yet he made a strong case for the educational benefits of testing and became the key force behind American schools' widespread adoption of IQ tests. As a result of his efforts,

TABLE 8.1 Calculating the Intelligence Quotient

Measure	Child 1	Child 2	Child 3	Child 4
Mental age (MA)	6 years	6 years	9 years	12 years
Chronological age (CA)	6 years	9 years	12 years	9 years
$IQ = \dfrac{MA}{CA} \times 100$	$\dfrac{6}{6} \times 100 = 100$	$\dfrac{6}{9} \times 100 = 67$	$\dfrac{9}{12} \times 100 = 75$	$\dfrac{12}{9} \times 100 = 133$

the Stanford-Binet quickly became the world's foremost intelligence test and the standard of comparison for virtually all intelligence tests that followed. Today, it remains one of the world's most widely used psychological tests.

Further advances in intelligence testing came from the work of David Wechsler (1939), who published the first high-quality IQ test designed specifically for *adults* in 1939. His test, the Wechsler Adult Intelligence Scale (WAIS), introduced two major innovations. First, Wechsler made his test less dependent on subjects' verbal ability than the Stanford-Binet. He included many items that required nonverbal reasoning. To highlight the distinction between verbal and nonverbal ability, he formalized the computation of separate scores for verbal IQ, performance (nonverbal) IQ, and full-scale (total) IQ. Second, Wechsler discarded the intelligence quotient in favor of a new scoring scheme based on the *normal distribution*. This scoring system has since been adopted by most other IQ tests, including the Stanford-Binet. Although the term *intelligence quotient* lingers on in our vocabulary, scores on intelligence tests are no longer based on an actual quotient (Urbina, 2011).

What Do Modern IQ Scores Mean?

As we discussed, scores on intelligence tests once represented a ratio of mental age to chronological age. However, this system has given way to one based on the normal distribution and the *standard deviation*, a statistical index of variability in a data distribution, which is explained in Appendix B. **The *normal distribution* is a symmetrical, bell-shaped curve that represents the pattern in which many characteristics are dispersed in the population.** When a trait is normally distributed, most cases fall near the center

In American culture, most people become familiar with standardized testing during their grade school years because they are repeatedly asked to take IQ tests and various other types of achievement tests. Standardized testing is a huge enterprise in the United States.

iStockphoto.com/Susan Chiang

of the distribution. The number of cases then gradually declines as one moves away from the center in either direction. The normal distribution provides a precise way to measure how people stack up in comparison to one another. The scores under the normal curve are dispersed in a fixed pattern, with the standard deviation serving as the unit of measurement (see **Figure 8.16**). About 68% of the scores in the distribution fall within one standard deviation of the mean, whereas 95% of the scores fall within two standard deviations of the mean.

Psychologists eventually recognized that intelligence scores fall into a normal distribution. This insight permitted David Wechsler to devise a more sophisticated scoring system for his tests that was eventually adopted by all modern IQ tests. In this system, raw scores are translated into ***deviation IQ scores* that locate respondents precisely within the normal distribution.** For most IQ tests, the mean of the distribution is set at 100 and the standard deviation (SD) is set at 15. These choices were made to provide continuity with the original IQ ratio (mental age to chronological age) that was centered at 100. In this system, which is shown in **Figure 8.16**, a score of 115 means that a person scored exactly one SD (15 points) above the mean. A score of 85 means that a person scored one SD below the mean. A score of 100 means that a person showed average performance. *The key point is that modern IQ scores indicate exactly where you fall in the normal distribution of intelligence.* Thus, a score of 120 does not indicate that you answered 120 questions correctly. Nor does it mean that you have 120 "units" of intelligence. A deviation IQ score places you at a specific point in the normal distribution of intelligence (based on the norms for your age group). Deviation IQ scores can be converted into *percentile scores,* as shown in **Figure 8.16**. **A *percentile score* indicates the percentage of people who score at or below the score one has obtained.**

FIGURE 8.16

The normal distribution. Many characteristics are distributed in a pattern represented by this bell-shaped curve. The horizontal axis shows how far above or below the mean a score is (measured in plus or minus standard deviations). The vertical axis is used to graph the number of cases obtaining each score. In a normal distribution, the cases are distributed in a fixed pattern. For instance, 68.26% of the cases fall between −1 and +1 standard deviation. Modern IQ scores indicate where a person's measured intelligence falls in the normal distribution. On most IQ tests, the mean is set at an IQ of 100 and the standard deviation at 15. Any deviation IQ score can be converted into a percentile score. The mental classifications at the bottom of the figure are descriptive labels that roughly correspond to ranges of IQ scores.

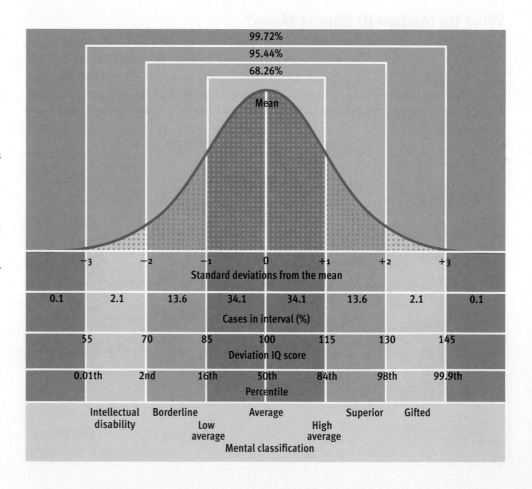

Do Intelligence Tests Have Adequate Reliability?

In the jargon of psychological testing, *reliability* **refers to the measurement consistency of a test.** A reliable test is one that yields similar scores upon repetition. Like other types of measuring devices, such as a stopwatch or a tire gauge, psychological tests need to be reasonably reliable (Geisinger, 2013). Estimates of reliability require the computation of correlation coefficients, which we introduced in Chapter 2. As you may recall, a *correlation coefficient* **is a numerical index of the degree of relationship between two variables** (see **Figure 8.17**). In gauging a test's reliability, the two variables that are correlated are typically two sets of scores from two administrations of the test. Do IQ tests produce consistent results when people are retested? Yes. Most IQ tests report commendable reliability estimates. The correlations generally range into the .90s (Kaufman, 2000), which is very high. In comparison with most other types of psychological tests, IQ tests are exceptionally reliable.

However, like other tests, they *sample* behavior, and a specific testing may yield an unrepresentative score. Variations in examinees' motivation to take an IQ test or in their anxiety about the test can sometimes produce misleading scores (Duckworth et al., 2011; Hopko et al., 2005). The most common problem is that low motivation or high anxiety can drag a person's score down on a particular occasion. Although the reliability of IQ tests is excellent, caution is always in order in interpreting test scores.

Do Intelligence Tests Have Adequate Validity?

Even if a test is quite reliable, we still need to be concerned about its validity. *Validity* **refers to the ability of a test to measure what it was designed to measure.** Validity can be estimated in several ways, depending on the nature of the test (Sireci & Sukin, 2013). In measuring an abstract personal quality, such as intelligence, one needs to be concerned about the test's *construct validity*. Do intelligence tests measure what they're supposed to measure? Yes, but this answer has to be qualified very carefully. IQ tests are valid measures of the kind of intelligence necessary to do well in academic work. But if the purpose is to assess intelligence in a broader sense, the validity of IQ tests is questionable.

As you may recall, intelligence tests were originally designed with a relatively limited purpose in mind: to predict school performance. This has continued to be the principal purpose of IQ testing. Efforts to document the validity of IQ tests have usually concentrated on their relationship to grades in school. Typically, positive correlations in the .40s

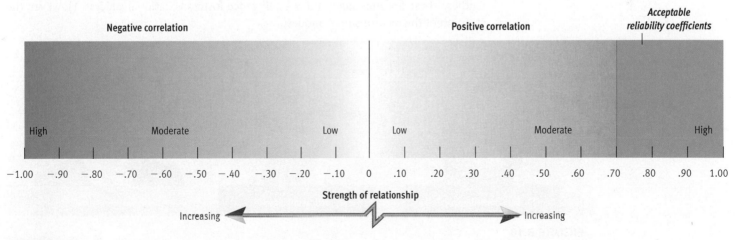

FIGURE 8.17

Correlation and reliability. As explained in Chapter 2, a positive correlation means that two variables co-vary in the *same* direction; a negative correlation means that two variables co-vary in the *opposite* direction. The closer the correlation coefficient gets to either −1.00 or +1.00, the stronger the relationship. At a minimum, reliability estimates for psychological tests must be moderately high positive correlations. Most reliability coefficients fall between .70 and .95.

and .50s are found between IQ scores and school grades (Mackintosh, 1998). Moreover, one huge study of more than 70,000 children in England found an even stronger relationship between intelligence and educational achievement. When Deary and colleagues (2007) used a composite measure of intelligence (based on several tests) to predict a composite estimate of educational progress (based on 25 achievement tests) 5 years later, they found correlations in the vicinity of .70.

These correlations are about as high as one could expect, given that many factors besides a person's intelligence are likely to affect grades and school progress. For example, school grades may be influenced by a student's motivation or personality, not to mention teachers' subjective biases. Indeed, one study reported that measures of students' *self-discipline* are surprisingly strong predictors of students' performance (Duckworth & Seligman, 2005). Thus, given all the other factors likely to influence performance in school, IQ tests appear to be reasonably valid indexes of school-related intellectual ability, or academic intelligence.

But the abilities assessed by IQ tests are not as broad or general as widely assumed by the public. When Robert Sternberg and his colleagues (1981) asked people to list examples of intelligence, they found that the examples fell into three categories: (1) *verbal intelligence,* (2) *practical intelligence,* and (3) *social intelligence* (see **Figure 8.18**). Thus, people generally recognize three basic components of intelligence. For the most part, IQ tests assess only the first of these three components, focusing somewhat narrowly on academic/verbal intelligence (Sternberg, 2003b).

Do Intelligence Tests Predict Vocational Success?

The data relating IQ to occupational attainment are pretty clear. *People who score high on IQ tests are more likely than those who score low to end up in high-status jobs* (Gottfredson, 2003b; Schmidt & Hunter, 2004). Because IQ tests measure school ability fairly well and school performance is important in attaining certain occupations, this link between IQ scores and job status makes sense. Of course, the correlation between IQ and occupational attainment is moderate. For example, in a meta-analysis of many studies of the issue, Strenze (2007) found a correlation of .37 between IQ and occupational status. That figure means there are plenty of exceptions to the general trend. Some people probably outperform brighter colleagues through bulldog determination and hard work. The relationship between IQ and income appears to be somewhat weaker. The meta-analysis by Strenze (2007) reported a correlation of .21 between IQ and income based on thirty-one studies. These findings suggest that intelligence fosters vocational success. However, the strength of the relationship is modest.

Verbal intelligence   Practical intelligence   Social intelligence

FIGURE 8.18

Laypersons' conceptions of intelligence. Robert Sternberg and his colleagues (1981) asked participants to list examples of behaviors characteristic of intelligence. The examples tended to sort into three groups that represent the three types of intelligence recognized by the average person: verbal intelligence, practical intelligence, and social intelligence. The three well-known individuals shown here are prototype examples of verbal intelligence (J. K. Rowling), practical intelligence (Jeff Bezos), and social intelligence (Jimmy Fallon).

There is far more debate about whether IQ scores are effective predictors of performance *within* a particular occupation. On the one hand, research suggests that (a) there is a substantial correlation (about .50) between IQ scores and job performance, and (b) this correlation varies somewhat depending on the complexity of a job's requirements, but does not disappear even for low-level jobs (Kuncel & Hezlett, 2010; Ones, Viswesvaran, Dilchert, 2005). On the other hand, critics argue that the reported correlations have usually been corrected for statistical artifacts and that the raw, uncorrected correlations are lower (.30s) (Outtz, 2002). They also note that even a correlation of .50 would provide only modest accuracy in prediction (accounting for about 25% of the variation in job performance). Concerns have also been raised that when IQ tests are used for job selection, they can have an adverse impact on employment opportunities for those in minority groups that tend to score somewhat lower (on average) on such tests (Murphy, 2002). In the final analysis, there is no question that intelligence is associated with vocational success. There is, however, room for argument about whether this association is strong enough to justify reliance on IQ testing in hiring employees.

Are IQ Tests Widely Used in Other Cultures?

In other Western cultures with European roots the answer is yes. In most non-Western cultures, the answer is only very little. IQ testing has a long history and continues to be a major enterprise in many Western countries, such as Britain, France, Norway, Canada, and Australia (Irvine & Berry, 1988). However, efforts to export IQ tests to non-Western societies have met with mixed results. The tests have been well received in some non-Western cultures, such as Japan, where the Binet-Simon scales were introduced as early as 1908 (Iwawaki & Vernon, 1988). But they have been met with indifference or resistance in other cultures, such as China and India. One reason is that some cultures have different conceptions of what intelligence is, and value different mental skills (Niu & Brass, 2011; Sternberg, 2007). Thus, the bottom line is that Western IQ tests do not translate well into the language and cognitive frameworks of many non-Western cultures (Sternberg, 2004).

Wigbert Röth/imageBROKER/Alamy

The skills and knowledge that are crucial to success vary from one culture to the next. IQ tests were designed to assess the skills and knowledge valued in modern, Western cultures. They have proven useful in some non-Western cultures that value similar sets of skills, but have also proven irrelevant in many cultures.

Key Learning Goals

- Summarize evidence that heredity affects intelligence, and discuss the concept of heritability.
- Describe various lines of research that indicate that environment affects intelligence.
- Evaluate heredity and socioeconomic disadvantage as explanations for cultural differences in IQ.

8.5 HEREDITY AND ENVIRONMENT AS DETERMINANTS OF INTELLIGENCE

Most early pioneers of intelligence testing maintained that intelligence is inherited (Mackintosh, 2011). Small wonder, then, that this view lingers in our society. Gradually, however, it has become clear that both heredity and environment influence intelligence (Tucker-Drob, Briley, & Harden, 2013; Davis, Arden, & Plomin, 2008). Does this mean that the nature versus nurture debate has been settled with respect to intelligence? Absolutely not. Theorists and researchers continue to argue vigorously about which is more important, in part because the issue has such far-reaching social and political implications.

Theorists who believe that intelligence is largely inherited downplay the value of special educational programs for underprivileged groups (Herrnstein & Murray, 1994; Kanazawa, 2006; Rushton & Jensen, 2005). They assert that a child's intelligence cannot be increased noticeably because genetic destiny cannot be altered. Other theorists take issue with this argument, pointing out that traits with a strong genetic component are not necessarily unchangeable (Flynn, 2007; Sternberg, Grigorenko, & Kidd, 2005). The people in this camp maintain that even more funds should be devoted to remedial education programs, improved schooling in lower-class neighborhoods, and college financial aid for the underprivileged. Because the debate over the role of heredity in intelligence has direct relevance to important social issues and political decisions, we'll take a detailed look at this complex controversy.

Evidence for Hereditary Influence

Researchers have long been aware that intelligence runs in families. However, *family studies* can determine only whether genetic influence on a trait is *plausible,* not whether it is certain. Family members share not just genes, but similar environments. If high intelligence (or low intelligence) appears in a family over several generations, this consistency could reflect the influence of either shared genes or shared environment. Because of this problem, researchers must turn to *twin studies* and *adoption studies* to obtain more definitive evidence on whether heredity affects intelligence.

Twin Studies

The best evidence regarding the role of genetic factors in intelligence comes from studies that compare identical and fraternal twins. The rationale for twin studies is that both identical and fraternal twins normally develop under similar environmental conditions. However, identical twins share more genetic kinship than fraternal twins. Thus, if pairs of identical twins are more similar in intelligence than pairs of fraternal twins, it's presumably because of their greater genetic similarity. (See Chapter 3 for a more detailed explanation of the logic underlying twin studies.)

What are the findings of twin studies regarding intelligence? McGue and colleagues (1993) reviewed the results of more than 100 studies of intellectual similarity for various kinds of kinship relations and childrearing arrangements. The key findings from their review are highlighted in **Figure 8.19**. This figure plots the average correlation observed for various types of relationships. As you can see, the average reported for identical twins (.86) is very high. This indicates that identical twins tend to be quite similar in intelligence. The average for fraternal twins (.60) is significantly lower. This correlation indicates that fraternal twins also tend to be similar in intelligence, but noticeably less similar than identical twins. These results support the notion that intelligence is inherited to a considerable degree (Plomin & Spinath, 2004).

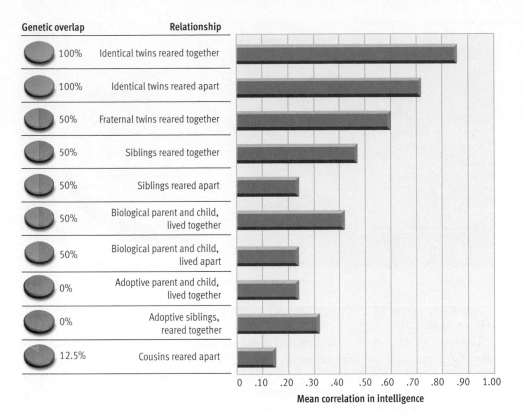

Genetic overlap	Relationship
100%	Identical twins reared together
100%	Identical twins reared apart
50%	Fraternal twins reared together
50%	Siblings reared together
50%	Siblings reared apart
50%	Biological parent and child, lived together
50%	Biological parent and child, lived apart
0%	Adoptive parent and child, lived together
0%	Adoptive siblings, reared together
12.5%	Cousins reared apart

0   .10   .20   .30   .40   .50   .60   .70   .80   .90   1.00
Mean correlation in intelligence

FIGURE 8.19

Studies of IQ similarity. The graph shows the mean correlations of IQ scores for people of various types of relationships, as obtained in studies of IQ similarity. Higher correlations indicate greater similarity. The results show that greater genetic similarity is associated with greater similarity in IQ, suggesting that intelligence is partly inherited (compare, for example, the correlations for identical and fraternal twins). However, the results also show that living together is associated with greater IQ similarity, suggesting that intelligence is partly governed by environment (compare, for example, the scores of siblings reared together and reared apart). (Data from McGue et al., 1993).

Of course, critics have tried to poke holes in this line of reasoning. They argue that identical twins are more alike in IQ because parents and others treat them more similarly than they treat fraternal twins. This environmental explanation of the findings has some merit. After all, identical twins are always the same gender, and gender influences how a child is raised. However, this explanation seems unlikely in light of the evidence on identical twins reared apart as a result of family breakups or adoption (Bouchard, 1997). *Although reared in different environments,* these identical twins still display greater similarity in IQ (average correlation: .72) than fraternal twins reared together (average correlation: .60).

Adoption Studies

Research comparing adopted children with their biological parents also provides evidence about the effects of heredity (and of environment, as we shall see). If adopted children resemble their biological parents in intelligence even though they were not reared by these parents, this finding supports the genetic hypothesis. The relevant studies indicate that there is indeed some measurable similarity between adopted children and their biological parents (refer again to **Figure 8.19**).

Heritability Estimates

Various experts have sifted through mountains of correlational evidence to estimate the *heritability* of intelligence. **A *heritability ratio* is an estimate of the proportion of trait variability in a population that is determined by variations in genetic inheritance.** Heritability can be estimated for any trait. For example, the heritability of height is estimated to be around 90% (Plomin, 2013). Heritability estimates for intelligence vary (see **Figure 8.20**). At the high end, some theorists estimate that the heritability of IQ ranges as high as 80%. That is, they believe that only about 20% of the variation in intelligence is attributable to environmental factors. Estimates at the low end of the spectrum suggest that the heritability of intelligence is around 40%. *In recent years,*

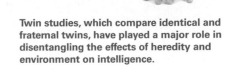

Twin studies, which compare identical and fraternal twins, have played a major role in disentangling the effects of heredity and environment on intelligence.

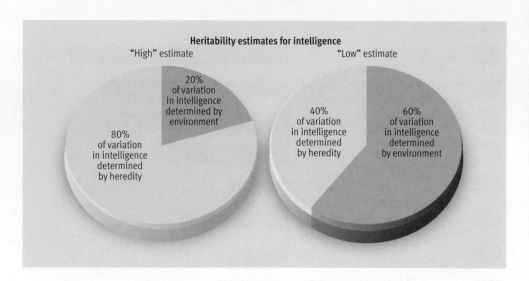

FIGURE 8.20

The concept of heritability. A heritability ratio is an estimate of the portion of variation in a trait determined by heredity—with the remainder presumably determined by environment—as these pie charts illustrate. Heritability estimates for intelligence range between a high of 80% and a low of 40%. The consensus estimate tends to hover around 50%. Bear in mind that heritability ratios are *estimates* and have certain limitations, which are discussed in the text.

the consensus estimates of the experts tend to hover around 50% (Petrill, 2005; Plomin, DeFries, et al., 2013).

However, it's important to understand that heritability estimates have certain limitations (Grigorenko, 2000; Johnson et al., 2009). First, a heritability estimate is a *group statistic* based on studies of trait variability within a specific group. A heritability estimate cannot be applied meaningfully to *individuals*. In other words, even if the heritability of intelligence truly is 60%, this does not mean that each individual's intelligence is 60% inherited. Second, the heritability of a trait can fluctuate over the life span. For example, recent research has demonstrated that the heritability of intelligence increases with age. In other words, heritability estimates in young children start out relatively low, increase considerably by adolescence, and continue to escalate gradually through middle age (Briley & Tucker-Drob, 2013). Third, the heritability of a specific trait can vary from one group to another depending on a variety of factors (Mandelman & Grigorenko, 2011). For example, evidence suggests that the heritability of intelligence is notably lower in samples drawn from lower socioeconomic strata than it is in samples drawn from middle- and upper-class homes (Nisbett et al., 2012). It appears that heritability is suppressed by the negative environmental conditions associated with poverty.

Although the concept of heritability is not as simple as it first appears, it is absolutely clear that IQ is influenced by heredity. New approaches to analyzing molecular genetics data, which have permitted scientists to quantify heritability in entirely different ways, have yielded heritability estimates that converge nicely with the estimates based on decades of twin and adoptions studies (Davies et al., 2011; Plomin, Haworth, et al., 2013). That said, molecular genetics research that has attempted to identify the specific genes that shape intelligence has yielded disappointing findings (Deary, 2012). Candidate genes discovered thus far have been found to have miniscule effects on intelligence, accounting for only tiny portions (well under 1% each) of the variation in cognitive ability (Plomin, 2013). Moreover, many of the reported associations between genetic variants and intelligence have proven difficult to replicate in subsequent studies (Chabris et al., 2012). Although researchers remain hopeful, efforts to map out the specific genes that govern intelligence have a long way to go.

Evidence for Environmental Influence

Heredity unquestionably influences intelligence, but a great deal of evidence indicates that upbringing also affects mental ability. We'll examine three lines of research—concerning adoption, environmental deprivation or enrichment, and generational changes in IQ—that show how life experiences shape intelligence.

Adoption Studies

Research with adopted children provides useful evidence about the impact of experience as well as heredity on intelligence (Nisbett et al., 2012). Many of the correlations in **Figure 8.19** reflect the influence of the environment. For example, adopted children show some resemblance to their foster parents in IQ. This similarity is usually attributed to the fact that their foster parents shape their environment. Adoption studies also indicate that siblings reared together are more similar in IQ than siblings reared apart. This is true even for identical twins. Moreover, entirely unrelated children who are raised in the same home also show a significant resemblance in IQ. All of these findings indicate that environment influences intelligence.

Environmental Deprivation and Enrichment

If environment affects intelligence, then children who are raised in substandard circumstances should experience a gradual decrease in IQ as they grow older (since other children will be progressing more rapidly). This *cumulative deprivation hypothesis* was tested decades ago. Researchers studied children consigned to understaffed orphanages and children raised in the poverty and isolation of the back hills of Appalachia (Sherman & Key, 1932; Stoddard, 1943). Generally, investigators *did* find that environmental deprivation led to the predicted decline in IQ scores.

Conversely, children who are removed from a deprived environment and placed in circumstances more conducive to learning tend to benefit from their environmental enrichment (Schiff & Lewontin, 1986). For example, a meta-analysis of relevant studies found that adopted children scored notably higher on IQ tests than siblings or peers "left behind" in institutions or disadvantaged homes (van IJzendoorn & Juffer, 2005). These gains are sometimes reduced if children suffer from severe, lengthy deprivation prior to their adoptive placement. But the overall trends clearly demonstrate that improved environments lead to increased IQ scores for most adoptees (Grotevant & McDermott, 2014). These findings show that IQ scores are not unchangeable and that they are sensitive to environmental influences.

Generational Changes: The Flynn Effect

The most interesting, albeit perplexing, evidence showcasing the importance of environment is the finding that performance on IQ tests has steadily increased over generations. This trend was not widely appreciated until relatively recently because the tests are revised periodically with new samples and scoring adjustments so that the mean IQ always remains at 100. However, in a study of the IQ tests used by the U.S. military, James Flynn noticed that the level of performance required to earn a score of 100 jumped upward every time the scoring was adjusted. Curious about this unexpected finding, he eventually gathered extensive data from twenty nations and demonstrated that IQ performance has been rising steadily all over the industrialized world since the 1930s (Flynn, 1987, 2003, 2011). Researchers who study intelligence are now scrambling to explain this trend, which has been dubbed the "Flynn effect." About the only thing they mostly agree on is that the Flynn effect has to be attributed to environmental factors because the modern world's gene pool could not have changed overnight (in evolutionary terms, 80 years is like a fraction of a second) (Dickens & Flynn, 2001; Sternberg et al., 2005).

At this point, the proposed explanations for the Flynn effect are conjectural, but it is worth reviewing some of them because they highlight the diversity of environmental factors that may shape IQ performance. Some theorists attribute generational gains in IQ test performance to reductions in the prevalence of severe malnutrition among children (Lynn, 2009). Others attribute the Flynn effect to increased access to schooling and more demanding curricula in schools over the course of the last century (Rönnlund & Nilsson, 2009). W. M. Williams (1998) discusses the importance of a constellation of factors, including improved schools, smaller families, better-educated parents, and higher-quality parenting. All of these speculations have some plausibility and are not mutually exclusive (R. L. Williams, 2013). Thus, the causes of the Flynn effect remain under investigation.

The Interaction of Heredity and Environment

Clearly, heredity and environment both influence intelligence to a significant degree (Petrill, 2005). And their effects involve intricate, dynamic, reciprocal interactions (Johnson, 2010; Tucker-Drob et al., 2013). Thus, many theorists now assert that the question of which is more important ought to take a backseat to the question of *how they interact* to govern IQ.

One line of thinking is that heredity sets certain limits on intelligence and that environmental factors determine where individuals fall within these limits (Bouchard, 1997; Hunt, 2011). According to this model, genetic makeup places an upper limit on a person's IQ that can't be exceeded even when environment is ideal. Heredity is also thought to place a lower limit on an individual's IQ, although extreme circumstances (for example, being locked in an attic for years) could drag a person's IQ beneath this boundary. Theorists use the term **reaction range to refer to these genetically determined limits on IQ (or other traits).**

According to the reaction-range model, children reared in high-quality environments that promote the development of intelligence should score near the top of their potential IQ range. Children reared under less ideal circumstances should score lower in their reaction range. The reaction range for most people is *estimated* to be around 20–25 points on the IQ scale (Weinberg, 1989). The concept of a reaction range can explain why high-IQ children sometimes come from poor environments. It can also explain why low-IQ children sometimes come from very good environments (see **Figure 8.21**). Moreover, it can explain these apparent paradoxes without discounting the importance of the environment.

CONCEPT CHECK 8.3

Understanding Correlational Evidence of the Heredity-Environment Question

Check your understanding of how correlational findings relate to the nature versus nurture issue by indicating how you would interpret the meaning of each "piece" of evidence described below. The figures inside the parentheses are the median IQ correlations observed for the relationships described (based on McGue et al., 1993), which are shown in **Figure 8.19**.

In the spaces on the left, enter the letter H if the findings suggest that intelligence is shaped by heredity, enter the letter E if the findings suggest that intelligence is shaped by the environment, and enter the letter B if the findings suggest that intelligence is shaped by both (or either) heredity and environment. The answers can be found in Appendix A.

_____ 1. Identical twins reared apart are more similar (.72) than fraternal twins reared together (.60).

_____ 2. Identical twins reared together are more similar (.86) than identical twins reared apart (.72).

_____ 3. Siblings reared together are more similar (.47) than siblings reared apart (.24).

_____ 4. Biological parents and the children they rear are more similar (.42) than unrelated persons who are reared apart (no correlation if sampled randomly).

_____ 5. Adopted children show similarity to their biological parents (.24) and to their adoptive parents (.24).

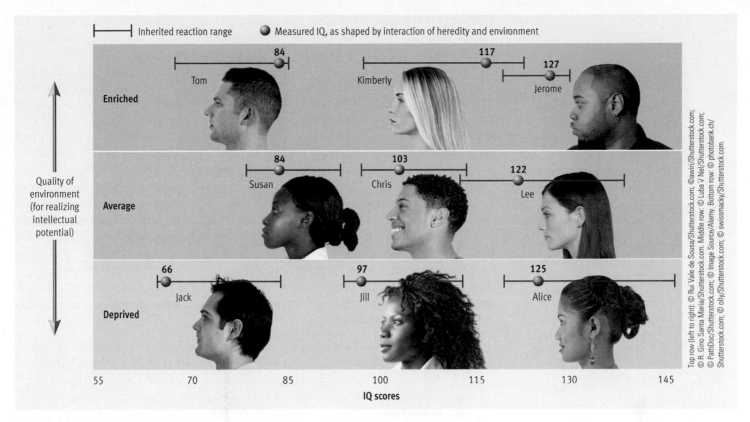

FIGURE 8.21

Reaction range. The concept of reaction range posits that heredity sets limits on one's intellectual potential (represented by the horizontal bars), while the quality of one's environment influences where one scores within this range (represented by the dots on the bars). People raised in enriched environments should score near the top of their reaction range, whereas people raised in poor-quality environments should score near the bottom of their range. Genetic limits on IQ can be inferred only indirectly, so theorists aren't sure whether reaction ranges are narrow (like Jerome's) or wide (like Kimberly's). The concept of reaction range can explain how two people with similar genetic potential can be quite different in intelligence (compare Tom and Jack) and how two people reared in environments of similar quality can score quite differently (compare Alice and Jack).

Cultural Differences in IQ Scores

Although the full range of IQ scores is seen in all ethnic groups, the average IQ for many of the larger minority groups in the United States (such as blacks, Native Americans, and Hispanics) is somewhat lower than the average for whites. The typical disparity is around 10 to 15 points, depending on the group tested and the IQ scale used (Hunt & Carlson, 2007; Nisbett, 2005). However, newer data suggest that the gap has shrunk in recent decades (Suzuki, Short, & Lee, 2011). There is relatively little argument about the existence of these group differences, variously referred to as racial, ethnic, or cultural differences in intelligence. The controversy concerns *why* the differences are found. A vigorous debate continues about whether cultural differences in intelligence are due to the influence of heredity or of environment.

Heritability as an Explanation

In 1969, Arthur Jensen sparked a heated war of words by arguing that racial differences in average IQ are largely due to heredity. The cornerstone for Jensen's argument was his analysis suggesting that the heritability of intelligence is about 80%. Essentially, he asserted that (1) intelligence is largely genetic in origin, and (2) therefore, genetic factors are "strongly implicated" as the cause of ethnic differences in intelligence. Jensen's article triggered bitter criticism in many quarters, as well as a great deal of additional research on the determinants of intelligence. Twenty-five years later, Richard Herrnstein and Charles

Murray (1994) reignited the same controversy with the publication of their widely discussed book *The Bell Curve*. They argued that ethnic differences in average intelligence are substantial, not easily reduced, and at least partly genetic in origin. The implicit message throughout *The Bell Curve* was that disadvantaged groups cannot avoid their fate because it is their genetic destiny. And as recently as 2010, based on an extensive review of statistical evidence, J. Phillipe Rushton and Arthur Jensen (2010) argued that genetic factors account for the bulk of the gap between races in average IQ.

As you might guess, these analyses and conclusions have elicited many lengthy and elaborate rebuttals. Critics argue that heritability explanations for ethnic differences in IQ have a variety of flaws and weaknesses (Brody, 2003; Horn, 2002; Nisbett, 2009; Sternberg, 2005a). For example, as noted earlier, the heritability of intelligence appears to be lower in the lower socioeconomic classes as opposed to higher socioeconomic classes (Tucker-Drob et al., 2011). Hence, there is doubt about the validity of applying heritability estimates based on the general population to cultural groups that are overrepresented in the lower classes.

Moreover, even if one accepts the assumption that the heritability of IQ is very high, it does not follow logically that differences in group averages must be due largely to heredity. Leon Kamin presents a compelling analogy that highlights the logical fallacy in this reasoning (see **Figure 8.22**):

> We fill a white sack and a black sack with a mixture of different genetic varieties of corn seed. We make certain that the proportions of each variety of seed are identical in each sack. We then plant the seed from the white sack in fertile Field A, while that from the black sack is planted in barren Field B. We will observe that within Field A, as within Field B, there is considerable variation in the height of individual corn plants. This variation will be due largely to genetic factors (seed differences). We will also observe, however, that the average height of plants in Field A is greater than that in Field B. That difference will be entirely due to environmental factors (the soil). The same is true of IQs: differences in the average IQ of various human populations could be entirely due to environmental differences, even if within each population all variation were due to genetic differences! (Eysenck & Kamin, 1981, p. 97)

Kamin's analogy shows that even if the heritability of intelligence is high, group differences in average IQ *could* still be caused entirely (or in part) by environmental factors (Block, 2002). For decades, critics of Jensen's thesis have relied on this analogy rather than actual data to make the point that between-groups differences in IQ do not necessarily reflect genetic differences. They depended on the analogy because no relevant data were available. However, the discovery of the Flynn effect has provided compelling data that are directly relevant (Flynn, 2003). Generational gains in IQ scores show that a between-groups disparity in average IQ (in this case the gap is between generations rather than ethnic groups) can be environmental in origin, even though intelligence is highly heritable.

Socioeconomic Disadvantage as an Explanation

Many social scientists argue that minority students' IQ scores are depressed because these children tend to grow up in deprived environments that create a disadvantage—both in school and on IQ tests. There is no question that, on the average, whites and minorities tend to be raised in very different circumstances. Most minority groups have endured a long history of economic discrimination and are greatly overrepresented in the lower social classes. A lower-class upbringing tends to carry a number of disadvantages that work against the development of a youngster's full intellectual potential (Bigelow, 2006; Dupere et al., 2010; Evans, 2004; Noble, McCandliss, & Farah, 2007; Yoshikawa, Aber, & Beardslee, 2012). In comparison with children from the middle and upper classes, lower-class children tend to be exposed to fewer books, to have fewer learning supplies and less access to computers, to have less privacy for concentrated study, and to get less parental

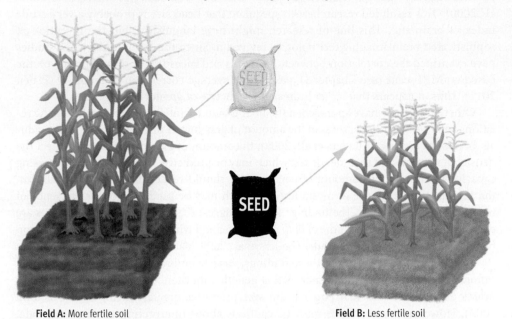

Individual variation in corn plant heights within each group (cause: genetic variation in the seeds)

Field A: More fertile soil

Field B: Less fertile soil

Differences in average corn plant height between groups
(cause: the soils in which the plants were grown)

FIGURE 8.22

Genetics and between-group differences on a trait. Leon Kamin's analogy (see text) shows how between-group differences on a trait (the average height of corn plants) could be due to environment, even if the trait is largely inherited. The same reasoning presumably applies to ethnic group differences in average intelligence.

assistance in learning. Typically, they also have poorer role models for language development, experience less pressure to work hard on intellectual pursuits, have less access to quality day care, and attend poorer-quality schools. Poor children (and their parents) also are exposed to far greater levels of neighborhood stress, which may disrupt parenting efforts and undermine youngsters' learning. Children growing up in poverty also suffer from greater exposure to environmental risks that may undermine intellectual development, such as poor prenatal care, lead poisoning, pollution, nutritional deficiencies, and substandard medical care (Daley & Onwuegbuzie, 2011; Suzuki et al., 2011).

In light of these disadvantages, it's not surprising that average IQ scores among children from lower social classes tend to run about 15 points below the average scores obtained by children from middle- and upper-class homes (Seifer, 2001; Williams & Ceci, 1997). This is the case even if race is factored out of the picture by studying whites exclusively. Admittedly, there is room for argument about the direction of the causal relationships underlying this association between social class and intelligence. Nonetheless, given the overrepresentation of minorities in the lower classes, many researchers argue that ethnic differences in intelligence are really social class differences in disguise.

8.6 NEW DIRECTIONS IN THE STUDY OF INTELLIGENCE

8.6

Key Learning Goals

- Understand evidence of the brain correlates of intelligence and the link between IQ and mortality.
- Explain Sternberg's cognitive analysis of intelligence and Gardner's theory of multiple intelligences.

Intelligence testing has been through a period of turmoil, and changes are on the horizon. In fact, many changes have occurred already. Let's look at some of the major new trends and projections for the future.

Exploring Biological Correlates of Intelligence

Researchers have begun to explore the relations between variations in intelligence and variations in specific characteristics of the brain. The early studies in this area used various measures of head size as an indicator of brain size. These studies generally found positive but very small correlations (average = .15) between head size and IQ (Vernon et al., 2000). This result led researchers to speculate that head size is probably a very crude index of brain size. This line of research might have languished, but the invention of sophisticated brain-imaging technologies revived it. Since the 1990s, quite a few studies have examined the correlation between IQ scores and measures of overall brain volume based on MRI scans (see Chapter 3), yielding an average correlation of about .40 (Haier, 2011). Thus, it appears that larger brains are predictive of greater intelligence.

Other researchers have approached the neural bases of intelligence by analyzing the relations between IQ and measures of the amount of gray matter or white matter in individuals' brains. According to Luders et al. (2009), the amount of gray matter should reflect the density of neurons and their dendrites, which may be predictive of information-processing capacity. In contrast, the amount of white matter should reflect the quantity of axons in the brain and their degree of myelinization, which may be predictive of the efficiency of neuronal communication. The findings thus far suggest that higher intelligence scores are correlated with increased volume of *both* gray matter and white matter, with the association being a little stronger for gray matter (Luders et al., 2009; Narr et al., 2007, Taki et al., 2012).

One obvious implication of these findings, eagerly embraced by those who tout the influence of heredity on intelligence, is that genetic inheritance gives some people larger brains than others and that larger brain size promotes greater intelligence (Rushton, 2003). However, as always, we must be cautious about interpreting correlational data. As discussed in Chapter 3, research has demonstrated that an enriched environment can produce denser neural networks and heavier brains in laboratory rats (Rosenzweig & Bennett, 1996). Thus, it is also possible that causation runs in the opposite direction— that developing greater intelligence promotes larger brain size, much like weightlifting can promote larger muscles (Nisbett et al., 2012).

Research on the biological correlates of intelligence has turned up another interesting finding. IQ scores measured in childhood correlate with physical health and even longevity decades later (Deary & Batty, 2011; Wrulich et al., 2014). Quite a number of studies have arrived at the conclusion that *smarter people tend to be healthier and live longer than others* (see **Figure 8.23**). Why is higher IQ linked to increased longevity? Researchers

FIGURE 8.23

The relationship between childhood IQ and mortality. Leon et al. (2009) examined the association between IQ measured at age 7 and mortality through the age of 57 in a sample of more than 11,000 people in the UK. The data in the graph are age-adjusted *relative* mortality rates in comparison with the reference group of people scoring near average (90–109) in intelligence. Thus, in comparison with the reference group, people who scored 70–79 were 22% more likely to die by age 57, and people who scored over 130 were less than half as likely to die by age 57. As you can see, there is a clear trend. As IQ scores go up, mortality rates decline.

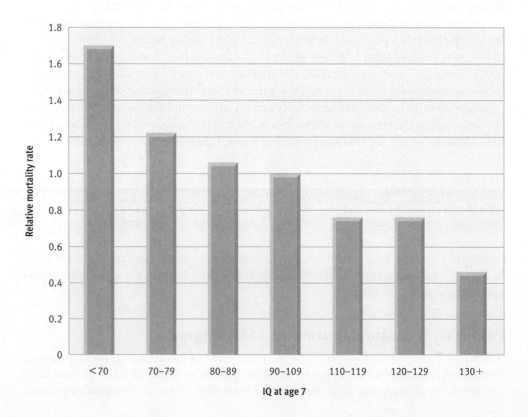

have offered a variety of explanations (Arden, Gottfredson, & Miller, 2009; Batterham, Christensen, & Mackinnon, 2009; Wrulich et al., 2013). One possibility is that good genes could foster both higher intelligence and resilient health. A second possibility is that health self-care is a complicated lifelong mission, for which brighter people are better prepared. In other words, smarter people may be more likely to avoid health-impairing habits (such as smoking and overeating), to be proactive about health (such as exercising and taking vitamins), and to use medical care more effectively (such as knowing when to seek treatment). A third possibility is that intelligence fosters educational and career success, which means that brighter people are more likely to end up in higher socioeconomic strata. People in higher socioeconomic classes tend to have less-stressful jobs with lower accident risks, reduced exposure to toxins and pathogens, better health insurance, and greater access to medical care. Thus, affluence could be the key factor linking intelligence to longevity. These explanations are not mutually exclusive. They might all contribute to the association between IQ and longevity.

Investigating Cognitive Processes in Intelligent Behavior

Investigators interested in intelligence and scholars who have studied cognition have traditionally pursued separate lines of research that only rarely intersected. However, since the mid-1980s, Robert Sternberg (1985, 1991) has spearheaded an effort to apply a cognitive perspective to the study of intelligence. His cognitive approach emphasizes the need to understand how people use their intelligence.

In recent versions of his *triarchic theory of successful intelligence,* Sternberg (1999, 2005b; 2012) asserts there are three aspects, or facets, of intelligence: analytical intelligence, creative intelligence, and practical intelligence (see **Figure 8.24**). *Analytical intelligence* involves abstract reasoning, evaluation, and judgment. It is the type of intelligence that is crucial to most schoolwork and that is assessed by conventional IQ tests. *Creative intelligence* involves the ability to generate new ideas and to be inventive in dealing with novel problems. *Practical intelligence* involves the ability to deal effectively with the kinds of problems people encounter in everyday life, such as on the job or at home. A big part of practical intelligence involves acquiring *tacit knowledge*—what one needs to know in a particular environment in order to work efficiently, but that is not explicitly taught and often is not even verbalized. According to Sternberg, *successful intelligence* consists of individuals' ability to harness their analytical, creative, and practical intelligence to achieve their life goals within their cultural context by taking advantage of their strengths and compensating for their weaknesses.

In a series of studies, Sternberg and his colleagues gathered data suggesting that (1) all three facets of intelligence can be measured reliably, (2) the three facets of intelligence are relatively independent (uncorrelated), and (3) the assessment of all three aspects of intelligence can improve the prediction of intelligent behavior in the real world (Henry, Sternberg, & Grigorenko, 2005; Sternberg, 2011). Some critics doubt that Sternberg's measures will facilitate better prediction of meaningful outcomes than done by traditional IQ tests (Gottfredson, 2003a), but that is an empirical question that should be resolved by future research. In any event, Sternberg certainly has been an articulate voice arguing for a broader, expanded concept of intelligence, which is a theme that has been echoed by others.

Expanding the Concept of Intelligence

In recent years, many theorists have concluded that traditional IQ tests are too narrow in focus. This view has been articulated particularly well by Howard Gardner (1983, 1999, 2006; Davis et al., 2011). According to Gardner, IQ tests have generally emphasized verbal and mathematical skills, to the exclusion of other important skills. He suggests the existence of a number of relatively independent *human intelligences,* which are listed in **Figure 8.25**. To build his list of separate intelligences, Gardner reviewed the evidence of cognitive capacities in normal individuals; people suffering from brain damage; and

Researchers are not sure why higher intelligence is associated with greater longevity. Several processes may be at work. All we know at this point is that extremely bright people, such as Warren Buffett, have a better chance of living into their eighties and nineties than their less intelligent counterparts.

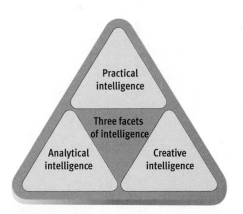

FIGURE 8.24

Sternberg's theory of intelligence. Sternberg's (2003a, 2005b) model of intelligence proposes that there are three aspects or types of intelligence: analytical intelligence, practical intelligence, and creative intelligence. According to Sternberg, traditional IQ tests focus almost exclusively on analytical intelligence. He believes that the prediction of real-world outcomes could be improved by broadening intelligence assessments to tap practical and creative intelligence.

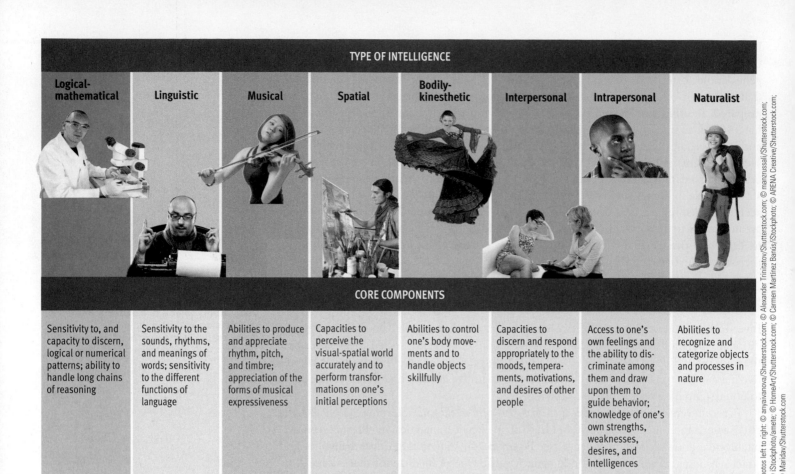

FIGURE 8.25

Gardner's eight intelligences. Howard Gardner argues for an expanded view of intelligence. He asserts that humans display eight very different forms of intelligence, which he maintains are largely independent of one another.

special populations, such as prodigies and idiot savants. He concluded that humans exhibit eight largely independent intelligences: logical-mathematical, linguistic, musical, spatial, bodily-kinesthetic, interpersonal, intrapersonal, and naturalist. These intelligences obviously include a variety of talents that are not assessed by conventional IQ tests. Gardner is investigating the extent to which these intelligences are largely independent, as his theory asserts. For the most part, he has found that people tend to display a mixture of strong, intermediate, and weak abilities, which is consistent with the idea that the various types of intelligence are independent.

Gardner's books have been very popular, and his theory clearly resonates with many people (Shearer, 2004). His ideas have had an enormous impact on educators' attitudes and beliefs around the world (Kaufman, Kaufman, & Plucker, 2013). He has raised thought-provoking questions about what abilities should be included under the rubric of intelligence. However, he has his critics (Hunt, 2001; Visser, Ashton, & Vernon, 2006; Waterhouse, 2006; White, 2006). Some argue that his use of the term *intelligence* is so broad, encompassing virtually any valued human ability, that the term is almost meaningless (Davidson & Kemp, 2011). These critics wonder whether there is any advantage to relabeling talents such as musical ability and motor coordination as forms of intelligence. Critics also note that Gardner's theory has not generated much research on the predictive value of measuring individual differences in the eight intelligences he has described. This research would require the development of tests to measure the eight intelligences, but Gardner is not particularly interested in the matter of assessment, and he loathes conventional testing. This situation makes it difficult to predict where his theory will lead, as research is crucial to the evolution of a theory.

8.7

Key Learning Goals
- Identify the five unifying themes highlighted in this chapter.

Five of our unifying themes surfaced in this chapter. The first is the empirical nature of psychology. For many decades, psychologists paid little attention to cognitive processes because most of them assumed that thinking is too private to be studied scientifically. During the 1950s and 1960s, however, psychologists began to devise creative new ways to measure mental processes. These innovations, which fueled the cognitive revolution, show that empirical methods are the lifeblood of the scientific enterprise.

Second, our review of cognition and intelligence demonstrated the importance of cultural factors. For example, we learned that there are striking cultural variations in cognitive style. We also saw that intelligence testing is largely a Western phenomenon and that ethnic differences in average intelligence may be largely cultural in origin. Thus, we see once again that if we hope to achieve a sound understanding of behavior, we need to appreciate the cultural contexts in which behavior unfolds.

Third, our coverage showed that intelligence is shaped by a complex interaction of hereditary and environmental factors. We've drawn a similar conclusion before in other chapters where we examined other topics. However, this chapter should have enhanced your appreciation of this idea by illustrating in detail how scientists arrive at this conclusion.

Fourth, we saw more evidence that psychology evolves in a sociohistorical context. Prevailing social attitudes have always exerted some influence on testing practices and the interpretation of test results. In the first half of the 20th century, a strong current of racial and class prejudice was apparent in the United States and Britain. This prejudice supported the idea that IQ tests measured innate ability and that "undesirable" groups scored poorly because of their genetic inferiority. Although these beliefs did not go unchallenged within psychology, their widespread acceptance in the field reflected the social values of the time. Today, the continuing, ferocious debate about the roots of cultural differences in intelligence shows that issues in psychology often have far-reaching social and political implications.

The final theme apparent in this chapter was the subjective nature of human experience, which was prominent in our discussion of peculiarities in human decision making.

 Empiricism

 Cultural Heritage

 Heredity & Environment

 Sociohistorical Context

 Subjectivity of Experience

CONCEPT CHECK 8.4

Recognizing Conceptions of Intelligence

Check your understanding of various theories on the nature of intelligence by matching the names of their originators with the brief descriptions of the theories' main themes that appear below. Choose from the following theorists: (a) Alfred Binet, (b) Howard Gardner, (c) Arthur Jensen, (d) Lewis Terman, (e) Robert Sternberg, and (f) David Wechsler. The answers are in Appendix A.

_____ 1. This psychologist developed the Stanford-Binet Intelligence Scale, which originally described children's scores in terms of an intelligence quotient.

_____ 2. This theorist posited eight human intelligences: logical-mathematical, linguistic, musical, spatial, bodily-kinesthetic, interpersonal, intrapersonal, and naturalist.

_____ 3. This person distinguished between verbal and nonverbal ability, and discarded the intelligence quotient in favor of a scoring scheme based on the normal distribution.

_____ 4. This theorist stated that the heritability of intelligence is very high and that IQ differences between ethnic groups are mainly due to genetics.

_____ 5. This French psychologist devised the first successful intelligence test, which expressed a child's score in terms of mental age.

_____ 6. This person's theory posits that there are three facets of intelligence: analytical, practical, and creative intelligence.

8.8

Key Learning Goals
- Evaluate the role of insight and divergent thinking in creativity, and discuss creativity tests.
- Clarify the associations between creativity and personality, intelligence, and mental illness.

8.8 PERSONAL APPLICATION
Measuring and Understanding Creativity

Answer the following "true" or "false":

____ 1 Creative ideas often come out of nowhere.

____ 2 Creativity usually occurs in a burst of insight.

____ 3 Creativity and intelligence are unrelated.

Intelligence is not the only type of mental ability that psychologists have studied. They have devised tests to explore a variety of mental abilities. Among these, creativity is certainly one of the most interesting. People tend to view creativity as an essential trait for artists, musicians, and writers. However, it is important in *many* walks of life. In this Application, we'll discuss psychologists' efforts to measure and understand creativity. As we progress, you'll learn that all the statements above are false.

The Nature of Creativity

What makes thought creative? *Creativity* **involves the generation of ideas that are original, novel, and useful.** Creative thinking is fresh, innovative, and inventive. But novelty by itself is not enough. In addition to being unusual, creative thinking must be adaptive. It must be appropriate to the situation and problem.

Does Creativity Occur in a Burst of Insight?

It is widely believed that creativity usually involves sudden flashes of insight and great leaps of imagination. Robert Weisberg (1986) calls this belief the "Aha! myth." Undeniably, creative bursts of insight do occur (Feldman, 1988). However, the evidence suggests that major creative achievements generally are logical extensions of existing ideas, involving long,

hard work and many small, faltering steps forward. Creative ideas do not come out of nowhere. They come from a deep well of experience and training in a specific area, whether it's music, painting, business, or science (Weisberg, 1999, 2006). For example, one recent study of an engineering team's brainstorming sessions found that progress toward creative solutions tended to be incremental (Chan & Schunn, 2014).

Does Creativity Depend on Divergent Thinking?

According to many theorists, the key to creativity lies in *divergent thinking*—thinking "that goes off in different directions," as J. P. Guilford (1959) put it. Guilford distinguished between convergent thinking and divergent thinking. **In** *convergent thinking* **one tries to narrow down a list of alternatives to converge on a single correct answer.** For example, when you take a multiple-choice exam, you try to eliminate incorrect options until you hit on the correct response. Most training in school encourages convergent thinking. **In** *divergent thinking* **one tries to expand the range of alternatives by generating many possible solutions.** Imagine that you work for an advertising agency. To come up with as many slogans as possible for a client's product, you must use divergent thinking. Some of your slogans may be clear losers, and eventually you will have to engage in convergent thinking to pick the best. But coming up with the range of new possibilities depends on divergent thinking.

Thirty years of research on divergent thinking has yielded mixed results. As a whole, the evidence suggests that divergent thinking contributes to creativity. However, it clearly does not represent the essence of creativity, as originally proposed (Runco, 2010; Weisberg, 2006). In retrospect, it was unrealistic to

expect creativity to depend on a single cognitive skill.

Measuring Creativity

Although its nature may be elusive, creativity clearly is important in today's world. Creative masterpieces in the arts and literature enrich human existence. Creative inventions fuel technological progress. Thus, it is understandable that psychologists have been interested in measuring creativity with psychological tests.

How Do Psychological Tests Assess Creativity?

A diverse array of psychological tests have been devised to measure individuals' creativity (Plucker & Makel, 2010). Usually, the items on creativity tests give respondents a specific starting point and then require them to generate as many possibilities as they can in a short period of time. Typical items on a creativity test might include the following: (1) List as many uses as you can for a newspaper. (2) Think of as many fluids that burn as you can. (3) Imagine that people no longer need sleep and think of as many consequences as you can. Participants' scores on these tests depend on the *number* of alternatives they generate and on the *originality* and *usefulness* of the alternatives.

How Well Do Tests Predict Creative Productivity?

In general, studies indicate that creativity tests are mediocre predictors of creative achievement in the real world (Plucker & Makel, 2010; Zeng, Proctor, & Salvendy, 2011). Why? One reason is that these tests measure creativity in the abstract, as a *general trait*. However, the accumulation of evidence suggests that, to a large degree, *creativity is specific to particular domains* (Baer, 2013; Feist, 2004; Kaufman

& Baer, 2004). Despite some rare exceptions, creative people usually excel in a single field, in which they typically have considerable training and expertise. An innovative physicist might have no potential to be a creative poet. Measuring this person's creativity outside of physics may be meaningless.

Correlates of Creativity

What are creative people like? Are they brighter or less well adjusted than average? A great deal of research has been conducted on the correlates of creativity.

Is There a Creative Personality?

There is no single personality profile that accounts for creativity (Weisberg, 2006). However, investigators have found modest correlations between certain personality characteristics and creativity. Research suggests that highly creative people tend to be more independent, nonconforming, introverted, open to new experiences, self-confident, persistent, ambitious, dominant, and impulsive (Feist, 1998, 2010). At the core of this set of personality characteristics are the related traits of nonconformity and openness to new experiences. Creative people tend to think for themselves and are less easily influenced by the opinions of others than the average person is. The importance of openness to new experiences can be seen in a new line of research suggesting that living abroad enhances creativity.

Although living abroad has long been viewed as a rite of passage for creative artists and writers, no one thought to take an empirical look at its impact until relatively recently. In a series of studies, Maddux and Galinsky (2009) found that the amount of time spent living abroad correlated positively with measures of creativity. Interestingly, time spent in tourist travel did *not* predict creativity. The contrasting effects of living and traveling abroad seem to depend on acculturation. Maddux and Galinsky found that the degree to which people adapted to foreign cultures was responsible for the association between living abroad and creativity. A subsequent study found that individuals who identify with both their home culture and their temporary host culture benefit the most from living abroad (Tadmor, Galinsky, & Maddux, 2012). Apparently, a bicultural mentality fosters an enhanced ability to view problems from multiple perspectives and to integrate those perspectives, thus fostering more flexible, creative thinking.

Are Creativity and Intelligence Related?

Are creative people exceptionally smart? Conceptually, creativity and intelligence represent different types of mental ability. Thus, it's not surprising that correlations between measures of creativity and measures of intelligence are generally weak (Kaufman & Plucker, 2011). For example, a meta-analysis of many studies reported a correlation of only .17 (Kim, 2005).

Is There a Connection Between Creativity and Mental Illness?

There may be a connection between truly exceptional creativity and mental illness—in particular, mood disorders, such as depression. When Nancy Andreasen studied thirty accomplished writers who had been invited as visiting faculty to the prestigious Iowa Writers Workshop, she found that 80% of her sample had suffered a mood disorder at some point in their lives (Andreasen, 1987, 2005). In a similar study of fifty-nine female writers from another writers'

conference, Ludwig (1994) found that 56% had experienced depression. These figures are far above the base rate (roughly 15%) for mood disorders in the general population. Other studies have also found an association between creativity and the prevalence of psychological disorders (Jamison, 1988; Kyaga et al., 2013; Silvia & Kaufman, 2010). Perhaps the most ambitious examination of the issue has been Arnold Ludwig's (1995) analyses of the biographies of 1004 people who achieved eminence in eighteen fields. He found greatly elevated rates of depression and other disorders among eminent writers, artists, and composers (see **Figure 8.26**). Thus, accumulating empirical data tentatively suggest a correlation between major creative achievement and vulnerability to mental disorders.

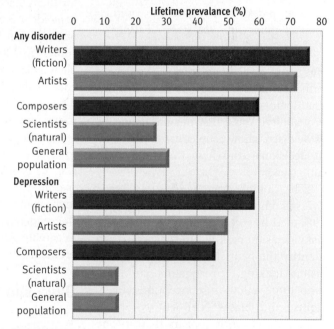

FIGURE 8.26

Estimated prevalence of psychological disorders among people who achieved creative eminence. Ludwig (1995) studied biographies of 1004 people who had clearly achieved eminence in one of eighteen fields and tried to determine whether each person suffered from any specific mental disorders in his or her lifetime. The data summarized here show the prevalence rates for depression and for a mental disorder of any kind for four fields in which creativity is often the key to achieving eminence. As you can see, the estimated prevalence of mental illness was extremely elevated among eminent writers, artists, and composers (but not natural scientists) in comparison with the general population, with depression accounting for much of this elevation.

Key Learning Goals
* Describe the gambler's fallacy, the tendency to overestimate the improbable, framing effects, and loss aversion.

8.9 CRITICAL THINKING APPLICATION
Understanding Pitfalls in Reasoning About Decisions

Consider the following scenario:

Laura is in a casino watching people play roulette. The thirty-eight slots in the roulette wheel include eighteen black numbers, eighteen red numbers, and two green numbers. Hence, on any one spin, the probability of red or black is slightly less than 50–50 (.474, to be exact). Although Laura hasn't been betting, she has been following the pattern of results in the game very carefully. The ball has landed in red seven times in a row. Laura concludes that black is long overdue, and she jumps into the game, betting heavily on black.

Has Laura made a good bet? Do you agree with Laura's reasoning? Or do you think that Laura misunderstands the laws of probability? You'll find out momentarily, as we discuss how people reason their way to decisions—and how their reasoning can go awry.

The pioneering work of Amos Tversky and Daniel Kahneman (1974, 1982) led to an explosion of research on risky decision making. In their efforts to identify the heuristics people use in decision making, investigators stumbled onto quite a few misconceptions, oversights, and biases (LeBoeuf & Shafir, 2012). Moreover, it appears that no one is immune to these errors in thinking. Research indicates that extremely bright people are just as vulnerable to irrational thinking as everyone else is (Stanovich, 2012). Fortunately, however, some research suggests that increased awareness of common shortcomings in reasoning about decisions can lead to improved decision making (Lilienfeld, Ammirati, & Landfield, 2009). With this goal in mind, let's look at some common pitfalls in decision making.

The Gambler's Fallacy

Laura's reasoning in our opening scenario is flawed. Laura's behavior illustrates **the gambler's fallacy—the belief that the odds of a chance event increase if the event hasn't occurred recently.** People believe that the laws of probability should yield fair results. If they believe that a process is random, they expect the process to be self-correcting (Burns & Corpus, 2004). These aren't bad assumptions in the long run. However, they don't apply to individual, independent events.

The roulette wheel does not remember its recent results and make adjustments for them. Each spin of the wheel is an independent event. The probability of black on each spin remains at .474, even if red comes up 100 times in a row! The gambler's fallacy reflects the pervasive influence of the *representativeness heuristic*. In betting on black, Laura is predicting that future results will be more representative of a random process. This logic can be used to estimate the probability of black across a *string of spins*. But it doesn't apply to a *specific spin* of the roulette wheel. Interestingly, some recent research suggests that the tendency to perceive illusory streaks in gambling situations might contribute to problem gambling (Wilke et al., 2014).

Overestimating the Improbable

Let's examine another issue that frequently crops up in working with probabilities.

Various causes of death are paired up below. In each pairing, which is the more likely cause of death?

Asthma or tornadoes?
Accidental falls or gun accidents?
Tuberculosis or floods?
Suicide or murder?

Table 8.2 shows the actual fatality numbers for each of the causes of death just listed. As you can see, the first choice in each pair is the more common cause of death. If you guessed wrong for several pairings, don't feel bad. Like many other people, you may be a victim of the tendency to *overestimate the improbable*. People tend to greatly overestimate the likelihood of dramatic, vivid—but infrequent—events that receive heavy media coverage. Thus, the number of fatalities due to tornadoes, shooting accidents, floods, and murders is usually overestimated (Slovic, Fischhoff, & Lichtenstein, 1982). Fatalities due to asthma and other common diseases that receive less media coverage tend to be underestimated. For instance, even though tuberculosis has largely been eradicated and garners no attention in the press, deaths from this disease outnumber flood deaths by about 18 to 1! This tendency to exaggerate the improbable has generally been attributed to operation of the *availability heuristic* (Reber, 2004). Instances of floods, tornadoes, and such are readily available in memory because people are

TABLE 8.2 Annual Deaths for Selected Causes

Cause of Death	Number	Cause of Death	Number
Asthma	3345	Tornadoes	70
Accidental falls	27,483	Firearms accidents	591
Tuberculosis	539	Floods	29
Suicide	39,518	Homicide	16,238

Note: All data are for the United States in 2011 based on Mortality Multiple Cause Micro-Data Files from the CDC (http://www.cdc.gov/nchs/data_access/Vitalstatsonline.htm), except for tornadoes and floods, which are based on National Weather Service statistics for 2012.

exposed to a great deal of media coverage of such events. As a general rule, people's beliefs about what they should fear tend to be surprisingly inconsistent with actual probabilities (Glassner, 1999).

The Effects of Framing

Another consideration in making decisions involving risks is the framing of questions (Tversky & Kahneman, 1988, 1991). *Framing refers to how decision issues are posed or how choices are structured.* People often allow a decision to be shaped by the language or context in which it's presented, rather than explore it from different perspectives. Consider the following scenario adapted from Kahneman and Tversky (1984, p. 343):

> Imagine that the United States is preparing for the outbreak of a dangerous disease, which is expected to kill 600 people. Two alternative programs to combat the disease have been proposed. Assume that the exact scientific estimates of the consequences of the programs are as follows.

- If Program A is adopted, 200 people will be saved.
- If Program B is adopted, there is a one-third probability that all 600 people will be saved and a two-thirds probability that no people will be saved.

Kahneman and Tversky found that 72% of their subjects chose the "sure thing" (Program A) over the "risky gamble" (Program B). However, they obtained different results when the alternatives were reframed as follows:

- If Program C is adopted, 400 people will die.
- If Program D is adopted, there is a one-third probability that nobody will die and a two-thirds probability that all 600 people will die.

Although framed differently, Programs A and B represent exactly the same probability situation as Programs C and D (see **Figure 8.27**). In spite of this, 78% of the subjects chose Program D. Thus, subjects chose the sure thing when the decision was framed in terms of lives saved. They went with the risky gamble, however, when the decision was framed in terms of lives lost. Obviously, sound decision making should yield consistent decisions that are not altered dramatically by superficial changes in how options are presented.

Loss Aversion

Another interesting phenomenon is *loss aversion*—in general, losses loom larger than gains of equal size (Novemsky & Kahneman, 2005). Thus, most people expect that the negative impact of losing $1000 will be greater than the positive impact of winning $1000. Loss aversion can lead people to pass up excellent opportunities. For instance, subjects tend to decline a theoretical gamble in which

they are given an 85% chance of doubling their life savings versus a 15% chance of losing their life savings, which mathematically is vastly more attractive than any bet one could place in a casino (Gilbert, 2006). Loss aversion can influence decisions in many areas of life, including choices of consumer goods, investments, business negotiations, and approaches to health care (Camerer, 2005). The problem with loss aversion is that people generally overestimate the intensity and duration of the negative emotions they will experience after all sorts of losses, ranging from losing a job or romantic partner to botching an interview or watching one's team lose in a big game (Kermer et al., 2006; see Chapter 9).

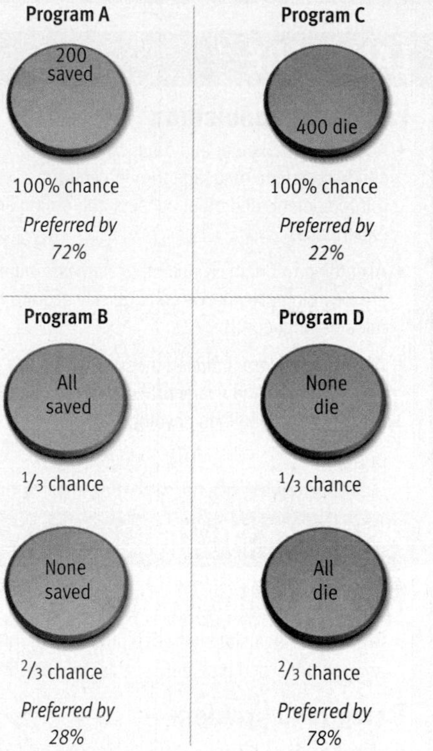

FIGURE 8.27

The framing of questions. This chart shows that Programs A and B are parallel in probability to Programs C and D, but these parallel pairs of alternatives lead subjects to make different choices. Studies show that when choices are framed in terms of possible gains, people prefer the safer plan. However, when choices are framed in terms of losses, people are more willing to take a gamble.

TABLE 8.3 Critical Thinking Skills Discussed in This Application

Skill	Description
Understanding the limitations of the representativeness heuristic	The critical thinker understands that focusing on prototypes can lead to inaccurate probability estimates.
Understanding the limitations of the availability heuristic	The critical thinker understands that the ease with which examples come to mind may not be an accurate guide to the probability of an event.
Recognizing framing effects	The critical thinker is aware that how choices are posed or structured can influence subjective perceptions of probabilities.
Understanding loss aversion	The critical thinker appreciates that losses subjectively seem larger than gains of equal size.

LANGUAGE

Language acquisition

- According to Skinner and other *behaviorists*, children acquire language through imitation, reinforcement, and other aspects of learning and experience.
- According to Chomsky and other *nativists*, humans are neurologically prewired to quickly acquire the rules of language.
- According to *interactionist* theories, an innate predisposition and a supportive environment both contribute to language development.

Bilingualism

- There is little empirical support for the belief that bilingualism slows language development.
- Bilinguals have a slight handicap in processing speed, but they have advantages in attention, working memory capacity, and reasoning.

Language and thought

- The *linguistic relativity hypothesis* asserts that one's language shapes the nature of one's thought processes.
- Empirical support for the linguistic relativity hypothesis has increased considerably in recent years.

© Ton Koene photography/Getty Images

PROBLEM SOLVING

Types of problems

- Greeno distinguished between problems of inducing structure, problems of arrangement, and problems of transformation.

Barriers to problem solving

- People are often distracted by irrelevant information.
- *Functional fixedness* is the tendency to perceive an item only in terms of its most common use.
- A *mental set* exists when people persist in using strategies that have worked in the past but are no longer optimal.
- People often impose unnecessary constraints on their possible solutions.

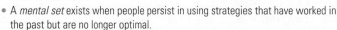

Approaches to problem solving

- *Trial and error* is a common, albeit primitive, approach to problem solving.
- A *heuristic* is a rule of thumb or mental shortcut used in solving problems or making decisions.
- It is often useful to formulate intermediate subgoals.
- If you can spot an analogy between one problem and another, a solution may become apparent.
- When progress is stalled, changing the representation of a problem often helps.
- Research on *incubation effects* suggests that taking a break from a problem can sometimes enhance problem-solving efforts.

Culture and problem solving

- Cross-cultural disparities have been observed in problem-solving style.
- Research suggests that Eastern cultures exhibit a more holistic cognitive style, whereas Western cultures display a more analytical cognitive style.

DECISION MAKING

Basic strategies

- Simon's *theory of bounded rationality* asserts that people tend to use simple decision strategies that often yield seemingly irrational results because they can only juggle so much information at once.
- Schwartz argues that in modern societies, people suffer from choice overload, which leads to rumination, regret, and diminished well-being.
- Research suggests that intuitive, unconscious decisions often are more satisfying than those based on conscious deliberation.
- Risky decision making involves making choices under conditions of uncertainty.

© Les and Dave Jacobs/Cultura/Getty Images

Common heuristics and flaws

- The *availability heuristic* involves basing the estimated probability of an event on the ease with which relevant instances come to mind.
- The *representative heuristic* involves basing the estimated probability of an event on how similar it is to the typical prototype of that event.
- In estimating probabilities, people often ignore base rates because of the influence of the representativeness heuristic.
- The *conjunction fallacy* occurs when people estimate that the odds of two uncertain events happening together are greater than the odds of either event happening alone.
- Evolutionary psychologists argue that humans seem irrational because cognitive psychologists have been asking questions that have nothing to do with the adaptive problems the human mind has evolved to solve.
- According to Gigerenzer, people mostly depend on *fast and frugal heuristics* that are much simpler than the complicated inferential processes studied in traditional cognitive research.
- Dual-process theories assert that people depend on both quick, automatic, intuitive thinking and slower, effortful, controlled thinking.

MEASURING INTELLIGENCE

History of intelligence tests

- Modern intelligence testing was launched in 1905 by Binet, who devised a scale to measure a child's mental age.
- Terman revised the Binet scale to produce the Stanford-Binet in 1916, which introduced the *intelligence quotient (IQ)*.
- In 1939, Wechsler published an improved measure of intelligence for adults, which introduced the *deviation IQ score* based on the normal distribution.

Essentials of intelligence testing

- Modern deviation IQ scores indicate where people fall in the normal distribution for their age.
- Individuals' IQ scores can vary across testing occasions, but intelligence tests tend to have very high reliability.
- There is ample evidence that IQ tests are valid measures of academic/verbal intelligence, but they do not tap social or practical intelligence.
- IQ scores are correlated with occupational attainment, but doubts have been raised about how well they predict performance within a specific occupation.
- IQ tests are not widely used in most non-Western cultures.

HEREDITY AND ENVIRONMENT AS DETERMINANTS OF INTELLIGENCE

Evidence for hereditary influence

- *Twin studies* show that identical twins are more similar in intelligence than fraternal twins, suggesting that intelligence is at least partly inherited.
- Even more impressive, identical twins reared apart are more similar in intelligence than fraternal twins reared together.
- *Adoption studies* show that adopted children resemble their biological parents in intelligence.
- A *heritability ratio* is an estimate of the proportion of trait variability in a population that is determined by genetic variations.
- Estimates of the heritability of intelligence range from 40% to 80%, and mostly converge around 50%, but heritability ratios have limitations.

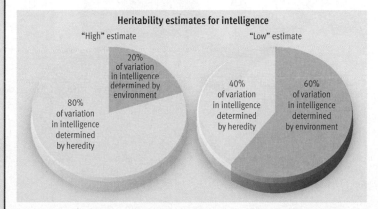

Heritability estimates for intelligence

"High" estimate
- 20% of variation in intelligence determined by environment
- 80% of variation in intelligence determined by heredity

"Low" estimate
- 40% of variation in intelligence determined by heredity
- 60% of variation in intelligence determined by environment

Evidence for environmental influence

- *Adoption studies* find that adopted children show some IQ resemblance to their foster parents and to their adoptive siblings.
- Studies of *environmental deprivation and enrichment* show that children's IQ scores change in response to altered circumstances.
- The *Flynn effect* refers to the finding that performance on IQ tests has steadily increased over generations.

The interaction of heredity and environment

- Evidence clearly shows that intelligence is shaped by both heredity and environment, and that these influences interact.
- The *reaction range model* posits that heredity sets limits to one's intelligence, and that environmental factors determine where people fall within these limits.

The debate about cultural differences in IQ scores

- Jensen and others have argued that cultural differences in IQ scores are largely due to heredity.
- Even if the heritability of IQ is high, group differences in IQ could be entirely environmental in origin.
- Many scientists believe that cultural differences in IQ are attributable to socioeconomic disadvantage.

NEW DIRECTIONS

- Recent research has uncovered moderate positive correlations between IQ and overall brain volume and the volume of gray and white matter.
- Researchers have found that IQ measured in childhood correlates with longevity decades later.
- Sternberg's theory uses a cognitive perspective, which emphasizes the need to understand how people use their intelligence.
- According to Sternberg, the three facets of successful intelligence are analytical, creative, and practical intelligence.
- Gardner argues that the concept of intelligence should be expanded to encompass a diverse set of eight types of abilities, which are independent of one another.

APPLICATIONS

- Creativity does not usually involve sudden insight; creativity tests are mediocre predictors of creative productivity.
- The association between creativity and intelligence is weak; creative geniuses may exhibit heightened vulnerability to psychological disorders.
- The *gambler's fallacy* is the belief that the odds of a chance event increase if the event hasn't occurred recently.
- People tend to inflate estimates of improbable events that garner heavy media coverage, because of the availability heuristic.
- Research shows that people overestimate the negative impact of losses.

CHAPTER 9

MOTIVATION AND EMOTION

© Alinute Silzeviciute/Shutterstock.com

Themes in this Chapter

Cultural Heritage   Sociohistorical Context   Theoretical Diversity   Heredity & Environment

Multifactorial Causation

It was a bright afternoon in May 1996, and 41-year-old Jon Krakauer was on top of the world—literally. Krakauer had just fulfilled a boyhood dream by climbing Mount Everest, the tallest peak on Earth. Clearing the ice from his oxygen mask, he looked down on a sweeping vista of ice, snow, and majestic mountains. His triumph should have brought him intense joy. Yet, he felt strangely detached. "I'd been fantasizing about this moment, and the release of emotion that would accompany it, for many years," he wrote later. "But now that I was finally here, standing on the summit of Mount Everest, I just couldn't summon the energy to care" (Krakauer, 1998, p. 6).

Why were Krakauer's emotions so subdued? A major reason was that he was physically exhausted. Climbing Mount Everest is an incredibly grueling experience. At just over 29,000 feet, the mountain's peak is at the altitude flown by jumbo jets. Because such high altitudes wreak havoc on the human body, Krakauer and his fellow climbers couldn't even approach the summit until they had spent 6 weeks acclimating at Base Camp, 17,600 feet above sea level.

From Base Camp, it's another 2 vertical miles through the aptly named Death Zone to the summit. By the time Krakauer reached the summit, every step was labored, every gasping breath hurt. He was bitterly cold. He was utterly exhausted. Instead of elation, he felt only apprehension because he understood that getting down from the summit would be just as dangerous as getting up. During Krakauer's descent, a sudden, howling storm hit the mountain. Krakauer barely escaped with his life. Twelve men and women were not as fortunate. They died on the mountain, including several in Krakauer's own party.

The saga of Jon Krakauer and the other climbers is packed with motivation riddles. Why would people push on toward a goal even at the risk of their lives? Why endure such a punishing and hazardous ordeal? In the case of Mount Everest, perhaps the most obvious motive is simply the satisfaction of conquering the world's tallest peak. When British climber George Leigh Mallory was asked why he wanted to climb Everest in the 1920s, his famous reply was, "Because it is there." Some

Christian Kober/Getty Images

Climbing to the summit of Mount Everest is always a daunting and dangerous challenge, as Jon Krakauer's story demonstrates.

people seem to have an intense desire to take on the toughest challenges imaginable.

Krakauer's story is also filled with strong emotions. He anticipated that he would experience a transcendent emotional high when he reached the summit of Mount Everest. As it turned out, his triumph was accompanied more by anxiety than by ecstasy. The harrowing events that followed left him emotionally numb at first. However, he was soon flooded with intense feelings of despair, grief, and guilt over the deaths of his companions. His tale illustrates the intimate connection between motivation and emotion—the topics we'll examine in this chapter.

9.1 MOTIVATIONAL THEORIES

Motives are the needs, wants, interests, and desires that propel people in certain directions. In short, *motivation* **involves goal-directed behavior.** Psychologists have devised a number of theoretical approaches to motivation. Let's look at some of these theories and related concepts.

Drive Theories

Many theories view motivational forces in terms of *drives*. The concept of drive was derived from Walter Cannon's (1932) observation that organisms seek to maintain *homeostasis,* **a state of physiological equilibrium or stability.** The body maintains homeostasis in various ways. For example, human body temperature normally fluctuates around 98.6 degrees Fahrenheit (see **Figure 9.1**). If your body temperature rises or drops noticeably, automatic responses occur: If your temperature goes up, you'll perspire. If your temperature goes down, you'll shiver. These reactions are designed to move your temperature back toward 98.6 degrees. Thus, your body reacts to many disturbances in physiological stability by trying to restore equilibrium.

Drive theories apply the concept of homeostasis to behavior. **A *drive* is a hypothetical, internal state of tension that motivates an organism to engage in activities that should reduce this tension.** These unpleasant states of tension are viewed as disruptions of the preferred equilibrium. According to drive theories, when individuals experience a drive, they're motivated to pursue actions that will lead to *drive reduction.* For example, the hunger motive has usually been viewed as a drive system. If you go without food for a while, you begin to experience some discomfort. This internal tension (the drive) motivates you to obtain food. Eating reduces the drive and restores physiological equilibrium.

Drive theories have been very influential, and the drive concept continues to be widely used in modern psychology. *However, drive theories cannot explain all motivation* (Berridge, 2004). Homeostasis appears irrelevant to some human motives, such as a "thirst for knowledge." And think of all the times that you've eaten when you weren't the least bit hungry. Drive theories can't explain this behavior very well.

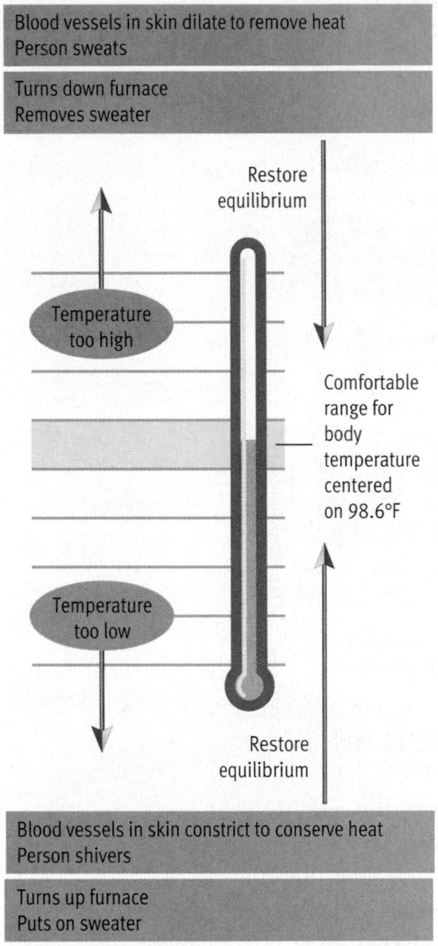

Incentive Theories

Incentive theories propose that external stimuli regulate motivational states (Bolles, 1975; McClelland, 1975). **An *incentive* is an external goal that has the capacity to motivate behavior.** Ice cream, a juicy steak, a monetary prize, approval from friends, an A on an exam, and a promotion at work are all incentives. Some of these incentives may reduce drives, but others may not.

Drive and incentive models of motivation are often contrasted as *push versus pull* theories. Drive theories emphasize how *internal* states of tension *push* people in certain directions. Incentive theories emphasize how *external* stimuli *pull* people in certain directions. According to drive theories, the source of motivation lies *within* the organism. According to incentive theories, the source of motivation lies *outside* the organism, in the environment. Thus, incentive models emphasize the role of environmental factors rather than the principle of homeostasis.

Evolutionary Theories

Psychologists who take an evolutionary perspective assert that the motives of humans and of other species are the products of evolution, just as anatomical characteristics are. They argue that natural selection favors behaviors that maximize reproductive success;

Blood vessels in skin dilate to remove heat
Person sweats

Turns down furnace
Removes sweater

Restore equilibrium

Temperature too high

Comfortable range for body temperature centered on 98.6°F

Temperature too low

Restore equilibrium

Blood vessels in skin constrict to conserve heat
Person shivers

Turns up furnace
Puts on sweater

FIGURE 9.1

Temperature regulation as an example of homeostasis. The regulation of body temperature provides a simple example of how organisms often seek to maintain homeostasis, or a state of physiological equilibrium. When your temperature moves out of an acceptable range, automatic bodily reactions (such as sweating or shivering) occur that help restore equilibrium. Of course, these automatic reactions may not be sufficient by themselves, so you may have to take other actions (such as turning a furnace up or down) to bring your body temperature back into its comfort zone.

that is, passing on genes to the next generation. Thus, they explain motives such as affiliation, achievement, dominance, aggression, and sex drive in terms of their adaptive value (Durrant & Ellis, 2013).

Evolutionary analyses of motivation are based on the premise that motives can best be understood in terms of the adaptive problems they have solved over the course of human history. For example, the need for dominance is thought to be greater in men than in women because it could facilitate males' reproductive success in a variety of ways. For instance, females may prefer mating with dominant males, dominant males may poach females from subordinate males, dominant males may intimidate male rivals in competition for sexual access, and dominant males may acquire more material resources that may increase mating opportunities (Buss, 2014). Consider, also, the *affiliation motive,* or need for belongingness. The adaptive benefits of affiliation for our ancestors probably included help with offspring, collaboration in hunting and gathering, mutual defense, opportunities for sexual interaction, and so forth (Griskevicius, Haselton, & Ackerman, 2015). Hence, humans developed a strong need to belong and a strong aversion to rejection (Neuberg & Schaller, 2015). David Buss (1995) points out that it is not by accident that achievement, power (dominance), and intimacy are among the most heavily studied motives because the satisfaction of each of these motives is likely to affect one's reproductive success.

Motivational theorists of all persuasions agree on one point: humans display an enormous diversity of motives. These include a host of *biological motives,* such as hunger, thirst, and sex, and a variety of *social motives,* such as the needs for achievement, affiliation, autonomy, dominance, and order. Given the range and diversity of human motives, we can only examine a handful in depth. To a large degree, our choices reflect the motives psychologists have studied the most: hunger, sex, and achievement. After our discussion of these motivational systems, we will explore the elements of emotional experience and discuss various theories of emotion.

9.2 THE MOTIVATION OF HUNGER AND EATING

9.2

Key Learning Goals

- Summarize evidence of the physiological factors implicated in the regulation of hunger.
- Explain how food availability, culture, and learning influence hunger.
- Describe evidence of the prevalence, health consequences, and roots of obesity.

Why do people eat? Because they're hungry. What makes them hungry? A lack of food. Any grade-school child can explain these basic facts. So hunger is a simple motivational system, right? Wrong! Hunger is deceptive. It only looks simple. Actually, it's a puzzling and complex motivational system.

Biological Factors in the Regulation of Hunger

You have probably had embarrassing occasions when your stomach growled loudly at an untimely moment. Someone may have commented, "You must be starving!" Most people equate a rumbling stomach with hunger, and in fact, the first scientific theories of hunger were based on this simple equation. In an elaborate 1912 study, Walter Cannon and A. L. Washburn verified what most people have noticed based on casual observation: there is an association between stomach contractions and the experience of hunger.

Based on this correlation, Cannon theorized that stomach contractions *cause* hunger. However, as we've seen before, correlation is no assurance of causation. His theory was eventually discredited. Stomach contractions often accompany hunger, but they don't cause it. How do we know? Because later research showed that people continue to experience hunger even after their stomachs have been removed out of medical necessity (Wangensteen & Carlson, 1931). If hunger can occur without a stomach, then stomach contractions can't be the cause of hunger. This realization led to more elaborate theories of hunger that focus on (1) the role of the brain, (2) digestive factors, and (3) hormones.

Brain Regulation

Research with lab animals eventually suggested that the experience of hunger is controlled in the brain—specifically, in the hypothalamus. As we have noted before, the *hypothalamus* is a tiny structure involved in the regulation of a variety of biological needs related to survival (see **Figure 9.2**). In the 1940s and 1950s, researchers found that when they surgically destroyed animals' *lateral hypothalamus* (*LH*), the animals showed little or no interest in eating, as if their hunger center had been wiped out (Anand & Brobeck, 1951). In contrast, when researchers destroyed animals' *ventromedial nucleus of the hypothalamus* (*VMH*), the animals ate excessively and gained weight rapidly, as if their ability to recognize satiety (fullness) had been neutralized (Brobeck, Tepperman, & Long, 1943). These results led to the conclusion that the lateral hypothalamus and ventromedial nucleus of the hypothalamus were the brain's on-off switches for the control of hunger (Stellar, 1954).

However, over the course of several decades, a variety of empirical findings undermined the dual-centers model of hunger (Winn, 1995). The current thinking is that the lateral and ventromedial areas of the hypothalamus are elements in the neural circuitry that regulates hunger. However, they are not the key elements, nor simple on-off centers (Meister, 2007). Today, scientists believe that two other areas of the hypothalamus—the *arcuate nucleus* and the *paraventricular nucleus*—play a larger role in the modulation of hunger (Scott, McDade, & Luckman, 2007; see **Figure 9.2**). In recent years, the arcuate nucleus has been singled out as especially important (Moran & Sakai, 2013).

Contemporary theories of hunger focus more on *neural circuits* that pass through areas of the hypothalamus rather than on *anatomical centers* in the brain. These circuits depend on a large variety of neurotransmitters and they appear to be much more complicated than anticipated. Evidence suggests that the neural circuits regulating hunger are massively and reciprocally interconnected with extensive parallel processing (Powley, 2009). This complex neural circuitry is sensitive to a diverse range of physiological processes.

Digestive and Hormonal Regulation

The digestive system includes a variety of mechanisms that influence hunger (Ritter, 2004). It turns out that Walter Cannon was not entirely wrong in hypothesizing that the stomach regulates hunger. After you have consumed food, the stomach can send a variety of signals to the brain that inhibit further eating (Woods & Stricker, 2008). For instance, the vagus nerve carries information about the stretching of the stomach walls that indicates when the stomach is full. Other nerves carry satiety messages that depend on how rich in nutrients the contents of the stomach are.

A variety of hormones circulating in the bloodstream appear to contribute to the regulation of hunger (Schwartz, 2012). For example, after the body goes without food for a while, the stomach secretes *ghrelin,* which causes stomach contractions and promotes hunger. In contrast, after food is consumed, the upper intestine releases a hormone called *CCK* that delivers satiety signals to the brain, thus reducing hunger.

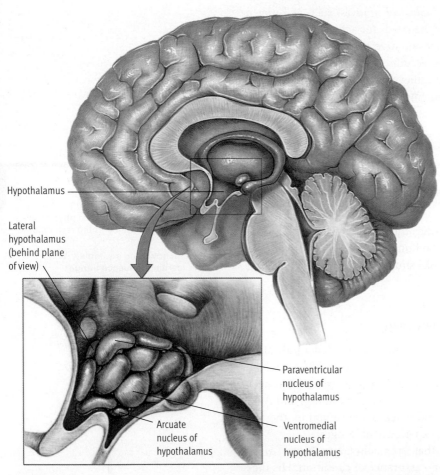

FIGURE 9.2

The hypothalamus. This small structure at the base of the forebrain plays a role in regulating a variety of human biological needs, including hunger. The detailed blow-up shows that the hypothalamus is made up of a variety of discrete areas. Scientists used to believe that the lateral and ventromedial areas were the brain's on-off centers for eating. However, more recent research suggests that the arcuate and paraventricular areas may be more crucial to the regulation of hunger and that thinking in terms of neural circuits rather than anatomical centers makes more sense.

Finally, evidence indicates that a hormone called *leptin* contributes to the long-term regulation of hunger, as well as the regulation of numerous other bodily functions (Ramsay & Woods, 2012). Leptin is produced by fat cells throughout the body and released into the bloodstream. Leptin circulates through the bloodstream and ultimately provides the hypothalamus with information about the body's fat stores (Dietrich & Horvath, 2012). When leptin levels are high, the propensity to feel hungry diminishes. When leptin levels are low, signals arriving in the brain promote increased hunger. *Insulin,* a hormone secreted by the pancreas, is also sensitive to fluctuations in the body's fat stores. The hormonal signals that influence hunger (the fluctuations of insulin, ghrelin, CCK, and leptin) all seem to converge in the hypothalamus, especially the arcuate and paraventricular nuclei (Moran & Sakai, 2013).

Environmental Factors in the Regulation of Hunger

Hunger clearly is a biological need. But eating is not regulated by biological factors alone. Studies show that social and environmental factors govern eating to a considerable extent.

Food Availability and Related Cues

Most of the research on the physiological regulation of hunger has been based on the assumption that hunger operates as a drive system in which homeostatic mechanisms are at work. However, some theorists emphasize the incentive value of food. They argue that humans and other animals are often motivated to eat not by the need to compensate for energy deficits but by the anticipated pleasure of eating (Finlayson, Dalton, & Blundell, 2012; Johnson, 2013). This perspective has been bolstered by evidence that a variety of environmental variables exert significant influence over food consumption:

- *Palatability.* As you might expect, the better food tastes, the more of it people consume (de Castro, 2010). This principle is not limited to humans. The eating behavior of rats and other animals is also influenced by palatability.
- *Quantity available.* A powerful determinant of the amount eaten is the amount available. People tend to consume what is put in front of them. The more food people are served, the more they eat (Rolls, 2012). For example, one study found that people consumed 45% more popcorn when it was served in larger containers (Wansink & Kim, 2005). In another study, young children requested almost twice as much cereal when it was served into a large bowl as opposed to a small one (Wansink, van Ittersum, & Payne, 2014). Similarly, diners at a buffet with large plates consumed 45% more (and wasted 135% more!) than diners given smaller plates (Wansink & van Ittersum, 2013). Unfortunately, in recent decades, the size of grocery store packages, restaurant portions, and dinnerware has increased steadily (Wansink, 2012). These bloated cues about what represents "normal" food consumption clearly fuel increased eating.
- *Variety.* Humans and animals increase their consumption when a greater variety of foods are available (Temple et al., 2008). As you eat a specific food, its incentive value declines. This phenomenon is called *sensory-specific satiety* (Meillon et al., 2013). If only a few foods are available, the appeal of all of them can decline quickly. But if many foods are available, people can keep shifting to new foods and end up eating more overall. This principle explains why people are especially likely to overeat at buffets, where many foods are available.
- *Presence of others.* On average, individuals eat 44% more when they eat with other people as opposed to eating alone. The more people present, the more food people tend to eat (de Castro, 2010). When two people eat together, they tend to reciprocally adjust their intake, eating roughly the same amount (Hermans et al., 2012). When asked afterward, people seem oblivious of the fact that their eating is influenced by the presence of others.
- *Stress.* Stress has varied effects on eating, as some individuals eat less, but estimates suggest that roughly 40%–50% of people increase their food consumption in times of stress (Sproesser, Schupp, & Renner, 2014). In many people, stress also appears to foster a shift toward less healthy food choices, such as loading up on sweets and fatty foods (Michels et al., 2012).

The more food people are served, the more they tend to consume. Hence, the gradual increase in the size of food servings clearly contributes to increased eating.

According to incentive models of hunger, the availability and palatability of food are key factors regulating hunger. An abundance of diverse foods tends to lead to increased eating.

RosalreneBetancourt 5/Alamy

- *Exposure to food cues.* Eating can be triggered by exposure to cues that have been associated with food (Wansink & Chandon, 2014). You have no doubt had your hunger aroused by television commercials for delicious-looking meals or by seductive odors coming from the kitchen. Consistent with this observation, studies have shown that exposure to food advertisements incites hunger and leads to increased food intake (Harris, Bargh, & Brownell, 2009). Unfortunately, the mere sight or smell of tasty food can lead people to think how pleasurable it would be to consume the food and undermine their willpower (Stroebe et al., 2013).

Learned Preferences and Habits

Are you fond of eating calves' brains? How about eel or snake? Could I interest you in a grasshopper or some dog meat? Probably not. Yet these are delicacies in some regions of the world. Arctic Eskimos like to eat maggots! You probably prefer chicken, apples,

Food preferences are influenced greatly by culture. For example, the fried grasshoppers shown here would not be a treat for most Americans, but they are a delicacy in some cultures.

© Don Mammoser/Shutterstock.com

eggs, lettuce, potato chips, pizza, cornflakes, or ice cream. These preferences are acquired through learning. People from different cultures display very different patterns of food consumption (Rozin, 2007). If you doubt this fact, just visit an ethnic grocery store.

Taste preferences are partly a function of learned associations formed through *classical conditioning* (Appleton, Gentry, & Shepherd, 2006). For instance, youngsters can be conditioned to prefer flavors paired with pleasant events. Of course, as we learned in Chapter 6, taste aversions can also be acquired through conditioning when foods are followed by nausea (Reilly & Schachtman, 2009). Eating habits are also shaped by *observational learning* (see Chapter 6). To a large degree, food preferences are a matter of exposure (Cooke, 2007). People generally prefer familiar foods. Geographical, cultural, religious, and ethnic factors limit people's access to certain foods, but repeated exposures to a new food usually lead to increased liking. However, as many parents have learned the hard way, forcing a child to eat a specific food can backfire and have a negative effect on the youngster's preference for the required food (Benton, 2004).

Eating and Weight: The Roots of Obesity

As we've seen, hunger is regulated by a complex interaction of biological and psychological factors. The same kinds of complexities emerge when investigators explore the roots of *obesity,* **the condition of being overweight.** Most experts assess obesity in terms of *body mass index (BMI)*—**weight (in kilograms) divided by height (in meters) squared (kg/m²).** This index of weight controls for variations in height. A BMI of 25.0–29.9 is typically regarded as overweight, and a BMI over 30 is generally considered obese. American culture seems to be obsessed with slimness, but surveys show surprisingly sharp increases in the incidence of obesity in recent decades. In one highly regarded study of a nationally representative U.S. sample, 40% of the subjects were found to be overweight and another 28.5% were obese (Flegal et al., 2010). Overweight adults have plenty of company from their children, as weight problems have tripled among children and adolescents (Ogden et al., 2012). Moreover, the obesity epidemic has become a global problem, spreading from affluent countries to much of the world, including many relatively poor countries (Popkin, 2012).

Theorists have a plausible explanation for the dramatic increase in the prevalence of obesity (Blass, 2012; King, 2013). They point out

---

CONCEPT CHECK 9.1

Understanding Factors in the Regulation of Hunger

Check your understanding of the effects of the various factors that influence hunger by indicating whether hunger and eating would tend to increase or decrease in each of the situations described below. Indicate your choice by marking an I (increase), a D (decrease), or a ? (can't be determined without more information) next to each situation. You'll find the answers in Appendix A.

_____ 1. Jameer's stomach has just secreted the hormone ghrelin.

_____ 2. The leptin levels in Marlene's bloodstream have increased in recent weeks.

_____ 3. Norman wasn't hungry, but his roommate just brought home a delicious-looking pizza that smells great.

_____ 4. You're offered an exotic, strange-looking food from another culture and told that everyone in that culture loves it.

_____ 5. Darius is eating at a huge buffet where an enormous variety of foods is available.

_____ 6. You have just been served your meal at a new restaurant. You are astonished by the enormous size of the meal.

© Christo/Shutterstock.com

Many theorists maintain that the increased prevalence of obesity is due to the fact that modern societies are characterized by obesogenic environments where tasty, tempting food is everywhere around us.

Lynne Sutherland/Alamy

that, over the course of history, most humans lived in environments characterized by fierce competition for limited, unreliable food resources. Thus, they evolved a propensity to consume more food than immediately necessary when the opportunity presented itself because food might not be available later. Excess calories were stored in the body (as fat) to prepare for future food shortages. However, in today's modern, industrialized societies, the vast majority of humans live in environments that provide an abundant, reliable supply of highly palatable food. In these environments, the evolved tendency to overeat when food is plentiful leads many people down a path of chronic, excessive food consumption. Of course, because of variations in genetics, metabolism, and other factors, only some become overweight.

If obesity merely affected people's vanity, there would be little cause for concern. Unfortunately, obesity is a big health problem that elevates one's mortality risk. Obese individuals are more vulnerable than others to coronary disease, stroke, hypertension, diabetes, respiratory problems, gallbladder disease, arthritis, muscle and skeletal pain, sleep apnea, and some types of cancer (Corsica & Perri, 2013; Ogden, 2010). Moreover, recent evidence suggests that obesity may foster inflammatory and metabolic changes that contribute to the development of Alzheimer's disease (Letra, Santana, & Seica, 2014; Spielman, Little, & Klegeris, 2014). **Figure 9.3** shows how the prevalence of diabetes, hypertension, coronary heart disease, and musculoskeletal pain are elevated as BMI increases. Clearly, obesity is a significant health problem. Hence, scientists have devoted a great deal of attention to the causes of obesity. Let's look at some of the factors they have identified.

Genetic Predisposition

Research suggests that obesity is partly a matter of hereditary influence (Price, 2012). In an influential *twin study,* Stunkard and colleagues (1990) found that identical twins reared apart were far more similar in BMI than fraternal twins reared together (see **Figure 9.4**). In another study of over 4000 twins, Allison and colleagues (1994) estimated that genetic factors account for 61% of the variation in weight among men and 73% among women.

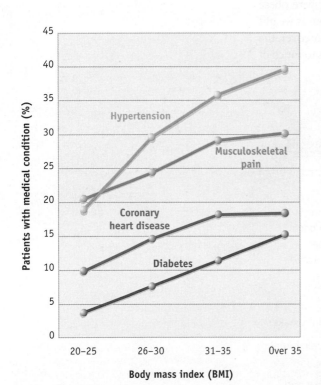

FIGURE 9.3

Weight and the prevalence of various diseases. This graph shows how obesity, as indexed by BMI, is related to the prevalence of four common types of illness. The prevalences of diabetes, heart disease, muscle pain, and hypertension increase as BMI goes up, suggesting that obesity is a significant health risk. (Based on data in Brownell & Wadden, 2000).

Thus, it appears that some people inherit a genetic *vulnerability* to obesity (Chung & Leibel, 2012).

Excessive Eating and Inadequate Exercise

The bottom line for overweight people is that they eat too much in relation to their level of exercise. In modern America, the tendency to overeat and exercise too little is easy to understand (Henderson & Brownell, 2004). Tasty, high-calorie, high-fat foods and sugar-sweetened drinks are readily available nearly everywhere—not just in restaurants and grocery stores, but in shopping malls, airports, gas stations, schools, and workplaces. Today, Americans spend almost one-half of their food dollars in restaurants, where they tend to eat more than they typically consume at home (Corsica & Perri, 2013). Unhealthy foods are heavily advertised, and these marketing efforts are very effective in getting people to increase their consumption of such foods (Horgen, Harris, & Brownell, 2012). The inability to control overeating has become so common that some theorists are coming around to the view that highly processed, high-fat, high-sugar foods may literally be addictive (Ahmed, 2012; Gearhardt & Corbin, 2012). Modern societies are thought to create a toxic, "obesogenic" environment for eating. Unfortunately, the rise of this obesogenic environment has been paralleled by a significant decline in physical activity (Corsica & Perri, 2013). Modern conveniences, such as cars and elevators; and changes in the world of work, such as the shift to more desk jobs; and increases in TV viewing and video-gaming have conspired to make American lifestyles more sedentary than ever before.

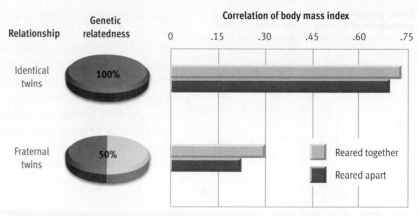

FIGURE 9.4

The heritability of weight. These data from a twin study by Stunkard et al. (1990) reveal that identical twins are much more similar in body mass index than fraternal twins, suggesting that genetic factors account for much of the variation among people in the propensity to become overweight.

Inadequate Sleep

Sleep deprivation, which has increased in modern societies in recent decades, is another factor that is thought to contribute to obesity. Sleep seems to be linked with weight regulation, and insufficient rest has been associated with weight gain. One recent study found that sleeping less than 6 hours per night at age 16 was associated with a 20% increase in the probability of being obese at age 21 (Suglia, Kara, & Robinson, 2014). Another study found that even after controlling for seventeen possible confounding variables, a significant relationship remained between short sleep and elevated obesity (Di Milia, Vandelanotte, & Duncan, 2013). What's the causal culprit? Sleep deprivation appears to alter the hormonal balances involved in regulating appetite, eating, and satiety (Knutson & Van Cauter, 2008).

The Concept of Set Point

People who lose weight on a diet have a rather strong tendency to gain back all the weight they lose, suggesting that homeostatic mechanisms defend against weight loss (Berthoud, 2012). It appears that a constellation of metabolic and neuroendocrine processes work to resist weight loss. For example, after significant weight loss, individuals' energy expenditure tends to decline (Goldsmith et al., 2010); that is they burn calories more slowly, which gradually fosters weight gain. Even more important, reduced fat stores result in reduced levels of the hormone leptin. Low levels of leptin fuel increased hunger and blunt some of the satiety signals that normally keep a lid on eating, thus promoting increased food consumption (Kissilef et al., 2012). Obviously, these biological adaptations to weight loss eventually lead most people to regain the weight they have lost. Interestingly, the human body is also wired to resist weight gain. People who have to work to put weight on often have trouble keeping it on. The adaptive mechanisms that tend to maintain a fairly stable body weight suggest that everyone may have a *set point* for weight. This set point is each individual's natural point of stability for weight. Originally viewed as a

▶ **REALITY CHECK**

Misconception

Skipping breakfast and eating at night will lead to extra weight gain.

Reality

Changes in weight depend on one's caloric intake in relation to one's energy expenditure from physical activities and metabolic processes. *When* you consume your calories is irrelevant. Calories consumed at night are not processed differently than calories consumed earlier in the day. That said, there is some evidence that people who eat a late supper tend to consume more calories during supper than those who have supper earlier, perhaps because of a circadian influence on hunger (Baron et al., 2011; Scheer, Morris, & Shea, 2013).

specific point of balance, it is now viewed as a narrow range of weight around that point (Pinel, Assanand, & Lehman, 2000). The set point concept raises a perplexing question: If the human body is wired to keep weight within a narrow range, why has obesity increased dramatically in recent decades? It turns out that the physiological processes that defend against weight loss are much stronger than those that defend against weight gain (Berthoud, 2012). Why? Probably because in ancestral environments where food resources were limited and unreliable, defending against weight loss would have been more adaptive for survival than defending against weight gain (Rosenbaum et al., 2010). Thus, another consideration promoting obesity is that the human body has been sculpted by evolution to defend against weight loss more effectively than against weight gain.

9.3 SEXUAL MOTIVATION AND BEHAVIOR

How does sex resemble food? Sometimes it seems that people are obsessed with both. People joke and gossip about sex constantly. Magazines, novels, movies, and television shows are saturated with sexual activity and innuendo. The advertising industry uses sex to sell everything from mouthwash to designer jeans to automobiles. This intense interest in sex reflects the importance of sexual motivation.

The Human Sexual Response

Assuming people are motivated to engage in sexual activity, exactly what happens to them physically? This may sound like a simple question, but scientists really knew very little about the physiology of the human sexual response before William Masters and Virginia Johnson did groundbreaking research in the 1960s. Their work yielded a detailed description of the human sexual response that eventually won them widespread acclaim. Masters and Johnson (1966, 1970) divided the sexual response cycle into four stages: excitement, plateau, orgasm, and resolution. **Figure 9.5** shows how the intensity of sexual arousal changes as women and men progress through these stages.

During the *excitement phase,* the level of physical arousal usually escalates rapidly. In both genders, muscle tension, respiration rate, heart rate, and blood pressure increase quickly. *Vasocongestion*—engorgement of blood vessels—produces penile erection and swollen testes in males. In females, vasocongestion leads to a swelling and hardening of the clitoris, expansion of the vaginal lips, and vaginal lubrication. During the *plateau phase,* physiological arousal usually continues to build, but at a much slower pace. When foreplay is lengthy, arousal tends to fluctuate in both genders.

Orgasm occurs when sexual arousal reaches its peak intensity and is discharged in a series of muscular contractions that pulsate through the pelvic area. The subjective experience of orgasm is very similar for men and women, but women are more likely than men to experience more than one orgasm in a brief time period (pattern C in **Figure 9.5**). That said,

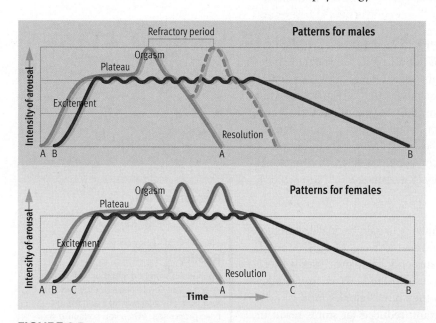

FIGURE 9.5

The human sexual response cycle. There are similarities and differences between men and women in patterns of sexual arousal. Pattern A, which culminates in orgasm and resolution, is the modal sequence for both genders, but not something one can count on. Pattern B, which involves sexual arousal without orgasm followed by a slow resolution, is seen in both genders, but is more common among women. Pattern C, which involves multiple orgasms, is seen almost exclusively in women because men go through a refractory period before they are capable of another orgasm.

SOURCE: Based on Masters, W. H., & Johnson, V. E. (1966). *Human sexual response.* Boston: Little, Brown. Copyright © 1966 Little, Brown and Company.

women are also more likely than men to engage in intercourse without experiencing an orgasm (Katz-Wise & Hyde, 2014). When respondents are asked whether they *always* have an orgasm with their partner, the gender gap in orgasmic consistency looks quite large. For example, among respondents ages 35–39, Laumann et al. (1994) found that 78% of men but only 28% of women reported always having an orgasm. However, a more recent, major survey of sexual behavior approached the issue in a different way and found a smaller gender gap. Herbenick et al. (2010) asked respondents about many of the details of their *most recent sexual interaction* (what they did, how pleasurable it was, whether they had an orgasm, and so forth). As you can see in **Figure 9.6**, men were more likely to report having an orgasm, but the disparity was not nearly as huge as when respondents were asked about *always* having an orgasm.

Whether this gender gap reflects attitudes and sexual practices or physiological processes is open to debate. On the one hand, it's easy to argue that males' greater orgasmic consistency must be a product of evolution because it would have obvious adaptive significance for promoting men's reproductive fitness. On the other hand, gender differences in the socialization of guilt feelings about sex, as well as sexual scripts and practices that are less than optimal for women, could play a part (Katz-Wise & Hyde, 2014).

During the *resolution phase,* the physiological changes produced by sexual arousal gradually subside. If orgasm has not occurred, the reduction in sexual tension may be relatively slow. After orgasm, men experience a *refractory period,* a time following orgasm during which they are largely unresponsive to further stimulation. The length of the refractory period varies from a few minutes to a few hours, and increases with age.

Evolutionary Analyses of Human Sexual Motivation

The task of explaining sexual behavior is obviously crucial to evolutionary psychologists, given their fundamental thesis that natural selection is fueled by variations in reproductive success. The thinking in this area has been guided by Robert Trivers's (1972) *parental investment theory.* **Parental investment refers to what each sex has to invest—in terms of time, energy, survival risk, and forgone opportunities (to pursue other goals)—to produce and nurture offspring.** For example, the efforts required to guard eggs, build nests, and nourish offspring represent parental investments. In most species, striking disparities exist between males and females in their parental investment, and these discrepancies shape mating strategies. So how does this theory apply to humans?

As with many mammalian species, human males are *required* to invest little in the production of offspring beyond the act of copulation. Hence, their reproductive potential is maximized by mating with as many females as possible. The situation for females is quite different. Females have to invest nine months in pregnancy, and our female ancestors typically had to devote at least several additional years to nourishing offspring through breastfeeding. These realities place a ceiling on the number of offspring women can produce, regardless of how many males they mate with. Hence, females have little or no incentive for mating with many males. Instead, females can optimize their reproductive potential by being selective in mating. Thus, in humans, males are thought to compete with other males for the relatively scarce and valuable "commodity" of reproductive opportunities.

Parental investment theory predicts that in comparison with women, men will show more interest in sexual activity, more desire for variety in sexual partners, and more willingness to engage in uncommitted sex (Durrant & Ellis, 2013). In contrast, females are thought to be conservative and highly selective in choosing partners (see **Figure 9.7**). This selectivity supposedly involves seeking partners who have the greatest ability to contribute toward feeding and caring for offspring. Why? Because in the world of our ancient ancestors, males' greater strength, agility, and access to economic resources would have been crucial assets in the never-ending struggle to find food and shelter and defend territory.

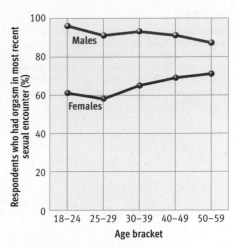

FIGURE 9.6

The gender gap in orgasm consistency. In their sexual interactions, men reach orgasm more reliably than women. When respondents are asked whether they *always* have an orgasm, the gender gap is huge. But the data shown here, which indicate whether people had an orgasm in their most recent sexual encounter, suggest that the gender gap is quite a bit smaller, although not insignificant. The data also indicate that the gender gap diminishes in older age groups. (Data from Herbenick et al., 2010).

FIGURE 9.7

Parental investment theory and mating preferences. Parental investment theory suggests that basic differences between males and females in parental investment have great adaptive significance and lead to gender differences in mating tendencies and preferences, as outlined here.

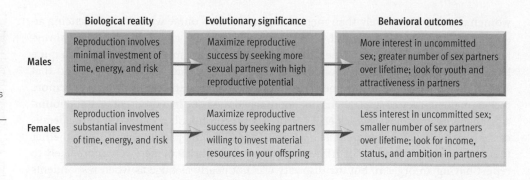

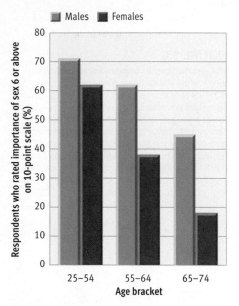

FIGURE 9.8

The gender gap in interest in sex. Lindau and Gavrilova (2010) summarized data from a nationally representative sample of over 3000 participants. In the survey, respondents were asked to rate how much thought and effort they put into the sexual aspect of their lives. The rating scale ranged from 0 (none) to 10 (very much). The graph shows the percentage of respondents who gave a rating of 6 or greater. As you can see, males generally expressed a greater interest in sex than females. The gender gap was modest, in the 25–54 age range, but widened considerably in older age groups.

Gender Differences in Patterns of Sexual Activity

Consistent with evolutionary theory, males generally show a greater interest in sex than females do. Men think about sex more often than women, initiate sex more often, and have more frequent and varied sexual fantasies (Baumeister, Catanese, & Vohs, 2001). Men are also much more likely to view and enjoy pornographic materials (Buss & Schmitt, 2011). Males masturbate quite a bit more than females and they are somewhat more likely to have extramarital affairs (Petersen & Hyde, 2011). When heterosexual couples are asked about their sex lives, male partners are more likely than their female counterparts to report that they would like to have sex more often. The findings of one study suggest that this disparity in sexual motivation only widens when people reach middle age (Lindau & Gavrilova, 2010). As you can see in **Figure 9.8**, in the 55–64 age bracket, 62% of men but only 38% of women report that they are still very interested in sex.

Men are also more motivated than women to pursue sex with a greater variety of partners (Buss & Schmitt, 2011). For example, Buss and Schmitt (1993) found that college men indicated that they would ideally like to have eighteen sex partners across their lives. College women, on the other hand, reported that they would prefer only five partners. Similar findings were observed in a follow-up study that examined desire for sexual variety in over 16,000 subjects from ten major regions of the world (Schmitt et al., 2003). Males expressed a desire for more partners than did females in all ten world regions. In most cases, the differences were substantial.

Clear gender disparities are also seen in regard to people's willingness to engage in casual or uncommitted sex. For example, in a compelling field study, Clark and Hatfield (1989) had average-looking men approach female (college-age) strangers and ask if they would go back to the man's apartment to have sex with him. None of the women agreed to this proposition. But when Clark and Hatfield had average-looking women approach males with the same proposition, 75% of the men eagerly agreed! Similar findings were seen in a more recent study that also looked at whether the person approached was in a relationship (Hald & Høgh-Olesen, 2010). Among those who were not in a relationship, 59% of the men and none of the women agreed to the invitation for casual sex. When the approached people *were* in a relationship, acceptance of the proposition declined considerably in men, and the gender gap shrank, with 18% of men and 4% of women agreeing to casual sex.

Gender Differences in Mate Preferences

Parental investment theory suggests some glaring disparities should exist between men and women in what they look for in a long-term mate (see **Figure 9.7** again). The theory predicts that men should place more emphasis than women on such partner characteristics as youthfulness (which allows for more reproductive years) and attractiveness (which is assumed to be correlated with health and fertility). In contrast, parental investment theory predicts that women should place more emphasis than men on partner characteristics such as intelligence, ambition, education, income, and social status (which are associated with the ability to provide more material resources). If these evolutionary analyses of sexual motivation are on the mark, gender differences in mating preferences should be virtually universal and thus transcend culture.

To test this hypothesis, David Buss (1989) and fifty scientists from around the world surveyed more than 10,000 people from thirty-seven cultures about what they looked for in a mate. As predicted by parental investment theory, they found that women placed a higher value than men on potential partners' status, ambition, and financial prospects (see **Figure 9.9**). These priorities were apparent in third-world cultures, socialist countries, and all varieties of economic systems. In contrast, men around the world consistently showed more interest than women in potential partners' youthfulness and physical attractiveness. A number of studies, using diverse samples and a variety of research methods, have replicated these findings (Li et al., 2013; Schmitt, 2014).

Criticism and Alternative Explanations

So, the findings on gender differences in sexual behavior and mating priorities mesh nicely with predictions derived from evolutionary theory. But, evolutionary theory has its share of critics. Some skeptics argue that there are alternative explanations for the findings. For example, women's emphasis on males' material resources could be a by-product of cultural and economic forces rather than the result of biological imperatives (Eagly & Wood, 1999). Women may have learned to value males' economic clout because their own economic potential has historically been limited in virtually all cultures (Kasser & Sharma, 1999). In a similar vein, Baumeister and Twenge (2002) argue that the gender disparity in sexual motivation may be largely attributable to extensive cultural processes that serve to suppress female sexuality. Recent research found some support for the idea that gender disparities in mating preferences are influenced by culture (Zentner & Mitura, 2012). The study found that the size of the gender gap in mating preferences is smaller in nations that exhibit greater gender equality. To some extent, this finding undermines analyses that attribute the gender gap in mating preferences to how males' and females' brains have been wired by evolution.

The Mystery of Sexual Orientation

Sex must be a contentious topic, as the controversy swirling around evolutionary explanations of gender differences in sexuality is easily equaled by the controversy surrounding the determinants of *sexual orientation*. **Sexual orientation refers to a person's preference for emotional and sexual relationships with individuals of the same sex, the other sex, or either sex.** *Heterosexuals* **seek emotional-sexual relationships with members of the other sex,** *bisexuals* **with members of either sex, and** *homosexuals* **with members of the same sex.** The terms *gay* and *straight* have become widely used to refer to homosexuals and heterosexuals, respectively. Although *gay* can refer to homosexuals of either sex, most homosexual women prefer to call themselves *lesbians*.

People tend to view heterosexuality and homosexuality as an all-or-none distinction. However, in a large-scale survey of sexual behavior, Alfred Kinsey and his colleagues (1948, 1953) discovered that many people who define themselves as heterosexuals have had homosexual experiences, and vice versa. Thus, Kinsey and others concluded that it is more accurate to view heterosexuality and homosexuality as end points on a continuum. Indeed, Kinsey devised a seven-point scale, shown in **Figure 9.10**, that can be used to characterize individuals' sexual orientation.

How common is homosexuality? No one knows for sure. Part of the problem is that this question is vastly more complex than it appears at first glance (Savin-Williams, 2006). Given that sexual orientation is best represented as a continuum, where do you draw the lines between heterosexuality, bisexuality, and homosexuality? And how do you handle the distinction between overt behavior and latent desire? Many surveys simply ask

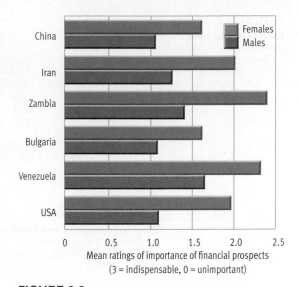

FIGURE 9.9

Gender and potential mates' financial prospects. Consistent with evolutionary theory, Buss (1989) found that females place more emphasis on potential partners' financial prospects than males do. Moreover, he found that this trend transcended culture. The specific results for six of the thirty-seven cultures studied by Buss are shown here.

Evolutionary theory posits that men can maximize their reproductive fitness by seeking youthful partners, whereas women can maximize their reproductive success by searching for mates who are rich in material resources that can be invested in children. Obviously, this theory can explain why attractive young women sometimes become romantically involved with much older men who happen to be wealthy.

0	1	2	3	4	5	6
Exclusively heterosexual	Predominantly heterosexual, only incidentally homosexual	Predominantly heterosexual, more than incidentally homosexual	Equally heterosexual and homosexual	Predominantly homosexual, more than incidentally heterosexual	Predominantly homosexual, only incidentally heterosexual	Exclusively homosexual

FIGURE 9.10

Homosexuality and heterosexuality as end points on a continuum. Sex researchers view heterosexuality and homosexuality as falling on a continuum, rather than make an all-or-none distinction. Kinsey and his associates (1948, 1953) created this seven-point scale (from 0 to 6) to describe people's sexual orientation.

people whether they identify as heterosexual, homosexual, or bisexual, but one survey that dug deeper found that roughly three-quarters of those who acknowledged at least some same-sex attractions or behavior did not self-identify as gay or bisexual (Chandra et al., 2011). So, self-identification and behavior are two different things. Small wonder then that estimates of the portion of the population that is homosexual vary widely. In U.S. surveys, about 3.5% of people self-identify as gay or bisexual, whereas 8.2% acknowledge that they have engaged in sexual activity with a same-sex partner, and 11% acknowledge at least some attraction to people of the same sex (Gates, 2011, 2013).

Although Kinsey's continuum was proposed long ago, the conventional thinking on sexual orientation has been that the vast majority of people are either straight or gay. Hence, it has been widely assumed that most of those who report some same-sex attractions are exclusively homosexual—with bisexuals presumed to be infrequent exceptions who are often viewed skeptically as gays in denial about their homosexuality. In reality, recent, more fine-grained data from a variety of surveys suggest that among those who are not exclusively heterosexual (especially women), only a minority are exclusively homosexual (Diamond, 2014). These data suggest that bisexuality is much more common than previously appreciated, but Diamond points out that the term *bisexuality* suggests an equal attraction to both genders, whereas many of the people in this category are predominantly, but not exclusively, attracted to one sex or the other. She argues that it is probably more accurate to characterize these individuals as nonexclusive in their sexuality, as opposed to bisexual. As you can see, the data on the demographics of sexual orientation are complicated.

Environmental Theories of Homosexuality

Over the years, many environmental theories have been floated to explain the origins of homosexuality. However, when tested empirically, these theories have received remarkably little support. For example, psychoanalytic and behavioral theorists—who usually agree on very little—both proposed environmental explanations for the development of

The prevalence of homosexuality is a complex and hotly debated issue. And, although much has been learned, the roots of homosexuality remain something of a mystery.

homosexuality. The Freudian theorists argued that a male is likely to become gay when raised by a weak, detached, ineffectual father who is a poor heterosexual role model and by an overprotective, overly attached mother, with whom the boy identifies. Behavioral theorists argued that homosexuality is a learned preference acquired when same-sex stimuli have been paired with sexual arousal, perhaps through chance seductions by adult homosexuals. Extensive research on homosexuals' upbringing and childhood experiences has failed to support either of these theories (Bell, Weinberg, & Hammersmith, 1981). Similarly, there is no evidence that parents' sexual orientation is linked to that of their children (Gato & Fontaine, 2013); that is, homosexual parents are no more likely to produce homosexual offspring than heterosexual parents are.

However, efforts to research homosexuals' personal histories have yielded a number of interesting insights. Extremely feminine behavior in young boys or masculine behavior in young girls does predict the subsequent development of homosexuality (Mustanski, Kuper & Greene, 2014). For example, Rieger and colleagues (2008) asked homosexual and heterosexual adults to supply childhood home videos. Independent judges were asked to rate how gender nonconforming the young children were in the videos. Rieger and colleagues found that children who would eventually identify as homosexual in adulthood were more gender nonconforming than those who identified as heterosexual. This finding held for both males and females. Consistent with this finding, most gay men and women report that they can trace their homosexual leanings back to their early childhood, even before they understood what sex was really about (Bailey, 2003). Most also report that because of negative parental and societal attitudes about homosexuality, they initially struggled to deny their sexual orientation. Thus, they felt that their homosexuality was not a matter of choice and not something they could readily change. Although people's subjective recollections of the past need to be interpreted with caution, these findings suggest that the roots of homosexuality are more biological than environmental.

Biological Theories of Homosexuality

Like environmental theorists, biological theorists were frustrated for quite a while in their efforts to explain the roots of homosexuality. However, that picture changed dramatically in the 1990s. In one landmark investigation, Bailey and Pillard (1991) studied gay men who had either a twin brother or an adopted brother. They found that 52% of the participants' identical twins were gay, that 22% of their fraternal twins were gay, and that 11% of their adoptive brothers were gay. A companion study (Bailey et al., 1993) of lesbians yielded a similar pattern of results (see **Figure 9.11**). Given that identical twins share more genetic overlap than fraternal twins, who share more genes than unrelated adoptive siblings, these results suggest a genetic predisposition to homosexuality (Hill, Dawood, & Puts, 2013). The heritability of sexual orientation appears to be similar in men and women (Rosario & Scrimshaw, 2014). Research also suggests that epigenetic processes that dampen or silence specific genes' effects may influence sexual orientation (Rice, Friberg, & Gavrilets, 2012; see Chapter 3 for an explanation of epigenetics).

Many theorists suspect that the roots of homosexuality may lie in the organizing effects of prenatal hormones on neurological development

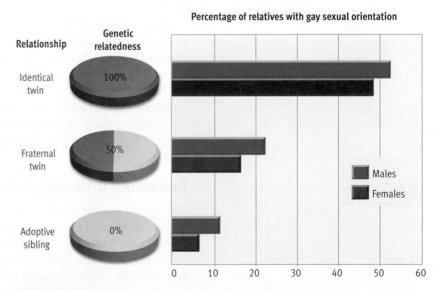

FIGURE 9.11

Genetics and sexual orientation. If relatives who share more genetic relatedness show greater similarity on a trait than relatives who share less genetic overlap, this evidence suggests a genetic predisposition to the characteristic. Studies of both gay men and lesbian women have found a higher prevalence of homosexuality among their identical twins than their fraternal twins, who, in turn, are more likely to be homosexual than their adoptive siblings. These findings suggest that genetic factors influence sexual orientation. (Data from Bailey & Pillard, 1991; Bailey et. al., 1993)

 AP Images/Peter Kramer

Some people were baffled when actress Lindsay Lohan became involved with DJ Samantha Ronson after a history of heterosexual relationships. Although shifts in sexual orientation like this are uncommon among males, research has shown that females' sexual orientation tends to be characterized by more plasticity than that of males.

(James, 2005). Several lines of research suggest that hormonal secretions during critical periods of prenatal development may shape sexual development, organize the brain in a lasting manner, and influence subsequent sexual orientation (Berenbaum & Snyder, 1995). For example, researchers have found elevated rates of homosexuality among women exposed to abnormally high androgen levels during prenatal development (because their mothers had an adrenal disorder or were given a synthetic hormone to reduce the risk of miscarriage) (Rosario & Scrimshaw, 2014). Several other independent lines of research suggest that abnormalities in prenatal hormonal secretions may foster a predisposition to homosexuality (Mustanski, Kuper, & Greene, 2014).

Despite this progress, much remains to be learned about the determinants of sexual orientation. One complication that has emerged relatively recently is that the pathways to homosexuality may be somewhat different for males than for females. Females' sexuality appears to be characterized by more *plasticity* than males' sexuality (Baumeister, 2000, 2004). In other words, women's sexual behavior may be more easily shaped and modified by sociocultural factors. For example, although sexual orientation is assumed to be a stable characteristic, research shows that lesbian and bisexual women often change their sexual orientation over the course of their adult years (Diamond, 2008, 2013). And, in comparison with gay males, lesbians are less likely to trace their homosexuality back to their childhood and are more likely to indicate that their attraction to the same sex emerged during adulthood (Diamond, 2013). These findings suggest that sexual orientation may be more fluid and malleable in women than in men.

9.4

Key Learning Goals

- Describe the need for achievement and how it has been measured.

- Explain how the need for achievement and situational factors influence achievement strivings.

9.4 THE ACHIEVEMENT MOTIVE

At the beginning of this chapter, we discussed Jon Krakauer's laborious, grueling effort to reach the summit of Mount Everest. What motivates people to push themselves so hard? In all likelihood, it's a strong need for achievement. **The *achievement motive* is the need to master difficult challenges, to outperform others, and to meet high standards of excellence.** Above all else, the need for achievement involves the desire to excel, especially in competition with others.

Research on achievement motivation was pioneered by David McClelland and his colleagues (McClelland, 1985; McClelland et al., 1953). McClelland argued that achievement motivation is of the utmost importance—that it is the spark that ignites economic growth, scientific progress, inspirational leadership, and masterpieces in the creative arts.

Individual Differences in the Need for Achievement

The need for achievement is a fairly stable aspect of personality. Thus, research on in achievement motivation has focused mostly on variations among individuals. In this research, investigators usually measure participants' need for achievement with some variant of the Thematic Apperception Test (TAT) (Spangler, 1992). The TAT is a *projective* test, one that requires subjects to respond to vague, ambiguous stimuli in ways that may reveal personal motives and traits (see Chapter 11). The stimulus materials for the TAT are pictures of people in ambiguous scenes open to interpretation. Examples include a man working at a desk and a woman seated in a chair staring off into space. Participants are asked to write or tell stories about what's happening in the scenes and what the characters are feeling. The themes of these stories are then scored to measure the strength of various needs. **Figure 9.12** shows examples of stories dominated by themes of achievement, and as another example, affiliation needs.

Affiliation arousal
George is an engineer who is working late. He is *worried that his wife will be annoyed* with him for neglecting her. She has been *objecting* that he cares more about his work than his wife and family. He seems *unable to satisfy* both his boss and his wife, but he *loves her* very much and will do his best to *finish up* fast and get home to her.

Achievement arousal
George is an engineer who *wants to win* a competition in which the man with the *most practicable drawing* will be awarded the contract to build a bridge. He is taking a moment to think *how happy he will be* if he wins. He has been *baffled by how to make such a long span strong*, but he remembers to *specify a new steel alloy* of great strength, submits his entry, but does not win, and is *very unhappy*.

FIGURE 9.12

Measuring motives with the Thematic Apperception Test (TAT). Subjects taking the TAT tell or write stories about what is happening in a scene, such as this one showing a man at work. The two stories shown here illustrate strong affiliation motivation and strong achievement motivation. The italicized parts of the stories are thematic ideas that would be identified by a TAT scorer.

SOURCE: Stories reprinted by permission of Dr. David McClelland.

The research on individual differences in achievement motivation has yielded interesting findings on the characteristics of people who score high in the need for achievement. For instance, they tend to work harder and more persistently on tasks than people low in the need for achievement (Brown, 1974). They are also more likely than others to delay gratification in order to pursue long-term goals (Raynor & Entin, 1982). As you might guess, given these characteristics, a high need for achievement correlates with higher educational attainment (Hustinx et al., 2009) and greater success in business (Winter, 2010). In terms of careers, those with a high achievement need typically go into competitive occupations that provide them with an opportunity to excel (Stewart & Roth, 2007). In the workplace, high need for achievement has its upside and its downside. On the one hand, it appears to provide some protection against the burnout syndrome that is seen in many lines of work (Moneta, 2011). On the other hand, it contributes to the tendency for some people to become workaholics (Mazzetti, Schaufeli, & Guglielmi, 2014).

Do people high in achievement need always tackle the biggest challenges available? Not necessarily. A curious finding has emerged in laboratory studies in which subjects were asked to choose the difficulty level of a task to work on. Participants high in the need for achievement tended to select tasks of intermediate difficulty (McClelland & Koestner, 1992). Research on the situational determinants of achievement behavior has suggested a reason, as we will see in the next section.

Situational Determinants of Achievement Behavior

Your achievement drive is not the only determinant of how hard you work. Situational factors can also influence achievement strivings. John Atkinson (1974, 1981, 1992) has elaborated extensively on McClelland's original theory of achievement motivation and identified some important situational determinants of achievement behavior. Atkinson theorizes that the tendency to pursue achievement in a particular situation depends on:

• The strength of one's *motivation* to *achieve* success, which is viewed as a stable aspect of personality
• One's estimate of the *probability of success* for the task at hand; such estimates vary from task to task
• The *incentive value* of success, which depends on the tangible and intangible rewards for success on the specific task

The last two variables are situational determinants of achievement behavior; that is, they vary from one situation to another. According to Atkinson, the pursuit of achievement increases as the probability of success and incentive value of success go up. Let's apply Atkinson's model to a simple example. Given a certain motivation to achieve success, you

Misconception

People with high achievement motivation are risk takers who prefer very challenging tasks.

Reality

People who score high in achievement motivation seem to *need* to experience success; many of them fear failure. Hence, they tend to select tasks that are moderately challenging and pursue goals that are reasonably realistic. They are not necessarily the most daring risk takers.

will pursue a good grade in calculus less vigorously if your professor gives impossible exams (thus lowering your expectancy of success) or if a good grade in calculus is not required for your major (lowering the incentive value of success).

The joint influence of these situational factors may explain why high achievers prefer tasks of intermediate difficulty. Atkinson notes that the probability of success and the incentive value of success on tasks are interdependent to some degree. As tasks get easier, success becomes less satisfying. As tasks get harder, success becomes more satisfying but becomes less likely. When the probability and incentive value of success are weighed together, moderately challenging tasks seem to offer the best overall value.

We turn next to the study of emotion. Motivation and emotion are often intertwined (Zurbriggen & Sturman, 2002). On the one hand, *emotion can cause motivation*. For example, *anger* about your work schedule may motivate you to look for a new job. *Jealousy* of an ex-girlfriend may motivate you to ask out her roommate. On the other hand, *motivation can cause emotion*. For example, your motivation to win a photography contest may lead to great *anxiety* during the judging and either *elation* if you win or *gloom* if you don't. Although motivation and emotion are closely related, they're *not* the same thing. We'll analyze the nature of emotion in the next section.

9.5

Key Learning Goals

• Describe the cognitive and physiological components of emotion.

• Explain how emotions are reflected in facial expressions, and describe the facial feedback hypothesis.

• Review cross-cultural similarities and variations in emotional experience.

9.5 ELEMENTS OF EMOTIONAL EXPERIENCE

The most profound and important experiences in life are saturated with emotion. Think of the *joy* that people feel at weddings, the *grief* they feel at funerals, the *ecstasy* they feel when they fall in love. Emotions also color everyday experiences. For instance, you might experience *anger* when a waiter treats you rudely, *dismay* when you learn that your car needs expensive repairs, and *happiness* when you see that you aced your economics exam. Clearly, emotions play an important role in people's lives.

Exactly what is an emotion? Everyone has plenty of personal experience with emotion, but it's an elusive concept to define (LeDoux, 1995). Emotion includes cognitive, physiological, and behavioral

CONCEPT CHECK 9.2

Understanding the Determinants of Achievement Behavior

According to John Atkinson, one's pursuit of achievement in a particular situation depends on several factors. Check your understanding of these factors by identifying each of the following vignettes as an example of one of the following three determinants of achievement behavior: (a) need for achievement, (b) perceived probability of success, and (c) incentive value of success. The answers can be found in Appendix A.

_____ 1. Belinda is nervously awaiting the start of the finals of the 200-meter dash in the last meet of her high school career. "I've gotta win this race! This is the most important race of my life!"

_____ 2. Corey grins as he considers the easy time he's going to have this semester. "This class is supposed to be a snap. I hear the professor gives A's and B's to nearly everyone."

_____ 3. Diana's just as hard-charging as ever. She's gotten the highest grade on every test throughout the semester, yet she's still up all night studying for the final. "I know I've got an A in the bag, but I want to be the best student Dr. McClelland's ever had!"

components, which are summarized in the following definition: ***Emotion* involves (1) a subjective conscious experience (the cognitive component), accompanied by (2) bodily arousal (the physiological component) and (3) characteristic overt expressions (the behavioral component).** That's a pretty complex definition. Let's take a closer look at each of these three components.

The Cognitive Component

In studying the cognitive component of emotions, psychologists generally rely on individuals' highly subjective verbal reports of what they're experiencing. These reports indicate that emotions are potentially intense internal feelings that sometimes seem to have a life of their own. People can't switch their emotions on and off like a bedroom light. If it were that simple, you could choose to be happy whenever you wanted. As Joseph LeDoux puts it, "Emotions are things that happen to us rather than things we will to occur" (1996, p. 19).

People's cognitive appraisals of events in their lives are key determinants of the emotions they experience (Ellsworth, 2013). A specific event, such as giving a speech, may be a highly threatening and thus anxiety-arousing occasion for one person but a routine matter for another. The conscious experience of emotion includes an *evaluative* aspect. People characterize their emotions as pleasant or unpleasant (Shuman, Sander, & Scherer, 2013). These evaluative reactions can be automatic and subconscious (Keltner & Horberg, 2015). Of course, individuals often experience "mixed emotions," which include both pleasant and unpleasant qualities (Larsen & McGraw, 2011). For example, an executive just given a promotion with challenging new responsibilities may experience both happiness and anxiety.

In recent years, a curious finding has emerged regarding people's cognitive assessments of their emotions: they are not very good at anticipating their emotional responses to future events. Research on *affective forecasting—* **efforts to predict one's emotional reactions to future events**—demonstrates that people reliably mispredict their future feelings in response to good and bad events, such as getting a promotion at work, taking a long-awaited vacation, or getting a poor grade in an important class (Wilson & Gilbert, 2003, 2005, 2013). People tend to be reasonably accurate in anticipating whether events will generate positive or negative emotions, but they often are way off in predicting the intensity and duration of their emotional reactions.

For example, Dunn, Wilson, and Gilbert (2003) asked college students to predict what their overall level of happiness would be if a campus housing lottery assigned them to a desirable or an undesirable dormitory. The students expected that their dormitory assignments would have a pretty dramatic effect on their well-being. But when their happiness was assessed a year after actually being assigned to the good or bad dorms, it was clear that their happiness was not affected by their dorm assignments (see **Figure 9.13**). In a similar vein, research shows that young professors overestimate the happiness they will feel 5 years after being granted tenure, college students overestimate how despondent they will be after the breakup of a romantic relationship, and job applicants overestimate how distressed they will feel after being rejected for a job (Kushlev & Dunn, 2012).

Why are our predictions of our emotional reactions surprisingly inaccurate? Many factors can contribute (Hoerger et al., 2009; Schwartz & Sommers, 2013). One consideration is that most of us do not fully appreciate how effective people tend to be in rationalizing, discounting, and overlooking failures and mistakes. Another issue is that people's predictions about the future are based on their memories of the past, but these recollections are often distorted and inaccurate. Yet another issue is that when anticipating an event, people

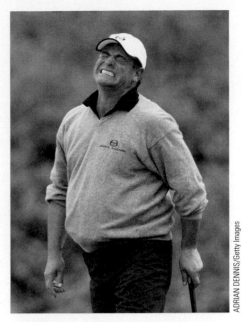

Emotions involve automatic reactions that can be difficult to control.

ADRIAN DENNIS/Getty Images

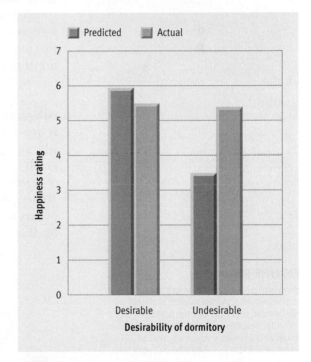

FIGURE 9.13

The inaccuracy of affective forecasting. Using a seven-point scale (where 1 = unhappy and 7 = happy), college students predicted how happy they would be a year later if they were randomly assigned to live in a desirable or an undesirable dormitory. Students anticipated that their dorm assignment would have a pronounced positive or negative impact on their overall happiness (blue bars); however a year later, those who ended up living in undesirable versus desirable dorms showed nearly identical levels of happiness (green bars).

SOURCE: Wilson, T. D., & Gilbert, D. T. (2005). Affective forecasting: Knowing what to want. *Current Directions in Psychological Science, 14,* 131-134. Figure 1. Copyright 2006 Blackwell Publishing. Reprinted by permission of Sage Publications.

focus on aspects of their lives that will change, while ignoring a host of other aspects of their lives that will remain the same. As you can see, emotions are not only hard to regulate, they are also hard to predict.

The Physiological Component

Emotional processes are closely tied to physiological processes, but the interconnections are enormously complex. The biological bases of emotions are diffuse and multifaceted, involving many areas in the brain, as well as the autonomic nervous system and the endocrine system.

Autonomic Arousal

Imagine your reaction as your car spins out of control on an icy highway. Your fear is accompanied by a variety of physiological changes. Your heart rate and breathing accelerate. Your blood pressure surges, and your pupils dilate. The hairs on your skin stand erect, giving you goosebumps, and you start to perspire. Although your reactions may not always be as obvious as in this scenario, *emotions are accompanied by physical arousal* (Larsen et al., 2008). Surely you've experienced a "knot in your stomach" or a "lump in your throat" thanks to anxiety.

Much of the physiological arousal associated with emotion occurs through the actions of the *autonomic nervous system* (Levenson, 2014). This system regulates the activity of glands, smooth muscles, and blood vessels (see **Figure 9.14**). As you may recall from Chapter 3, the autonomic nervous system is responsible for the highly emotional *fight-or-flight response,* which is largely controlled by the release of adrenal *hormones* that radiate throughout the body. Hormonal changes clearly play a crucial role in emotional responses to stress and may contribute to many other emotions as well (Wirth & Gaffey, 2013).

The connection between emotion and autonomic arousal provides the basis for the **polygraph, or *lie detector,* a device that records autonomic fluctuations while a subject is questioned.** The polygraph was invented in 1915 by psychologist William Marston—who also dreamed up the comic book superhero Wonder Woman (Knight, 2004). A polygraph can't actually detect lies. It's really an emotion detector. It monitors key indicators of autonomic arousal, typically heart rate; blood pressure; respiration rate; and *galvanic skin response* (GSR), which is an increase in the electrical conductivity of the skin that occurs when sweat glands increase their activity. The assumption is that when people lie, they experience emotion (presumably anxiety) that produces noticeable changes in

FIGURE 9.14

Emotion and autonomic arousal. The autonomic nervous system (ANS) is composed of the nerves that connect to the heart, blood vessels, smooth muscles, and glands (consult Chapter 3 for more information). The ANS is divided into the *sympathetic division,* which mobilizes bodily resources in response to stress, and the *parasympathetic division,* which conserves bodily resources. Emotions are frequently accompanied by sympathetic ANS activation, which leads to goosebumps, sweaty palms, and the other physical responses listed on the left side of the diagram.

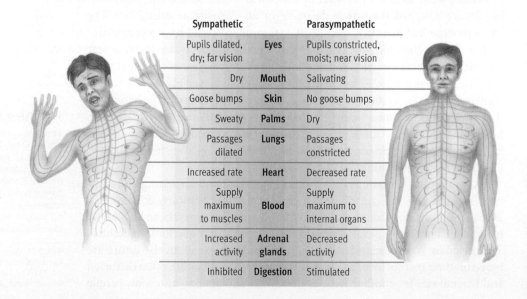

Sympathetic		Parasympathetic
Pupils dilated, dry; far vision	Eyes	Pupils constricted, moist; near vision
Dry	Mouth	Salivating
Goose bumps	Skin	No goose bumps
Sweaty	Palms	Dry
Passages dilated	Lungs	Passages constricted
Increased rate	Heart	Decreased rate
Supply maximum to muscles	Blood	Supply maximum to internal organs
Increased activity	Adrenal glands	Decreased activity
Inhibited	Digestion	Stimulated

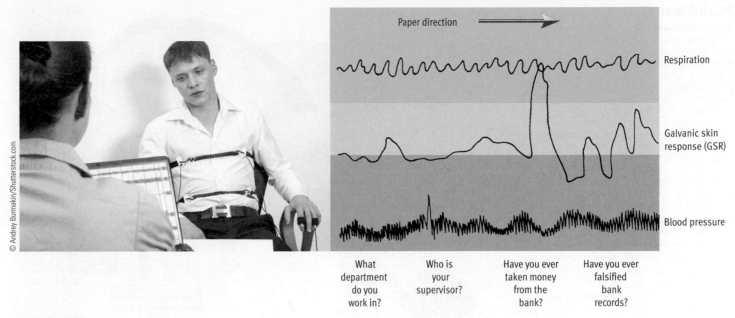

FIGURE 9.15

Emotion and the polygraph. A lie detector measures the autonomic arousal that most people experience when they tell a lie. After using nonthreatening questions to establish a baseline, a polygraph examiner looks for signs of arousal (such as the sharp change in GSR shown here) on incriminating questions. Unfortunately, as your text explains, the polygraph is not a very dependable index of whether people are lying.

these physiological indicators (see **Figure 9.15**). The polygraph examiner asks a subject a number of nonthreatening questions to establish the person's baseline on these indicators. Then the examiner asks the critical questions (for example, "Were you at home on the night of the burglary?") and observes whether the subject's autonomic arousal changes.

The polygraph has been controversial since its invention (Grubin & Madsen, 2005). Polygraph advocates claim that lie detector tests are about 85%–90% accurate and that the validity of polygraph testing has been demonstrated in empirical studies. However, these claims clearly are not supported by the evidence (Iacono, 2008). Methodologically sound research on the validity of polygraph testing is surprisingly sparse (largely because it is difficult research to do), and the limited evidence is not very impressive (Branaman & Gallagher, 2005). Part of the problem is that people who are telling the truth may experience emotional arousal when they respond to incriminating questions. Another problem is that some people can lie without experiencing anxiety or autonomic arousal. The polygraph *is* a potentially useful tool that can help police check out leads and alibis. However, polygraph results are not reliable enough to be submitted as evidence in most types of courtrooms.

Neural Circuits

The autonomic responses that accompany emotions are ultimately controlled in the brain. The hypothalamus, amygdala, and adjacent structures in the *limbic system* have long been viewed as the seat of emotions in the brain (MacLean, 1993).

Evidence suggests that the *amygdala* plays a particularly central role in the acquisition of conditioned fears (Armony, 2013). According to Joseph LeDoux (2000), sensory inputs capable of eliciting emotions arrive in the thalamus, which simultaneously routes the information along two separate pathways: to the nearby amygdala and to areas in the cortex (see **Figure 9.16**). The amygdala processes the information very quickly. If it detects a threat, it almost instantly triggers activity in the hypothalamus, which leads to autonomic arousal and hormonal responses. The processing in this pathway is extremely fast, so that emotions can be triggered even before the cortex has had a chance to really

> ▶ **REALITY CHECK**

Misconception

The lie detector is an accurate, reliable method for identifying dishonest responses.

Reality

The accuracy of the polygraph has long been exaggerated. For example, one influential study (Kleinmuntz & Szucko, 1984) found that lie detector tests would have led to incorrect verdicts for about one-third of the suspects who were proven innocent and about one-fourth of those who eventually confessed.

FIGURE 9.16

The amygdala and fear. Emotions are controlled by a constellation of interacting brain systems, but the amygdala appears to play a particularly crucial role. According to LeDoux (1996), sensory inputs that can trigger fear (such as seeing a snake while out walking) arrive in the thalamus and then are routed along a fast pathway (shown in red) directly to the amygdala, and along a slow pathway (shown in blue), which allows the cortex time to think about the situation. Activity in the fast pathway also elicits the autonomic arousal and hormonal responses that are part of the physiological component of emotion. (Adapted from LeDoux, 1994).

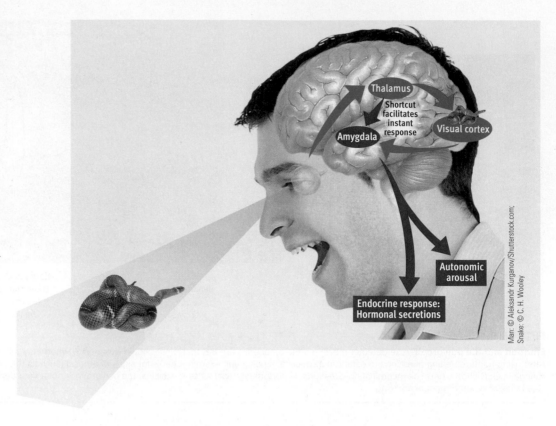

"think" about the input. LeDoux believes that this rapid-response pathway evolved because it is a highly adaptive warning system that can "be the difference between life and death." As LeDoux's theory would predict, evidence indicates that the amygdala can process emotion independent of cognitive awareness (Phelps, 2005). Consistent with the notion that the amygdala is the brain's fear center, a recent study found that highly anxious children tend to have an enlarged amygdala, with increased connectivity to other brain regions (Qin et al., 2014). Although the amygdala clearly plays a role in fear, some theorists believe that it is merely a key part of a neural network that underlies the experience of fear. According to this view, various emotions depend on activity in neural networks that are broadly distributed across various regions of the brain, rather than that are discrete structures in the brain (Lindquist et al., 2012).

The Behavioral Component

At the behavioral level, people reveal their emotions through characteristic overt expressions, such as smiles, frowns, furrowed brows, clenched fists, and slumped shoulders. In other words, *emotions are expressed in "body language," or nonverbal behavior.*

Facial expressions can reveal a variety of basic emotions. In an extensive research project, Paul Ekman and Wallace Friesen asked participants to identify what emotion a person was experiencing on the basis of facial cues in photographs. They found that subjects are generally successful in identifying six fundamental emotions: happiness, sadness, anger, fear, surprise, and disgust (Ekman & Friesen, 1975, 1984).

Some theorists believe that muscular feedback from one's own facial expressions contributes to one's conscious experience of emotions (Izard, 1990; Tomkins, 1991). Proponents of the *facial-feedback hypothesis* assert that facial muscles send signals to the brain and that these signals help the brain recognize the emotion that one is experiencing (see **Figure 9.17**). According to this view, smiles, frowns, and furrowed brows help create the experience of various emotions. Consistent with this idea, studies show that if subjects

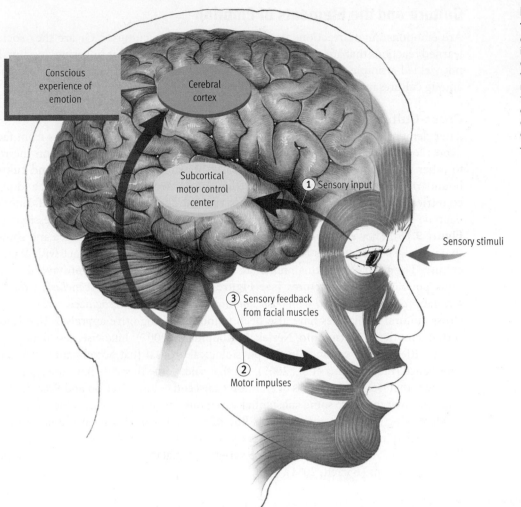

Conscious experience of emotion

Cerebral cortex

Subcortical motor control center

① Sensory input

Sensory stimuli

③ Sensory feedback from facial muscles

② Motor impulses

FIGURE 9.17

The facial feedback hypothesis. According to the facial feedback hypothesis, inputs to subcortical centers automatically evoke facial expressions associated with certain emotions, and the facial muscles then feed signals to the cortex that help it recognize the emotion that one is experiencing. In this view, facial expressions help create the subjective experience of various emotions.

are instructed to contract their facial muscles to mimic facial expressions associated with certain emotions, they tend to report that they actually experience these emotions to some degree (Dimberg & Söderkvist, 2011). Based on the facial-feedback hypothesis, researchers developed a novel treatment for depression involving the injection of Botox into the forehead to paralyze the facial muscles responsible for frowning. The assumption is that the feedback from constant frowning contributes to feelings of depression. A significant reduction in depressive symptoms was seen within 6 weeks, providing fascinating support for the facial-feedback hypothesis (Wollmer et al., 2012, 2014).

The facial expressions that go with various emotions may be largely innate (Eibl-Eibesfeldt, 1975; Izard, 1994). For the most part, people who have been blind since birth smile and frown much like everyone else, even though they've never seen a smile or frown (Galati, Scherer, & Ricci-Bitti, 1997). In an influential study, David Matsumoto and Bob Willingham (2009) carefully photographed the facial expressions of congenitally blind judo athletes in the Paralympic Games and sighted judo athletes in the Olympic Games. The photos for comparison were taken just after the athletes had won or lost their crucial final matches (for gold, silver, or bronze medals). The analysis of thousands of photos of numerous athletes yielded clear results: the facial expressions of sighted and blind athletes were indistinguishable. These findings suggest that the facial expressions that go with emotions are wired into the human brain (Matsumoto & Hwang, 2011).

In a creative application of naturalistic observation, Matsumoto and Willingham (2009) shot photos of the award ceremonies for congenitally blind and sighted athletes to gain insight into whether facial expressions of emotion are innate.

Culture and the Elements of Emotion

Are emotions innate reactions that are universal across cultures? Or are they socially learned reactions that are culturally variable? The research on this lingering question has not yielded a simple answer. Investigators have found both similarities and differences among cultures in the experience of emotion.

Cross-Cultural Similarities in Emotional Experience

After demonstrating that Western subjects could discern specific emotions from facial expressions, Ekman and Friesen (1975) took their facial-cue photographs on the road to other societies to see whether nonverbal expressions of emotion transcend cultural boundaries. For example, they tested participants in Argentina, Spain, Japan, and other countries. They found considerable cross-cultural agreement in the identification of happiness, sadness, anger, fear, surprise, and disgust based on facial expressions (see **Figure 9.18**). They even took their photos to a remote area in New Guinea and showed them to a group of natives (the Fore) who had had virtually no contact with Western culture. The people from this preliterate culture did a fair job of identifying the emotions portrayed in the pictures (see **Figure 9.18**), *leading to the conclusion that the facial expressions associated with basic emotions are universally recognized across cultures.* Cross-cultural similarities have also been found in the cognitive appraisals that lead to certain emotions (Matsumoto, Nezlek, & Koopmann, 2007). Likewise, researchers have found little cultural variance in the physiological arousal that accompanies emotional experience (Breugelmans et al., 2005). All that said, some theorists have questioned the assertion that facial expressions of emotion transcend culture. Nelson and Russell (2013) point out that there are some substantial variations across cultures in subjects' accuracy in identifying specific emotions. This line of research has also been criticized on the grounds that it has depended on a rather small set of artificial, highly posed, caricature-like photos that do not do justice to the variety of facial expressions that can accompany specific emotions (Barrett, 2011).

Cross-Cultural Differences in Emotional Experience

The cross-cultural similarities in emotional experience are impressive. Yet, researchers have also found many cultural disparities in how people think about and express their emotions (Mesquita & Leu, 2007). For example, fascinating variations have been observed in how cultures categorize emotions. Some basic categories of emotion that are universally understood in Western cultures appear to go unrecognized—or at least unnamed—in

FIGURE 9.18

Cross-cultural comparisons of people's ability to recognize emotions from facial expressions. Ekman and Friesen (1975) found that people in highly disparate cultures showed fair agreement on the emotions portrayed in these photos. This consensus across cultures suggests that facial expressions of emotions may be universal and that they have a strong biological basis.

SOURCE: Data from Ekman, P., & Friesen, W. V. (1975). *Unmasking the Face.* Englewood Cliffs, NJ: Prentice-Hall. © 1975 by Paul Ekman, photographs courtesy of Paul Ekman.

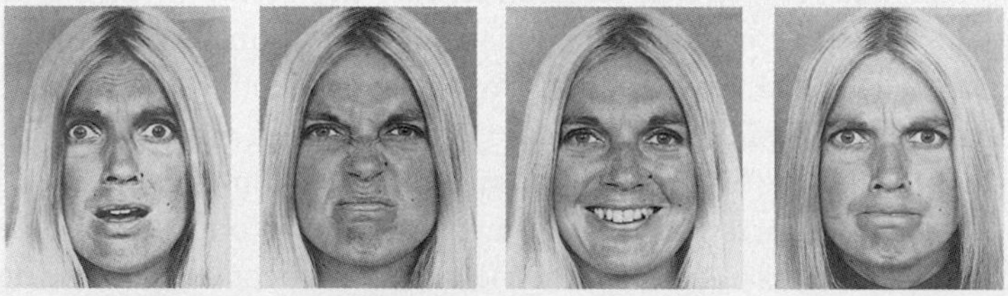

Country	Fear	Disgust	Happiness	Anger
	Agreement in judging photos (%)			
United States	85	92	97	67
Brazil	67	97	95	90
Chile	68	92	95	94
Argentina	54	92	98	90
Japan	66	90	100	90
New Guinea	54	44	82	50

From Unmasking the Face, © 1975 by Paul Ekman, photographs courtesy of Paul Ekman

some non-Western cultures (Russell, 1991). For example, some cultures have no word that corresponds to *sadness*. Others lack words for *depression, anxiety,* or *remorse*.

Cultural disparities have also been found in regard to nonverbal expressions of emotion. ***Display rules* are norms that regulate the appropriate expression of emotions.** They prescribe when, how, and to whom people can show various emotions. These norms vary from one culture to another (Ekman, 1992). The Ifaluk of Micronesia, for instance, severely restrict expressions of happiness because they believe that this emotion often leads people to neglect their duties. Japanese culture emphasizes the suppression of negative emotions in public. More so than in many other cultures, the Japanese are socialized to mask emotions such as anger, sadness, and disgust with stoic facial expressions or polite smiling. Thus, nonverbal expressions of emotions vary somewhat across cultures.

9.6 THEORIES OF EMOTION

9.6

Key Learning Goals

- Compare the James-Lange and Cannon-Bard theories of emotion.
- Explain the two-factor theory of emotion and evolutionary theories of emotion.

How do psychologists explain the experience of emotion? A variety of theories and conflicting models exist. Some have been vigorously debated for over a century. Indeed, the debate continues in contemporary psychology (see Dror, 2014; Ellsworth, 2014; Laird & Lacasse, 2014; Reisenzein & Stephan, 2014).

James-Lange Theory

As we noted in Chapter 1, William James was an early theorist who urged psychologists to explore the functions of consciousness. James (1884) developed a theory of emotion over 130 years ago that remains influential today. At about the same time, he and Carl Lange (1885) independently proposed that the *conscious experience of emotion results from one's perception of autonomic arousal.* Their theory stood common sense on its head. Everyday logic suggests that when you stumble onto a rattlesnake in the woods, the conscious experience of fear leads to autonomic arousal (the fight-or-flight response). The James-Lange theory of emotion asserts the opposite. It posits that the perception of autonomic arousal leads to the conscious experience of fear (see **Figure 9.19**). In other words, while you might assume that your pulse is racing because you're fearful, James and Lange argue that you're fearful because your pulse is racing. According to James-Lange theory, *different patterns of autonomic activation lead to the experience of different emotions.* Hence, people supposedly distinguish emotions—such as fear, joy, and anger—on the basis of the exact configuration of physical reactions they experience.

Cannon-Bard Theory

Walter Cannon (1927) found the James-Lange theory unconvincing. Cannon pointed out that physiological arousal can occur without the experience of emotion (if one exercises vigorously, for instance). He also argued that visceral changes are too slow to precede the conscious experience of emotion. Finally, he argued that people experiencing very different emotions, such as fear, joy, and anger, exhibit patterns of autonomic arousal that are too similar to be readily distinguished.

Thus, Cannon espoused a different explanation of emotion. Later, Philip Bard (1934) elaborated on it. The resulting Cannon-Bard theory argues that emotion occurs when the *thalamus* sends signals *simultaneously* to the cortex (creating the conscious experience of emotion) and to the autonomic nervous system (creating visceral arousal). The Cannon-Bard model is compared to the James-Lange model in **Figure 9.19**. Cannon and Bard were off the mark a bit in pinpointing the thalamus as the neural center for emotion. However, many modern theorists agree with the Cannon-Bard view that emotions originate in subcortical brain structures (LeDoux, 1996; Panksepp, 1991). Likewise, most

FIGURE 9.19

Theories of emotion. Three influential theories of emotion are contrasted with one another and with the common sense view. The James-Lange theory was the first to suggest that feelings of arousal cause emotion, rather than vice versa. Schachter built on this idea by adding a second factor—interpretation (appraisal and labeling) of arousal.

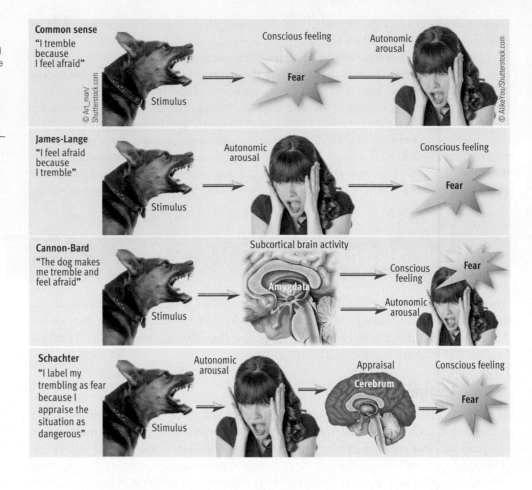

modern theorists accept the notion that people do *not* infer their emotions from different patterns of autonomic activation (Frijda, 1999).

Schachter's Two-Factor Theory

In another influential analysis, Stanley Schachter asserted that people look at situational cues to differentiate between alternative emotions. According to Schachter (1964), the experience of emotion depends on two factors: (1) autonomic arousal and (2) cognitive interpretation of that arousal. Schachter proposed that when you experience physiological arousal, you search your environment for an explanation (see **Figure 9.19** again). If you're stuck in a traffic jam, you'll probably label your arousal as anger. If you're taking an important exam, you'll probably label it as anxiety. If you're celebrating your birthday, you'll probably label it as happiness.

Schachter agrees with the James-Lange view that emotion is inferred from arousal. However, he also agrees with the Cannon-Bard position that different emotions yield indistinguishable patterns of arousal. He reconciles these views by arguing that people look to external rather than internal cues to differentiate and label their specific emotions. In essence, Schachter suggests that people think along the following lines: "If I'm aroused and you're obnoxious, I must be angry."

In a classic test of the two-factor theory, Dutton and Aron (1974) arranged for young men crossing a footbridge in a park to encounter a young woman who asked them to stop briefly to fill out a questionnaire. The woman offered to explain the research at some future time and gave the men her phone number. Autonomic arousal was manipulated by enacting this scenario on two very different bridges. One was a long suspension bridge that swayed precariously 230 feet above a river. The other bridge was a solid, safe structure

above a small stream. The experimenters reasoned that the men crossing the frightening bridge would be experiencing emotional arousal and that some of them might attribute that arousal to the woman rather than to the bridge. If so, they might mislabel their emotion as lust rather than fear and infer that they were attracted to the woman. The dependent variable was how many of the men later called the woman to pursue a date. As predicted, more of the men who met the woman on the precarious bridge called her for a date. Thus, the findings supported the theory that people often infer emotion from their physiological arousal and label that emotion in accordance with their cognitive explanation for it.

Evolutionary Theories of Emotion

In recent decades, some theorists interested in emotion have returned to ideas espoused by Charles Darwin over a century ago. Darwin (1872) believed that emotions developed because of their adaptive value. Fear, for instance, would help an organism avoid danger and hence would aid in survival. Thus, Darwin viewed human emotions as a product of evolution. This premise serves as the foundation for several modern theories of emotion developed independently by S. S. Tomkins (1980, 1991); Carroll Izard (1984, 1991); and Robert Plutchik (1984, 1993).

These *evolutionary theories* consider emotions to be largely innate reactions to certain stimuli. As such, emotions should be immediately recognizable under most conditions, without much thought. After all, primitive animals that are incapable of complex thought seem to have little difficulty recognizing their emotions. Evolutionary theorists believe that emotion evolved before thought. These theories generally assume that emotions originate in subcortical brain structures (such as the hypothalamus and most of the limbic system) that evolved before the higher brain areas (in the cortex) associated with complex thought.

Evolutionary theories also assume that natural selection has equipped humans with a small number of innate emotions with proven adaptive value. Thus, the principal question that evolutionary theories of emotion wrestle with is what are the *fundamental emotions* that are universal across cultures? **Figure 9.20** summarizes the conclusions of the leading theorists in this area. As you can see, Tomkins, Izard, and Plutchik have not come up with identical lists. However, there is considerable agreement. All three conclude that people exhibit eight to ten primary emotions. Moreover, six of these emotions appear on all three lists: fear, anger, joy, disgust, interest, and surprise.

Silvan Tomkins	Carroll Izard	Robert Plutchik
Fear	Fear	Fear
Anger	Anger	Anger
Enjoyment	Joy	Joy
Disgust	Disgust	Disgust
Interest	Interest	Anticipation
Surprise	Surprise	Surprise
Contempt	Contempt	
Shame	Shame	
	Sadness	Sadness
Distress		
	Guilt	
		Acceptance

FIGURE 9.20

Primary emotions. Evolutionary theories of emotion attempt to identify primary emotions. Three leading theorists—Silvan Tomkins, Carroll Izard, and Robert Plutchik—compiled different lists of primary emotions, but this chart shows great overlap among the basic emotions identified by these theorists. (Based on Mandler, 1984)

© Ienetstan/Shutterstock.com

CONCEPT CHECK 9.3

Understanding Theories of Emotion

Check your understanding of theories of emotion by matching the theories we discussed with the statements below. Let's borrow William James's classic example: assume that you just stumbled onto a bear in the woods. The first statement expresses the common sense explanation of your fear. Each of the remaining statements expresses the essence of a different theory; indicate which theory in the spaces provided. The answers are provided in Appendix A.

1. You tremble because you're afraid.

   _____ *Common sense* _____

2. You're afraid because you're trembling.

   _____

3. You're afraid because situational cues (the bear) suggest that's why you're trembling.

   _____

4. You're afraid because the bear has elicited an innate primary emotion.

   _____

Key Learning Goals

- Identify the five unifying themes highlighted in this chapter.

 Cultural Heritage

 Sociohistorical Context

 Theoretical Diversity

 Heredity & Environment

 Multifactorial Causation

9.7 REFLECTING ON THE CHAPTER'S THEMES

Five of our organizing themes were particularly prominent in this chapter: the influence of cultural contexts, the dense connections between psychology and society at large, psychology's theoretical diversity, the interplay of heredity and environment, and the multiple causes of behavior.

Our discussion of motivation and emotion demonstrated once again that there are both similarities and differences across cultures in behavior. The neural, biochemical, genetic, and hormonal processes underlying hunger and eating, for instance, are universal. However, cultural factors influence what people prefer to eat and how much they eat. In a similar vein, researchers have found a great deal of cross-cultural similarity in the cognitive, physiological, and expressive elements of emotional experience, but they have also found cultural variations in how people think about and express their emotions.

Our discussion of the controversies surrounding evolutionary theory and the determinants of sexual orientation show once again that psychology is not an ivory tower enterprise. It evolves in a sociohistorical context that helps shape the debates in the field, and these debates often have far-reaching social and political ramifications for society at large. We ended the chapter with a discussion of various theories of emotion, which showed once again that psychology is characterized by great theoretical diversity.

Finally, we repeatedly saw that biological and environmental factors jointly govern behavior. For example, we learned that eating behavior, sexual desire, and the experience of emotion all depend on complicated interactions between biological and environmental determinants. Indeed, complicated interactions permeated the entire chapter. Thus, if we want to fully understand behavior, we have to take multiple causes into account.

9.8 PERSONAL APPLICATION
Exploring the Ingredients of Happiness

Answer the following "true" or "false."

___ 1 The empirical evidence indicates that most people are relatively unhappy.

___ 2 Although wealth doesn't *guarantee* happiness, very wealthy people are much more likely to be happy than the rest of the population.

___ 3 People who have children are happier than people without children.

___ 4 Good health is an essential requirement for happiness.

The answer to all these questions is "false." These assertions are all reasonable and widely believed hypotheses about the prevalence and correlates of happiness. Yet, they have *not* been supported by empirical research. Recent years have brought a surge of interest in the correlates of *subjective well-being*—individuals' **personal perceptions of their overall happiness and life satisfaction.** The findings of this research are quite interesting.

How Happy Are People?

One of these inaccuracies is the apparently widespread assumption that most people are relatively unhappy. Writers, social scientists, and the general public seem to believe that people around the world are predominantly dissatisfied and unhappy. However, empirical surveys consistently find that the vast majority of respondents characterize themselves as fairly happy (Pavot & Diener, 2013). When people are asked to rate their happiness, only a small minority place themselves below the neutral point on the various scales used (see **Figure 9.21**). When the average subjective well-being of entire nations is computed, based on almost 1000 surveys, the means cluster toward the positive end of the scale (Tov & Diener, 2007). That's not to say that everyone is equally happy. Researchers find substantial disparities in subjective well-being,

which we will analyze momentarily. The overall picture, though, seems rosier than anticipated. This is an encouraging finding, as subjective well-being tends to be relatively stable over the course of people's lives, and higher levels of happiness are predictive of better social relationships, greater career satisfaction, better physical health, and greater longevity (Lucas & Diener, 2015). Thus, one's subjective well-being can have important consequences.

Weak Predictors of Happiness

Let's begin our discussion of individual differences in happiness by highlighting those things that turn out to be relatively unimportant determinants of subjective well-being. Quite a number of factors that you might expect to be influential appear to bear little or no relationship to general happiness.

Money

There *is* a positive correlation between income and subjective feelings of happiness. The association is surprisingly weak, however. Within specific nations, the correlation between income and happiness tends to fall somewhere between .12 and .20 (Diener & Biswas-Diener, 2002; Johnson & Krueger, 2006). Obviously, being poor can contribute to unhappiness. Yet it seems once people ascend above a certain level of income, additional wealth does not appear to foster greater happiness. One study in the United States estimated that once people exceed an income of around $75,000, little relation is seen between wealth and emotional well-being (Kahneman & Deaton, 2010).

Why isn't money a better predictor of happiness? One reason is that there seems to be a disconnect between actual income and how people feel about their financial situation. Research (Johnson & Krueger, 2006) suggests that the correlation between actual wealth and people's subjective

perceptions of whether they have enough money to meet their needs is surprisingly modest (around .30). Another problem is that pervasive advertising fuels escalating material desires that often outstrip what people can afford, causing dissatisfaction (Norris & Larsen, 2011). Thus, complaints about not having enough money are routine even among people who are very affluent by objective standards. Interestingly, there is some evidence that people who place an especially strong emphasis on materialistic goals tend to be somewhat less happy than others (Ahuvia & Izberk-Bilgin, 2013). Evidence also suggests that living in wealthy neighborhoods fuels increased materialism (Zhang, Howell, & Howell, 2014), providing yet another reason wealth does not necessarily foster happiness. Unfortunately, research suggests that levels of materialism in the United States have been rising in

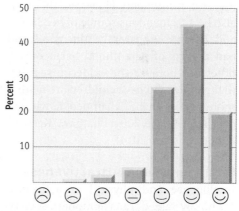

Which of these faces represents the way you feel about life as a whole?

FIGURE 9.21

Measuring happiness with a nonverbal scale. Researchers have used a variety of methods to estimate the distribution of happiness. For example, in one study in the United States, respondents were asked to examine the seven facial expressions shown and select the one that "comes closest to expressing how you feel about your life as a whole." As you can see, the vast majority of participants chose happy faces. (Data adapted from Myers, 1992)

recent decades to historically high levels (Twenge & Kasser, 2013).

Recent studies have provided some other interesting and unexpected insights about money and happiness. First, studies suggest that money spent purchasing *experiences,* such as concerts, travel, and outdoor activities, promotes more happiness than money spent purchasing *material goods,* such as clothes, jewelry, and appliances (Pchelin & Howell, 2014). Second, research indicates that across many cultures of varied wealth, people derive more happiness from money spent to help others than from money spent on themselves (Dunn, Aknin, & Norton, 2014).

Age
Age and happiness are consistently found to be unrelated. For example, a study of over 7000 adults concluded that levels of happiness did not vary with age (Cooper et al., 2011). The key factors influencing subjective well-being may shift some as people grow older—work becomes less important, health more so. But people's average level of happiness tends to remain fairly stable over the life span.

Parenthood
Children can be a tremendous source of joy and fulfillment. However, they can also be a tremendous source of headaches and hassles. Apparently, the good and bad aspects of parenthood balance each other out because the evidence suggests that people who have children are neither more nor less happy than people without children (Argyle, 2001; Bhargava, Kassam, & Loewenstein, 2014).

Intelligence and Attractiveness
Intelligence and physical attractiveness are highly valued traits in modern society. But researchers have *not* found an association between either characteristic and happiness (Diener, Wolsic, & Fujita, 1995; Diener, Kesebir, & Tov, 2009).

Moderately Good Predictors of Happiness
Research has identified some facets of life that appear to have a *moderate* association

with subjective well-being: health, social activity, and religious belief.

Health
Good physical health would seem to be an essential requirement for happiness, but people adapt to health problems. Research reveals that individuals who develop serious, disabling health conditions aren't as unhappy as one might guess (Myers, 1992; Riis et al., 2005). Furthermore, it appears that people tend to take good health for granted. Considerations such as these may help to explain why researchers find only a moderate positive correlation (average = .32) between health status and subjective well-being (Argyle, 1999).

Social Activity
Humans are social animals, and interpersonal relations do appear to contribute to people's happiness. Those who are satisfied with their social support and friendship networks and those who are socially active report somewhat higher levels of happiness than others do (Demir, Orthel, & Andelin, 2013; Lakey, 2013). One study found that at age 50, people with larger friendship networks reported greater psychological well-being than did those with fewer friends (Cable et al., 2013).

Religious Belief
The link between religiosity and subjective well-being is modest. However, a number of surveys suggest that people with heartfelt religious convictions are more likely to be happy than people who characterize themselves as nonreligious (Myers, 2013). Researchers aren't sure how religious faith fosters happiness, but Myers (1992) offers some interesting conjectures. He discusses how religion can give people a sense of purpose and meaning in their lives. It can help them accept their setbacks gracefully. It can connect them to a caring, supportive community. Finally, it can comfort them by putting their mortality in perspective.

Stronger Predictors of Happiness
The list of factors that turn out to have fairly strong associations with happiness is

surprisingly short. The key ingredients of happiness appear to involve relationship satisfaction, work, and personality.

Relationship Satisfaction
Romantic relationships can be stressful, but people consistently rate being in love as one of the critical ingredients of happiness. Furthermore, although people complain a lot about their marriages, research consistently finds that married people tend to be happier than people who are single or divorced (Saphire-Bernstein & Taylor, 2013). This relationship holds around the world in widely different cultures (Diener et al., 2000). And among married people, level of marital satisfaction predicts personal well-being (Proulx, Helms, & Buehler, 2007). The research in this area has used marital status as a crude but easily measured marker of relationship satisfaction. In all likelihood, it is *relationship satisfaction* that fosters happiness. Relationship satisfaction probably has the same association with happiness in cohabiting heterosexual couples and gay couples. In support of this line of thinking, one study found that both married and cohabiting people were happier than those who remained single (Musick & Bumpass, 2012).

Work
People often complain about their jobs. Hence, one might not expect work to be a key source of happiness, but it is. Although less critical than love and marriage, job satisfaction has a substantial association with general happiness (Judge & Klinger, 2008). Studies also show that unemployment has strong negative effects on subjective well-being (Lucas et al., 2004). It is difficult to sort out whether job satisfaction causes happiness or vice versa, but evidence suggests that causation flows both ways (Argyle, 2001).

Genetics and Personality
The best predictor of individuals' future happiness is their past happiness (Pavot & Diener, 2013). Some people seem destined to be happy and others unhappy, regardless of their triumphs

or setbacks. Evidence suggests that happiness does not depend on external circumstances—buying a nice house, getting promoted—as much as internal factors, such as one's outlook on life (Lyubomirsky, Sheldon, & Schkade, 2005). With this reality in mind, researchers investigated whether there might be a hereditary basis for variations in happiness. These studies suggest that people's genetic predispositions account for a substantial portion of the variance in happiness, perhaps as much as 50% (Stubbe et al., 2005). How can one's genes influence one's happiness? Presumably by shaping one's temperament and personality, which are known to be heritable. Indeed, personality traits show some of the strongest correlations with subjective well-being (Lucas & Diener, 2015). For example, *extraversion* is one of the better predictors of happiness. People who are outgoing and sociable tend to be happier than others (Gale et al., 2013). In contrast, those who score high in *neuroticism*—the tendency to be anxious, hostile, and insecure—tend to be less happy than others (Zhang & Howell, 2011).

Conclusions About Subjective Well-Being

We must be cautious in drawing inferences about the *causes* of happiness because the available data are correlational (see **Figure 9.22**). Nonetheless, the empirical findings suggest a number of worthwhile insights about the roots of happiness.

First, research on happiness shows that the determinants of subjective well-being are precisely that: subjective. *Objective realities are not as important as subjective feelings.* In other words, your health, your wealth, your job, and your age are not as influential as how you *feel* about your health, wealth, job, and age

Research shows that happiness does not depend on people's positive and negative experiences as much as one would expect. Some people, presumably because of their personality, seem destined to be happy in spite of major setbacks, and others seem destined to cling to unhappiness even though their lives seem reasonably pleasant.

Insadco Photography/Alamy

(Schwarz & Strack, 1999). Second, *when it comes to happiness, everything is relative* (Argyle, 1999; Hagerty, 2000). In other words, you evaluate what you have relative to what the people around you have and relative to what you expected to have. Generally, we compare ourselves to others who are similar to us. Thus, people who are wealthy assess what they have by comparing themselves to their wealthy friends and neighbors, and their *relative* standing is crucial (Boyce, Brown, & Moore, 2010). This is yet another reason underlying the low correlation between wealth and happiness.

Third, *research on subjective well-being indicates that people often adapt to their circumstances.* This adaptation effect is one reason that increases in income don't necessarily bring increases

in happiness. ***Hedonic adaptation* occurs when the mental scale that people use to judge the pleasantness-unpleasantness of their experiences shifts so that their neutral point, or baseline for comparison, changes.** Unfortunately, when people's experiences improve, hedonic adaptation can *sometimes* put them on a *hedonic treadmill.* Their neutral point moves upward, so that the improvements yield no real benefits (Kahneman, 1999). However, when people have to grapple with major setbacks, hedonic adaptation probably helps protect their mental and physical health. For example, people who are sent to prison and people who develop debilitating diseases are not as unhappy as one might assume because they adapt to their changed situations and evaluate events from a shifted baseline (Frederick & Loewenstein, 1999). That's not to say that hedonic adaptation in the face of life's difficulties is inevitable or complete, but a substantial portion of people appear to adapt to setbacks much better than widely assumed (Lucas, 2007).

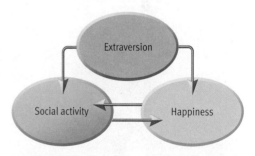

FIGURE 9.22

Possible causal relations among the correlates of happiness. Although we have considerable data on the correlates of happiness, it is difficult to untangle the possible causal relationships. For example, we know that there is a moderate positive correlation between social activity and happiness, but we can't say for sure whether high social activity causes happiness or whether happiness causes people to be more socially active. Moreover, in light of the research showing that a third variable—extraversion—correlates with both variables, we have to consider the possibility that extraversion causes both greater social activity and greater happiness.

9.9

Key Learning Goals

• Identify the key elements in arguments, and recognize common fallacies in arguments.

9.9 CRITICAL THINKING APPLICATION
Analyzing Arguments: Making Sense out of Controversy

Consider the following argument: "Dieting is harmful to your health because the tendency to be obese is largely inherited." What is your reaction to this reasoning? Do you find it convincing? Hopefully not because this argument is seriously flawed. Can you see what's wrong? There is no relationship between the conclusion that "dieting is harmful to your health" and the reason given that "the tendency to be obese is largely inherited." The argument is initially seductive because most people know that obesity *is* largely inherited. So, the reason provided represents a true statement. But the reason is unrelated to the conclusion advocated. This scenario may strike you as odd. But if you start listening carefully to discussions about controversial issues, you will probably notice that people often cite irrelevant considerations in support of their favored conclusions.

This chapter is loaded with controversial issues that sincere, well-meaning people could argue about for weeks. Are gender differences in mating preferences a product of evolution or of modern economic realities? Is there a biological basis for homosexuality? Unfortunately, arguments about issues such as these are typically unproductive in terms of moving toward a resolution because most people know little about the rules of argumentation. In this application, we will explore what makes arguments sound or unsound in the hope of improving your ability to analyze and think critically about arguments.

The Anatomy of an Argument

In everyday usage, the word *argument* is used to refer to a dispute or disagreement between two or more people. However, in the technical language of rhetoric, **an argument consists of one or more premises that are used to provide support for a conclusion.** *Premises* **are the reasons that are presented to persuade someone that a conclusion is true or probably true.** *Assumptions* **are premises for which no proof or evidence is offered.** Assumptions are often left unstated. For example, suppose your doctor tells you that you should exercise regularly because regular exercise is good for your heart. In this simple argument, the conclusion is "You should exercise regularly." The premise that leads to this conclusion is the idea that "exercise is good for your heart." An unstated assumption is that everyone wants a healthy heart. In the language of argument analysis, premises are said to support (or not support) conclusions. A conclusion may be supported by one reason or by many reasons.

Arguments can get pretty complicated because they usually have more parts than just premises and conclusions. In addition, there often are *counterarguments,* which are reasons that take support away from a conclusion. And sometimes the most important part of an argument is something that is not there—reasons that have been omitted, either deliberately or not, that would lead to a different conclusion if they were supplied. Given all the complex variations that can occur in arguments, it is impossible to give you simple rules for judging arguments, but we can highlight some common fallacies and then provide some criteria you can apply in thinking critically about arguments.

Common Fallacies

As noted in previous chapters, cognitive scientists have compiled lengthy lists of fallacies that people frequently display in their arguments. This section describes five common fallacies (drawn from Halpern, 2014). To illustrate each one, we will analyze some arguments asserting that pornographic material on the Internet (cyberporn) should be banned or heavily regulated.

Irrelevant Reasons

Reasons cannot provide support for an argument unless they are relevant to the conclusion. Arguments that depend on irrelevant reasons—either intentionally

Arguments about controversial issues occur all the time. It pays to be aware of some common fallacies in argumentation.

or inadvertently—are quite common. You already saw one example at the beginning of this application. The Latin term for this fallacy is *non sequitur*, which literally translates to "it doesn't follow." In other words, the conclusion does not follow from the premise. For example, in the debate about Internet pornography, you might hear the following *non sequitur*: "We need to regulate cyberporn because research has shown that most date rapes go unreported."

Circular Reasoning

In *circular reasoning*, the premise and conclusion are simply restatements of each other. People vary their wording a little so it isn't obvious, but when you look closely, the conclusion is the premise. For example, in arguments about Internet pornography you might hear someone assert, "We need to control cyberporn because it is currently unregulated."

Slippery Slope

The concept of *slippery slope* argumentation takes its name from the notion that if you are on a slippery slope and you don't dig your heels in, you will slide and slide until you reach bottom. A slippery slope argument typically asserts that if you allow X to happen, things will spin out of control and far worse events will follow. The trick is that no inherent connection exists between X and the events that are predicted to follow. For example, in the debate about medical marijuana, opponents have argued, "If you legalize medical marijuana, the next thing you know cocaine and heroin will be legal." In the debate about cyberporn, a slippery slope argument might go, "If we don't ban cyberporn, the next thing you know, grade school children will be watching smut in their school libraries."

Weak Analogies

An *analogy* asserts that two concepts or events are similar in some way. Hence, you can draw conclusions about event B because of its similarity to event A. Analogies can be very useful in thinking about complex issues. However, some analogies are weak or inappropriate because the similarity between A and B is superficial, minimal, or irrelevant to the issue at hand. For example, in the debate about Internet erotica, someone might argue, "Cyberporn is morally offensive, just like child molestation. We wouldn't tolerate child molestation, so we shouldn't permit cyberporn."

False Dichotomy

A *false dichotomy* creates an either-or choice between two outcomes: the outcome advocated and some obviously horrible outcome that any sensible person would want to avoid. These outcomes are presented as the only possible ones, when in reality many other outcomes are possible, including some that lie between the extremes depicted in the false dichotomy. In the debate about Internet pornography, someone might argue, "We can ban cyberporn, or we can hasten the moral decay of modern society."

Evaluating the Strength of Arguments

In everyday life, you frequently need to assess the strength of arguments made by friends, family, co-workers, politicians, media pundits, and so forth. You may also want to evaluate your own arguments when you write papers or speeches for school or prepare presentations for your work. The following questions can help you to make systematic evaluations of arguments (adapted from Halpern, 2014):

- What is the conclusion?
- What are the premises provided to support the conclusion? Are the premises valid?
- Does the conclusion follow from the premises? Are there any fallacies in the chain of reasoning?
- What assumptions have been made? Are they valid assumptions? Should they be stated explicitly?
- What are the counterarguments? Do they weaken the argument?
- Is there anything that has been omitted from the argument?

TABLE 9.1 Critical Thinking Skills Discussed in This Application

Skill	Description
Understanding the elements of an argument	The critical thinker understands that an argument consists of premises and assumptions that are used to support a conclusion.
Recognizing and avoiding common fallacies, such as irrelevant reasons, circular reasoning, slippery slope reasoning, weak analogies, and false dichotomies	The critical thinker is vigilant about conclusions based on unrelated premises, conclusions that are rewordings of premises, unwarranted predictions that things will spin out of control, superficial analogies, and contrived dichotomies.
Evaluating arguments systematically	The critical thinker carefully assesses the validity of the premises, assumptions, and conclusions in an argument, and considers counterarguments and missing elements.

MOTIVATIONAL THEORIES AND CONCEPTS

- *Drive theories* emphasize how *internal* states of tension (due to disruptions of homeostasis) *push* organisms in certain directions.

- *Incentive theories* emphasize how *external goals pull* organisms in certain directions.

- Evolutionary theories assert that motives are a product of *natural selection* that have had adaptive value in terms of fostering reproductive fitness.

- Humans display an enormous diversity of *biological* and *social* motives.

© Christian Kober/Getty Images

MOTIVATION OF HUNGER

Biological factors regulating hunger

- Research originally suggested that the *lateral* and *ventromedial areas of the hypothalamus* were the brain's on-off switches for hunger, but the dual-centers model proved too simple.

- Today scientists think that *neural circuits* passing through the *arcuate* and *paraventricular* areas of the hypothalamus play a larger role in the regulation of hunger.

- In the digestive system, the stomach can send various types of satiety signals to the brain.

- Secretions of the hormone *ghrelin* cause stomach contractions and increased hunger.

- Secretions of the hormone *CCK* carry satiety signals from the intestine to the brain.

- The hormone *leptin* provides the hypothalamus with information about the body's fat stores.

© Picturepartners/Shutterstock.com

Environmental factors regulating hunger

- Organisms consume more food when it is palatable, when more is available, and when there is greater variety.

- People tend to eat more in the presence of others and in response to food advertisements.

- Stressful events can increase food consumption in about 40%–50% of people.

- Classical conditioning and observational learning shape what people prefer to eat.

- Food preferences are also governed by exposure, which is why there are huge cultural variations in eating habits.

The roots of obesity

- Surveys show surprisingly sharp increases in the incidence of obesity in recent decades.

  - Obesity is associated with an increased incidence of many health problems and elevated risk of mortality.

  - Some people inherit a genetic vulnerability to obesity.

  - Obesity is attributable to excessive eating and inadequate exercise.

  - Increased sleep deprivation in modern society probably fuels increased obesity.

  - The concept of a *set point* suggests that each individual has a natural range of stability for weight.

SEXUAL MOTIVATION

The human sexual response

- Masters and Johnson showed that the sexual response cycle consists of four stages: excitement, plateau, orgasm, and resolution.

- Intercourse leads to orgasm in women less consistently than in men, but women are much more likely to be multiorgasmic.

Evolutionary analyses

- According to *parental investment theory*, the gender that makes the smaller investment in offspring will compete for mating opportunities with the gender that makes the larger investment, which will be more discriminating in selecting partners.

- Human males are required to invest little in offspring, so their reproductive potential is maximized by mating with as many partners as possible.

- Human females have to invest months to years in carrying and nourishing offspring, so they maximize their reproductive potential by mating with males who are able to invest more resources in their offspring.

© Lisa F. Young/Shutterstock.com

Sexual orientation

- People tend to view heterosexuality and homosexuality as an all-or-none distinction, but it is more accurate to view them as endpoints on a continuum.

- Environmental explanations of sexual orientation have not been supported by research.

- Biological explanations have fared better in recent years, as twin studies have shown that genetic factors influence sexual orientation.

- Research also suggests that idiosyncrasies in prenatal hormonal secretions can influence sexual orientation.

- Females' sexual orientation appears to be characterized by more *plasticity* than that of males.

ACHIEVEMENT MOTIVATION

- David McClelland pioneered the use of the TAT to measure individual differences in *need for achievement*.

- People who score high in the need for achievement tend to work harder and more persistently than others and are more likely to delay gratification.

- However, people high in the need for achievement tend to choose challenges of intermediate difficulty.

- The pursuit of achievement goals tends to increase when the probability of success on a task and the incentive value of the success are higher.

Gender differences in sexual activity

- Males think about sex and initiate sex more often than females do.

- Males are more willing to engage in casual sex and tend to have more partners than females do.

Gender differences in mate preferences

- Males around the world place more emphasis than females do on potential partners' youthfulness and attractiveness.

- Females around the world place more emphasis than males do on partners' status, intelligence, and financial prospects.

APPLICATIONS

- Income, age, parenthood, intelligence, and attractiveness are largely uncorrelated with happiness.

- Physical health, good social relationships, and religious convictions have a modest association with happiness.

- Stronger predictors of happiness include love and marriage, work satisfaction, and personality and genetics.

- Subjective well-being is a relative concept, and people adapt to their circumstances.

- Arguments are often marred by fallacies, such as irrelevant reasons, weak analogies, circular reasoning, slippery slope scenarios, and false dichotomies.

EMOTION

Cognitive component

- The cognitive component of emotion consists of subjective feelings that are often intense and difficult to control.

- Cognitive appraisals of events influence the emotions people experience.

- Research on *affective forecasting* shows that people are surprisingly bad at predicting the intensity and duration of their emotional reactions to events.

Physiological component

- The physiological component of emotion is dominated by autonomic arousal.

- A *polygraph* detects emotional arousal, which is far from a perfect index of lying.

- According to Joseph LeDoux, the *amygdala* lies at the core of a complex set of neural circuits that process emotion, especially fear.

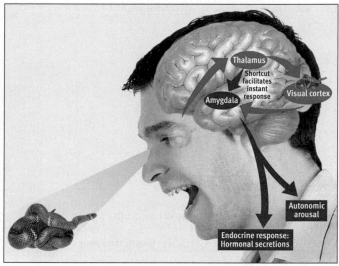

Man: © Aleksandr Kurganov/Shutterstock.com; Snake: © C. H. Wooley

Behavioral component

- At the behavioral level, emotions are revealed through body language.

- People can identify at least six emotions based on facial expressions.

- According to the *facial feedback hypothesis*, facial muscles send signals to the brain that aid in the recognition of emotions.

Cultural considerations

- Ekman and Friesen found cross-cultural agreement in the identification of emotions based on facial expressions.

- Cross-cultural similarities have also been found in the cognitive and physiological components of emotion.

- However, there are cultural disparities in how emotions are categorized and in public displays of emotions.

Theoretical views

- The *James-Lange theory* asserts that the conscious experience of emotion results from one's perception of autonomic arousal.

- The *Cannon-Bard theory* asserts that emotions originate in subcortical areas of the brain.

- According to the *two-factor theory*, people infer emotion from autonomic arousal and then label it in accordance with their cognitive explanation for the arousal.

- *Evolutionary theories of emotion* assert that emotions are innate reactions that do not depend on cognitive processes.

CHAPTER 10

HUMAN DEVELOPMENT ACROSS THE LIFE SPAN

Themes in this Chapter

Theoretical
Diversity

Sociohistorical
Context

Multifactorial
Causation

Cultural
Heritage

Heredity &
Environment

© RonTech3000/Shutterstock.com

In high school, kids called her "catfish" because of her outsized lips. Her attempts at modeling brought more than 100 rejections—she was too short, too skinny, too scarred. Today, she's been named "Most Beautiful Woman in the World" by *People* magazine, is one of the highest-paid actors in the world, and is known for her humanitarian work for the United Nations. Let's take a closer look at the life of Angelina Jolie.

After her parents divorced, Angelina's childhood was marked by frequent moves to rented and ever-smaller houses as her mother struggled to make ends meet. Attending Beverly Hills High School, Angelina felt out of place among the well-scrubbed rich kids in preppy clothes. Taken on modeling calls by her mother, Angelina was self-conscious and nervous. Although her father, Jon Voigt, was a famous Oscar-winning actor, she didn't want to be an actress. She wanted to be a funeral director. She hung out at the arcade with the outcasts, experimenting with drugs. At 14, she dyed her hair purple and went slam-dancing with her live-in punk boyfriend. She continued to rebel against convention when, at her wedding to actor Jonny Lee Miller, she wore black rubber pants and a white shirt with the groom's name written in her blood across the back. The media couldn't write enough about the "wild child."

But in her mid-20s, Angelina underwent a transformation. Filming *Lara Croft: Tomb Raider* in Cambodia, she saw conditions that would change her forever. The plight of displaced people in Cambodia affected her deeply. She contacted the United Nations to learn more and asked to help. The U.N. sent her to paparazzi-free zones: trouble spots in Sierra Leone and Tanzania. In 2001, the U.N. High Commissioner for Refugees made Angelina an official Goodwill Ambassador. Since then, Angelina has been on many daunting U.N. field missions to places such as Thailand, Sudan, and Ecuador, where she often has had to endure extremely primitive living conditions.

Angelina's transition from an insecure teenager to a self-assured adult and from a wild child to humanitarian was startling. Yet there was also a strong element of continuity in her life. Consider, for instance, her rebelliousness. When Angelina was young, she was quite a rebel. As she matured, Angelina remained a rebel, vigorously fighting for more-humane treatment of oppressed refugee populations. In a sense, she rechanneled her defiance. As she puts it, "Now I take that punk in me to Washington, and I fight for something important" (Swibel, 2006).

The story of Angelina Jolie's metamorphosis from an awkward, insecure "wild child" into an elegant, self-assured public figure provides a dramatic demonstration of how human development is marked by both continuity and transition.

Another personality trait that has remained constant throughout her life is empathy. Perhaps because of her own uprooted childhood, Angelina was always maternal to younger children. From the age of 12, Angelina knew that she wanted to adopt underprivileged children. As an adult, she followed through on this desire, adopting three orphans from far-flung corners of the globe. And, of course, her continued empathy for the plight of the world's downtrodden is manifested in her unselfish commitment to humanitarian missions.

What does Angelina Jolie have to do with developmental psychology? Although her story is obviously unique in many ways, it provides an interesting illustration of the two themes that permeate the study of human development: *transition* and *continuity*. In investigating human development, psychologists study how people evolve through transitions over time. In looking at these transitions, developmental psychologists inevitably find continuity with the past.

Development **is the sequence of age-related changes that occur as a person progresses from conception to death.** It is a reasonably orderly, cumulative process that includes both the biological and behavioral changes that take place as people grow older. An infant's newfound ability to grasp objects, a child's gradual mastery of grammar, an adolescent's spurt in physical growth, a young adult's increasing commitment to a vocation, and an older adult's transition into the role of grandparent all represent development. These transitions are predictable changes that are related to age.

Traditionally, psychologists have been most interested in development during childhood. Our coverage reflects this emphasis. However, decades of research have clearly shown that development is a lifelong process. In this chapter, we divide the life span into four broad periods: the prenatal period between conception and birth, childhood, adolescence, and adulthood. We examine aspects of development that are especially dynamic during each period. Let's begin by looking at events that occur before birth, during prenatal development.

10.1

Key Learning Goals
- Outline the major events of the three stages of prenatal development.
- Summarize the impact of environmental factors on prenatal development.

10.1 PROGRESS BEFORE BIRTH: PRENATAL DEVELOPMENT

The ***prenatal period*** **extends from conception to birth, usually encompassing nine months of pregnancy.** Significant development occurs before birth. In fact, development during the prenatal period is remarkably rapid. If you were an average-sized newborn and your physical growth had continued during the first year of your life at a prenatal pace, by your first birthday you would have weighed 200 pounds! Fortunately, you didn't grow at that rate because in the final weeks before birth the frenzied pace of prenatal development tapers off dramatically.

In this section, we'll examine the usual course of prenatal development and discuss how environmental events can leave their mark on development even before birth exposes the newborn to the outside world.

The Course of Prenatal Development

The prenatal period is divided into three phases: (1) the germinal stage (the first 2 weeks), (2) the embryonic stage (2 weeks to 2 months), and (3) the fetal stage (2 months to birth). Some key developments in these phases are outlined here.

Germinal Stage

The ***germinal stage*** **is the first phase of prenatal development, encompassing the first 2 weeks after conception.** This brief stage begins when a zygote is created through fertilization. Within 36 hours, rapid cell division begins. The zygote becomes a microscopic mass of multiplying cells. This mass slowly migrates along the mother's fallopian tube to the uterine cavity. On about the seventh day, the cell mass begins to implant itself in the uterine wall. This process takes about a week and is far from automatic. Many zygotes are rejected at this point. As many as one in five pregnancies ends with the woman never being aware that conception has occurred (Simpson & Jauniaux, 2012).

During the implantation process, the placenta begins to form. **The *placenta* is a structure that allows oxygen and nutrients to pass into the fetus from the mother's bloodstream and bodily wastes to pass out to the mother.** This critical exchange takes place across thin membranes that block the passage of blood cells, keeping the fetal and maternal bloodstreams separate.

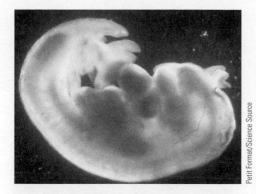

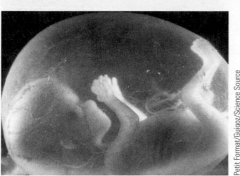

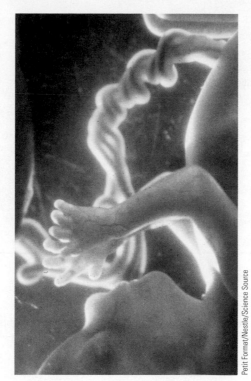

Prenatal development is remarkably rapid. Top left: This 30-day-old embryo is just 6 millimeters in length. Bottom left: At 14 weeks, the fetus is approximately 2 inches long. Note the well-developed fingers. The fetus can already move its legs, feet, hands, and head and displays a variety of basic reflexes. Right: After 4 months of prenatal development, facial features are beginning to emerge.

Embryonic Stage

The *embryonic stage* **is the second stage of prenatal development, lasting from 2 weeks until the end of the second month.** During this stage, most of the vital organs and bodily systems begin to form in the developing organism, which is now called an *embryo*. Structures such as the heart, spine, and brain emerge gradually as cell division becomes more specialized. Although the embryo is typically only about an inch long at the end of this stage, it's already beginning to look human. Arms, legs, hands, feet, fingers, toes, eyes, and ears are already discernible.

The embryonic stage is a period of great vulnerability because virtually all the basic physiological structures are being formed. If anything interferes with normal development during the embryonic phase, the effects can be devastating. Most miscarriages occur during this period (Simpson & Jauniaux, 2012). Most major structural birth defects also result from problems that occur during the embryonic stage (Niebyl & Simpson, 2012).

Fetal Stage

The *fetal stage* **is the third stage of prenatal development, lasting from 2 months through birth.** Some highlights of fetal development are summarized in **Figure 10.1**. The first 2 months of the fetal stage bring rapid bodily growth, as muscles and bones begin to form (Moore, Persaud, & Torchia, 2013). The developing organism, now called a *fetus,* becomes capable of physical movements as skeletal structures harden. Organs formed in the embryonic stage continue to grow and gradually begin to function. The sense of hearing, for example, is functional by around 20–24 weeks (Hepper, 2003).

During the final 3 months of the prenatal period, brain cells multiply at a brisk pace. A layer of fat is deposited under the skin to provide insulation, and the respiratory and digestive systems mature (Adolph & Berger, 2011). Sometime between 23 weeks and 25 weeks, the fetus reaches the *threshold of viability*—the age at which a baby can survive in the event of a premature birth. At 23 weeks, the probability of survival is still slim (about 20%), but it climbs rapidly to around a 67% survival rate at 25 weeks (Seaton et al., 2013). Unfortunately, a great many of the premature infants born near the threshold of viability go on to experience a wide range of developmental problems (Cunningham et al., 2010).

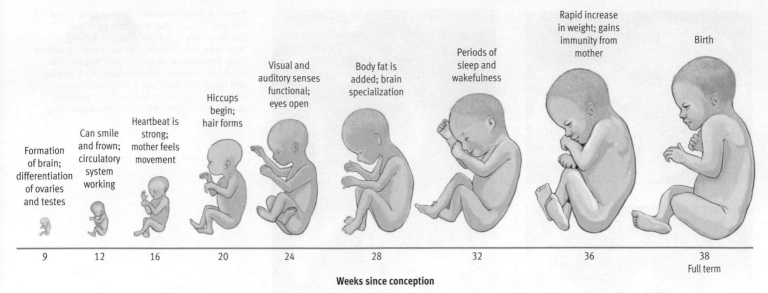

Weeks since conception

FIGURE 10.1
Overview of fetal development. This chart outlines some of the highlights of development during the fetal stage.

Environmental Factors and Prenatal Development

Although the fetus develops within the protective buffer of the womb, events in the external environment can affect it indirectly through the mother, as the developing organism and its mother are linked via the placenta.

Nutrition

Maternal nutrition is very important because the developing fetus needs a variety of essential nutrients. Severe maternal malnutrition increases the risk of birth complications and neurological deficits for the newborn (Coutts, 2000). The impact of moderate malnutrition is more difficult to gauge because it is often confounded with other risk factors associated with poverty, such as drug abuse and limited access to health care (Guerrini, Thomson, & Gurling, 2007).

CONCEPT CHECK 10.1

Understanding the Stages of Prenatal Development

Check your understanding of the stages of prenatal development by filling in the blanks in the chart below. The first column contains descriptions of a main event from each of the three stages. In the second column, write the name of the stage; in the third column, write the term used to refer to the developing organism during that stage; and in the fourth column, write the time span (in terms of weeks or months) covered by the stage. The answers are in Appendix A.

Event	Stage	Term for organism	Time span
1. Uterine implantation	_____	_____	_____
2. Muscle and bone begin to form	_____	_____	_____
3. Vital organs and body systems begin to form	_____	_____	_____

© Supri Suharjoto/Shutterstock.com

Still, even when pregnant women have ample access to food, it is important for them to consume a balanced diet that includes essential vitamins and minerals (Monk, Georgieff, & Osterholm, 2013).

Stress and Emotion

Recent studies suggest that maternal emotions in reaction to stressful events can have an impact on prentatal development. For example, elevated levels of prenatal stress have been found to be associated with increased stillbirths (Hogue et al., 2013); impaired immune response (Veru et al, 2014); heightened vulnerability to infectious disease (Nielsen et al., 2010); slowed motor development (Cao et al., 2014); below-average cognitive development (Tarabulsy et al, 2014); and social deficits (Walder et al., 2014). Why is prenatal stress so harmful? Research suggests that prospective mothers' emotional reactions to stressful events can disrupt the delicate hormonal balance that fosters healthy prenatal development (Douglas, 2010).

Drug Use

Another major source of concern is the mother's consumption of drugs. Unfortunately, most drugs consumed by a pregnant woman can slip through the membranes of the placenta. Virtually all "recreational" drugs can be harmful, with sedatives, narcotics, cocaine, and methamphetamine being particularly dangerous (Kaltenbach & Jones, 2011). Thanks to their mothers' drug abuse, more than 13,000 babies in the United States are born addicted to narcotics each year (Patrick et al., 2012). Problems can even be caused by drugs prescribed for legitimate medical reasons and by some over-the-counter drugs (Niebyl & Simpson, 2012). Tobacco use during pregnancy is also problematic. Smoking appears to increase a mother's risk for miscarriage, stillbirth, and prematurity, as well as newborns' risk for sudden infant death syndrome (Shea & Steiner, 2008) and for attention deficits, hyperactivity, and conduct problems (Wehby et al., 2011).

Alcohol Consumption

Alcohol consumption during pregnancy carries serious risks. It has long been clear that *heavy* drinking by a mother can be hazardous to a fetus. **Fetal alcohol syndrome is a collection of congenital (inborn) problems associated with excessive alcohol use during pregnancy.** Typical problems manifesting in childhood include microcephaly (a small head), heart defects, irritability, hyperactivity, and delayed motor development (Dörrie et al., 2014). Fetal alcohol syndrome is the most common known cause of intellectual disability (Niccols, 2007). Even moderate drinking during pregnancy can have enduring and substantial negative effects (Flak et al., 2014). Research on pregnant women's drinking has found that moderate alcohol intake is associated with an elevated risk for deficits in IQ, motor skills, and attention span, and with increased impulsive, antisocial, and delinquent behavior (Lewis et al., 2012; Streissguth, 2007).

Maternal Illness

The placenta screens out quite a number of infectious agents, but not all. Thus, many maternal illnesses can interfere with prenatal development. Diseases such as measles, rubella (German measles), syphilis, and chickenpox can be hazardous to the fetus (Bernstein, 2007); the nature of any damage depends, in part, on when the mother contracts the illness. The HIV virus that causes AIDS can also be transmitted by pregnant women to their offspring. The transmission of AIDS can occur prenatally through the placenta, during delivery, or through breastfeeding. Up through the mid-1990s, about 20%–30% of HIV-positive pregnant women passed the virus on to their babies, but improved antiretroviral drugs (given to the mother) and more cautious obstetrical care have reduced this figure to about 2% in the United States (Cotter & Potter, 2006).

© Samuel Borges Photography/Shutterstock.com

A surprising number of environmental factors can influence the course of prenatal development and have enduring effects on children. In some cases, these effects may not be apparent until decades later.

▷ **REALITY CHECK**

Misconception

It is safe for pregnant women to engage in moderate social drinking.

Reality

Not really. Studies have linked social drinking during pregnancy to a variety of enduring problems for children. We have no clear evidence on what would represent a safe amount of drinking. Lacking that evidence, the only safe course of action is to completely abstain from alcohol during pregnancy.

Environmental Toxins

Research also suggests that babies in the womb are exposed to a surprising variety of *environmental toxins* that can affect them (Houlihan et al., 2005). For example, prenatal exposure to air pollution has been linked to impairments in cognitive development at age 5 (Edwards et al., 2010) and increased obesity at age 7 (Rundle et al., 2012). In a similar vein, exposure to the chemicals used in flame-retardant materials correlates with slower mental and physical development up through age 6 (Herbstman et al., 2010).

Fetal Origins of Adult Disease

Research on prenatal development has generally focused on its connection to the risk for birth defects and adverse outcomes that are apparent during early childhood. However, researchers have begun to explore the links between prenatal factors and *adults'* physical and mental health. Evidence suggests that events during prenatal development can "program" the fetal brain in ways that influence the person's vulnerability to various types of illness decades later (Barker, 2013; Skogen & Overland, 2012). For example, prenatal malnutrition has been linked to vulnerability to schizophrenia, which usually emerges in late adolescence or early adulthood (A. S. Brown, 2012a). Low birth weight, which is a marker for a variety of prenatal disruptions, has been found to be associated with an increased risk of heart disease many decades later in adulthood (Roseboom, de Rooij, & Painter, 2006). Studies have also linked aspects of prenatal development to adults' risk for depression and bipolar disorders (Bale et al., 2010; Talati et al., 2013), as well as obesity, diabetes, and some types of cancer (Calkins & Devaskar, 2011). These findings on the fetal origins of disease have provoked a dramatic reassessment of the factors that influence health and illness.

10.2 MOTOR, SOCIAL, AND LANGUAGE DEVELOPMENT IN CHILDHOOD

10.2

Key Learning Goals

- Understand the role of maturation and cultural variations in motor development.
- Describe Harlow's and Bowlby's views on attachment, and discuss research on patterns of attachment.
- Trace the development of human language during childhood.

A certain magic is associated with childhood. Young children have an extraordinary ability to captivate adults' attention as helpless infants become curious toddlers almost overnight. In this section you'll see what psychologists have learned about the development of motor skills, attachment relationships, and language.

Exploring the World: Motor Development

Motor development **refers to the progression of muscular coordination required for physical activities.** Basic motor skills include grasping and reaching for objects, manipulating objects, sitting up, crawling, walking, and running. Historically, a great deal of attention has been focused on walking, which is typically mastered around 12 months of age. One study of the transition to walking revealed that infants get an enormous amount of experience in short bursts of walking activity as they average 2368 steps and 17 falls per hour during free play (Adolph et al., 2012). Extrapolating from the hourly data suggests that infants may walk more than 14,000 steps per day, traveling the length of forty-six football fields! Small wonder then that infants' walking improves rapidly.

Early motor development depends in part on physical growth, which is not only rapid during infancy but also more uneven than previously appreciated. Research has shown that in the first couple years of life, lengthy periods of no growth are punctuated by sudden bursts of growth. These growth spurts tend to be accompanied by restlessness, irritability, and increased sleep (Lampl & Johnson, 2011; Lampl, Veldhuis, & Johnson, 1992). Thus, parents who sometimes feel that their children are changing overnight may not be imagining it.

Early progress in motor skills has traditionally been attributed almost entirely to the process of maturation (Adolph & Berger, 2011). *Maturation* **is development that reflects the gradual unfolding of one's genetic blueprint.** It is a product of genetically programmed physical changes that come with age, rather than through experience and learning. However, research that has taken a closer look at the *process* of motor development suggests that infants are active agents, not passive organisms waiting for their brain and limbs to mature (Adolph & Berger, 2011; Thelen, 1995). According to this view, the driving force behind motor development is infants' ongoing exploration of their world and their need to master specific tasks (such as grasping a larger toy or looking out a window).

Understanding Developmental Norms

Parents often pay close attention to early motor development, comparing their child's progress with developmental norms. *Developmental norms* **indicate the typical (median) age at which individuals display various behaviors and abilities.** Developmental norms are useful benchmarks as long as parents don't expect their children to progress exactly at the pace specified in the norms. Some parents get unnecessarily alarmed when their children fall behind developmental norms. What these parents overlook is that developmental norms are group *averages*. Variations from the average are entirely normal. This normal variation stands out in **Figure 10.2**, which indicates the age at which 25%, 50%, and 90% of youngsters can demonstrate various motor skills. As **Figure 10.2** shows, a substantial portion of children don't achieve a particular milestone until long after the average time cited in norms.

Cultural Variations and Their Significance

Cross-cultural research has highlighted the dynamic interplay between experience and maturation in motor development. Relatively rapid motor development has been observed in some cultures that provide special practice in basic motor skills (Adolph, Karasik, & Tamis-Lemonda, 2010). For example, the Kipsigis people of Kenya begin active efforts to train their infants to sit up, stand, and walk soon after birth. Thanks to this training, Kipsigis children achieve these developmental milestones (but not others) about a month earlier than babies in the United States (Super, 1976). In contrast, relatively slow motor development has been found in some cultures that discourage motor exploration

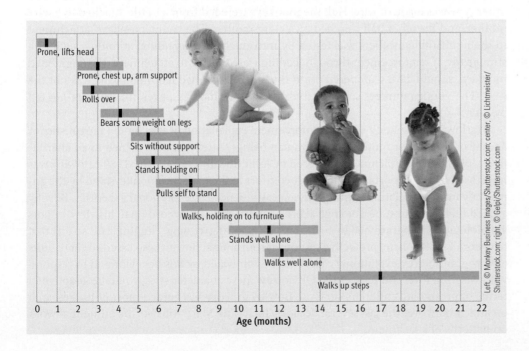

FIGURE 10.2

Milestones in motor development. The left edge, interior mark, and right edge of each bar indicate the age at which 25%, 50%, and 90% of infants have mastered each motor skill shown. Developmental norms typically report only the median age of mastery (the interior mark), which can be misleading in light of the variability in age of mastery apparent in this chart.

Tribes across the world use a variety of methods to foster rapid development of motor abilities in their children. The Kung San of the Kalahari, Botswana, teach their young to dance quite early, using poles to develop the kinesthetic sense of balance.

Even if fed by a wire surrogate mother, Harlow's infant monkeys cuddled up with a terry cloth surrogate that provided contact comfort. When threatened by a frightening toy, the monkeys sought security from their terry cloth mothers.

(Adolph et al., 2010). Cultural variations in the emergence of basic motor skills show that environmental factors can accelerate or slow early motor development.

Early Emotional Development: Attachment

Attachment **refers to the close emotional bonds of affection that develop between infants and their caregivers.** Researchers have shown a keen interest in how infant-mother attachments are formed early in life. Children eventually form attachments to many people, including their fathers, siblings, grandparents, and others (Cassidy, 2008; Easterbrooks et al., 2013). However, a child's first important attachment usually occurs with his or her mother because she is typically the main caregiver in the early months of life (Lamb & Lewis, 2011).

Initially, babies show relatively little in the way of a special preference for their mother. At 2–3 months of age, infants may smile and laugh more when they interact with their mother, but they can be handed over to strangers such as babysitters with relatively little difficulty. This situation gradually changes. By about 6–8 months of age, infants begin to show a pronounced preference for their mother's company and often protest when separated from her (Lamb, Ketterlinus, & Fracasso, 1992). This is the first manifestation of *separation anxiety*—**emotional distress seen in many infants when they are separated from people with whom they have formed an attachment.** Separation anxiety may occur with other familiar caregivers as well as the mother. It typically peaks at around 14–18 months and then begins to decline.

Theories of Attachment

Why do children gradually develop a special attachment to their mothers? This question sounds simple enough; however, it has been the subject of a lively theoretical dialogue. Behaviorists have argued that the infant-mother attachment develops because mothers are associated with the powerful, reinforcing event of being fed. Thus, the mother becomes a conditioned reinforcer. However, this reinforcement theory of attachment came into question as a result of Harry Harlow's famous studies of attachment in infant rhesus monkeys (Harlow, 1958, 1959).

Harlow removed monkeys from their mothers at birth and raised them in the laboratory with two types of artificial "substitute mothers." One type of artificial mother was made of terrycloth and could provide "contact comfort" (see the adjacent photo). The other type was made of wire. Half the monkeys were fed from a bottle attached to a wire mother, and the other half were fed by a cloth mother. The young monkeys' attachment to their substitute mothers was tested by introducing a frightening stimulus, such as a strange toy. If reinforcement through feeding were the key to attachment, the frightened monkeys should have scampered off to the mother that had fed them. This was not the case. The young monkeys scrambled for their cloth mothers, even if they were *not* fed by them.

Harlow's work made a simple reinforcement explanation of attachment unrealistic for animals, let alone for more complex human beings. Attention then turned to an alternative explanation of attachment proposed by John Bowlby (1969, 1973, 1980). Bowlby was impressed by the importance of contact comfort to the Harlows' monkeys and by the apparently unlearned nature of this preference. Influenced by evolutionary theories, Bowlby argued that there must be a biological basis for attachment. According to his view, infants are biologically programmed to emit behavior (smiling, cooing, clinging, and so on) that triggers an affectionate, protective response from adults. Bowlby also asserted that adults are programmed by evolutionary forces to be captivated by this behavior and to respond with warmth, love, and protection. Obviously, these characteristics would be adaptive in terms of promoting children's survival. Bowlby's theory has guided most of the research on attachment over the last several decades, including Mary Ainsworth's influential work on patterns of attachment.

Patterns of Attachment

Infant-mother attachments vary in quality. Mary Ainsworth and her colleagues (1978) found that these attachments fall into three categories. Fortunately, most infants develop a *secure attachment*. They play and explore comfortably with their mother present, become visibly upset when she leaves, and are quickly calmed by her return. However, some children display a pattern called *anxious-ambivalent attachment* (also called *resistant attachment*). They appear anxious even when their mothers are near and protest excessively when she leaves, but they are not particularly comforted when she returns. Children in the third category seek little contact with their mothers and often are not distressed when she leaves. This condition is labeled *avoidant attachment*.

Although quite a variety of factors can shape the type of attachment that emerges between an infant and mother, maternal sensitivity appears to be especially influential (Posada et al., 2007; Thompson, 2013). Mothers who are sensitive and responsive to their children's needs are more likely to promote secure attachments than mothers who are relatively insensitive or inconsistent in their responding (Easterbrooks et al., 2013). However, infants are not passive bystanders as this process unfolds. They are active participants who influence the process with their crying, smiling, fussing, and babbling. Difficult infants who spit up most of their food, make bathing a major battle, and rarely smile may sometimes slow the process of attachment (van IJzendoorn & Bakermans-Kranenburg, 2004). Thus, the type of attachment that emerges between an infant and mother can depend on the nature of the infant's temperament as well as the mother's sensitivity (Kagan & Fox, 2006).

Evidence suggests that the quality of the attachment relationship can have important consequences for children's subsequent development. Based on their attachment experiences, children develop *internal working models* of the dynamics of close relationships that influence their future interactions with a wide range of people (Bretherton & Munholland, 2008). Infants with a relatively secure attachment *tend* to become resilient, socially competent toddlers with high self-esteem (Thompson, 2013) and more advanced language development (Moullin, Waldfogel, & Washbrook, 2014). In their preschool years, such children display more persistence, curiosity, self-reliance, and leadership and have better peer relations (Weinfeld et al., 2008). As these children mature, they exhibit fewer problems with anger, defiance, and aggression, as well as less anxiety and depression (Moullin et al., 2014).

Day Care and Attachment

The impact of day care on attachment has been the subject of some debate. The crucial question is whether frequent infant-mother separations might disrupt the attachment process. The issue is an important one, given that about half of infants and toddlers in the United States receive some nonparental care (Berlin, 2012). For the most part, the evidence suggests that day care does not have a harmful effect on children's attachment relationships (Friedman & Boyle, 2008). When mothers are sensitive to their children, the amount and quality of day care tend to be unrelated to attachment security (Thompson, 2008). However, decreases in attachment security have been seen when mothers are relatively insensitive and their children experience low-quality day care (Vermeer & Bakermans-Kranenburg, 2008). Some studies suggest that infants with a "difficult" temperament may be particularly vulnerable to the potential negative effects of low-quality day care (Pluess & Belsky, 2010; Burchinal, Lowe Vandell, & Belsky, 2014). So, there may be reasons for concern about children placed in understaffed, low-quality day care who get little personal attention.

Culture and Attachment

Separation anxiety emerges in children at about 6–8 months and peaks at about 14–18 months in cultures around the world (Grossmann & Grossmann, 1990). These findings, which have been replicated in quite a variety of non-Western cultures, suggest that

The quality of the attachment relationship between an infant and its mother can have lasting effects on the child's development. A secure attachment tends to foster healthier outcomes than an avoidant or anxious-ambivalent attachment.

▶ **REALITY CHECK**

Misconception

A strong attachment relationship depends on infant-mother bonding during the first few hours after birth.

Reality

Bonding immediately after birth can be a magic moment for mothers and probably should be encouraged for their sake. But there is no empirical evidence that this practice leads to healthier attachment relationships in the long run.

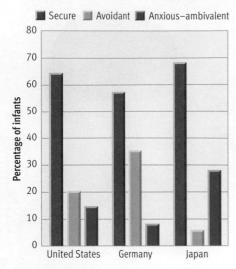

■ Secure ■ Avoidant ■ Anxious–ambivalent

FIGURE 10.3

Cultural variations in attachment patterns.
This graph shows the prevalence of secure, avoidant, and anxious-ambivalent attachment patterns found in specific studies in Germany, Japan, and the United States. As you can see, secure attachment is the most common pattern in all three societies, as it is around the world. However, there are some modest cultural differences in the prevalence of each pattern of attachment, which are probably attributable to cultural variations in childrearing practices. (Data from van IJzendoorn & Kroonenberg, 1988)

attachment is a universal feature of human development. However, studies have found some modest cultural variations in the proportion of infants who fall into the three attachment categories described by Ainsworth, as you can see in **Figure 10.3**, which shows data for Japan, Germany, and the United States (Thompson, 2013; van IJzendoorn & Sagi-Schwartz, 2008). Although secure attachment appears to be the predominant type of attachment around the world, researchers have found that the factors that promote secure attachment and the outcomes associated with secure attachment vary some across cultures (Molitor & Hsu, 2011).

Learning to Communicate: Language Development

The early course of language development is similar across very different cultures (Gleitman & Newport, 1996), and language development tends to unfold at *roughly* the same pace for most children, even though children obviously are reared in diverse environments (Wagner & Hoff, 2013). These findings suggest that language development is determined by biological maturation more than by personal experience. That said, there are variations among children in the pace of language acquisition, and experience is *not* irrelevant (Parish-Morris, Golinkoff, & Hirsh-Pasek, 2013). Parents who are more responsive to infants' attempts at communication foster more rapid early language development (Tamis-LeMonda, Kuchirko, & Song, 2014). Even listening and responding to early babbling, which may seem nonsensical, can promote communication efforts and speed up language acquisition (Gros-Louis, West, & King, 2014). It is also important for parents to talk to their infant children. The amount and diversity of child-directed speech experienced during infancy predicts vocabulary growth and other aspects of language development (Goldin-Meadow et al., 2014; Weisleder & Fernald, 2013).

Moving Toward Producing Words

Long before infants utter their first words, they are making progress in learning the sound structure of their native language. Research suggests that babies start learning basic vowel sounds while still in their mothers' womb (Moon, Lagercrantz, & Kuhl, 2012). During the first 6 months of life, a baby's vocalizations are dominated by crying, cooing, and laughter, which have limited value as a means of communication. Soon, infants are *babbling*. Their babbling gradually becomes more complex and increasingly resembles the language spoken by parents and others in the child's environment (Hoff, 2014). Infants start learning the meaning of some words as early as 6–9 months of age, well before they are capable of producing words (Parise & Csibra, 2012).

Around 10–13 months of age, most children begin to utter sounds that correspond to words. Most infants' first words are similar in phonetic form and meaning—even in different languages (Waxman, 2002). The initial words resemble the syllables that infants most often babble spontaneously. For example, words such as *dada, mama,* and *papa* are names for parents in many languages because they consist of sounds that are easy to produce.

Using Words

After children utter their first words, their vocabulary grows slowly for the next few months. Toddlers typically can say between three and fifty words by 18 months. However, their *receptive vocabulary* is larger than their *productive vocabulary.* That is, they can comprehend more words spoken by others than they can actually produce to express themselves (Pan & Uccelli, 2009). Thus, toddlers can *understand* fifty words months before they can *say* fifty words.

Youngsters' vocabularies soon begin to grow at a dizzying pace, as a *vocabulary spurt* often begins at around 18 months, when toddlers realize that everything has a name (Camaioni, 2001). By the first grade, the average child has a vocabulary of approximately 10,000 words, which builds to an astonishing 40,000 words by the fifth grade (Anglin, 1993). *Fast mapping* appears to be one factor underlying this rapid growth of vocabulary

(Carey, 2010). *Fast mapping* **is the process by which children map a word onto an underlying concept after only one exposure.** Thus, children often add words such as *tank, board,* and *tape* to their vocabularies after their first encounter with objects that illustrate these concepts. Building a vocabulary in the preschool years is an important process, as vocabulary growth at 30 months predicts vocabulary size when children enter kindergarten (Rowe, Raudenbush, & Goldin-Meadow, 2012). Vocabulary knowledge is a crucial building block for the development of reading comprehension skills (Lervag & Aukrust, 2010).

Of course, children's efforts to learn new words are not flawless. Toddlers often make errors, such as overextensions and underextensions (Harley, 2008). **An *overextension* occurs when a child incorrectly uses a word to describe a wider set of objects or actions than it is meant to.** For example, a child might use the word *ball* for anything round— oranges, apples, even the moon. Overextensions usually appear in children's speech between ages 1 and 2 1/2. Specific overextensions typically last up to several months. Toddlers also tend to be guilty of *underextensions,* **which occur when a child incorrectly uses a word to describe a narrower set of objects or actions than it is meant to.** For example, a child might use the word *doll* to refer only to a single, favorite doll. Overextensions and underextensions show that toddlers are actively trying to learn the rules of language, albeit with mixed success.

Combining Words

Children typically begin to combine words into sentences near the end of their second year. Early sentences are characterized as "telegraphic" because they resemble old-fashioned telegrams, which omitted nonessential words because senders were charged by the word (Bochner & Jones, 2003). *Telegraphic speech* **consists mainly of content words; articles, prepositions, and other less critical words are omitted.** Thus, a child might say, "Give doll" rather than "Please give me the doll." Although not unique to the English language, telegraphic speech is not cross-culturally universal, as was once thought (de Villiers & de Villiers, 1999).

By the end of their third year, most children can express complex ideas, such as ideas requiring use of plurals or the past tense. However, their efforts to learn language continue to generate revealing mistakes. *Overregularizations* **occur when grammatical rules are incorrectly generalized to irregular cases where they do not apply.** For example, children will say things such as "The girl goed home" or "I hitted the ball." Children don't learn the fine points of grammar and usage in a single leap, but gradually acquire them in small steps. Youngsters make their largest strides in language development in their first 4–5 years. However, they continue to refine their language skills during their school-age years.

10.3 PERSONALITY, COGNITIVE, AND MORAL DEVELOPMENT IN CHILDHOOD

Many other aspects of development are especially dynamic during childhood. In this section we'll examine personality development; cognitive development; and the development of moral reasoning, which is closely tied to cognitive development. We begin with a look at the work of Erik Erikson and introduce the concept of developmental stages.

Becoming Unique: Personality Development

How do individuals develop their unique sets of personality traits over time? The first major theory of personality development was put together by Sigmund Freud around the turn of the 20th century. As we'll discuss in Chapter 11, he claimed that the basic

FIGURE 10.4

Stage theories of development. Some theories view development as a relatively continuous process, albeit not as smooth and perfectly linear as shown on the left **(a)**. In contrast, stage theories assume that development is marked by major discontinuities, as shown on the right **(b)**, that bring fundamental, qualitative changes in capabilities or characteristic behavior.

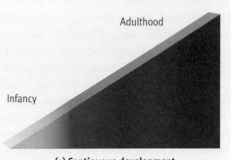

Adulthood

Infancy

(a) Continuous development

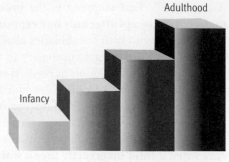

Adulthood

Infancy

(b) Discontinuous development (stages)

foundation of an individual's personality is firmly laid down by age 5. Half a century later, Erik Erikson (1963) proposed a sweeping revision of Freud's theory that has proven influential. Like Freud, Erikson concluded that events in early childhood leave a permanent stamp on adult personality. However, unlike Freud, Erikson theorized that personality continues to evolve over the entire life span.

Building on Freud's earlier work, Erikson devised a stage theory of personality development. As you'll see in this chapter, many theories describe development in terms of stages. **A *stage* is a developmental period during which characteristic patterns of behavior are exhibited and certain capacities become established.** Stage theories assume that (1) individuals must progress through specified stages in a particular order because each stage builds on the previous stage, (2) progress through these stages is strongly related to age, and (3) development is marked by discontinuities that usher in dramatic transitions in behavior (see **Figure 10.4**).

Erikson's Stage Theory

Erikson divided the life span into eight stages. Each stage brings a *psychosocial crisis* involving transitions in important social relationships. According to Erikson, personality is shaped by how individuals deal with these psychosocial crises. Each crisis is a potential turning point that can yield different outcomes. Erikson described the stages in terms of these alternative outcomes, which represent personality traits that people display over the remainder of their lives. All eight stages in Erikson's theory are charted in **Figure 10.5**. We describe the first four childhood stages here and discuss the remaining stages in the upcoming sections on adolescence and adulthood.

Trust versus mistrust Erikson's first stage encompasses the first year of life. During this time, an infant has to depend completely on adults to take care of its basic needs for such necessities as food, a warm blanket, and changed diapers. If an infant's basic biological needs are adequately met by its caregivers and sound attachments are formed, the child should develop an optimistic, trusting attitude toward the world. However, if the infant's basic needs are taken care of poorly, a more distrusting, insecure personality may result.

Autonomy versus shame and doubt Erikson's second stage unfolds during the second and third years of life. During this time, parents begin toilet training and other efforts to regulate the child. The child must begin to take some personal responsibility for feeding, dressing, and bathing. If all goes well, he or she acquires a sense of self-sufficiency, or autonomy. But if parents are never satisfied with the child's efforts and if parent-child conflicts are constant, the child may develop a sense of personal shame and self-doubt.

Initiative versus guilt In Erikson's third stage, roughly from ages 3 to 6, the challenge facing children is to function socially within their families. If children think only of their

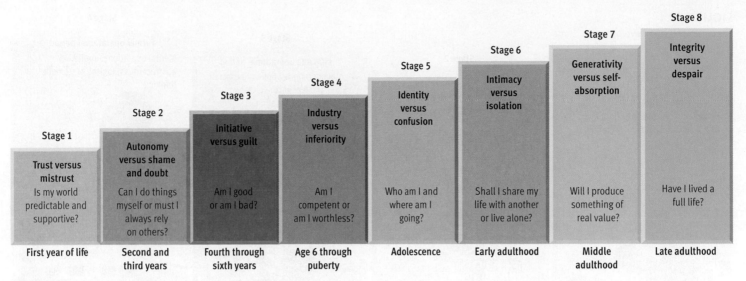

FIGURE 10.5

Erikson's stage theory. Erikson's theory of personality development asserts that people evolve through eight stages over the life span. Each stage is marked by a *psychosocial crisis* that involves confronting a fundamental question, such as "Who am I and where am I going?" The stages are described in terms of alternative traits that are potential outcomes from the crises. Development is enhanced when a crisis is resolved in favor of the healthier alternative (which is listed first for each stage).

own needs and desires, family members may begin to instill feelings of guilt, and self-esteem may suffer. But if children learn to get along well with siblings and parents, a sense of initiative and self-confidence should begin to grow.

Industry versus inferiority In the fourth stage (age 6 through puberty), the challenge of learning to function socially is extended beyond the family to the broader social realm of the neighborhood and school. Children who are able to function effectively in this less nurturant social sphere where productivity is highly valued should develop a sense of competence.

The Growth of Thought: Cognitive Development

Cognitive development **refers to transitions in youngsters' patterns of thinking, including reasoning, remembering, and problem solving.** The investigation of cognitive development has been dominated by the theory of Jean Piaget. Much of our discussion of cognitive development is devoted to Piaget's theory and the research it generated, although we'll also delve into other approaches to cognitive development.

Overview of Piaget's Stage Theory

Noting that children actively explore the world around them, Swiss scholar Jean Piaget (1929, 1952, 1983) asserted that interaction with the environment and maturation gradually alter the way children think. Like Erikson's theory, Piaget's model is a *stage theory* of development. Piaget proposed that children's thought processes go through a series of four major stages: (1) the *sensorimotor period* (birth to age 2), (2) the *preoperational period* (ages 2–7), (3) the *concrete operational period* (ages 7–11), and (4) the *formal operational period* (age 11 onward). **Figure 10.6** provides an overview of each of these periods. Piaget regarded his age norms as approximations and acknowledged that transitional ages can vary from one child to another.

Sensorimotor period The first stage in Piaget's theory is the *sensorimotor period,* lasting from birth to about age 2. Piaget called this stage *sensorimotor* because infants

FIGURE 10.6

Piaget's stage theory. Piaget's theory of cognitive development identifies four stages marked by fundamentally different modes of thinking through which youngsters evolve. The approximate age norms and some key characteristics of thought at each stage are summarized here.

are developing the ability to coordinate their sensory input with their motor actions. The major development during the sensorimotor stage is the gradual appearance of symbolic thought. At the beginning of this stage, a child's behavior is dominated by innate reflexes; infants aren't "thinking" as much as they are simply responding to stimuli. But by the end of the stage, the child can use mental symbols to represent objects (for example, a mental image of a favorite toy). The key to this transition is the acquisition of the concept of object permanence.

Object permanence **develops when a child recognizes that objects continue to exist even when they are no longer visible.** Although you surely take the permanence of objects for granted, infants aren't aware of this permanence at first. If you show a 3-month-old child an eye-catching toy and then cover the toy with a pillow, the child will not attempt to search for the toy. Piaget inferred from this observation that the child does not understand that the toy continues to exist under the pillow. According to Piaget, children gradually acquire the concept of object permanence between 4 and 18 months of age.

Preoperational period The *preoperational period* extends roughly from age 2 to age 7. Although progress in symbolic thought continues, Piaget emphasized the *shortcomings* in preoperational thought. Consider a simple problem that Piaget presented to youngsters. He would take two identical beakers and fill each with the same amount of water. After a child had agreed that the two beakers contained the same amount of water, he would pour the water from one of the beakers into a much taller and thinner beaker (see **Figure 10.7**). He would then ask the child whether the two differently shaped beakers still contained the same amount of water. Confronted with a problem like this, children in the preoperational period generally said "no." They typically focused on the higher water line in the taller beaker and insisted that there was more water in it. They had not yet mastered the principle of conservation. *Conservation* **is Piaget's term for the awareness that physical quantities remain constant in spite of changes in their shape or appearance.**

Why are preoperational children unable to solve conservation problems? According to Piaget, their inability to understand conservation is the result of some basic flaws in preoperational thinking. These flaws include centration, irreversibility, and egocentrism.

Centration **is the tendency to focus on just one feature of a problem, neglecting other important aspects.** When working on the conservation problem with water, preoperational children tend to concentrate on the height of the water while ignoring the width. They have difficulty focusing on several aspects of a problem at once.

Irreversibility **is the inability to envision reversing an action.** Preoperational children can't mentally "undo" something. For instance, in grappling with the conservation of water, they don't think about what would happen if the water were poured back from the tall beaker into the original beaker.

Egocentrism **in thinking is characterized by a limited ability to share another person's viewpoint.** Indeed, Piaget felt that preoperational children fail to appreciate that there are points of view other than their own. For instance, if you ask a preoperational girl whether her sister has a sister, she'll probably say "no" if they are the only two girls in the family. She's unable to view sisterhood from her sister's perspective (this example also shows irreversibility). A notable feature of egocentrism is *animism—***the belief that all things are living,** just like oneself. Thus, youngsters attribute lifelike, human qualities to inanimate objects, asking questions such as, "When does the ocean stop to rest?" or "Why does the wind get so mad?"

Step 1
The child agrees that beakers A and B contain the same amount of water.

Step 2
The child observes as the water from beaker B is poured into beaker C, which is shaped differently.

Step 3
The child is asked: "Do beakers A and C contain the same amount of water?"

FIGURE 10.7

Piaget's conservation task. After watching the transformation shown, a preoperational child will usually answer that the taller beaker contains more water. In contrast, the child in the concrete operations period tends to respond correctly, recognizing that the amount of water in beaker C remains the same as the amount in beaker A.

Concrete operational period   The *concrete operational period* usually lasts from about age 7 to age 11. Piaget called this stage *concrete* operations because children can perform operations only on images of tangible objects and actual events. Among the operations that children master during this stage are reversibility and decentration. *Reversibility* permits a child to mentally undo an action. *Decentration* allows the child to focus on more than one feature of a problem simultaneously. The newfound ability to coordinate several aspects of a problem helps the child appreciate that there are several ways to look at things. This ability in turn leads to a *decline in egocentrism* and to a *gradual mastery of conservation,* as it applies to liquid, mass, number, volume, area, and length.

As children master concrete operations, they develop a variety of new problem-solving capacities. Let's examine another problem studied by Piaget. Give a preoperational child seven carnations and three daisies. Tell the child the names for the two types of flowers. Then ask the child to sort them into carnations and daisies. That should be no problem. Now ask the child whether there are more carnations or more daisies. Most children will correctly respond that there are more carnations. Now ask the child whether there are more carnations or more flowers. At this point, most preoperational children will stumble and respond incorrectly that there are more carnations than flowers. Generally, preoperational children can't handle *hierarchical classification* problems that require them to focus simultaneously on two levels of classification. However, the child who has advanced to the concrete operational stage is not as limited by centration and can work successfully with hierarchical classification problems.

Formal operational period   The final stage in Piaget's theory is the *formal operational period,* which is supposed to begin around 11 years of age. In this stage, children begin to apply their operations to *abstract* concepts in addition to concrete objects. Indeed, during this stage, youngsters come to *enjoy* the contemplation of abstract concepts. Many adolescents spend hours mulling over hypothetical possibilities related to abstractions, such as justice, love, and free will. Thought processes in the formal operational period can be characterized as relatively systematic, logical, and reflective.

According to Piaget, youngsters graduate to relatively adult modes of thinking in the formal operations stage. He did *not* mean to suggest that no further cognitive development occurs once children reach this stage. However, he believed that after children achieve formal operations, further developments in thinking are changes in *degree* rather than fundamental changes in the *nature* of thinking.

Evaluating Piaget's Theory

Jean Piaget made a landmark contribution to psychology's understanding of children in general and their cognitive development in particular (Beilin, 1992). Piaget's theory guided an enormous volume of productive research that continues through today (Feldman, 2013). This research has supported many of Piaget's central ideas (Flavell, 1996). In such a far-reaching theory, however, there are bound to be some weak spots. Here are some criticisms of Piaget's theory:

1. In many aspects, Piaget appears to have underestimated young children's cognitive development (Birney et al., 2005). For example, researchers have found evidence that children understand object permanence and are capable of some symbolic thought much earlier than Piaget thought (Birney & Sternberg, 2011). Similarly, some evidence suggests that preoperational children are not as egocentric as Piaget believed (Moll & Meltzoff, 2011).

2. Another problem is that children often simultaneously display patterns of thinking that are characteristic of several stages. This "mixing" of stages and the fact that the transitions between stages are gradual rather than abrupt call into question the value of organizing cognitive development in terms of stages (Bjorklund, 2012). Progress in children's thinking appears to occur in overlapping waves rather than distinct stages with clear boundaries.

3. Piaget believed that his theory described universal processes that should lead children everywhere to progress through uniform stages of thinking at roughly the same ages. Subsequent research has shown

---

CONCEPT CHECK 10.2

Recognizing Piaget's Stages

Check your understanding of Piaget's theory by indicating the stage of cognitive development illustrated by each of the examples below. For each scenario, fill in the letter for the appropriate stage in the space on the left. The answers are in Appendix A.

a. Sensorimotor period

c. Concrete operational period

b. Preoperational period

d. Formal operational period

_____ 1. Upon seeing a glass lying on its side, Sammy says, "Look, the glass is tired. It's taking a nap."

_____ 2. Maria is told that a farmer has nine cows and six horses. The teacher asks, "Does the farmer have more cows or more animals?" Maria answers, "More animals."

_____ 3. Alice is playing in the living room with a small red ball. The ball rolls under the sofa. She stares for a moment at the place where the ball vanished and then turns her attention to a toy truck sitting in front of her.

that the *sequence* of stages is largely invariant, but the *timetable* that children follow in passing through these stages varies considerably across cultures (Molitor & Hsu, 2011; Rogoff, 2003). Thus, Piaget underestimated the influence of cultural factors on cognitive development.

Vygotsky's Sociocultural Theory

In recent decades, as the limitations and weaknesses of Piaget's ideas have become more apparent, some developmental researchers have looked elsewhere for theoretical guidance. Ironically, the theory that has inspired the greatest interest—Lev Vygotsky's *sociocultural theory*—dates back to around the same time that Piaget began formulating his theory (1920s–1930s). Vygotsky was a prominent Russian psychologist whose research ended prematurely in 1934 when he died of tuberculosis at the age of 37. Vygotsky's and Piaget's perspectives on cognitive development have much in common, but they differ in some important respects (Lourenco, 2012; Rowe & Wertsch, 2002). First, in Piaget's theory, cognitive development is primarily fueled by individual children's active exploration of the world around them. In contrast, Vygotsky places enormous emphasis on how children's cognitive development is fueled by social interactions with parents, teachers, and older children who can provide invaluable guidance (Hedegaard, 2005). Second, Piaget viewed children's gradual mastery of language as just another aspect of cognitive development, whereas Vygotsky argued that language acquisition plays a crucial, central role in fostering cognitive development (Kozulin, 2005).

According to Vygotsky, children acquire most of their culture's cognitive skills and problem-solving strategies through collaborative dialogues with more experienced members of their society. Vygotsky's emphasis on the primacy of language is reflected in his discussion of *private speech.* Preschool children talk aloud to themselves a lot as they go about their activities. Piaget viewed this speech as egocentric and insignificant. Vygotsky argued that children use this private speech to plan their strategies, regulate their actions, and accomplish their goals. As children grow older, this private speech is internalized and becomes the normal verbal dialogue that people have with themselves as they go about their business. Thus, language increasingly serves as the *foundation* for youngsters' cognitive processes. Vygotsky's sociocultural theory has provided influential guidance for contemporary research on cognitive development and learning (Mahn & John-Steiner, 2013).

Are Some Cognitive Abilities Innate?

The finding that Piaget underestimated infants' cognitive abilities has led to a rash of studies suggesting that infants have a surprising grasp of many complex concepts. Studies have shown that infants understand basic properties of objects and some of the rules that govern them (Baillargeon, 2002, 2004). At 3–4 months of age, infants understand that objects are distinct entities with boundaries, that objects move in continuous paths, that one solid object cannot pass through another, that an object cannot pass through an opening that is smaller than the object, and that objects on slopes roll down rather than up (Baillargeon, 2008; Spelke & Newport, 1998). Infants also understand that liquids are different from objects. For example, 5-month-old infants expect that liquids will change shape as they move and that they can be penetrated by solid objects (Hespos, Ferry, & Rips, 2009). In a similar vein, a recent study showed that 6-month-old infants appear to understand that dried fruits derived from plants are more likely to be edible than dried fruits derived from artificial objects (Wertz & Wynn, 2014). In other words, they preferentially identify plants as sources of food at a surprisingly young age.

In this line of research, perhaps the most stunning discovery has been the finding that *infants seem to exhibit surprisingly sophisticated numerical abilities* (Wood & Spelke, 2005). If 5-month-old infants are shown a sequence of events in which one object is added to another behind a screen, they expect to see two objects when the screen is removed, and they exhibit surprise when their expectation is violated. This expectation suggests that they understand that 1 + 1 = 2 (Wynn, 1992, 1996). Similar manipulations suggest

Vygotsky and Piaget differ about the importance of private speech—young children's tendency to talk to themselves as they go about their business. Piaget views private speech as insignificant, whereas Vygotsky asserts that children use private speech to regulate their actions and plan their strategies.

that infants also understand that 2 – 1 = 1; that 2 + 1 = 3; that 3 – 1 = 2, and other, more complicated calculations (Hauser & Carey, 1998; McCrink & Wynn, 2004). Although these findings have been replicated many times, some theorists argue that the results can be explained by simple perceptual reactions to stimuli rather than infants' understanding of numerical relations (Colombo, Brez, & Curtindale, 2013).

Again and again, research has shown that infants appear to understand surprisingly complex concepts that they have had virtually no opportunity to learn about. These findings have led some theorists to conclude that certain basic cognitive abilities are biologically prewired into humans' neural architecture (Spelke & Kinzler, 2007). As you might anticipate, evolutionary theorists maintain that this prewiring is a product of natural selection, and they strive to understand its adaptive significance for our ancient ancestors (Hauser & Carey, 1998; Wynn, 1998).

The Development of Moral Reasoning

> *In Europe, a woman was near death from cancer. One drug might save her, a form of radium that a druggist in the same town had recently discovered. The druggist was charging $2,000, ten times what the drug cost him to make. The sick woman's husband, Heinz, went to everyone he knew to borrow the money, but he could only get together about half of what it cost. He told the druggist that his wife was dying and asked him to sell it cheaper or let him pay later. But the druggist said, "No." The husband got desperate and broke into the man's store to steal the drug for his wife. Should the husband have done that? Why? (Kohlberg, 1969, p. 379)*

What's your answer to Heinz's dilemma? Would you have answered the same way 5 years ago? Can you guess what you might have said at age 6? By presenting similar dilemmas to participants and studying their responses, Lawrence Kohlberg (1976, 1984) developed a model of *moral development*.

Kohlberg's Stage Theory

Kohlberg's model is the most influential of a number of competing theories that attempt to explain how youngsters develop a sense of right and wrong (Magun-Jackson & Burgette, 2013). Kohlberg's theory focuses on moral *reasoning* rather than overt *behavior*. This point is best illustrated by describing Kohlberg's method of investigation. He presented his participants with thorny moral questions, such as Heinz's dilemma. He then asked them what the actor in the dilemma should do, and more important, why. It was the *why* that interested Kohlberg. He examined the nature and progression of subjects' moral reasoning.

The result of this work is the stage theory of moral reasoning outlined in **Figure 10.8**. Kohlberg found that individuals progress through a series of three levels

FIGURE 10.8

Kohlberg's stage theory. Kohlberg's model describes three levels of moral reasoning, each of which can be divided into two stages. This chart summarizes some of the key facets in how individuals think about right and wrong at each stage.

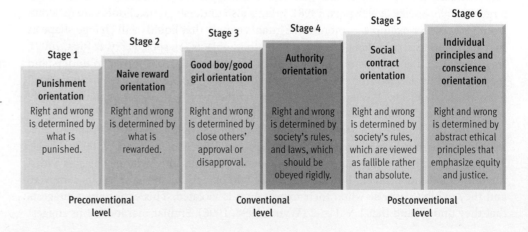

Stage 1	Stage 2	Stage 3	Stage 4	Stage 5	Stage 6
Punishment orientation	Naive reward orientation	Good boy/good girl orientation	Authority orientation	Social contract orientation	Individual principles and conscience orientation
Right and wrong is determined by what is punished.	Right and wrong is determined by what is rewarded.	Right and wrong is determined by close others' approval or disapproval.	Right and wrong is determined by society's rules, and laws, which should be obeyed rigidly.	Right and wrong is determined by society's rules, which are viewed as fallible rather than absolute.	Right and wrong is determined by abstract ethical principles that emphasize equity and justice.

Preconventional level   Conventional level   Postconventional level

of moral development. Each of these levels can be broken into two sublevels, yielding a total of six stages. Each stage represents a different approach to thinking about right and wrong.

Younger children at the *preconventional level* think in terms of external authority. Acts are wrong because they are punished, or right because they lead to positive consequences. Older children who have reached the *conventional level* of moral reasoning see rules as necessary for maintaining social order. They therefore accept these rules as their own. They "internalize" these rules not to avoid punishment, but to be virtuous and win approval from others. Moral thinking at this stage is relatively inflexible. Rules are viewed as absolute guidelines that should be enforced rigidly.

During adolescence, some youngsters move on to the *postconventional level.* This level involves working out a personal code of ethics. Acceptance of rules is less rigid, and moral thinking shows some flexibility. Subjects at the postconventional level allow for the possibility that someone might not comply with some of society's rules if they conflict with personal ethics. For example, participants at this level might applaud a newspaper reporter who goes to jail rather than reveal a source of information who was promised anonymity.

Evaluating Kohlberg's Theory

How has Kohlberg's theory fared in research? The central ideas have received reasonable support. Studies have shown that youngsters generally do move through Kohlberg's stages of moral reasoning in the order he proposed (Walker, 1989). Furthermore, relations between age and level of moral reasoning are in the predicted directions (Rest, 1986; see **Figure 10.9**). Although these findings

---

CONCEPT CHECK 10.3

Analyzing Moral Reasoning

Check your understanding of Kohlberg's theory of moral development by analyzing hypothetical responses to the following moral dilemma.

A Midwest biologist has conducted numerous studies demonstrating that simple organisms, such as worms and paramecia, can learn through conditioning. It occurs to her that perhaps she could condition fertilized human ova to provide a dramatic demonstration that abortions destroy adaptable, living human organisms. This possibility appeals to her because she is ardently opposed to abortion. However, there is no way to conduct the necessary research on human ova without sacrificing the lives of potential human beings. She desperately wants to conduct the research, but obviously the sacrifice of human ova is fundamentally incompatible with her belief in the sanctity of human life. What should she do? Why? [Submitted by a student (age 13) to Professor Barbara Banas at Monroe Community College]

In the spaces on the left of each numbered response, indicate the level of moral reasoning shown, choosing from the following: (a) preconventional level, (b) conventional level, or (c) postconventional level. The answers are in Appendix A.

_____ 1. She should do the research. Although it's wrong to kill, there's a greater good that can be realized through the research.

_____ 2. She shouldn't do the research because people will think that she's a hypocrite and condemn her.

_____ 3. She should do the research because she may become rich and famous as a result.

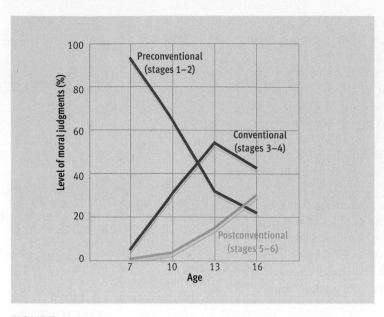

FIGURE 10.9

Age and moral reasoning. The percentages of different types of moral judgments made by subjects at various ages are graphed here (based on Kohlberg, 1963, 1969). As predicted, preconventional reasoning declines as children mature, conventional reasoning increases during middle childhood, and postconventional reasoning begins to emerge during adolescence. But at each age, children display a mixture of various levels of moral reasoning.

support Kohlberg's model, critics note that it is not unusual to find that a person shows signs of several adjacent levels of moral reasoning at a particular point in development (Krebs & Denton, 2005). As we noted in the critique of Piaget, this mixing of stages is a problem for virtually all stage theories. Evidence is also mounting that Kohlberg's theory reflects an individualistic ideology characteristic of modern Western nations that is much more culture specific than Kohlberg appreciated (Miller, 2006). Finally, a consensus is building that Kohlberg's theory has led to a constricted focus on reasoning about interpersonal conflicts, while ignoring many other important aspects of moral development (Walker, 2007). Contemporary theorists note that moral behavior depends on many factors besides reasoning, including emotional reactions, variations in temperament, and cultural background (Haidt & Kesebir, 2010).

Building on this insight, Haidt (2007, 2013) argues that many moral judgments involve immediate, automatic emotional reactions to people's behavior ("How dare he!"), which he calls *moral intuitions.* After making these gut judgments, people turn to reasoning to justify their instant emotional reactions. Thus, Haidt maintains that moral behavior is much more emotional, intuitive, and irrational than Kohlberg envisioned.

10.4 THE TRANSITION OF ADOLESCENCE

Key Learning Goals

- Review the physiological changes of puberty, and summarize research on neural development in adolescence.
- Discuss identity formation in adolescence and the stage of emerging adulthood.

Adolescence is a bridge between childhood and adulthood. During this time, individuals continue to experience significant changes in cognitive, moral, and social development. However, the most dynamic areas of development during adolescence are physical changes and related transitions in emotional and personality development.

Physiological Changes

Recall for a moment your junior high school days. Didn't it seem that your body grew so fast that your clothes just couldn't "keep up"? This phase of rapid growth in height and weight is called the *adolescent growth spurt.* Brought on by hormonal changes, it typically starts at about age 9–10 in girls and 10–12 in boys (Peper & Dahl, 2013). In addition to growing taller and heavier, children begin to develop the **secondary sex characteristics—physical features that distinguish one sex from the other but that are not essential for reproduction,** such as facial hair and broader shoulders in males, and breast growth and wider hips in females (Susman & Dorn, 2013; see **Figure 10.10**).

Soon, youngsters reach *puberty—***the stage during which sexual functions reach maturity, which marks the beginning of adolescence.** It is during puberty that the *primary sex characteristics—*the structures necessary for reproduction—develop fully. In the male, these include the testes, penis, and related internal structures. Primary sex characteristics in the female include the ovaries, vagina, uterus, and other internal structures.

In females, puberty is typically signaled by *menarche—***the first occurrence of menstruation,** which reflects the culmination of a series of hormonal changes. American girls

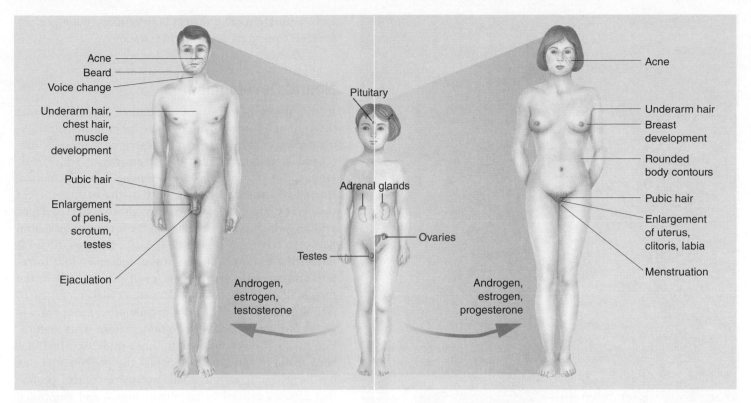

FIGURE 10.10

Physical development at puberty. Hormonal changes during puberty lead not only to a growth spurt but also to the development of secondary sex characteristics. The pituitary gland sends signals to the adrenal glands and gonads (ovaries and testes), which secrete hormones responsible for various physical changes that differentiate males and females.

typically reach menarche at age 12–13, with further sexual maturation continuing until approximately age 16. American boys typically experience *spermarche*—**the first occurrence of ejaculation**—at age 13–14, with further sexual maturation continuing until approximately age 18.

Interestingly, *generational* changes have occurred in the timing of puberty over the last 150 years. Today's adolescents begin puberty at a younger age, and complete it more rapidly, than their counterparts in earlier generations (Lee & Styne, 2013; Talma et al., 2013). This trend appears to be occurring in both genders. The reasons for this trend are the subject of debate. It seems likely that multiple factors have contributed (Bellis, Downing, & Ashton. 2006; Susman & Dorn, 2013). The most obvious potential causes are widespread improvements in nutrition and medical care, which would probably explain why the trend toward younger puberty has mostly been seen in modern, "developed" countries. Some theorists also believe that a variety of environmental pollutants serve as "endocrine disrupters" that hasten the onset of puberty (Lee & Styne, 2013).

The timing of puberty varies from one adolescent to the next. Generally, girls who mature early and boys who mature late seem to experience more subjective distress with the transition to adolescence (Susman, Dorn, & Schiefelbein, 2003). This experience of subjective stress may contribute to the elevated prevalence of psychological disorders seen in both groups, but especially females (Graber, 2013). However, in both males and females, early maturation is associated with greater use of tobacco, alcohol, and other drugs; more high-risk behavior; greater aggression; and more trouble with the law (Lynne et al., 2007; Steinberg & Morris, 2001). Among females, early maturation is also correlated with a greater risk for eating problems (Klump, 2013). Thus, we might speculate that

The timing of sexual maturation can have important implications for adolescents. Youngsters who mature unusually early or unusually late often feel uneasy about this transition.

Prefrontal cortex

FIGURE 10.11

The prefrontal cortex. Recent research suggests that neural development continues throughout adolescence. Moreover, the chief site for much of this development is the prefrontal cortex, which appears to be the last area of the brain to mature fully. This discovery may have fascinating implications for understanding the adolescent brain, as the prefrontal cortex appears to play a key role in emotional regulation and self-control.

early maturation often thrusts both genders (but especially females) toward the adult world too soon.

Neural Development

In recent years, brain-imaging studies have shown that the volume of white matter in the brain grows throughout adolescence, while the volume of gray matter declines (Giedd & Rapoport, 2010). The growth of white matter suggests that *neurons are becoming more myelinated,* leading to enhanced connectivity in the brain, whereas the decrease in gray matter is thought to reflect *synaptic pruning,* which plays a key role in the formation of neural networks (Geier, 2013; see Chapter 3). Perhaps the most interesting discovery has been that increased myelinization and synaptic pruning are most pronounced in the *prefrontal cortex* (Sebastian, Burnett, & Blakemore, 2010) (see **Figure 10.11**). Thus, *the prefrontal cortex appears to be the last area of the brain to fully mature.* This maturation may not be complete until one's mid-20s. Much has been made of this finding because the prefrontal cortex has been characterized as an "executive control center" that appears crucial to cognitive control and emotional regulation (Casey et al., 2005). Theorists have suggested that the immaturity of the prefrontal cortex may explain why risky behavior (such as reckless driving, experimentation with drugs, dangerous stunts, unprotected sex, and so forth) peaks during adolescence and then declines in adulthood (Steinberg, 2008).

More recent research has suggested that the role of the prefrontal cortex in adolescent risk taking has been exaggerated, as other features of neural development also contribute (Casey & Caudle, 2013). Studies have demonstrated that adolescents exhibit heightened sensitivity to various types of rewards, such as the pleasures associated with tasty foods, financial payoffs, psychoactive drugs, and thrilling adventures (Galvan, 2013). This elevated sensitivity to reward is attributed to relatively early maturation of the subcortical dopamine circuits that mediate the experience of pleasure (Luna et al., 2013). Thus, the current thinking is that adolescent risk taking is fueled by a mismatch in the maturation of subcortical reward centers in relation to the prefrontal areas underlying cognitive control (Mills et al., 2014). In other words, the brain's early-maturing reward system overpowers the late-maturing prefrontal cortex.

That said, other factors also contribute to risky behavior during adolescence. Evidence suggests that teenagers are particularly sensitive to the social evaluations of others (Somerville, 2013). Adolescents spend a great deal of time with their peers. Hence, susceptibility to peer influence may also contribute to adolescent risk taking (Albert, Chein, & Steinberg, 2013). One elegant lab study found that the presence of peers more than doubled the number of risks taken by teenagers in a video game involving in-the-moment decisions about crash risks (Gardner & Steinberg, 2005). In contrast, older adults' risk taking was not elevated by the presence of peers (see **Figure 10.12**).

The Search for Identity

Erik Erikson was especially interested in personality development during adolescence, which is the fifth of the eight major life stages he described. The psychosocial crisis during this stage pits *identity* against *confusion* as potential outcomes. According to Erikson (1968), the main challenge of adolescence is the struggle to form a clear sense of identity. This struggle involves working out a stable concept of oneself as a unique individual and embracing an ideology or system of values that provides a sense of direction. In Erikson's view, adolescents grapple with questions such as "Who am I?" and "Where am I going in life?" Recent research has focused on the consequences of identity confusion. Studies have found that identity confusion is associated with an increased risk for substance abuse, unprotected sexual activity, anxiety, low self-worth, and eating disorders (Schwartz et al., 2013).

Adolescents deal with identity formation in a variety of ways. Building on Erikson's insights, James Marcia (1966, 1980, 1994) proposed that the presence or absence of a sense of commitment (to life goals and values) and a sense of crisis (active questioning and exploration) can combine to produce four different *identity statuses*. In order of increasing maturity, Marcia's four identity statuses begin with *identity diffusion,* a state of rudderless apathy, with no commitment to an ideology. *Identity foreclosure* is a premature commitment to visions, values, and roles—typically those prescribed by one's parents. Foreclosure is associated with conformity and not being very open to new experiences (Kroger, 2003). An *identity moratorium* involves delaying commitment for a while to experiment with alternative ideologies and careers. *Identity achievement* involves arriving at a sense of self and direction after some consideration of alternative possibilities.

Identity achievement is associated with higher self-esteem, conscientiousness, security, achievement motivation, and capacity for intimacy (Kroger, 2003; Kroger & Marcia, 2011). However, research suggests that people tend to reach identity achievement at later ages than originally envisioned by Marcia. In one large-scale study (Meeus et al., 2010), by late adolescence only 22%–26% of the sample had reached identity achievement. Thus, the struggle for a sense of identity routinely extends into young adulthood. Indeed, some people continue to struggle with identity issues well into middle and even late adulthood (Newton & Stewart, 2012).

Emerging Adulthood as a New Developmental Stage

The finding that the search for identity routinely extends into adulthood is one of many considerations that led Jeffrey Arnett to make the radical claim that we ought to recognize the existence of a new developmental stage in modern societies. He calls this stage *emerging adulthood.* According to Arnett (2000, 2006), the years between ages 18 and 25 (roughly) have become a distinct, new transitional stage of life. He attributes the rise of this new developmental period to a variety of demographic trends. For example, more people are delaying marriage and parenthood until their late 20s or early 30s. More people stay in school for lengthier periods, and young people face more barriers to financial independence.

Arnett (2000, 2006, 2011) maintains that emerging adulthood is marked by a number of distinct features. A central feature is the subjective feeling that one is in between adolescence and adulthood. Emerging adults don't feel like adolescents, but most don't see themselves as adults, either (see **Figure 10.13**). Another feature of emerging adulthood is that it is an age of possibilities. It tends to be a time of great optimism about one's personal future. A third aspect of emerging adulthood is that it is a self-focused time of life. Finally, Arnett found that emerging adulthood is a period of continued struggles with identity issues. Arnett's provocative theory has already inspired a good deal of research on the dynamics and developmental significance of emerging adulthood (Chow & Ruhl, 2014; Chung et al., 2014; Claxton & van Dulmen, 2013).

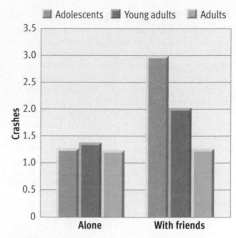

FIGURE 10.12

Peer influence on risk taking. Gardner and Steinberg (2005) had adolescents, young adults, and adults play a video game involving simulated driving in which participants had to make quick decisions about crash risks. The dependent variable, which indexed subjects' risk taking, was the number of crashes experienced. Some participants played the video game alone, whereas others played in the presence of peers. The data showed that the presence of peers increased risk taking by young adults moderately and by adolescents considerably, but adults' risk taking was unaffected. These findings suggest that susceptibility to peer influence may increase risky behavior among adolescents and young adults.

SOURCE: Adapted from Steinberg, L. (2007). Risk taking in adolescence: New perspectives from brain and behavioral science. *Current Directions in Psychological Science,* 16, 55–59. Copyright © 2007 Blackwell Publishing.

FIGURE 10.13

Emerging adulthood as a phase in between adolescence and adulthood. Arnett (2006) characterizes emerging adulthood as an "age of feeling in-between." This characterization comes from a study in which he asked participants of various ages "Do you feel like you have reached adulthood?" As you can see in the data shown here, the dominant response in the 18–25 age group was an ambivalent "Yes and no," but it shifted to predominantly "Yes" in the 26–35 age group.

SOURCE: Arnett, J. J. (2006). Emerging adulthood: Understanding the new way of coming of age. In J. J. Arnett & J. L. Tanner (Eds.), *Emerging adults in America: Coming of age in the 21st century* (p. 11). Washington, DC: American Psychological Association.

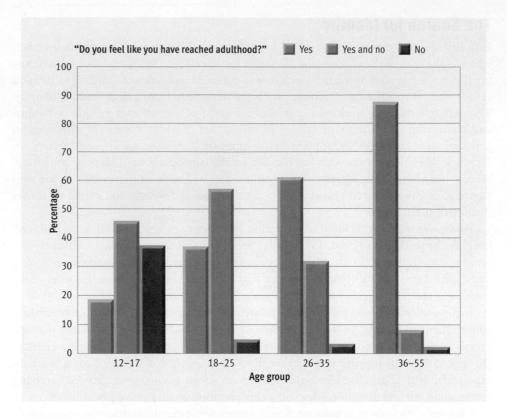

10.5 THE EXPANSE OF ADULTHOOD

10.5

Key Learning Goals

- Discuss personality development in adulthood, and trace typical transitions in family relations during the adult years.
- Describe the physical changes associated with aging, and summarize information on Alzheimer's disease.
- Understand how memory and mental speed change in later adulthood.
- Discuss attitudes about death, the process of dying, and variations in how people cope with bereavement.

The concept of development was once associated almost exclusively with childhood and adolescence. Today, however, development is widely recognized as a lifelong journey. Interestingly, patterns of development during the adult years are becoming increasingly diverse. The boundaries between young, middle, and late adulthood are becoming blurred as more and more people have children later than one is "supposed" to, retire earlier than one is "supposed" to, and so forth.

Personality Development

Research on adult personality development has been dominated by one key question: How stable is personality over the life span? We'll look at this issue and Erikson's view of adulthood in our discussion of personality development in the adult years.

The Question of Stability

How common are significant personality changes in adulthood? Is a grouchy 20-year-old going to be a grouchy 40-year-old and a grouchy 65-year-old? After tracking subjects through adulthood, many researchers have been impressed by the amount of change observed (Helson, Jones, & Kwan, 2002; Whitbourne et al., 1992). In contrast, many other researchers have concluded that personality tends to be quite stable over periods of 20 to 40 years (Costa & McCrae, 1994, 1997; Roberts & DelVecchio, 2000).

Clearly, researchers assessing the stability of personality in adulthood have reached very different conclusions. How can these contradictory conclusions be reconciled? It appears that *both* are accurate—they just reflect different ways of looking at the data (Bertrand, Graham, & Lachman, 2013). As noted in Chapter 8, psychological test scores are *relative* measures. They show how one scores *relative to other people*. Raw scores are converted into *percentile scores* that indicate the precise degree to which one is above or below average on a particular trait. The data indicate that these percentile scores tend to be fairly stable over lengthy spans of time—people's relative standing on personality traits doesn't tend to change much (Allemand, Steiger, & Hill, 2013). Furthermore, the stability in relative measures of personality traits tends to increase with age (Roberts, Donnellan, & Hill, 2013).

However, if we examine participants' raw scores on fundamental personality traits, we can see meaningful developmental trends. Although adults' mean raw scores on extraversion remain pretty stable, neuroticism scores tend to decline moderately with increasing age, while agreeableness, openness to experience, and conscientiousness tend to increase gradually (Soto et al., 2011; see **Figure 10.14**). Moreover, studies show that (1) there are variations among people in the extent to which they experience personality change, (2) the biggest changes in raw scores tend to occur between the ages of 20 and 40, (3) significant changes can even occur in old age, and (4) the typical developmental trends represent "positive" changes that move people toward great social maturity (Donnellan, Hill, & Roberts, 2015). In sum, it appears that personality in adulthood is characterized by *both* stability and change.

Erikson's View of Adulthood

Insofar as personality changes during the adult years, Erik Erikson's (1963) theory offers some clues about the kinds of changes people can expect. In his eight-stage model of development over the life span, Erikson divided adulthood into three stages (see again **Figure 10.5**):

Intimacy versus isolation In early adulthood, the key concern is whether one can develop the capacity to share intimacy with others. Successful resolution of the challenges in this stage should promote empathy and openness, rather than shrewdness and manipulativeness.

Generativity versus self-absorption In middle adulthood, the key challenge is to acquire a genuine concern for the welfare of future generations, which results in providing unselfish guidance to younger people. Self-absorption is characterized by self-indulgent concerns with meeting one's own needs and desires.

Integrity versus despair During the retirement years, the challenge is to avoid the tendency to dwell on the mistakes of the past and on one's imminent death. People need to find meaning and satisfaction in their lives, rather than wallow in bitterness and resentment.

Transitions in Family Life

Many of the important transitions in adulthood involve changes in family responsibilities and relationships. Everyone emerges from a family, and most people go on to form their own families. However, the transitional period during which young adults are "between families" until they form a new family is being prolonged by more and more people. The percentage of young adults who are postponing marriage until their late 20s or early 30s has risen

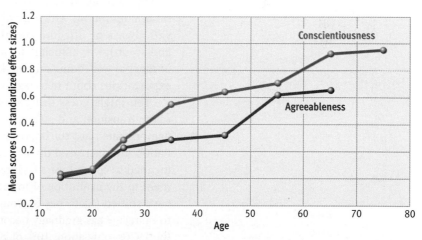

FIGURE 10.14

Examples of personality trends in the adult years. According to Roberts and Mroczek (2008), when researchers examine participants' mean raw scores on personality measures, they find meaningful trends over the decades of adulthood. The trends for two specific traits—agreeableness and conscientiousness—are shown here as examples. Using subjects' test scores in adolescence as a baseline, you can see how measures of agreeableness and conscientiousness increase substantially over the decades.

SOURCE: Roberts, B. W., & Mroczek, D. (2008). Personality trait change in adulthood. *Current Directions in Psychological Science, 17*, 31–35. Copyright © 2008 Blackwell Publishing.

FIGURE 10.15

Median age at first marriage. The median age at which people in the United States marry for the first time has been creeping up for both males and females since the mid-1960s. This trend indicates that more people are postponing marriage. (Data from the U.S. Bureau of the Census).

steadily (see **Figure 10.15**). This trend is probably the result of a number of factors. Chief among them are the availability of new career options for women, increased educational requirements in the world of work, and increased emphasis on personal autonomy. Nonetheless, more than 90% of adults eventually marry.

Adjusting to Marriage

Most new couples are pretty happy, but 8%–14% of newlyweds score in the distressed range on measures of marital satisfaction, with the most commonly reported problems being difficulties balancing work and marriage and financial concerns (Schramm et al., 2005). Optimism can help, but it depends on the nature of one's optimism. One recent study found that the *personality trait of optimism,* which involves a general tendency to expect good outcomes, fosters constructive problem solving and marital well-being (Neff & Geers, 2013). However, this study found that *relationship-specific optimism,* which involves idealistic expectations about marriage (my partner will always be affectionate, always communicate well, never intentionally hurt me, and so on), was associated with less constructive problem solving and steep declines in marital well-being during the first year of marriage. So, it may help to have realistic expectations about marriage.

You might guess that partners who cohabit prior to getting married would have an easier transition and greater marital success. However, until relatively recently, research demonstrated just the opposite. Studies found an association between premarital cohabitation and increased divorce rates (Teachman, 2003). Theorists speculated that people inclined to cohabit were less traditional, more individualistic, and had a weaker commitment to the institution of marriage. However, the findings on the effects of cohabitation have shifted (Liefbroer & Dourleijn, 2006). One reason may be that cohabitation prior to marriage has gradually become the norm rather than the exception (Cohan, 2013). In the 1970s, only about 10% of couples lived together before marriage, but that figure has risen to 66% (Manning, Brown, & Payne, 2014; Tach & Halpern-Meekin, 2009). A large-scale study in Australia that looked at trends over decades (from 1945 to 2000) found that cohabitants had higher rates of marital dissolution up through 1988, but then the trend started to gradually reverse itself, with cohabitants showing lower rates of divorce (Hewitt & de Vaus, 2009). In the United States, studies focusing on more recent marriages also failed to find cohabitation associated with marital instability (Manning & Cohen, 2012; Reinhold, 2010).

One major source of conflict in many new marriages is the negotiation of marital roles in relation to career commitments. More and more women are aspiring to demanding careers. However, research shows that husbands' careers continue to take priority over their wives' career ambitions (Cha, 2010). Moreover, many husbands maintain traditional role expectations about housework, child care, and decision making. Men's contribution to housework/child care *has* increased noticeably since the 1960s. But studies of couples with children indicate that wives are still doing about twice as much housework/child care as their husbands (Bianchi et al., 2012; see **Figure 10.16**). This is true even among highly paid and highly stressed female executives. Miller Burke and Attridge (2011a, 2011b) interviewed 106 successful men and women from the world of business who were mostly worth over a million dollars. Among the women, 44% reported they did most of the housework/child care, whereas only 4% of the men reported shouldering the bulk of housework/child care. All that said, husbands still put in more hours of paid work than wives on average, and most wives do not view their larger share of housework as unfair because most women don't expect a 50–50 split (Braun et al., 2008).

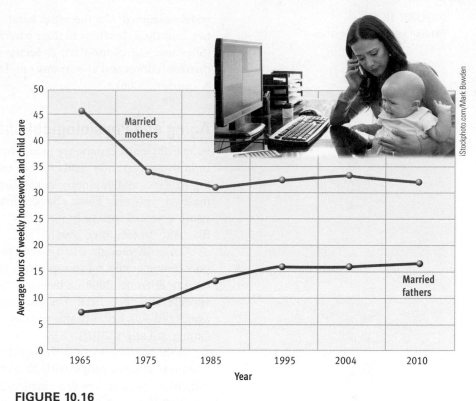

FIGURE 10.16

Housework trends since the 1960s. As these data show, the gap between husbands and wives in hours devoted to housework/child care has narrowed in recent decades. Married fathers have doubled their contribution since the 1960s, but married mothers still allocate about twice as many hours to housework/child care. (Data from Bianchi et al., 2012)

Adjusting to Parenthood

Although an increasing number of people are choosing to remain childless, the vast majority of married couples continue to have children. Most couples are happy with their decision to have children. However, the arrival of the first child represents a major transition, and the disruption of routines can be emotionally draining. The transition to parenthood tends to have more impact on mothers than on fathers (Nomaguchi & Milkie, 2003). One carefully designed study found steep declines in relationship quality after the birth of a first child (Doss et al., 2009). A review of decades of research on parenthood and marital satisfaction found that (1) parents exhibit lower marital satisfaction than comparable nonparents; (2) mothers of infants report the steepest decline in marital satisfaction; and (3) the more children couples have, the lower their marital satisfaction tends to be (Twenge, Campbell, & Foster, 2003). Although these findings are distressing, crisis during the transition to first parenthood is far from universal. One recent study found that average relationship satisfaction after the transition to parenthood showed the usual decline, but further analyses revealed that the average was dragged down by subgroups of parents who experienced steep decreases in satisfaction (Don & Mickelson, 2014). It turned out that relationship satisfaction held up pretty well for about one-half of the fathers and three-quarters of the mothers. So, as is often true, averages can be deceiving.

As children grow up, parental influence over them tends to decline. As this happens, the early years of parenting—that once seemed so difficult—are often recalled with fondness. When youngsters reach adolescence and seek to establish their own identities, gradual realignments occur in parent-child relationships (Bornstein, Jager, & Steinberg, 2013). On the one hand, these relations generally are not as bitter or contentious as

> **REALITY CHECK**

Misconception

Children are a key ingredient of marital bliss.

Reality

Children can be a source of great joy, but they also are a source of considerable stress. Although other factors are also at work, and there are many exceptions, studies show that marital satisfaction generally declines after the arrival of children and often increases after grown children leave home.

widely assumed. On the other hand, adolescents do spend less time in family activities, and their closeness to their parents declines while conflicts become more frequent (Smetana, Campione-Barr, & Metzger, 2006). The conflicts tend to involve everyday matters (chores and appearance) more than substantive issues (sex and drugs) (Collins & Laursen, 2006).

Aging and Physiological Changes

People obviously experience many physical changes as they progress through adulthood. In both genders, hair tends to thin out and become gray. Many males confront receding hairlines and baldness. To the dismay of many, the proportion of body fat tends to increase with age. These changes have relatively little functional significance. In our youth-oriented society, however, they often lead people to view themselves as unattractive (Aldwin & Gilmer, 2004).

Curiously though, when elderly people are asked how old they feel, they mostly report feeling quite a bit younger than they actually are (Kleinspehn-Ammerlahn, Kotter-Grühn, & Smith, 2008). Obviously, there is some wishful thinking at work here, but it appears to be beneficial. Evidence suggests that feeling younger than one's real age is associated with better health and cognitive functioning and reduced mortality risk (Hsu, Chung, & Langer, 2010).

In the sensory domain, the key developmental changes occur in vision and hearing. The proportion of people with 20/20 visual acuity declines with age. Farsightedness and difficulty seeing in low illumination become more common (Schieber, 2006). Hearing sensitivity begins declining gradually in early adulthood, but usually isn't noticeable until after age 50. Even mild hearing loss can undermine speech perception and put an added burden on cognitive processing (Wingfield, Tun, & McCoy, 2005). These sensory losses would be more problematic, but in modern society they can usually be partially compensated for with eyeglasses, contacts, and hearing aids.

Age-related changes also occur in hormonal functioning during adulthood. Among women, these changes lead to *menopause*. This ending of menstrual periods, accompanied by a loss of fertility, typically occurs at around age 50 (Grady, 2006). Most women experience at least some unpleasant symptoms—such as hot flashes, headaches, night sweats, mood changes, sleep difficulties, and reduced sex drive—but the degree of discomfort varies considerably (Grady, 2006; Williams et al., 2007). Not long ago, menopause was thought to be almost universally accompanied by severe emotional strain. However, it is now clear that most women experience relatively modest psychological distress (George, 2002; Walter, 2000).

Overall, the physiological changes brought on by aging tend to decrease functional capabilities, reduce biological resilience in the face of stress, and increase susceptibility to acute and chronic diseases (Freund, Nikitin, & Riediger, 2013). Hence, as you might guess, the proportion of people with chronic diseases climbs steadily with increased age (Ward, Schiller, & Goodman, 2014) (see **Figure 10.17**). That said, some people exhibit more "successful aging" than others do. Although people tend to assume that good health in old age depends primarily on physiological factors, such as good genes, quite a variety of *psychological factors* seem to have protective value in diminishing the deleterious effects of aging. For example, in Chapter 8, we noted that higher *intelligence* is associated with greater health and longevity (Wrulich et al., 2014). In Chapter 13, we will discuss how health and longevity are associated with the personality traits of *optimism* (Carver & Scheier, 2014) and *conscientiousness* (Friedman et al., 2014). Research has also linked high *self-esteem* and the tendency to experience *positive emotions* to successful aging (Vondracek & Crouter, 2013). And, of course, healthy aging depends on *behavioral habits*, such as consuming a nutritious diet, getting adequate exercise, avoiding smoking and substance use, and being proactive about one's health by getting regular medical checkups and screenings

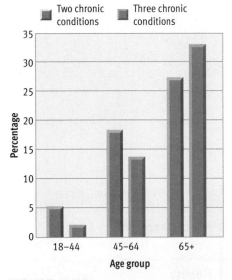

FIGURE 10.17

Age and chronic health conditions. As people grow older, they do tend to experience more chronic health problems. This graph shows the percentage of people in three age brackets who wrestle with either two or three chronic health problems. (Data from Ward, Schiller, & Goodman, 2014).

(CDC, 2009). Thus, good health in old age may be as much about psychological processes as physiological processes.

Aging and Neural Changes

The amount of brain tissue and the brain's weight decline gradually in late adulthood, mostly after age 60 (Victoroff, 2005). These trends appear to reflect both a decrease in the number of active neurons in some areas of the brain and shrinkage of still-active neurons, with neuron loss perhaps being less important than once believed. Although this gradual loss of brain tissue sounds alarming, it is a normal part of the aging process. Its functional significance is the subject of some debate, but it doesn't appear to be a key factor in any of the age-related dementias. **A *dementia* is an abnormal condition marked by multiple cognitive deficits that include memory impairment.** Dementia can be caused by quite a variety of diseases, such as Alzheimer's disease, Parkinson's disease, Huntington's disease, and AIDS, to name a few (Bourgeois, Seaman, & Servis, 2008). The prevalence of many of these diseases increases with age. Thus, dementia is seen in about 5%–8% of people ages 65–70, and 15%–20% of those ages 75–80 (Richards & Sweet, 2009). However, it is important to emphasize that dementia and "senility" are not part of the normal aging process.

Alzheimer's disease accounts for roughly 60%–80% of all cases of dementia (Thies & Bleiler, 2013). The disease is accompanied by major structural deterioration in the brain. Alzheimer's patients exhibit profound and widespread loss of neurons and brain tissue, especially in the hippocampal region known to play a key role in memory (Braskie & Thompson, 2013). The hallmark early symptom is the forgetting of newly learned information after surprisingly brief periods of time. Impairments of working memory, attention, and executive function (planning, staying on task) are also quite common (Storandt, 2008). The course of the disease is one of progressive deterioration, typically over a period of 8–10 years, ending in death (Albert, 2008). Families of Alzheimer's patients experience enormous stress as they grapple with caregiving challenges and watch their loved ones slowly deteriorate (Thies & Bleiler, 2013).

The causes that launch this debilitating neural meltdown are not well understood. Genetic factors clearly contribute (Kauwe et al., 2013). Their exact role, though, remains unclear (Guerreiro, Gustafson, & Hardy, 2012). Recent evidence implicates chronic inflammation as a contributing factor (Obulesu & Jhansilakshmi, 2014). Some "protective" factors that diminish vulnerability to Alzheimer's disease have been identified. For example, risk is reduced among those who engage in regular exercise (Smith, et al., 2013) and those with lower cardiovascular risk factors, such as absence of high blood pressure and no history of smoking or diabetes (Prince et al., 2014). Decreased vulnerability to Alzheimer's is also associated with frequent participation in stimulating cognitive activities (Landau et al., 2012) and maintenance of active social engagement with friends and family (James et al., 2011).

Contrary to widespread stereotypes, many people remain active and productive well into their 70s and 80s and even beyond. This "successful aging" appears to depend to a considerable degree on a variety of psychological factors.

Aging and Cognitive Changes

Numerous studies report decreases in older adults' memory capabilities (Dixon et al., 2013). Some researchers maintain that the memory losses associated with normal aging tend to be moderate and are *not* experienced by everyone (Dixon & Cohen, 2003). However, Salthouse (2003, 2004) takes a much more pessimistic view, arguing that age-related decreases in memory are substantial in magnitude, that they begin in early adulthood, and that they affect everyone. One reason for these varied conclusions may be that a variety of memory types can be assessed (see Chapter 7), such as semantic, episodic, and procedural memory (Small et al., 2012). Episodic memory appears to be more vulnerable than semantic memory to age-related decline (Nyberg et al., 2012).

FIGURE 10.18

Age and mental speed. Many studies have found that mental speed decreases with age. The data shown here, from Salthouse (2000), are based on two perceptual speed tasks. The data points are means for large groups of subjects expressed in terms of how many standard deviations (see Appendix B) they are above or below the mean for all ages (which is set at 0). Similar age-related declines are seen on many tasks that depend on mental speed.

SOURCE: Adapted from Salthouse, T. A. (2000). Aging and measures of processing speed. *Biological Psychology, 54,* 35–54. Reproduced by permission of Elsevier Science.

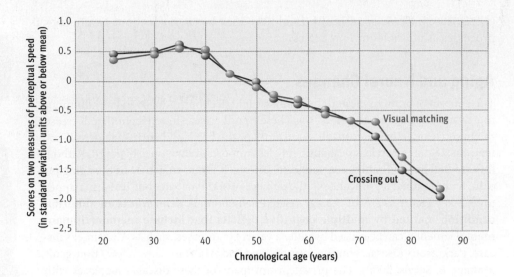

In the cognitive domain, aging seems to take its toll on *speed* first. Many studies indicate that speed in learning, solving problems, and processing information tends to decline with age (Salthouse, 1996, 2000). The evidence suggests that the erosion of processing speed may be a gradual, lengthy trend beginning in middle adulthood (see **Figure 10.18**). Although mental speed declines with age, problem-solving ability remains largely unimpaired if older people are given adequate time to compensate for their reduced speed.

A hot issue in recent years has been whether high levels of mental activity in late adulthood can delay the typical age-related declines in cognitive functioning. This possibility is sometimes referred to as the "use it or lose it" hypothesis. Several lines of evidence seem to provide support for this notion. For example, people who continue to work further into old age, especially people who remain in mentally demanding jobs, tend to show smaller decrements in cognitive abilities than their age-mates (Schooler, 2007). Other studies suggest that continuing to engage in intellectually challenging activities in late adulthood serves to buffer against cognitive declines (Nyberg et al., 2012). For example, one recent study of older individuals (average age = 72) found that 3 months of sustained engagement in learning new skills (quilting or digital photography) enhanced episodic memory (Park et al., 2014).

With findings such as these in mind, some scientists have developed elaborate and challenging cognitive training programs for elderly people that are intended to slow their cognitive decline. Studies of these interventions have yielded some promising, albeit moderate, improvements in aspects of memory performance (Kanaan et al., 2014; Miller et al., 2013). That said, the evidence on memory training in the elderly is a mixed bag. It remains to be seen whether modest training effects can delay the onset or slow the progress of Alzheimer's disease.

Death and Dying

Life is indeed a journey, and death is the ultimate destination. Dealing with the deaths of close friends and loved ones is an increasingly frequent problem as people move through adulthood. Moreover, the final challenge of life is to confront one's own death.

Because death is a taboo topic in modern Western society, the most common strategy for dealing with it is *avoidance.* People often use euphemisms such as "passed away" to avoid even the word itself. Attitudes about death vary from culture to culture. Negativism and avoidance are *not* universal. For example, in Mexican culture, death is discussed frequently and is even celebrated on a national feast day, the Day of the Dead (DeSpelder & Strickland, 1983).

Anxiety about death typically declines from early to late adulthood (Thorson & Powell, 2000). Elderly adults are more likely to fear the period of uncertainty that comes before death than death itself. They worry about where they will live, who will take care of them, and how they will cope.

Pioneering research on the experience of dying was conducted by Elisabeth Kübler-Ross (1969, 1970) during the 1960s. Based on interviews with terminally ill patients, she concluded that people evolve through a series of five stages as they confront their own death: (1) denial, (2) anger, (3) bargaining (with God for more time), (4) depression, and (5) acceptance. Subsequent studies of dying patients have not all observed the same five emotions or the same progression of emotions she described (Corr, 1993; Friedman & James, 2008). But Kübler-Ross deserves credit for launching empirical research on death and dying.

When a friend, spouse, or relative dies, individuals must cope with *bereavement*. Considerable variation exists among cultures in how people tend to deal with this highly stressful event. In America and western European countries, the bereaved are typically encouraged to break their emotional ties with the deceased relatively quickly and to return to their regular routines. In Asian, African, and Hispanic cultures, the bereaved are encouraged to maintain emotional ties to their dead loved ones (Bonanno, 1998). For example, almost all Japanese homes have altars dedicated to family ancestors, and family members routinely talk to the deceased. Regardless of the particular form that mourning takes, all such rituals are designed to make death meaningful and to help the bereaved cope with the pain and disruption of death.

Studies of bereaved spouses suggest that grief reactions fall into five patterns (Bonanno, Wortman, & Neese, 2004). *Absent grief* or the *resilient pattern* is characterized by low levels of depression before and after the spouse's death. In *chronic grief*, low pre-loss depression is followed by sustained depression after the spouse's death. *Common grief* is characterized by a spike in depression shortly after the spouse's death and a decline in depression over time. In the *depressed-improved* pattern, high pre-loss depression is followed by a relatively quick and sustained decline in depression after the spouse's death. *Chronic depression* describes those who experience high levels of depression both before and long after spousal loss. Surprisingly, absent grief/resilience is the most common pattern, exhibited by roughly one-half of bereaved spouses. Many people believe that individuals who fail to engage in "grief work" will suffer long-term adjustment problems. However, this view has been contradicted by many studies (Bonanno et al., 2002; Wortman, Wolff, & Bonanno, 2004).

10.6 REFLECTING ON THE CHAPTER'S THEMES

Five of our seven integrative themes surfaced to some degree in our coverage of human development. We saw theoretical diversity in our discussions of cognitive development and personality development. We saw that psychology evolves in a sociohistorical context, investigating complex, real-world issues—such as the controversy surrounding gender differences—that emerge as our society changes. We encountered multifactorial causation of behavior in the development of attachment, among other things. We saw cultural invariance and cultural diversity in our examination of attachment, motor development, cognitive development, and moral development.

But above all else, we saw how heredity and environment jointly mold behavior. We've encountered the dual influence of heredity and environment before, but this theme is rich in complexity, and each chapter draws out different aspects and implications. Our discussion of development amplified the point that genetics and experience work *interactively* to shape behavior. What does it mean to say that heredity and environment interact?

Theoretical Diversity

Sociohistorical Context

Multifactorial Causation

Cultural Heritage

 Heredity & Environment

In the language of science, an interaction means that the effects of one variable depend on the effects of another. In other words, heredity and environment do not operate independently. Children with "difficult" temperaments will elicit different reactions from different parents, depending on the parents' personalities and expectations. Likewise, a particular pair of parents will affect different children in different ways, depending on the inborn characteristics of the children. An interplay, or feedback loop, exists between biological and environmental factors.

All aspects of development are shaped jointly by heredity and experience. We often estimate their relative weight or influence as if we could cleanly divide behavior into genetic and environmental components. Although we can't really carve up behavior that neatly, such comparisons can be of great theoretical interest, as you'll see in our upcoming Personal Application, which discusses the nature and origins of gender differences in behavior.

10.7

Key Learning Goals

- Summarize evidence on gender differences in behavior, and assess the significance of these differences.
- Explain how biological and environmental factors are thought to contribute to gender differences.

10.7 PERSONAL APPLICATION
Understanding Gender Differences

Answer the following "true" or "false."

____ 1 Females are more socially oriented than males.

____ 2 Males outperform females on most spatial tasks.

____ 3 Females are more irrational than males.

____ 4 Males are less sensitive to nonverbal cues than females are.

____ 5 Females are more emotional than males.

Are there genuine behavioral differences between the genders similar to those mentioned above? If so, why do these differences exist? How do they develop? These are the complex and controversial questions that we'll explore in this Personal Application.

How Do the Genders Differ in Behavior?

Gender differences **are disparities between males and females in typical behavior or average ability.** Mountains of research, literally thousands of studies, exist on gender differences. What does this research show? Are the stereotypes of males and females accurate? Well, the

findings are a mixed bag. The research indicates that genuine behavioral differences *do* exist between genders and that people's stereotypes are not entirely inaccurate. But the differences are fewer in number, smaller in size, and more complex than stereotypes suggest (Hyde, 2014; Leaper, 2013). As you'll see, only two of the differences mentioned in our opening true-false questions (the even-numbered items) are largely supported by the research.

Cognitive Abilities

In the cognitive domain, it appears that there are three genuine—albeit very small—gender differences. First, on the average, females tend to exhibit slightly better *verbal skills* than males (Leaper, 2013). For example, girls score higher in reading achievement around the world (Stoet & Geary, 2013). The size of females' advantage varies depending on the nature of the task, but the gender gaps generally are quite small (Halpern, 2012). Second, starting during high school, males show a slight advantage on tests of *mathematical ability*. When all students are compared, males' advantage is quite small. Indeed, it appears that the gender gap in math has disappeared in the general population in the United States (Hyde, 2014). Around the world, though, small to modest

gender disparities are still seen in many countries, and these differences usually favor males (Else-Quest, Hyde, & Linn, 2010; Stoet & Geary, 2013). Also, at the high end of the ability distribution, a gender gap is still found in the United States. About three to four times as many males as females manifest exceptional math skills (Wai, Putallaz, & Makel, 2012). Third, starting in the grade-school years, males tend to score higher than females on most measures of *visual-spatial ability* (Hines, 2013). Tasks requiring mental rotations in space and perception of movement in space tend to generate the biggest gender disparities (Halpern, 2012).

Social Behavior

In regard to social behavior, research findings support the existence of some additional gender differences. First, studies indicate that males tend to be much more *physically aggressive* than females (Archer, 2005; Card et al., 2008). This disparity shows up early in childhood. Its continuation into adulthood is supported by the fact that men account for a grossly disproportionate number of the violent crimes in our society (Kenrick, Trost, & Sundie, 2004). Contrary to popular belief, females and males seem pretty similar in their level of *verbal or relational aggression* (snide remarks and so forth), but this is the type of aggression females use most commonly, resulting in the "mean girls" stereotype (Leaper, 2013). Second, there are gender differences in *nonverbal communication*. The evidence indicates that females are more sensitive than males to subtle nonverbal cues (Hampson, van Anders, & Mullin, 2006; Schmid et al., 2011) and that they pay more attention to interpersonal information (Hall & Mast, 2008). Third, males are more *sexually active* than females in a variety of ways. For example, males are more likely to engage in casual and premarital sex, masturbation, and the use of pornography (Petersen & Hyde, 2011; see Chapter 9).

Some Qualifications

Although research has identified some genuine gender differences in behavior, bear in mind that these are group differences that indicate nothing about individuals. Essentially, research results compare the "average man" with the "average woman." However, you are—and every individual is—unique. The average female and male are ultimately figments of our imagination. Furthermore, the genuine group differences noted are relatively small (Hyde, 2014). **Figure 10.19** shows how scores on a trait, perhaps verbal ability, might be distributed for men and women. Although the group averages are detectably different, you can see the great variability within each group (gender) and the huge overlap between the two group distributions.

Biological Origins of Gender Differences

What accounts for the development of gender differences? To what degree are they the product of learning or of biology? This question is yet another manifestation of the *nature versus nurture* issue. Investigations of the biological origins of gender differences have centered on the evolutionary bases of behavior, hormones, and brain organization.

Evolutionary Explanations

Evolutionary psychologists argue that gender differences in behavior reflect different natural selection pressures operating on males and females over the course of human history (Archer, 1996; Geary, 2007). For example, as we discussed in Chapter 9, males supposedly are more sexually active and permissive because they invest less than females in the process of procreation and can maximize their reproductive success by seeking many sexual partners (Schmitt, 2005; Webster, 2009). The gender gap in aggression is also explained in terms of reproductive fitness. Because females are more selective about mating than males are, males have to engage in more competition for sexual partners than females do. Greater aggressiveness is thought to be adaptive for males in this competition for sexual access because it should foster social dominance over other males. It should also facilitate the acquisition

of the material resources emphasized by females when evaluating potential partners (Campbell, 2005; Cummins, 2005). Evolutionary theorists assert that gender differences in spatial ability reflect the division of labor in ancestral hunting-and-gathering societies, in which males typically handled the hunting and females the gathering. Males' superiority on most spatial tasks has been attributed to the adaptive demands of hunting (Silverman & Choi, 2005; see Chapter 1).

Evolutionary analyses of gender differences are interesting and plausible, but critics argue that evolutionary hypotheses are speculative and that there are alternative explanations (Eagly & Wood, 1999, 2013). The crucial problem for some critics is that evolutionary analyses are so "flexible" that they can be used to explain almost anything. For example, if the situation regarding spatial ability were reversed— if females scored higher than males— evolutionary theorists might attribute females' superiority to the adaptive demands of gathering food, weaving baskets, and making clothes—and it would be difficult to prove otherwise (Cornell, 1997).

The Role of Hormones

The potential role of prenatal hormones becomes apparent when something interferes with normal prenatal hormonal secretions. About half a dozen endocrine disorders can cause overproduction or underproduction of specific gonadal hormones during prenatal development. The general trend in this research is that females exposed prenatally to abnormally high levels of androgens exhibit more male-typical behavior than other females do. Likewise, males exposed prenatally to abnormally low levels of androgens exhibit more female-typical behavior than other males (Hines, 2004, 2013). These findings suggest that prenatal hormones contribute to the shaping of gender differences in humans. But the evidence is much stronger for females than for males, and it's always dangerous to draw conclusions about the general population based on small samples of people who have abnormal conditions (Basow, 1992; Jordan-Young, 2010).

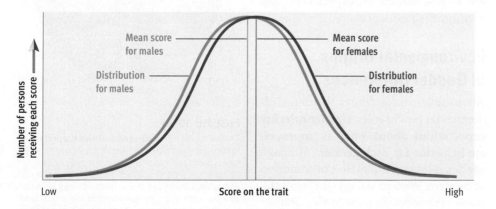

FIGURE 10.19

The nature of gender differences. Gender differences are group differences that indicate little about individuals because of the great overlap between the groups. For a given trait, one gender may score higher on the average, but far more variation occurs within each gender than between the genders.

The socialization of gender roles begins very early, as parents dress their infants in gendered clothing, buy them gender-driven toys, and encourage them to participate in "gender-appropriate" activities.

Differences in Brain Organization

Gender differences have also been linked to specialization of the cerebral hemispheres in the brain (see **Figure 10.20**). As you may recall from Chapter 3, in most people, the left hemisphere is more actively involved in verbal processing, whereas the right hemisphere is more active in visual-spatial processing (Gazzaniga, Ivry, & Mangum, 2009). After these findings surfaced, theorists began to wonder whether this division of labor in the brain might be related to gender differences in verbal and spatial skills.

Some thought-provoking findings *have* been reported. For instance, some studies have found that *males tend to exhibit more cerebral specialization than females* (Boles, 2005). Other studies suggest that *females tend to have a larger corpus callosum* (Gur & Gur, 2007), the band of fibers that connects the two hemispheres of the brain. Thus, some theorists have concluded that differences between the genders in brain organization are responsible for gender differences in verbal and spatial ability (Clements et al., 2006; Hines, 2013).

This idea is intriguing, but studies have not been consistent in finding that males have more specialized brain organization than females do (Kaiser et al., 2009), and doubts have been raised about the finding that females have a larger corpus callosum (Halpern et al., 2007). Moreover, even if these findings were replicated consistently, no one is really sure just how they would account for the observed gender differences in cognitive abilities (Fine, 2010).

In summary, researchers have made some intriguing progress in their efforts to document the biological roots of gender differences in behavior. However, the idea that "anatomy is destiny" has proven difficult to demonstrate. Many theorists remain convinced that gender differences are largely shaped by experience. Let's examine their evidence.

Environmental Origins of Gender Differences

All societies make efforts to train children about gender roles. ***Gender roles are expectations about what is appropriate behavior for each gender.*** Although gender roles are in a period of transition in modern Western society, there are still many disparities in how males and females are brought up. Investigators have identified three key processes involved in the development of gender roles: operant conditioning, observational learning, and self-socialization. First we'll examine these processes. Then we'll look at the principal sources of gender-role socialization: families, schools, and the media.

Operant Conditioning

In part, gender roles are shaped by the power of reward and punishment—the key processes in *operant conditioning* (see Chapter 6). Parents, teachers, peers, and others often reinforce (usually with tacit approval) "gender-appropriate" behavior and respond negatively to "gender-inappropriate" behavior (Bussey & Bandura, 1999; Matlin, 2008). If you're a man, you might recall getting hurt as a young boy and being told that "big boys don't cry." If you succeeded in inhibiting your crying, you may have earned an approving smile or even something tangible, such as an ice cream cone. The reinforcement probably strengthened your tendency to "act like a man" and suppress emotional displays. Studies suggest that fathers encourage

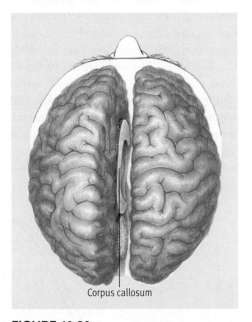

Corpus callosum

FIGURE 10.20

The cerebral hemispheres and the corpus callosum. In this drawing the cerebral hemispheres have been "pulled apart" to reveal the corpus callosum, the band of fibers that connects the right and left halves of the brain. Research has shown that the right and left hemispheres are specialized to handle different types of cognitive tasks (see Chapter 3), leading some theorists to speculate that patterns of hemispheric specialization might contribute to gender differences in verbal and spatial abilities.

and reward gender-appropriate behavior in their youngsters more than mothers do and that boys experience more pressure to behave in gender-appropriate ways than girls do (Levy, Taylor, & Gelman, 1995).

Observational Learning

Observational learning (see Chapter 6) by children can lead to the imitation of adults' gender-appropriate behavior. Children imitate both males and females, but most children tend to imitate same-sex role models more than opposite-sex role models (Bussey & Bandura, 1984; Frey & Ruble, 1992). Thus, imitation often leads young girls to play with dolls, dollhouses, and toy stoves, while young boys are more likely to tinker with toy trucks, miniature gas stations, and tool kits.

Self-Socialization

Children themselves are active agents in their own gender-role socialization. Several *cognitive theories* of gender-role development emphasize self-socialization (Bem, 1985; Martin & Ruble, 2004). According to this view, young children strive to bring their behavior in line with what is considered gender-appropriate in their culture. In other words, children work diligently to discover the rules that are supposed to govern their behavior.

Sources of Gender-Role Socialization

There are three main sources of influence in gender-role socialization: families, schools, and the media. Of course, we are now in an era of transition in gender roles. Thus, the generalizations that follow may say more about how you were socialized than about how children will be socialized in the future.

Families A great deal of gender-role socialization takes place in the home (Berenbaum, Martin, & Ruble, 2008). For example, fathers engage in more "rough-housing" play with their sons than with their daughters, even in infancy (McBride-Chang & Jacklin, 1993). As children grow, boys and girls are encouraged to play with different types of toys (Hines, 2013). Generally, boys have less leeway to play with "feminine" toys than girls do with "masculine" toys. When children are old enough to help with household chores, the assignments tend to depend on gender (Cunningham, 2001). For example, girls wash dishes and boys mow the lawn.

Schools Schools and teachers clearly contribute to the socialization of gender roles (Berenbaum et al., 2008). The books that children use in learning to read can influence their ideas about what is suitable behavior for males and females (McCabe et al., 2011). Traditionally, males have been more likely to be portrayed as clever, heroic, and adventurous in these books, while females have been more likely to be shown doing domestic chores. Preschool and grade-school teachers frequently reward gender-appropriate behavior in their pupils (Ruble & Martin, 1998). Interestingly, teachers tend to pay greater attention to males—helping them, praising them, and scolding them more than they do females (Jones & Dindia, 2004).

Schools may play a key role in the gender gap in outstanding math performance. For example, Hyde and Mertz (2009) note that girls traditionally have been much less likely than boys to be encouraged to enroll in advanced math, chemistry, and physics courses.

Media Television and other mass media are another source of gender-role socialization (Bussey & Bandura, 2004). Although some improvement has occurred in recent years, television shows have traditionally depicted men and women in stereotypical ways (Galambos, 2004; Signorielli, 2001). Women are often portrayed as submissive, passive, and emotional. Men are more likely to be portrayed as independent, assertive, and competent. Research *has* found an association between children's exposure to gender stereotyping in the media and their beliefs about gender roles (Oppliger, 2007).

Conclusion

As you can see, the findings on gender and behavior are complex and confusing. Nonetheless, the evidence does permit one very general conclusion—a conclusion that you have seen before and will see again. Taken as a whole, the research in this area suggests that biological factors and environmental factors both contribute to gender differences in behavior—as they do to all other aspects of development. And these biological and environmental influences interact in very complex ways (Miller & Halpern, 2014).

10.8

Key Learning Goals
- Clarify and critique the argument that fathers are essential for healthy development.

10.8 CRITICAL THINKING APPLICATION
Are Fathers Essential to Children's Well-Being?

Are fathers essential for children to experience normal, healthy development? This question is currently the subject of heated debate. A number of social scientists have mounted a thought-provoking argument that father absence is the chief factor underlying a variety of modern social ills. For example, David Blankenhorn (1995) argues that "fatherlessness is the most harmful demographic trend of this generation. It is the leading cause of declining child well-being in our society" (p. 1). Expressing a similar view, David Popenoe (2009) maintains that "today's fatherlessness has led to social turmoil—damaged children, unhappy children, aimless children, children who strike back with pathological behavior and violence" (p. 192). The belief that fathers are crucial to healthy development has become widely accepted. This conventional wisdom has been strongly endorsed by both President George W. Bush and President Barack Obama, and it has guided government policy in a variety of areas.

The Basic Argument

What is the evidence for the proposition that fathers are essential to healthy development? Over the last 40 years, the proportion of children growing up without a father in the home has more than doubled. During the same time, we have seen dramatic increases in teenage pregnancy, juvenile delinquency, violent crime, drug abuse, eating disorders, teen suicide, and family dysfunction. Moreover, mountains of studies have demonstrated an association between father absence and an elevated risk for these problems. Summarizing this evidence, Popenoe (2009) asserts that "fatherless children have a risk factor two to three times that of fathered children for a wide range of negative outcomes, including dropping out of high school, giving birth as a teenager, and

becoming a juvenile delinquent" (p. 192). This leads him to infer that "fathers have a unique and irreplaceable role to play in child development" (p. 197). Working from this premise, Popenoe concludes, "If present trends continue, our society could be on the verge of committing social suicide" (p. 192). Echoing this dire conclusion, Blankenhorn (1995) comments that "to tolerate the trend of fatherlessness is to accept the inevitability of continued societal recession" (p. 222).

You might be thinking, "What's all the fuss about?" Surely, proclaiming the importance of fatherhood ought to be no more controversial than advocacy for motherhood or apple pie. But the assertion that a father is *essential* to a child's well-being has some interesting political implications. It suggests that heterosexual marriage is the only appropriate context in which to raise children and that other family configurations are fundamentally deficient. Based on this line of reasoning, some people have argued for new laws that would make it more difficult to obtain a divorce and have advocated other policies and programs that would favor traditional families over families headed by single mothers, cohabiting parents, and gay and lesbian parents (Silverstein & Auerbach, 1999). Not surprisingly, the belief that children need both a mother and a father has surfaced repeatedly in the legal wrangling over same-sex marriage. Thus, the question about the importance of fathers is creating a great deal of controversy because it is really a question about alternatives to traditional family structure.

Evaluating the Argument

In light of the far-reaching implications of the view that fathers are essential to normal

development, it makes sense to subject this view to critical scrutiny. How could you use critical thinking skills to evaluate this argument? At least three previously discussed ideas seem pertinent.

First, it is important to recognize that the position that fathers are essential for healthy development rests on a foundation of correlational evidence. As we have seen repeatedly, *correlation is no assurance of causation*. Yes, there has been an increase in fatherlessness that has been paralleled by increases in teenage pregnancy, drug abuse, eating disorders, and other disturbing social problems. But think of all the other changes that have occurred in American culture over the last 40 years, such as the decline of organized religion, the growth of mass media, dramatic shifts in sexual mores, and so forth. Increased fatherlessness has co-varied with a host of other cultural trends. Thus, it is highly speculative to infer that father absence is the chief cause of most modern social problems.

Second, it always pays to think about whether there are *alternative explanations* for findings that you might have doubts about. What other factors might account for the association between father absence and children's maladjustment? Think for a moment: What is the most frequent

Are fathers crucial to children's well-being? This seemingly simple question has sparked heated debate.

cause of father absence? Obviously, it is divorce. Divorces tend to be highly stressful events that disrupt children's entire lives. Although the evidence suggests that a majority of children seem to survive divorce without lasting detrimental effects, it is clear that divorce elevates youngsters' risk for a wide range of negative developmental outcomes (Amato & Dorius, 2010; Ehrenberg et al., 2014; Greene et al., 2012). Given that father absence and divorce are often intertwined, it is possible that the negative effects of divorce account for much of the association between father absence and social problems.

Are there any other alternative explanations for the correlation between fatherlessness and social maladies? Yes, critics point out that the prevalence of father absence co-varies with socioeconomic status: Father absence is much more common in low-income families (Anderson, Kohler, & Letiecq, 2002). Thus, the effects of father absence are entangled to some extent with the many powerful, malignant effects of poverty, which might account for much of the correlation between fatherlessness and negative outcomes (McLoyd, 1998).

A third possible strategy in thinking critically about the effects of father absence would be to ask *if there is contradictory evidence*. Once again, the answer is yes. Biblarz and Stacey (2010) reviewed studies comparing pairs of heterosexual parents against pairs of lesbian parents. If fathers are essential, the adjustment of children raised by heterosexual parents should be superior to that of children raised by lesbian parents. But the studies found negligible differences between these parental configurations.

A fourth possible strategy in thinking critically about the effects of father absence would be to look for some of the *fallacies in reasoning* introduced in Chapter 9 (irrelevant reasons, circular reasoning, slippery slope, weak analogies, and false dichotomy). A couple of the quotes from Popenoe and Blankenhorn were chosen to give you an opportunity to detect two of these fallacies in a new context. Take a look at the quotes again and see whether you can spot the fallacies.

Popenoe's assertion that "if present trends continue, our society could be on the verge of social suicide" is an example of *slippery slope argumentation*, which involves predictions that if one allows X to happen, things will spin out of control and catastrophic events will follow. "Social suicide" is a little vague, but it sounds as if Popenoe is predicting that father absence will lead to the destruction of modern American culture. The other fallacy you might have spotted is the *false dichotomy* apparent in Blankenhorn's assertion that "to tolerate the trend of fatherlessness is to accept the inevitability of continued societal recession." A false dichotomy creates an either-or choice between the position one wants to advocate (in this case, new social policies to reduce father absence) and some obviously horrible outcome that any sensible person would want to avoid (social decay), while ignoring other possible outcomes that might lie between these extremes.

In summary, we can find a number of flaws and weaknesses in the argument that fathers are *essential* to normal development. However, our critical evaluation of this argument *does not mean that fathers are unimportant*. Many types of evidence suggest that fathers generally make significant contributions to their children's development (McLanahan, Tach, & Schneider, 2013; Ramchandani et al., 2013). We could argue with merit that fathers typically provide a substantial advantage for children that fatherless children do not have. But there is a crucial distinction between arguing that fathers *promote* normal, healthy development and arguing that fathers are *necessary* for normal, healthy development. If fathers are *necessary*, children who grow up without them could not achieve the same level of well-being as those who have fathers. It is clear, however, that a great many children from single-parent homes turn out just fine.

Fathers surely are important, and it seems likely that father absence *contributes* to a variety of problems in modern society. So, why do Blankenhorn (1995) and Popenoe (2009) argue for the much stronger conclusion—that fathers are *essential*? They appear to prefer the stronger conclusion because it raises much more serious questions about the viability of nontraditional family forms. Thus, they seem to want to advance a *political agenda* that champions traditional family values. They are certainly entitled to do so, but when research findings are used to advance a political agenda—whether conservative or liberal—a special caution alert should go off in your head. When a political agenda is at stake, it pays to scrutinize arguments with extra care because research findings are more likely to be presented in a slanted fashion. The field of psychology deals with a host of complex questions that have profound implications for a wide range of social issues. The skills and habits of critical thinking can help you find your way through the maze of reasons and evidence that holds up the many sides of these complicated issues.

TABLE 10.1 Critical Thinking Skills Discussed in This Application

Skill	Description
Understanding the limitations of correlational evidence	The critical thinker understands that a correlation between two variables does not demonstrate that there is a causal link between the variables.
Looking for alternative explanations for findings and events	In evaluating explanations, the critical thinker explores whether there are other explanations that could also account for the findings or events under scrutiny.
Recognizing and avoiding common fallacies, such as irrelevant reasons, circular reasoning, slippery slope reasoning, weak analogies, and false dichotomies	The critical thinker is vigilant about conclusions based on unrelated premises, conclusions that are rewordings of premises, unwarranted predictions that things will spin out of control, superficial analogies, and contrived dichotomies.

PRENATAL DEVELOPMENT

Stages

- During the *germinal stage*, a zygote becomes a mass of cells that implants in the uterine wall and the placenta begins to form.

- During the *embryonic stage*, most vital organs and bodily systems begin to form, making it a period of great vulnerability.

- During the *fetal stage*, organs continue to grow and gradually begin to function; the fetus reaches the *threshold of viability* around 23–25 weeks.

© Samuel Borges Photography/Shutterstock.com

Environmental influences

- Maternal malnutrition during the prenatal period has been linked to birth complications and other problems, and maternal emotions can have an impact on prenatal development.

- Maternal use of illicit drugs can be dangerous to the unborn child. Even normal social drinking and routine tobacco use can be hazardous.

- A variety of maternal illnesses can interfere with prenatal development, and environmental toxins are also a source of concern.

- Recent evidence suggests that prenatal development can "program" the fetal brain in ways that influence one's vulnerability to various types of illness decades later.

DEVELOPMENT IN CHILDHOOD

Motor development

- Physical growth is rapid and uneven during infancy, as there are sudden bursts of growth.

- Early progress in motor skills has traditionally been attributed to *maturation*, but recent research suggests that infants' exploration is also important.

- Researchers have found cultural variations in the pacing of motor development, which demonstrates the potential importance of learning.

Attachment

- *Attachment* refers to the close emotional bonds that develop between infants and caregivers.

- Harlow's studies of infant monkeys showed that reinforcement is not the key to attachment.

- Bowlby argued that attachment has a biological and evolutionary basis.

- Research by Ainsworth showed that infant-mother attachments fall into three categories: secure, anxious-ambivalent, and avoidant.

- Infants with a relatively secure attachment tend to become resilient, competent toddlers with high self-esteem.

- Cultural variations in child rearing influence the patterns of attachment seen in a society.

Language development

- Language development tends to unfold at *roughly* the same pace for most children.

- The initial vocalizations by infants are similar across languages, but their babbling gradually begins to resemble the sounds from their surrounding language.

- Children typically utter their first words around their first birthday.

- Vocabulary growth is slow at first, but *fast mapping* contributes to a vocabulary spurt that often begins around 18 months.

- Children begin to combine words by the end of their second year, exhibiting *telegraphic speech*.

- Over the next several years, children gradually learn the complexities of grammar, but they exhibit many *overregularizations*.

Personality development

- Erikson's theory proposes that individuals evolve through eight stages over the life span, with each stage marked by a specific *psychosocial crisis*.

- *Stage theories* assume that individuals progress through stages in a particular order, that progress is strongly related to age, and that new stages bring major changes.

- Erikson's four childhood stages are trust versus mistrust, autonomy versus shame and doubt, initiative versus guilt, and industry versus inferiority.

Cognitive development

- Piaget proposed that children evolve through four stages of cognitive development.

- The major achievement of the *sensorimotor period* (birth to age 2) is the development of object permanence.

- Children's thought during the *preoperational period* (ages 2–7) is marked by centration, animism, irreversibility, and egocentrism.

- In the *concrete operational period* (ages 7–11), children develop the ability to perform operations on mental representations.

- In the *formal operational stage* (age 11 onward), thought becomes more systematic, abstract, and logical.

- Piaget may have underestimated some aspects of children's cognitive development, the mixing of stages, and the impact of culture.

- Vygotsky's sociocultural theory asserts that children's cognitive development is shaped by social interactions, language progress, and cultural factors.

- Researchers have found that infants understand complex concepts, such as addition, that they have had little opportunity to acquire through learning.

- These findings have led some theorists to conclude that some basic cognitive abilities are wired into humans' neural architecture.

Moral development

- Kohlberg's theory proposes that individuals progress through three levels of moral reasoning.

- *Preconventional reasoning* focuses on acts' consequences, *conventional reasoning* on the need to maintain social order, and *postconventional reasoning* on working out a personal code of ethics.

- Age-related progress in moral reasoning has been found in research, but there is a lot of overlap between stages.

DEVELOPMENT IN ADOLESCENCE

Physiological and neural development

- Brought on by hormonal changes, the *adolescent growth spurt* typically begins at about age 9–10 in girls and age 10–12 in boys.

- Puberty is the stage during which *primary sex characteristics* develop fully.

- Today's adolescents tend to begin puberty at an earlier age than previous generations, perhaps because of improvements in nutrition and medical care.

- Girls who reach puberty early and boys who mature relatively late have a greater risk for psychological and social difficulties.

- The *prefrontal cortex* appears to be the last area of the brain to fully mature, and this maturation is not complete until early adulthood.

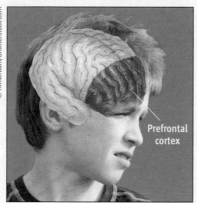

Prefrontal cortex

© RimDream/Shutterstock.com

The search for identity

- According to Erikson, the main challenge of adolescence is the struggle for a sense of identity.

- Marcia asserted that adolescents deal with their identity crisis in four ways: *foreclosure, moratorium, identity diffusion,* and *identity achievement.*

- Arnett argued for the existence of a new developmental stage in modern societies, called *emerging adulthood.*

APPLICATIONS

- Genuine gender differences have been found in verbal ability, math ability, spatial ability, aggression, nonverbal communication, and sexual behavior.

- However, many gender stereotypes are inaccurate, and most gender differences in behavior are very small in magnitude.

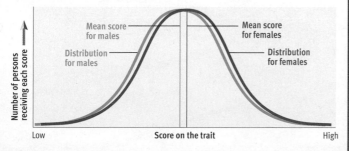

- Evolutionary theorists attribute gender differences to natural selection based on different adaptive demands confronted by males and females.

- Evidence suggests that prenatal hormones contribute to gender differences, but the hypotheses on cerebral specialization have been highly speculative.

- Operant conditioning, observational learning, and self-socialization contribute to the development of gender differences.

- There are contradictory data and alternative explanations for the association between father absence and negative developmental outcomes.

DEVELOPMENT IN ADULTHOOD

Personality development

- During adulthood, personality is marked by both stability and change, as percentile scores remain stable but mean raw scores change in predictable ways.

- The adult years tend to bring gradual increases in agreeableness, openness to experience, and conscientiousness.

- According to Erikson, people evolve through three stages of development in the adult years: intimacy versus isolation, generativity versus self-absorption, and integrity versus despair.

Family transitions

- Optimism can ease the transition into marriage, but idealistic expectations about marriage are associated with steep declines in well-being.

- Premarital cohabitation used to be predictive of an increased likelihood of marital dissolution, but the situation seems to be changing.

- Adjusting to marriage is more likely to be difficult when spouses have different expectations about marital roles.

- Most parents are happy with their decision to have children, but the arrival of the first child represents a major transition, and the disruption of routines can be draining.

- Parent-adolescent relations are not as contentious as widely assumed, but conflicts do increase.

Physiological and neural changes

- In the sensory domain, vision and hearing acuity tend to decline, but glasses and hearing aids can compensate for these losses.

- Women's reactions to menopause vary, and menopause is not as stressful as widely believed.

- The proportion of people with chronic diseases climbs steadily with age, but some people exhibit more successful aging than others.

- Brain tissue and weight tend to decline after age 60, but this loss does not appear to be the key to age-related dementias.

- *Dementias* are seen in about 15%–20% of people over age 75, but they are not part of the normal aging process.

- Alzheimer's patients exhibit profound loss of brain tissue and the accumulation of characteristic neural abnormalities.

Cognitive changes

- Many studies have found decreases in older adults' memory capabilities; there is debate about the severity of these memory losses.

- Speed in cognitive processing tends to begin a gradual decline during middle adulthood.

- Some studies suggest that high levels of mental activity in late adulthood can delay the typical age-related declines in cognitive functioning.

Death and dying

- Kübler-Ross concluded that people evolve through a series of five stages as they confront their death, but some subsequent studies did not find the same progression.

- Considerable variation exists among cultures in how people tend to deal with bereavement.

- Studies of bereaved spouses suggest that grief reactions fall into five patterns, with absent grief/resilience the most common pattern.

CHAPTER 11

PERSONALITY

Themes in this Chapter

Cultural
Heritage

Theoretical
Diversity

Sociohistorical
Context

John Shaw/Science Source

Richard Branson was sure that he was about to die. He was high above the Atlantic Ocean, alone in a capsule attached to the biggest balloon in the world. Per Lindstrand, the balloon's pilot, was somewhere in the icy waves far below. He and Branson had just become the first people ever to cross the Atlantic in a hot-air balloon. But when an emergency landing at sea failed, Lindstrand had leaped into the water. Before Branson could follow, the balloon had shot back up into the sky. Branson had never flown a balloon before his all-too-brief training for the trip. Now he was stranded in midair with no idea how to save himself.

Hastily Branson scribbled a note to his family. Then he began trying to vent the huge balloon in a desperate attempt to guide it safely earthward. Much to his own surprise, he was able to get close enough to the sea to jump for it. A rescue helicopter plucked him out of the waves.

After this brush with death, Branson swore that he would never risk his life so foolishly again. Yet 3 years later, he and Lindstrand were at it again. This time they attempted to become the first people to cross the Pacific in a hot-air balloon. The trip turned into another terrifying ordeal, and once again they were nearly killed. But that didn't stop them from planning their next exploit—trying to become the first hot-air balloonists to fly completely around the world (Branson, 2005; Brown, 1998).

When people describe Richard Branson, they are apt to use words such as *adventurous, brave, daring, impulsive,* and *reckless.* These are the kinds of words used to characterize what we call "personality." And Branson—a self-made billionaire and one of the richest people in the world—may be as famous for his exuberant personality as he is for his immense wealth.

Branson is the founder of the Virgin group of companies, including the Virgin Atlantic airline and Virgin Galactic, which aims to become the first company to fly tourists into space. Branson is a brash, shrewd, and relentless entrepreneur who loves cutting a deal. But he also loves parties, practical jokes, and flamboyant publicity stunts. Most of all, he relishes finding new fields to conquer.

Most people would agree that Richard Branson has an unusual personality. But what exactly *is* personality? And why are personalities so different? Why is one person daring, while another is timid? Was Richard Branson born with the self-confidence and daring he is renowned for, or were environment and learning critical in shaping his personality? Consider that Branson's parents stressed the importance

Richard Branson, the founder of the Virgin group of companies, clearly manifests a powerful and unusual personality. But everyone has his or her own unique personality, which makes the study of personality a fascinating area of inquiry in psychology.

of being strong and independent, starting at an early age. But perhaps the roots of Branson's personality lie in biological inheritance. Branson (2005) describes his mother as a woman of dazzling energy and fierce determination who also had a taste for adventure. During World War II, she talked her way into pilot training on the condition that she disguise herself as a boy. Maybe Branson's genetic makeup is responsible for his being an "adrenaline junkie."

Psychologists have approached questions such as these from a variety of perspectives. Traditionally, the study of personality has been dominated by "grand theories" that attempt to explain a great many facets of behavior. Our discussion will reflect this emphasis, as we'll devote most of our time to the sweeping theories of Freud, Skinner, Rogers, and several others. In recent decades, however, the study of personality has shifted toward narrower research programs that examine specific issues related to personality. This trend is reflected in our review of biological, cultural, and other contemporary approaches to personality in the last several sections of the chapter. In the Personal Application, we'll examine how psychological tests are used to measure aspects of personality. The Critical Thinking Application will explore how hindsight bias can taint people's analyses of personality.

11.1

Key Learning Goals

- Clarify the meaning of personality and personality traits.
- Describe the five-factor model of personality and the relationship between the Big Five traits and life outcomes.

11.1 THE NATURE OF PERSONALITY

Personality is a complex hypothetical construct that has been defined in a variety of ways. Let's take a closer look at the concepts of personality and personality traits.

Defining Personality: Consistency and Distinctiveness

What does it mean to say that someone has an optimistic personality? This assertion indicates that the person has a fairly *consistent tendency* to behave in a cheerful, hopeful, enthusiastic way, looking at the bright side of things across a wide variety of situations. Although no one is entirely consistent in behavior, this quality of *consistency across situations* lies at the core of the concept of personality.

Distinctiveness is also central to the concept of personality. Personality is used to explain why everyone does not act the same way in similar situations. If you were stuck in an elevator with three people, each might react differently. One might crack jokes to relieve tension. Another might make ominous predictions that "we'll never get out of here." The third person might calmly think about how to escape. These varied reactions to the same situation occur because each person has a different personality. Each person has traits that are seen in other people, but each individual has his or her own distinctive *set* of personality traits.

In summary, the concept of personality is used to explain (1) the stability in a person's behavior over time and across situations (consistency) and (2) the behavioral differences among people reacting to the same situation (distinctiveness). We can combine these ideas into the following definition: **Personality refers to an individual's unique set of consistent behavioral traits.** Let's explore the concept of *traits* in more detail.

Personality Traits: Dispositions and Dimensions

When describing another person, we tend to make remarks like "Jan is very *conscientious.*" Or we might assert that "Jamaal is too *timid* to succeed in that job." These descriptive statements refer to personality traits. **A *personality trait* is a durable disposition to behave in a particular way in a variety of situations.** Adjectives such as *honest, dependable, moody, impulsive, suspicious, domineering,* and *friendly* describe dispositions that represent personality traits. People use an enormous number of these trait terms to describe one another's personality. One prominent personality theorist, Gordon Allport (1937, 1961), went through an unabridged dictionary and identified more than 4500 personality traits!

Most approaches to personality assume that some traits are more basic than others (Paunonen & Hong, 2015). According to this notion, a small number of fundamental traits determine other, more superficial traits. For example, a person's tendency to be impulsive, restless, irritable, boisterous, and impatient might all be derived from a more basic tendency to be excitable.

A number of theorists have taken on the challenge of identifying the basic traits that form the core of personality. These theorists depend on a statistical procedure called *factor analysis* (Cai, 2013). **In *factor analysis,* correlations among many variables are analyzed to identify closely related clusters of variables.** If the measurements of a number of variables (in this case, personality traits) correlate highly with one another, the assumption is that a single factor is influencing all of them. Factor analysis is used to identify these hidden factors. In factor analyses of personality traits, these hidden factors are viewed as basic, higher-order traits that determine less basic, more specific traits. In recent decades, the most influential model of personality structure has been the *five-factor model of personality,* which we turn to next.

The Five-Factor Model of Personality Traits

Based on factor analyses, Robert McCrae and Paul Costa (1987, 1997, 2008) maintain that most personality traits are derived from just five higher-order traits that have come to be known as the "Big Five" (see **Figure 11.1**):

- *Extraversion.* People who score high in extraversion are characterized as outgoing, sociable, upbeat, friendly, assertive, and gregarious. They also have a more positive outlook on life and are motivated to pursue social contact, intimacy, and interdependence (Wilt & Revelle, 2009).
- *Neuroticism.* People who score high in neuroticism tend to be anxious, hostile, self-conscious, insecure, and vulnerable. They also tend to exhibit more impulsiveness and emotional instability than others (Widiger, 2009).
- *Openness to experience.* Openness is associated with curiosity, flexibility, imaginativeness, intellectual pursuits, interests in new ideas, and unconventional attitudes. People who are high in openness also tend to be tolerant of ambiguity (McCrae & Sutin, 2009).
- *Agreeableness.* Those who score high in agreeableness tend to be sympathetic, trusting, cooperative, modest, and straightforward. Agreeableness is also correlated with empathy and helping behavior (Graziano & Tobin, 2009).
- *Conscientiousness.* Conscientious people tend to be diligent, well-organized, punctual, and dependable. Conscientiousness is associated with strong self-discipline and the ability to regulate oneself effectively (Roberts et al., 2009).

Correlations have been found between the Big Five traits and quite a variety of important life outcomes. For instance, higher grades in college are associated with higher conscientiousness (McAbee & Oswald, 2013), perhaps because conscientious students work harder (Noftle & Robins, 2007). Several of the Big Five traits are associated with career success. Extraversion and conscientiousness are positive predictors of occupational attainment, whereas neuroticism is a negative predictor (Miller Burke & Attridge, 2011; Roberts, Caspi, & Moffitt, 2003). Agreeableness is negatively associated with income, especially among men (Judge, Livingston, & Hurst, 2012). The likelihood of divorce can also be predicted by personality traits because neuroticism elevates the probability of divorce, whereas agreeableness and conscientiousness reduce it (Roberts et al., 2007). Finally, and perhaps most important, several of the Big Five traits are related to health and mortality. Neuroticism is associated with an elevated prevalence of physical and mental disorders (Smith, Williams, & Segerstrom, 2015), whereas conscientiousness is correlated with the experience of less illness and with greater longevity (Friedman & Kern, 2014). Recent research suggests that openness to experience may also foster longevity (DeYoung, 2015).

Advocates of the five-factor model maintain that personality can be described adequately by measuring the basic traits they've identified. Their bold claim has been supported in many studies, and the Big Five model has become the dominant conception of personality structure in contemporary psychology (McCrae, Gaines, & Wellington, 2013). However, some theorists argue that only two or three traits are necessary to account for most of the variation seen in human personality, while others suggest that more than five traits are needed to describe personality adequately (Saucier & Srivastava, 2015).

The debate about how many dimensions are necessary to describe personality is likely to continue. As you'll see throughout the chapter, the study of personality is an area in psychology that has a long history of "dueling theories." We'll divide these diverse personality theories into four broad groups that each share certain assumptions, emphases, and interests: (1) psychodynamic perspectives, (2) behavioral perspectives, (3) humanistic perspectives, and (4) biological perspectives. We'll begin our discussion of personality theories by examining the ideas of Sigmund Freud.

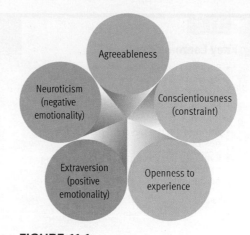

FIGURE 11.1

The five-factor model of personality. Trait models attempt to break personality down into its basic dimensions. McCrae and Costa (1985, 1987, 1997) maintain that personality can be described adequately with the five higher-order traits identified here, which are widely referred to as the "Big Five."

Key Learning Goals

- Explain Freud's view of personality structure and the role of conflict and anxiety.
- Identify key defense mechanisms, and outline Freud's view of development.
- Summarize the psychodynamic theories proposed by Jung and Adler.
- Evaluate the strengths and weaknesses of the psychodynamic approach to personality.

Psychodynamic theories include all the diverse theories descended from the work of Sigmund Freud that focus on unconscious mental forces. Freud inspired many scholars who followed in his intellectual footsteps. Some of these followers simply refined and updated Freud's theory. Others veered off in new directions and established independent, albeit related, schools of thought. Today, the psychodynamic umbrella covers a large collection of loosely related theories. In this section, we'll examine the ideas of Sigmund Freud in some detail. Then we'll take a briefer look at the psychodynamic theories of Carl Jung and Alfred Adler.

Freud's Psychoanalytic Theory

Sigmund Freud was a physician specializing in neurology when he began his medical practice in Vienna toward the end of the 19th century. Like other neurologists in his era, he often treated people troubled by nervous problems, such as irrational fears, obsessions, and anxieties. Eventually he devoted himself to the treatment of mental disorders using an innovative procedure he had developed, which he called *psychoanalysis.* It required lengthy verbal interactions with patients, during which Freud probed deeply into their lives (see Chapter 15). Freud's (1901, 1924, 1940) *psychoanalytic theory* grew out of his decades of interactions with his clients. Psychoanalytic theory attempts to explain personality by focusing on the influence of early childhood experiences, unconscious conflicts, and sexual urges.

Although Freud's theory gradually gained prominence, most of Freud's contemporaries were uncomfortable with his theory, for at least three reasons. First, in arguing that people's behavior is governed by unconscious factors of which they are unaware, Freud made the disconcerting suggestion that individuals are not masters of their own minds. Second, in claiming that adult personalities are shaped by childhood experiences and other factors beyond one's control, he suggested that people are not masters of their own destinies. Third, by emphasizing the importance of how people cope with their sexual urges, he offended those who held the conservative, Victorian values of his time. Let's examine the ideas that generated so much controversy.

Structure of Personality

Freud divided personality structure into three components: the id, the ego, and the superego. He saw a person's behavior as the outcome of interactions among these three components.

The *id* **is the primitive, instinctive component of personality that operates according to the pleasure principle.** Freud referred to the id as the reservoir of psychic energy. By this he meant that the id houses the raw biological urges (to eat, sleep, defecate, copulate, and so on) that energize human behavior. The id operates according to **the pleasure principle, which demands immediate gratification of its urges.** The id engages in *primary-process thinking,* which is primitive, illogical, irrational, and fantasy oriented.

The *ego* **is the decision-making component of personality that operates according to the reality principle.** The ego mediates between the id, with its forceful desires for immediate satisfaction, and the external social world, with its expectations and norms regarding suitable behavior. The ego considers social realities—society's norms, etiquette, rules, and customs—in deciding how to behave. The ego is guided by **the reality principle, which seeks to delay gratification of the id's urges until appropriate outlets and situations can be found.** In short, to stay out of trouble, the ego often works to tame the unbridled desires of the id.

In the long run, the ego wants to maximize gratification, just as the id does. However, the ego engages in *secondary-process thinking,* which is relatively rational, realistic, and oriented toward problem solving. Thus, the ego strives to avoid negative consequences from society and its representatives (for example, punishment by parents or teachers) by behaving "properly." It also attempts to achieve long-range goals, which sometimes require putting off gratification.

While the ego concerns itself with practical realities, **the *superego* is the moral component of personality that incorporates social standards about what represents right and wrong.** Throughout their lives, but especially during childhood, people receive training about what constitutes good and bad behavior, and many social norms regarding morality are eventually internalized. The superego emerges out of the ego at around 3–5 years of age. In some people, the superego can become irrationally demanding in its striving for moral perfection, and they become plagued by excessive feelings of guilt.

According to Freud, the id, ego, and superego are distributed differently across three levels of awareness, which we'll describe next.

Freud's psychoanalytic theory was based on decades of clinical work. He treated a great many patients in the consulting room pictured here. The room contains numerous artifacts from other cultures—and the original psychoanalytic couch.

Peter Aprahamian/Encyclopedia/Corbis

Levels of Awareness

Perhaps Freud's most enduring insight was his recognition of how unconscious forces can influence behavior. He inferred the existence of the unconscious from a variety of observations that he made with his patients. For example, he noticed that "slips of the tongue" often revealed a person's true feelings (hence the expression "Freudian slip"). He also realized that his patients' dreams often expressed hidden desires. Most important, through psychoanalysis, he often helped patients discover feelings and conflicts they had previously been unaware of.

Freud contrasted the unconscious with the conscious and preconscious, creating three levels of awareness. **The *conscious* consists of whatever one is aware of at a particular point in time.** For example, at this moment, your conscious may include the train of thought in this text and a dim awareness in the back of your mind that your eyes are getting tired and you're beginning to get hungry. **The *preconscious* contains material just beneath the surface of awareness that can easily be retrieved.** Examples might include your middle name, what you had for supper last night, or an argument you had with a friend yesterday. **The *unconscious* contains thoughts, memories, and desires that are well below the surface of conscious awareness, but that nonetheless exert great influence on behavior.** Examples of material that might be found in your unconscious include a forgotten trauma from childhood, hidden feelings of hostility toward a parent, and repressed sexual desires.

Freud's conception of the mind is often compared to an iceberg that has most of its mass hidden beneath the water's surface (see **Figure 11.2**). He believed that the unconscious (the mass below the surface) is much larger than the conscious or preconscious. As you can see in **Figure 11.2**, he proposed that the ego and superego operate at all three levels of awareness. In contrast, the id is entirely unconscious, expressing its urges at a conscious level through the ego.

Conflict and the Tyranny of Sex and Aggression

Freud assumed that behavior is the outcome of an ongoing series of internal conflicts. He saw internal battles among the id, ego, and superego as routine. Why? Because the id wants to gratify its urges immediately, but the norms of civilized society frequently dictate otherwise. For example, your id might feel an urge to clobber a co-worker who constantly irritates you. However, society frowns on such behavior, so your ego would try to hold this urge in check. Hence, you would find yourself in conflict.

Freud believed that internal conflicts are a routine part of people's lives. He asserted that conflicts centering on sexual and aggressive impulses are especially likely to have far-reaching consequences. Why did he emphasize sex and aggression? Two reasons were

FIGURE 11.2

Freud's model of personality structure. Freud theorized that people have three levels of awareness: the conscious, the preconscious, and the unconscious. The enormous size of the unconscious is often dramatized by comparing it to the portion of an iceberg that lies beneath the water's surface. Freud also divided personality structure into three components—id, ego, and superego—that operate according to different principles and exhibit different modes of thinking. In Freud's model, the id is entirely unconscious, but the ego and superego operate at all three levels of awareness.

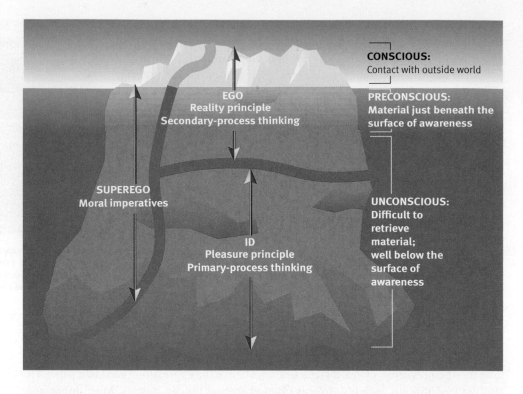

CONSCIOUS: Contact with outside world

EGO Reality principle Secondary-process thinking

PRECONSCIOUS: Material just beneath the surface of awareness

SUPEREGO Moral imperatives

UNCONSCIOUS: Difficult to retrieve material; well below the surface of awareness

ID Pleasure principle Primary-process thinking

prominent in his thinking. First, he thought that sex and aggression are subject to more complex and ambiguous social controls than other basic motives. Thus, people often get inconsistent messages about what's appropriate. Second, he noted that the aggressive and sexual drives are thwarted more regularly than other basic, biological urges. Think about it: If you get hungry or thirsty, you can simply head for a nearby vending machine or a drinking fountain. But when you see an attractive person who inspires lustful urges, you don't normally walk over and propose hooking up in a nearby broom closet. Freud ascribed great importance to these needs because social norms dictate that they're routinely frustrated.

Anxiety and Defense Mechanisms

Most internal conflicts are trivial and are quickly resolved. Occasionally, however, a conflict will linger for days, months, or even years, creating internal tension. More often than not, such prolonged and troublesome conflicts involve sexual and aggressive impulses that society wants to tame. These conflicts are often played out entirely in the unconscious. Although you may not be aware of these unconscious battles, they can produce *anxiety* that slips to the surface of conscious awareness.

The arousal of anxiety is a crucial event in Freud's theory of personality functioning. Anxiety is distressing, so people try to rid themselves of this unpleasant emotion any way they can. This effort to ward off anxiety often involves the use of defense mechanisms (see **Figure 11.3**). ***Defense mechanisms** are largely unconscious reactions that protect a person from unpleasant emotions, such as anxiety and guilt.* Typically, they're mental maneuvers that work through self-deception (see **Table 11.1**). Consider ***rationalization,***

FIGURE 11.3

Freud's model of personality dynamics. According to Freud, unconscious conflicts between the id, ego, and superego sometimes lead to anxiety. This discomfort can lead to the use of defense mechanisms, which can temporarily relieve anxiety.

Intrapsychic conflict (between id, ego, and superego) → Anxiety → Reliance on defense mechanisms

TABLE 11.1 Defense Mechanisms, with Examples

Defense Mechanism	Definition	Example
Repression	Keeping distressing thoughts and feelings buried in the unconscious	A traumatized soldier has no recollection of the details of a close brush with death.
Projection	Attributing one's own thoughts, feelings, or motives to another	A woman who dislikes her boss thinks she likes her boss but feels that the boss doesn't like her.
Displacement	Diverting emotional feelings (usually anger) from their original source to a substitute target	After a parental scolding, a young girl takes her anger out on her little brother.
Reaction formation	Behaving in a way that is exactly the opposite of one's true feelings	A parent who unconsciously resents a child spoils the child with outlandish gifts.
Regression	A reversion to immature patterns of behavior	An adult has a temper tantrum when he doesn't get his way.
Rationalization	Creating false but plausible excuses to justify unacceptable behavior	A student watches TV instead of studying, saying that "additional study wouldn't do any good anyway."
Identification	Bolstering self-esteem by forming an imaginary or real alliance with some person or group	An insecure young man joins a fraternity to boost his self-esteem.

which is creating false but plausible excuses to justify unacceptable behavior. For example, after cheating someone in a business transaction, you might reduce your guilt by rationalizing that "everyone does it."

According to Freud, the most basic and widely used defense mechanism is repression. *Repression* is keeping distressing thoughts and feelings buried in the unconscious. People tend to repress desires that make them feel guilty, conflicts that make them anxious, and memories that are painful. If you forget a dental appointment or the name of someone you don't like, repression may be at work.

Self-deception can also be seen in projection and displacement. *Projection* is attributing one's own thoughts, feelings, or motives to another. Usually, the thoughts one projects onto others are those that would make one feel guilty. For example, if lusting for a co-worker makes you feel guilty, you might attribute any latent sexual tension between the two of you to the *other person's* desire to seduce you. *Displacement* is diverting emotional feelings (usually anger) from their original source to a substitute target. If your boss gives you a hard time at work and you come home and slam the door, kick the dog, and scream at your spouse, you're displacing your anger onto irrelevant targets. Unfortunately, social constraints often force people to hold back their anger, and they end up lashing out at the people they love the most.

Other prominent defense mechanisms include reaction formation, regression, and identification. *Reaction formation* is behaving in a way that's exactly the opposite of one's true feelings. Guilt about sexual desires often leads to reaction formation. Freud theorized that many homophobic males who ridicule homosexuals are defending against their own latent homosexual impulses. The telltale sign of reaction formation is the exaggerated quality of the opposite behavior. *Regression* is a reversion to immature patterns of behavior. When anxious about their self-worth, some adults respond with childish boasting and bragging (as opposed to subtle efforts to impress others). For example, a fired executive having difficulty finding a new job might start making ridiculous statements about his incomparable talents and achievements. Such bragging is regressive when it's marked by massive exaggerations that virtually anyone can see through. *Identification* is bolstering self-esteem by forming an imaginary or real alliance with some person or group. Young people often shore up fragile feelings of self-worth by identifying with rock stars, movie stars, or famous athletes. Adults may join exclusive country clubs or civic organizations as a means of boosting their self-esteem via identification.

Recent decades have brought a revival of interest in research on defense mechanisms. For example, a series of studies identified a *repressive coping style* and showed that "repressors" have an impoverished memory for events that are likely to trigger unpleasant emotions and that they avoid negative information regarding themselves (Myers, 2010; Saunders, Worth, & Fernandes, 2012). Moreover, studies have found a link between repressive coping and poor physical health, including heart disease (Denollet et al., 2008; Myers et al., 2007). In another line of recent research, support was found for the Freudian hypothesis that reaction formation underlies *homophobia,* **which involves an intense fear and intolerance of homosexuality** (Weinstein et al., 2012). This research found that people who report that they are straight but show an unconscious attraction to the same sex on subtle psychological tests, tend to exhibit elevated hostility toward gays and endorse anti-gay policies. The research suggests that homophobics are threatened by gays because gays remind them of latent homosexual desires within themselves. Hence, they lash out with hostility toward gays to mask their conflicting feelings about homosexuality.

According to Freud, everyone uses defense mechanisms to some extent. They become problematic only when a person depends on them excessively. The seeds for psychological disorders are sown when defenses lead to wholesale distortion of reality. Research provides some support for Freud's belief that mental health depends in part on the extent to which people rely on defense mechanisms. A study of patients undergoing long-term psychoanalytic therapy found that reductions in their reliance on defense mechanisms were associated with improvements in life functioning and decreases in psychiatric symptoms (Perry & Bond, 2012).

Development: Psychosexual Stages

Freud made the rather startling claim that the basic foundation of an individual's personality has been laid down by the tender age of 5. To shed light on these crucial early years, Freud formulated a stage theory of development. He emphasized how young children deal with their immature but powerful sexual urges (he used the term *sexual* in a general way to refer to many urges for physical pleasure). According to Freud, these urges shift in focus as children progress from one stage of development to another. Indeed, the names for the stages (oral, anal, genital, and so on) are based on where children are focusing their erotic

CONCEPT CHECK 11.1

Identifying Defense Mechanisms

Check your understanding of defense mechanisms by identifying specific defenses in the story below. Each example of a defense mechanism is underlined, with a number beneath it. Write in the defense at work in each case in the numbered spaces after the story. The answers are in Appendix A.

My boyfriend recently broke up with me after we had dated seriously for several years. At first, I cried a great deal and <u>locked myself in my room, where I pouted endlessly.</u> [1] I was sure that my former boyfriend felt as miserable as I did. <u>I told several friends that he was probably lonely and depressed.</u> [2] Later, I decided that I hated him. <u>I was happy about the breakup and talked about how much I was going to enjoy my newfound freedom.</u> [3] I went to parties and socialized a great deal and just forgot about him. <u>It's funny—at one point I couldn't even remember his phone number!</u> [4] Then I started pining for him again. But eventually I began to look at the situation more objectively. I realized that he had many faults and that <u>we were bound to break up sooner or later, so I was better off without him.</u> [5]

1. _____   4. _____

2. _____   5. _____

3. _____

TABLE 11.2 Freud's Stages of Psychosexual Development

Stage	Approximate Ages	Erotic Focus	Key Tasks and Experiences
Oral	0–1	Mouth (sucking, biting)	Weaning (from breast or bottle)
Anal	2–3	Anus (expelling or retaining feces)	Toilet training
Phallic	4–5	Genitals (masturbating)	Identifying with adult role models; coping with Oedipal crisis
Latency	6–12	None (sexually repressed)	Expanding social contacts
Genital	Puberty onward	Genitals (being sexually intimate)	Establishing intimate relationships; contributing to society through working

energy during that period. Thus, ***psychosexual stages* are developmental periods with a characteristic sexual focus that leave their mark on adult personality.**

Freud theorized that each psychosexual stage has its own unique developmental challenges or tasks (see **Table 11.2**). The way these challenges are handled supposedly shapes personality. The notion of *fixation* plays an important role in this process. ***Fixation* involves a failure to move forward from one stage to another, as expected.** Fixation can be caused by excessive *gratification* of needs at a particular stage or by excessive *frustration* of those needs. Either way, fixations left over from childhood affect adult personality. Freud described a series of five psychosexual stages. Let's examine some of the highlights in this sequence and how fixation might occur.

Oral stage The oral stage encompasses the first year of life. During this period, the main source of erotic stimulation is the mouth (in biting, sucking, chewing, and so on). In Freud's view, the way the child's feeding experience is handled is crucial to subsequent development. He attributed considerable importance to the manner in which the child is weaned from the breast or the bottle. According to Freud, fixation at the oral stage could form the basis for obsessive eating or smoking (among many other things) later in life.

Anal stage In their second year, children get their erotic pleasure from their bowel movements, through either the expulsion or retention of feces. The significant event at this time is toilet training, which represents society's first systematic effort to regulate the child's biological urges. Severely punitive toilet training leads to a variety of possible outcomes. For example, excessive punishment might produce a latent feeling of hostility toward the "trainer," usually the mother. This hostility might generalize to women as a class. Another possibility is that heavy reliance on punitive measures could lead to an association between genital concerns and the anxiety that the punishment arouses. This genital anxiety derived from severe toilet training could evolve into anxiety about sexual activities later in life.

Phallic stage In the third through fifth years, the genitals become the focus for the child's erotic energy, largely through self-stimulation. During this pivotal stage, the *Oedipal complex* emerges. That is, little boys develop an erotically tinged preference for their mother. They also feel hostility toward their father, whom they view as a competitor for mom's affection. Similarly, little girls develop a special attachment to their father. Around the same time, they learn that little boys have different genitals, and they supposedly develop *penis envy*. According to Freud, young girls feel hostile toward their mother because they blame her for their anatomical "deficiency." To summarize, in the ***Oedipal complex,* children manifest erotically tinged desires for their opposite-sex parent, accompanied by feelings of hostility toward their same-sex parent.** The name for this syndrome was taken from the Greek myth in which

According to Freud, early childhood experiences, such as toilet training (a parental attempt to regulate a child's biological urges), can influence an individual's personality, with consequences lasting throughout adulthood.

Oedipus, not knowing the identity of his real parents, inadvertently kills his father and marries his mother.

According to Freud, the way parents and children deal with the sexual and aggressive conflicts inherent in the Oedipal complex is of paramount importance. The child has to resolve the Oedipal dilemma by purging the sexual longings for the opposite-sex parent and by crushing the hostility felt toward the same-sex parent. In Freud's view, healthy psychosexual development hinges on the resolution of the Oedipal conflict. Why? Because continued hostility toward the same-sex parent can prevent the child from identifying adequately with that parent. Freudian theory predicts that without such identification, many aspects of the child's development won't progress as they should.

Latency and genital stages   From around age 5 through puberty, the child's sexuality is largely suppressed—it becomes *latent*. Important events during this *latency stage* center on expanding social contacts beyond the immediate family. With the advent of puberty, the child progresses into the *genital stage*. Sexual urges reappear and focus on the genitals once again. At this point, sexual energy is normally channeled toward peers of the other sex, rather than toward oneself as in the phallic stage.

In arguing that the early years shape personality, Freud did not mean that personality development comes to an abrupt halt in middle childhood. However, he did believe that the foundation for adult personality is solidly entrenched by this time. He maintained that future developments are rooted in early, formative experiences and that significant conflicts in later years are replays of crises from childhood.

In fact, Freud believed that unconscious sexual conflicts rooted in childhood experiences cause most personality disturbances. His steadfast belief in the psychosexual origins of psychological disorders eventually led to bitter theoretical disputes with two of his most brilliant colleagues: Carl Jung and Alfred Adler. Jung and Adler both argued that Freud overemphasized sexuality. Freud summarily rejected their ideas. Hence, Jung and Adler felt compelled to go their own way, with each developing his own psychodynamic theory of personality.

Jung's Analytical Psychology

Carl Jung was an established young psychiatrist in Switzerland when he began to write to Freud in 1906. They exchanged 359 letters before their friendship and theoretical alliance were torn apart in 1913. Jung called his new approach *analytical psychology* to differentiate it from Freud's psychoanalytic theory. Like Freud, Jung (1921, 1933) emphasized the unconscious determinants of personality. However, he proposed that the unconscious consists of two layers. The first layer, called the *personal unconscious,* is essentially the same as Freud's version of the unconscious. The personal unconscious houses material that is not within one's conscious awareness because it has been repressed or forgotten. In addition, Jung theorized the existence of a deeper layer that he called the collective unconscious. **The collective unconscious is a storehouse of latent memory traces inherited from people's ancestral past.** According to Jung, each person shares the collective unconscious with the entire human race (see **Figure 11.4**).

Jung called these ancestral memories *archetypes.* They are not memories of actual, personal experiences. Instead, *archetypes* **are emotionally charged images and thought forms that have universal meaning.** These archetypal images and ideas show up frequently in dreams and are often manifested in a culture's use of symbols in art, literature, and religion. According to Jung, symbols from very different cultures often show striking similarities because they emerge from archetypes that are shared by the entire human race. For instance, Jung found numerous cultures in which the *mandala,* or "magic circle," has served as a symbol of the unified wholeness of the self. Jung felt that an understanding of archetypal symbols helped him make sense of his patients' dreams. He thought that dreams contain important messages from the unconscious, and like Freud, depended extensively on dream analysis in his treatment of patients.

Adler's Individual Psychology

Growing up in Vienna, Alfred Adler was a sickly child who was overshadowed by an exceptionally successful older brother. Nonetheless, he went on to earn his medical degree and gradually became interested in psychiatry. He was a charter member of Freud's inner circle—the Vienna Psychoanalytic Society. However, he soon began to develop his own approach to personality, which he called *individual psychology.*

Like Jung, Adler (1917, 1927) argued that Freud had gone overboard in centering his theory on sexual conflicts. According to Adler, the foremost source of human motivation is a *striving for superiority.* Adler saw striving for superiority as a universal drive to adapt, improve oneself, and master life's challenges. He noted that young children understandably feel weak and helpless in comparison with more competent older children and adults. These early inferiority feelings supposedly motivate them to acquire new skills and develop new talents.

Adler asserted that everyone has to work to overcome some feelings of inferiority. He called this process compensation. **Compensation involves efforts to overcome imagined or real inferiorities by developing one's abilities.** Adler believed that compensation is entirely normal. However, in some people, inferiority feelings can become excessive, which can result in what is widely known today as an *inferiority complex*—exaggerated feelings of weakness and inadequacy. Adler thought that either parental pampering or

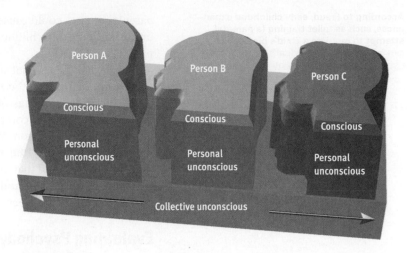

FIGURE 11.4

Jung's vision of the collective unconscious. Much like Freud, Jung theorized that each person has conscious and unconscious levels of awareness. However, he also proposed that the entire human race shares a collective unconscious, which exists in the deepest reaches of everyone's awareness. He saw the collective unconscious as a storehouse of hidden ancestral memories, called *archetypes.*

Adler's theory has been used to analyze the tragic life of the legendary actress Marilyn Monroe (Ansbacher, 1970). During her childhood, Monroe suffered from parental neglect that left her with acute feelings of inferiority. Her inferiority feelings led her to overcompensate by flaunting her beauty, marrying celebrities (Joe DiMaggio and Arthur Miller), keeping film crews waiting for hours, and seeking the adoration of her fans.

parental neglect could cause an inferiority complex. Thus, he agreed with Freud on the importance of early childhood experiences. However, he focused on different aspects of parent-child relations.

Adler maintained that some people engage in *overcompensation* in order to conceal, even from themselves, their feelings of inferiority. These people work to acquire status, power, and the trappings of success (fancy clothes, impressive cars) to cover up their underlying inferiority complex. Adler's theory stressed the social context of personality development (Carlson & Englar-Carlson, 2013). For instance, it was Adler who first focused attention on the possible importance of *birth order* as a factor governing personality. He noted that first-borns, second children, and later-born children enter varied home environments and are treated differently by parents and that these experiences are likely to affect their personality (Eckstein & Kaufman, 2012).

Evaluating Psychodynamic Perspectives

Psychodynamic theories yielded some bold new insights when they were first presented. Although one might argue about the exact details of interpretation, decades of research have demonstrated that (1) unconscious forces can influence behavior, (2) internal conflict often plays a key role in generating psychological distress, (3) early childhood experiences can influence adult personality, and (4) people use defense mechanisms to reduce their experience of unpleasant emotions (Bornstein, Denckla, & Chung, 2013; Westen, Gabbard, & Ortigo, 2008).

In addition to being praised, psychodynamic formulations have also been criticized on several grounds, including the following (Crews, 2006; Kramer, 2006; Torrey, 1992):

1. *Poor testability.* Scientific investigations require testable hypotheses. Psychodynamic ideas have often been too vague and conjectural to permit a clear scientific test. For instance, how would you prove or disprove the assertion that the id is entirely unconscious?

2. *Unrepresentative samples.* Freud's theories were based on an exceptionally narrow sample of upper-class, neurotic, sexually repressed Viennese women. They were not even remotely representative of western European culture, let alone other cultures or other times.

3. *Overemphasis on case studies.* Psychodynamic theories depend too heavily on clinical case studies in which it's much too easy for clinicians to see what they expect to see. Reexaminations of Freud's own clinical work suggest that he frequently distorted his patients' case histories to make them mesh with his theory (Esterson, 2001) and that there were substantial disparities between Freud's writings and his actual therapeutic methods (Lynn & Vaillant, 1998). Moreover, Freud's ideas were based on his adult patients' *recollections* of their childhood experiences, which contemporary memory research suggests were probably distorted, incomplete, and inaccurate.

4. *Contradictory evidence.* Although studies have supported some insights from psychodynamic theories, the weight of empirical evidence has contradicted many of the central hypotheses (Westen, Gabbard, & Ortigo, 2008; Wolitzky, 2006). For example, we now know that development is a lifelong journey and that Freud overemphasized the importance of the first 5 years. The Oedipal complex is neither as universal nor as important as Freud believed. Struggles with sexuality are *not* the root cause of most disorders. Freud's theory of dreams has garnered modest support, at best.

5. *Sexism.* Many critics have argued that psychodynamic theories are characterized by a sexist bias against women. Freud believed that females' penis envy made them feel inferior to men. He also thought that females tended to develop weaker superegos and to be more prone to psychological distress than men. The gender bias in modern psychodynamic theories has been reduced considerably. Nonetheless, the psychodynamic approach has generally provided a rather male-centered point of view (Lerman, 1986; Person, 1990).

It's easy to ridicule Freud for concepts such as penis envy, and it's easy to point to Freudian ideas that have turned out to be wrong. However, psychodynamic theories have had extraordinary impact on modern intellectual thought. In psychology as a whole, no other school of thought has been so influential—with the exception of behaviorism, to which we turn next.

11.3 BEHAVIORAL PERSPECTIVES

11.3

Key Learning Goals

- Understand Skinner's and Bandura's contributions to behavioral views of personality.
- Identify Mischel's principal thesis, and evaluate the behavioral approach to personality.

Behaviorism is a theoretical orientation based on the premise that scientific psychology should study only observable behavior. As we saw in Chapter 1, behaviorism has been a major school of thought in psychology since 1913, when John B. Watson argued that psychology should abandon its earlier focus on the mind and mental processes, and focus exclusively on overt behavior. In this section, we'll examine three behavioral views of personality: those of B. F. Skinner, Albert Bandura, and Walter Mischel. For the most part, you'll see that behaviorists explain personality the same way they explain everything else—in terms of learning.

Skinner's Ideas Applied to Personality

As we noted in Chapters 1 and 6, modern behaviorism's most prominent theorist has been B. F. Skinner, an American psychologist who lived from 1904 to 1990. Working at Harvard University, Skinner achieved renown for his research on learning in lower organisms, mostly rats and pigeons. Skinner's (1953, 1957) principles of *operant conditioning* were never meant to be a theory of personality. However, his ideas have affected thinking in all areas of psychology and have been applied to the explanation of personality. Here we'll examine Skinner's views as they relate to personality structure and development.

Personality Structure: A View from the Outside

Skinner made no provision for internal personality structures similar to Freud's id, ego, and superego because such structures can't be observed. Following in the tradition of Watson, Skinner showed little interest in what goes on "inside" people. Instead, he focused on how the external environment molds overt behavior. Indeed, he argued for a strong brand of *determinism,* asserting that behavior is fully determined by environmental stimuli.

How can Skinner's theory explain the consistency that can be seen in individuals' behavior? According to his view, people show some consistent patterns of behavior because they have some stable *response tendencies* that they have acquired through experience. These response tendencies may change in the future as a result of new experience. But they're enduring enough to create a certain degree of consistency in a person's behavior. Implicitly, then, Skinner viewed an individual's personality as a *collection of response tendencies that are tied to various stimulus situations.* A specific situation may be associated with a number of response tendencies that vary in strength, depending on past conditioning (see **Figure 11.5**).

Personality Development as a Product of Conditioning

Skinner's theory accounts for personality development by explaining how various response tendencies are acquired through learning (Bolling, Terry, & Kohlenberg, 2006). He believed that most human responses are shaped by the type of conditioning that he described: *operant conditioning.* As we discussed in Chapter 6, Skinner maintained that environmental consequences—reinforcement, punishment, and extinction—determine people's patterns of responding. On the one hand, when responses are

FIGURE 11.5

A behavioral view of personality. Staunch behaviorists devote little attention to the structure of personality because it is unobservable, but they implicitly view personality as an individual's collection of response tendencies. A possible hierarchy of response tendencies for a particular person in specific stimulus situation (a large party) is shown here.

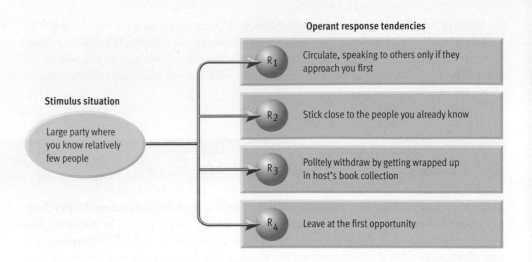

Stimulus situation

Large party where you know relatively few people

Operant response tendencies

R₁ Circulate, speaking to others only if they approach you first

R₂ Stick close to the people you already know

R₃ Politely withdraw by getting wrapped up in host's book collection

R₄ Leave at the first opportunity

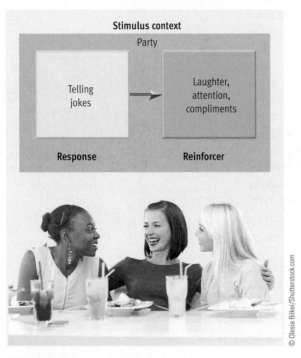

Stimulus context

Party

Telling jokes

Laughter, attention, compliments

Response   **Reinforcer**

© Olesia Bilkei/Shutterstock.com

FIGURE 11.6

Personality development and operant conditioning. According to Skinner, people's characteristic response tendencies are shaped by reinforcers and other consequences that follow behavior. Thus, if your joking leads to attention and compliments, your tendency to be witty and humorous will be strengthened.

followed by favorable consequences (reinforcement), they are strengthened. For example, if your joking around friends pays off with favorable attention, your tendency to joke will increase (see **Figure 11.6**). On the other hand, when responses lead to negative consequences (punishment), they are weakened. Thus, if your impulsive decisions always backfire, your tendency to be impulsive will decline.

Response tendencies are constantly being strengthened or weakened by new experiences. Because of this, Skinner's theory views personality development as a continuous, lifelong journey. Unlike Freud and many other theorists, Skinner saw no reason to break the developmental process into stages. Nor did he attribute special importance to early childhood experiences.

Bandura's Social Cognitive Theory

Albert Bandura (1986, 2012) is one of several behaviorists who have added a cognitive flavor to behaviorism since the 1960s. These theorists take issue with Skinner's "pure" behaviorism. They point out that humans obviously are conscious, thinking, feeling beings. Moreover, they argue that in neglecting cognitive processes, Skinner ignored the most distinctive and important feature of human behavior. Bandura and like-minded theorists originally called their modified brand of behaviorism *social learning theory*. Today, Bandura refers to his model as *social cognitive theory*.

Bandura (1999, 2006) agrees with the fundamental thrust of behaviorism in that he believes that personality is largely shaped through learning. However, he contends that conditioning is not a mechanical process in which people are passive participants. Instead, he maintains that people actively seek out and process information about their environment to maximize favorable outcomes. In focusing on information processing, he brings unobservable cognitive events into the picture.

Observational Learning

Bandura's foremost theoretical contribution has been his description of observational learning, which we introduced in Chapter 6. **Observational learning occurs when an organism's responding is influenced by the observation of others.** According to Bandura, both classical and operant conditioning can occur indirectly when one person observes another's conditioning. For example, watching your sister get burned by a bounced check upon selling her old smart phone could strengthen your tendency to be suspicious of others. Although your sister would be the one actually experiencing the negative consequences, they might also influence you through observational learning. Bandura maintains that people's characteristic patterns of behavior are shaped by the *models* they're exposed to. In observational learning, **a *model* is a person whose behavior is observed by another.** At one time or another, everyone serves as a model for others. Bandura's key point is that many response tendencies are the product of imitation. According to Bandura, children learn to be assertive, conscientious, self-sufficient, dependable, easygoing, and so forth by observing parents, teachers, relatives, siblings, and peers behaving in these ways.

Self-Efficacy

Bandura discusses how a variety of personal factors (aspects of personality) govern behavior. The factor he emphasized most is self-efficacy (Bandura, 1990, 1993, 1995). *Self-efficacy* **refers to one's belief about one's ability to perform behaviors that should lead to expected outcomes.** When self-efficacy is high, individuals feel confident that they can execute the responses necessary to earn reinforcers. When self-efficacy is low, individuals worry that the necessary responses may be beyond their abilities. Perceptions of self-efficacy are subjective and specific to certain kinds of tasks. For instance, you might feel extremely confident about your ability to handle difficult social situations. On the other hand, you might be doubtful about your ability to handle academic challenges.

Perceptions of self-efficacy can influence which challenges people tackle and how well they perform. Studies have found that feelings of greater self-efficacy are associated with reduced procrastination (Wäschle et al., 2014); greater success in giving up smoking (Perkins et al., 2012); greater adherence to an exercise regimen (Ayotte, Margrett, & Hicks-Patrick, 2010); more effective weight-loss efforts (Byrne, Barry, & Petry, 2012); higher quality of life after a heart attack (Brink et al., 2012); greater physical activity among adolescents (Rutkowski & Connelly, 2012); reduced psychological distress among rheumatoid arthritis patients (Benka et al., 2014); better study habits (Prat-Sala & Redford, 2010); higher levels of academic engagement and performance (Ouweneel, Schaufeli, & Le Blanc, 2013); enhanced athletic performance (Gilson, Chow, & Feltz, 2012); more effective work performance (Tims, Bakker, & Derks, 2014); more proactive customer care by employees in the service industry (Raub & Liao, 2012); and reduced vulnerability to burnout among teachers (C. G. Brown, 2012) among many other things.

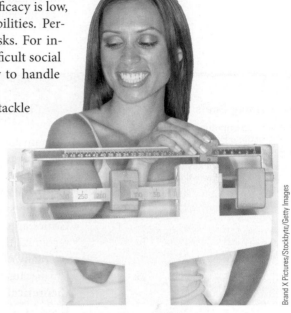

Perceptions of self-efficacy can influence which challenges people pursue and how well they perform. For example, research has linked self-efficacy to job performance and success in adhering to an exercise regime.

Mischel and the Person-Situation Controversy

Walter Mischel is another prominent social learning theorist. Mischel's (1973, 1984) chief contribution to personality theory has been to focus attention on the extent to which situational factors govern behavior. According to Mischel, people make responses they think will lead to reinforcement in the situation at hand. For example, if you believe hard work in your job will pay off by leading to raises and promotions, you'll probably be diligent and industrious. But if you think hard work in your job is unlikely to be rewarded, you may behave in a lazy and irresponsible manner. Thus, Mischel's version of social learning theory predicts people will often behave differently in different situations. Mischel (1968, 1973) reviewed decades of research and concluded that, indeed, people exhibit far less consistency across situations than had been widely assumed. For example, a person who is shy in one context might be quite outgoing in another. Other models of personality largely ignore this inconsistency. Mischel's provocative theories sparked a robust debate about the relative importance of the *person* as opposed to the *situation* in determining behavior. The ensuing research led to a growing recognition that *both* personality and situational factors are important determinants of behavior (Reis & Holmes, 2012).

> **▸ REALITY CHECK**
>
> **Misconception**
>
> People's behavior is largely determined by their personality and character.
>
> **Reality**
>
> Mischel's argument that situational forces shape much of our behavior has proven compelling. That is not to say that personality is irrelevant. But research has shown again and again that situational factors are more powerful determinants of behavior than laypersons or scientists would have guessed (Benjamin & Simpson, 2009; Ross & Nisbett, 1991; Zimbardo, 2004).

Evaluating Behavioral Perspectives

Behavioral theories are firmly rooted in extensive empirical research. Skinner's ideas have shed light on how environmental consequences and conditioning mold people's characteristic behavior. Bandura's social cognitive theory has shown how learning from others can mold personality. Mischel deserves credit for increasing psychology's awareness of how situational factors shape behavior.

Of course, each theoretical approach has its shortcomings, and the behavioral approach is no exception. The behaviorists used to be criticized because they neglected cognitive processes. The rise of social cognitive theory blunted this criticism. However, social cognitive theory undermines the foundation on which behaviorism was built—the idea that psychologists should study only observable behavior. Thus, some critics complain that behavioral theories aren't very behavioral anymore. Other critics argue that behaviorists have indiscriminately generalized from animal research to human behavior (Burger, 2015). Humanistic theorists, whom we shall cover next, have been particularly vocal in criticizing behavioral views.

Key Learning Goals

- Explain the impetus for humanism, and articulate Rogers's views on the self-concept.
- Describe Maslow's key insights, and evaluate the humanistic approach to personality.

11.4 HUMANISTIC PERSPECTIVES

Humanistic theory emerged in the 1950s as something of a backlash against the behavioral and psychodynamic theories we have just discussed (Cassel, 2000). The principal charge hurled at these two models was that they are dehumanizing. Freudian theory was criticized for its belief that behavior is dominated by primitive, animalistic drives (sex and aggression). Behaviorism was criticized for its preoccupation with animal research. Critics argued that both schools of thought were too deterministic—that they failed to recognize that humans are free to chart their own courses of action.

Many of these critics blended into a loose alliance that came to be known as humanism because of its exclusive focus on human behavior. In psychology, *humanism* **is a theoretical orientation that emphasizes the unique qualities of humans, especially their freedom and their potential for personal growth.** In contrast with most psychodynamic and behavioral theorists, humanistic theorists, such as Carl Rogers and Abraham Maslow, take an optimistic view of human nature. They assume that people (1) can rise above their primitive animal heritage; (2) are largely conscious and rational beings who are not dominated by unconscious, irrational conflicts; and (3) are not helpless pawns of deterministic forces. Humanistic theorists also maintain that a person's subjective view of the world is more important than objective reality (Wong, 2006). According to this notion, if you think that you're homely or bright or sociable, then this belief will influence your behavior more than the realities of how homely, bright, or sociable you actually are.

Rogers's Person-Centered Theory

Carl Rogers (1951, 1961, 1980) was one of the fathers of the human potential movement. This movement emphasizes self-realization through sensitivity training, encounter groups, and other exercises intended to foster personal growth. Like Freud, Rogers based his personality theory on his extensive therapeutic interactions with many clients. Because of its emphasis on a person's subjective point of view, Rogers called his approach a *person-centered theory.*

The Self

Rogers viewed personality structure in terms of just one construct. He called this construct the *self,* although it's more widely known today as the *self-concept.* **A *self-concept*** is a collection of beliefs about one's own nature, unique qualities, and typical behavior. Your self-concept is your own mental picture of yourself. It's a collection of self-perceptions. For example, a self-concept might include beliefs such as "I'm easygoing" or "I'm sly and crafty" or "I'm pretty" or "I'm hardworking."

Rogers stressed the subjective nature of the self-concept. Your self-concept may not be entirely consistent with your experiences. Most people tend to distort their experiences to some extent to promote a relatively favorable self-concept. For example, you may believe that you're quite bright, but your grade transcript might suggest otherwise. Rogers called the gap between self-concept and reality "incongruence." *Incongruence* is the degree of disparity between one's self-concept and one's actual experience. In contrast, if a person's self-concept is reasonably accurate, it's said to be *congruent* with reality (see **Figure 11.7**). Everyone experiences a certain amount of incongruence. The crucial issue is how much. As we'll see, Rogers held that too much incongruence undermines one's psychological well-being.

Development of the Self

In terms of personality development, Rogers was concerned with how childhood experiences promote a congruent or incongruent self-concept. According to Rogers, people have a strong need for affection and acceptance from others. Early in life, parents provide most of this affection. Rogers maintained that some parents make their affection *conditional*. That is, it depends on the child's behaving well and living up to expectations. When parental love seems conditional, children often block out of their self-concept those experiences that make them feel unworthy of love. They do so because they're worried about parental acceptance, which appears precarious. At the other end of the spectrum, some parents make their affection *unconditional*. Their children have less need to block out unworthy experiences because they've been assured that they're worthy of affection no matter what they do.

Rogers believed that unconditional love from parents fosters congruence and that conditional love fosters incongruence. He further theorized that if individuals grow up believing that affection from others is highly conditional, they will go on to distort more and more of their experiences in order to feel worthy of acceptance from a wider and wider array of people.

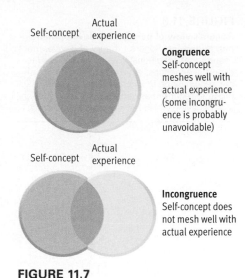

Self-concept | Actual experience

Congruence
Self-concept meshes well with actual experience (some incongruence is probably unavoidable)

Self-concept | Actual experience

Incongruence
Self-concept does not mesh well with actual experience

FIGURE 11.7
Rogers's view of personality structure. In Rogers's model, the self-concept is the only important structural construct. However, Rogers acknowledges that one's self-concept may not be consistent with the realities of one's actual experience—a condition called *incongruence*.

According to Carl Rogers, unconditional love from parents tends to foster an accurate self-concept that is congruent with reality.

© Dereje/Shutterstock.com

FIGURE 11.8

Rogers's view of personality development and dynamics. Rogers's theory of development asserts that conditional love leads to a need to distort experiences, which fosters an incongruent self-concept. Incongruence makes one prone to recurrent anxiety, which triggers defensive behavior, which fuels more incongruence.

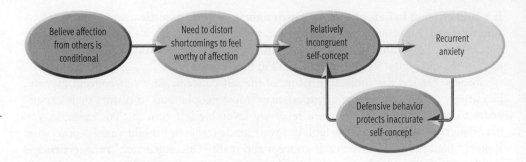

Anxiety and Defense

According to Rogers, experiences that threaten people's personal views of themselves are the principal cause of troublesome anxiety. Thus, people with highly incongruent self-concepts are especially likely to be plagued by recurrent anxiety (see **Figure 11.8**). To ward off this anxiety, individuals often behave defensively in an effort to reinterpret their experience so that it appears consistent with their self-concept. Thus, they ignore, deny, or twist reality to protect and perpetuate their self-concept. For example, a young woman who is selfish but unable to face that reality might attribute friends' comments about her selfishness to their jealousy of her good looks.

Maslow's Theory of Self-Actualization

Abraham Maslow (1970) was a prominent humanistic theorist who argued that psychology should take a greater interest in the nature of the healthy personality instead of dwelling on the causes of disorders. "To oversimplify the matter somewhat," he said, "it is as if Freud supplied to us the sick half of psychology and we must now fill it out with the healthy half" (Maslow, 1968, p. 5). Maslow's key contributions were his analysis of how motives are organized hierarchically and his description of the healthy personality.

Hierarchy of Needs

Maslow proposed that human motives are organized into a *hierarchy of needs—a systematic arrangement of needs, according to priority, in which basic needs must be met before less basic needs are aroused.* This hierarchical arrangement is usually portrayed as a pyramid (see **Figure 11.9**). The needs toward the bottom of the pyramid, such as physiological or security needs, are the most basic. Higher levels in the pyramid consist of progressively less basic needs. When a person manages to satisfy a level of needs

FIGURE 11.9

Maslow's hierarchy of needs. According to Maslow, human needs are arranged in a hierarchy, and people must satisfy their basic needs before they can satisfy higher needs. In the diagram, higher levels in the pyramid represent progressively less basic needs. Individuals progress upward in the hierarchy when lower needs are satisfied reasonably well, but they may regress back to lower levels if basic needs are no longer satisfied.

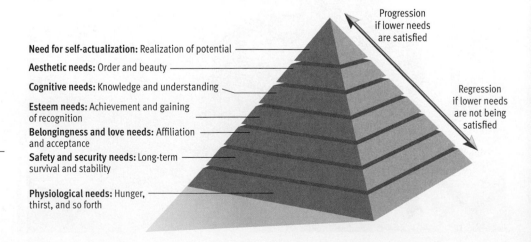

reasonably well (complete satisfaction is not necessary), *this satisfaction activates needs at the next level.*

Maslow argued that humans have an innate drive toward personal growth—that is, evolution toward a higher state of being. Thus, he described the needs in the uppermost reaches of his hierarchy as *growth needs.* These include the needs for knowledge, understanding, order, and aesthetic beauty. Foremost among them is the **need for self-actualization, which is the need to fulfill one's potential.** It is the highest need in Maslow's motivational hierarchy. Maslow summarized this concept with a simple statement: "What a man *can* be, he *must* be." According to Maslow, individuals will be frustrated if they are unable to fully utilize their talents or pursue their true interests. For example, if you have great musical talent but must work as an accountant, your need for self-actualization will be thwarted.

Maslow's hierarchy of needs has proven to be a challenging subject for empirical study. However, a recent study that measured the satisfaction of various levels of needs in the hierarchy found that the satisfaction of needs at each level was predicted by satisfaction at the level just below it (Taormina & Gao, 2013). This finding provides some support for Maslow's thesis that satisfaction of needs at each level activates needs at the next level.

Maslow's pyramid has penetrated popular culture to a remarkable degree (Peterson & Park, 2009). But more recently, almost 70 years after Maslow first proposed his influential pyramid of needs, theorists have proposed a major renovation. Working from an evolutionary perspective, Kenrick and colleagues (2010) argue for a reworking of the upper levels of Maslow's hierarchy. They acknowledge that research and theory provide support for the priority of the first four levels of needs. But they contend that the higher needs in the pyramid are not that fundamental and that they are really pursued in service of esteem needs—that people seek knowledge, beauty, and self-actualization to impress others. After grouping Maslow's higher needs with the esteem needs, Kenrick et al. (2010) fill in the upper levels of their revised hierarchy with needs related to reproductive fitness—that is, passing on one's genes. Specifically, they propose that the top three needs in the pyramid should be the need to find a mate, the need to retain a mate, and the need to successfully parent offspring (see **Figure 11.10**). It hard to say whether this sweeping revision of Maslow's pyramid will gain traction (Kesebir, Graham, & Oishi, 2010).

The Healthy Personality

Because of his interest in self-actualization, Maslow conducted research to analyze the nature of the healthy personality. He called people with exceptionally healthy personalities *self-actualizing persons* because of their commitment to continued personal growth. Maslow identified various traits characteristic of self-actualizing people. Many of these

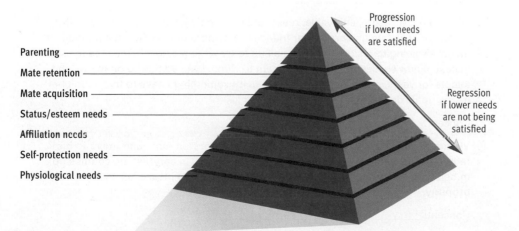

Parenting
Mate retention
Mate acquisition
Status/esteem needs
Affiliation needs
Self-protection needs
Physiological needs

Progression if lower needs are satisfied

Regression if lower needs are not being satisfied

FIGURE 11.10

Proposed revision of Maslow's pyramid.
According to Kenrick and colleagues (2010), the lower levels of needs in Maslow's hierarchy have been supported by research, but the needs in the upper portion of his pyramid should be replaced. Working from an evolutionary perspective, Kenrick et al. argue that humans' highest needs involve motives related to reproductive fitness, as shown here.

Characteristics of self-actualizing people	
• Clear, efficient perception of reality and comfortable relations with it	• Mystical and peak experiences
	• Feelings of kinship and identification with the human race
• Spontaneity, simplicity, and naturalness	• Strong friendships, but limited in number
• Problem centering (having something outside themselves they "must" do as a mission)	• Democratic character structure
	• Ethical discrimination between good and evil
• Detachment and need for privacy	• Philosophical, unhostile sense of humor
• Autonomy, independence of culture and environment	
• Continued freshness of appreciation	• Balance between polarities in personality

FIGURE 11.11

Maslow's view of the healthy personality.
Humanistic theorists emphasize psychological health instead of maladjustment. Maslow's description of characteristics of self-actualizing people evokes a picture of the healthy personality.

SOURCE: Adapted from Potkay, C. R., & Allen, B. P. (1986). *Personality: Theory, research and application.* Pacific Grove, CA: Brooks/Cole. Copyright © 1986 by C. R. Potkay & B. P. Allen. Adapted by permission of the author.

traits are listed in **Figure 11.11**. In brief, Maslow found that self-actualizers are accurately tuned in to reality and that they're at peace with themselves. He found that they're open and spontaneous and that they retain a fresh appreciation of the world around them. Socially, they're sensitive to others' needs and enjoy rewarding interpersonal relations. However, they're not dependent on others for approval or uncomfortable with solitude. They thrive on their work, and they enjoy their sense of humor. Maslow also noted that they have "peak experiences" (profound emotional highs) more often than others do. Finally, he found that they strike a nice balance between many polarities in personality. For instance, they can be both childlike and mature, both rational and intuitive, both conforming and rebellious.

Evaluating Humanistic Perspectives

The humanistic approach deserves credit for making the self-concept an important construct in psychology. The insight that a person's subjective views may be more important than objective reality has also proven compelling. One could argue that the humanists' optimistic, health-oriented approach laid the foundation for the emergence of the positive psychology movement that is increasingly influential today (Sheldon & Kasser, 2001; Taylor, 2001).

Of course, the balance sheet has a negative side, as well (Burger, 2015; Wong, 2006). Critics argue that (1) many aspects of humanistic theory are difficult to put to a scientific test, (2) humanists have been unrealistically optimistic in their assumptions about human nature and their descriptions of the healthy personality, and (3) more empirical research is needed to solidify the humanistic view.

CONCEPT CHECK 11.2

Recognizing Key Concepts in Personality Theories

Check your understanding of psychodynamic, behavioral, and humanistic personality theories by identifying key concepts from these theories in the scenarios below. The answers can be found in Appendix A.

1. Thirteen-year-old Sarah watches a TV show in which the leading female character manipulates her boyfriend by acting helpless and purposely losing a tennis match against him. The female lead repeatedly expresses her slogan, "Never let them [men] know you can take care of yourself." Sarah becomes more passive and less competitive around boys her own age.

   Concept: _____

2. Yolanda has a secure, enjoyable, reasonably well-paid job as a tenured English professor at a state university. Her friends are dumbfounded when she announces that she's going to resign and give it all up to try writing a novel. She tries to explain, "I need a new challenge, a new mountain to climb. I've had this lid on my writing talents for years, and I've got to break free. It's something I have to try. I won't be happy until I do."

   Concept: _____

3. Vladimir, who is 4, seems to be emotionally distant from and inattentive to his father. He complains whenever he's left with his dad. In contrast, he cuddles up in bed with his mother frequently and tries very hard to please her by behaving properly.

   Concept: _____

Key Learning Goals

- Outline Eysenck's view of personality, and summarize behavioral genetics research on personality.
- Articulate evolutionary explanations for why the Big Five traits are important, and evaluate the biological approach to personality.

Could personality be a matter of genetic inheritance? This possibility was largely ignored for many decades of personality research until Hans Eysenck made a case for genetic influence in the 1960s. In this section, we'll discuss Eysenck's theory and look at more-recent behavioral genetics research on the heritability of personality. We'll also examine evolutionary perspectives on personality.

Eysenck's Theory

Hans Eysenck was born in Germany but fled to London during the era of Nazi rule. He went on to become one of Britain's most prominent psychologists. Eysenck (1967, 1982, 1990) views personality structure as a hierarchy of traits, in which many superficial traits are derived from a smaller number of more basic traits, which are derived from a handful of fundamental higher-order traits, as shown in **Figure 11.12**.

According to Eysenck, personality is largely shaped by one's genes. How is heredity linked to personality in Eysenck's model? In part, through conditioning concepts borrowed from behavioral theory (consult Chapter 6 for an overview of classical conditioning). Eysenck theorizes that some people can be conditioned more readily than others because of inherited differences in their physiological functioning. These variations are assumed to influence the personality traits people acquire through conditioning processes.

Eysenck showed a special interest in explaining variations in *extraversion-introversion*. He proposed that introverts are more easily aroused by events, which make them more easily conditioned than extraverts. According to Eysenck, such people acquire more conditioned inhibitions than others do. These inhibitions make them more bashful, tentative, and uneasy in social situations, leading them to turn inward.

Behavioral Genetics and Personality

Recent research in behavioral genetics has provided impressive support for the idea that genetic blueprints shape the contours of an individual's personality (South et al., 2015). For instance, in twin studies of the Big Five personality traits, identical twins were found to be much more similar than fraternal twins on all five traits (Zuckerman, 2013; see

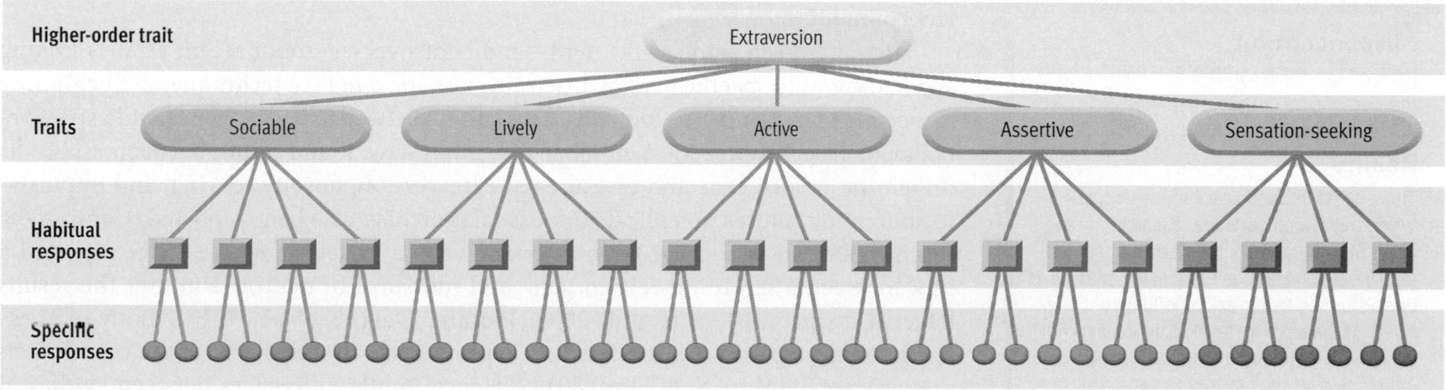

FIGURE 11.12

Eysenck's model of personality structure. Eysenck described personality structure as a hierarchy of traits. In this scheme, a few higher-order traits, such as extraversion, determine a host of lower-order traits, which determine a person's habitual responses.

SOURCE: Eysenck, H. J. (1976). *The biological basis of personality*. Springfield, IL: Charles C. Thomas. Reprinted by permission of the publisher.

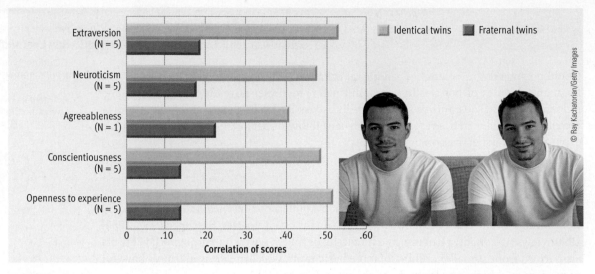

FIGURE 11.13

Twin studies of personality. Loehlin (1992) summarized the results of twin studies that examined the Big Five personality traits. The N under each trait indicates the number of twin studies that examined that trait. The chart plots the average correlations obtained for identical and fraternal twins in these studies. As you can see, identical twins show greater resemblance in personality than do fraternal twins, suggesting that personality is partly inherited. (Based on data from Loehlin, 1992)

Figure 11.13). Especially telling is the finding that this is true even when the identical twins are reared in different homes. The latter finding argues against the possibility that environmental factors (rather than heredity) could be responsible for identical twins' greater personality resemblance. Overall, five decades of research on the determinants of the Big Five traits suggests that the heritability (see Chapter 8) of each trait is in the vicinity of 50% (South et al., 2013).

Research on the heritability of personality has inadvertently turned up a surprising finding: *shared family environment* appears to have remarkably little impact on personality. This unexpected finding has been observed quite consistently in behavioral genetics research (South et al., 2015). It is surprising in that social scientists have long assumed that the family environment shared by children growing up together led to some personality resemblance among them. This finding has led researchers to explore how children's subjective environments vary *within* families. But scientists continue to be perplexed by the minimal impact of shared family environment.

There has been some excitement—and controversy—about recent reports linking specific genes to specific personality traits. *Genetic mapping* techniques are beginning to permit investigators to look for associations between specific genes and aspects of behavior (see Chapter 3). A number of studies have found a link between a specific dopamine-related gene and measures of extraversion, novelty seeking, and impulsivity, but many failures to replicate this association have also been reported (Canli, 2008; Plomin, DeFries et al., 2013). In a similar vein, a variety of studies have reported a link between a serotonin-related gene and measures of neuroticism, but the results have been inconsistent (Canli, 2008; Plomin, DeFries et al., 2013). Both of these links could be genuine, but difficult to replicate consistently because the correlations are very weak (Munafò & Flint, 2011). Hence, subtle differences between studies in sampling or the specific personality tests used can lead to inconsistent findings (South et al., 2015). The ultimate problem, however, is probably that specific personality traits may be influenced by *hundreds, if not thousands,* of genes, each of which may have a very tiny effect that is difficult to detect (Krueger & Johnson, 2008; Munafò & Flint, 2011).

The Evolutionary Approach to Personality

In the realm of biological perspectives on personality, the most recent development has been the emergence of evolutionary theory. Evolutionary theorists assert that personality has a biological basis because natural selection has favored certain traits over the course of human history (Figueredo et al., 2005, 2009). Thus, evolutionary analyses focus on how various personality traits—and the ability to recognize these traits in others—may have contributed to reproductive fitness in ancestral human populations.

For example, David Buss (1991, 1995, 1997) argues that the Big Five personality traits stand out as important dimensions of personality across a variety of cultures because those traits have had significant adaptive implications. Buss points out that humans historically have depended heavily on groups, which afford protection from predators or enemies, opportunities for sharing food, and a diverse array of other benefits. In the context of these group interactions, people have had to make difficult but crucial judgments about the characteristics of others, asking such questions as: Who can I depend on when in need? Who will share their resources? According to Buss, the Big Five emerge as fundamental dimensions of personality because humans have evolved special sensitivity to variations in the ability to bond with others (extraversion), the willingness to cooperate and collaborate (agreeableness), the tendency to be reliable and ethical (conscientiousness), the capacity to be an innovative problem solver (openness to experience), and the ability to handle stress (low neuroticism). In a nutshell, Buss argues that the Big Five reflect the most salient features of others' adaptive behavior over the course of evolutionary history.

Daniel Nettle (2006) takes this line of thinking one step further. He asserts that the traits themselves (as opposed to the ability to recognize them in others) are products of evolution that were adaptive in ancestral environments. For example, he discusses how extraversion could have promoted mating success, how agreeableness could have fostered the effective building of coalitions, and so forth. Consistent with this analysis, a variety of personality traits are associated with variations in lifetime reproductive success (Berg et al., 2014; Buss & Penke, 2015).

One article informed by this view hypothesized that variations in extraversion may be shaped by variations in attractiveness and physical strength, two traits that could have influenced the reproductive value of extraversion in human ancestral environments (Lukaszewski & Roney, 2011). The authors assert that over the course of human history, the reproductive payoffs of extraverted behavior probably were higher for men and women who exhibited greater physical attractiveness, and for men who exhibited greater physical strength. Hence, they theorize that, to some extent, indviduals learn to adjust or calibrate their level of extraversion to reflect their levels of attractiveness and strength. Thus, they predict attractiveness should correlate positively with extraversion in both genders, and that strength should be predictive of extraversion in men. This is what they found in two studies. Thus, in addition to explaining why certain traits are important dimensions of personality, evolutionary analyses may be able to help explain the origins of individual variations on these dimensions.

Evaluating Biological Perspectives

Researchers have compiled convincing evidence that biological factors help shape personality, and findings on the meager effects of shared family environment have launched intriguing new approaches to the investigation of personality development. Nonetheless, we must take note of some weaknesses in biological approaches to personality. Critics assert that too much emphasis has been placed on heritability estimates, which vary depending on sampling and statistical procedures (Funder, 2001). Critics also argue that efforts to carve behavior into genetic and environmental components ultimately lead to artificial results. The effects of nature and nurture are twisted together in complicated interactions that can't be separated cleanly (Asbury & Plomin, 2014; Rutter, 2012). For example, a genetically influenced trait, such as a young child's surly, sour temperament, might evoke a particular style of parenting. In essence then, the child's genes have molded his or her environment. Thus, genetic and environmental influences on personality are not entirely independent.

11.6

Key Learning Goals

- Understand the nature, correlates, and social consequences of narcissism.
- Describe the chief concepts of terror management theory.

11.6 CONTEMPORARY EMPIRICAL APPROACHES TO PERSONALITY

So far, our coverage has been devoted to grand, panoramic theories of personality. In this section, we'll examine some contemporary empirical approaches that are narrower in scope. In modern personality research programs, investigators typically attempt to describe and measure an important personality trait and ascertain its relationship to other traits and specific behaviors. To get a sense of this kind of research, we'll take a look at research on a trait called *narcissism*. We'll also look at an influential new approach called *terror management theory,* which focuses on personality dynamics rather than personality traits.

Narcissism

Narcissism is a personality trait marked by an inflated sense of importance, a need for attention and admiration, a sense of entitlement, and a tendency to exploit others. The term is drawn from the Greek myth of Narcissus, who was an attractive young

---

CONCEPT CHECK 11.3

Understanding the Implications of Major Theories: Who Said This?

Check your understanding of the implications of the personality theories we've discussed by indicating which theorist is likely to have made the statements below. The answers are in Appendix A.

Choose from the following theorists: (a) Alfred Adler, (b) Albert Bandura, (c) Hans Eysenck, (d) Sigmund Freud, (e) Abraham Maslow, (f) Walter Mischel.

_____ 1. "If you deliberately plan to be less than you are capable of being, then I warn you that you'll be deeply unhappy for the rest of your life."

_____ 2. "I feel that the major, most fundamental dimensions of personality are likely to be those on which [there is] strong genetic determination of individual differences."

_____ 3. "People are in general not candid over sexual matters . . . they wear a heavy overcoat woven of a tissue of lies, as though the weather were bad in the world of sexuality."

© Supri Suharjoto/Shutterstock.com

man in search of love. In the mythical tale, he eventually saw his reflection in water, fell in love with his own image, and gazed at it until he died, thus illustrating the perils of excessive self-love. The concept of narcissism was originally popularized over a century ago by pioneering sex researcher Havelock Ellis (1898) and Sigmund Freud (1914).

Narcissism was not widely discussed outside psychoanalytic circles until the 1980s, when some researchers developed scales intended to assess narcissism as a normal personality trait (as opposed to a pathological syndrome). Of these scales, the Narcissistic Personality Inventory (NPI) (Raskin & Hall, 1979, 1981; Raskin & Terry, 1988) has become the most widely used measure of narcissism.

Studies have painted an interesting portrait of those who score high in narcissism (Rhodewalt & Peterson, 2009). Narcissists have highly positive but easily-threatened self-concepts. Above all else, their behavior is driven by a need to maintain their fragile self-esteem. They display a craving for approval and admiration that resembles an addiction (Baumeister & Vohs, 2001). Hence, they tend to obsess about their looks and are prone to preening. And they work overtime to impress people by bragging about their accomplishments. As you might guess, in this era of social networking via the Internet, those who are high in narcissism tend to post relatively blatant self-promotional content on Facebook and similar websites (Buffardi & Campbell, 2008; Carpenter, 2012). Research also suggests that narcissists like to purchase products that make them stand out in a crowd; thus they prefer products that are exclusive, distinctive, and personalized (Lee, Gregg, & Park, 2013). Because they are self-centered, they tend to show relatively little empathy for people in distress (Heppner, Hart, & Sedikides, 2014). Narcissism is not distributed equally across socioeconomic classes; it is found more among the upper classes (Piff, 2014).

When they first meet people, narcissists are often perceived as charming, self-assured, humorous, and perhaps even charismatic. Initially, they tend to be well liked. With repeated exposure, however, their need for attention, brazen boasting, and sense of entitlement tend to wear thin. Eventually, they tend to be viewed as arrogant, selfish, and unlikable (Back, Schmukle, & Egloff, 2010). Interestingly, research has shown that narcissists have some awareness of the fact that they make favorable first impressions that deteriorate over time (Carlson, Vazire, & Oltmanns, 2011).

Based on a variety of social trends, Jean Twenge and colleagues (2008) suspected that narcissism might be increasing in recent generations. To test this hypothesis, they gathered data from eighty-five studies dating back to the 1980s in which American college students had been given the NPI. Their analysis revealed that NPI scores have been rising, going from a mean of about 15.5 in the 1980s to almost 17.5 in 2005–2006. This finding was replicated and extended in several subsequent studies (Twenge, Gentile, & Campbell, 2015). In a discussion of the possible implications of this trend, Twenge and Campbell (2009) argue that rising narcissism has fueled an obsessive concern about being physically attractive in young people, leading to unhealthy dieting, overuse of cosmetic surgery, and steroid-fueled body building. They also assert that narcissists' "me-first" attitude has led to increased materialism and overconsumption of the Earth's resources.

Although research has emphasized the dark side of narcissism, there is some evidence that narcissism is associated with entrepreneurial activity and successful leadership. Entrepreneurs tend to score higher on narcissism than others (Mathieu & St-Jean, 2013), and businesses led

Fjeraku/Getty, Images

Narcissists, who have a need for attention and an inflated sense of importance, like to stand out in a crowd. They tend to obsess about their appearance and engage in frequent preening.

Illustrated Overview **Major Theories of Personality**

THEORIST AND ORIENTATION	SOURCE OF DATA AND OBSERVATIONS	KEY ASSUMPTIONS

A PSYCHODYNAMIC VIEW

Sigmund Freud

Case studies from clinical practice of psychoanalysis

© Peter Aprahamian/Corbis

Past events in childhood determine our adult personality.

Our behavior is dominated by unconscious, irrational wishes, needs, and conflicts.

Personality development progresses through stages.

A BEHAVIORAL VIEW

B. F. Skinner

Laboratory experiments, primarily with animals

Courtesy of Professor Rick Stalling and Bradley University. Photo by Duane Zehr

Behavior is determined by the environment, although this view was softened by Bandura's social cognitive theory.

Nurture (learning and experience) is more influential than nature (heredity and biological factors).

Situational factors exert great influence over behavior.

A HUMANISTIC VIEW

Carl Rogers

© Zigy Kaluzny/Getty Images

Case studies from clinical practice of client-centered therapy

People are free to chart their own courses of action; they are not hapless victims governed by the environment.

People are largely conscious, rational beings who are not driven by unconscious needs.

A person's subjective view of the world is more important than objective reality.

A BIOLOGICAL VIEW

Hans Eysenck

Twin, family, and adoption studies of heritability; factor analysis studies of personality structure

© Ray Kachatorian/Getty Images

Behavior is largely determined by evolutionary adaptations, the wiring of the brain, and heredity.

Nature (heredity and biological factors) is more influential than nurture (learning and experience).

MODEL OF PERSONALITY STRUCTURE

Three interacting components (id, ego, super-ego) operating at three levels of consciousness

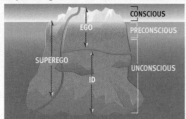

Collections of response tendencies tied to specific stimulus situations

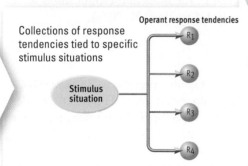

Self-concept, which may or may not mesh well with actual experience

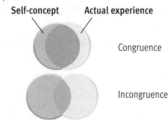

Hierarchy of traits, with specific traits derived from more fundamental, general traits

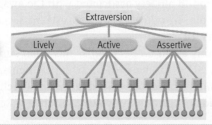

VIEW OF PERSONALITY DEVELOPMENT

Emphasis on fixation or progress through psychosexual stages; experiences in early childhood (such as toilet training) can leave lasting mark on adult personality

Personality evolves gradually over the life span (not in stages); responses (such as extraverted joking) followed by reinforcement (such as appreciative laughter) become more frequent

Children who receive unconditional love have less need to be defensive; they develop more accurate, congruent self-concept; conditional love fosters incongruence

Emphasis on unfolding of genetic blueprint with maturation; inherited predispositions interact with learning experiences

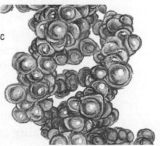

ROOTS OF DISORDER

Unconscious fixations and unresolved conflicts from childhood, usually centering on sex and aggression

Maladaptive behavior due to faulty learning; the "symptom" is the problem, not a sign of under-lying disease

Incongruence between self and actual experience (inaccurate self-concept); over-dependence on others for approval and sense of worth

Genetic vulnera-bility activated in part by environ-mental factors

by narcissistic CEOs tend to exhibit a strong entrepreneurial orientation (Wales, Patel, & Lumpkin, 2013). Narcissists tend to emerge as leaders in newly formed groups (Brunell et al., 2008). Narcissistic leaders tend to be viewed as charismatic and tend to articulate bold visions for the future (Galvin, Waldman, & Balthazard, 2010). Under some circumstances, narcissism seems to foster more effective leadership in the world of business (Reina, Zhang, & Peterson, 2014). Moreover, a study of American presidents found that higher levels of narcissism (as estimated by experts) were positively associated with independent assessments of the presidents' public persuasiveness, crisis management, legislative success, and overall greatness (Watts et al., 2013) But let's return to the dark side. Studies also suggest that narcissistic leaders tend to respond poorly to criticism, manipulate situations to make themselves look good, and are prone to ethical lapses (Reina et al., 2014). Indeed, the study of American presidents found that higher narcissism was associated with more unethical behavior, and a recent study found that companies led by narcissistic leaders were more likely to be investigated for fraud (Rijsenbilt & Commandeur, 2013).

Some theorists argue that there are two types of narcissism: *grandiose narcissism* and *vulnerable narcissism* (Houlcroft, Bore, & Munro, 2012; Miller, Gentile et al., 2013). Thus far, we have been discussing grandiose narcissism, which is characterized by arrogance, extraversion, immodesty, and aggressiveness. In contrast, vulnerable narcissism is characterized by hidden feelings of inferiority, introversion, neuroticism, and a need for recognition. To date, the vast majority of research has focused on grandiose narcissism, but recently there has been a surge of interest in the roots and ramifications of vulnerable narcissism (Czarna, Dufner, & Clifton, 2014; Lamkin et al., 2014).

Terror Management Theory

Terror management theory emerged as an influential perspective in the 1990s. Although the theory borrows from Freudian and evolutionary formulations, it provides its own unique analysis of the human condition. Developed by Sheldon Solomon, Jeff Greenberg, and Tom Pyszczynski (1991, 2004), this fresh perspective is currently generating a huge volume of research.

One of the chief goals of terror management theory is to explain why people need self-esteem. Unlike other animals, humans have evolved complex cognitive abilities that permit self-awareness and contemplation of the future. These cognitive capacities make humans keenly aware that life can be snuffed out at any time. The collision between humans' self-preservation instinct and their awareness of the inevitability of death creates the potential for experiencing anxiety, alarm, and terror when people think about their mortality (see **Figure 11.14**).

How do humans deal with this potential for terror? According to terror management theory, "What saves us is culture. Cultures provide ways to view the world—worldviews—that 'solve' the existential crisis engendered by the awareness of death" (Pyszczynski, Solomon, & Greenberg, 2003, p. 16). Cultural worldviews diminish anxiety by providing answers to universal questions, such as: Why am I here? What is the meaning of life? Cultures create stories, traditions, and institutions that give their members a sense of being part of an enduring legacy and thus soothe their fear of death.

Where does self-esteem fit into the picture? Self-esteem is viewed as a sense of personal worth that depends on one's confidence in the validity of one's cultural worldview and the belief that one is living up to the standards prescribed by that worldview. Hence, self-esteem buffers people from the profound anxiety associated with the awareness that they are transient animals destined to die. In other words, self-esteem serves a *terror management* function (refer to **Figure 11.14**).

The notion that self-esteem functions as an *anxiety buffer* has been supported by numerous studies (Landau & Sullivan, 2015). In many of these experiments, researchers manipulated what they call **mortality salience—the degree to which subjects' mortality is prominent in their minds.** Typically, mortality salience is temporarily

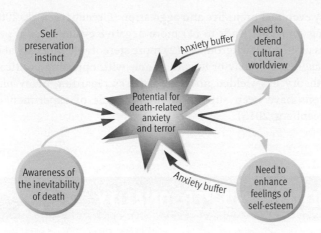

FIGURE 11.14

Overview of terror management theory. This graphic maps out the relations among the key concepts proposed by terror management theory. The theory asserts that humans' unique awareness of the inevitability of death fosters a need to defend one's cultural worldview and one's self-esteem, which serve to protect one from mortality-related anxiety.

increased by asking participants to briefly think about their own future death. Consistent with the anxiety buffer hypothesis, reminding people of their mortality leads subjects to engage in a variety of behaviors that are likely to bolster their self-esteem, thus reducing anxiety.

Increasing mortality salience also leads people to work harder at defending their cultural worldview (Landau & Sullivan, 2015). For instance, after briefly pondering their mortality, research participants (1) hand out harsher penalties to moral transgressors; (2) respond more negatively to people who criticize their country; and (3) show more respect for cultural icons, such as a flag. This need to defend one's cultural

According to terror management theory, events that remind people of their mortality motivate them to defend their cultural worldview. One manifestation of this process is an increased interest in and respect for cultural icons, such as flags.

worldview may even fuel prejudice and aggression (Greenberg et al., 2009). Reminding subjects of their mortality leads to (1) more negative evaluations of people from different religious or ethnic backgrounds, (2) more stereotypic thinking about minorities, and (3) more aggressive behavior toward people with opposing political views. Terror management theory has yielded novel hypotheses regarding many phenomena, and these predictions have been supported in hundreds of experiments (Pyszczynski, Sullivan, & Greenberg, 2015).

11.7

Key Learning Goals

- Clarify how researchers have found both cross-cultural similarities and disparities in personality.

11.7 CULTURE AND PERSONALITY

Are there connections between culture and personality? Psychology's new interest in cultural factors has led to a renaissance of culture-personality research (Church, 2010). This research has sought to determine whether Western personality constructs are relevant to other cultures.

For the most part, continuity has been apparent in cross-cultural comparisons of the *trait structure* of personality. When translated versions of the scales that tap the Big Five personality traits are administered and subjected to factor analysis in other cultures, the usual five traits typically surface (Chiu, Kim, & Wan, 2008; McCrae & Costa, 2008). Admittedly, the results are not *always* consistent with the five-factor model (Kwan & Herrmann, 2015). The most common inconsistency is that a clear factor for the trait of openness to experience does not emerge in some cultures (Saucier & Srivastava, 2015). Still, overall, the research tentatively suggests the basic dimensions of personality trait structure may be nearly universal.

On the other hand, some cross-cultural variability is seen when researchers compare the average trait scores of samples from various cultural groups. For example, in a study comparing fifty-one cultures, McCrae et al. (2005) found that Brazilians scored relatively high in neuroticism, Australians in extraversion, Germans in openness to experience, Czechs in agreeableness, and Malaysians in conscientiousness, to give but a handful of examples. These findings suggest there may be genuine cultural differences on some personality traits, although the cultural disparities that were observed were modest in size.

The availability of the data from the McCrae et al. (2005) study allowed Terracciano et al. (2005) to evaluate the concept of *national character*—the idea that various cultures have widely recognized prototype personalities. Terracciano and his colleagues asked subjects from many cultures to describe the *typical* member of *their* culture on rating forms guided by the five-factor model. Generally, subjects displayed substantial agreement on these ratings of what was typical for their culture. The averaged ratings, which served as the measures of each culture's national character, were then correlated with the actual mean trait scores for various cultures compiled in the McCrae et al. (2005) study. The results were definitive: the vast majority of correlations were extremely low and often even negative. In other words, there was little or no relationship between perceptions of national character and actual trait scores for various cultures (see **Figure 11.15**). People's beliefs about national character, which often fuel cultural prejudices, turned out to be profoundly inaccurate stereotypes (McCrae & Terracciano, 2006). Although some doubts have been raised about this conclusion (Heine, Buchtel, & Norenzayan, 2008), a recent replication found once again that perceptions of national character tend to be largely inaccurate (McCrae et al., 2013). Although the replication collected more fine-grained data on beliefs about national character (taking gender and age group into account) than the original study, these beliefs still showed little or no correlation with actual trait scores.

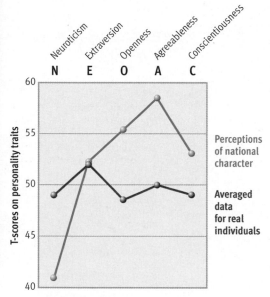

FIGURE 11.15

An example of inaccurate perceptions of national character. Terracciano et al. (2005) found that perceptions of national character (the prototype or typical personality for a particular culture) are largely inaccurate. The data shown here for one culture—Canadians—illustrate this inaccuracy. Averaged perceptions of national character for Canadians are graphed in blue. Mean scores on the Big Five traits for a sample of real individuals from Canada are graphed in red. The discrepancy between perception and reality is obvious. Terracciano et al. found similar disparities between views of national character and actual trait scores for a majority of the cultures they studied. (Adapted from McCrae & Terracciano, 2006)

Perhaps the most interesting and influential work on culture and personality has been that of Hazel Markus and Shinobu Kitayama (1991, 1994, 2003). Their research has compared American and Asian conceptions of the self. According to Markus and Kitayama, American parents teach their children to be self-reliant, to feel good about themselves, and to view themselves as special individuals. Children are encouraged to excel in competitive endeavors and to strive to stand out from the crowd. They are told that "the squeaky wheel gets the grease" and that "you have to stand up for yourself." Thus, Markus and Kitayama argue that *American culture fosters an independent view of the self.* American youngsters learn to define themselves in terms of their personal attributes, abilities, accomplishments, and possessions. Their unique strengths and achievements become the basis for their sense of self-worth. Thus, they are prone to emphasize their uniqueness.

Most of us take this individualistic mentality for granted. However, Markus and Kitayama marshal convincing evidence that this view is *not* universal. They argue that in Asian cultures, such as Japan and China, socialization practices foster a more *interdependent view of the self* that emphasizes the fundamental connectedness of people to one another (see **Figure 11.16**). In these cultures, parents teach their children that they can rely on family and friends, that they should be modest about their personal accomplishments so they don't diminish others' achievements, and that they should view themselves as part of a larger social matrix. Children are encouraged to fit in with others and to avoid standing out from the crowd. A popular adage in Japan reminds children that "the nail that stands out gets pounded down." Hence, Markus and Kitayama assert that Asian youngsters typically learn to define themselves in terms of the groups they belong to. Their harmonious relations with others and their pride in group achievements become the basis for their sense of self-worth. Thus, Asian and American conceptions of self appear to be noticeably different.

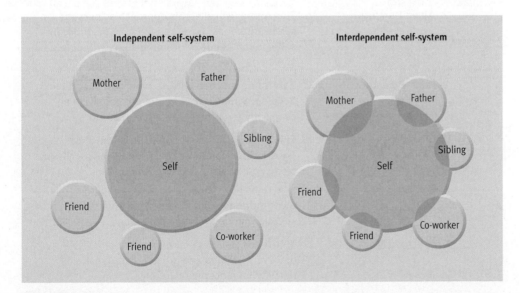

FIGURE 11.16

Culture and conceptions of self. According to Markus and Kitayama (1991), Western cultures foster an independent view of the self as a unique individual who is separate from others, as diagrammed on the left. In contrast, Asian cultures encourage an interdependent view of the self as part of an interconnected social matrix, as diagrammed on the right. The interdependent view leads people to define themselves in terms of their social relationships (for instance, as someone's daughter, employee, colleague, or neighbor).

11.8

Key Learning Goals

• Identify the three unifying themes high-lighted in this chapter.

Cultural Heritage

Theoretical Diversity

Sociohistorical Context

11.8 REFLECTING ON THE CHAPTER'S THEMES

The preceding discussion of culture and personality obviously highlighted the text's theme that people's behavior is influenced by their cultural heritage. This chapter has also been ideally suited for embellishing on two other unifying themes: psychology's theoretical diversity and the idea that psychology evolves in a sociohistorical context.

No other area of psychology is characterized by as much theoretical diversity as the study of personality, where there are literally dozens of insightful theories. Some of this diversity exists because different theories attempt to explain different facets of behavior. Of course, much of this diversity reflects genuine disagreements on basic questions about personality. These disagreements should be apparent on pages 404–405, where you'll find an Illustrated Overview of the ideas of Freud, Skinner, Rogers, and Eysenck, as representatives of the psychodynamic, behavioral, humanistic, and biological approaches to personality.

CONCEPT CHECK 11.4

Identifying the Contributions of Major Personality Theorists

Check your recall of the principal ideas of important personality theorists covered in this chapter by matching the people listed on the left with the appropriate contributions described on the right. Fill in the letters for your choices in the spaces provided on the left. You'll find the answers in Appendix A.

Major Theorists

_____ 1. Alfred Adler

_____ 2. Albert Bandura

_____ 3. Hans Eysenck

_____ 4. Sigmund Freud

_____ 5. Carl Jung

_____ 6. Abraham Maslow

_____ 7. Walter Mischel

_____ 8. Carl Rogers

_____ 9. B. F. Skinner

Key Ideas and Contributions

a. This humanistic theorist is famous for his hierarchy of needs and his work on self-actualizing persons.

b. This humanist called his approach a "person-centered theory." He argued that an incongruent self-concept tends to promote anxiety and defensive behavior.

c. This influential behaviorist explained personality development in terms of operant conditioning, especially the process of reinforcement.

d. This theorist emphasized the importance of unconscious conflicts, anxiety, defense mechanisms, and psychosexual development.

e. This behaviorist sparked a robust debate about the importance of the person, as opposed to the situation, in determining behavior.

f. This theorist views personality structure as a hierarchy of traits and argues that personality is heavily influenced by heredity.

g. This theorist clashed with Freud and argued that the foremost source of human motivation is a striving for superiority.

h. This psychodynamic theorist is famous for the concepts of the collective unconscious and archetypes.

i. This theorist's social cognitive theory emphasizes observational learning and self-efficacy.

The study of personality also highlights the sociohistorical context in which psychology evolves. Personality theories have left many marks on modern culture. The theories of Freud, Adler, and Skinner have had an enormous impact on childrearing practices. The ideas of Freud and Jung have found their way into literature (influencing the portrayal of fictional characters) and the visual arts, whereas Maslow's hierarchy of needs and Skinner's affirmation of the value of positive reinforcement have given rise to new approaches to management in the world of business and industry.

Sociohistorical forces also leave their imprint on psychology. This chapter provided many examples of how personal experiences, prevailing attitudes, and historical events have contributed to the evolution of ideas in psychology. For example, Freud's emphasis on sexuality was surely influenced by the Victorian climate of sexual repression that existed in his youth. Adler's views also reflected the social context in which he grew up. His interest in inferiority feelings and compensation appears to have sprung from his own sickly childhood and the difficulties he had to overcome.

Progress in the study of personality has also been influenced by developments in other areas of psychology. For instance, the enterprise of psychological testing originally emerged out of efforts to measure general intelligence. Eventually, however, the principles of psychological testing were applied to the challenge of measuring personality. In the upcoming Personal Application we discuss the logic and limitations of personality tests.

11.9 PERSONAL APPLICATION
Understanding Personality Assessment

11.9

Key Learning Goals
- Explain how personality inventories and projective tests work, and evaluate their strengths and weaknesses.

Answer the following "true" or "false."

____ 1 Responses to personality tests are subject to unconscious distortion.

____ 2 The results of personality tests are often misunderstood.

____ 3 Personality test scores should be interpreted with caution.

____ 4 Personality tests serve many important functions.

If you answered "true" to all four questions, you earned a perfect score. Yes, personality tests are subject to distortion. Admittedly, test results are often misunderstood, and they should be interpreted cautiously. In spite of these problems, however, psychological tests can be quite useful.

Personality tests can be helpful in (1) making clinical diagnoses of psychological disorders, (2) vocational counseling, (3) personnel selection in business and industry, and (4) measuring specific personality traits for research purposes. Personality tests can be divided into two broad categories: *self-report inventories* and *projective tests*. In this Personal Application, we'll discuss some representative tests from both categories. We'll also discuss their strengths and weaknesses.

Self-Report Inventories

Self-report inventories **are personality tests that ask individuals to answer a series of questions about their characteristic behavior.** The logic underlying this approach is very simple. Who knows you better? Who has known you longer? Who has more access to your private feelings? Imperfect though they may be, self-ratings remain the gold standard for personality assessment (Paunonen & Hong, 2015). We'll look at two examples of self-report scales, the MMPI and the NEO Personality Inventory.

The MMPI

The most widely used self-report inventory is the Minnesota Multiphasic Personality Inventory (MMPI) (Butcher, 2011). The MMPI was originally designed to aid clinicians in the diagnosis of psychological disorders. It measures ten personality traits that, when manifested to an extreme degree, are thought to be symptoms of disorders. Examples include traits such as paranoia, depression, and hysteria.

Are the MMPI clinical scales valid? That is, do they measure what they were designed to measure? Originally, it was assumed that the ten clinical subscales would provide direct indexes of specific types of disorders. In other words, a high score on the depression scale would be indicative of depression, a high score on the paranoia scale would be indicative of a paranoid disorder, and so forth. However, research revealed that the relations between MMPI scores and various types of mental illness are much more complex than originally anticipated. People with most types of disorders show elevated scores on *several* MMPI subscales. This means that certain score *profiles* are indicative of specific disorders (see **Figure 11.17**). Thus, the interpretation of

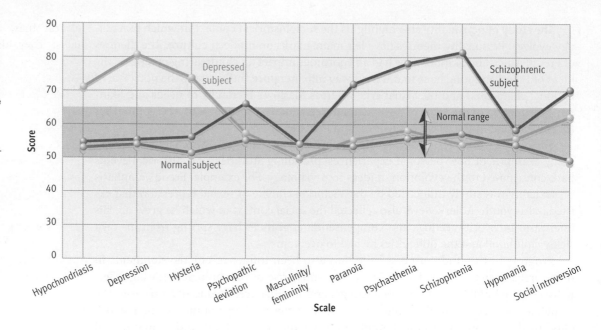

FIGURE 11.17

MMPI profiles. Scores on the ten clinical scales of the MMPI are often plotted as shown here to create a profile for a client. The normal range for scores on each subscale is 50 to 65. People with disorders frequently exhibit elevated scores on several clinical scales rather than just one.

the MMPI is quite complicated—perhaps overly complicated, according to some critics (Helmes, 2008). Still, the MMPI can be a helpful diagnostic tool for the clinician. The fact that the inventory has been translated into more than 115 languages is a testimonial to its usefulness.

The NEO Personality Inventory

As we noted in the main body of the chapter, many theorists believe that only five trait dimensions are required to provide a full description of personality. This view led to the creation of the NEO Personality Inventory. Developed by Paul Costa and Robert McCrae (1985, 1992), the NEO Inventory is designed to measure the Big Five traits: neuroticism, extraversion, openness to experience, agreeableness, and conscientiousness. In spite of its relatively short life span, the NEO inventory is widely used in research and clinical work, and updated revisions of the scale have been released (McCrae & Costa, 2007, 2010). An example of a NEO personality profile (averaged from many respondents) was shown in our discussion of culture and personality (see **Figure 11.15**).

Strengths and Weaknesses of Self-Report Inventories

To appreciate the strengths of self-report inventories, consider how else you might inquire about an individual's personality.

For instance, if you want to know how assertive someone is, why not just ask the person? Why administer an elaborate fifty-item personality inventory that measures assertiveness? The advantage of the personality inventory is that it can provide a more objective and more precise estimate of the person's assertiveness. Self-report inventories are used for many purposes in a broad range of settings, and they have well-documented value in providing useful information about individuals (Ben-Porath, 2013; Krug, 2013).

Of course, self-report inventories are only as accurate as the information that respondents provide (Butcher, Bubany, & Mason, 2013). They are susceptible to several sources of error, including the following:

1. *Deliberate deception.* Some self-report inventories include many questions whose purpose is easy to figure out. This problem makes it possible for some respondents to intentionally fake particular personality traits (Rees & Metcalfe, 2003). Some studies suggest that deliberate faking is a serious problem when personality scales are used to evaluate job applicants (Birkeland et al., 2006). Other studies, however, suggest that the problem is not all that significant (Hogan & Chamorro-Premuzic, 2015).

2. *Social desirability bias.* Without realizing it, some people consistently respond to questions in ways that make them look good. This social desirability bias, which isn't a matter of deception so much as wishful thinking, can distort test results to some degree (Paunonen & LeBel, 2012).

3. *Response sets.* A response set is a systematic tendency to respond to test items in a particular way that is unrelated to the content of the items. For instance, some people, called "yea-sayers," tend to agree with virtually every statement on a test. Other people, called "nay-sayers," tend to disagree with nearly every statement.

Test developers have devised a number of strategies to reduce the impact of deliberate deception, social desirability bias, and response sets (Paunonen & Hong, 2015; Hough & Connelly, 2013). One strategy is to insert a validity scale into a test to assess the likelihood that a respondent is engaging in intentional deception (Ellingson, Heggestad, & Makarius, 2012). For instance, the MMPI contains several scales that are very sensitive in detecting various types of deceptive responding (Butcher, 2013). The best way to reduce the impact of social desirability bias is to identify items that are sensitive to this bias and drop them from the test. Problems with response sets can be reduced by systematically varying the way in which test items are worded.

Projective Tests

Projective tests, which take a rather indirect approach to the assessment of personality, are used extensively in clinical work. *Projective tests ask participants to respond to vague, ambiguous stimuli in ways that can reveal the subjects' needs, feelings, and personality traits.* The Rorschach test, for instance, consists of a series of ten inkblots. Respondents are asked to describe what they see in the blots. In the Thematic Apperception Test (TAT), a series of pictures of simple scenes is presented to individuals who are asked to tell stories about what is happening in the scenes and what the characters are feeling. For instance, one TAT card shows a young boy contemplating a violin resting on a table in front of him.

The Projective Hypothesis

The "projective hypothesis" is that ambiguous materials can serve as a blank screen onto which people project their characteristic concerns, conflicts, and desires (Frank, 1939). Thus, a competitive person who is shown the TAT card of the boy at the table with the violin might concoct a story about how the boy is contemplating an upcoming musical competition at which he hopes to excel. The same card shown to a person high in impulsiveness might elicit a story about how the boy is planning to sneak out the door to go dirt-bike riding with friends.

The scoring and interpretation of projective tests is very complicated. Rorschach responses can be analyzed in terms of content, originality, the feature of the inkblot that determined the response, and the amount of the inkblot used, among other criteria. In fact, six different systems exist for scoring the Rorschach (Adams & Culbertson, 2005). TAT stories are examined in terms of heroes, needs, themes, and outcomes.

Strengths and Weaknesses of Projective Tests

Proponents of projective tests assert that the tests have two unique strengths. First, they are not transparent to respondents. That is, the subject doesn't know how the test provides information to the tester. Hence, it may be difficult for people to engage in intentional deception (Weiner, 2013a). Second, the indirect approach used in these tests may make them especially sensitive to unconscious, latent features of personality (Meyer & Viglione, 2008).

Unfortunately, the scientific evidence on projective measures is unimpressive (Garb et al., 2005; Wood et al., 2010). In a thorough review of the relevant research, Lilienfeld, Wood, and Garb (2000) conclude that projective tests tend to be plagued by inconsistent scoring, low reliability, inadequate test norms, cultural bias, and poor validity estimates. They also assert that, contrary to advocates' claims, projective tests are susceptible to some types of intentional deception (primarily, faking poor mental health). Based on their analysis, Lilienfeld and his colleagues argue that projective tests should be referred to as projective "techniques" or "instruments" rather than tests because "most of these techniques as used in daily clinical practice do not fulfill the traditional criteria for psychological tests" (p. 29). Another problem specific to the Rorschach is that all the inkblots have been posted on Wikipedia, along with common responses and their interpretation. Although psychologists have vigorously protested, the copyright for the test has expired, and the images are in the public domain. Clinicians are concerned that this exposure of the inkblots could compromise the utility of the test (Hartmann & Hartmann, 2014; Schultz & Brabender, 2013).

In spite of these problems, projective tests, such as the Rorschach, continue to be used by many clinicians (Weiner & Meyer, 2009). Although the questionable scientific status of these techniques is a very real problem, their continued popularity suggests that they yield subjective information that many clinicians find useful (Meyer et al., 2013).

11.10

Key Learning Goals
- Understand how hindsight bias affects everyday analyses and theoretical analyses of personality.

11.10 CRITICAL THINKING APPLICATION
Hindsight in Everyday Analyses of Personality

Consider the case of two close sisters who grew up together: Lorena and Christina. Lorena grew into a frugal adult who is careful about spending her money, only shops when there are sales, and saves every penny she can. In contrast, Christina became an extravagant spender who lives to shop and never saves any money. How do the sisters explain their striking personality differences? Lorena attributes her thrifty habits to the fact that her family was so poor when she was a child that she learned the value of being careful with money. Christina attributes her extravagant spending to the fact that her family was so poor that she learned to really enjoy any money that she might have. Now, it *is* possible that two sisters could react to essentially the same circumstances quite differently. But the more likely explanation is that both sisters have been influenced by *hindsight bias*—**the tendency to mold one's interpretation of the past to fit how events actually turned out.** We saw how hindsight can distort memory in Chapter 7. Here, we will see how hindsight tends to make people feel as if they are personality experts and how it creates interpretive problems even for scientific theories of personality.

The Prevalence of Hindsight Bias

Hindsight bias is *ubiquitous,* which means that it occurs in many settings, with all sorts of people (Bernstein et al., 2011). Most of the time, people are not aware of the way their explanations are skewed by the fact that the outcome is already known. The experimental literature on hindsight bias offers a rich array of findings on how the knowledge of an outcome biases the way people think about its causes (Fischhoff, 2007; Guilbault et al., 2004). For example, when college students were told the results of a hypothetical experiment, each group of students could "explain" why the studies turned out the way they did, even though different groups were given opposite results to explain (Slovic & Fischhoff, 1977). The students believed that the results of the studies were obvious when they were told what the experimenter found. Yet, when they were given only the information that was available before the outcome was known, it was not obvious at all. This bias is also called the "I knew it all along" effect because that is the typical refrain of people when they have the luxury of hindsight.

Indeed, afterward, people often act as if events that would have been difficult to predict had in fact been virtually *inevitable* and *foreseeable* (Roese & Vohs, 2012). Looking back at the 2008 crash of the U.S. mortgage system and ensuing financial meltdown, for instance, many people today act as though these events were bound to happen. In reality, though, these landmark events were predicted by almost no one. It appears that outcome knowledge warps judgments in two ways (Erdfelder, Brandt, & Bröder, 2007). First, knowing the outcome of an event impairs one's recall of earlier, more naïve expectations about the event. Second, outcome knowledge shapes how people reconstruct their thinking about the event.

Hindsight bias shows up in many contexts. For example, when a couple announces that they are splitting up, many people in their social circle will typically claim they "saw it coming." When a football team loses in a huge upset, you will hear many fans claim, "I knew they were overrated and vulnerable." When public authorities make a difficult decision that leads to a disastrous outcome—such as officials' decision not to evacuate New Orleans in preparation for Hurricane Katrina until relatively late—many of the pundits in the press are quick to criticize, often asserting that only incompetent fools could have failed to foresee the catastrophe. Interestingly, people are not much kinder to themselves when they make ill-fated decisions. When individuals make tough calls that lead to negative results—such as buying a car that turns out to be a lemon or investing in a stock that plummets—they often say things like, "Why did I ignore the obvious warning signs?" or "How could I have been such an idiot?"

Hindsight and Personality

Hindsight bias can influence everyday analyses of personality (Nestler et al., 2012). Think about it: if you attempt to explain why you are so suspicious, why your mother is so domineering, or why your best friend is so insecure, the starting point in each case will be the personality outcome. It would probably be impossible to reconstruct the past without being swayed by your knowledge of these outcomes. Thus, hindsight makes everybody an expert on personality, as we can all come up with plausible explanations for the personality traits of people we know well. Perhaps this is why Judith Harris (1998) ignited a firestorm of protest when she wrote a book arguing that parents have relatively little effect on their children's personalities, beyond the genetic material that they supply.

In her book *The Nurture Assumption,* Harris summarizes behavioral genetics research (which we discussed in the main body of the chapter; see pp. 399–400) and other evidence suggesting that family environment has surprisingly little impact on children's personality. There is room for debate on this complex issue (Kagan, 1998; Tavris, 1998). Our chief interest here, though, is that Harris made a cogent, compelling argument that attracted extensive coverage in the press, which generated an avalanche of commentary from angry parents who argued that *parents do matter.* For example, *Newsweek*

Bill Clark/Getty Images

With the luxury of hindsight, it is easy to second-guess officials, such as then Secretary of State Hilary Clinton, who failed to foresee the 2012 attack on the U.S. diplomatic compound in Benghazi, Libya.

magazine received 350 letters, mostly from parents who provided examples of how they thought they had influenced their children's personalities. However, parents' retrospective analyses of their children's personality development have to be treated with great skepticism. These analyses are likely to be distorted by hindsight bias (not to mention the selective recall commonly seen in anecdotal reports).

Unfortunately, hindsight bias is so prevalent that it also presents a problem for scientific theories of personality. For example, the issue of hindsight bias has been raised in many critiques of psychoanalytic theory (Torrey, 1992). Freudian theory was originally built mainly on a foundation of case studies of patients in therapy. Obviously, Freudian therapists who knew what their patients' adult personalities were like probably went looking for the types of childhood experiences hypothesized by Freud (oral fixations, punitive toilet training, Oedipal conflicts, and so forth) in their efforts to explain their patients' personalities.

Another problem with hindsight bias is that once researchers know an outcome, more often than not they can fashion some plausible explanation for it. For instance, Torrey (1992) describes a study inspired by Freudian theory that examined breast-size preferences among men.

The original hypothesis was that men who scored higher in dependence—thought to be a sign of oral fixation—would manifest a stronger preference for women with large breasts. When the actual results of the study showed just the opposite—that dependence was associated with a preference for smaller breasts—the finding was attributed to reaction formation (the defense mechanism that involves behaving in a way opposite of one's true feelings). Instead of failing to support Freudian theory, the unexpected findings were simply reinterpreted in a way that was consistent with Freudian theory.

Hindsight bias also presents thorny problems for evolutionary theorists, who generally work backward from known outcomes to reason out how adaptive pressures in humans' ancestral past may have led to those outcomes (Cornell, 1997). Consider, for instance, evolutionary theorists' assertion that the Big Five traits are found to be fundamental dimensions of personality around the world because those specific traits have had major adaptive implications over the course of human history (Buss, 1995; Nettle, 2006). Their explanation makes sense, but what would have happened if some *other traits* had shown up in the Big Five? Would the evolutionary view have been weakened if dominance or paranoia had turned up in the Big Five? Probably not. With the luxury of hindsight, evolutionary theorists surely could have constructed plausible explanations for how these traits promoted reproductive success in the distant past. Thus, hindsight bias is a fundamental feature of human cognition and the scientific enterprise is not immune to this problem.

Other Implications of "20-20 Hindsight"

Our discussion of hindsight has focused on its implications for thinking about personality, but there is ample evidence

that hindsight can bias thinking in all sorts of domains. For example, consider the practice of obtaining second opinions on medical diagnoses. The doctor providing the second opinion usually is aware of the first physician's diagnosis, which creates a hindsight bias (Arkes et al., 1981). Second opinions would probably be more valuable if the doctors rendering them were not aware of previous diagnoses. Hindsight bias frequently taints decision making in medicine, not to mention verdicts in malpractice cases (Arkes, 2013). Indeed, hindsight has the potential to distort legal decisions in many types of cases where jurors evaluate defendants' responsibility for known outcomes, such as a faulty braking system (Harley, 2007). For example, in trials involving allegations of negligence, jurors' natural tendency to think "how could they have failed to foresee this problem?" may exaggerate the appearance of negligence. The ultimate problem with hindsight bias is that it tends to promote single-cause thinking and overconfidence when people analyze decisions that went awry (Roese & Vohs, 2012). In both medical and legal contexts these cognitive biases can have important consequences.

Hindsight bias is powerful. The next time you hear of an unfortunate outcome to a decision made by a public official, carefully examine the way news reporters describe the decision. You will probably find that they believe the disastrous outcome should have been obvious because they can clearly see what went wrong after the fact. Similarly, if you find yourself thinking, "Only a fool would have failed to anticipate this disaster" or "I would have foreseen this problem," take a deep breath and try to review the decision *using only information that was known at the time the decision was being made*. Sometimes good decisions based on the best available information can have terrible outcomes. Unfortunately, the clarity of "20-20 hindsight" makes it difficult for people to learn from their own and others' mistakes.

TABLE 11.3 Critical Thinking Skill Discussed in This Application

Skill	Description
Recognizing the bias in hindsight analysis	The critical thinker understands that knowing the outcome of events biases one's recall and interpretation of the events.

CHAPTER 11 CONCEPT CHART

THE NATURE OF PERSONALITY

- A *personality trait* is a durable disposition to behave in a particular way across a variety of situations.

- According to the *five-factor model*, most aspects of personality are derived from five crucial traits: neuroticism, extraversion, openness to experience, agreeableness, and conscientiousness.

- The Big Five traits are predictive of important life outcomes, such as grades, occupational attainment, divorce, health, and mortality.

PSYCHODYNAMIC PERSPECTIVES

Freud's theory

- Freud's *psychoanalytic theory* grew out of his therapeutic work with clients and emphasized the importance of the unconscious.

- Freud divided personality structure into three components: the id, ego, and superego.

- The *id* is the instinctive component that follows the pleasure principle, the *ego* is the decision-making component that follows the reality principle, and the *superego* is the moral component.

- Freud described three levels of awareness: the *conscious* (current awareness), the *preconscious* (material just beneath the surface of awareness), and the *unconscious* (material well below the surface of awareness).

- Freud theorized that conflicts centering on sex and aggression are especially likely to lead to significant anxiety.

- According to Freud, anxiety and other unpleasant emotions are often warded off with *defense mechanisms*, which work through self-deception.

- Freud proposed that children evolve through five stages of psychosexual development: the oral, anal, phallic, latency, and genital stages.

- Certain experiences during these stages, such as handling of the *Oedipal complex*, can shape subsequent adult personality.

Jung's theory

- Jung's *analytical psychology* emphasized unconscious determinants of personality, but he divided the unconscious into the personal and collective unconscious.

- The *collective unconscious* is a storehouse of latent memory traces inherited from people's ancestral past.

- These memories consist of *archetypes*, which are emotionally charged thought forms that have universal meaning.

Adler's theory

- Adler's *individual psychology* emphasized how social forces shape personality development.

- Adler argued that *striving for superiority* is the foremost motivational force in people's lives.

- Adler attributed personality disturbances to excessive inferiority feelings that can pervert the normal process of striving for superiority and can result in *overcompensation*.

BEHAVIORAL PERSPECTIVES

Skinner's theory

- Skinner's work on *operant conditioning* was not meant to be a theory of personality, but it has been applied to personality.

- Skinner's followers view personality as a collection of response tendencies that are tied to specific situations.

- Skinnerians view personality development as a lifelong process in which response tendencies are shaped by reinforcement.

Bandura's theory

- Bandura's *social cognitive theory* emphasizes how cognitive factors shape personality.

- According to Bandura, people's response tendencies are largely acquired through *observational learning*.

- Bandura stressed the role of *self-efficacy*—one's belief about one's ability to perform behaviors that should lead to expected outcomes.

Mischel's theory

- Mischel's brand of social learning theory emphasizes how people behave differently in different situations.

- His theory sparked debate about the relative importance of the person versus the situation in determining behavior.

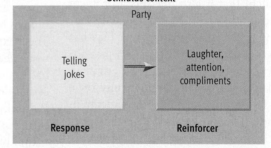

Stimulus context

Party

| Telling jokes | → | Laughter, attention, compliments |

Response | | **Reinforcer**

Defense Mechanism	Definition
Repression	Keeping distressing thoughts and feelings buried in the unconscious
Projection	Attributing one's own thoughts, feelings, or motives to another
Displacement	Diverting emotional feelings (usually anger) from their original source to a substitute target
Reaction formation	Behaving in a way that is exactly the opposite of one's true feelings
Regression	A reversion to immature patterns of behavior
Rationalization	Creating false but plausible excuses to justify unacceptable behavior
Identification	Bolstering self-esteem by forming an imaginary or real alliance with some person or group

HUMANISTIC PERSPECTIVES

Rogers's theory

- Rogers's *person-centered theory* focuses on the *self-concept*—a collection of subjective beliefs about one's nature.
- *Incongruence* is the degree of disparity between one's self-concept and one's actual experiences.
- According to Rogers, unconditional love during childhood fosters congruence, while conditional love fosters incongruence.
- Rogers asserted that people with highly incongruent self-concepts are prone to recurrent anxiety.

Need for self-actualization

Maslow's theory

- Maslow proposed that human motives are organized into a *hierarchy of needs*, in which basic needs must be met before less basic needs are aroused.
- At the top of Maslow's hierarchy of needs is the need for *self-actualization*—the need to fulfill one's potential.
  - Recently, theorists have proposed a major revision of Maslow's pyramid of needs in which the higher, growth needs are replaced by motives related to reproductive fitness.
  - According to Maslow, *self-actualizing persons* are people with very healthy personalities, marked by continued personal growth.

BIOLOGICAL PERSPECTIVES

Eysenck's theory

- Eysenck viewed personality structure as a hierarchy of traits in which many superficial traits are derived from a handful of fundamental traits.
- According to Eysenck, personality is largely determined by genetic inheritance.
- Eysenck theorized that introversion and extraversion are shaped by inherited differences in ease of conditioning.

Behavioral genetics research

- Identical twins reared apart tend to be more similar in personality than fraternal twins reared together, which suggests that genetics shape personality.
- *Heritability estimates* for personality tend to hover around 50%.
- Behavioral genetics research revealed that *shared family environment* has surprisingly little impact on personality.
- Genetic mapping studies on personality yielded inconsistent, difficult to replicate findings.

The evolutionary approach

- According to Buss, the ability to recognize and judge other's status on the Big Five traits may have contributed to reproductive fitness.
- Nettle argues that the Big Five traits themselves (rather than the ability to recognize them) are products of evolution that were adaptive in ancestral times.

CONTEMPORARY EMPIRICAL APPROACHES TO PERSONALITY

Narcissism

- *Narcissism* is a trait marked by an inflated sense of self, need for attention, and a sense of entitlement.
- Narcissists work overtime trying to impress others with self-aggrandizing tales of their accomplishments to protect their fragile self-esteem.
- Narcissists often are well-liked at first, but eventually are seen as arrogant and self-centered. Research suggests that levels of narcissism have been increasing.

Terror management theory

- The collision between humans' self-preservation instinct and their awareness of death creates the potential for terror when people think about their mortality.
- Cultural worldviews and self-esteem buffer people from the anxiety associated with their awareness of their mortality.
- Increasing morality salience leads people to work harder at defending their cultural worldview and their self-esteem.
- Manipulations of mortality salience lead to harsh treatment for moral transgressions, elevated respect for cultural icons, and increased prejudice.

CULTURE AND PERSONALITY

- The basic trait structure of personality may be much the same across cultures because the Big Five traits usually emerge in cross-cultural studies.
- However, some cultural variability has been seen when researchers compare average trait scores for various cultural groups.
- Studies showed that perceptions of national character tend to be inaccurate stereotypes.
- Markus and Kitayama asserted that American culture fosters an *independent view* of the self, whereas Asian cultures foster an *interdependent view* of the self.

APPLICATIONS

- *Self-report inventories*, such as the MMPI and NEO, ask subjects to describe themselves.
- Self-report inventories are valuable assessment devices, but they are vulnerable to sources of error, including deception, the social desirability bias, and response sets.
- *Projective tests*, which depend on subjects' responses to ambiguous stimuli, have poor reliability and validity.
- *Hindsight bias* often leads people to assert that "I knew it all along" in discussing outcomes they did not actually predict.

SOCIAL BEHAVIOR

Themes in this Chapter

Empiricism   Cultural Heritage   Multifactorial Causation   Subjectivity of Experience

W2 Photography/Fancy/Corbis

Audrey, a 16-year-old junior in high school, takes her cell phone with her everywhere, yet she is loathe to actually talk on her phone. She will do anything to avoid phone conversations. The immediacy of real-time conversation intimidates her. It's not that her phone goes unused. She uses it constantly for texting, which she prefers because she can take time to think and edit her thoughts. She also uses her phone's camera all day long. She snaps away and posts many pictures to Facebook. "I like to feel that my life is up there," she says. But the life depicted on her Facebook profile is a carefully crafted one. She agonizes over which photos to post. Which ones will portray her in the best light?

The comments Audrey gets about what she posts shape what she does next. Say Audrey experiments with a flirty style on Facebook. If she gets a good response from her Facebook friends, she'll escalate the flirty tone. One day, she tries out "an ironic, witty" tone in her wall posts. The response is not particularly enthusiastic, so she backs off. Friends who know Audrey in real life give her some leeway as she bends reality a bit. She reciprocates by not challenging their self-presentations.

But sometimes a little spat online can spin out of control. Audrey clashed with a classmate, Logan, in a chat room one day. Feeling she'd been wrong, she apologized to him the next day at school. But Logan wasn't satisfied. He brought the quarrel back online, this time posting his side of the story on Audrey's Facebook page, where all her friends would see it. Audrey felt she had to fight back to counter his smoldering version of what had happened. Even six months later, she and Logan, who had been "really good friends" avoided each other in the hall. Eventually, Logan apologized, but it was "an online apology. It's cheap. It's easy. All you have to do is type 'I'm sorry.'" With an online apology, there are still unanswered questions.

Despite her own beliefs about doing certain things in person, Audrey acknowledges that she once broke up with a boyfriend online. She readily admits that she endorses the norm that one should not break off a relationship via text or other online communication, but she claims she just couldn't help herself. "I felt so bad, because I really did care for him, and I couldn't get myself to say it. . . . I wasn't trying to chicken out, I just couldn't form the words, so I had to do it online, and I wish I hadn't. He deserved to have me do it in person. . . . I'm very sorry for it. I just think it was a really cold move, and kind of lame."

SOURCE: Turkle, S. (2011). *Alone together*. New York: Basic Books, pp. 189–197.

The preceding account is a real story, taken from Sherry Turkle's book *Alone Together* (2011), which provides a fascinating analysis of how modern technology is altering the fabric of our social relationships. Audrey's story illustrates something that you probably already know: social relationships assume enormous importance in our lives. Audrey, like most of us, is deeply concerned about how others perceive her. She agonizes over the demise of her friendship with Logan and her inability to break up with her boyfriend face-to-face. Audrey's story also illustrates how advances in technology are reshaping the nature of our social behavior. More and more of our social interactions are migrating onto the Internet. Intimate relationships are increasingly forged at online dating sites. Work groups are conducting more and more of their business from distant locations via the Internet. People routinely form their impressions of others from what is posted on social networking sites. Whether these shifts will prove to be fundamental or superficial alterations in our social landscape remains to be seen.

In any event, in this chapter we take a look at our social world. *Social psychology* **is the branch of psychology concerned with the way individuals' thoughts, feelings, and behaviors are influenced by others.** Social psychologists study how people are affected by the actual, imagined, or implied presence of others. Their interest is not limited to individuals' interactions with others because people can engage in social behavior even when they're alone. For instance, if you were driving by yourself on a deserted highway and tossed your trash out your car window, your littering would still be a social action. It would defy social norms, reflect your socialization and attitudes, and have repercussions (albeit, small) for other people in your society. Social psychologists often study individual behavior in a social context.

Key Learning Goals

- Understand how physical appearance and stereotypes can influence impressions of others.

- Discuss the subjectivity of social perception and evolutionary explanations for bias in person perception.

12.1 PERSON PERCEPTION: FORMING IMPRESSIONS OF OTHERS

Can you remember the first meeting of your introductory psychology class? What kind of impression did your professor make on you that day? Did your instructor appear to be confident? Easygoing? Pompous? Open-minded? Cynical? Friendly? Were your first impressions supported or undermined by subsequent observations? When you interact with people, you're constantly engaged in *person perception—***the process of forming impressions of others.** In this section, we consider some of the factors that influence, and often distort, people's perceptions of others.

Effects of Physical Appearance

"Don't judge a book by its cover." People know better than to let physical attractiveness determine their perceptions of others' personal qualities. Or do they? Recent studies have found that good-looking people command more of our attention than less-attractive individuals do (Lorenzo, Biesanz, & Human, 2010). And a number of studies have shown that judgments of others' personality are often swayed by their appearance, especially their physical attractiveness. People tend to ascribe desirable personality characteristics to those who are good looking. This phenomenon has been referred to as the *attractiveness stereotype* or the *what is beautiful is good effect.* Attractive people tend to be seen as more sociable, friendly, poised, warm, and well adjusted than those who are less attractive (Macrae & Quadflieg, 2010). One recent study, focusing on the Big Five personality traits, found that attractive women were viewed as more agreeable, extraverted, conscientious, open to experience, and emotionally stable (lower in neuroticism) than less attractive women (Segal-Caspi, Roccas, & Sagiv, 2012). In reality, research findings suggest that little correlation exists between attractiveness and personality traits (Segal-Caspi et al., 2012).

You might guess that physical attractiveness would influence perceptions of competence less than perceptions of personality, but the data suggest otherwise. People have a surprisingly strong tendency to view good-looking individuals as more competent than less-attractive individuals (Langlois et al., 2000). This bias pays off for good-looking people because they tend to secure better jobs and earn higher salaries than less-attractive individuals (Senior et al., 2007). For example, a recent study found that real estate agents who were rated as highly attractive were able to secure home listings with higher prices than their less attractive competitors, which presumably translates into higher commissions and greater income (Salter, Mixon, & King, 2012). Aware of findings such as these, Judge, Hurst, and Simon (2009) set out to compare the impact of brains versus beauty on income. As one would expect (and hope), intelligence was more strongly related to earnings (correlation = .50) than good looks were. But the correlation of .24 between attractiveness and income was not trivial. Of course, the tragic flipside of the attractiveness stereotype is that unattractive people are often viewed in a negative light, and this bias can have unfortunate consequences. For instance, one recent study in the workplace found that unattractive employees face more hostile and abusive behavior (hurtful comments, rude actions, making fun of them) than their more attractive counterparts (Scott & Judge, 2013).

Perceptions of people's faces are particularly influential. Based on a split-second glance at someone's face, people routinely draw inferences about the person's personality, social dominance, and sexual orientation (Uleman & Saribay, 2012). Even 3- to 4-year-old children make characters judgments based on faces that resemble those made by adults (Cogsdill et al., 2014). These findings suggest that our reactions to faces may have evolutionary roots (Zebrowitz & Montepare, 2015).

These gut reactions appear to have important consequences in the real world. For example, studies show that perceptions of competence based solely on facial appearance predict outcomes in U.S. elections surprisingly well (Olivola & Todorov, 2010). However, U.S. elections typically involve only two candidates, who to some extent have been prescreened by their political parties for attractiveness, which may limit the generalizability of these results. Hence, one recent study examined a presidential election in Bulgaria, where there were eighteen candidates (Sussman, Petkova, & Todorov, 2013). More than 200 U.S. residents rated the competence (and other qualities) of these eighteen candidates, based on head shots. These competence ratings correlated .77 with where the candidates finished in the actual election! Thus, voters' decisions, which ought to be based on multifaceted assessments of candidates' abilities, values, and political positions, appear to be swayed considerably by intuitive judgments of candidates' faces.

Stereotypes

Stereotypes can have a dramatic effect on the process of person perception. **Stereotypes are widely held beliefs that people have certain characteristics because of their membership in a particular group.** The most common stereotypes in our society are those based on gender, age, and membership in ethnic or occupational groups. People who subscribe to traditional *gender stereotypes* tend to assume that women are emotional, submissive, illogical, and passive, while men are unemotional, dominant, logical, and aggressive. Preconceived notions that Jews are mercenary, blacks have rhythm, Germans are methodical, and Italians are passionate are examples of common *ethnic stereotypes*. *Occupational stereotypes* suggest that lawyers are manipulative, computer programmers are nerdy, accountants are conforming, artists are moody, and so forth.

People have a tendency to view good-looking men and women as warm, friendly, bright, and competent. This stereotype of attractive people can work to their advantage in the workplace and other spheres of life.

Stereotyping is a normal cognitive process that is often automatic and that saves on the time and effort required to get a handle on people individually (Fiske & Russell, 2010). Stereotypes save energy by simplifying our social world. However, this conservation of energy often comes at some cost in terms of accuracy. Stereotypes tend to be broad overgeneralizations that ignore the diversity within social groups and foster inaccurate perceptions of people (Bodenhausen & Morales, 2013). Obviously, not all males, Jews, and lawyers behave alike. Most people who subscribe to stereotypes realize that not all members of a group are identical. However, people may still tend to assume that males, Jews, and lawyers are *more likely* than others to have certain characteristics.

Subjectivity in Person Perception

Stereotypes create biases in person perception that often lead to confirmation of people's expectations about others. If any ambiguity exists in someone's behavior, people are likely to interpret what they see in a way that's consistent with their expectations (Olson, Roese, & Zanna, 1996). People not only see what they expect to see, they also tend to overestimate how often they see it (Risen, Gilovich, & Dunning, 2007). **The *illusory correlation* occurs when people estimate that they have encountered more confirmations of an association between social traits than they have actually seen.** People also tend to underestimate the number of disconfirmations they have encountered, as illustrated by statements such as "I've never met an honest lawyer."

Memory processes can contribute to confirmatory biases in person perception in a variety of ways. Often, individuals selectively recall facts that fit with their stereotypes (Quinn, Macrae, & Bodenhausen, 2003). Evidence for such a tendency was found in a study by Cohen (1981). In this experiment, subjects watched a videotape of a woman, described as either a waitress or a librarian, who engaged in a variety of activities, including listening to classical music, drinking beer, and watching TV. When asked to recall what the woman did during the filmed sequence, participants tended to remember activities consistent with their stereotypes of waitresses and librarians. For instance, participants who thought the woman was a waitress tended to recall her drinking beer, whereas subjects who thought she was a librarian tended to recall her listening to classical music.

An Evolutionary Perspective on Bias in Person Perception

Why is the process of person perception riddled with bias? Evolutionary psychologists argue that many of the biases seen in social perception were adaptive in humans' ancestral environment (Krebs & Denton, 1997). For example, they argue that person perception is swayed by physical attractiveness because attractiveness was associated with reproductive potential in women and with health, vigor, and the accumulation of material resources in men.

Evolutionary theorists attribute the human tendency to automatically categorize others to our distant ancestors' need to quickly separate friend from foe (Park, 2012). They assert that humans are programmed by evolution to immediately classify people as members of an *ingroup*—**a group that one belongs to and identifies with,** or as members of an *outgroup*—**a group that one does not belong to or identify with.** This crucial categorization is thought to structure subsequent perceptions. Ingroup members tend to be viewed in a favorable light, whereas outgroup members tend to be viewed in terms of various negative stereotypes ("They are inferior; they are all alike"). In addition, in some circumstances, there are automatic biases toward viewing outgroup members as hostile and threatening (Park, 2012). Thus, evolutionary psychologists assert that much of the bias in person perception is due to cognitive mechanisms that have been wired into the human brain by natural selection.

12.2 ATTRIBUTION PROCESSES: EXPLAINING BEHAVIOR

12.2

Key Learning Goals

- Distinguish between internal and external attributions, and summarize Weiner's theory of attributions for success and failure.
- Identify some types of bias in patterns of attribution, including cultural variations.

It's Friday evening and you're sitting around at home feeling bored. You call a few friends to see whether they'd like to go out. They all say that they'd love to go, but they have other commitments and they can't. Their commitments sound vague, and you feel that their reasons for not going out with you are rather flimsy. How do you explain these rejections? Do your friends really have commitments? Are they worn out by school and work? Are they just lazy and apathetic about going out? These questions illustrate a process that people engage in routinely: the explanation of behavior. *Attributions* play a key role in these explanatory efforts, and they have significant effects on social relations.

What are attributions? *Attributions* **are inferences that people draw about the causes of events, others' behavior, and their own behavior.** If you conclude that a friend turned down your invitation because she's overworked, you've made an attribution about the cause of her behavior. If you conclude that you're stuck at home with nothing to do because you failed to plan ahead, you've made an attribution about the cause of an event (being stuck at home). *Why do people make attributions?* Individuals make attributions because they have a strong need to understand their experiences. They want to make sense out of their own behavior, others' actions, and the events in their lives.

Internal Versus External Attributions

Fritz Heider (1958) was the first to describe how people make attributions. He asserted that people tend to locate the cause of behavior either *within a person,* attributing it to personal factors, or *outside a person,* attributing it to environmental factors.

Elaborating on Heider's insight, various theorists have agreed that explanations of behavior and events can be categorized as internal or external attributions (Jones & Davis, 1965; Kelley, 1967). *Internal attributions* **ascribe the causes of behavior to personal dispositions, traits, abilities, and feelings.** *External attributions* **ascribe the causes of behavior to situational demands and environmental constraints.** For example, if a friend's business fails, you might attribute it to your friend's lack of business knowledge (an internal, personal factor) or to negative trends in the nation's economic climate (an external, situational explanation). Parents who find out that their teenage son has just banged up the car may blame it on his carelessness (an internal attribution) or on slippery road conditions (an external attribution).

Internal and external attributions can have a tremendous impact on everyday interpersonal interactions. Blaming a friend's business failure on poor business smarts as opposed to a poor economy will have a great impact on how you view your friend—not to mention on whether you'll lend him or her money in the future. Likewise, if parents attribute their son's automobile accident to slippery road conditions, they're likely to deal with the event very differently than if they attribute it to his carelessness.

Attributions for Success and Failure

Some psychologists have sought to discover additional dimensions of attributional thinking besides the internal-external dimension. After studying the attributions that people make in explaining success and failure, Bernard Weiner (1980, 1994, 2012) concluded that people often focus on the *stability* of the causes underlying behavior. According to Weiner, the stable-unstable dimension in attribution cuts across the internal-external dimension, creating four types of attributions for success and failure, as shown in **Figure 12.1**.

FIGURE 12.1

Weiner's model of attributions for success and failure. Weiner's model assumes that people's explanations for success and failure emphasize internal versus external causes and stable versus unstable causes. Examples of causal factors that fit into each of the four cells in Weiner's model are shown in the diagram.

SOURCE: Weiner, B., Friese, I., Kukla, A., Reed, L., & Rosenbaum, R. M. (1972). Perceiving the causes of success and failure. In E. E. Jones, D. E. Kanouse, H. H. Kelley, R. E. Nisbett, S. Valins, & B. Weiner (Eds.) *Perceiving the causes of behavior.* Morristown, NJ: General Learning Press. Used by permission of Bernard Weiner.

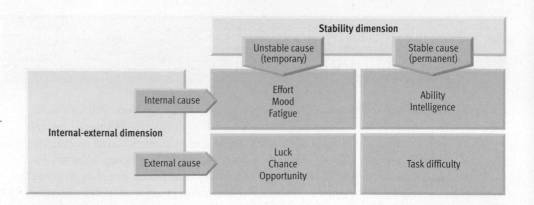

	Stability dimension	
	Unstable cause (temporary)	Stable cause (permanent)
Internal cause	Effort Mood Fatigue	Ability Intelligence
External cause	Luck Chance Opportunity	Task difficulty

Internal-external dimension

Let's apply Weiner's model to a concrete event. Imagine that you're contemplating why you failed to get a job you wanted. You might attribute your setback to internal factors that are stable (lack of ability) or unstable (inadequate effort to put together an eye-catching résumé). Or you might attribute your setback to external factors that are stable (too much outstanding competition) or unstable (bad luck). If you got the job, the explanations you might offer for your success would fall into the same four categories: internal-stable (your excellent ability), internal-unstable (your hard work to assemble a superb résumé), external-stable (lack of top-flight competition), and external-unstable (good luck).

Weiner's model can be used to understand complex issues in the real world. For example, when people analyze the causes of poverty, their explanations tend to fit neatly into the cells of Weiner's model: internal-stable (laziness, lack of thrift); internal-unstable (financially draining illness); external-stable (discrimination, inadequate government programs for training); and external-unstable (bad luck, economic recession) (Weiner, Osborne, & Rudolph, 2011) Moreover, using an

CONCEPT CHECK 12.1

Analyzing Attributions

Check your understanding of attribution processes by analyzing possible explanations for an athletic team's success. Imagine that the women's track team at your school has just won a regional championship that qualifies them for the national tournament. Around the campus, you hear people attribute the team's success to a variety of factors. Examine the attributions shown below and place each of them in one of the cells of Weiner's model of attribution (just record the letter inside the cell). The answers are in Appendix A.

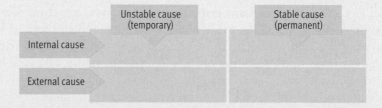

	Unstable cause (temporary)	Stable cause (permanent)
Internal cause		
External cause		

a. "They won only because the best two athletes on Central State's team were out with injuries—talk about good fortune!"

b. "They won because they have some of the best talent in the country."

c. "Anybody could win this region; the competition is far below average in comparison with the rest of the country."

d. "They won because they put in a great deal of last-minute effort and practice, and they were incredibly fired up for the regional tourney after last year's near miss."

© Christo/Shutterstock.com

attributional framework, research has shed light on why people disagree about how to reduce poverty. Liberals tend to attribute poverty to external causes, such as discrimination, poorly crafted government policies, recessions, and so forth (Weiner, 2006). In contrast, conservatives tend to attribute poverty to internal causes, such as laziness, lack of thrift, elevated alcoholism/drug abuse, and so forth. These differences in attributions for poverty go a long way toward explaining why liberals tend to favor increased public assistance for the poor, whereas conservatives tend to be less enthusiastic about such programs. Thus, the attributions we make can shape our thinking on complex, important issues.

Bias in Attribution

Attributions are only inferences. Your attributions may not be the correct explanations for events. Paradoxical as it may seem, people often arrive at inaccurate explanations even when they contemplate the causes of *their own behavior*. Attributions ultimately represent guesswork about the causes of events, and these guesses tend to be slanted in certain directions. Let's look at the principal biases seen in attribution.

Actor-Observer Bias

Your view of your own behavior can be quite different from the view of someone else observing you. When an actor (the person exhibiting the behavior) and an observer draw inferences about the causes of the actor's behavior, they often make different attributions. **The *fundamental attribution error* refers to observers' bias in favor of internal attributions in explaining others' behavior.** Of course, in many instances, an internal attribution may not be an "error." However, observers have a curious tendency to overestimate the likelihood that an actor's behavior reflects personal qualities rather than situational factors (Krull, 2001). Why? Primarily because attributing others' behavior to their dispositions is a relatively effortless, almost automatic process. In contrast, explaining people's behavior in terms of situational factors requires more thought and effort (see **Figure 12.2**; Krull & Erickson, 1995).

To illustrate the gap that often exists between actors' and observers' attributions, imagine you're visiting your bank and you fly into a rage over a mistake made on your account. Observers who witness your rage are likely to make an internal attribution and infer that you are surly, temperamental, and quarrelsome. They may be right, but if asked, you'd probably attribute your rage to the frustrating situation. Perhaps you're normally a calm, easygoing person, but today you've been in line for 20 minutes, you just straightened out a similar error by the same bank last week, and you're being treated rudely by the teller. Observers often are unaware of situational considerations such as these. Hence, they tend to make internal attributions for another's behavior (Gilbert, 1998).

In contrast, the circumstances that have influenced an actor's behavior tend to be more salient to the actor. Hence, actors are more likely than observers to locate the cause of their behavior in the situation. In general, then, *actors favor external attributions for their behavior, while observers are more likely to explain the same behavior with internal attributions* (Jones & Nisbett, 1971; Krueger, Ham, & Linford, 1996).

Self-Serving Bias

The self-serving bias in attribution comes into play when people attempt to explain success and failure (Mezulis et al., 2004). **The *self-serving bias* is the tendency to attribute one's successes to personal factors and one's failures to situational factors.** In explaining *failure*, the usual actor-observer biases are apparent. But in explaining *success*, the usual actor-observer differences are reversed to some degree: actors prefer internal attributions so they can take credit for their triumphs. Interestingly, this bias grows stronger as time passes after an event, so that people tend to take progressively more credit for their successes and less blame for their failures (Burger, 1986). The self-serving bias is intended to bolster self-esteem and subjective well-being, and the evidence suggests that it is at least partially successful in this regard (Sanjuan & Magallares, 2014).

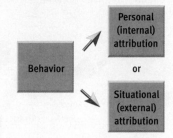

Traditional model of attribution

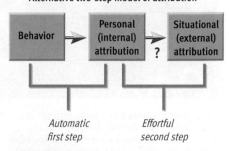

Alternative two-step model of attribution

Automatic first step   Effortful second step

FIGURE 12.2

An alternative view of the fundamental attribution error. According to Gilbert (1989) and others, the nature of attribution processes favors the *fundamental attribution error.* Traditional models of attribution assume that internal and external attributions are an either-or proposition requiring equal amounts of effort. In contrast, the two-step model of attribution posits that people tend to automatically make internal attributions with little effort, then *may* expend additional effort to adjust for the influence of situational factors, which can lead to an external attribution. Thus, external attributions for others' behavior require more thought and effort, which makes them less common than personal attributions.

Culture and Attributions

Do the patterns of attribution observed in subjects from Western societies transcend culture? Perhaps not. Some interesting cultural disparities have emerged in attribution processes.

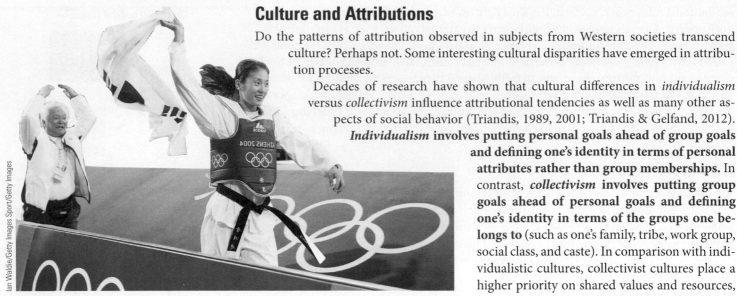

Decades of research have shown that cultural differences in *individualism* versus *collectivism* influence attributional tendencies as well as many other aspects of social behavior (Triandis, 1989, 2001; Triandis & Gelfand, 2012). *Individualism* **involves putting personal goals ahead of group goals and defining one's identity in terms of personal attributes rather than group memberships.** In contrast, *collectivism* **involves putting group goals ahead of personal goals and defining one's identity in terms of the groups one belongs to** (such as one's family, tribe, work group, social class, and caste). In comparison with individualistic cultures, collectivist cultures place a higher priority on shared values and resources, cooperation, mutual interdependence, and concern for how one's actions will affect other group members. Generally speaking, North American and Western European cultures tend to be individualistic, whereas Asian, African, and Latin American cultures tend to be collectivistic (Hofstede, 1980, 1983, 2001).

Triumphant athletes from cultures high in collectivism typically exhibit different attributional biases than winning athletes from Western societies that are high in individualism. Collectivist cultures tend to promote a self-effacing bias in explaining success, rather than a self-serving bias.

How does individualism versus collectivism relate to patterns of attribution? The evidence suggests that collectivist cultures may promote different attributional biases than individualistic cultures do. For example, although people from collectivist societies are not immune to the *fundamental attribution error,* they appear to be less susceptible to it than those from individualistic societies (Koenig & Dean, 2011). Research also suggests that *self-serving bias* may be particularly prevalent in individualistic, Western societies, where an emphasis on competition and high self-esteem motivates people to try to impress others, as well as themselves (Mezulis et al., 2004). Like the fundamental attribution error, the self-serving bias *is* seen in collectivist cultures, but not as frequently as in Western societies (Koenig & Dean, 2011).

CONCEPT CHECK 12.2

Recognizing Bias in Social Cognition

Check your understanding of bias in social cognition by identifying various types of errors that are common in person perception and attribution. Imagine that you're a nonvoting student member of a college committee at Southwest State University that is hiring a new political science professor. As you listen to the committee's discussion, you hear examples of (a) the illusory correlation effect, (b) stereotyping, and (c) the fundamental attribution error. Indicate which of these is at work in the excerpts from committee members' deliberations below. The answers are in Appendix A.

_____ 1. "I absolutely won't consider the fellow who arrived 30 minutes late for his interview. Anybody who can't make a job interview on time is either irresponsible or hopelessly disorganized. I don't care what he says about the airline messing up his reservations."

_____ 2. "You know, I was very, very impressed with the young female applicant, and I would love to hire her, but every time we add a young woman to the faculty in liberal arts, she gets pregnant within the first year." The committee chairperson, who has heard this line from this professor before replies, "You always say that, so I finally did a systematic check of what's happened in the past. Of the last fourteen women hired in liberal arts, only one has become pregnant within a year."

_____ 3. "The first one I want to rule out is the guy who's been practicing law for the last 10 years. Although he has an excellent background in political science, I just don't trust lawyers. They're all ambitious, power hungry, manipulative cutthroats. He'll be a divisive force in the department."

12.3
Key Learning Goals
- Understand the role of physical attractiveness, similarity, and reciprocity in attraction.
- Discuss theoretical views of love and how culture and the Internet relate to romantic relationships.
- Understand evolutionary analyses of mating preferences.

"I just don't know what she sees in him. She could do so much better for herself. I suppose he's a nice guy, but they're just not right for each other." Can't you imagine someone in your social circle making these comments in discussing a mutual friend's new boyfriend? You've probably heard similar remarks on many occasions. These comments illustrate people's interest in analyzing the dynamics of attraction. *Interpersonal attraction refers to positive feelings toward another person.* Social psychologists use this term broadly to encompass a variety of experiences, including liking, friendship, admiration, lust, and love.

Key Factors in Attraction

Many factors influence who is attracted to whom. Here we'll discuss factors that promote the development of liking, friendship, and love. Although these are different types of attraction, the interpersonal dynamics at work in each are surprisingly similar.

Physical Attractiveness

It is often said that "beauty is only skin deep." But the empirical evidence suggests that most people don't behave in a manner that is consistent with this saying. Research shows that the key determinant of romantic attraction for both genders is the physical attractiveness of the other person (Sprecher & Duck, 1994). Many studies have demonstrated the singular prominence of physical attractiveness in the initial stage of dating and have shown that it continues to influence the course of commitment as relationships evolve (Sprecher et al., 2015). In the realm of romance, being physically attractive appears to be more important for females' desirability (Regan, 2008). For example, in a study of college students (Speed & Gangestad, 1997), the correlation between romantic popularity (assessed by peer ratings) and physical attractiveness was higher for females (.76) than for males (.47).

Although people prefer physically attractive partners in romantic relationships, they may consider their own level of attractiveness in pursuing dates. *The matching hypothesis proposes that males and females of approximately equal physical attractiveness are likely to select each other as partners.* The matching hypothesis is supported by evidence that dating and married couples tend to be similar in level of physical attractiveness (Regan, 2008). There is some debate, however, about whether people match up by mutual choice. Some theorists believe that individuals mostly pursue highly attractive partners and that their matching is the result of social forces beyond their control, such as rejection by more attractive others (Taylor et al., 2011).

Similarity Effects

Is it true that "birds of a feather flock together," or do "opposites attract"? Research provides far more support for the former than the latter (Sprecher et al., 2015). One study found that people sit closer to others who are similar to them on simple physical traits, such as hair length, hair color, and whether they wear glasses (Mackinnon, Jordan, & Wilson, 2011). Married and dating couples tend to be similar in age, race, religion, social class, education, intelligence, physical attractiveness, and attitudes (Kalmijn, 1998; Watson et al., 2004). The similarity principle operates in both friendships and romantic relationships regardless of sexual orientation (Fehr, 2008; Morry, 2009). The most obvious explanation for these correlations is that similarity causes attraction (Byrne, 1997), perhaps because we assume that similar others will like us (Montoya & Horton, 2012). However, research also suggests that attraction can foster similarity (Sprecher, 2014) because people who are close gradually modify their attitudes in ways that make them more congruent, a phenomenon called *attitude alignment.*

According to the matching hypothesis, males and females who are similar in physical attractiveness are likely to be drawn together. This type of matching can also influence the formation of friendships.

© Warren Goldswain/Shutterstock.com

▶ **REALITY CHECK**

Misconception

In the realm of romance, opposites attract.

Reality

There is absolutely no empirical evidence to support this folklore. Research consistently shows that couples tend to be similar in intelligence, education, social status, ethnicity, physical attractiveness, and attitudes. Dissimilarity does not foster attraction.

Reciprocity Effects

In interpersonal attraction, *reciprocity* **involves liking those who show that they like us.** In general, research indicates that we tend to like those who show that they like us and that we tend to see others as liking us more if we like them. Thus, it appears that liking breeds liking, and loving promotes loving (Whitchurch, Wilson, & Gilbert, 2011). Reciprocating attraction generally entails providing friends and intimate partners with positive feedback that results in a *self-enhancement* effect—in other words, you help them feel good about themselves (Sedikides & Strube, 1997).

Perspectives on the Mystery of Love

Love has proven to be an elusive subject. It's difficult to define and study because there are many types of love. Nonetheless, psychologists have begun to make some progress in their study of love.

Passionate and Companionate Love

In an influential analysis, some theorists have proposed that romantic relationships are characterized by two kinds of love: passionate love and companionate love (Berscheid, 1988; Hatfield & Rapson, 1993). *Passionate love* **is a complete absorption in another that includes tender sexual feelings and the agony and ecstasy of intense emotion.** Passionate love has its ups and downs. It's associated with large swings in positive and negative emotions (Reis & Aron, 2008). *Companionate love* **is warm, trusting, tolerant affection for another whose life is deeply intertwined with one's own.** Passionate and companionate love *can* coexist. They don't, however, necessarily go hand in hand. Initially, it was thought that passionate love peaks in intensity early in relationships and then declines significantly over time. However, more recent research suggests that in relationships that remain intact, the erosion of passionate love tends to be gradual and modest, with levels remaining fairly high in most couples (Fehr, 2015; O'Leary et al., 2012).

Research demonstrates that passionate love is a powerful motivational force that produces profound changes in people's thinking, emotion, and behavior (Acevedo & Aron, 2014). Interestingly, brain-imaging research indicates that when people think about someone they are passionately in love with, these thoughts light up the dopamine circuits in the brain that are known to be activated by cocaine and other addictive drugs (Acevedo & Aron, 2014). Perhaps that explains why passionate love sometimes resembles an addiction.

Love as Attachment

In another groundbreaking analysis of love, Hazan and Shaver (1987) looked at similarities between adult love and attachment relationships in infancy. We noted in Chapter 10 that infant-caregiver bonding, or *attachment*, emerges in the first year of life. Early attachments vary in quality, and infants tend to fall into three groups (Ainsworth et al., 1978). Most infants develop a *secure attachment*. However, some are very anxious when separated from their caregiver, a syndrome called *anxious-ambivalent attachment*. A third group of infants, characterized by *avoidant attachment*, never bond very well with their caregiver.

According to Hazan and Shaver, romantic love is an attachment process, and people's intimate relationships in adulthood follow the same form as their attachments in infancy. In their theory, a person who had an anxious-ambivalent attachment in infancy will tend to have romantic relations marked by anxiety and ambivalence in adulthood. In other words, people relive their early bonding experiences with their parents in their romantic relationships in adulthood.

Hazan and Shaver's (1987) initial survey study provided striking support for their theory. They found that adults' love relationships could be sorted into groups that paralleled the three patterns of attachment seen in infants (see **Figure 12.3**). *Secure adults* found it relatively easy to get close to others and described their love relations as trusting.

Adult attachment style

Secure
I find it relatively easy to get close to others and am comfortable depending on them and having them depend on me. I don't often worry about being abandoned or about someone getting too close to me.

Avoidant
I am somewhat uncomfortable being close to others; I find it difficult to trust them, difficult to allow myself to depend on them. I am nervous when anyone gets too close, and often love partners want me to be more intimate than I feel comfortable being.

Anxious/ambivalent
I find that others are reluctant to get as close as I would like. I often worry that my partner doesn't really love me or won't want to stay with me. I want to merge completely with another person, and this desire sometimes scares people away.

FIGURE 12.3

Attachment and romantic relationships.
According to Hazan and Shaver (1987), people's romantic relationships in adulthood are similar in form to their attachment patterns in infancy, which fall into three categories. The three attachment styles seen in adult intimate relations are described here. (Based on Hazan and Shaver, 1986, 1987)

Anxious-ambivalent adults reported a preoccupation with love, accompanied by expectations of rejection, and they described their love relations as volatile and marked by jealousy. *Avoidant adults* found it difficult to get close to others and described their love relations as lacking intimacy and trust. Research eventually showed that attachment patterns are reasonably stable over time and that people's working models of attachment are carried forward from one relationship to the next (Simpson & Winterheld, 2012). These findings supported the notion that individuals' infant attachment experiences shape their intimate relations in adulthood.

Research on the correlates of adult attachment styles has grown exponentially since the mid-1990s. Consistent with the original theory, research has shown that securely attached individuals have more committed, satisfying, intimate, well-adjusted, and longer-lasting relationships than do people with anxious-ambivalent or avoidant attachment styles (Pietromonaco & Beck, 2015). Moreover, studies have shown that people with different attachment styles are predisposed to think, feel, and behave differently in their relationships (Mikulincer & Shaver, 2013). For example, people high in attachment anxiety tend to behave in awkward ways that undermine their dating success. Worried about the likelihood of rejection, they end up courting rejection by acting cold, wary, disengaged, and preoccupied with themselves (McClure & Lydon, 2014). When they *do* get involved in romantic relationships, people high in attachment anxiety tend to overreact emotionally to conflict with their partners. Their exaggerated expressions of hurt and vulnerability are designed to make their partners feel guilty, but these manipulative efforts end up having a negative impact on their relationship (Overall et al., 2014).

Culture and Close Relationships

The limited evidence available suggests both similarities and differences among cultures in romantic relationships (Schmitt, 2005). For the most part, similarities have been seen when research has focused on what people look for in prospective mates—such as mutual attraction, kindness, and intelligence (Fehr, 2013). Cultures vary, however, in their emphasis on love—especially passionate love—as a prerequisite for marriage. Passionate love as the basis for marriage is an 18th-century invention of individualistic Western culture (Stone, 1977). In contrast, marriages arranged by families and other go-betweens remain common in cultures high in collectivism, including India, Japan, China, and many Middle East countries (Eastwick, 2013). In collectivist societies, people contemplating marriage tend to think in terms of "What will my parents and other people say?" rather than "What does my heart say?" Although romantic love is routinely seen in collectivist societies (Fehr, 2013), subjects from those societies are less likely than subjects from cultures high in individualism to report that romantic love is important for marriage (Fehr, 2015).

People from Western societies are often dumbfounded by collectivist cultures' deemphasis on love and their penchant for arranged marriages. Most of us assume that our modern conception of love as the basis for marriage must result in better marital relationships than collectivist cultures' "antiquated" beliefs. However, the limited evidence available is a mixed bag and provides little empirical support for this ethnocentric view (Eastwick, 2013; Triandis, 1994).

The Internet and Close Relationships

In recent years, the Internet has dramatically expanded opportunities for people to meet and develop close relationships through social networking sites (Google+, Facebook), online dating services, email, and chat rooms. Critics are concerned that Internet relationships tend to be superficial. Research, however, suggests that virtual relationships can be just as intimate as face-to-face ones and are sometimes even closer (Bargh, McKenna, & Fitzsimons, 2002). Moreover, many virtual relationships evolve into face-to-face interactions (Boase & Wellman, 2006).

Marriages based on romantic love are the norm in individualistic, Western cultures. However, in more collectivistic cultures, arranged marriages are common.

Facebook and similar social networking websites are changing patterns of social interaction. Research suggests that Facebook usage can help some people forge social connections, but it can foster feelings of social isolation in other people.

Facebook appears to fulfill two important motives: the need to belong and the need to engage in self-presentation or impression management (Nadkarni & Hofmann, 2012). Research on Facebook users suggests that people's profiles are reasonably accurate self-presentations (Wilson, Gosling, & Graham, 2012). Obviously, people try to portray themselves in a positive light, but so do people in offline interactions. Some theorists have expressed concern that as people spend more time in online interactions, they will spend less time with each other, resulting in loneliness and isolation (Turkle, 2011). Research suggests, paradoxically, that people's level of Facebook usage is correlated with both an increased sense of connection and disconnection (Sheldon, Abad, & Hinsch, 2011). On the one hand, feelings of loneliness appear to motivate greater dependence on Facebook as a coping strategy, but on the other hand, people who rely heavily on Facebook do forge rewarding connections with others. The benefits of Facebook are seen primarily in those who engage in active interaction with others (leaving wall posts, messaging friends), as opposed to those who passively view others' content and updates (Burke, Marlow, & Lento, 2010). That said, a recent study found that Facebook use was associated with temporary decreases in subjective well-being (Kross et al., 2013), perhaps because people feel envious of their friends' good news and impressive-looking self-presentations. Another study found that heavy use of Facebook sometimes caused conflicts between romantic partners (Clayton, Nagurney, & Smith, 2013).

The power of similarity effects provides the foundation for some of the Internet's most successful online dating sites. Prior to 2000, web dating sites were basically just an electronic variation on the personal ads that had been around for decades—with the addition of sophisticated search capabilities. But in 2000, eHarmony.com launched the first matching website. This site claims to use a "scientific approach" to matching people, based on compatibility. Members fill out lengthy questionnaires about their attitudes, values, interests, and so forth, and then matching algorithms are used to identify people who exhibit promising similarity. The commercial success of eHarmony.com has led many other online dating sites to add matching services. The architects of eHarmony claim that their services account for 5% of newlywed couples in the United States (Martin, 2011).

Online matching sites clearly have altered the landscape of dating and mating (Finkel et al., 2012). Online sites offer individuals access to vastly more dating candidates than they could ever meet in bars, churches, classes, and parties. The process of getting acquainted has become information-rich in unprecedented ways, as potential partners typically learn a great deal about each other before meeting face-to-face. Online matching sites claim they help people meet their "soul mates," and that their matching formulas lead to more successful romantic relationships than result from traditional dating. Is there any evidence to support these bold claims? For the most part, no (Sprecher et al., 2015). For business reasons, the competing matching sites have generally been unwilling to reveal the details of their matching algorithms and have chosen to not publish any internal research they may have conducted (Finkel et al., 2012). The notion that matching based on compatibility might foster romantic success is plausible, but with the exception of one recent study, there has been no published research. However, that single study, conducted with the cooperation of eHarmony, did yield surprisingly promising results (Cacioppo et al., 2013). Working with a sample of more than 19,000 respondents who married between 2005 and 2012, the researchers found that a marital breakup had occurred in a lower portion of those who met online (5.96%) than those who met in traditional offline venues (7.67%). A single study does not settle the issue by any means, but the initial findings are encouraging.

An Evolutionary Perspective on Attraction

Evolutionary psychologists have a great deal to say about heterosexual attraction. For example, they assert that physical appearance is an influential determinant of attraction because certain aspects of good looks can be indicators of sound health, good genes, and high fertility, all of which can contribute to reproductive potential (Maner & Ackerman, 2013). Consistent with the evolutionary view, research has found that some standards of attractiveness are more consistent across cultures than previously believed (Sugiyama, 2005). For example, *facial symmetry* seems to be a key element of attractiveness in highly diverse cultures. Facial symmetry is thought to be valued because a variety of environmental insults and developmental abnormalities are associated with physical asymmetries, which can serve as markers of relatively poor genes or health (Fink et al., 2006). Another facet of appearance that may transcend culture is *women's waist-to-hip ratio* (Singh et al., 2010). Around the world, men seem to prefer women with a moderately low waist-to-hip ratio (in the vicinity of .70), which roughly corresponds to an "hourglass figure." This appears to be a meaningful correlate of females' reproductive potential (Gallup & Frederick, 2010), as it signals that a woman is healthy, young, and not pregnant.

The most thoroughly documented findings on the evolutionary bases of heterosexual attraction are those on gender differences in mating preferences, which appear to be consistent across highly varied cultures (Neuberg, Kenrick, & Schaller, 2010). In keeping with the notion that humans are programmed by evolution to behave in ways that enhance their reproductive fitness, evidence indicates that men generally are more interested than women in seeking youthfulness and physical attractiveness in their mates because these traits should be associated with greater reproductive potential (see Chapter 9). On the other hand, research shows that women place a greater premium on prospective mates' ambition, social status, and financial potential because these traits should be associated with the ability to invest material resources in children (Griskevicius, Haselton, & Ackerman, 2015; Kenrick, Neuberg, & White, 2013).

These findings have been questioned in some studies of speed dating, which found that dating prospects' physical attractiveness did not differentially predict males' and females' romantic interest (Asendorpf, Penke, & Back, 2011; Eastwick et al., 2011). However, critics have noted that the speed dating situation may evoke short-term mating strategies (Meltzer et al., 2014), and it has long been known that when women are asked about what they prefer in a short-term partner (for casual sex), they value physical attractiveness just as much as men do (Maner & Ackerman, 2013). Critics have also wondered whether the speed dating studies included enough variation in social status and attractiveness to provide a sensitive test of the impact of these variables (Li et al., 2013). A recent study that included more people at the low end of the spectrum in terms of attractiveness and social status (thus increasing the variation on these dimensions) yielded results consistent with evolutionary theory: men placed more emphasis on the attractiveness of dating prospects, whereas women emphasized social status more (Li et al., 2013). Moreover, another study that focused on couples in their first 4 years of marriage found that partners' physical attractiveness influenced the relationship satisfaction of husbands more than wives (Meltzer et al., 2014).

Evolutionary analyses also make some interesting predictions about how women's menstrual cycles may influence their mating preferences and tactics. When women are in mid-cycle approaching ovulation—that is, when they are most fertile—their preferences shift to favor men who exhibit masculine facial and bodily features, attractiveness, and dominance (Gangestad et al., 2007; Little, Jones, & Burriss, 2007). Women's mating strategies also change when their fertility is at its peak, as they tend to wear more provocative clothing and they are more flirtatious in the presence of attractive men (Cantu et al., 2014; Durante, Li, & Haselton, 2008). Interestingly, although ovulation is far from obvious in human females, strippers earn 58% more tip money per night when they are in their most fertile period (see **Figure 12.4**; Miller, Tybur, & Jordan, 2007). Researchers aren't sure whether male patrons are "detecting" the strippers' heightened fertility or whether the ovulating dancers come on to the customers more because they are more sexually motivated.

Does the gender gap in mating priorities influence the tactics people actually use in pursuing romantic relationships? Yes, evidence indicates that during courtship, men tend

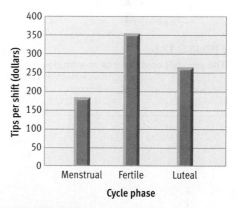

FIGURE 12.4

The menstrual cycle and strippers' earnings. Miller et al. (2007) found that strippers' tips were influenced by their menstrual cycle. As you can see in this graph, which shows the data for strippers who were not using hormonal contraception, the dancers' tips per shift were 58% higher when they were in their fertile period than when they were in their menstrual or luteal periods. (Based on Miller et al., 2007)

to emphasize their material resources, whereas women are more likely to work at enhancing their appearance (Buss, 1988). For example, men often use conspicuous consumption (the purchase of luxury goods, such as expensive cars) to signal their wealth and success to potential mating partners (Sundie et al., 2011). In a similar vein, when compared with men, women invest more time trying to enhance their attractiveness and they allocate more of their income to goods and services intended to enhance their looks (Hill et al., 2012). Furthermore, during economic downturns—when there presumably is a smaller pool of financially stable males, making competition for them tougher—women boost their spending on beauty products (Hill et al., 2012).

Another gender disparity consistent with evolutionary theory is that men show a tendency to overestimate women's sexual interest, whereas women tend to underestimate men's sexual interest (Perilloux, 2014; Perilloux, Easton, & Buss, 2012). These cognitive biases seem to be designed to reduce the probability that men will overlook sexual opportunities, while helping women to avoid being viewed as "promiscuous" (Neuberg & Schaller, 2015).

12.4 ATTITUDES: MAKING SOCIAL JUDGMENTS

Key Learning Goals

- Analyze the structure of attitudes and the link between attitudes and behavior.
- Distinguish between explicit and implicit attitudes, and explain how implicit attitudes are measured.
- Summarize how source, message, and receiver factors influence the process of persuasion.
- Clarify various theories of attitude formation and change.

What are attitudes? *Attitudes* **are positive or negative evaluations of objects of thought.** "Objects of thought" may include social issues (capital punishment or gun control, for example); groups (liberals, farmers); institutions (the Lutheran church, the Supreme Court); consumer products (yogurt, computers); and people (the president, your next-door neighbor).

Components and Dimensions of Attitudes

Attitudes can include up to three components (Briñol & Petty, 2012). The *cognitive component* of an attitude is made up of the beliefs people hold about the object of an attitude. The *affective component* consists of the *emotional feelings* stimulated by an object of thought. The *behavioral component* consists of *predispositions to act* in certain ways toward an attitude object. **Figure 12.5** provides concrete examples of how someone's attitude about gun control might be divided into its components.

FIGURE 12.5

The possible components of attitudes.
Attitudes can include cognitive, affective, and behavioral components, as illustrated here for a hypothetical person's attitude about gun control.

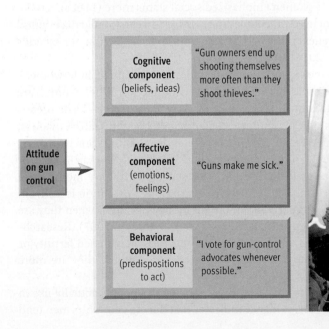

Attitude on gun control

Cognitive component (beliefs, ideas) — "Gun owners end up shooting themselves more often than they shoot thieves."

Affective component (emotions, feelings) — "Guns make me sick."

Behavioral component (predispositions to act) — "I vote for gun-control advocates whenever possible."

© Timothy A. Clary/AFP/Getty Images

Attitudes also vary along several crucial dimensions. These include their *strength, accessibility,* and *ambivalence* (Maio, Olson, & Cheung, 2013). Definitions of *attitude strength* differ. However, strong attitudes are generally viewed as ones that are firmly held (resistant to change), that are durable over time, and that have a powerful impact on behavior (Petty, Wheeler, & Tormala, 2013). The *accessibility* of an attitude refers to how often one thinks about it and how quickly it comes to mind. Highly accessible attitudes are quickly and readily available (Fabrigar, MacDonald, & Wegener, 2005). *Ambivalent attitudes* are conflicted evaluations that include both positive and negative feelings about an object of thought. When ambivalence is high, an attitude tends to be more pliable in the face of persuasion (Fabrigar & Wegener, 2010).

How well do attitudes predict actual behavior? Research on attitudes has yielded a surprising answer to this question. Studies have repeatedly shown that attitudes are mediocre predictors of people's behavior (Ajzen & Fishbein, 2005). When Wallace and colleagues (2005) reviewed 797 attitude-behavior studies, they found that the average correlation between attitudes and behavior was .41. That correlation is high enough to conclude that attitudes are a meaningful predictor of actual behavior, but they do not predict behavior nearly as well as most people assume.

Why aren't attitude-behavior relations more consistent? One consideration is that people fail to factor in the influence of attitude strength (Fabrigar & Wegener, 2010). Although strong attitudes predict behavior reasonably well (Ajzen, 2012), many attitudes are not strongly held and are only weak predictors of behavior. Inconsistent relations between attitudes and behavior are also seen because behavior depends on situational constraints (Ajzen & Fishbein, 2000, 2005). Your subjective perceptions of how people expect you to behave are especially important. For instance, you may be strongly opposed to marijuana use. However, you may not say anything when friends start passing a joint around at a party because you don't want to turn the party into an argument. In another situation, though, governed by different norms, such as a class discussion, you may speak out forcefully against marijuana use.

Implicit Attitudes: Looking Beneath the Surface

In recent years, theorists have begun to make a distinction between explicit and implicit attitudes (Blair, Dasgupta, & Glaser, 2015). **Explicit attitudes are attitudes that one holds consciously and can readily describe.** For the most part, these overt attitudes are what social psychologists have always studied until fairly recently. **Implicit attitudes are covert attitudes that are expressed in subtle automatic responses over which one has little conscious control.** It was only in the mid-1990s that social psychologists started digging beneath the surface to explore the meaning and importance of implicit attitudes. Implicit attitudes were discovered in research on prejudice, and their role in various types of prejudice continues to be the main focus of current inquiry.

Why are implicit attitudes a central issue in the study of prejudice? Because in modern societies most people have been taught that prejudicial attitudes are inappropriate, but negative stereotypes about certain groups are still widely disseminated. Although most people want to be unbiased, research has shown that these negative ideas can seep into one's subconscious mind and contaminate one's reactions to others. Thus, many people express explicit attitudes that condemn prejudice but unknowingly harbor implicit attitudes that reflect subtle forms of prejudice (Devine & Sharp, 2009; Dovidio & Gaertner, 2008).

How are implicit attitudes measured? A number of techniques have been developed, but the most widely used is the Implicit Association Test (IAT) (Greenwald, McGhee, & Schwartz, 1998). This computer-administered test measures how quickly people associate carefully chosen pairs of concepts. Let's consider how the IAT would be used to assess implicit prejudice against blacks. A series of words and pictures is presented on-screen, and subjects are urged to respond to these stimuli as quickly and as accurately as possible. In the first series of trials, respondents are instructed to press a specific

> ▶ **REALITY CHECK**

Misconception

People's attitudes are excellent predictors of their behavior.

Reality

Decades of research have shown that attitudes are undependable predictors of behavior. For a variety of reasons, the correlation between attitudes and behavior is surprisingly modest. Thus, a favorable attitude about a specific product or candidate does not necessarily translate into a purchase or vote.

FIGURE 12.6

Measuring implicit attitudes. The IAT assesses implicit prejudice against blacks by tracking how quickly subjects respond to images of black and white people paired with positive or negative words. If participants are prejudiced against African Americans, they will react more quickly to the pairings in the condition on the right. The IAT has been used to measure implicit attitudes toward a variety of groups.

key with their left hand if the stimulus is a black person or a positive word and to press another key with their right hand if the stimulus is a white person or a negative word (see **Figure 12.6**). In the second series of trials, the instructions are changed and participants are told to press the left-hand key if the stimulus is a black person or a negative word and to press the right-hand key if the stimulus is a white person or positive word. The various types of stimuli are presented in quick succession, and the computer records precise reaction times. Research shows that reaction times are quicker when liked faces are paired with positive words and disliked faces with negative words. So, if respondents have negative implicit attitudes about African Americans, the second series of trials will yield shorter average reaction times. And if this is so, the size of the difference between average reaction times in the two series provides an index of the strength of participants' implicit racism.

Since 1998, millions of people have responded to a web-based version of the IAT (Nosek, Greenwald, & Banaji, 2007). Although surveys of people's explicit attitudes suggest that prejudice has declined considerably, the IAT results show that more than 80% of respondents, both young and old, show negative implicit attitudes about the elderly. And about three-quarters of white respondents exhibit implicit prejudice against blacks. The findings also indicate that implicit prejudice against gays, the disabled, and the obese is common.

Do IAT scores based on tiny differences in reaction times predict prejudicial behavior in the real world? Yes, IAT scores are predictive of subtle but potentially important differences in behavior (Greenwald et al., 2009; Greenwald, Banaji, & Nosek, 2015). For instance, white participants' degree of implicit racial prejudice predicts how far they choose to sit from a black partner whom they expect to work with on a task (Amodio & Devine, 2006). Higher implicit racism scores in white subjects are also associated with decreased smiling, reduced eye contact, and shorter speaking time in interracial interactions (Devos, 2008). Implicit prejudice also predicts discrimination in hiring, negative attitudes about immigration, and aggression in response to provocation (Fiske & Tablante, 2015). Beyond the realm of prejudice, implicit attitudes about math predict interest and performance in math, and implicit attitudes about political candidates predict voting behavior (Blair et al., 2015).

Trying to Change Attitudes: Factors in Persuasion

Every day you're bombarded by efforts to alter your attitudes. In light of this reality, let's examine some of the factors that determine whether persuasion works. The process of persuasion includes four basic elements: the source, receiver, message, and channel (see **Figure 12.7**). **The *source* is the person who sends a communication, and the *receiver* is the person to whom the message is sent.** Thus, if you watch a presidential news

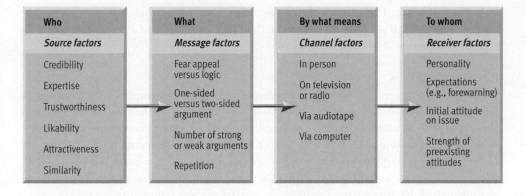

Who	What	By what means	To whom
Source factors	**Message factors**	**Channel factors**	**Receiver factors**
Credibility	Fear appeal versus logic	In person	Personality
Expertise	One-sided versus two-sided argument	On television or radio	Expectations (e.g., forewarning)
Trustworthiness		Via audiotape	Initial attitude on issue
Likability	Number of strong or weak arguments	Via computer	
Attractiveness			Strength of preexisting attitudes
Similarity	Repetition		

FIGURE 12.7

Overview of the persuasion process. The process of persuasion essentially boils down to *who* (the source) communicates *what* (the message) *by what means* (the channel) *to whom* (the receiver). Thus, four sets of variables influence the process of persuasion: source, message, channel, and receiver factors. The diagram lists some of the more important factors in each category (including some that are not discussed in the text due to space limitations). (Adapted from Lippa, 1994).

conference on TV, the president is the source, and you and millions of other viewers are the receivers. **The *message* is the information transmitted by the source, and the *channel* is the medium through which the message is sent.** Although the research on communication channels is interesting, we'll confine our discussion to source, message, and receiver variables.

Source Factors

Occasional exceptions to the general rule are seen, but persuasion tends to be more successful when the source has high *credibility* (Petty & Brinol, 2015). What gives a person credibility? Either expertise or trustworthiness. People try to convey their *expertise* by mentioning their degrees, their training, and their experience or by showing an impressive grasp of the issue at hand. Expertise is a plus, but *trustworthiness* can be even more important. Many people tend to accept messages from trustworthy sources with little scrutiny (Priester & Petty, 2003). Trustworthiness is undermined when a source appears to have something to gain. *Likability* also increases the effectiveness of a persuasive source (Neal et al., 2012). In addition, people respond better to sources who share *similarity* with them in ways that are relevant to the issue at hand (Petty & Brinol, 2015).

Message Factors

If you were going to give a speech to a local community group advocating a reduction in state taxes on corporations, you'd probably wrestle with a number of questions about how to structure your message. Should you look at both sides of the issue or should you just present your side? Should you deliver a low-key, logical speech? Or should you try to strike fear into the hearts of your listeners? These questions are concerned with message factors in persuasion.

In general, two-sided arguments seem to be more effective than one-sided presentations (Petty & Wegener, 1998). Just mentioning that an issue has two sides can increase your credibility with an audience. Fear appeals appear to work—if the message is successful in arousing fear. Research reveals that many messages intended to induce fear fail to do so. Fear appeals are most likely to work when your listeners think the dire consequences you describe as exceedingly unpleasant are fairly probable if they don't take your advice and are avoidable if they do (Das, de Wit, & Stroebe, 2003).

Frequent repetition of a message also seems to be an effective strategy (Dechêne et al., 2010), probably because of the mere exposure effect first described by Robert Zajonc. **The *mere exposure effect* is the finding that repeated exposures to a stimulus promotes greater liking of the stimulus.** In a groundbreaking study (Zajonc, 1968), participants were exposed to unfamiliar Turkish words 0, 1, 2, 5, 10, or 25 times. Subsequently, the subjects were asked to rate the degree to which they thought the words referred to something good or bad. The more subjects had been exposed to a specific word, the more favorably they rated it. Zajonc observed remarkably similar findings when participants rated the favorability of selected Chinese pictographs (the symbols used in

> **REALITY CHECK**

Misconception

Familiarity breeds contempt: the more we are exposed to something, the less we like it.

Reality

People often comment that they are sick of an incessant commercial or overexposed celebrity, but a large body of research shows that repeated exposures to something, even neutral as opposed to favorable exposures, generally lead to increased liking.

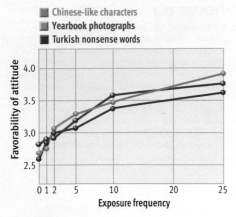

Legend:
- Chinese-like characters
- Yearbook photographs
- Turkish nonsense words

FIGURE 12.8

The mere exposure effect. In seminal research on the mere exposure effect, Robert Zajonc (1968) manipulated how often participants were exposed to various unfamiliar, neutral stimuli. As the data show here, he found that increased exposures led to increased liking. The mere exposure effect may shed light on why repetition is an effective strategy in persuasion.

Chinese writing) and when they rated the likability of people shown in yearbook photos (see **Figure 12.8**). The mere exposure effect has been replicated with many types of stimuli (Albarracin & Vargas, 2010).

Receiver Factors

What about the receiver of the persuasive message? Are some people easier to persuade than others? Undoubtedly, but transient factors, such as the forewarning a receiver gets about a persuasive effort, seem to be more influential than the receiver's personality. Consider, for instance, the old adage that "to be forewarned is to be forearmed." The value of *forewarning* does apply to targets of persuasive efforts (Janssen, Fennis, & Pruyn, 2010). When you shop for a new car, you *expect* the salespeople to work at persuading you, and to some extent this forewarning reduces the impact of their arguments.

Furthermore, studies show that *stronger attitudes are more resistant to change* (Miller & Peterson, 2004). Strong attitudes may be tougher to alter because they tend to be embedded in networks of beliefs and values that might also require change. Finally, *resistance can promote resistance.* That is, when people successfully resist persuasive efforts to change specific attitudes, they often become more certain about those attitudes (Tormala & Petty, 2002, 2004).

Theories of Attitude Formation and Change

Many theories have been proposed to explain the mechanisms at work in attitude change, whether or not it occurs in response to persuasion. We'll look at three theoretical perspectives: learning theory, dissonance theory, and the elaboration likelihood model.

CONCEPT CHECK 12.3

Understanding Attitudes and Persuasion

Check your understanding of the components of attitudes and the elements of persuasion by analyzing hypothetical political strategies. Imagine you're working on a political campaign and you're invited to join the candidate's inner circle in strategy sessions, as staff members prepare the candidate for upcoming campaign stops. During the meetings, you hear various strategies discussed. For each strategy below, indicate which component of voters' attitudes (cognitive, affective, or behavioral) is being targeted for change, and indicate which element in persuasion (source, message, or receiver factors) is being manipulated. The answers are in Appendix A.

1. "You need to convince this crowd that your program for regulating nursing homes is sound. Whatever you do, don't acknowledge the two weaknesses in the program that we've been playing down. I don't care if you're asked point blank. Just slide by the question and keep harping on the program's advantages."

    _____
    _____

2. "You haven't been smiling enough lately, especially when the TV cameras are rolling. Remember, you can have the best ideas in the world, but if you don't seem likable, you're not gonna get elected. By the way, I think I've lined up some photo opportunities that should help us create an image of sincerity and compassion."

    _____
    _____

3. "This crowd is already behind you. You don't have to alter their opinions on any issue. Get right to work convincing them to contribute to the campaign. I want them lining up to donate money."

    _____
    _____

Learning Theory

Attitudes can be learned from parents, peers, the media, cultural traditions, and other social influences (Banaji & Heiphetz, 2010). The affective, or emotional, component in an attitude can be created through a special subtype of *classical conditioning*, called evaluative conditioning (Walther & Langer, 2008). As we discussed in Chapter 6, *evaluative conditioning* consists of efforts to transfer the emotion attached to an unconditioned stimulus (US) to a new conditioned stimulus (CS) (De Houwer, 2011). Advertisers routinely try to take advantage of evaluative conditioning by pairing their products with stimuli that elicit pleasant emotional responses, such as extremely attractive models; highly likable spokespersons; and cherished events, such as the Olympics (Schachtman, Walker, & Fowler, 2011). This conditioning process is diagrammed in **Figure 12.9**. Evaluative conditioning may occur without awareness and seems to be exceptionally resistant to extinction (Balas & Sweklej, 2012).

Operant conditioning can come into play when you openly express an attitude, such as "I believe that husbands should do more housework." Agreement from other people generally functions as a reinforcer. It strengthens your tendency to express a specific attitude (Bohner & Schwarz, 2001). Disagreement often functions as a form of punishment. Thus, it may gradually weaken your commitment to your viewpoint.

Another person's attitudes can rub off on you through *observational learning* (Banaji & Heiphetz, 2010). If you hear your uncle say, "Republicans are nothing but puppets of big business" and your mother heartily agrees, your exposure to your uncle's attitude and your mother's reinforcement of your uncle may influence your attitude toward the Republican Party. The opinions of teachers, coaches, co-workers, talk-show hosts, rock stars, and so forth are also likely to sway people's attitudes through observational learning.

Dissonance Theory

Leon Festinger's *dissonance theory* assumes that inconsistency among attitudes propels people in the direction of attitude change. In a landmark study of dissonance, Festinger and Carlsmith (1959) had male college students come to a laboratory and work on excruciatingly dull tasks, such as turning pegs repeatedly. When a subject's hour was over, the experimenter confided that some participants' motivation was being manipulated by telling them that the task was interesting and enjoyable before they started it. Then, after a moment's hesitation, the experimenter asked if the subject could help him out of a jam. His usual helper was delayed, and he needed someone to testify to the next "subject" (really an accomplice) that the experimental task was interesting. He offered to pay the subject if he would tell the person in the adjoining waiting room that the task was enjoyable and involving.

This entire scenario was enacted to coax participants into doing something that was inconsistent with their true feelings. Some subjects received a token payment of $1 for their effort, while others received a more substantial payment of $20 (an amount equivalent to about $120 today, in light of inflation). Later, a second experimenter inquired about the participants' true feelings regarding the dull experimental task. **Figure 12.10** summarizes the design of the Festinger and Carlsmith study.

Who do you think rated the task more favorably: the subjects who were paid $1 or those who were paid $20? Both common sense and learning theory would predict that the subjects who received the greater reward ($20) should come to like the task more. In reality, however, the participants who were paid $1 exhibited more favorable attitude change—just as Festinger and Carlsmith had predicted. Why? Dissonance theory provides an explanation.

According to Festinger (1957), **cognitive dissonance exists when related attitudes or beliefs are inconsistent; that is, when they contradict each other.** When cognitions are related, they may be consonant ("I am hardworking" and "I'm staying overtime to get an important job done") or dissonant ("I am hardworking" and "I'm playing hooky from work"). When aroused, cognitive dissonance is supposed to create an unpleasant state of tension that motivates people to reduce their dissonance—usually by altering their cognitions.

FIGURE 12.9

Classical conditioning of attitudes in advertising. Advertisers routinely pair their products with likable celebrities in the hope that their products will come to elicit pleasant emotional responses. As discussed in Chapter 6, this special type of classical conditioning is called *evaluative conditioning*. See the Critical Thinking Application in Chapter 6 for a more in-depth discussion of this practice.

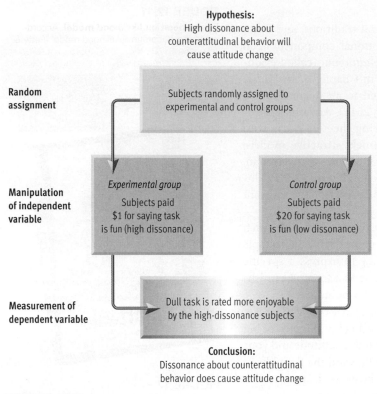

Hypothesis:
High dissonance about counterattitudinal behavior will cause attitude change

Random assignment

Subjects randomly assigned to experimental and control groups

Manipulation of independent variable

Experimental group
Subjects paid $1 for saying task is fun (high dissonance)

Control group
Subjects paid $20 for saying task is fun (low dissonance)

Measurement of dependent variable

Dull task is rated more enjoyable by the high-dissonance subjects

Conclusion:
Dissonance about counterattitudinal behavior does cause attitude change

FIGURE 12.10

Design of the Festinger and Carlsmith (1959) study. The manipulations of variables and the results of Festinger and Carlsmith's (1959) landmark study of cognitive dissonance and attitude change are outlined here.

When political candidates use music, flags, and slogans to influence voters, they are using the peripheral route to persuasion. When they try to sway voters with their analyses of complex political issues, they are using the central route to persuasion.

In the study by Festinger and Carlsmith (1959), the subjects' contradictory cognitions were "The task is boring" and "I told someone the task was enjoyable." The participants who were paid $20 for lying had an obvious reason for behaving inconsistently with their true attitudes, so these subjects experienced little dissonance. In contrast, the participants paid $1 had no readily apparent justification for their lie and experienced high dissonance. To reduce it, they tended to persuade themselves that the task was more enjoyable than they had originally thought. *Thus, dissonance theory sheds light on why people sometimes come to believe their own lies.*

Cognitive dissonance is also at work when people turn attitude somersaults to justify efforts that haven't panned out, a syndrome called *effort justification*. Aronson and Mills (1959) studied effort justification by putting college women through a "severe initiation" before they could qualify to participate in what promised to be an interesting discussion of sexuality. In the initiation, the women had to read obscene passages out loud to a male experimenter. After all that, the highly touted discussion of sexuality turned out to be a boring, taped lecture on reproduction in lower animals. Subjects in the severe initiation condition experienced highly dissonant cognitions ("I went through a lot to get here" and "This discussion is terrible"). How did they reduce their dissonance? Apparently, by changing their attitude about the discussion because they rated it more favorably than did participants in two control conditions. Effort justification may be at work in many facets of everyday life. For example, music fans who pay hundreds of dollars for scalped concert tickets will tend to view the concert favorably, even if the artists show up in a stupor and play out of tune.

Dissonance theory has been tested in hundreds of studies with mixed, but largely favorable, results (Petty et al., 2013). The dynamics of dissonance appear to underlie many important types of attitude changes. And research has largely supported Festinger's claim that dissonance involves genuine psychological discomfort and even physiological arousal (Cooper, 2012).

Elaboration Likelihood Model

The *elaboration likelihood model* of attitude change, originally proposed by Richard Petty and John Cacioppo (1986), asserts that there are two basic "routes" to persuasion (Petty & Briñol, 2012). The *central route* is taken when people carefully ponder the content and logic of persuasive messages. The *peripheral route* is taken when persuasion depends on nonmessage factors, such as the attractiveness and credibility of the source, or on conditioned emotional responses (see **Figure 12.11**). For example, a politician who campaigns by delivering carefully researched speeches that thoughtfully analyze complex issues is following the central route to persuasion. In contrast, a politician who depends on marching bands, flag waving, celebrity endorsements, and emotional slogans is following the peripheral route.

Both routes can lead to effective persuasion and attitude change. However, according to the elaboration likelihood model, the durability of attitude change depends on the extent to which people elaborate on (think about) the contents of persuasive communications. Studies suggest that the central route to persuasion leads to more enduring attitude change than the peripheral route (Petty & Briñol, 2010). Research also suggests that attitudes changed through central processes are more resistant to change and predict behavior better than do attitudes changed through peripheral processes (Petty & Briñol, 2015).

Photodisc/Digital Vision/Getty Images

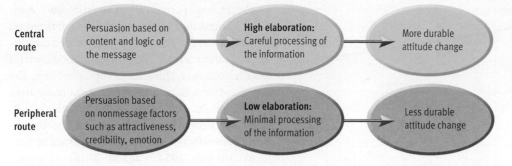

| Central route | Persuasion based on content and logic of the message | → | High elaboration: Careful processing of the information | → | More durable attitude change |
| Peripheral route | Persuasion based on nonmessage factors such as attractiveness, credibility, emotion | → | Low elaboration: Minimal processing of the information | → | Less durable attitude change |

FIGURE 12.11

The elaboration likelihood model. According to the elaboration likelihood model (Petty & Cacioppo, 1986), the central route to persuasion leads to more elaboration of message content and more enduring attitude change than the peripheral route to persuasion.

12.5 CONFORMITY AND OBEDIENCE: YIELDING TO OTHERS

12.5

Key Learning Goals

- Understand Asch's work on conformity and Milgram's research on obedience.
- Discuss cultural variations in conformity and obedience, and describe the Stanford Prison Simulation.

Since the 1950s, social psychologists have shown an enduring fascination with the subject of social influence. Work in this area has yielded some of the most famous and influential studies in the history of psychology. Let's look at this research.

Conformity

If you keep a well-manicured lawn and praise the music of Coldplay, are you exhibiting conformity? According to social psychologists, it depends on whether your behavior is the result of group pressure. *Conformity* **occurs when people yield to real or imagined social pressure.** For example, if you maintain a well-groomed lawn only to avoid complaints from your neighbors, you're yielding to social pressure. If you like Coldplay because you genuinely enjoy their music, that's *not* conformity. However, if you like Coldplay because doing so is "hip" and your friends would question your taste if you didn't, then you're conforming. That said, conformity lies in the eye of the beholder, as people have a curious tendency to see others as more conforming than themselves (Pronin, Berger, & Molouki, 2007). For example, when *your friends* buy iPhones, you may see their choices as mindless conformity, but when *you* buy an iPhone, you may see your choice as a sensible decision based on the features you need. Thus, people tend to believe they are "alone in a crowd of sheep" because everyone else is so conforming.

In the 1950s, Solomon Asch (1951, 1955, 1956) devised a clever procedure that minimized ambiguity about whether subjects were conforming, allowing him to investigate the variables that govern conformity. Let's re-create one of Asch's (1955) classic experiments. The participants are male undergraduates recruited for a study of visual perception. A group of seven subjects are shown a large card with a vertical line on it. They are then are asked to indicate which of three lines on a second card matches the original "standard line" in length (see **Figure 12.12**). All seven participants are given a turn at the task. They each announce their choice to the group. The subject in the sixth chair doesn't know it, but everyone else in the group is an accomplice of the experimenter. They're about to make him wonder whether he has taken leave of his senses.

The accomplices give accurate responses on the first two trials. On the third trial, line number 2 clearly is the correct response, but the first five "subjects" all say that line number 3 matches the standard line. The genuine subject is bewildered and can't believe his ears. Over the course of the next fifteen trials, the accomplices all give the same incorrect response on eleven of them. How does the real subject respond? The line judgments are easy and unambiguous. So, if the participant consistently agrees with the accomplices, he isn't making honest mistakes—he's conforming.

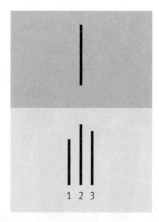

FIGURE 12.12

Stimuli used in Asch's conformity studies. Subjects were asked to match a standard line (top) with one of three other lines displayed on another card (bottom). The task was easy—until experimental accomplices started responding with obviously incorrect answers, creating a situation in which Asch evaluated subjects' conformity.

SOURCE: Adapted from Asch, S. (1955). Opinion and social pressure. *Scientific American, 193* (5), 31–35. Based on illustrations by Sara Love. Copyright © 1955 by Scientific American, Inc. All rights reserved.

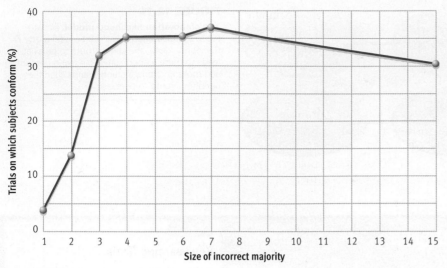

FIGURE 12.13

Conformity and group size. This graph shows the percentage of trials on which participants conformed as a function of group size in Asch's research. Asch found that conformity became more frequent as group size increased up to about seven, and then the amount of conformity leveled off.

Averaging across all fifty subjects, Asch (1955) found that the young men conformed on 37% of the trials. The participants varied considerably in their tendency to conform, however. Of the fifty subjects, thirteen never caved in to the group, while fourteen conformed on more than half the trials. One could argue that the results show that people confronting a unanimous majority generally tend to *resist* the pressure to conform (Hodges, 2014; Padalia, 2014). However, given how clear and easy the line judgments were, most social scientists view the findings as a dramatic demonstration of humans' propensity to conform (Prislin & Crano, 2012).

In subsequent studies, *group size* and *group unanimity* turned out to be key determinants of conformity (Asch, 1956). To examine the impact of group size, Asch repeated his procedure with groups that included from one to fifteen accomplices. Little conformity was seen when a subject was pitted against just one person, but conformity increased rapidly as group size went from two to four, peaked at a group size of seven, and then leveled off (see **Figure 12.13**). Thus, Asch reasoned that as groups grow larger, conformity increases—up to a point—a conclusion that has been echoed by other researchers (Cialdini & Trost, 1998).

However, group size made little difference if just one accomplice "broke" with the others, wrecking their unanimous agreement. The presence of another dissenter lowered conformity to about one-quarter of its peak, even when the dissenter made *inaccurate* judgments that happened to conflict with the majority view. Apparently, the participants just needed to hear someone else question the accuracy of the group's perplexing responses. The importance of unanimity in fostering conformity has been replicated in subsequent research (Forsyth, 2013).

Why do people tend to conform in certain situations? Two key processes appear to contribute: normative influence and informational influence (Levine & Tindale, 2015). *Normative influence* **operates when people conform to social norms for fear of negative social consequences.** In other words, people often conform because they are afraid of being criticized or rejected. People are also likely to conform when they are uncertain how to behave. *Informational influence* **operates when people look to others for guidance about how to behave in ambiguous situations.** Thus, if you're at a nice restaurant and don't know which fork to use for a specific course, you may watch others to see what they're doing. In situations like this, using others as a source of information about appropriate behavior is a sensible strategy. Ultimately, informational influence is all about being right, whereas normative influence is all about being liked.

Obedience

Obedience **is a form of compliance that occurs when people follow direct commands, usually from someone in a position of authority.** To a surprising extent, when an authority figure says, "Jump!" many people simply ask, "How high?"

Milgram's Studies

Stanley Milgram wanted to study this tendency to obey authority figures. Like many other people after World War II, he was troubled by how readily the citizens of Germany

Conformity may be more common than most people appreciate. We all conform to social expectations in myriad ways. There is nothing inherently good or bad about conforming; it all depends on the situation.

followed the orders of dictator Adolf Hitler, even when the orders required shockingly immoral actions, such as the slaughter of millions of Jews. Milgram, who had worked with Solomon Asch, set out to design a standard laboratory procedure for the study of obedience, much like Asch's procedure for studying conformity. The clever experiment that Milgram devised became one of the most famous and controversial studies in the annals of psychology (Blass, 2009).

Milgram's (1963) participants were a diverse collection of forty men from the local community. They were told that they would be participating in a study concerned with the effects of punishment on learning. When they arrived at the lab, they drew slips of paper from a hat to get their assignments. The drawing was rigged so that the subject always became the "teacher" and an experimental accomplice (a likable 47-year-old accountant) became the "learner."

The learner was strapped into an electrified chair through which a shock could be delivered whenever he made a mistake on the task (see **Figure 12.14**). The subject was then taken to an adjoining room that housed the shock generator that he would control in his role as the teacher. Although the apparatus looked and sounded realistic, it was a fake and the learner was never shocked.

As the "learning experiment" proceeded, the accomplice made many mistakes that necessitated shocks. The teacher was instructed to increase the shock level after each wrong answer. At 300 volts, the learner began to pound on the wall between the two rooms in protest and soon stopped responding to the teacher's questions. From this point forward, participants frequently turned to the experimenter for guidance. Whenever they did so, the experimenter firmly indicated that the teacher should continue to give stronger and stronger shocks to the now-silent learner. The dependent variable was the maximum shock the participant was willing to administer before refusing to go on.

As **Figure 12.14** shows, twenty-six of the forty subjects (65%) administered all thirty levels of shock. Although they tended to obey the experimenter, many subjects voiced and displayed considerable distress about harming the learner. The horrified participants groaned, bit their lips, stuttered, trembled, and broke into a sweat, but continued administering the shocks. Based on these results, Milgram concluded that obedience to authority was even more common than he or others anticipated. Before the study was conducted, Milgram had described it to forty psychiatrists and had asked them to predict how much shock subjects would be willing to administer to their innocent victims. Most

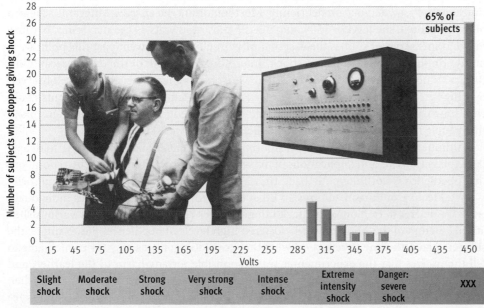

FIGURE 12.14

Milgram's experiment on obedience. The photo on the left shows the "learner" being connected to the shock generator during one of Milgram's experimental sessions. The photo on the right shows the fake shock generator used in the study. The surprising results of the Milgram (1963) study are summarized in the bar graph. Although subjects frequently protested, the vast majority (65%) delivered the entire series of shocks to the learner.

SOURCE: Photos Copyright © 1965 by Stanley Milgram. From the film *Obedience,* distributed by The Pennsylvania State University. Reprinted by permission of Alexandra Milgram.

of the psychiatrists had predicted that fewer than 1% of the subjects would continue to the end of the series of shocks!

In interpreting his results, Milgram argued that strong pressure from an authority figure can make decent people do indecent things to others. Applying this insight to Nazi war crimes and other travesties, Milgram asserted that some sinister actions may not be due to actors' evil character as much as to situational pressures that can lead normal people to engage in acts of treachery and violence. Thus, he arrived at the disturbing conclusion that given the right circumstances, any of us might obey orders to inflict harm on innocent strangers.

The Ensuing Controversy

Milgram's study evoked a controversy that continues through today (Benjamin & Simpson, 2009; Reicher, Haslam, & Miller, 2014). Some critics argued that Milgram's results wouldn't generalize to the real world (Orne & Holland, 1968). For example, Baumrind (1964) asserted that subjects who agree to participate in a scientific study *expect to obey* orders from an experimenter. Milgram (1964, 1968) replied by pointing out that so do soldiers and bureaucrats in the real world who are accused of villainous acts performed in obedience to authority. Overall, the weight of evidence supports the generalizability of Milgram's results. They were consistently replicated for many years, in diverse settings, with a variety of subjects and procedural variations (Blass, 1999, 2009; Miller, 1986).

Critics also questioned the ethics of Milgram's experimental procedures (Baumrind, 1964; Kelman, 1967). They noted that without prior consent, participants were exposed to extensive deception that could undermine their trust in people and severe stress that could leave emotional scars. Milgram's defenders argued that the brief distress experienced by his subjects was a small price to pay for the insights that emerged from his obedience studies. Looking back, however, many psychologists seem to share the critics' concerns about the ethical implications of Milgram's groundbreaking work. His procedure is questionable by contemporary standards of research ethics, and no replications of his obedience study were conducted in the United States from the mid-1970s until relatively recently (Elms, 2009), when Jerry Burger (2009) crafted a very cautious, *partial* replication that incorporated a variety of additional safeguards to protect the welfare of the participants.

To accommodate modern ethical standards, Burger (2009) screened participants with great care, excluding those who seemed likely to experience excessive stress; he emphasized repeatedly that participants could withdraw from the study without penalty at any time; and he provided instant debriefing. Most important, he enacted Milgram's scenario only up through the level of 150 volts. Burger chose 150 volts as the maximum because in Milgram's series of studies the vast majority of subjects who went past this point went on to administer all the levels of shock. Interestingly, in spite of the extra precautions, Burger's study yielded obedience rates that were only slightly lower than those observed by Milgram 45 years earlier. Given Burger's repeated assurances that participants could withdraw from the study (which one would expect to reduce obedience), it seems likely that people today are just as prone to obedience as they were 45 years ago.

Although Milgram's research has stood the test of time, theorists continue to debate the explanations for and implications of his findings. Ent and Baumeister (2014) point out that obedience is not inherently bad. They assert that obedience to legitimate authority is a vital feature of human cultures and that this obedience often suppresses individuals' reflexive desires to lash out and attack others. Burger (2014) discusses how various situational factors in the Milgram study fostered high levels of obedience. For example, the subjects had little time to reflect on what they were doing; it was easy for participants to tell themselves that the experimenter was responsible for any harm to the learner; and the small, incremental steps toward maximum shock seemed inconsequential. Reicher, Haslam, and Smith (2012) take issue with the widespread inference from Milgram's research that people's natural inclination is to exhibit blind obedience to authority figures.

They argue for a much more disturbing thesis—that oppressive behavior in the real world usually is not a matter of blind obedience, but rather a function of people actively identifying with their leaders and proactively working to fulfill their leaders' oppressive goals. Other theorists take issue with the notion that Milgram's obedience research can explain the Holocaust and other episodes of genocide (Miller, 2014; Overy, 2014; Staub, 2014). These theorists typically give Milgram credit for showing that obedience to authority was an important contributing factor to the Holocaust, but they maintain that it was only one of many factors. They assert that the Holocaust was a product of a complex constellation of economic, political, societal, cultural, and psychological forces, and not just blind obedience to authority.

Cultural Variations in Conformity and Obedience

Are conformity and obedience unique to American culture? By no means. The Asch and Milgram experiments have been repeated in many other societies, where they have yielded results roughly similar to those seen in the United States. Thus, the phenomena of conformity and obedience seem to transcend culture.

The replications of Milgram's obedience study have largely been limited to industrialized nations similar to the United States. Many of these studies have reported even *higher* obedience rates than those seen in Milgram's American samples (Blass, 2012). The Asch experiment has been repeated in a more diverse range of societies than the Milgram experiment. Various theorists have hypothesized that collectivistic cultures—which emphasize respect for group norms, cooperation, and harmony—encourage more conformity than do individualistic cultures, with their emphasis on independence (Kim & Markus, 1999). Consistent with this analysis, replications of the Asch experiment have tended to find somewhat higher levels of conformity in collectivistic cultures than in individualistic cultures (Forsyth, 2013).

The Power of the Situation: The Stanford Prison Simulation

The research of Asch and Milgram provided dramatic demonstrations of the potent influence that situational factors can have on social behavior. The power of the situation was underscored once again, about a decade after Milgram's obedience research, in a landmark study conducted by Philip Zimbardo, who, ironically, was a high school classmate of Milgram's. Zimbardo and his colleagues designed the Stanford Prison Simulation to investigate why prisons tend to become abusive, degrading, violent environments (Haney, Banks, & Zimbardo, 1973; Zimbardo, Haney, & Banks, 1973).

The participants were college students recruited for a study of prison life through a newspaper ad. After seventy volunteers were given an extensive battery of tests and interviews, the researchers chose twenty-four students who appeared to be physically healthy and psychologically stable to be the subjects. A coin flip determined which of them would be "guards" and which would be "prisoners" in a simulated prison set up at Stanford University. The prisoners were "arrested" at their homes, handcuffed, and transported to a mock prison on the Stanford campus. Upon arrival, they were ordered to strip, sprayed with a delousing agent, given prison uniforms (smocks), assigned numbers as their identities, and locked up in iron-barred cells. The subjects assigned to be guards were given khaki uniforms, billy clubs, whistles, and reflective sunglasses. They were told that they could run their prison in whatever way they wanted, except that they were not allowed to use physical punishment.

What happened? In short order, confrontations occurred between the guards and prisoners, and the guards quickly devised a variety of sometimes cruel strategies to maintain total control over their prisoners. Meals, blankets, and bathroom privileges were selectively denied to some prisoners to achieve control. The prisoners were taunted, humiliated, and called demeaning names. Pointless, petty rules were strictly enforced. Difficult prisoners were punished with hard labor (doing pushups and jumping jacks, cleaning toilets with their bare hands). And the guards creatively turned a 2-foot by 2-foot closet into a "hole" for solitary confinement of rebellious prisoners. Although there was some variation among the guards, collectively they became mean, malicious, and abusive in fulfilling their responsibilities. How did the prisoners react? A few of them showed signs of emotional disturbance and had to be released early, but they mostly became listless, apathetic, and demoralized. The study was designed to run for 2 weeks, but Zimbardo decided to end it prematurely after just 6 days because he was concerned about the rapidly escalating abuse and degradation of the prisoners. The subjects were debriefed, offered counseling, and sent home.

How did Zimbardo and his colleagues explain the stunning transformations of their subjects? First, they attributed the participants' behavior to the enormous influence of social roles. **Social roles are widely shared expectations about how people in certain positions are supposed to behave.** We have role expectations for salespeople, waiters, ministers, medical patients, students, bus drivers, tourists, flight attendants, and, of course, prison guards and prisoners. The participants had a rough idea of what it meant to act like a guard or a prisoner, and they were gradually consumed by their roles (Haney & Zimbardo, 1998). Second, the researchers attributed their subjects' behavior to the compelling power of situational factors. Before the study began, the tests and interviews showed no measurable differences in personality or character between those randomly assigned to be guards or prisoners. The stark differences in their behavior had to be due to the radically different situations that they found themselves in. As a result, Zimbardo, like Milgram before him, concluded that situational pressures can lead normal, decent people to behave in sinister, repugnant ways.

Another parallel between Milgram's and Zimbardo's research is that both have proven controversial. Some critics argued that the Stanford Prison Simulation was more of an elaborate demonstration than an empirical study that collected precise data (Ribkoff, 2013). Other critics voiced concern that the guards were implicitly encouraged to be abusive, thus tainting the findings (Banuazizi & Movahedi, 1975; Haslam & Reicher, 2003). Still others questioned Zimbardo's explanation for the finding that people passively enact social roles dictated by situational factors (Reicher & Haslam, 2006; Turner, 2006).

12.6 BEHAVIOR IN GROUPS: JOINING WITH OTHERS

Key Learning Goals

- Describe the bystander effect and social loafing.
- Explain group polarization and groupthink.

In social psychologists' eyes, **a group consists of two or more individuals who interact and are interdependent.** Historically, most groups have interacted on a face-to-face basis, but advances in telecommunications are rapidly changing that situation. In the era of the Internet, people can interact, become interdependent, and develop a group identity without ever meeting in person. Indeed, Hackman and Katz (2010) assert that the nature of groups is evolving because of advances in technology. They note that groups traditionally tended to be intact and stable with clear boundaries, whereas membership in modern groups is often continuously changing. Traditional groups usually had a designated leader, whereas modern groups often are self-managing, with shared leadership. Similarly, traditional groups tended to be created in a top-down fashion, whereas modern groups often coalesce on their own to explore shared interests. It will be interesting to see whether these shifts have an impact on how groups function.

Behavior Alone and in Groups: The Case of the Bystander Effect

Imagine that you have a precarious medical condition and that you must go through life worrying about whether someone will leap forward to provide help if the need ever arises. Wouldn't you feel more secure around larger groups? After all, there's "safety in numbers." Logically, as group size increases, the probability of having a good Samaritan on the scene increases. Or does it? We've seen before that human behavior isn't necessarily logical. When it comes to helping behavior, many studies have uncovered an apparent paradox called the *bystander effect*: **people are less likely to provide needed help when they are in groups than when they are alone.**

Evidence that your probability of getting help *declines* as group size increases was first described by John Darley and Bibb Latané (1968), who were conducting research on the determinants of helping behavior. In the Darley and Latané study, students in individual cubicles connected by an intercom participated in discussion groups of three sizes. Early in the discussion, a student who was an experimental accomplice hesitantly mentioned that he was prone to seizures. Later in the discussion, the same accomplice faked a severe seizure and cried out for help. Although a majority of participants sought assistance for the student, the tendency to seek help *declined* with increasing group size.

Similar trends have been seen in many other experiments, in which subjects had opportunities to respond to apparent emergencies, including fires, asthma attacks, faintings, crashes, and flat tires, as well as less pressing needs to answer a door or to pick up objects dropped by a stranger (Fischer et al., 2011). Pooling the results of early research on the bystander effect, Latané and Nida (1981) estimated that participants who are alone provide help 75% of the time, whereas participants in the presence of others provide help only 53% of the time.

What accounts for the bystander effect? A number of factors may be at work, but the most important appears to be the *diffusion of responsibility* that occurs in a group situation. If you're by yourself when you encounter someone in need of help, the responsibility to provide help rests squarely on your shoulders. However, if other people are present, the responsibility is divided among you, and you may all say to yourselves, "Someone else will help." A reduced sense of responsibility may contribute to other aspects of behavior in groups, as we'll see in the next section.

Group Productivity and Social Loafing

Have you ever driven through a road construction project—at a snail's pace, of course—and become irritated because so many workers seem to be just standing around? Maybe the irony of the posted sign "Your tax dollars at work" made you imagine that they were all dawdling. And then again, perhaps not. Individuals' productivity often does decline in larger groups (Latané, Williams, & Harkins, 1979).

CONCEPT CHECK 12.4

Scrutinizing Common Sense

Check your understanding of the implications of research in social psychology by indicating whether the common sense assertions listed below have been supported by empirical findings. Do the trends in research summarized in this chapter indicate that the following statements are true or false? The answers are in Appendix A.

_____ 1. Generally, in forming their impressions of others, people don't judge a book by its cover.

_____ 2. When it comes to attraction, birds of a feather flock together.

_____ 3. In the realm of love, opposites attract.

_____ 4. If you're the target of persuasion, to be forewarned is to be forearmed.

_____ 5. When you need help, there's safety in numbers.

© Supri Suharjoto/Shutterstock.com

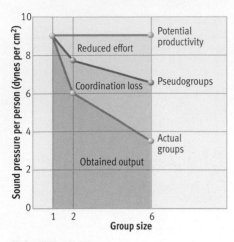

FIGURE 12.15

The effect of loss of coordination and social loafing on group productivity. The amount of sound produced per person declined noticeably when subjects worked in actual groups of two or six (orange line). This decrease in productivity reflects both loss of coordination and social loafing. Sound per person also declined when subjects merely thought they were working in groups of two or six (purple line). This smaller decrease in productivity is attributed to social loafing.

SOURCE: Adapted from Latané, B., Williams, K., & Harkins, S. (1979). Many hands make light the work: The causes and consequences of social loafing. *Journal of Personality and Social Psychology, 37,* 822–832. Copyright © 1979 by the American Psychological Association. Adapted by permission of the author.

Two factors appear to contribute to reduced individual productivity in larger groups. One factor is *reduced efficiency* resulting from the *loss of coordination* among workers' efforts. As you put more people on a yearbook staff, for instance, you'll probably create more and more duplication of effort and increase how often group members end up working at cross purposes.

The second factor contributing to low productivity in groups involves *effort* rather than efficiency. **Social loafing is a reduction in effort by individuals when they work in groups, as compared with when they work by themselves.** To investigate social loafing, Latané et al. (1979) measured the sound output produced by subjects who were asked to cheer or clap as loudly as they could. So they couldn't see or hear other group members, participants were told that the study concerned the importance of sensory feedback and were asked to don blindfolds and put on headphones through which loud noise was played. This maneuver permitted a simple deception: subjects were led to *believe* they were working alone or in a group of two or six, when in fact *individual* output was actually measured.

When subjects *thought* they were working in larger groups, their individual output declined. Because lack of coordination could not affect individual output, the participants' decreased sound production had to be attributable to reduced effort. Latané and his colleagues also had the same subjects clap and shout in genuine groups of two and six, and found an additional decrease in production that was attributed to loss of coordination. **Figure 12.15** shows how social loafing and loss of coordination combined to reduce productivity as group size increased.

Social loafing and the bystander effect appear to share a common cause: diffusion of responsibility in groups (Latané, 1981). As group size increases, the responsibility for getting a job done is divided among more people. Many group members then ease up because their individual contribution is less recognizable. Thus, social loafing occurs in situations where individuals can "hide in the crowd."

That said, social loafing is *not* inevitable. For example, social loafing is reduced when people work in smaller and more cohesive groups (Shiue, Chiu, & Chang, 2010). Social loafing is also less of a problem in newly formed groups (Worchel, Rothgerber, & Day, 2011), and among people who exhibit a "Protestant work ethic" (Smrt & Karau, 2011). Finally, research suggests that social loafing is less prevalent in collectivistic cultures, which place a high priority on meeting group goals and contributing to one's ingroups (Smith, 2001).

Decision Making in Groups

Productivity is not the only issue that commonly concerns groups. When people join together in groups, they often have to make decisions about what the group will do and how it will use its resources. Whether it's your study group deciding what type of pizza to order or a jury deciding on a verdict, groups make decisions. Social psychologists have discovered some interesting tendencies in group decision making. We'll take a brief look at two of these: *group polarization* and *groupthink*.

Group Polarization

Who leans toward more cautious decisions: individuals or groups? Common sense suggests that groups will work out compromises that cancel out members' extreme views. Hence, the collective wisdom of the group should yield relatively conservative choices. Is common sense correct? To investigate this question, Stoner (1961) asked individual participants to give their recommendations on tough decisions, and then asked the same subjects to engage in group discussion to arrive at joint recommendations. When Stoner compared individuals' average recommendation against their group decision generated through discussion, he found that groups arrived at *riskier* decisions than individuals did.

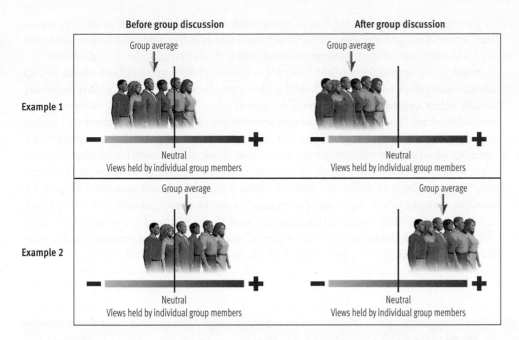

Before group discussion | After group discussion

Example 1

Group average

Group average

Neutral
Views held by individual group members

Neutral
Views held by individual group members

Example 2

Group average

Group average

Neutral
Views held by individual group members

Neutral
Views held by individual group members

FIGURE 12.16

Group polarization. Two examples of group polarization are diagrammed here. In the first example (top), a group starts out mildly opposed to an idea; however, after discussion, sentiment against the idea is stronger. In the second example (bottom), a group starts out with a favorable disposition toward an idea, and this disposition is strengthened by group discussion.

However, investigators eventually determined that groups can shift either way—toward risk or caution—depending on which way the group is leaning to begin with (Friedkin, 1999). A shift toward a more extreme position, an effect called *polarization,* is often the result of group discussion (Van Swol, 2009). Thus, ***group polarization* occurs when group discussion strengthens a group's dominant point of view and produces a shift toward a more extreme decision in that direction** (see **Figure 12.16**). Group polarization does not involve widening the gap between factions in a group, as its name might suggest. In fact, group polarization can contribute to consensus in a group. Group polarization can occur in all sorts of groups. For instance, recent studies have looked at how group polarization plays a role in the decision making of corporate boards (Zhu, 2013, 2014).

Groupthink

In contrast with group polarization, which is a normal process in group dynamics, groupthink is more like a "disease" that can infect decision making in groups. ***Groupthink* occurs when members of a cohesive group emphasize concurrence at the expense of critical thinking in arriving at a decision.** As you might imagine, groupthink doesn't produce very effective decision making. Indeed, groupthink often leads to major blunders that look incomprehensible after the fact. Irving Janis (1972) first described groupthink in his effort to explain how President John F. Kennedy and his advisers could have miscalculated so badly in deciding to invade Cuba at the Bay of Pigs in 1961. The attempted invasion failed miserably, and in retrospect, seemed remarkably ill-conceived. Applying his many years of research on group dynamics to the Bay of Pigs fiasco, Janis developed a model of groupthink.

When groups get caught up in groupthink, members suspend their critical judgment, and the group starts censoring dissent as the pressure to conform increases. Soon, everyone begins to think alike. Moreover, "mind guards" try to shield the group from information that contradicts the group's view. If the group's view

Many types of groups have to arrive at collective decisions. The social dynamics of group decisions are complicated, and a variety of factors can undermine effective decision making.

is challenged from outside, victims of groupthink tend to think in simplistic "us versus them" terms. Groupthink also promotes confirmation bias because members tend to seek and focus on information that supports their initial views (Schulz-Hardt et al., 2000).

What causes groupthink? One key precondition is high group cohesiveness. *Group cohesiveness* **refers to the strength of the liking relationships linking group members to each other and to the group itself.** Members of cohesive groups are close-knit, are committed, have "team spirit," and are loyal to the group. Cohesiveness itself isn't bad. It can help groups achieve great things. But Janis maintains that the danger of groupthink is greater when groups are highly cohesive. Groupthink is also more likely when a group works in relative isolation; when its power structure is dominated by a strong, directive leader; and when it is under pressure to make a major decision quickly. Groupthink can taint many kinds of decisions. For example, studies have analyzed how groupthink may have contributed to the calamitous decision to forge ahead on Mount Everest in 1996 (discussed at the beginning of Chapter 9) and to the abuse of prisoners at the Abu Ghraib prison camp in Iraq (Burnette, Pollack, & Forsyth, 2011; Post, 2011).

Key Learning Goals

- Identify the four unifying themes highlighted in this chapter.

 Empiricism

 Cultural Heritage

 Multifactorial Causation

 Subjectivity of Experience

12.7 REFLECTING ON THE CHAPTER'S THEMES

Our discussion of social psychology has provided a penetrating look at four of our seven unifying themes: psychology's commitment to empiricism, the importance of cultural factors, multifactorial causation, and the extent to which people's experience of the world is highly subjective. Let's consider the virtues of empiricism first.

It's easy to question the need to do scientific research on social behavior because studies in social psychology often seem to verify common sense. While most people wouldn't presume to devise their own theory of color vision or question the significance of REM sleep, everyone has beliefs about the nature of love, how to persuade others, and the limits of obedience. Thus, when studies show that credibility enhances persuasion or that good looks facilitate attraction, it's tempting to conclude that social psychologists go to great lengths to document the obvious, and some critics say, "Why bother?"

You saw why in this chapter. Research in social psychology has repeatedly shown that the predictions of logic and common sense are often wrong. Consider just a few examples. Even psychiatric experts failed to predict the remarkable obedience to authority uncovered in Milgram's research. The bystander effect in helping behavior violates cold-blooded mathematical logic. Dissonance research shows that after a severe initiation, the bigger the letdown, the more favorable people's feelings are. These unexpected findings provide dramatic illustrations of why psychologists put their faith in empiricism.

Our coverage of social psychology also showed once again that behavior is marked by both cultural variance and invariance. Although basic social phenomena—such as stereotyping, attraction, obedience, and conformity—probably occur all over the world, cross-cultural studies of social behavior show that research findings based on American samples may not generalize precisely to other cultures. Our discussion of social behavior also demonstrated once again that behavior is determined by multiple causes. For example, we saw how a variety of factors influence the processes of person perception, interpersonal attraction, and persuasion.

Research in social psychology is also uniquely suited for making the point that people's view of the world is highly personal and subjective. In this chapter we saw how physical appearance can color perceptions of a person's ability or personality, how people tend to see what they expect to see in their interactions with others, how pressure to conform can make people begin to doubt their senses, and how groupthink can lead group members down a perilous path of shared illusions.

12.8

Key Learning Goals
- Relate person perception processes and attributional bias to prejudice.
- Relate attitude formation, intergroup competition, and ingroups versus outgroups to prejudice.

Answer the following "true" or "false."

____ 1 Prejudice and discrimination amount to the same thing.

____ 2 Stereotypes are always negative or unflattering.

____ 3 Ethnic and racial groups are the only widespread targets of prejudice in modern society.

Prejudice is a major social problem. It can harms victims' self-concepts, suppress their potential, create enormous stress in their lives, cause depression and other mental health problems, and promote tension and strife between groups (Cox et al., 2012; Inzlicht & Kang, 2010). Far worse, racially based stereotypes can cause dangerous—and potentially horrific—split-second decisions in which people think they see a weapon that is not really there (Payne, 2006). In light of these problems, it is understandable that research on prejudice has grown dramatically in recent decades (Biernat & Danaher, 2013). The first step toward reducing prejudice is to understand its roots. Hence, in this Application, we'll strive to achieve a better understanding of why prejudice is so common. Along the way, you'll learn the answers to the true-false questions above.

In our modern society, prejudice often manifests in brief, everyday, apparently routine social interactions that subtly convey a particular group's perceived inferiority. These inconspicuous insults, which are sometimes unintentional, have been characterized as *microaggressions* (Sue, 2010). Examples include a white person providing friendlier service to a white customer than to a minority customer, or not sitting next to a minority person on a train or bus, or a man assuming a woman cannot do math, and so forth. Unfortunately, research indicates that these microaggressions can have substantial, cumulative effects on individuals' self-esteem and subjective well-being (Nadal et al., 2014; Ong et al., 2013).

Prejudice and discrimination are closely related, but not interchangeable concepts. ***Prejudice is a negative attitude held toward members of a group.*** Like other attitudes, prejudice can include three components (see **Figure 12.17**): beliefs ("Indians are mostly alcoholics"), emotions ("I despise Jews"), and behavioral dispositions ("I wouldn't hire a Mexican"). Racial and ethnic prejudice receives the lion's share of publicity, but prejudice is not limited to ethnic groups. Women, homosexuals, the aged, the disabled, the homeless, and the mentally ill are also targets of widespread prejudice (Fiske & Tablante, 2015). Thus, many people hold prejudicial attitudes toward one group or another, and many have been victims of prejudice.

Prejudice may lead to ***discrimination, which involves behaving differently, usually unfairly, toward the members of a group.*** Prejudice and discrimination tend to go hand in hand, but attitudes and behavior do not necessarily correspond (see **Figure 12.18**). In our discussion, we'll concentrate primarily on the attitude of prejudice.

Stereotyping

Perhaps no factor plays a larger role in prejudice than *stereotypes*. Although stereotypes are not inevitably negative, many people subscribe to derogatory stereotypes of various ethnic groups. Studies suggest that negative racial stereotypes have diminished over the last 50 years, but they're not a thing of the past. According to a variety of investigators, modern racism has merely become more subtle (Fiske & Tablante, 2015).

Indeed, research indicates that prejudicial stereotypes are so pervasive and insidious they often operate automatically, even in people who truly renounce prejudice (Forscher & Devine, 2014). Thus, a heterosexual man who rejects prejudice against homosexuals may still feel uncomfortable sitting next to a gay couple, even though he regards his reaction as inappropriate. Negative stereotypes not only can lead to prejudice and discrimination, but can also be used to justify or rationalize that prejudice and discrimination (Crandall et al., 2011). For example, a lack of minorities on a police force may be justified by asserting that they didn't score high enough on the selection test.

Stereotypes persist because the *subjectivity* of person perception makes it likely

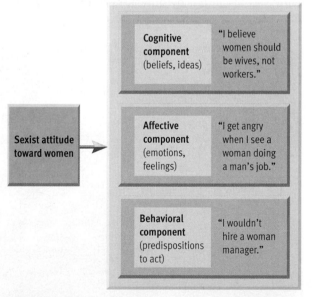

FIGURE 12.17

The three potential components of prejudice as an attitude. Attitudes can consist of up to three components. The tricomponent model of attitudes, applied to prejudice against women, would view sexism as negative beliefs about women (cognitive component) that lead to emotional reactions (affective component), and that promote a readiness to discriminate against women (behavioral component).

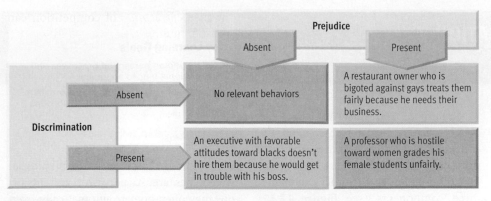

	Prejudice	
	Absent	**Present**
Discrimination **Absent**	No relevant behaviors	A restaurant owner who is bigoted against gays treats them fairly because he needs their business.
Present	An executive with favorable attitudes toward blacks doesn't hire them because he would get in trouble with his boss.	A professor who is hostile toward women grades his female students unfairly.

FIGURE 12.18

Relationship between prejudice and discrimination. As these examples show, prejudice can exist without discrimination, and discrimination without prejudice. In the green cells, there is a disparity between attitude and behavior.

that people will see what they expect to see when they actually come into contact with members of groups they view with prejudice (Fiske & Russell, 2010). For example, Duncan (1976) had white subjects watch and evaluate interactions on a TV monitor that was supposedly live (actually it was a videotape), and he varied the race of the person who got into an argument and gave another person a slight shove. The shove was coded as "violent behavior" by 73% of the participants when the actor was black, but by only 13% of the participants when the actor was white. As we've noted before, people's perceptions are highly subjective. Because of stereotypes, even "violence" may lie in the eye of the beholder.

Making Biased Attributions

Attribution processes can also help perpetuate stereotypes and prejudice. Research taking its cue from Weiner's (1980) model of attribution has shown that people often make *biased attributions for success and failure*. For example, men and women don't get equal credit for their successes (Swim & Sanna, 1996). Observers often discount a woman's success by attributing it to good luck, sheer effort, or the ease of the task (except on traditional feminine tasks). In comparison, a man's success is more likely to be attributed to his outstanding ability (see **Figure 12.19**). For example, one recent study found that when men and women collaborate on a stereotypically "male" task, both the men and the women tend downplay the women's contribution (Haynes & Heilman, 2013). These biased patterns of attribution help sustain the stereotype that men are more competent than women.

Recall that the *fundamental attribution error* is a tendency to explain events by pointing to the personal characteristics of the actors as causes (internal attributions). Research suggests that people are particularly likely to make this error when evaluating targets of prejudice (Hewstone, 1990). Thus, when people take note of ethnic neighborhoods dominated by crime and poverty, they blame the personal qualities of the residents for these problems, while downplaying or ignoring other explanations emphasizing situational factors (job discrimination, poor police service, and so on).

Forming and Preserving Prejudicial Attitudes

If prejudice is an attitude, where does it come from? Many prejudices appear to be handed down as a legacy from parents (Killen, Richardson, & Kelly, 2010). Research suggests that parents' racial attitudes often influence their children's racial attitudes, especially when the parents exhibit strong prejudice (Jackson, 2011). This transmission of prejudice across generations presumably depends to some extent on *observational learning*. For example, if a young boy hears his father ridicule homosexuals, his exposure to his father's attitude is likely to affect his attitude about gays. If the boy then goes to school and makes disparaging remarks about gays that are reinforced by approval from peers, his prejudice will be strengthened through *operant conditioning*. Although

Members of many types of groups are victims of prejudice. Besides racial minorities, others that have been stereotyped and discriminated against include gays and lesbians, women, the homeless, and those who are overweight.

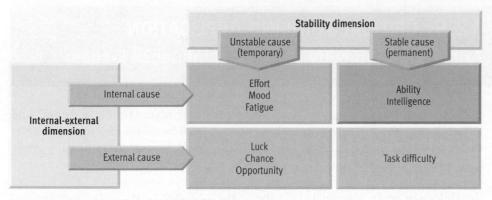

FIGURE 12.19
Bias in the attributions used to explain success and failure by men and women. Attributions about the two genders often differ. For example, men's successes tend to be attributed to their ability and intelligence (blue cell), whereas women's successes tend to be attributed to hard work, good luck, or low task difficulty (green cells). These attributional biases help to perpetuate the belief that men are more competent than women.

parents clearly are important, as children grow older, their peer groups may become more influential than parents and other authority figures (Killen, Hitti, & Mulvey, 2015). Like parents, peers can foster either prejudice or egalitarian attitudes, depending on the views they endorse. Of course, prejudicial attitudes are not acquired only through direct experience. Stereotypic portrayals of various groups in the media can also foster prejudicial attitudes (Mutz & Goldman, 2010).

Competition Between Groups

One of the oldest and simplest explanations for prejudice is that competition between groups can fuel animosity. If two groups compete for scarce resources, such as good jobs and affordable housing, one group's gain is the other's loss. *Realistic group conflict theory* asserts that intergroup hostility and prejudice are a natural outgrowth of fierce competition between groups.

A classic study at Robbers' Cave State Park in Oklahoma provided support for this theory many years ago (Sherif et al., 1961). The subjects were 11-year-old white boys attending a 3-week summer camp at the park. They did not know that the camp counselors were actually researchers (their parents knew). The boys were randomly assigned to one of two groups. During the first week, the boys got to know the other members of their own group through typical camp activities. They gradually developed group identities, choosing to call themselves the Rattlers and the Eagles. In the second week, the Rattlers and Eagles were put into a series of competitive situations—such as a football game, a treasure hunt, and a tug of war—with trophies and other prizes at stake. As predicted by realistic group conflict theory, hostile feelings quickly erupted between the two groups. Food fights broke out in the mess hall, cabins were ransacked, and group flags were burned.

If competition between innocent groups of children pursuing trivial prizes can foster hostility, you can imagine what is likely to happen when adults from very different backgrounds battle for genuinely important resources. Research has repeatedly shown that conflict over scarce resources can fuel prejudice and discrimination (Esses, Jackson, & Bennett-AbuAyyash, 2010). In fact, even the mere *perception* of competition can breed prejudice.

Dividing the World into Ingroups and Outgroups

As noted in the main body of the chapter, when people join together in groups, they sometimes divide the social world into "us versus them," or *ingroups versus outgroups*. This distinction has a profound impact on how people perceive, evaluate, and remember others (Dovidio & Gaertner, 2010). People tend to think simplistically about outgroups. They tend to see diversity among the members of their own group, but overestimate the homogeneity of the outgroup (Boldry, Gaertner, & Quinn, 2007). At a simple, concrete level, the essence of this process is captured by the statement "They all look alike." The illusion of homogeneity in the outgroup makes it easier to sustain stereotypic beliefs about its members (Rubin & Badea, 2012). Furthermore, as you might anticipate, people tend to evaluate outgroup members less favorably than they do ingroup members (Fiske & Tablante, 2015). People routinely engage in outgroup derogation—in other words, they "trash" outgroups so they can feel superior to them.

Although hostility toward outgroups certainly fuels a great deal of discrimination, a recent analysis made a convincing case for the assertion that the more subtle and seemingly less offensive phenomenon of ingroup favoritism actually accounts for even more of the discrimination that occurs in modern society (Greenwald & Pettigrew, 2014). Favoring one's ingroup a little in hiring, promotions, provision of housing opportunities, and so forth is extremely common. Because it is not driven by malice or contempt, it does not seem to be particularly objectionable. But the sheer frequency of ingroup favoritism may make it a more widespread source of discrimination than outgroup hostility.

12.9

Key Learning Goals
- Identify useful criteria for evaluating credibility, and recognize standard social influence strategies.

12.9 CRITICAL THINKING APPLICATION
Analyzing Credibility and Social Influence Tactics

There is no way to evade the constant, never-ending efforts of others to shape your attitudes and behavior. In this Application we will discuss two topics that can be useful in evaluating the credibility of a persuasive source. Second, we will describe some widely used social influence strategies that it pays to know about.

Evaluating Credibility

The salesperson at your local health food store swears that a specific herb combination improves memory and helps people stay healthy. A popular singer touts a psychic hotline where the operators can "really help" with the important questions in life. Speakers at a "historical society" meeting claim that the Holocaust never happened. These are just a few real-life examples of the pervasive attempts to persuade the public to believe something. In these examples, the "something" people are expected to believe runs counter to the conventional or scientific view, but who is to say who is right? After all, people are entitled to their own opinions, aren't they?

Yes, people *are* entitled to their own opinions, but that does not mean that all opinions are equally valid. In deciding what to believe, it is important to carefully examine the evidence presented and the logic of the argument that supports the conclusion (see the Critical Thinking Application for Chapter 9). In deciding what to believe, you also need to decide *whom* to believe, a task that requires assessing the *credibility* of the source of the information. Let's look at some questions that can provide guidance in this process.

Does the source have a vested interest in the issue at hand? If the source is likely to benefit in some way from convincing you of something, you need to take a skeptical attitude. In the examples provided here, it is easy to see how the sales clerk and popular singer will benefit if you buy the products they are selling. But what about the so-called historical society? How would members benefit by convincing large numbers of people that the Holocaust never happened? Like the sales clerk and singer, they are also selling something—in this case, a particular view of history they hope will influence future events in certain ways. Of course, the fact that sources have a vested interest does not necessarily mean their arguments are invalid. But a source's credibility needs to be evaluated with extra caution when the person or group has something to gain.

What are the source's credentials? Does the person have any special training, an advanced degree, or any other basis for claiming special knowledge about the topic? The usual training for a sales clerk or singer does not include how to assess research results in medical journals or to evaluate claims of psychic powers. The Holocaust deniers are more difficult to evaluate. Some of them have studied history and written books on the topic. However, the books are mostly self-published, and few of these "experts" hold positions at reputable universities where scholars are subject to peer evaluation. That's *not* to say that legitimate credentials *ensure* a source's credibility, but they tend to be associated with credibility.

Is the information grossly inconsistent with the conventional view on the issue? Just being different from the mainstream view certainly does *not* make a conclusion wrong. But claims that vary radically from most other information on a subject should raise a red flag that leads to careful scrutiny. Bear in mind that charlatans and hucksters are often successful because they typically try to persuade people to believe things that they already want to believe. Wouldn't it be great if we could effortlessly enhance our memory, foretell the future, eat all we want and still lose weight, and earn hundreds of dollars per hour working at home? And wouldn't it be nice if the Holocaust never happened? It is prudent to be wary of wishful thinking.

Recognizing Social Influence Strategies

It pays to understand social influence strategies because advertisers, salespeople, and fundraisers—not to mention friends and neighbors—frequently rely on them to manipulate people's behavior. Let's look at four basic strategies: the foot-in-the-door technique, misuse of the reciprocity norm, the lowball technique, and feigned scarcity.

Door-to-door salespeople have long recognized the importance of gaining a *little* cooperation from sales targets (getting a "foot in the door") before hitting them with the real sales pitch. **The *foot-in-the-door technique* involves getting people to agree to a small request to increase the chances they will agree to a larger request later.** This technique is widely used in all walks of life. For example, groups seeking donations often ask people to simply sign a petition first.

In an early study of the foot-in-the-door technique (Freedman & Fraser, 1966), the large request involved asking homemakers whether a team of six men doing consumer research could come into their home to classify *all* their household products. Only 22% of the control subjects agreed to this outlandish request. However, when the same request was made 3 days after a small request (to answer a few questions about soap preferences), 53% of the participants agreed to the larger request. Why does the foot-in-the-door technique work? According to Burger (1999), quite a variety of processes contribute to its effectiveness, including people's tendency to try to behave consistently (with their initial response) and their reluctance to renege on their sense of commitment to the person who made the initial request.

Most of us have been socialized to believe in the *reciprocity norm*—**the rule that we should pay back in kind what we receive from others.** Robert Cialdini (2008) has written extensively about how the reciprocity norm is used in social influence efforts. For example, groups seeking donations routinely send address labels, key rings, and other small gifts with their pleas. Salespeople using the reciprocity principle distribute free samples to prospective customers. When they return a few days later, most of the customers feel obligated to buy some of their products. The reciprocity rule is meant to promote fair exchanges in social interactions. However, when people manipulate the reciprocity norm, they usually give something of minimal value in the hopes of getting far more in return (Howard, 1995). Many Internet scams involve manipulations of reciprocity (Muscanell, Guadagno, & Murphy, 2014).

The lowball technique is even more deceptive. The name for this technique derives from a common practice in automobile sales, in which a customer is offered a terrific bargain on a car. The bargain price gets the customer to commit to buying the car. Soon after this commitment is made, however, the dealer starts revealing some hidden costs. Typically, the customer learns that options assumed to be included in the original price are actually going to cost extra or that a promised low loan rate has "fallen through." Once they have committed to buying a car, most customers

Advertisers often try to artificially create scarcity to make their products seem more desirable.

are unlikely to cancel the deal. Thus, **the *lowball technique* involves getting someone to commit to a seemingly attractive proposition before its hidden costs are revealed.** Car dealers aren't the only ones who use this technique, which is a surprisingly effective strategy (Cialdini & Griskevicius, 2010).

A number of years ago, Jack Brehm (1966) demonstrated that telling people they can't have something only makes them want it more. This phenomenon helps explain why companies often try to create the impression their products are in scarce supply. Scarcity threatens your freedom to choose a product, thus creating an increased desire for the scarce commodity. Advertisers frequently feign scarcity to drive up the demand for products. Thus, we constantly see ads that scream "limited supply available," "for a limited time only," "while they last," and "time is running out." Like genuine scarcity, feigned scarcity can enhance the desirability of a commodity (Cialdini & Griskevicius, 2010; van Herpen, Pieters, & Zeelenberg, 2014).

TABLE 12.1 Critical Thinking Skills Discussed in This Application

Skill	Description
Judging the credibility of an information source	The critical thinker understands that credibility and bias are central to determining the quality of information and looks at factors such as vested interests, credentials, and appropriate expertise.
Recognizing social influence strategies	The critical thinker is aware of manipulative tactics such as the foot-in-the-door and lowball techniques, misuse of the reciprocity norm, and feigned scarcity.

PERSON PERCEPTION

- Judgments of others can be distorted by their physical appearance, as we tend to ascribe desirable personality characteristics and competence to those who are good looking.

- Perceptions of faces are especially influential and shape perceptions of competence, which can even affect voters' reactions to candidates.

- *Stereotypes* are widely held beliefs that others will have certain characteristics because of their membership in a particular group.

- Evolutionary theorists attribute the tendency to categorize people into *ingroups* and *outgroups* to our ancestors' need to quickly separate friend from foe.

ATTRIBUTION

Basic processes

- *Attributions* are inferences that people draw about the causes of events and behaviors.

- *Internal attributions* ascribe the causes of behavior to personal traits, abilities, and feelings, whereas *external attributions* ascribe the causes of behavior to situational demands and environmental factors.

- According to Weiner, attributions for success and failure can be analyzed along the stable-unstable and internal-external dimensions.

Biases

- The *fundamental attribution error* refers to observers' bias in favor of internal attributions in explaining others' behavior.

- Actors favor external attributions in explaining their own behavior, whereas observers favor internal attributions.

- The *self-serving* bias is the tendency to explain one's successes with internal attributions and one's failures with external attributions.

Traditional model of attribution

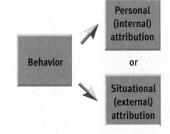

Behavior → Personal (internal) attribution

or

Situational (external) attribution

Alternative two-step model of attribution

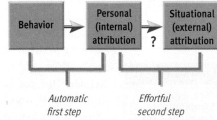

Behavior → Personal (internal) attribution → ? → Situational (external) attribution

Automatic first step   *Effortful second step*

Cultural influences

- Cultures vary in their emphasis on *individualism* (putting personal goals ahead of group goals) as opposed to *collectivism* (putting group goals ahead of personal goals), which influence attributional tendencies.

- People from collectivist cultures appear to be less prone to the fundamental attribution error and to the self-serving bias than are people from individualist cultures.

INTERPERSONAL ATTRACTION

Factors in attraction

- A key determinant of romantic attraction for both genders is the physical attractiveness of the other person.

- The *matching hypothesis* asserts that males and females of roughly equal physical attractiveness are likely to select each other as partners.

- Married and dating couples tend to be similar on many traits, probably because similarity causes attraction and attraction can foster similarity.

© Warren Goldswain/Shutterstock.com

- Research on *reciprocity* shows that liking breeds liking and that loving breeds loving.

Perspectives on love

- Some theorists distinguish between *passionate love* and *companionate love*.

- Another approach views romantic love as an *attachment process* and argues that love relationships in adulthood mimic attachment patterns in infancy, which fall into three categories: secure, anxious-ambivalent, and avoidant.

- The traits people seek in prospective mates seem to transcend culture, but societies vary in their emphasis on romantic love as a prerequisite for marriage.

© alphonsusjimos/Shutterstock.com

Influences on attraction

- Although critics are concerned that Internet relationships are superficial and plagued by deception, they appear to be just as intimate and stable as relationships forged offline.

- The power of similarity effects provides the foundation for online matching sites.

- According to evolutionary psychologists, some aspects of good looks influence attraction because they are indicators of reproductive fitness.

- Men tend to be more interested than women in seeking youthfulness and attractiveness in mates, whereas women tend to emphasize potential mates' financial prospects.

ATTITUDES

STRUCTURE OF ATTITUDES

Components

- The *cognitive component* of an attitude is made up of the beliefs that people hold about the object of an attitude.
- The *affective component* of an attitude consists of the emotional feelings stimulated by an object of thought.
- The *behavioral component* of an attitude consists of predispositions to act in certain ways toward an attitudinal object.

Dimensions

- *Attitude strength* refers to how firmly attitudes are held.
- *Attitude accessibility* refers to how often and how quickly an attitude comes to mind.
- *Attitude ambivalence* refers to how conflicted one feels about an attitude.

Relations to behavior

- Research demonstrates that attitudes are mediocre predictors of people's behavior.
- *Explicit attitudes* are attitudes that we hold consciously and can readily describe, whereas *implicit attitudes* are covert attitudes that are expressed in subtle automatic responses. Implicit attitudes *can* influence behavior.

TRYING TO CHANGE ATTITUDES

Source factors

- Persuasion tends to be more successful when a source has credibility, which may depend on expertise or trustworthiness.
- Likeability also tends to increase success in persuasion.

Message factors

- Two-sided arguments tend to be more effective than one-sided presentations.
- Fear appeals tend to work if they are successful in arousing fear.
- Repetition of a message can be effective, perhaps because of the mere exposure effect.

Receiver factors

- Persuasion is more difficult when the receiver is forewarned about the persuasive effort.
- Resistance is greater when strong attitudes are targeted.

THEORIES OF ATTITUDE CHANGE

Learning theory

- The affective component of an attitude can be shaped by classical conditioning.
- Attitudes can be strengthened by reinforcement or acquired through observational learning.

Dissonance theory

- According to Festinger, inconsistency between attitudes motivates attitude change.
- Dissonance theory can explain why people sometimes come to believe their own lies.

Elaboration likelihood model

- The *central route* to persuasion depends on the logic of one's message, whereas the *peripheral route* depends on nonmessage factors, such as emotions.
- Both routes can lead to effective persuasion, but the central route tends to produce more durable attitude change.

© Abdul Qaiyoom/Fotolia LLC

smartwater GLACÉAU
simplicity is delicious

YIELDING TO OTHERS

Conformity

- Research by Asch showed that people have a surprisingly strong tendency to conform.
- Asch found that conformity becomes more likely as group size increases up to a size of seven.
- However, the presence of another dissenter in the group greatly reduces the conformity observed.
- Asch's findings have been replicated in many cultures, with even higher levels of conformity observed in collectivist cultures.

Obedience

- In Milgram's landmark study, adult men drawn from the community showed a remarkable tendency to follow orders to shock an innocent stranger, with 65% delivering the maximum shock.
- The generalizability of Milgram's findings has stood the test of time, but his work helped stimulate stricter ethical standards for research.
- Milgram's findings have been replicated in many modern nations, and even higher rates of obedience have been seen in many places.

The power of the situation

- The Stanford Prison Stimulation demonstrated that social roles and other situational pressures can exert tremendous influence over social behavior.
- Like Milgram, Zimbardo showed that situational forces can lead normal people to exhibit surprisingly callous, abusive behavior.

BEHAVIOR IN GROUPS

- The *bystander effect* refers to the fact that people are less likely to provide help when they are in groups than when they are alone because of the diffusion of responsibility.
- Productivity often declines in groups because of loss of coordination and *social loafing*, which refers to the reduced effort seen when people work in groups.
- *Group polarization* occurs when discussion leads a group to shift toward a more extreme decision in the direction it was already leaning.
- In *groupthink*, a cohesive group suspends critical thinking in a misguided effort to promote agreement.

APPLICATIONS

- Modern prejudice tends to be subtle and often is manifested in inconspicuous microaggressions.
- Negative racial stereotypes have diminished, but they still can fuel automatic, subtle racism.
- Attributional biases, such as the tendency to assume that others' behavior reflects their disposition, can contribute to prejudice.
- Negative attitudes about groups are often acquired through observational learning and strengthened through operant conditioning.
- Realistic group conflict theory posits that competition between groups for scarce resources fosters prejudice
- Outgroup derogation and ingroup favoritism both appear to contribute to discrimination.
- To resist manipulative efforts, be aware of social influence tactics, such as the foot-in-the-door technique, misuse of the reciprocity norm, the lowball technique, and feigned scarcity.

CHAPTER 13

STRESS, COPING, AND HEALTH

Tony Latham/The Image Bank/Getty Images

Themes in this Chapter

Multifactorial
Causation

Subjectivity
of Experience

You're in your car headed home from school with a classmate. Traffic is barely moving. You gripe about the traffic as you fiddle impatiently with the radio dial. Another motorist nearly takes your fender off trying to cut into your lane. Your pulse quickens as you shout insults at the unknown driver, who can't even hear you. You think about the term paper you have to work on tonight. Your stomach knots up as you think about all the research you still have to do, not to mention study for your math test. Your classmate asks how you feel about the tuition increase that the college announced yesterday. You've been trying not to think about it. You're already in debt up to your ears. Your parents are bugging you about changing schools, but you don't want to leave your friends. Your heartbeat quickens as you contemplate the debate you're sure to have with your parents. You feel wired with tension as you realize that the stress in your life never seems to let up.

In this chapter, we'll discuss the nature of stress, how people cope with stress, and the potential effects of stress. Our examination of the relationship between stress and physical illness will lead us into a broader discussion of the psychology of health. The way people in health professions think about physical illness has changed considerably in the past 20 to 30 years. The traditional view of physical illness as a purely biological phenomenon has given way to a biopsychosocial model of illness (Friedman & Adler, 2007; Suls, Luger, & Martin, 2010). **The *biopsychosocial model* holds that physical illness is caused by a complex interaction of biological, psychological, and sociocultural factors.** This model does not suggest that biological factors are unimportant. It simply asserts that these factors operate in a psychological and social context that is also influential.

13.1 THE NATURE OF STRESS

13.1

Key Learning Goals

- Evaluate the impact of minor stressors and people's appraisals of stress.
- Identify four major types of stress.

The term *stress* has been used in different ways by different theorists. We'll define **stress as any circumstances that threaten or are perceived to threaten one's well-being and tax one's coping abilities.** The threat may be to immediate physical safety, long-range security, self-esteem, reputation, peace of mind, or many other things one values. This is a complex concept, so let's explore it a little further.

Stress as an Everyday Event

The word *stress* tends to spark images of overwhelming, traumatic crises. People may think of terrorist attacks, hurricanes, military combat, and nuclear accidents. Undeniably, major disasters of this sort are extremely stressful. Studies conducted in the aftermath of such traumas typically find elevated rates of psychological problems and physical illness in the affected communities and individuals (Dougall & Swanson, 2011). For example, 15 months after Hurricane Katrina devastated the New Orleans area, a survey of residents uncovered dramatic increases in physical and mental health problems (Kim et al., 2008). Even 6 *years* after Katrina, a study found that heart attack rates were three times higher than prior to the hurricane (Peters et al., 2014). However, major disasters are unusual events and represent only a small part of what constitutes stress. Many everyday events—such as waiting in line, having car trouble, shopping for Christmas presents, misplacing your checkbook, and staring at bills you can't pay—are also stressful.

You might guess that minor stresses would produce minor effects, but that isn't necessarily true. Research has shown that routine hassles can have significant harmful effects on mental and physical health (Delongis, Folkman, & Lazarus, 1988; Pettit et al., 2010). One recent study looked at whether everyday hassles and major stressful events, both measured over a period of 15 years, predicted mortality in an elderly sample of men (Aldwin et al., 2014). Elevated levels of both types of stress were associated with increased mortality, but the impact of hassles was somewhat greater than that of major stressors! Why would minor hassles be related to health outcomes? It may be because of the *cumulative* nature of stress (Seta, Seta, & McElroy, 2002). Stress adds up. Routine stresses at home, at school, and at work might be fairly benign individually, but collectively they can create great strain. Also, major stressful events are relatively rare, whereas hassles tend to be an incessant thorn in our sides.

Appraisal: Stress Lies in the Eye of the Beholder

The experience of feeling stressed depends on what events one notices and how one appraises them. Appraisals are particularly crucial determinants of stress reactions (Folkman, 2011; Gomes, Faria, & Goncalves, 2013). Events that are stressful for one person may be routine for another. For example, many people find flying in an airplane somewhat stressful, but frequent flyers may not be bothered at all. Some people enjoy the excitement of going out on a date with someone new; others find the uncertainty terrifying.

In discussing appraisals of stress, Lazarus and Folkman (1984) distinguish between primary and secondary appraisal (see **Figure 13.1**). *Primary appraisal* **is an initial evaluation of whether an event is (1) irrelevant to you, (2) relevant but not threatening, or (3) stressful.** When you view an event as stressful, you are likely to make **a** *secondary appraisal,* **which is an evaluation of your coping resources and options for dealing with the stress.** Thus, your primary appraisal would determine whether you saw an upcoming job interview as stressful. Your secondary appraisal would determine how stressful the interview appeared, in light of your assessment of your ability to deal with the event.

Often, people aren't very objective in their appraisals of potentially stressful events. A study of hospitalized patients awaiting surgery showed only a slight correlation between the objective seriousness of a person's upcoming surgery and the amount of fear the patient experienced (Janis, 1958). Clearly, some people are more prone than others to feel threatened by life's difficulties. A number of studies have shown that anxious, neurotic people report more stress than others (Smith, 2011; Espejo et al., 2011), as do people who are relatively unhappy (Cacioppo et al., 2008). Thus, stress lies in the eye (actually, the mind) of the beholder. People's appraisals of stressful events are highly subjective.

Major Types of Stress

An enormous variety of events can be stressful for one person or another. Although they're not entirely independent, the four principal types of stress are (1) frustration, (2) conflict, (3) change, and (4) pressure. As you read about each type, you'll surely recognize some familiar adversaries.

FIGURE 13.1

Primary and secondary appraisal of stress. *Primary appraisal* is an initial evaluation of whether an event is (1) irrelevant to you; (2) relevant, but not threatening; or (3) stressful. When you view an event as stressful, you are likely to make a *secondary appraisal,* which is an evaluation of your coping resources and options for dealing with the stress. (Based on Lazarus & Folkman, 1984)

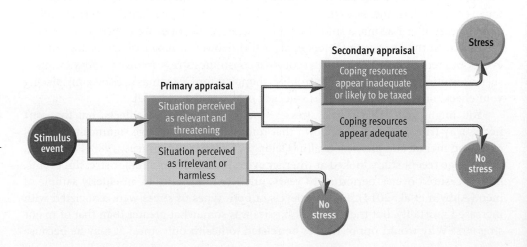

Frustration

As psychologists use the term, *frustration* **is experienced whenever the pursuit of some goal is thwarted.** In essence, you experience frustration when you want something and you can't have it. Everyone has to deal with frustration virtually every day. Traffic jams, difficult commutes, and annoying drivers, for instance, are a routine source of frustration that can elicit anger and aggression (Schaefer, 2005; Wener & Evans, 2011). Fortunately, most frustrations are brief and insignificant. You may be quite upset when you go to a repair shop to pick up your ailing laptop and find that it hasn't been fixed as promised. However, a week later, you'll probably have your computer back, and the frustration will be forgotten. Of course, some frustrations—such as failing to get a promotion at work or losing a boyfriend or girlfriend—can be sources of significant stress.

Internal Conflict

Like frustration, conflict is an unavoidable feature of everyday life. The perplexing question "Should I or shouldn't I?" comes up countless times in one's life. *Conflict* **occurs when two or more incompatible motivations or behavioral impulses compete for expression.** As we discussed in Chapter 11, Sigmund Freud proposed a century ago that internal conflicts generate considerable psychological distress.

Conflicts come in three types (Lewin, 1935; Miller, 1944, 1959). These three basic types of conflict—approach-approach, avoidance-avoidance, and approach-avoidance— are diagrammed in **Figure 13.2**.

In an *approach-approach conflict,* **a choice must be made between two attractive goals.** The problem, of course, is that you can choose just one of the two goals. For example, you have a free afternoon—should you play tennis or racquetball? You can't afford both the blue sweater and the gray jacket—which should you buy? Among the three kinds of conflict, the approach-approach type tends to be the least stressful. Nonetheless, approach-approach conflicts over important issues can sometimes be troublesome. If you're torn between two appealing college majors or two attractive boyfriends, for example, you may find the decision-making process quite stressful.

In an *avoidance-avoidance conflict,* **a choice must be made between two unattractive goals.** Forced to choose between two repellent alternatives, you are, as they say, "caught between a rock and a hard place." For example, should you continue to collect unemployment checks, or should you take that boring job at the car wash? Or suppose

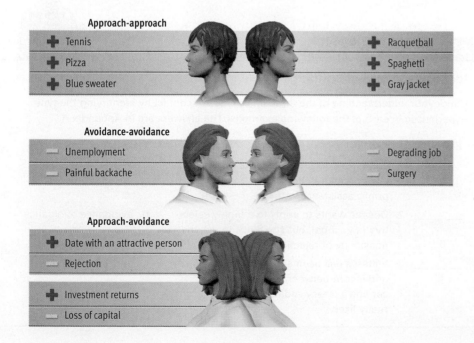

Approach-approach

✚ Tennis	✚ Racquetball
✚ Pizza	✚ Spaghetti
✚ Blue sweater	✚ Gray jacket

Avoidance-avoidance

— Unemployment	— Degrading job
— Painful backache	— Surgery

Approach-avoidance

✚ Date with an attractive person
— Rejection

✚ Investment returns
— Loss of capital

FIGURE 13.2

Types of conflict. Psychologists have identified three basic types of conflict. In approach-approach and avoidance-avoidance conflicts, a person is torn between two goals. In an approach-avoidance conflict, only one goal is under consideration, but it has both positive and negative aspects.

you have painful backaches. Should you submit to surgery that you dread, or should you continue to live with the pain? Obviously, avoidance-avoidance conflicts are most unpleasant and highly stressful.

In an *approach-avoidance conflict,* **a choice must be made about whether to pursue a single goal that has both attractive and unattractive aspects.** For instance, imagine that you're offered a promotion that will mean a large increase in pay, but you'll have to move to a city you hate. Approach-avoidance conflicts are common and can be quite stressful. Any time you have to take a risk to pursue some desirable outcome, you're likely to find yourself in an approach-avoidance conflict. Should you risk rejection by approaching that attractive person in class? Should you risk your savings by investing in a new business that could fail? Approach-avoidance conflicts often produce *vacillation* (Miller, 1944). That is, you go back and forth, beset by indecision. You decide to go ahead, then you decide not to, and then you decide to go ahead again.

Change

Thomas Holmes and Richard Rahe led the way in exploring the idea that life changes—including positive events, such as getting married or getting promoted—represent a key type of stress. *Life changes* **are any substantial alterations in one's living circumstances that require readjustment.** Based on their theory, Holmes and Rahe (1967) developed the Social Readjustment Rating Scale (SRRS) to measure life change as a form of stress. The scale assigns numerical values to forty-three major life events. These values are supposed to reflect the magnitude of the readjustment required by each change (see **Table 13.1**). In using the scale, respondents are asked to indicate how often they experienced any of these forty-three events during a certain time period (typically, the past year). The numbers associated with each checked event are then added. This total is an index of the amount of change-related stress the person has recently experienced.

The SRRS and similar scales based on it have been used in over 10,000 studies by researchers all over the world (Dohrenwend, 2006). Overall, these studies have shown that people with higher scores tend to be more vulnerable to many kinds of physical illness and to many types of psychological problems as well (Scully, Tosi, & Banning, 2000; Surtees & Wainwright, 2007). These results have attracted a great deal of attention. The SRRS has even been reprinted in many popular newspapers and magazines. The attendant publicity has led to the widespread conclusion that life change is inherently stressful.

CONCEPT CHECK 13.1

Identifying Types of Conflict

Check your understanding of the three basic types of conflict by identifying the type experienced in each of the following examples. The answers are in Appendix A.

Examples	Types of conflict
_____ 1. John can't decide whether to take a boring job in a car wash or apply for public assistance.	a. approach-approach
_____ 2. Desiree wants to apply to a highly selective law school, but she hates to risk the possibility of rejection.	b. avoidance-avoidance
_____ 3. Vanessa has been shopping for a new car and is torn between a nifty little sports car and a classy sedan, both of which she really likes.	c. approach-avoidance

© Orange Line Media/Shutterstock.com

TABLE 13.1 Social Readjustment Rating Scale

Life Event	Mean Value	Life Event	Mean Value
Death of a spouse	100	Son or daughter leaving home	29
Divorce	73	Trouble with in-laws	29
Marital separation	65	Outstanding personal achievement	28
Jail term	63	Spouse begins or stops work	26
Death of a close family member	63	Begin or end school	26
Personal injury or illness	53	Change in living conditions	25
Marriage	50	Revision of personal habits	24
Fired at work	47	Trouble with boss	23
Marital reconciliation	45	Change in work hours or conditions	20
Retirement	45	Change in residence	20
Change in health of family member	44	Change in school	20
Pregnancy	40	Change in recreation	19
Sex difficulties	39	Change in church activities	19
Gain of a new family member	39	Change in social activities	18
Business readjustment	39	Mortgage or loan for lesser purchase (car, TV, etc.)	17
Change in financial state	38	Change in sleeping habits	16
Death of a close friend	37	Change in number of family get-togethers	15
Change to a different line of work	36	Change in eating habits	15
Change in number of arguments with spouse	35	Vacation	13
Mortgage or loan for major purchase (home, etc.)	31	Christmas	12
Foreclosure of mortgage or loan	30	Minor violations of the law	11
Change in responsibilities at work	29		

SOURCE: Adapted from Holmes, T. H., & Rahe, R. (1967). The Social Readjustment Rating Scale. *Journal of Psychosomatic Research, 11,* 213–218. Copyright © 1967 by Elsevier Science Publishing Co. Reprinted by permission.

However, experts have criticized this research, citing problems with the methods used and problems in interpreting the findings (Anderson, Wethington, & Kamarck, 2011; Monroe, 2008). At this point, it's a key interpretive issue that concerns us. A variety of critics have collected evidence showing that the SRRS does not measure *change* exclusively (Turner & Wheaton, 1995). In reality, it assesses a wide range of kinds of stressful experiences. Thus, we have little reason to believe that change is *inherently* or *inevitably* stressful. Undoubtedly, some life changes may be quite challenging, but others may be quite benign.

Pressure comes in two varieties: pressure to perform and pressure to conform. For example, standup comedians are under intense pressure to make audiences laugh (pressure to perform), whereas corporate employees are often expected to dress in certain ways (pressure to conform).

Pressure

At one time or another, most people have remarked that they're "under pressure." What does this mean? **Pressure involves expectations or demands that one behave in a certain way.** You are under pressure to *perform* when you're expected to execute tasks and

Misconception

Stress is something that is imposed from outside forces.

Reality

It is hard to quantify, but a significant portion of people's stress is self-imposed. People routinely impose pressure on themselves by taking on extra work and new challenges. They court frustration by embracing unrealistic goals or engaging in self-defeating behavior. And people create stress by making unrealistic appraisals of adverse events.

responsibilities quickly, efficiently, and successfully. For example, salespeople are usually under pressure to move merchandise. Stand-up comedians are under intense pressure to make people laugh. Pressures to *conform* to others' expectations are also common. Businessmen are expected to wear suits and ties. Suburban homeowners are expected to keep their yards well groomed.

Although widely discussed by the general public, the concept of pressure has received scant attention from researchers. However, Weiten (1988, 1998) has devised a scale to measure pressure as a form of life stress. In research with this scale, a strong relationship has been found between pressure and a variety of psychological symptoms and problems. In fact, pressure turned out to be more strongly related to measures of mental health than was the SRRS and other established measures of stress. Additionally, a 15-year study of more than 12,000 nurses found that increased pressure at work was related to an increased risk for heart disease (Väänänen, 2010). Participants who reported that their pressure at work was much too high were almost 50% more likely to develop heart disease than subjects who experienced normal levels of pressure.

We tend to think of pressure as something imposed by outside forces. However, studies of high school and college students find that *pressure is often self-imposed* (Kouzma & Kennedy, 2004; Hamaideh, 2011). For example, you might sign up for extra classes to get through school quickly. Actually, self-imposed stress is not unique to pressure. Research suggests that other forms of stress can also be self-generated (Roberts & Ciesla, 2007). One implication of this finding is that people might have more control over a substantial portion of the stress in their lives than they realize.

13.2 RESPONDING TO STRESS

13.2

Key Learning Goals

- Discuss the role of positive emotions in response to stress, and describe the effects of emotional arousal.
- Describe Selye's general adaptation syndrome and other physiological responses to stress.
- Evaluate the adaptive value of common coping strategies.

The human response to stress is complex and multidimensional (Segerstrom & O'Connor, 2012). Stress affects the individual at several levels. Consider again the chapter's opening scenario. You're driving home in heavy traffic and thinking about overdue papers, tuition increases, and parental pressures. Let's look at some of the reactions that were mentioned. When you groan about the traffic, you're experiencing an *emotional response* to stress, in this case annoyance and anger. When your pulse quickens and your

CONCEPT CHECK 13.2

Recognizing Sources of Stress

Check your understanding of the major sources of stress by indicating which type or types of stress are at work in each of the examples below. Bear in mind that the four basic types of stress are not mutually exclusive. There's some potential for overlap, so a specific experience might include both change and pressure, for instance. The answers are in Appendix A.

Examples	Types of stress
_____ 1. Marie is stuck in line at the bank.	a. frustration
_____ 2. Tamika decides she won't be satisfied unless she gets straight A's this year.	b. conflict
_____ 3. Jose has just graduated from business school and has taken an exciting new job.	c. change
_____ 4. Morris has just been fired from his job and needs to find another.	d. pressure

© Christo/Shutterstock.com

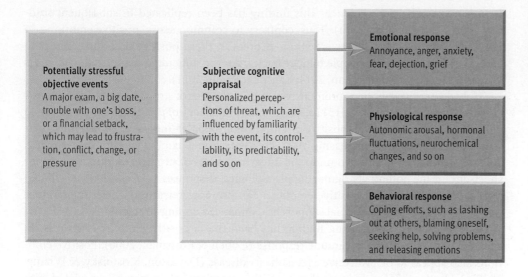

FIGURE 13.3

Overview of the stress process. A potentially stressful event, such as a major exam, elicits a subjective appraisal of how threatening the event is. If the event is viewed with alarm, the stress can trigger emotional, physiological, and behavioral reactions because people's response to stress is multidimensional.

stomach knots up, you're exhibiting *physiological responses* to stress. When you shout insults at another driver, your verbal aggression is a *behavioral response* to the stress at hand. Thus, we can analyze a person's reactions to stress at three levels: (1) emotional responses, (2) physiological responses, and (3) behavioral responses. **Figure 13.3** provides an overview of the stress process.

Emotional Responses

When people are under stress, they often react emotionally. Studies that have tracked stress and mood on a daily basis have found intimate relationships between the two (Kiang & Buchanan, 2014; van Eck, Nicolson, & Berkhof, 1998). Moreover, one recent study found that stress-induced negative moods can have long-term implications for mental health (Charles et al., 2013). In this study, heightened emotional reactivity to daily stress predicted the likelihood of experiencing mood disorders 10 years later.

Emotions Commonly Elicited

No simple one-to-one connections have been found between certain types of stressful events and particular emotions. However, researchers *have* begun to uncover some strong links between *specific cognitive reactions to stress* (appraisals) and specific emotions (Lazarus, 2006). For example, self-blame tends to lead to guilt, helplessness to sadness, and so forth. Many emotions can be evoked by stressful events, but some are certainly more likely than others. Common emotional responses to stress include (1) annoyance, anger, and rage; (2) apprehension, anxiety, and fear; and (3) dejection, sadness, and grief (Lazarus, 1993; Woolfolk & Richardson, 1978).

Investigators have tended to focus heavily on the connection between stress and negative emotions. However, research shows that positive emotions also occur during periods of stress (Moskowitz et al., 2012; Folkman, 2008). Although this finding seems counterintuitive, researchers have found that people experience a diverse array of pleasant emotions even while enduring the most dire of circumstances (Folkman et al., 1997). Consider, for example, a study that examined subjects' emotional functioning early in 2001 and again in the weeks following the 9/11 terrorist attacks in the United States (Fredrickson et al., 2003). Like most U.S. citizens, these subjects reported many negative emotions in the aftermath of 9/11, including anger, sadness, and fear. However, within this "dense cloud of anguish," positive emotions also emerged. For example, people felt gratitude for the safety of their loved ones, many took stock and counted their blessings, and quite a few reported renewed love for their friends and family. Fredrickson et al. (2003) also found that the frequency of pleasant emotions correlated positively with

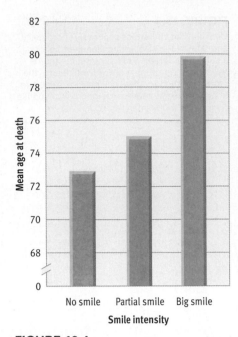

FIGURE 13.4

Positive emotions and longevity. To look at the relation between positive emotions and longevity, Abel and Kruger (2010) used the intensity of baseball players' smiles in photographs as a rough indicator of the players' characteristic emotional tone. All the photos in the *Baseball Register* for 1952 were reviewed and classified as showing no smile, a partial smile, or a big smile. Then the age at death was determined for the players (except the forty-six who were still alive in June 2009). As you can see, greater smile intensity was associated with living longer.

a measure of subjects' resilience. This finding has been replicated in subsequent studies (Gloria & Steinhardt, 2014). Thus, contrary to common sense, positive emotions do *not* vanish during times of severe stress. Moreover, these positive emotions appear to play a key role in helping people bounce back from the difficulties associated with stress (Tugade, Devlin, & Fredrickson, 2014; Zautra & Reich, 2011).

How do positive emotions promote resilience in the face of stress? Barbara Fredrickson's (2001, 2006; Conway et al., 2013) *broaden-and-build theory of positive emotions* can shed light on this question. First, positive emotions alter people's mindsets, broadening their scope of attention and increasing their creativity and flexibility in problem solving. Second, positive emotions can undo the lingering effects of negative emotions, and thus short-circuit the potentially damaging physiological responses to stress that we will discuss momentarily. Third, positive emotions can promote rewarding social interactions that help to build valuable social support and enhanced coping strategies.

One particularly interesting finding has been that a positive emotional style is associated with an enhanced immune response (Cohen & Pressman, 2006). Positive emotions also appear to be protective against heart disease (Davidson, Mostofsky, & Whang, 2010). Indeed, evidence suggests that a positive emotional style may be associated with enhanced physical health in general (Moskowitz & Saslow, 2014). These effects probably contribute to the recently discovered association between the tendency to report positive emotions and longevity (Ong, 2010; Pressman & Cohen, 2012). Yes, people who experience a high level of positive emotions appear to live longer than others! One study exploring this association looked at photos of major league baseball players taken from the *Baseball Register* for 1952. The intensity of the players' smiles was used as a crude index of their tendency to experience positive emotions, which was then related to how long they lived. As you can see in **Figure 13.4**, greater smile intensity predicted greater longevity (Abel & Kruger, 2010). A more recent study looked at the use of positive words in the autobiographies of eighty-eight well-known, deceased psychologists (Pressman & Cohen, 2012). Once again, the results suggest that a positive mentality was associated with greater longevity. Thus, it appears that the benefits of positive emotions may be more diverse and more far reaching than widely appreciated.

Effects of Emotional Arousal

Emotional responses are a natural and normal part of life. Even unpleasant emotions serve important purposes. Like physical pain, painful emotions can serve as warnings that one needs to take action. However, strong emotional arousal can also interfere with efforts to cope with stress. For example, there's evidence that high emotional arousal can interfere with attention and memory retrieval and can impair judgment and decision making (Lupien & Maheu, 2007; Mandler, 1993).

Although emotional arousal may hurt coping efforts, that isn't *necessarily* the case. The *inverted-U hypothesis* predicts that task performance should improve with increased emotional arousal—up to a point, after which further increases in arousal become disruptive and performance deteriorates (Anderson, 1990; Mandler, 1993). This idea is referred to as the inverted-U hypothesis because when performance is plotted as a function of arousal, the resulting graphs approximate an upside-down U (see **Figure 13.5**). In these graphs, the level of arousal at which performance peaks is characterized as the *optimal level of arousal* for a task.

This optimal level appears to depend in part on the complexity of the task at hand. The conventional wisdom is that *as a task becomes more complex, the optimal level of arousal (for peak performance) tends to decrease.* This relationship is depicted in **Figure 13.5**. As you can see, a fairly high level of arousal should be optimal on simple tasks (such as driving 8 hours to help a friend in a crisis). However, performance should peak at a lower level of arousal on complex tasks (such as making a major decision in which you have to weigh many factors). Thus, emotional arousal could have either beneficial or disruptive effects on coping, depending on the nature of the stressful demands one encounters.

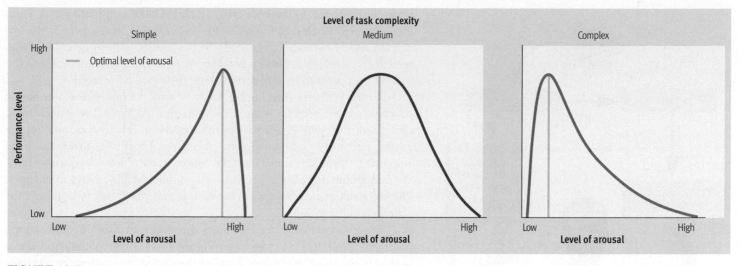

FIGURE 13.5

Arousal and performance. Graphs of the relationship between emotional arousal and task performance tend to resemble an inverted U, as increased arousal is associated with improved performance up to a point, after which higher arousal leads to poorer performance. The optimal level of arousal for a task depends on the complexity of the task. On complex tasks, a relatively low level of arousal tends to be optimal. On simple tasks, however, performance may peak at a much higher level of arousal.

Physiological Responses

As we just discussed, stress frequently elicits strong emotional responses. Now we'll look at the important physiological changes that often accompany these emotions.

The General Adaptation Syndrome

Concern about the physical effects of stress was first voiced by Hans Selye (1936, 1956, 1974), a Canadian scientist who coined the term *stress* while launching stress research many decades ago. Selye explained stress reactions in terms of what he called the *general adaptation syndrome*. The *general adaptation syndrome* **is a model of the body's stress response, consisting of three stages: alarm, resistance, and exhaustion** (see **Figure 13.6**). In the first stage, an *alarm reaction* occurs when an organism first recognizes the existence of a threat: Physiological arousal occurs as the body musters its resources to combat the challenge. Selye's alarm reaction is essentially the fight-or-flight response described in Chapters 3 and 9.

However, Selye took his investigation of stress a few steps further by exposing laboratory animals to *prolonged stress,* similar to the chronic stress often endured by humans. As stress continues, the organism may progress to the second phase of the general adaptation syndrome, the *stage of resistance.* During this phase, physiological changes stabilize as coping efforts get under way. Typically, physiological arousal continues to be higher than normal, although it may level off somewhat as the organism becomes accustomed to the threat.

If the stress continues over a substantial period of time, the organism may enter the third stage, the *stage of exhaustion.* According to Selye, the body's resources for fighting stress are limited. If the stress can't be overcome, the body's resources may be depleted. Eventually, he thought, the organism would experience hormonal exhaustion, although we now know that the crux of the problem is that chronic overactivation of the stress response can have damaging physiological effects on a variety of organ systems (Sapolsky, 2007). These harmful physiological effects can lead to what Selye called *diseases of adaptation.*

Brain-Body Pathways

Even in cases of moderate stress, you may notice that your heart has started beating faster, you've begun to breathe harder, and you're perspiring more than usual. How does all this (and much more) happen? It appears that there are two major pathways along which the

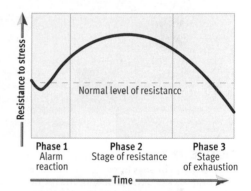

FIGURE 13.6

The general adaptation syndrome. According to Selye, the physiological response to stress can be broken into three phases. During the first phase, the body mobilizes its resources for resistance after a brief initial shock. In the second phase, resistance levels off and eventually begins to decline. If the third phase of the general adaptation syndrome is reached, resistance is depleted, leading to health problems and exhaustion.

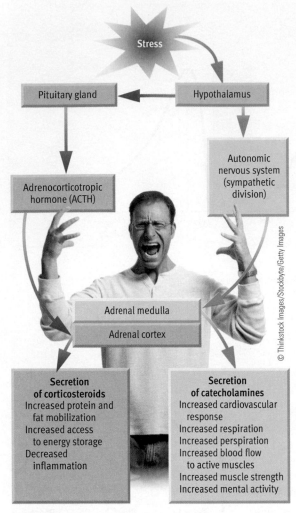

FIGURE 13.7
Brain-body pathways in stress. In times of stress, the brain sends signals along two pathways. The pathway through the autonomic nervous system controls the release of catecholamine hormones, which help mobilize the body for action. The pathway through the pituitary gland and the endocrine system controls the release of corticosteroid hormones, which increase energy and ward off tissue inflammation.

In the figure:

Stress

Pituitary gland ← Hypothalamus

Adrenocorticotropic hormone (ACTH)

Autonomic nervous system (sympathetic division)

Adrenal medulla
Adrenal cortex

Secretion of corticosteroids
Increased protein and fat mobilization
Increased access to energy storage
Decreased inflammation

Secretion of catecholamines
Increased cardiovascular response
Increased respiration
Increased perspiration
Increased blood flow to active muscles
Increased muscle strength
Increased mental activity

© Thinkstock Images/Stockbyte/Getty Images

brain sends signals to the endocrine system (Dallman, Bhatnagar, & Viau, 2007; Stowell, Robles, & Kane, 2013). As we noted in Chapter 3, the *endocrine system* consists of glands located at various sites in the body that secrete chemicals called *hormones*. The hypothalamus is the structure in the brain that appears to initiate action along these two pathways.

The first pathway (see **Figure 13.7**) is routed through the autonomic nervous system (ANS). Your hypothalamus activates the sympathetic division of the ANS. A key part of this activation involves stimulating the central part of the adrenal glands (the adrenal medulla) to release large amounts of *catecholamines* into the bloodstream. These hormones radiate throughout your body, producing a number of physiological changes. The net result of catecholamine elevation is that your body is mobilized for action (Lundberg, 2007).

The second pathway involves more direct communication between the brain and the endocrine system (see **Figure 13.7**). The hypothalamus sends signals to the so-called master gland of the endocrine system, the pituitary gland. In turn, the pituitary secretes a hormone (ACTH) that stimulates the outer part of the adrenal glands (the adrenal cortex) to release another important set of hormones—*corticosteroids*. These hormones stimulate the release of chemicals that help increase your energy and help inhibit tissue inflammation in case of injury (Munck, 2007).

An important new finding in research on stress and the brain is that stress can interfere with neurogenesis (Mahar et al., 2014; McEwen, 2009). As you may recall from Chapter 3, scientists have discovered that the adult brain is capable of **neurogenesis—the formation of new neurons,** primarily in key areas in the hippocampus. In Chapter 14 we will discuss evidence that suppressed neurogenesis may be a key cause of depression (Anacker, 2014). Thus, the capacity of stress to hinder neurogenesis may have important ramifications. This is currently the subject of intense research.

Behavioral Responses

People respond to stress at several levels. However, it's clear that behavior is the crucial dimension of their reactions. Most behavioral responses to stress involve coping. **Coping refers to efforts to master, reduce, or tolerate the demands created by stress.** Notice that this definition is neutral as to whether coping efforts are healthful or maladaptive. The popular use of the term often implies that coping is inherently healthful. When people say that someone "coped with her problems," the implication is that she handled them effectively.

In reality, however, coping responses can be adaptive or maladaptive (Folkman & Moskowitz, 2004; Kleinke, 2007). For example, if you were flunking a history course at midterm, you might cope with this stress by (1) increasing your study efforts, (2) seeking help from a tutor, (3) blaming your professor, or (4) giving up on the class without really trying. Clearly, the first two of these coping responses would be more adaptive than the last two. In this section we'll focus most of our attention on styles of coping that tend to be less than ideal. We'll discuss more healthful coping strategies in the Personal Application on stress management.

Giving Up and Blaming Oneself

When confronted with stress, people sometimes simply give up and withdraw from the battle. Some people routinely respond to stress with fatalism and resignation. They passively accept setbacks that could be dealt with effectively. This syndrome is referred to as *learned helplessness* (Seligman, 1974, 1992). **Learned helplessness is passive behavior produced by exposure to unavoidable aversive events.** Learned helplessness seems to occur when individuals come to believe that events are beyond their control. As you might guess, giving up is not a highly regarded method of coping. Consistent with this view, many studies suggest that learned helplessness can contribute to depression (Isaacowitz & Seligman, 2007).

Although giving up is clearly less than optimal in many contexts, research suggests that when people struggle to pursue goals that turn out to be unattainable, it sometimes makes sense for them to cut their losses and disengage from the goal (Wrosch et al., 2012). Studies have shown that people who are better able to disengage from unattainable goals report better health and exhibit lower levels of a key stress hormone (Wrosch, 2011; Wrosch et al., 2007). Given the way people in our competitive culture tend to disparage the concept of "giving up," the authors note that it might be better to characterize this coping tactic as "goal adjustment."

Blaming oneself is another common response when people are confronted by stressful difficulties. The tendency to become highly self-critical in response to stress has been noted by a number of influential theorists. Albert Ellis (1973, 1987, 2001) calls this phenomenon *catastrophic thinking*. According to Ellis, catastrophic thinking causes, aggravates, and perpetuates emotional reactions to stress that are often problematic (see the Personal Application for this chapter). Although there is something to be said for recognizing one's weaknesses and taking responsibility for one's failures, Ellis maintains that excessive self-blame can be very unhealthy.

Striking Out at Others

People often respond to stressful events by striking out at others with aggressive behavior. *Aggression* **is any behavior that is intended to hurt someone, either physically or verbally.** Many years ago, a team of psychologists (Dollard et al., 1939) proposed the *frustration-aggression hypothesis,* which held that aggression is always caused by frustration. Decades of research have supported this idea of a causal link between frustration and aggression (Berkowitz, 1989). However, this research has also shown that there isn't an inevitable, one-to-one correspondence between the two.

Sigmund Freud theorized that behaving aggressively could get pent-up emotion out of one's system and thus be adaptive. He coined the term *catharsis* **to refer to this release of emotional tension.**

CONCEPT CHECK 13.3

Tracing Brain-Body Pathways in Stress

Check your understanding of the two major pathways along which the brain sends signals to the endocrine system in the event of stress, by separating the eight terms below into two sets of four and arranging each set in the appropriate sequence. You'll find the answers in Appendix A.

ACTH

corticosteriods

adrenal cortex

hypothalamus

adrenal medulla

pituitary

catecholamines

sympathetic division of the ANS

Pathway 1	Pathway 2
_____	_____
_____	_____
_____	_____
_____	_____

Research suggests that lashing out at others is not cathartic and that it only fuels additional anger and stress.

The Freudian notion that it is a good idea to vent anger has become widely disseminated and accepted in modern society. Books, magazines, and self-appointed experts routinely advise that it is healthy to "blow off steam" and thereby release and reduce anger. However, experimental research generally has *not* supported the catharsis hypothesis. Indeed, *most studies find just the opposite: behaving in an aggressive manner tends to fuel more anger and aggression* (Bushman & Huesmann, 2012). Other behaviors, such as talking or writing about one's problems, may have some value in releasing pent-up emotions (see the Personal Application), but aggressive behavior is not cathartic.

Indulging Oneself

Stress sometimes leads to reduced impulse control, or *self-indulgence*. When troubled by stress, many people engage in unwise patterns of eating, drinking, spending money, and so forth. Thus, it's not surprising that studies have linked stress to increases in eating (O'Connor & Conner, 2011); smoking (Slopen et al., 2013); gambling (Elman, Tschibelu, & Borsook, 2010); and consumption of alcohol and drugs (Grunberg, Berger, & Hamilton, 2011). Another example of self-indulgence as a coping strategy is stress-induced shopping. One recent study examined the relations among stress, materialism, and compulsive shopping in two Israeli samples, one of which was under intense stress due to daily rocket attacks (Ruvio, Somer, & Rindfleisch, 2014). The findings indicated that stress increases compulsive consumption and that this coping strategy is particularly common among those who are highly materialistic. The authors essentially conclude that *when the going gets tough, the materialistic go shopping.*

A relatively new manifestation of this coping strategy that has attracted much attention is the tendency to immerse oneself in the online world of the Internet. Kimberly Young (2009, 2013) has called this syndrome *Internet addiction*. Internet addiction typically involves one of three subtypes: excessive gaming; preoccupation with sexual content; or obsessive socializing (via Facebook, texting, and so forth; Weinstein et al., 2014). All three subtypes exhibit (1) excessive time online; (2) anger and depression when thwarted from being online; (3) an escalating need for better equipment and connections; and (4) adverse consequences, such as arguments and lying about Internet use, social isolation, and reductions in academic or work performance. Estimates of the prevalence of Internet addiction vary considerably from one country to another, but a recent meta-analysis of

There is some debate about whether excessive Internet use should be characterized as an *addiction*. However, the inability to control online use clearly is a common and growing problem of international scope.

findings from thirty-one nations estimated that the average prevalence is around 6% of the population (Cheng & Li, 2014). The exact percentage is not as important as the recognition that the syndrome is *not* rare and that it is a global problem. Studies suggest that Internet addiction *is* fostered by high stress (Chen et al., 2014; Tang et al., 2014). Among other things, Internet addiction is associated with increased levels of anxiety, depression, and alcohol use (Ho et al., 2014). Although not all psychologists agree about whether excessive Internet use should be classified as an *addiction* (Hinic, 2011; Starcevic, 2013), it is clear that this coping strategy can be problematic (Muller et al., 2014).

Defensive Coping

Many people exhibit consistent styles of defensive coping in response to stress (Vaillant, 1994). We noted in Chapter 11 that Sigmund Freud originally developed the concept of the *defense mechanism*. Though rooted in the psychoanalytic tradition, this concept has gained widespread acceptance from psychologists of most persuasions (Cramer, 2000). Building on Freud's initial insights, modern psychologists broadened the scope of the concept and added to Freud's list of defense mechanisms.

Defense mechanisms **are largely unconscious reactions that protect a person from unpleasant emotions, such as anxiety and guilt.** Many specific defense mechanisms have been identified. For example, Laughlin (1979) lists forty-nine different defenses. We described seven common defense mechanisms in our discussion of Freud's theory in Chapter 11: repression, projection, displacement, reaction formation, regression, rationalization, and identification (consult **Table 11.1**).

The main purpose of defense mechanisms is to shield individuals from the unpleasant emotions so often elicited by stress (Cramer, 2008) They accomplish this purpose through *self-deception,* distorting reality so it doesn't appear so threatening. Defense mechanisms operate at varying levels of awareness, although they're largely unconscious (Cramer, 2001; Erdelyi, 2001).

Generally, defensive coping is less than optimal because avoidance and wishful thinking rarely solve personal problems (Grant et al., 2013; MacNeil et al., 2012). That said, there is some evidence that suggests that "positive illusions" can sometimes be adaptive for mental health (Taylor, 2011; Taylor & Brown, 1994). Some of the personal illusions people create through defensive coping can help them deal with life's difficulties. Roy Baumeister (1989) theorizes that it's all a matter of degree and that there is an "optimal margin of illusion." According to Baumeister, extreme distortions of reality are maladaptive, but small illusions can be beneficial.

Constructive Coping

Our discussion thus far has focused on coping strategies that are less than ideal. Of course, people also exhibit many healthful strategies for dealing with stress. We'll use the term *constructive coping* **to refer to relatively healthful efforts that people make to deal with stressful events.** Please bear in mind that no specific strategy of coping can *guarantee* a successful outcome. Even coping responses that generally tend to be adaptive can turn out to be ineffective in some circumstances (Bonanno & Burton, 2013). The efficacy of a coping response depends to some extent on the person, the nature of the stressful challenge, and the context of events. Thus, the concept of constructive coping is simply meant to convey a healthful, positive approach, without promising success.

What makes certain coping strategies constructive? Frankly, it's a gray area in which psychologists' opinions vary to some extent. Nonetheless, a consensus about the nature of constructive coping has emerged from the sizable literature on stress management. Key themes in this literature include the following:

1. Constructive coping involves confronting problems directly. It is task relevant and action oriented. It entails a conscious effort to rationally evaluate your options so you can try to solve your problems.

2. Constructive coping is based on reasonably realistic appraisals of your stress and coping resources. A little self-deception can sometimes be adaptive. However, excessive self-deception and highly unrealistic negative thinking clearly are not.

3. Constructive coping often involves reappraising stressful events in less threatening ways.

4. Constructive coping includes making efforts to ensure that your body is not especially vulnerable to the potentially damaging effects of stress.

The principles just described provide a rather general and abstract picture of constructive coping. We'll look at patterns of constructive coping in more detail in the Personal Application, which discusses various stress management strategies that people can use. We turn next to some of the possible outcomes of struggles with stress.

13.3 STRESS AND PHYSICAL HEALTH

People struggle with many stressors every day. Most stressors come and go without leaving any enduring imprint. However, when stress is severe or when many stressful demands pile up, one's mental or physical health can be affected. In Chapter 14 you'll learn that chronic stress contributes to many types of psychological disorders, including depression, schizophrenia, and anxiety disorders. In this section, we'll discuss the link between stress and physical illness.

Prior to the 1970s, it was thought that stress contributed to the development of only a few physical diseases, such as high blood pressure, ulcers, and asthma, which were called *psychosomatic diseases*. However, in the 1970s, research began to uncover new links between stress and a great variety of diseases previously believed to be purely physiological in origin (Carver & Vargas, 2011; Dougall & Baum, 2012). Let's look at some of this research.

Personality, Hostility, and Heart Disease

In spite of declines, heart disease remains the leading cause of death in the United States. *Coronary heart disease* involves a reduction in blood flow in the coronary arteries, which supply the heart with blood. This type of heart disease accounts for about 90% of heart-related deaths. Established risk factors for coronary disease include smoking, lack of exercise, high cholesterol levels, and high blood pressure (Bekkouche et al., 2011). Recently, attention has shifted to mounting evidence that *inflammation* plays a key role in the initiation and progression of coronary disease, as well as the acute complications that trigger heart attacks (Christodoulidis et al., 2014; Libby et al., 2014).

Research on the relationship between *psychological* factors and heart attacks began in the 1960s and 1970s, when a pair of cardiologists, Meyer Friedman and Ray Rosenman (1974), discovered an apparent connection between coronary risk and a syndrome they called the *Type A personality*, which involves self-imposed stress and intense reactions to stress. **The *Type A personality* includes three elements: (1) a strong competitive orientation, (2) impatience and time urgency, and (3) anger and hostility.** Type A's are ambitious, hard-driving perfectionists who are exceedingly time-conscious. Often they are highly competitive, irritable workaholics who drive themselves with many deadlines. In contrast, **the *Type B personality* is marked by relatively relaxed, patient, easygoing, amicable behavior.** Type B's are less hurried, less competitive, and less easily angered than Type A's.

Decades of research uncovered a relatively modest correlation between Type A behavior and increased coronary risk. More often than not, studies found a correlation between Type A personality and an elevated incidence of heart disease, but the findings were not as strong or as consistent as expected (Smith et al., 2012). However, in recent years, researchers have found a stronger link between personality and coronary risk by focusing on a specific component of the Type A personality: *anger and hostility* (Betensky, Contrada, & Glass, 2012; Smith, Williams, & Segerstrom, 2015). For example, in one study of almost 13,000 men and women who had no prior history of heart disease, investigators found an elevated incidence of heart attacks among participants who exhibited an angry temperament (Williams et al., 2000). Among participants with normal blood pressure, high-anger subjects experienced almost three times as many coronary events as low-anger subjects did (see **Figure 13.8**). The results of this study and many others suggest that hostility may be the crucial toxic element in the Type A syndrome.

Emotional Reactions, Depression, and Heart Disease

Recent studies suggest that people's emotions can also contribute to heart disease. *One line of research has supported the hypothesis that transient mental stress and the resulting emotions people experience can tax the heart* (Emery, Anderson, & Goodwin, 2013). Based on anecdotal evidence, cardiologists and laypersons have long voiced suspicions that strong emotional reactions might trigger heart attacks in individuals with coronary

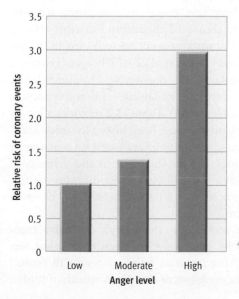

FIGURE 13.8

Anger and coronary risk. Working with a large sample of healthy men and women who were followed for a median of 4.5 years, Williams et al. (2000) found an association between participants' propensity to get angry and the likelihood of a coronary event. Among subjects who manifested normal blood pressure at the beginning of the study, a moderate anger level was associated with a 36% increase in coronary attacks. A high level of anger nearly tripled participants' risk for coronary disease.

disease, but it was difficult to document this connection. However, advances in cardiac monitoring have facilitated investigation of the issue.

As suspected, laboratory experiments with cardiology patients have shown that brief periods of mental stress can trigger sudden symptoms of heart disease (Baker, Suchday, & Krantz, 2007). Overall, the evidence suggests that mental stress can elicit cardiac symptoms in about 30%–70% of coronary patients (Emery et al., 2013). Outbursts of anger can be particularly dangerous. A recent meta-analysis of available evidence concluded that in the 2 hours immediately following an outburst of anger, there is nearly a fivefold jump in an individual's risk for a heart attack and a more than threefold increase in the risk for a stroke (Mostofsky, Penner, & Mittleman, 2014). These brief elevations in cardiovascular risk are transient, but in people who have frequent outbursts of anger, they can add up to significant increases in cardiovascular vulnerability.

Another line of research has implicated depression as a risk factor for heart disease (Glassman, Maj, & Sartorius, 2011). *Depressive disorders,* which are characterized by persistent feelings of sadness and despair, are a fairly common form of mental illness (see Chapter 14). In many studies, elevated rates of depression have been found among patients suffering from heart disease. Experts have tended to explain this correlation by asserting that being diagnosed with heart disease makes people depressed. However, recent evidence suggests that the causal relations may be just the opposite: *the emotional dysfunction of depression may cause heart disease* (Gustad et al., 2014; Brunner et al., 2014). For example, one study of almost 20,000 people who were initially free of heart disease reported striking results: Participants who suffered from depression were 2.7 times more likely to die of heart disease during the follow-up period than people who were not depressed (Surtees et al., 2008). Because the participants' depressive disorders preceded their heart attacks, it can't be argued that their heart disease caused their depression. Overall, studies suggest that depression roughly doubles one's chances of developing heart disease (Halaris, 2013; Herbst et al., 2007).

Stress, Other Diseases, and Immune Functioning

The development of questionnaires to measure life stress has allowed researchers to look for correlations between stress and a variety of diseases. These researchers have uncovered many connections between stress and physical illness. For example, researchers have found an association between life stress and the course of rheumatoid arthritis (Davis et al., 2013). Other studies have connected stress to the development of diabetes (Nezu et al., 2013); herpes (Pedersen, Bovbjerg, & Zachariae, 2011); fibromyalgia (Malin & Littlejohn, 2013); and flare-ups of inflammatory bowel syndrome (Keefer, Taft, & Kiebles, 2013). **Table 13.2** provides a longer list of health problems that have been linked to stress. Many of these stress-illness connections are based on tentative or inconsistent findings, but the sheer length and diversity of the list is remarkable. Why should stress increase the risk for so many kinds of illness? A partial answer may lie in the body's immune functioning.

The *immune response* is the body's defensive reaction to invasion by bacteria, viral agents, or other foreign substances. The immune response works to protect organisms from many forms of disease. A wealth of studies

TABLE 13.2 Health Problems that May Be Linked to Stress

Health Problem	Representative Evidence
AIDS	Perez, Cruess, & Kalichman (2010)
Asthma	Schmaling (2013)
Cancer	Dalton & Johansen (2005)
Chronic back pain	Mitchell et al. (2009)
Common cold	Cohen (2005)
Complications of pregnancy	Wakeel et al. (2013)
Diabetes	Nezu et al. (2013)
Epileptic seizures	Novakova et al. (2013)
Fibromyalgia	Malin & Littlejohn (2013)
Heart disease	Bekkouche et al. (2011)
Herpes virus	Pedersen, Bovbjerg, & Zachariae (2011)
Hypertension	Emery, Anderson, & Goodwin (2013)
Inflammatory bowel disease	Keefer, Taft, & Kiebles (2013)
Migraine headaches	Schramm et al. (2014)
Multiple sclerosis	Senders et al. (2014)
Periodontal disease	Parwani & Parwani (2014)
Premenstrual distress	Stanton et al. (2002)
Rheumatoid arthritis	Davis et al. (2013)
Skin disorders	Huynh, Gupta, & Koo (2013)
Stroke	Egido et al. (2012)
Ulcers	Kanno et al. (2013)

indicate that experimentally induced stress can impair immune functioning *in animals* (Ader, 2001; Kemeny, 2011). That is, stressors such as crowding, shock, food restriction, and restraint reduce various aspects of immune reactivity in laboratory animals (Prolo & Chiappelli, 2007).

Some studies have also related stress to suppressed immune activity *in humans* (Kiecolt-Glaser, 2009; Dhabhar, 2011). In one study, medical students provided researchers with blood samples so that their immune response could be assessed (Kiecolt-Glaser et al., 1984). They provided a baseline sample a month before final exams. They then contributed a high-stress sample on the first day of their finals. Reduced levels of immune activity were found during the extremely stressful finals week. Underscoring the practical significance of this immune suppression, studies have shown that when quarantined volunteers are exposed to respiratory viruses that cause the common cold, those who report high stress are more likely to be infected by the viruses (Marsland, Bachen, & Cohen, 2012).

Research in this area has mainly focused on the link between stress and immune suppression. However, recent studies have revealed other important connections between stress, immune function, and vulnerability to illness. Research suggests that exposure to long-term stress can sometimes promote chronic inflammation (Cohen et al., 2012; Gouin et al., 2012). Scientists have only begun to fully appreciate the potential ramifications of chronic inflammation. As we noted earlier, inflammation has recently been recognized as a factor in heart disease. But that's not all. Research has also demonstrated that chronic inflammation contributes to a diverse array of diseases, including arthritis, osteoporosis, respiratory diseases, diabetes, Alzheimer's disease, and some types of cancer (Gouin, Hantsoo, Kiecolt-Glaser, 2011). Thus, chronic inflammation resulting from immune system dysregulation may be another key mechanism underlying the association between stress and a wide variety of diseases.

Sizing Up the Link Between Stress and Illness

A wealth of evidence shows that stress is related to physical health. Converging lines of evidence suggest that stress contributes to the *causation* of illness (Cohen, Janicki-Deverts, & Miller, 2007; Pedersen et al., 2011). But we have to put this intriguing finding in perspective. Virtually all the relevant research is correlational, so it can't demonstrate conclusively that stress *causes* illness (Smith & Gallo, 2001; see Chapter 2 for a discussion of correlation and causation). Subjects' elevated levels of stress and illness could both be due to a third variable, perhaps some aspect of personality (see **Figure 13.9**). For instance, some evidence suggests that neuroticism can make people overly prone to interpret events as stressful and overly prone to interpret unpleasant sensations as symptoms of illness. Such a trend would inflate the correlation between stress and illness (Espejo et al., 2011).

In spite of methodological problems favoring inflated correlations, the research in this area consistently indicates that the *strength* of the relationship between stress and health is *modest*. The correlations typically fall in the .20s and .30s (Schwarzer & Luszczynska, 2013). Clearly, stress is not an irresistible force that produces inevitable effects on health. Actually, this fact should not come as a surprise because stress is but one factor operating in a complex network of biopsychosocial determinants of health. Other key factors include one's genetic endowment, exposure to infectious agents and environmental toxins, nutrition, exercise, alcohol and drug use, smoking, use of medical care, and cooperation with medical advice. Furthermore, some people handle stress better than others, which is the matter we turn to next.

Factors Moderating the Impact of Stress

Some people seem to be able to withstand the ravages of stress better than others (Smith, Epstein et al., 2013). Why? Because certain factors can lessen the impact of stress on physical and mental health. We'll look at several such factors to shed light on individual differences in how well people tolerate stress.

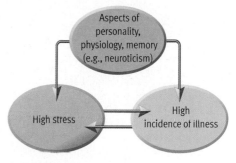

FIGURE 13.9

The stress-illness correlation. One or more aspects of personality, physiology, and memory could play the role of a postulated third variable in the relationship between high stress and a high incidence of illness. For example, neuroticism may lead some subjects to view more events as stressful and to remember more illness, thus inflating the apparent correlation between stress and illness.

> ▸ **REALITY CHECK**

Misconception

Stress is the leading cause of disease and poor health.

Reality

The contribution of stress to illness has probably been exaggerated in the popular press. Stress *can* be an important factor in health, but the correlations between stress and health outcomes are not all that strong, and there is room for some argument about whether these correlations reflect causal processes.

Social Support

Friends may be good for your health! This startling conclusion emerges from studies on social support as a moderator of stress. **Social support refers to various types of aid and emotional sustenance provided by members of one's social networks.** Many studies have found positive correlations between high social support and greater immune functioning (Stowell, Robles, & Kane, 2013). In contrast, the opposite of social support—loneliness and social isolation—is associated with immune dysregulation and increased inflammation (Jaremka et al., 2013). In recent decades, a vast number of studies have found evidence that social support is favorably related to overall physical health (Gleason & Masumi, 2015; Uchino & Birmingham, 2011). Meanwhile, studies have linked social isolation to poor health and increased mortality (Cacioppo & Cacioppo, 2014; Steptoe et al., 2013). The favorable effects of social support are strong enough to have an impact on mortality, increasing people's odds of survival by roughly 50% (Holt-Lunstad, Smith, & Layton, 2010). This surprising finding suggests that the negative effect of inadequate social support may be greater than the negative effects of being obese, not exercising, drinking excessively, and smoking.

Research suggests that cultural disparities exist in the type of social support that people prefer. Taylor et al. (2007) distinguish between *explicit social support* (overt emotional solace and instrumental aid from others) and *implicit social support* (the comfort that comes from knowing one has access to close others who will be supportive). Research has shown that Americans generally prefer and pursue explicit social support. In contrast, Asians do not feel comfortable seeking explicit social support because they worry about the strain it will place on their friends and family (Kim, Sherman, & Taylor, 2008; Taylor, 2015). But Asians do benefit from the implicit support that results when they spend time with close others and when they remind themselves that they belong to valued groups that would be supportive if needed.

Interestingly, a recent study suggests that even superficial social interactions with acquaintances and strangers—such as waiters, grocery store clerks, and people we see around our neighborhood—can be beneficial. Sandstrom and Dunn (2014) asked participants about their recent interactions involving people with whom they had either strong ties or weak ties. As expected, greater interactions with strong ties correlated with greater subjective well-being, but surprisingly, so did greater interactions with weak ties.

The availability of social support is a key factor influencing one's capacity to tolerate stress. Decades of research have shown that social support fosters resilience.

© Monkey Business Images/Shutterstock.com

Generally, researchers have assumed that our feelings of belongingness and social support are derived from our interactions with close friends and family, but the Sandstrom and Dunn study raises the possibility that weak ties can also contribute.

Optimism and Conscientiousness

Optimism **is as a general tendency to expect good outcomes.** Studies have found a correlation between optimism and relatively good physical health (Scheier, Carver, & Armstrong, 2012); more effective immune functioning (Segerstrom & Sephton, 2010); greater cardiovascular health (Hernandez et al., 2015); and increased longevity (Peterson et al., 1998). Why is optimism beneficial to health? Research suggests that optimists cope with stress in more adaptive ways than pessimists do (Carver, Scheier, & Segerstrom, 2010). Optimists are more likely to engage in action-oriented, problem-focused coping, and they are more likely to emphasize the positive in their appraisals of stressful events. Optimists also enjoy greater social support than pessimists, in part because they work harder on their relationships (Carver & Scheier, 2014). For the most part, research on optimism has been conducted in modern, industrialized societies. However, a recent study of representative samples from 142 countries yielded evidence that the link between optimism and health can be found around the world (Gallagher, Lopez, & Pressman, 2013).

Optimism is not the only personality trait that has been examined as a possible moderator of the relationship between stress and health. Research has shown that *conscientiousness,* one of the Big Five personality traits discussed in Chapter 11, is associated with good physical health and increased longevity (Friedman, 2011; Kern, Della Porta, & Friedman, 2014). Why does conscientiousness promote longevity? Several considerations appear to contribute (Shanahan et al., 2014). First, people who are high in conscientiousness are less likely than others to exhibit unhealthy habits, such as excessive drinking, drug abuse, dangerous driving, smoking, overeating, and risky sexual practices. Second, they tend to rely on constructive coping strategies and they are persistent in their efforts, so they may handle stressors better than others. Third, conscientiousness appears to promote better adherence to medical advice and more effective management of health problems. Fourth, conscientiousness is associated with higher educational attainment and job performance, which both foster career success and increased income, meaning that people high in conscientiousness tend to end up in the upper levels of socioeconomic status (SES). It may not be equitable, but a large body of research indicates that high SES confers a host of advantages that promote greater health and longevity. Age-adjusted mortality rates are 2–3 times higher among the poor than among the wealthy (Phelan, Link, & Tehranifar, 2010). These well-documented health disparities exist because wealthier people tend to endure lower levels of stress, benefit from better nutrition and more exercise, exhibit fewer unhealthy habits (see **Figure 13.10**), are exposed less to pollution and work in less toxic environments, and can afford easier access to higher-quality medical care (Ruiz, Prather, & Steffen, 2012).

Stress Mindset

Could your attitudes and beliefs about stress and its effects influence your capacity to handle stress effectively? Recent research by Crum, Salovey, and

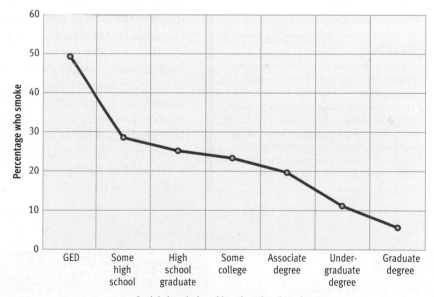

Social class indexed by educational attainment

FIGURE 13.10

Social class and smoking. Higher SES is associated with a lower prevalence of most unhealthy habits, such as smoking, excessive drinking, and failing to exercise. In many cases, these associations are surprisingly strong, as you can see in this graph, which depicts the relationship between social class and the likelihood of smoking. Using educational attainment as an indicator of SES, it is clear that smoking drops precipitously as SES increases. That is not to say that the upper classes have no bad health habits, but on average, they do appear to make far fewer unhealthy choices than the lower classes. (Based on Dube et al., 2010)

Achor (2013) suggests that the answer is yes. They argue that most people assume stress is generally harmful. They label this attitude a *stress-is-debilitating mindset*. However, they note that some people view stress as an invigorating challenge and opportunity for growth. They call this attitude a *stress-is-enhancing mindset*. They assert that people's stress mindset is likely to shape their psychological experience of stressful events, as well as their behavioral reactions. Specifically, they hypothesize that a stress-is-enhancing mindset should be associated with intermediate arousal in response to stress and more effective coping strategies. Their initial data provided some support for this line of thinking. A great deal of additional research is needed, but one's stress mindset may turn out to be another factor moderating the impact of stressful events.

Positive Effects of Stress

As just discussed, most people seem to operate under the impression that the effects of stress are entirely negative, but this most certainly is not the case. Recent decades have brought increased interest in the positive aspects of the stress process, including favorable outcomes that follow in the wake of stress (Folkman & Moskowitz, 2000). To some extent, the new focus on the possible benefits of stress reflects a new emphasis on "positive psychology." As we noted in Chapter 1, the advocates of positive psychology argue for increased research on well-being, courage, perseverance, tolerance, and other human strengths and virtues (Seligman, 2003). One of these strengths is resilience in the face of stress; in fact, studies indicate that resilience is not as uncommon as widely assumed (Bonanno, Westphal, & Mancini, 2012).

Research on resilience suggests that stress can promote personal growth or self-improvement (Calhoun & Tedeschi, 2008, 2013). For example, studies of people grappling with major health problems show that the majority of respondents report they derived benefits from their adversity (Lechner, Tennen, & Affleck, 2009). Stressful events sometimes force people to develop new skills, reevaluate priorities, learn new insights, and acquire new strengths. In other words, the adaptation process initiated by stress can lead to personal changes for the better. One study that measured participants' exposure to thirty-seven major negative events found a curvilinear relationship between lifetime adversity and mental health (Seery, 2011). High levels of adversity predicted poor mental health, as expected, but people who had faced intermediate levels of adversity were healthier than those who experienced little adversity, suggesting that moderate amounts of stress can foster resilience. A follow-up study found a similar link between the amount of lifetime adversity and subjects' responses to laboratory stressors (Seery et al., 2013). Intermediate levels of adversity were predictive of the greatest resilience. Thus, having to grapple with a moderate amount of stress may build resilience in the face of future stress.

13.4

Key Learning Goals

- Evaluate the negative health impact of smoking, substance abuse, and lack of exercise.
- Clarify the relationship between behavioral factors and AIDS.

13.4 HEALTH-IMPAIRING BEHAVIOR

Some people seem determined to dig an early grave for themselves. They do precisely those things that are bad for their health. For example, some people drink heavily even though they know they're damaging their liver. Others eat all the wrong foods even though they know they're increasing their risk of a second heart attack. Behavior that's downright *self-destructive* is surprisingly common. In this section, we'll discuss how health is affected by smoking, alcohol and drug use, and lack of exercise, and we'll look at behavioral factors in AIDS.

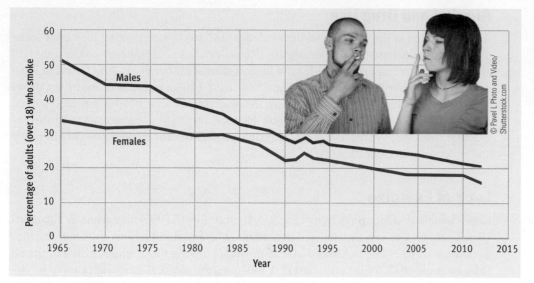

FIGURE 13.11
The prevalence of smoking in the United States. This graph shows how the percentage of U.S. adults who smoke has declined steadily since the mid-1960s. Although considerable progress has been made, smoking still accounts for a huge number of premature deaths in the United States each year. (Based on data from the Centers for Disease Control and Prevention)

Smoking

The smoking of tobacco is widespread in our culture. The percentage of people who smoke has declined noticeably since the mid-1960s (see **Figure 13.11**). Nonetheless, about 20.5% of adult men and 15.8% of adult women in the United States continue to smoke regularly. Smokers face a much greater risk of premature death than nonsmokers. For example, the average smoker has an estimated life expectancy *13 to 14 years shorter* than that of a similar nonsmoker (Grunberg, Berger, & Starosciak, 2012).

Why are mortality rates higher for smokers? Smoking increases the likelihood of developing a surprisingly large range of diseases (Thun, Apicella, & Henley, 2000; Thun et al., 2013). Lung cancer and heart disease kill the largest number of smokers. However, smokers also have an elevated risk for oral, bladder, and kidney cancer, as well as cancers of the larynx, esophagus, and pancreas; for arteriosclerosis, hypertension, stroke, and other cardiovascular diseases; and for bronchitis, emphysema, and other pulmonary diseases. Most smokers know about the risks associated with tobacco use. Interestingly, though, they tend to underestimate the risks as applied to themselves (Ayanian & Cleary, 1999).

Lamentably, the dangers of smoking are not limited to smokers themselves. Family members and co-workers who spend a lot of time around smokers are exposed to *second-hand smoke* or *environmental tobacco smoke*. Second-hand smoke can increase their risk for a variety of illnesses, including lung cancer (Vineis, 2005) and heart disease (Ding et al., 2009). Young children may be particularly vulnerable to the effects of second-hand smoke (Homa et al., 2015).

Studies show that if people can give up smoking, their health risks decline reasonably quickly (Kenfield et al., 2008). Evidence suggests that most smokers would like to quit but are reluctant to give up a major source of pleasure. They also worry about craving cigarettes, gaining weight, becoming anxious and irritable, and feeling less able to cope with stress (Grunberg, Faraday, & Rahman, 2001).

Unfortunately, it's difficult to give up cigarettes. People who enroll in formal smoking cessation programs are only slightly more successful than people who try to quit on their own (Swan, Hudman, & Khroyan, 2003). Long-term success rates peak in the vicinity of only 25%. Many studies report even lower figures. Nonetheless, the fact that there are roughly 50 million ex-smokers in the United States indicates that it *is* possible to quit smoking successfully. Interestingly, many people fail several times before they eventually succeed. Research suggests that the readiness to give up smoking builds gradually as people cycle through periods of abstinence and relapse (Prochaska et al., 2004).

> **► REALITY CHECK**
>
> **Misconception**
>
> If you can't quit smoking the first time you try, you are unlikely to succeed in the future.
>
> **Reality**
>
> People attempting to give up smoking usually fail several or more times before eventually succeeding. Hence, if your first effort to quit smoking ends in failure, you should not give up hope. Try again in a few weeks or a few months.

Alcohol and Drug Use

Although there is thought-provoking evidence that *moderate* drinking may offer some protection against cardiovascular disease (Ronksley et al., 2011), heavy consumption of alcohol clearly increases one's risk for a host of diseases (Sher et al., 2011). Recreational drug use is another common health-impairing habit. Unlike smoking or inactivity, drugs can kill directly and immediately. And in the long run, alcohol and various recreational drugs can elevate one's risk for infectious diseases; respiratory, pulmonary, and cardiovascular diseases; liver disease; gastrointestinal problems; cancer; neurological disorders; and pregnancy complications (see Chapter 5).

Lack of Exercise

Considerable evidence links lack of exercise to poor health (Wilson, Zarrett, & Kitzman-Ulrich, 2011). Conversely, studies have found substantial reductions in the prevalence of chronic diseases late in life and overall mortality among those who are high in fitness (Moore et al., 2012; Willis et al., 2012). Unfortunately, physical fitness appears to be declining in the United States. Only about one-third of American adults get an adequate amount of regular exercise (Carlson et al., 2010).

Why would exercise help people live longer? For one thing, an appropriate exercise program can enhance cardiovascular fitness and thereby reduce susceptibility to deadly cardiovascular problems (Brassington et al., 2012). Second, exercise can indirectly reduce one's risk for a variety of obesity-related health problems, such as diabetes and respiratory difficulties (Corsica & Perri, 2013). Third, recent studies suggest that exercise can help diminish chronic inflammation, which is thought to contribute to quite a variety of diseases (You et al., 2013). Fourth, exercise can serve as a buffer that reduces the potentially damaging physical effects of stress (Edenfield & Blumenthal, 2011). This buffering effect may occur because people high in fitness show less physiological reactivity to stress than do those who are less fit (Zschucke et al., 2015). Fifth, among the elderly, exercise is associated with a reduction in the brain shrinkage normally seen after age 60 (Gow et al., 2012) and a reduction in vulnerability to Alzheimer's disease (Radak et al., 2010).

Regular exercise has many diverse physical and psychological benefits that can promote enhanced health and greater longevity.

© Andrey_Popov/Shutterstock.com

Behavior and HIV/AIDS

At present, some of the most problematic links between behavior and health may be those related to AIDS. AIDS stands for *acquired immune deficiency syndrome,* **a disorder in which the immune system is gradually weakened and eventually disabled by the human immunodeficiency virus (HIV).** Being infected with the HIV virus is *not* equivalent to having AIDS, which is the final stage of the HIV infection process, typically manifesting about 7–10 years after the original infection. With the onset of AIDS, one is left virtually defenseless against numerous infectious agents. AIDS inflicts its harm indirectly by opening the door to other diseases. The symptoms of AIDS vary widely, depending on the specific constellation of diseases that one develops (Cunningham & Selwyn, 2005). Although the growth of the epidemic has leveled off in recent years and the number of AIDS-related deaths has declined, this deadly disease remains disproportionally prevalent in certain regions of Africa.

Prior to 1996–1997, the average length of survival for people after the onset of the AIDS syndrome was about 18–24 months. Encouraging advances in the treatment of AIDS with drug regimens, referred to as *highly active antiretroviral therapy (HAART),* hold out promise for *substantially* longer survival (Thompson et al., 2012). However, because these drug regimens are complicated to administer, have adverse side effects, are not effective for all patients, and are harder to obtain in poor nations, they have been used by a mere 10% of AIDS patients worldwide (Carey, Scott-Sheldon, & Vanable, 2013). Medical experts are concerned that the general public has gotten the impression that these treatments have transformed AIDS from a fatal disease to a manageable one. This may be a premature conclusion, as HIV strains are evolving and some strains are resistant to drug treatment (Temoshok, 2011).

The HIV virus is transmitted through person-to-person contact involving the exchange of bodily fluids, primarily semen and blood. The two principal modes of transmission in the United States have been sexual contact and the sharing of needles by intravenous (IV) drug users. In the United States, sexual transmission has occurred primarily among gay and bisexual men, but heterosexual transmission has increased in recent years (U.S. Centers for Disease Control, 2011). In the world as a whole, infection through heterosexual relations has been much more common from the beginning (Carey et al., 2013). In heterosexual relations, male-to-female transmission is estimated to be about eight times more likely than female-to-male transmission (Ickovics, Thayaparan, & Ethier, 2001). The HIV virus can be found in the tears and saliva of infected individuals, but the concentrations are low and there is no evidence that the infection can spread through casual contact. Even most forms of noncasual contact, including kissing, hugging, and sharing food with infected individuals, appear safe (Kalichman, 1995).

One problem related to transmission is that many young heterosexuals who are sexually active with a variety of partners foolishly downplay their risk of getting HIV. They greatly underestimate the probability that their sexual partners previously may have used IV drugs or had unprotected sex with an infected individual. Also, many young people inaccurately believe that prospective sexual partners who carry the HIV virus will exhibit telltale signs of illness. In reality, many HIV carriers do not know themselves that they are HIV-positive. In one study that screened more than 5000 men for HIV, 77% of those who tested HIV-positive were previously unaware of their infection (MacKellar et al., 2005).

13.5 REACTIONS TO ILLNESS

Some people respond to physical symptoms and illnesses by ignoring warning signs of developing diseases. In contrast, others actively seek to conquer their diseases. Let's examine the decision to seek medical treatment, communication with health providers, and factors that affect adherence to medical advice.

Key Learning Goals

- Discuss differences in the willingness to seek medical treatment and some barriers to effective patient-provider communication.
- Review the extent to which people tend to adhere to medical advice.

Deciding to Seek Treatment

Have you ever experienced nausea, diarrhea, stiffness, headaches, cramps, chest pains, or sinus problems? Of course you have; everyone experiences some of these problems periodically. However, whether someone views these sensations as *symptoms* is a matter of individual interpretation. When two people experience the same unpleasant sensations, one may shrug them off as a nuisance, while the other may rush to a physician (Martin & Leventhal, 2004). Studies suggest that people who are relatively high in anxiety and neuroticism tend to report more symptoms of illness than others do (Petrie & Pennebaker, 2004).

The biggest problem in regard to treatment seeking is the tendency of many people to delay the pursuit of needed professional consultation. Delays can be critical because early diagnosis and quick intervention may facilitate more effective treatment of many health problems (Petrie & Pennebaker, 2004). Unfortunately, procrastination is the norm even when people are faced with a medical emergency, such as a heart attack (Martin & Leventhal, 2004). Why do people dawdle in the midst of a crisis? Robin DiMatteo (1991), a leading expert on patient behavior, mentions a number of reasons, noting that people delay because they often (1) misinterpret and downplay the significance of their symptoms; (2) fret about looking silly if the problem turns out to be nothing; (3) worry about "bothering" their physician; (4) are reluctant to disrupt their plans (to go out to dinner, see a movie, and so forth); or (5) waste time on trivial matters (such as taking a shower, gathering personal items, or packing clothes) before going to a hospital emergency room.

Communicating with Health Providers

The quality of communication between patients and their health providers can influence individuals' health outcomes (Hall & Roter, 2011). A large portion of medical patients leave their doctors' offices not understanding what they have been told and what they are supposed to do (Johnson & Carlson, 2004). This situation is most unfortunate because good communication is a crucial requirement for sound medical decisions, informed choices about treatment, and appropriate follow-through by patients (Haskard et al., 2008).

There are many barriers to effective provider-patient communication (DiMatteo, 1997; Marteau & Weinman, 2004). Economic realities dictate that medical visits generally be quite brief, allowing little time for discussion. Many providers use too much medical jargon and overestimate their patients' understanding of technical terms. Patients who are upset and worried about their illness may simply forget to report some symptoms or to ask questions they meant to ask. Other patients are evasive about their real concerns because they fear a serious diagnosis. Many patients are reluctant to challenge doctors' authority and are too passive in their interactions with providers.

What can you do to improve your communication with health care providers? The key is to not be a passive consumer of medical services (Berger, 2013). Arrive at a medical visit on time, with your questions and concerns prepared in advance. Try to be accurate and candid in replying to your doctor's questions. If you don't understand something the doctor says, don't be embarrassed about asking for clarification. And if you have doubts about the suitability or feasibility of your doctor's recommendations, don't be afraid to voice them.

Adhering to Medical Advice

Many patients fail to follow the instructions they receive from physicians and other health care professionals. The evidence suggests that *nonadherence* to medical advice may occur 30% of the time when short-term treatments are prescribed for acute conditions and 50% of the time when long-term treatments are needed for chronic illness (Johnson &

Communication between health care providers and patients tends to be far from optimal, for a variety of reasons.

Carlson, 2004). Nonadherence takes many forms. Patients may fail to begin a treatment regimen, may stop the regimen early, may reduce or increase the levels of treatment that were prescribed, or may be inconsistent and unreliable in following treatment procedures (Dunbar-Jacob & Schlenk, 2001). Nonadherence has been linked to increased sickness, treatment failures, and higher mortality (Dunbar-Jacob, Schlenk, & McCall, 2012). Moreover, nonadherence wastes expensive medical visits and medications and increases hospital admissions, leading to enormous economic costs. DiMatteo (2004b) speculates that in the United States alone, nonadherence may be a $300 billion a year drain on the health care system.

Why don't people comply with the advice they've sought from highly regarded health care professionals? Physicians tend to attribute noncompliance to patients' personal characteristics, but research indicates that personality traits and demographic factors are surprisingly unrelated to adherence rates (DiMatteo, 2004b). The most commonly reported reason for poor adherence is simple forgetting (Dunbar-Jacob et al., 2012). One factor that *is* related to adherence is patients' *social support*. Adherence is improved when patients have family members, friends, or co-workers who remind them and help them comply with treatment requirements (DiMatteo, 2004a). Other considerations that influence the likelihood of adherence include the following (Hall & Roter, 2011; Johnson & Carlson, 2004):

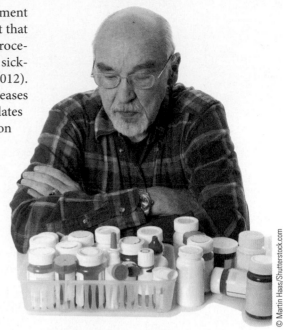

Nonadherence to medical advice and treatment regimens is a major problem in our health care system. For example, only about one-half of patients take their medications as prescribed.

1. Frequently, nonadherence occurs because the patient doesn't understand the instructions as given. Highly trained professionals often forget that what seems obvious and simple to them may be obscure and complicated to many of their patients.

2. Another key factor is how aversive or difficult the instructions are. If the prescribed regimen is unpleasant, adherence tends to decrease. And the more that following instructions interferes with routine behavior, the less probable it is that the patient will cooperate successfully.

3. If a patient has a negative attitude toward a physician, the probability of noncompliance increases. When patients are unhappy with their interactions with the doctor, they're more likely to ignore the medical advice provided, no matter how important it may be.

13.6 REFLECTING ON THE CHAPTER'S THEMES

13.6

Key Learning Goals

- Identify the two unifying themes highlighted in this chapter.

Which of our themes were prominent in this chapter? As you probably noticed, our discussion of stress and health illustrated multifactorial causation and the subjectivity of experience.

Our discussion of the psychology of health provided a particularly complex illustration of multifactorial causation. As we noted in Chapter 1, people are likely to think simplistically, in terms of single causes. In recent years, the highly publicized research linking stress to health has led many people to point automatically to stress as an explanation for illness. In reality, stress has only a modest impact on physical health. Stress can increase the risk for illness, but health is governed by a dense network of factors. Important factors include inherited vulnerabilities, exposure to infectious agents, health-impairing habits, reactions to symptoms, treatment-seeking behavior, compliance with medical advice, optimism, and social support. In other words, stress is but one actor on a crowded stage. This should be apparent in **Figure 13.12**, which shows the multitude of biopsychosocial factors that jointly influence physical health. It illustrates multifactorial causation in all its complexity.

 Multifactorial Causation

 Subjectivity of Experience

Biological factors

Environmental toxins

Genetic predisposition

Physiological reactivity

Immune response

Infectious agents

Social support

Physical health and illness

Stress

Health education

Coping tactics

Pollution control

Personality

Psychological (behavioral) factors

Health-related habits

Reactions to illness

Medical care

Sanitation

Social (system) factors

Steve Sant/Alamy

FIGURE 13.12

Biopsychosocial factors in health. Physical health can be influenced by a remarkably diverse set of variables, including biological, psychological, and social factors. The variety of factors that affect health provide an excellent example of multifactorial causation.

The subjectivity of experience was demonstrated by the frequently repeated point that stress lies in the eye of the beholder. The same job promotion may be stressful for one person and invigorating for another. One person's pressure is another's challenge. When it comes to stress, objective reality is not nearly as important as subjective perceptions. More than anything else, the impact of stressful events seems to depend on how people view them. The critical importance of stress appraisals will continue to be apparent in our Personal Application on stress management. Many stress-management strategies depend on altering one's appraisals of events.

Key Learning Goals

- Analyze the adaptive value of rational thinking, humor, and releasing pent-up emotions.
- Assess the adaptive value of forgiving others, relaxing, increasing fitness, and improving sleep habits.

Answer the following "true" or "false."

____ **1** The key to managing stress is to avoid or circumvent it.

____ **2** It's best to suppress emotional reactions to stress.

13.7 PERSONAL APPLICATION
Improving Coping and Stress Management

____ **3** Laughing at one's problems is immature.

____ **4** Exercise has little or no impact on stress resistance.

Courses and books on stress management have multiplied at a furious pace in recent decades. They summarize experts' advice on how to cope with stress more effectively. How do these experts feel about our four true/false statements? As you'll see in this Personal Application, most would agree that all four are false.

The key to managing stress does not lie in avoiding it. Stress is an inevitable element in the fabric of modern life. As

Hans Selye (1973) noted, "Contrary to public opinion, we must not—and indeed can't—avoid stress" (p. 693). Thus, most stress-management programs train people to use more effective coping strategies. In this Application, we'll examine a variety of constructive coping tactics, beginning with Albert Ellis's ideas about changing one's appraisals of stressful events.

Reappraisal: Ellis's Rational Thinking

Albert Ellis is a prominent theorist who believes that people can short-circuit their emotional reactions to stress by altering their appraisals of stressful events. Ellis's insights about stress appraisal are the foundation for a widely used system of therapy called *rational-emotive behavior therapy* (Ellis, 1977, 1987; Ellis & Ellis, 2011) and several popular books on effective coping (Ellis, 1985, 1999, 2001).

Ellis maintains that *you feel the way you think*. He argues that problematic emotional reactions are caused by negative self-talk, which he calls catastrophic thinking. **Catastrophic thinking involves unrealistically pessimistic appraisals of stress that exaggerate the magnitude of one's problems.** According to Ellis, people unwittingly believe that stressful events cause their emotional turmoil, but he maintains that emotional reactions to personal setbacks are actually caused by overly negative appraisals of stressful events (see **Figure 13.13**).

Ellis theorizes that unrealistic appraisals of stress are derived from irrational assumptions people hold. He maintains that if you scrutinize your catastrophic thinking, you'll find your reasoning is based on a logically indefensible premise, such as "I must have approval from everyone" or "I must perform well in all endeavors." These faulty assumptions, which people often hold unconsciously, generate catastrophic thinking and emotional turmoil. How can you reduce your unrealistic appraisals of stress? Ellis asserts that you must learn (1) how to detect catastrophic thinking and (2) how to dispute the irrational assumptions that cause it.

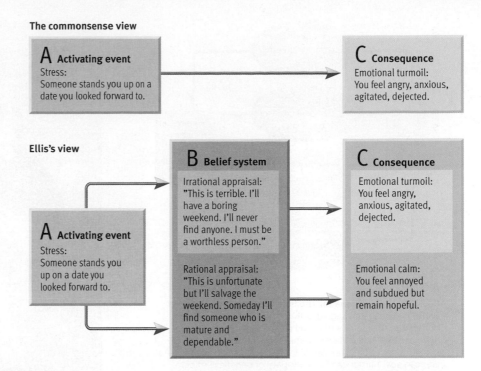

FIGURE 13.13

Albert Ellis's model of emotional reactions. Although most people attribute their negative emotional reactions directly to negative events they experience, Ellis argues that events themselves do *not* cause emotional distress; rather, distress is caused by the way people *think* about negative events. According to Ellis, the key to managing stress is to change one's appraisal of stressful events.

Humor as a Stress Reducer

A number of years ago, the Chicago suburbs experienced their worst flooding in about a century. Thousands of people saw their homes wrecked when two rivers spilled over their banks. As the waters receded, the flood victims returning to their homes were subjected to the inevitable TV interviews. A remarkable number of victims, surrounded by the ruins of their homes, *joked* about their misfortune. When the going gets tough, it may pay to laugh about it. In a study of coping styles, McCrae (1984) found that 40% of his subjects used humor to deal with stress.

Empirical evidence showing that humor moderates the impact of stress has been accumulating over the last 30 years (Abel, 2002; Lefcourt, 2001, 2005). For example, a review of forty-nine studies found that employees who used humor at work showed enhanced performance, satisfaction, and health, as well as decreased burnout and stress (Mesmer-Magnus, Glew, & Viswesvaran, 2012).

How does humor help to reduce the effects of stress and promote wellness? Several explanations have been proposed (see **Figure 13.14**). One possibility is that humor affects appraisals of stressful events (Abel, 2002). Jokes can help people put a less threatening spin on their trials and tribulations. Another possibility is that humor increases the experience of positive emotions (Martin, 2002). These emotions may help people bounce back from stressful events (Tugade & Fredrickson, 2004). Another hypothesis is that a good sense of humor facilitates rewarding social interactions, which promote social support, a factor known to buffer the effects of stress (Martin, 2002). Finally, Lefcourt and colleagues (1995) argue that high-humor people may benefit from not taking themselves as seriously as low-humor people do. As they put it, "If persons do not regard themselves too seriously and do not have an inflated sense of self-importance, then defeats, embarrassments, and even tragedies should have

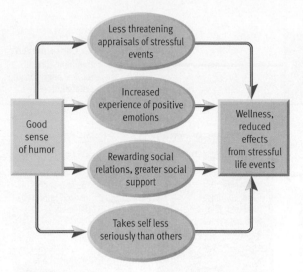

FIGURE 13.14

Possible explanations for the link between humor and wellness. Research suggests that a good sense of humor buffers the effects of stress and promotes wellness. Four hypothesized explanations for the link between humor and wellness are outlined in the middle column of this diagram. As you can see, humor can have a variety of beneficial effects.

In September 1994, Reg and Maggie Green were vacationing in Italy when their 7-year-old son Nicholas was shot and killed during a highway robbery. In an act of forgiveness that stunned Europe, the Greens chose to donate their son's organs, which went to seven Italians. The Greens, shown here 5 years after the incident, weathered their horrific loss better than most, perhaps in part because of their willingness to forgive.

less pervasive emotional consequences for them" (p. 375).

Releasing Pent-Up Emotions and Forgiving Others

Although there's no guarantee of it, you can sometimes reduce stress-induced physiological arousal by *expressing* your emotions. For instance, evidence is accumulating that writing or talking about life's difficulties can be valuable in dealing with stress (Smyth, Pennebaker, & Arigo, 2012). In one study of college students, half the subjects were asked to write three essays about their difficulties in adjusting to college, while the other half wrote three essays about superficial topics. The subjects who wrote about their personal problems enjoyed better health in the following months than the other subjects did (Pennebaker, Colder, & Sharp, 1990). Subsequent studies replicated this finding

and showed that emotional disclosure is associated with better immune functioning (Slatcher & Pennebaker, 2005). So, if you can find a good listener, you may be able to discharge problematic emotions by letting your fears, misgivings, and frustrations spill out in a candid conversation.

People tend to experience hostility and other negative emotions when they feel "wronged"; that is, when they believe the actions of another person were harmful, immoral, or unjust. People's natural inclination in such situations is either to seek revenge or to avoid further contact with the offender (McCullough, Kurzban, & Tabak, 2013). *Forgiving* someone involves counteracting these natural tendencies and releasing the person from further liability for his or her transgression. Research suggests that forgiving is associated with better adjustment and well-being (McCullough & Witvliet, 2002; Worthington & Scherer, 2004), as

well as reduced anger and physical symptoms (Bono, McCullough, & Root, 2008; McCullough et al., 2014). For example, in one study of divorced or permanently separated women reported by McCullough (2001), the extent to which the women had forgiven their former husbands was positively related to several measures of well-being.

Relaxing and Minimizing Physiological Vulnerability

Relaxation is a valuable stress-management technique that can soothe emotional turmoil and suppress problematic physiological arousal (McGuigan & Lehrer, 2007; Smith, 2007). The value of relaxation became apparent to Herbert Benson (1975) as a result of his research on meditation. Benson, a Harvard Medical School cardiologist, believes relaxation is the key to many of the beneficial effects of

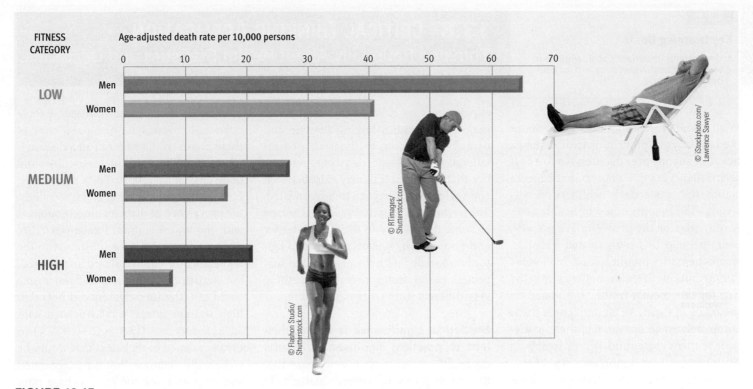

FIGURE 13.15

Physical fitness and mortality. Blair and colleagues (1989) studied death rates among men and women who exhibited low, medium, or high physical fitness. As you can see, fitness was associated with lower mortality rates in both genders.

meditation. Anything that relaxes you—whether it's music, meditation, prayer, or a warm bath—can be helpful. Experts have also devised a variety of systematic relaxation procedures that can make relaxation efforts more effective. You may want to learn about techniques such as *progressive relaxation* (Jacobson, 1938); *autogenic training* (Schultz & Luthe, 1959); and the *relaxation response* (Benson & Klipper, 1988).

As this chapter has made clear, the wear and tear of stress can be injurious to one's physical health. To combat this potential problem, it helps to keep your body in relatively sound shape. The potential benefits of regular exercise are substantial,

including increased longevity (Gremeaux et al., 2012). Moreover, research has shown that you don't have to be a dedicated athlete to benefit from exercise because even a moderate amount of exercise reduces your risk of disease (Richardson et al., 2004; see **Figure 13.15**).

Embarking on an exercise program is difficult for many people. Exercise is time-consuming, and if you're out of shape, your initial attempts may be painful and discouraging. To avoid these problems, it's wise to (1) select an activity you find enjoyable, (2) increase your participation gradually, (3) exercise regularly without overdoing it, and (4) reinforce yourself for your efforts (Greenberg, 2002).

Good sleep habits can also help in the effort to minimize physiological vulnerability to stress. As we discussed in Chapter 5, sleep loss can undermine immune system responding (Motivala & Irwin, 2007) and fuel inflammatory responses (Patel et al., 2009). Evidence also suggests that poor sleep quality is associated with poor health (Grandner et al., 2012, 2014) and that sleep loss can elevate the risk of mortality (Magee et al., 2013). Thus, sound sleep patterns can contribute to stress management. The results of one study suggest that people need to get a sufficient amount of sleep and should strive for consistency in their patterns of sleeping (Barber et al., 2010).

13.8

Key Learning Goals
- Understand important considerations in evaluating health statistics and making health decisions.

13.8 CRITICAL THINKING APPLICATION
Thinking Rationally About Health Statistics and Decisions

With so many conflicting claims about the best ways to prevent or treat diseases, how can anyone ever decide what to do? It seems that every day a report in the media claims that yesterday's health news was wrong. The inconsistency of health news is only part of the problem. We are also overwhelmed by health-related statistics. As mathematics pundit John Allen Paulos (1995) puts it, "Health statistics may be bad for our mental health. Inundated by too many of them, we tend to ignore them completely, to accept them blithely, to disbelieve them closemindedly, or simply to misinterpret their significance" (p. 133).

Making personal decisions about health-related issues may not be easy. Even medical personnel often struggle to make sense out of health statistics (Gigerenzer at al., 2007). Yet it's particularly important to try to think rationally and systematically about such issues. In this Application, we'll discuss a few insights that can help you to think critically about statistics on health risks. Then we'll briefly outline a systematic approach to thinking through health decisions.

Evaluating Statistics on Health Risks

News reports seem to suggest that there are links between virtually everything people do, touch, and consume and some type of physical illness. For example, media have reported that coffee consumption is related to hypertension, sleep loss is related to mortality, and a high-fat diet is related to heart disease. Such reports are enough to send even the most subdued person into a panic. Fortunately, your evaluation of data on health risks can become more sophisticated by considering the following factors.

Correlation is not an assurance of causation. It is not easy to conduct experiments on health risks, so the vast majority of studies linking lifestyle and demographic factors to diseases are correlational studies. Hence, it pays to remember that no causal link may exist between two variables that happen to be correlated. Thus, when you hear that a factor is related to some disease, try to dig a little deeper and find out *why* scientists think this factor is associated with the disease. The suspected causal factor may be something very different from what was measured.

Statistical significance is not equivalent to practical significance. Reports on health statistics often emphasize that the investigators uncovered "statistically significant" findings. Statistically significant findings are results that are not likely to be due to chance fluctuations. Statistical significance is a useful concept, but it can sometimes be misleading (Matthey, 1998). Medical studies are often based on rather large samples because they tend to yield more reliable conclusions than small samples. However, when a large sample is used, weak relationships and small differences between groups can turn out to be statistically significant, and these small differences may not have much practical importance. For example, in one study of sodium (salt) intake and cardiovascular disease, which used a sample of over 14,000 participants, He et al. (1999) found a statistically significant link between high sodium intake and the prevalence of hypertension among normal-weight subjects. However, this statistically significant difference was not particularly large. The prevalence of hypertension among subjects with the lowest sodium intake was 19.1%, compared with 21.8% for subjects with the highest sodium intake—not exactly a difference worthy of panic.

Base rates should be considered in evaluating probabilities. In evaluating whether a possible risk factor is associated with some disease, people often fail to consider the base rates of these events. If the base rate of a disease is relatively low, a small increase can sound quite large if it's reported as a percentage. For example, in the He et al. (1999) study, the prevalence of diabetes among subjects with the lowest sodium intake was 2.1%, compared with 3.8% for subjects with the highest sodium intake. Based on this small but statistically significant difference, one could say (the investigators did not) that high sodium intake was associated with an 81% increase ($[3.8 - 2.1] \div 2.1$) in the prevalence of diabetes. This would be technically accurate, but an exaggerated way of portraying the results. Base rates should also be considered when evaluating claims made about the value of medications and other medical treatments. If the base rate of a disease is low, a very modest decrease reported as a percentage can foster exaggerated perceptions of treatment benefits. For instance, Gigerenzer at al. (2007) describe an advertisement for Lipitor (a drug intended to lower cholesterol levels) claiming that Lipitor reduced the risk of stroke by 48%. Although this was technically accurate, in absolute terms the protective benefits of Lipitor were actually rather modest. After 4 years, 1.5% of those taking Lipitor had a stroke, versus 2.8% of those taking the placebo.

Thinking Systematically About Health Decisions

Health decisions are oriented toward the future, which means there are always uncertainties. And they usually involve weighing potential risks and benefits. None of these variables is unique to health decisions. Uncertainty, risks, and benefits play prominent roles in economic and political decisions as well as in personal decisions. To illustrate, let's apply some basic principles of quantitative reasoning to a treatment decision involving whether to

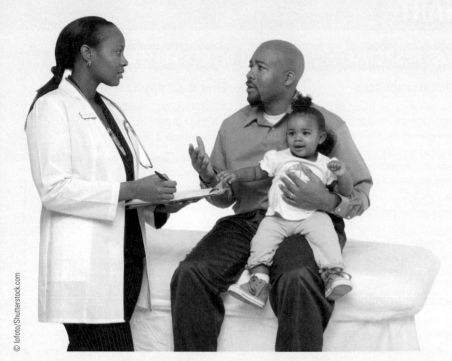

When you have to make decisions about medical issues for yourself or your family, it pays to think rationally. In particular, it is wise to remember that correlation is no assurance of causation.

prescribe Ritalin for a boy who has been diagnosed with attention deficit disorder. Keep in mind that the general principles applied in this example can be used for a wide variety of decisions.

Seek information to reduce uncertainty. Gather information and check it carefully for accuracy, completeness, and the presence or absence of conflicting information. For example, is the diagnosis of attention deficit correct? Look for conflicting information that does not fit with this diagnosis. If the child can sit and read for a long period of time, maybe the problem is an undetected hearing loss that makes him appear to be hyperactive in some situations. As you consider the additional information, begin quantifying the degree of uncertainty or its "flip side" (your degree of confidence that the diagnosis is correct). If you decide that you are not confident about the diagnosis, you may be trying to solve the wrong problem.

Make risk-benefit assessments. What are the risks and benefits of Ritalin? How likely is this child to benefit from Ritalin, and just how much improvement can be expected? If the child is 8 years old and unable to read and is miserable in school and at home, any treatment that could reduce his problems deserves serious consideration. As in the first step, the quantification is at an approximate level.

List alternative courses of action. What are the alternatives to Ritalin? How well do they work? What are the risks associated with the alternatives, including the risk of falling further behind in school? Consider the pros and cons of each alternative. A special diet that sometimes works might be a good first step, along with the decision to start drug therapy if the child does not show improvement over some time period. What are the relative success rates for different types of treatment for children like the one being considered? To answer these questions, you will need to use probability estimates in your decision making.

As you can see from this example, many parts of the problem have been quantified (confidence in the diagnosis, likelihood of improvement, probability of negative outcomes, and so forth). Precise probability values were not used because often the actual numbers are not known. Some of the quantified values reflect value judgments, others reflect likelihoods, and yet others assess the degree of uncertainty. If you are thinking that the quantification of many unknowns in decision making is a lot of work, you are right. But it is work worth doing. Whenever there are important decisions to be made about health, the ability to think with numbers will help you reach a better decision. And yes, that assertion is a virtual certainty.

TABLE 13.3 Critical Thinking Skills Discussed in This Application

Skill	Description
Understanding the limitations of correlational evidence	The critical thinker understands that a correlation between two variables does not demonstrate that there is a causal link between the variables.
Understanding the limitations of statistical significance	The critical thinker understands that weak relationships can be statistically significant when large samples are used in research.
Utilizing base rates in making predictions and evaluating probabilities	The critical thinker appreciates that the initial proportion of some group or event needs to be considered in weighing probabilities.
Seeking information to reduce uncertainty	The critical thinker understands that gathering more information can often decrease uncertainty, and reduced uncertainty can facilitate better decisions.
Making risk-benefit assessments	The critical thinker is aware that most decisions have risks and benefits that need to be weighed carefully.
Generating and evaluating alternative courses of action	In problem solving and decision making, the critical thinker knows the value of generating as many alternatives as possible and assessing their advantages and disadvantages.

© Iofoto/Shutterstock.com

CHAPTER 13 CONCEPT CHART

STRESS

- Stress is a common, everyday event, and even routine hassles can have harmful effects.
- People's *primary appraisals* of events determine what they find stressful.
- People's *secondary appraisals* assess their coping resources and influence the degree of stress experienced.

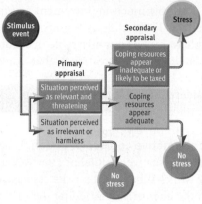

MAJOR TYPES OF STRESS

Frustration

- *Frustration* occurs when the pursuit of some goal is thwarted.

Conflict

- In an *approach-approach conflict*, a choice must be made between two attractive goals.
- In an *avoidance-avoidance conflict*, a choice must be made between two unattractive goals.
- In an *approach-avoidance conflict*, a choice must be made about whether to pursue a goal that has positive and negative aspects.

Change

- *Life changes* are alterations in living circumstances, including positive changes, that require adjustment.
- The Social Readjustment Rating Scale (SRRS) purports to measure change-related stress, but actually taps many types of stressful experiences.
- Many studies have shown that high scores on the SRRS are associated with increased vulnerability to physical illness and psychological problems.

Pressure

- People may be under *pressure* to perform well or to conform to others' expectations.
- Pressure is a predictor of psychological symptoms and heart disease.

STRESS RESPONSE

Emotional responses

- Many emotions can be evoked by stress, but anger-rage, anxiety-fear, and sadness-grief are especially common.
- Investigators tend to focus on negative emotions, but research shows that positive emotions also occur during periods of stress.
- Emotional arousal can interfere with coping efforts.
- The *inverted-U hypothesis* posits that as tasks become more complex, the optimal level of arousal decreases.

Physiological responses

- The *general adaptation syndrome* is Hans Selye's model of the body's response to stress, which can progress through three stages: alarm, resistance, and exhaustion.
- Prolonged stress can lead to what Selye called diseases of adaptation.
- Stress can cause the brain to send signals to the endocrine system along two pathways.

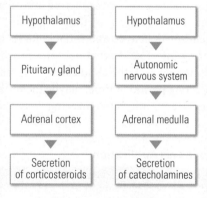

Behavioral responses

- Coping efforts intended to master or reduce stress can be healthy or unhealthy.
- *Giving up and blaming oneself* are less than optimal methods of coping with stress.
- Another unhealthy response is to strike out at others with acts of *aggression*.
- *Indulging oneself* is another common response to stress that tends to be less than optimal.
- *Defensive coping* protects against emotional distress, but it depends on self-deception and avoidance.
- However, small positive illusions about one's life can be adaptive for mental health.
- *Constructive coping* refers to relatively healthful efforts to handle the demands of stress.

STRESS EFFECTS

Effects on physical health

- Stress appears to contribute to many types of physical illness and not just *psychosomatic diseases*.
- The *Type A personality* has been identified as a contributing factor in coronary heart disease.
- Research suggests that *hostility* is the most toxic element of the Type A syndrome.
- Recent evidence suggests that strong emotional reactions can precipitate heart attacks.
- Research indicates that depression roughly doubles one's chances of developing heart disease.
- The association between stress and vulnerability to many diseases may reflect the negative impact of stress on immune function.
- The correlation between stress and illness is modest in strength because stress is only one of many factors that influence health.

Variations in stress tolerance

- There are individual differences in how much stress people can tolerate without negative effects.
- Strong *social support* appears to buffer the impact of stress, and thus promote physical and psychological health.
- Asians prefer *implicit* social support, whereas Americans prefer *explicit* social support.
- Two personality traits, *optimism* and *conscientiousness*, appear to promote health.
- A *stress-is-enhancing mindset* may be associated with reduced stress arousal and more effective coping.
- Research on resilience suggests that stress can promote personal growth, self-improvement, and other benefits.

HEALTH-IMPAIRING BEHAVIOR

Smoking

- Smokers have much higher mortality rates than nonsmokers because smoking elevates the risk for a wide range of diseases, including lung cancer and heart disease.

- When people quit smoking, their health risks decline fairly quickly.

- Long-term success rates for giving up smoking are only 25% or less.

Alcohol and drug use

- Moderate drinking may offer some protection against cardiovascular disease, but heavy consumption clearly increases one's risk for a host of diseases.

- Recreational drug use also elevates people's vulnerability to various types of illness.

Lack of exercise

- Research indicates that regular exercise is associated with increased longevity.

- Physical fitness can reduce vulnerability to deadly cardiovascular diseases, obesity-related problems, and chronic inflammation.

Behavior and AIDS

- Behavioral patterns influence one's risk for AIDS, which is transmitted through person-to-person contact involving the exchange of bodily fluids, primarily semen and blood.

- In the world as a whole, sexual transmission has mostly taken place through heterosexual relations.

- Many young heterosexuals naïvely downplay their risk for HIV.

REACTIONS TO ILLNESS

The decision to seek treatment

- Whether people view physical sensations as symptoms of an illness depends on subjective interpretation.

- The biggest problem in regard to treatment seeking is the common tendency to delay the pursuit of needed treatment.

- People procrastinate because they worry about looking silly or bothering their physician or because they are reluctant to disrupt their plans.

Communicating with health providers

- A large portion of patients depart medical visits not understanding what they have been told.

- Barriers to effective provider-patient communication include short visits, overuse of medical jargon, and patients' reluctance to challenge physicians' authority.

- The key to improving communication is to be an active, not passive, consumer.

© lofoto/Shutterstock.com

Adherence to medical advice

- Nonadherence to advice from health providers is very common.

- Nonadherence is often due to forgetting or the patient's failure to understand instructions.

- If a prescribed regimen is unpleasant or difficult to follow, compliance tends to decline.

- Noncompliance increases when patients have negative attitudes toward their health providers.

APPLICATIONS

- Ellis emphasized the importance of reappraising stressful events and rational thinking.

- Humor can dampen stress appraisals, increase positive emotions, and enhance social support.

- Releasing pent-up emotions, especially through writing about one's difficulties, can foster better health.

- Stress can be reduced by learning to be more forgiving.

- Relaxation, exercise, and good sleep habits can reduce vulnerability to the physical effects of stress.

- Evaluations of health risks can be enhanced by remembering that correlation is not an assurance of causation and that statistical significance is not equivalent to practical significance.

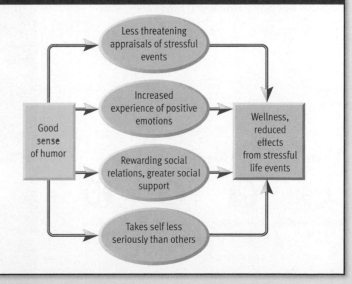

CHAPTER 14

PSYCHOLOGICAL DISORDERS

Michael Cogliantry/The Image Bank/Getty Images

Themes in this Chapter

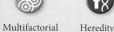

 Multifactorial
Causation

 Heredity &
Environment

 Sociohistorical
Context

 Cultural
Heritage

Actress Jessica Alba used to unplug every single appliance in her house because she worried it would catch fire. She would also check and recheck her doors to ensure that they were locked.

Soccer star David Beckham acknowledges more elaborate concerns that involve symmetry and matching. He is not comfortable unless everything is arranged in straight lines or in pairs. For instance, if he has five cans of Pepsi in a refrigerator, he has to get rid of one to restore even pairs. When he enters a hotel room, he immediately has to put away all the leaflets and books to restore order to the room.

For Alba and Beckham, these aren't just little eccentricities of being a celebrity. They're manifestations of obsessive-compulsive disorder (OCD). Comedian and talk show host Howie Mandel explains the disorder in his 2009 autobiography, *Here's the Deal: Don't Touch Me*. Mandel doesn't shake hands because of his fear of germs, but "it's not just that I'm scared of germs," he says. There's nothing wrong with shaking hands with someone and then washing your hands. But "there *is* something wrong with being totally consumed that you didn't get everything off your hand, that there's things crawling, so you wash it again, and you're so consumed that you wash it again, and you wash it again and you wash it again and you wash it again," Mandel says. "When you can't get past that, that's obsessive-compulsive disorder. It's not that you're afraid of germs, it's that you obsess about that thought and have to do things like handwashing to relieve the worry. I always have intrusive thoughts and rituals."

What causes such abnormal behavior? Does Mandel have a mental illness, or does he just behave strangely? What is the basis for judging behavior as normal versus abnormal? How common are such disorders? Can they be cured? These are just a few of the questions we will address in this chapter as we discuss psychological disorders and their complex causes.

Howie Mandel has written an insightful and amusing account of his struggles with obsessive-compulsive disorder.

14.1 GENERAL CONCEPTS

14.1

Key Learning Goals

- Evaluate the medical model of psychological disorders, and identify the key criteria of abnormality.
- Describe recent developments and issues related to the DSM-5 diagnostic system.

Misconceptions about abnormal behavior are common. Consequently, we need to clear up some preliminary issues before we describe the various types of disorders. In this section, we will discuss (1) the medical model of abnormal behavior, (2) the criteria of abnormal behavior, and (3) the classification of psychological disorders.

The Medical Model Applied to Abnormal Behavior

There's no question that Howie Mandel's extreme fear of germs is abnormal. But does it make sense to view his unusual and irrational behavior as an illness? This is a controversial question. **The *medical model* proposes that it is useful to think of abnormal behavior as a disease.** This point of view is the basis for many of the terms used to refer to

491

abnormal behavior, including mental *illness,* psychological *disorder,* and *psychopathology* (*pathology* refers to manifestations of disease). The medical model gradually became the dominant way of thinking about abnormal behavior during the 18th and 19th centuries. Its influence remains very strong today.

The medical model clearly represented progress over earlier models of abnormal behavior. Prior to the 18th century, most conceptions of abnormal behavior were based on superstition. People who behaved strangely were thought to be possessed by demons, to be witches in league with the devil, or to be victims of God's punishment. The rise of the medical model brought improvements in the treatment of those who exhibited abnormal behavior. As victims of an illness, they were viewed with more sympathy and less hatred and fear. Although living conditions in early asylums were often deplorable, gradual progress was made toward more humane care of the mentally ill.

However, in recent decades, some critics have suggested that the medical model may have outlived its usefulness (Deacon, 2013; Glasser, 2005; Rosemond, 2005). Some critics are troubled because medical diagnoses of abnormal behavior pin potentially derogatory labels on people (Hinshaw, 2007). Being labeled as psychotic, schizophrenic, or mentally ill carries a social stigma that can be difficult to shake. Those characterized as mentally ill are viewed as erratic, dangerous, incompetent, and inferior (Corrigan & Larson, 2008). These stereotypes promote distancing, disdain, and rejection. This prejudice is a significant source of stress for people who suffer from mental illness (Rüsch et al., 2014). Perhaps even more important, the stigma associated with psychological disorders prevents many people from seeking the mental health care they need and could benefit from (Corrigan, Druss, & Perlick, 2014). Unfortunately, the stigma associated with psychological disorders appears to be deeply rooted. In recent decades, research has increasingly demonstrated that many psychological disorders are at least partly attributable to genetic and biological factors, making them appear more similar to physical illnesses, which carry far less stigma (Pescosolido, 2010). You would think that these trends would lead to a reduction in the stigma associated with mental illness, but research suggests that the stigmatization of mental disorders has remained stable or perhaps even increased (Hinshaw & Stier, 2008; Schnittker, 2008).

Another line of criticism has been voiced by Thomas Szasz (1974, 1990). He asserts that "strictly speaking, disease or illness can affect only the body; hence there can be no mental illness. . . . Minds can be 'sick' only in the sense that jokes are 'sick' or economies are 'sick'" (1974, p. 267). He further argues that abnormal behavior usually involves a deviation from social norms rather than an illness. He contends that such deviations are "problems in living" rather than medical problems. According to Szasz, the medical model's disease analogy converts moral and social questions about what is acceptable behavior into medical questions.

The criticism of the medical model has some merit, and it is important to recognize the social roots and ramifications of the medical model. However, the bottom line is that the medical model continues to dominate thinking about psychological disorders. Medical concepts such as *diagnosis, etiology,* and *prognosis* have proven valuable in the treatment and study of abnormality. **Diagnosis involves distinguishing one illness from another. Etiology refers to the apparent causation and developmental history of an illness. A *prognosis* is a forecast about the probable course of an illness.** These medically based concepts have widely shared meanings that permit clinicians, researchers, and the public to communicate more effectively in their discussions about abnormal behavior.

Criteria of Abnormal Behavior

If your next-door neighbor scrubs his front porch twice every day and spends virtually all his time cleaning and recleaning his house, is he normal? If your sister-in-law goes to one physician after another seeking treatment for ailments that appear imaginary, is she psychologically healthy? How are we to judge what's normal and what's abnormal? More important, who's to do the judging?

These are complex questions. In a sense, *all* people make judgments about normality in that they all express opinions about others' (and perhaps their own) mental health. Of course, formal diagnoses of psychological disorders are made by mental health professionals. In making these diagnoses, clinicians rely on a variety of criteria, the foremost of which are the following:

1. *Deviance.* As Szasz pointed out, people are often said to have a disorder because their behavior deviates from what their society considers acceptable. What constitutes normality varies somewhat from one culture to another. However, all cultures have such norms. When people violate these standards and expectations, they may be labeled mentally ill. For example, *transvestic fetishism* is a sexual disorder in which a man achieves sexual arousal by dressing in women's clothing. This behavior is regarded as disordered because a man who wears a dress, brassiere, and nylons is deviating from our culture's norms. This example illustrates the somewhat arbitrary nature of cultural standards regarding normality, as the same overt behavior (cross-sex dressing) is considered acceptable for women but deviant for men.

2. *Maladaptive behavior.* In many cases, people are judged to have a psychological disorder because their everyday adaptive behavior is impaired. This is the key criterion in the diagnosis of substance use (drug) disorders. In and of itself, alcohol and drug use is not terribly unusual or deviant. However, when the use of cocaine, for instance, begins to interfere with a person's social or occupational functioning, a substance use disorder exists. In such cases, it is the maladaptive quality of the behavior that makes it disordered.

3. *Personal distress.* Frequently, the diagnosis of a psychological disorder is based on an individual's report of great personal distress. This is usually the criterion met by people who are troubled by depression or anxiety disorders. Depressed people, for instance, may or may not exhibit deviant or maladaptive behavior. Such people are usually labeled as having a disorder when they describe their subjective pain and suffering to friends, relatives, and mental health professionals.

Although two or three criteria may apply in a particular case, people are often viewed as disordered when only one criterion is met. As you may have already noticed, diagnoses of psychological disorders involve *value judgments* about what represents normal or abnormal behavior (Sadler, 2005; Widiger & Sankis, 2000). These judgments reflect prevailing

► **REALITY CHECK**

Misconception

People with psychological disorders typically exhibit highly bizarre behavior.

Reality

This is true only in a small minority of cases, usually involving relatively severe disorders. The vast majority of people with psychological disorders do not display strange behavior. On the surface, most are indistinguishable from those without disorders.

Sandy Huffaker/Getty Images

Hoarding behavior clearly represents a certain type of deviance, but should it be regarded as a mental disorder? The criteria of mental illness are subjective and complicated. Hoarding *is* viewed as a disorder, but as with any disorder, it is a matter of degree. In many cases, it can be very difficult to draw a line between normality and abnormality.

FIGURE 14.1
Normality and abnormality as a continuum.
No sharp boundary exists between normal and abnormal behavior. Behavior is normal or abnormal in degree, depending on the extent to which one's behavior is deviant, personally distressing, or maladaptive.

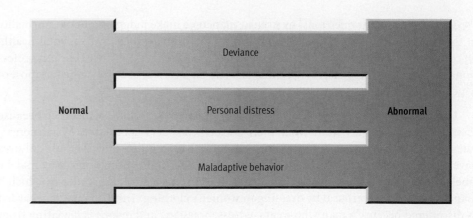

cultural values, social trends, and political forces, as well as scientific knowledge (Frances & Widiger, 2012; Kirk, Gomory, & Cohen, 2013).

Antonyms such as *normal* versus *abnormal* and *mental health* versus *mental illness* imply that people can be divided neatly into two distinct groups: those who are normal and those who are not. In reality, it is often difficult to draw a line that clearly separates normality from abnormality. On occasion, everyone acts in deviant ways, everyone displays some maladaptive behavior, and everyone experiences personal distress. People are judged to have psychological disorders only when their behavior becomes *extremely* deviant, maladaptive, or distressing. Thus, normality and abnormality exist on a continuum. It's a matter of degree, not an either-or proposition (see **Figure 14.1**).

CONCEPT CHECK 14.1

Applying the Criteria of Abnormal Behavior

Check your understanding of the criteria of abnormal behavior by identifying the criteria met by each of the examples below and checking them off in the table provided. Remember, a specific behavior may meet more than one criterion. The answers are in Appendix A.

Behavioral Examples

1. Alan's performance at work has suffered because he has been drinking alcohol to excess. Several co-workers have suggested he seek help for his problem, but he thinks they're getting alarmed over nothing. "I just enjoy a good time once in a while," he says.

2. Monica has gone away to college and feels lonely, sad, and dejected. Her grades are fine, and she gets along okay with the other students in the dormitory, but inside she's choked with gloom, hopelessness, and despair.

3. Boris believes that he's Napoleon reborn. He believes he is destined to lead the U.S. military forces into a great battle to recover California from space aliens.

4. Natasha panics with anxiety whenever she leaves her home. Her problem escalated gradually until she was absent from work so often that she was fired. She hasn't been out of her house in 9 months and is deeply troubled by her problem.

Criteria Met by Each Example

	Maladaptive behavior	*Deviance*	*Personal distress*
1. Alan	_____	_____	_____
2. Monica	_____	_____	_____
3. Boris	_____	_____	_____
4. Natasha	_____	_____	_____

© lenetstan/Shutterstock.com

Psychodiagnosis: The Classification of Disorders

Lumping all psychological disorders together would make it extremely difficult to understand them better. A sound taxonomy of mental disorders can facilitate empirical research and enhance communication among scientists and clinicians (First, 2008; Widiger & Crego, 2013). Thus, a great deal of effort has been invested in devising an elaborate system for classifying psychological disorders. This classification system, published by the American Psychiatric Association, is outlined in a book titled the *Diagnostic and Statistical Manual of Mental Disorders*. The fourth edition, titled DSM-IV, was used from 1994 until 2013, when the current fifth edition was released. The fifth edition is titled DSM-5 (instead of DSM-V) to facilitate incremental updates (such as DSM 5.1). It is the product of more than a decade of research (Kupfer, Kuhl, & Regier, 2013). Clinical researchers collected extensive data; held numerous conferences; and engaged in heated debates about whether various syndromes should be added, eliminated, redefined, or renamed (Sachdev, 2013).

One major issue in the development of DSM-5 was whether to reduce the system's commitment to a *categorical approach*. In recent years, many critics of the DSM system have questioned the fundamental axiom that the diagnostic system is built on: the assumption that people can reliably be placed in discontinuous (nonoverlapping) diagnostic categories (Helzer et al., 2008). These critics note that there is enormous overlap among various disorders' symptoms, making the boundaries between diagnoses much fuzzier than would be ideal. Critics have also pointed out that people often qualify for more than one diagnosis (Lilienfeld & Landfield, 2008).

Because of problems such as these, some theorists argue that the traditional categorical approach to diagnosis should be replaced by a *dimensional approach*. A dimensional approach would describe disorders in terms of how people score on a limited number of continuous dimensions, such as the degree to which they exhibit anxiety, depression, agitation, anger, hypochondria, rumination, paranoia, and so forth (Kraemer, 2008; Widiger, Livesley, & Clark, 2009). The practical logistics of shifting to a dimensional approach to psychological disorders proved formidable and controversial (Blashfield et al., 2014). Experts would have had to agree about which dimensions to assess and how to measure them. Because of difficulties such as these, the authorities developing DSM-5 chose to retain a categorical approach, although they supplemented the traditional system with dimensional approaches in some areas (Burke & Kraemer, 2014; Krueger & Markon, 2014).

Another area of concern related to the DSM has been its nearly exponential growth. The number of specific diagnoses in the DSM increased from 128 in the first edition to 541 in the current edition (Blashfield et al., 2014) (see **Figure 14.2**). Some of this growth was due to splitting existing disorders into narrower subtypes, but much of it was due to adding entirely new disorders. Some of the new disorders encompass behavioral patterns that used to be regarded as mundane, everyday adjustment problems, rather than mental disorders. For example, DSM-5 includes diagnoses for caffeine intoxication (getting really buzzed from coffee), tobacco use disorder (inability to control smoking), disruptive mood dysregulation disorder (problems with recurrent temper tantrums in youngsters), binge-eating disorder (gluttonous overeating more than once a week for at least 3 months), and gambling disorder (inability to control gambling). Some of these syndromes can be serious problems for which people might want to seek treatment, but should they merit a formal designation

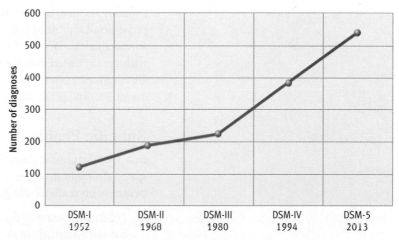

FIGURE 14.2

Growth of the DSM diagnostic system. Published by the American Psychiatric Association, the *Diagnostic and Statistical Manual of Mental Disorders* has grown dramatically with each new edition. The number of specific diagnoses has more than quadrupled since the first edition was released. (Based on Blashfield et al., 2014)

as a mental illness? Some critics of the DSM argue that this approach "medicalizes" everyday problems and casts the stigma of pathology on normal self-control issues (Frances, 2013; Kirk et al., 2013). Critics also worry that turning everyday problems into mental disorders could trivialize the concept of mental illness.

We are now ready to start examining the specific types of psychological disorders. Obviously, in this chapter, we cannot cover all of the hundreds of specific diagnoses listed in DSM-5. However, we will introduce most of the major categories of disorders to give you an overview of the many forms abnormal behavior takes. In discussing each set of disorders, we will begin with brief descriptions of the specific subtypes that fall in the category. If data are available, we will discuss the *prevalence* of the disorders in that category (how common the disorders are in the population). Then we'll focus on the *etiology* of that set of disorders.

14.2 ANXIETY DISORDERS, OCD, AND PTSD

Key Learning Goals

- Describe the symptoms of generalized anxiety disorder, specific phobia, panic disorder, agoraphobia, OCD, and PTSD.
- Discuss how biology, conditioning, cognition, and stress can contribute to the development of anxiety-dominated disorders.

In DSM-IV, *anxiety disorders* was a very broad category of disorders, including generalized anxiety disorder, specific phobia, panic disorder, obsessive-compulsive disorder (OCD), and posttraumatic stress disorder (PTSD). In DSM-5, OCD was removed from the anxiety disorders category and put in its own special category with other compulsive problems, such as hoarding disorder. Similarly, PTSD was shifted into a new category for trauma-related disorders. There were compelling reasons for this reorganization (Stein et al., 2014), but for our level of analysis, it still makes sense to cover these anxiety-dominated disturbances together.

Generalized Anxiety Disorder

Generalized anxiety disorder **is marked by a chronic, high level of anxiety that is not tied to any specific threat.** People with this disorder worry constantly about yesterday's mistakes and tomorrow's problems. They worry about minor matters related to family, finances, work, and personal illness. Their anxiety is often accompanied by physical symptoms, such as trembling, muscle tension, diarrhea, dizziness, faintness, sweating, and heart palpitations. They hope their worrying will prepare them for the worst that could possibly happen, but the net result is they just generate negative emotions and prolonged physiological arousal (Newman & Llera, 2011). People with generalized anxiety disorder sound like the "worried well," but the disorder can be very disabling and is associated with an increased risk for a variety of physical health problems (Newman et al., 2013). Generalized anxiety disorder tends to have a gradual onset, has a lifetime prevalence of about 5%, and is seen about twice as much in females as males (Schneier et al., 2014).

Specific Phobia

In a specific phobic disorder, an individual's troublesome anxiety has a precise focus. **A** *specific phobia* **involves a persistent and irrational fear of an object or situation that presents no realistic danger.** The following case provides an example of a specific phobia:

> *Hilda is 32 years of age and has a rather unusual fear. She is terrified of snow. She cannot go outside in the snow. She cannot even stand to see snow or hear about it on the weather report. Her phobia severely constricts her day-to-day behavior. Probing in therapy revealed that her phobia was caused by a traumatic experience at age 11. Playing at a ski lodge, she was buried briefly by a small avalanche of snow. She had no recollection of this experience until it was recovered in therapy. (Adapted from Laughlin, 1967, p. 227)*

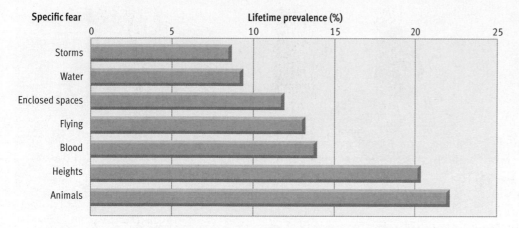

FIGURE 14.3

Common specific phobias. This graph shows the lifetime prevalence of the most common types of phobic fears reported by participants in a study by Curtis et al. (1998). As you can see, a very substantial number of people struggle with a variety of specific fears. Bear in mind that only a portion of these people qualify for a *diagnosis* of specific phobia, which is merited only if individuals' phobias seriously impair their everyday functioning.

As Hilda's unusual snow phobia illustrates, people can develop phobic responses to virtually anything. Nonetheless, certain types of phobias are relatively common, including acrophobia (fear of heights), claustrophobia (fear of small, enclosed places), brontophobia (fear of storms), hydrophobia (fear of water), and various animal and insect phobias (McCabe & Antony, 2008; see **Figure 14.3**). People troubled by phobias typically realize that their fears are irrational, but still are unable to calm themselves when confronted by a phobic object. Phobic fears appear to be quite common, as the lifetime prevalence of specific phobias is estimated to be around 10%; two-thirds of the victims are females (Sadock, Sadock, & Ruiz, 2015).

Panic Disorder

A *panic disorder* **is characterized by recurrent attacks of overwhelming anxiety that usually occur suddenly and unexpectedly.** These paralyzing attacks are accompanied by physical symptoms of anxiety and are sometimes misinterpreted as heart attacks. After a number of anxiety attacks, victims often become apprehensive and hypervigilant, wondering when their next panic attack will occur. About two-thirds of people who are diagnosed with panic disorder are female, and the onset of the disorder typically occurs during late adolescence or early adulthood (Schneier et al., 2014).

Agoraphobia

People with panic disorder often become increasingly concerned about exhibiting panic in public, to the point where they are afraid to leave home. This fear creates a condition called *agoraphobia,* **which is a fear of going out to public places** (its literal meaning is "fear of the marketplace or open places"). Because of this fear, some people become prisoners confined to their homes, although many will venture out if accompanied by a trusted companion (Hollander & Simeon, 2008). As its name suggests, agoraphobia was originally viewed as a phobic disorder. However, in DSM-III and DSM-IV, it was characterized as a common complication of panic disorder. In DSM-5, it is listed as a separate anxiety disorder that may or may not co-exist with panic disorder; as it turns out, it can co-exist with a variety of disorders (Asmundson, Taylor, & Smits, 2014). Like other disorders, agoraphobia can vary in severity, but it can be a very disabling condition.

Obsessive-Compulsive Disorder

Obsessions are *thoughts* that repeatedly intrude on one's consciousness in a distressing way. Compulsions are *actions* one feels forced to carry out. Thus, *obsessive-compulsive disorder (OCD)* **is marked by persistent, uncontrollable intrusions of unwanted**

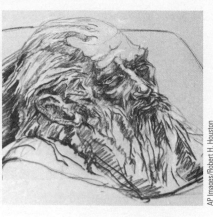

As a young man (shown in the photo), Howard Hughes was a handsome, dashing daredevil pilot and movie producer who appeared to be reasonably well adjusted. However, as the years went by, his behavior gradually became more and more maladaptive, as obsessions and compulsions came to dominate his life. In his later years (shown in the drawing), he spent most of his time in darkened rooms, naked, unkempt, and dirty, following bizarre rituals to alleviate his anxieties. (The drawing was done by an NBC artist and was based on descriptions from men who had seen Hughes.)

thoughts (obsessions) and urges to engage in senseless rituals (compulsions). To illustrate, let's examine the bizarre behavior of a man once reputed to be the wealthiest person in the world:

> *The famous industrialist Howard Hughes was obsessed with the possibility of being contaminated by germs. This led him to devise extraordinary rituals to minimize the possibility of such contamination. He would spend hours methodically cleaning a single telephone. He once wrote a three-page memo instructing assistants on exactly how to open cans of fruit for him. (Adapted from Barlett & Steele, 1979, pp. 227–237)*

Obsessions often center on inflicting harm on others, personal failures, suicide, or sexual acts. People troubled by obsessions may feel they have lost control of their mind. Compulsions usually involve stereotyped rituals that may temporarily relieve the anxiety produced by one's obsessions. As we saw at the beginning of the chapter, common examples include constant handwashing; repetitive cleaning and ordering of things; and endless rechecking of locks, faucets, and such. Many of us can be compulsive at times. Indeed, in samples of people without a mental disorder, many individuals report significant obsessions or compulsions (Clark et al., 2014). However, full-fledged obsessive-compulsive *disorders* occur in roughly 2%–3% of the population (Zohar, Fostick, & Juven-Wetzler, 2009). OCD can be a particularly severe disorder and is often associated with serious social and occupational impairments (Dougherty, Wilhelm, & Jenike, 2014). OCD is unusual among anxiety-related problems in that it is seen in males and females in roughly equal numbers (Gallo et al., 2013).

Handwashing is one of the most common compulsions among OCD patients, second only to checking and rechecking. Some theorists believe these compulsions are driven by a need to reduce irrational feelings of guilt.

Posttraumatic Stress Disorder

Posttraumatic stress disorder (PTSD) **involves enduring psychological disturbance attributed to the experience of a major traumatic event.** PTSD was first recognized as a disorder in the 1970s in the aftermath of the Vietnam War, when a great many veterans were traumatized by their combat experiences. Research eventually showed that PTSD can be caused by a variety of traumatic events besides harrowing war experiences. For example, PTSD is often seen after a rape or assault, a severe automobile accident, a natural disaster, or the witnessing of someone's death. Although people tend to assume that such events are relatively uncommon, research shows that a majority of adults have been exposed to one or more serious traumatic events (Ogle et al., 2013). Common symptoms of PTSD include reexperiencing the event in the form of nightmares and flashbacks; emotional numbing; alienation; problems in social relations; an increased sense of vulnerability; and elevated arousal, anxiety, anger, and guilt (Stoddard, Simon, & Pitman,

2014). Research suggests that about 7% of people have suffered from PTSD at some point in their lives (Resick, Monson, & Rizvi, 2008). Currently, there is great concern and some debate about the prevalence of PTSD among military returnees from the Afghanistan and Iraq wars (Berntsen et al., 2012; Fisher, 2014; Hines et al., 2014).

A variety of factors are predictors of individuals' risk for PTSD (McNally, 2009). For example, people who were exposed to a high level of stress and adversity in childhood tend to be especially vulnerable to PTSD (Yehuda et al., 2010). As you might expect, increased vulnerability is associated with greater personal injuries and losses due to the traumatic event, greater intensity of exposure to the traumatic event, and more exposure to the grotesque aftermath of the event. One key predictor of vulnerability is the *intensity of one's reaction at the time of the traumatic event* (Ozer et al., 2003). Individuals who have especially intense emotional reactions during or immediately after the traumatic event go on to show elevated vulnerability to PTSD.

There are concerns that many military personnel who served in the wars in Iraq and Afghanistan will suffer from PTSD. There also is some debate about the prevalence rates of PTSD due to these wars.

Etiology of Anxiety-Related Disturbances

Like most psychological disorders, anxiety-dominated disorders develop out of complicated interactions between a variety of biological and psychological factors.

Biological Factors

In studies that assess the impact of heredity on psychological disorders, investigators look at *concordance rates*. **A *concordance rate* indicates the percentage of twin pairs or other pairs of relatives who exhibit the same disorder.** If relatives who share more genetic similarity show higher concordance rates than relatives who share less genetic overlap, this finding supports the genetic hypothesis. The results of both *twin studies* (see **Figure 14.4**) and *family studies* (see Chapter 3 for discussions of both methods) suggest a moderate genetic predisposition to anxiety disorders (Fyer, 2009).

Recent evidence suggests that a link may exist between anxiety disorders and neurochemical activity in the brain. As you learned in Chapter 3, *neurotransmitters* are chemicals that carry signals from one neuron to another. Therapeutic drugs (such as Valium or Xanax) that reduce excessive anxiety appear to alter neurotransmitter activity at synapses that release a neurotransmitter called *GABA*. This finding and other lines of evidence suggest that disturbances in the neural circuits using GABA may play a role in some types of anxiety disorders (Rowa & Antony, 2008). Abnormalities in neural circuits using serotonin have been implicated in obsessive-compulsive disorders (Sadock et al., 2015).

Conditioning and Learning

Many anxiety responses can be *acquired through classical conditioning* and *maintained through operant conditioning* (see Chapter 6). According to Mowrer (1947), an originally neutral stimulus (the snow in Hilda's case, for instance) can be paired with a frightening event (the avalanche) so that it becomes a conditioned stimulus eliciting anxiety (see **Figure 14.5**). Once a fear is acquired through classical conditioning, the person may start avoiding the anxiety-producing stimulus. The avoidance response is negatively reinforced because it is followed by a reduction in anxiety. This process involves operant conditioning (see **Figure 14.5**). Thus, separate conditioning processes can create and then sustain specific anxiety responses (Levis, 1989). Consistent with this view, studies find that a substantial portion of people suffering from phobias can identify a traumatic

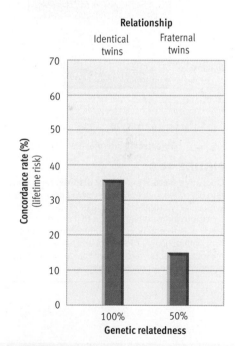

FIGURE 14.4

Twin studies of anxiety-related disorders. The concordance rate for anxiety-related disorders in identical twins is higher than that for fraternal twins, who share less genetic overlap. These results suggest there is a genetic predisposition to anxiety-dominated disturbances. (Data based on Noyes et al., 1987; Slater & Shields, 1969; Torgersen, 1979, 1983)

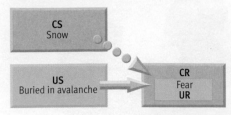

(a) Classical conditioning: Acquisition of phobic fear

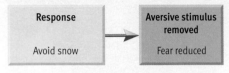

(b) Operant conditioning: Maintenance of phobic fear
(negative reinforcement)

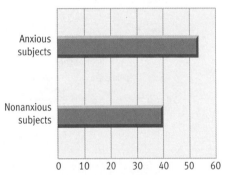

FIGURE 14.5

Conditioning as an explanation for phobias.
(a) Many phobias appear to be acquired through classical conditioning when a neutral stimulus is paired with an anxiety-arousing stimulus. **(b)** Once acquired, a phobia may be maintained through operant conditioning. Avoidance of the phobic stimulus reduces anxiety, resulting in negative reinforcement.

FIGURE 14.6

Cognitive factors in anxiety disorders. Eysenck and his colleagues (1991) compared how subjects with anxiety problems and nonanxious subjects tended to interpret sentences that could be viewed as threatening or nonthreatening. Consistent with cognitive models of anxiety disorders, anxious subjects were more likely to interpret the sentences in a threatening light.

conditioning experience that probably contributed to their anxiety disorder (McCabe & Antony, 2008). The acquisition of conditioned fears is far from automatic, however. For a variety of reasons, people vary in how easily they develop conditioned fears that may evolve into anxiety problems (Mineka, 2013).

The tendency to develop phobias of certain types of objects and situations can be explained by Martin Seligman's (1971) concept of *preparedness*. Like many theorists, Seligman believes that classical conditioning creates most phobic responses. *However, he suggests that people are biologically prepared by their evolutionary history to acquire some fears much more easily than others.* His theory would explain why people develop phobias of ancient sources of threat (such as snakes and spiders) much more readily than modern sources of threat (such as electrical outlets or hot irons). Arne Öhman and Susan Mineka (2001) updated the notion of preparedness, which they call an *evolved module for fear learning.* They maintain that this evolved module is automatically activated by stimuli related to past survival threats in evolutionary history and that it is relatively resistant to intentional efforts to suppress the resulting fears. Consistent with this view, phobic stimuli associated with evolutionary threats tend to produce more rapid conditioning of fears and stronger fear responses (Mineka & Öhman, 2002).

Cognitive Factors

Cognitive theorists maintain that certain styles of thinking make some people particularly vulnerable to anxiety disorders (Ferreri, Lapp, & Peretti, 2011). According to these theorists, some people are more likely to suffer from anxiety problems because they tend to (1) misinterpret harmless situations as threatening, (2) focus excessive attention on perceived threats, and (3) selectively recall information that seems threatening (Clark & Beck, 2010). In one intriguing test of the cognitive view, anxious and nonanxious subjects were asked to read thirty-two sentences that could be interpreted in either a threatening or a nonthreatening manner (Eysenck et al., 1991). For instance, one such sentence was "The doctor examined little Emma's growth," which could mean that the doctor checked her height or the growth of a tumor. As **Figure 14.6** shows, the anxious participants interpreted the sentences in a threatening way more often than the nonanxious participants did. Thus, consistent with our theme that human experience is highly subjective, the cognitive view holds that some people are prone to anxiety disorders because they see threat in every corner of their lives (Riskind, 2005).

Stress

Obviously, cases of posttraumatic stress disorder are attributed to individuals' exposure to extremely stressful incidents. Research has also demonstrated that other types of anxiety disorders can be stress related (Beidel & Stipelman, 2007). For instance, Faravelli and Pallanti (1989) found that patients with panic disorder had experienced a dramatic increase in stress in the month prior to the onset of their disorder. Other studies found that stress levels are predictive of the severity of OCD patients' symptoms (Lin et al., 2007; Morgado et al., 2013). Thus, there is reason to believe that high stress often helps to precipitate or to aggravate anxiety disorders.

Key Learning Goals

- Describe dissociative amnesia and dissociative identity disorder.
- Discuss the etiology of dissociative identity disorder.

14.3 DISSOCIATIVE DISORDERS

Dissociative disorders are probably the most controversial set of disorders in the diagnostic system, sparking heated debate among normally subdued researchers and clinicians. ***Dissociative disorders* are a class of disorders in which people lose contact with portions of their consciousness or memory, resulting in disruptions in their sense of identity.** We'll describe two dissociative syndromes: dissociative amnesia and dissociative identity disorder. Both of these disorders are relatively uncommon.

Description

Dissociative amnesia **is a sudden loss of memory for important personal information that is too extensive to be due to normal forgetting.** Memory losses can occur for a single traumatic event (such as an automobile accident or home fire) or for an extended period of time surrounding the event. Cases of amnesia have been observed after people have experienced disasters, accidents, combat stress, physical abuse, and rape, among other things (Cardeña & Gleaves, 2007). In some cases, having forgotten their name, their family, where they live, and where they work, these people wander away from their home area. In spite of this wholesale forgetting, they remember matters unrelated to their identity, such as how to drive a car and how to do math.

Dissociative identity disorder (DID) **involves a disruption of identity marked by the experience of two or more largely complete, and usually very different, personalities.** The name for this disorder used to be *multiple personality disorder,* which still enjoys informal usage. The name for the disorder was changed because the old name seemed to imply that different people inhabited the same body, whereas the modern view is that these individuals fail to integrate incongruent aspects of their personality into a normal, coherent whole (Cardeña et al., 2013). In dissociative identity disorder, the divergences in behavior go far beyond those that people normally display in adapting to different roles in life. People with "multiple personalities" feel they have more than one

---

CONCEPT CHECK 14.2

Distinguishing Among Anxiety Disorders, OCD, and PTSD

Check your understanding of the nature of anxiety disorders, OCD, and PTSD by making preliminary diagnoses for the cases described below. Read each case summary and write your tentative diagnosis in the space provided. The answers are in Appendix A.

1. Malcolm religiously follows an exact schedule every day. His showering and grooming ritual takes 2 hours. He follows the same path in walking to his classes every day, and he always sits in the same seat in each class. He can't study until his apartment is arranged perfectly. Although he tries not to, he thinks constantly about flunking out of school. Both his grades and his social life are suffering from his rigid routines.

   Preliminary diagnosis:

   _____

2. Jane has an intense fear of thunderstorms. Lightning and thunder terrify her. If she is home when a thunderstorm hits, she drops everything she is doing and runs to her basement. If she is out and about when a thunderstorm hits, she goes into a panic. She carefully monitors weather predictions to avoid this calamity. Because of her fear of thunderstorms, she often misses work and is worried she may be fired.

   Preliminary diagnosis:

   _____

3. Nathan recently returned from a 6-month tour of military duty in Afghanistan, where he saw a close friend die in combat. He keeps reliving the nightmare of seeing his friend die. He reports chronic feelings of anxiety, anger, and emotional numbing.

   Preliminary diagnosis:

   _____

identity. Each identity has his or her own name, memories, traits, physical mannerisms, and autonomy. Although it is relatively infrequent, this syndrome is often portrayed in novels, movies, and television shows, such as the satirical film *Me, Myself, and Irene,* a 2000 release starring Jim Carrey, and more recently the Showtime series the *United States of Tara.* In popular media portrayals, the syndrome is often mistakenly called *schizophrenia.* As you will see later, schizophrenic disorders are entirely different.

In dissociative identity disorder, the various personalities generally report that they are unaware of each other, although objective measures of memory suggest otherwise (Huntjens et al., 2006). The alternate personalities commonly display traits that are quite foreign to the original personality. For instance, a shy, inhibited person might develop a flamboyant, extraverted alternate personality. Transitions between identities often occur suddenly. Dissociative identity disorder is seen more often in women than in men (Simeon & Loewenstein, 2009).

Starting in the 1970s, a dramatic increase was seen in the diagnosis of DID. Only seventy-nine well-documented cases had accumulated up through 1970, but by the late-1990s, about 40,000 cases were estimated to have been reported (Lilienfeld & Lynn, 2003). Some theorists believe that the disorder used to be underdiagnosed (Maldonado & Spiegel, 2014). However, other theorists argue that a handful of clinicians have begun overdiagnosing the condition and that some clinicians unwittingly reinforce patients for progressively showing a seemingly exotic or exciting disorder (Boysen & VanBergen, 2013; Powell & Gee, 1999). Consistent with this view, a survey of all the psychiatrists in Switzerland found that 90% had never seen a case of DID, and six (of the 655 surveyed) accounted for two-thirds of the dissociative identity disorder diagnoses in Switzerland (Modestin, 1992).

Etiology of Dissociative Disorders

Dissociative amnesia is usually attributed to excessive stress. However, relatively little is known about why this extreme reaction to stress occurs in a tiny minority of people, but not in the vast majority who are subjected to similar stress.

The causes of dissociative identity disorder are particularly obscure. Some skeptical theorists (Lilienfeld et al., 1999; Lynn et al., 2012) believe that people with multiple identities come to believe, thanks in part to book and movie portrayals of dissociative identity disorder and reinforcement from their therapists, that independent entities within them are to blame for their peculiar behaviors, unpredictable moods, and ill-advised actions. Gradually, aided by subtle encouragement from their therapists and a tendency to fantasize, they come to attribute unique traits and memories to imaginary alternate personalities. Theorists who favor this line of thinking also note that recent research suggests that sleep disturbances can amplify dissociative symptoms (van der Kloet et al., 2012).

In spite of these concerns, many clinicians are convinced that dissociative identity disorder is an authentic disorder (Dorahy et al., 2014; van der Hart & Nijenhuis, 2009). They argue that there is no incentive for either patients or therapists to manufacture cases of multiple personalities, which are often greeted with skepticism and outright hostility. They maintain that most cases of dissociative identity disorder are rooted in severe emotional trauma that occurred during childhood (Maldonado & Spiegel, 2014). A substantial majority of people with dissociative identity disorder report a childhood history of rejection from parents and of physical and sexual abuse (van der Hart & Nijenhuis, 2009). However, this abuse typically has not been independently verified (Ross & Ness, 2010). In the final analysis, little is known about the causes of dissociative identity disorder, which remains a controversial diagnosis (Lilienfeld & Arkowitz, 2011).

14.4 DEPRESSIVE AND BIPOLAR DISORDERS

Key Learning Goals

- Describe the symptoms of major depressive disorder and bipolar disorder and their relation to suicide.
- Understand how genetic, neural, hormonal, cognitive, social, and stress factors are related to the development of depressive and bipolar disorders.

What do Abraham Lincoln, Marilyn Monroe, Kurt Cobain, Vincent van Gogh, Ernest Hemingway, Winston Churchill, Ted Turner, Alec Baldwin, Catherine Zeta-Jones, Sting, Billy Joel, Jim Carrey, Jon Hamm, Ben Stiller, and Anne Hathaway have in common? Yes, they all achieved great prominence, albeit in different ways at different times. But, more pertinent to our interest, they all suffered from severe emotional dysfunction, or mood disorders. Although emotional disorders can be crippling, people with mood disorders can still achieve greatness because such disorders tend to be *episodic*. In other words, mood disturbances often come and go, interspersed between periods of normality.

In DSM-III and DSM-IV, *major depressive disorder* and *bipolar disorder* were lumped together in a category called *mood disorders*. In DSM-5, they each get their own chapter or category, but we will discuss them together here. **Figure 14.7** depicts the main way in which these disorders differ. People with major depressive disorder experience emotional extremes at just one end of the mood continuum because they experience periodic bouts of depression. People with bipolar disorders generally experience emotional extremes at both ends of the mood continuum, going through periods of both *depression* and *mania* (excitement and elation). Actually, although the name for the disorder suggests that all bipolar individuals experience both depression and mania, a minority of people with bipolar disorder do not report episodes of depression (Johnson, Cuellar, & Peckham, 2014).

Major Depressive Disorder

The line between normal and abnormal depression can be difficult to draw (Bebbington, 2013). The *depressive disorders* category includes a number of milder syndromes, but the most common disorder in this domain is *major depressive disorder*. **In *major depressive disorder*, people show persistent feelings of sadness and despair and a loss of interest in previous sources of pleasure.** Negative emotions form the heart of this syndrome, but many other symptoms can also appear. The most common symptoms

Mood disorders are common and have affected many successful, well-known people, such as Jon Hamm and Catherine Zeta-Jones.

FIGURE 14.7

Episodic patterns in depressive and bipolar disorders. Time-limited episodes of emotional disturbance come and go unpredictably. People with major depression suffer from bouts of depression only, whereas people with bipolar disorder usually experience both manic and depressive episodes. The time between episodes of disturbance and the length of the episodes vary greatly.

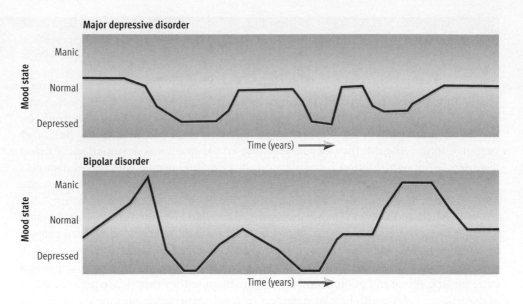

of depression are summarized and compared with the symptoms of mania in **Table 14.1**. A central feature of major depression is ***anhedonia*—a diminished ability to experience pleasure.** Depressed people lack energy and motivation. Hence, they often give up things they used to enjoy, such as hobbies, favorite foods, or spending time with friends. Reduced appetite and insomnia are common. They tend to move sluggishly and talk slowly. Anxiety, irritability, and brooding are commonly observed. Depression plunges people into feelings of hopelessness, dejection, and boundless guilt.

The onset of depression can occur at any point in the life span. However, a substantial majority of cases emerge before age 40. Depression occurs in children and adolescents, as well as adults, although rates of depression are notably lower in children and somewhat lower in adolescents (Rohde et al., 2013). The vast majority of people who suffer from major depression experience more than one episode over the course of their lifetime (McInnis, Ribia, & Greden, 2014). The average number of depressive episodes is five to six. The average length of these episodes is about 5–7 months (Keller et al., 2013). An earlier age of onset is associated with more recurrences, more severe symptoms, and a worse prognosis (Hammen & Keenan-Miller, 2013). Although depression tends to be episodic, some people suffer from chronic major depression that may persist for many years (Klein & Allmann, 2014). Such chronic depression is associated with a particularly severe impairment of functioning. Depression is associated with an elevated risk for a variety of physical health problems and increases mortality by about 50% (Cuijpers et al., 2014).

TABLE 14.1 Comparison of Depressive and Manic Symptoms

Symptoms	Depressive Episode	Manic Episode
Emotional symptoms	Dysphoric, gloomy mood Diminished ability to experience pleasure Sense of hopelessness	Euphoric, enthusiastic mood Excessive pursuit of pleasurable activities Unwarranted optimism
Behavioral symptoms	Fatigue, loss of energy Insomnia Slowed speech and movement Social withdrawal	Energetic, tireless, hyperactive Decreased need for sleep Rapid speech and agitation Increased sociability
Cognitive symptoms	Impaired ability to think and make decisions Slowed thought processes Excessive worry, rumination Guilt, self-blame, unrealistic negative evaluations of one's worth	Grandiose planning, indiscriminate decision making Racing thoughts, easily distracted Impulsive behavior Inflated self-esteem and self-confidence

How common are depressive disorders? Lifetime prevalence is estimated to be around 13%–16% (Hammen & Keenan-Miller, 2013). At the low end, that estimate suggests that roughly 40 million people in the United States have suffered or will suffer from depression! If this news isn't sufficiently depressing, there is new evidence that the prevalence of depression may be on the rise in recent birth cohorts (Twenge, 2015).

Research indicates that the prevalence of depression is about twice as high in women as it is in men (Gananca, Kahn, & Oquendo, 2014). The many possible explanations for this gender gap are the subject of considerable debate. The gap does *not* appear to be attributable to differences in genetic makeup (Franić et al., 2010). A portion of the disparity may be the result of women's elevated vulnerability to depression at certain points in their reproductive life cycle (Hilt & Nolen-Hoeksema, 2014). Obviously, only women have to worry about postpartum and postmenopausal depression. Susan Nolen-Hoeksema (2001) argues that women experience more depression than men because they are far more likely to be victims of sexual abuse and somewhat more likely to endure poverty, sexual harassment, and excessive pressure to be thin and attractive. In other words, she attributes a portion of the higher prevalence of depression among women to their experience of greater stress and adversity. Nolen-Hoeksema also believes that women have a greater tendency than men to ruminate about setbacks and problems. Evidence suggests that this tendency to dwell on one's difficulties elevates vulnerability to depression, as we will discuss momentarily.

Bipolar Disorder

Bipolar disorder **is marked by the experience of both depressed and manic periods.** The symptoms seen in manic periods generally are the opposite of those seen in depression (see **Table 14.1** for a comparison). In a manic episode, a person's mood becomes elevated to the point of euphoria. Self-esteem skyrockets as the person bubbles over with optimism, energy, and extravagant plans. He or she becomes hyperactive and may go for days without sleep. The individual talks rapidly and shifts topics wildly, as his or her mind races at breakneck speed. Judgment is often impaired. Some people in manic periods gamble impulsively, spend money frantically, or become sexually reckless. Like depressive disorders, bipolar disorders vary considerably in severity (Youngstrom & Algorta, 2014).

You may be thinking that the euphoria in manic episodes sounds appealing. If so, you are not entirely wrong. In their milder forms, manic states can seem attractive. The increases in energy, self-esteem, and optimism can be deceptively seductive (Goodwin & Jamison, 2007). However, manic periods often carry a paradoxical negative undercurrent of uneasiness, irritability, and anger. Moreover, mild manic episodes often escalate to higher levels that become scary and disturbing. Impaired judgment leads many victims to do things they greatly regret later, as you can see in the following case history:

> *Robert, a dentist, awoke one morning with the idea that he was the most gifted dental surgeon in his tri-state area. He decided that he should try to provide services to as many people as possible, so that more people could benefit from his talents. Thus, he decided to remodel his two-chair dental office so that he could simultaneously attend to twenty patients. That same day, impatient to get rolling on his remodeling, he rolled up his sleeves, got himself a sledgehammer, and began to knock down the walls in his office. Annoyed when that didn't go so well, he smashed his dental tools, washbasins, and X-ray equipment. Later, Robert's wife became concerned about his behavior and summoned two of her adult daughters for assistance. The daughters responded quickly, arriving at the family home with their husbands. In the ensuing discussion, Robert made sexual advances toward his daughters. He had to be subdued by their husbands. (Adapted from Kleinmuntz, 1980, p. 309)*

Although not rare, bipolar disorder is much less common than depression. Bipolar disorder affects about 1% of the population, and unlike depression, it is seen equally often

Suicide Prevention Tips

1. *Take suicidal talk seriously.* When people talk about suicide in vague generalities, it's easy to dismiss it as idle talk and let it go. However, people who talk about suicide are a high-risk group, and their veiled threats should not be ignored. The first step in suicide prevention is to directly ask such people if they're contemplating suicide.

2. *Provide empathy and social support.* It is important to show the suicidal person that you care. People often contemplate suicide because they see the world around them as indifferent and uncaring. Thus, you must demonstrate to the suicidal person that you are genuinely concerned. Suicide threats are often a last-ditch cry for help. It is therefore imperative that you offer to help.

3. *Identify and clarify the crucial problem.* The suicidal person is often confused and feels lost in a sea of frustration and problems. It is a good idea to try to help sort through this confusion. Encourage the person to try to identify the crucial problem. Once it is isolated, the problem may not seem quite so overwhelming.

4. *Do not promise to keep someone's suicidal ideation secret.* If you really feel like someone's life is in danger, don't agree to keep his or her suicidal plans secret to preserve your friendship.

5. *In an acute crisis, do not leave a suicidal person alone.* Stay with the person until additional help is available. Try to remove any guns, drugs, sharp objects, and so forth that might provide an available means to commit suicide.

6. *Encourage professional consultation.* Most mental health professionals have some experience in dealing with suicidal crises. Many cities have suicide prevention centers with 24-hour hotlines. These centers are staffed with people who have been specially trained to deal with suicidal problems. It is important to try to get a suicidal person to seek professional assistance.

FIGURE 14.8

Preventing suicide. As Sudak (2005) notes, "It is not possible to prevent all suicides or to totally and absolutely protect a given patient from suicide. What is possible is to reduce the likelihood of suicide" (p. 2449). Hence, the advice summarized here may prove useful if you ever have to help someone through a suicidal crisis. (Based on Fremouw, de Perczel, & Ellis, 1990; Rosenthal, 1988; Shneidman, Farberow, & Litman, 1994)

in males and females (Jauhar & Cavanagh, 2013). The onset of bipolar disorder is age related. The typical age of onset is in the late teens or early twenties (Ketter & Chang, 2014).

Mood Dysfunction and Suicide

A tragic, heartbreaking problem associated with mood disorders is suicide. Suicide is the tenth leading cause of death in the United States, accounting for about 40,000 deaths annually. Official statistics may underestimate the scope of the problem. Many suicides are disguised as accidents, either by the suicidal person or by the survivors, who try to cover up afterward. Moreover, experts estimate that suicide attempts may outnumber completed suicides by a ratio of as much as 25 to 1 (Rothberg & Feinstein, 2014). Women *attempt* suicide three times more often than men, but men are more likely to actually kill themselves in an attempt, so they *complete* four times as many suicides as women (Rothberg & Feinstein, 2014).

With the luxury of hindsight, it is recognized that about 90% of the people who complete suicide suffer from some type of psychological disorder, although this disorder may not be readily apparent beforehand in some cases (Nock et al., 2014). As you might expect, suicide rates are highest for people with depressive and bipolar disorders. They account for about 50%–60% of completed suicides (Nock et al., 2014). The likelihood of a suicide attempt increases as the severity of individuals' depression increases (MacLeod, 2013). Still, suicide is notoriously difficult to predict. Perhaps the best predictor is when one expresses a sense of hopelessness about the future, but even that can be difficult to gauge (MacLeod, 2013). Unfortunately, there is no foolproof way to prevent suicidal persons from taking their own lives. But some useful tips are compiled in **Figure 14.8**.

Etiology of Depressive and Bipolar Disorders

Quite a bit is known about the etiology of depressive and bipolar disorders, although the puzzle hasn't been assembled completely. There appear to be a number of routes into these disorders, involving intricate interactions among psychological and biological factors.

Genetic Vulnerability

The evidence strongly suggests that genetic factors influence the likelihood of developing major depression (Lau et al., 2014) and bipolar disorder (Macritchie & Blackwood, 2013). *Twin studies* have found a huge disparity between identical and fraternal twins in concordance rates for mood disorders. The concordance rate for identical twins is much higher (see **Figure 14.9**). This evidence suggests that heredity can create a *predisposition* to mood dysfunction. Environmental factors probably determine whether this predisposition is converted into an actual disorder.

Neurochemical and Neuroanatomical Factors

Correlations have been found between mood disorders and abnormal levels of two neurotransmitters in the brain—norepinephrine and serotonin—although other neurotransmitter disturbances may also contribute (Thase, Hahn, & Berton, 2014). The details remain elusive, but low levels of serotonin appear to be a crucial factor underlying most forms of depression.

Studies have also found some interesting correlations between mood disorders and a variety of structural abnormalities in the brain (Kempton et al., 2011). Perhaps the best-documented correlation is the association between depression and *reduced hippocampal* volume, especially in the dentate gyrus of the hippocampus (Treadway et al., 2015). A relatively new theory of the biological bases of depression may be able to account for this finding. The springboard for this theory is the discovery that the human brain continues to generate new neurons (neurogenesis) in adulthood, especially in the hippocampal formation which was discussed in Chapter 3 (Kozorovitskiy & Gould, 2007, 2008). Recent evidence suggests that depression occurs when major life stress causes neurochemical reactions that suppress this neurogenesis, resulting in reduced hippocampal volume (Mahar et al., 2014). According to this view, the suppression of neurogenesis is the central cause of depression, and antidepressant drugs are successful because they promote neurogenesis (Boldrini et al., 2013). A great deal of additional research will be required to fully test this innovative model of the biological bases of depressive disorders.

Hormonal Factors

In recent years, researchers have begun to focus on how hormonal changes may contribute to the emergence of depression. As we discussed in Chapter 13, in times of stress, the brain sends signals along two pathways. One of these runs from the hypothalamus to the pituitary gland to the adrenal cortex, which releases corticosteroid hormones (refer back to **Figure 13.7**). This pathway is often referred to as the hypothalamic-pituitary-adrenocortical (HPA) axis. Evidence suggests that overactivity along the HPA axis in response to stress can often play a role in the development of depression (Goodwin, 2009). Consistent with this hypothesis, a substantial portion of depressed patients show elevated levels of cortisol, a key stress hormone produced by HPA activity (Cleare & Rane, 2013). Some theorists believe that these hormonal changes eventually have an impact in the brain, where they may be the trigger for the suppression of neurogenesis that we just discussed (Duman, Polan, & Schatzberg, 2008).

Cognitive Factors

A variety of theories emphasize how cognitive factors contribute to depressive disorders (Clasen, Disner, & Beevers, 2013). For example, based largely on animal research, Seligman (1974) proposed that depression is caused by *learned helplessness*—passive "giving up" behavior produced by exposure to unavoidable aversive events (such as uncontrollable shock in the lab). He originally considered learned helplessness to be a product of conditioning, but eventually revised his theory to give it a cognitive slant. The reformulated theory of learned helplessness asserts that the roots of depression lie in how people explain the setbacks and other negative events they experience (Abramson, Seligman, & Teasdale, 1978). According to Seligman (1990), people who exhibit a *pessimistic explanatory style* are especially vulnerable to depression. These people tend to attribute their setbacks to their personal flaws instead of to situational factors. Moreover, they tend to draw global, far-reaching conclusions about their personal inadequacies based on these setbacks.

In accord with this line of thinking, Susan Nolen-Hoeksema (1991, 2000) found that depressed people who *ruminate* about their depression remain depressed longer than those who try to distract themselves. People who respond to depression with rumination repetitively focus their attention on their feelings of depression. They think constantly about how sad, lethargic, and unmotivated they are. Excessive rumination tends to foster and amplify episodes of depression by increasing negative thinking, impairing problem solving, and undermining social support (Nolen-Hoeksema, Wisco, & Lyubomirsky, 2008). As we noted earlier, Nolen-Hoeksema believes women have a greater tendency to ruminate than men, and that this disparity may be a major reason depression is more prevalent in women.

In sum, cognitive models of depression maintain that negative thinking is what leads to depression in many people. The principal problem with cognitive theories is their difficulty in separating cause from effect. Does negative thinking cause depression? Or does depression cause negative thinking (see **Figure 14.10**)? Strong evidence favoring a causal role for negative thinking comes from a study by Alloy and colleagues (1999),

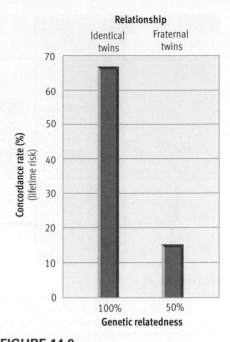

FIGURE 14.9

Twin studies of mood disorders. The concordance rate for mood disorders in identical twins is much higher than that for fraternal twins, who share less genetic overlap. These results suggest that there is a genetic predisposition to mood disorders. (Data from Berrettini, 2006)

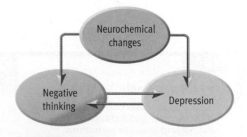

FIGURE 14.10

Interpreting the correlation between negative thinking and depression. Cognitive theories of depression assume that consistent patterns of negative thinking cause depression. Although these theories are highly plausible, depression could cause negative thoughts, or both could be caused by a third factor, such as neurochemical changes in the brain.

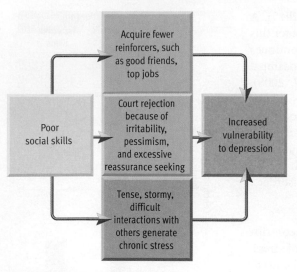

FIGURE 14.11

Interpersonal factors in depression. Behavioral theories about the etiology of depression emphasize how inadequate social skills and other interpersonal quirks may contribute to the development of the disorder through several mechanisms, as diagrammed here.

who assessed explanatory style in first-year college students who were not depressed at the outset of the study, which followed students for 2.5 years. They found that a negative explanatory style predicted vulnerability to depression, with major depression emerging in 17% of students who exhibited negative thinking, but only 1% of those who did not.

Interpersonal Roots

Behavioral approaches to understanding depression emphasize how social difficulties put people on the road to depressive disorders (see **Figure 14.11**; Ingram, Scott, & Hamill, 2009). According to this notion, depression-prone people tend to lack the social finesse needed to acquire many important kinds of reinforcers, such as good friends, top jobs, and desirable spouses. This lack of reinforcers could understandably lead to negative emotions and depression. Consistent with this theory, researchers have found correlations between poor social skills and depression (Petty, Sachs-Ericsson, & Joiner, 2004). Evidence also suggests that depressed people unintentionally court rejection from others because they tend to be irritable, pessimistic, unpleasant companions (Joiner & Timmons, 2009). They also alienate people by constantly asking for reassurances about their relationships and their worth. This excessive reassurance seeking ends up fostering rejection and is predictive of depression (Hames, Hagan, & Joiner, 2013). Yet another issue is that complicated and difficult social relations can greatly increase the level of stress in one's life. Insofar as depressed people are prone to experience awkward, tense, stormy, and frustrating interactions with family, friends, and colleagues, they are likely to generate chronic stress for themselves (Hammen & Shih, 2014), and as we will discuss next, stress can be a factor in mood dysfunction.

Precipitating Stress

Mood disorders sometimes appear mysteriously in people who are leading benign, nonstressful lives (Monroe & Harkness, 2005). For this reason, experts used to believe that stress had little influence on mood disorders. However, advances in the measurement of personal stress altered this picture. The evidence available today suggests the existence of a moderately strong link between stress and the onset of both major depression (Monroe, Slavich, & Georgiades, 2014) and bipolar disorder (Johnson et al., 2014). Of course, the vast majority of people who experience significant stress do not develop a mood disorder, so one's vulnerability to both stress and mood disorders must play a role (Bifulco, 2013). Unfortunately, vulnerability to depression seems to increase as people go through more recurrences of depressive episodes. Studies show that stress is less of a factor in triggering depression as episodes of depression accumulate over the years (Monroe et al., 2014).

14.5

Key Learning Goals

- Identify the general characteristics of schizophrenia, and distinguish between positive and negative symptoms.
- Explain how genetic and neural factors can contribute to the development of schizophrenia.
- Understand the neurodevelopmental hypothesis and how family dynamics and stress can play a role in schizophrenia.

14.5 SCHIZOPHRENIC DISORDERS

Literally, *schizophrenia* means "split mind." However, when Eugen Bleuler coined the term in 1911, he was referring to the fragmentation of thought processes seen in the disorder—not to a "split personality." Unfortunately, writers in the popular media often assume that the split-mind notion, and thus schizophrenia, refers to the rare syndrome in which a person manifests two or more personalities. As you have already learned, this syndrome is actually called *dissociative identity disorder*. Schizophrenia is a much more common, and altogether different, type of disorder.

Schizophrenia is a disorder marked by delusions, hallucinations, disorganized thinking and speech, and deterioration of adaptive behavior. Schizophrenia usually emerges during adolescence or early adulthood. About 75% of cases manifest by the age of 30 (Perkins, Miller-Anderson, & Lieberman, 2006). Prevalence estimates suggest that about 1% of the population may suffer from schizophrenia (Sadock et al., 2015). That may not sound like much, but it means that in the United States alone, several million people may be troubled by schizophrenic disturbances. Schizophrenia is an extremely costly illness for society because it is a severe, debilitating illness that tends to have an early onset and often requires lengthy hospital care (Samnaliev & Clark, 2008). Moreover, individuals suffering from schizophrenia show an increased risk for suicide and for premature mortality (early death) from natural causes (Nielsen et al., 2013).

Symptoms

Schizophrenia is a severe disorder that wreaks havoc in victims' lives. Many of the key symptoms of schizophrenia are apparent in the following case history, adapted from Sheehan (1982). Sylvia was first diagnosed as schizophrenic at age 15. She has been in and out of many types of psychiatric facilities since then. She has never been able to hold a job for any length of time. During severe flare-ups of her disorder, her personal hygiene deteriorates. She rarely washes, she wears clothes that neither fit nor match, and she smears makeup on heavily but randomly. Sylvia occasionally hears voices talking to her. She tends to be argumentative, aggressive, and emotionally volatile. Over the years, she has been involved in innumerable fights with fellow patients, psychiatric staff members, and strangers. Her thoughts can be highly irrational, as is apparent from the following quote:

> "Mick Jagger wants to marry me. If I have Mick Jagger, I don't have to covet Geraldo Rivera. Mick Jagger is St. Nicholas and the Maharishi is Santa Claus. I want to form a gospel rock group called the Thorn Oil, but Geraldo wants me to be the music critic on Eyewitness News, so what can I do? Got to listen to my boyfriend. Teddy Kennedy cured me of my ugliness. I'm pregnant with the son of God. They're eating the patients here. I'm Joan of Arc. I'm Florence Nightingale. The door between the ward and the porch is the dividing line between New York and California. Forget about zip codes. I need shock treatments. The body is run by electricity. My wiring is all faulty." (Adapted from Sheehan, 1982; quotation from pp. 104–105)

Sylvia's case clearly shows that schizophrenic thinking can be bizarre and that schizophrenia can be a severe and crippling disorder. Although no single symptom is inevitably present, the following symptoms are commonly seen in schizophrenia (Arango & Carpenter, 2011; Liddle, 2009).

Delusions and Irrational Thought

Cognitive deficits and disturbed thought processes are the central, defining feature of schizophrenia (Heinrichs et al., 2013). Various kinds of delusions are common. **Delusions are false beliefs that are maintained even though they clearly are out of touch with reality.** For example, one patient's delusion that he was a tiger (with a deformed body) persisted for 15 years (Kulick, Pope, & Keck, 1990). More typically, affected persons believe that their private thoughts are being broadcast to other people, that thoughts are being injected into their mind against their will, or that their thoughts are being controlled by some external force (Maher, 2001). In *delusions of grandeur,* people maintain that they are famous or important. Sylvia expressed an endless array of grandiose delusions, such as thinking that Mick Jagger wanted to marry her, that she had dictated the hobbit stories to J. R. R. Tolkien, and that she was going to win the Nobel Prize for medicine. In addition to delusions, the schizophrenic person's train of thought deteriorates. Thinking becomes chaotic rather than logical and linear. A "loosening of associations" occurs as the person shifts topics in disjointed ways. The quotation from Sylvia illustrates this symptom dramatically. The entire quote involves a wild flight of ideas in which the thoughts mostly have no apparent connection to one another.

> **REALITY CHECK**

Misconception

Schizophrenia refers to the syndrome in which a person manifests two or more personalities.

Reality

Literally, *schizophrenia* means "split mind." However, when Eugen Bleuler coined the term in 1911, he was referring to the fragmentation of thought processes seen in the disorder—not to a "split personality." Unfortunately, writers in the popular media often erroneously equate the split-mind notion with split personality. As you have already learned, this syndrome is actually called *dissociative identity disorder.*

Deterioration of Adaptive Behavior

Schizophrenia usually involves a noticeable deterioration in the quality of the person's routine functioning in work, social relations, and personal care (Harvey & Bowie, 2013). Friends often make remarks such as "Hal just isn't himself anymore." This deterioration is readily apparent in Sylvia's inability to get along with others or to function in the work world. It's also apparent in her neglect of personal hygiene.

Distorted Perception

A variety of perceptual distortions can occur with schizophrenia, the most common being auditory hallucinations, which are reported by about 75% of patients (Combs & Mueser, 2007). *Hallucinations* **are sensory perceptions that occur in the absence of a real, external stimulus or are gross distortions of perceptual input.** People with schizophrenia commonly report that they hear voices of nonexistent or absent people talking to them. Sylvia, for instance, said she heard messages from former Beatle Paul McCartney. These voices often provide an insulting, running commentary on the person's behavior ("You're an idiot for shaking his hand"). They may be argumentative ("You don't need a bath"), or they may issue commands ("Prepare your home for visitors from outer space").

Disturbed Emotion

Normal emotional tone can be disrupted in a variety of ways. Some victims show a flattening of emotions. In other words, they show little emotional responsiveness. Others show inappropriate emotional responses that don't jell with the situation or with what they are saying. People with schizophrenia can also become emotionally volatile. Because of this volatility, acts of aggression can be a problem with some schizophrenic patients (Serper, 2011).

Traditionally, four subtypes of schizophrenic disorders were recognized: paranoid, catatonic, disorganized, and undifferentiated schizophrenia (Minzenberg, Yoon, & Carter, 2008). As its name implies, *paranoid schizophrenia* was thought to be dominated by delusions of persecution, along with delusions of grandeur. *Catatonic schizophrenia* was marked by striking motor disturbances, ranging from the muscular rigidity seen in a withdrawn state called a *catatonic stupor* to random motor activity seen in a state of *catatonic excitement*. *Disorganized schizophrenia* was viewed as a particularly severe syndrome marked by frequent incoherence, obvious deterioration in adaptive behavior, and virtually complete social withdrawal. People who were clearly schizophrenic but who could not be placed into any of the three previous categories were said to have *undifferentiated schizophrenia,* which involved idiosyncratic mixtures of schizophrenic symptoms.

However, in a radical departure from tradition, DSM-5 discarded the four subtypes of schizophrenia. Why? For many years, researchers pointed out that there were not meaningful differences between the classic subtypes in etiology, prognosis, or response to treatment. The absence of such differences cast doubt on the value of distinguishing among the subtypes. Critics also noted that the catatonic and disorganized subtypes were rarely seen in contemporary clinical practice and that undifferentiated cases did not represent a subtype as much as a hodgepodge of "leftovers." Finally, researchers had stopped focusing their studies on the specific subtypes of schizophrenia (Braff et al., 2013).

Another approach to understanding and describing schizophrenia is to distinguish between the *positive symptoms* and *negative symptoms* of the disorder (Stroup et al., 2014; see **Figure 14.12**). *Negative symptoms* involve behavioral deficits, such as flattened emotions, social withdrawal, apathy, impaired attention, poor grooming, lack of persistence at work or school, and poverty of speech. *Positive symptoms* involve behavioral excesses or peculiarities, such as hallucinations, delusions, incoherent thought, agitation, bizarre behavior, and wild flights of ideas. Most patients exhibit both types of symptoms, but vary in the *degree* to which positive or negative symptoms dominate (Andreasen, 2009). A relative

Positive and Negative Symptoms in Schizophrenia

Negative symptoms	Percent of patients	Positive symptoms	Percent of patients
Few friendship relationships	96	Delusions of persecution	81
Few recreational interests	95	Auditory hallucinations	75
Lack of persistence at work or school	95	Delusions of being controlled	46
Impaired grooming or hygiene	87	Derailment of thought	45
Paucity of expressive gestures	81	Delusions of grandeur	39
Social inattentiveness	78	Bizarre social, sexual behavior	33
Emotional nonresponsiveness	64	Delusions of thought insertion	31
Inappropriate emotion	63	Aggressive, agitated behavior	27
Poverty of speech	53	Incoherent thought	23

FIGURE 14.12

Positive and negative symptoms in schizophrenia. Some theorists believe that schizophrenic disorders can be best understood by thinking in terms of two kinds of symptoms: positive symptoms (behavioral excesses) and negative symptoms (behavioral deficits). The percentages shown here, based on a sample of 111 schizophrenic patients studied by Andreasen (1987), provide an indication of how common each specific symptom is.

predominance of negative symptoms is associated with less effective social functioning (Robertson et al., 2014), and poorer overall treatment outcomes (Fervaha et al., 2014).

Etiology of Schizophrenia

You can probably identify, at least to some extent, with people who suffer from mood disorders and anxiety disorders. You can probably imagine events that could unfold that might leave you struggling with depression or grappling with anxiety. But what could possibly account for Sylvia's

CONCEPT CHECK 14.3

Distinguishing Among Depressive, Bipolar, and Schizophrenic Disorders

Check your understanding of the nature of depressive, bipolar, and schizophrenic disorders by making preliminary diagnoses for the cases described below. Read each case summary and write your tentative diagnosis in the space provided. The answers are in Appendix A.

1. Max hasn't slept in 4 days. He's determined to write the "great American novel" before his class reunion, which is a few months away. He expounds eloquently on his novel to anyone who will listen, talking at such a rapid pace that no one can get a word in edgewise. He feels like he's wired with energy, and is supremely confident about the novel, even though he's only written 10–20 pages. Last week, he charged $2000 worth of new computer equipment, which is supposed to help him write his book.

   Preliminary diagnosis: _____

2. Eduardo maintains that he invented the atomic bomb, even though he was born after its invention. He says he invented it to punish homosexuals, Nazis, and short people. It's short people he's most afraid of. He's sure that all the short people on TV are talking about him. He thinks short people are conspiring to make him look like a Republican. Eduardo frequently gets in arguments with people and is emotionally volatile. His grooming is poor, but he says it's okay because he's the secretary of state.

   Preliminary diagnosis: _____

3. Margaret has hardly gotten out of bed for weeks, although she's troubled by insomnia. She doesn't feel like eating and has absolutely no energy. She feels dejected, discouraged, spiritless, and apathetic. Friends stop by to try to cheer her up, but she tells them not to waste their time on "pond scum."

   Preliminary diagnosis: _____

© Orange Line Media/Shutterstock.com

John Nash, the Nobel Prize–winning mathematician whose story was told in the film *A Beautiful Mind,* struggled with paranoid schizophrenia dating back to 1959.

thinking that she was Joan of Arc or had dictated the hobbit novels to Tolkien? As mystifying as these delusions may seem, you'll see that the etiology of schizophrenic disorders is not all that different from the etiology of other psychological disorders. We'll begin our discussion by examining the matter of genetic vulnerability.

Genetic Vulnerability

Evidence is plentiful that hereditary factors play a role in the development of schizophrenic disorders (Riley & Kendler, 2011). For instance, in twin studies, concordance rates average around 48% for identical twins, in comparison with about 17% for fraternal twins (Gottesman, 1991, 2001). Studies also indicate that a child born to two schizophrenic parents has about a 46% probability of developing a schizophrenic disorder (as compared with the probability in the general population of about 1%). These and other findings that show the genetic roots of schizophrenia are summarized in **Figure 14.13**. Some theorists suspect that genetic factors may account for as much as 80% of the variability in susceptibility to schizophrenia (Pogue-Geile & Yokley, 2010). After years of inconsistent findings and difficulties in replicating results, genetic mapping studies are finally beginning to yield some promising insights regarding the specific combinations of genes and genetic mutations that increase individuals' risk for schizophrenia (Gelernter, 2015; Gershon & Alliey-Rodriguez, 2013; Hall et al., 2015).

Neurochemical Factors

Like depressive and bipolar disorders, schizophrenic disorders appear to be accompanied by changes in the activity of one or more neurotransmitters in the brain. The *dopamine hypothesis* asserts that excess dopamine activity is the neurochemical basis for schizophrenia. This hypothesis makes sense because most of the drugs that are useful in the treatment of schizophrenia are known to dampen dopamine activity in the brain (Stroup et al., 2014). Research suggests that increased dopamine *synthesis* and *release* in specific regions of the brain may be the crucial factor that triggers schizophrenic illness in vulnerable individuals (Howes et al., 2011; Winton-Brown et al., 2014). In recent years, the dopamine hypothesis has become more nuanced and complex. Researchers believe that dysregulation occurs in dopamine circuits and that the nature of this dysregulation may vary in different regions of the brain (Abi-Dargham & Grace, 2011).

Recent research has suggested that marijuana use *during adolescence* may help precipitate schizophrenia in young people who have a *genetic vulnerability* to the disorder (van Winkel & Kuepper, 2014). For example, a meta-analysis of eighty-three studies found that the onset of psychotic disorder tended to occur 2.7 years earlier in cannabis users than in non-users (Large et al., 2011). This unexpected finding has generated

FIGURE 14.13

Genetic vulnerability to schizophrenic disorders. Relatives of schizophrenic patients have an elevated risk for schizophrenia. This risk is greater among closer relatives. Although environment also plays a role in the etiology of schizophrenia, the concordance rates shown here suggest that there is a genetic vulnerability to the disorder. These concordance estimates are based on pooled data from forty studies conducted between 1920 and 1987. (Data adapted from Gottesman, 1991)

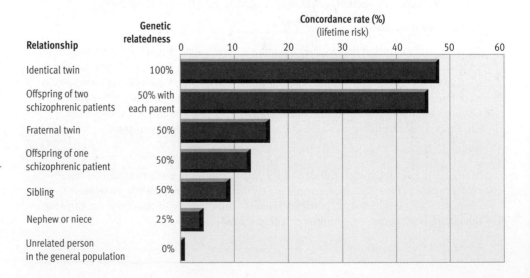

Relationship	Genetic relatedness	Concordance rate (%) (lifetime risk)
Identical twin	100%	
Offspring of two schizophrenic patients	50% with each parent	
Fraternal twin	50%	
Offspring of one schizophrenic patient	50%	
Sibling	50%	
Nephew or niece	25%	
Unrelated person in the general population	0%	

AP Images/Charles Rex Arbogast

512   CHAPTER 14

considerable debate about whether and how cannabis might contribute to the emergence of schizophrenia. Some critics suggest that schizophrenia could lead to cannabis use, rather than vice versa. In other words, emerging psychotic symptoms may prompt young people to turn to marijuana to self-medicate. However, carefully controlled studies have not supported the self-medication explanation (van Winkel & Kuepper, 2014). The evidence suggests a causal link between marijuana use and the emergence of schizophrenia, but the mechanism at work remains a mystery. Research suggests there may also be an association between methamphetamine use and the emergence of schizophrenia (Callaghan et al., 2012).

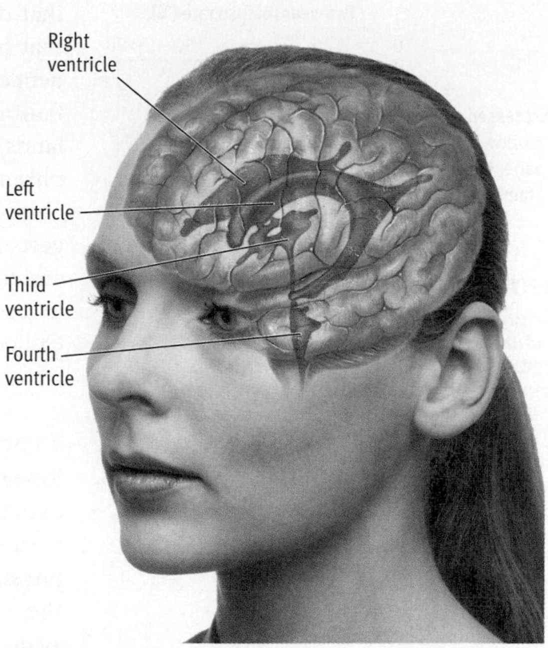

Structural Abnormalities in the Brain

Individuals with schizophrenia exhibit a variety of deficits in attention, perception, and information processing (Goldberg, David, & Gold, 2011). These cognitive deficits suggest that schizophrenic disorders may be caused by neurological defects. Brain-imaging studies have yielded intriguing findings that are consistent with this idea. The most reliable finding is that CT scans and MRI scans (see Chapter 3) suggest an association between enlarged brain ventricles (the hollow, fluid-filled cavities in the brain depicted in **Figure 14.14**) and schizophrenic disturbance (Lawrie & Pantelis, 2011). Enlarged ventricles are assumed to reflect the degeneration of nearby brain tissue. The significance of enlarged ventricles is hotly debated, however. This structural deterioration could be a *consequence* of schizophrenia, or it could be a contributing *cause* of the illness. Brain-imaging studies have also uncovered other structural abnormalities, including reductions in both gray matter and white matter in specific brain regions (Cannon et al., 2015; White et al., 2013).

The Neurodevelopmental Hypothesis

The *neurodevelopmental hypothesis* of schizophrenia asserts that schizophrenia is caused in part by various disruptions in the normal maturational processes of the brain before or at birth (Rapoport, Giedd, & Gogtay, 2012). According to this hypothesis, insults to the brain during sensitive phases of prenatal development or during birth can cause subtle neurological damage that elevates individuals' vulnerability to schizophrenia years later in adolescence and early adulthood (see **Figure 14.15**). What are the sources of these early insults to the brain? Thus far, research has focused on viral infection or malnutrition during prenatal development and on obstetrical complications during the birth process.

Quite a number of studies have found a link between exposure to influenza and other infections during prenatal development and an increased prevalence of schizophrenia (Brown & Derkits, 2010), with inflammation thought to be the critical process

Right ventricle
Left ventricle
Third ventricle
Fourth ventricle

photo: © RimDream/Shutterstock.com; art: © Cengage Learning

FIGURE 14.14

Schizophrenia and the ventricles of the brain. Cerebrospinal fluid (CSF) circulates around the brain and spinal cord. The hollow cavities in the brain filled with CSF are called *ventricles*. The four ventricles in the human brain are depicted here. Studies with CT scans and MRI scans suggest an association between enlarged ventricles in the brain and the occurrence of schizophrenic disturbance.

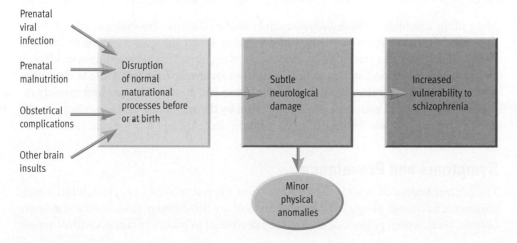

Prenatal viral infection
Prenatal malnutrition
Obstetrical complications
Other brain insults

Disruption of normal maturational processes before or at birth

Subtle neurological damage

Increased vulnerability to schizophrenia

Minor physical anomalies

FIGURE 14.15

The neurodevelopmental hypothesis of schizophrenia. Recent findings suggest that insults to the brain sustained during prenatal development or at birth can disrupt crucial maturational processes in the brain, resulting in subtle neurological damage that gradually becomes apparent as youngsters develop. This neurological damage is believed to increase both vulnerability to schizophrenia and the incidence of minor physical anomalies (slight anatomical defects of the head, face, hands, and feet).

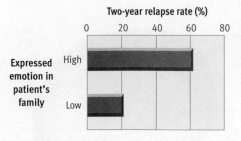

Two-year relapse rate (%)

FIGURE 14.16

Expressed emotion and relapse rates in schizophrenia. Schizophrenic patients who return to a home that is high in expressed emotion have higher relapse rates than those who return to a home low in expressed emotion. Thus, unhealthy family dynamics can influence the course of schizophrenia. (Data adapted from Leff & Vaughn, 1981)

that disrupts neural maturation (Miller, Culpepper et al., 2013). Additionally, a study that investigated the possible impact of prenatal malnutrition found an elevated incidence of schizophrenia in a group of people who were prenatally exposed to a severe famine in 1944–1945, resulting from a Nazi blockade of food deliveries in the Netherlands during World War II (Susser et al., 1996). Other research has shown that schizophrenic patients are more likely than control subjects to have experienced obstetrical complications when they were born (McGrath & Murray, 2011). Finally, research suggests that minor physical anomalies (slight anatomical defects of the head, hands, feet, and face) that would be consistent with prenatal neurological damage are more common in people with schizophrenia than in others (Akabaliev, Sivkov, & Mantarkov, 2014). Collectively, these diverse studies argue for a relationship between early neurological trauma and a predisposition to schizophrenia (Rapoport et al., 2012).

Expressed Emotion

Research on expressed emotion has primarily focused on how this element of family dynamics influences the *course* of schizophrenic illness, after the onset of the disorder (Leff & Vaughn, 1985). ***Expressed emotion* is the degree to which a relative of a schizophrenic patient displays highly critical or emotionally overinvolved attitudes toward the patient.** Audiotaped interviews of relatives' communication have been carefully evaluated for critical comments; resentment toward the patient; and excessive emotional involvement (overprotective, overconcerned attitudes) (Hooley, 2004). Studies show that a family's expressed emotion is a good predictor of the course of a schizophrenic patient's illness (Hooley, 2007). After release from a hospital, schizophrenic patients who return to a family high in expressed emotion show relapse rates three times those of patients who return to a family low in expressed emotion (Hooley, 2009; see **Figure 14.16**). Part of the problem for patients returning to homes high in expressed emotion is that their families probably are sources of stress rather than of social support (Bebbington & Kuipers, 2011).

Stress

Most theories of schizophrenia assume that stress plays a key role in triggering schizophrenic disorders (Walker & Tessner, 2008). According to this notion, various biological and psychological factors influence individuals' *vulnerability* to schizophrenia. High stress may then serve to precipitate a schizophrenic disorder in someone who is vulnerable (Bebbington & Kuipers, 2011). Research indicates that high stress can also trigger relapses in patients who have made progress toward recovery (Walker, Mittal, & Tessner, 2008).

14.6

14.6 AUTISM SPECTRUM DISORDERS

Key Learning Goals

- Describe the symptoms, prevalence, and etiology of autism spectrum disorder.

Many of the disorders we have discussed can be seen in children. For example, phobic disorders, obsessive-compulsive disorders, and depression are routinely seen among children, as well as adults. However, our next disorder, *autism,* is diagnosed exclusively during childhood, and very early childhood at that. ***Autism,* or *autism spectrum disorder (ASD),* is characterized by profound impairment of social interaction and communication and severely restricted interests and activities, usually apparent by the age of 3.** Originally called *infantile autism,* this disorder was first described by child psychiatrist Leo Kanner in the 1940s.

Symptoms and Prevalence

The central feature of ASD is the child's lack of interest in other people. Children with autism act as though people in their environment are not different than nearby inanimate objects, such as toys, pillows, or chairs. They don't tend to make eye contact with others or need physical contact with their caregivers. They make no effort to connect with people and fail to bond with their parents or to develop normal peer relationships. Verbal communication can be greatly impaired, as about one-third of ASD children fail to develop speech (Wetherby & Prizant, 2005). Among those who do develop speech, their ability to initiate and sustain a conversation is limited, and their use of language tends to be marked by peculiarities, such as *echolalia,* which involves rote repetition of others' words. Autistic children's interests are restricted in that they tend to become preoccupied with objects or repetitive body movements (spinning, body rocking, playing with their hands, and so forth). They can also be extremely inflexible, and minor changes in their environment can trigger rages and tantrums. Some ASD children exhibit self-injurious behavior, such as banging their heads, pulling their hair, or hitting themselves. About one-half of children with autism exhibit subnormal IQ scores (Volkmar et al., 2009).

Parents of autistic children typically become concerned about their child's development by about 15–18 months of age and usually seek professional consultation by about 24 months. The diagnosis of ASD is almost always made before affected children reach age 3. More often than not, autism turns out to be a lifelong affliction, requiring extensive family and institutional support throughout adulthood. However, with early and effective intervention, around 15%–20% of individuals with ASD are able to live independently in adulthood, and another 20%–30% approach this level of functioning (Volkmar et al., 2009). Moreover, recent research suggests that a small minority experience a full recovery in adulthood (Fein et al., 2013).

Until relatively recently, the prevalence of autism was thought to be well under 1% (Newschaffer, 2007). Since the mid-1990s, however, there has been a dramatic (roughly fourfold) increase in the diagnosis of autism, with prevalence estimates approaching and even exceeding 1% (Brugha et al., 2011; Idring et al., 2014; Zahorodny et al., 2014). Most experts believe that this surge in ASD is largely due to greater awareness of the syndrome and the use of broader diagnostic criteria (Abbeduto et al., 2014). Contemporary prevalence estimates usually include related syndromes, such as *Asperger's disorder,* that are milder forms of the disease that used to go uncounted, but are now included within the broadly defined DSM-5 version of autism *spectrum* disorder. Although these explanations make sense, scientists have not ruled out the possibility of a genuine increase in the prevalence of autism (Weintraub, 2011). Males account for about 80% of autism diagnoses, although curiously, females tend to exhibit more severe impairments (Ursano et al., 2008).

Children with autism often fail to make eye contact with others, as you can see in this photo of a boy with autism participating in a behavior therapy session.

DIAGNOSTIC CATEGORIES

SUBTYPES

PREVALENCE/ WELL-KNOWN VICTIMS

ANXIETY-RELATED DISORDERS

Evelyn Williams's *People Waiting* expresses overwhelming feelings of anxiety.

© Evelyn Williams/Bridgeman Art Library

Generalized anxiety disorder: Chronic, high level of anxiety not tied to any specific threat

Specific phobia: Persistent, irrational fear of object or situation that presents no real danger

Panic disorder: Recurrent attacks of overwhelming anxiety that occur suddenly and unexpectedly

Agoraphobia: Fear of going out to public places

Obsessive-compulsive disorder: Persistent, uncontrollable intrusions of unwanted thoughts and urges to engage in senseless rituals

Post-traumatic stress disorder: Enduring psychological disturbance attributable to the experience of a major traumatic event

0 2 4 6 8 10 12 14 16 18 20

19%

Prevalence

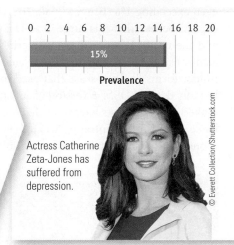

Comedian Howie Mandel suffers from obsessive-compulsive disorder.

© Dennis Van Tine/ABACAUSA.COM/Newscom

MOOD-RELATED DISORDERS

Vincent Van Gogh's *Portrait of Dr. Gachet* captures the profound dejection experienced in depressive disorders.

Musee d'Orsay, Paris. © Erich Lessing/Art Resource, NY

Major depressive disorder: Two or more major depressive episodes marked by feelings of sadness, worthlessness, despair

Bipolar disorder: One or more manic episodes marked by inflated self-esteem, grandiosity, and elevated mood and energy, usually accompanied by major depressive episodes

0 2 4 6 8 10 12 14 16 18 20

15%

Prevalence

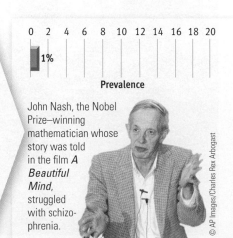

Actress Catherine Zeta-Jones has suffered from depression.

© Everett Collection/Shutterstock.com

SCHIZOPHRENIC DISORDERS

The perceptual distortions seen in schizophrenia probably contributed to the bizarre imagery apparent in this portrait of a cat painted by Louis Wain.

© *Kaleidoscope Cats IV* (colored pencil on paper), Wain, Louis (1860–1939)/Bethlem Royal Hospital Museum, Beckenham, Kent/Bridgeman Images

Distinctions between paranoid, catatonic, disorganized, and undifferentiated schizophrenia were discarded in DSM-5

Negative symptoms involve behavioral deficits, such as flattened emotions, social withdrawal, apathy, and poverty of speech

Positive symptoms involve behavioral excesses or peculiarities, such as hallucinations, delusions, agitation, and bizarre behavior

A predominance of negative symptoms is associated with a worse prognosis

0 2 4 6 8 10 12 14 16 18 20

1%

Prevalence

John Nash, the Nobel Prize–winning mathematician whose story was told in the film *A Beautiful Mind*, struggled with schizophrenia.

© AP Images/Charles Rex Arbogast

ETIOLOGY: BIOLOGICAL FACTORS

Genetic vulnerability: Twin studies and other evidence suggest a mild genetic predisposition to anxiety-related disorders.

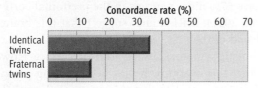

Concordance rate (%)

	0	10	20	30	40	50	60	70

Identical twins
Fraternal twins

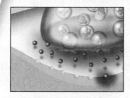

Neurochemical bases: Disturbances in neural circuits releasing GABA may contribute to some disorders; abnormalities at serotonin synapses have been implicated in obsessive-compulsive disorders.

Genetic vulnerability: Twin studies and other evidence suggest a genetic predisposition to mood-related disorders.

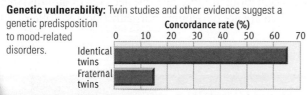

Concordance rate (%)

	0	10	20	30	40	50	60	70

Identical twins
Fraternal twins

Suppressed neurogenesis: Disruption of neurogenesis may lead to reduced volume in the hippocampus and to depression.

Neurochemical bases: Disturbances in neural circuits releasing norepinephrine may contribute to some mood-related disorders; abnormalities at serotonin synapses have also been implicated as a factor in depression.

Genetic vulnerability: Twin studies and other evidence suggest a genetic predisposition to schizophrenic disorders.

Concordance rate (%)

	0	10	20	30	40	50	60	70

Identical twins
Fraternal twins

Neurochemical bases: Overactivity in neural circuits releasing dopamine is associated with schizophrenia; but abnormalities in other neurotransmitter systems may also contribute.

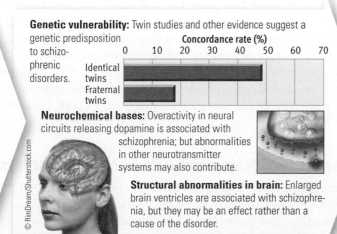

Structural abnormalities in brain: Enlarged brain ventricles are associated with schizophrenia, but they may be an effect rather than a cause of the disorder.

© RimDream/Shutterstock.com

ETIOLOGY: PSYCHOLOGICAL FACTORS

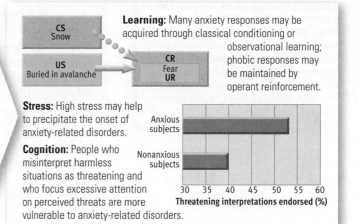

CS Snow

US Buried in avalanche

CR Fear UR

Learning: Many anxiety responses may be acquired through classical conditioning or observational learning; phobic responses may be maintained by operant reinforcement.

Stress: High stress may help to precipitate the onset of anxiety-related disorders.

Cognition: People who misinterpret harmless situations as threatening and who focus excessive attention on perceived threats are more vulnerable to anxiety-related disorders.

Anxious subjects
Nonanxious subjects

30	35	40	45	50	55	60

Threatening interpretations endorsed (%)

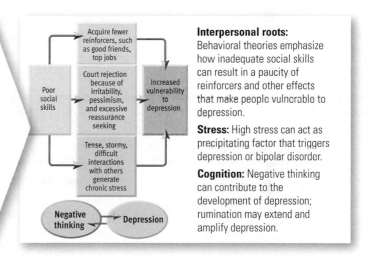

Poor social skills → Acquire fewer reinforcers, such as good friends, top jobs → Increased vulnerability to depression

Court rejection because of irritability, pessimism, and excessive reassurance seeking

Tense, stormy, difficult interactions with others generate chronic stress

Negative thinking → Depression

Interpersonal roots: Behavioral theories emphasize how inadequate social skills can result in a paucity of reinforcers and other effects that make people vulnerable to depression.

Stress: High stress can act as precipitating factor that triggers depression or bipolar disorder.

Cognition: Negative thinking can contribute to the development of depression; rumination may extend and amplify depression.

Expressed emotion: A family's expressed emotion is a good predictor of the course of a schizophrenic patient's illness.

Stress: High stress can precipitate schizophrenic disorder in people who are vulnerable to schizophrenia.

The neurodevelopmental hypothesis: Insults to the brain sustained during prenatal development or at birth may disrupt maturational processes in the brain resulting in elevated vulnerability to schizophrenia.

Two-year relapse rate (%)

20	40	60	80

Expressed emotion in patient's family — High
Low

Disruption of normal maturational processes before or at birth → Subtle neurological damage → Increased vulnerability to schizophrenia

Misconception

Autism can be caused by childhood vaccinations.

Reality

Many people continue to cling to this belief, even though the 1998 study that first reported a link between vaccinations and autism has been discredited as fraudulent (Deer, 2011; Godlee et al., 2011). Moreover, independent efforts to replicate the purported association between vaccinations and autism have consistently failed. Hence, the available evidence suggests that vaccinations do not play a role in the development of autistic disorder.

Etiology of ASD

Autism was originally blamed on cold, aloof parenting (Bettelheim, 1967), but that view was eventually discredited by research (Bhasin & Schendel, 2007). Given its appearance so early in life, most theorists today view autism as a disorder that originates in biological dysfunctions. Consistent with that viewpoint, twin studies and family studies have demonstrated that genetic factors make a major contribution to ASD (Abbeduto et al., 2014; Risch et al., 2014). Many theorists believe that autism must be attributable to some sort of brain abnormality, but until recently there was relatively little progress in pinpointing the nature of this abnormality. The most reliable finding has been that ASD is associated with generalized brain enlargement that is apparent by age 2 (Hazlett et al., 2011). Children with autism appear to have 67% more neurons in the prefrontal cortex than other children do (Courchesne et al., 2011). MRI studies suggest that this brain overgrowth begins some time around the end of the first year, which, with the luxury of hindsight, is right around the time that autistic symptoms usually start to surface. However, a more recent study found evidence that this overgrowth may begin during prenatal development (Stoner et al., 2014). Theorists speculate that this overgrowth probably produces disruptions in neural circuits.

One hypothesis that has garnered a great deal of publicity is the idea that autism may be caused by the mercury used as a preservative in some childhood vaccines (Kirby, 2005). However, the 1998 study that first reported a link between vaccinations and autism has been discredited as fraudulent (Deer, 2011; Godlee, Smith, & Marcovitch, 2011). Moreover, independent efforts to replicate the purported association between vaccinations and ASD have consistently failed (Paul, 2009; Wing & Potter, 2009). Widespread belief in the apparently spurious relationship between autism and vaccinations may simply be due to the fact that children get scheduled vaccinations around the same age (12–15 months) that parents first start to realize their children are not developing normally (Doja & Roberts, 2006).

14.7

Key Learning Goals

- Discuss the nature of personality disorders; the symptoms of antisocial, borderline, and narcissistic personality disorders; and their etiology.

14.7 PERSONALITY DISORDERS

Personality disorders **are a class of disorders marked by extreme, inflexible personality traits that cause subjective distress or impaired social and occupational functioning.** Personality disorders generally become recognizable during adolescence or early adulthood. One conservative estimate pegged the lifetime prevalence of personality disorders at around 12% (Caligor, Yeomans, & Levin, 2014).

DSM-5 lists ten personality disorders. They are grouped into three related clusters: anxious/fearful, odd/eccentric, and dramatic/impulsive. These disorders are described briefly in **Table 14.2**. If you examine this table, you will find a diverse collection of maladaptive personality syndromes. You may also notice that some personality disorders essentially are milder versions of more severe disorders that we have already covered. For example, the schizoid and schizotypal personality disorders are milder cousins of schizophrenic disorders. Although personality disorders tend to be relatively mild disorders in comparison with anxiety, mood, and schizophrenic disorders, they often are associated with significant impairments of social and occupational functioning (Trull, Carpenter, & Widiger, 2013).

Antisocial, Borderline, and Narcissistic Personality Disorders

Given the sheer number of personality disorders, we can only provide brief descriptions of a few of the more interesting syndromes in this category. Hence, we will take a quick look at the antisocial, borderline, and narcissistic personality disorders.

TABLE 14.2 Personality Disorders

Cluster	Disorder	Description
Anxious/fearful	Avoidant personality disorder	Excessively sensitive to potential rejection, humiliation, or shame; socially withdrawn in spite of desire for acceptance from others
	Dependent personality disorder	Excessively lacking in self-reliance and self-esteem; passively allowing others to make all decisions; constantly subordinating own needs to others' needs
	Obsessive-compulsive personality disorder	Preoccupied with organization, rules, schedules, lists, trivial details; extremely conventional, serious, and formal; unable to express warm emotions
Odd/eccentric	Schizoid personality disorder	Defective in capacity for forming social relationships; showing absence of warm, tender feelings for others
	Schizotypal personality disorder	Showing social deficits and oddities of thinking, perception, and communication that resemble schizophrenia
	Paranoid personality disorder	Showing pervasive and unwarranted suspiciousness and mistrust of people; overly sensitive; prone to jealousy
Dramatic/ impulsive	Histrionic personality disorder	Overly dramatic; tending to exaggerated expressions of emotion; egocentric, seeking attention
	Narcissistic personality disorder	Grandiosely self-important; preoccupied with success fantasies; expecting special treatment; lacking interpersonal empathy
	Borderline personality disorder	Unstable in self-image, mood, and interpersonal relationships; impulsive and unpredictable
	Antisocial personality disorder	Chronically violating the rights of others; failing to accept social norms, to form attachments to others, or to sustain consistent work behavior; exploitive and reckless

Antisocial Personality Disorder

People with this disorder are *antisocial* in the sense that they choose to *reject widely accepted social norms* regarding moral principles. People with antisocial personalities chronically exploit others. The *antisocial personality disorder* **is marked by impulsive, callous, manipulative, aggressive, and irresponsible behavior.** Since they haven't accepted the social norms they violate, people with antisocial personalities rarely feel guilty about their transgressions. Essentially, they lack an adequate conscience. The antisocial personality disorder occurs much more frequently among males than females (Torgersen, 2012). Many people with antisocial personalities get involved in illegal activities (Porter & Porter, 2007). However, some people with antisocial personalities keep their exploitive behavior channeled within the boundaries of the law. Such people may even enjoy high status in our society (Babiak & Hare, 2006). In other words, the concept of the antisocial personality disorder can apply to cut-throat business executives and scheming politicians, as well as to con artists, drug dealers, and petty thieves. People with antisocial personalities exhibit quite a variety of maladaptive traits (Hare, 2006; Hare & Neumann, 2008). Among other things, they rarely experience genuine affection for others. Sexually, they are predatory and promiscuous. They can tolerate little frustration, and they pursue immediate gratification. These characteristics make them unreliable employees, unfaithful spouses, inattentive parents, and undependable friends. Many people with antisocial personalities have a checkered history of divorce, child abuse, and job instability.

Borderline Personality Disorder

The *borderline personality disorder* **is marked by instability in social relationships, self-image, and emotional functioning.** This disorder appears to be somewhat more common in females than males (Tomko et al., 2014). These individuals tend to have turbulent interpersonal relationships marked by fears of abandonment (Hooley, Cole, & Gironde, 2012). They often switch back and forth between idealizing people and devaluing them. They tend to be intense, with frequent anger issues and poor control of their emotions. They tend to be moody, shifting among panic, despair, and feelings of emptiness. They are prone to impulsive behavior, such as reckless spending, drug use, or sexual behavior. Individuals with borderline personality disorder often exhibit fragile, unstable self-concepts, as their goals, values, opinions, and career plans shift suddenly. Borderline personality disorder is also associated with an elevated risk for self-injurious behavior, such as cutting or burning oneself and with an increased risk for suicide (Caligor et al., 2014).

Narcissistic Personality Disorder

We discussed the personality trait of *narcissism* in Chapter 11. As you might guess, people with narcissistic personality disorder exhibit this trait to a very extreme degree. Hence, **the *narcissistic personality disorder* is marked by a grandiose sense of self-importance, a sense of entitlement, and an excessive need for attention and admiration.** This syndrome is more common in males (Trull et al., 2010). People with this disorder think they are unique and superior to others. They tend to be boastful and pretentious. Although they seem self-assured and confident, their self-esteem is actually quite fragile, leading them to fish for compliments and to be easily threatened by criticism. Their sense of entitlement manifests in arrogant expectations that they should merit special treatment and extra privileges. Their need for admiration is hard to fulfill. They routinely complain that others do not appreciate their accomplishments or give them the respect they deserve. Some critics have argued that the current diagnostic criteria for narcissistic personality disorder focus too much on the overt, grandiose presentation of the disorder and too little on its covert, vulnerable side (Levy, 2012; Skodol, Bender, & Morey, 2014).

Etiology of Personality Disorders

Like other disorders, the personality disorders all surely involve interactions between genetic predispositions and environmental factors, such as cognitive styles, coping patterns, and exposure to stress. As noted in Chapter 11, personality traits are shaped to a significant degree by heredity (South et al., 2013). Given that personality disorders consist of extreme manifestations of personality traits, it stands to reason that these disorders are also influenced by heredity, and the data from twin and family studies support this line of reasoning (Skodol et al., 2014). The environmental factors implicated in personality disorders vary considerably from one disorder to another, which makes sense given the diversity of the personality disorders. For example, contributing factors to antisocial personality disorder include dysfunctional family systems; erratic discipline; parental neglect; and parental modeling of exploitive, amoral behavior (Farrington, 2006; Sutker & Allain, 2001). In contrast, borderline personality disorder has been attributed primarily to a history of early trauma, including physical and sexual abuse (Ball & Links, 2009; Widom, Czaja, & Paris, 2009). Different constellations of environmental factors have been implicated for each of the other eight personality disorders.

14.8

Key Learning Goals

- Identify the subtypes of eating disorders, and discuss their prevalence.
- Outline how genetic factors, personality, culture, family dynamics, and disturbed thinking contribute to eating disorders.

14.8 EATING DISORDERS

Most people don't seem to take eating disorders as seriously as they take other types of psychological disorders. Yet, you will see that these disorders are dangerous and debilitating, and that no other types of psychological disorders are associated with a greater elevation in mortality.

Description

Eating disorders **are severe disturbances in eating behavior characterized by preoccupation with weight concerns and unhealthy efforts to control weight.** The three syndromes are: anorexia nervosa, bulimia nervosa, and a new syndrome added to DSM-5 called binge-eating disorder.

Anorexia Nervosa

Anorexia nervosa **involves intense fear of gaining weight, disturbed body image, refusal to maintain normal weight, and use of dangerous measures to lose weight.** Two subtypes have been observed. In *restricting type anorexia nervosa,* people drastically reduce their intake of food, sometimes literally starving themselves. In *binge-eating/purging type anorexia nervosa,* individuals attempt to lose weight by forcing themselves to vomit after meals, by misusing laxatives and diuretics, and by engaging in excessive exercise.

Anorexics suffer from a disturbed body image. No matter how frail they become, they insist that they are too fat. Their morbid fear of obesity means that they are never satisfied with their weight. If they gain a pound or two, they panic. The only thing that makes them happy is to lose more weight. The common result is a relentless decline in body weight. Because of their disturbed body image, individuals suffering from anorexia generally do *not* appreciate the maladaptive quality of their behavior. Hence, they rarely seek treatment on their own. They are typically coaxed or coerced into treatment by friends or family members who are alarmed by their appearance.

Anorexic patients frequently endure other psychological disorders, as well. More than half suffer from depressive disorders or anxiety disorders (Sadock et al., 2015). Anorexia nervosa eventually leads to a cascade of medical problems. These problems may include *amenorrhea* (a loss of menstrual cycles in women), gastrointestinal problems, low blood pressure, *osteoporosis* (a loss of bone density), and metabolic disturbances that can lead to cardiac arrest or circulatory collapse (Mitchell & Wonderlich, 2014). Anorexia is a debilitating illness that is associated with greatly elevated mortality rates (Franko et al., 2013).

Eating disorders have become distressingly common among young women in Western cultures. No matter how frail they become, people suffering from anorexia insist they are too fat.

Bulimia Nervosa

Bulimia nervosa **involves habitually engaging in out-of-control overeating, followed by unhealthy compensatory efforts, such as self-induced vomiting, fasting, abuse of laxatives and diuretics, and excessive exercise.** The eating binges are usually carried out in secret and are followed by intense guilt and concern about gaining weight. These feelings motivate ill-advised strategies to undo the effects of the overeating. However, vomiting prevents the absorption of only about half of recently consumed food, and laxatives and diuretics have negligible impact on caloric intake. So, individuals suffering from bulimia nervosa typically maintain a reasonably normal weight (Fairburn, Cooper, & Murphy, 2009). Medical problems associated with bulimia nervosa include cardiac arrythmias, dental problems, metabolic deficiencies, and gastrointestinal problems (Mitchell & Wonderlich, 2014).

Obviously, bulimia nervosa shares many features with anorexia nervosa, such as a morbid fear of becoming obese; preoccupation with food; and rigid, maladaptive approaches to controlling weight that are grounded in naïve all-or-none thinking. However, the syndromes also differ in crucial ways. First and foremost, bulimia is a much less life-threatening condition. Second, although their appearance is usually more "normal" than that seen with anorexia, people with bulimia are much more likely to recognize that their eating behavior is pathological and are more likely to cooperate with treatment (Guarda et al., 2007). Nonetheless, like anorexia, bulimia is associated with elevated mortality rates, although this elevation is only about one-third as great as that seen for anorexia (Arcelus et al., 2011).

Binge-Eating Disorder

Binge-eating disorder **involves distress-inducing eating binges that are not accompanied by the purging, fasting, and excessive exercise seen in bulimia.** Obviously, this syndrome resembles bulimia, but it is a less severe disorder. Still, this disorder creates great distress, as these people tend to be disgusted by their bodies and distraught about their overeating. People with binge-eating disorder are frequently overweight. Their excessive eating is often triggered by stress (Gluck, 2006). This comparatively mild syndrome is more common than anorexia or bulimia (Hudson et al., 2007).

Prevalence and Cultural Roots

Eating disorders are a product of modern, affluent Western culture, in which food is generally plentiful and the desirability of being thin is widely endorsed. Until recent decades, these disorders were not seen outside Western cultures (Hoek, 2002). However, advances in communication have exported Western culture to far-flung corners of the globe. Hence, eating disorders have started showing up in many non-Western societies, especially affluent Asian countries (Becker & Fay, 2006).

There are huge gender gaps in the likelihood of developing eating disorders. About 90%–95% of individuals with anorexia nervosa and bulimia nervosa are female, and about 60% of those with binge-eating disorder are female (Devlin & Steinglass, 2014). The staggering gender disparities in the prevalence of the more serious eating disorders appear to be a result of cultural pressures rather than biological factors (Smolak & Murnen, 2001). Western standards of attractiveness emphasize slenderness more for females than for males, and women generally experience greater pressure to be physically attractive than men do (Strahan et al., 2008). Eating disorders mostly afflict *young* women. The typical age of onset for anorexia is 14–18; for bulimia it is 15–21 (see **Figure 14.17**).

How common are eating disorders in Western societies? Research suggests that among females, about 1% develop anorexia nervosa, roughly 1.5% develop bulimia nervosa, and about 3.5% exhibit binge-eating disorder (Hudson et al., 2007). In some respects, these figures may only scratch the surface of the problem (Keel et al., 2012). Evidence suggests that another 2%–4% of people may struggle with serious eating problems that do not quite qualify for a formal diagnosis (Swanson et al., 2011). And community surveys suggest that there may be more undiagnosed eating disorders among men than generally appreciated (Field et al., 2014).

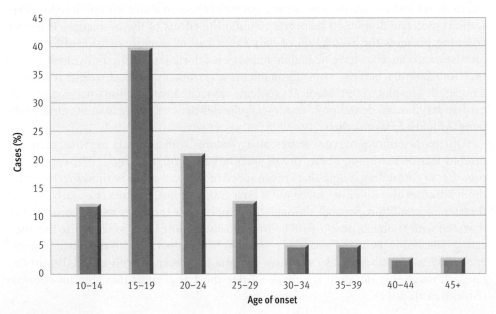

FIGURE 14.17

Age of onset for anorexia nervosa. Eating disorders mostly emerge during adolescence, as these data for anorexia nervosa show. This graph shows how age of onset was distributed in a sample of 166 female patients from Minnesota. As you can see, more than half the patients experienced the onset of their illness before the age of 20, with vulnerability clearly peaking between the ages of 15 and 19. (Based on data from Lucas et al., 1991)

Etiology of Eating Disorders

Like other types of psychological disorders, eating disorders are caused by multiple determinants that work interactively. Let's take a brief look at some of the factors that contribute to the development of anorexia nervosa and bulimia nervosa.

Genetic Vulnerability

The stockpile of research findings is not as large as it is for many other types of psychopathology (such as anxiety, mood, and schizophrenic disorders), but some people may inherit a genetic vulnerability to eating disorders. There is convincing evidence for a hereditary component in both anorexia nervosa and bulimia nervosa, with genetics probably playing a stronger role in anorexia (Trace et al., 2013). A genetic predisposition also appears to contribute to binge-eating disorder, but there are fewer studies of this newer diagnosis.

Personality Factors

Certain personality traits may increase vulnerability to eating disorders. There are innumerable exceptions, but victims of anorexia nervosa tend to be obsessive, rigid, and emotionally restrained, whereas victims of bulimia nervosa tend to be impulsive, overly sensitive, and low in self-esteem (Anderluh, Tchauturia, & Rube-Hesketh, 2003; Wonderlich, 2002). Research also suggests that perfectionism is a risk factor for anorexia (Keel et al., 2012).

Cultural Values

The contribution of cultural values to the increased prevalence of eating disorders can hardly be overestimated (Striegel-Moore & Bulik, 2007). In Western society, young women are socialized to believe they must be attractive. To be attractive, they think they must be as thin as the actresses and fashion models who dominate the media (Fox-Kales, 2011; Levine & Harrison, 2004). Thanks to this cultural milieu, many young women are dissatisfied with their weight because the societal ideals promoted by the media are unattainable for most of them (Thompson & Stice, 2001). Unfortunately, in a small portion of these women, the pressure to be thin, in combination with genetic vulnerability, family pathology, and other factors, leads to unhealthy efforts to control weight.

The Role of the Family

Quite a number of theorists stress how family dynamics can contribute to the development of anorexia and bulimia in young women (Haworth-Hoeppner, 2000). The principal issue appears to be that some mothers contribute to eating disorders simply by endorsing society's message that "you can never be too thin" and by modeling unhealthy dieting behaviors of their own (Francis & Birch, 2005). In conjunction with media pressures, this role modeling leads many daughters to internalize the idea that the thinner you are, the more attractive you are. Of course, peers can also endorse beliefs and model behaviors that promote eating disorders (Keel et al., 2013). Another potentially family-related issue is that there is an association between childhood sexual and physical abuse and an elevated risk for eating disorders (Steiger, Bruce, & Israël, 2013).

Cognitive Factors

Many theorists emphasize the role of disturbed thinking in the etiology of eating disorders (Williamson et al., 2001). For example, anorexic patients' typical belief that they are fat when they are really wasting away is a dramatic illustration of how thinking goes awry. Patients with eating disorders display rigid, all-or-none thinking and many maladaptive beliefs (Roberts, Tchanturia, & Treasure, 2010). Such thoughts may include "I must be thin to be accepted"; "If I am not in complete control, I will lose all control"; "If I gain one pound, I'll go on to gain enormous weight." Additional research is needed to determine whether distorted thinking is a *cause* or merely a *symptom* of eating disorders.

14.9

Key Learning Goals
• Describe two recent findings on pathology that transcend specific diagnoses.

14.9 NEW DIRECTIONS IN THE STUDY OF PSYCHOLOGICAL DISORDERS

Recent years have brought to light two interesting new findings regarding psychological disorders that largely transcend specific diagnoses; they are tentative insights that apply to a wide range of disorders. The first is that early-life stress may elevate vulnerability to a host of very diverse disorders. The second is that a number of severe disorders that have long been presumed to be distinct and unrelated may share more genetic and neurobiological roots than previously appreciated. Let's take a brief look at these findings.

The Role of Early-Life Stress in Adult Disorders

Until relatively recently, interest in the connection between stress and various disorders was largely limited to how adverse events in adolescence or adulthood might contribute to provoking the onset of certain disorders soon after the stress. However, in recent years, there has been a surge of research on how severe stress in early childhood may increase individuals' vulnerability to various disorders many years later. These studies have looked at many forms of early childhood trauma, such as physical abuse, sexual abuse, emotional neglect, parental death, childhood illness, and so forth. Two systematic reviews of this burgeoning research literature show that numerous studies have linked early-life stress to an increased prevalence of anxiety disorders, dissociative disorders, depressive disorders, bipolar disorders, schizophrenic disorders, personality disorders, and eating disorders (Carr et al., 2013; Martins et al., 2011). Admittedly, these studies have varied considerably in methodological quality. Many have relied on retrospective recollections of childhood trauma from patients and have not incorporated non-patient comparison groups (Bendall et al., 2008). These are weak correlational methods that could inflate the apparent effects of childhood adversity and that do not permit conclusions about causality. So, more evidence is needed to establish causality, but the sheer number and consistency of the findings suggest that childhood trauma may have long-term ripple effects that heighten individuals' vulnerability to a broad range of psychological disorders. Why would this be so? The thinking is that adversity during childhood may alter critical features of developing brain structure and the reactivity of the HPA axis that regulates hormonal responses to stressors (Aust et al., 2014; Juruena, 2014).

Genetic Overlap Among Major Disorders

Depression, bipolar disorder, schizophrenia, and autism have been viewed as independent disorders for many, many decades. They all are relatively severe mental disorders, but each involves a different course of illness, a different constellation of symptoms, different etiological factors, and different treatments. But recent findings suggest they may share more lineage than most experts would have guessed. One line of research suggests an overlap between autism and schizophrenia. For example, one family study found that having close relatives who were diagnosed with schizophrenia was associated with an increased risk for autism (Sullivan et al., 2012). Another review noted that autism and schizophrenia appear to involve similar neurodevelopmental abnormalities and that recently discovered genetic mutations elevate the risk for both disorders (De Lacy & King, 2013). Another line of research highlighted the overlap between schizophrenia and bipolar disorder. For example, recent studies demonstrated that schizophrenia and bipolar disorder share genetic vulnerabilities (Cardno & Owen, 2014); reductions in the volume of the hippocampus in the brain (Haukvik et al., 2015); and abnormalities in prefrontal white matter (Hercher, Chopra, & Beasley, 2014). The most interesting and influential research in this area is a study that used cutting-edge genetic mapping technology to quantify the hereditary covariation among depression, bipolar disorder, schizophrenia, autism, and attention-deficit/hyperactivity disorder (Cross-Disorder Group of the Psychiatric Genomics Consortium, 2013). More than 300 scientists at eighty research centers worked on this massive project. The findings suggest that the genetic overlap between schizophrenia and bipolar disorder is high; the overlap between schizophrenia and depression is moderate; the overlap between depression and bipolar disorder is moderate; and there is some overlap between autism and schizophrenia, but it is relatively low. It is hard to say where these findings will lead. These disorders will surely continue to be viewed as distinct entities, but the genetic and neurobiological overlap among the disorders is likely to be a lively area of research in the years to come. Depending on what that research reveals, these disorders may come to be seen as related disorders existing on a spectrum.

14.10 REFLECTING ON THE CHAPTER'S THEMES

Key Learning Goals

- Identify the four unifying themes highlighted in this chapter.

Our examination of abnormal behavior and its roots has highlighted four of our organizing themes: multifactorial causation, the interplay of heredity and environment, the sociohistorical context in which psychology evolves, and the influence of culture on psychological phenomena.

We can safely assert that every disorder described in this chapter has multiple causes. The development of mental disorders involves an interplay among a variety of psychological, biological, and social factors. We also saw that most psychological disorders depend on an interaction of genetics and experience. This interaction shows up most clearly in the *stress-vulnerability models* for mood disorders and schizophrenic disorders. *Vulnerability* to these disorders seems to depend primarily on heredity, whereas *stress* is largely a function of the environment. According to stress-vulnerability theories, disorders emerge when high vulnerability intersects with high stress. Thus, the impact of heredity depends on the environment, and the effect of the environment depends on heredity.

This chapter also demonstrated that psychology evolves in a sociohistorical context. We saw that modern conceptions of normality and abnormality are largely shaped by empirical research, but social trends, prevailing values, and political realities also play a role. Finally, our discussion of psychological disorders showed once again that psychological phenomena are shaped to some degree by cultural parameters, as cultural norms influence what is regarded as abnormal.

 Multifactorial Causation

 Heredity & Environment

 Sociohistorical Context

 Cultural Heritage

14.11

Key Learning Goals

- Articulate the legal concepts of insanity and competency, and clarify the grounds for involuntary commitment.

14.11 PERSONAL APPLICATION
Understanding Psychological Disorders and the Law

Answer the following "true" or "false."

____ 1 Insanity is frequently used as a defense in criminal proceedings.

____ 2 When the insanity defense is used, it is successful fairly often.

____ 3 Final decisions about involuntary commitment to a mental hospital are made by psychiatrists and psychologists.

All of the above statements are false, as you will see in this Application. Societies use laws to enforce their norms regarding appropriate behavior. Given this function, the law in our society has something to say about many issues related to abnormal behavior. In this section, we examine the concepts of insanity, competency, and involuntary commitment.

Insanity

Insanity is *not* a diagnosis; it's a legal concept. **Insanity is a legal status indicating that a person cannot be held responsible for his or her actions because of mental illness.** Why is this an issue in the courtroom? Because criminal acts must be intentional. The law reasons that people who are "out of their mind" may not be able to appreciate the significance of what they're doing. The insanity defense is used in criminal trials by defendants who admit they committed the crime, but claim they lacked intent.

No simple relationship exists between specific diagnoses of mental disorders and court judgments of insanity, or what is sometimes called *criminal responsibility*. The vast majority of people with diagnosed psychological disorders would *not* qualify as insane. The people most likely to qualify are those troubled by severe disturbances that display delusional behavior. The courts apply various rules in making judgments about a defendant's sanity, depending on the jurisdiction

(Packer, 2015). According to one widely used rule, called the *M'naghten rule*, *insanity exists when a mental disorder makes a person unable to distinguish right from wrong*. As you can imagine, evaluating insanity as defined in the M'naghten rule can be difficult for judges and jurors, and even for the psychologists and psychiatrists who are called into court as expert witnesses.

Although highly publicized and controversial, the insanity defense is actually used less frequently and less successfully than widely believed (see **Figure 14.18**). One study found that the general public estimates the insanity defense is used in 37% of felony cases, when in fact it's used in less than 1% (Silver, Cirincione, & Steadman, 1994). Another study of over 60,000 indictments in Baltimore found that only 190 defendants (0.31%) pleaded insanity. Of these, only eight were successful (Janofsky et al., 1996).

Competency

Competency (or "fitness" in some states) **refers to a defendant's capacity to stand trial.** To be competent, defendants must

be able to understand the nature and purpose of the legal proceedings and be able to assist their attorney. If they're not able, they're declared incompetent and can't be brought to trial unless they become competent once again.

What's the difference between insanity and incompetence? Insanity refers to a defendant's mental state *at the time of the alleged crime*. Competency refers to a defendant's mental state *at the time of the trial*. Given the potential for delay in our legal system, the crime and the trial may take place many months or even years apart. Insanity can't even become an issue unless a defendant is competent to stand trial. Far more people are found to be incompetent than insane. As with insanity, no simple relationship exists between specific diagnoses and being declared incompetent (Simon & Shuman, 2008).

What happens to defendants who are declared incompetent or insane? Essentially, they're turned over to the mental health system for treatment. However, this simple statement masks immense variability in the handling of their cases. What happens to a defendant depends on

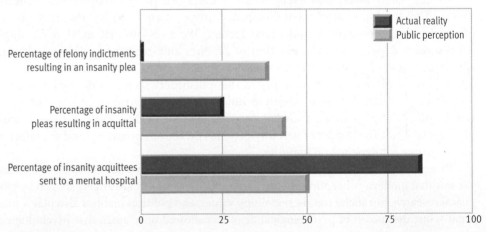

FIGURE 14.18

The insanity defense: Public perceptions and actual realities. Silver et al. (1994) collected data on the general public's beliefs about the insanity defense and the realities of how often it is used and how often it is successful (based on a large-scale survey of insanity pleas in eight states). Because of highly selective media coverage, dramatic disparities are seen between public perceptions and actual realities, as the insanity defense is used less frequently and less successfully than widely assumed.

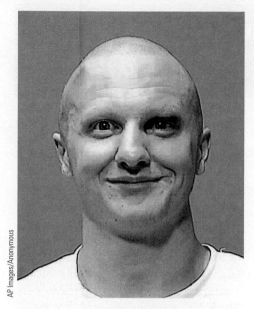

Jared Lee Loughner, who gunned down Congresswoman Gabrielle Giffords and many innocent bystanders in January 2011, apparently showed many signs of psychological deterioration in the months leading up to the shootings. Given his struggles with psychological disturbance, many people were baffled by why he had not been subjected to involuntary commitment. What most people do not understand is that laws in the United States generally set the bar very high for involuntary commitment. Why? Because predictions of dangerousness are not very accurate and because our legal system is reluctant to incarcerate people for what they *might* do. Unfortunately, our conservative approach to involuntary commitment sometimes has tragic consequences.

the nature of the offense, the rules applied in the specific jurisdiction, the nature of the mental disorder, the likelihood of recovery and a return to competence, and a host of other factors.

Involuntary Commitment

The issue of insanity surfaces only in *criminal* proceedings. Far more people are affected by *civil* proceedings relating to involuntary commitment. **In *involuntary commitment,* people are hospitalized in psychiatric facilities against their will.** What are the grounds for such a dramatic action? They vary some from state to state. Generally, people are subject to involuntary commitment when mental health professionals and legal authorities believe that a mental disorder makes them (1) dangerous to themselves (usually suicidal), (2) dangerous to others (potentially violent), or (3) unable to provide for their own basic care (Simon & Shuman, 2014). In emergency situations, psychologists and psychiatrists can authorize *temporary* commitment, usually for 24 to 72 hours. Orders for long-term involuntary commitment are usually set up for renewable 6-month periods and can be issued by a court only after a formal hearing. Mental health professionals provide extensive input in these hearings. The courts, however, make the final decisions.

Most involuntary commitments occur because people appear to be dangerous to themselves or others. The real difficulty, though, is in predicting dangerousness (Freedman et al., 2007). Studies suggest that clinicians' short-term predictions about which patients are likely to become violent are only moderately accurate. Moreover, their long-term predictions of violent behavior are largely inaccurate (Simon & Shuman, 2008). Overall, individuals with psychological disorders are not nearly as prone to violence as the public assumes. They are *somewhat* more likely to be violent than the general population. For example, in one recent year, 2.9% of people with serious mental illness committed violent acts, compared with 0.8% of people without mental disorders (Swanson et al., 2014). But a history of violent behavior is a much stronger predictor of future violence than is a psychiatric diagnosis.

This inaccuracy in predicting dangerousness is unfortunate. Detaining a person is no small matter. And involuntary commitment involves the detention of people for what they *might* do in the future, not necessarily for what they did do. Such detention goes against the grain of the American legal principle that people are *innocent until proven guilty*. The inherent difficulty in predicting dangerousness makes involuntary commitment a complex and controversial issue.

> **REALITY CHECK**

Misconception

People with psychological disorders are often violent and dangerous.

Reality

Overall, only a modest association has been found between mental illness and violence-prone tendencies (Elbogen & Johnson, 2009; Swanson et al., 2014). This stereotype exists because incidents of violence involving the mentally ill tend to command media attention and warp people's views of the mentally ill (McGinty, Webster, & Barry, 2013). However, the individuals involved in these incidents are not representative of the large number of people who have struggled with psychological disorders.

14.12

Key Learning Goals
• Understand how mental heuristics can distort estimates of cumulative and conjunctive probabilities.

14.12 CRITICAL THINKING APPLICATION
Working with Probabilities in Thinking About Mental Illness

As you read about the various types of psychological disorders, did you think to yourself that you or someone you know was being described? On the one hand, there is no reason to be alarmed. The tendency to see yourself and your friends in descriptions of pathology is a common response. It is sometimes called the *medical students' syndrome* because beginning medical students often erroneously believe they or their friends have whatever diseases they are currently learning about. On the other hand, realistically speaking, it *is* quite likely that you know *many* people with psychological disorders. Recent data on the prevalence of psychological disorders—which are summarized in **Figure 14.19**—suggest that the likelihood of anyone having at least one DSM disorder at some point during his or her life is about 44%.

This estimate strikes most people as surprisingly high. Why is this so? One reason is that when people think about psychological disorders, they tend to think of severe disorders, such as bipolar disorder or schizophrenia (which are relatively infrequent), rather than "ordinary" disturbances, such as anxiety and depressive disorders (which are much more common). When it comes to mental illness, people tend to think of patients in straightjackets or of obviously psychotic homeless people, who do not reflect the broad and diverse population of people who suffer from psychological disorders. In other words, their *prototypes,* or "best examples," of mental illness consist of severe disorders that are infrequent. Hence, they underestimate the prevalence of mental disorders. This distortion illustrates the influence of the ***representativeness heuristic,*** which is basing the estimated probability of an event on how similar it is to the typical prototype of that event (see Chapter 8).

Do you still find it hard to believe that the overall prevalence of psychological disorders is about 44%? Another reason this number seems surprisingly high is that many people do not understand that the probability of having *at least one* disorder is much higher than the probability of having the most prevalent disorder by itself. For example, the probability of having a substance use disorder, the single most common type of disorder, is approximately 24%, but the probability of having a substance use disorder *or* an anxiety disorder *or* a mood disorder *or* a schizophrenic disorder jumps to 44%. These "or" relationships represent *cumulative probabilities.*

What about "and" relationships—that is, relationships in which we want to know the probability of someone having condition A *and* condition B? For example, given the lifetime prevalence estimates (from **Figure 14.19**) for each category of disorder, which are shown in the parentheses, what is the probability of someone having a substance use disorder (24% prevalence) *and* an anxiety disorder (19%) *and* a mood disorder (15%) *and* a schizophrenic disorder (1%) during his or her lifetime? Such "and" relationships represent *conjunctive probabilities.* Stop and think: What must be true about the probability of having all four types of disorders? Will this probability be less than 24%, between 24% and 44%, or greater than 44%? You may be surprised to learn that this figure is under 1%. You can't have all four disorders unless you have the least frequent disorder (schizophrenia), which has a prevalence of 1%, so the answer *must* be 1% or less. Moreover, of all of the people with schizophrenia, only a tiny subset are likely to have all three of the other disorders, so the answer is surely well under 1% (see **Figure 14.20**). If this type of question strikes you as contrived, think again. Epidemiologists have devoted an enormous amount of research to the estimation of *comorbidity*—the coexistence of two or more disorders—because it can greatly complicate treatment issues.

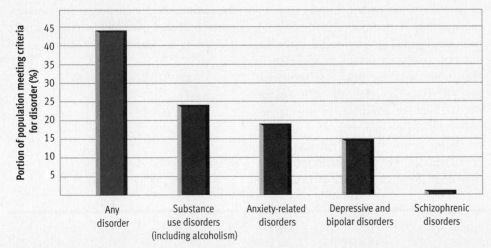

FIGURE 14.19

Lifetime prevalence of psychological disorders. The estimated percentages of people who have, at any time in their life, suffered from one of four types of psychological disorders or from a disorder of any kind (blue bar) are shown here. Prevalence estimates vary somewhat from one study to the next, depending on the exact methods used in sampling and assessment. The estimates shown here are based on pooling data from Wave 1 and 2 of the Epidemiological Catchment Area studies and the National Comorbidity Study, as summarized by Regier and Burke (2000) and Dew, Bromet, and Switzer (2000). These studies collectively evaluated more than 28,000 subjects.

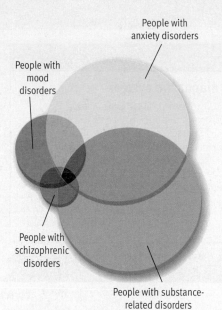

FIGURE 14.20

Conjunctive probabilities. The probability of someone having all four disorders depicted here cannot be greater than the probability of the least common condition by itself, which is 1% for schizophrenia. The intersection of all four disorders (shown in black) has to be a subset of schizophrenic disorders and has to be well under 1%. Efforts to think about probabilities can sometimes be facilitated by creating diagrams that show the relationships and overlap between various events.

Labels in figure: People with anxiety disorders; People with mood disorders; People with schizophrenic disorders; People with substance-related disorders

These are two examples of using statistical probabilities as a critical thinking tool. Let's apply this type of thinking to another problem dealing with physical health. Here is a problem used in a study by Tversky and Kahneman (1983, p. 308) that many physicians got wrong:

A health survey was conducted in a sample of adult males in British Columbia, of all ages and occupations. Please give your best estimate of the following values:

What percentage of the men surveyed have had one or more heart attacks?_____

What percentage of the men surveyed both are over 55 years old and have had one or more heart attacks? _____

Fill in the blanks above with your best guesses. Of course, you probably have only a very general idea about the prevalence of heart attacks, but go ahead and fill in the blanks anyway.

The actual values are not as important in this example as the relative values are. More than 65% of the physicians who participated in the experiment by Tversky and Kahneman gave a higher percentage value for the second question than for the first. What is wrong with their answers? The second question is asking about the conjunctive probability of two events. Hopefully, you see why this figure *must* be less than the probability of either one of these events occurring alone. Of all the men in the survey who had had a heart attack, only some are also over 55, so the second number must be smaller than the first. As we saw in Chapter 8, this common error in thinking is called the *conjunction fallacy.* **The conjunction fallacy occurs when people estimate that the odds of two uncertain events happening together are greater than the odds of either event happening alone.**

Why did so many physicians get this problem wrong? They were vulnerable to the conjunction fallacy because they were influenced by the *representativeness heuristic,* or the power of prototypes. When physicians think "heart attack," they tend to envision a man over the age of 55. Hence, the second scenario fit so well with their prototype of a heart attack victim that they carelessly overestimated its probability.

Let's consider some additional examples of erroneous reasoning about probabilities involving how people think about psychological disorders. Many people tend to stereotypically assume that mentally ill people are likely to be violent. People also tend to wildly overestimate (thirty-sevenfold in one study) how often the insanity defense is used in criminal trials (Silver et al., 1994). These mistaken beliefs reflect the influence of **the availability heuristic, which is basing the estimated probability of an event on the ease with which relevant instances come to mind.** Because of the availability heuristic, people tend to overestimate the probability of dramatic events that receive heavy media coverage, even when these events are rare, because examples of the events are easy to retrieve from memory. Violent acts by former psychiatric patients tend to get lots of attention in the press. And because of the *hindsight bias,* journalists tend to question why authorities couldn't foresee and prevent the violence (see the Critical Thinking Application for Chapter 11), so the mental illness angle tends to be emphasized. In a similar vein, press coverage is usually intense when a defendant in a murder trial mounts an insanity defense.

In sum, the various types of statistics that come up in thinking about psychological disorders demonstrate that we are constantly working with probabilities, even though we may not realize it. Critical thinking requires a good understanding of the laws of probability because there are very few certainties in life.

TABLE 14.3 Critical Thinking Skills Discussed in This Application

Skill	Description
Understanding the limitations of the representativeness heuristic	The critical thinker understands that focusing on prototypes can lead to inaccurate probability estimates.
Understanding cumulative probabilities	The critical thinker understands that the probability of at least one of several events occurring is additive and increases with time and the number of events.
Understanding conjunctive probabilities	The critical thinker appreciates that the probability of two uncertain events happening together is less than the probability of either event happening alone.
Understanding the limitations of the availability heuristic	The critical thinker understands that the ease with which examples come to mind may not be an accurate guide to the probability of an event.

CHAPTER 14 CONCEPT CHART

GENERAL CONCEPTS

The medical model

- The *medical model*, which assumes it is useful to view abnormal behavior as a disease, led to more humane treatment for people who exhibit abnormal behavior.
- However, mental illness carries a *stigma* that can be difficult to shake and creates difficulties for those who suffer from psychological disorders.
- The medical model has also been criticized on the grounds that it converts moral and social questions into medical questions.

Criteria of abnormality

- Judgments of abnormality are based on three criteria: deviance from social norms, maladaptive behavior, and reports of personal distress.
- Judgments about mental illness reflect prevailing cultural values, social trends, and political forces, as well as scientific knowledge.
- Normality and abnormality exist on a continuum.

The diagnostic system

- DSM-5, released in 2013, is the official psychodiagnostic classification system in the United States.
- The practical logistics of shifting to a *dimensional approach* to diagnosis proved controversial, so DSM-5 retained a *categorical approach* to disorders.
- The number of diagnoses in the DSM increased from 128 in the first edition to 541 in the current edition.

ANXIETY DISORDERS, OCD, AND PTSD

Types

- *Generalized anxiety disorder* is marked by chronic high anxiety not tied to a specific threat.
- *Specific phobia* is marked by a persistent, irrational fear of an object or situation that is not dangerous.
- *Panic disorder* involves recurrent, sudden anxiety attacks that occur unexpectedly.
- *Agoraphobia* is a fear of going out to public places; it can coexist with various disorders, but especially panic disorder.
- *Obsessive-compulsive disorder (OCD)* is marked by uncontrollable intrusions of unwanted thoughts and urges to engage in senseless rituals.
- *Posttraumatic stress disorder (PTSD)* involves enduring psychological disturbance attributable to the experience of a major traumatic event.

Etiology

- Twin studies suggest a *genetic predisposition* to anxiety disorders.
- Disturbances in the neural circuits using *GABA* and *serotonin* may play a role in some anxiety disorders.
- Many anxiety responses can be acquired through classical conditioning and maintained through operant conditioning.
- Cognitive theorists assert that the tendency to misinterpret harmless situations as threatening leads to anxiety disorders.
- Exposure to great stress can contribute to the emergence of some anxiety disorders.

DISSOCIATIVE DISORDERS

Types

- *Dissociative amnesia* is a sudden loss of memory for personal information that is too extensive to be due to normal forgetting.
- *Dissociative identity disorder (DID)* involves the coexistence of two or more largely complete and usually very different personalities.

Etiology

- Dissociative amnesia is usually attributed to extreme stress.
- Some theorists maintain that people with DID gradually come to believe that independent entities within them are to blame for their problems.
- Other theorists maintain that DID is rooted in severe emotional trauma that occurred during childhood.

DEPRESSIVE AND BIPOLAR DISORDERS

Types

- *Major depressive disorder* is marked by persistent feelings of sadness and despair, loss of interest in previous sources of pleasure, slowed thought processes, and self-blame.
- *Bipolar disorder* is marked by the experience of depressed and manic episodes, with the latter involving irrational euphoria, racing thoughts, impulsive behavior, and increased energy.
- Both major depression and bipolar disorder are associated with substantial elevations in suicide rates.

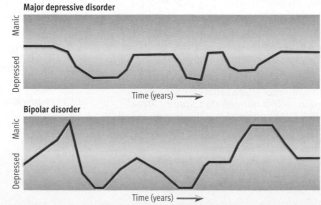

Etiology

- Twin studies suggest a *genetic predisposition* to depression and bipolar disorder.
- Disturbances in the neural circuits using *serotonin* and *norepinephrine* appear to contribute to depressive disorders.
- Researchers have found a correlation between depression and *reduced hippocampal volume*, which may reflect *suppressed neurogenesis* due to stress.
- Hormonal overactivity along the HPA axis in response to stress may play a role in depression.
- Cognitive theorists assert that people who exhibit a *pessimistic explanatory style* are especially vulnerable to depression.
- Behavioral theories emphasize how inadequate social skills increase vulnerability to depression.
- High stress is associated with increased vulnerability to both depression and bipolar disorder.

SCHIZOPHRENIC DISORDERS

Symptoms

- Symptoms of schizophrenia include irrational thought, delusions, deterioration of adaptive behavior, distorted perception, hallucinations, and disturbed emotion.

- The distinctions between schizophrenic subtypes (paranoid, catatonic, disorganized, and undifferentiated) were discarded in DSM-5.

- A newer approach to describing schizophrenia looks at the balance between the positive and negative symptoms of the disorder.

Etiology

- Twin studies and adoption studies suggest a *genetic vulnerability* to schizophrenia.

- Disturbances at *dopamine* synapses have been implicated as a possible cause of schizophrenia.

- Research uncovered an association between *enlarged brain ventricles* and schizophrenic disturbance.

- The *neurodevelopmental hypothesis* posits that vulnerability to schizophrenia is increased by disruptions of normal brain maturational processes during prenatal development or at birth.

- Schizophrenic patients from families high in *expressed emotion* have elevated relapse rates.

- High stress is associated with increased vulnerability to schizophrenic disorders.

AUTISM SPECTRUM DISORDERS

- *Autism spectrum disorder* is characterized by profound impairment of social communication and severely restricted interests and activities, apparent by age 3.

- Autism tends to be a lifelong affliction requiring extensive family and institutional support.

- The recent increase in the diagnosis of autism is probably due to greater awareness of the syndrome and the use of broader diagnostic criteria.

© ITAR-TASS Photo Agency/Alamy

- Genetic factors contribute to autistic disorders and brain overgrowth may play a role.

- Research has failed to find an association between vaccinations and the development of autism.

PERSONALITY DISORDERS

- *Personality disorders* are marked by extreme personality traits that cause subjective distress or impaired social and occupational functioning.
- *Antisocial personality disorder* is characterized by manipulative, impulsive, exploitive, aggressive behavior.
- *Borderline personality disorder* is marked by instability in social relationships, self-concept, and emotional functioning.
- *Narcissistic personality disorder* involves a grandiose sense of self-importance, a sense of entitlement, and an excessive need for attention.

EATING DISORDERS

© LEVINE/SIPA/Newscom

- The eating disorders include anorexia nervosa, bulimia nervosa, and binge-eating disorder.

- Anorexia and bulimia tend to develop in late adolescence; 90%–95% of victims are female.

- A genetic predisposition and certain personality traits can increase vulnerability to eating disorders.

- Rigid, disturbed thinking, cultural values, and family pathology can also contribute to eating disorders.

NEW DIRECTIONS

- New research suggests that significant stress early in life can increase vulnerability to a wide range of psychological disorders.

- Some severe disorders that have long been viewed as distinct and unrelated appear to share more genetic and neurobiological roots than expected.

APPLICATIONS

- The *insanity* defense is used less frequently and less successfully than widely believed.

- *Competency* refers to defendants' capacity to understand the nature and purpose of legal proceedings and assist their attorney.

- People are subject to *involuntary commitment* in a hospital when they appear to be dangerous to themselves or others.

- Due to the representativeness heuristic, people equate mental disorders with severe disorders, and hence underestimate the prevalence of mental disorders.

- The availability heuristic leads people to overestimate the likelihood that the mentally ill will be violent because such incidents receive heavy media coverage.

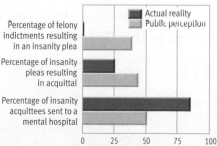

	Actual reality	Public perception
Percentage of felony indictments resulting in an insanity plea		
Percentage of insanity pleas resulting in acquittal		
Percentage of insanity acquittees sent to a mental hospital		

0   25   50   75   100

CHAPTER 15

TREATMENT OF PSYCHOLOGICAL DISORDERS

Themes in this Chapter

Cultural
Heritage

Theoretical
Diversity

2 Todd Pearson/Ocean/Corbis

What do you picture when you hear the term *psychotherapy*? Unless you've had some personal exposure to therapy, your image of it has likely been shaped by portrayals you've seen on television or in the movies. A good example is the 1999 film *Analyze This,* a comedy starring Billy Crystal as psychiatrist Ben Sobol and Robert De Niro as Paul Vitti, a mob boss who is suffering from "panic attacks." Complications develop when Vitti—a man no one says "no" to—demands Dr. Sobol cure him of his problem before his rivals in crime turn his "weakness" against him.

With his glasses and beard, Billy Crystal's Dr. Sobol resembles many people's picture of a therapist. Like many movie therapists, Dr. Sobol practices "talk therapy." He listens attentively as his patients talk about what is troubling them. Occasionally, he offers comments that reflect their thoughts and feelings back to them or that offer some illuminating insight into their problems. We can get a feeling for his approach from a funny scene in which the uneducated Vitti turns Dr. Sobol's techniques on him:

VITTI: Hey, let's see how you like it. Let's talk about your father.

SOBOL: Let's not.

VITTI: What kind of work does your father do?

SOBOL: It's not important.

VITTI: You paused.

SOBOL: I did not.

VITTI: You just paused. That means you had a feeling, like a thought . . .

SOBOL: You know, we're running out of time. Let's not waste it talking about my problems.

VITTI: Your father's a problem?

SOBOL: No!

VITTI: That's what you just said.

SOBOL: I did not!

VITTI: Now you're upset.

SOBOL: (getting upset) I am not upset!

VITTI: Yes you are.

SOBOL: Will you stop it!

VITTI: You know what, I'm getting good at this.

As in this scene, the film derives much of its humor from popular conceptions—and misconceptions—about therapy. The technique that Vitti

The popular film *Analyze This* derived much of its humor from common misconceptions about the process of psychotherapy.

makes fun of does resemble one type of therapeutic process. Like Vitti, many people associate needing therapy with having a shameful weakness. Furthermore, therapy is often of considerable benefit in helping people make significant changes in their lives—even if those changes are not as dramatic as Vitti's giving up his life of crime at the end of the movie. On the other hand, the film's comic exaggerations also highlight some misconceptions about therapy, including the following:

- Vitti is driven to see a "shrink" because he feels like he's "falling apart." In fact, therapists help people with all kinds of problems. People need not have severe symptoms of mental illness to benefit from therapy.
- Dr. Sobol is a psychiatrist, but most therapists are not. And although Dr. Sobol quotes Freud, and the film's plot turns on interpreting a dream (in this case, it's the psychiatrist's dream!), most therapists make little or no use of Freudian techniques.
- Dr. Sobol relies on talk therapy to produce insights that will help his patients overcome their troubles. In reality, this approach is only one of the many techniques used by therapists.
- Dr. Sobol "cures" Vitti by getting him to acknowledge a traumatic event in his childhood (the death of his father) that is at the root of his problems. But only rarely does therapy produce a single dramatic insight that results in wholesale change for the client.

In this chapter, we'll take a down-to-earth look at *psychotherapy,* using the term in its broadest sense, to refer to all the diverse approaches used in the treatment of mental disorders and psychological problems. We'll start by discussing some general questions about how treatment is provided. After considering these issues, we'll examine the goals, techniques, and effectiveness of some of the more widely used approaches to therapy and discuss recent trends in treatment, including changes in institutional treatment. In the Personal Application, we'll look at practical questions related to finding and choosing a therapist. And in the Critical Thinking Application we'll address problems involved in determining whether therapy actually helps.

Key Learning Goals
- Identify the three major categories of therapy, and discuss patterns of treatment seeking.
- Identify the various types of mental health professionals involved in the provision of therapy.

15.1 ELEMENTS OF THE TREATMENT PROCESS

Sigmund Freud is widely credited with launching modern psychotherapy around 1880. Freud and a colleague discovered that a patient's symptoms cleared up when she was encouraged to talk about emotionally charged experiences from her past. Freud speculated that talking things through had enabled the patient to drain off bottled up emotions that had caused her symptoms. This insight led him to develop a new treatment procedure, which he called *psychoanalysis*. Freud's breakthrough ushered in a century of progress for psychotherapy. Psychoanalysis spawned many offspring, as Freud's followers developed their own systems of treatment. Since then, approaches to psychotherapy have steadily grown more numerous, more diverse, and more effective.

Treatments: How Many Types Are There?

In their efforts to help people, psychotherapists use many treatment methods. One expert (Kazdin, 1994) estimates that there may be more than 400 different approaches to treatment! Fortunately, we can impose some order on this chaos. As varied as therapists' procedures are, approaches to treatment can be classified into three major categories:

1. *Insight therapies.* Insight therapy is talk therapy in the tradition of Freud's psychoanalysis. In insight therapies, clients engage in complex, often lengthy verbal interactions with their therapist. The goal in these discussions is to pursue increased insight regarding the nature of the client's difficulties and to sort through possible solutions.

2. *Behavior therapies.* Behavior therapies are based on the principles of learning, which were introduced in Chapter 6. Instead of emphasizing personal insights, behavior therapists make direct efforts to alter problematic responses (phobias, for instance) and maladaptive habits (drug use, for instance).

3. *Biomedical therapies.* Biomedical approaches to therapy involve interventions into a person's biological functioning. The most widely used procedures are drug therapy and electroconvulsive (shock) therapy. In recent decades, drug therapy has become the dominant mode of treatment for psychological disorders. As **Figure 15.1** shows, one large-scale study found that 57% of mental health patients were treated with medication only, up from 44% just 9 years earlier (Olfson & Marcus, 2010). As the name bio*medical* therapies suggests, these treatments have traditionally been provided only by physicians with a medical degree (usually psychiatrists). This situation is changing, however, as psychologists have been campaigning for prescription privileges and have obtained prescription authority in three states.

Clients: Who Seeks Therapy?

People seeking mental health treatment represent the full range of human problems: anxiety, depression, unsatisfactory interpersonal relations, troublesome habits, poor self-control, low self-esteem, marital conflicts, self-doubt, a sense of emptiness, and feelings

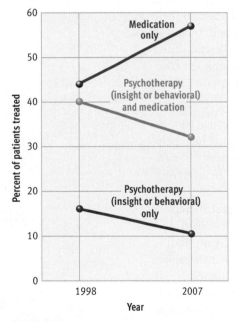

FIGURE 15.1

Escalating reliance on drug therapy. Using data from an ongoing national survey focusing on patterns of health care, Olfson and Marcus (2010) found some interesting trends in outpatient treatment for psychological disorders. Comparing treatment procedures in 1998 and 2007, they found that the percentage of patients treated with medication exclusively increased from 44% to 57%. During the same time period, the percentage of patients treated with insight or behavior therapy alone, or in combination with drug therapy, declined.

of personal stagnation. Among adults, the two most common presenting problems are depression and anxiety disorders (Olfson & Marcus, 2010).

People vary considerably in their willingness to seek psychotherapy. People often delay for many years before finally seeking treatment for their psychological problems (Wang, Berglund et al., 2005). As you can see in **Figure 15.2**, women are more likely than men to receive therapy. In terms of ethnicity, whites are more likely to pursue treatment than blacks or Hispanics. Treatment is also more likely when people have medical insurance and when they have more education (Olfson & Marcus, 2010).

Unfortunately, it appears that many people who need therapy don't receive it (Kazdin & Rabbitt, 2013). People who could benefit from therapy do not seek it for a variety of reasons. Lack of health insurance and cost concerns appear to be major barriers to obtaining needed care for many people. Perhaps the biggest roadblock is the stigma surrounding the receipt of mental health treatment (Corrigan, Druss, & Perlick, 2014). Unfortunately, many people equate seeking therapy with admitting personal weakness (Clement et al., 2015).

Therapists: Who Provides Professional Treatment?

Friends and relatives may provide you with excellent advice about your personal problems, but their assistance does not qualify as therapy. Psychotherapy refers to *professional* treatment by someone with special training. However, a common source of confusion about psychotherapy is the variety of "helping professions" involved. Psychology and psychiatry are the principal professions involved in the delivery of psychotherapy. However, treatment is also provided by other types of therapists (see **Table 15.1**). Let's look at these mental health professions.

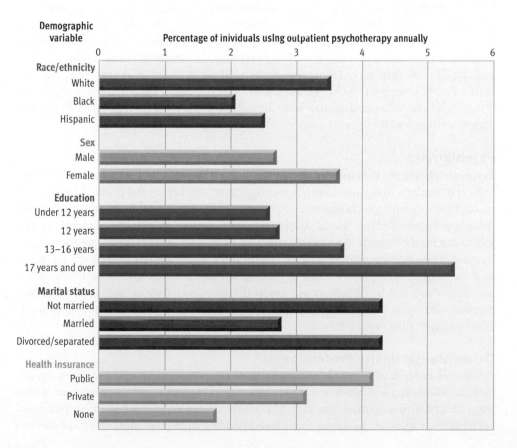

FIGURE 15.2

Therapy utilization rates. Olfson and Marcus (2010) analyzed data on the use of outpatient mental health services in the United States in relation to various demographic variables. In regard to marital status, utilization rates are particularly high among those who are divorced or not married. The use of therapy is also greater among those who have more education. Females are more likely to pursue therapy than males are, but utilization rates are relatively low among ethnic minorities and those who lack health insurance.

TABLE 15.1 Types of Therapists

Profession	Degree	Education beyond Bachelor's degree	Typical roles and activities
Clinical psychologist	PhD or PsyD	5–7 years	Psychological testing, diagnosis, treatment with insight or behavior therapy
Counseling psychologist	PhD, PsyD, or EdD	5–7 years	Similar to clinical psychologist, but more focus on work, career, and adjustment problems
Psychiatrist	MD	8 years	Diagnosis and treatment, primarily with biomedical therapies, but also insight therapies
Clinical social worker	MSW, DSW	2–5 years	Insight and behavior therapy, often help inpatients with their return to the community
Psychiatric nurse	RN, MA, or PhD	0–5 years	Inpatient care, insight and behavior therapy
Counselor	BA or MA	0–2 years	Vocational counseling, drug counseling, rehabilitation counseling
Marriage and family therapist	MA or PhD	2–5 years	Marital/couples therapy, family therapy

Psychologists

Two types of psychologists may provide therapy, although the distinction between them is more theoretical than real. *Clinical psychologists* and *counseling psychologists* **specialize in the diagnosis and treatment of psychological disorders and everyday behavioral problems.** In theory, clinical psychologists' training emphasizes the treatment of full-fledged disorders. In contrast, counseling psychologists' training is supposed to be slanted toward the treatment of everyday adjustment problems in normal people. In practice, however, clinical and counseling psychologists overlap greatly in training, skills, and the clientele they serve (Morgan & Cohen, 2008). Both types of psychologists must earn a doctoral degree (Ph.D., Psy.D., or Ed.D.). In providing therapy, psychologists use either insight or behavioral approaches. Clinical and counseling psychologists do psychological testing as well as psychotherapy, and many also conduct research.

Psychiatrists

Psychiatrists **are physicians who specialize in the diagnosis and treatment of psychological disorders.** Many psychiatrists also treat everyday behavioral problems. However, in comparison with psychologists, psychiatrists devote more time to relatively severe disorders (schizophrenia, mood disorders) and less time to everyday marital, family, job, and school problems. Psychiatrists have an M.D. degree. Their graduate training requires 4 years of coursework in medical school and a 4-year apprenticeship in a residency at a hospital. In comparison with psychologists, psychiatrists are more likely to use psychoanalysis and less likely to use group therapies or behavior therapies. That said, contemporary psychiatrists increasingly depend on medication as their principal mode of treatment (Olfson et al., 2014).

Other Mental Health Professionals

Several other kinds of mental health professions provide psychotherapy services. *Psychiatric social workers* and *psychiatric nurses* often work as part of a treatment team with a psychologist or psychiatrist. Social workers have traditionally worked in hospitals and social service agencies. However, many also provide a wide range of therapeutic services as independent practitioners. Many kinds of *counselors* also provide therapeutic services. They often specialize in particular types of problems, such as vocational counseling, marital counseling, rehabilitation counseling, and drug counseling.

Marriage and family therapists (MFTs) generally have a master's degree that prepares them to work with couples experiencing relationship problems or with dysfunctional families. Marital and family therapy has experienced enormous growth since the 1980s (Lebow, 2008), and MFTs are licensed as independent practitioners in all fifty states.

There are clear differences among the helping professions in their education, training, and approach to therapy. That said, their roles in the treatment process overlap considerably. In this chapter, we will refer to psychologists or psychiatrists as needed, but otherwise we'll use the terms *clinician, therapist,* and *mental health professional* to refer to psychotherapists of all kinds, regardless of their professional degree.

Now that we have discussed the basic elements in psychotherapy, we can examine specific approaches to treatment in terms of their goals, procedures, and effectiveness. We'll begin with some representative insight therapies.

15.2 INSIGHT THERAPIES

Many schools of thought offer ideas about how to conduct insight therapy. Therapists with various theoretical orientations use different methods to pursue different kinds of insights. These varied approaches have in common is that *insight therapies* **involve verbal interactions intended to enhance clients' self-knowledge, and thus promote healthful changes in personality and behavior.** In this section, we'll delve into psychoanalysis, client-centered therapy, group therapy, and couples and family therapy.

Psychoanalysis

Sigmund Freud worked as a psychotherapist for almost 50 years in Vienna. Through a painstaking process of trial and error, he developed innovative techniques for the treatment of psychological disorders and distress. His system of *psychoanalysis* came to dominate psychiatry for many decades. Although this dominance eventually eroded, a diverse collection of psychoanalytic approaches to therapy remain influential today (Luborsky, O'Reilly-Landry, & Arlow, 2011; Ursano & Carr, 2014).

Psychoanalysis **is an insight therapy that emphasizes the recovery of unconscious conflicts, motives, and defenses through techniques such as free association and transference.** To appreciate the logic of psychoanalysis, we have to look at Freud's thinking about the roots of mental disorders. Freud mostly treated anxiety-dominated disturbances—such as phobic, panic, obsessive-compulsive, and conversion disorders, which were then called *neuroses.*

Freud believed that neurotic problems are caused by unconscious conflicts left over from early childhood. As explained in Chapter 11, he thought that people depend on defense mechanisms to avoid confronting these conflicts, which remain hidden in the depths of the unconscious (see **Figure 15.3**). However, he noted that defensive maneuvers tend to be only partially successful in alleviating anxiety, guilt, and other distressing emotions. With this model in mind, let's take a look at the therapeutic procedures used in psychoanalysis.

Probing the Unconscious

Given Freud's assumptions, we can see that the logic of psychoanalysis is quite simple. The analyst attempts to probe the murky depths of the unconscious to discover the

Key Learning Goals

- Explain the logic of psychoanalysis and the techniques by which analysts probe the unconscious.
- Understand the role of therapeutic climate and therapeutic process in client-centered therapy.
- Explain how group therapy, couples therapy, and family therapy are generally conducted.
- Assess the efficacy of insight therapies and the role of common factors in therapy.

FIGURE 15.3

Freud's view of the roots of disorders. According-ing to Freud, unconscious conflicts between the id, ego, and superego sometimes lead to anxiety. This discomfort can lead to pathological reliance on defensive behavior.

unresolved conflicts causing the client's neurotic behavior. In this effort to explore the unconscious, the therapist relies on two techniques: free association and dream analysis.

In *free association,* **clients spontaneously express their thoughts and feelings exactly as they occur, with as little censorship as possible.** In free associating, clients talk about anything that comes to mind, no matter how trivial, silly, or embarrassing it might be. The analyst studies these free associations for clues about what is going on in the unconscious. In *dream analysis,* **the therapist interprets the symbolic meaning of the client's dreams.** For Freud, dreams were the "royal road to the unconscious," the most direct means of access to patients' innermost conflicts, wishes, and impulses. Psycho-analytic clients are encouraged and trained to remember their dreams, which they then describe in therapy.

To better illustrate these matters, let's look at an actual case treated through psycho-analysis (adapted from Greenson, 1967, pp. 40–41). Mr. N was troubled by an unsat-isfactory marriage. He claimed to love his wife, but he preferred sexual relations with prostitutes. Mr. N reported that his parents also endured lifelong marital difficulties. His childhood conflicts about their relationship appeared to be related to his problems. Both dream analysis and free association can be seen in the following description of a session in Mr. N's treatment:

> Mr. N reported a fragment of a dream. All that he could remember is that he was waiting for a red traffic light to change, when he felt that someone had bumped into him from behind. . . . The associations led to Mr. N's love of cars, especially sports cars. He loved the sensation, in particular, of whizzing by those fat, old expensive cars. . . . His father always hinted that he had been a great athlete, but he never substantiated it. . . . Mr. N doubted whether his father could really perform. His father would flirt with a waitress in a cafe or make sexual remarks about women passing by, but he seemed to be showing off. If he were really sexual, he wouldn't resort to that.

As is characteristic of free association, Mr. N's train of thought meandered about with little direction. Nonetheless, clues about his unconscious conflicts were apparent. What did Mr. N's therapist extract from this session? The therapist saw sexual overtones in the dream fragment, where Mr. N was bumped from behind. The therapist also inferred that Mr. N had a competitive orientation toward his father, based on the free association about whizzing by fat, old expensive cars. As you can see, analysts must *interpret* their clients' dreams and free associations. Contrary to popular belief, analysts generally don't try to dazzle clients with startling revelations. Instead, analysts move forward inch by inch, offering interpretations that should be just out of the client's own reach. Mr. N's therapist eventually offered the following interpretations to his client:

> I said to Mr. N near the end of the hour that I felt he was struggling with his feelings about his father's sexual life. He seemed to be saying that his father was sexually not a very potent man. . . . He also recalls that he once found a packet of condoms under his father's pillow when he was an adolescent and he thought, "My father must be going to prostitutes." I then intervened and pointed out that the condoms under his father's pillow seemed to indicate more obviously that his father used the condoms with his mother, who slept in the same bed. However, Mr. N wanted to believe his wish-fulfilling fantasy: mother doesn't want sex with father and father is not very potent. The patient was silent and the hour ended.

As you may have already guessed, the therapist concluded that Mr. N's difficulties were rooted in an *Oedipal complex* (see Chapter 11). The patient had unresolved sexual feelings toward his mother and hostile feelings about his father. These unconscious conflicts, rooted in Mr. N's childhood, were distorting his intimate relations as an adult.

Resistance and Transference

How would you expect Mr. N to respond to the therapist's suggestion that he was in competition with his father for the sexual attention of his mother? Obviously, most clients would have great difficulty accepting such an interpretation. Freud fully expected clients to display some resistance to therapeutic efforts. ***Resistance* refers to largely unconscious defensive maneuvers intended to hinder the progress of therapy.** Resistance is assumed to be an inevitable part of the psychoanalytic process (Samberg & Marcus, 2005). Why would clients try to resist the helping process? Because they don't want to face the painful, disturbing conflicts that they have buried in their unconscious. Although they have sought help, they are reluctant to confront their real problems. Analysts use a variety of strategies to deal with clients' resistance. Often, a key consideration is the handling of transference.

***Transference* occurs when clients start relating to their therapists in ways that mimic critical relationships in their lives.** Thus, a client might start relating to a therapist as if the therapist were an overprotective mother, a rejecting brother, or a passive spouse. In a sense, the client *transfers* conflicting feelings about important people onto the therapist (Høglend et al., 2011). Psychoanalysts often encourage transference so that clients can reenact relations with crucial people in the context of therapy. These reenactments can help bring repressed feelings and conflicts to the surface, allowing the client to work through the conflicts.

Undergoing psychoanalysis is not easy. It can be a slow, painful process of self-examination that routinely requires 3–5 years of hard work. It tends to be a lengthy process because patients need time to gradually work through their problems and genuinely accept unnerving revelations (Williams, 2005). Ultimately, if resistance and transference can be handled effectively, the therapist's interpretations should lead the client to profound insights. For instance, Mr. N eventually admitted, "The old boy is probably right, it does tickle me to imagine that my mother preferred me and I could beat out my father. Later, I wondered whether this had something to do with my own screwed-up sex life with my wife." According to Freud, once clients recognize the unconscious sources of conflicts, they can resolve these conflicts and discard their neurotic defenses.

Modern Psychodynamic Treatments

Though still available, classical psychoanalysis as done by Freud is not widely practiced anymore. Freud's psychoanalytic method was geared to a particular kind of clientele he was seeing in Vienna a century ago. As his followers fanned out across Europe and America, many found it necessary to adapt psychoanalysis to different cultures, changing times, and new kinds of patients (Karasu, 2005). Thus, many variations on Freud's original approach to psychoanalysis have developed over the years. These descendants of psychoanalysis are collectively known as *psychodynamic approaches* to therapy.

As a result, today we have a rich diversity of psychodynamic approaches (Magnavita, 2008). Recent reviews of these treatments suggest that interpretation, resistance, and transference continue to play key roles in therapeutic effects (Høglend et al., 2008; Luborsky & Barrett, 2006). Other central features of modern psychodynamic therapies

© Photos 12/Alamy

In psychoanalysis, the therapist encourages the client to reveal thoughts, feelings, dreams, and memories, which can then be interpreted in relation to the client's current problems.

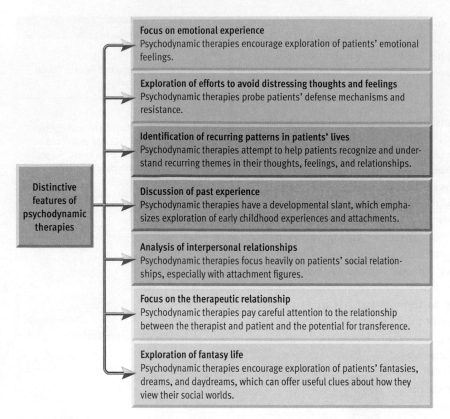

Focus on emotional experience
Psychodynamic therapies encourage exploration of patients' emotional feelings.

Exploration of efforts to avoid distressing thoughts and feelings
Psychodynamic therapies probe patients' defense mechanisms and resistance.

Identification of recurring patterns in patients' lives
Psychodynamic therapies attempt to help patients recognize and understand recurring themes in their thoughts, feelings, and relationships.

Discussion of past experience
Psychodynamic therapies have a developmental slant, which emphasizes exploration of early childhood experiences and attachments.

Analysis of interpersonal relationships
Psychodynamic therapies focus heavily on patients' social relationships, especially with attachment figures.

Focus on the therapeutic relationship
Psychodynamic therapies pay careful attention to the relationship between the therapist and patient and the potential for transference.

Exploration of fantasy life
Psychodynamic therapies encourage exploration of patients' fantasies, dreams, and daydreams, which can offer useful clues about how they view their social worlds.

Distinctive features of psychodynamic therapies

FIGURE 15.4

Core features of psychodynamic therapies. In an article on the efficacy of psychodynamic therapies, Jonathan Shedler (2010) outlined the distinctive aspects of modern psychodynamic techniques and processes. The seven features described here represent the core of contemporary psychodynamic treatment.

include (1) a focus on emotional experience, (2) exploration of efforts to avoid distressing thoughts and feelings, (3) identification of recurring patterns in patients' life experiences, (4) discussion of past experience, especially events in early childhood, (5) analysis of interpersonal relationships, (6) a focus on the therapeutic relationship itself, and (7) exploration of dreams and other aspects of fantasy life (Shedler, 2010; see **Figure 15.4**). Recent research suggests that psychodynamic approaches can be helpful in the treatment of a diverse array of disorders (Josephs & Weinberger, 2013; Barber et al., 2013).

Client-Centered Therapy

You may have heard of people going into therapy to "find themselves" or to "get in touch with their real feelings." These now-popular phrases emerged out of the *human potential movement*. This movement was stimulated in part by the work of Carl Rogers (1951, 1986). Using a humanistic perspective, Rogers devised client-centered therapy (also known as person-centered therapy) in the 1940s and 1950s.

Client-centered therapy **is an insight therapy that emphasizes providing a supportive emotional climate for clients, who play a major role in determining the pace and direction of their therapy.** Rogers's theory about the principal causes of neurotic anxieties is quite different from the Freudian explanation. As discussed in Chapter 11, Rogers maintains that most personal distress is to the result of inconsistency, or "incongruence," between a person's self-concept and reality (see **Figure 15.5**). According to his theory, incongruence makes people feel threatened by realistic feedback about themselves from others. According to Rogers, anxiety about such feedback often leads to reliance on defense mechanisms, to distortions of reality, and to stifled personal growth. Excessive incongruence is thought to be rooted in clients' overdependence on others for approval and acceptance.

Given Rogers's theory, client-centered therapists stalk insights that are quite different from the repressed conflicts that psychoanalysts go after. Client-centered therapists help clients realize that they do not have to worry constantly about pleasing others and winning acceptance. These clinicians help people restructure their self-concept to correspond better to reality. Ultimately, they try to foster self-acceptance and personal growth.

FIGURE 15.5

Rogers's view of the roots of disorders.
Rogers's theory asserts that anxiety and self-defeating behavior are rooted in an incongruent self-concept that makes one prone to recurrent anxiety, which triggers defensive behavior, which fuels more incongruence.

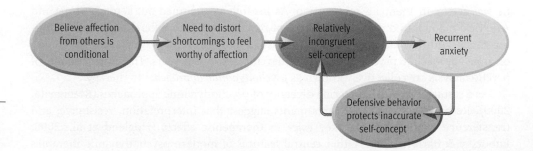

Therapeutic Climate

According to Rogers, the *process* of therapy is not as important as the emotional *climate* in which the therapy takes place. He believes that it is critical for the therapist to provide a warm, supportive climate that creates a safe environment in which clients can confront their shortcomings without feeling threatened. The lack of threat should reduce clients' defensive tendencies and thus help them open up. To create this supportive atmosphere, client-centered therapists must provide three conditions: (1) *genuineness* (honest communication), (2) *unconditional positive regard* (nonjudgmental acceptance of the client), and (3) *accurate empathy* (understanding of the client's point of view). Consistent with Rogers's view of the vital importance of therapeutic climate, research has found that measures of therapists' empathy and unconditional positive regard correlate with positive patient outcomes (Elliott et al., 2011; Farber & Doolin, 2011).

Therapeutic Process

In client-centered therapy, the client and therapist work together as equals. The therapist provides relatively little guidance and keeps interpretation and advice to a minimum (Raskin, Rogers, & Witty, 2011). The therapist's key task is *clarification*. The client-centered therapist tries to function like a human mirror, reflecting statements back to the client, but with enhanced clarity. He or she helps clients become more aware of their true feelings by highlighting themes that may be obscure in the clients' rambling discourse.

By working with clients to clarify their feelings, client-centered therapists hope to gradually build toward more far-reaching insights. In particular, they try to help clients better understand their interpersonal relationships and become more comfortable with their genuine selves. Obviously, these are ambitious goals. Client-centered therapy resembles psychoanalysis in that both seek to achieve a major reconstruction of a client's personality.

Client-centered therapists emphasize the importance of a supportive emotional climate in therapy. They also work to clarify, rather than interpret, the feelings expressed by their patients.

Group Therapy

Many approaches to insight therapy can be conducted on either an individual or group basis. **Group therapy is the simultaneous treatment of several clients in a group.** Because of economic pressures in mental health care, the use of group therapy appears likely to grow in future years (Burlingame & Baldwin, 2011). Although group therapy can be conducted in a variety of ways, we can provide a general overview of the process (see Piper & Hernandez, 2013; Spitz, 2009).

A therapy group typically consists of four to twelve people, with six to eight participants regarded as ideal (Cox et al., 2008). The therapist usually screens the participants, excluding persons who seem likely to be disruptive. Some theorists maintain that judicious selection of participants is crucial to effective group treatment (Schachter, 2011). In group therapy, participants essentially function as therapists for one another (Stone, 2008). Group members describe their problems, trade viewpoints, share experiences, and discuss coping strategies. Most important, they provide acceptance and emotional support for one another. In this atmosphere, group members work at peeling away the social masks that cover their insecurities. As members come to value one another's opinions, they work hard to display healthy changes. In group treatment, the therapist's responsibilities include selecting participants, setting goals for the group, initiating and maintaining the therapeutic process, and preventing interactions among group members that might be psychologically harmful (Cox et al., 2008). The therapist often plays a relatively subtle role in group therapy, staying in the background and focusing mainly on promoting group cohesiveness.

Group therapies obviously save time and money, which can be critical in understaffed mental hospitals and other institutional settings (Cox et al., 2008). Therapists in private practice usually charge less for group than individual therapy, making therapy affordable for more people. However, group therapy is *not* just a less costly substitute for individual

therapy (Knauss, 2005; Stone, 2008). Group therapy has unique strengths of its own, and certain kinds of problems are especially well suited to group treatment. Group treatments are being used successfully for an increasingly diverse collection of problems and disorders in contemporary clinical practice (Burlingame, Strauss, & Joyce, 2013).

Couples and Family Therapy

Like group therapy, marital and family therapy rose to prominence after World War II. As their names suggest, these interventions are defined in terms of who is being treated. *Couples* or *marital therapy* **involves the treatment of both partners in a committed, intimate relationship, in which the main focus is on relationship issues.** Couples therapy is not limited to married couples. It is frequently provided to cohabiting couples, including same-sex couples. *Family therapy* **involves the treatment of a family unit as a whole, in which the main focus is on family dynamics and communication.** Family therapy often emerges out of efforts to treat children or adolescents with individual therapy. A child's therapist, for instance, might come to the realization that treatment is likely to fail because the child returns to a home environment that contributes to the child's problems and so proposes a broader family intervention.

As with other forms of insight therapy, there are different schools of thought about how to conduct couples and family therapy (Goldenberg, Goldenberg, & Pelavin, 2011). Some of these diverse systems are extensions of influential approaches to individual therapy, including psychodynamic, humanistic, and behavioral treatments. Other approaches are based on innovative models of families as complex systems and are an explicit rejection of individual models of treatment. Although the various approaches to couples and family therapy differ in terminology and in their theoretical models of relationship and family dysfunction, they tend to share two common goals.

Marital therapists attempt to help partners to clarify their needs and desires in the relationship, appreciate their mutual contribution to problems, enhance their communication patterns, increase role flexibility and tolerance of differences, work out their balance of power, and learn to deal with conflict more constructively.

First, they seek to understand the entrenched patterns of interaction that produce distress. In this endeavor, they view individuals as parts of a family ecosystem, and they assume that people behave as they do because of their role in the system (Lebow & Stroud, 2013). Second, they seek to help couples and families improve their communication and move toward healthier patterns of interaction.

Understanding Therapists' Conceptions of Disorders

Check your understanding of the three approaches to insight therapy covered in the text by matching each approach with the appropriate explanation of the typical origins of clients' psychological disorders. The answers are in Appendix A.

Theorized Causes of Disorders	Therapy
_____ 1. Problems rooted in families' or couples' social ecosystem	a. Psychoanalysis
_____ 2. Problems rooted in unconscious conflicts left over from childhood	b. Client-centered therapy
_____ 3. Problems rooted in inaccurate self-concept and excessive concern about pleasing others	c. Couples and family therapy

How Effective Are Insight Therapies?

Evaluating the effectiveness of any approach to psychotherapy is a complex matter (Comer & Kendall, 2013; Lilienfeld et al., 2014; Ogles, 2013). For one thing, psychological disorders sometimes clear up on their own, a phenomenon called *spontaneous remission*. If a client experiences a recovery after treatment, we can't automatically assume the recovery was due to the treatment (see the Critical Thinking Application). Evaluations of insight therapies are especially complicated given that various schools of thought pursue entirely different goals. Judgments of therapeutic outcome in insight therapy tend to be subjective, with little consensus about the best way to assess therapeutic progress. Moreover, people enter therapy with diverse problems of varied severity, which further complicates the evaluation process.

Despite these difficulties, thousands of outcome studies have been conducted to evaluate the effectiveness of insight therapy. These studies have examined a broad range of clinical problems and used a variety of methods to assess therapeutic outcomes, including looking at scores on psychological tests and ratings by family members, as well as therapists' and clients' ratings. These studies consistently indicate that insight therapy *is* superior to no treatment or to placebo treatment and that the effects of therapy are reasonably durable (Lambert, 2011, 2013). And when insight therapies are compared head-to-head against drug therapies, they usually show roughly equal efficacy (Arkowitz & Lilienfeld, 2007; Wampold, 2013). Studies generally find the greatest improvement early in treatment (roughly the first ten to twenty weekly sessions), with further gains gradually diminishing over time (Lambert, 2013), as the data from one study show in **Figure 15.6**. Of course, these broad generalizations mask considerable variability in outcome, but the general trends are encouraging.

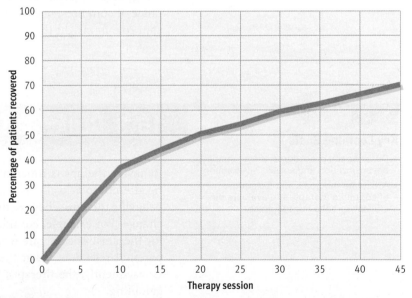

FIGURE 15.6

Recovery as a function of number of therapy sessions. Based on a national sample of over 6000 patients, Lambert, Hansen, and Finch (2001) mapped out the relationship between recovery and the duration of treatment. These data show that about half the patients experienced a clinically significant recovery after 20 weekly sessions of therapy. After 45 sessions of therapy, about 70% recovered.

SOURCE: Adapted from Lambert, M. J., Hansen, N. B., & Finch, A. E. (2001). Patient-focused research: Using patient outcome data to enhance treatment effects. *Journal of Consulting and Clinical Psychology, 69,* 159–172. Copyright © 2001 by the American Psychological Association. Used by permission of the authors.

How Do Insight Therapies Work?

Although there is considerable evidence that insight therapy tends to produce positive effects for a sizable majority of clients, vigorous debate continues about the *mechanisms of action* underlying these positive effects (Duncan & Reese, 2013). The advocates of various therapies tend to attribute the benefits of therapy to the particular methods used by each specific approach. In essence, they argue that different therapies achieve similar benefits through different processes. An alternative view espoused by many theorists is that the diverse approaches to therapy share certain *common factors* that account for much of the improvement experienced by clients (Wampold, 2001). Evidence supporting the common factors view has mounted in recent years (Lambert & Ogles, 2014; Sparks, Duncan, & Miller, 2008).

What are the common denominators that lie at the core of diverse approaches to therapy? The models proposed to answer this question vary considerably, but the most widely cited common factors include (1) the development of a therapeutic alliance with a professional helper; (2) the provision of emotional support and empathy; (3) the cultivation of hope and positive expectations in the client; (4) the provision of a rationale for the client's problems and a plausible method for reducing them; and (5) the opportunity to express feelings, confront problems, and gain new insights (Laska, Gurman, & Wampold, 2014; Weinberger, 1995). How important are these factors in therapy? Some theorists argue that common factors account for virtually *all* the progress that clients make in therapy (Wampold, 2001). It seems more likely that the benefits of therapy represent the combined effects of common factors and specific procedures. One study attempted to quantify the influence of common factors in an analysis of thirty-one studies that focused on the treatment of depression. When the variance in patient outcomes was partitioned among various influences, the researchers estimated that 49% of this variance was attributable to common factors (Cuijpers et al., 2012). Admittedly, this is just one estimate based on one form of treatment for one specific disorder, so it does not provide a definitive answer regarding the importance of common factors. But it certainly suggests that common factors play a significant role in insight therapy.

15.3

Key Learning Goals

- Describe the procedures of systematic desensitization and social skills training.
- Articulate the goals and techniques of cognitive therapy, and evaluate the efficacy of behavior therapies.

15.3 BEHAVIOR THERAPIES

Behavior therapy is different from insight therapy in that behavior therapists make no attempt to help clients achieve grand insights about themselves. Why not? Because behavior therapists believe that such insights aren't necessary to produce constructive change. For example, consider a client troubled by compulsive gambling. The behavior therapist doesn't care whether this behavior is rooted in unconscious conflicts or parental rejection. What the client needs is to get rid of the maladaptive behavior. Consequently, the therapist simply designs a program to eliminate the compulsive gambling.

Behavior therapies **involve the application of the principles of learning and conditioning to direct efforts to change clients' maladaptive behaviors.** Behavior therapies are based on two main assumptions (Stanley & Beidel, 2009). *First, it is assumed that behavior is a product of learning.* No matter how self-defeating or pathological a client's behavior might be, the behaviorist believes it is the result of past conditioning. *Second, it is assumed that what has been learned can be unlearned.* Thus, behavior therapists attempt to change clients' behavior by applying the principles of classical conditioning, operant conditioning, and observational learning (see Chapter 6). Behavior therapy involves designing specific procedures for specific types of problems, as you'll see in our discussion of systematic desensitization.

Systematic Desensitization

Devised by Joseph Wolpe (1958), systematic desensitization revolutionized psychotherapy by giving therapists their first useful alternative to traditional "talk therapy" (Fishman, Rego, & Muller, 2011). *Systematic desensitization* **is a behavior therapy used to reduce clients' phobic responses.** The treatment assumes that most anxiety responses are acquired through classical conditioning (as discussed in Chapter 14). According to this model, a harmless stimulus (for instance, a bridge) can be paired with a fear-arousing event (lightning striking it), so that it becomes a conditioned stimulus eliciting anxiety. The goal of systematic desensitization is to weaken the association between the conditioned stimulus (the bridge) and the conditioned response of anxiety (see **Figure 15.7**).

Systematic desensitization involves three steps. *In the first step, the therapist helps the client build an anxiety hierarchy.* This is a list of anxiety-arousing stimuli related to the specific source of anxiety, such as flying, academic tests, or snakes. The client ranks the stimuli from the least anxiety arousing to the most anxiety arousing. *The second step involves training the client in deep muscle relaxation.* This second phase may begin during early sessions while the therapist and client are still constructing the anxiety hierarchy. *In the third step, the client tries to work through the hierarchy, learning to remain relaxed while imagining each stimulus.* Starting with the least anxiety-arousing stimulus, the client imagines the situation as vividly as possible while relaxing. If the client experiences strong anxiety, he or she drops the imaginary scene and concentrates on relaxation. The client keeps repeating this process until he or she can imagine a scene with little or no anxiety. After a particular scene is conquered, the client moves on to the next stimulus situation in the anxiety hierarchy. Gradually, over a number of therapy sessions, the client progresses through the hierarchy, unlearning troublesome anxiety responses.

The effectiveness of systematic desensitization in reducing phobic responses is well documented (Spiegler, 2016). However, interventions emphasizing real-life, *direct*

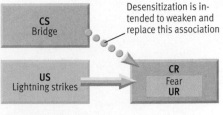

FIGURE 15.7

The logic underlying systematic desensitization. Behaviorists argue that many phobic responses are acquired through classical conditioning. For example, a person traumatized by a lightning strike while crossing a bridge might develop a phobia of bridges, as diagrammed here. Systematic desensitization targets the conditioned associations between phobic stimuli and fear responses.

Systematic desensitization is a behavioral treatment for phobias. Early studies of the procedure's efficacy often used people who had snake phobias as research subjects because people with snake phobias were relatively easy to find. This research showed that systematic desensitization is generally an effective treatment.

exposures to anxiety-arousing situations have become behavior therapists' treatment of choice for phobic and other anxiety disorders (Rachman, 2009). **In *exposure therapies*, clients are confronted with situations they fear so they learn that these situations are really harmless.** The exposures take place in a controlled setting and often involve a gradual progression from less-feared to more-feared stimuli. These real-life exposures to anxiety-arousing situations usually prove harmless, and individuals' anxiety responses decline. In recent decades, some therapists have resorted to highly realistic virtual-reality presentations of feared situations via computer-generated imagery (Meyerbröker & Emmelkamp, 2010; Reger et al., 2011). Exposure therapies are versatile in that they can be used with the full range of anxiety disorders, including obsessive-compulsive disorder, posttraumatic stress disorder, and panic disorder.

Social Skills Training

Many psychological problems grow out of interpersonal difficulties. Behavior therapists point out that people are not born with social finesse—they acquire social skills through learning. Unfortunately, some people have not learned how to be friendly, how to make conversation, how to express anger appropriately, and so forth. As a result, behavior therapists are increasingly using social skills training to improve clients' social abilities. This approach has yielded promising results in the treatment of depression (Thase, 2012), autism (Otero et al., 2015), and schizophrenia (Mueser et al., 2013).

Social skills training **is a behavior therapy designed to improve interpersonal skills that emphasizes modeling, behavioral rehearsal, and shaping.** With *modeling,* clients are encouraged to watch socially skilled friends and colleagues so they can acquire appropriate responses (eye contact, active listening, and so on) through observation. In *behavioral rehearsal,* clients practice social techniques in structured role-playing exercises. The therapist provides corrective feedback and uses approval to reinforce progress. Eventually, of course, clients try their newly acquired skills in real-world interactions. Usually, they are given specific homework assignments. *Shaping* is used so clients can gradually handle more complicated and delicate social situations. For example, a nonassertive client may begin by working on making requests of friends. Only much later will the client be asked to tackle standing up to his or her boss at work.

Cognitive-Behavioral Treatments

In Chapter 14, we learned that cognitive factors play a key role in the development of many anxiety and mood disorders. Citing the importance of such findings, in the 1970s, behavior therapists started to focus more attention on their clients' cognitions. ***Cognitive-behavioral treatments*** **use combinations of verbal interventions and behavior modification techniques to help clients change maladaptive patterns of thinking.** Some of these treatments, such as Albert Ellis's (1973) *rational-emotive behavior therapy* and Aaron Beck's (1976) *cognitive therapy,* have proven extremely influential. We will focus on Beck's cognitive therapy as an example of a cognitive-behavioral treatment (see Chapter 13 for a discussion of some of Ellis's ideas).

Cognitive therapy **uses specific strategies to correct habitual thinking errors that underlie various types of disorders.** Cognitive therapy was originally devised as a treatment for depression. However, in recent decades, cognitive therapy has been applied fruitfully to an increasingly wide range of disorders (Hollon & Beck, 2013; Wright, Thase, & Beck, 2014). According to cognitive therapists, depression and other disorders are caused by "errors" in thinking (see **Figure 15.8**). For example, they assert that depression-prone people tend to (1) blame their setbacks on personal inadequacies, without considering circumstantial explanations; (2) focus selectively on negative

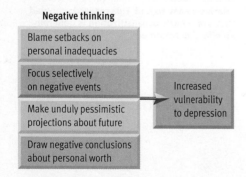

Negative thinking

Blame setbacks on personal inadequacies

Focus selectively on negative events

Make unduly pessimistic projections about future

Draw negative conclusions about personal worth

→ Increased vulnerability to depression

FIGURE 15.8

Beck's view of the roots of disorders. Beck's theory initially focused on the causes of depression, although it was gradually broadened to explain other disorders. According to Beck, depression is caused by the types of negative thinking shown here.

events, while ignoring positive events; (3) make unduly pessimistic projections about the future; and (4) draw negative conclusions about their worth as a person, based on insignificant events. For instance, imagine you got a low grade on a minor quiz in a class. If you made the kinds of errors in thinking just described, you might blame the grade on your woeful stupidity, dismiss comments from a classmate that it was an unfair test, gloomily predict that you will surely flunk the course, and conclude you are not genuine college material.

The goal of cognitive therapy is to change clients' negative thoughts and maladaptive beliefs (Wright et al., 2014). To begin, clients are taught to detect their automatic negative thoughts—the self-defeating statements that people are prone to make when analyzing problems. Examples include "I'm just not smart enough," "No one really likes me," and "It's all my fault." Clients are then trained to subject these automatic thoughts to reality testing. The therapist helps them see how unrealistically negative the thoughts are.

Cognitive therapy uses a variety of behavioral techniques, such as modeling, systematic monitoring of one's behavior, and behavioral rehearsal (Beck & Weishaar, 2011). For example, cognitive therapists often give their clients "homework assignments" that focus on changing clients' overt behaviors. Clients may be instructed to engage in overt responses on their own, outside the clinician's office.

How Effective Are Behavior Therapies?

Behavior therapists have historically placed more emphasis on the importance of measuring therapeutic outcomes than insight therapists have. Thus, there has been a good deal of research on the effectiveness of behavior therapy (Stanley & Beidel, 2009). Of course, behavior therapies are not well suited to the treatment of some types of problems (vague feelings of discontent, for instance). Furthermore, it's misleading to make global statements about the effectiveness of behavior therapies because they include many types of procedures designed for very different purposes. For example, the value of systematic desensitization for phobias has no bearing on the value of aversion therapy for sexual deviance. For our purposes, it is sufficient to note that there is favorable evidence on the efficacy of most of the widely used behavioral interventions (Zinbarg & Griffith, 2008). Behavior therapies can make important contributions to the treatment of phobias, obsessive-compulsive disorders, sexual dysfunction, schizophrenia, drug-related problems, eating disorders, psychosomatic disorders, hyperactivity, autism, and mental retardation (Craighead et al., 2013; Emmelkamp, 2013; Wilson, 2011).

CONCEPT CHECK 15.2

Understanding Therapists' Goals

Check your understanding of therapists' goals by matching various therapies with the appropriate description. The answers are in Appendix A.

Principal Therapeutic Goals	Therapy
_____ 1. Elimination of maladaptive behaviors or symptoms	a. Psychoanalysis
_____ 2. Acceptance of genuine self, personal growth	b. Client-centered therapy
_____ 3. Recovery of unconscious conflicts	c. Cognitive therapy
_____ 4. Detection and reduction of negative thinking	d. Behavior therapy

Key Learning Goals

- Summarize the therapeutic actions and side effects of four categories of psychiatric drugs.
- Evaluate the overall efficacy of drug treatments, and discuss controversies surrounding pharmaceutical research.
- Describe electroconvulsive therapy, and assess its therapeutic effects and risks.

Biomedical therapies **are physiological interventions intended to reduce symptoms associated with psychological disorders.** These therapies assume that psychological disorders are caused, at least in part, by biological malfunctions. As we discussed in the previous chapter, this assumption clearly has merit for many disorders, especially the more severe ones.

Treatment with Drugs

Therapeutic drugs for mental disorders fall into four major groups: antianxiety drugs, antipsychotic drugs, antidepressant drugs, and mood stabilizers. As you can see in **Figure 15.9**, the rate at which psychiatrists prescribe these drugs has increased since the mid-1990s for all four of these drug classes (Olfson et al., 2014).

Antianxiety Drugs

Antianxiety drugs **reduce tension, apprehension, and nervousness.** The most popular of these drugs are Valium and Xanax (trade names for the generic drugs diazepam and alprazolam, respectively). Valium, Xanax, and other similar drugs are often called *tranquilizers.* These drugs exert their effects almost immediately. They can be fairly effective in relieving feelings of anxiety (Dubovsky, 2009). However, their effects are measured in hours, so their impact is relatively short lived. Antianxiety drugs are routinely prescribed for people with anxiety disorders, but they are also given to millions of people who simply suffer from chronic nervous tension.

All the drugs used to treat psychological disorders have potentially troublesome side effects that show up in some patients but not others. The most common side effects of Valium and Xanax are drowsiness, lightheadedness, cottonmouth, depression, nausea, and constipation. These drugs also have potential for abuse, drug dependence, and overdose, although these risks have probably been exaggerated in the press (Martinez, Marangell, & Martinez, 2008). Another drawback is that patients who have been on antianxiety drugs for a while often experience unpleasant withdrawal symptoms when their drug treatment is stopped (Ferrando, Owen, & Levenson, 2014).

Antipsychotic Drugs

Antipsychotic drugs are used primarily in the treatment of schizophrenia. They are also given to people with severe mood disorders who become delusional. *Antipsychotic drugs* **are used to gradually reduce psychotic symptoms, including hyperactivity, mental confusion, hallucinations, and delusions.** The traditional antipsychotics appear to decrease activity at dopamine synapses. However, the exact relationship between their neurochemical effects and their clinical effects remains obscure (Miyamoto et al., 2008).

Studies suggest that antipsychotic drugs reduce psychotic symptoms in about 70% of patients, albeit in varied degrees (Kane, Stroup, & Marder, 2009). When antipsychotic drugs are effective, they work their magic gradually, as shown in **Figure 15.10**. Patients usually begin to respond within 2 days to a week. Further improvement can occur over several months. Many schizophrenic patients are placed on antipsychotics indefinitely because these drugs can reduce the likelihood of a relapse into an active schizophrenic episode.

Antipsychotic drugs undeniably make a major contribution to the treatment of severe mental disorders, and psychiatrists' reliance on antipsychotic

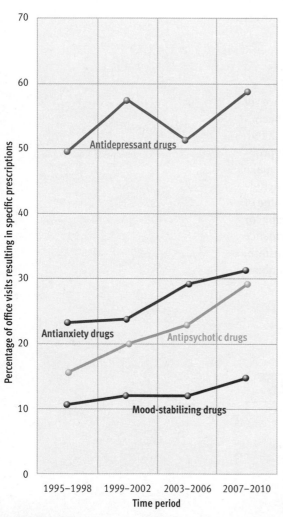

FIGURE 15.9

Increasing prescription of psychiatric drugs. Olfson et al. (2014) tracked prescription trends for psychiatric drugs over a period of 15 years. These data show the percentage of office visits to psychiatrists that resulted in prescriptions for various types of drugs. As you can see, reliance on all four categories of psychiatric drugs increased over this time period. (Based on data from Olfson et al., 2014)

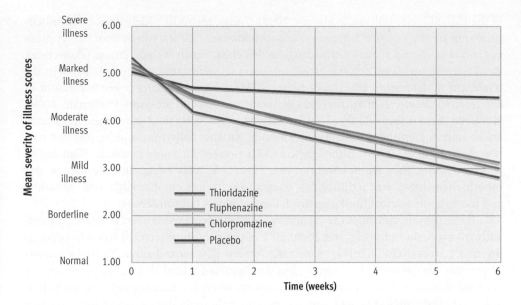

FIGURE 15.10

The time course of antipsychotic drug effects.
Antipsychotic drugs reduce psychotic symptoms
gradually, over a span of weeks, as graphed
here. In contrast, patients given placebo medication show little improvement.

SOURCE: Cole, J. O., Goldberg, S. C., & Davis, J. M.
(1966). Drugs in the treatment of psychosis. In P.
Solomon (Ed.), *Psychiatric drugs.* New York: Grune &
Stratton. From data in the NIMH-PSC Collaborative
Study I. Reprinted by permission of J. M. Davis.

medications has increased dramatically in recent decades (Olfson et al., 2012). However, antipsychotic drugs present their share of problems. They have many unpleasant side effects (Ferrando et al., 2014). Drowsiness, constipation, and cottonmouth are common. Tremors, muscular rigidity, and impaired coordination can also occur. After being released from a hospital, many patients who have been placed on antipsychotics stop their drug regimen because of the side effects. Unfortunately, after patients stop taking antipsychotic medication, about 70% relapse within a year (van Kammen, Hurford, & Marder, 2009). One study found that even brief periods of partial noncompliance with one's drug regimen increased the risk of relapse (Subotnik et al., 2011). Another 10-year study showed that noncompliance was associated with increased mortality among schizophrenic patients (Cullen et al., 2013). In addition to their nuisance side effects, antipsychotics can cause a more severe and lasting problem called *tardive dyskinesia,* which is seen in about 15%–25% of patients who receive long-term treatment with traditional antipsychotics (Stewart, Russakoff, & Stewart, 2014). ***Tardive dyskinesia* is a neurological disorder marked by involuntary writhing and tic-like movements of the mouth, tongue, face, hands, or feet.** Once this debilitating syndrome emerges, there is no cure, although spontaneous remission sometimes occurs after the discontinuation of antipsychotic medication.

Psychiatrists currently rely primarily on a newer class of antipsychotic agents called *second-generation antipsychotic drugs* (Marder, Hurford, & van Kammen, 2009). These drugs appear to be roughly similar to the first-generation antipsychotics in therapeutic effectiveness, but they offer several advantages (Meltzer & Bobo, 2009). For instance, they can help some treatment-resistant patients who do not respond to traditional antipsychotics, and they produce fewer unpleasant side effects and carry less risk for tardive dyskinesia. Of course, like all powerful drugs, they carry some risks: Second-generation antipsychotics appear to increase patients' vulnerability to diabetes and cardiovascular problems. In the hopes of reducing drug discontinuation by patients and associated high relapse rates, psychiatrists are experimenting with long-acting, injectable antipsychotic medications that only need to be administered on a monthly basis. However, the early research results on this new approach have not yielded the increases in efficacy clinicians hoped to see (Goff, 2014; McEvoy et al., 2014).

Antidepressant Drugs

As their name suggests, *antidepressant drugs* **gradually elevate mood and help bring people out of a depression.** Reliance on antidepressants has increased dramatically in recent years, as these drugs have become the most frequently prescribed class of medication

in the United States (Olfson & Marcus, 2009). Today, the most widely prescribed antidepressants are the *selective serotonin reuptake inhibitors (SSRIs)*, which slow the reuptake process at serotonin synapses. The drugs in this class, which include Prozac (fluoxetine), Paxil (paroxetine), and Zoloft (sertraline), seem to yield rapid therapeutic gains in the treatment of depression (Boland & Keller, 2008), while producing fewer unpleasant or dangerous side effects than previous generations of antidepressants (Sussman, 2009). However, there is some doubt about how effective the SSRIs (and other antidepressants) are in relieving episodes of depression among patients suffering from bipolar disorder (Pacchiarotti et al., 2013). Although the SSRIs present far fewer problems than earlier antidepressants, they are not without side effects. Adverse effects include nausea, dry mouth, drowsiness, sexual difficulties, weight gain, feeling emotionally numb, agitation, and increases in suicidal thinking (Read, Cartwright, & Gibson, 2014).

Like antipsychotic drugs, the various types of antidepressants exert their effects gradually over a period of weeks, but about 60% of patients' improvement tends to occur in the first 2 weeks (Gitlin, 2014). A research review that looked carefully at the *severity* of patients' depression when medication was initiated found that people with serious depression benefit the most from antidepressants, whereas antidepressants appear to provide a relatively modest benefit for patients with mild to moderate depression (Fournier et al, 2010).

A major concern in recent years has been evidence from a number of studies that SSRIs may increase the risk for suicide, especially in adolescents and young adults (Healy & Whitaker, 2003; Holden, 2004). The challenge of collecting definitive data on this issue is much more daunting than one might guess. The crux of the problem is that suicide rates are already elevated among people who exhibit the disorders for which SSRIs are prescribed (Berman, 2009). The research findings on this issue are complicated and contradictory. One influential meta-analysis concluded that antidepressants lead to a slight elevation in the risk of suicidal behavior (Bridge et al., 2007). However, a more recent analysis of forty-one antidepressant drug trials failed to find an increase in suicidal risk (Gibbons et al., 2012). Regulatory warnings from the U.S. Food and Drug Administration (FDA) have led to a decline in the prescription of SSRIs among adolescents (Nemeroff et al., 2007). This trend has prompted concern that the well-intended warnings may have backfired and led to increases in suicide among untreated individuals (Dudley et al., 2008). A recent study yielded disturbing evidence that bolsters this concern. C. Y. Lu et al. (2014) found that in the second year after the FDA warnings, antidepressant use declined by 31% among adolescents and by 24% among young adults, while apparent suicide attempts via drug overdose (a method of suicide that was relatively easy to track in medical databases) increased by 22% among adolescents and by 34% among young adults. The association between reduced antidepressant use and increased suicide may not reflect a causal relationship, but the findings are worrisome. Clearly, the risks of putting young patients on antidepressants need to be weighed against the risks of not putting them on antidepressants. In the final analysis, this is a complex issue, but the one thing experts seem to agree on is that adolescents starting on SSRIs should be monitored closely by their families and physicians.

Mood Stabilizers

Mood stabilizers **are drugs used to control mood swings in patients with bipolar mood disorders.** The principal drugs in this category are *lithium* and *valproate*. Both have proven valuable in preventing *future* episodes of both mania and depression in patients with bipolar illness (Miklowitz, 2014; Post & Altshuler, 2009). They can also be used in efforts to bring patients with bipolar illness out of *current* manic or depressive episodes. On the negative side of the ledger, lithium has some dangerous side effects if its use isn't managed skillfully (Ferrando et al., 2014). Lithium levels in the patient's blood must be monitored carefully because high concentrations can be toxic and even fatal. Kidney and thyroid gland complications are the other major problems associated with lithium therapy.

▶ **REALITY CHECK**

Misconception

Psychological disorders are largely chronic and incurable.

Reality

Admittedly, there are mentally ill people for whom treatment is a failure. However, they are greatly outnumbered by people who do get better, either spontaneously or through formal treatment. The vast majority of people who are diagnosed as mentally ill eventually improve and lead normal, productive lives. Even the most severe psychological disorders can be treated successfully.

Evaluating Drug Therapies

Drug therapies can produce clear therapeutic gains for many kinds of patients. What's especially impressive is that they can be effective with severe disorders that often defy therapeutic endeavors. Nonetheless, drug therapies are controversial. Critics have raised a number of issues (Bentall, 2009; Breggin, 2008; Healy, 2004; Kirsch, 2010; Spielmans & Kirsch, 2014; Whitaker, 2002). First, some critics argue that drug therapies are not as effective as advertised and that they often produce superficial, short-lived curative effects. For example, Valium does not really solve problems with anxiety; it merely provides temporary relief from an unpleasant symptom. Moreover, relapse rates are substantial when drug regimens are discontinued. Second, critics charge that many drugs are overprescribed and many patients overmedicated. According to these critics, a number of physicians routinely hand out prescriptions without giving adequate consideration to more complicated and difficult interventions. Consistent with this line of criticism, a study of office visits to psychiatrists found that they increasingly prescribe two and even three medications to patients, even though relatively little is known about the interactive effects of psychiatric drugs (Mojtabai & Olfson, 2010). Moreover, the growing reliance on medication has undermined the provision of insight and behavioral interventions. Although the empirical evidence on the value of insight and behavioral therapies has never been greater, the medicalization of psychological disorders has led to a decline in the use of psychosocial interventions that may be just as effective and safer than drug therapies (Gaudiano & Miller, 2013). Third, some critics charge that the damaging side effects of therapeutic drugs are underestimated by psychiatrists and that these side effects are often worse than the illnesses the drugs are supposed to cure. Some critics also have argued that psychiatric drugs may be helpful in the short-term but that they disrupt neurotransmitter systems in ways that actually *increase* patients' vulnerability to psychological disorders in the long-term picture (Andrews et al., 2011).

Critics maintain that the negative effects of psychiatric drugs are not fully appreciated because the pharmaceutical industry has managed to gain undue influence over the research enterprise as it relates to drug testing (Angell, 2004; Healy, 2004; Insel, 2010). Today, most researchers who investigate the benefits and risks of medications and write treatment guidelines have lucrative financial arrangements with the pharmaceutical industry (Bentall, 2009; Cosgrove & Krimsky, 2012). Their studies are funded by drug companies, and they often receive substantial consulting fees. Unfortunately, these financial ties appear to undermine the objectivity required in scientific research because studies funded by drug companies are far less likely to report unfavorable results than are nonprofit-funded studies (Bekelman, Li, & Gross, 2003; Perlis et al., 2005). Industry-financed drug trials also tend to be too brief to detect the long-term risks associated with new drugs (Vandenbroucke & Psaty, 2008). Additionally, positive findings on drugs are almost always published, whereas when unfavorable results emerge, the data are often withheld from publication (Spielmans & Kirsch, 2014; Turner et al., 2008). Also, research designs are often slanted in a variety of ways to exaggerate the positive effects and minimize the negative effects of the drugs under scrutiny (Carpenter, 2002; Chopra, 2003; Spielmans & Kirsch, 2014). The conflicts of interest that appear to be pervasive in contemporary drug research raise grave concerns that require attention from researchers, universities, and federal agencies.

Electroconvulsive Therapy (ECT)

In the 1930s, a Hungarian psychiatrist named Ladislas von Meduna speculated that epilepsy and schizophrenia could not coexist in the same body. On the basis of this observation, which turned out to be inaccurate, von Meduna theorized that it might be useful to induce epileptic-like seizures in schizophrenic patients. Initially, a drug was used to trigger these seizures. However, by 1938, a pair of Italian psychiatrists (Cerletti & Bini, 1938) had demonstrated that it was safer to elicit the seizures with electric shock. Thus, modern electroconvulsive therapy was born.

Electroconvulsive therapy (*ECT*) **is a biomedical treatment in which electric shock is used to produce a cortical seizure accompanied by convulsions.** In ECT, electrodes are attached to the skull over the temporal lobes of the brain. A light anesthesia is administered, and the patient is given a variety of drugs to minimize the likelihood of complications, such as spinal fractures. An electric current is then applied for about a second. The current triggers a brief (5–20 seconds) convulsive seizure, during which the patient usually loses consciousness. The patient normally awakens in an hour or two. People typically receive three treatments a week over a period of 2–7 weeks (Fink, 2009).

The clinical use of ECT peaked in the 1940s and 1950s, before effective drug therapies were widely available. ECT is not a rare treatment today, but its use has been declining. A recent study reported that the portion of hospitals with psychiatric units that offered ECT declined from 55% in 1993 to 35% in 2009 (Case et al., 2013). During the same time period, the number of patients treated with ECT decreased 43%. ECT advocates argue that ECT is underutilized because the public harbors many misconceptions about its risks and side effects (Fink, Kellner, & McCall, 2014; Kellner et al., 2012). Conversely, some critics of ECT have argued that it is overused because it is a lucrative procedure that consumes relatively little time in comparison with insight therapy (Frank, 1990).

Effectiveness of ECT

The evidence of the therapeutic efficacy of ECT is open to varied interpretations. Proponents maintain that it is a remarkably effective treatment for major depression (Fink, 2014; Prudic, 2009). Moreover, they note that many patients who do not benefit from antidepressant medication improve in response to ECT (Nobler & Sackeim, 2006). However, opponents argue that the available studies are flawed and inconclusive and that ECT is probably no more effective than a placebo (Rose et al., 2003). Overall, there does seem to be enough favorable evidence to justify *conservative* use of ECT in treating severe mood disorders in patients who have not responded to medication (Kellner et al., 2012). ECT patients who recover from their depression and do not relapse report great improvements in the quality of their lives (McCall et al., 2013). Unfortunately, relapse rates after ECT are distressingly high. A review of thirty-two studies found that the risk of relapse into depression was 38% after 6 months and 51% after 1 year (Jelovac, Kolshus, & McLoughlin, 2013). However, these high relapse rates may occur because ECT is largely reserved for patients who have severe, chronic depression that has not responded to drug treatment (Fekadu et al., 2009). In other words, if ECT is only used for the toughest cases, high relapse rates are to be expected.

CONCEPT CHECK 15.3

Understanding Biomedical Therapies

Check your understanding of biomedical therapies by matching each treatment with its chief use. The answers are in Appendix A.

Treatment	Chief Purpose
_____ 1. Antianxiety drugs	a. To reduce psychotic symptoms
_____ 2. Antipsychotic drugs	b. To bring a major depression to an end
_____ 3. Antidepressant drugs	c. To suppress tension, nervousness, and apprehension
_____ 4. Mood stabilizers	d. To prevent future episodes of mania or depression in bipolar disorders
_____ 5. Electroconvulsive therapy (ECT)	

Risks Associated with ECT

Even ECT proponents acknowledge that memory losses, impaired attention, and other cognitive deficits are common short-term side effects of electroconvulsive therapy (Rowny & Lisanby, 2008; Sackeim et al., 2007). However, advocates assert that these deficits are mild and usually disappear within a month or two (Fink, 2004; Glass, 2001). In contrast, ECT critics maintain that ECT-induced cognitive deficits are often significant and sometimes permanent (Breggin, 1991; Rose et al., 2003). A recent, thorough review of the evidence concluded that retrograde amnesia for autobiographical information is a common side effect of ECT and that these memory losses can be persistent and sometimes permanent (Sackeim, 2014). Given the doubts that have been raised about the efficacy and risks of electroconvulsive therapy, it appears that this treatment will remain controversial for some time to come.

15.5 CURRENT TRENDS IN TREATMENT

15.5

Key Learning Goals

- Analyze the barriers that lead to underutilization of mental health services by ethnic minorities and possible solutions.
- Discuss efforts to expand the delivery of clinical services through technology and the merits of blending approaches to therapy.

As we saw in our discussion of insight, behavioral, and drug therapy, recent decades have brought many changes in the world of mental health care. In this section, we'll discuss three trends that are not tied to a particular mode of treatment. Specifically, we'll look at efforts to respond more effectively to increasing cultural diversity, initiatives to increase the availability of psychotherapy through the use of technology, and the trend toward blending various approaches to therapy.

Increasing Multicultural Sensitivity in Treatment

Modern psychotherapy was spawned in a cultural milieu that viewed the person as an independent, reflective, rational being, capable of self-improvement (Cushman, 1992). Psychological disorders were assumed to have natural causes like physical diseases do and to be susceptible to treatments derived from scientific research. But the individualized, medicalized institution of modern psychotherapy reflects Western cultural values that are far from universal (Sue & Sue, 1999). In many nonindustrialized societies, psychological disorders are attributed to supernatural forces (possession, witchcraft, angry gods, and so forth), and victims seek help from priests, shamans, and folk healers, rather than doctors (Wittkower & Warnes, 1984). Thus, efforts to export Western psychotherapies to non-Western cultures have met with mixed success. Indeed, the highly culture-bound origins of modern therapies have raised questions about their applicability to ethnic minorities *within* Western culture (Falicov, 2014; Miranda et al., 2005).

Research on how cultural factors influence the process and outcome of psychotherapy has increased in recent years. Its growth has been motivated in part by the need to improve mental health services for ethnic minority groups in American society (Gunthert, 2014; Worthington, Soth-McNett, & Moreno, 2007). Studies suggest that American minority groups generally underutilize therapeutic services (López et al., 2012; Snowden, 2012; Sue et al., 2012). Why? A variety of barriers appear to contribute to this problem (Snowden & Yamada, 2005; F. G. Lu et al., 2014; Zane et al., 2004). One major consideration is that many members of minority groups have a history of frustrating interactions with government bureaucracies. Hence, they tend to be distrusting of large, intimidating institutions, such as hospitals and community mental health centers (Henderson et al., 2014). Another issue is that most hospitals and mental health agencies are not adequately staffed with therapists who speak the languages used by minority groups in their service areas. Yet another problem is that the vast majority of therapists have been trained almost exclusively in the treatment of white, middle-class Americans. As a result, they often are not familiar with the cultural backgrounds and unique characteristics of various ethnic groups. This

Illustrated Overview Five Major Approaches to Treatment

THERAPY/FOUNDER

ROOTS OF DISORDERS

PSYCHOANALYSIS

Developed by **Sigmund Freud** in Vienna, from the 1890s through the 1930s

National Library of Medicine

Intrapsychic conflict (among id, ego, and superego) → Anxiety → Reliance on defense mechanisms

Unconscious conflicts resulting from fixations in earlier development cause anxiety, which leads to defensive behavior. The repressed conflicts typically center on sex and aggression.

CLIENT-CENTERED THERAPY

Courtesy of Carl Rogers Memorial Library

Created by **Carl Rogers** at the University of Chicago during the 1940s and 1950s

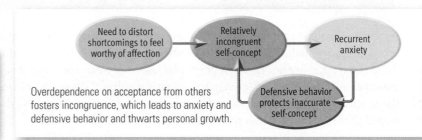

Need to distort shortcomings to feel worthy of affection → Relatively incongruent self-concept → Recurrent anxiety

Defensive behavior protects inaccurate self-concept

Overdependence on acceptance from others fosters incongruence, which leads to anxiety and defensive behavior and thwarts personal growth.

BEHAVIOR THERAPY

Launched primarily by South African **Joseph Wolpe**'s description of systematic desensitization in 1958

Courtesy of Dr. Joseph Wolpe

CS
Bridge

US
Lightning strikes

CR
Fear
UR

Maladaptive patterns of behavior are acquired through learning. For example, many phobias are thought to be created through classical conditioning and maintained by operant conditioning.

COGNITIVE-BEHAVIORAL TREATMENTS

Courtesy of Aaron T. Beck

One approach devised by **Aaron Beck** at the University of Pennsylvania in the 1960s and 1970s

Pervasive negative thinking about events related to self fosters anxiety and depression, and other forms of pathology.

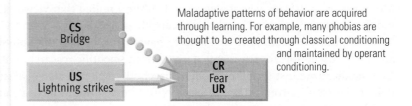

Blame setbacks on personal inadequacies

Focus selectively on negative events

Make unduly pessimistic projections about future

Draw negative conclusions about personal worth

→ Increased vulnerability to depression

BIOMEDICAL THERAPY

Many researchers contributed; key breakthroughs in drug treatment made around 1950 by John Cade in Australia, Henri Laborit in France, and Jean Delay and Pierre Deniker, also in France

Most disorders are attributed to genetic predisposition and physiological malfunctions, such as abnormal neurotransmitter activity.

For example, schizophrenia appears to be associated with overactivity at dopamine synapses.

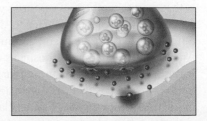

THERAPEUTIC GOALS

THERAPEUTIC TECHNIQUES

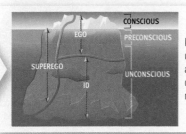

Insights regarding unconscious conflicts and motives; resolution of conflicts; personality reconstruction

Free association, dream analysis, interpretation, transference

Increased congruence between self-concept and experience; acceptance of genuine self; self-determination and personal growth

Genuineness, empathy, unconditional positive regard, clarification, reflecting back to client

Elimination of maladaptive symptoms; acquisition of more adaptive responses

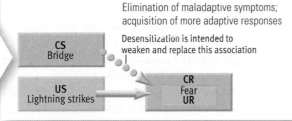

Desensitization is intended to weaken and replace this association

Classical and operant conditioning, systematic desensitization, aversive conditioning, social skills training, reinforcement, shaping, punishment, extinction, biofeedback

Reduction of negative thinking; substitution of more realistic thinking

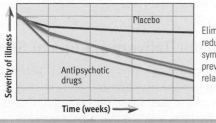

Thought stopping, recording of automatic thoughts, refuting of negative thinking, homework assignments

Elimination or reduction of symptoms; prevention of relapse

Antianxiety, antidepressant, antipsychotic, and mood-stabilizing drugs, electroconvulsive therapy

Research indicates that ethnic minorities tend to feel more comfortable with therapists who share their ethnicity. Unfortunately, there is a shortage of minority therapists in the United States.

culture gap often leads to misunderstandings, ill-advised treatment strategies, and reduced rapport. Consistent with this assertion, recent research found that psychiatrists spend less time with African American patients than with white patients (Olfson, Cherry, & Lewis-Fernandez, 2009). Another study of more than 15,000 people suffering from depression found that Mexican Americans and African Americans were notably less likely to receive treatment than whites, as can be seen in **Figure 15.11** (González et al., 2010).

What can be done to improve mental health services for American minority groups? Researchers in this area have offered a variety of suggestions (Berger, Zane, & Hwang, 2014; Hansen et al., 2013; Hong, Garcia, & Soriano, 2000; Miranda et al., 2005). Discussions of possible solutions usually begin with the need to recruit and train more ethnic minority therapists. Studies show that ethnic minorities are more likely to go to mental health facilities staffed by a higher proportion of people who share their ethnic background (Snowden & Hu, 1996; Sue, Zane, & Young, 1994). Research has also shown that outcomes tend to be better and client satisfaction higher when clients see a therapist of similar ethnicity (Meyer, Zane, & Cho, 2011). Therapists who are similar in ethnicity are perceived as having more similar experiences and greater credibility. White therapists working with non-white clients have been urged to work harder at building a vigorous *therapeutic alliance* (a strong supportive bond) with their ethnic clients. A strong therapeutic alliance is associated with better therapeutic outcomes, regardless of ethnicity (Crits-Christoph, Gibbons, & Mukherjee, 2013), but some studies suggest it is especially crucial for minority clients (Bender et al., 2007; Comas-Diaz, 2006). Finally, most authorities urge further investigation of how traditional approaches to therapy can be modified and tailored to be more compatible with specific cultural groups' attitudes, values, norms, and traditions (Hwang, 2006). A recent review of research that has examined the effects of culturally adapted interventions found evidence that this tailoring process often yields positive effects, although the evidence was mixed (Huey et al., 2014).

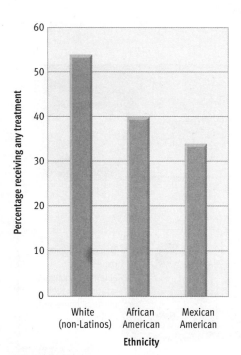

FIGURE 15.11

Ethnicity and treatment for depression. In a nationally representative sample of almost 16,000 subjects, González and colleagues (2010) identified participants suffering from depression and ascertained what types of treatment they received. When they analyzed these data in relation to ethnicity, they found that members of minority groups were less likely than whites to get treatment. The data graphed here show the percentage of patients receiving treatment of any kind.

Using Technology to Expand the Delivery of Clinical Services

Although the problem is especially acute among ethnic minorities, inadequate availability of mental health care is a broad problem that reaches into every corner of our society. In an influential article, Alan Kazdin and Stacey Blase (2011) argue that there just are not enough clinicians and treatment facilities available to meet America's mental health needs. This shortage of clinicians is particularly serious in small towns and rural areas. Moreover, Kazdin and Blase note that the traditional model of one-on-one therapy imposes constraints on the availability of treatment. To address these problems, clinicians are increasingly attempting to harness technology to expand the delivery of mental health services and to reduce the costs of therapy.

These efforts to use technology to create new platforms for the delivery of therapeutic services have taken many forms. One of the simpler approaches is to deliver both individual and group therapy over the phone. For example, this method has been used in the treatment of elderly clients with anxiety problems (Brenes, Ingram, & Danhauer, 2012) and veterans suffering from loneliness and depression (Davis, Guyker, & Persky, 2012). Another relatively simple innovation has been to use videoconferencing technology to provide both individual and group therapy. A review of research on this approach to treatment concluded that clinical outcomes are about the same as in face-to-face therapy and that clients tend to report high satisfaction (Backhaus et al., 2012).

Interventions delivered via the Internet hold promise for reaching larger swaths of people who might otherwise go untreated. For example, software programs have been created for the treatment of substance abuse (Campbell et al., 2014); generalized anxiety disorder (Amir & Taylor, 2012); obsessive-compulsive disorder (Andersson et al., 2011); and phobic disorders (Opriş et al., 2012). Most of these treatments involve online, interactive, multimedia adaptations of cognitive-behavioral therapies. The computerized treatments typically consist of a series of modules that educate individuals about the nature and causes of their disorder and cognitive strategies for ameliorating their problems, along with practice exercises and homework assignments. In most cases, the interventions include limited access to an actual therapist through the Internet, but some programs are fully automated, with no therapist contact. Studies of computerized therapies suggest they can be effective for many types of disorders, but more research and higher-quality research are needed before solid conclusions can be drawn regarding their value (Kiluk et al., 2011). Thus, it appears likely that the future will see increased efforts to improve access to treatment through innovations in technology.

Blending Approaches to Treatment

In this chapter, we have reviewed many approaches to treatment. However, there is no rule that a client must be treated with just one approach. Often, a clinician will use several techniques in working with a client. For example, a depressed person might receive cognitive therapy, social skills training, and antidepressant medication. Studies suggest that combining approaches to treatment has merit (Glass, 2004; Szigethy & Friedman, 2009). In particular, combining medication with insight or behavioral treatments tends to yield modest improvements in outcomes, although not for all types of disorders (Forand, DeRubeis, & Amsterdam, 2013).

The value of multiple approaches to treatment may explain why a significant trend seems to have crept into the field of psychotherapy. There's now a movement *away* from strong loyalty to individual schools of thought and a corresponding move toward integrating various approaches to therapy (Gold & Stricker, 2013). Many clinicians used to depend exclusively on one system of therapy while rejecting the utility of all others, but in recent years a growing number of clinicians characterize themselves as using an *eclectic* approach (see **Figure 15.12**). **Eclecticism in the practice of therapy involves drawing ideas from two or more systems of therapy instead of committing to just one system.** Advocates of eclecticism, such as Arnold Lazarus (2008), maintain that therapists should ask themselves, "What is the best approach for this specific client, problem, and situation?" and then adjust their strategy accordingly.

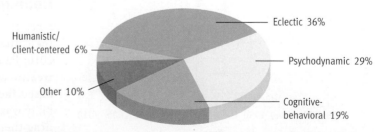

FIGURE 15.12

The leading approaches to therapy among psychologists. These data, from a survey of 531 psychologists who belong to the American Psychological Association's Division of Psychotherapy, provide some indication of how common an eclectic approach to therapy has become. The findings suggest that the most widely used approaches to therapy are eclectic, psychodynamic, and cognitive-behavioral treatments. (Based on data from Norcross, Hedges, & Castle, 2002)

15.6

Key Learning Goals

- Explain why people grew disenchanted with mental hospitals, and discuss the resultant change in mental health care.
- Assess the effects of the deinstitutionalization movement.

Traditionally, much of the treatment of mental illness was carried out in institutional settings, primarily in mental hospitals. **A *mental hospital* is a medical institution specializing in providing inpatient care for psychological disorders.** In the United States, a national network of state-funded mental hospitals started to emerge in the 1840s through the efforts of Dorothea Dix and other reformers. Prior to these reforms, the mentally ill who were poor were housed in jails and poorhouses or were left to wander the countryside. Today, mental hospitals continue to play a role in the delivery of mental health services. However, since World War II, institutional care for mental illness has undergone a series of major transitions—and the dust hasn't settled yet. Let's look at how institutional care has evolved in recent decades.

Disenchantment with Mental Hospitals

By the 1950s, it had become apparent that public mental hospitals were not fulfilling their goals very well (Mechanic, 1980; Menninger, 2005). Experts began to realize that hospitalization often *contributed* to the development of pathology instead of curing it.

What were the causes of these unexpected negative effects? Part of the problem was that the facilities were usually underfunded (Hogan & Morrison, 2008). The lack of adequate funding meant that the facilities were overcrowded and understaffed. Hospital personnel were undertrained and overworked, making them hard pressed to deliver minimal custodial care. Despite gallant efforts at treatment, the demoralizing conditions made most public mental hospitals decidedly nontherapeutic (Scull, 1990). These problems were aggravated by the fact that state mental hospitals served large geographic regions, but were rarely placed near major population centers. As a result, most patients were uprooted from their community and isolated from their social support networks.

Disenchantment with the public mental hospital system inspired the *community mental health movement* that emerged in the 1960s (Duckworth & Borus, 1999; Huey et al., 2009). The community mental health movement emphasizes (1) local, community-based care; (2) reduced dependence on hospitalization; and (3) the prevention of psychological disorders. Community mental health centers were intended to supplement mental hospitals with decentralized and more accessible services. However, they have had their own funding struggles (Dixon & Goldman, 2004).

Deinstitutionalization

Since the 1960s, a policy of deinstitutionalization has been followed in the United States, as well as in most other Western countries (Novella, 2010; Paulson, 2012). ***Deinstitutionalization* refers to transferring the treatment of mental illness from inpatient institutions to community-based facilities that emphasize outpatient care.** This shift in responsibility was facilitated by two developments: (1) the emergence of effective drug therapies for severe disorders and (2) the anticipated deployment of community mental health centers to coordinate local care (Goff & Gudeman, 1999).

The exodus of patients from mental hospitals was dramatic. The average inpatient population in state and county mental hospitals dropped from a peak of around 550,000 in the mid-1950s to around 40,000 by 2010, as shown in **Figure 15.13**. This trend does not mean that

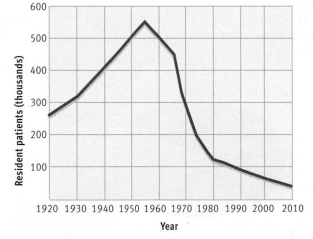

FIGURE 15.13

Declining inpatient population at state and county mental hospitals. The inpatient population in public mental hospitals has declined dramatically since the late 1950s, as a result of deinstitutionalization and the development of effective antipsychotic medication.

hospitalization for mental illness has become a thing of the past. A great many people are still hospitalized, but the shift has been toward placing them in local general hospitals for brief periods instead of distant psychiatric hospitals for long periods (Hogan & Morrison, 2008). In keeping with the philosophy of deinstitutionalization, these local facilities try to get patients stabilized and back into the community as swiftly as possible.

How has deinstitutionalization worked out? It gets mixed reviews. On the positive side, many people have benefited by avoiding disruptive and unnecessary hospitalization. Ample evidence suggests that alternatives to hospitalization can be as effective as inpatient care, while costing less (Hamden et al., 2011; Kunitoh, 2013). Moreover, follow-up studies of discharged patients reveal that a substantial majority prefer the greater freedom provided by community-based treatment (Leff, 2006).

Nonetheless, some unanticipated problems have arisen (Elpers, 2000; Novella, 2010; Talbott, 2004). Many patients suffering from chronic psychological disorders had nowhere to go when they were released. They had no families, friends, or homes to return to. Many had no work skills and were poorly prepared to live on their own. These people were supposed to be absorbed by "halfway houses," sheltered workshops, and other types of intermediate care facilities. Unfortunately, many communities were never able to fund and build the planned facilities (Hogan & Morrison, 2008). Thus, commenting on the unintended effects of deinstitutionalization, Novella (2010, p. 228) concludes that it "frequently resulted in destroying a needed sanctuary, particularly for those patients requiring the highest degree of support." Ultimately, deinstitutionalization left two major problems in its wake: a "revolving door" population of people who flow in and out of psychiatric facilities, and a sizable population of homeless mentally ill people.

Mental Illness, the Revolving Door, and Homelessness

Most of the people caught in the mental health system's revolving door suffer from chronic, severe disorders (usually schizophrenia) that often require hospitalization (Machado, Leonidas, & Santos, 2012). They respond to drug therapies in the hospital; however, after they're stabilized through drug therapy, they no longer qualify for expensive hospital treatment according to the new standards mandated by deinstitutionalization and managed care. Thus, they're sent back out the door, into communities that often aren't prepared to provide adequate outpatient care. Because they lack appropriate care and support, their condition deteriorates, and they soon require readmission to a hospital, where the cycle begins once again (Botha et al., 2010). Overall, around the world, about one in seven psychiatric inpatients is readmitted within 30 days (Vigod et al., 2015), with 40%–50% of patients rehospitalized within a year of their release (Bridge & Barbe, 2004). Readmission rates are particularly high among patients who have a concurrent substance abuse problem (Frick et al., 2013).

Deinstitutionalization has been blamed for contributing to the growing population of homeless people. Homelessness has many causes, but inadequately treated mental illness appears to be a key factor that increases individuals' vulnerability to homelessness. Studies have consistently found elevated rates of mental illness among the homeless. Taken as a whole, the evidence suggests that roughly one-third of homeless people suffer from severe mental illness (schizophrenic and mood disorders), that another one-third or more are struggling with alcohol and drug problems, that many qualify for multiple diagnoses, and that the prevalence of mental illness among the homeless may be increasing (Bassuk et al., 1998; Hodgson, Shelton, & Bree, 2015; North et al., 2004; Viron et al., 2014). In essence, homeless shelters have become a *de facto* element of America's mental health care system (Callicutt, 2006). So too, by the way, have our jails and prisons because the homeless mentally ill are frequently incarcerated, leading to an epidemic of psychological disorders in the U.S. prison system (Baillargeon et al.,

2009). Indeed, the revolving door for some mentally ill individuals refers to their frequently being reincarcerated.

Ultimately, it's clear that our society is not providing adequate care for a sizable segment of the mentally ill population (Appelbaum, 2002; Gittelman, 2005; Torrey, 2014). That's not a new development. Inadequate care for mental illness has always been the norm. Societies always struggle with the problem of what to do with the mentally ill and how to pay for their care (Duckworth & Borus, 1999). Ours is not different. Unfortunately, in recent years, the situation has deteriorated rather than improved. Although overall health care spending has been increasing steadily in recent years, funding for mental health care has diminished dramatically (Geller, 2009). Today, most states have a shortage of psychiatric beds, resulting in waiting lists for admission, overcrowding, and increasingly brief hospitalizations (Geller, 2009). Lamentably, the situation has deteriorated to the point where the *Journal of the American Medical Association* recently published an opinion piece that advocated for a partial rollback of deinstitutionalization. In arguing for the return of the abandoned mental asylums, the authors assert that "the choice is between the prison-homelessness-acute hospitalization-prison cycle or long-term psychiatric institutionalization" (Sisti, Segal, & Emanuel, 2015; p. 244).

15.7 REFLECTING ON THE CHAPTER'S THEMES

15.7

Key Learning Goals
- Identify the two unifying themes highlighted in this chapter.

Cultural Heritage

Theoretical Diversity

In our discussion of psychotherapy, one of our unifying themes—the value of theoretical diversity—was particularly prominent, and one other theme—the importance of culture—surfaced briefly. Let's discuss the latter theme first. The approaches to psychotherapy described in this chapter are products of modern, white, middle-class Western culture. Some of these therapies have proven useful in some other cultures, but many have turned out to be irrelevant or counterproductive when used with different cultural groups. Thus, we have seen once again that Western psychology cannot assume that its theories and practices have universal applicability.

As for theoretical diversity, its value can be illustrated with a rhetorical question: Can you imagine what the state of modern psychotherapy would be if everyone in psychology and psychiatry had simply accepted Freud's theories about the nature and treatment of psychological disorders? If not for theoretical diversity, mental health treatment might still be in the dark ages. Psychoanalysis can be a useful method of therapy, but we would have a tragic state of affairs if that were the *only* treatment available to people experiencing psychological distress. Multitudes of people have benefited from alternative approaches to treatment that emerged out of tension between psychoanalytic theory and various other theoretical perspectives.

Given that people have diverse problems, rooted in varied origins, it is fortunate they can choose from a diverse array of approaches to treatment. The illustrated overview on pages 554–555 summarizes and compares the approaches we've discussed in this chapter. This overview shows that all the major approaches to therapy have their own vision of the nature of human discontent and the ideal remedy.

Of course, diversity can be confusing. The range and variety of available treatments in modern psychotherapy leaves many people puzzled about their options. Thus, in our Personal Application we'll sort through the practical issues involved in selecting a therapist.

15.8

Key Learning Goals
- Discuss some practical considerations in seeking therapy, including the importance of therapists' theoretical approach.

Answer the following "true" or "false."

____**1** Psychotherapy is an art as well as a science.

____**2** Psychotherapy can be harmful or damaging to a client.

____**3** Mental health treatment does not have to be expensive.

____**4** The type of professional degree that a therapist holds is relatively unimportant.

All of these statements are true. Do any of them surprise you? If so, you're in good company. Many people know relatively little about the practicalities of selecting a therapist.

The task of finding an appropriate therapist is no less complex than shopping for any other major service. Should you see a psychologist or a psychiatrist? Should you opt for individual therapy or group therapy? Should you see a client-centered therapist or a behavior therapist? The unfortunate part of this complexity is that people seeking psychotherapy often feel overwhelmed by personal difficulties. The last thing they need is to be confronted by yet another complex problem.

Nonetheless, the importance of finding a good therapist cannot be overestimated. Therapy can sometimes have harmful rather than helpful effects. We have already discussed how drug therapies and ECT can sometimes be damaging. But problems are not limited to biological interventions. Talking about your problems with a therapist may sound pretty harmless, but studies indicate that insight therapies can also backfire (Lambert, 2013; Lilienfeld, 2007). Although a great many talented therapists are available, psychotherapy, like any other profession, has mediocre and incompetent practitioners, as well. Therefore, you should shop for a skilled therapist, just as you would for a good attorney or a good mechanic.

In this Application, we'll go over some information that should be helpful if you ever have to look for a therapist for yourself or for a friend or family member (based on Beutler, Bongar, & Shurkin, 2001; Ehrenberg & Ehrenberg, 1994; Pittman, 1994; Zimmerman & Strouse, 2002).

Where Do You Find Therapeutic Services?

Psychotherapy can be found in a variety of settings. Contrary to general belief, most therapists are not in private practice. Many work in institutional settings, such as community mental health centers, hospitals, and human service agencies. The principal sources of therapeutic services are described in **Table 15.2**. The exact collection of therapeutic services available varies from one community to another. To find out what your community has to offer, it is a good idea to conduct an online search or consult your friends, your local phonebook, or your local community mental health center.

Is the Therapist's Profession or Gender Important?

Psychotherapists may be trained in psychology, psychiatry, social work, counseling, psychiatric nursing, or marriage and family therapy. Researchers have *not* found any reliable associations between therapists' professional background and therapeutic efficacy (Beutler et al., 2004). This is probably because many talented therapists can be found in all of these professions. Thus, the type of degree a

Finding the right therapist is no easy task. You need to take into account the therapist's training and orientation, fees charged, and personality. An initial visit should give you a good idea of what a particular therapist is like.

TABLE 15.2 Principal Sources of Therapeutic Services

Source	Comments
Private practitioners	Self-employed therapists are listed in the Yellow Pages under their professional category, such as psychologists or psychiatrists. Private practitioners tend to be relatively expensive, but they also tend to be highly experienced therapists.
Community mental health centers	Community mental health centers have salaried psychologists, psychiatrists, and social workers on staff. The centers provide a variety of services and often have staff available on weekends and at night to deal with emergencies.
Hospitals	Several kinds of hospitals provide therapeutic services. There are both public and private mental hospitals that specialize in the care of people with psychological disorders. Many general hospitals have a psychiatric ward, and those that do not usually have psychiatrists and psychologists on staff and on call. Although hospitals tend to concentrate on in-patient treatment, many provide outpatient therapy as well.
Human service agencies	Various social service agencies employ therapists to provide short-term counseling. Depending on your community, you may find agencies that deal with family problems, juvenile problems, drug problems, and so forth.
Schools and workplaces	Most high schools and colleges have counseling centers where students can get help with personal problems. Similarly, some large businesses offer in-house counseling to their employees.

therapist holds doesn't need to be a crucial consideration in your selection process. It *is* true that currently only psychiatrists can prescribe drugs in most states. However, critics argue that many psychiatrists are too quick to use drugs to solve problems (Breggin, 2008; Whitaker, 2009). In any case, other types of therapists can refer you to a psychiatrist if they think drug therapy would be helpful.

Whether a therapist's gender is important depends on your attitude (Nadelson, Notman, & McCarthy, 2005). If *you* feel that the therapist's gender is important, then for you it is. The therapeutic relationship must be characterized by trust and rapport. Feeling uncomfortable with a therapist of one gender or the other could inhibit the therapeutic process. Thus, you should feel free to look for a male or female therapist if you prefer to do so.

Is Treatment Always Expensive?

Psychotherapy does not have to be prohibitively expensive. Private practitioners tend to be the most expensive, charging between $75 and $150 per (50-minute) hour. These fees may seem high, but they are in line with those of similar professionals, such as

dentists and attorneys. Community mental health centers and social service agencies are usually supported by tax dollars. Consequently, they can charge lower fees than most therapists in private practice. Many of these organizations use a sliding scale, so that clients are charged according to how much they can afford to pay. Thus, most communities have inexpensive opportunities for treatment. Moreover, many health insurance plans provide at least partial reimbursement for the cost of psychotherapy.

Is the Therapist's Theoretical Approach Important?

Logically, you might expect that the diverse approaches to therapy would vary in effectiveness. For the most part, that is *not* what researchers find. After reviewing many studies of therapeutic efficacy, Jerome Frank (1961) and Lester Luborsky and his colleagues (1975) both quote the dodo bird who has just judged a race in *Alice in Wonderland:* "Everybody has won, and *all* must have prizes." Improvement rates for various theoretical orientations usually come out pretty close in most studies (Lambert, 2013; Laska et al., 2014; see **Figure 15.14**).

However, these findings are a little misleading because these estimates of overall effectiveness have been averaged across many types of patients and many types of problems. Many experts seem to think that *for certain types of problems, some approaches to therapy are more*

Therapy is both a science and an art. It is scientific in that practitioners are guided in their work by a huge body of empirical research. It is an art in that therapists often have to be creative in adapting their treatment procedures to individual patients and their idiosyncrasies.

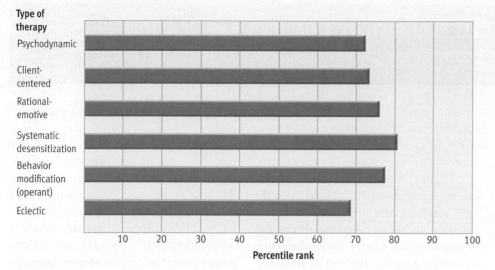

FIGURE 15.14

Estimates of the effectiveness of various approaches to psychotherapy. Smith and Glass (1977) reviewed nearly 400 studies in which clients who were treated with a specific type of therapy were compared with a control group made up of individuals with similar problems who went untreated. The bars indicate the percentile rank (on outcome measures) attained by the average client treated with each type of therapy when compared with control subjects. The higher the percentile, the more effective the therapy was. As you can see, the various approaches were fairly similar in their overall effectiveness.

SOURCE: Adapted from Smith, M. L., & Glass, G. V. (1977). Meta-analysis of psychotherapy outcome series. *American Psychologist, 32,* 752–760. Copyright © 1977 by the American Psychological Association. Adapted by permission of the author.

effective than others (Beutler, 2002; Barlow et al., 2013; Hofmann & Barlow, 2014). It is also important to point out that the finding that different approaches to therapy are roughly equal in overall efficacy does not mean all *therapists* are created equal. Some therapists unquestionably are more effective than others, and the differences can be sizable (Baldwin & Imel, 2013; Castonguay et al., 2013). However, these variations in effectiveness appear to depend on individual therapists' personal skills rather than on their theoretical orientation (Beutler et al., 2004). Good, bad, and mediocre therapists are found within each school of thought.

The key point is that effective therapy requires skill and creativity. Arnold Lazarus (1987, p. 167), who devised multimodal therapy, emphasizes that therapists "straddle the fence between science and art." Therapy is scientific in that interventions are based on extensive theory and empirical research (Forsyth & Strong, 1986). Ultimately, though, each client is a unique human being, and the therapist has to creatively fashion a treatment program that will help that individual (Goodheart, 2006).

What Is Therapy Like?

It is important to have realistic expectations about therapy. Otherwise, you may be unnecessarily disappointed. Some people expect miracles. They expect to turn their life around quickly with little effort. Others expect their therapist to run their lives for them. These are unrealistic expectations.

Therapy usually is a slow process. Your problems are not likely to melt away quickly. Moreover, therapy is hard work, and your therapist is only a facilitator. Ultimately, you have to confront the challenge of changing your behavior, your patterns of thinking, your feelings, or your personality. This process may not be pleasant. You may have to face painful truths about yourself. As Ehrenberg and Ehrenberg (1994, p. 5) point out, "Psychotherapy takes time, effort, and courage."

15.9

Key Learning Goals
- Understand how placebo effects and regression toward the mean can complicate the evaluation of therapy.

15.9 CRITICAL THINKING APPLICATION
From Crisis to Wellness—But Was It the Therapy?

It often happens that problems seem to go from bad to worse. The trigger could be severe pressures at work, an emotional fight with your spouse, or a child's unruly behavior spiraling out of control. At some point, you recognize that it might be wise to seek professional assistance from a therapist, but where do you turn? If you are like most people, you will probably hesitate before actively seeking professional help. People hesitate because therapy carries a stigma, because the task of finding a therapist is daunting, and because they hope their psychological problems will clear up on their own—which *does* happen with some regularity. When people finally decide to pursue mental health care, it is often because they feel they have reached rock bottom in terms of their functioning and have no choice. Motivated by their crisis, they enter into treatment, looking for a ray of hope. Will therapy help them feel better?

It may surprise you to learn that the answer *generally* is yes, even if the professional treatment itself was utterly worthless. People entering therapy are likely to get better, regardless of whether their treatment is effective, for two major reasons: placebo effects and regression toward the mean. **Placebo effects occur when people's expectations lead them to experience some change even though they receive a fake treatment** (such as getting a sugar pill instead of a real drug). Clients generally enter therapy with expectations that it will have positive effects, and as we have emphasized throughout this text, *people have a remarkable tendency to see what they expect to see.* Because of this factor, studies of the efficacy of medical drugs usually include a placebo condition in which subjects are given fake medication (see Chapter 2). Researchers are often surprised by just how much the placebo subjects improve (Fisher & Greenberg, 1997; Walsh et al., 2002).

Placebo effects can be powerful and should be taken into consideration whenever efforts are made to evaluate the efficacy of an approach to treatment.

The other factor at work is the main focus in this Application. It is an interesting statistical phenomenon we have not discussed previously. *Regression toward the mean* **occurs when people who score extremely high or low on a trait are measured a second time, and their new scores fall closer to the mean (average).** Regression effects work in both directions. On the second measurement, high scorers tend to fall back toward the mean, and low scorers tend to creep upward toward the mean. For example, let's say we wanted to evaluate the effectiveness of a 1-day coaching program intended to improve performance on the SAT test. We reason that coaching is most likely to help students who have performed poorly on the test. So, we recruit a sample of high school students who have previously scored in the bottom 20% on the SAT. Thanks to regression toward the mean, most of these students will score higher if they take the SAT a second time, so our coaching program may *look* effective even if it has no value. By the way, if we set out to see whether our coaching program could increase the performance of high scorers, regression effects would be working *against* us. The processes underlying regression toward the mean are complex matters of probability, but they can be understood through a simple principle: if you are near the bottom, you have almost nowhere to go but up, and if you are near the top, you have almost nowhere to go but down.

What does all of this have to do with the effects of professional treatment for psychological problems and disorders? Well, recall that most people enter psychotherapy during a time of severe crisis, when they are at a really low point in their lives. If you measure the mental health

of a group of people entering therapy, most will get relatively low scores. If you measure their mental health again a few months later, chances are that most of them will score higher—with or without therapy—because of regression toward the mean. This is not a matter of idle speculation. In studies of therapeutic efficacy, data on *untreated (control group) subjects* demonstrate that poor scores on measures of mental health regress toward the mean when participants are assessed a second time (Flett, Vredenburg, & Krames, 1995; Hsu, 1995).

Does the fact that most people will get better even without therapy mean there is no sound evidence that psychotherapy works? No. Regression effects, along with placebo effects, do create major headaches for researchers evaluating the efficacy of various therapies, but these problems *can* be neutralized. Control groups, random assignment, placebo conditions, and statistical adjustments can be used to control for regression and placebo effects, as well as for other threats to validity. As discussed in the main body of the chapter, researchers have accumulated rigorous evidence that most approaches to therapy have efficacy. However, our discussion of placebo and regression effects shows you some of the complexities that make this type of research far more complicated than might be anticipated.

Recognizing how regression toward the mean can occur in a variety of contexts is an important critical thinking skill, so let's look at some additional examples. Think about an outstanding young pro baseball player who has a fabulous first season and is named Rookie of the Year. Statistically speaking, our Rookie of the Year is likely to perform well above average the next year, but not as well as he did in his first year. If you are a sports fan, you may recognize this pattern as the "sophomore slump," which is often blamed on an athlete's

© Mangostock/Shutterstock.com

Placebo effects and regression toward the mean are two prominent factors that make it difficult to evaluate the efficacy of various approaches to therapy.

Tony Freeman/PhotoEdit

Placebo effects and regression toward the mean can help explain why phony, worthless treatments can have sincere supporters who really believe that the bogus interventions are effective.

personality or motivation ("He got lazy," or "He got cocky"), when it may just reflect regression toward the mean. Of course, sometimes the Rookie of the Year performs even better during his second year. Thus, our baseball example can be used to emphasize an important point. Regression toward the mean is not an inevitability. It is a statistical tendency that predicts what will happen far more often than not, but it is merely a matter of probability.

People who do not understand regression toward the mean can make some interesting mistakes in their efforts to improve task performance. For instance,

Kahneman and Tversky (1973) worked with Israeli flight instructors who, logically enough, praised students when they handled a difficult maneuver well and criticized students when they exhibited poor performance. Because of regression toward the mean, the students' performance tended to decline after they earned praise for good work and to improve after they earned criticism for bad work. Taking note of this trend, the flight instructors erroneously concluded that praise led to poorer performance and criticism led to improved performance—until the concept of regression toward the mean was explained to them.

Let's return to the world of therapy for one last thought about the significance of both regression and placebo effects. Over the years, a host of quacks, charlatans, con artists, herbalists, and faith healers have marketed an endless array of worthless treatments for both psychological problems and physical maladies. In many instances, people who have been treated with these phony therapies have expressed satisfaction or even praise and gratitude. People are often puzzled by glowing testimonials for treatments they believe to be worthless. Well, you now have two explanations for why people can honestly believe they have derived great benefit from harebrained, bogus treatments: placebo effects and regression effects. The people who provide testimonials for worthless treatments may have experienced *genuine* improvements in their conditions, but those improvements may have been the result of placebo effects or regression toward the mean. Placebo and regression effects add to the many reasons you should always be skeptical about anecdotal evidence. And they help explain why charlatans can be so successful and why ineffective treatments can have sincere proponents.

TABLE 15.3 Critical Thinking Skills Discussed in This Application

Skill	Description
Recognizing situations in which placebo effects might occur	The critical thinker understands that if people have expectations that a treatment will produce a certain effect, they may experience that effect even if the treatment was fake or ineffectual.
Recognizing situations in which regression toward the mean may occur	The critical thinker understands that when people are selected for their extremely high or low scores on some trait, their subsequent scores will probably fall closer to the mean.
Recognizing the limitations of anecdotal evidence	The critical thinker is wary of anecdotal evidence, which consists of personal stories used to support one's assertions. Anecdotal evidence tends to be unrepresentative, inaccurate, and unreliable.

CHAPTER 15 CONCEPT CHART

ELEMENTS OF TREATMENT

Treatment approaches

Insight therapies involve verbal interactions intended to enhance clients' self-knowledge and thus promote healthful changes.

Behavior therapies involve the application of the principles of learning and conditioning to direct efforts to change clients' maladaptive behaviors.

Biomedical therapies are physiological interventions intended to reduce symptoms associated with psychological disorders.

INSIGHT THERAPIES

Psychoanalysis

- Freud believed that neuroses are caused by *unconscious conflicts* regarding sex and aggression left over from childhood.
- In psychoanalysis, *dream analysis* and *free association* are used to explore the unconscious.
- When an analyst's interpretations touch on sensitive issues, *resistance* can be expected.
- The *transference* relationship can be used to overcome resistance and promote insight.
- Classical psychoanalysis is not widely practiced today, but a diverse array of psychodynamic therapies remain in use.

Client-centered therapy

- According to Rogers, neurotic anxieties are due to *incongruence* between one's self-concept and reality.
- Rogers maintained that the *process* of therapy is not as crucial as the therapeutic *climate*.
- To create a healthy climate, therapists must be genuine and provide unconditional positive regard and empathy.
- The key process at work in client-centered therapy is the *clarification* of clients' feelings.

Group therapy

- Most insight therapies can be conducted on a group basis, which involves the simultaneous treatment of several or more clients.
- In group therapy, participants essentially function as therapists for one another as they share experiences, coping strategies, and support.
- Group therapists usually play a subtle role, staying in the background and working to promote group cohesiveness and supportive interactions.

Couples and family therapy

- *Couples*, or *marital*, *therapy* involves the treatment of both partners in a committed, intimate relationship, focusing on relationship issues.
- *Family therapy* involves the treatment of a family unit as a whole, focusing on family dynamics and communication.
- Marital and family therapists seek to understand the entrenched patterns of interaction that produce distress for their clients.

BEHAVIOR THERAPIES

General principles

- Behaviorists assume that even pathological behavior is a product of learning and that what has been learned can be unlearned.
- In behavior therapy, different procedures are used for different types of clinical problems.

Systematic desensitization and exposure therapies

- Wolpe's *systematic desensitization*, a treatment for phobias, involves the construction of an anxiety hierarchy, relaxation training, and movement through the hierarchy pairing relaxation with each phobic stimulus.
- In *exposure therapies*, clients are confronted with situations they fear so they learn that these situations are really harmless.
- Exposure therapy can be conducted with virtual reality presentations.

Social skills training

- Many psychological problems grow out of interpersonal difficulties attributable to deficits in social skills.
- *Social skills training* is designed to improve clients' interpersonal interactions through modeling, behavioral rehearsal, and shaping.

Cognitive-behavioral treatments

- Cognitive-behavioral treatments combine verbal interventions and behavior modification techniques to help clients change maladaptive patterns of thinking.
- *Cognitive therapy* was devised by Aaron Beck as a treatment for depression, but is now used for a variety of disorders.
- Beck asserts that most disorders are caused by irrational, rigid, negative thinking.

Evaluating behavior therapies

- There has been extensive research on the effectiveness of various behavior therapies.
- Favorable evidence exists for the efficacy of most of the widely used behavioral interventions.

Evaluating insight therapies

- Evaluating the effectiveness of any approach to treatment is extremely complicated and subjective.
- Hundreds of outcome studies collectively suggest that insight therapy is superior to placebo treatment and that the beneficial effects of therapy are reasonably durable.
- Many theorists believe that common factors account for much of the improvement seen in insight therapies.

Clients

- Clients bring a wide variety of problems to therapy and do not necessarily have a disorder.

- The likelihood of receiving treatment is greater among women, whites, those who are well-educated, and those who have insurance.

- People vary in their willingness to seek therapy, and many who need therapy don't receive it.

Therapists

- *Clinical* and *counseling psychologists* specialize in the diagnosis and treatment of mental disorders and everyday problems.

- *Psychiatrists* are physicians who specialize in the diagnosis and treatment of mental disorders.

- *Psychiatric social workers, psychiatric nurses, counselors,* and *marriage and family therapists* also provide psychotherapy services.

© Phase4Photography/Shutterstock.com

BIOMEDICAL THERAPIES

Drug treatments

- *Antianxiety drugs*, which are used to relieve nervousness, are effective in the short term.

- *Antipsychotic drugs* can gradually reduce psychotic symptoms, but they have many unpleasant side effects.

- *Antidepressant drugs* can gradually relieve episodes of depression, but even the newer SSRIs are not free of side effects.

- *Mood stabilizers*, such as lithium, can help to prevent future episodes of both mania and depression in bipolar patients.

- Drug therapies can lead to impressive positive effects, but critics worry that drugs produce short-lived gains, are overprescribed, and more dangerous than widely appreciated.

- Critics also argue that conflicts of interest are a pervasive problem in research on new medications, leading to overestimates of drugs' efficacy and underestimates of their negative side effects.

ECT

- In *electroconvulsive therapy (ECT)*, electric shock is used to produce a cortical seizure and convulsions, which are believed to be beneficial in the treatment of depression.

- Proponents of ECT maintain that it is a very effective treatment, but critics have raised doubts, and its use has declined.

- Memory losses are a short-term side effect of ECT, but there is debate about whether ECT carries significant long-term risks.

CURRENT ISSUES IN TREATMENT

- The culture-bound origins of Western therapies have raised doubts about their applicability to other cultures and even to ethnic groups in Western societies.

- Ethnic minorities in America underutilize mental health services because of cultural distrust, language difficulties, and institutional barriers.

- Clinicians are increasingly attempting to harness technology to expand the delivery of mental health services and to reduce the costs of therapy.

- Combinations of insight, behavioral, and biomedical therapies are often used fruitfully in treatment.

INSTITUTIONAL TREATMENT IN TRANSITION

- Disenchantment with traditional mental hospitals led to the *community mental health movement*, which advocates local, community-based care and prevention of mental disorders.

- *Deinstitutionalization* refers to the transfer of mental health care from inpatient institutions to community-based outpatient facilities.

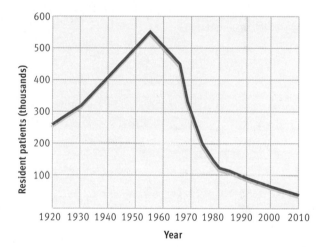

- Deinstitutionalization has worked for some patients, but it has contributed to the *revolving door problem*.

- Deinstitutionalization has also contributed to the growth of homelessness and the increased incidence of mental illness among the homeless.

- It is clear that our society is not providing adequate care for a sizable segment of the mentally ill population, and the situation is only getting worse.

APPLICATIONS

- Therapists' personal skills are more important than their professional degree.

- Various theoretical approaches to therapy appear to be roughly similar in overall effectiveness.

- However, for certain types of problems, some approaches are probably more effective than others.

- Regression toward the mean and placebo effects can help explain why people often are deceived by phony, ineffectual treatments.

PART 1: CHAPTER PRACTICE TESTS

Chapter 1 Practice Test

1. For which of the following is Wilhelm Wundt primarily known?
   A. The establishment of the first formal laboratory for research in psychology
   B. The distinction between mind and body as two separate entities
   C. The discovery of how signals are conducted along nerves in the body
   D. The development of the first formal program for training in psychotherapy

2. Which of the following approaches might William James criticize for examining a movie frame by frame instead of seeing the motion in the motion picture?
   A. Structuralism
   B. Functionalism
   C. Dualism
   D. Humanism

3. Fred, a tennis coach, insists that he can make any reasonably healthy individual into an internationally competitive tennis player. Fred is echoing the thoughts of:
   A. Sigmund Freud.
   B. John B. Watson.
   C. Abraham Maslow.
   D. William James.

4. Which of the following is a statement with which Skinner's followers would agree?
   A. The whole is greater than the sum of its parts.
   B. The goal of behavior is self-actualization.
   C. Nature is more influential than nurture.
   D. Free will is an illusion.

5. Which of the following approaches has the most optimistic view of human nature?
   A. Humanism   C. Psychoanalysis
   B. Behaviorism   D. Structuralism

6. Which of the following historical events created a demand for clinicians that was far greater than the supply?
   A. World War I   C. World War II
   B. The Depression   D. The Korean War

7. _____ psychology examines behavioral processes in terms of their adaptive value for a species over the course of many generations.
   A. Clinical   C. Evolutionary
   B. Cognitive   D. Physiological

8. The study of the endocrine system and genetic mechanisms would most likely be undertaken by a:
   A. clinical psychologist.
   B. physiological psychologist.
   C. social psychologist.
   D. educational psychologist.

9. A multifactorial causation approach to behavior suggests that:
   A. most behaviors can be explained best by single-cause explanations.
   B. most behavior is governed by a complex network of interrelated factors.
   C. data need to be analyzed by the statistical technique called factor analysis for the data to make sense.
   D. explanations of behavior tend to build up from the simple to the complex in a hierarchical manner.

10. Psychology's answer to the question of whether we are "born" or "made" tends to be that:
    A. we are "born."
    B. we are "made."
    C. we are both "born" and "made."
    D. neither is correct.

11. A good reason for taking notes in your own words, rather than verbatim, is that:
    A. most lecturers are quite wordy.
    B. "translating" on the spot is good mental exercise.
    C. it reduces the likelihood that you'll later engage in plagiarism.
    D. it forces you to assimilate the information in a way that makes sense to you.

12. Critical thinking skills:
    A. are abstract abilities that cannot be identified.
    B. usually develop spontaneously through normal content instruction.
    C. usually develop spontaneously without any instruction.
    D. need to be deliberately taught because they often do not develop by themselves with standard content instruction.

Answers

1.	A	pp. 3–4	7.	C	p. 14
2.	A	pp. 4–5	8.	B	p. 17
3.	B	pp. 7–8	9.	B	pp. 20–21
4.	D	pp. 8–9	10.	C	p. 22
5.	A	pp. 10–11	11.	D	p. 25
6.	C	p. 12	12.	D	p. 26

Chapter 2 Practice Test

1. Theories permit researchers to move from:
   A. understanding to application.
   B. concept to description.
   C. application to control.
   D. description to understanding.

2. Researchers must describe the actions that will be taken to measure or control each variable in their studies. In other words, they must:
   A. provide operational definitions of their variables.
   B. decide whether their studies will be experimental or correlational.
   C. use statistics to summarize their findings.
   D. decide how many subjects should participate in their studies.

3. A researcher found that clients who were randomly assigned to same-sex groups participated more in group therapy sessions than clients who were randomly assigned to coed groups. In this experiment, the independent variable was:
   A. the amount of participation in the group therapy sessions.
   B. whether or not the group was same-sex or coed.
   C. the clients' attitudes toward group therapy.
   D. how much the clients' mental health improved.

4. In a study of the effect of a new teaching technique on students' achievement test scores, an important extraneous variable would be the students':
   A. hair color.
   B. athletic skills.
   C. IQ scores.
   D. sociability.

5. Whenever you have a cold, you rest in bed, take aspirin, and drink plenty of fluids. You can't determine which remedy is most effective because of which of the following problems?
   A. Sampling bias
   B. Distorted self-report data
   C. Confounding of variables
   D. Experimenter bias

6. Which of the following correlation coefficients would indicate the strongest relationship between two variables?
   A. .58
   B. .19
   C. −.97
   D. −.05

7. A psychologist monitors a group of nursery school children during the school day, recording each instance of helping behavior as it occurs, without any intervention. The psychologist is using:
   A. the experimental method.
   B. naturalistic observation.
   C. case studies.
   D. the survey method.

8. Among the advantages of descriptive/correlational research is (are):
   A. it can often be used in circumstances in which an experiment would be unethical or impossible.
   B. it permits researchers to examine subjects' behavior in natural, real-world circumstances.
   C. it can demonstrate conclusively that two variables are causally related.
   D. both A and B.

9. Sampling bias exists when:
   A. the sample is representative of the population.
   B. the sample is not representative of the population.
   C. two variables are confounded.
   D. the effect of the independent variable can't be isolated.

10. Critics of deception in research have assumed that deceptive studies are harmful to subjects. The empirical data on this issue suggest that:
    A. many deceptive studies do have significant negative effects on subjects.
    B. most participants in deceptive studies report that they enjoyed the experience and didn't mind being misled.
    C. deceptive research seriously undermines subjects' trust in others.
    D. both A and C.

11. Which of the following would *not* be included in the results section of a journal article?
    A. Descriptive statistics summarizing the data
    B. Statistical analysis of the data
    C. Graphs and/or tables presenting the data pictorially
    D. Interpretation, evaluation, and implications of the data

12. Anecdotal evidence:
    A. is often concrete, vivid, and memorable.
    B. tends to influence people.
    C. is fundamentally flawed and unreliable.
    D. is all of the above.

Answers

1. D   p. 32
2. A   p. 33
3. B   pp. 37–38
4. C   pp. 39–40
5. C   p. 39
6. C   p. 43
7. B   p. 45
8. D   p. 48
9. B   p. 49
10. B   p. 53
11. D   p. 59
12. D   pp. 60–61

Chapter 3 Practice Test

1. A neural impulse is initiated when a neuron's charge momentarily becomes less negative, or even positive. This event is called:
   A. an action potential.
   B. a resting potential.
   C. impulse facilitation.
   D. neuromodulation.

2. Neurons convey information about the strength of stimuli by varying:
   A. the size of their action potentials.
   B. the speed of their action potentials.
   C. the rate at which they fire action potentials.
   D. all of the above.

3. Alterations in activity at dopamine synapses have been implicated in the development of:
   A. anxiety.
   B. schizophrenia.
   C. Alzheimer's disease.
   D. nicotine addiction.

4. Jim has just barely avoided a head-on collision on a narrow road. With heart pounding, hands shaking, and body perspiring, Jim recognizes that these are signs of the body's fight-or-flight response, which is controlled by the:
   A. empathetic division of the peripheral nervous system.
   B. parasympathetic division of the autonomic nervous system.
   C. somatic division of the peripheral nervous system.
   D. sympathetic division of the autonomic nervous system.

5. The thalamus can be characterized as:
   A. a regulatory mechanism.
   B. the consciousness switch of the brain.
   C. a relay station.
   D. a bridge between the two cerebral hemispheres.

6. The _____ lobe is to hearing what the occipital lobe is to vision.
   A. frontal
   B. temporal
   C. parietal
   D. cerebellar

7. The scientist who won a Nobel Prize for his work with split-brain patients is:
   A. Walter Cannon.
   B. Paul Broca.
   C. Roger Sperry.
   D. James Olds.

8. In people whose corpus callosums have not been severed, verbal stimuli are identified more quickly and more accurately:
   A. when sent to the right hemisphere first.
   B. when sent to the left hemisphere first.
   C. when presented to the left visual field.
   D. when presented auditorally rather than visually.

9. Hormones are to the endocrine system what _____ are to the nervous system.
   A. nerves
   B. synapses
   C. neurotransmitters
   D. action potentials

10. Adopted children's similarity to their biological parents is generally attributed to _____; adopted children's similarity to their adoptive parents is generally attributed to _____.
    A. heredity; the environment
    B. the environment; heredity
    C. the environment; the environment
    D. heredity; heredity

11. In evolutionary theory, *fitness* refers to:
    A. the ability to survive.
    B. the ability to adapt to environmental demands.
    C. reproductive success.
    D. the physical skills necessary for survival.

12. For which of the following assertions is the empirical evidence strongest?
    A. The two cerebral hemispheres are specialized to handle different types of cognitive tasks.
    B. Schools should be reformed to better educate the right hemisphere.
    C. Each hemisphere has its own cognitive style.
    D. Some people are right-brained, while others are left-brained.

Answers

1. A   p. 68
2. C   pp. 68–69
3. B   pp. 71, 73
4. D   p. 76
5. C   pp. 79, 81
6. B   pp. 82–83
7. C   p. 86
8. B   pp. 88–89
9. C   p. 89
10. A   pp. 93–94
11. C   p. 96
12. A   pp. 100–101

Chapter 4 Practice Test

1. The term used to refer to the stimulation of the sense organs is:
   A. sensation.
   B. perception.
   C. transduction.
   D. adaptation.

2. Perception of the brightness of a color is affected mainly by:
   A. the wavelength of light waves.
   B. the amplitude of light waves.
   C. the purity of light waves.
   D. the saturation of light waves.

3. In farsightedness:
   A. close objects are seen clearly, but distant objects appear blurry.
   B. the focus of light from close objects falls behind the retina.
   C. the focus of light from distant objects falls a little short of the retina.
   D. both A and B occur.
   E. both A and C occur.

4. The collection of rod and cone receptors that funnel signals to a particular visual cell in the retina make up that cell's:
   A. blind spot.
   B. optic disk.
   C. opponent process field.
   D. receptive field.

5. The primary visual cortex is located in the:
   A. occipital lobe.
   B. temporal lobe.
   C. parietal lobe.
   D. frontal lobe.

6. Which theory would predict that the American flag has a green, black, and yellow afterimage?
   A. Subtractive color mixing
   B. Opponent process theory
   C. Additive color mixing
   D. Trichromatic theory

7. A readiness to perceive a stimulus in a particular way is referred to as (a):
   A. Gestalt.
   B. feature analysis.
   C. perceptual set.
   D. congruence.

8. In a painting, train tracks may look as if they go off into the distance because the artist draws the tracks as converging lines, a monocular cue to depth known as:
   A. interposition.
   B. texture gradient.
   C. relative size.
   D. linear perspective.

9. Perception of pitch can best be explained by:
   A. place theory.
   B. frequency theory.
   C. both A and B.
   D. none of the above.

10. In what way(s) is the sense of taste like the sense of smell?
    A. There are four primary stimulus groups for both senses.
    B. Both systems are routed through the thalamus on the way to the cortex.
    C. The physical stimuli for both senses are chemical substances dissolved in fluid.
    D. All of the above.
    E. None of the above.

11. The fact that theories originally seen as being incompatible, such as the trichromatic and opponent process theories of color vision, are now seen as both being necessary to explain sensory processes illustrates:
    A. that psychology evolves in a sociohistorical context.
    B. the subjectivity of experience.
    C. the value of psychology's theoretical diversity.
    D. the nature-nurture controversy.

12. In the study by Kenrick and Gutierres (1980), exposing male subjects to a TV show dominated by extremely beautiful women:
    A. had no effect on their ratings of the attractiveness of a prospective date.
    B. increased their ratings of the attractiveness of a prospective date.
    C. decreased their ratings of the attractiveness of a prospective date.
    D. decreased their ratings of their own attractiveness.

Answers

1. A   p. 107
2. B   p. 108
3. B   p. 110
4. D   p. 112
5. A   pp. 113–114
6. B   pp. 116–117
7. C   p. 118
8. D   p. 123
9. C   pp.130–131
10. C   pp. 133–134
11. C   pp. 138–139
12. C   p. 143

Chapter 5 Practice Test

1. An EEG would indicate primarily _____ activity while you take this test.
   A. alpha
   B. beta
   C. delta
   D. theta

2. Readjusting your biological clock would be most difficult under which of the following circumstances?
   A. Flying west from New York to Los Angeles
   B. Flying north from Miami to New York
   C. Flying east from Los Angeles to New York
   D. Flying south from New York to Miami

3. As the sleep cycle evolves through the night, people tend to:
   A. spend more time in REM sleep and less time in non-REM sleep.
   B. spend more time in non-REM sleep and less time in REM sleep.
   C. spend a more or less equal amount of time in REM sleep and non-REM sleep.
   D. spend more time in slow-wave sleep and less time in REM sleep.

4. Newborn infants spend about _____ % of their sleep time in REM, and adults spend about _____ % of their sleep time in REM.
   A. 20; 50
   B. 50; 20
   C. 20; 20
   D. 50; 50

5. After being selectively deprived of REM sleep, people typically experience:
   A. hypochondriasis.
   B. non-REM dysfunction.
   C. emotional breakdowns.
   D. a temporary increase in time spent in REM.

6. Which of the following is *not* true of sleeping pills?
   A. Sleeping pills are an excellent long-range solution for all types of insomnia.
   B. There is some danger of overdose.
   C. Sleeping pills can make people sluggish and drowsy the next day.
   D. Use of sleeping pills is associated with elevated mortality.

7. The activation-synthesis theory of dreaming contends that:
   A. dreams are simply the by-product of bursts of activity in the brain.
   B. dreams provide an outlet for energy invested in socially undesirable impulses.
   C. dreams represent the brain's attempt to purge information taken in during waking hours.
   D. dreams are an attempt to restore a neurotransmitter balance within the brain.

8. A common driving experience is "highway hypnosis," in which one's consciousness seems to be divided between the driving itself and one's conscious train of thought. This phenomenon has been cited to support the idea that hypnosis is:
   A. an exercise in role playing.
   B. a dissociated state of consciousness.
   C. a goal-directed fantasy.
   D. not an altered state of consciousness.

9. Amphetamines work by increasing activity at _____ synapses in a variety of ways.
   A. GABA and glycine
   B. serotonin and dopamine
   C. acetylcholine
   D. norepinephrine and dopamine

10. Which of the following drugs would be most likely to result in a fatal overdose?
    A. LSD
    B. Mescaline
    C. Marijuana
    D. Narcotics

11. Which of the following is a true statement about naps?
    A. Daytime naps invariably lead to insomnia.
    B. Daytime naps are invariably refreshing and an efficient way to rest.
    C. Daytime naps are not very efficient ways to sleep, but their effects are variable and they can be beneficial.
    D. Taking many naps during the day can substitute for a full night's sleep.

12. Definitions:
    A. generally emerge out of research.
    B. often have great explanatory value.
    C. generally exert little influence over how people think.
    D. are usually constructed by experts or authorities in a specific field.

Answers

1. B   pp. 148–149
2. C   pp. 150–151
3. A   pp. 152–153
4. B   pp. 154–155
5. D   p. 157
6. A   p. 160
7. A   pp. 164–165
8. B   p. 167
9. D   p. 172
10. D   pp. 172–173
11. C   p. 176
12. D   pp. 178–179

Chapter 6 Practice Test

1. After repeated pairings of a tone with meat powder, Pavlov found that a dog will salivate when the tone is presented. Salivation to the tone is a(n):
   A. unconditioned stimulus.
   B. unconditioned response.
   C. conditioned stimulus.
   D. conditioned response.

2. Sam's wife always wears the same black nightgown whenever she is in the mood for sexual relations. Sam becomes sexually aroused as soon as he sees his wife in the nightgown. For Sam, the nightgown is a(n):
   A. unconditioned stimulus.
   B. unconditioned response.
   C. conditioned stimulus.
   D. conditioned response.

3. Watson and Rayner (1920) conditioned "Little Albert" to fear white rats by banging a hammer on a steel bar as he played with a white rat. Later, it was discovered that Albert feared not only white rats but white stuffed toys and Santa's beard, as well. Albert's fear of these other objects can be attributed to:
   A. shaping.
   B. stimulus generalization.
   C. stimulus discrimination.
   D. an overactive imagination.

4. The phenomenon of higher-order conditioning shows that:
   A. only a genuine, natural US can be used to establish a CR.
   B. auditory stimuli are easier to condition than visual stimuli.
   C. visual stimuli are easier to condition than auditory stimuli.
   D. an already established CS can be used in the place of a natural US.

5. In a Skinner box, the dependent variable is usually:
   A. the force with which the lever is pressed or the disk is pecked.
   B. the schedule of reinforcement used.
   C. the rate of responding.
   D. the speed of the cumulative recorder.

6. A primary reinforcer has _____ reinforcing properties; a secondary reinforcer has _____ reinforcing properties.
   A. biological; acquired
   B. conditioned; unconditioned
   C. weak; potent
   D. immediate; delayed

7. The steady, rapid responding of a person playing a slot machine is an example of the pattern of responding typically generated on a _____ schedule of reinforcement.
   A. fixed-ratio
   B. variable-ratio
   C. fixed-interval
   D. variable-interval

8. Positive reinforcement _____ the rate of responding; negative reinforcement _____ the rate of responding.
   A. increases; decreases
   B. decreases; increases
   C. increases; increases
   D. decreases; decreases

9. Research on avoidance learning suggests that conditioned fear acquired through _____ conditioning plays a key role.
   A. classical
   B. operant
   C. reinforcement
   D. intermittent

10. The studies by Garcia and his colleagues demonstrate that rats easily learn to associate a taste CS with a(n) _____ US.
    A. shock
    B. visual
    C. auditory
    D. nausea-inducing

11. Albert Bandura:
    A. was the first to describe species-specific learning tendencies.
    B. was the founder of behaviorism.
    C. pioneered the study of classical conditioning.
    D. pioneered the study of observational learning.

12. In designing a self-modification program, control of antecedents should be used:
    A. by people who are in poor physical condition.
    B. only when your usual reinforcers are unavailable.
    C. when you want to decrease the frequency of a response.
    D. when you are initially not capable of making the target response.

Answers

1.	D	pp. 185–186	7.	B	pp. 199–201
2.	C	pp. 186–187	8.	C	p. 201
3.	B	pp. 190–191	9.	A	p. 202
4.	D	p. 192	10.	D	pp. 206–207
5.	C	p. 194	11.	D	p. 210
6.	A	p. 198	12.	C	p. 217

Chapter 7 Practice Test

1. Getting information into memory is called _____; getting information out of memory is called _____.
   A. storage; retrieval
   B. encoding; storage
   C. encoding; retrieval
   D. storage; encoding

2. The word *big* is flashed on a screen. A mental picture of the word *big* represents a _____ code; the definition "large in size" represents a _____ code; "sounds like pig" represents a _____ code.
   A. structural; phonemic; semantic
   B. phonemic; semantic; structural
   C. structural; semantic; phonemic
   D. phonemic; structural; semantic

3. The capacity of short-term memory is:
   A. about 50,000 words.
   B. unlimited.
   C. about 25 stimuli.
   D. thought to be 7 plus or minus 2 chunks of information, although some theorists suggest it may be 4 plus or minus 1 chunks.

4. Which statement best represents current evidence on the durability of long-term storage?
   A. All forgetting involves breakdowns in retrieval.
   B. LTM is like a barrel of marbles in which none of the marbles ever leak out.
   C. There is no convincing evidence that all of one's memories are stored away permanently.
   D. All long-term memories gradually decay at a constant rate.

5. An organized cluster of knowledge about a particular object or sequence of events is called a:
   A. semantic network.
   B. conceptual hierarchy.
   C. schema.
   D. retrieval cue.

6. The tip-of-the-tongue phenomenon:
   A. is a temporary inability to remember something you know, accompanied by a feeling that it's just out of reach.
   B. is clearly due to a failure in retrieval.
   C. reflects a permanent loss of information from LTM.
   D. is both A and B.

7. Loftus's work on eyewitness testimony demonstrated that:
   A. memory errors are surprisingly infrequent.
   B. memory errors are mainly due to repression.
   C. information given after an event can alter a person's memory of the event.
   D. information given after an event cannot alter a person's memory of the event.

8. If decay theory is correct:
   A. information can never be permanently lost from long-term memory.
   B. forgetting is simply a case of retrieval failure.
   C. the principal cause of forgetting should be the passage of time.
   D. all of the above.

9. Amnesia in which people lose memories for events that occurred prior to their injury is called _____ amnesia.
   A. anterograde
   B. retrospective
   C. retrograde
   D. episodic

10. Your knowledge that birds fly, that the sun rises in the east, and that 2 + 2 = 4 is contained in your _____ memory.
    A. episodic
    B. procedural
    C. implicit
    D. semantic

11. Dorothy memorized her shopping list. When she got to the store, however, she found she had forgotten many of the items from the middle of the list. This is an example of:
    A. inappropriate encoding.
    B. retrograde amnesia.
    C. proactive interference.
    D. the serial-position effect.

12. The tendency to mold one's interpretation of the past to fit how events actually turned out is called:
    A. the overconfidence effect.
    B. selective amnesia.
    C. retroactive interference.
    D. the hindsight bias.

Answers

1. C   pp. 223–224
2. C   pp. 225–226
3. D   p. 229
4. C   p. 232
5. C   p. 233
6. D   p. 235
7. C   pp. 236–237
8. C   p. 240
9. C   p. 245
10. D   p. 250
11. D   p. 253
12. D   p. 256

Chapter 8 Practice Test

1. Chomsky proposed that children learn language swiftly:
   A. because they possess an innate language acquisition device.
   B. through imitation, reinforcement, and shaping.
   C. because the quality of their thought improves with age.
   D. because they need to in order to get their increasingly complex needs met.

2. Problems that require a common object to be used in an unusual way may be difficult to solve because of:
   A. mental set.
   B. irrelevant information.
   C. unnecessary constraints.
   D. functional fixedness.

3. The nine-dot problem is:
   A. the basis for the saying "think outside the box."
   B. difficult because people assume constraints that are not part of the problem.
   C. solved through forming subgoals.
   D. both A and B.

4. A heuristic is a:
   A. flash of insight.
   B. guiding principle, or "rule of thumb," used in problem solving or decision making.
   C. methodical procedure for trying all possible solutions to a problem.
   D. way of making a compensatory decision.

5. According to Nisbett, Eastern cultures tend to favor a(n) _____ cognitive style, whereas Western cultures tend to display a(n) _____ cognitive style.
   A. analytic; holistic
   B. holistic; analytic
   C. logical; emotional
   D. emotional; logical

6. The work of Herbert Simon on decision making showed that:
   A. people generally make rational choices that maximize their gains.
   B. people can evaluate an unlimited number of alternatives effectively.
   C. people tend to focus on only a few aspects of their available options and often make "irrational" decisions as a result.
   D. the more options people consider, the better their decisions tend to be.

7. When you estimate the probability of an event by judging the ease with which relevant instances come to mind, you are relying on:
   A. an additive decision-making model.
   B. the representativeness heuristic.
   C. the availability heuristic.
   D. a noncompensatory model.

8. On most modern IQ tests, a score of 115 would be:
   A. about average.
   B. about 15% higher than the average of one's age-mates.
   C. an indication of genius.
   D. one standard deviation above the mean.

9. IQ tests have proven to be good predictors of:
   A. social intelligence.
   B. practical problem-solving intelligence.
   C. school performance.
   D. all of the above.

10. Saying that the heritability of intelligence is 60% would mean that:
    A. 60% of a person's intelligence is due to heredity.
    B. 60% of the variability in intelligence scores in a group is estimated to be due to genetic variations.
    C. intelligence is 40% inherited.
    D. heredity affects intelligence in 60% of the members of the group.

11. According to theories that use the concept of reaction range, the upper limits of an individual's intellectual potential are:
    A. determined during the first year of life.
    B. largely set by heredity.
    C. determined by a person's unique experiences.
    D. determined by one's heritability quotient.

12. The belief that the probability of heads is higher after a long string of tails:
    A. is rational and accurate.
    B. is an example of the "gambler's fallacy."
    C. reflects the influence of the representativeness heuristic.
    D. is both B and C.

Answers

1. A   p. 262
2. D   p. 267
3. D   p. 268
4. B   p. 269
5. B   p. 272
6. C   p. 273
7. C   p. 274
8. D   pp. 279–280
9. C   pp. 281–282
10. B   pp. 285–286
11. B   pp. 288–289
12. D   p. 298

Chapter 9 Practice Test

1. Although Jackson had a huge breakfast and felt stuffed, he ate three of the donuts that a colleague brought to a morning meeting. His behavior is consistent with:
   A. incentive theories of motivation.
   B. drive theories of motivation.
   C. evolutionary theories of motivation.
   D. the Cannon-Bard theory of motivation.

2. Based on modern research, which two areas of the hypothalamus appear to have the most influence in regulating hunger?
   A. Lateral and ventromedial
   B. Arcuate and paraventricular
   C. Ventromedial and arcuate
   D. Lateral and paraventricular

3. Which of the following statements is false?
   A. Insulin is a hormone secreted by the pancreas.
   B. CCK delivers satiety signals to the brain.
   C. Leptin levels correlate with levels of the body's fat stores.
   D. Ghrelin secretions are associated with decreased hunger.

4. Which of the following has *not* been found in research on gender differences in sexual interest?
   A. Men think about sex more than women do.
   B. Men are more likely to view pornography than women are.
   C. Women are more interested in having many partners than men are.
   D. Men are more interested in uncommitted/casual sex than women are.

5. Kinsey maintained that sexual orientation:
   A. depends on early classical conditioning experiences.
   B. should be viewed as a continuum.
   C. depends on normalities and abnormalities in the amygdala.
   D. should be viewed as an either-or distinction.

6. One's need for achievement is usually assessed using the:
   A. McClelland Achievement Inventory.
   B. MMPI.
   C. Thematic Apperception Test.
   D. Atkinson Manifest Needs Scale.

7. A polygraph (lie detector) works by:
   A. monitoring physiological indexes of autonomic arousal.
   B. directly assessing the truthfulness of a person's statements.
   C. monitoring the person's facial expressions.
   D. doing all of the above.

8. Which of the following statements about emotional experience is true?
   A. The facial expressions associated with various emotions vary widely across cultures.
   B. Some basic emotions go unnamed in some cultures.
   C. People can identify eleven fundamental emotions from others' facial expressions.
   D. Display rules do not vary across different cultures.

9. According to the James-Lange theory of emotion:
   A. the experience of emotion depends on autonomic arousal and on one's cognitive interpretation of that arousal.
   B. emotion results from the perception of autonomic arousal.
   C. emotion occurs when the thalamus sends signals simultaneously to the cortex and to the autonomic nervous system.
   D. emotions develop because of their adaptive value.

10. The fact that eating behavior, sexual behavior, and the experience of emotion all depend on interactions between biological and environmental determinants lends evidence to which of the text's organizing themes?
    A. Psychology's theoretical diversity
    B. Psychology's empiricism
    C. People's experience of the world is subjective
    D. The joint influence of biology and environment

11. Which of the following statements is (are) true?
    A. For the most part, people are pretty happy.
    B. Age is largely unrelated to happiness.
    C. Income is only weakly related to happiness.
    D. All of the above.

12. The sales pitch "We're the best dealership in town because the other dealerships just don't stack up against us" is an example of:
    A. a false dichotomy.
    B. semantic slanting.
    C. circular reasoning.
    D. slippery slope.

Answers

1.	A	p. 304	**7.**	A	pp. 322–323
2.	B	p. 306	**8.**	B	pp. 326–327
3.	D	pp. 306–307	**9.**	B	pp. 327–328
4.	C	p. 314	**10.**	D	p. 330
5.	B	pp. 315–316	**11.**	D	pp. 331–332
6.	C	pp. 318–319	**12.**	C	p. 335

Chapter 10 Practice Test

1. The stage of prenatal development during which the developing organism is most vulnerable to injury is the:
   A. zygotic stage.
   B. germinal stage.
   C. fetal stage.
   D. embryonic stage.
2. Developmental norms:
   A. can be used to make extremely precise predictions about the age at which an individual child will reach various developmental milestones.
   B. indicate the maximum age at which a child can reach a particular developmental milestone and still be considered "normal."
   C. indicate the average age at which individuals reach various developmental milestones.
   D. involve both A and B.
3. The behavioral, reinforcement explanation of the basis for infant-caregiver attachment was undermined by the research of:
   A. Erik Erikson.
   B. Harry Harlow.
   C. Lawrence Kohlberg.
   D. Lev Vygotsky.
4. The quality of infant-caregiver attachment depends:
   A. on the quality of bonding in the first few hours of life.
   B. exclusively on the infant's temperament.
   C. on the interaction between the infant's temperament and the caregiver's responsiveness.
   D. on how stranger anxiety is handled.
5. The 2-year-old child who refers to every four-legged animal as "doggie" is making which of the following errors?
   A. Underextension
   B. Overextension
   C. Overregularization
   D. Underregularization
6. During the second year of life, toddlers begin to take some personal responsibility for feeding, dressing, and bathing themselves in an attempt to establish what Erikson calls a sense of:
   A. superiority.
   B. industry.
   C. generativity.
   D. autonomy.
7. Five-year-old David watches as you pour water from a short, wide glass into a tall, narrow one. He says there is now more water than before. This response demonstrates that:
   A. David understands the concept of conservation.
   B. David does not understand the concept of conservation.
   C. David's cognitive development is "behind" for his age.
   D. both B and C are happening.

8. Which of the following is *not* one of the criticisms of Piaget's theory of cognitive development?
   A. Piaget may have underestimated the cognitive skills of children in some areas.
   B. Piaget may have underestimated the influence of cultural factors on cognitive development.
   C. The simultaneous mixing of stages raises questions about the value of analyzing development in terms of stages
   D. Evidence for the theory is based on children's answers to questions.
9. If a child's primary reason for not drawing pictures on the living room wall with crayons is to avoid the punishment that would inevitably follow this behavior, the child would be said to be at which level of moral development?
   A. Conventional
   B. Postconventional
   C. Preconventional
   D. Unconventional
10. Girls who mature _____ and boys who mature _____ feel more subjective distress about the transition of puberty.
    A. early; early
    B. early; late
    C. late; early
    D. late; late
11. Two cognitive areas that may decline at around 60 years of age are:
    A. verbal and math test scores.
    B. cognitive speed and episodic memory.
    C. vocabulary scores and abstract reasoning.
    D. none of the above.
12. Males have been found to differ slightly from females in three well-documented areas of mental abilities. Which of the following is *not* one of these?
    A. Verbal ability
    B. Mathematical ability
    C. Intelligence
    D. Visual-spatial ability

Answers

1. D   pp. 340–341
2. C   p. 345
3. B   p. 346
4. C   p. 347
5. B   p. 349
6. D   pp. 350–351
7. B   pp. 352–353
8. D   pp. 354–355
9. C   pp. 356–357
10. B   p. 359
11. B   pp. 367–368
12. C   p. 370

Chapter 11 Practice Test

1. Harvey Hedonist devoted his life to the search for physical pleasure and immediate need gratification. Freud would say that Harvey is dominated by his:
   A. ego.
   B. superego.
   C. id.
   D. preconscious.

2. Furious at her boss for what she considers to be unjust criticism, Clara turns around and takes out her anger on her subordinates. Clara may be using the defense mechanism of:
   A. displacement.
   B. reaction formation.
   C. identification.
   D. replacement.

3. Freud believed that most personality disturbances are due to:
   A. the failure of parents to reinforce healthy behavior.
   B. a poor self-concept resulting from excessive parental demands.
   C. unconscious and unresolved sexual conflicts rooted in childhood experiences.
   D. the exposure of children to unhealthy role models.

4. According to Alfred Adler, the prime motivating force in a person's life is:
   A. physical gratification.
   B. existential anxiety.
   C. striving for superiority.
   D. the need for power.

5. Which of the following learning mechanisms does B. F. Skinner see as being the major means by which behavior is learned?
   A. Classical conditioning
   B. Operant conditioning
   C. Observational learning
   D. Insight learning

6. Always having been a good student, Irving is confident he will do well in his psychology course. According to Bandura's social cognitive theory, Irving would be said to have:
   A. strong feelings of self-efficacy.
   B. a sense of superiority.
   C. strong feelings of narcissism.
   D. strong defense mechanisms.

7. Which of the following did Carl Rogers believe fosters a congruent self-concept?
   A. Conditional love
   B. Appropriate role models
   C. Immediate need gratification
   D. Unconditional love

8. What need was Abraham Maslow expressing when he said, "What a man can be, he must be"?
   A. The need for superiority
   B. The need for unconditional love
   C. The need for self-actualization
   D. The need to achieve

9. The most convincing evidence for the theory that personality is heavily influenced by genetics is provided by strong personality similarity between:
   A. identical twins reared together.
   B. identical twins reared apart.
   C. fraternal twins reared together.
   D. nontwins reared together.

10. In which of the following cultures is an independent view of the self most likely to be the norm?
    A. China
    B. Japan
    C. Korea
    D. United States

11. Which of the following is *not* a shortcoming of self-report personality inventories?
    A. The accuracy of the results is a function of the honesty of the respondent.
    B. Respondents may attempt to answer in a way that makes them look good.
    C. There is sometimes a problem with "yea-sayers" or "nay-sayers."
    D. They are objective measures.

12. In *The Nurture Assumption,* Judith Harris argues that the evidence indicates that family environment has _____ on children's personalities.
    A. largely positive effects
    B. largely negative effects
    C. surprisingly little effect
    D. a powerful effect

Answers

1. C   pp. 382–383
2. A   p. 385
3. C   p. 388
4. C   p. 389
5. B   pp. 391–392
6. A   p. 393
7. D   p. 395
8. C   p. 397
9. B   p. 400
10. D   pp. 408–409
11. D   p. 412
12. C   p. 414–415

Chapter 12 Practice Test

1. Stereotypes:
   A. reflect normal cognitive processes that frequently are automatic.
   B. are widely held beliefs that people have certain characteristics because of their membership in a particular group.
   C. tend to be broad overgeneralizations that ignore the diversity within social groups.
   D. are all of the above.

2. You believe that short men have a tendency to be insecure. The concept of illusory correlation implies that you will:
   A. overestimate how often you meet short men who are insecure.
   B. underestimate how often you meet short men who are insecure.
   C. overestimate the frequency of short men in the population.
   D. falsely assume that shortness in men causes insecurity.

3. A father suggests that his son's low marks in school are due to the child's laziness. The father has made _____ attribution.
   A. an external
   B. an internal
   C. a situational
   D. a high consensus

4. The fundamental attribution error refers to the tendency of:
   A. observers to favor external attributions in explaining the behavior of others.
   B. observers to favor internal attributions in explaining the behavior of others.
   C. actors to favor external attributions in explaining the behavior of others.
   D. actors to favor internal attributions in explaining their behavior.

5. Which of the following factors is **not** one that influences interpersonal attraction?
   A. Physical attractiveness
   B. Similarity
   C. Reciprocity
   D. Latitude of acceptance

6. According to Hazan and Shaver (1987):
   A. romantic relationships in adulthood follow the same form as attachment relationships in infancy.
   B. those who had ambivalent attachments in infancy are doomed never to fall in love as adults.
   C. those who had avoidant attachments in infancy often overcompensate by becoming excessively intimate in their adult love relationships.
   D. all of the above are the case.

7. Which of the following variables does **not** tend to facilitate persuasion?
   A. Source credibility
   B. Source trustworthiness
   C. Forewarning of the receiver
   D. A two-sided argument

8. Cognitive dissonance theory predicts that after people engage in behavior that contradicts their true feelings, they will:
   A. convince themselves they really didn't perform the behavior.
   B. change their attitude to make it more consistent with their behavior.
   C. change their attitude to make it less consistent with their behavior.
   D. do nothing.

9. The elaboration likelihood model of attitude change suggests that:
   A. the peripheral route results in more enduring attitude change.
   B. the central route results in more enduring attitude change.
   C. only the central route to persuasion can be effective.
   D. only the peripheral route to persuasion can be effective.

10. The results of Milgram's (1963) study imply that:
    A. in the real world, most people will refuse to follow orders to inflict harm on a stranger.
    B. many people will obey an authority figure even if innocent people get hurt.
    C. most people are willing to give obviously wrong answers when ordered to do so.
    D. most people stick to their own judgment, even when group members unanimously disagree.

11. It appears that social loafing is due to:
    A. social norms that stress the importance of positive interactions between group members.
    B. duplication of effort between group members.
    C. diffusion of responsibility in groups.
    D. a bias toward making internal attributions about the behavior of others.

12. Groupthink occurs when members of a cohesive group:
    A. are initially unanimous about an issue.
    B. stress the importance of caution in group decision making.
    C. emphasize concurrence at the expense of critical thinking in arriving at a decision.
    D. shift toward a less extreme position after group discussion.

Answers

1. D   pp. 421–422
2. A   p. 422
3. B   p. 423
4. B   p. 425
5. D   pp. 427–428
6. A   pp. 428–429
7. C   pp. 435–436
8. B   pp. 437–438
9. B   pp. 438–439
10. B   pp. 441–442
11. C   p. 446
12. C   p. 447

Chapter 13 Practice Test

1. The notion that health is governed by a complex interaction of biological, psychological, and sociocultural factors is referred to as the:
   A. medical model.
   B. multifactorial model.
   C. biopsychosocial model.
   D. interactive model.

2. The four principal types of stress are:
   A. frustration, conflict, pressure, and anxiety.
   B. frustration, anger, pressure, and change.
   C. anger, anxiety, depression, and annoyance.
   D. frustration, conflict, pressure, and change.

3. You want very badly to ask someone for a date, but you are afraid to risk rejection. You are experiencing:
   A. an approach-avoidance conflict.
   B. an avoidance-avoidance conflict.
   C. optimized arousal.
   D. conformity pressure.

4. Research suggests that a high level of arousal may be most optimal for the performance of a task when:
   A. the task is complex.
   B. the task is simple.
   C. the rewards are high.
   D. an audience is present.

5. The alarm stage of Hans Selye's general adaptation syndrome is essentially the same as:
   A. the fight-or-flight response.
   B. constructive coping.
   C. approach-avoidance conflict.
   D. secondary appraisal.

6. In response to stress, the brain structure responsible for initiating action along the two major pathways through which the brain sends signals to the endocrine system is the:
   A. hypothalamus.
   B. thalamus.
   C. corpus callosum.
   D. medulla.

7. Which of the following is accurate in regard to defense mechanisms?
   A. There are many different defense mechanisms.
   B. They are used to ward off unpleasant emotions.
   C. They work through self-deception.
   D. All of the above are accurate.

8. Which element of the Type A personality seems to be most strongly related to increased coronary risk?
   A. Time consciousness
   B. Perfectionism
   C. Ambitiousness
   D. Hostility

9. All of the following are associated with high conscientiousness *except*:
   A. reliance on persistent, constructive coping strategies.
   B. lower levels of unhealthy habits, such as smoking.
   C. relatively poor adherence to medical advice.
   D. higher probability of ending up in higher socioeconomic strata.

10. Which of the following has *not* been found to be a mode of transmission for the HIV virus?
    A. Sexual contact among homosexual men
    B. The sharing of needles by intravenous drug users
    C. Heterosexual contact
    D. Sharing food

11. The fact that health is governed by a dense network of factors is an illustration of the theme of:
    A. psychology in a sociohistorical context.
    B. the phenomenology of experience.
    C. multifactorial causation.
    D. empiricism.

12. In evaluating health statistics, it is useful to:
    A. remember that statistical significance is equivalent to practical significance.
    B. remember that correlation is a reliable indicator of causation.
    C. consider base rates in thinking about probabilities.
    D. do all of the above.

Answers

1. C   p. 457
2. D   p. 458
3. A   p. 459
4. B   pp. 464–465
5. A   p. 465
6. A   p. 466
7. D   p. 469
8. D   p. 471
9. C   p. 475
10. D   p. 479
11. C   pp. 481–482
12. C   pp. 486–487

Chapter 14 Practice Test

1. According to Thomas Szasz, abnormal behavior usually involves:
   A. behavior that is statistically unusual.
   B. behavior that deviates from social norms.
   C. a disease of the mind.
   D. a biological imbalance.

2. Although Sue always feels a high level of dread, worry, and anxiety, she still manages to meet her daily responsibilities. Sue's behavior:
   A. should not be considered abnormal because her adaptive functioning is not impaired.
   B. should not be considered abnormal because everyone sometimes experiences worry and anxiety.
   C. can still be considered abnormal because she feels great personal distress.
   D. both A and B.

3. A concordance rate indicates:
   A. the percentage of relatives who exhibit the same disorder.
   B. the percentage of people with a given disorder who are currently receiving treatment.
   C. the prevalence of a given disorder in the general population.
   D. the rate of cure for a given disorder.

4. The observation that people acquire phobias of ancient sources of threat (such as snakes) much more readily than modern sources of threat (such as electrical outlets) can best be explained by:
   A. classical conditioning.
   B. operant conditioning.
   C. observational learning.
   D. preparedness/an evolved module for fear learning.

5. Which of the following statements about dissociative identity disorder is true?
   A. The original personality is always aware of the alternate personalities.
   B. Dissociative identity disorder is an alternate name for schizophrenia.
   C. The personalities are typically all quite similar to one another.
   D. Starting in the 1970s, there was a dramatic increase in the diagnosis of dissociative identity disorder.

6. The estimated prevalence of bipolar disorder is about _____ and the typical age of onset is _____.
   A. 1%; late teens or early 20s
   B. 1%; mid-30s
   C. 10%; late teens or early 20s
   D. 10%; after age 40

7. People who consistently come up with _____ explanations for negative events are more prone to depression.
   A. overly optimistic
   B. pessimistic
   C. delusional
   D. dysthymic

8. Mary believes that while she sleeps at night, space creatures are attacking her and invading her uterus, where they will multiply until they are ready to take over the world. Mary was chosen for this task, she believes, because she is the only one with the power to help the space creatures succeed. Mary would most likely be diagnosed with:
   A. schizophrenia
   B. major depression
   C. bipolar disorder
   D. PTSD

9. Most of the drugs that are useful in the treatment of schizophrenia are known to dampen _____ activity in the brain, suggesting that disruptions in the activity of this neurotransmitter may contribute to the development of the disorder.
   A. norepinephrine
   B. serotonin
   C. acetylcholine
   D. dopamine

10. Research suggests that there is an association between schizophrenia and:
    A. atrophied brain ventricles.
    B. enlarged brain ventricles.
    C. hippocampal degeneration.
    D. abnormalities in the cerebellum.

11. The syndrome characterized by manipulative, aggressive, exploitive behavior and a lack of conscience is:
    A. borderline personality disorder.
    B. narcissistic personality disorder.
    C. histrionic personality disorder.
    D. antisocial personality disorder.

12. Victims of _____ are more likely to recognize that their eating behavior is pathological; the more life-threatening eating disorder is

    _____.
    A. anorexia nervosa; bulimia nervosa
    B. bulimia nervosa; anorexia nervosa
    C. anorexia nervosa; anorexia nervosa
    D. bulimia nervosa; bulimia nervosa

Answers

1. B   p. 492
2. C   p. 493
3. A   p. 499
4. D   p. 500
5. D   pp. 501–502
6. A   pp. 505–506
7. B   p. 507
8. A   pp. 509–510
9. D   p. 512
10. B   p. 513
11. D   p. 519
12. B   p. 521

Chapter 15 Practice Test

1. One key problem with the provision of psychotherapy is that there are:
   A. too many different approaches to treatment.
   B. too many different professions involved.
   C. too few professions involved.
   D. many people who need therapy but do not receive treatment.
2. After undergoing psychoanalysis for several months, Karen suddenly started "forgetting" to attend her therapy sessions. Karen's behavior is most likely a form of:
   A. resistance.
   B. transference.
   C. insight.
   D. catharsis.
3. The key task of the client-centered therapist is:
   A. interpretation of the client's thoughts, feelings, memories, and behaviors.
   B. clarification of the client's feelings.
   C. confrontation of the client's irrational thoughts.
   D. modification of the client's problematic behaviors.
4. Evaluating the effectiveness of psychotherapy is complicated and difficult because:
   A. disorders sometimes clear up on their own.
   B. different approaches to treatment pursue entirely different goals.
   C. clients' problems vary in severity.
   D. all of the above are involved.
5. Systematic desensitization is particularly effective for the treatment of _____ disorders.
   A. generalized anxiety
   B. panic
   C. obsessive-compulsive
   D. phobic
6. Linda's therapist has her practice active listening skills in structured role-playing exercises. Later, Linda is gradually asked to practice these skills with family members; friends; and finally, her boss. Linda is undergoing:
   A. systematic desensitization.
   B. cognitive restructuring.
   C. a token economy.
   D. social skills training.
7. After being released from a hospital, many schizophrenic patients stop taking their antipsychotic medication because:
   A. their mental impairment causes them to forget.
   B. of the unpleasant side effects.
   C. most schizophrenics don't believe they are ill.
   D. all of the above are involved.
8. Selective serotonin reuptake inhibitors (SSRIs) appear to have value for the treatment of _____ disorders.
   A. depressive
   B. schizophrenic
   C. dissociative
   D. alcoholic
9. Modern psychotherapy:
   A. was spawned by a cultural milieu that viewed the self as an independent, rational being.
   B. embraces universal cultural values.
   C. has been successfully exported to most non-Western cultures.
   D. both B and C.
10. Many people repeatedly go in and out of mental hospitals. Typically, such people are released because _____; they are eventually readmitted because _____.
    A. they have been stabilized through drug therapy; their condition deteriorates once again because of inadequate outpatient care
    B. they run out of funds to pay for hospitalization; they once again can afford it
    C. they have been cured of their disorder; they develop another disorder
    D. they no longer want to be hospitalized; they voluntarily recommit themselves
11. The type of professional training a therapist has:
    A. is the most important indicator of his or her competence.
    B. should be the major consideration in choosing a therapist.
    C. is not all that important because talented therapists can be found in all the mental health professions.
    D. both A and B are true.
12. Which of the following could be explained by regression toward the mean?
    A. You get an average bowling score in one game and a superb score in the next game.
    B. You get an average bowling score in one game and a very low score in the next game.
    C. You get an average bowling score in one game and another average score in the next game.
    D. You get a terrible bowling score in one game and an average score in the next game.

Answers

1. D pp. 534–536
2. A p. 539
3. B p. 541
4. D p. 543
5. D p. 545
6. D p. 546
7. B p. 549
8. A p. 550
9. A p. 553
10. A p. 559
11. C pp. 561–562
12. D pp. 564–565

PART 2: ANSWERS TO THE CONCEPT CHECKS

Chapter 1

CONCEPT CHECK 1.1

1. c. Sigmund Freud (1905, pp. 77–78) arguing that it is possible to probe into the unconscious depths of the mind.

2. a. Wilhelm Wundt (1904 revision of an earlier text, p. v) campaigning for a new, independent science of psychology.

3. b. William James (1890) commenting negatively on the structuralists' efforts to break consciousness into its elements and his view of consciousness as a continuously flowing stream.

CONCEPT CHECK 1.2

1. b. B. F. Skinner (1971, p. 17) explaining why he believes that freedom is an illusion.

2. c. Carl Rogers (1961, p. 27) commenting on others' assertion that he had an overly optimistic (Pollyannaish) view of human potential and discussing humans' basic drive toward personal growth.

3. a. John B. Watson (1930, p. 103) dismissing the importance of genetic inheritance while arguing that traits are shaped entirely by experience.

CONCEPT CHECK 1.3

1. c. Thomas and Chess's (1977) well-known New York Longitudinal Study is a landmark in developmental psychology.

2. a. Olds and Milner (1954) made this discovery by accident and thereby opened up a fascinating line of inquiry in physiological psychology.

3. e. Zuckerman (1971) pioneered the study of sensation seeking as a personality trait.

Chapter 2

CONCEPT CHECK 2.1

1. IV: Film violence (present versus absent).
   DV: Heart rate and blood pressure (there are two DVs).

2. IV: Courtesy training (training versus no training).
   DV: Number of customer complaints.

3. IV: Stimulus complexity (high versus low) and stimulus contrast (high versus low) (there are two IVs).
   DV: Length of time spent staring at the stimuli.

4. IV: Group size (large versus small).
   DV: Conformity.

CONCEPT CHECK 2.2

1. b and e. The other three conclusions all equate correlation with causation.

2. a. Negative. As age increases, more people tend to have visual problems and acuity tends to decrease.

   b. Positive. Studies show that highly educated people tend to earn higher incomes and that people with less education tend to earn lower incomes.

   c. Negative. As shyness increases, the size of one's friendship network should decrease. However, research suggests that this inverse association may be weaker than widely believed.

CONCEPT CHECK 2.3

Methodological flaw	Study 1	Study 2
Sampling bias	✓	✓
Placebo effects	✓	
Confounding of variables	✓	
Distortions in self-report data		✓
Experimenter bias	✓	

Explanations for Study 1. Sensory deprivation is an unusual kind of experience that may intrigue certain potential subjects, who may be more adventurous or more willing to take risks than the population at large. Using the first 80 students who sign up for this study may not yield a sample that is representative of the population. Assigning the first 40 subjects who sign up to the experimental group may confound these extraneous variables with the treatment (students who sign up most quickly may be the most adventurous). In announcing that he will be examining the detrimental effects of sensory deprivation, the experimenter has created expectations in the subjects. These expectations could lead to placebo effects that have not been controlled for with a placebo group. The experimenter has also revealed that he has a bias about the outcome of the study. Because he supervises the treatments, he knows which subjects are in the experimental and control groups, thus aggravating potential problems with experimenter bias. For example, he might unintentionally give the control group subjects better instructions on how to do the pursuit-rotor task and thereby slant the study in favor of finding support for his hypothesis.

Explanations for Study 2. Sampling bias is a problem because the researcher has sampled only subjects from a low-income, inner-city neighborhood. A sample obtained in this way is not likely to be representative of the population at large. People are sensitive about the issue of racial prejudice, so distortions in self-report data are also likely. Many subjects may be swayed by social desirability bias and rate themselves as less prejudiced than they really are.

Chapter 3

CONCEPT CHECK 3.1

1. d. Serotonin.

2. b and d. Norepinephrine and serotonin.

3. e. Endorphins.

4. c. Dopamine.

5. a. Acetylcholine.

CONCEPT CHECK 3.2

1. Left hemisphere damage, probably to Wernicke's area.

2. Deficit in dopamine synthesis in an area of the midbrain.

3. Deterioration of myelin sheaths surrounding axons.

4. Disturbance in dopamine activity.

Please note that neuropsychological assessment is not as simple as this introductory exercise may suggest. There are many possible causes of most disorders, and we discussed only a handful of leading causes for each.

CONCEPT CHECK 3.3

1. Closer relatives; more distant relatives.
2. Identical twins; fraternal twins.
3. Biological parents; adoptive parents.
4. Genetic overlap or closeness; trait similarity.

Chapter 4

CONCEPT CHECK 4.1

Dimension	Rods	Cones
1. Physical shape	Elongated	Stubby
2. Number in the retina	100 million	6 million
3. Area of the retina in which they are dominant receptor	Periphery	Center/fovea
4. Critical to color vision	No	Yes
5. Critical to peripheral vision	Yes	No
6. Sensitivity to dim light	Strong	Weak
7. Speed of dark adaptation	Slow	Rapid

CONCEPT CHECK 4.2

✓ 1. **Interposition.** Some of the columns cut off parts of the statues behind them.

✓ 2. **Height in plane.** The back of the corridor is higher on the horizontal plane than the front of the corridor is.

✓ 3. **Texture gradient.** The squares on the floor become denser and less distinct with increasing distance.

✓ 4. **Relative size.** The statues and columns in the distance are smaller than those in the foreground.

✓ 5. **Light and shadow.** Light shining in from the windows on the right contrasts with shadow elsewhere.

✓ 6. **Linear perspective.** The lines of the corridor converge in the distance.

CONCEPT CHECK 4.3

Dimension	Vision	Hearing
1. Stimulus	Light waves	Sound waves
2. Elements of the stimulus and related perceptions	Wavelength/hue Amplitude/brightness Purity/saturation	Frequency/pitch Amplitude/loudness Purity/timbre
3. Receptors	Rods and cones	Hair cells
4. Location of receptors	Retina	Basilar membrane
5. Main location of processing in brain	Occipital lobe, visual cortex	Temporal lobe, auditory cortex

Chapter 5

CONCEPT CHECK 5.1

Characteristic	REM sleep	Non-REM sleep
1. Type of EEG activity	"Wide awake" brain waves, mostly beta	Varied, lots of delta waves
2. Eye movements	Rapid, lateral	Slow or absent
3. Dreaming	Frequent, vivid	Less frequent
4. Depth (difficulty in awakening)	Difficult to awaken	Varied, generally easier to awaken
5. Percentage of total sleep (in adults)	About 20%	About 80%
6. Increases or decreases (as percentage of sleep) during childhood	Percent decreases	Percent increases
7. Timing in sleep (dominates early or late)	Dominates later in cycle	Dominates early in cycle

CONCEPT CHECK 5.2

1. Beta. Video games require alert information processing, which is associated with beta waves.
2. Alpha. Meditation involves relaxation, which is associated with alpha waves, and studies show increased alpha in meditators.
3. Theta. In stage 1 sleep, theta waves tend to be prevalent.
4. Beta. Dreams are associated with REM sleep, which paradoxically produces "wide awake" beta waves.
5. Beta. If you're a beginner, typing will require alert, focused attention, which should generate beta waves.

CONCEPT CHECK 5.3

1. c. Stimulants.
2. d. Hallucinogens.
3. b. Sedatives.
4. f. Alcohol.
5. a. Narcotics.
6. e. Cannabis.

Chapter 6

CONCEPT CHECK 6.1

1. CS: Fire in fireplace
   US: Pain from burn CR/UR: Fear
2. CS: Brake lights in rain
   US: Car accident CR/UR: Tensing up
3. CS: Sight of cat
   US: Cat dander CR/UR: Wheezing

CONCEPT CHECK 6.2

1. FR. Each sale is a response and every third response earns reinforcement.
2. VI. A varied amount of time elapses before the response of doing yard work can earn reinforcement.
3. VR. Reinforcement occurs after a varied number of unreinforced casts (time is irrelevant; the more casts Martha makes, the more reinforcers she will receive).
4. CR. The designated response (reading a book) is reinforced (with a gold star) each and every time.
5. FI. A fixed time interval (3 years) has to elapse before Skip can earn a salary increase (the reinforcer).

CONCEPT CHECK 6.3

1. Punishment.

2. Positive reinforcement.

3. Punishment.

4. Negative reinforcement (for Audrey); the dog is positively reinforced for its whining.

5. Negative reinforcement.

6. Extinction. When Sharma's co-workers start to ignore her complaints, they are trying to extinguish the behavior (which had been positively reinforced when it won sympathy).

CONCEPT CHECK 6.4

1. Classical conditioning. Midori's blue windbreaker is a CS eliciting excitement in her dog.

2. Operant conditioning. Playing new songs leads to negative consequences (punishment), which weaken the tendency to play new songs. Playing old songs leads to positive reinforcement, which gradually strengthens the tendency to play old songs.

3. Classical conditioning. The song was paired with the passion of new love so that it became a CS eliciting emotional, romantic feelings.

4. Both. Ralph's workplace is paired with criticism so that his workplace becomes a CS eliciting anxiety. Calling in sick is operant behavior that is strengthened through negative reinforcement (because it reduces anxiety).

Chapter 7
CONCEPT CHECK 7.1

Feature	Sensory memory	Short-term memory	Long-term memory
1. Main encoding format	Copy of input	Largely phonemic	Largely semantic
2. Storage	Limited capacity	Small	No known limit
3. Storage duration	About ¼ second	Up to 20 seconds	Minutes to years

CONCEPT CHECK 7.2

1. c. Ineffective encoding due to lack of attention.

2. f. Retrieval failure due to motivated forgetting.

3. d. Proactive interference (previous learning of Justin Timberlake's name interferes with new learning).

4. e. Retroactive interference (new learning of sociology interferes with older learning of history).

CONCEPT CHECK 7.3

1. d. Declarative memory.

2. c. Long-term memory.

3. a. Sensory memory.

4. f. Episodic memory.

5. e. Nondeclarative memory.

6. g. Semantic memory.

7. i. Prospective memory.

8. b. Short-term memory.

Chapter 8
CONCEPT CHECK 8.1

1. Functional fixedness.

2. Forming subgoals.

3. Insight.

4. Searching for analogies.

5. Arrangement problem.

CONCEPT CHECK 8.2

1. c. Tendency to ignore base rates.

2. a. Availability heuristic leads to overestimation of the improbable.

3. b. Representativeness heuristic leads to inaccurate probability estimate.

CONCEPT CHECK 8.3

1. H. Given that the identical twins were reared apart, their greater similarity in comparison to fraternals reared together can only be due to heredity. This comparison is probably the most important piece of evidence supporting the genetic determination of IQ.

2. E. We tend to associate identical twins with evidence supporting heredity, but in this comparison genetic similarity is held constant because both sets of twins are identical. The only logical explanation for the greater similarity in identicals reared together is the effect of their being reared together (environment).

3. E. This comparison is similar to the previous one. Genetic similarity is held constant and a shared environment produces greater similarity than being reared apart.

4. B. This is nothing more than a quantification of the observation that intelligence runs in families. Because families share both genes and environment, either or both could be responsible for the observed correlation.

5. B. The similarity of adopted children to their biological parents can only be due to shared genes, and the similarity of adopted children to their foster parents can only be due to shared environment, so these correlations show the influence of both heredity and environment.

CONCEPT CHECK 8.4

1. d. Lewis Terman
2. b. Howard Gardner
3. f. David Wechsler
4. c. Arthur Jensen
5. a. Alfred Binet
6. e. Robert Sternberg

Chapter 9
CONCEPT CHECK 9.1

1. I. The secretion of ghrelin by the stomach tends to trigger stomach contractions and promote hunger.

2. D. When leptin levels increase, the tendency to feel hunger declines.

3. I or ?. Food cues generally trigger hunger and eating, but reactions vary among individuals.

4. D. Food preferences are mostly learned, and we tend to like what we are accustomed to eating. Most people will not be eager to eat a strange-looking food.

5. I. People tend to eat more when a variety of foods are available.

6. I. The more people are served, the more they tend to eat. Large portions tend to increase eating.

CONCEPT CHECK 9.2

1. c. Incentive value of success.
2. b. Perceived probability of success.
3. a. Need for achievement.

CONCEPT CHECK 9.3

2. James-Lange theory
3. Schachter's two-factor theory
4. Evolutionary theories

Chapter 10

CONCEPT CHECK 10.1

Event	Stage	Organism	Time span
1. Uterine implantation	Germinal	Zygote	0–2 weeks
2. Muscle and bone begin to form	Fetal	Fetus	2 months to birth
3. Vital organs and body systems begin to form	Embryonic	Embryo	2 weeks to 2 months

CONCEPT CHECK 10.2

1. b. Animism is characteristic of the preoperational period.
2. c. Mastery of hierarchical classification occurs during the concrete operational period.
3. a. Lack of object permanence is characteristic of the sensorimotor period.

CONCEPT CHECK 10.3

1. c. Commitment to personal ethics is characteristic of postconventional reasoning.
2. b. Concern about approval of others is characteristic of conventional reasoning.
3. a. Emphasis on positive or negative consequences is characteristic of preconventional reasoning.

Chapter 11

CONCEPT CHECK 11.1

1. Regression.
2. Projection.
3. Reaction formation.
4. Repression.
5. Rationalization.

CONCEPT CHECK 11.2

1. Bandura's observational learning. Sarah imitates a role model from television.
2. Maslow's need for self-actualization. Yolanda is striving to realize her fullest potential.
3. Freud's Oedipal complex. Vladimir shows preference for his opposite-sex parent and emotional distance from his same-sex parent.

CONCEPT CHECK 11.3

1. e. Maslow (1971, p. 36) commenting on the need for self-actualization.
2. c. Eysenck (1977, pp. 407–408) commenting on the biological roots of personality.
3. d. Freud (in Malcolm, 1980) commenting on the repression of sexuality.

CONCEPT CHECK 11.4

1. g
2. i
3. f
4. d
5. h
6. a
7. e
8. b
9. c

Chapter 12

CONCEPT CHECK 12.1

	Unstable	Stable
Internal	d	b
External	a	c

CONCEPT CHECK 12.2

1. c. Fundamental attribution error (assuming that arriving late reflects personal qualities).
2. a. Illusory correlation effect (overestimating how often one has seen confirmations of the assertion that young, female professors get pregnant soon after being hired).
3. b. Stereotyping (assuming that all lawyers have certain traits).

CONCEPT CHECK 12.3

1. *Target:* Cognitive component of attitudes (beliefs about program for regulating nursing homes).

   Persuasion: Message factor (advice to use one-sided instead of two-sided arguments).

2. *Target:* Affective component of attitudes (feelings about candidate).

   Persuasion: Source factor (advice on appearing likable, sincere, and compassionate).

3. *Target:* Behavioral component of attitudes (making contributions).

   Persuasion: Receiver factor (considering audience's initial position regarding the candidate).

CONCEPT CHECK 12.4

1. False.
2. True.
3. False.
4. True.
5. False.

Chapter 13

CONCEPT CHECK 13.1

1. b. A choice between two unattractive options.
2. c. Weighing the positive and negative aspects of a single goal.
3. a. A choice between two attractive options.

CONCEPT CHECK 13.2

1. a. Frustration due to delay.
2. d. Pressure to perform.
3. c. Change associated with leaving school and taking a new job.
4. a. Frustration due to loss of job.

   c. Change in life circumstances.

   d. Pressure to perform (in quickly obtaining new job).

CONCEPT CHECK 13.3

Pathway 1: hypothalamus, sympathetic division of the ANS, adrenal medulla, catecholamines.

Pathway 2: pituitary, ACTH, adrenal cortex, corticosteroids.

Chapter 14

CONCEPT CHECK 14.1

		Deviance	Maladaptive behavior	Personal distress
1.	Alan	____	✓	____
2.	Monica	____	____	✓
3.	Boris	✓	____	____
4.	Natasha	✓	✓	✓

CONCEPT CHECK 14.2

1. Obsessive-compulsive disorder (key symptoms: frequent rituals, obsession with ordering things).
2. Specific phobia (key symptoms: persistent and irrational fear of thunderstorms, interference with work functioning).
3. Posttraumatic stress disorder (key symptoms: enduring disturbance due to exposure to traumatic event, nightmares, emotional numbing).

CONCEPT CHECK 14.3

1. Bipolar disorder, manic episode (key symptoms: extravagant plans, hyperactivity, reckless spending).
2. Schizophrenia (key symptoms: delusions of persecution and grandeur along with deterioration of adaptive behavior).
3. Major depression (key symptoms: feelings of despair, low self-esteem, lack of energy).

Chapter 15

CONCEPT CHECK 15.1

1. c. Client-centered therapy
2. a. Psychoanalysis
3. b. Couples and family therapy

CONCEPT CHECK 15.2

1. d. Behavior therapy
2. b. Client-centered therapy
3. a. Psychoanalysis
4. c. Cognitive therapy

CONCEPT CHECK 15.3

1. c.
2. a.
3. b.
4. d.
5. b.

Empiricism depends on observation; precise observation depends on measurement; and measurement requires numbers. Thus, scientists routinely analyze numerical data to arrive at their conclusions. Over 3000 empirical studies are cited in this text, and all but a few of the simplest ones required a statistical analysis. ***Statistics* is the use of mathematics to organize, summarize, and interpret numerical data.** We discussed correlation briefly in Chapter 2, but in this appendix we look at a variety of statistics.

To illustrate statistics in action, let's assume that we want to test a hypothesis that has generated quite an argument in your psychology class. The hypothesis is that college students who watch a great deal of television aren't as bright as those who watch TV infrequently. For the fun of it, your class decides to conduct a correlational study of itself, collecting survey and psychological test data. Your classmates all agree to respond to a short survey on their TV viewing habits. Because everyone at your school has had to take the SAT, the class decides to use scores on the SAT verbal subtest as an index of how bright students are. All of them agree to allow the records office at the college to furnish their SAT scores to the professor, who replaces each student's name with a subject number (to protect students' right to privacy). Let's see how we could use statistics to analyze the data collected in our pilot study (a small, preliminary investigation).

Graphing Data

After collecting our data, our next step is to organize the data to get a quick overview of our numerical results. Let's assume that there are 20 students in your class, and when they estimate how many hours they spend per day watching TV, the results are as follows:

3	2	0	3	1
3	4	0	5	1
2	3	4	5	2
4	5	3	4	6

One of the simpler things that we can do to organize data is to create a *frequency distribution*—**an orderly arrangement of scores indicating the frequency of each score or group of scores. Figure B.1(a)** shows a frequency distribution for our data on TV viewing. The column on the left lists the possible scores (estimated hours of TV viewing) in order, and the column on the right lists the number of subjects with each score. Graphs can provide an even better overview of the data. One approach is to portray the data in a *histogram*, **which is a bar graph that presents data from a frequency distribution.** Such a histogram, summarizing our TV viewing data, is presented in **Figure B.1(b)**.

Another widely used method of portraying data graphically is the *frequency polygon*—**a line figure used to present data from a frequency distribution. Figures B.1(c)** and **B.1(d)** show how our TV viewing data can be converted from a histogram to a frequency polygon. In both the bar graph and the line figure, the horizontal axis lists the possible scores and the vertical axis is used to indicate the frequency of each score. This use of the axes is nearly universal for frequency

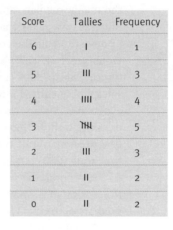

Score	Tallies	Frequency
6	I	1
5	III	3
4	IIII	4
3	IIII I	5
2	III	3
1	II	2
0	II	2

(a) Frequency distribution

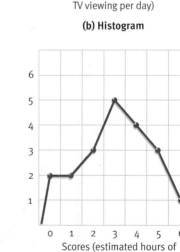

(b) Histogram

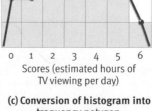

(c) Conversion of histogram into frequency polygon

(d) Frequency polygon

FIGURE B.1

Graphing data. (a) Our raw data are tallied into a frequency distribution. **(b)** The same data are portrayed in a bar graph called a histogram. **(c)** A frequency polygon is plotted over the histogram. **(d)** The resultant frequency polygon is shown by itself.

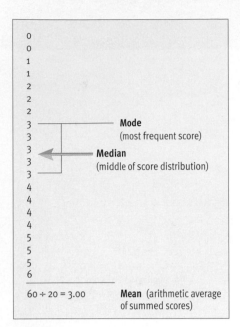

0
0
1
1
2
2
2
3 ── **Mode** (most frequent score)
3
3
3 ← **Median** (middle of score distribution)
3
3
4
4
4
4
5
5
5
6

60 ÷ 20 = 3.00   **Mean** (arithmetic average of summed scores)

FIGURE B.2

Measures of central tendency. The mean, median, and mode sometimes yield different results, but they usually converge, as in the case of our TV viewing data.

polygons, although sometimes it is reversed in histograms (the vertical axis lists possible scores, so the bars become horizontal).

Our graphs improve on the jumbled collection of scores that we started with, but ***descriptive statistics,*** **which are used to organize and summarize data,** provide some additional advantages. Let's see what the three measures of central tendency tell us about our data.

Measuring Central Tendency

In examining a set of data, it's routine to ask "What is a typical score in the distribution?" For instance, in this case we might compare the average amount of TV watching in our sample against national estimates to determine whether our subjects appear to be representative of the population. The three measures of central tendency, the median, the mean, and the mode, give us indications regarding the typical score in a data set. The ***median* is the score that falls in the center of a distribution, the *mean* is the arithmetic average of the scores,** and **the *mode* is the score that occurs most frequently.**

All three measures of central tendency are calculated for our TV viewing data in **Figure B.2**. As you can see, in this set of data, the mean, median, and mode all turn out to be the same score, which is 3. The correspondence among the three measures of central tendency seen in our TV viewing data is quite common, but there are situations in which the mean, median, and mode can yield very different estimates of central tendency. To illustrate, imagine that you're interviewing for a sales position at a company. Unbeknownst to you, the company's five salespeople earned the following incomes in the previous year: $20,000, $20,000, $25,000, $35,000, and $200,000. You ask how much the typical salesperson earns in a year. The sales director proudly announces that her five salespeople earned *a mean* income of $60,000 last year. However, before you order that expensive, new sports car, you had better inquire about the *median* and *modal* income for the sales staff. In this case, one extreme score ($200,000) has inflated the mean, making it unrepresentative of the sales staff's earnings. In this instance, the median ($25,000) and the mode ($20,000) both provide better estimates of what you are likely to earn.

In general, the mean is the most useful measure of central tendency because additional statistical manipulations can be performed on it that are not possible with the median or mode. However, the mean is sensitive to extreme scores in a distribution, which can sometimes make the mean misleading. Thus, lack of agreement among the three measures of central tendency usually occurs when a few extreme scores pull the mean away from the center of the distribution, as shown in **Figure B.3**. The curves

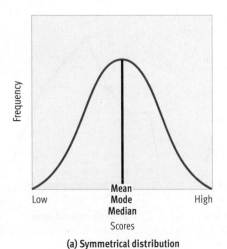

(a) Symmetrical distribution

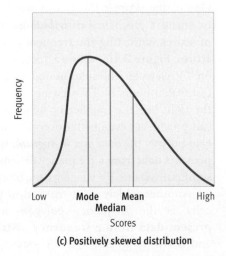

(b) Negatively skewed distribution

(c) Positively skewed distribution

FIGURE B.3

Measures of central tendency in skewed distributions. In a symmetrical distribution (**a**), the three measures of central tendency converge. However, in a negatively skewed distribution (**b**) or in a positively skewed distribution (**c**), the mean, median, and mode are pulled apart as shown here. Typically, in these situations the median provides the best index of central tendency.

plotted in **Figure B.3** are simply "smoothed out" frequency polygons based on data from many subjects. They show that when a distribution is symmetric, the measures of central tendency fall together, but this is not true in skewed or unbalanced distributions.

Figure B.3(b) shows a *negatively skewed distribution,* **in which most scores pile up at the high end of the scale** (the negative skew refers to the direction in which the curve's "tail" points). A *positively skewed distribution,* **in which scores pile up at the low end of the scale,** is shown in **Figure B.3(c)**. In both types of skewed distributions, a few extreme scores at one end pull the mean, and to a lesser degree the median, away from the mode. In these situations, the mean may be misleading and the median usually provides the best index of central tendency.

In any case, the measures of central tendency for our TV viewing data are reassuring because they all agree and they fall reasonably close to national estimates regarding how much young adults watch TV. Given the small size of our group, this agreement with national norms doesn't *prove* that our sample is representative of the population, but at least there's no obvious reason to believe that they're unrepresentative.

Measuring Variability

Of course, everyone in our sample did not report identical TV viewing habits. Virtually all data sets are characterized by some variability. *Variability* **refers to how much the scores tend to vary or depart from the mean score.** For example, the distribution of golf scores for a mediocre, erratic golfer would be characterized by high variability, while scores for an equally mediocre but more consistent golfer would show less variability.

The *standard deviation* **is an index of the amount of variability in a set of data.** It reflects the dispersion of scores in a distribution. This principle is portrayed graphically in **Figure B.4**, where the two distributions of golf scores have the same mean but the one on the left has less variability because the scores are bunched up in the center (for the consistent golfer). The distribution in **Figure B.4(b)** is characterized by more variability, as the erratic golfer's scores are more spread out. This distribution will yield a higher standard deviation than the distribution in **Figure B.4(a)**.

The formula for calculating the standard deviation is shown in **Figure B.5**, where d stands for each score's deviation from the mean and Σ stands for summation. A step-by-step application of this formula to our TV viewing data, shown in **Figure B.5**, reveals that the standard deviation for our TV viewing data is 1.64. The standard deviation has a variety of uses. One of these uses will surface in the next section, where we discuss the normal distribution.

TV viewing score (X)	Deviation from mean (d)	Deviation squared (d^2)
0	−3	9
0	−3	9
1	−2	4
1	−2	4
2	−1	1
2	−1	1
2	−1	1
3	0	0
3	0	0
3	0	0
3	0	0
3	0	0
4	+1	1
4	+1	1
4	+1	1
4	+1	1
5	+2	4
5	+2	4
5	+2	4
$N = 20$ 6	+3	9
$\Sigma X = 60$		$\Sigma d^2 = 54$

$$\text{Mean} = \frac{\Sigma X}{N} = \frac{60}{20} = 3.0$$

$$\text{Standard deviation} = \sqrt{\frac{\Sigma d^2}{N}} = \sqrt{\frac{54}{20}}$$

$$= \sqrt{2.70} = 1.64$$

FIGURE B.5

Steps in calculating the standard deviation. (1) Add the scores (ΣX) and divide by the number of scores (N) to calculate the mean (which comes out to 3.0 in this case). (2) Calculate each score's deviation from the mean by subtracting the mean from each score (the results are shown in the second column). (3) Square these deviations from the mean and total the results to obtain (Σd^2) as shown in the third column. (4) Insert the numbers for N and Σd^2 into the formula for the standard deviation and compute the results.

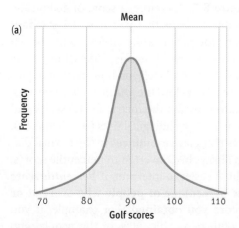

(a)

Mean

Frequency

70   80   90   100   110

Golf scores

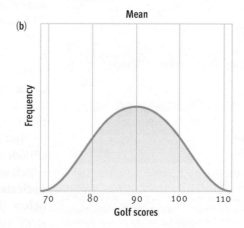

(b)

Mean

Frequency

70   80   90   100   110

Golf scores

FIGURE B.4

The standard deviation and dispersion of data. Although both these distributions of golf scores have the same mean, their standard deviations will be different. In (**a**) the scores are bunched together and there is less variability than in (**b**), yielding a lower standard deviation for the data in distribution (**a**).

The Normal Distribution

The hypothesis in our study is that brighter students watch less TV than relatively dull students. To test this hypothesis, we're going to correlate TV viewing with SAT scores. But to make effective use of the SAT data, we need to understand what SAT scores mean, which brings us to the normal distribution.

The *normal distribution* **is a symmetrical, bell-shaped curve that represents the pattern in which many human characteristics are dispersed in the population.** A great many physical qualities (for example, height, nose length, and running speed) and psychological traits (intelligence, spatial reasoning ability, introversion) are distributed in a manner that closely resembles this bell-shaped curve. When a trait is normally distributed, most scores fall near the center of the distribution (the mean) and the number of scores gradually declines as one moves away from the center in either direction (see **Figure B.6**). The normal distribution is *not* a law of nature. It's a mathematical function, or theoretical curve, that approximates the way nature seems to operate.

The normal distribution is the bedrock of the scoring system for most psychological tests, including the SAT. As we discuss in Chapter 8, psychological tests are *relative measures;* they assess how people score on a trait in comparison to other people. The normal distribution gives us a precise way to measure how people stack up in comparison to one another. The scores under the normal curve are dispersed in a fixed pattern, with the standard deviation serving as the unit of measurement, as shown in **Figure B.6**. About 68% of the scores in the distribution fall within plus or minus 1 standard deviation of the mean, while 95% of the scores fall within plus or minus 2 standard deviations of the mean. Given this fixed pattern, if you know the mean and standard deviation of a normally distributed trait, you can tell where any score falls in the distribution for the trait.

Although you may not have realized it, you probably have taken many tests in which the scoring system is based on the normal distribution. On the SAT, for instance, raw scores (the number of items correct on each subtest) are converted into standard scores that indicate where you fall in the normal distribution for the trait measured. In this conversion, the mean is set arbitrarily at 500 and the standard deviation at 100, as shown in **Figure B.7**. Therefore, a score of 400 on the SAT verbal subtest means that you scored 1 standard deviation below the mean, while an SAT score of 600 indicates that you scored 1 standard deviation above the mean. Thus, SAT scores tell you how many standard deviations above or below the mean your score was. This system also provides the metric for IQ scales and many other types of psychological tests (see Chapter 8).

Test scores that place examinees in the normal distribution can always be converted to percentile scores, which are a little easier to interpret. A *percentile score* **indicates the percentage of people who score at or below the score you obtained.** For example, if you score at the 60th percentile, 60% of the people who take the test score the same or below you, while the remaining 40% score above you. There are tables available that permit us to convert any standard deviation

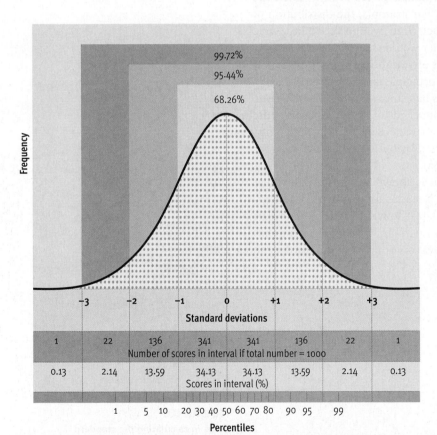

FIGURE B.6

The normal distribution. Many characteristics are distributed in a pattern represented by this bell-shaped curve (each dot represents a case). The horizontal axis shows how far above or below the mean a score is (measured in plus or minus standard deviations). The vertical axis shows the number of cases obtaining each score. In a normal distribution, most cases fall near the center of the distribution, so that 68.26% of the cases fall within plus or minus 1 standard deviation of the mean. The number of cases gradually declines as one moves away from the mean in either direction, so that only 13.59% of the cases fall between 1 and 2 standard deviations above or below the mean, and even fewer cases (2.14%) fall between 2 and 3 standard deviations above or below the mean.

placement in a normal distribution into a precise percentile score. **Figure B.6** gives some percentile conversions for the normal curve.

Of course, not all distributions are normal. As we saw in **Figure B.3**, some distributions are skewed in one direction or the other. As an example, consider what would happen if a classroom exam were much too easy or much too hard. If the test were too easy, scores would be bunched up at the high end of the scale, as in **Figure B.3(b)**. If the test were too hard, scores would be bunched up at the low end, as in **Figure B.3(c)**.

Measuring Correlation

To determine whether TV viewing is related to SAT scores, we have to compute a *correlation coefficient*—**a numerical index of the degree of relationship that exists between two variables.** As discussed in Chapter 2, a *positive* correlation means that the two variables—say X and Y—covary together. This means that high scores on variable X are associated with high scores on variable Y and that low scores on X are associated with low scores on Y. A *negative* correlation indicates that there is an inverse relationship between two variables. This means that people who score high on variable X tend to score low on variable Y, whereas those who score low on X tend to score high on Y. In our study, we hypothesized that as TV viewing increases, SAT scores will decrease, so we should expect a negative correlation between TV viewing and SAT scores.

The *magnitude* of a correlation coefficient indicates the *strength* of the association between two variables. This coefficient can vary between 0 and ± 1.00. The coefficient is usually represented by the letter r (for example, $r = .45$). A coefficient near 0 tells us that there is no relationship between two variables. A coefficient of $+1.00$ or -1.00 indicates that there is a perfect, one-to-one correspondence between two variables. A perfect correlation is found only rarely when working with real data. The closer the coefficient is to either -1.00 or $+1.00$, the stronger the relationship is.

The direction and strength of correlations can be illustrated graphically in scatter diagrams. A *scatter diagram* **is a graph in which paired X and Y scores for each subject are plotted as single points. Figure B.8** below shows scatter diagrams for positive correlations in the upper half and for negative correlations in the bottom half. A perfect positive correlation and a perfect negative correlation are shown on the far left. When a correlation

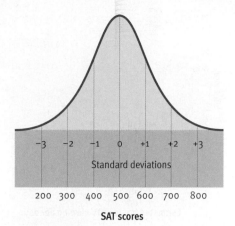

FIGURE B.7

The normal distribution and SAT scores. The normal distribution is the basis for the scoring system on many standardized tests. For example, on the SAT, the mean is set at 500 and the standard deviation at 100. Hence, an SAT score tells you how many standard deviations above or below the mean you scored. For example, a score of 700 means you scored 2 standard deviations above the mean.

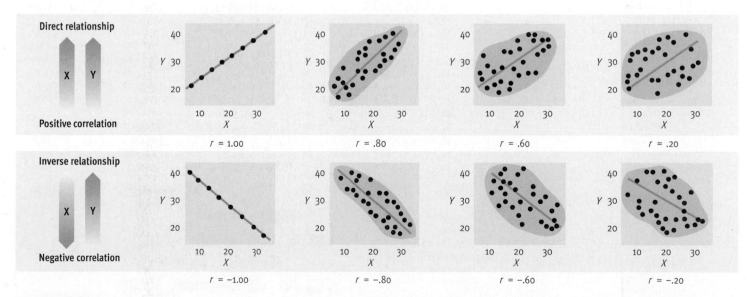

FIGURE B.8

Scatter diagrams of positive and negative correlations. Scatter diagrams plot paired *X* and *Y* scores as single points. Score plots slanted in the opposite direction result from positive (top row) as opposed to negative (bottom row) correlations. Moving across both rows (to the right), you can see that progressively weaker correlations result in more and more scattered plots of data points.

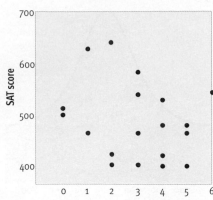

FIGURE B.9

Scatter diagram of the correlation between TV viewing and SAT scores. Our hypothetical data relating TV viewing to SAT scores are plotted in this scatter diagram. Compare it to the scatter diagrams seen in **Figure B.8** and see whether you can estimate the correlation between TV viewing and SAT scores in our data (see the text for the answer).

FIGURE B.10

Computing a correlation coefficient. The calculations required to compute the Pearson product-moment coefficient of correlation are shown here. The formula looks intimidating, but it's just a matter of filling in the figures taken from the sums of the columns shown above the formula.

is perfect, the data points in the scatter diagram fall exactly in a straight line. However, positive and negative correlations yield lines slanted in the opposite direction because the lines map out opposite types of associations. Moving to the right in **Figure B.8**, you can see what happens when the magnitude of a correlation decreases. The data points scatter farther and farther from the straight line that would represent a perfect relationship.

What about our data relating TV viewing to SAT scores? **Figure B.9** shows a scatter diagram of these data. Having just learned about scatter diagrams, perhaps you can estimate the magnitude of the correlation between TV viewing and SAT scores. The scatter diagram of our data looks a lot like the one seen in the bottom right corner of **Figure B.8**, suggesting that the correlation will be in the vicinity of −.20.

The formula for computing the most widely used measure of correlation—the Pearson product-moment correlation—is shown in **Figure B.10**, along with the calculations for our data on TV viewing and SAT scores. The data yield a correlation of $r = -.24$. This coefficient of correlation reveals that we have found a weak inverse association between TV viewing and performance on the SAT. Among our subjects, as TV viewing increases, SAT scores decrease, but the trend isn't very strong. We can get a better idea of how strong this correlation is by examining its predictive power.

Correlation and Prediction

As the magnitude of a correlation increases (gets closer to either −1.00 or +1.00), our ability to predict one variable based on knowledge of the other variable steadily increases. This relationship between the magnitude of a correlation and predictability can be

Subject number	TV viewing score (X)	X^2	SAT score (Y)	Y^2	XY
1	0	0	500	250,000	0
2	0	0	515	265,225	0
3	1	1	450	202,500	450
4	1	1	650	422,500	650
5	2	4	400	160,000	800
6	2	4	675	455,625	1350
7	2	4	425	180,625	850
8	3	9	400	160,000	1200
9	3	9	450	202,500	1350
10	3	9	500	250,000	1500
11	3	9	550	302,500	1650
12	3	9	600	360,000	1800
13	4	16	400	160,000	1600
14	4	16	425	180,625	1700
15	4	16	475	225,625	1900
16	4	16	525	275,625	2100
17	5	25	400	160,000	2000
18	5	25	450	202,500	2250
19	5	25	475	225,625	2375
20	6	36	550	302,500	3300
$N = 20$	$\Sigma X = 60$	$\Sigma X^2 = 234$	$\Sigma Y = 9815$	$\Sigma Y^2 = 4,943,975$	$\Sigma XY = 28,825$

Formula for Pearson product-moment correlation coefficient

$$r = \frac{(N)\,\Sigma XY - ((\Sigma X)\,\Sigma Y)}{\sqrt{[(N)\,\Sigma X^2 - (\Sigma X)^2][(N)\,\Sigma Y^2 - (\Sigma Y)^2]}}$$

$$= \frac{(20)\,(28,825) - (60)\,(9815)}{\sqrt{[(20)\,(234) - (60)^2][(20)\,(4,943,975) - (9815)^2]}}$$

$$= \frac{-12,400}{\sqrt{[1080][2,545,275]}}$$

$$= -.237$$

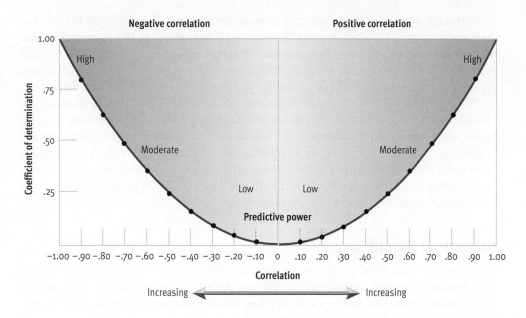

FIGURE B.11

Correlation and the coefficient of determination. The coefficient of determination is an index of a correlation's predictive power. As you can see, whether positive or negative, stronger correlations yield greater predictive power.

quantified precisely. All we have to do is square the correlation coefficient (multiply it by itself) and this gives us the *coefficient of determination,* **the percentage of variation in one variable that can be predicted based on the other variable.** Thus, a correlation of .70 yields a coefficient of determination of .49 (.70 × .70 = .49), indicating that variable *X* can account for 49% of the variation in variable *Y*. **Figure B.11** shows how the coefficient of determination goes up as the magnitude of a correlation increases.

Unfortunately, a correlation of −.24 doesn't give us much predictive power. We can account for only a little over 6% of the variation in variable *Y*. So, if we tried to predict individuals' SAT scores based on how much TV they watched, our predictions wouldn't be very accurate. Although a low correlation doesn't have much practical, predictive utility, it may still have theoretical value. Just knowing that there is a relationship between two variables can be theoretically interesting. However, we haven't yet addressed the question of whether our observed correlation is strong enough to support our hypothesis that there is a relationship between TV viewing and SAT scores. To make this judgment, we have to turn to inferential statistics and the process of hypothesis testing.

Hypothesis Testing

Inferential statistics go beyond the mere description of data. *Inferential statistics* **are used to interpret data and draw conclusions.** They permit researchers to decide whether their data support their hypotheses.

In our study of TV viewing we hypothesized that we would find an inverse relationship between amount of TV watched and SAT scores. Sure enough, that's what we found. However, we have to ask ourselves a critical question: Is this observed correlation large enough to support our hypothesis, or might a correlation of this size have occurred by chance?

We have to ask a similar question nearly every time we conduct a study. Why? Because we are working only with a sample. In research, we observe a limited *sample* (in this case, 20 subjects) to draw conclusions about a much larger *population* (college students in general). There's always a possibility that if we drew a different sample from the population, the results might be different. Perhaps our results are unique to our sample and not generalizable to the larger population. If we were able to collect data on the entire population, we would not have to wrestle with this problem, but our dependence on a sample necessitates the use of inferential statistics to precisely evaluate the likelihood that our results are due to chance factors in sampling. Thus, inferential statistics are the key to making the inferential leap from the sample to the population (see **Figure B.12**).

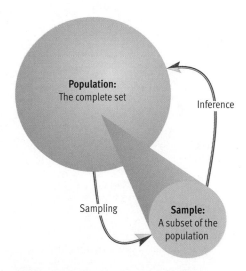

FIGURE B.12

The relationship between the population and the sample. In research, we are usually interested in a broad population, but we can observe only a small sample from the population. After making observations of our sample, we draw inferences about the population, based on the sample. This inferential process works well as long as the sample is reasonably representative of the population.

Although it may seem backward, in hypothesis testing we formally test the *null* hypothesis. As applied to correlational data, the **null hypothesis is the assumption that there is no true relationship between the variables observed.** In our study, the null hypothesis is that there is no genuine association between TV viewing and SAT scores. We want to determine whether our results will permit us to *reject* the null hypothesis and thus conclude that our *research hypothesis* (that there is a relationship between the variables) has been supported. Why do we test the null hypothesis instead of the research hypothesis? Because our probability calculations depend on assumptions tied to the null hypothesis. Specifically, we compute the probability of obtaining the results that we have observed if the null hypothesis is indeed true. The calculation of this probability hinges on a number of factors. A key factor is the amount of variability in the data, which is why the standard deviation is an important statistic.

Statistical Significance

When we reject the null hypothesis, we conclude that we have found *statistically significant* results. **Statistical significance is said to exist when the probability that the observed findings are due to chance is very low, usually less than 5 chances in 100.** This means that if the null hypothesis is correct and we conduct our study 100 times, drawing a new sample from the population each time, we will get results such as those observed only 5 times out of 100. If our calculations allow us to reject the null hypothesis, we conclude that our results support our research hypothesis. Thus, statistically significant results typically are findings that *support* a research hypothesis.

The requirement that there be less than 5 chances in 100 that research results are due to chance is the *minimum* requirement for statistical significance. When this requirement is met, we say the results are significant at the .05 level. If researchers calculate that there is less than 1 chance in 100 that their results are due to chance factors in sampling, the results are significant at the .01 level. If there is less than a 1 in 1000 chance that findings are attributable to sampling error, the results are significant at the .001 level. Thus, there are several *levels* of significance that you may see cited in scientific articles.

Because we are only dealing in matters of probability, there is always the possibility that our decision to accept or reject the null hypothesis is wrong. The various significance levels indicate the probability of erroneously rejecting the null hypothesis (and inaccurately accepting the research hypothesis). At the .05 level of significance, there are 5 chances in 100 that we have made a mistake when we conclude that our results support our hypothesis, and at the .01 level of significance the chance of an erroneous conclusion is 1 in 100. Although researchers hold the probability of this type of error quite low, the probability is never zero. This is one of the reasons that competently executed studies of the same question can yield contradictory findings. The differences may be due to chance variations in sampling that can't be prevented.

What do we find when we evaluate our data linking TV viewing to students' SAT scores? The calculations indicate that, given our sample size and the variability in our data, the probability of obtaining a correlation of −.24 by chance is greater than 20%. That's not a high probability, but it's not low enough to reject the null hypothesis. Thus, our findings are not strong enough to allow us to conclude that we have supported our hypothesis.

Statistics and Empiricism

In summary, conclusions based on empirical research are a matter of probability, and there's always a possibility that the conclusions are wrong. However, two major strengths of the empirical approach are its precision and its intolerance of error. Scientists can give you precise estimates of the likelihood that their conclusions are wrong, and because they're intolerant of error, they hold this probability extremely low. It's their reliance on statistics that allows them to accomplish these goals.

GLOSSARY

A

Absolute refractory period The minimum length of time after an action potential during which another action potential cannot begin.

Achievement motive The need to master difficult challenges, to outperform others, and to meet high standards of excellence.

Acquired immune deficiency syndrome (AIDS) A disorder in which the immune system is gradually weakened and eventually disabled by the human immunodeficiency virus (HIV).

Acquisition The initial stage of learning a new response tendency.

Action potential A brief shift in a neuron's electrical charge that travels along an axon.

Adaptation An inherited characteristic that increased in a population (through natural selection) because it helped solve a problem of survival or reproduction during the time it emerged. See also *Sensory adaptation*.

Additive color mixing Formation of colors by superimposing lights, putting more light in the mixture than exists in any one light by itself.

Adoption studies Research studies that assess hereditary influence by examining the resemblance between adopted children and both their biological and their adoptive parents.

Affective forecasting Efforts to predict one's emotional reactions to future events.

Afferent nerve fibers Axons that carry information inward to the central nervous system from the periphery of the body.

Afterimage A visual image that persists after a stimulus is removed.

Aggression Any behavior that is intended to hurt someone, either physically or verbally.

Agoraphobia A fear of going out to public places.

Alcohol A variety of beverages containing ethyl alcohol.

Amnesia See *Anterograde amnesia, Retrograde amnesia*.

Anecdotal evidence Personal stories about specific incidents and experiences.

Anhedonia A diminished ability to experience pleasure.

Animism The belief that all things are living.

Anorexia nervosa Eating disorder characterized by intense fear of gaining weight, disturbed body image, refusal to maintain normal weight, and use of dangerous measures to lose weight.

Anterograde amnesia Loss of memories for events that occur after a head injury.

Antianxiety drugs Medications that reduce tension, apprehension, and nervousness.

Antidepressant drugs Medications that gradually elevate mood and help bring people out of a depression.

Antipsychotic drugs Medications used to gradually reduce psychotic symptoms, including hyperactivity, mental confusion, hallucinations, and delusions.

Antisocial personality disorder A disorder marked by impulsive, callous, manipulative, aggressive, and irresponsible behavior.

Approach-approach conflict A conflict situation in which a choice must be made between two attractive goals.

Approach-avoidance conflict A conflict situation in which a choice must be made about whether to pursue a single goal that has both attractive and unattractive aspects.

Archetypes According to Jung, emotionally charged images and thought forms that have universal meaning.

Argument One or more premises used to provide support for a conclusion.

Assumptions Premises for which no proof or evidence is offered.

Attachment A close, emotional bond of affection between infants and their caregivers.

Attention Focusing awareness on a narrowed range of stimuli or events.

Attitudes Positive or negative evaluations of objects of thought.

Attributions Inferences that people draw about the causes of events, others' behavior, and their own behavior.

Auditory localization Locating the source of a sound in space.

Autism, or autism spectrum disorder (ASD) Childhood psychological disorder characterized by profound impairment of social interaction and severely restricted interests and activities, usually apparent by the age of 3.

Autonomic nervous system (ANS) The system of nerves that connect to the heart, blood vessels, smooth muscles, and glands.

Availability heuristic Basing the estimated probability of an event on the ease with which relevant instances come to mind.

Avoidance-avoidance conflict A conflict situation in which a choice must be made between two unattractive goals.

Avoidance learning Learning that has occurred when an organism engages in a response that prevents aversive stimulation from occurring.

Axon A long, thin fiber that transmits signals away from the neuron cell body (soma) to other neurons or to muscles or glands.

B

Basilar membrane A structure that runs the length of the cochlea in the inner ear and holds the auditory receptors, called *hair cells*.

Behavior Any overt (observable) response or activity by an organism.

Behavior modification A systematic approach to changing behavior through the application of the principles of conditioning.

Behavior therapies Application of the principles of learning and conditioning to direct efforts to change clients' maladaptive behaviors.

Behaviorism A theoretical orientation based on the premise that scientific psychology should study only observable behavior.

Bilingualism The acquisition of two languages that use different speech sounds, vocabulary, and grammatical rules.

Binge-eating disorder Eating disorder characterized by distress-inducing eating binges that are not accompanied by the purging, fasting, and excessive exercise seen in bulimia.

Binocular depth cues Clues about distance based on the differing views of the two eyes.

Biological rhythms Periodic fluctuations in physiological functioning.

Biomedical therapies Physiological interventions intended to reduce symptoms associated with psychological disorders.

Biopsychosocial model A model of illness that holds that physical illness is caused by a complex interaction of biological, psychological, and sociocultural factors.

Bipolar disorder Mood disorder marked by the experience of both depressed and manic periods. Formerly known as *manic-depressive disorder*.

Bisexuals Persons who seek emotional-sexual relationships with members of either sex.

Body mass index (BMI) A weight-to-height ratio calculated as weight (in kilograms) divided by height (in meters) squared (kg/m^2).

Borderline personality disorder A disorder marked by instability in social relationships, self-image, and emotional functioning.

Bottom-up processing In form perception, progression from individual elements to the whole.

Bounded rationality See *Theory of bounded rationality*.

Bulimia nervosa Eating disorder characterized by habitually engaging in out-of-control overeating, followed by unhealthy compensatory efforts, such as self-induced vomiting, fasting, abuse of laxatives and diuretics, and excessive exercise.

Bystander effect A paradoxical social phenomenon in which people are less likely to provide needed help when they are in groups than when they are alone.

C

Cannabis The hemp plant from which marijuana, hashish, and THC are derived.

Case study An in-depth investigation of an individual subject.

Catastrophic thinking Unrealistically pessimistic appraisals of stress that exaggerate the magnitude of one's problems.

Catharsis The release of emotional tension.

Central nervous system (CNS) The brain and the spinal cord.

Centration The tendency to focus on just one feature of a problem, neglecting other important aspects.

Cerebellum A relatively large and deeply folded structure located adjacent to the back surface of the brainstem.

Cerebral cortex The convoluted outer layer of the cerebrum.

Cerebral hemispheres The right and left halves of the cerebrum.

Channel The medium through which a message is sent.

Chromosomes Threadlike strands of DNA (deoxyribonucleic acid) molecules that carry genetic information.

Chunk A group of familiar stimuli stored as a single unit.

Circadian rhythms The 24-hour biological cycles found in humans and many other species.

Classical conditioning A type of learning in which a neutral stimulus acquires the ability to evoke a response that was originally evoked by another stimulus (also called *Pavlovian conditioning*).

Client-centered therapy An insight therapy that emphasizes providing a supportive emotional climate for clients, who play a major role in determining the pace and direction of their therapy.

Clinical psychologists Psychologists who specialize in the diagnosis and treatment of psychological disorders and everyday behavioral problems.

Clinical psychology The branch of psychology concerned with the diagnosis and treatment of psychological problems and disorders.

Cochlea The fluid-filled, coiled tunnel in the inner ear that contains the receptors for hearing.

Coefficient of determination The percentage of variation in one variable that can be predicted based on the other variable.

Cognition The mental processes involved in acquiring knowledge.

Cognitive-behavioral treatments A varied combination of verbal interventions and behavioral modification techniques used to help clients change maladaptive patterns of thinking.

Cognitive development Transitions in youngsters' patterns of thinking, including reasoning, remembering, and problem solving.

Cognitive dissonance A psychological state that exists when related attitudes or beliefs contradict one another.

Cognitive therapy An insight therapy that uses specific strategies to correct habitual thinking errors that underlie various types of disorders.

Collective unconscious According to Jung, a storehouse of latent memory traces inherited from people's ancestral past.

Collectivism Putting group goals ahead of personal goals and defining one's identity in terms of the groups one belongs to.

Color blindness Deficiency in the ability to distinguish among colors.

Comorbidity The coexistence of two or more disorders.

Companionate love Warm, trusting, tolerant affection for another whose life is deeply intertwined with one's own.

Comparators People, objects, events, and other standards that are used as a baseline for comparisons in making judgments.

Compensation According to Adler, efforts to overcome imagined or real inferiorities by developing one's abilities.

Competency A defendant's capacity to stand trial, called *fitness* in some states.

Complementary colors Pairs of colors that produce gray tones when added together.

Conceptual hierarchy A multilevel classification system based on common properties among items.

Concordance rate The percentage of twin pairs or other pairs of relatives that exhibit the same disorder.

Conditioned reinforcers See *Secondary reinforcers*.

Conditioned response (CR) A learned reaction to a conditioned stimulus that occurs because of previous conditioning.

Conditioned stimulus (CS) A previously neutral stimulus that has, through conditioning, acquired the capacity to evoke a conditioned response.

Conditioning Learning associations between events that occur in an organism's environment.

Cones Specialized visual receptors that play a key role in daylight vision and color vision.

Conflict A state that occurs when two or more incompatible motivations or behavioral impulses compete for expression.

Conformity The tendency for people to yield to real or imagined social pressure.

Confounding of variables A condition that exists whenever two variables are linked together in a way that makes it difficult to sort out their specific effects.

Conjunction fallacy An error that occurs when people estimate that the odds of two uncertain events happening together are greater than the odds of either event happening alone.

Conscious Whatever one is aware of at a particular point in time.

Consciousness One's awareness of internal and external stimuli.

Conservation Piaget's term for the awareness that physical quantities remain constant in spite of changes in their shape or appearance.

Consolidation A hypothetical process involving the gradual conversion of new, unstable memories into stable, durable memory codes stored in long-term memory.

Constructive coping Relatively healthful efforts that people make to deal with stressful events.

Continuous reinforcement Reinforcing every instance of a designated response.

Control group Subjects in a study who do not receive the special treatment given to the experimental group.

Convergent thinking Narrowing down a list of alternatives to converge on a single correct answer.

Coping Active efforts to master, reduce, or tolerate the demands created by stress.

Corpus callosum The major structure that connects the two cerebral hemispheres.

Correlation A correlation exists when two variables are related to each other.

Correlation coefficient A numerical index of the degree of relationship between two variables.

Counseling psychologists Psychologists who specialize in the diagnosis and treatment of psychological disorders and everyday behavioral problems.

Couples therapy The treatment of both partners in a committed, intimate relationship, in which the main focus is on relationship issues. Also called *marital therapy*.

Creativity The generation of ideas that are original, novel, and useful.

Critical period A limited time span in the development of an organism when it is optimal for certain capacities to emerge because the organism is especially responsive to certain experiences.

Critical thinking Purposeful, reasoned, goal-directed thinking that involves solving problems, formulating inferences, working with probabilities, and making carefully thought-out decisions.

Culture The widely shared customs, beliefs, values, norms, institutions, and other products of a community that are transmitted socially across generations.

Culture-bound disorders Abnormal syndromes found only in a few cultural groups.

Cumulative recorder A graphic record of reinforcement and responding in a Skinner box as a function of time.

D

Dark adaptation The process in which the eyes become more sensitive to light in low illumination.

Data collection techniques Procedures for making empirical observations and measurements.

Decay theory The idea that forgetting occurs because memory traces fade with time.

Decision making The process of evaluating alternatives and making choices among them.

Declarative memory system Memory for factual information.

Defense mechanisms Largely unconscious reactions that protect a person from unpleasant emotions, such as anxiety and guilt.

Deinstitutionalization Transferring the treatment of mental illness from inpatient institutions to community-based facilities that emphasize outpatient care.

Delusions False beliefs that are maintained even though they are clearly out of touch with reality.

Dementia An abnormal condition marked by multiple cognitive defects that include memory impairment.

Dendrites Branchlike parts of a neuron that are specialized to receive information.

Dependent variable In an experiment, the variable that is thought to be affected by the manipulation of the independent variable.

Depth perception Interpretation of visual cues that indicate how near or far away objects are.

Descriptive statistics Statistics that are used to organize and summarize data.

Development The sequence of age-related changes that occur as a person progresses from conception to death.

Developmental norms The average age at which individuals display various behaviors and abilities.

Deviation IQ scores Scores that locate subjects precisely within the normal distribution, using the standard deviation as the unit of measurement.

Diagnosis Distinguishing one illness from another.

Discrimination Behaving differently, usually unfairly, toward the members of a group.

Discriminative stimuli In operant conditioning, cues that influence operant behavior by indicating the probable consequences (reinforcement or nonreinforcement) of a response.

Displacement Diverting emotional feelings (usually anger) from their original source to a substitute target.

Display rules Cultural norms that regulate the appropriate expressions of emotions.

Dissociation A splitting off of mental processes into two separate, simultaneous streams of awareness.

Dissociative amnesia A sudden loss of memory for important personal information that is too extensive to be due to normal forgetting.

Dissociative disorders A class of disorders in which people lose contact with portions of their consciousness or memory, resulting in disruptions in their sense of identity.

Dissociative identity disorder A type of dissociative disorder characterized by the coexistence in one person of two or more largely complete, and usually very different, personalities. Formerly called *multiple-personality disorder*.

Divergent thinking Trying to expand the range of alternatives by generating many possible solutions.

Door-in-the-face technique Making a large request that is likely to be turned down as a way to increase the chances that people will agree to a smaller request later.

Double-blind procedure A research strategy in which neither subjects nor experimenters know which subjects are in the experimental or control groups.

Dream analysis A psychoanalytic technique in which the therapist interprets the symbolic meaning of the client's dreams.

Drive An internal state of tension that motivates an organism to engage in activities that should reduce the tension.

Dual-coding theory Paivio's theory that memory is enhanced by forming semantic and visual codes because either can lead to recall.

E

Eating disorders Severe disturbances in eating behavior characterized by preoccupation with weight concerns and unhealthy efforts to control weight.

Eclecticism In psychotherapy, drawing ideas from two or more systems of therapy instead of committing to just one system.

Efferent nerve fibers Axons that carry information outward from the central nervous system to the periphery of the body.

Ego According to Freud, the decision-making component of personality that operates according to the reality principle.

Egocentrism A limited ability to share another person's viewpoint.

Elaboration Linking a stimulus to other information at the time of encoding.

Electrical stimulation of the brain (ESB) Sending a weak electric current into a brain structure to stimulate (activate) it.

Electrocardiograph (EKG) A device that records the contractions of the heart.

Electroconvulsive therapy (ECT) A biomedical treatment in which electric shock is used to produce a cortical seizure accompanied by convulsions.

Electroencephalograph (EEG) A device that monitors the electrical activity of the brain over time by means of recording electrodes attached to the surface of the scalp.

Electromyograph (EMG) A device that records muscular activity and tension.

Electrooculograph (EOG) A device that records eye movements.

Elicit To draw out or bring forth.

Embryonic stage The second stage of prenatal development, lasting from two weeks until the end of the second month.

Emit To send forth.

Emotion A subjective conscious experience (the cognitive component) accompanied by bodily arousal (the physiological component) and by characteristic overt expression (the behavioral component).

Empiricism The premise that knowledge should be acquired through observation.

Encoding Forming a memory code.

Encoding specificity principle The idea that the value of a retrieval cue depends on how well it corresponds to the memory code.

Endocrine system A group of glands that secrete chemicals into the bloodstream that help control bodily functioning.

Endorphins The entire family of internally produced chemicals that resemble opiates in structure and effects.

Epigenetics The study of heritable changes in gene expression that do not involve modifications to the DNA sequence.

Episodic memory system Chronological, or temporally dated, recollections of personal experiences.

Escape learning A type of learning in which an organism acquires a response that decreases or ends some aversive stimulation.

Etiology The apparent causation and developmental history of an illness.

Evaluative conditioning Changes in the liking of a stimulus that result from pairing that stimulus with other positive or negative stimuli.

Evolutionary psychology Theoretical perspective that examines behavioral processes in terms of their adaptive value for a species over the course of many generations.

Experiment A research method in which the investigator manipulates a variable under carefully controlled conditions and observes whether any changes occur in a second variable as a result.

Experimental group The subjects in a study who receive some special treatment in regard to the independent variable.

Experimenter bias A phenomenon that occurs when a researcher's expectations or preferences about the outcome of a study influence the results obtained.

Explicit attitude Attitudes that people hold consciously and can readily describe.

Exposure therapies An approach to behavior therapy in which clients are confronted with situations they fear so they learn these situations are really harmless.

Expressed emotion The degree to which a relative of a schizophrenic patient displays highly critical or emotionally overinvolved attitudes toward the patient.

External attributions Ascribing the causes of behavior to situational demands and environmental constraints.

Extinction The gradual weakening and disappearance of a conditioned response tendency.

Extraneous variables Any variables other than the independent variable that seem likely to influence the dependent variable in a specific experiment.

F

Factor analysis Statistical analysis of correlations among many variables to identify closely related clusters of variables.

Family studies Scientific studies in which researchers assess hereditary influence by examining blood relatives to see how much they resemble each other on a specific trait.

Family therapy The treatment of a family unit as a whole, in which the main focus is on family dynamics and communication.

Farsightedness A visual deficiency in which distant objects are seen clearly but close objects appear blurry.

Fast mapping The process by which children map a word onto an underlying concept after only one exposure.

Feature analysis The process of detecting specific elements in visual input and assembling them into a more complex form.

Feature detectors Neurons that respond selectively to very specific features of more complex stimuli.

Fetal alcohol syndrome A collection of congenital (inborn) problems associated with excessive alcohol use during pregnancy.

Fetal stage The third stage of prenatal development, lasting from two months through birth.

Fitness The reproductive success (number of descendants) of an individual organism relative to the average reproductive success of the population.

Fixation According to Freud, failure to move forward from one psychosexual stage to another as expected.

Fixed-interval (FI) schedule A reinforcement schedule in which the reinforcer is given for the first response that occurs after a fixed time interval has elapsed.

Fixed-ratio (FR) schedule A reinforcement schedule in which the reinforcer is given after a fixed number of nonreinforced responses.

Flashbulb memories Unusually vivid and detailed recollections of momentous events.

Foot-in-the-door technique Getting people to agree to a small request to increase the chances that they will agree to a larger request later.

Forebrain The largest and most complicated region of the brain, encompassing a variety of structures, including the thalamus, hypothalamus, limbic system, and cerebrum.

Forgetting curve A graph showing retention and forgetting over time.

Fovea A tiny spot in the center of the retina that contains only cones; visual acuity is greatest at this spot.

Framing In decision making, refers to how decision issues are posed or how choices are structured.

Free association A psychoanalytic technique in which clients spontaneously express their thoughts and feelings exactly as they occur, with as little censorship as possible.

Frequency distribution An orderly arrangement of scores indicating the frequency of each score or group of scores.

Frequency polygon A line figure used to present data from a frequency distribution.

Frequency theory Theory holding that perception of pitch corresponds to the rate, or frequency, at which the entire basilar membrane vibrates.

Frustration The feeling that people experience in any situation in which their pursuit of some goal is thwarted.

Functional fixedness The tendency to perceive an item only in terms of its most common use.

Functionalism A school of psychology based on the belief that psychology should investigate the function or purpose of consciousness, rather than its structure.

Fundamental attribution error Observers' bias in favor of internal attributions in explaining others' behavior.

G

Galvanic skin response (GSR) An increase in the electrical conductivity of the skin that occurs when sweat glands increase their activity.

Gambler's fallacy The belief that the odds of a chance event increase if the event hasn't occurred recently.

Gender differences Disparities between the sexes in typical behavior or average ability.

Gender roles Expectations about what is appropriate behavior for each sex.

Gender stereotypes Widely held beliefs about males' and females' abilities, personality traits, and behavior.

General adaptation syndrome Selye's model of the body's stress response, consisting of three stages: alarm, resistance, and exhaustion.

Generalized anxiety disorder A psychological disorder marked by a chronic, high level of anxiety that is not tied to any specific threat.

Genes DNA segments that serve as the key functional units in hereditary transmission.

Germinal stage The first phase of prenatal development, usually encompassing the first two weeks after conception.

Glia Cells found throughout the nervous system that provide various types of support for neurons.

Group Two or more individuals who interact and are interdependent.

Group cohesiveness The strength of the liking relationships linking group members to each other and to the group itself.

Group polarization A phenomenon that occurs when group discussion strengthens a group's dominant point of view and produces a shift toward a more extreme decision in that direction.

Group therapy The simultaneous treatment of several clients in a group.

Groupthink A process in which members of a cohesive group emphasize concurrence at the expense of critical thinking in arriving at a decision.

Gustatory system The sensory system for taste.

H

Hallucinations Sensory perceptions that occur in the absence of a real, external stimulus, or gross distortions of perceptual input.

Hallucinogens A diverse group of drugs that have powerful effects on mental and emotional functioning, marked most prominently by distortions in sensory and perceptual experience.

Halo effect Phenomenon that occurs in self-reports when someone's overall evaluation of a person, object, or institution spills over to influence more specific ratings.

Hedonic adaptation An effect that occurs when the mental scale that people use to judge the pleasantness-unpleasantness of their experiences shifts so that their neutral point, or baseline for comparison, changes.

Heritability ratio An estimate of the proportion of trait variability in a population that is determined by variations in genetic inheritance.

Heterosexuals Persons who seek emotional-sexual relationships with members of the other sex.

Heuristic A strategy, guiding principle, or rule of thumb used in solving problems or making decisions.

Hierarchy of needs Maslow's systematic arrangement of needs, according to priority, which assumes that basic needs must be met before less basic needs are aroused.

Higher-order conditioning A type of conditioning in which a conditioned stimulus functions as if it were an unconditioned stimulus.

Hindbrain The part of the brain that includes the cerebellum and two structures found in the lower part of the brainstem: the medulla and the pons.

Hindsight bias The tendency to mold one's interpretation of the past to fit how events actually turned out.

Histogram A bar graph that presents data from a frequency distribution.

Homeostasis A state of physiological equilibrium or stability.

Homophobia An intense fear and intolerance of homosexuality.

Homosexuals Persons who seek emotional-sexual relationships with members of the same sex.

Hormones The chemical substances released by the endocrine glands.

Humanism A theoretical orientation that emphasizes the unique qualities of humans, especially their freedom and their potential for personal growth.

Hypnosis A systematic procedure that typically produces a heightened state of suggestibility.

Hypothalamus A structure found near the base of the forebrain that is involved in the regulation of basic biological needs.

Hypothesis A tentative statement about the relationship between two or more variables.

I

Id According to Freud, the primitive, instinctive component of personality that operates according to the pleasure principle.

Identification Bolstering self-esteem by forming an imaginary or real alliance with some person or group.

Illusory correlation A misperception that occurs when people estimate that they have encountered more confirmations of an association between social traits than they have actually seen.

Immune response The body's defensive reaction to invasion by bacteria, viral agents, or other foreign substances.

Implicit attitudes Covert attitudes that are expressed in subtle automatic responses that people have little conscious control over.

Inattentional blindness The failure to see fully visible objects or events in a visual display because one's attention is focused elsewhere.

Incentive An external goal that has the capacity to motivate behavior.

Incongruence The degree of disparity between one's self-concept and one's actual experience.

Incubation effect A phenomenon that occurs when new solutions surface for a previously unsolved problem after a period of not consciously thinking about the problem.

Independent variable In an experiment, a condition or event that a researcher varies in order to see its impact on another variable.

Individualism Putting personal goals ahead of group goals and defining one's identity in terms of personal attributes rather than group memberships.

Inferential statistics Statistics that are used to interpret data and draw conclusions.

Informational influence An effect that often contributes to conformity in which people look to others for guidance about how to behave in ambiguous situations.

Ingroup The group that people belong to and identify with.

Insanity A legal status indicating that a person cannot be held responsible for his or her actions because of mental illness.

Insight In problem solving, the sudden discovery of the correct solution following incorrect attempts based primarily on trial and error.

Insight therapies Psychotherapy methods characterized by verbal interactions intended to enhance clients' self-knowledge and thus promote healthful changes in personality and behavior.

Insomnia Chronic problems in getting adequate sleep that result in daytime fatigue and impaired functioning.

Intelligence quotient (IQ) A child's mental age divided by chronological age, multiplied by 100.

Interference theory The idea that people forget information because of competition from other material.

Intermittent reinforcement A reinforcement schedule in which a designated response is reinforced only some of the time.

Internal attributions Ascribing the causes of behavior to personal dispositions, traits, abilities, and feelings.

Interpersonal attraction Positive feelings toward another.

Introspection Careful, systematic observation of one's own conscious experience.

Involuntary commitment When people are hospitalized in psychiatric facilities against their will.

Irreversibility The inability to envision reversing an action.

J

Journal A periodical that publishes technical and scholarly material, usually in a narrowly defined area of inquiry.

L

Language acquisition device (LAD) According to Chomsky, an innate mechanism or process that facilitates the learning of language.

Latent content According to Freud, the hidden or disguised meaning of the events in a dream.

Latent learning Learning that is not apparent from behavior when it first occurs.

Learned helplessness Passive behavior produced by exposure to unavoidable aversive events.

Learning A relatively durable change in behavior or knowledge that is due to experience.

Lens The transparent eye structure that focuses the light rays falling on the retina.

Lesioning Destroying a piece of the brain.

Levels-of-processing theory The theory holding that deeper levels of mental processing result in longer-lasting memory codes.

Lie detector See *Polygraph.*

Life changes Any substantial alterations in one's living circumstances that require readjustment.

Light adaptation The process whereby the eyes become less sensitive to light in high illumination.

Limbic system A loosely connected network of structures roughly located along the border between the cerebral cortex and deeper subcortical areas.

Linguistic relativity The hypothesis that one's language determines the nature of one's thoughts.

Link method A mnemonic device that involves forming a mental image of items to be remembered in a way that links them together.

Long-term memory (LTM) An unlimited capacity store that can hold information over lengthy periods of time.

Lowball technique Getting someone to commit to a seemingly attractive proposition before revealing the hidden costs.

M

Major depressive disorder Mood disorder characterized by persistent feelings of sadness and despair and a loss of interest in previous sources of pleasure.

Manic-depressive disorder See *Bipolar disorder.*

Manifest content According to Freud, the plot of a dream at a surface level.

Marital therapy See *couples therapy.*

Matching hypothesis The idea that males and females of approximately equal physical attractiveness are likely to select each other as partners.

Maturation Development that reflects the gradual unfolding of one's genetic blueprint.

Mean The arithmetic average of the scores in a distribution.

Median The score that falls exactly in the center of a distribution of scores.

Medical model The view that it is useful to think of abnormal behavior as a disease.

Meditation A family of practices that train attention to heighten awareness and bring mental processes under greater voluntary control.

Menarche The first occurrence of menstruation.

Mental age In intelligence testing, a score that indicates that a child displays the mental ability typical of a child of that chronological (actual) age.

Mental hospital A medical institution specializing in providing inpatient care for psychological disorders.

Mental set Persisting in using problem-solving strategies that have worked in the past.

Mere exposure effect The finding that repeated exposures to a stimulus promotes greater liking of the stimulus.

Message In persuasion, the information transmitted by a source to a receiver.

Meta-analysis A research technique that combines the statistical results of many studies of the same question, yielding an estimate of the size and consistency of a variable's effects.

Method of loci A mnemonic device that involves taking an imaginary walk along a familiar path where images of items to be remembered are associated with certain locations.

Midbrain The segment of the brain stem that lies between the hindbrain and the forebrain.

Mirror neurons Neurons that are activated by performing an action or by seeing another monkey or person perform the same action.

Misinformation effect Phenomenon that occurs when participants' recall of an event they witnessed is altered by introducing misleading post-event information.

Mnemonic devices Strategies for enhancing memory.

Mode The score that occurs most frequently in a distribution.

Model In observational learning, a person whose behavior is observed by another.

Monocular depth cues Clues about distance based on the image from either eye alone.

Mood disorders A class of disorders marked by emotional disturbances of varied kinds that may spill over to disrupt physical, perceptual, social, and thought processes.

Mortality salience The degree to which subjects' mortality is prominent in their minds.

Motivation Goal-directed behavior.

Motor development The progression of muscular coordination required for physical activities.

Multiple-personality disorder See *Dissociative identity disorder.*

Myelin sheath Insulating material derived from glial cells that encases some axons of neurons.

Narcissism A personality trait marked by an inflated sense of importance, a need for attention and admiration, a sense of entitlement, and a tendency to exploit others.

Narcissistic personality disorder A disorder marked by grandiose sense of self-importance, a sense of entitlement, and an excessive need for attention and admiration.

Narcolepsy A disease marked by sudden and irresistible onsets of sleep during normal waking periods.

Narcotics (opiates) Drugs derived from opium that are capable of relieving pain.

Natural selection Principle stating that inherited characteristics that provide a survival or reproductive advantage are more likely than alternative characteristics to be passed on to subsequent generations and thus come to be "selected" over time.

Naturalistic observation A descriptive research method in which the researcher engages in careful, usually prolonged, observation of behavior without intervening directly with the subjects.

Nearsightedness A visual deficiency in which close objects are seen clearly but distant objects appear blurry.

Need for self-actualization According to Maslow, the need to fulfill one's potential.

Negative reinforcement The strengthening of a response because it is followed by the removal of an aversive (unpleasant) stimulus.

Negatively skewed distribution A distribution in which most scores pile up at the high end of the scale.

Neurogenesis The formation of new neurons.

Neurons Individual cells in the nervous system that receive, integrate, and transmit information.

Neurotransmitters Chemicals that transmit information from one neuron to another.

Nerves Bundles of neuron fibers (axons) that are routed together in the peripheral nervous system.

Nondeclarative memory system The repository for memories for actions, skills, conditioned responses, and emotional memories. Also called *procedural memory*.

Non-REM (NREM) sleep Sleep stages 1 through 3, which are marked by an absence of rapid eye movements, relatively little dreaming, and varied EEG activity.

Nonsense syllables Consonant-vowel-consonant arrangements that do not correspond to words.

Normal distribution A symmetric, bell-shaped curve that represents the pattern in which many characteristics are dispersed in the population.

Normative influence An effect that promotes conformity to social norms for fear of negative social consequences.

Null hypothesis In inferential statistics, the assumption that there is no true relationship between the variables being observed.

Obedience A form of compliance that occurs when people follow direct commands, usually from someone in a position of authority.

Obesity The condition of being overweight.

Object permanence Recognizing that objects continue to exist even when they are no longer visible.

Observational learning A type of learning that occurs when an organism's responding is influenced by the observation of others, who are called *models*.

Obsessive-compulsive disorder (OCD) A disorder marked by persistent, uncontrollable intrusions of unwanted thoughts (obsessions) and urges to engage in senseless rituals (compulsions).

Oedipal complex According to Freud, children's manifestation of erotically tinged desires for their opposite-sex parent, accompanied by feelings of hostility toward their same-sex parent.

Olfactory system The sensory system for smell.

Operant conditioning A form of learning in which voluntary responses come to be controlled by their consequences.

Operational definition In empirical research, a definition that describes the actions or operations that will be used to measure or control a variable.

Opiates See *Narcotics*.

Opponent process theory The idea that color perception depends on receptors that make antagonistic responses to three pairs of colors.

Optic chiasm The point at which the axons from the inside half of each eye cross over and then project to the opposite half of the brain.

Optimism A general tendency to expect good outcomes.

Outgroup People who are not part of one's ingroup.

Overextension Mistake in language learning that occurs when a child incorrectly uses a word to describe a wider set of objects or actions than it is meant to.

Overregulation Mistake in language learning in which a child incorrectly generalizes grammatical rules to irregular cases where they do not apply.

Oxytocin A hormone released by the pituitary gland that regulates reproductive behaviors.

Panic disorder A type of anxiety disorder characterized by recurrent attacks of overwhelming anxiety that usually occur suddenly and unexpectedly.

Parasympathetic division The branch of the autonomic nervous system that generally conserves bodily resources.

Parental investment What each sex invests—in terms of time, energy, survival risk, and forgone opportunities—to produce and nurture offspring.

Participants The persons or animals whose behavior is systematically observed in a study.

Passionate love A complete absorption in another that includes tender sexual feelings and the agony and ecstasy of intense emotion.

Pavlovian conditioning See *Classical conditioning*.

Percentile score A figure that indicates the percentage of people who score at or below the score any one individual has obtained.

Perception The selection, organization, and interpretation of sensory input.

Perceptual constancy A tendency to experience a stable perception in the face of continually changing sensory input.

Perceptual hypothesis An inference about what form could be responsible for a pattern of sensory stimulation.

Perceptual set A readiness to perceive a stimulus in a particular way.

Peripheral nervous system All the nerves that lie outside the brain and spinal cord.

Person perception The process of forming impressions of others.

Personality An individual's unique set of consistent behavioral traits.

Personality disorders A class of disorders marked by extreme, inflexible personality traits that cause subjective distress or impaired social and occupational functioning.

Personality trait A durable disposition to behave in a particular way in a variety of situations.

Phi phenomenon The illusion of movement created by presenting visual stimuli in rapid succession.

Physical dependence The condition that exists when a person must continue to take a drug to avoid withdrawal illness.

Pictorial depth cues Clues about distance that can be given in a flat picture.

Pituitary gland The "master gland" of the endocrine system; it releases a great variety of hormones that fan out through the body, stimulating actions in the other endocrine glands.

Place theory The idea that perception of pitch corresponds to the vibration of different portions, or places, along the basilar membrane.

Placebo effects Occur when subjects' expectations lead them to experience some change even though they receive an empty, fake, or ineffectual treatment.

Placenta A structure that allows oxygen and nutrients to pass into the fetus from the mother's bloodstream and bodily wastes to pass out to the mother.

Pleasure principle According to Freud, the principle upon which the id operates, demanding immediate gratification of its urges.

Polygenic traits Characteristics that are influenced by more than one pair of genes.

Polygraph A device that records autonomic fluctuations while a subject is questioned, in an effort to determine whether the subject is telling the truth.

Population The larger collection of animals or people from which a sample is drawn and that researchers want to generalize about.

Positive psychology Approach to psychology that uses theory and research to better understand the positive, adaptive, creative, and fulfilling aspects of human existence.

Positive reinforcement Reinforcement that occurs when a response is strengthened because it is followed by the presentation of a rewarding stimulus.

Positively skewed distribution A distribution in which scores pile up at the low end of the scale.

Postsynaptic potential (PSP) A voltage change at the receptor site on a postsynaptic cell membrane.

Posttraumatic stress disorder (PTSD) Psychological disturbance that is attributed to a major stressful event but that emerges after the stress is over.

Preconscious According to Freud, the level of awareness that contains material just beneath the surface of conscious awareness that can easily be retrieved.

Prejudice A negative attitude held toward members of a group.

Premises The reasons presented to persuade someone that a conclusion is true or probably true.

Prenatal period The period from conception to birth, usually encompassing nine months of pregnancy.

Preparedness Species-specific predisposition to be conditioned in certain ways and not others.

Pressure Expectations or demands that one behave in a certain way.

Primary appraisal An initial evaluation of whether an event is (1) irrelevant to you, (2) relevant but not threatening, or (3) stressful.

Primary reinforcers Events that are inherently reinforcing because they satisfy biological needs.

Primary sex characteristics The sexual structures necessary for reproduction.

Proactive interference A source of forgetting that occurs when previously learned information interferes with the retention of new information.

Problem solving Active efforts to discover what must be done to achieve a goal that is not readily available.

Procedural memory system See *Nondeclarative memory system.*

Prognosis A forecast about the probable course of an illness.

Projection Attributing one's own thoughts, feelings, or motives to another.

Projective tests Psychological tests that ask subjects to respond to vague, ambiguous stimuli in ways that may reveal the subjects' needs, feelings, and personality traits.

Prospective memory The ability to remember to perform actions in the future.

Psychiatrists Physicians who specialize in the diagnosis and treatment of psychological disorders.

Psychiatry A branch of medicine concerned with the diagnosis and treatment of psychological problems and disorders.

Psychoactive drugs Chemical substances that modify mental, emotional, or behavioral functioning.

Psychoanalysis An insight therapy that emphasizes the recovery of unconscious conflicts, motives, and defenses through techniques such as free association and transference.

Psychoanalytic theory A theory developed by Freud that attempts to explain personality, motivation, and mental disorders by focusing on unconscious determinants of behavior.

Psychological dependence The condition that exists when a person must continue to take a drug in order to satisfy intense mental and emotional craving for the drug.

Psychology The science that studies behavior and the physiological and cognitive processes that underlie it, and the profession that applies the accumulated knowledge of this science to practical problems.

Psychosexual stages According to Freud, developmental periods with a characteristic sexual focus that leave their mark on a person's adult personality.

Puberty The stage during which sexual functions reach maturity, which marks the beginning of adolescence.

Punishment An event that follows a response that weakens or suppresses the tendency to make that response.

Pupil The opening in the center of the iris that helps regulate the amount of light passing into the rear chamber of the eye.

R

Random assignment A procedure in which all subjects in a study have an equal chance of being assigned to any group or condition.

Rationalization Creating false but plausible excuses to justify unacceptable behavior.

Reaction formation Behaving in a way that's exactly the opposite of one's true feelings.

Reaction range Genetically determined limits on IQ or other traits.

Reactivity Alteration of a subject's behavior due to the presence of an observer.

Reality principle According to Freud, the principle on which the ego operates, which seeks to delay gratification of the id's urges until appropriate outlets and situations can be found.

Recall measure A memory test that requires subjects to reproduce information on their own without any cues.

Receiver In persuasion, the person to whom an attitude-change message is sent from a source.

Receptive field of a visual cell The retinal area that, when stimulated, affects the firing of that cell.

Reciprocity Liking those who show that they like you.

Reciprocity norm The rule that people should pay back in kind what they receive from others.

Recognition measure A memory test that requires subjects to select previously learned information from an array of options.

Regression A reversion to immature patterns of behavior.

Regression toward the mean Effect that occurs when people who score extremely high or low on some trait are measured a second time and their new score falls closer to the mean (average).

Rehearsal The process of repetitively verbalizing or thinking about information to be stored in memory.

Reinforcement An event following a response that strengthens the tendency to make that response.

Reinforcement contingencies The circumstances or rules that determine whether responses lead to the presentation of reinforcers.

Relearning measure A memory test that requires a subject to memorize information a second time to determine how much time or effort is saved by having learned it before.

Reliability The measurement consistency of a psychological test (or of other kinds of measurement techniques).

REM sleep A deep stage of sleep marked by rapid eye movements, high-frequency brain waves, and dreaming.

REM sleep behavior disorder (RBD) A sleep disorder marked by potentially troublesome dream enactments during REM periods.

Renewal effect Refers to the phenomenon that occurs if a response is extinguished in a different environment than it was acquired; the extinguished response will reappear if the animal is returned to the original environment where acquisition took place.

Replication The repetition of a study to see whether the earlier results are duplicated.

Representativeness heuristic Basing the estimated probability of an event on how similar it is to the typical prototype of that event.

Repression Keeping distressing thoughts and feelings buried in the unconscious.

Research methods Differing approaches to the observation, measurement, manipulation, and control of variables in empirical studies.

Resistance Largely unconscious defensive maneuvers a client uses to hinder the progress of therapy.

Resistance to extinction In operant conditioning, the phenomenon that occurs when an organism continues to make a response after delivery of the reinforcer for it has been terminated.

Response See *Conditioned response, Unconditioned response.*

Resting potential The stable, negative charge of a neuron when it is inactive.

Retention The proportion of material retained (remembered).

Retina The neural tissue lining the inside back surface of the eye; it absorbs light, processes images, and sends visual information to the brain.

Retinal disparity A cue used in depth perception based on the fact that objects within 25 feet project images to slightly different locations on the left and right retinas, so the right and left eyes see slightly different views of the object.

Retrieval Recovering information from memory stores.

Retroactive interference A source of forgetting that occurs when new information impairs the retention of previously learned information.

Retrograde amnesia Loss of memories for events that occurred prior to a head injury.

Retrospective memory The ability to remember events from the past or previously learned information.

Reuptake A process in which neurotransmitters are sponged up from the synaptic cleft by the presynaptic membrane.

Reversible figure A drawing that is compatible with two different interpretations that can shift back and forth.

Risky decision making Making choices under conditions of uncertainty.

Rods Specialized visual receptors that play a key role in night vision and peripheral vision.

S

Sample The collection of subjects selected for observation in an empirical study.

Sampling bias A problem that occurs when a sample is not representative of the population from which it was drawn.

Scatter diagram A graph in which paired X and Y scores for each subject are plotted as single points.

Schedule of reinforcement A specific pattern of presentation of reinforcers over time.

Schema An organized cluster of knowledge about a particular object or sequence of events.

Schizophrenia A disorder marked by delusions, hallucinations, disorganized thinking and speech, and deterioration of adaptive behavior.

Secondary appraisal An evaluation of your coping resources and options for dealing with a stressful event.

Secondary (conditioned) reinforcers Stimulus events that acquire reinforcing qualities by being associated with primary reinforcers.

Secondary sex characteristics Physical features that are associated with gender but that are not directly involved in reproduction.

Sedatives Sleep-inducing drugs that tend to decrease central nervous system activation and behavioral activity.

Self-concept A collection of beliefs about one's own nature, unique qualities, and typical behavior.

Self-efficacy One's belief about one's ability to perform behaviors that should lead to expected outcomes.

Self-report inventories Personality tests that ask individuals to answer a series of questions about their characteristic behavior.

Self-serving bias The tendency to attribute one's successes to personal factors and one's failures to situational factors.

Semantic memory system General knowledge that is not tied to the time when the information was learned.

Semantic network Concepts joined together by links that show how the concepts are related.

Sensation The stimulation of sense organs.

Sensory adaptation A gradual decline in sensitivity to prolonged stimulation.

Sensory memory The preservation of information in its original sensory form for a brief time, usually only a fraction of a second.

Separation anxiety Emotional distress seen in many infants when they are separated from people with whom they have formed an attachment.

Serial-position effect In memory tests, the fact that subjects show better recall for items at the beginning and end of a list than for items in the middle.

Sexual orientation A person's preference for emotional and sexual relationships with individuals of the same sex, the other sex, or either sex.

Shaping The reinforcement of closer and closer approximations of a desired response.

Short-term memory (STM) A limited-capacity store that can maintain unrehearsed information for up to about 20 seconds.

Skinner box A small enclosure in which an animal can make a specific response that is systematically recorded while the consequences of the response are controlled.

Sleep apnea A sleep disorder characterized by frequent reflexive gasping for air that awakens the sleeper and disrupts sleep.

Social desirability bias A tendency to give socially approved answers to questions about oneself when responding to surveys.

Social loafing A reduction in effort by individuals when they work in groups as compared to when they work by themselves.

Social psychology The branch of psychology concerned with the way individuals' thoughts, feelings, and behaviors are influenced by others.

Social roles Widely shared expectations about how people in certain positions are supposed to behave.

Social skills training A behavior therapy designed to improve interpersonal skills that emphasizes shaping, modeling, and behavioral rehearsal.

Social support Various types of aid and emotional sustenance provided by members of one's social networks.

Soma The cell body of a neuron; it contains the nucleus and much of the chemical machinery common to most cells.

Somatic nervous system The system of nerves that connect to voluntary skeletal muscles and to sensory receptors.

Somnambulism Arising and walking about while remaining asleep; sleepwalking.

Source In persuasion, the person who sends a message intended to produce attitude change to a receiver.

Source monitoring The process of making attributions about the origins of memories.

Source-monitoring error An error that occurs when a memory derived from one source is misattributed to another source.

Specific phobia A persistent and irrational fear of an object or situation that presents no realistic danger.

Spermarche The first occurrence of ejaculation.

Split-brain surgery A procedure in which the bundle of fibers that connects the cerebral hemispheres (the corpus callosum) is cut to reduce the severity of epileptic seizures.

Spontaneous recovery In classical conditioning, the reappearance of an extinguished response after a period of nonexposure to the conditioned stimulus.

Stage A developmental period during which characteristic patterns of behavior are exhibited and certain capacities become established.

Standard deviation An index of the amount of variability in a set of data.

Statistical significance The condition that exists when the probability that the observed findings are due to chance is very low.

Statistics The use of mathematics to organize, summarize, and interpret numerical data. See also *Descriptive statistics, Inferential statistics*.

Stereotypes Widely held beliefs that people have certain characteristics because of their membership in a particular group.

Stimulants Drugs that tend to increase central nervous system activation and behavioral activity.

Stimulus See *Conditioned stimulus, Unconditioned stimulus*.

Stimulus discrimination The phenomenon that occurs when an organism that has learned a response to a specific stimulus does not respond in the same way to stimuli that are similar to the original stimulus.

Stimulus generalization The phenomenon that occurs when an organism that has learned a response to a specific stimulus responds in the same way to new stimuli that are similar to the original stimulus.

Storage Maintaining encoded information in memory over time.

Stress Any circumstances that threaten or are perceived to threaten one's well-being and that thereby tax one's coping abilities.

Structuralism A school of psychology based on the notion that the task of psychology is to analyze consciousness into its basic elements and to investigate how these elements are related.

Subjective well-being Individuals' perceptions of their overall happiness and life satisfaction.

Subjects See *participants*.

Subtractive color mixing Formation of colors by removing some wavelengths of light, leaving less light than was originally there.

Superego According to Freud, the moral component of personality that incorporates social standards about what represents right and wrong.

Survey A descriptive research method in which researchers use questionnaires or interviews to gather information about specific aspects of participants' background, attitudes, beliefs, or behavior.

Sympathetic division The branch of the autonomic nervous system that mobilizes the body's resources for emergencies.

Synapse A junction where information is transmitted from one neuron to the next.

Synaptic cleft A microscopic gap between the terminal button of a neuron and the cell membrane of another neuron.

Systematic desensitization A behavior therapy used to reduce clients' phobic responses.

T

Tardive dyskinesia A neurological disorder marked by involuntary writhing and tic-like movements of the mouth, tongue, face, hands, or feet.

Telegraphic speech Refers to a child's early sentences, which consist mainly of content words; articles, prepositions, and other less critical words are omitted.

Terminal buttons Small knobs at the end of axons that secrete chemicals called *neurotransmitters.*

Thalamus A structure in the forebrain through which all sensory information (except smell) must pass to get to the cerebral cortex.

Theory A system of interrelated ideas that is used to explain a set of observations.

Theory of bounded rationality The idea that people tend to use simple strategies in decision making that focus on only a few facets of available options and often result in "irrational" decisions that are less than optimal.

Tip-of-the-tongue phenomenon The temporary inability to remember something you know, accompanied by a feeling that it's just out of reach.

Tolerance A progressive decrease in a person's responsiveness to a drug as a result of continued use.

Top-down processing In form perception, a progression from the whole to the elements.

Transference In therapy, the phenomenon that occurs when clients start relating to their therapists in ways that mimic critical relationships in their lives.

Trial In classical conditioning, any presentation of a stimulus or pair of stimuli.

Trial and error Trying possible solutions sequentially and discarding those that are in error until one works.

Trichromatic theory The idea that the human eye has three types of receptors with differing sensitivities to different light wavelengths.

Twin studies A research design in which hereditary influence is assessed by comparing the resemblance of identical twins and fraternal twins with respect to a trait.

Type A personality Personality characterized by (1) a strong competitive orientation, (2) impatience and time urgency, and (3) anger and hostility.

Type B personality Personality characterized by relatively relaxed, patient, easygoing, amicable behavior.

U

Unconditioned response (UR) An unlearned reaction to an unconditioned stimulus that occurs without previous conditioning.

Unconditioned stimulus (US) A stimulus that evokes an unconditioned response without previous conditioning.

Unconscious According to Freud, thoughts, memories, and desires that are well below the surface of conscious awareness, but that nonetheless exert great influence on behavior.

Underextension Mistake in language learning that occurs when a child incorrectly uses a word to describe a narrower set of objects or actions than it is meant to.

V

Validity The ability of a psychological test to measure what it was designed to measure.

Variability The extent to which the scores in a data set tend to vary from one another and from the mean score.

Variable-interval (VI) schedule A reinforcement schedule in which the reinforcer is given for the first response after a variable time interval has elapsed.

Variable-ratio (VR) schedule A reinforcement schedule in which the reinforcer is given after a variable number of nonreinforced responses.

Variables Any measurable conditions, events, characteristics, or behaviors that are controlled or observed in a study.

Visual illusion An apparently inexplicable discrepancy between the appearance of a visual stimulus and its physical reality.

W

Working memory A model of short-term memory consisting of a modular system for temporary storage and manipulation of information.

Working memory capacity (WMC) One's ability to hold and manipulate information in working memory.

Z

Zygote A one-celled organism formed by the union of a sperm and an egg.

REFERENCES

Abbeduto, L., Ozonoff, S., Thurman, A. J., McDuffie, A., & Schweitzer, J. (2014). Neurodevelopmental disorders. In R. E. Hales, S. C. Yudofsky, & L. W. Roberts (Eds.), *The American Psychiatric Publishing textbook of psychiatry* (6th ed.). Washington, DC: American Psychiatric Publishing.

Abel, E. L., & Kruger, M. L. (2010). Smile intensity in photographs predicts longevity. *Psychological Science, 21*(4), 542–544.

Abel, M. H. (2002). Humor, stress, and coping strategies. *Humor: International Journal of Humor Research, 15,* 365–381.

Abi-Dargham, A., & Grace, A. (2011). Dopamine and schizophrenia. In D. R. Weinberger & P. Harrison (Eds.), *Schizophrenia* (3rd ed.). Malden, MA: Wiley-Blackwell.

Abraham, A., Thybusch, K., Pieritz, K., & Hermann, C. (2014). Gender differences in creative thinking: Behavioral and fMRI findings. *Brain Imaging and Behavior, 8*(1), 39–51. doi:org/10.1007/s11682-013-9241-4

Abramov, I., Gordon, J., Feldman, O., & Chavarga, A. (2012). Sex and vision II: Color appearance of monochromatic lights. *Biology of Sex Differences, 3*(1), 21.

Abramson, L. Y., Seligman, M. E. P., & Teasdale, J. (1978). Learned helplessness in humans: Critique and reformulation. *Journal of Abnormal Psychology, 87,* 32–48.

Accardi, M., Cleere, C., Lynn, S. J., & Kirsch, I. (2013). Placebo versus "standard" hypnosis rationale: Attitudes, expectancies, hypnotic responses, and experiences. *American Journal of Clinical Hypnosis, 56,* 103–114. doi:10.1080/00029157.2013.769087

Acevedo, B. P., & Aron, A. P. (2014). Romantic love, pair-bonding, and the dopaminergic reward system. In M. Mikulincer & P. R. Shaver (Eds.), *Mechanisms of social connection: From brain to group.* Washington, DC: American Psychological Association.

Achermann, P., & Borbely, A. A. (2011). Sleep homeostasis and models of sleep regulation. In M. H. Kryger, T. Roth, & W. C. Dement (Eds.), *Principles and practice of sleep medicine* (5th ed.). Saint Louis, MO: Elsevier Saunders.

Adam, T. C., & Epel, E. (2007). Stress, eating and the reward system. *Physiology and Behavior, 91,* 449–458.

Adams, R. L., & Culbertson, J. L. (2005). Personality assessment: Adults and children. In B. J. Sadock & V. A. Sadock (Eds.), *Kaplan & Sadock's comprehensive textbook of psychiatry.* Philadelphia, PA: Lippincott Williams & Wilkins.

Ader, R. (2001). Psychoneuroimmunology. *Current Directions in Psychological Science, 10*(3), 94–98.

Ader, R., & Cohen, N. (1993). Psychoneuroimmunology: Conditioning and stress. *Annual Review of Psychology, 44,* 53–85.

Adesope, O. O., Lavin, T., Thompson, T., & Ungerleider, C. (2010). A systematic review and meta-analysis of the cognitive correlates of bilingualism. *Review of Educational Research, 80*(2), 207–245. doi:10.3102/0034654310368803

Adler, A. (1917). *Study of organ inferiority and its psychical compensation.* New York, NY: Nervous and Mental Diseases Publishing Co.

Adler, A. (1927). *Practice and theory of individual psychology.* New York, NY: Harcourt, Brace & World.

Adler, L. L. (Ed.). (1993). *International handbook on gender roles.* Westport, CT: Greenwood.

Adolph, K. E., & Berger, S. E. (2011). Physical and motor development. In M. H. Bornstein & M. E. Lamb (Eds.), *Developmental science: An advanced textbook* (pp. 109–198). New York, NY: Psychology Press.

Adolph, K. E., Cole, W. G., Komati, M., Garciaguirre, J. S., Badaly, D., Lingeman, J. M., . . . Sotsky, R. B. (2012). How do you learn to walk? Thousands of steps and dozens of falls per day. *Psychological Science, 23,* 1387–1394. doi:10.1177/0956797612446346

Adolph, K. E., Karasik, L. B., & Tamis-Lemonda, C. S. (2010). Motor skills. In M. H. Bornstein (Ed.), *Handbook of cultural developmental science* (pp. 61–88). New York, NY: Psychology Press.

Agid, O., Siu, C. O., Potkin, S. G., Kapur, S., Watsky, E., Vanderburg, D., . . . Remington, G. (2013). Meta-regression analysis of placebo response in antipsychotic trials, 1970–2010. *The American Journal of Psychiatry, 170,* 1335–1344.

Ahmed, S. H. (2012). Is sugar as addictive as cocaine. In K. D. Brownell, & M. S. Gold (Eds.), *Food and addiction: A comprehensive handbook.* New York, NY: Oxford University Press.

Ahuvia, A., & Izberk-Bilgin, E. (2013). Well-being in consumer societies. In S. A. David, I. Boniwell, & A. Conley Ayers (Eds.), *The Oxford handbook of happiness.* New York, NY: Oxford University Press.

Ainsworth, M. D. S., Blehar, M. C., Waters, E., & Wall, S. (1978). *Patterns of attachment: A psychological study of the strange situation.* Hillsdale, NJ: Erlbaum.

Ajzen, I. (2012). Attitudes and persuasion. In K. Deaux & M. Snyder (Eds.), *Oxford handbook of personality and social psychology.* New York, NY: Oxford University Press.

Ajzen, I., & Fishbein, M. (2000). Attitudes and the attitude-behavior relation: Reasoned and automatic processes. In W. Stroebe & M. Hewstone (Eds.), *European review of social psychology* (Vol. 11). Chichester, UK: Wiley.

Ajzen, I., & Fishbein, M. (2005). The influence of attitudes on behavior. In D. Albarracin, B. T. Johnson, & M. P. Zanna (Eds.), *The handbook of attitudes.* Mahwah, NJ: Erlbaum.

Akabaliev, V. H., Sivkov, S. T., & Mantarkov, M. Y. (2014). Minor physical anomalies in schizophrenia and bipolar I disorder and the neurodevelopmental continuum of psychosis. *Bipolar Disorders, 16,* 633–641. doi:10.1111/bdi.12211

Akerstedt, T., Hume, K., Minors, D., & Waterhouse, J. (1997). Good sleep: Its timing and physiological sleep characteristics. *Journal of Sleep Research, 6,* 221–229.

Akerstedt, T., & Kecklund, G. (2012). Sleep, work, and occupational stress. In C. M. Morin, & C. A. Espie (Eds.), *Oxford handbook of sleep and sleep disorders.* New York, NY: Oxford University Press.

Akins, C. K., & Panicker, S. (2012). Ethics and regulation of research with nonhuman animals. In H. Cooper, P. M. Camic, D. L. Long, A. T. Panter, D. Rindskopf, & K. J. Sher (Eds.), *APA handbook of research methods in psychology: Vol. 1. Foundations, planning, measures, and psychometrics.* Washington, DC: American Psychological Association.

Albarracin, D., & Vargas, P. (2010). Attitudes and persuasion: From biology to social responses to persuasive intent. In S. T. Fiske, D. T. Gilbert, G. Lindzey, & S. T. Fiske (Eds.), *Handbook of social psychology,* (5th ed., Vol. 1, pp. 353–393). Hoboken, NJ: Wiley.

Albert, D., Chein, J., & Steinberg, L. (2013). The teenage brain: Peer influences on adolescent decision making. *Current Decisions in Psychological Science, 22,* 114–120. doi:10.1177/0963721412471347

Albert, M. A. (2008). Neuropsychology of the development of Alzheimer's disease. In F. I. M. Craik & T. A. Salthouse (Eds.), *Handbook of aging and cognition* (2nd ed., pp. 97–132). New York, NY: Psychology Press.

Albouy, G., King, B. R., Maquet, P., & Doyon, J. (2013). Hippocampus and striatum: Dynamics and interaction during acquisition and sleep-related motor sequence memory consolidation. *Hippocampus, 23*(11), 985–1004. doi:org/10.1002/hipo.22183

Alcock, J. (2005). *Animal behavior.* Sunderland, MA: Sinauer Associates.

Aldington, S., Harwood, M., Cox, B., Weatherall, M., Beckert, L., Hansell, A., . . . Cannabis and Respiratory Disease Research Group. (2008). Cannabis use and risk of lung cancer: A case-control study. *European Respiratory Journal, 31,* 280–286.

Aldwin, C. M., & Gilmer, D. F. (2004). *Health, illness, and optimal aging: Biological and psychosocial perspectives.* Thousand Oaks, CA: Sage.

Aldwin, C. M., Jeong, Y., Igarashi, H., Choun, S., & Spiro III, A. (2014). Do hassles mediate between life events mortality in older men? Longitudinal findings from the VA Normative Aging Study. *Experimental Gerontology, 59,* 74–80.

Ale, C. M., Arnold, E. B., Whiteside, S. P. H., & Storch, E. A. (2014). Family-based behavioral treatment of pediatric compulsive hoarding: A case example. *Clinical Case Studies, 13*(1), 9–21. doi:10.1177/1534650113504487

Allemand, M., Steiger, A. E., & Hill, P. L. (2013). Stability of personality traits in adulthood: Mechanisms and implications. *GeroPsych: The Journal of Gerontology and Geriatric Psychiatry, 26,* 5–13. doi:10.1024/1662-9647/a000080

Allison, D. B., Heshka, S., Neale, M. C., Lykken, D. T., & Heymsfield, S. B. (1994). A genetic analysis of relative weight among 4,020 twin pairs, with an emphasis on sex effects. *Health Psychology, 13,* 362–365.

Alloy, L. B., Abramson, L. Y., Whitehouse, W. G., Hogan, M. E., Tashman, N. A., Steinberg, D. L., . . . Donovan, P. (1999). Depressogenic cognitive styles: Predictive validity, information processing and personality characteristics, and developmental origins. *Behavioral Research and Therapy, 37,* 503–531.

Allport, G. W. (1937). *Personality: A psychological interpretation.* New York, NY: Holt.

Allport, G. W. (1961). *Pattern and growth in personality.* New York, NY: Holt.

Altman, I. (1990). Centripetal and centrifugal trends in psychology. In L. Brickman & H. Ellis (Eds.), *Preparing psychologists for the 21st century: Proceedings of the National Conference on Graduate Education in Psychology.* Hillsdale, NJ: Erlbaum.

Amato, P. R., & Dorius, C. (2010). Fathers, children, and divorce. In M. Lamb (Ed.), *The role of the father in child development* (5th ed., pp. 177–200). Hoboken, NJ: Wiley.

Amedi, A., Floel, A., Knecht, S., Zohary, E., & Cohen, L. G. (2004). Transcranial magnetic stimulation of the occipital pole interferes with verbal processing in blind subjects. *Nature Neuroscience, 7,* 1266–1270.

American Psychological Association. (1984). *Behavioral research with animals.* Washington, DC: Author.

American Psychological Association. (2002). Ethical principles of psychologists and code of conduct. *American Psychologist, 57,* 1060–1073.

Amir, N., & Taylor, C. T. (2012). Combining computerized home-based treatments for generalized anxiety disorder: An attention modification program and cognitive behavioral therapy. *Behavior Therapy, 43,* 546–559. doi:10.1016/j.beth.2010.12.008

Amodio, D. M., & Devine, P. G. (2006). Stereotyping and evaluation in implicit race bias: Evidence for independent constructs and unique effects on behavior. *Journal of Personality and Social Psychology, 91*(4), 652–661. doi:10.1037/0022-3514.91.4.652

Anacker, C. (2014). Adult hippocampal neurogenesis in depression: Behavioral implications and regulation by the stress system. In C. M. Pariante & M. D. Lapiz-Bluhm (Eds.), *Behavioral neurobiology of stress-related disorders.* New York, NY: Springer-Verlag Publishing.

Anand, B. K., & Brobeck, J. R. (1951). Hypothalamic control of food intake in rats and cats. *Yale Journal of Biology and Medicine, 24,* 123–140.

Anderluh, M. B., Tchanturia, K., & Rabe-Hesketh, S. (2003). Childhood obsessive-compulsive personality traits in adult women with eating disorders: Defining a broader eating disorder phenotype. *American Journal of Psychiatry, 160,* 242–247.

Anderson, B., Wethington, E., & Kamarck, T. W. (2011). Interview assessment of stressor exposure. In R. J. Contrada & A. Baum (Eds.), *Handbook of stress science: Biology, psychology and health.* New York, NY: Spring Publishing Company.

Anderson, C. A., Shibuya, A., Ihori, N., Swing, E. L., Bushman, B. J., Sakamoto, A., . . . Saleem, M. (2010). Violent video game effects on aggression, empathy, and prosocial behavior in Eastern and Western countries: A meta-analytic review. *Psychological Bulletin, 136,* 151–173. doi:10.1037/a0018251

Anderson, E. A., Kohler, J. K., & Letiecq, B. L. (2002). Low-income fathers and "Responsible Fatherhood" programs: A qualitative investigation of participants' experiences. *Family Relations, 51,* 148–155.

Anderson, K. J. (1990). Arousal and the inverted-U hypothesis: A critique of Neiss's "reconceptualizing arousal." *Psychological Bulletin, 107,* 96–100.

Anderson, M. C., & Huddleston, E. (2012). Towards a cognitive and neurobiological model of motivated forgetting. In R. F. Belli (Ed.), *True and false recovered memories: Toward a reconciliation of the debate.* New York, NY: Springer.

Anderson, M. C., & Neely, J. H. (1996). Interference and inhibition in memory retrieval. In E. L. Bjork & R. A. Bjork (Eds.), *Memory.* San Diego, CA: Academic Press.

Andersson, E., Ljótsson, B., Hedman, E., Kaldo, V., Paxling, B., Andersson, G., . . . Rück, C. (2011). Internet-based cognitive behavior therapy for obsessive compulsive disorder: A pilot study. *BMC Psychiatry, 11*(125), 1–10. doi:10.1186/1471-244X-11-125

Andreasen, N. C. (1987). The diagnosis of schizophrenia. *Schizophrenia Bulletin, 13*(1), 9–22.

Andreasen, N. C. (1990). Positive and negative symptoms: Historical and conceptual aspects. In N. C. Andreasen (Ed.), *Modern problems of pharmacopsychiatry: Positive and negative symptoms and syndromes.* Basel: Karger.

Andreasen, N. C. (2005). *The creating brain: The neuroscience of genius.* New York, NY: Dana Press.

Andreasen, N. C. (2009). Schizophrenia: A conceptual history. In M. C. Gelder, N. C. Andreasen, J. J. Lopez-Ibor, Jr., & J. R. Geddes (Eds.), *New Oxford textbook of psychiatry* (2nd ed., Vol. 1). New York, NY: Oxford University Press.

Andrews, P. W., Kornstein, S. G., Halberstadt, L. J., Gardner, C. O., & Neale, M. C. (2011). Blue again: perturbational effects of antidepressants suggest monoaminergic homeostasis in major depression. *Frontiers in Psychology, 2*(159), 1–24. doi:10.3389/fpsyg.2011.00159

Angell, M. (2004). *The truth about the drug companies: How they deceive us and what to do about it.* New York, NY: Random House.

Anglin, J. M. (1993). Vocabulary development: A morphological analysis. *Monographs of the Society for Research in Child Development, 58.*

Annese, J., Schenker-Ahmed, N. M., Bartsch, H., Maechler, P., Sheh, C., Thomas, N., . . . Corkin, S. (2014). Postmortem examination of patient HM's brain based on histological sectioning and digital 3D reconstruction. *Nature Communications, 5,* 3122. doi:10.1038/ncomms4122

Ansbacher, H. (1970, February). Alfred Adler, individual psychology. *Psychology Today, 66,* 42–44.

Appelbaum, P. S. (2002). Responses to the presidential debate: The systematic defunding of psychiatric care: A crisis at our doorstep. *American Journal of Psychiatry, 159,* 1638–1640.

Appleton, K. M., Gentry, R. C., & Shepherd, R. (2006). Evidence of a role for conditioning in the development of liking for flavours in humans in everyday life. *Physiology & Behavior, 87,* 478–486.

Arango, C., & Carpenter, W. T. (2011). The schizophrenia construct: Symptomatic presentation. In D. R. Weinberger & P. Harrison (Eds.), *Schizophrenia* (3rd ed.). Malden, MA: Wiley-Blackwell.

Arcelus, J., Mitchell, A. J., Wales, J., & Nielsen, S. (2011). Mortality rates in patients with anorexia nervosa and other eating disorders: A meta-analysis of 36 studies. *Archives of General Psychiatry, 68,* 724–731. doi:10.1001/archgenpsychiatry.2011.74

Arcelus, J., Whight, D., Langham, C., Baggott, J., McGrain, L., Meadows, L., & Meyer, C. (2009). A case series evaluation of the modified version of interpersonal psychotherapy (IPT) for the treatment of bulimic eating disorders: A pilot study. *European Eating Disorders Review, 17*(4), 260–268. doi:10.1002/(ISSN)1099-096810.1002/erv.v17:410.1002/erv.932.

Archer, J. (1996). Sex differences in social behavior: Are the social role and evolutionary explanations compatible? *American Psychologist, 51,* 909–917.

Archer, J. (2005). Are women or men the more aggressive sex? In S. Fein, G. R. Goethals, & M. J. Sansdtrom (Eds.), *Gender and aggression: Interdisciplinary perspectives.* Mahwah, NJ: Erlbaum.

Arden, R., Gottfredson, L. S., & Miller, G. (2009). Does a fitness factor contribute to the association between intelligence and health outcomes? Evidence from medical abnormality counts among 3654 U.S. veterans. *Intelligence, 37*(6), 581–591. doi:10.1016/j.intell.2009.03.008

Arendt, J. (2009). Managing jet lag: Some of the problems and possible new solutions. *Sleep Medicine Reviews, 13*(4), 249–256. doi:10.1016/j.smrv.2008.07.011

Arendt, J. (2010). Shift work: Coping with the biological clock. *Occupational Medicine, 60*(1), 10–20. doi:10.1093/occmed/kqp162

Argyle, M. (1999). Causes and correlates of happiness. In D. Kahneman, E. Diener, & N. Schwarz (Eds.), *Well-being: The foundations of hedonic psychology.* New York, NY: Russell Sage Foundation.

Argyle, M. (2001). *The psychology of happiness.* New York, NY: Routledge.

Arkes, H. R. (2013). The consequences of the hindsight bias in medical decision making. *Current Directions in Psychological Science, 22,* 356–360. doi:10.1177/0963721413489988

Arkes, H. R., Wortmann, R. L., Saville, P. D., & Harkness, A. R. (1981). Hindsight bias among physicians weighing the likelihood of diagnoses. *Journal of Applied Psychology, 66,* 252–254.

Arkowitz, H., & Lilienfeld, S. O. (2007). The best medicine? How drugs stack up against talk therapy for the treatment of depression. *Scientific American Mind, 18*(5), 80–83.

Armbruster, B. B. (2000). Taking notes from lectures. In R. F. Flippo & D. C. Caverly (Eds.), *Handbook of college reading and study strategy research.* Mahwah, NJ: Erlbaum.

Armony, J. L. (2013). Current emotion research in behavioral neuroscience: The role(s) of the amygdala. *Emotion Review, 5*(1), 104–115. doi:10.1177/1754073912457208

Arnett, J. J. (2000). Emerging adulthood: A theory of development from the late teens through the twenties. *American Psychologist, 55,* 469–480.

Arnett, J. J. (2006). Emerging adulthood: Understanding the new way of coming of age. In J. J. Arnett & J. L. Tanner (Eds.), *Emerging adults in America: Coming of age in the 21st century.* Washington, DC: American Psychological Association.

Arnett, J. J. (2008). The neglected 95%: Why American psychology needs to become less American. *American Psychologist, 63*(7), 602–614. doi:10.1037/0003-066X.63.7.602.

Arnett, J. J. (2011). Emerging adulthood(s): The cultural psychology of a new life stage. In L. A. Jensen (Ed.), *Bridging cultural and development approaches to psychology: New syntheses in theory, research, and policy.* New York, NY: Oxford University Press.

Arnold, E. M., Greco, E., Desmond, K., & Rotheram-Borus, M. J. (2014). When life is a drag: Depressive symptoms associated with early adolescent smoking. *Vulnerable Children and Youth Studies, 9*(1), 1–9. doi:10.1080 /17450128.2013.797129.

Aronson, E., & Mills, J. (1959). The effect of severity of initiation on liking for a group. *Journal of Abnormal and Social Psychology, 59*, 177–181.

Arrazola, R. A., Kuiper, N. M., & Dube, S. R. (2014). Patterns of current use of tobacco products among U.S. high school students for 2000–2012: Findings from the National Youth Tobacco Survey. *Journal of Adolescent Health, 54*(1), 54–60. doi:10.1016 /j.jadohealth.2013.08.003.

Asbridge, M., Hayden, J. A., & Cartwright, J. L. (2012). Acute cannabis consumption and motor vehicle collision risk: Systematic review of observational studies and meta-analysis. *British Medical Journal, 344*, e536. doi:10.1136/bmj.e536

Asbury, K., & Plomin, R. (2014). *G is for genes: The impact of genetics on education and achievement.* Malden, MA: Wiley-Blackwell.

Asch, S. E. (1951). Effects of group pressure on the modification and distortion of judgments. In H. Guetzkow (Ed.), *Groups, Leadership and men.* Pittsburgh, PA: Carnegie Press.

Asch, S. E. (1955). Opinions and social pressures. *Scientific American, 193*(5), 31–35.

Asch, S. E. (1956). Studies of independence and conformity: A minority of one against a unanimous majority. *Psychological Monographs, 70*(9, Whole No. 416).

Asendorpf, J. B., Penke, L., & Back, M. D. (2011). From dating to mating and relating: Predictors of initial and long-term outcomes of speed-dating in a community sample. *European Journal of Personality, 25*, 16–30. doi:10.1002/per.768

Asmundson, G. G., Taylor, S., & Smits, J. J. (2014). Panic disorder and agoraphobia: An overview and commentary on DSM-5 changes. *Depression and Anxiety, 31*(6), 480–486. doi:10.1002 /da.22277

Assefi, S. L., & Garry, M. (2003). Absolut® memory distortions: Alcohol placebos influence the misinformation effect. *Psychological Science, 14*(1), 77–80.

Atkinson, J. W. (1974). The main springs of achievement-oriented activity. In J. W. Atkinson & J. O. Raynor (Eds.), *Motivation and achievement.* New York, NY: Wiley.

Atkinson, J. W. (1981). Studying personality in the context of an advanced motivational psychology. *American Psychologist, 36*, 117–128.

Atkinson, J. W. (1992). Motivational determinants of thematic apperception. In C. P. Smith (Ed.), *Motivation and personality: Handbook of thematic content analysis.* New York, NY: Cambridge University Press.

Atkinson, R. C., & Shiffrin, R. M. (1968). Human memory: A proposed system and its control processes. In K. W. Spence & J. T. Spence (Eds.), *The psychology of learning and motivation* (Vol. 2). New York, NY: Academic Press.

Atkinson, R. C., & Shiffrin, R. M. (1971). The control of short-term memory. *Scientific American, 225*, 82–90.

Aust, S., Stasch, J., Jentschke, S., Härtwig, E. A., Koelsch, S., Heuser, I., & Bajbouj, M. (2014). Differential effects of early life stress on hippocampus and amygdala volume as a function of emotional abilities. *Hippocampus, 24*, 1094–1101. doi:10.1002 /hipo.22293

Axel, R. (1995). The molecular logic of smell. *Scientific American, 273*, 154–159.

Ayanian, J. Z., & Cleary, P. D. (1999). Perceived risks of heart disease and cancer among cigarette smokers. *JAMA, 281*, 1019–1021.

Ayotte, B. J., Margrett, J. A., & Hicks-Patrick, J. (2010). Physical activity in middle-aged and young-old adults: The roles of self-efficacy, barriers, outcome expectancies, self-regulatory behaviors and social support. *Journal of Health Psychology, 15*(2), 173–185. doi:10.1177/1359105309342283

Azevedo, F. C., Carvalho, L. B., Grinberg, L. T., Farfel, J. M., Ferretti, R. L., Leite, R. P., . . . Herculano-Houzel, S. (2009). Equal numbers of neuronal and nonneuronal cells make the human brain an isometrically scaled-up primate brain. *The Journal of Comparative Neurology, 513*, 532–541. doi:10.1002/cne.21974

Baars, B. J. (1986). *The cognitive revolution in psychology.* New York, NY: Guilford Press.

Babiak, P., & Hare, R. D. (2006). *Snakes in suits: When psychopaths go to work.* New York, NY: Regan Books/Harper Collins Publishers.

Back, M. D., Schmukle, S. C., & Egloff, B. (2010). Why are narcissists so charming at first sight? Decoding the narcissism-popularity link at zero acquaintance. *Journal of Personality and Social Psychology, 98*(1), 132–145. doi:10.1037/a0016338

Backhaus, A., Agha, Z., Maglione, M. L., Repp, A., Ross, B., Zuest, D., . . . Thorp, S. R. (2012). Videoconferencing psychotherapy: A systematic review. *Psychological Services, 9*(2), 111–131. doi:10.1037/a0027924

Baddeley, A. D. (1986). *Working memory.* New York, NY: Oxford University Press.

Baddeley, A. D. (1992). Working memory. *Science, 255*, 556–559.

Baddeley, A. D. (2001). Is working memory still working? *American Psychologist, 56*, 851–864.

Baddeley, A. D. (2003). Working memory: Looking back and looking forward. *Nature Reviews Neuroscience, 4*, 829–839.

Baddeley, A. D. (2012). Working memory: Theories, models, and controversies. *Annual Review of Psychology, 631–29.* doi:10.1146 /annurev-psych-120710-100422

Baddeley, A. D., & Hitch, G. (1974). Working memory. In G. H. Bower (Ed.), *The psychology of learning and motivation* (Vol. 8). New York, NY: Academic Press.

Baddeley, J. L., Pennebaker, J. W., & Beevers, C. G. (2013). Everyday social behavior during a major depressive episode. *Social Psychology and Personality Science, 4*(4), 445–452. doi:10.1177/1948550612461654.

Baer, J. (2013). Teaching for creativity: Domains and divergent thinking, intrinsic motivation, and evaluation. In M. Banks Gregerson, H. T. Snyder, & J. C. Kaufman (Eds.), *Teaching creatively and teaching creativity.* New York, NY: Springer Science + Business Media. doi:10.1007/978-1-4614 -5185-3_13

Bahrick, H. P. (2000). Long-term maintenance of knowledge. In E. Tulving & F. I. M. Craik (Eds.), *The Oxford handbook of memory* (pp. 347–362). New York, NY: Oxford University Press.

Bailey, C. H., & Kandel, E. R. (2009). Synaptic and cellular basis of learning. In G. G. Berntson & J. T. Cacioppo (Eds.), *Handbook of neuroscience for the behavioral sciences* (Vol. 1, pp. 528–551). Hoboken, NJ: Wiley.

Bailey, J. M. (2003). Biological perspectives on sexual orientation. In L. D. Garnets & D. C. Kimmel (Eds.), *Psychological perspectives on lesbian, gay, and bisexual experiences.* New York, NY: Columbia University Press.

Bailey, J. M., & Pillard, R. C. (1991). A genetic study of male sexual orientation. *Archives of General Psychology, 48*, 1089–1096.

Bailey, J. M., Pillard, R. C., Neale, M. C. I., & Agyei, Y. (1993). Heritable factors influence sexual orientation in women. *Archives of General Psychiatry, 50*, 217–223.

Baillargeon, J., Binswanger, I. A., Penn, J. V., Williams, B. A., & Murray, O. J. (2009). Psychiatric disorders and repeat incarcerations: The revolving prison door. *The American Journal of Psychiatry, 166*(1), 103–109. doi:10.1176/appi.ajp.2008.08030416

Baillargeon, R. (2002). The acquisition of physical knowledge in infancy: A summary in eight lessons. In U. Goswami (Ed.), *Blackwell handbook of childhood cognitive development.* Malden, MA: Blackwell.

Baillargeon, R. (2004). Infants' physical world. *Current Directions in Psychological Science, 13*(3), 89–94.

Baillargeon, R. (2008). Innate ideas revisited: For a principle of persistence in infants' physical reasoning. *Perspectives on Psychological Science, 3*(1), 2–13.

Baird, A. D., Scheffer, I. E., & Wilson, S. J. (2011). Mirror neuron system involvement in empathy: A critical look at the evidence. *Social Neuroscience, 6*, 327–335. doi:10.1080/174709 19.2010.547085

Baird, B., Smallwood, J., Mrazek, M. D., Kam, J. Y., Franklin, M. S., & Schooler, J. W. (2012). Inspired by distraction: Mind wandering facilitates creative incubation. *Psychological Science, 23*, 1117–1122. doi:10.1177/0956797612446024

Baker, C. I. (2013). Visual processing in the primate brain. In R. J. Nelson, S. J. Y. Mizumori, & I. B. Weiner (Eds.), *Handbook of psychology: Vol. 3. Behavioral neuroscience* (2nd ed.). New York, NY: Wiley.

Baker, G. J., Suchday, S., & Krantz, D. S. (2007). Heart disease/attack. In G. Fink (Ed.), *Encyclopedia of stress.* San Diego, CA: Elsevier.

Balas, R., & Sweklej, J. (2012). Evaluative conditioning may occur with and without contingency awareness. *Psychological Research, 76*, 304–310. doi:10.1007/s00426-011-0336-5

Balas, R., & Sweklej, J. (2013). Changing prejudice with evaluative conditioning. *Polish Psychological Bulletin, 44*, 379–383. doi:10.2478 /ppb-2013-0041

Balcetis, E., & Dunning, D. (2006). See what you want to see: The impact of motivational states on visual perception. *Journal of Personality and Social Psychology, 91*, 612–625.

Baldwin, E. (1993). The case for animal research in psychology. *Journal of Social Issues, 49*(1), 121–131.

Baldwin, S. A., & Imel, Z. E. (2013). Therapist effects: Findings and methods. In M. J. Lambert (Ed.). *Bergin and Garfield's handbook of psychotherapy and behavior change* (6th ed.). New York, NY: Wiley.

Baldwin, W. (2000). Information no one else knows: The value of self-report. In A. A. Stone, J. S. Turkkan, C. A. Bachrach, J. B. Jobe, H. S. Kurtzman, & V. Cain

(Eds.), *The science of self-report: Implications for research and practice.* Mahwah, NJ: Erlbaum.

Bale, T. L., Baram, T. Z., Brown, A. S., Goldstein, J. M., Insel, T. R., McCarthy, . . . Nestler, E. J. (2010). Early life programming and neurodevelopmental disorders. *Biological Psychiatry, 68*(4), 314–319. doi:10.1016/j.biopsych.2010.05.028

Ball, J. S., & Links, P. S. (2009). Borderline personality disorder and childhood trauma: evidence for a causal relationship. *Current Psychiatry Reports, 11*(1), 63–68. doi:10.1007/s11920-009-0010-4

Balter, M. (2010). Did working memory spark creative culture? *Science, 328*(5975), 160–163. doi:10.1126/science.328.5975.160

Bamidis, P., Vivas, A., Styliadis, C., Frantzidis, C., Klados, M., Schlee, W., . . . Papageorgiou, S. (2014). A review of physical and cognitive interventions in aging. *Neuroscience and Biobehavioral* Reviews, *44*, 206–220. doi:10.1016/j.neubiorev.2014.03.019

Banaji, M. R., & Heiphetz, L. (2010). Attitudes. In S. T. Fiske, D. T. Gilbert, & G. Lindzey (Eds.), *Handbook of social psychology* (Vol. 1, 5th ed., pp. 353–393). Hoboken, NJ: Wiley.

Bandura, A. (1977). *Social learning theory.* Englewood Cliffs, NJ: Prentice-Hall.

Bandura, A. (1986). *Social foundations of thought and action: A social-cognitive theory.* Englewood Cliffs, NJ: Prentice-Hall.

Bandura, A. (1990). Perceived self-efficacy in the exercise of personal agency. *Journal of Applied Sport Psychology, 2*(2), 128–163.

Bandura, A. (1993). Perceived self-efficacy in cognitive development and functioning. *Educational Psychologist, 28*(2), 117–148.

Bandura, A. (1995). Exercise of personal and collective efficacy in changing societies. In A. Bandura (Ed.), *Self-efficacy in changing societies.* New York, NY: Cambridge University Press.

Bandura, A. (1999). Social cognitive theory of personality. In L. A. Pervin & O. P. John (Eds.), *Handbook of personality: Theory and research.* New York, NY: Guilford Press.

Bandura, A. (2006). Toward a psychology of human agency. *Perspectives on Psychological Science, 1,* 164–180.

Bandura, A. (2012). Social cognitive theory. In P. A. Van Lange, A. W. Kruglanski, & E. T. Higgins (Eds.), *Handbook of theories of social psychology* (Vol. 1). Los Angeles, CA: Sage.

Bandura, A., Ross, D., & Ross, S. A. (1963). Imitation of film-mediated aggressive models. *Journal of Abnormal and Social Psychology, 66,* 3–11.

Banks, S., & Dinges, D. F. (2011). Chronic sleep deprivation. In M. H. Kryger, T. Roth, & W. C. Dement (Eds.), *Principles and practice of sleep medicine* (5th ed.). Saint Louis, MO: Elsevier Saunders.

Banuazizi, A., & Movahedi, S. (1975). Interpersonal dynamics in a simulated prison: A methodological analysis. *American Psychologist, 30,* 152–160.

Banyard, V. L., & Williams, L. M. (1999). Memories for child sexual abuse and mental health functioning: Findings on a sample of women and implications for future research. In L. M. Williams & V. L. Banyard (Eds.), *Trauma & memory.* Thousand Oaks, CA: Sage.

Bar, M., & Bubic, A. (2013). Top-down effects in visual perception. In K. N. Ochsner & S. Kosslyn (Eds.), *The oxford handbook of cognitive neuroscience: Vol.1. Core topics.* doi:10.1093/oxfordhb/9780199988693.013.0004

Barber, J. P., Muran, C., McCarthy, K. S., & Keefe, J. R. (2013). Research on dynamic therapies. In M. J. Lambert (Ed.). *Bergin and Garfield's handbook of psychotherapy and behavior change* (6th ed.). New York, NY: Wiley.

Barber, L., Munz, D., Bagsby, P., & Powell, E. (2010). Sleep consistency and sufficiency: Are both necessary for less psychological strain? *Stress & Health: Journal of the International Society for the Investigation of Stress, 26*(3), 186–193.

Bard, P. (1934). On emotional experience after decortication with some remarks on theoretical views. *Psychological Review, 41,* 309–329.

Bargh, J. A., Gollwitzer, P. M., & Oettingen, G. (2010). Motivation. In S. T. Fiske, D. T. Gilbert, & G. Lindzey (Eds*.), Handbook of social psychology* (5th ed., Vol. 1, pp. 268–316). New York, NY: Wiley.

Bargh, J. A., McKenna, K. Y. A., & Fitzsimons, G. M. (2002). Can you see the real me? Activation and expression of the "true self" on the Internet. *Journal of Social Issues, 58,* 33–48.

Barker, D. J. P. (2013). The developmental origins of chronic disease. In N. S. Landale, S. M. McHale, & A. Booth (Eds.), *Families and child health: National Symposium on family issues* (Vol. 3). New York, NY: Spring Science + Business Media. doi:10.1007/978-1-4614-6194-4_1

Barlett, D. L., & Steele, J. B. (1979). *Empire: The life, legend and madness of Howard Hughes.* New York, NY: Norton.

Barlow, D. H., Bullis, J. R., Comer, J. S., & Ametaj, A. A. (2013). Evidence-based psychological treatments: an update and a way forward. *Annual Review of Clinical Psychology, 9,* 1–27. doi:10.1146/annurev-clinpsy-050212-185629

Barnier, A. J., Cox, R. E., & McConkey, K. M. (2014). The province of "highs": The high hypnotizable person in the science of hypnosis and in psychological science. *Psychology of Consciousness: Theory, Research, and Practice, 1,* 168–183. doi:10.1037/cns0000018

Baron, K. G., Reid, K. J., Kern, A. S., & Zee, P. C. (2011). Role of sleep timing in caloric intake and BMI. *Obesity, 19,* 1374–1381. doi:10.1038/oby.2011.100

Barrett, L. F. (2011). Was Darwin wrong about emotional expressions? *Current Directions in Psychological Science, 20,* 400–406. doi:10.1177/0963721411429125

Barrios-Miller, N. L., & Siefferman, L. (2013). Evidence that fathers, but not mothers, respond to mate and offspring coloration by favouring high-quality offspring. *Animal Behaviour, 85*(6), 1377–1383. doi:10.1016/j.anbehav.2013.03.029

Bartoshuk, L. M. (1993). Genetic and pathological taste variation: What can we learn from animal models and human disease? In D. Chadwick, J. Marsh, & J. Goode (Eds.), *The molecular basis of smell and taste transduction.* New York, NY: Wiley.

Bartoshuk, L. M., Duffy, V. B., & Miller, I. J. (1994). PTC/PROP taste: Anatomy, psychophysics, and sex effects. *Physiology & Behavior, 56,* 1165–1171.

Basbaum, A. I., & Jessell, T. M. (2013). Pain. In E. R. Kandel, J. H. Schwartz, T. M. Jessell, S. A. Siegelbaum, & A. J. Hudspeth (Eds.), *Principles of neural science* (5th ed.). New York, NY: McGraw-Hill.

Basow, S. A. (1992). *Gender: Stereotypes and roles.* Pacific Grove, CA: Brooks/Cole.

Bassok, M., & Novick, L. R. (2012). Problem solving. In K. J. Holyoak, & R. G. Morrison (Eds.), *Oxford handbook of thinking and reasoning.* New York, NY: Oxford University Press.

Bassuk, E. L., Buckner, J. C., Perloff, J. N., & Bassuk, S. S. (1998). Prevalence of mental health and substance use disorders among homeless and low-income housed mothers. *American Journal of Psychiatry, 155,* 1561–1564.

Bates, E. (1999). Plasticity, localization, and language development. In S. H. Broman & J. M. Fletcher (Eds.), *The changing nervous system: Neurobehavioral consequences of early brain disorders* (pp. 214–247). New York, NY: Oxford University Press.

Bateson, P. (2011). Ethical debates about animal suffering and the use of animals in research. *Journal of Consciousness Studies, 18*(9–10), 186–208.

Batterham, P. J., Christensen, H., & Mackinnon, A. J. (2009). Fluid intelligence is independently associated with all-cause mortality over 17 years in an elderly community sample: An investigation of potential mechanisms. *Intelligence, 37*(6), 551–560. doi:10.1016/j.intell.2008.10.004

Baumeister, R. F. (1989). The optimal margin of illusion. *Journal of Social and Clinical Psychology, 8,* 176–189.

Baumeister, R. F. (2000). Gender differences in erotic plasticity: The female sex drive as socially flexible and responsive. *Psychological Bulletin, 126,* 347–374.

Baumeister, R. F. (2004). Gender and erotic plasticity: Sociocultural influences on the sex drive. *Sexual and Relationship Therapy, 19,* 133–139.

Baumeister, R. F., Catanese, K. R., & Vohs, K. D. (2001). Is there a gender difference in strength of sex drive? Theoretical views, conceptual distinctions, and a review of relevent evidence. *Personality and Social Psychology Review, 5*(3), 242–273. doi:10.1207/S15327957PSPR0503_5

Baumeister, R. F., & Twenge, J. M. (2002). Cultural suppression of female sexuality. *Review of General Psychology, 6,* 166–203.

Baumeister, R. F., & Vohs, K. D. (2001). Narcissism as addiction to esteem. *Psychological Inquiry, 12*(4), 206–210.

Baumrind, D. (1964). Some thoughts on the ethics of reading Milgram's "Behavioral study of obedience." *American Psychologist, 19,* 421–423.

Baumrind, D. (1985). Research using intentional deception: Ethical issues revisited. *American Psychologist, 40,* 165–174.

Bebbington, P. (2013). The classification and epidemiology of unipolar depression. In M. Power (Ed.), *The Wiley-Blackwell handbook of mood disorders* (2nd ed.). Malden, MA: Wiley-Blackwell.

Bebbington, P. E., & Kuipers, E. (2011). Schizophrenia and psychosocial stress. In D. R. Weinberger & P. Harrison (Eds.), *Schizophrenia* (3rd ed.). Malden, MA: Wiley-Blackwell.

Beck, A. T. (1976). *Cognitive therapy and the emotional disorders.* New York, NY: International Universities Press.

Beck, A. T., & Weishaar, M. E. (2011). Cognitive therapy. In R. J. Corsini & D. Wedding (Eds.), *Current psychotherapies* (9th ed.). Belmont, CA: Brooks/Cole.

Becker, A. E., & Fay, K. (2006). Socio-cultural issues and eating disorders. In S. Wonderlich, J. Mitchell, M. de Zwaan, & H. Steiger (Eds.), *Annual review of eating disorders*. Oxon, UK: Radcliffe.

Becker, A. L. (2009, November 29). Science of memory: Researchers to study pieces of unique brain. *The Hartford Courant*. Retrieved from www.courant.com

Beer, J. S., Shimamura, A. P., & Knight, R. T. (2004). Frontal lobe contributions to executive control of cognitive and social behavior. In M. S. Gazzaniga (Ed.), *The cognitive neurosciences*. Cambridge, MA: MIT Press.

Behrens, R. R. (2010). Ames demonstration in perception. In E. B. Goldstein (Ed.), *Encyclopedia of perception*. Thousand Oaks, CA: Sage.

Beidel, D. C., & Stipelman, B. (2007). Anxiety disorders. In M. Hersen, S. M. Turner, & D. C. Beidel (Eds.), *Adult psychopathology and diagnosis*. New York, NY: Wiley.

Beilin, H. (1992). Piaget's enduring contribution to developmental psychology. *Developmental Psychology, 28*, 191–204.

Bekelman, J. E., Li, Y., & Gross, C. P. (2003). Scope and impact of financial conflicts of interest in biomedical research. *JAMA, 289*, 454–465.

Bekkouche, N. S., Holmes, S., Whittaker, K. S., & Krantz, D. S. (2011). Stress and the heart: Psychosocial stress and coronary heart disease. In R. J. Contrada & A. Baum (Eds.), *The handbook of stress science: Biology, psychology, and health* (pp. 111–121). New York, NY: Springer Publishing.

Bell, A. P., Weinberg, M. S., & Hammersmith, S. K. (1981). *Sexual preference: Its development in men and women*. Bloomington: IN: University Press.

Bellis, M. A., Downing, J., & Ashton, J. R. (2006). Adults at 12? Trends in puberty and their public health consequences. *Journal of Epidemiology and Community Health, 60*, 910–911.

Bem, S. L. (1985). Androgyny and gender schema theory: A conceptual and empirical integration. In T. B. Sonderegger (Ed.), *Nebraska symposium on motivation, 1984: Psychology and gender* (Vol. 32). Lincoln, NE: University of Nebraska Press.

Benarroch, E. E. (2013). Adult neurogenesis in the dentate gyrus: General concepts and potential implications. *Neurology, 81*, 1443–1452. doi:10.1212/WNL.0b013e3182a9a156

Bendall, S., Jackson, H. J., Hulbert, C. A., & McGorry, P. D. (2008).

Childhood trauma and psychotic disorders: A systematic, critical review of the evidence. *Schizophrenia Bulletin, 34*, 568–579. doi:10.1093/schbul/sbm121

Bender, D. S., Skodol, A. E., Dyck, I. R., Markowitz, J. C., Shea, M. T., Yen, S., . . . Grilo, C. M. (2007). Ethnicity and mental health treatment utilization by patients with personality disorders. *Journal of Consulting and Clinical Psychology, 75*, 992–999.

Benedetti, F. (2009). *Placebo effects: Understanding the mechanisms in health and disease*. New York, NY: Oxford University Press.

Benedetti, F. (2013). Placebo and the new physiology of the doctor-patient relationship. *Physiological Reviews, 93*(3), 1207–1246. doi:10.1152/physrev.00043.2012.

Benjamin, L. T., Jr. (2000). The psychology laboratory at the turn of the 20th century. *American Psychologist, 55*, 318–321.

Benjamin, L. T., Jr. (2014). *A brief history of modern psychology* (2nd ed.). New York, NY: Wiley.

Benjamin, L. T., Jr., & Baker, D. B. (2004). *From seance to science: A history of the profession of psychology in America*. Belmont, CA: Wadsworth.

Benjamin, L. T., Jr., & Simpson, J. A. (2009). The power of the situation: The impact of Milgram's obedience studies on personality and social psychology. *American Psychologist, 64*, 12–19. doi:10.1037/a0014077

Benka, J., Nagyova, I., Rosenberger, J., Macejova, Z., Lazurova, I., Van der Klink, J., . . . Van Dijk, J. (2014). Is coping self-efficacy related to psychological distress in early and established rheumatoid arthritis patients? *Journal of Developmental and Physical Disabilities, 26*(3), 285–297. doi:10.1007/s10882-013-9364-y

Bennett, A. J. (2012). Animal research: The bigger picture and why we need psychologists to speak out. *Psychological Science Agenda, 26*(4). doi:10.1037/e553492012-010

Ben-Porath, Y. S. (2013). Self-report inventories: Assessing personality and psychopathology. In J. R. Graham, J. A. Naglieri, & I. B. Weiner (Eds.), *Handbook of psychology: Vol. 10. Assessment psychology* (2nd ed.). Hoboken, NJ: Wiley.

Benson, H. (1975). *The relaxation response*. New York, NY: Morrow.

Benson, H., & Klipper, M. Z. (1988). *The relaxation response*. New York, NY: Avon.

Bentall, R. P. (2009). *Doctoring the mind: Is our current treatment of mental illness really any good?* New York, NY: New York University Press.

Benton, D. (2004). Role of parents in the determination of the food preferences of children and the development of obesity. *International Journal of Obesity, 28*, 858–869.

Berenbaum, S. A., Martin, C. L., & Ruble, D. N. (2008). Gender development. In W. Damon & R. M. Lerner (Eds.), *Child and adolescent development: An advanced course* (pp. 647–681). New York, NY: Wiley.

Berenbaum, S. A., & Snyder, E. (1995). Early hormonal influences on childhood sex-typed activity and playmate preferences: Implications for the development of sexual orientation. *Developmental Psychology, 31*, 31–42.

Berent, I., Pan, H., Zhao, X., Epstein, J., Bennett, M. L., Deshpande, V., . . . Stern, E. (2014). Language universals engage Broca's area. *PloS One, 9*(4), e95155. doi:10.1371/journal.pone.009515

Berg, V., Lummaa, V., Lahdenperä, M., Rotkirch, A., & Jokela, M. (2014). Personality and long-term reproductive success measured by the number of grandchildren. *Evolution and Human Behavior, 35*, 533–539. doi:10.1016/j.evolhumbehav.2014.07.006

Berger, L. K., Zane, N., & Hwang, W. (2014). Therapist ethnicity and treatment orientation differences in multicultural counseling competencies. *Asian American Journal of Psychology, 5*(1), 53–65. doi:10.1037/a0036178

Berger, Z. (2013). *Talking to your doctor: A patient's guide to communication in the exam room and beyond*. Lanham, MD: Rowman & Littlefield Publishers.

Berghmans, R. L. P. (2007). Misleading research participants: Moral aspects of deception in psychological research. *Netherlands Journal of Psychology, 63*(1), 14–20.

Berkowitz, L. (1989). Frustration-aggression hypothesis: Examination and reformulation. *Psychological Bulletin, 106*, 59–73.

Berlin, B., & Kay, P. (1969). *Basic color terms: Their universality and evolution*. Berkeley, CA: University of California Press.

Berlin, L. J. (2012). Leveraging attachment research to re-vision infant/toddler care for poor families. In S. L. Odom, P. E. Pungello, & N. Gardner-Neblett (Eds.), *Infants, toddlers, and families in poverty: Research implications for early child care*. New York, NY: Guilford Press.

Berman, A. L. (2009). Depression and suicide. In I. H. Gotlib & C. L. Hammen (Eds.), *Handbook of depression* (2nd ed.). New York, NY: Guilford Press.

Bernstein, D. M., Erdfelder, E., Meltzoff, A. N., Peria, W., & Loftus, G. R. (2011). Hindsight bias from 3 to 95 years of age. *Journal of Experimental Psychology: Learning, Memory, and Cognition, 37*, 378–391. doi:10.1037/a0021971

Bernstein, D. M., & Loftus, E. F. (2009). The consequences of false memories for food preferences and choices. *Perspectives on Psychological Science, 4*(2), 135–139. doi:10.1111/j.1745-6924.2009.01113.x-7

Bernstein, H. (2007). Maternal and perinatal infection-viral. In S. G. Gabbe, J. R. Niebyl, & J. L. Simpson (Eds.), *Obstetrics: Normal and problem pregnancies* (5th ed., pp. 1203–1232). Philadelphia, PA: Elsevier.

Berntsen, D., Johannessen, K. B., Thomsen, Y. D., Bertelsen, M., Hoyle, R. H., & Rubin, D. C. (2012). Peace and war: Trajectories of posttraumatic stress disorder symptoms before, during, and after military deployment in Afghanistan. *Psychological Science, 23*, 1557–1565. doi:10.1177/0956797612457389

Berrettini, W. (2006). Genetics of bipolar and unipolar disorders. In D. J. Stein, D. J. Kupfer, & A. F. Schatzberg (Eds.), *Textbook of mood disorders*. Washington, DC: American Psychiatric Publishing.

Berridge, K. C. (2004). Motivation concepts in behavioral neuroscience. *Physiology and Behavior, 81*(2), 179–209.

Berry, C. M., & Sackett, P. R. (2009). Individual differences in course choice result in underestimation of the validity of college admissions systems. *Psychological Science, 20*(7), 822–830. doi:10.1111/j.1467-9280.2009.02368.x.

Berry, J. W., Poortinga, Y., Segall, M., & Dasen, P. (1992). *Cross-cultural psychology*. New York, NY: Cambridge University Press.

Berscheid, E. (1988). Some comments on love's anatomy: Or, whatever happened to old-fashioned lust. In R. J. Sternberg & M. L. Barnes (Eds.), *The psychology of love*. New Haven: Yale University Press.

Berthoud, H. (2012). Central regulation of hunger, satiety, and body weight. In K. D. Brownell, & M. S. Gold (Eds.), *Food and addiction: A comprehensive handbook*. New York, NY: Oxford University Press.

Bertrand, R. M., Graham, E. K., & Lachman, M. E. (2013). Personality development in adulthood and old age. In R. M. Lerner, M. A. Easterbrooks, J. Mistry, & I. B. Weiner (Eds.), *Handbook of psychology: Vol. 6. Developmental psychology*. New York, NY: Wiley.

Betensky, J. D., Contrada, R. J., & Glass, D. C. (2012). Psychosocial factors in cardiovascular disease: Emotional states, conditions, and attributes. In A. Baum, T. A. Revenson, & J. Singer (Eds.), *Handbook of health psychology* (2nd ed.). New York, NY: Psychology Press.

Bettelheim, B. (1967). *The empty fortress.* New York, NY: Free Press.

Beutler, L. E. (2002). The dodo bird is extinct. *Clinical Psychology: Science & Practice, 9*(1), 30–34.

Beutler, L. E., Bongar, B., & Shurkin, J. N. (2001). *A consumer's guide to psychotherapy.* New York, NY: Oxford University Press.

Beutler, L. E., Malik, M., Alimohamed, S., Harwood, T. M., Talebi, H., Noble, S., & Wong, E. (2004). Therapist variables. In M. J. Lambert (Ed.), *Bergin and Garfield's handbook of psychotherapy and behavior change.* New York, NY: Wiley.

Bhanpuri, N. H., Okamura, A. M., & Bastian, A. J. (2013). Predictive modeling by the cerebellum improves proprioception. *The Journal of Neuroscience, 33,* 14301–14306. doi:10.1523/JNEUROSCI.0784-13.2013

Bhargava, S., Kassam, K. S., & Loewenstein, G. (2014). A reassessment of the defense of parenthood. *Psychological Science, 25,* 299–302. doi:10.1177/0956797613503348

Bhasin, T., & Schendel, D. (2007). Sociodemographic risk factors for autism in a U.S. metropolitan area. *Journal of Autism and Developmental Disorders, 37,* 667–677.

Bialystok, E., Craik, F. M., Binns, M. A., Ossher, L., & Freedman, M. (2014). Effects of bilingualism on the age of onset and progression of MCI and AD: Evidence from executive function tests. *Neuropsychology, 28,* 290–304. doi:10.1037/neu0000023

Bianchi, M. T., Williams, K. L., McKinney, S., & Ellenbogen, J. M. (2013). The subjective-objective mismatch in sleep perception among those with insomnia and sleep apnea. *Journal of Sleep Research, 22,* 557–568. doi:10.1111/jsr.12046

Bianchi, S. M., Sayer, L. C., Milkie, M. A., & Robinson, J. P. (2012). Housework: Who did, does or will do it, and how much does it matter? *Social Forces, 91,* 55–63. doi:10.1093/sf/sos120

Biblarz, T. J., & Stacey, J. (2010). How does the gender of parents matter? *Journal of Marriage and Family, 72*(1), 3–22. doi:10.1111/j.1741-3737.2009.00678.x

Biermann, T., Estel, D., Sperling, W., Bleich, S., Kornhuber, J., & Reulbach, U. (2005). Influence of lunar phases on suicide: The end of a myth? A population-based study. *Chronobiology International, 22,* 1137–1143.

Biernat, M., & Danaher, K. (2013). Prejudice. In H. Tennen, J. Suls, & I. B. Weiner (Eds.), *Handbook of psychology: Vol. 5. Personality and social psychology* (2nd ed.). New York, NY: Wiley.

Bifulco, A. (2013). Psychosocial models and issues in major depression. In M. Power (Ed.), *The Wiley-Blackwell handbook of mood disorders* (2nd ed.). Malden, MA: Wiley-Blackwell.

Bigelow, B. J. (2006). There's an elephant in the room: The impact of early poverty and neglect on intelligence and common learning disorders in children, adolescents, and their parents. *Developmental Disabilities Bulletin, 34*(1–2), 177–215.

Bilali_, M., McLeod, P., & Gobet, F. (2010). The mechanism of the Einstellung (set) effect: A pervasive source of cognitive bias. *Current Directions in Psychological Science, 19*(2), 111–115. doi:10.1177/0963721410363571

Birkeland, S. A., Manson, T. M., Kisamore, J. L., Brannick, M. T., & Smith, M. A. (2006). A meta-analytic investigation of job applicant faking on personality measures. *International Journal of Selection and Assessment, 14,* 317–335.

Birney, D. P., Citron-Pousty, J. H., Lutz, D. J., & Sternberg, R. J. (2005). The development of cognitive and intellectual abilities. In M. H. Bornstein & M. E. Lamb (Eds.), *Developmental science: An advanced textbook.* Mahwah, NJ: Erlbaum.

Birney, D. P., & Sternberg, R. J. (2011). The development of cognitive abilities. In M. H. Bornstein & M. E. Lamb (Eds.), *Developmental science: An advanced textbook* (pp. 353–388). New York, NY: Psychology Press.

Bjork, R. A. (1992). Interference and forgetting. In L. R. Squire (Ed.), *Encyclopedia of learning and memory.* New York, NY: Macmillan.

Bjork, R. A., Dunlosky, J., & Kornell, N. (2013). Self-regulated learning: Beliefs, techniques, and illusions. *Annual Review of Psychology, 64,* 417–444.

Bjorklund, D. F. (2012). *Children's thinking: Cognitive development and individual differences* (5th ed.). Belmont, CA: Wadsworth.

Blair, I. V., Dasgupta, N., & Glaser, J. (2015). Implicit attitudes. In M. Mikulincer, P. R. Shaver, E. Borgida, & J. A. Bargh (Eds.), *APA handbook of personality and social psychology: Vol. 1. Attitudes and social cognition.* Washington, DC: American Psychological Association.

Blair, S. N., Kohl, H. W., Paffenbarger, R. S., Clark, D. G., Cooper, K. H., &

Gibbons, L. W. (1989). Physical fitness and all-cause mortality: A prospective study of healthy men and women. *JAMA, 262,* 2395–2401.

Blankenhorn, D. (1995). *Fatherless America: Confronting our most urgent social problem.* New York, NY: Basic Books.

Blashfield, R. K., Keeley, J. W., Flanagan, E. H., & Miles, S. R. (2014). The cycle of classification: DSM-I through DSM-5. *Annual Review of Clinical Psychology, 10,* 25–51. doi:10.1146/annurev-clinpsy-032813-153639

Blass, E. M. (2012). Phylogenic and ontogenetic contributions to today's obesity quagmire. In K. D. Brownell, & M. S. Gold (Eds.), *Food and addiction: A comprehensive handbook.* New York, NY: Oxford University Press.

Blass, T. (1999). The Milgram Paradigm after 35 years: Some things we now know about obedience to authority. *Journal of Applied Social Psychology, 29,* 955–978.

Blass, T. (2009). From New Haven to Santa Clara: A historical perspective on the Milgram obedience experiments. *American Psychologist, 64*(1), 37–45. doi:10.1037/a0014434

Bleak, J., & Frederick, C. M. (1998). Superstitious behavior in sport: Levels of effectiveness and determinants of use in three collegiate sports. *Journal of Sport Behavior, 21,* 1–15.

Bleuler, E. (1911). *Dementia praecox or the group F schizophrenias.* New York, NY: International Universities Press.

Bliwise, D. L. (2011). Normal aging. In M. H. Kryger, T. Roth, & W. C. Dement (Eds.), *Principles and practice of sleep medicine* (5th ed.). Saint Louis, MO: Elsevier Saunders.

Block, J. R., & Yuker, H. E. (1992). *Can you believe your eyes?: Over 250 illusions and other visual oddities.* New York, NY: Brunner/Mazel.

Block, N. (2002). How heritability misleads us about race. In J. Fish (Ed.), *Race and intelligence: Separating science from myth.* Mahwah, NJ: Erlbaum.

Boase, J., & Wellman, B. (2006). Personal relationships: On and off the Internet. In A. L. Vangelisti & D. Perlman (Eds.), *The Cambridge handbook of personal relationships.* New York, NY: Cambridge University Press.

Bochner, S., & Jones, J. (2003). *Child language development: Learning to talk.* London, UK: Whurr Publishers.

Bodenhausen, G. V., & Morales, J. R. (2013). Social cognition and perception. In H. Tennen, J. Suls, & I. B. Weiner (Eds.), *Handbook of psychology: Vol. 5. Personality and social*

psychology (2nd ed.). New York, NY: Wiley.

Boecker, H., Sprenger, T., Spilker, M. E., Henriksen, G., Koppenhoefer, M., & Wagner, K. J., . . . Tolle, T. R. (2008). The runner's high: Opioidergic mechanisms in the human brain. *Cerebral Cortex, 18*(11), 2523–2531. doi:10.1093/cercor/bhn013

Bohacek, J., Gapp, K., Saab, B. J., & Mansuy, I. M. (2013). Transgenerational epigenetic effects on brain functions. *Biological Psychiatry, 73,* 313–320. doi:10.1016/j.biopsych.2012.08.019

Bohannon, J. N., III., & Bonvillian, J. D. (2009). Theoretical approaches to language acquisition. In J. B. Gleason & N. B. Ratner (Eds.), *The development of language.* Boston, MA: Pearson.

Bohner, G., & Schwarz, N. (2001). Attitudes, persuasion, and behavior. In A. Tesser & N. Schwarz (Eds.), *Blackwell handbook of social psychology: Intraindividual processes.* Malden, MA: Blackwell.

Boland, R. J., & Keller, M. B. (2008). Antidepressants. In A. Tasman, J. Kay, J. A. Lieberman, M. B. First, & M. Maj (Eds.), *Psychiatry* (3rd ed.). New York, NY: Wiley-Blackwell.

Boldrini, M., Santiago, A. N., Hen, R., Dwork, A. J., Rosoklija, G. B., Tamir, H., . . . Mann, J. J. (2013). Hippocampal granule neuron number and denate gyrus volume in antidepressant-treated and untreated major depression. *Neuropsychopharmacology, 38,* 1068–1077. doi:10.1038/npp.2013.5

Boldry, J. G., Gaertner, L., & Quinn, J. (2007). Measuring the measures: A meta-analytic investigation of the measures of outgroup homogeneity. *Group Processes & Intergroup Relations, 10,* 157–178.

Boles, D. B. (2005). A large-sample study of sex differences in functional cerebral lateralization. *Journal of Clinical and Experimental Neuropsychology, 27*(6), 759–768. doi:10.1081/13803390590954263

Bolles, R. C. (1975). *Theory of motivation.* New York, NY: Harper & Row.

Bolling, M. Y., Terry, C. M., & Kohlenberg, R. J. (2006). Behavioral theories. In J. C. Thomas & D. L. Segal (Eds.), *Comprehensive handbook of personality and psychopathology.* New York, NY: Wiley.

Boly, M., Faymonville, M.-E., Vogt, B. A., Maquet, P., & Laureys, S. (2007). Hypnotic regulation of consciousness and the pain neuromatrix. In G. A. Jamieson (Ed.), *Hypnosis and conscious states: The cognitive neuroscience perspective.* New York, NY: Oxford University Press.

Bonanno, G. A. (1998). The concept or "working through" loss: A critical evaluation of the cultural, historical, and empirical evidence. In A. Maercker, M. Schuetzwohl, & Z. Solomon (Eds.), *Posttraumatic stress disorder: Vulnerability and resilience in the lifespan*. Gottingen, Germany: Hogrefe and Huber.

Bonanno, G. A., & Burton, C. L. (2013). Regulatory flexibility: An individual differences perspective on coping and emotion regulation. *Perspectives on Psychological Science, 8*, 591–612. doi:10.1177/1745691613504116

Bonanno, G., Westphal, M., & Mancini, A. D. (2012). Loss, trauma, and resilience in adulthood. In B. Hayslip, Jr., & G. C. Smith (Eds.), *Annual review of gerontology and geriatrics: Vol. 32. Emerging perspectives on resilience in adulthood and later life*. New York, NY: Springer Publishing Co.

Bonanno, G. A., Wortman, C. B., Lehman, D. R., Tweed, R. G., Harrig, M., Sonnega, J., . . . Nesse, R. M. (2002). Resilience to loss and chronic grief: A prospective study from preloss to 18-months postloss. *Journal of Personality and Social Psychology, 83*, 1150–1164.

Bonanno, G. A., Wortman, C. B., & Nesse, R. M. (2004). Prospective patterns of resilience and maladjustment during widowhood. *Psychology and Aging, 19*, 260-271. doi:10.1037/0882-7974.19.2.260

Bonnet, M. H. (2005). Acute sleep deprivation. In M. H. Kryger, T. Roth, & W. C. Dement (Eds.), *Principles and practice of sleep medicine*. Philadelphia, PA: Elsevier Saunders.

Bono, G., McCullough, M. E., & Root, L. M. (2008). Forgiveness, feeling connected to others, and well-being: Two longitudinal studies. *Personality and Social Psychology Bulletin, 34*, 182–195.

Boot, W. R., Simons, D. J., Stothart, C., & Stutts, C. (2013). The pervasive problems with placebos in psychology: Why active control groups are not sufficient to rule out placebo effects. *Perspective on Psychological Science, 8*(4), 445–454. doi:10.1177/1745691613491271

Borgida, E., & Nisbett, R. E. (1977). The differential impact of abstract vs. concrete information on decisions. *Journal of Applied Social Psychology, 7*, 258–271.

Boring, E. G. (1966). A note on the origin of the word *psychology*. *Journal of the History of the Behavioral Sciences, 2*, 167.

Born, J., & Wilhelm, I. (2012). System consolidation of memory during sleep. *Psychological Research, 76*, 192–203. doi:10.1007/s00426-011-0335-6

Bornstein, M. H., Jager, J., & Steinberg, L. D. (2013). Adolescents, parents, friends/peers: A relationships model. In R. M. Lerner, M. A. Easterbrooks, J. Mistry, & I. B. Weiner (Eds.), *Handbook of psychology: Vol. 6. Developmental psychology*. New York, NY: Wiley.

Bornstein, R. F., Denckla, C. A., & Chung, W.-J. (2013). Psychodynamic models of personality. In H. Tennen, J. Suls, & I. B. Weiner (Eds.), *Handbook of psychology, Vol. 5. Personality and social psychology* (2nd ed.; pp. 43-64). Hoboken, NJ: Wiley.

Boroditsky, L. (2001). Does language shape thought? Mandarin and English speakers' conceptions of time. *Cognitive Psychology, 43*(1), 1–22.

Botha, U. A., Koen, L., Joska, J. A., Parker, J. S., Horn, N., Hering, L. M., & Oosthuizen, P. P. (2010). The revolving door phenomenon in psychiatry: Comparing low-frequency and high-frequency users of psychiatric inpatient services in a developing country. *Social Psychiatry and Psychiatric Epidemiology, 45*, 461–468. doi:10.1007/s00127-009-0085-6

Bottoms, H. C., Eslick, A. N., & Marsh, E. J. (2010). Memory and the Moses illusion: Failures to detect contradictions with stored knowledge yield negative memorial consequences. *Memory, 18*(6), 670–678. doi:org/10.1080/09658211.2010.501558

Bouchard, T. J., Jr. (1997). IQ similarity in twins reared apart: Findings and responses to critics. In R. J. Sternberg, & E. L. Grigorenko (Eds.), *Intelligence, heredity, and environment*. New York, NY: Cambridge University Press.

Bourgeois, J. A., Seaman, J. S., & Servis, M. E. (2008). Delirium, dementia, and amnestic and other cognitive disorders. In R. E. Hales, S. C. Yudofsky, & G. O. Gabbard (Eds.), *The American Psychiatric Publishing textbook of psychiatry* (5th ed.). Washington, DC: American Psychiatric Publishing.

Bourguignon, E. (1972). Dreams and altered states of consciousness in anthropological research. In F. L. K. Hsu (Ed.), *Psychological anthropology* (2nd ed.). Cambridge, MA: Schenkman.

Bousfield, W. A. (1953). The occurrence of clustering in the recall of randomly arranged associates. *Journal of General Psychology, 49*, 229–240. doi:10.1080/00221309.1953.9710088

Bouton, M. E., & Todd, T. P. (2014). A fundamental role for context in instrumental learning and extinction. *Behavioural Processes, 104*, 13–19. doi:10.1016/j.beproc.2014.02.012

Bouton, M. E., Todd, T. P., Vurbic, D., & Winterbauer, N. E. (2011). Renewal after the extinction of free operant behavior. *Learning & Behavior, 39*, 57–67.

Bouton, M. E., & Woods, A. M. (2009). Extinction: Behavioral mechanisms and their implications. In J. H. Byrne (Ed.), *Concise learning and memory: The editor's selection*. San Diego, CA: Elsevier.

Bowd, A. D., & Shapiro, K. J. (1993). The case against laboratory animal research in psychology. *Journal of Social Issues, 49*(1), 133–142.

Bower, G. H. (1970a). Analysis of a mnemonic device. *American Scientist, 58*, 496–499.

Bower, G. H. (1970b). Organizational factors in memory. *Cognitive Psychology, 1*(1), 18–46. doi:10.1016/0010-0285(70)90003-4

Bower, G. H., Clark, M. C., Lesgold, A. M., & Winzenz, D. (1969). Hierarchical retrieval schemes in recall of categorized word lists. *Journal of Verbal Learning and Verbal Behavior, 8*, 323–343.

Bower, G. H., & Springston, F. (1970). Pauses as recoding points in letter series. *Journal of Experimental Psychology, 83*, 421–430.

Bowlby, J. (1969). *Attachment and loss: Vol. 1. Attachment*. New York, NY: Basic Books.

Bowlby, J. (1973). *Attachment and loss: Vol. 2. Separation, anxiety and anger*. New York, NY: Basic Books.

Bowlby, J. (1980). *Attachment and loss: Vol. 3. Sadness and depression*. New York, NY: Basic Books.

Boyce, C. J., Brown, G. A., & Moore, S. C. (2010). Money and happiness: Rank of income, not income, affects life satisfaction. *Psychological Science, 21*(4), 471–475.

Boysen, G. A., & VanBergen, A. (2013). A review of published research on adult dissociative identity disorder: 2000–2010. *Journal of Nervous and Mental Disease, 201*(1), 5–11. doi:10.1097/NMD.0b013e31827aaf81

Bradshaw, J. L. (1989). *Hemispheric specialization and psychological function*. New York, NY: Wiley.

Braff, D. L., Ryan, J., Rissling, A. J., & Carpenter, W. T. (2013). Lack of use in the literature from the last 20 years supports dropping traditional schizophrenia subtypes from DSM-5 and ICD-11. *Schizophrenia Bulletin, 39*, 751-753. doi:10.1093/schbul/sbt068

Brainerd, C. J., & Reyna, V. F. (2005). *The science of false memory*. New York, NY: Oxford University Press.

Branaman, T. F., & Gallagher, S. N. (2005). Polygraph testing in sex offender treatment: A review of limitations. *American Journal of Forensic Psychology, 23*(1), 45–64.

Branson, R. (2005). *Losing my virginity: The autobiography*. London, UK: Virgin.

Braskie, M. N., & Thompson, P. M. (2013). Understanding cognitive deficits in Alzheimer's disease based on neuroimaging findings. *Trends in Cognitive Sciences, 17*, 510–516. doi:10.1016/j.tics.2013.08.007

Brassington, G. S., Hekler, E. B., Cohen, Z., & King, A. C. (2012). Health-enhancing physical activity. In A. Baum, T. A. Revenson, & J. Singer (Eds.), *Handbook of health psychology* (2nd ed.). New York, NY: Psychology Press.

Braun, M., Lewin-Epstein, N., Stier, H., & Baumgärtner, M. K. (2008). Perceived equity in the gendered division of household labor. *Journal of Marriage and Family, 70*(5), 1145–1156. doi:10.1111/j.1741-3737.2008.00556.x

Bravo, M. (2010). Context effects in perception. In E. B. Goldstein (Ed.), *Encyclopedia of perception*. Thousand Oaks, CA: Sage.

Breggin, P. R. (1991). *Toxic psychiatry*. New York, NY: St. Martin's Press.

Breggin, P. R. (2008). *Medication madness: A psychiatrist exposes the dangers of mood-altering medications*. New York, NY: St. Martin's Press.

Brehm, J. W. (1966). *A theory of psychological reactance*. New York, NY: Academic Press.

Breland, K., & Breland, M. (1961). The misbehavior of organisms. *American Psychologist, 16*, 681–684.

Brenes, G. A., Ingram, C. W., & Danhauer, S. C. (2012). Telephone-delivered psychotherapy for late-life anxiety. *Psychological Services, 9*(2), 219–220. doi:10.1037/a0025950

Bretherton, I., & Munholland, K. A. (2008). Internal working models in attachment relationships: Conceptual and empirical aspects of security. In J. Cassidy & P. R. Shaver (Eds.), *Handbook of attachment: Theory, research, and clinical applications* (2nd ed., pp. 102–130). New York, NY: Guilford Press.

Breugelmans, S. M., Poortinga, Y. H., Ambadar, Z., Setiadi, B., Vaca, J. B., Widiyanto, P., et al. (2005). Body sensations associated with emotions in Raramuri Indians, rural Javanese, and three student samples. *Emotion, 5*, 166–174.

Brewer, C. L. (1991). Perspectives on John B. Watson. In G. A. Kimble, M. Wertheimer, & C. White (Eds.), *Portraits of pioneers in psychology*. Hillside, NJ: Erlbaum.

Brewer, W. F. (2000). Bartlett, functionalism, and modern schema theories. *Journal of Mind and Behavior, 21,* 37–44.

Brewer, W. F., & Treyens, J. C. (1981). Role of schemata in memory for places. *Cognitive Psychology, 13,* 207–230.

Brewin, C. R. (2012). A theoretical framework for understanding recovered memory experiences. In R. F. Belli (Ed.), *True and false recovered memories: Toward a reconciliation of the debate.* New York, NY: Springer.

Bridge, J. A., & Barbe, R. P. (2004). Reducing hospital readmission in depression and schizophrenia: Current evidence. *Current Opinion in Psychiatry, 17,* 505–511.

Bridge, J. A., Iyengar, S., Salary, C. B., Barbe, R. P., Birmaher, B., Pincus, H. A., . . . Brent, D. A. (2007). Clinical response and risk for reported suicidal ideation and suicide attempts in pediatric antidepressant treatment: A meta-analysis of randomized controlled trials. *JAMA, 297,* 1683–1969.

Briere, J., & Conte, J. R. (1993). Self-reported amnesia for abuse in adults molested as children. *Journal of Traumatic Stress, 6*(1), 21–31.

Briley, D. A., & Tucker-Drob, E. M. (2013). Explaining the increasing heritability of cognitive ability across development: A meta-analysis of longitudinal twin and adoption studies. *Psychological Science, 24,* 1704–1713. doi:10.1177/0956797613478618

Brink, E., Alsén, P., Herlitz, J., Kjellgren, K., & Cliffordson, C. (2012). General self-efficacy and health-related quality of life after myocardial infarction. *Psychology, Health & Medicine, 17,* 346–355. doi:10.1080/13548506.2011.608807

Briñol, P., & Petty, R. E. (2012). A history of attitudes and persuasion research. In A. W. Kruglanski & W. Stroebe (Eds.), *Handbook of the history of social psychology.* New York, NY: Psychology Press.

Brislin, R. (2000). *Understanding culture's influence on behavior.* Belmont, CA: Wadsworth.

Broadbent, D. E. (1958). *Perception and communication.* New York, NY: Pergamon Press.

Brobeck, J. R., Tepperman, T., & Long, C. N. (1943). Experimental hypothalamic hyperphagia in the albino rat. *Yale Journal of Biology and Medicine, 15,* 831–853.

Bröder, A. (1998). Deception can be acceptable. *American Psychologist, 53,* 805–806.

Brody, N. (2003). Jensen's genetic interpretation of racial differences in intelligence: Critical evaluation. In

H. Nyborg (Ed.), *The scientific study of general intelligence: Tribute to Arthur R. Jensen.* Oxford, UK: Pergamon.

Brown, A. S. (2012a). Epidemiological studies of exposure to prenatal infection and risk of schizophrenia and autism. *Developmental Neurobiology, 72,* 1272–1276. doi:10.1002/dneu.22024

Brown, A. S. (2012b). *The tip of the tongue state.* New York, NY: Psychology Press.

Brown, A. S., & Derkits, E. J. (2010). Prenatal infection and schizophrenia: A review of epidemiologic and translational studies. *American Journal of Psychiatry, 167*(3), 261–280. doi:10.1176/appi.ajp.2009.09030361

Brown, C. G. (2012). A systematic review of the relationship between self-efficacy and burnout in teachers. *Educational and Child Psychology, 29*(4), 47–63.

Brown, M. (1974). Some determinants of persistence and initiation of achievement-related activities. In J. W. Atkinson & J. O. Raynor (Eds.), *Motivation and achievement.* Washington, DC: Halsted.

Brown, M. (1998). *Richard Branson: The inside story.* London: Headline.

Brown, R., & Kulik, J. (1977). Flashbulb memories. *Cognition, 5,* 73–79.

Brown, R., & McNeill, D. (1966). The "tip-of-the-tongue" phenomenon. *Journal of Verbal Learning and Verbal Behavior, 5*(4), 325–337.

Brown, R. D., Goldstein, E., & Bjorklund, D. F. (2000). The history and zeitgeist of the repressed–false-memory debate: Scientific and sociological perspectives on suggestibility and childhood memory. In D. F. Bjorklund (Ed.), *False-memory creation in children and adults* (pp. 1–30). Mahwah, NJ: Erlbaum.

Brown, S. C., & Craik, F. I. M. (2000). Encoding and retrieval of information. In E. Tulving & F. I. M. Craik (Eds.), *The Oxford handbook of memory* (pp. 93–108). New York, NY: Oxford University Press.

Brownell, K. D., & Wadden, T. A. (2000). Obesity. In B. J. Sadock & V. A. Sadock (Eds.), *Kaplan and Sadock's comprehensive textbook of psychiatry* (7th ed., Vol. 2, pp. 1787–1796). Philadelphia, PA: Lippincott Williams & Wilkins.

Bruer, J. T. (1999). *The myth of the first three years: A new understanding of early brain development and life-long learning.* New York, NY: Free Press.

Bruer, J. T. (2002). Avoiding the pediatrician's error: How neuroscientists can help educators (and themselves). *Nature Neuroscience, 5,* 1031–1033.

Brugha, T. S., McManus, S., Bankart, J., Scott, F., Purdon, S., Smith, J., Bebbington, P., Jenkins, R., & Meltzer, H. (2011). Epidemiology of autism spectrum disorders in adults in the community in England. *Archives of General Psychiatry, 68*(5), 459–466. doi:10.1001/archgenpsychiatry.2011.38

Brunell, A. B., Gentry, W. A., Campbell, W. K., Hoffman, B. J., Kuhnert, K. W., & DeMarree, K. G. (2008). Leader emergence: The case of the narcissistic leader. *Personality and Social Psychology Bulletin, 34,* 1663–1676. doi:10.1177/0146167208324101

Brunner, E. J., Shipley, M. J., Britton, A. R., Stansfeld, S. A., Heuschmann, P. U., Rudd, A. G., . . . & Kivimaki, M. (2014). Depressive disorder, coronary heart disease, and stroke: Dose-response and reverse causation effects in the Whitehall II cohort study. *Preventive Cardiology, 21,* 340–346. doi:10.1177/2047487314520785

Buccino, G., & Riggio, L. (2006). The role of the mirror neuron system in motor learning. *Kinesiology, 38*(1), 5–15.

Buck, L. B. (2004). Olfactory receptors and coding in mammals. *Nutrition Reviews, 62,* S184–S188.

Buck, L. B., & Bargmann, C. I. (2013). Smell and taste: The chemical senses. In E. R. Kandel, J. H. Schwartz, T. M. Jessell, S. A. Siegelbaum, & A. J. Hudspeth (Eds.), *Principles of neural science* (5th ed.). New York, NY: McGraw-Hill.

Buckley, K. W. (1982). The selling of a psychologist: John Broadus Watson and the application of behavioral techniques to advertising. *Journal of the History of Behavioral Sciences, 18*(3), 207–221. doi:10.1002/1520-6696(198207)18:3<207::AID-JHBS2300180302>3.0.CO;2–8

Buckley, K. W. (1994). Misbehaviorism: The case of John B. Watson's dismissal from Johns Hopkins University. In J. T. Todd & E. K. Morris (Eds.), *Modern perspectives on John B. Watson and classical behaviorism.* Westport, CT: Greenwood.

Budney, A. J., Vandrey, R. L., & Fearer, S. (2011). Cannabis. In P. Ruiz, & E. C. Strain (Eds.), *Lowinson and Ruiz's substance abuse: A comprehensive textbook* (5th ed.). Philadelphia, PA: Wolters Kluwer Lippincott Williams & Wilkins.

Buffardi, L. E., & Campbell, W. (2008). Narcissism and social networking web sites. *Personality and Social Psychology Bulletin, 34*(10), 1303–1314. doi:10.1177/0146167208320061

Bühler, C., & Allen, M. (1972). *Introduction to humanistic psychology.* Pacific Grove, CA: Brooks/Cole.

Burchinal, M. R., Lowe Vandell, D., & Belsky, J. (2014). Is the prediction of adolescent outcomes from early child care moderated by later maternal sensitivity? Results from the NICHD Study of Early Child Care and Youth Development. *Developmental Psychology, 50,* 542–553. doi:10.1037/a0033709

Burger, J. M. (1986). Temporal effects on attributions: Actor and observer differences. *Social Cognition, 4,* 377–387.

Burger, J. M. (1999). The foot-in-the-door compliance procedure: A multiple process analysis review. *Personality and Social Psychology Review, 3,* 303–325.

Burger, J. M. (2009). Replicating Milgram: Would people still obey today? *American Psychologist, 64*(1), 1–11. doi:10.1037/a0010932

Burger, J. M. (2014). Situational features in Milgram's experiment that kept his participants shocking. *Journal of Social Issues, 70,* 489–500. doi:10.1111/josi.12073

Burger, J. M. (2015). *Personality* (9th ed.). San Francisco, CA: Cengage Learning.

Burgess, A. (2007). On the contribution of neurophysiology to hypnosis research: Current state and future directions. In G. A. Jamieson (Ed.), *Hypnosis and conscious states: The cognitive neuroscience perspective.* New York, NY: Oxford University Press.

Burke, A., Kandler, A., & Good, D. (2012). Women who know their place: Sex-based differences in spatial abilities and their evolutionary significance. *Human Nature, 23,* 133–148. doi:10.1007/s12110-012-9140-1

Burke, J. D., & Kraemer, H. C. (2014). DSM-5 as a framework for psychiatric diagnosis. In R. E. Hales, S. C. Yudofsky, L. W. Roberts, R. E. Hales, S. C. Yudofsky, & L. W. Roberts (Eds.), *The American Psychiatric Publishing textbook of psychiatry* (6th ed.). Washington, DC: American Psychiatric Publishing.

Burke, M., Marlow, C., & Lento, T. (2010). Social network activity and social well-being. *Postgraduate Medical Journal, 85,* 455–459.

Burkhardt, D. A. (2010). Visual processing: Retinal. In E. B. Goldstein (Ed.), *Encyclopedia of perception.* Thousand Oaks, CA: Sage.

Burlingame, G. M., & Baldwin, S. (2011). Group therapy. In J. C. Norcross, G. R. Vandenbos, & D. K. Freedheim (Eds.), *History of psychotherapy: Continuity and change* (2nd ed.). Washington, DC: American Psychological Association.

Burlingame, G. M., Strauss, B., & Joyce, A. S. (2013). Change mechanisms and effectiveness of small group treatments. In M. J. Lambert (Ed.). *Bergin and Garfield's handbook of psychotherapy and behavior change* (6th ed.). New York, NY: Wiley.

Burnette, J. L., Pollack, J. M., & Forsyth, D. R. (2011). Leadership in extreme contexts: A groupthink analysis of the May 1996 Mount Everest disaster. *Journal of Leadership Studies, 4,* 29–40. doi:10.1002/jls.20190

Burns, B. D., & Corpus, B. (2004). Randomness and inductions from streaks: "Gambler's fallacy" versus "hot hand." *Psychonomic Bulletin & Review, 11*(1), 179–184.

Burns, J. K. (2013). Pathways from cannabis to psychosis: A review of the evidence. *Frontiers in Psychiatry, 4,* 128. doi:10.3389/fpsyt.2013.00128

Burton, C., Campbell, P., Jordan, K., Strauss, V., & Mallen, C. (2013). The association of anxiety and depression with future dementia diagnosis: A case-control study in primary care. *Family Practice, 30*(1), 25–30. doi:10.1093/fampra/cms044

Bushdid, C., Magnasco, M. O., Vosshall, L. B., & Keller, A. (2014). Humans can discriminate more than 1 trillion olfactory stimuli. *Science, 343,* 1370–1372.

Bushman, B. J., & Anderson, C. A. (2001). Media violence and the American public: Scientific facts versus media misinformation. *American Psychologist, 56,* 477–489.

Bushman, B. J., & Anderson, C. A. (2009). Comfortably numb: Desensitizing effects of violent media on helping others. *Psychological Science, 20*(3), 273–277. doi:10.1111/j.1467-9280.2009.02287.x

Bushman, B. J., & Huesmann, L. R. (2012). Effects of violent media on aggression. In D. G. Singer, & J. L. Singer (Eds.), *Handbook of children and the media* (2nd ed.). Thousand Oaks, CA: Sage.

Bushman, B. J., & Huesmann, L. R. (2014). Twenty-five years of research on violence in digital games and aggression revisited: A reply to Elson and Ferguson (2013). *European Psychologist, 19,* 47–55. doi:10.1027/1016-9040/a000164

Buss, D. M. (1985). Human mate selection. *American Scientist, 73,* 47–51.

Buss, D. M. (1988). The evolution of human intrasexual competition: Tactics of mate attraction. *Journal of Personality and Social Psychology, 54,* 616–628.

Buss, D. M. (1989). Sex differences in human mate preferences: Evolutionary hypotheses tested in 37 cultures. *Behavioral and Brain Sciences, 12,* 1–49.

Buss, D. M. (1991). Evolutionary personality psychology. *Annual Review of Psychology, 42,* 459–491.

Buss, D. M. (1995). Evolutionary psychology: A new paradigm for psychological science. *Psychological Inquiry, 6,* 1–30.

Buss, D. M. (1997). Evolutionary foundation of personality. In R. Hogan, J. Johnson, & S. Briggs (Eds.), *Handbook of personality psychology.* San Diego, CA: Academic Press.

Buss, D. M. (2009). The great struggles of life: Darwin and the emergence of evolutionary psychology. *American Psychologist, 64*(2), 140–148. doi:10.1037/a0013207

Buss, D. M. (2014). *Evolutionary psychology: The new science of the mind* (5th ed.). Boston, MA: Pearson.

Buss, D. M., & Penke, L. (2015). Evolutionary personality psychology. In M. Mikulincer, P. R. Shaver, M. L. Cooper, & R. J. Larsen (Eds.), *APA handbook of personality and social psychology: Vol. 4. Personality processes and individual differences.* Washington, DC: American Psychological Association.

Buss, D. M., & Schmitt, D. P. (1993). Sexual strategies theory: A contextual evolutionary analysis of human mating. *Psychological Review, 100,* 204–232.

Buss, D. M., & Schmitt, D. P. (2011). Evolutionary psychology and feminism. *Sex Roles, 64,* 768–787. doi:10.1007/s11199-011-9987-3

Bussey, K., & Bandura, A. (1984). Influence of gender constancy and social power on sex-linked modeling. *Journal of Personality and Social Psychology, 47,* 1292–1302.

Bussey, K., & Bandura, A. (1999). Social cognitive theory of gender development and differentiation. *Psychological Review, 106,* 676–713.

Bussey, K., & Bandura, A. (2004). Social cognitive theory of gender development and functioning. In A. H. Eagly, A. E. Beall, & R. J. Sternberg (Eds.), *The psychology of gender.* New York, NY: Guilford Press.

Butcher, J. N. (2011). *A beginner's guide to the MMPI-2* (3rd ed.). Washington, DC: American Psychological Association.

Butcher, J. N. (2013). Assessing MMPI-2 profile validity. In G. P. Koocher, J. C. Norcross, & B. A. Greene (Eds.), *Psychologists' desk reference* (3rd ed.). New York, NY: Oxford University Press.

Butcher, J. N., Bubany, S., & Mason, S. N. (2013). Assessment of personality and psychopathology with self-report inventories. In K. F. Geisinger, B. A. Bracken, J. F. Carlson, J. C. Hansen, N. R. Kuncel, S. P. Reise, & M. C. Rodriguez, *APA handbook of testing and assessment in psychology: Vol. 2. Testing and assessment in clinical and counseling psychology.* Washington, DC: American Psychological Association. doi:10.1037/14048-011

Buysse, D. J. (2011). Clinical pharmacology of other drugs used as hypnotics. In M. H. Kryger, T. Roth, & W. C. Dement (Eds.), *Principles and practice of sleep medicine* (5th ed.). Saint Louis, MO: Elsevier Saunders.

Buzan, D. S. (2004, March 12). I was not a lab rat. *The Guardian.* Retrieved from www.guardian.co.uk/education/2004/mar/12/highereducation.uk

Byrne, D. (1997). An overview (and underview) of research and theory within the attraction paradigm. *Journal of Social and Personal Relationships, 14,* 417–431.

Byrne, S., Barry, D., & Petry, N. M. (2012). Predictors of weight loss success. Exercise vs. dietary self-efficacy and treatment attendance. *Appetite, 58,* 695–698. doi:10.1016/j.appet.2012.01.005

Cable, N., Bartley, M., Chandola, T., & Sacker, A. (2013). Friends are equally important to men and women, but family matters more for men's well-being. *Journal of Epidemiology And Community Health, 67*(2), 166–171. doi:10.1136/jech-2012-201113

Cacioppo, J. T., & Cacioppo, S. (2014). Social relationships and health: The toxic effects of perceived social isolation. *Social and Personality Psychology Compass, 8,* 58–72. doi:10.1111/spc3.12087

Cacioppo, J. T., Cacioppo, S., Gonzaga, G. C., Ogburn, E. L., & VanderWeele, T. J. (2013). Marital satisfaction and break-ups differ across on-line and off-line meeting venues. *PNAS Proceedings of the National Academy of Sciences of the United States of America, 110,* 10135–10140. doi:10.1073/pnas.1222447110

Cacioppo, J. T., Hawkley, L. C., Kalil, A., Hughes, M. E., Waite, L., & Thisted, R. A. (2008). Happiness and the invisible threads of social connection: The Chicago health, aging, and social relations study. In M. Eid & R. J. Larsen (Eds.), *The science of subjective well-being.* New York, NY: Guilford Press.

Cahn, B. R., & Polich, J. (2006). Meditation states and traits: EEG, ERP, and neuroimaging studies. *Psychological Bulletin, 132,* 180–211.

Cai, D. J., Mednick, S. A., Harrison, E. M., Kanady, J. C., & Mednick, S. C. (2009). REM, not incubation, improves creativity by priming associative networks. *PNAS Proceedings of the National Academy of Sciences of the United States of America, 106*(25), 10130–10134. doi:10.1073/pnas.0900271106

Cai, L. (2013). Factor analysis of tests and items. In K. F. Geisinger, B. A. Bracken, J. F. Carlson, J. C. Hansen, N. R. Kuncel, S. P. Reise, & M. C. Rodriguez (Eds.), *APA handbook of testing and assessment in psychology: Vol. 1. Test theory and testing and assessment in industrial and organizational psychology.* Washington, DC: American Psychological Association. doi:10.1037/14047-005

Cain, W. S. (1988). Olfaction. In R. C. Atkinson, R. J. Herrnstein, G. Lindzey, & R. D. Luce (Eds.), *Stevens' handbook of experimental psychology: Perception and motivation* (Vol. 1). New York, NY: Wiley.

Calhoun, L. G., & Tedeschi, R. G. (2008). The paradox of struggling with trauma: Guidelines for practice and directions for research. In S. Joseph & P. A. Linley (Eds.), *Trauma, recovery, and growth: Positive psychological perspectives on posttraumatic stress.* Hoboken, NJ: Wiley.

Calhoun, L. G., & Tedeschi, R. G. (2013). *Posttraumatic growth in clinical practice.* New York, NY: Routledge/Taylor & Francis Group.

Caligor, E., Yeomans, F., & Levin, Z. (2014). Feeding and eating disorders. In J. L. Cutler (Ed.), *Psychiatry* (3rd ed.). New York, NY: Oxford University Press.

Calkins, K., & Devaskar, S. U. (2011). Fetal origins of adult disease. *Current Problems in Pediatric and Adolescent Health Care, 41,* 158–176. doi:10.1016/j.cppeds.2011.01.001

Callaghan, R C., Allebeck, P., & Sidorchuk, A. (2013). Marijuana use and risk of lung cancer: A 40-year cohort study. *Cancer Causes & Control, 24,* 1811–1820.

Callaghan, R. C., Cunningham, J. K., Allebeck, P., Arenovich, T., Sajeev, G., Remington, G., . . . Kish, S. J. (2012). Methamphetamine use and schizophrenia: a population-based cohort study in California. *American Journal of Psychiatry, 169,* 389–396.

Callicutt, J. W. (2006). Homeless shelters: An uneasy component of the de facto mental health system. In J. Rosenberg & S. Rosenberg (Eds.), *Community mental health: Challenges for the 21st century.* New York, NY: Routledge.

Camaioni, L. (2001). Early language. In G. Bremner & A. Fogel (Eds.), *Blackwell handbook of infant development.* Malden, MA: Blackwell.

Camerer, C. (2005). Three cheers—psychological, theoretical, empirical—for loss aversion. *Journal of Marketing Research, 42*(2), 129–133.

Campbell, A. (2005). Aggression. In D. M. Buss (Ed.), *The handbook of evolutionary psychology*. New York, NY: Wiley.

Campbell, A. C., Nunes, E. V., Matthews, A. G., Stitzer, M., Miele, G. M., Polsky, D., . . . Ghitza, U. E. (2014). Internet-delivered treatment for substance abuse: A multisite randomized controlled trial. *The American Journal of Psychiatry, 171,* 683–690. doi:10.1176/appi.ajp.2014 .13081055

Canli, T. (2008). Toward a "molecular psychology" of personality. In O. P. John, R. W. Robbins, & L. A. Pervin (Eds.), *Handbook of personality: Theory and research* (Vol. 3, pp. 311–327). New York, NY: Guilford Press.

Cannon, T. D., Chung, Y., He, G., Sun, D., Jacobson, A., van Erp, T. G., . . . Heinssen, R. (2015). Progressive reduction in cortical thickness as psychosis develops: A multisite longitudinal neuroimaging study of youth at elevated clinical risk. *Biological Psychiatry, 77*(2), 147–157. doi:10.1016 /j.biopsych.2014.05.023

Cannon, W. B. (1927). The James-Lange theory of emotions: A critical examination and an alternate theory. *American Journal of Psychology, 39,* 106–124.

Cannon, W. B. (1932). *The wisdom of the body.* New York, NY: Norton.

Cannon, W. B., & Washburn, A. L. (1912). An explanation of hunger. *American Journal of Physiology, 29,* 444–454.

Canter, P. H. (2003). The therapeutic effects of meditation. *British Medical Journal, 326,* 1049–1050.

Cantu, S. M., Simpson, J. A., Griskevicius, V., Weisberg, Y. J., Durante, K. M., & Beal, D. J. (2014). Fertile and selectively flirty: Women's behavior toward men changes across the ovulatory cycle. *Psychological Science, 25,* 431–438. doi:10.1177/0956797613508413

Cao, M. T., Guilleminault, C., & Kushida, C. A. (2011). Clinical features and evaluation of obstructive sleep apnea and upper airway resistance syndrome. In M. H. Kryger, T. Roth, & W. C. Dement (Eds.), *Principles and practice of sleep medicine* (5th ed.). Saint Louis, MO: Elsevier Saunders.

Cao, X., Laplante, D. P., Brunet, A., Ciampi, A., & King, S. (2014). Prenatal maternal stress affects motor function in 5 1/2-year-old children: Project ice storm. *Developmental Psychobiology, 56,* 117–125. doi:10.1002 /dev.21085

Card, N. A., Stucky, B. D., Sawalani, G. M., & Little, T. D. (2008). Direct and indirect aggression during childhood and adolescence: A meta-analytic review of gender differences, intercorrelations, and relations to maladjustment. *Child Development, 79,* 1185–1229.

Cardeña, E., Butler, L. D., Reijman, S., & Spiegel, D. (2013). Disorders of extreme stress. In T. A. Widiger, G. Stricker, I. B. Weiner, G. Stricker, T. A. Widiger, & I. B. Weiner (Eds.), *Handbook of psychology: Vol. 8. Clinical psychology* (2nd ed.). New York, NY: Wiley.

Cardeña, E., & Gleaves, D. H. (2007). Dissociative disorders. In M. Hersen, S. M. Turner, & D. C. Beidel (Eds.), *Adult psychopathology and diagnosis.* New York, NY: Wiley.

Cardno, A. G., & Owen, M. J. (2014). Genetic relationships between schizophrenia, bipolar disorder, and schizoaffective disorder. *Schizophrenia Bulletin, 40,* 504–515. doi:10.1093/ schbul/sbu016

Cardoso, C., Ellenbogen, M. A., & Linnen, A. (2012). Acute intranasal oxytocin improves positive self-perceptions of personality. *Psychopharmacology, 220,* 741–749. doi:10.1007 /s00213-011-2527-6

Carey, B. (2009, December 21). Building a search engine of the brain, slice by slice. *The New York Times.* Retrieved from www.newyorktimes.com

Carey, M. P., Scott-Sheldon, L. A. J., & Vanable, P. A. (2013). HIV/AIDS. In A. M. Nezu, C. M. Nezu, P. A. Geller, & I. B. Weiner (Eds.), *Handbook of psychology: Vol. 9. Health psychology* (2nd ed.). New York, NY: Wiley.

Carey, S. (2010). Beyond fast mapping. *Language Learning and Development, 6*(3), 184–205. doi:10.1080/15475441 .2010.484379

Carlson, E. N., Vazire, S., & Oltmanns, T. F. (2011). You probably think this paper is about you: Narcissists' perceptions of their personality and reputation. *Journal of Personality and Social Psychology, 101,* 185–201. doi:10.1037/a0023781

Carlson, J. D., & Englar-Carlson, M. (2013). Adlerian therapy. In J. Frew, & M. D. Spiegler (Eds.), *Contemporary psychotherapies for a diverse world* (1st rev. ed.). New York, NY: Routledge/Taylor & Francis Group.

Carlson, S. A., Fulton, J. E., Schoenborn, C. A., & Loustalot, F. (2010). Trend and prevalence estimates based on the 2008 Physical Activity Guidelines for Americans. *American Journal of Preventive Medicine, 39*(4), 305–313.

Carpenter, C. J. (2012). Narcissism on Facebook: Self-promotional and anti-social behavior. *Personality and Individual Differences, 52,* 482–486. doi:10.1016/j.paid.2011.11.011

Carpenter, S. K. (2012). Testing enhances the transfer of learning. *Current Directions in Psychological Science, 21,* 279–283. doi:10.1177/0963721412452728

Carpenter, S. K. (2014). Spacing and interleaving of study and practice. In V. A. Benassi, C. E. Overson, & C. M. Hakala (Eds.), *Applying science of learning in education: Infusing psychological science into the curriculum.* Washington, DC: Society for the Teaching of Psychology.

Carpenter, W. T. (2002). From clinical trial to prescription. *Archives of General Psychology, 59,* 282–285.

Carr, C. P., Martins, C. S., Stingel, A. M., Lemgruber, V. B., & Juruena, M. F. (2013). The role of early life stress in adult psychiatric disorders: A systematic review according to childhood trauma subtypes. *Journal of Nervous and Mental Disease, 201,* 1007–1020. doi:10.1097 /NMD.0000000000000049

Carroll, M. E., & Overmier, J. B. (2001). *Animal research and human health.* Washington, DC: American Psychological Association.

Carskadon, M. A., & Dement, W. C. (2011). Normal human sleep: An overview. In M. H. Kryger, T. Roth, & W. C. Dement (Eds.), *Principles and practice of sleep medicine* (5th ed.). Saint Louis, MO: Elsevier Saunders.

Carter, C. S. (2014). Oxytocin pathways and the evolution of human behavior. *Annual Review of Psychology, 65,* 17–39. doi:10.1146/annurev -psych-010213-115110

Cartwright, R. D. (2004). The role of sleep in changing our minds: A psychologist's discussion of papers on memory reactivation and consolidation in sleep. *Learning & Memory, 11,* 660–663.

Cartwright, R. D. (2006). Sleepwalking. In T. Lee-Chiong (Ed.), *Sleep: A comprehensive handbook.* Hoboken, NJ: Wiley-Liss.

Cartwright, R. D. (2011). Dreaming as a mood-regulation system. In M. H. Kryger, T. Roth, & W. C. Dement (Eds.), *Principles and practice of sleep medicine* (5th ed.). Saint Louis, MO: Elsevier Saunders.

Cartwright, R. D., & Lamberg, L. (1992). *Crisis dreaming.* New York, NY: HarperCollins.

Carver, C. S., & Scheier, M. F. (2014). Dispositional optimism. *Trends in Cognitive Sciences, 18,* 293–299. doi:10.1016/j.tics.2014.02.003

Carver, C. S., Scheier, M. F., & Segerstrom, S. C. (2010). Optimism. *Clinical Psychology Review, 30*(7), 879–889.

Carver, C. S., & Vargas, S. (2011). Stress, coping, and health. In H. S. Friedman (Ed.), *The Oxford handbook of health psychology.* New York, NY: Oxford University Press.

Casanova, C., Merabet, L., Desautels, A., & Minville, K. (2001). Higher-order motion processing in the pulvinar. *Progress in Brain Research, 134,* 71–82.

Case, B. G., Bertollo, D. N., Laska, E. M., Price, L. H., Siegel, C. E., Olfson, M., & Marcus, S. C. (2013). Declining use of electroconvulsive therapy in United States general hospitals. *Biological Psychiatry, 73*(2), 119–126. doi:10.1016/j.biopsych.2012.09.005

Casey, B. J., & Caudle, K. (2013). The teenage brain: Self control. *Current Directions in Psychological Science, 22,* 82–87. doi:10.1177/0963721413480170

Casey, B. J., Tottenham, N., Listen, C., & Durston, S. (2005). Imaging the developing brain: What have we learned about cognitive development? *Trends in Cognitive Sciences, 9*(3), 104–110. doi:10.1016/j.tics.2005.01.011

Caspi, O., & Burleson, K. O. (2005). Methodological challenges in meditation research. *Advances in Mind-Body Medicine, 21*(1), 4–11.

Cassel, R. N. (2000). Third force psychology and person-centered theory: From ego-status to ego-ideal. *Psychology: A Journal of Human Behavior, 37*(3), 44–48.

Cassidy, J. (2008). The nature of the child's ties. In J. Cassidy & P. R. Shaver (Eds.), *Handbook of attachment: Theory, research, and clinical applications* (2nd ed., pp. 3–22). New York, NY: Guilford Press.

Castonguay, L., Barkham, M., Lutz, W., & McAleavey, A. (2013). Practice-oriented research: Approaches and applications. In M. J. Lambert (Ed.). *Bergin and Garfield's handbook of psychotherapy and behavior change* (6th ed.). New York, NY: Wiley.

Catania, A. C. (1992). Reinforcement. In L. R. Squire (Ed.), *Encyclopedia of learning and memory.* New York, NY: Macmillan.

Catrambone, R. (1998). The subgoal learning model: Creating better examples so that students can solve novel problems. *Journal of Experimental Psychology: General, 127,* 355–376.

Cautin, R. L., Freedheim, D. K., & DeLeon, P. H. (2013). Psychology as a profession. In D. K. Freedheim & I. B. Weiner (Eds.), *Handbook of psychology: Vol. 1. History of psychology* (2nd ed., pp. 32–54). New York, NY: Wiley.

Caverly, D. C., Orlando, V. P., & Mullen, J. L. (2000). Textbook study reading. In R. F. Flippo & D. C. Caverly (Eds.), *Handbook of college reading and study strategy research*. Mahwah, NJ: Erlbaum.

Cepeda, N. J., Pashler, H., Vul, E., Wixted, J. T., & Roher, D. (2006). Distributed practice in verbal recall tasks: A review and quantitative synthesis. *Psychological Bulletin, 132*, 354–380.

Cerletti, U., & Bini, L. (1938). Un nuovo metodo di shockterapie "L'elettro-shock." *Boll. Acad. Med. Roma, 64*, 136–138.

Cetinkaya, H., & Domjan, M. (2006). Sexual fetishism in a quail (*Coturnix japonica*) model system: Test of reproductive success. *Journal of Comparative Psychology, 120*(4), 427–432. doi:10.1037/0735-7036.120.4.427

Cha, Y. (2010). Reinforcing separate spheres: The effect of spousal overwork on men's and women's employment in dual-earner households. *American Sociological Review, 75*(2), 303–329. doi:10.1177/000312241036530

Chabris, C. F., Hebert, B. M., Benjamin, D. J., Beauchamp, J., Cesarini, D., van der Loos, M., . . . Laibson, D. (2012). Most reported genetic associations with general intelligence are probably false positives. *Psychological Science, 23*, 1314–1323. doi:10.1177/0956797611435528

Chan, J., & Schunn, C. (2014). The impact of analogies on creative concept generation: Lessons from an in vivo study in engineering design. *Cognitive Science*, 1–30. doi:10.1111/cogs.12127

Chance, P. (2001, September/October). The brain goes to school: Why neuroscience research is going to the head of the class. *Psychology Today*, p. 72.

Chandra, A., Copen, C. E., & Mosher, W. D. (2011). Sexual behavior, sexual attraction, and sexual identity in the United States: Data from the 2006-2008 National Survey of Family Growth. *National Health Statistics Reports, 3*, 1–36.

Chapman, C. D., Nilsson, E. K., Nilsson, V. C., Cedernaes, J., Rangtell, F. H., Vogel, H., . . . Benedict, C. (2013). Acute sleep deprivation increases food purchasing in men. *Obesity, 21*, E555–E560. doi:10.1002/oby.20579

Charles, S. T., Piazza, J. R., Mogle, J., Sliwinski, M. J., & Almeida, D. M. (2013). The wear and tear of daily stressors on mental health. *Psychological Science, 24*, 733–741. doi:10.1177/0956797612462222

Chen, M. C., Yu, H., Huang, Z., & Lu, J. (2013). Rapid eye movement sleep behavior disorder. *Current Opinion in Neurobiology, 23*, 793–798.

Chen, Q., & Yan, Z. (2013). New evidence of impacts of cell phone use on driving performance: A review. *International Journal of Cyber Behavior, Psychology and Learning, 3*(3), 46–61. doi:10.4018/ijcbpl.2013070104

Chen, S., Gau, S. F., Pikhart, H., Peasey, A., Chen, S., & Tsai, M. (2014). Work stress and subsequent risk of Internet addiction among information technology engineers in Taiwan. *Cyberpsychology, Behavior, and Social Networking, 17*, 542–550. doi:10.1089/cyber.2013.0686

Cheng, C., & Li, A. Y-I. (2014). Internet addiction prevalence and quality of (real) life: A meta-analysis of 31 nations across seven world regions. *Cyberpsychology, Behavior, and Social Networking, 17*, 755–760. doi:10.1089/cyber.2014.0317

Chew, S. L. (2014). Helping students to get the most out of studying. In V. A. Benassi, C. E. Overson, & C. M. Hakala (Eds.), *Applying science of learning in education: Infusing psychological science into the curriculum*. Washington, DC: Society for the Teaching of Psychology.

Chiriboga, D. A. (1989). Mental health at the midpoint: Crisis, challenge, or relief? In S. Hunter & M. Sundel (Eds.), *Sage sourcebooks for the human services series: Vol. 7. Midlife myths: Issues, findings, and practice implications* (pp. 116–144). Thousand Oaks, CA: Sage.

Chiu, C., Kim, Y., & Wan, W. W. N. (2008). Personality: Cross-cultural perspectives. In G. J. Boyles, G. Matthews, & D. H. Saklofskc (Eds.), *The Sage handbook of personality theory and assessment: Personality theories and models* (Vol. 1, pp. 124–144). Los Angles, CA: Sage.

Chiu, C. Y., Leung, A. K. Y., & Kwan, L. (2007). Language, cognition, and culture: Beyond the Whorfian hypothesis. In S. Kitayama & D. Cohen (Eds.), *Handbook of cultural psychology* (pp. 668–690). New York, NY: Guilford Press.

Cholewiak, R. W., & Cholewiak, S. A. (2010). Pain: Physiological mechanisms. In E. B. Goldstein (Ed.), *Encyclopedia of perception*. Thousand Oaks, CA: Sage.

Chomsky, N. (1959). A review of B. F. Skinner's "Verbal Behavior." *Language, 35*, 26–58.

Chomsky, N. (1965). *Aspects of theory of syntax*. Cambridge, MA: MIT Press.

Chomsky, N. (1975). *Reflections on language*. New York, NY: Pantheon.

Chomsky, N. (1986). *Knowledge of language: Its nature, origins, and use*. New York, NY: Praeger.

Chomsky, N. (2006). *Language and mind* (3rd ed.). New York, NY: Cambridge University Press.

Chopra, S. S. (2003). Industry funding of clinical trials: Benefit of bias? *JAMA, 290*, 113–114.

Chow, C. M., & Ruhl, H. (2014). Friendship and romantic stressors and depression in emerging adulthood: Mediating and moderating roles of attachment representations. *Journal of Adult Development, 21*, 106–115. doi:10.1007/s10804-014-9184-z

Christensen, B. T., & Schunn, C. D. (2007). The relationship of analogical distance to analogical function and preinventive structure: The case of engineering design. *Memory & Cognition, 35*(1), 29–38.

Christensen, C. C. (2005). Preferences for descriptors of hypnosis: A brief communication. *International Journal of Clinical and Experimental Hypnosis, 53*, 281–289.

Christensen, L. (1988). Deception in psychological research: When is its use justified? *Personality and Social Psychology Bulletin, 14*, 664–675.

Christodoulidis, G., Vittorio, T. J., Fudim, M., Lerakis, S., & Kosmas, C. E. (2014). Inflammation in coronary artery disease. *Cardiology Review, 22*, 279–288. doi:10.1097/CRD.0000000000000006

Chrobak, Q. M., & Zaragoza, M. S. (2013). The misinformation effect: Past research and recent advances. In A. M. Ridley, F. Gabbert, & D. J. La Rooy (Eds.), *Suggestibility in legal contexts: Psychological research and forensic implications*. Malden, MA: Wiley-Blackwell.

Chu, J. A., Frey, L. M., Ganzel, B. L., & Matthews, J. A. (1999). Memories of childhood abuse: Dissociation, amnesia, and corroboration. *American Journal of Psychiatry, 156*, 749–755.

Chudler, E. H. (2007). The power of the full moon. Running on empty? In S. Della Sala (Ed.), *Tall tales about the mind & brain: Separating fact from fiction* (pp. 401–410). New York, NY: Oxford University Press.

Chung, J. M., Robins, R. W., Trzesniewski, K. H., Noftle, E. E., Roberts, B. W., & Widaman, K. F. (2014). Continuity and change in self-esteem during emerging adulthood. *Journal of Personality and Social Psychology, 106*, 469–483. doi:10.1037/a0035135

Chung, W. K., & Leibel, R. L. (2012). Genetics of body weight regulation. In K. D. Brownell, & M. S. Gold (Eds.), *Food and addiction: A comprehensive handbook*. New York, NY: Oxford University Press.

Church, A. (2010). Current perspectives in the study of personality across cultures. *Perspectives on Psychological Science, 5*(4), 441–449. doi:10.1177/1745691610375559

Cialdini, R. B. (2007). *Influence: Science and practice*. New York, NY: HarperCollins.

Cialdini, R. B. (2008). *Influence: Science and practice* (5th ed.). Boston, MA: Allyn & Bacon.

Cialdini, R. B., & Griskevicius, V. (2010). Social influence. In R. F. Baumeister & E. J. Finkel (Eds.), *Advanced social psychology: The state of the science* (pp. 385–417). New York, NY: Oxford University Press.

Cialdini, R. B., & Trost, M. R. (1998). Social influence: Social norms, conformity, and compliance. In D. T. Gilbert, S. T. Fiske, & G. Lindzey (Eds.), *The handbook of social psychology*. New York, NY: McGraw-Hill.

Ciborowski, T. (1997). "Superstition" in the collegiate baseball player. *Sport Psychologist, 11*, 305–317.

Clark, D. A., Abramowitz, J., Alcolado, G. M., Alonso, P., Belloch, A., Bouvard, M., . . . Wong, W. (2014). Part 3. A question of perspective: The association between intrusive thoughts and obsessionality in 11 countries. *Journal of Obsessive-Compulsive and Related Disorders, 3*(3), 292–299. doi:10.1016/j.jocrd.2013.12.006

Clark, D. A., & Beck, A. T. (2010). *Cognitive Therapy of Anxiety Disorders: Science and practice*. New York, NY: Guilford Press.

Clark, R. D., & Hatfield, E. (1989). Gender differences in receptivity to sexual offers. *Journal of Psychology & Human Sexuality, 2*(1), 39–55.

Clark, R. E., Hales, J. B., Zola, S. M., & Thompson, R. F. (2013). Biological psychology. In D. K. Freedheim, & I. B. Weiner (Eds.), *Handbook of psychology: Vol. 1. History of psychology* (2nd ed., pp. 55–78). New York, NY: Wiley.

Clasen, P. C., Disner, S. G., & Beevers, C. G. (2013). Cognition and depression: Mechanisms associated with the onset and maintenance of emotional disorder. In M. D. Robinson, E. Watkins, & E. Harmon-Jones (Eds.), *Handbook of cognition and emotion*. New York, NY: Guilford Press.

Claxton, S. E., & van Dulmen, M. H. M. (2013). Casual sexual relationships and experiences in emerging adulthood. *Emerging Adulthood, 1*, 138–150.

Clayton, R. B., Nagurney, A., & Smith, J. R. (2013). Cheating, breakup, and divorce: Is Facebook use to blame? *Cyberpsychology, Behavior, and Social Networking, 16*, 717–720. doi:10.1089/cyber.2012.0424

Cleare, A. J., & Rane, L. J. (2013). Biological models of unipolar depression. In M. Power (Ed.), *The Wiley-Blackwell handbook of mood* disorders (2nd ed.). Malden, MA: Wiley-Blackwell.

Clement, S., Schauman, O., Graham, T., Maggioni, F., Evans-Lacko, S., Bezborodovs, N., . . . Thornicroft, G. (2015). What is the impact of mental health–related stigma on help-seeking? A systematic review of quantitative and qualitative studies. *Psychological Medicine, 45*(1), 11–27. doi:10.1017/S0033291714000129

Clements, A. M., Rimrodt, S. L., Abel, J. R., Blankner, J. G., Mostofsky, S. H., Pekar, J. J., . . . Cutting, L. E. (2006). Sex differences in cerebral laterality of language and visuospatial processing. *Brain and Language, 98*(2), 150–158. doi:10.1016/j.bandl.2006.04.007

Clint, E. K., Sober, E., Garland Jr, T., & Rhodes, J. S. (2012). Male superiority in spatial navigation: Adaptation or side effect? *The Quarterly Review of Biology, 87,* 289–313. doi:10.1086/668168

Clow, A. (2001). The physiology of stress. In F. Jones & J. Bright (Eds.), *Stress: Myth, theory, and research.* Harlow, UK: Pearson.

Coderre, T. J., Mogil, J. S., & Bushnell, M. C. (2003). The biological psychology of pain. In M. Gallagher & R. J. Nelson (Eds.), *Handbook of psychology: Vol. 3, Biological psychology.* New York, NY: Wiley.

Cogsdill, E. J., Todorov, A. T., Spelke, E. S., & Banaji, M. R. (2014). Inferring character from faces: A developmental study. *Psychological Science, 25,* 1132–1139. doi:10.1177/0956797614523297

Cohan, C. L. (2013). The cohabitation conundrum. In M. A. Fine & F. D. Fincham (Eds.), *Handbook of family theories: A content-based approach.* New York, NY: Routledge/Taylor & Francis Group.

Cohen, C. E. (1981). Person categories and social perception: Testing some boundaries of the processing effects of prior knowledge. *Journal of Personality and Social Psychology, 40,* 441–452.

Cohen, D. B. (1999). *Stranger in the nest: Do parents really shape their child's personality, intelligence, or character?* New York, NY: Wiley.

Cohen, S. (2005). Pittsburgh common cold studies: Psychosocial predictors of susceptibility to respiratory infectious illness. *International Journal of Behavioral Medicine, 12*(3), 123–131.

Cohen, S., Janicki-Deverts, D., Doyle, W. J., Miller, G. E., Frank, E., Rabin, B. S., & Turner, R. B. (2012). Chronic stress, glucocorticoid receptor resistance, inflammation, and disease risk. *PNAS Proceedings of the National Academy of Sciences in the United States of America, 109,* 5995–5999. doi:10.1073/pnas.1118355109

Cohen, S., Janicki-Deverts, D., & Miller, G. E. (2007). Psychological stress and disease. *JAMA, 298,* 1685–1687.

Cohen, S., & Pressman, S. D. (2006). Positive affect and health. *Current Directions in Psychological Science, 15*(3), 122–125.

Colagiuri, B., & Boakes, R. A. (2010). Perceived treatment, feedback, and placebo effects in double-blind RCTs: An experimental analysis. *Psychopharmacology, 208*(3), 433–441. doi:10.1007/s00213-009-1743-9

Colangelo, J. J. (2009). Case study: The recovered memory controversy: A representative case study. *Journal of Child Sexual Abuse: Research, Treatment, & Program Innovations For Victims, Survivors, & Offenders, 18,* 103–121. doi:10.1080/10538710802584601

Cole, M., & Packer, M. (2011). Culture and cognition. In K. D. Keith (Ed.), *Cross-cultural psychology: Contemporary themes and perspectives.* Malden, MA: Wiley-Blackwell.

Collins, A. M., & Loftus, E. F. (1975). A spreading-activation theory of semantic processing. *Psychological Review, 82,* 407–428. doi:10.1037/0033-295X.82.6.407

Collins, W. A., & Laursen, B. (2006). Parent-adolescent relationships. In P. Noller & J. A. Feeney (Eds.), *Close relationships: Functions, forms and processes.* Hove, England: Psychology Press.

Colombo, J., Brez, C. C., & Curtindale, L. M. (2013). Infant perception and cognition. In R. M. Lerner, M. A. Easterbrooks, J. Mistry, & I. B. Weiner (Eds.), *Handbook of psychology: Vol. 6. Developmental psychology.* New York, NY: Wiley.

Colwill, R. M. (1993). An associative analysis of instrumental learning. *Current Directions in Psychological Science, 2*(4), 111–116.

Comas-Diaz, L. (2006). Cultural variation in the therapeutic relationship. In C. D. Goodheart, A. E. Kazdin, & R. J. Sternberg (Eds.), *Evidence-based psychotherapy: Where practice and research meet.* Washington, DC: American Psychological Association.

Combs, D. R., & Mueser, K. T. (2007). Schizophrenia. In M. Hersen, S. M. Turner, & D. C. Beidel (Eds.), *Adult psychopathology and diagnosis.* New York, NY: Wiley.

Comer, J. S., & Kendall, P. C. (2013). Methodology, design, and evaluation in psychotherapy research. In M. J. Lambert (Ed.), *Bergin and Garfield's handbook of psychotherapy and behavior change* (6th ed.). New York, NY: Wiley.

Connell, J. D. (2005). *Brain-based strategies to reach every learner.* New York, NY: Scholastic.

Connor, C. E., Pasupathy, A., Brincat, S., & Yamane, Y. (2009). Neural transformation of object information by ventral pathway visual cortex. In M. S. Gazzaniga (Ed.), *The cognitive neurosciences.* Cambridge, MA: MIT Press.

Conway, A. M., Tugade, M. M., Catalino, L. I., & Fredrickson, B. L. (2013). The broaden-and-build theory of positive emotions: Form, function, and mechanisms. In S. A. David, I. Boniwell, & A. Conley Ayers (Eds.), *Oxford handbook of happiness.* New York, NY: Oxford University Press.

Cooke, L. (2007). The importance of exposure for healthy eating in childhood: A review. *Journal of Human Nutrition and Dietetics, 20,* 294–301.

Coolidge, F. L., & Wynn, T. (2009). *The rise of homo sapiens: The evolution of modern thinking.* Malden, MA: Wiley-Blackwell. doi:10.1002/9781444308297

Cooper, C., Bebbington, P., King, M., Jenkins, R., Farrell, M., Brugha, T., . . . Livingston, G. (2011). Happiness across age groups: Results from the 2007 National Psychiatric Morbidity Survey. *International Journal of Geriatric Psychiatry, 26,* 608–614. doi:10.1002/gps.2570

Cooper, J. (2012). Cognitive dissonance theory. In P. A. M. Van Lange, A. W. Kruglanski, & E. T. Higgins (Eds.), *Handbook of theories of social psychology: Vol. 1.* Los Angeles, CA: Sage.

Corballis, M. C. (1991). *The lopsided ape.* New York, NY: Oxford University Press.

Corballis, M. C. (2007). The dual-brain myth. In S. Della Sala (Ed.), *Tall tales about the mind & brain: Separating fact from fiction* (pp. 291–313). New York, NY: Oxford University Press.

Corballis, P. M. (2003). Visuospatial processing and the right-hemisphere interpreter. *Brain & Cognition, 53*(2), 171–176.

Coren, S. (1992). *The left-hander syndrome: The causes and consequences of left-handedness.* New York, NY: Free Press.

Coren, S., & Girgus, J. S. (1978). *Seeing is deceiving: The psychology of visual illusions.* Hillsdale, NJ: Erlbaum.

Corkin, S. (1984). Lasting consequences of bilateral medial temporal lobectomy: Clinical course and experimental findings in H. M. *Seminars in Neurology, 4,* 249–259.

Corkin, S. (2002). What's new with the amnesic patient H. M.? *Nature Reviews Neuroscience, 3,* 153–159.

Cornell, D. G. (1997). Post hoc explanation is not prediction. *American Psychologist, 52,* 1380.

Corr, C. A. (1993). Coping with dying: Lessons that we should and should not learn from the work of Elisabeth Kubler-Ross. *Death Studies, 17,* 69–83.

Corrigan, P. W., Druss, B. G., & Perlick, D. A. (2014). The impact of mental illness stigma on seeking and participating in mental health care. *Psychological Science in the Public Interest, 15*(2), 37–70. doi:10.1177/1529100614531398

Corrigan, P. W., & Larson, J. E. (2008). Stigma. In K. T. Mueser & D. V. Jeste (Eds.), *Clinical handbook of schizophrenia* (pp. 533–540). New York, NY: Guilford Press.

Corsica, J. A., & Perri, M. G. (2013). Understanding and managing obesity. In A. M. Nezu, C. M. Nezu, P. A. Geller, & I. B. Weiner (Eds.), *Handbook of psychology: Vol. 9. Health psychology* (2nd ed.). Hoboken, NJ: Wiley.

Cosgrove, L., & Krimsky, S. (2012). A comparison of DSM-IV and DSM-5 panel members' financial associations with industry: a pernicious problem persists. *PLoS Medicine, 9*(3), e1001190. doi:10.1371/journal.pmed.1001190

Cosmides, L. L., & Tooby, J. (1989). Evolutionary psychology and the generation of culture. Part II. Case study: A computational theory of social exchange. *Ethology and Sociobiology, 10,* 51–97.

Cosmides, L. L., & Tooby, J. (1996). Are humans good intuitive statisticians after all? Rethinking some conclusions from the literature on judgment under uncertainty. *Cognition, 58,* 1–73.

Costa, A., & Sebastián-Gallés, N. (2014). How does the bilingual experience sculpt the brain? *Nature Reviews Neuroscience, 15,* 336–345. doi:10.1038/nrn3709

Costa, P. T., Jr., & McCrae, R. R. (1985). *NEO Personality Inventory.* Odessa, FL: Psychological Assessment Resources.

Costa, P. T., Jr., & McCrae, R. R. (1992). *Revised NEO Personality Inventory: NEO PI and NEO Five-Factor Inventory* (professional manual). Odessa, FL: Psychological Assessment Resources.

Costa, P. T., Jr., & McCrae, R. R. (1994). Set like plaster? Evidence for the stability of adult personality. In T. F. Heatherton & J. L. Weinberger (Eds.), *Can personality change?*

Washington, DC: American Psychological Association.

Costa, P. T., Jr., & McCrae, R. R. (1997). Longitudinal stability of adult personality. In R. Hogan, J. Johnson, & S. Briggs (Eds.), *Handbook of personality psychology*. San Diego, CA: Academic Press.

Cotter, A., & Potter, J. E. (2006). Mother to child transmission. In J. Beal, J. J. Orrick, & K. Alfonso (Eds.), *HIV/AIDS: Primary care guide*. Norwalk, CT: Crown House.

Courchesne, E., Mouton, P. R., Calhoun, M. E., Semendeferi, K., Ahrens-Barbeau, C., Hallet, M. J., . . . Pierce, K. (2011). Neuron number and size in prefrontal cortex of children with autism. *JAMA, 306*, 2001–2010. doi:10.1001/jama.2011.1638

Coutts, A. (2000). Nutrition and the life cycle. 1: Maternal nutrition and pregnancy. *British Journal of Nursing, 9*, 1133–1138.

Cowan, N. (2005). *Working memory capacity*. New York, NY: Psychology Press.

Cowan, N. (2010). The magical mystery four: How is working memory capacity limited, and why? *Current Directions in Psychological Science, 19*(1), 51–57. doi:10.1177/0963721409359277

Cowart, B. J. (2005). Taste, our body's gustatory gatekeeper. *Cerebrum, 7*(2), 7–22.

Cowart, B. J., & Rawson, N. E. (2001). Olfaction. In E. B. Goldestein (Ed.), *Blackwell handbook of perception*. Malden, MA: Blackwell.

Cox, D., Meyers, E., & Sinha, P. (2004). Contextually evoked object-specific responses in human visual cortex. *Science, 304,* 115–117.

Cox, P. D., Vinogradov, S., & Yalom, I. D. (2008). Group therapy. In R. E. Hales, S. C. Yudofsky, & G. O. Gabbard (Eds.), *The American Psychiatric Publishing textbook of psychiatry* (pp. 1329–1376). Washington, DC: American Psychiatric Publishing.

Cox, R. E., & Bryant, R. A. (2008). Advances in hypnosis research: Methods, designs and contributions of intrinsic and instrumental hypnosis. In M. R. Nash & A. J. Barnier (Eds.). *The Oxford Handbook of Hypnosis: Theory, research and practice* (pp. 311–336). New York, NY: Oxford University Press.

Cox, W. T. L., Abramson, L. Y., Devine, P. G., & Hollon, S. D. (2012). Stereotypes, prejudice, and depression: The integrated perspective. *Perspective on Psychological Science, 7*, 427–449. doi:10.1177/1745691612455204

Craighead, W. E., Craighead, L. W., Ritschel, L. A., & Zagoloff, A. (2013).

Behavior therapy and cognitive-behavioral therapy. In G. Stricker & T. A. Widiger (Eds.), *Handbook of psychology: Vol. 8. Clinical psychology* (2nd ed.). New York, NY: Wiley.

Craik, F. I. M. (2001). Effects of dividing attention on encoding and retrieval processes. In H. L. Roediger III, J. S. Nairne, I. Neath, & A. M. Surprenant (Eds.), *The nature of remembering: Essays in honor of Robert G. Crowder* (pp. 55–68). Washington, DC: American Psychological Association.

Craik, F. I. M. (2002). Levels of processing: Past, present . . . and future? *Memory, 10*(5–6), 305–318.

Craik, F. I. M., & Lockhart, R. S. (1972). Levels of processing: A framework for memory research. *Journal of Verbal Learning and Verbal Behavior, 11,* 671–684.

Craik, F. I. M., & Tulving, E. (1975). Depth of processing and the retention of words in episodic memory. *Journal of Experimental Psychology: General, 104*, 268–294.

Cramer, P. (2000). Defense mechanisms in psychology today: Further processes for adaptation. *American Psychologist, 55*(6), 637–646.

Cramer, P. (2001). The unconscious status of defense mechanisms. *American Psychologist, 56*, 762–763.

Cramer, P. (2008). Seven pillars of defense mechanism theory. *Social and Personality Psychology Compass, 2*(5), 1963 1981. doi:org/10.1111/j.1751-9004.2008.00135.x

Crandall, C. S., Bahns, A. J., Warner, R., & Schaller, M. (2011). Stereotypes as justifications of prejudice. *Personality and Social Psychology Bulletin, 37*, 1488–1498. doi:10.1177/0146167211411723

Crede, M., & Kuncel, N. R. (2008). Study habits, skills, and attitudes: The third pillar supporting collegiate academic performance. *Perspectives on Psychological Science, 3*(6), 425–453. doi:10.1111/j.1745-6924.2008.00089.x

Creswell, J. D., Bursley, J. K., & Satpute, A. B. (2013). Neural reactivation links unconscious thought to decision-making performance. *Social Cognitive and Affective Neuroscience, 8*, 863–869. doi:10.1093/scan/nst004

Crews, F. (2006). *Follies of the wise: Dissenting essays*. Emeryville, CA: Shoemaker & Hoard.

Crits-Christoph, P., Gibbons, M. B., & Mukherjee, D. (2013). Psychotherapy process-outcome research. In M. J. Lambert (Ed.). *Bergin and Garfield's handbook of psychotherapy and behavior change* (6th ed.). New York, NY: Wiley.

Cross-Disorder Group of the Psychiatric Genomics Consortium. (2013). Genetic relationship between five psychiatric disorders estimated from genome-wide SNPs. *Nature Genetics, 45*, 1371–1379. doi:10.1038/ng.2711

Crowder, R. G., & Greene, R. L. (2000). Serial learning: Cognition and behavior. In E. Tulving & F. I. M. Craik (Eds.), *The Oxford handbook of memory* (pp. 125–136). New York, NY: Oxford University Press.

Crum, A. J., Salovey, P., & Achor, S. (2013). Rethinking stress: The role of mindsets in determining stress response. *Journal of Personality and Social Psychology, 104*, 716–733. doi:10.1037/a0031201

Cuijpers, P., Driessen, E., Hollon, S. D., van Oppen, P., Barth, J., & Andersson, G. (2012). The efficacy of non-directive supportive therapy for adult depression: A meta-analysis. *Clinical Psychology Review, 32*(4), 280–291. doi:10.1016/j.cpr.2012.01.003

Cuijpers, P., Vogelzangs, N., Twisk, J., Kleiboer, A., Li, J., & Penninx, B. W. (2014). Comprehensive meta-analysis of excess mortality in depression in the general community versus patients with specific illnesses. *The American Journal of Psychiatry, 171*, 453–462. doi:10.1176/appi.ajp.2013.13030325

Cullen, B. A., McGinty, E. E., Zhang, Y., dosReis, S. C., Steinwachs, D. M., Guallar, E., & Daumit, G. L. (2013). Guideline-concordant antipsychotic use and mortality in schizophrenia. *Schizophrenia Bulletin, 39*, 1159–1168. doi:10.1093/schbul/sbs097

Cummins, D. (2005). Dominance, status, and social hierarchies. In D. M. Buss (Ed.), *The handbook of evolutionary psychology*. New York, NY: Wiley.

Cunningham, C. O., & Selwyn, P. A. (2005). HIV-related medical complications and treatment. In J. H. Lowinson, P. Ruiz, R. B. Millman, & J. G. Langrod (Eds.), *Substance abuse: A comprehensive textbook*. Philadelphia, PA: Lippincott Williams & Wilkins.

Cunningham, F., Leveno, K., Bloom, S., Hauth, J., Rouse, D., & Spong, C. (2010). *Williams obstetrics* (23rd ed.). New York, NY: McGraw-Hill.

Cunningham, J. B., & MacGregor, J. N. (2014). Productive and re-productive thinking in solving insight problems. *Journal of Creative Behavior, 48*(1), 44–63. doi:10.1002/jocb.40

Cunningham, M. (2001). The influence of parental attitudes and behaviors on children's attitudes toward gender and household labor in early adulthood. *Journal of Marriage and the Family, 63*, 111–122.

Curci, A., Lanciano, T., Soleti, E., & Rimé, B. (2013). Negative emotional experiences arouse rumination and affect working memory capacity. *Emotion, 13*, 867–880. doi:10.1037/a0032492

Curtis, G. C., Magee, W. J., Eaton, W. W., Wittchen, H., & Kessler, R. C. (1998). Specific fears and phobias: Epidemiology and classification. *British Journal of Psychiatry, 173*, 212–217. doi:10.1192/bjp.173.3.212

Cushman, P. (1992). Psychotherapy to 1992: A historically situated interpretation. In D. K. Freedheim (Ed.), *History of psychotherapy: A century of change*. Washington, DC: American Psychological Association.

Czarna, A. Z., Dufner, M., & Clifton, A. D. (2014). The effects of vulnerable and grandiose narcissism on liking-based and disliking-based centrality in social networks. *Journal of Research in Personality, 50*, 42–45. doi:10.1016/j.jrp.2014.02.004

Dager, A. D., Anderson, B. M., Rosen, R., Khadka, S., Sawyer, B., Jiantonio-Kelly, R. E., . . . Pearson, G. D. (2014). Functional magnetic resonance imaging (fMRI) response to alcohol pictures predicts subsequent transition to heavy drinking in college students. *Addiction, 109*, 585–595. doi:10.1111/add.12437

Daiek, D. B., & Anter, N. M. (2004). *Critical reading for college and beyond*. New York, NY: McGraw-Hill.

Daley, C. E., & Onwuegbuzie, A. J. (2011). Race and intelligence. In R. J. Sternberg, & S. B. Kaufman (Eds.), *Cambridge handbook of intelligence*. New York, NY: Cambridge University Press.

Dallman, M. F., Bhatnagar, S., & Viau, V. (2007). Hypothalamic-pituitary-adrenal axis. In G. Fink (Ed.), *Encyclopedia of stress*. San Diego, CA: Elsevier.

Dalton, S. O., & Johansen, C. (2005). Stress and cancer: The critical research. In C. L. Cooper (Ed.), *Handbook of stress medicine and health*. Boca Raton, FL: CRC Press.

Daly, M., & Wilson, M. (1985). Child abuse and other risks of not living with both parents. *Ethology and Sociobiology, 6*, 197–210.

Dang-Vu, T. T., Schabus, M., Cologan, V., & Maquet, P. (2009). Sleep: Implications for theories of dreaming and consciousness. In W. P. Banks (Ed.), *Encyclopedia of Consciousness* (pp. 357–374). San Diego, CA: Academic Press.

Danziger, K. (1990). *Constructing the subject: Historical origins of psychological research*. Cambridge, UK: Cambridge University Press.

Darley, J. M., & Latané, B. (1968). Bystander intervention in emergencies: Diffusion of responsibility. *Journal of Personality and Social Psychology, 8,* 377–383.

Darling-Kuria, N. (2010). *Brain-based early learning activities: Connecting theory and practice.* St. Paul, MN: Redleaf Press.

Darwin, C. (1859). *The origin of species.* London, UK: Murray.

Darwin, C. (1872). *The expression of emotions in man and animals.* New York, NY: Philosophical Library.

Das, E. H. H. J., de Wit, J. B. F., & Stroebe, W. (2003). Fear appeals motivate acceptance of action recommendations: Evidence for a positive bias in the processing of persuasive messages. *Personality and Social Psychology Bulletin, 29*(5), 650–664. doi:org/10.1177/0146167203029005009

David, E. R., Okazaki, S., & Giroux, D. (2014). A set of guiding principles to advance multicultural psychology and its major concepts. In F. L. Leong, L. Comas-Díaz, G. C. Nagayama Hall, V. C. McLoyd, & J. E. Trimble (Eds.), *APA handbook of multicultural psychology: Vol. 1. Theory and research.* Washington, DC: American Psychological Association. doi:10.1037/14189-005

Davidoff, J. (2001). Language and perceptual categorization. *Trends in Cognitive Sciences, 5,* 382–387.

Davidoff, J. (2004). Coloured thinking. *Psychologist, 17,* 570–572.

Davidson, J. E., & Kemp, I. A. (2011). Contemporary models of intelligence. In R. J. Sternberg, & S. B. Kaufman (Eds.), *Cambridge handbook of intelligence.* New York, NY: Cambridge University Press.

Davidson, K. W., Mostofsky, E., & Whang, W. (2010). Don't worry, be happy: Positive affect and reduced 10-year incident coronary heart disease: The Canadian Nova Scotia Health Survey. *European Heart Journal, 31,* 1065–1070.

Davidson, R. J., Kabat-Zinn, J., Schumacher, J., Rosenkranz, M., Muller, D., Santorelli, . . . Sheridan, J. F. (2003a). Alterations in brain and immune function produced by mindfulness meditation. *Psychosomatic Medicine, 65,* 564–570.

Davies, G., Tenesa, A., Payton, A., Yang, J., Harris, S. E., Liewald, D., . . . Deary, I. J. (2011). Genome-wide association studies establish that human intelligence is highly heritable and polygenic. *Molecular Psychiatry, 16,* 996–1005. doi:10.1038/mp.2011.85

Davies, I. R. L. (1998). A study of colour in three languages: A test of linguistic relativity hypothesis. *British Journal of Psychology, 89,* 433–452.

Davis, A., & Bremner, G. (2006). The experimental method in psychology. In G. M. Breakwell, S. Hammond, C. Fife-Schaw, & J. A. Smith (Eds.), *Research methods in psychology* (3rd ed.). London, UK: Sage.

Davis, A. S., & Dean, R. S. (2005). Lateralization of cerebral functions and hemispheric specialization: Linking behavior, structure, and neuroimaging. In R. C. D'Amato, E. Fletcher-Janzen, & C. R. Reynolds (Eds.), *Handbook of school neuropsychology.* Hoboken, NJ: Wiley.

Davis, D., & Loftus, E. F. (2007). Internal and external sources of misinformation in adult witness memory. In M. P. Toglia, J. D. Read, D. F. Ross, & R. C. L. Lindsay (Eds.), *Handbook of eyewitness psychology: Vol. 1. Memory for events.* Mahwah, NJ: Erlbaum.

Davis, K., Christodoulou, J., Seider, S., & Gardner, H. (2011). The theory of multiple intelligences. In R. J. Sternberg, & S. B. Kaufman (Eds.), *Cambridge handbook of intelligence.* New York, NY: Cambridge University Press.

Davis, M., Guyker, W., & Persky, I. (2012). Uniting veterans across distance through a telephone-based reminiscence group therapy intervention. *Psychological Services, 9*(2), 206–208. doi:10.1037/a0026117

Davis, M. C., Burke, H. M., Zautra, A. J., & Stark, S. (2013). Arthritis and musculoskeletal conditions. In A. M. Nezu, C. M. Nezu, P. A. Geller, & I. B. Weiner (Eds.), *Handbook of psychology: Vol. 9. Health psychology* (2nd ed.). New York, NY: Wiley.

Davis, O. S. P., Arden, R., & Plomin, R. (2008). *g* in middle childhood: Moderate genetic and shared environmental influence using diverse measures of general cognitive ability at 7, 9 and 10 years in a large population sample of twins. *Intelligence, 36,* 68–80.

Day, R. H. (1965). Inappropriate constancy explanation of spatial distortions. *Nature, 207,* 891–893.

Deacon, B. J. (2013). The biomedical model of mental disorder: A critical analysis of its validity, utility, and effects on psychotherapy research. *Clinical Psychology Review, 33,* 846–861. doi:10.1016/j.cpr.2012.09.007

Deary, I. J. (2012). Intelligence. *Annual Review of Psychology, 63,* 453–482. doi:10.1146/annurev-psych-120710-100353

Deary, I. J., & Batty, G. D. (2011). Intelligence as a predictor of health, illness; and death. In R. J. Sternberg, & S. B. Kaufman (Eds.), *Cambridge handbook of intelligence.* New York, NY: Cambridge University Press.

Deary, I. J., Strand, S., Smith, P., & Fernandes, C. (2007). Intelligence and educational achievement. *Intelligence, 35,* 13–21.

de Castro, J. M. (2010). The control of food intake of free-living humans: Putting the pieces back together. *Physiology & Behavior, 100*(5), 446–453. doi:10.1016/j.physbeh.2010.04.028

Dechêne, A., Stahl, C., Hansen, J., & Wänke, M. (2010). The truth about the truth: A meta-analytic review of the truth effect. *Personality and Social Psychology Review, 14*(2), 238–257. doi:10.1177/1088868309352251

Deer, B. (2011). How the case against the MMR vaccine was fixed. *British Medical Journal, 342,* 77–82.

Deese, J. (1959). On the prediction of occurrence of particular verbal intrusions in immediate recall. *Journal of Experimental Psychology, 58,* 17–22.

De Houwer, J. (2011). Evaluative conditioning: A review of functional knowledge and mental process theories. In T. R. Schachtman, & S. Reilly (Eds.), *Associative learning and condition theory: Human and non-human applications.* New York, NY: Oxford University Press.

Deitmer, J. W., & Rose, C. R. (2010). Ion changes and signaling in perisynaptic glia. *Brain Research Reviews, 63*(1–2), 113–129. doi:10.1016/j.brainresrev.2009.10.006

De Koninck, J. (2000). Waking experiences and dreaming. In M. H. Kryger, T. Roth, & W. C. Dement (Eds.), *Principles and practice of sleep medicine.* Philadelphia, PA: Saunders.

De Lacy, N., & King, B. H. (2013). Revisiting the relationship between autism and schizophrenia: toward an integrated neurobiology. *Annual Review of Clinical Psychology, 9,* 555–587. doi:10.1146/annurev-cinpsy-050212-185627

Delis, D. C., & Lucas, J. A. (1996). Memory. In B. S. Fogel, R. B. Schiffer, & S. M. Rao (Eds.), *Neuropsychiatry.* Baltimore: Williams & Wilkins.

DeLongis, A., Folkman, S., & Lazarus, R. S. (1988). The impact of daily stress on health and mood: Psychological and social resources as mediators. *Journal of Personality and Social Psychology, 54,* 486–495.

Dement, W. C. (1992). *The sleepwatchers.* Stanford, CA: Stanford Alumni Association.

Dement, W. C., & Wolpert, E. (1958). The relation of eye movements, bodily motility, and external stimuli to dream content. *Journal of Experimental Psychology, 53,* 543–553.

Demir, M., Orthel, H., & Andelin, A. K. (2013). Friendship and happiness. In S. A. David, I. Boniwell, & A. Conley Ayers (Eds.), *The Oxford handbook of happiness.* New York, NY: Oxford University Press.

Dempster, E. L., Pidsley, R., Schalkwyk, L. C., Owens, S., Georgiades, A., Kane, F., . . . Mill, J. (2011). Disease-associated epigenetic changes in monozygotic twins discordant for schizophrenia and bipolar disorder. *Human Molecular Genetics.* doi:10.1093/hmg/ddr416

Denollet, J., Martens, E. J., Nyklicek, I., Conraads, V., & de Gelder, B. (2008). Clinical events in coronary patients who report low distress: Adverse effect of repressive coping. *Health Psychology, 27,* 302–308. doi:10.1037/0278-6133.27.3.302

DePrince, A. P., Brown, L. S., Cheit, R. E., Freyd, J. J., Gold, S. N., Pezdek, K., & Quina, K. (2012). Motivated forgetting and misremembering: Perspectives from betrayal trauma theory. In R. F. Belli (Ed.), *True and false recovered memories: Toward a reconciliation of the debate.* New York, NY: Springer.

Derevensky, J. L., & Gupta, R. (2004). Preface. In J. L. Derevensky & R. Gupta (Eds.), *Gambling problems in youth: Theoretical and applied perspectives* (pp. xxi–xxiv). New York, NY: Kluwer/Plenum.

Desmurget, M., Song, Z., Mottolese, C., & Sirigu, A. (2013). Re-establishing the merits of electrical brain stimulation. *Trends in Cognitive Sciences, 17,* 442–449. doi:10.1016/j.tics.2013.07.002

DeSpelder, L. A., & Strickland, A. L. (1983). *The last dance: Encountering death and dying.* Palo Alto, CA: Mayfield.

Deutch, A. Y., & Roth, R. H. (2008). Neurotransmitters. In L. Squire, D. Berg, F. Bloom, S. Du Lac, A. Ghosh, & N. Spitzer (Eds.), *Fundamental neuroscience* (3rd ed., pp. 133–156). San Diego, CA: Elsevier.

de Villiers, J. G., & de Villiers, P. A. (1999). Language development. In M. H. Bornstein & M. E. Lamb (Eds.), *Developmental psychology: An advanced textbook.* Mahwah, NJ: Erlbaum.

de Villiers, P. (1977). Choice in concurrent schedules and a quantitative formulation of the law of effect. In W. K. Honig & J. E. R. Staddon (Eds.), *Handbook of operant behavior.* Englewood Cliffs, NJ: Prentice-Hall.

Devine, P. G., & Sharp, L. B. (2009). Automaticity and control in stereotyping and prejudice. In T. D. Nelson (Ed.), *Handbook of prejudice, stereotyping, and discrimination* (pp. 1–22). New York, NY: Psychology Press.

Devlin, M. J., & Steinglass, J. E. (2014). Feeding and eating disorders. In J. L. Cutler (Ed.), *Psychiatry* (3rd ed.). New York, NY: Oxford University Press.

Devos, T. (2008). Implicit attitudes 101: Theoretical and empirical insights. In W. D. Crano, & R. Prislin (Eds.), *Attitudes and attitude change* (pp. 61–84). New York, NY: Psychology Press.

Dew, M. A., Bromet, E. J., & Switzer, G. E. (2000). Epidemiology. In M. Hersen & A. S. Bellack (Eds.), *Psychopathology in adulthood*. Boston, MA: Allyn & Bacon.

De Waal, F. (2001). *The ape and the sushi master: Cultural reflections of a primatologist*. New York, NY: Basic Books.

Dewald, J. F., Meijer, A. M., Oort, F. J., Kerkhof, G. A., & Bogels, S. M. (2010). The influence of sleep quality, sleep duration and sleepiness on school performance in children and adolescents: A meta-analytic review. *Sleep Medicine Reviews, 14*, 179–189. doi:10.1016/j.smrv.2009.10.004

de Wit, J. B. F., Das, E., & Vet, R. (2008). What works best: Objective statistics or a personal testimonial? An assessment of the persuasive effects of different types of message evidence on risk perception. *Health Psychology, 27*(1), 110–115. doi:10.1037/0278 -6133.27.1.110

Dewsbury, D. A. (2009). Charles Darwin and psychology at the bicentennial and sesquicentennial: An introduction. *American Psychologist, 64*(2), 67–74. doi:10.1037/a0013205

DeYoung, C. G. (2015). Openness/intellect: A dimension of personality reflecting. In M. Mikulincer, P. R. Shaver, M. L. Cooper, & R. J. Larsen (Eds.), *APA handbook of personality and social psychology: Vol. 4. Personality processes and individual differences*. Washington, DC: American Psychological Association.

Dhabhar, F. S. (2011). Effects of stress on immune function: Implications for immunoprotection and immunopathology. In R. J. Contrada & A. Baum (Eds.), *Handbook of stress science: Biology, psychology, and health*. New York, NY: Springer Publishing Company.

Diamond, L. M. (2008). Female bisexuality from adolescence to adulthood: Results from a 10-year longitudinal study. *Developmental Psychology, 44*(1), 5–14. doi:10.1037/0012 -1649.44.1.5

Diamond, L. M. (2013). Concepts of female sexual orientation. In C. J. Patterson, & A. R. D'Augelli (Eds.), *Handbook of psychology and sexual orientation*. New York, NY: Oxford University Press.

Diamond, L. M. (2014). Gender and same-sex sexuality. In D. L. Tolman, L.

M. Diamond, J. A. Bauermeister, W. H. George, J. G. Pfaus, & L. M. Ward (Eds.), *APA handbook of sexuality and psychology: Vol. 1. Person-based approaches*. Washington, DC: American Psychological Association.

DiCicco-Bloom, E., & Falluel-Morel, A. (2009). Neural development & neurogenesis. In B. J. Sadock, V. A. Sadock, & P. Ruiz (Eds.), *Kaplan & Sadock's comprehensive textbook of psychiatry* (9th ed., Vol. 1, pp. 42–64). Philadelphia, PA: Lippincott Williams & Wilkins.

Dick, D. M., & Rose, R. J. (2002). Behavior genetics: What's new? What's next? *Current Directions in Psychological Science, 11*(2), 70–74.

Dickens, W. T., & Flynn, J. R. (2001). Heritability estimates versus large environmental effects: The IQ paradox resolved. *Psychological Review, 108*, 346–369.

Diener, E., & Biswas-Diener, R. (2002). Will money increase subjective well-being? *Social Indicators Research, 57*(2), 119–169. doi:10.1023/A:1014411319119

Diener, E., Gohm, C. L., Suh, E., & Oishi, S. (2000). Similarity of the relations between marital status and subjective well-being across cultures. *Journal of Cross-Cultural Psychology, 31*, 419–436.

Diener, E., Kesebir, P., & Tov, W. (2009). Happiness. In M. R. Leary & R. H. Hoyle (Eds.), *Handbook of individual differences in social behavior* (pp. 147–160). New York, NY: Guilford Press.

Diener, E., Wolsic, B., & Fujita, F. (1995). Physical attractiveness and subjective well-being. *Journal of Personality and Social Psychology, 69*, 120–129.

Dietrich, M. O., & Horvath T. L. (2012). Neuroendocrine regulation of energy balance. In K. D. Brownell, & M. S. Gold (Eds.), *Food and addiction: A comprehensive handbook*. New York, NY: Oxford University Press.

Dijk, D., & Lazar, A. S. (2012). The regulation of human sleep and wakefulness: Sleep homeostasis and circadian rhythmicity. In C. M. Morin, & C. A. Espie (Eds.), *Oxford handbook of sleep and sleep disorders*. New York, NY: Oxford University Press.

Dijksterhuis, A. (2010). Automaticity and the unconscious. In S. T. Fiske, D. T. Gilbert, & G. Lindzey (Eds.), *Handbook of social psychology* (5th ed., Vol. 1, pp. 228–267). New York, NY: Wiley.

Dijksterhuis, A., Bos, M. W., Nordgren, L. F., & van Baaren, R. B. (2006). On making the right choice: The deliberation-without-attention effect. *Science, 311*, 1005–1007.

Dijksterhuis, A., & Nordgren, L. F. (2006). A theory of unconscious thought. *Perspectives on Psychological Science, 1*(2), 95–109.

Dijksterhuis, A., & van Olden, Z. (2006). On the benefits of thinking unconsciously: Unconscious thought can increase post-choice satisfaction. *Journal of Experimental Social Psychology, 42*, 627–631.

Di Lorenzo, P. M., & Youngentob, S. L. (2003). Olfaction and taste. In M. Gallagher & R. J. Nelson (Eds.), *Handbook of psychology: Vol. 3. Biological psychology*. New York, NY: Wiley.

Di Lorenzo, P. M., & Youngentob, S. L. (2013). Taste and olfaction. In R. J. Nelson, S. J. Y. Mizumori, & I. B. Weiner (Eds.), *Handbook of psychology: Vol. 3. Behavioral neuroscience* (2nd ed.). New York, NY: Wiley.

DiMatteo, M. R. (1991). *The psychology of health, illness, and medical care: An individual perspective*. Pacific Grove, CA: Brooks/Cole.

DiMatteo, M. R. (1997). Health behaviors and care decisions: An overview of professional-patient communication. In D. S. Gochman (Ed.), *Handbook of health behavior research II: Provider determinants*. New York, NY: Plenum.

DiMatteo, M. R. (2004a). Social support and patient adherence to medical treatment: A meta analysis. *Health Psychology, 23*, 207–218.

DiMatteo, M. R. (2004b). Variations in patients' adherence to medical recommendations: A quantitative review of 50 years of research. *Medical Care, 42*, 200–209.

Dimberg, U., & Söderkvist, S. (2011). The voluntary facial action technique: A method to test the facial feedback hypothesis. *Journal of Nonverbal Behavior, 35*(1), 17–33. doi:10.1007 /s10919-010-0098-6

Di Milia, L., Vandelanotte, C., & Duncan, M. J. (2013). The association between short sleep and obesity after controlling for demographic, lifestyle, work and health related factors. *Sleep Medicine, 14*, 319–323. doi:10.1016/ j.sleep.2012.12.007

Ding, D., Fung, J. W., Zhang, Q., Yip, G. W., Chang, C., & Yu, C. (2009). Effect of household passive smoking exposure on the risk of ischaemic heart disease in never-smoke female patients in Hong Kong. *Tobacco Control: An International Journal, 18*, 354–357. doi:10.1136/tc.2008.026112

Dinsmoor, J. A. (1998). Punishment. In W. O'Donohue (Ed.), *Learning and behavior therapy*. Boston, MA: Allyn & Bacon.

Dinsmoor, J. A. (2004). The etymology of basic concepts in the experimental

analysis of behavior. *Journal of the Experimental Analysis of Behavior, 82*, 311–316.

Dismukes, R. K. (2012). Prospective memory in workplace and everyday situations. *Current Directions in Psychological Science, 21*, 215–220. doi:10.1177/0963721412447621

Dissell, R. (2005, December 14). Student from Ohio robbed bank to feed gambling habit, lawyer says. *The Plain Dealer*.

Dixon, L., & Goldman, H. (2004). Forty years of progress in community mental health: The role of evidence-based practices. *Administration & Policy in Mental Health, 31*(5), 381–392.

Dixon, R. A., & Cohen, A. (2003). Cognitive development in adulthood. In R. M. Lerner, M. A. Easterbrooks, & J. Mistry (Eds.), *Handbook of psychology: Vol. 6. Developmental psychology*. New York, NY: Wiley.

Dixon, R. A., McFall, G. P., Whitehead, B. P., & Dolcos, S. (2013). Cognitive development in adulthood and aging. In R. M. Lerner, M. A. Easterbrooks, J. Mistry, & I. B. Weiner (Eds.), *Handbook of psychology: Vol. 6. Developmental psychology*. New York, NY: Wiley.

Dobzhansky, T. (1937). *Genetics and the origin of species*. New York, NY: Columbia University Press.

Dodds, R. A., Ward, T. B., & Smith, S. M. (2011). A review of experimental literature on incubation in problem solving and creativity. In M. A. Runco (Ed.), *Creativity research handbook* (Vol. 3). Cresskill, NJ: Hampton. doi:10.1016/j.neuroimage.2010.01.021

Dohrenwend, B. P. (2006). Inventorying stressful life events as risk factors for psychopathology: Toward resolution of the problem of intracategory variability. *Psychological Bulletin, 132*, 477–495.

Doja, A., & Roberts, W. (2006). Immunizations and autism: A review of the literature. *Canadian Journal of Neurological Sciences, 33*(4), 341–346.

Dollard, J., Doob, L. W., Miller, N. E., Mowrer, O. H., & Sears, R. R. (1939). *Frustration and aggression*. New Haven: Yale University Press.

Domhoff, G. W. (2005a). The content of dreams: Methodologic and theoretical implications. In M. H. Kryger, T. Roth, & W. C. Dement (Eds.), *Principles and practice of sleep medicine*. Philadelphia, PA: Elsevier Saunders.

Domhoff, G. W. (2005b). Refocusing the neurocognitive approach to dreams: A critique of the Hobson versus Solms debate. *Dreaming, 15*(1), 3–20.

Domjan, M. (1994). Formulation of a behavior system for sexual conditioning. *Psychonomic Bulletin & Review, 1,* 421–428.

Domjan, M., & Atkins, C. K. (2011). Applications of Pavlovian conditioning to sexual behavior and reproduction. In T. R. Schachtman, & S. Reilly (Eds.), *Associative learning and condition theory: Human and non-human applications.* New York, NY: Oxford University Press.

Domjan, M., & Purdy, J. E. (1995). Animal research in psychology: More than meets the eye of the general psychology student. *American Psychologist, 50,* 496–503.

Don, B. P., & Mickelson, K. D. (2014). Relationship satisfaction trajectories across the transition to parenthood among low-risk parents. *Journal of Marriage and Family, 76,* 677–692. doi:10.1111/jomf.12111

Donnellan, M. B., Hill, P. L., & Roberts, B. W. (2015). Personality development across the life span: Current findings and future directions. In M. Mikulincer, P. R. Shaver, M. L. Cooper, & R. J. Larsen (Eds.), *APA handbook of personality and social psychology: Vol. 4. Personality processes and individual differences.* Washington, DC: American Psychological Association.

Dorahy, M. J., Brand, B. L., şar, V., Krüger, C., Stavropoulos, P., Martínez-Taboas, A., . . . Middleton, W. (2014). Dissociative identity disorder: An empirical overview. *Australian and New Zealand Journal of Psychiatry, 48,* 402–417. doi:10.1177/0004867414527523

Doron, K. W., Bassett, D. S., & Gazzaniga, M. S. (2012). Dynamic network structure of interhemispheric coordination. *PNAS Proceedings of the National Academy of Sciences of the United States of America, 109,* 18661–18668. doi:10.1073/pnas.1216402109

Dörrie, N., Focker, M., Freunscht, I., & Hebebrand, J. (2014). Fetal alcohol spectrum disorders. *European Child & Adolescent Psychiatry, 23,* 863–875. doi:10.1007/s00787-014-0571-6

Doss, B. D., Rhoades, G. K., Stanley, S. M., & Markman, H. J. (2009). The effect of the transition to parenthood on relationship quality: An 8-year prospective study. *Journal of Personality and Social Psychology, 96,* 601–619. doi:10.1037/a0013969

Doty, R. L. (2010). Olfaction. In E. B. Goldstein (Ed.), *Encyclopedia of perception.* Thousand Oaks, CA: Sage.

Dougall, A. L., & Baum, A. (2012). Stress, health, and illness. In A. Baum, T. A. Revenson, & J. Singer (Eds.), *Handbook of health psychology* (2nd ed.). New York, NY: Psychology Press.

Dougall, A. L., & Swanson, J. N. (2011). Physical health outcomes of trauma. In R. J. Contrada & A. Baum (Eds.), *Handbook of stress science: Biology, psychology and health.* New York, NY: Spring Publishing Company.

Dougherty, D. D., Wilhelm, S., & Jenike, M. A. (2014). Obsessive-compulsive and related disorders. In R. E. Hales, S. C. Yudofsky, & L. W. Roberts (Eds.), *The American Psychiatric Publishing textbook of psychiatry* (6th ed.). Washington, DC: American Psychiatric Publishing.

Douglas, A. J. (2010). Baby on board: Do responses to stress in the maternal brain mediate adverse pregnancy outcome? *Frontiers in Neuroendocrinology, 31*(3), 359–376. doi:10.1016/j.yfrne.2010.05.002

Dovidio, J. F., & Gaertner, S. L. (2008). New directions in aversive racism research: Persistence and pervasiveness. In C. Willis-Esqueda (Ed.), *Motivational aspects of prejudice and racism* (pp. 43–67). New York, NY: Springer Science & Business Media. doi:10.1007/978-0-387-73233-6_3

Dovidio, J. F., & Gaertner, S. L. (2010). Intergroup bias. In S. T. Fiske, D. T. Gilbert, & G. Lindzey (Eds.), *Handbook of social psychology* (5th ed., Vol. 1, pp. 353–393). Hoboken, NJ: Wiley.

Dowling, K. W. (2005). The effect of lunar phases on domestic violence incident rates. *The Forensic Examiner, 14*(4), 13–18.

Downey, C. A., & Chang, E. C. (2014). Positive psychology: Current knowledge, multicultural considerations, and the future of the movement. In F. L. Leong, L. Comas-Díaz, G. C. Nagayama Hall, V. C. McLoyd, & J. E. Trimble (Eds.), *APA handbook of multicultural psychology: Vol. 2. Applications and training.* Washington, DC: American Psychological Association. doi:10.1037/14187-008

Draganski, B., Gaser, C., Busch, V., Schuierer, G., Bogdahn, U., & May, A. (2004). Changes in grey matter induced by training. *Nature, 427,* 311–312.

Drake, C. L., & Wright, Jr., K. P. (2011). Shift work, shift-work disorder, and jet lag. In M. H. Kryger, T. Roth, & W. C. Dement (Eds.), *Principles and practice of sleep medicine* (5th ed.). Saint Louis, MO: Elsevier Saunders.

Drew, L. J., Fusi, S., & Hen, R. (2013). Adult neurogenesis in the mammalian hippocampus: Why the dentate gyrus? *Learning & Memory, 20,* 710–729. doi:10.1101/lm.026542.112

Drews, F. A., Pasupathi, M., & Strayer, D. L. (2008). Passenger and cell phone conversations in simulated driving. *Journal of Experimental Psychology: Applied, 14*(4), 392–400. doi:10.1037/a0013119

Drews, F. A., Yazdani, H., Godfrey, C. N., Cooper, J. M., & Strayer, D. L. (2009). Text messaging during simulated driving. *Human Factors, 51*(5), 762–770. doi:10.1177/0018720809353319

Dror, O. E. (2014). The Cannon-Bard thalamic theory of emotions: A brief genealogy and reappraisal. *Emotion Review, 6*(1), 13–20. doi:10.1177/1754073913494898

DuBois, G. E. (2010). Taste stimuli: Chemical and food. In E. B. Goldstein (Ed.), *Encyclopedia of perception.* Thousand Oaks, CA: Sage.

Dubovsky, S. L. (2009). Benzodiazepine receptor agonists and antagonists. In B. J. Sadock, V. A. Sadock, & P. Ruiz (Eds.), *Kaplan & Sadock's comprehensive textbook of psychiatry* (pp. 3044–3055). Philadelphia, PA: Lippincott Williams & Wilkins.

Duckworth, A. L., Quinn, P. D., Lynam, D. R., Loeber, R., & Stouthamer-Loeber, M. (2011). Role of test motivation in intelligence testing. *PNAS Proceedings of the National Academy of Sciences of the United States of America, 108,* 7716–7720. doi:10.1073/pnas.1018601108

Duckworth, A. L., & Seligman, M. E. P. (2005). Self-discipline outdoes IQ in predicting academic performance of adolescents. *Psychological Science, 16,* 939–944.

Duckworth, K., & Borus, J. F. (1999). Population-based psychiatry in the public sector and managed care. In A. M. Nicholi (Ed.), *The Harvard guide to psychiatry.* Cambridge, MA: Harvard University Press.

Dudai, Y. (2004). The neurobiology of consolidation, or, how stable is the engram? *Annual Review of Psychology, 55,* 51–86.

Dudley, M., Hadzi-Pavlovic, D., Andrews, D., & Perich, T. (2008). New-generation antidepressants, suicide and depressed adolescents: How should clinicians respond to changing evidence? *Australian and New Zealand Journal of Psychiatry, 42*(6), 456–466. doi:10.1080/00048670802050538

Duffy, V. B., Hayes, J. E., Davidson, A. C., Kidd, J. R., Kidd, K. K, & Bartoshuk, L. M. (2010). Vegetable intake in college-aged adults is explained by oral sensory phenotypes and TAS2R38 genotype. *Chemosensory Perception, 3*(3–4), 137–148. doi:10.1007/s12078-010-9079-8

Duffy, V. B., Lucchina, L. A., & Bartoshuk, L. M. (2004). Genetic variation in taste: Potential biomarker for cardiovascular disease risk? In J. Prescott & B. J. Tepper (Eds.), *Genetic variations in taste sensitivity: Measurement, significance, and implications* (pp. 195–228). New York, NY: Dekker.

Duke, A. A., Bègue, L., Bell, R., & Eisenlohr-Moul, T. (2013). Revisiting the serotonin–aggression relation in humans: A meta-analysis. *Psychological Bulletin, 139,* 1148–1172. doi:10.1037/a0031544

Dum, R. P., & Strick, P. L. (2009). Basal ganglia and cerebellar circuits with the cerebral cortex. In M. S. Gazzangia (Ed.), *The cognitive neurosciences* (4th ed., pp. 553–564). Cambridge, MA: MIT Press.

Duman, R. S., Polan, H. J., & Schatzberg, A. (2008). Neurobiologic foundations of mood disorders. In A. Tasman, J. Kay, J. A. Lieberman, M. B. First, & M. Maj (Eds.), *Psychiatry* (3rd ed.). New York, NY: Wiley-Blackwell.

Dunbar-Jacob, J., & Schlenk, E. (2001). Patient adherence to treatment regimen. In A. Baum, T. A. Revenson, & J. E. Singer (Eds.), *Handbook of health psychology.* Mahwah, NJ: Erlbaum.

Dunbar-Jacob, J., Schlenk, E., & McCall, M. (2012). Patient adherence to treatment regimen. In A. Baum, T. A. Revenson, & J. Singer (Eds.), *Handbook of health psychology* (2nd ed.). New York, NY: Psychology Press.

Duncan, B. L. (1976). Differential social perception and attribution of intergroup violence: Testing the lower limits of stereotyping of blacks. *Journal of Personality and Social Psychology, 34,* 590–598.

Duncan, B. L., & Reese, R. J. (2013). Empirically supported treatments, evidence-based treatments, and evidence-based practice. In G. Stricker & T. A. Widiger (Eds.), *Handbook of psychology: Vol. 8. Clinical psychology* (2nd ed.). New York, NY: Wiley.

Dunlosky, J., Rawson, K. A., Marsh, E. J., Nathan, M. J., & Willingham, D. T. (2013). Improving students' learning with effective learning techniques: Promising directions from cognitive and educational psychology. *Psychological Science in the Public Interest, 14*(1), 4–58. doi:10.1177/1529100612453266

Dunn, E. W., Aknin, L. B., & Norton, M. I. (2014). Prosocial spending and happiness: Using money to benefit others pays off. *Current Directions in Psychological Science, 23*(1), 41–47. doi:10.1177/0963721413512503

Dunn, E. W., Wilson, T. D., & Gilbert, D. T. (2003). Location, location, location: The misprediction of satisfaction in housing lotteries. *Personality and Social Psychology*

Bulletin, 29(11), 1421–1432. doi:10.1177/0146167203256867

Dunning, D., & Balcetis, E. (2013). Wishful seeing: How preferences shape visual perception. *Current Directions in Psychological Science, 22*(1), 33–37. doi:10.1177/0963721412463693

Dupere, V., Leventhal, T., Crosnoe, R., & Dion, E. (2010). Understanding the positive role of neighborhood socio-economic advantage in achievement: The contribution of the home, child care, and school environments. *Developmental Psychology, 46*, 1227–1244. doi:10.1037/a0020211

Durante, K. M., Li, N. P., & Haselton, M. G. (2008). Changes in women's choice of dress across the ovulatory cycle: Naturalistic and laboratory task-based evidence. *Personality and Social Psychology Bulletin, 34*, 1451–1460.

Durrant, J., & Ensom, R. (2012). Physical punishment of children: Lessons from 20 years of research. *Canadian Medical Association Journal*, 1373–1377. doi:10.1503/cmaj.101314

Durrant, R., & Ellis, B. J. (2013). Evolutionary psychology. In R. J. Nelson, S. Y. Mizumori, & I. B. Weiner (Eds.), *Handbook of psychology: Vol. 3. Behavioral neuroscience* (2nd ed.). New York, NY: Wiley.

Dutton, D. G., & Aron, A. P. (1974). Some evidence for heightened sexual attraction under conditions of high anxiety. *Journal of Personality and Social Psychology, 30*, 510–517. doi:10.1037/h0037031

Eagle, M. N. (2013). The implications of conceptual critiques and empirical research on unconscious processes for psychoanalytic theory. *Psychoanalytic Review, 100*, 881–917. doi:10.1521/prev.2013.100.6.881

Eagly, A. H., & Wood, W. (1999). The origins of sex differences in human behavior: Evolved dispositions versus social roles. *American Psychologist, 54*, 408–423.

Eagly, A. H., & Wood, W. (2013). The nature-nurture debates: 25 years of challenges in understanding the psychology of gender. *Perspectives on Psychological Science, 8*, 340–357. doi:10.1177/1745691613484767

Easterbrooks, M. A., Bartlett, J. D., Beeghly, M., & Thompson, R. A. (2013). Social and emotional development in infancy. In R. M. Lerner, M. A. Easterbrooks, J. Mistry, & I. B. Weiner (Eds.), *Handbook of psychology: Vol. 6. Developmental psychology.* New York, NY: Wiley.

Eastwick, P. W. (2013). Cultural influences on attraction. In J. A. Simpson & L. Campbell (Eds.), *Oxford handbook of close relationships.* New York, NY: Oxford University Press.

Eastwick, P. W., Eagly, A. H., Finkel, E. J., & Johnson, S. E. (2011). Implicit and explicit preferences for physical attractiveness in a romantic partner: A double dissociation in predictive validity. *Journal of Personality and Social Psychology, 101*, 993–1011. doi:10.1037/a0024061

Ebbinghaus, H. (1885/1964). *Memory: A contribution to experimental psychology* (H. A. Ruger & E. R. Bussemius, Trans.). New York, NY: Dover.

Ebrahim, I. O., Shapiro, C. M., Williams, A. J., & Fenwick, P. B. (2013). Alcohol and sleep I: Effects on normal sleep. *Alcoholism: Clinical and Experimental Research, 37*, 539–549. doi:10.1111/acer.12006

Eckstein, D., & Kaufman, J. A. (2012). The role of birth order in personality: An enduring intellectual legacy of Alfred Adler. *The Journal of Individual Psychology, 68*(1), 60–61.

Edenfield, T. M., & Blumenthal, J. A. (2011). Exercise and stress reduction. In R. J. Contrada & A. Baum (Eds.), *Handbook of stress science: Biology, psychology, and health.* New York, NY: Spring Publishing Company.

Edwards, S., Jedrychowski, W., Butscher, M., Camann, D., Kieltyka, A., Mroz, E., . . . Perera, F. (2010). Prenatal exposure to airborne polycyclic aromatic hydrocarbons and children's intelligence at 5 years of age in a prospective cohort study in Poland. *Environmental Health Perspectives, 118*(9), 1326–1331. doi:10.1289/ehp.0901070

Egido, J. A., Castillo, O., Roig, B., Sanz, I., Herrero, M. R., Garay, M. T., . . . Fernandez, C. (2012). Is psychophysical stress a risk factor for stroke? A case-control study. *Journal of Neurology, Neurosurgery, & Psychiatry, 83*, 1104–1110. doi:10.1136/jnnp-2012-302420

Ehrenberg, M., Regev, R., Lazinski, M., Behrman, L. J., & Zimmerman, J. (2014). Adjustment to divorce for children. In L. Grossman & S. Walfish (Eds.), *Translating psychological research into practice.* New York, NY: Spring Publishing Co.

Ehrenberg, O., & Ehrenberg, M. (1994). *The psychotherapy maze: A consumer's guide to getting in and out of therapy.* Northvale, NJ: Jason Aronson.

Eibl-Eibesfeldt, I. (1975). *Ethology: The biology of behavior.* New York, NY: Holt, Rinehart, & Winston.

Eichenbaum, H. (2013). Memory systems. In R. J. Nelson, S. Y. Mizumori, & I. B. Weiner (Eds.), *Handbook of psychology: Vol. 3. Behavioral neuroscience* (2nd ed.). New York, NY: Wiley.

Eichenlaub, J., Nicolas, A., Jerome, D., Redoute, J., Costes, N., & Ruby, P. (2014). Resting brain activity varies with dream recall frequency between subjects. *Neuropsychopharmacology, 39*, 1594–1602. doi:10.1038/npp.2014.6

Einstein, G. O., & McDaniel, M. A. (2004). *Memory fitness: A guide for successful aging.* New Haven, CT: Yale University Press.

Eippert, F., Bingel, U., Schoell, E. D., Yacubian, J., Klinger, R., Lorenz, J., & Büchel, C. (2009). Activation of the opioidergic descending pain control system underlies placebo analgesia. *Neuron, 63*(4), 533–543.

Ekman, P. (1992). Facial expressions of emotion: New findings, new questions. *Psychological Science, 3*, 34–38.

Ekman, P., & Friesen, W. V. (1975). *Unmasking the face.* Englewood Cliffs, NJ: Prentice-Hall.

Ekman, P., & Friesen, W. V. (1984). *Unmasking the face.* Palo Alto, CA: Consulting Psychologists Press.

Elbogen, E. B., & Johnson, S. C. (2009). The intricate link between violence and mental disorder: Results from the national epidemiologic survey on alcohol and related conditions. *Archives of General Psychiatry, 66*(2), 152–161. doi:10.1001/archgenpsychiatry.2008.537

Ellingson, J. E., Heggestad, E. D., & Makarius, E. E. (2012). Personality retesting for managing intentional distortion. *Journal of Personality and Social Psychology, 102*, 1063–1076. doi:10.1037/a0027327

Elliot, A. J., & Maier, M. A. (2012). Color-in-context theory. In P. Devine & A. Plant (Eds.), *Advances in experimental social psychology.* San Diego, CA: Academic Press.

Elliot, A. J., & Maier, M. A. (2014). Color psychology: Effects of perceiving color on psychological functions in humans. *Annual Review of Psychology, 65*, 95–120.

Elliot, A. J., Maier, M. A., Moller, A. C., Friedman, R., & Meinhardt, J. (2007). Color and psychological functioning: The effect of red on performance attainment. *Journal of Experimental Psychology: General, 136*(1), 154–168. doi:10.1037/0096-3445.136.1.154

Elliot, A. J., & Niesta, D. (2008). Romantic red: Red enhances men's attraction to women. *Journal of Personality and Social Psychology, 95*(5), 1150–1164. doi:10.1037/0022-3514.95.5.1150

Elliott, R., Bohart, A. C., Watson, J. C., & Greenberg, L. S. (2011). Empathy. *Psychotherapy, 48*(1), 43–49.

Ellis, A. (1973). *Humanistic psychotherapy: The rational-emotive approach.* New York, NY: Julian Press.

Ellis, A. (1977). *Reason and emotion in psychotherapy.* Seacaucus, NJ: Lyle Stuart.

Ellis, A. (1985). *How to live with and without anger.* New York, NY: Citadel Press.

Ellis, A. (1987). The evolution of rational-emotive therapy (RET) and cognitive behavior therapy (CBT). In J. K. Zeig (Ed.), *The evolution of psychotherapy.* New York, NY: Brunner/Mazel.

Ellis, A. (1999). *How to make yourself happy and remarkably less disturbable.* Atascadero, CA: Impact Publishers.

Ellis, A. (2001). *Feeling better, getting better: Profound self-help therapy for your emotions.* Atascadero, CA: Impact Publishers.

Ellis, A., & Ellis, D. (2011). *Rational emotive behavior therapy.* Washington, DC: American Psychological Association.

Ellis, H. H. (1898). Autoerotism: A psychological study. *Alienist and Neurologist, 19*, 260–299.

Ellsworth, P. C. (2013). Appraisal theory: Old and new questions. *Emotion Review, 5*(2), 125–131. doi:10.1177/1754073912463617

Ellsworth, P. C. (2014). Basic emotions and the rocks of New Hampshire. *Emotion Review, 6*(1), 21–26. doi:10.1177/1754073913494897

Ellwood, S., Pallier, G., Snyder, A., & Gallate, J. (2009). The incubation effect: Hatching a solution? *Creativity Research Journal, 21*(1), 6–14. doi:10.1080/10400410802633368

Elman, I., Tschibelu, E., & Borsook, D. (2010). Psychosocial stress and its relationship to gambling urges in individuals with pathological gambling. *The American Journal on Addictions, 19*, 332–339.

Elms, A. C. (2009). Obedience lite. *American Psychologist, 64*(1), 32–36. doi:10.1037/a0014473

Elpers, J. R. (2000). Public psychiatry. In B. J. Sadock & V. A. Sadock (Eds.), *Kaplan and Sadock's comprehensive textbook of psychiatry* (7th ed., Vol. 2). Philadelphia, PA: Lippincott Williams & Wilkins.

Else-Quest, N. M., Hyde, J., & Linn, M. C. (2010). Cross-national patterns of gender differences in mathematics: A meta-analysis. *Psychological Bulletin, 136*(1), 103–127. doi:10.1037/a0018053

Elson, M., & Ferguson, C. J. (2014). Twenty-five years of research on violence in digital games and aggression: Empirical evidence, perspectives, and a debate gone astray. *European Psychologist, 19,* 33–46. doi:10.1027/1016-9040/a000147

Emery, C. F., Anderson, D. R., & Goodwin, C. L. (2013). Coronary heart disease and hypertension. In A. M. Nezu, C. M. Nezu, P. A. Geller, & I. B. Weiner (Eds.), *Handbook of psychology: Vol. 9. Health psychology* (2nd ed.). New York, NY: Wiley.

Emmelkamp, P. M. (2013). Behavior therapy with adults. In M. J. Lambert (Ed.). *Bergin and Garfield's handbook of psychotherapy and behavior change* (6th ed.). New York, NY: Wiley.

Endeshaw, Y., Rice, T. B., Schwartz, A. V., Stone, K. L., Manini, T. M., & Satterfield, S., . . . Pahor, M. (2013). Snoring, daytime sleepiness, and incident cardiovascular disease in the Health, Aging, and Body Composition study. *Sleep: Journal of Sleep and Sleep Disorders Research, 36,* 1737–1745.

Ent, M. R., & Baumeister, R. F. (2014). Obedience, self-control, and the voice of culture. *Journal of Social Issues, 70,* 574–586. doi:10.1111/josi.12079

Epley, N., & Huff, C. (1998). Suspicion, affective response, and educational benefit as a result of deception in psychology research. *Personality and Social Psychology Bulletin, 24,* 759–768.

Epstein, D. H., Phillips, K. A., & Preston, K. L. (2011). Opioids. In P. Ruiz, & E. C. Strain (Eds.), *Lowinson and Ruiz's substance abuse: A comprehensive textbook* (5th ed.). Philadelphia, PA: Lippincott Williams & Wilkins.

Epstein, L., & Mardon, S. (2007). *The Harvard medical school guide to a good night's sleep.* New York, NY: McGraw-Hill.

Erdelyi, M. H. (2001). Defense processes can be conscious or unconscious. *American Psychologist, 56,* 761–762.

Erdfelder, E., Brandt, M., & Bröder, A. (2007). Recollection biases in hindsight judgments. *Social Cognition, 25,* 114–131.

Erikson, E. (1963). *Childhood and society.* New York, NY: Norton.

Erikson, E. (1968). *Identity: Youth and crisis.* New York, NY: Norton.

Espejo, E., Ferriter, C., Hazel, N., Keenan-Miller, D., Hoffman, L., & Hammen, C. (2011). Predictors of subjective ratings of stressor severity: The effects of current mood and neuroticism. *Stress & Health: Journal of the International Society for the Investigation of Stress, 27*(1), 23–33.

Esses, V. M., Jackson, L. M., & Bennett-AbuAyyash, C. (2010). Intergroup competition. In J. F. Dovidio,

M. Hewstone, P. Glick, & V. M. Esses (Eds.), *The Sage handbook of prejudice, stereotyping, and discrimination.* Los Angeles, CA: Sage.

Esterson, A. (2001). The mythologizing of psychoanalytic history: Deception and self-deception in Freud's accounts of the seduction theory episode. *History of Psychiatry, 7,* 329–352.

Estes, W. K. (1999). Models of human memory: A 30-year retrospective. In C. Izawa (Ed.), *On human memory: Evolution, progress, and reflections on the 30th anniversary of the Atkinson-Shiffrin model.* Mahwah, NJ: Erlbaum.

Evans, G. W. (2004). The environment of childhood poverty. *American Psychologist, 59*(2), 77–92.

Evans, J. T. (2012). Dual-process theories of deductive reasoning: Facts and fallacies. In K. J. Holyoak, & R. G. Morrison (Eds.), *Oxford handbook of thinking and reasoning.* New York, NY: Oxford University Press.

Evans, J. T., & Stanovich, K. E. (2013). Dual-process theories of higher cognition: Advancing the debate. *Perspectives on Psychological Science, 8,* 223–241. doi:10.1177/1745691612460685

Eysenck, H. J. (1967). *The biological basis of personality.* Springfield, IL: Charles C. Thomas.

Eysenck, H. J. (1982). *Personality, genetics and behavior: Selected papers.* New York, NY: Praeger.

Eysenck, H. J. (1990). Biological dimensions of personality. In L. A. Pervin (Ed.), *Handbook of personality: Theory and research.* New York, NY: Guilford Press.

Eysenck, H. J., & Kamin, L. (1981). *The intelligence controversy.* New York, NY: Wiley.

Eysenck, M. W., Mogg, K., May, J., Richards, A., & Mathews, A. (1991). Bias in interpretation of ambiguous sentences related to threat in anxiety. *Journal of Abnormal Psychology, 100,* 144–150.

Faber Taylor, A., & Kuo, F. E. (2009). Children with attention deficits concentrate better after walk in the park. *Journal of Attention Disorders, 12,* 402–409.

Fabrigar, L. R., MacDonald, T. K., & Wegener, D. T. (2005). The structure of attitudes. In D. Albarracin, B. T. Johnson, & M. P. Zanna (Eds.), *The handbook of attitudes.* Mahwah, NJ: Erlbaum.

Fabrigar, L. R., & Wegener, D. T. (2010). Attitude structure. In R. F. Baumeister & E. J. Finkel (Eds.), *Advanced social psychology: The state of the science* (pp. 177–216). New York, NY: Oxford University Press.

Fairburn, C. G., Cooper, Z., & Murphy, R. (2009). Bulimia nervosa.

In M. C. Gelder, N. C. Andreasen, J. J. López-Ibor, Jr., & J. R. Geddes (Eds.). *New Oxford textbook of psychiatry* (2nd ed., Vol. 1). New York, NY: Oxford University Press.

Falicov, C. J. (2014). Psychotherapy and supervision as cultural encounters: The multidimensional ecological comparative approach framework. In C. A. Falender, E. P. Shafranske, & C. J. Falicov, (Eds.), *Multiculturalism and diversity in clinical supervision: A competency-based approach.* (pp. 29–58). Washington, DC: American Psychological Association.

Falls, W. A. (1998). Extinction: A review of therapy and the evidence suggesting that memories are not erased with nonreinforcement. In W. O'Donohue (Ed.), *Learning and behavior therapy.* Boston, MA: Allyn & Bacon.

Faraday, A. (1974). *The dream game.* New York, NY: Harper & Row.

Faravelli, C., & Pallanti, S. (1989). Recent life events and panic disorders. *American Journal of Psychiatry, 146,* 622–626.

Farber, B. A., & Doolin, E. M. (2011). Positive regard and affirmation. In J. C. Norcross (Ed.), *Psychotherapy relationships that work: Evidence-based responsiveness* (2nd ed.). New York, NY: Oxford University Press. doi:10.1093/acprof:oso/9780199737208.003.0008

Farrington, D. P. (2006). Family background and psychopathy. In C. J. Patrick, & C. J. Patrick (Eds.), *Handbook of psychopathy* (pp. 229–250). New York, NY: Guilford Press.

Fazio, L. K., Barber, S. J., Rajaram, S., Ornstein, P. A., & Marsh, E. J. (2013). Creating illusions of knowledge: Learning errors that contradict prior knowledge. *Journal of Experimental Psychology: General, 142*(1), 1–5. doi:10.1037/a0028649

Fehr, B. (2008). Friendship formation. In S. Sprecher, A. Wenzel, & J. Harvey (Eds.), *Handbook of relationship initiation* (pp. 235–247). New York, NY: Psychology Press.

Fehr, B. (2013). The social psychology of love. In J. A. Simpson & L. Campbell (Eds.), *Oxford handbook of close relationships.* New York, NY: Oxford University Press.

Fehr, B. (2015). Love: Conceptualization and experience. In M. Mikulincer, P. R. Shaver, J. A. Simpson, & J. F. Dovidio (Eds.), *APA handbook of personality and social psychology Vol. 3: Interpersonal relations.* Washington, DC: American Psychological Association.

Fein, D., Barton, M., Eigsti, I., Kelley, E., Naigles, L., Schultz, R. T., & . . . Tyson, K. (2013). Optimal outcome in

individuals with a history of autism. *Journal of Child Psychology and Psychiatry, 54*(2), 195–205. doi:10.1111/jcpp.12037

Feinstein, J. S., Adolphs, R., Damasio, A., & Tranel, D. (2011). The human amygdala and the induction and experience of fear. *Current Biology, 21,* 34–38. doi:10.1016/j.cub.2010.11.042

Feist, G. J. (1998). A meta-analysis of personality in scientific and artistic creativity. *Personality and Social Psychology Review, 2,* 290–309.

Feist, G. J. (2004). The evolved fluid specificity of human creativity talent. In R. J. Sternberg, E. L. Grigorenko, & J. L. Singer (Eds.), *Creativity: From potential to realization.* Washington, DC: American Psychological Association.

Feist, G. J. (2010). The function of personality in creativity: The nature and nurture of the creative personality. In J. C. Kaufman & R. J. Sternberg (Eds.), *The Cambridge handbook of creativity* (pp. 113–130). New York, NY: Cambridge University Press.

Fekadu, A., Wooderson, S. C., Markopoulo, K., Donaldson, C., Papadopoulos, A., & Cleare, A. J. (2009). What happens to patients with treatment-resistant depression? A systematic review of medium to long term outcome studies. *Journal of Affective Disorders, 116*(1–2), 4–11. doi:10.1016/j.jad.2008.10.014

Feldman, D. H. (1988). Creativity: Dreams, insights, and transformations. In R. J. Sternberg (Ed.), *The nature of creativity: Contemporary psychological perspectives.* Cambridge: Cambridge University Press.

Feldman, D. H. (2013). Cognitive development in childhood: A contemporary perspective. In R. M. Lerner, M. A. Easterbrooks, J. Mistry, & I. B. Weiner (Eds.), *Handbook of psychology: Vol. 6. Developmental psychology.* New York, NY: Wiley.

Feng, J., Spence, I., & Pratt, J. (2007). Playing an action video game reduces gender differences in spatial cognition. *Psychological Science, 18*(10), 850–855. doi:10.1111/j.1467-9280.2007.01990.x

Ferguson, C. J. (2013). Violent video games and the Supreme Court: Lessons for the scientific community in the wake of Brown v. Entertainment Merchants Association. *American Psychologist, 68,* 57–74. doi:10.1037/a0030597

Ferguson, C. J., & Savage, J. (2012). Have recent studies addressed methodological issues raised by five decades of television violence research? A critical review. *Aggression and Violent Behavior, 17,* 129–139. doi:10.1016/j.avb.2011.11.001

Ferrando, S. J., Owen, J. A., & Levenson, J. L. (2014). Psychopharmacology. In R. E. Hales, S. C. Yudofsky, & L. W. Roberts (Eds.), *The American Psychiatric Publishing textbook of psychiatry* (6th ed.). Washington, DC: American Psychiatric Publishing.

Ferreri, F., Lapp, L. K., & Peretti, C. (2011). Current research on cognitive aspects of anxiety disorders. *Current Opinion in Psychiatry, 24*(1), 49-54. doi:10.1097/YCO.0b013e32833f5585

Ferster, C. S., & Skinner, B. F. (1957). *Schedules of reinforcement.* New York, NY: Appleton-Century-Crofts.

Fervaha, G., Foussias, G., Agid, O., & Remington, G. (2014). Impact of primary negative symptoms on functional outcomes in schizophrenia. *European Psychiatry, 29*, 449–455. doi:10.1016/j.eurpsy.2014.01.007

Festinger, L. (1957). *A theory of cognitive dissonance.* Stanford, CA: Stanford University Press.

Festinger, L., & Carlsmith, J. M. (1959). Cognitive consequences of forced compliance. *Journal of Abnormal and Social Psychology, 58*, 203–210.

Ficca, G., Axelsson, J., Mollicone, D. J., Muto, V., & Vitiello, M. V. (2010). Naps, cognition and performance. *Sleep Medicine Reviews, 14*(4), 249–258. doi:10.1016/j.smrv.2009.09.005

Field, A. E., Sonneville, K. R., Crosby, R. D., Swanson, S. A., Eddy, K. T., Camargo, C. A., . . . Micali, N. (2014). Prospective associations of concerns about physique and the development of obesity, binge drinking, and drug use among adolescent boys and young adult men. *JAMA Pediatrics, 168*(1), 34–39. doi:10.1001/jamapediatrics.2013.2915

Field, A. P., & Purkis, H. M. (2012). Associating learning and phobias. In M. Haselgrove, & L. Hogarth (Eds.), *Clinical applications of learning theory.* New York, NY: Psychology Press.

Fields, R. (2011, May 1). The hidden brain. *Scientific American: Mind, 22*(2), 52–59.

Fields, R. D. (2014). Myelin: More than insulation. *Science, 344*, 264–266.

Figueredo, A. J., Gladden, P., Vásquez, G., Wolf, P. S. A., & Jones, D. N. (2009). Evolutionary theories of personality. In P. J. Corr & G. Matthews (Eds.), *Cambridge handbook of personality psychology* (pp. 265–274). New York, NY: Cambridge University Press.

Figueredo, A. J., Sefcek, J. A., Vasquez, G., Brumbach, B. H., King, J. E., & Jacobs, W. J. (2005). Evolutionary personality psychology. In D. M. Buss (Ed.), *The handbook of evolutionary psychology.* New York, NY: Wiley.

Fine, C. (2010). From scanner to sound bite: Issues in interpreting and reporting sex differences in the brain. *Current Directions in Psychological Science, 19*(5), 280–283. doi:10.1177/0963721410383248

Fink, B., Neave, N., Manning, J. T., & Grammer, K. (2006). Facial symmetry and judgments of attractiveness, health and personality. *Personality and Individual Differences, 41*, 1253–1262.

Fink, M. (2004). *Electroshock: Healing mental illness.* New York, NY: Oxford University Press.

Fink, M. (2014). What was learned: Studies by the consortium for research in ECT (CORE) 1997–2011. *Acta Psychiatrica Scandinavica, 129*(6), 417–426. doi:10.1111/acps.12251

Fink, M., Kellner, C. H., & McCall, W. V. (2014). The role of ECT in suicide prevention. *The Journal of ECT, 30*(1), 5–9. doi:10.1097/YCT.0b013e3182a6ad0d

Fink, M. F. (2009). Non-pharmacological somatic treatments: Electroconvulsive therapy. In M. C. Gelder, N. C. Andreasen, J. J. López-Ibor, Jr., & J. R. Geddes (Eds.), *New Oxford textbook of psychiatry* (2nd ed., Vol. 1). New York, NY: Oxford University Press.

Finkel, E. J., Eastwick, P. W., Karney, B. R., Reis, H. T., & Sprecher, S. (2012). Online dating: A critical analysis from the perspective of psychological science. *Psychological Science in the Public Interest, 13*, 3–66. doi:10.1177/1529100612436522

Finlayson, G., Dalton, M., & Blundell, J. E. (2012). Liking versus wanting food in human appetite: Relation to craving. In K. D. Brownell, & M. S. Gold (Eds.), *Food and addiction: A comprehensive handbook.* New York, NY: Oxford University Press.

Firestein, S. (2001). How the olfactory system makes sense of scents. *Nature, 413*, 211–218.

First, M. B. (2008). Psychiatric classification. In A. Tasman, J. Kay, J. A. Lieberman, M. B. First, & M. Maj (Eds.), *Psychiatry* (3rd ed.). New York, NY: Wiley-Blackwell.

Fischer, P., Krueger, J. I., Greitemeyer, T., Vogrincic, C., Kastenmuller, A., Frey, D., . . . Kainbacher, M. (2011). The bystander-effect: A meta-analytic review on bystander intervention in dangerous and non-dangerous emergencies. *Psychological Bulletin, 137*, 517–537. doi:10.1037/a0023304

Fischhoff, B. (2007). An early history of hindsight research. *Social Cognition, 25*(1), 10–13.

Fisher, M. P. (2014). PTSD in the U.S. military, and the politics of prevalence. *Social Science & Medicine, 115*, 1–9. doi:10.1016/j.socscimed.2014.05.051

Fisher, S., & Greenberg, R. P. (1996). *Freud scientifically reappraised: Testing the theories and therapy.* New York, NY: Wiley.

Fisher, S., & Greenberg, R. P. (1997). The curse of the placebo: Fanciful pursuit of a pure biological therapy. In S. Fisher & R. P. Greenberg (Eds.), *From placebo to panacea: Putting psychiatric drugs to the test.* New York, NY: Wiley.

Fishman, D. B., Rego, S. A., & Muller, K. L. (2011). Behavioral theories of psychotherapy. In J. C. Norcross, G. R. VandenBos, & D. K. Freedheim, (Eds.), *History of psychotherapy: Continuity and change* (2nd ed.). Washington, DC: American Psychological Association. doi:10.1037/12353-004

Fiske, S. T. (2004). Mind the gap: In praise of informal sources of formal theory. *Personality and Social Psychology Review, 8*(2), 132–137.

Fiske, S. T., & Russell, A. M. (2010). Cognitive processes. In J. F. Dovidio, M. Hewstone, P. Glick, & V. M. Esses (Eds.), *The Sage handbook of prejudice, stereotyping, and discrimination.* Los Angeles, CA: Sage.

Fiske, S. T., & Tablante, C. B. (2015). Stereotyping: Process and content. In M. Mikulincer, P. R. Shaver, E. Borgida, & J. A. Bargh (Eds.), *APA handbook of personality and social psychology Vol. 1: Attitudes and social cognition.* Washington, DC: American Psychological Association.

Flak, A. L., Su, S., Bertrand, J., Denny, C. H., Kesmodel, U. S., & Cogswell, M. E. (2014). The association of mild, moderate, and binge prenatal alcohol exposure and child neuropsychological outcomes: A meta-analysis. *Alcoholism: Clinical and Experimental Research, 38*, 214–226. doi:10.1111/acer.12214

Flausino, N. H., Da Silva Prado, J. M., De Queiroz, S. S., Tufik, S., & De Mello, M. T. (2012). Physical exercise performed before bedtime improves the sleep pattern of healthy young good sleepers. *Psychophysiology, 49*(2), 186–192. doi:10.1111/j.1469-8986.2011.01300.x

Flavell, J. H. (1996). Piaget's legacy. *Psychological Science, 7*, 200–203.

Flegal, K. M., Carroll, M., Ogden, C., & Curtin, L. (2010). Prevalence and trends in obesity among U.S. adults, 1999–2008. *JAMA, 303*(3), 235–241.

Flett, G. L., Vredenburg, K., & Krames, L. (1995). The stability of depressive symptoms in college students: An empirical demonstration of regression to the mean. *Journal of Psychopathology & Behavioral Assessment, 17*, 403–415.

Florentine, M., & Heinz, M. (2010). Audition: Loudness. In E. B. Goldstein (Ed.), *Encyclopedia of perception.* Thousand Oaks, CA: Sage.

Flynn, J. R. (1987). Massive IQ gains in 14 nations: What IQ tests really measure. *Psychological Bulletin, 101*, 171–191.

Flynn, J. R. (2003). Movies about intelligence: The limitations of g. *Current Directions in Psychological Science, 12*(3), 95–99.

Flynn, J. R. (2007). *What is intelligence? Beyond the Flynn effect.* New York, NY: Cambridge University Press.

Flynn, J. R. (2011). Secular changes in intelligence. In R. J. Sternberg, & S. B. Kaufman (Eds.), *Cambridge handbook of intelligence.* New York, NY: Cambridge University Press.

Folkman, S. (2008). The case for positive emotions in the stress process. *Anxiety, Stress and Coping: An International Journal, 21*(1), 3–14.

Folkman, S. (2011). Stress, health, and coping: Synthesis, commentary, and future directions. In S. Folkman (Ed.), *Oxford handbook of stress, health, and coping.* New York, NY: Oxford University Press.

Folkman, S., & Moskowitz, J. T. (2000). Positive affect and the other side of coping. *American Psychologist, 55*, 647–654.

Folkman, S., & Moskowitz, J. T. (2004). Coping: Pitfalls and promise. *Annual Review of Psychology, 55*, 745–774.

Folkman, S., Moskowitz, J. T., Ozer, E. M., & Park, C. L. (1997). Positive meaningful events and coping in the context of HIV/AIDS. In B. H. Gottlieb (Ed.), *Coping with chronic stress* (pp. 293–314). New York, NY: Plenum.

Follette, W. C., & Davis, D. (2009). Clinical practice and the issue of repressed memories: Avoiding an ice patch on the slippery slope. In W. O'Donohue & S. R. Graybar (Eds.), *Handbook of contemporary psychotherapy: Toward an improved understanding of effective psychotherapy* (pp. 47–73). Thousand Oaks, CA: Sage.

Forand, N. R., DeRubeis, R. J., & Amsterdam, J. D. (2013). Combining medication and psychotherapy in the treatment of major mental disorders. In M. J. Lambert (Ed.), *Bergin and Garfield's handbook of psychotherapy and behavior change* (6th ed.). New York, NY: Wiley.

Forscher, P. S., & Devine, P. G. (2014). Breaking the prejudice habit: Automaticity and control in the context of a long-term goal. In J. W. Sherman, B. Gawronski, & Y. Trope (Eds.), *Dual-process theories of the social mind*. New York, NY: Guilford Press.

Forsyth, D. R. (2013). Social influence and group behavior. In H. Tennen, J. Suls, & I. B. Weiner (Eds.), *Handbook of psychology: Vol. 5. Personality and social psychology* (2nd ed.). New York, NY: Wiley.

Forsyth, D. R., & Strong, S. R. (1986). The scientific study of counseling and psychotherapy: A unificationist view. *American Psychologist, 41,* 113–119.

Foulkes, D. (1985). *Dreaming: A cognitive-psychological analysis.* Hillsdale, NJ: Erlbaum.

Fournier, J. C., DeRubeis, R. J., Hollon, S. D., Dimidjian, S., Amsterdam, J. D., Shelton, R. C., & Fawcett, J. (2010). Antidepressant drug effects and depression severity: A patient-level meta-analysis. *JAMA, 303*(1), 47–53.

Fox-Kales, E. (2011). *Body shots: Hollywood and the culture of eating disorders.* Albany, NY: State University of New York Press.

Frances, A. (2013). *Saving normal: An insider's revolt against out-of-control psychiatric diagnosis, DSM-5, Big Pharma, and the medicalization of ordinary life.* New York, NY: Morrow.

Frances, A. J., & Widiger, T. (2012). Psychiatric diagnosis: Lessons from the DSM-IV past and cautions for the DSM-5 future. *Annual Review of Clinical Psychology, 8,* 109–130. doi:10.1146/annurev-clinpsy-032511-143102

Francis, G. (1999). Spatial frequency and visual persistence: Cortical reset. *Spatial Vision, 12,* 31–50.

Francis, L. A., & Birch, L. L. (2005). Maternal influences on daughters' restrained eating behavior. *Health Psychology, 24,* 548–554.

Frani_, S., Middeldorp, C. M., Dolan, C. V., Ligthart, L., & Boomsma, D. I. (2010). Childhood and adolescent anxiety and depression: beyond heritability. *Journal of the American Academy of Child & Adolescent Psychiatry, 49,* 820–829.

Frank, J. D. (1961). *Persuasion and healing.* Baltimore: Johns Hopkins University Press.

Frank, L. K. (1939). Projective methods for the study of personality. *Journal of Psychology, 8,* 343–389.

Frank, L. R. (1990). Electroshock: Death, brain damage, memory loss, and brainwashing. *The Journal of Mind and Behavior, 11*(3/4), 489–512.

Frankland, P. W., Köhler, S., & Josselyn, S. A. (2013). Hippocampal neurogenesis and forgetting. *Trends in Neurosciences, 36,* 497–503. doi:10.1016/j.tins.2013.05.002

Franko, D. L., Keshaviah, A., Eddy, K. T., Krishna, M., Davis, M. C., Keel, P. K., & Herzog, D. B. (2013). A longitudinal investigation of mortality in anorexia nervosa and bulimia nervosa. *The American Journal of Psychiatry, 170,* 917–925. doi:10.1176/appi.ajp.2013.12070868

Frederick, S., & Loewenstein, G. (1999). Hedonic adaptation. In D. Kahneman, E. Diener, & N. Schwarz (Eds.), *Well-being: The foundations of hedonic psychology.* New York, NY: Russell Sage Foundation.

Fredrickson, B. L. (2001). The role of positive emotions in positive psychology: The broaden-and-build theory of positive emotions. *American Psychologist, 56,* 218–226.

Fredrickson, B. L. (2006). The broaden-and-build theory of positive emotions. In M. Csikszentmihalyi, & I. S. Csikszentmihalyi (Eds.), *A life worth living: Contributions to positive psychology.* New York, NY: Oxford University Press.

Fredrickson, B. L., Tugade, M. M., Waugh, C. E., & Larkin, G. R. (2003). What good are positive emotions in crises? A prospective study of resilience and emotions following the terrorist attacks on the United States on September 11, 2001. *Journal of Personality and Social Psychology, 84,* 365–376.

Freedman, J. L., & Fraser, S. C. (1966). Compliance without pressure: The foot-in-the-door technique. *Journal of Personality and Social Psychology, 4,* 195–202.

Freedman, R., Ross, R., Michels, R., Appelbaum, P., Siever, L., Binder, R., et al. (2007). Psychiatrists, mental illness, and violence. *American Journal of Psychiatry, 164*(9), 1315–1317. doi:10.1176/appi.ajp.2007.07061013

Fremouw, W. J., de Perczel, M., & Ellis, T. E. (1990). *Suicide risk: Assessment and response guidelines.* Elmsford, NY: Pergamon.

Frenda, S. J., Knowles, E. D., Saletan, W., & Loftus, E. F. (2013). False memories of fabricated political events. *Journal of Experimental Social Psychology, 49,* 280–286. doi:10.1016/j.jesp.2012.10.013

Frenda, S. J., Nichols, R. M., & Loftus, E. F. (2011). Current issues and advances in misinformation research. *Current Directions in Psychological Science, 20*(1), 20-23. doi:10.1177/0963721410396620

Freud, S. (1900/1953). *The interpretation of dreams.* In J. Strachey (Ed.), *The standard edition of the complete psychological works of Sigmund Freud* (Vols. 4 and 5). London UK: Hogarth. (Original work published 1900.)

Freud, S. (1901/1960). *The psychopathology of everyday life.* In J. Strachey (Ed.), *The standard edition of the complete psychological works of Sigmund Freud* (Vol. 6). London, UK: Hogarth. (Original work published 1900.)

Freud, S. (1914/1953). On narcissism: An introduction. In J. Strachey (Ed., Trans.), *The standard edition of the complete psychological works of Sigmund Freud* (Vol. 1). London, UK: Hogarth Press. (Original work published 1914.)

Freud, S. (1924). *A general introduction to psychoanalysis.* New York, NY: Boni & Liveright.

Freud, S. (1933/1964). *New introductory lectures on psychoanalysis.* In J. Strachey (Ed.), *The standard edition of the complete psychological works of Sigmund Freud* (Vol. 22). London, UK: Hogarth.

Freud, S. (1940). An outline of psychoanalysis. *International Journal of Psychoanalysis, 21,* 27–84.

Freund, A. M., Nikitin, J., & Riediger, M. (2013). Successful aging. In R. M. Lerner, M. A. Easterbrooks, J. Mistry, & I. B. Weiner (Eds.), *Handbook of psychology: Vol. 6. Developmental psychology.* New York, NY: Wiley.

Frey, K. S., & Ruble, D. N. (1992). Gender constancy and the cost of sex-typed behavior: A test of the conflict hypothesis. *Developmental Psychology, 28,* 714–721.

Frick, U., Frick, H., Langguth, B., Landgrebe, M., Hübner-Liebermann, B., & Hajak, G. (2013). The revolving door phenomenon revisited: Time to readmission in 17,415 patients with 37,697 hospitalisations at a German psychiatric hospital. *Plos ONE, 8*(10). Article ID e75612.

Fried, A. L. (2012). Ethics in psychological research: Guidelines and regulations. In H. Cooper, P. M. Camic, D. L. Long, A. T. Panter, D. Rindskopf, & K. J. Sher (Eds.), *APA handbook of research methods in psychology: Vol. 1. Foundations, planning, measures, and psychometrics.* Washington, DC: American Psychological Association.

Friedkin, N. E. (1999). Choice shift and group polarization. *American Sociological Review, 64,* 856–875.

Friedman, H. S. (2011). Personality, disease, and self-healing. In H. S. Friedman (Ed.), *Oxford handbook of health psychology.* New York, NY: Oxford University Press.

Friedman, H. S., & Adler, N. E. (2007). The history and background of health psychology. In H. S. Friedman & R. C. Silver (Eds.), *Foundations of health psychology.* New York, NY: Oxford University Press.

Friedman, H. S., & Kern, M. L. (2014). Personality, well-being, and health. *Annual Review of Psychology, 65,* 719–742. doi:10.1146/annurev-psych-010213-115123

Friedman, H. S., Kern, M. L., Hampson, S. E., & Duckworth, A. L. (2014). A new life-span approach to conscientiousness and health: Combining the pieces of the causal puzzle. *Developmental Psychology, 50,* 1377–1389. doi:10.1037/a0030373

Friedman, M., & Rosenman, R. F. (1974). *Type A behavior and your heart.* New York, NY: Knopf.

Friedman, R., & James, J. W. (2008). The myth of the sages of dying, death and grief. *Skeptic, 14,* 37–41.

Friedman, S. L., & Boyle, D. E. (2008). Attachment in U.S. children experiencing nonmaternal care in the early 1990s. *Attachment & Human Development, 10,* 225–261. doi:10.1080/14616730802113570

Frijda, N. H. (1999). Emotions and hedonic experience. In D. Kahneman, E. Diener, & N. Schwarz (Eds.), *Well-being: The foundations of hedonic psychology.* New York, NY: Russell Sage Foundation.

Fuchs, A. H., & Evans, R. B. (2013). Psychology as a science. In D. K. Freedheim, & I. B. Weiner (Eds.), *Handbook of psychology Vol. 1: History of psychology* (2nd ed., pp. 1–31). New York, NY: Wiley.

Funder, D. C. (2001). Personality. *Annual Review of Psychology, 52,* 197–221.

Furumoto, L., & Scarborough, E. (1986). Placing women in the history of psychology: The first American women psychologists. *American Psychologist, 41,* 35–42.

Fyer, A. J. (2009). Anxiety disorders: Genetics. In B. J. Sadock, V. A. Sadock, & P. Ruiz (Eds.), *Kaplan & Sadock's comprehensive textbook of psychiatry* (9th ed., pp. 1898–1905). Philadelphia, PA: Lippincott Williams & Wilkins.

Gaddis, C. (1999, August 8). A Boggs life. *Tampa Tribune.* Retrieved from http://rays.tbo.com/rays/MGBWZ4RSL3E.html

Gaeth, G. J., & Shanteau, J. (2000). Reducing the influence of irrelevant information on experienced decision makers. In T. Connolly, H. R. Arkes, & K. R. Hammond (Eds.), *Judgment and decision making: An interdisciplinary reader* (2nd ed., pp. 305–323). New York, NY: Cambridge University Press.

Gage, F. H. (2002). Neurogenesis in the adult brain. *Journal of Neuroscience, 22,* 612–613.

Galambos, N. L. (2004). Gender and gender role development in adolescence. In R. M. Lerner & L. Steinberg (Eds.), *Handbook of adolescent psychology.* New York, NY: Wiley.

Galati, D., Scherer, K. R., & Ricci-Bitti, P. E. (1997). Voluntary facial expression of emotion: Comparing congenitally blind with normally sighted encoders. *Journal of Personality and Social Psychology, 73*(6), 1363–1379. doi:10.1037/0022-3514.73.6.1363

Gale, C. R., Booth, T., Mõttus, R., Kuh, D., & Deary, I. J. (2013). Neuroticism and extraversion in youth predict mental well-being and life satisfaction 40 years later. *Journal of Research in Personality, 47,* 687–697. doi:10.1016/j.jrp.2013.06.005

Gallagher, M. W., Lopez, S. J., Pressman, S. D. (2013). Optimism is universal: Exploring the presence and benefits of optimism in a representative sample of the world. *Journal of Personality, 81,* 429–440. doi:10.1111/jopy.12026

Gallese, V., Fadiga, L., Fogassi, L., & Rizzolatti, G. (1996). Action recognition in the premotor cortex. *Brain, 119,* 593–609.

Gallo, D. A., & Wheeler, M. E. (2013). Episodic memory. In D. Reisberg (Ed.), *Oxford handbook of cognitive psychology.* New York, NY: Oxford University Press.

Gallo, K. P., Thompson-Hollands, J., Pincus, D. B., & Barlow, D. H. (2013). Anxiety disorders. In T. A. Widiger, G. Stricker, I. B. Weiner, G. Stricker, T. A. Widiger, & I. B. Weiner (Eds.), *Handbook of psychology: Vol. 8. Clinical psychology* (2nd ed.). New York, NY: Wiley.

Gallup, G. G., Jr., & Frederick, D. A. (2010). The science of sex appeal: An evolutionary perspective. *Review of General Psychology, 14*(3), 240–250.

Galvan, A. (2013). The teenage brain: Sensitivity to rewards. *Current Directions in Psychological Science, 22,* 88–93. doi:10.1177/0963721413480859

Galvin, B. M., Waldman, D. A., & Balthazard, P. (2010). Visionary communication qualities as mediators of the relationship between narcissism and attributions of leader charisma. *Personnel Psychology, 63,* 509–537. doi:10.1111/j.1744-6570.2010.01179.x

Gananca, L., Kahn, D. A., & Oquendo, M. A. (2014). Mood disorders. In J. L. Cutler (Ed.), *Psychiatry* (3rd ed.). New York, NY: Oxford University Press.

Gangestad, S. W., & Garver-Apgar, C. E., Simpson, J. A., & Cousins, A.

J. (2007). Changes in women's mate preferences across the ovulatory cycle. *Journal of Personality and Social Psychology, 92,* 151–163.

Garb, H. N., Wood, J. M., Lilienfeld, S. O., & Nezworski, M. T. (2005). Roots of the Rorschach controversy. *Clinical Psychology Review, 25*(1), 97–118. doi:10.1016/j.cpr.2004.09.002

Garcia, J. (1989). Food for Tolman: Cognition and cathexis in concert. In T. Archer & L. G. Nilsson (Eds.), *Aversion, avoidance, and anxiety: Perspectives on aversively motivated behavior.* Hillsdale, NJ: Erlbaum.

Garcia, J., Clarke, J. C., & Hankins, W. G. (1973). Natural responses to scheduled rewards. In P. P. G. Bateson & P. Klopfer (Eds.), *Perspectives in ethology.* New York, NY: Plenum.

Garcia, J., & Rusiniak, K. W. (1980). What the nose learns from the mouth. In D. Muller-Schwarze & R. M. Silverstein (Eds.), *Chemical signals.* New York, NY: Plenum.

Gardner, H. (1983). *Frames of mind: The theory of multiple intelligences.* New York, NY: Basic Books.

Gardner, H. (1985). *The mind's new science: A history of the cognitive revolution.* New York, NY: Basic Books.

Gardner, H. (1999). *Intelligence reframed: Multiple intelligences for the 21st century.* New York, NY: Basic Books.

Gardner, H. (2006). *Multiple intelligences: New horizons.* New York, NY: Basic Books.

Gardner, M., & Steinberg, L. (2005). Peer influence on risk-taking, risk preference, and risky decision-making in adolescence and adulthood: An experimental study. *Developmental Psychology, 41,* 625–635.

Garrett, B. L. (2011). *Convicting the innocent.* Cambridge, MA: Harvard University Press.

Gaskin, D. J., & Richard, P. (2012). The economic costs of pain in the United States. *The Journal of Pain, 13*(8), 715–724. doi:10.1016/j.jpain.2012.03.009

Gast, A., Gawronski, B., & De Houwer, J. (2012). Evaluative conditioning: Recent developments and future directions. *Learning and Motivation, 43,* 79–88. doi:10.1016/j.lmot.2012.06.004

Gatchel, R. J., McGeary, D. D., McGeary, C. A., & Lippe, B. (2014). Interdisciplinary chronic pain management: Past, present, and future. *American Psychologist, 69*(2), 119–130. doi:10.1037/a0035514

Gates, G. J. (2011). *How many people are lesbian, gay, bisexual and*

transgender? Los Angeles, CA: The Williams Institute, UCLA School of Law.

Gates, G. J. (2013). Demographic perspectives on sexual orientation. In C. J. Patterson, & A. R. D'Augelli (Eds.), *Handbook of psychology and sexual orientation.* New York, NY: Oxford University Press.

Gato, J., & Fontaine, A. M. (2013). Anticipation of the sexual and gender development of children adopted by same-sex couples. *International Journal of Psychology, 48,* 244–253. doi:10.1080/00207594.2011.645484

Gaudiano, B. A., & Miller, I. W. (2013). The evidence-based practice of psychotherapy: Facing the challenges that lie ahead. *Clinical Psychology Review, 33,* 813–824. doi:10.1016/j.cpr.2013.04.004

Gazzaniga, M. S. (1970). *The bisected brain.* New York, NY: Appleton-Century-Crofts.

Gazzaniga, M. S. (2005). Forty-five years of split-brain research and still going strong. *Nature Reviews Neuroscience, 6,* 653–659.

Gazzaniga, M. S. (2008). Spheres of influence. *Scientific American Mind, 19*(2), 32–39.

Gazzaniga, M. S., Bogen, J. E., & Sperry, R. W. (1965). Observations on visual perception after disconnection of the cerebral hemispheres in man. *Brain, 88,* 221–236.

Gazzaniga, M. S., Ivry, R. B., & Mangum, G. R. (2009). *Cognitive neuroscience: The biology of the mind* (3rd ed.). New York, NY: Norton.

Gearhardt, A. N., & Corbin, W. R. (2012). Food addiction and diagnostic criteria for dependence. In K. D. Brownell, & M. S. Gold (Eds.), *Food and addiction: A comprehensive handbook.* New York, NY: Oxford University Press.

Geary, D. C. (2007). An evolutionary perspective on sex difference in mathematics and the sciences. In S. J. Ceci & W. M. Williams (Eds.), *Why aren't more women in science?* (pp. 173–188). Washington, DC: American Psychological Association.

Gegenfurtner, K. (2010). Color perception: Physiological. In E. B. Goldstein (Ed.), *Encyclopedia of perception.* Thousand Oaks, CA: Sage.

Gehrman, P., Findley, J., & Perlis, M. (2012). Insomnia I: Etiology and conceptualization. In C. M. Morin, & C. A. Espie (Eds.), *Oxford handbook of sleep and sleep disorders.* New York, NY: Oxford University Press.

Geier, C. F. (2013). Adolescent cognitive control and reward processing: Implications for risk taking and substance use. *Hormones and*

Behavior, 64, 333–342. doi:10.1016/j.yhbeh.2013.02.008

Geisinger, K. F. (2013). Reliability. In K. F. Geisinger, B. A. Bracken, J. F. Carlson, J. C. Hansen, N. R. Kuncel, S. P. Reise, & M. C. Rodriguez (Eds.), *APA handbook of testing and assessment in psychology: Vol. 1. Test theory and testing and assessment in industrial and organizational psychology.* Washington, DC: American Psychological Association. doi:10.1037/14047-002

Gelernter, J. (2015). Genetics of complex traits in psychiatry. *Biological Psychiatry, 77*(1), 36–42. doi:10.1016/j.biopsych.2014.08.005

Geller, J. L. (2009). The role of the hospital in the care of the mentally ill. In B. J. Sadock, V. A. Sadock, & P. Ruiz (Eds.), *Kaplan & Sadock's comprehensive textbook of psychiatry* (9th ed., pp. 4299–4314). Philadelphia, PA: Lippincott Williams & Wilkins.

Geng, L., Liu, L., Xu, J., Zhou, K., & Fang, Y. (2013). Can evaluative conditioning change implicit attitudes towards recycling? *Social Behavior and Personality, 41,* 947–956.

Gennari, S. P., Sloman, S. A., Malt, B. C., & Fitch, W. T. (2002). Motion events in language and cognition. *Cognition, 83*(1), 49–79.

Gentile, B., Grabe, S., Dolan-Pascoe, B., Twenge, J. M., Wells, B. E., & Maitino, A. (2009). Gender differences in domain-specific self-esteem: A meta-analysis. *Review of General Psychology, 13*(1), 34–45. doi:10.1037/a0013689

Gentile, D. A., & Bushman, B. J. (2012). Reassessing media violence effects using a risk and resilience approach to understanding aggression. *Psychology of Popular Media Culture, 1,* 138–151. doi:10.1037/a0028481

Gentner, D., & Smith, L. A. (2013). Analogical learning and reasoning. In D. Reisberg (Ed.), *Oxford handbook of cognitive psychology.* New York, NY: Oxford University Press.

George, S. A. (2002). The menopause experience: A woman's perspective. *Journal of Obstetric, Gynecologic, and Neonatal Nursing, 31,* 71–85.

Geraerts E. (2012). Cognitive underpinnings of recovered memories of childhood abuse. In R. F. Belli (Ed.), *True and false recovered memories: Toward a reconciliation of the debate.* New York, NY: Springer.

Gershoff, E. T. (2002). Parental corporal punishment and associated child behaviors and experiences: A meta-analytic and theoretical review. *Psychological Bulletin, 128,* 539–579.

Gershoff, E. T. (2013). Spanking and child development: We know enough now to stop hitting our children. *Child Development Perspectives, 7,* 133–137. doi:10.1111/cdep.12038

Gershoff, E. T., Lansford, J. E., Sexton, H. R., Davis-Kean, P., & Sameroff, A. J. (2012). Longitudinal links between spanking and children's externalizing behaviors in a national sample of white, black, Hispanic, and Asian American families. *Child Development, 83,* 838–843. doi:10.1111/j.1467-8624.2011.01732.x

Gershon, E. S., & Alliey-Rodriguez, N. (2013). New ethical issues for genetic counseling in common mental disorders. *The American Journal of Psychiatry, 170,* 968–976. doi:10.1176/appi.ajp.2013.12121558

Gibbons, D. E., & Lynn, S. J. (2010). Hypnotic inductions: A primer. In S. J. Lynn, J. W. Rhue, & I. Kirsch (Eds.), *Handbook of Clinical Hypnosis* (2nd ed., pp. 267–292). Washington, DC: American Psychological Association.

Gibbons, R. D., Brown, C. H., Hur, K., Davis, J. M., & Mann, J. J. (2012). Suicidal thoughts and behavior with antidepressant treatment: Reanalysis of the randomized placebo-controlled studies of fluoxetine and venlafaxine. *Archives of General Psychiatry, 69*(6), 580–587. doi:10.1001/archgenpsychiatry.2011.2048

Gibson, C., Folley, B. S., & Park, S. (2009). Enhanced divergent thinking and creativity in musicians: A behavioral and near-infrared spectroscopy study. *Brain and Cognition, 69*(1), 162–169. doi:10.1016/j.bandc.2008.07.009

Giedd, J. N., Rapoport, J. L. (2010). Structural MRI of pediatric brain development: What have we learned and where are we going? *Neuron, 67,* 728–734.

Gigerenzer, G. (2008). Why heuristics work. *Perspective on Psychological Science, 3*(1), 20–29.

Gigerenzer, G., Gaissmaier, W., Kurz-Milcke, E., Schwartz, L. M., & Woloshin, S. (2007). Helping doctors and patients make sense of health statistics. *Psychological Science in the Public Interest, 8*(2), 53–96. doi:10.1111/j.1539-6053.2008.00033.x

Gilbert, D. T. (1989). Thinking lightly about others: Automatic components of the social inference process. In J. S. Uleman & J. A. Bargh (Eds.), *Unintended thought: Limits of awareness, intention, and control.* New York, NY: Guilford Press.

Gilbert, D. T. (1998). Speeding with Ned: A personal view of the correspondence bias. In J. M. Darley & J. Cooper (Ed.), *Attribution and social interaction: The legacy of Edward E. Jones.* Washington, DC: American Psychological Association.

Gilbert, D. T. (2006). *Stumbling on happiness.* New York, NY: Alfred A. Knopf.

Gilgen, A. R. (1982). *American psychology since World War II: A profile of the discipline.* Westport, CT: Greenwood.

Gillen-O'Neel, C., Huynh, V. W., & Fuligni, A. J. (2013). To study or sleep? The academic costs of extra studying at the expense of sleep. *Child Development, 84,* 133–142.

Gilovich, T. D., & Griffin, D. W. (2010). Judgment and decision making. In S. T. Fiske, D. T. Gilbert, & G. Lindzey (Eds.), *Handbook of social psychology* (5th ed., Vol. 1, pp. 542–588). Hoboken, NJ: Wiley.

Gilson, T. A., Chow, G. M., & Feltz, D. L. (2012). Self-efficacy and athletic squat performance: Positive or negative influences at the within—and between—levels of analysis. *Journal of Applied Social Psychology, 42,* 1467–1485. doi:10.1111/j.1559-1816.2012.00908.x

Gimmig, D., Huguet, P., Caverni, J., & Cury, F. (2006). Choking under pressure and working memory capacity: When performance pressure reduces fluid intelligence. *Psychonomic Bulletin & Review, 13*(6), 1005–1010.

Gitlin, M. J. (2014). Pharmacotherapy and other somatic treatments for depression. In I. H. Gotlib & C. L. Hammen, (Eds.), *Handbook of depression* (3rd ed.) New York, NY: Guilford Press.

Gittelman, M. (2005). The neglected disaster. *International Journal of Mental Health, 34*(2), 9–21.

Gläscher, J., Adolphs, R., Damasio, H., Bechara, A., Rudrauf, D., Calamia, M., . . . Tranel, D. (2012). Lesion mapping of cognitive control and value-based decision making in the prefrontal cortex. *PNAS Proceedings of The National Academy of Sciences of the United States of America, 109,* 14681–14686. doi:10.1073/pnas.1206608109

Glass, R. M. (2001). Electroconvulsive therapy. *JAMA, 285,* 1346–1348.

Glass, R. M. (2004). Treatment of adolescents with major depression: Contributions of a major trial. *JAMA, 292,* 861–863.

Glasser, W. (2005). Warning: Psychiatry can be hazardous to your mental health. In R. H. Wright & N. A. Cummings (Eds.), *Destructive trends in mental health: The well-intentioned path to harm.* New York, NY: Routledge.

Glassman, A., Maj, M., & Sartorius, N. (2011). *Depression and heart disease.* Hoboken, NJ: Wiley.

Glassner, B. (1999). *The culture of fear: Why Americans are afraid of the wrong things.* New York, NY: Perseus Books Group.

Gleason, M. E. J., & Masumi, I. (2015). Social support. In M. Mikulincer, P. R. Shaver, E. Borgida, & J. A. Bargh (Eds.), *APA handbook of personality and social psychology: Vol. 3. Interpersonal relations.* Washington, DC: American Psychological Association.

Gleitman, L., & Newport, E. (1996). *The invention of language by children.* Cambridge, MA: MIT Press.

Gleitman, L., & Papafragou, A. (2005). Language and thought. In K. J. Holyoak & R. G. Morrison (Eds.), *The Cambridge handbook of thinking and reasoning.* New York, NY: Cambridge University Press.

Gloria, C. T., & Steinhardt, M. A. (2014). Relationships among positive emotions, coping, resilience, and mental health. *Stress and Health: Journal of the International Society for the Investigation of Stress.* Advance online publication. doi:10.1002/smi.2589

Gluck, M. E. (2006). Stress response and binge eating disorder. *Appetite, 46*(1), 26–30.

Godlee, F., Smith, J., & Marcovitch, H. (2011). Wakefield's article linking MMR vaccine and autism was fraudulent. *British Medical Journal, 342,* 64–66.

Goff, D. C. (2014). Maintenance treatment with long-acting injectable antipsychotics: Comparing old with new. *JAMA, 311,* 1973–1974.

Goff, D. C., & Gudeman, J. E. (1999). The person with chronic mental illness. In A. M. Nicholi (Ed.), *The Harvard guide to psychiatry.* Cambridge, MA: Harvard University Press.

Gold, J., & Stricker, G. (2013). Psychotherapy integration and integrative psychotherapies. In G. Stricker & T. A. Widiger (Eds.), *Handbook of psychology: Vol. 8. Clinical psychology* (2nd ed.). New York, NY: Wiley.

Goldberg, T. E., David, A., & Gold, J. M. (2011). Neurocognitive impairments in schizophrenia: Their character and their role in symptom formation. In D. R. Weinberger & P. Harrison (Eds.), *Schizophrenia* (3rd ed.). Malden, MA: Wiley-Blackwell.

Goldenberg, H. (1983). *Contemporary clinical psychology.* Pacific Grove, CA: Brooks/Cole.

Goldenberg, I., Goldenberg, H., & Pelavin, E. G. (2011). Family therapy. In R. J. Corsini & D. Wedding (Eds.), *Current psychotherapies* (9th ed.). Belmont, CA: Brooks/Cole.

Goldin-Meadow, S., Levine, S. C., Hedges, L. V., Huttenlocher, J., Raudenbush, S. W., & Small, S. L. (2014). New evidence about language and cognitive development based on a longitudinal study: Hypotheses for intervention. *American Psychologist, 69,* 588–599. doi:10.1037/a0036886

Goldsmith, R., Joanisse, D. R., Gallagher, D., Pavlovich, K., Shamoon, E., Leibel, R. L., & Rosenbaum, M. (2010). Effects of experimental weight perturbation on skeletal muscle work efficiency, fuel utilization, and biochemistry in human subjects. *American Journal of Physiology-Regulatory, Integrative and Comparative Physiology, 298,* R79–R88.

Goldstein, D. G., & Gigerenzer, G. (2002). Models of ecological rationality: The recognition heuristic. *Psychological Review, 109,* 75–90.

Goldstein, E. B. (2001). Pictorial perception and art. In E. B. Goldstein (Ed.), *Blackwell handbook of perception.* Malden, MA: Blackwell.

Goldstein, E. B. (2010). Constancy. In E. B. Goldstein (Ed.), *Encyclopedia of perception.* Thousand Oaks, CA: Sage.

Gomes, A. R., Faria, S., & Goncalves, A. M. (2013). Cognitive appraisal as a mediator in the relationship between stress and burnout. *Work & Stress, 27,* 351–367. doi:10.1080/02678373.2013.840341

Gómez, D. M., Berent, I., Benavides-Varela, S., Bion, R. H., Cattarossi, L., Nespor, M., & Mehler, J. (2014). Language universals at birth. *PNAS Proceedings of the National Academy of Sciences of the United States of America, 111,* 5837–5841. doi:10.1073/pnas.1318261111

González, H. M., Vega, W. A., Williams, D. R., Tarraf, W., West, B. T., & Neighbors, H. W. (2010). Depression care in the United States: Too little for too few. *Archives of General Psychiatry, 67*(1), 37–46.

Goodall, J. (1986). Social rejection, exclusion, and shunning among the Gombe chimpanzees. *Ethology & Sociobiology, 7,* 227–236.

Goodall, J. (1990). *Through a window: My thirty years with the chimpanzees of Gombe.* Boston, MA: Houghton, Mifflin.

Goodheart, C. D. (2006). Evidence, endeavor, and expertise in psychology practice. In C. D. Goodheart, A. E. Kazdin, & R. J. Sternberg (Eds.), *Evidence-based psychotherapy: Where practice and research meet* (pp. 37–62). Washington, DC: American Psychological Association.

Goodie, A. S., & Fortune, E. E. (2013). Measuring cognitive distortions in pathological gambling: Review and meta-analyses. *Psychology of Addictive Behaviors, 27,* 730–743. doi:10.1037/a0031892

Goodwin, C. J. (1991). Misportraying Pavlov's apparatus. *American Journal of Psychology, 104*(1), 135–141.

Goodwin, F. K., & Jamison, K. R. (2007). *Manic-depressive illness: Bipolar disorders and recurrent depression.* New York, NY: Oxford University Press.

Goodwin, G. (2009). Neurobiological aetiology of mood disorders. In M. C. Gelder, N. C. Andreasen, J. J. Lopez-Ibor, Jr., & J. R. Geddes (Eds.). *New Oxford textbook of psychiatry* (2nd ed., Vol. 1). New York, NY: Oxford University Press.

Gopnik, A., Meltzoff, A. N., & Kuhl, P. K. (1999). *The scientist in the crib: Minds, brains, and how children learn.* New York, NY: Morrow.

Gordon, J., & Abramov, I. (2001). Color vision. In E. B. Goldstein (Ed.), *Blackwell handbook of perception.* Malden, MA: Blackwell.

Goswami, U. (2006). Neuroscience and education: From research to practice? *Nature Reviews Neuroscience, 7*(5), 2–7.

Gottesman, I. I. (1991). *Schizophrenia genesis: The origins of madness.* New York, NY: W. H. Freeman.

Gottesman, I. I. (2001). Psychopathology through a life span–genetic prism. *American Psychologist, 56,* 867–878.

Gottesmann, C. (2009). Discovery of the dreaming sleep stage: A recollection. *Sleep: Journal of Sleep and Sleep Disorders Research, 32*(1), 15–16.

Gottfredson, L. S. (2003a). Dissecting practical intelligence theory: Its claims and evidence. *Intelligence, 31,* 343–397.

Gottfredson, L. S. (2003b). G, jobs and life. In H. Nyborg (Ed.), *The scientific study of general intelligence: Tribute to Arthur R. Jensen.* Oxford, UK: Pergamon.

Gouin, J., Glaser, R., Malarkey, W. B., Beversdorf, D., & Kiecolt-Glaser, J. (2012). Chronic stress, daily stressors, and circulating inflammatory markers. *Health Psychology, 31,* 264–268. doi:10.1037/a0025536

Gouin, J., Hantsoo, L. V., & Keicolt-Glaser, J. K. (2011). Stress, negative emotions, and inflammation. In J. T. Cacioppo & J. Decety (Eds.), *Oxford handbook of social neuroscience.* New York, NY: Oxford University Press.

Gould, E. (2004). Stress, deprivation, and adult neurogenesis. In M. S. Gazzaniga (Ed.), *The cognitive neurosciences* (pp. 139–148). Cambridge, MA: MIT Press.

Gow, A. J., Bastin, M. E., Munoz Maniega, S., Valdes Hernandez, M. C., Morris, Z., Murray, C., . . . Wardlaw, J. M. (2012). Neuroprotective lifestyles and the aging brain: Activity, atrophy, and white matter integrity. *Neurology, 23,* 1802–1808. doi:10.1212/WNL.0b013e3182703fd2

Goyal, M., Singh, S., Sibinga, E. M. S., Gould, N. F., Rowland-Seymour, A., Sharma, R., . . . Haythornthwaite, J. A. (2014). Meditation programs for psychological stress and well-being: A systematic review and meta-analysis. *JAMA Internal Medicine, 174,* 357–368. doi:10.1001/jamainternmed.2013.13018

Graber, J. A. (2013). Pubertal timing and the development of psychopathology in adolescence and beyond. *Hormones and Behavior, 64,* 262–269. doi:10.1016/j.yhbeh.2013.04.003

Grady, D. (2006). Management of menopausal symptoms. *New England Journal of Medicine, 355,* 2338–2347.

Granberg, G., & Holmberg, S. (1991). Self-reported turnout and voter validation. *American Journal of Political Science, 35,* 448–459.

Grandner, M. A., Chakravorty, S., Perlis, M. L., Oliver, L., & Gurubhagavatula, I. (2014). Habitual sleep duration associated with self-reported and objectively determined cardiometabolic risk factors. *Sleep Medicine, 15,* 42–50. doi:10.1016/j.sleep.2013.09.012

Grandner, M. A., Hale, L., Moore, M., & Patel, N. P. (2010). Mortality associated with short sleep duration: The evidence, the possible mechanisms, and the future. *Sleep Medicine Reviews, 14*(3), 191–203. doi:10.1016/j.smrv.2009.07.006

Grandner, M. A., Jackson, N. J., Pak, V. M., & Gehrman, P. R. (2012). Sleep disturbance is associated with cardiovascular and metabolic disorders. *Journal of Sleep Research, 21,* 427–433. doi:10.1111/j.1365-2869.2011.00990.x

Granic, I., Lobel, A., & Engels, R. C. M. E. (2014). The benefits of playing video games. *American Psychologist, 69,* 66–78. doi:10.1037/a0034857

Grant, D. A., Bieling, P. J., Segal, Z. V., & Cochrane, M. M. (2013). Cognitive models and issues. In M. Power (Ed.), *The Wiley-Blackwell handbook of mood disorders* (2nd ed.). Malden, MA: Wiley-Blackwell.

Grant, J. A., Courtemanche, J., Duerden, E. G., Duncan, G. H., & Rainville, P. (2010). Cortical thickness and pain sensitivity in zen meditators. *Emotion, 10*(1), 43–53. doi:10.1037/a0018334

Grant, J. A., & Rainville, P. (2009). Pain sensitivity and analgesic effects of mindful states in Zen meditators: A cross-sectional study. *Psychosomatic Medicine, 71*(1), 106–114. doi:10.1097/PSY.0b013e31818f52ee

Gray, C., & Della Sala, S. (2007). The Mozart effect: It's time to face the music! In S. Della Sala (Ed.), *Tall tales about the mind & brain: Separating fact from fiction* (pp. 148–157). New York, NY: Oxford University Press.

Graziano, W. G., & Tobin, R. M. (2009). Agreeableness. In M. R. Leary & R. H. Hoyle (Eds.), *Handbook of individual differences in social behavior* (pp. 46–61). New York, NY: Guilford Press.

Green, C. D. (2009). Darwinian theory, functionalism, and the first American psychological revolution. *American Psychologist, 64*(2), 75–83. doi:10.1037/a0013338

Green, J. P. (1999). Hypnosis, context effects, and recall of early autobiographical memories. *International Journal of Clinical & Experimental Hypnosis, 47,* 284–300.

Green, J. P., Laurence, J., & Lynn, S. J. (2014). Hypnosis and psychotherapy: From Mesmer to mindfulness. *Psychology of Consciousness: Theory, Research, and Practice, 1,* 199–212. doi:10.1037/cns0000015

Greenberg, J., Landau, M., Kosloff, S., & Solomon, S. (2009). How our dreams of death transcendence breed prejudice, stereotyping, and conflict: Terror management theory. In T. D. Nelson (Ed.), *Handbook of prejudice, stereotyping, and discrimination* (pp. 309–332). New York, NY: Psychology Press.

Greenberg, J. S. (2002). *Comprehensive stress management: Health and human performance.* New York, NY: McGraw-Hill.

Greene, S. M., Anderson, E. R., Forgatch, M. S., DeGarmo, D. S., & Hetherington, E. M. (2012). Risk and resilience after divorce. In F. Walsh (Ed.), *Normal family processes: Growing diversity and complexity* (4th ed.). New York, NY: Guilford Press.

Greeno, J. G. (1978). Nature of problem-solving abilities. In W. K. Estes (Ed.), *Handbook of learning and cognitive processes* (Vol. 5). Hillsdale, NJ: Erlbaum.

Greenough, W. T. (1975). Experiential modification of the developing brain. *American Scientist, 63,* 37–46.

Greenough, W. T., & Volkmar, F. R. (1973). Pattern of dendritic branching in occipital cortex of rats reared in complex environments. *Experimental Neurology, 40,* 491–504.

Greenson, R. R. (1967). *The technique and practice of psychoanalysis* (Vol. 1). New York, NY: International Universities Press.

Greenwald, A. G., Banaji, M. R., & Nosek, B. A. (2015). Statistically small effects of the implicit association test can have societally large effects. *Journal of Personality and Social Psychology, 108*(4), 553–561. doi:10.1037/pspa0000016

Greenwald, A. G., McGhee, D. E., & Schwartz, J. K. (1998). Measuring individual differences in implicit cognition: The Implicit Association Test. *Journal of Personality and Social Psychology, 74*(6), 1464–1480. doi:10.1037/0022-3514.74.6.1464

Greenwald, A. G., & Pettigrew, T. F. (2014). With malice toward none and charity for some: Ingroup favoritism enables discrimination. *American Psychologist, 69,* 669–684. doi:10.1037/a0036056

Greenwald, A. G., Poehlman, T., Uhlmann, E., & Banaji, M. R. (2009). Understanding and using the Implicit Association Test: III. Meta-analysis of predictive validity. *Journal of Personality and Social Psychology, 97*(1), 17–41. doi:10.1037/a0015575

Gregory, R. L. (1973). *Eye and brain.* New York, NY: McGraw-Hill.

Gregory, R. L. (1978). *Eye and brain* (2nd ed.). New York, NY: McGraw-Hill.

Greiner, E., Ryan, M., Mithani, Z., & Junquera, P. (2013). Cannabis use and psychosis: Current perspectives. *Addictive Disorders & Their Treatment, 12,* 136–139. doi:10.1097/ADT.0b013e3182624271

Greitemeyer, T. (2014). Intense acts of violence during video game play make daily life aggression appear innocuous: A new mechanism of why violent video games increase aggression. *Journal of Experimental Social Psychology, 50,* 52–56. doi:10.1016/j.jesp.2013.09.004

Gremeaux, V., Gayda, M., Lepers, R., Sosner, P., Juneau, M., & Nigam, A. (2012). Exercise and longevity. *Maturitas, 73,* 312–317. doi:10.1016/j.maturitas.2012.09.012

Griffin, D. W., Gonzalez, R., Koehler, D. J., & Gilovich, T. (2012). Judgmental heuristics: A historical overview. In K. J. Holyoak, & R. G. Morrison (Eds.), *Oxford handbook of thinking and reasoning.* New York, NY: Oxford University Press.

Grigorenko, E. L. (2000). Heritability and intelligence. In R. J. Sternberg (Ed.), *Handbook of intelligence* (pp. 53–91). New York, NY: Cambridge University Press.

Grinspoon, L., Bakalar, J. B., & Russo, E. (2005). Marihuana: Clinical aspects. In J. H. Lowinson, P. Ruiz, R. B. Millman, & J. G. Langrod (Eds.), *Substance abuse: A comprehensive textbook.* Philadelphia, PA: Lippincott Williams & Wilkins.

Griskevicius, V., Haselton, M. G., & Ackerman, J. M. (2015). Evolution and close relationships. In M. Mikulincer, P. R. Shaver, J. A. Simpson, & J. F. Dovidio (Eds.), *APA handbook of personality and social psychology*

Vol. 3: Interpersonal relations. Washington, DC: American Psychological Association.

Gros-Louis, J.,West, M. J., & King, A. P. (2014). Maternal responsiveness and the development of directed vocalizing in social interactions. *Infancy, 19,* 385–408. doi:10.1111/infa.12054

Gross, A. L., Brandt, J., Bandeen-Roche, K., Carlson, M. C., Stuart, E. A., Marsiske, M., & Rebok, G. W. (2014). Do older adults use the method of loci? Results from the active study. *Experimental Aging Research, 40,* 140–163. doi:10.1080 /0361073X.2014.882204

Gross, C. G. (2000). Neurogenesis in the adult brain: Death of a dogma. *Nature Reviews Neuroscience, 1,* 67–73.

Grossmann, K. E., & Grossmann, K. (1990). The wider concept of attachment in cross-cultural research. *Human Development, 33,* 31–47.

Grotevant, H. D., & McDermott, J. M. (2014). Adoption: Biological and social processes linked to adaptation. *Annual Review of Psychology, 65,* 235–265. doi:10.1146/annurev-psych-010213-115020

Grubin, D., & Madsen, L. (2005). Lie detection and the polygraph: A historical review. *Journal of Forensic Psychiatry & Psychology, 16,* 357–369.

Grunberg, N. E., Berger, S. S., & Hamilton, K. R. (2011). Stress and drug use. In R. J. Contrada & A. Baum (Eds.), *The handbook of stress science: Biology, psychology, and health* (pp. 111–121). New York, NY: Springer Publishing.

Grunberg, N. E., Shafer Berger, S., & Starosciak, A. K. (2012). Tobacco use: Psychology, neurobiology and clinical implications. In A. Baum, T. A. Revenson, & J. Singer (Eds.), *Handbook of health psychology* (2nd ed., pp. 311–332). New York, NY: Psychology Press.

Grunberg, N. E., Faraday, M. M., & Rahman, M. A. (2001). The psychobiology of nicotine self-administration. In A. Baum, T. A. Revenson, & J. E. Singer (Eds.), *Handbook of health psychology* (pp. 249–262). Mahwah, NJ: Erlbaum.

Grundgeiger, T., Bayen, U. J., & Horn, S. S. (2014). Effects of sleep deprivation on prospective memory. *Memory, 22,* 679–686. doi:10.1080/09658211 .2013.812220

Guarda, A. S., Pinto, A. M., Coughlin, J. W., Hussain, S., Haug, N. A., & Heinberg, L. J. (2007). Perceived coercion and change in perceived need for admission in patients hospitalized for eating disorders. *American Journal of Psychiatry, 164,* 108–114.

Guardiola-Lemaitre, B., & Quera-Salva, M. A. (2011). Melatonin and the regulation of sleep and circadian rhythms. In M. H. Kryger, T. Roth, & W. C. Dement (Eds.), *Principles and practice of sleep medicine* (5th ed.). Saint Louis, MO: Elsevier Saunders.

Guenther, K. (1988). Mood and memory. In G. M. Davies & D. M. Thomson (Eds.), *Memory in context: Context in memory.* New York, NY: Wiley.

Guerreiro, R. J., Gustafson, D. R., & Hardy, J. (2012). The genetic architecture of Alzheimer's disease: Beyond APP, PSENs and APOE. *Neurogbiology of Aging, 33,* 437–456. doi:10.1016/j.neurobiolaging.2010 .03.025

Guerrini, I., Thomson, A. D., & Gurling, H. D. (2007). The importance of alcohol misuse, malnutrition, and genetic susceptibility on brain growth and plasticity. *Neuroscience & Biobehavioral Reviews, 31,* 212–220.

Guilbault, R. L., Bryant, F. B., Brockway, J. H., & Posavac, E. J. (2004). A meta-analysis of research on hindsight bias. *Basic & Applied Social Psychology, 26*(2–3), 103–117.

Guilford, J. P. (1959). Three faces of intellect. *American Psychologist, 14,* 469–479.

Guilleminault, C., & Cao, M. T. (2011). Narcolepsy: Diagnosis and management. In M. H. Kryger, T. Roth, & W. C. Dement (Eds.), *Principles and practice of sleep medicine* (5th ed.). Saint Louis, MO: Elsevier Saunders.

Gullifer, J. W., Kroll, J. F., & Dussias, P. E. (2013). When language switching has no apparent cost: Lexical access in sentence context. *Frontiers in Psychology, 4,* 1–13. doi:10.3389 /fpsyg.2013.00278

Gunn, S. R., & Gunn, W. S. (2006). Are we in the dark about sleepwalking's dangers? *Cerebrum,* 1–12.

Gunthert, K. (2014). Special series: Part I. Cultural competence at the intersection of research, practice, and training. *The Behavior Therapist, 37*(5), 100–101.

Gur, R. C., & Gur, R. E. (2007). Neural substrates for sex differences in cognition. In S. J. Ceci & W. M. Williams (Eds.), *Why aren't more women in science?* (pp. 189–198). Washington, DC: American Psychological Association.

Gustad, L. T., Laugsand, L. E., Janszky, I., Dalen, H., & Bjerkeset, O. (2014). Symptoms of anxiety and depression and risk of heart failure: The HUNT study. *European Journal of Heart Failure, 16,* 861–870. doi:10.1002 /ejhf.133

Guzmán-Vélez, E., & Tranel, D. (2015). Does bilingualism contribute to cognitive reserve? Cognitive and neural perspectives. *Neuropsychology, 29,* 139–150. doi:10.1037 /neu0000105

Hackman, J. R., & Katz, N. (2010). Attitudes. In S. T. Fiske, D. T. Gilbert, & G. Lindzey (Eds.), *Handbook of social psychology* (5th ed., Vol. 1, pp. 353–393). Hoboken, NJ: Wiley.

Hadar, L., & Sood, S. (2014). When knowledge is demotivating: Subjective knowledge and choice overload. *Psychological Science, 25,* 1739–1747. doi:10.1177/0956797614539165

Hadaway, C. K., Marler, P. L., & Chaves, M. (1993). What the polls don't show: A closer look at U.S. church attendance. *American Sociological Review, 58,* 741–752.

Hagerty, M. R. (2000). Social comparisons of income in one's community: Evidence from national surveys of income and happiness. *Journal of Personality and Social Psychology, 78,* 764–771.

Haidt, J. (2007). The new synthesis in moral psychology. *Science, 316,* 998–1002.

Haidt, J. (2013). Moral psychology for the twenty-first century. *Journal of Moral Education, 42,* 281–297. doi:10.1080/03057240.2013.817327

Haidt, J., & Kesebir, S. (2010). Morality. In S. T. Fiske, D. T. Gilbert, & G. Lindzey (Eds.), *Handbook of social psychology* (Vol. 2, 5th ed.). Hoboken NJ: Wiley.

Haier, R. J. (2011). Biological basis of intelligence. In R. J. Sternberg, & S. B. Kaufman (Eds.), *Cambridge handbook of intelligence.* New York, NY: Cambridge University Press.

Halaris, A. (2013). Inflammation, heart disease, and depression. *Current Psychiatry Reports, 15,* 400. doi:10.1007/s11920-013-0400-5

Halassa, M. M., & Haydon, P. G. (2010). Integrated brain circuits: astrocytic networks modulate neuronal activity and behavior. *Annual Review of Physiology,72,* 335–355.

Hald, G. M., & Høgh-Olesen, H. (2010). Receptivity to sexual invitations from strangers of the opposite gender. *Evolution and Human Behavior, 31,* 453–458. doi:10.1016 /j.evolhumbehav.2010.07.004

Haleem, D. J. (2012). Serotonin neurotransmission in anorexia nervosa. *Behavioural Pharmacology, 23,* 478–495. doi:10.1097/FBP.0b013e328357440d

Hall, C. I. (2014). The evolution of the revolution: The successful establishment of multicultural psychology. In F. L. Leong, L. Comas-Díaz, G. C. Nagayama Hall, V. C. McLoyd, & J. E. Trimble (Eds.), *APA handbook of multicultural psychology: Vol. 1. Theory and research.* Washington, DC: American Psychological Association. doi:10.1037/14189-001.

Hall, C. S. (1966). *The meaning of dreams.* New York, NY: McGraw-Hill.

Hall, C. S. (1979). The meaning of dreams. In D. Goleman & R. J. Davidson (Eds.), *Consciousness: Brain, states of awareness, and mysticism.* New York, NY: Harper & Row.

Hall, J., Trent, S., Thomas, K. L., O'Donovan, M. C., & Owen, M. J. (2015). Genetic risk for schizophrenia: Convergence on synaptic pathways involved in plasticity. *Biological Psychiatry, 77*(1), 52–58. doi:10.1016 /j.biopsych.2014.07.011

Hall, J. A., & Mast, M. S. (2008). Are women always more interpersonally sensitive than men? Impact of goals and content domain. *Personality and Social Psychology Bulletin, 34,* 144–155.

Hall, J. A., & Roter, D. L. (2011). Physician-patient communication. In H. S. Friedman (Ed.), *Oxford handbook of health psychology.* New York, NY: Oxford University Press.

Hall, J. E. (2011). *Guyton and Hall textbook of medical physiology* (12th ed.). Philadelphia, PA: Elsevier Saunders.

Hall, W. D., & Degenhardt, J. (2009). Cannabis-related disorders. In B. J. Sadock, V. A. Sadock, & P. Ruiz (Eds)., *Kaplan & Sadock's comprehensive textbook of psychiatry* (9th ed.). Philadelphia, PA: Lippincott Williams & Wilkins.

Halpern, C., Hurtig, H., Jaggi, J., Grossman, M., Won, M., & Baltuch, G. (2007). Deep brain stimulation in neurologic disorders. *Parkinsonism & Related Disorders, 13*(1), 1–16.

Halpern, D. F. (1994). A national assessment of critical thinking skills in adults: Taking steps toward the goal. In A. Greenwood (Ed.), *The national assessment of college student learning: Identification of the skills to be taught, learned, and assessed.* Washington, DC: US Department of Education. National Center for Education Statistics.

Halpern, D. F. (1998). Teaching critical thinking for transfer across domains: Dispositions, skills, structure training, and metacognitive monitoring. *American Psychologist, 53,* 449–455.

Halpern, D. F. (2012). *Sex differences in cognitive abilities* (4th ed.). New York, NY: Psychology Press.

Halpern, D. F. (2014). *Thought and knowledge: An introduction to critical thinking* (5th ed.). New York, NY: Psychology Press.

Hamaideh, S. H. (2011). Stressors and reactions to stressors among university students. *International Journal* of *Social Psychiatry, 57,* 69–80. doi:10.1177/0020764010348442

Hambrick, D. Z., & Meinz, E. J. (2013). Working memory capacity and musical skill. In T. Packiam Alloway, & R. G. Alloway (Eds.), *Working memory: The connected intelligence.* New York, NY: Psychology Press.

Hamden, A., Newton, R., McCauley-Elsom, K., & Cross, W. (2011). Is deinstitutionalization working in our community? *International Journal of Mental Health Nursing, 20*(4), 274–283. doi:10.1111/j.1447-0349.2010.00726.x

Hames, J. L., Hagan, C. R., & Joiner, T. E. (2013). Interpersonal processes in depression. *Annual Review of Clinical Psychology, 9,* 355–377. doi:10.1146/annurev-clinpsy-050212-185553

Hammen, C., & Keenan-Miller, D. (2013). Mood disorders. In T. A. Widiger, G. Stricker, I. B. Weiner, G. Stricker, T. A. Widiger, & I. B. Weiner (Eds.), *Handbook of psychology: Vol. 8. Clinical psychology* (2nd ed.). New York, NY: Wiley.

Hammen, C. L., & Shih, J. (2014). Depression and interpersonal processes. In I. H. Gotlib & C. L. Hammen (Eds.), *Handbook of depression* (3rd ed.). New York, NY: Guilford Press.

Hampson, E., van Anders, S. M., & Mullin, L. I. (2006). A female advantage in the recognition of emotional facial expressions: Test of an evolutionary hypothesis. *Evolution and Human Behavior, 27,* 401–416.

Hanczakowski, M., Zawadzka, K., & Coote, L. (2014). Context reinstatement in recognition: Memory and beyond. *Journal of Memory and Language, 72,* 85–97. doi:10.1016/j.jml.2014.01.001

Haney, C., Banks, W. C., & Zimbardo, P. G. (1973). Interpersonal dynamics in a simulated prison. *International Journal of Criminology and Penology, 1,* 69–97.

Haney, C., & Zimbardo, P. G. (1998). The past and future of U.S. prison policy: Twenty-five years after the Stanford Prison Experiment. *American Psychologist, 53,* 709–727.

Hanna-Pladdy, B., & MacKay, A. (2011). The relation between instrumental musical activity and cognitive aging. *Neuropsychology, 25,* 378–386. doi:10.1037/a0021895

Hansen, H., Dugan, T. M., Becker, A. E., Lewis-Fernández, R., Lu, F. G., Oquendo, M. A., . . . Trujillo, M. (2013). Educating psychiatry residents about cultural aspects of care: A qualitative study of approaches used by U.S. expert faculty. *Academic Psychiatry, 37,* 412–416. doi:10.1176/appi.ap.12080141

Hanson, K., Windward, J., Schweinsburg, A., Medina, K., Brown, S., & Tapert, S. (2010). Longitudinal study of cognition among adolescent marijuana users over three weeks of abstinence. *Addictive Behaviors, 35,* 970–976.

Hardt, O., Einarsson, E. Ö., & Nader, K. (2010). A bridge over troubled water: Reconsolidation as a link between cognitive and neuroscientific memory research traditions. *Annual Review of Psychology, 61,* 141–167. doi:10.1146/annurev.psych.093008.100455

Hardt, O., Nader, K., & Nadel, L. (2013). Decay happens: The role of active forgetting in memory. *Trends in Cognitive Sciences, 17,* 111–120. doi:10.1016/j.tics.2013.01.001

Hare, R. D. (2006). Psychopathy: A clinical and forensic overview. *Psychiatric Clinics of North America, 29,* 709–724. doi:10.1016/j.psc.2006.04.007

Hare, R. D., & Neumann, C. S. (2008). Psychopathy as a clinical and empirical construct. *Annual Review of Clinical Psychology, 4,* 217–246. doi:10.1146/annurev.clinpsy.3.022806.091452

Harley, E. M. (2007). Hindsight bias in legal decision making. *Social Cognition, 25,* 48–63.

Harley, T. A. (2008). *The psychology of language: From data to theory.* New York, NY: Psychology Press.

Harlow, H. F. (1958). The nature of love. *American Psychologist, 13,* 673–685.

Harlow, H. F. (1959). Love in infant monkeys. *Scientific American, 200*(6), 68–74.

Harris, J. E. (1984). Remembering to do things: A forgotten topic. In J. E. Harris & P. E. Morris (Eds.), *Everyday memory, actions, and absent-mindedness.* New York, NY: Academic Press.

Harris, J. L., Bargh, J. A., & Brownell, K. D. (2009). Priming effects of television food advertising on eating behavior. *Health Psychology, 28*(4), 404–413. doi:10.1037/a0014399

Harris, J. R. (1998). *The nurture assumption: Why children turn out the way they do.* New York, NY: Free Press.

Harte, J. L., & Eifert, G. H. (1995). The effects of running, environment, and attentional focus on athletes' catecholamine and cortisol levels and mood. *Psychophysiology, 32*(1), 49–54. doi:10.1111/j.1469-8986.1995.tb03405.x

Hartmann, E., & Hartmann, T. (2014). The impact of exposure to Internet-based information about the Rorschach and the MMPI–2 on psychiatric outpatients' ability to simulate mentally healthy test performance. *Journal of Personality Assessment, 96,* 432–444. doi:10.1080/00223891.2014.882342

Harvey, P. D., & Bowie, C. R. (2013). Schizophrenia spectrum disorders. In T. A. Widiger, G. Stricker, I. B. Weiner, G. Stricker, T. A. Widiger, & I. B. Weiner (Eds.), *Handbook of psychology: Vol. 8. Clinical psychology* (2nd ed.). New York, NY: Wiley.

Haskard, K. B., Williams, S. L., DiMatteo, M., Rosenthal, R., White, M., & Goldstein, M. G. (2008). Physician and patient communication training in primary care: Effects on participation and satisfaction. *Health Psychology, 27*(5), 513–522. doi:10.1037/0278-6133.27.5.513

Haslam, S. A., & Reicher, S. (2003). Beyond Stanford: Questioning a role-based explanation of tyranny. *Dialogue, 18,* 22–25.

Hastorf, A., & Cantril, H. (1954). They saw a game: A case study. *Journal of Abnormal and Social Psychology, 49,* 129–134.

Hatfield, E., & Rapson, R. L. (1993). *Love, sex, and intimacy: Their psychology, biology, and history.* New York, NY: HarperCollins.

Haukvik, U. K., Westlye, L. T., Mørch-Johnsen, L., Jørgensen, K. N., Lange, E. H., Dale, A. M., . . . Agartz, I. (2015). In vivo hippocampal subfield volumes in schizophrenia and bipolar disorder. *Biological Psychiatry, 77*(6), 581–588. doi:10.1016/j.biopsych.2014.06.020

Hauser, M., & Carey, S. (1998). Building a cognitive creature from a set of primitives: Evolutionary and developmental insights. In D. D. Cummins & C. Allen (Eds.), *The evolution of mind.* New York, NY: Oxford University Press.

Havens, J. R., Leukefeld, C. G., DeVeaugh-Geiss, A. M., Coplan, P., & Chilcoat, H. D. (2014). The impact of a reformulation of extended-release oxycodone designed to deter abuse in a sample of prescription opioid abusers. *Drug and Alcohol Dependence, 139,* 9–17. doi:10.1016/j.drugalcdep.2014.02.018

Haworth-Hoeppner, S. (2000). The critical shapes of body image: The role of culture and family in the production of eating disorders. *Journal of Marriage and the Family, 62,* 212–227.

Hayati, A. M., & Shariatifar, S. (2009). Mapping strategies. *Journal of College Reading and Learning, 39,* 53–67.

Haynes, M. C., & Heilman, M. E. (2013). It had to be you (not me)! Women's attributional rationalization of their contribution to successful joint work outcomes. *Personality and Social Psychology Bulletin, 39,* 956–969. doi:10.1177/0146167213486358

Hazan, C., & Shaver, P. (1986). *Parental caregiving style questionnaire.* Unpublished questionnaire.

Hazan, C., & Shaver, P. (1987). Romantic love conceptualized as an attachment process. *Journal of Personality and Social Psychology, 52,* 511–524.

Hazlett, H. C., Poe, M. D., Gerig, G., Styner, M., Chappell, C., Smith, R. G., & . . . Piven, J. (2011). Early brain overgrowth in autism associated with an increase in cortical surface area before age 2 years. *Archives of General Psychiatry, 68*(5), 467–476. doi:10.1001/archgenpsychiatry.2011.39

He, J., Ogden, L. G., Vupputuri, S., Bazzano, L. A., Loria, C., & Whelton, P. K. (1999). Dietary sodium intake and subsequent risk of cardiovascular disease in overweight adults. *JAMA, 282,* 2027–2034.

Healy, D. (2004). *Let them eat Prozac: The unhealthy relationship between the pharmaceutical industry and depression.* New York, NY: NYU Press.

Healy, D., & Whitaker, C. (2003). Antidepressants and suicide: Risk-benefit conundrums. *Journal of Psychiatry & Neuroscience, 28*(5), 28.

Heaps, C. M., & Nash, M. (2001). Comparing recollective experience in true and false autobiographical memories. *Journal of Experimental Psychology: Learning, Memory, and Cognition, 27,* 920–930.

Heavey, C. L., & Hurlburt, R. T. (2008). The phenomena of inner experience. *Consciousness and Cognition, 17,* 798–810. doi:10.1016/j.concog.2007.12.006

Hedegaard, M. (2005). The zone of proximal development as basis for instruction. In H. Daniels (Ed.), *An introduction to Vygotsky.* New York, NY: Routledge.

Heider, F. (1958). *The psychology of interpersonal relations.* New York, NY: Wiley.

Heine, S. J., Buchtel, E. E., & Norenzayan, A. (2008). What do cross-national comparisons of personality traits tell us? The case of conscientiousness. *Psychological Science, 19,* 309–313. doi:10.1111/j.1467-9280.2008.02085.x

Heinrichs, R. W., Miles, A. A., Ammari, N., & Muharib, E. (2013). Cognition as a central illness feature in schizophrenia. In P. D. Harvey (Ed.), *Cognitive impairment in schizophrenia: Characteristics, assessment and treatment.* New York, NY: Cambridge University Press. doi:10.1017/CBO9781139003872.002

Helmes, E. (2008). Modern applications of the MMPI/MMPI-2 in assessment. In G. J. Boyle, G. Matthews, & D. H. Saklofske (Eds.), *The Sage handbook of personality theory and assessment: Personality measurement and testing* (Vol. 2, pp. 589–607). Los Angeles, CA: Sage.

Helmholtz, H. von. (1852). On the theory of compound colors. *Philosophical Magazine, 4,* 519–534.

Helson, R., Jones, C., & Kwan, V. S. Y. (2002). Personality change over 40 years of adulthood: Hierarchical linear modeling analyses of two longitudinal studies. *Journal of Personality & Social Psychology, 83,* 752–766.

Helzer, J. E., Wittchen, H.-U., Krueger, R. F., & Kraemer, H. C. (2008). Dimensional options for DSM-V: The way forward. In J. E. Helzer, H. C. Kraemer, R. F. Krueger, H.-U, Wittchen, P. J. Sirovatka, et al. (Eds.), *Dimensional approaches in diagnostic classification: Refining the research agenda for DSM-V* (pp. 115–127). Washington, DC: American Psychiatric Association.

Henderson, K. E., & Brownell, K. D. (2004). The toxic environment and obesity: Contribution and cure. In J. K. Thompson (Ed.), *Handbook of eating disorders and obesity.* New York, NY: Wiley.

Henderson, R. C., Williams, P., Gabbidon, J., Farrelly, S., Schauman, O., Hatch, S., . . . Clement, S. (2014, March). Mistrust of mental health services: Ethnicity, hostpital admission and unfair treatment. *Epidemiological and Psychiatric Sciences,* 1–8.

Henry, P. J., Sternberg, R. J., & Grigorenko, E. L. (2005). Capturing successful intelligence through measures of analytic, creative, and practical skills. In O. Wilhelm & R. W. Engle (Eds.), *Handbook of understanding and measuring intelligence.* Thousand Oaks, CA: Sage.

Hepper, E. G., Hart, C. M., & Sedikides, C. (2014). Moving narcissus: Can narcissists be empathic? *Personality and Social Psychology Bulletin, 40,* 1079–1091. doi:10.1177/0146167214535812

Hepper, P. (2003). *Prenatal psychological and behavioural development.* Thousand Oaks, CA: Sage.

Herbenick, D., Reece, M., Schick, V., Sanders, S. A., Dodge, B., & Fortenberry, J. (2010). An event-level analysis of the sexual characteristics and composition among adults ages 18 to 59: Results from a national probability sample in the United States. *Journal of Sexual Medicine, 7* (Suppl 5), 346–361. doi:10.1111/j.1743-6109 .2010.02020.x

Herbst, S., Pietrzak, R. H., Wagner, J., White, W. B., & Petry, N. M. (2007). Lifetime major depression is associated with coronary heart disease in older adults: Results from the national epidemiologic survey on alcohol and related conditions. *Psychosomatic Medicine, 69,* 729–734.

Herbstman, J., Sjodin, A., Kurzon, M., Lederman, S., Jones, R., Rauh, V., . . . Perera, F. (2010). Prenatal exposure to PBDEs and neurodevelopment. *Environmental Health Perspectives, 118*(5), 712–719. doi:10.1289/ehp.0901340

Hercher, C., Chopra, V., & Beasley, C. L. (2014). Evidence for morphological alterations in prefrontal white matter glia in schizophrenia and bipolar disorder. *Journal of Psychiatry & Neuroscience, 39,* 376–385. doi:10.1503/jpn.130277

Hermann, D., Raybeck, D., & Gruneberg, M. (2002). *Improving memory and study skills: Advances in theory and practice.* Ashland, OH: Hogrefe & Huber.

Hermans, H. J. M., & Kempen, H. J. G. (1998). Moving cultures: The perilous problems of cultural dichotomies in a globalizing society. *American Psychologist, 53,* 1111–1120.

Hermans, R. C., Lichtwarck-Aschoff, A., Bevelander, K. E., Herman, C. P., Larsen, J. K., & Engels, R. C. (2012). Mimicry of food intake: the dynamic interplay between eating companions. *PloS One, 7*(2), e31027. doi:10.1371 /journal.pone.0031027

Hernandez, R., Kershaw, K. N., Siddique, J., Boehm, J. K., Kubzansky, L. D., Diez-Roux, A., . . . Lloyd-Jones, D. M. (2015). Optimism and cardiovascular health: Multi-Ethnic Study of Atherosclerosis (MESA). *Health Behavior and Policy Review, 2,* 62–73. doi:10.14485/HBPR.2.1.6

Hernandez-Avila, C. A., & Kranzler, H. R. (2011). Alcohol use disorders. In P. Ruiz, & E. C. Strain (Eds.), *Lowinson and Ruiz's substance abuse: A comprehensive textbook* (5th ed.). Philadelphia, PA: Wolters Kluwer Lippincott Williams & Wilkins.

Herrnstein, R. J., & Murray, C. (1994). *The bell curve: Intelligence and class structure in American life.* New York, NY: Free Press.

Hervé, P., Zago, L., Petit, L., Mazoyer, B., & Tzourio-Mazoyer, N. (2013). Revisiting human hemispheric specialization with neuroimaging. *Trends in Cognitive Sciences, 17*(2), 69–80. doi:10.1016/j.tics.2012.12.004

Hespos, S. J., Ferry, A. L., & Rips, L. J. (2009). Five-month-old infants have different expectations for solids and liquids. *Psychological Science, 20*(5), 603–611. doi:10.1111/j.1467 -9280.2009.02331.x

Hewitt, B., & de Vaus, D. (2009). Change in the association between premarital cohabitation and separation, Australia 1945–2000. *Journal of Marriage and Family, 71*(2), 353–361. doi:10.1111/j.1741-3737.2009 .00604.x

Hewstone, M. (1990). The "ultimate attribution error"? A review of the literature on intergroup causal attribution. *European Journal of Social Psychology, 20,* 311–335.

Heyman, R. E., Lorber, M. F., Eddy, J. M., & West, T. V. (2014). Behavioral observation and coding. In H. T. Reis & C. M. Judd (Eds.), *Handbook of research methods in social and personality psychology* (2nd ed.). New York, NY: Cambridge University Press.

Higgins, E. T. (2004). Making a theory useful: Lessons handed down. *Personality and Social Psychology Review, 8*(2), 138–145.

Hilgard, E. R. (1986). *Divided consciousness: Multiple controls in human thought and action.* New York, NY: Wiley.

Hilgard, E. R. (1987). *Psychology in America: A historical survey.* San Diego, CA: Harcourt Brace Jovanovich.

Hilgard, E. R. (1992). Dissociation and theories of hypnosis. In E. Fromm & M. R. Nash (Eds.), *Contemporary hypnosis research.* New York, NY: Guilford Press.

Hill, A. K., Dawood, K, & Puts, D. A. (2013). Biological foundations of sexual orientation. In C. J. Patterson, & A. R. D'Augelli (Eds.), *Handbook of psychology and sexual orientation.* New York, NY: Oxford University Press.

Hill, S. E., Rodeheffer, C. D., Griskevicius, V., Durante, K., & White, A. E. (2012). Boosting beauty in an economic decline: Mating, spending, and the lipstick effect. *Journal of Personality and Social Psychology, 2,* 275–291. doi:10.1037/a0028657

Hilt, L. M., & Nolen-Hoeksema, S. (2014). Gender differences in depression. In I. H. Gotlib & C. L. Hammen (Eds.), *Handbook of depression* (3rd ed.). New York, NY: Guilford Press.

Hines, L. A., Sundin, J., Rona, R. J., Wessely, S., & Fear, N. T. (2014). Posttraumatic stress disorder post Iraq and Afghanistan: Prevalence among military subgroups. *The Canadian Journal of Psychiatry / La Revue Canadienne de Psychiatrie, 59,* 468–479.

Hines, M. (2004). Androgen, estrogen, and gender: Contributions of the early hormone environment to gender-related behavior. In A. H. Eagly, A. E. Beall, & R. J. Sternberg (Eds.), *The psychology of gender.* New York, NY: Guilford Press.

Hines, M. (2013). Sex and sex differences. In P. D. Zelazo (Ed.), *Oxford handbook of developmental psychology: Vol. 1. Body and mind.* New York, NY: Oxford University Press.

Hingson, R., & Sleet, D. A. (2006). Modifying alcohol use to reduce motor vehicle injury. In A. C. Gielen, D. A. Sleet, & R. J. DiClemente (Eds.), *Injury and violence prevention: Behavioral science theories, methods, and applications.* San Francisco, CA: Jossey-Bass.

Hinic, D. (2011). Problems with "Internet addiction" diagnosis and classification. *Psychiatria Danubina, 23,* 145–151.

Hinshaw, S. P. (2007). *The mark of shame: Stigma of mental illness and an agenda for change.* New York, NY: Oxford University Press.

Hinshaw, S. P., & Stier, A. (2008). Stigma as related to mental disorders. *Annual Review of Clinical Psychology, 4,* 367–393.

Hinvest, N. S., Brosnan, M. J., Rogers, R. D., & Hodgson, T. L. (2014). fMRI evidence for procedural invariance underlying gambling preference reversals. *Journal of Neuroscience, Psychology, and Economics, 7*(1), 48–63. doi:10.1037/npe0000007

Hirst, W., Phelps, E. A., Buckner, R. L., Budson, A. E., Cuc, A., Gabrieli, J. E., et al. (2009). Long-term memory for the terrorist attack of September 11: Flashbulb memories, event memories, and the factors that influence their retention. *Journal of Experimental Psychology: General, 138*(2), 161–176. doi:10.1037/a0015527

Ho, R. C., Zhang, M. W. B., Tsang, T. Y., Toh, A. H., Pan, F., Lu, Y., . . . Mak, K. (2014). The association between Internet addiction and psychiatric co-morbidity: A meta-analysis. *BMC Psychiatry, 14,* 183.

Hobson, J. A. (1989). *Sleep.* New York, NY: Scientific American Library.

Hobson, J. A. (2007). Current understanding of cellular models of REM expression. In D. Barrett & P. McNamara (Eds.), *The new science of dreaming.* Westport, CT: Praeger.

Hobson, J. A., & McCarley, R. W. (1977). The brain as a dream state generator: An activation-synthesis hypothesis of the dream process. *American Journal of Psychiatry, 134,* 1335–1348.

Hodges, B. H. (2014). Rethinking conformity and imitation: Divergence, convergence, and social understanding. *Frontiers in Psychology, 5,* 726.

Hodgins, D. C., & Racicot, S. (2013). The link between drinking and gambling among undergraduate university students. *Psychology of Addictive Behaviors, 27,* 885–892. doi:10.1037/a0032866.

Hodgkin, A. L., & Huxley, A. F. (1952). Currents carried by sodium and potassium ions through the membrane of the giant axon of Loligo. *Journal of Physiology, 116,* 449–472.

Hodgson, K. J., Shelton, K. H., & Bree, M. M. (2015). Psychopathology among young homeless people: Longitudinal mental health outcomes for different subgroups. *British Journal of Clinical* Psychology. Advance online publication. doi:10.1111/bjc.12075

Hoek, H. W. (2002). Distribution of eating disorders. In C. G. Fairburn & K. D. Brownell (Eds.), *Eating disorders and obesity: A comprehensive handbook.* New York, NY: Guilford Press.

Hoerger, M., Quirk, S. W., Lucas, R. E., & Carr, T. H. (2009). Immune neglect in affective forecasting. *Journal of Research in Personality, 43(1),* 91–94. doi:10.1016/j.jrp.2008.10.001

Hoff, E. (2014). *Language development* (5th ed.). Belmont, CA: Wadsworth.

Hofmann, S. G., & Barlow, D. H. (2014). Evidence-based psychological interventions and the common factors approach: The beginnings of a rapprochement? *Psychotherapy, 51,* 510–513. doi:10.1037/a0037045

Hofmann, W., De Houwer, J., Perugini, M., Baeyens, F., & Crombez, G. (2010). Evaluative conditioning in humans: A meta-analysis. *Psychological Bulletin, 136,* 390–421. doi:10.1037/a0018916

Hofstede, G. (1980). *Culture's consequences: International differences in work-related values.* Beverly Hills, CA: Sage.

Hofstede, G. (1983). Dimensions of national cultures in fifty countries and three regions. In J. Deregowski, S. Dziurawiec, & R. Annis (Eds.), *Explications in cross-cultural psychology.* Lisse: Swets and Zeitlinger.

Hofstede, G. (2001). *Culture's consequences: Comparing values, behaviors, institutions, and organizations across nations.* Thousand Oaks, CA: Sage.

Hogan, M. F., & Morrison, A. K. (2008). Organization and economics of mental health treatment. In A. Tasman, J. Kay, J. A. Lieberman, M. B. First, & M. Maj (Eds.), *Psychiatry* (3rd ed.). New York, NY: Wiley-Blackwell.

Hogan, R., & Chamorro-Premuzic, T. (2015). Personality and career success. In M. Mikulincer, P. R. Shaver, M. L. Cooper, & R. J. Larsen (Eds.), *APA handbook of personality and social psychology, Volume 4: Personality processes and individual differences.*

Washington, DC: American Psychological Association.

Høglend, P., Bøgwald, K.-P., Amlo, S., Marble, A., Ulberg, R., Sjaastad, M. C., . . . Johansson, P. (2008). Transference interpretations in dynamic psychotherapy: Do they really yield sustained effects? *American Journal of Psychiatry, 165,* 763–771.

Høglend, P., Hersoug, A. G., Bøgwald, K., Amlo, S., Marble, A., Sørbye, Ø., . . . Crits-Christoph, P. (2011). Effects of transference work in the context of therapeutic alliance and quality of object relations. *Journal of Consulting and Clinical Psychology, 79,* 697–706. doi:10.1037/a0024863

Hogue, C. J. R., Parker, C. B., Willinger, J. R., Temple, C. M., Bann, R. M., Silver, D. J., . . . Goldenberg, R. L. (2013). A population-based case-control study of stillbirth: The relationship of significant life events to the racial disparity for African American. *American Journal of Epidemiology, 177,* 755–767. doi:10.1093/aje/kws381

Holden, C. (1986, October). The rational optimist. *Psychology Today,* pp. 55–60.

Holden, C. (2004). FDA weighs suicide risk in children on antidepressants. *Science, 303,* 745.

Holden, G. W., Williamson, P. A., & Holland, G. W. O. (2014). Eavesdropping on the family: A pilot investigation of corporal punishment in the home. *Journal of Family Psychology, 28,* 401–406. doi:10.1037/a0036370

Hollander, E., & Simeon, D. (2008). Anxiety disorders. In R. E. Hales, S. C. Yudofsky, & G. O. Gabbard (Eds.), *The American Psychiatric Publishing textbook of psychiatry.* Washington, DC: American Psychiatric Publishing.

Hollands, C. (1989). Trivial and questionable research on animals. In G. Langley (Ed.), *Animal experimentation: The consensus changes.* New York, NY: Chapman & Hall.

Hollands, G. J., Prestwich, A., & Marteau, T. M. (2011). Using aversive images to enhance healthy food choices and implicit attitudes: An experimental test of evaluative conditioning. *Health Psychology, 30,* 195–203. doi:10.1037/a0022261

Hollingworth, L. S. (1914). *Functional periodicity: An experimental study of the mental and motor abilities of women during menstruation.* New York, NY: Teachers College, Columbia University.

Hollingworth, L. S. (1916). Sex differences in mental tests. *Psychological Bulletin, 13,* 377–383.

Hollon, S. D., & Beck, A. T. (2013). Cognitive and cognitive-behavioral

therapies. In M. J. Lambert (Ed.), *Bergin and Garfield's handbook of psychotherapy and behavior change* (6th ed.). New York, NY: Wiley.

Holmes, T. H., & Rahe, R. H. (1967). The Social Readjustment Rating Scale. *Journal of Psychosomatic Research, 11,* 213–218.

Holtgraves, T. (2004). Social desirability and self-reports: Testing models of socially desirable responding. *Personality and Social Psychology Bulletin, 30,* 161–172.

Holt-Lunstad, J., Smith, T. B., & Layton, J. B. (2010). Social relationships and mortality risk: A meta-analytic review. *PLoS Medicine, 7(7),* 1–20.

Holyoak, K. J. (2012). Analogy and relational reasoning. In K. J. Holyoak, & R. G. Morrison (Eds.), *Oxford handbook of thinking and reasoning.* New York, NY: Oxford University Press.

Homa, D., Neff, L. J., King, B. A., Caraballo, R. S., Bunnell, R. E., Babb, S. S., . . . Centers for Disease Control and Prevention (CDC). (2015). Vital signs: Disparities in nonsmokers' exposure to secondhand smoke—United States, 1999–2012. *MMWR Morbidity and Mortality Weekly Report, 64(4),* 103–108.

Hong, G. K., Garcia, M., & Soriano, M. (2000). Responding to the challenge: Preparing mental health professionals for the new millennium. In I. Cuellar & F. A. Paniagua (Eds.), *Handbook of multicultural mental health: Assessment and treatment of diverse populations.* San Diego, CA: Academic Press.

Hooley, J. M. (2004). Do psychiatric patients do better clinically if they live with certain kinds of families? *Current Directions in Psychological Science, 13(5),* 202–205.

Hooley, J. M. (2007). Expressed emotion and relapse of psychopathology. *Annual Review of Clinical Psychology, 3,* 329–352.

Hooley, J. M. (2009). Schizophrenia: Interpersonal functioning. In P. H. Blaney & T. Millon (Eds.), *Oxford textbook of psychopathology* (2nd ed., pp. 333–360). New York, NY: Oxford University Press.

Hooley, J. M., Cole, S. H., & Gironde, S. (2012). Borderline personality disorder. In T. A. Widiger, & T. A. Widiger (Eds.), *The Oxford handbook of personality disorders.* New York, NY: Oxford University Press. doi:10.1093/oxfordhb/9780199735013.013.0020

Hooper, J., & Teresi, D. (1986). *The 3-pound universe: The brain.* New York, NY: Laurel.

Hopko, D. R., Crittendon, J. A., Grant, E., & Wilson, S. A. (2005). The impact of anxiety on performance IQ. *Anxiety,*

Stress, and Coping: An International Journal, 18(1), 17–35.

Horgen, K. B., Harris, J. L., & Brownell, K. D. (2012). Food marketing: Targeting young people in a toxic environment. In D. G. Singer, & J. L. Singer (Eds.), *Handbook of children and the media* (2nd ed.). Thousand Oaks, CA: Sage.

Horn, J. L. (2002). Selections of evidence, misleading assumptions, and oversimplifications: The political message of The Bell Curve. In J. M. Fish (Ed.), *Race and intelligence: Separating science from myth* (pp. 297–326). Mahwah, NJ: Erlbaum.

Horn, J. P., & Swanson, L. W. (2013). The autonomic motor system and the hypothalamus. In E. R. Kandel, J. H. Schwartz, T. M. Jessell, S. A. Siegelbaum, & A. J. Hudspeth (Eds.), *Principles of neural science* (5th ed.). New York, NY: McGraw-Hill.

Horowitz, F. D. (1992). John B. Watson's legacy: Learning and environment. *Developmental Psychology, 28,* 360–367.

Houben, K., Schoenmakers, T. M., & Wiers, R. W. (2010). I didn't feel like drinking but I don't know why: The effects of evaluative conditioning on alcohol-related attitudes, craving and behavior. *Addictive Behaviors, 35,* 1161–1163. doi:10.1016/j.addbeh.2010.08.012

Hough, L. M., & Connelly, B. S. (2013). Personality measurement and use in industrial and organizational psychology. In K. F. Geisinger, B. A. Bracken, J. F. Carlson, J. C. Hansen, N. R. Kuncel, S. P. Reise, & M. C. Rodriguez (Eds.), *APA handbook of testing and assessment in psychology: Vol. 1. Test theory and testing and assessment in industrial and organizational psychology.* Washington, DC: American Psychological Association. doi:10.1037/14047-028

Houlcroft, L., Bore, M., & Munro, D. (2012). Three faces of narcissism. *Personality and Individual Differences, 53(3),* 274–278. doi:10.1016/j.paid.2012.03.036

Houlihan, J., Kropp, T., Wiles, R., Gray, S., & Campbell, C. (2005). *Body burden: The pollution in newborns.* Washington, DC: Environmental Working Group.

Howard, D. J. (1995). "Chaining" the use of influence strategies for producing compliance behavior. *Journal of Social Behavior and Personality, 10,* 169–185.

Howes, O. D., Bose, S. K., Turkheimer, F., Valli, I., Egerton, A., Valmaggia, L. R., . . . McGuire, P. (2011). Dopamine synthesis capacity before onset of psychosis: A prospective [18F]-DOPA PET imaging study. *The American*

Journal of Psychiatry, 168(12), 1311–1317.

Hsu, L. M. (1995). Regression toward the mean associated with measurement error and the identification of improvement and deterioration in psychotherapy. *Journal of Consulting and Clinical Psychology, 63*(1), 141–144. doi:org/10.1037/0022-006X.63.1.141

Hsu, L. M., Chung, J., & Langer, E. J. (2010). The influence of age-related cues on health and longevity. *Perspectives on Psychological Science, 5*, 632–648. doi:10.1177/1745691610388762

Hubel, D. H., & Wiesel, T. N. (1962). Receptive fields, binocular interaction and functional architecture in the cat's visual cortex. *Journal of Physiology, 160*, 106–154.

Hubel, D. H., & Wiesel, T. N. (1963). Receptive fields of cells in striate cortex of very young visually inexperienced kittens. *Journal of Neurophysiology, 26*, 994–1002.

Hubel, D. H., & Wiesel, T. N. (1979). Brain mechanisms of vision. In *Scientific American* (Eds.), *The brain*. San Francisco, CA: W. H. Freeman.

Huber, R., & Tononi, G. (2009). Sleep and waking across the lifespan. In G. G. Berntson & J. T. Cacioppo (Eds.), *Handbook of neuroscience for the behavioral sciences* (Vol. 1, pp. 461–481). New York, NY: Wiley.

Hudson, J. I., Hiripi, E., Pope Jr., Harrison, G., & Kessler, R. C. (2007). The prevalence and correlates of eating disorders in the national comorbidity survey replication. *Biological Psychiatry, 61*, 348–358.

Hudson, W. (1960). Pictorial depth perception in sub-cultural groups in Africa. *Journal of Social Psychology, 52*, 183–208.

Hudson, W. (1967). The study of the problem of pictorial perception among unacculturated groups. *International Journal of Psychology, 2*, 89–107.

Hudspeth, A. J. (2013). The inner ear. In E. R. Kandel, J. H. Schwartz, T. M. Jessell, S. A. Siegelbaum, & A. J. Hudspeth (Eds.), *Principles of neural science* (5th ed.). New York, NY: McGraw-Hill.

Huey, E. D., Krueger, F., & Grafman, J. (2006). Representations in the human prefrontal cortex. *Current Directions in Psychological Science, 15*, 167–171.

Huey, L. Y., Cole, S., Cole, R. F., Daniels, A. S., & Katzelnick, D. J. (2009). Health care reform. In B. J. Sadock, V. A. Sadock, & P. Ruiz (Eds.), *Kaplan & Sadock's comprehensive textbook of psychiatry* (pp. 4282–4298). Philadelphia, PA: Lippincott Williams & Wilkins.

Huey, S. J., Tilley, J. L., Jones, E. O., & Smith, C. A. (2014). The contribution of cultural competence to evidence-based care for ethnically diverse populations. *Annual Review of Clinical Psychology, 10*, 305–338. doi:10.1146/annurev-clinpsy-032813-153729

Huma, D. M., Neff, L. J., King, B. A., Caraballo, R. S., Bunnell, R. E., Babb, S. D., . . . Wang, L. (2015). Vital signs: Disparities in nonsmokers' exposure to secondhand smoke—United States, 1999–2012. *Morbidity and Mortality Weekly Report, 64*, 103–108.

Hughes, J., Smith, T. W., Kosterlitz, H. W., Fothergill, L. A., Morgan, B. A., & Morris, H. R. (1975). Identification of two related pentapeptides from the brain with the potent opiate agonist activity. *Nature, 258*, 577–579.

Hunt, E. (2001). Multiple views of multiple intelligence [review of the book *Intelligence reframed: Multiple intelligence in the 21st century*]. *Contemporary Psychology, 46*, 5–7.

Hunt, E. (2011). Where are we? Where are we going? Reflections on the current and future state of research on intelligence. In R. J. Sternberg, & S. B. Kaufman (Eds.), *Cambridge handbook of intelligence*. New York, NY: Cambridge University Press.

Hunt, E., & Carlson, J. (2007). Considerations relating to the study of group differences in intelligence. *Perspectives on Psychological Science, 2*(2), 194–213. doi:10.1111/j.1745-6916.2007.00037.x

Huntjens, R. C., Peters, M. L., Woertman, L., Bovenschen, L. M., Martin, R. C., & Postma, A. (2006). Inter-identity amnesia in dissociative identity disorder: A simulated memory impairment? *Psychological Medicine, 36*, 857–863. doi:10.1017/S0033291706007100

Hustinx, P. J., Kuyper, H., van der Werf, M. C., & Dijkstra, P. (2009). Achievement motivation revisited: New longitudinal data to demonstrate its predictive power. *Educational Psychology, 29*(5), 561–582. doi:10.1080/01443410903132128

Huttenlocher, P. R. (1994). Synaptogenesis in human cerebral cortex. In G. Dawson & K. W. Fischer (Eds.), *Human behavior and the developing brain*. New York, NY: Guilford Press.

Huttenlocher, P. R. (2002). *Neural plasticity: The effects of environment on the development of the cerebral cortex*. Cambridge, MA: Harvard University Press.

Hutter, M., Sweldens, S., Stahl, C., Unkelbach, C., & Klauer, K. C. (2012). Dissociating contingency awareness and conditioned attitudes: Evidence of contingency-unaware evaluative conditioning. *Journal of Experimental Psychology: General, 141*, 539–557. doi:10.1037/a0026477

Huynh, M., Gupta, R., & Koo, J. Y. (2013). Emotional stress as a trigger for inflammatory skin disorders. *Seminars in Cutaneous Medicine and Surgery, 32*, 68–72.

Hwang, W. C. (2006). The psychotherapy adaptation and modification framework: Application to Asian Americans. *American Psychologist, 61*, 702–715.

Hyde, J. S. (2014). Gender similarities and differences. *Annual Review of Psychology, 65*, 373–398. doi:10.1146/annurev-psych-010213-115057

Hyde, J. S., & Mertz, J. E. (2009). Gender, culture, and mathematics performance. *Proceedings of the National Academy of Sciences of the United States of America, 106*(22), 8801–8807. doi:10.1073/pnas.0901265106

Hyman, I. E., Jr., & Kleinknecht, E. E. (1999). False childhood memories: Research, theory, and applications. In L. M. Williams, & V. L. Banyard (Eds.), *Trauma & memory*. Thousand Oaks, CA: Sage.

Iacoboni, M. (2012). The human mirror neuron system and its role in imitation and empathy. In F. M. de Waal, & P. F. Ferrari (Eds.), *The primate mind: Built to connect with other minds* (pp. 32–47). Cambridge, MA: Harvard University Press. doi:10.4159/harvard.9780674062917.c3

Iacoboni, M., & Dapretto, M. (2006). The mirror neuron system and the consequences of its dysfunction. *Nature Reviews Neuroscience, 7*, 942–951.

Iacono, W. G. (2008). Effective policing: Understanding how polygraph tests work and are used. *Criminal Justice and Behavior, 35*, 1295–1308. doi:10.1177/0093854808321529

Ickovics, J. R., Thayaparan, B., & Ethier, K. A. (2001). Women and AIDS: A contextual analysis. In A. Baum, T. A. Revenson, & J. E. Singer (Eds.), *Handbook of health psychology* (pp. 817–840). Mahwah, NJ: Erlbaum.

Idring, S., Lundberg, M., Sturm, H., Dalman, C., Gumpert, C., Rai, D., . . . Magnusson, C. (2014). Changes in prevalence of autism spectrum disorders in 2001–2011: Findings from the Stockholm youth cohort. *Journal of Autism and Developmental Disorders*. Advance online publication. doi:10.1007/s10803-014-2336-y

Infante, J. R., Torres-Avisbal, M., Pinel, P., Vallejo. J. A., Peran, F., Gonzalez, F., Contreras, P., Pacheco, C., Roldan, A., & Latre, J. M. (2001). Catecholamine levels in practitioners of the transcendental meditation technique. *Physiology & Behavior, 72*(1–2), 141–146.

Ingram, R. E., Scott, W. D., & Hamill, S. (2009). Depression: Social and cognitive aspects. In P. H. Blaney & T. Millon (Eds.), *Oxford textbook of psychopathology* (2nd ed., pp. 230–252). New York, NY: Oxford University Press.

Insel, T. R. (2010). Psychiatrists' relationships with pharmaceutical companies: Part of the problem or part of the solution? *JAMA, 303*(12), 1192–1193. doi:10.1001/jama.2010.317

Inzlicht, M., & Kang, S. K. (2010). Stereotype threat spillover: How coping with threats to social identity affects aggression, eating, decision making, and attention. *Journal of Personality and Social Psychology, 99*(3), 467–481. doi:10.1037/a0018951

Iredale, S. K., Nevill, C. H., & Lutz, C. K. (2010). The influence of observer presence on baboon (*Papio spp.*) and rhesus macaque (*Macaca mulatta*) behavior. *Applied Animal Behaviour Science, 122*(1), 53–57. doi:10.1016/j.applanim.2009.11.002.

Ireland, M. (2012). Meditation and psychological health and functioning: A descriptive and critical review. *Scientific Review of Mental Health Practice: Objective Investigations of Controversial and Unorthodox Claims in Clinical Psychology, Psychiatry, and Social Work, 9*, 4–19.

Irvine, S. H., & Berry, J. W. (1988). *Human abilities in cultural context*. New York, NY: Cambridge University Press.

Isaacowitz, D. M., & Seligman, M. E. P. (2007). Learned helplessness. In G. Fink (Ed.), *Encyclopedia of stress*. San Diego, CA: Elsevier.

Israel, S., Hart, E., & Winter, E. (2013). Oxytocin decreases accuracy in the perception of social deception. *Psychological Science, 25*, 293–295. doi:10.1177/0956797613500794

Iwawaki, S., & Vernon, P. E. (1988). Japanese abilities and achievements. In S. H. Irvine & J. W. Berry (Eds.), *Human abilities in cultural context*. New York, NY: Cambridge University Press.

Izard, C. E. (1984). Emotion-cognition relationships and human development. In C. E. Izard, J. Kagan, & R. B. Zajonc (Eds.), *Emotions, cognition and behavior*. Cambridge, England: Cambridge University Press.

Izard, C. E. (1990). Facial expressions and the regulation of emotions. *Journal of Personality and Social Psychology, 58*, 487–498.

Izard, C. E. (1991). *The psychology of emotions*. New York, NY: Plenum.

Izard, C. E. (1994). Innate and universal facial expressions: Evidence from developmental and cross-cultural research. *Psychological Bulletin, 115,* 288–299.

Jackson, L. M. (2011). *The psychology of prejudice: From attitudes to social action.* Washington, DC: American Psychological Association.

Jacobs, D. F. (2004). Youth gambling in North America: Long-term trends and future prospects. In J. L. Derevensky & R. Gupta (Eds.), *Gambling problems in youth: Theoretical and applied perspectives* (pp. 1-24). New York, NY: Kluwer/Plenum.

Jacobson, E. (1938). *Progressive relaxation.* Chicago, IL: University of Chicago Press.

James, B. D., Wilson, R. S., Barnes, L. L., & Bennett, D. A. (2011). Late-life social activity and cognitive decline in old age. *Journal of International Neuropsychological Society, 17,* 998–1005. doi:10.1017/S1355617711000531

James, C. E., Oechslin, M. S., Van De Ville, D., Hauert, C., Descloux, C., & Lazeyras, F. (2014). Musical training intensity yields opposite effects on grey matter density in cognitive versus sensorimotor networks. *Brain Structure & Function, 219,* 353–366. doi:10.1007/s00429-013-0504-z

James, W. (1884). What is emotion? *Mind, 19,* 188–205.

James, W. (1890). *The principles of psychology.* New York, NY: Holt.

James, W. (1902). *The varieties of religious experience.* New York, NY: Modern Library.

James, W. H. (2005). Biological and psychosocial determinants of male and female human sexual orientation. *Journal of Biosocial Science, 37,* 555–567.

Jamison, K. R. (1988). Manic-depressive illness and accomplishment: Creativity, leadership, and social class. In F. K. Goodwin & K. R. Jamison (Eds.), *Manic-depressive illness.* Oxford, England: Oxford University Press.

Janis, I. L. (1958). *Psychological stress.* New York, NY: Wiley.

Janis, I. L. (1972). *Victims of groupthink.* Boston, MA: Houghton Mifflin.

Janofsky, J. S., Dunn, M. H., Roskes, E. J., Briskin, J. K., & Rudolph, M. L. (1996). Insanity defense pleas in Baltimore City: An analysis of outcome. *The American Journal of Psychiatry, 153,* 1464–1468.

Janssen, L., Fennis, B. M., & Pruyn, A. H. (2010). Forewarned is forearmed: Conserving self-control strength to resist social influence. *Journal of Experimental Social Psychology, 46*(6), 911–921. doi:10.1016/j.jesp.2010.06.008

Jaremka, L. M., Fagundes, C. P., Glaser, R., Bennett, J. M., Malarkey, W. B., & Kiecolt-Glaser, J. K. (2013). Loneliness predicts pain, depression, and fatigue: Understanding the role of immune dysregulation. *Psychoneuroendocrinology, 38,* 1310–1317. doi:10.1016/j.psyneuen.2012.11.016

Jauhar, S., & Cavanagh, J. (2013). Classification and epidemiology of bipolar disorder. In M. Power (Ed.), *The Wiley-Blackwell handbook of mood disorders* (2nd ed.). Malden, MA: Wiley-Blackwell.

Jellinger, K. A. (2013). Organic bases of late-life depression: A critical update. *Journal of Neural Transmission, 120,* 1109–1125. doi:10.1007/s00702-012-0945-1

Jelovac, A., Kolshus, E., & McLoughlin, D. M. (2013). Relapse following successful electroconvulsive therapy for major depression: A meta-analysis. *Neuropsychopharmacology, 38,* 2467–2474. doi:10.1038/npp.2013.149

Jensen, A. R. (1969). How much can we boost IQ and scholastic achievement? *Harvard Educational Review, 39,* 1–23.

Jensen, M. P., & Patterson, D. R. (2014). Hypnotic approaches for chronic pain management: Clinical implications of recent research findings. *American Psychologist, 69,* 167–177. doi:10.1037/a0035644

Jensen, M. P., & Turk, D. C. (2014). Contributions of psychology to the understanding and treatment of people with chronic pain: Why it matters to all psychologists. *American Psychologist, 69*(2), 105–118. doi:10.1037/a0035641

Jessberger, S., Aimone, J. B., & Gage, F. H. (2009). Neurogenesis. In J. H. Byrne (Ed.), *Concise learning and memory: The editor's selection.* San Diego, CA: Elsevier.

Jessup, R. K., Veinott, E. S., Todd, P. M., & Busemeyer, J. R. (2009). Leaving the store empty-handed: Testing explanations for the too-much-choice effect using decision field theory. *Psychology & Marketing, 26*(3), 299–320. doi:10.1002/mar.20274

Ji, R. R., Berta, T., & Nedergaard, M. (2013). Glia and pain: Is chronic pain a gliopathy? *Pain, 154,* S10–28. doi:10.1016/j.pain.2013.06.022

Joffe, R. T. (2009). Neuropsychiatric aspects of multiple sclerosis and other demyelinating disorders. In B. J. Sadock, V. A. Sadock, & P. Ruiz (Eds.), *Kaplan & Sadock's comprehensive textbook of psychiatry* (9th ed., Vol. 1, pp. 248–272). Philadelphia, PA: Lippincott Williams & Wilkins.

John, U., Rumpf, H., Bischof, G., Hapke, U., Hanke, M., & Meyer, C. (2013). Excess mortality of alcohol-dependent individuals after 14 years and mortality predictors based on treatment participation and severity of alcohol dependence. *Alcoholism: Clinical and Experimental Research, 37*(1), 156–163. doi:10.1111/j.1530-0277.2012.01863.x

Johnson, A. W. (2003). Procedural memory and skill acquisition. In A. F. Healy & R. W. Proctor (Eds.), *Handbook of psychology: Vol. 4. Experimental psychology.* New York, NY: Wiley.

Johnson, A. W. (2013a). Eating beyond metabolic need: How environmental cues influence feeding behavior. *Trends in Neurosciences, 36*(2), 101–109. doi:10.1016/j.tins.2013.01.002

Johnson, A. W. (2013b). Procedural memory and skill acquisition. In A. F. Healy, R. W. Proctor, & I. B. Weiner (Eds.), *Handbook of psychology: Vol. 4. Experimental psychology* (2nd ed.). New York, NY: Wiley.

Johnson, B. T., & Eagly, A. H. (2014). Meta-analysis of research in social psychology and personality psychology. In H. T. Reis & C. M. Judd (Eds.), *Handbook of research methods in social and personality psychology* (2nd ed.). New York, NY: Cambridge University Press.

Johnson, J. (2013). Vulnerable subjects? The case of nonhuman animals in experimentation. *Journal of Bioethical Inquiry, 10*(4), 497–504. doi:10.1007/s11673-013-9473-4

Johnson, M. K. (1996). Fact, fantasy, and public policy. In D. J. Herrmann, C. McEvoy, C. Hertzog, P. Hertel, & M. K. Johnson (Eds.), *Basic and applied memory research: Theory in context* (Vol. 1). Mahwah, NJ: Erlbaum.

Johnson, M. K. (2006). Memory and reality. *American Psychologist, 61,* 760–771.

Johnson, M. K., Raye, C. L., Mitchell, K. J., & Ankudowich, E. (2012). The cognitive neuroscience of the true and false memories. In R. F. Belli (Ed.), *True and false recovered memories: Toward a reconciliation of the debate.* New York, NY: Springer.

Johnson, S. B., & Carlson, D. N. (2004). Medical regimen adherence: Concepts, assessment, and interventions. In J. M. Raczynski & L. C. Leviton (Eds.), *Handbook of clinical health psychology: Vol 2. Disorders of behavior and health.* Washington, DC: American Psychological Association.

Johnson, S. L., Cuellar, A. K., & Peckham, A. D. (2014). Risk factors for bipolar disorder. In I. H. Gotlib & C. L. Hammen (Eds.), *Handbook of depression* (3rd ed.). New York, NY: Guilford Press.

Johnson, W. (2010). Understanding the genetics of intelligence: Can height help? Can corn oil? *Current Directions in Psychological Science, 19*(3), 177–182. doi:10.1177/0963721410370136

Johnson, W., & Krueger, R. F. (2006). How money buys happiness: Genetic and environmental processes linking finances and life satisfaction. *Journal of Personality and Social Psychology, 90,* 680–691.

Johnson, W., Turkheimer, E., Gottesman, I. I., & Bouchard, T. R. (2009). Beyond heritability: Twin studies in behavioral research. *Current Directions in Psychological Science, 18*(4), 217–220. doi:10.1111/j.1467-8721.2009.01639.x

Johnston, J. C., & McClelland, J. L. (1974). Perception of letters in words: Seek not and ye shall find. *Science, 184,* 1192–1194.

Joiner, T. E., Jr., & Timmons, K. A. (2009). Depression in its interpersonal context. In I. H. Gotlib & C. L. Hammen (Eds.), *Handbook of depression* (2nd ed., pp. 322–339). New York, NY: Guilford Press.

Jones, E. E., & Davis, K. E. (1965). From acts to dispositions: The attribution process in person perception. In L. Berkowitz (Ed.), *Advances in experimental social psychology* (Vol. 2). New York, NY: Academic Press.

Jones, E. E., & Nisbett, R. E. (1971). The actor and the observer: Divergent perceptions of the causes of behavior. In E. E. Jones, D. E. Kanouse, H. H. Kelley, R. E. Nisbett, S. Valins, & B. Weiner (Eds.), *Attribution: Perceiving the causes of behavior.* Morristown, NJ: General Learning Press.

Jones, S. G., & Benca, R. M. (2013). Sleep and biological rhythms. In R. J. Nelson, S. Y. Mizumori, & I. B. Weiner (Eds.), *Handbook of psychology: Vol. 3. Behavioral neuroscience* (2nd ed., pp. 365–394). New York, NY: Wiley.

Jones, S. M., & Dindia, K. (2004). A meta-analytic perspective on sex equity in the classroom. *Review of Educational Research, 74,* 443–471.

Jordan-Young, R. M. (2010). *Brainstorm: The flaws in the science of sex differences.* Cambridge, MA: Harvard University Press.

Josephs, L., & Weinberger, J. (2013). Psychodynamic psychotherapy. In G. Stricker & T. A. Widiger (Eds.), *Handbook of psychology: Vol. 8. Clinical psychology* (2nd ed.). New York, NY: Wiley.

Josse, G., & Tzourio-Mazoyer, N. (2004). Hemispheric specialization for language. *Brain Research Reviews, 44,* 1–12.

Judge, T. A., Hurst, C., & Simon, L. S. (2009). Does it pay to be smart, attractive, or confident (or all three)? Relationships among general mental ability, physical attractiveness, core self-evaluations, and income. *Journal of Applied Psychology, 94*(3), 742–755. doi:10.1037/a0015497

Judge, T. A., & Klinger, R. (2008). Job satisfaction: Subjective well-being at work. In M. Eid & R. J. Larsen (Eds.), *The science of subjective well-being.* New York, NY: Guilford Press.

Judge, T. A., Livingston, B. A., & Hurst, C. (2012). Do nice guys—and gals—really finish last? The joint effects of sex and agreeableness on income. *Journal of Personality and Social Psychology, 102,* 390–407. doi:10.1037/a0026021

Jung, C. G. (1921/1960). *Psychological types.* In H. Read, M. Fordham, & G. Adler (Eds.), *Collected works of C. G. Jung* (Vol. 6). Princeton, NJ: Princeton University Press.

Jung, C. G. (1933). *Modern man in search of a soul.* New York, NY: Harcourt, Brace & World.

Juruena, M. F. (2014). Early-life stress and HPA axis trigger recurrent adulthood depression. *Epilepsy & Behavior, 38,* 148–159. doi:10.1016/j.yebeh.2013.10.020

Kaas, J. H. (2000). The reorganization of sensory and motor maps after injury in adult mammals. In M. S. Gazzaniga (Ed.), *The new cognitive neurosciences.* Cambridge, MA: The MIT Press.

Kaas, J. H., O'Brien, B. M. J., & Hackett, T. A. (2013). Auditory processing in primate brains. In R. J. Nelson, S. J. Y. Mizumori, & I. B. Weiner (Eds.), *Handbook of psychology: Vol. 3. Behavioral neuroscience* (2nd ed.). New York, NY: Wiley.

Kagan, J. (1998, November/December). A parent's influence is peerless. *Harvard Education Letter.*

Kagan, J., & Fox, A. (2006). Biology, culture, and temperamental biases. In N. Eisenberg, W. Damon, & R. M. Lerner (Eds.), *Handbook of child psychology: Social, emotional, and personality development.* Hoboken, NJ: Wiley.

Kahn, D. (2007). Metacognition, cognition, and reflection while dreaming. In D. Barrett & P. McNamara (Eds.), *The new science of dreaming.* Westport, CT: Praeger.

Kahneman, D. (1999). Objective happiness. In D. Kahneman, E. Diener, & N. Schwarz (Eds.), *Well-being: The foundations of hedonic psychology.* New York, NY: Russell Sage Foundation.

Kahneman, D. (2011). *Thinking, fast and slow.* New York, NY: Farrar, Straus, and Giroux.

Kahneman, D., & Deaton, A. (2010). High income improves evaluation of life but not emotional well-being. *Proceedings of the National Academy of Sciences of the United States of America, 107*(38), 16489–16493. doi:10.1073/pnas.1011492107

Kahneman, D., & Tversky, A. (1973). On the psychology of prediction. *Psychological Review, 80,* 237–251.

Kahneman, D., & Tversky, A. (1982). Subjective probability: A judgment of representativeness. In D. Kahneman, P. Slovic, & A. Tversky (Eds.), *Judgment under uncertainty: Heuristics and biases.* Cambridge: Cambridge University Press.

Kahneman, D., & Tversky, A. (1984). Choices, values, and frames. *American Psychologist, 39,* 341–350.

Kahneman, D., & Tversky, A. (2000). *Choices, values, and frames.* New York, NY: Cambridge University Press.

Kaiser, A., Haller, S., Schmitz, S., & Nitsch, C. (2009). On sex/gender related similarities and differences in fMRI language research. *Brain Research Reviews, 61*(2), 49–59. doi:10.1016/j.brainresrev.2009.03.005

Kakizaki, M., Kuriyama, S., Nakaya, N., Sone, T., Nagai, M., Sugawara, Y., . . . Tsuji, I. (2013). Long sleep duration and cause-specific mortality according to physical function and self-rated health: The Oshaki Cohort Study. *Journal of Sleep Research, 22,* 209–216. doi:10.1111/j.1365-2869.2012.01053.x

Kalat, J. W. (2013). *Biological psychology* (11th ed.). Belmont, CA: Wadsworth Cengage Learning.

Kalichman, S. C. (1995). *Understanding AIDS: A guide for mental health professionals.* Washington, DC: American Psychological Association.

Kalmijn, M. (1998). Intermarriage and homogamy: Causes, patterns, trends. *Annual Review of Sociology, 24,* 395–421.

Kaltenbach, K., & Jones, H. (2011). Maternal and neonatal complications of alcohol and other drugs. In P. Ruiz & E. C. Strain (Eds.), *Lowinson and Ruiz's substance abuse: A comprehensive textbook* (5th ed.). Philadelphia, PA: Lippincott Williams & Wilkins.

Kanaan, S. F., McDowd, J. M., Colgrove, Y., Burns, J. M., Gajewski, B., & Pohl, P. S. (2014). Feasibility and efficacy of intensive cognitive training in early-stage Alzheimer's disease. *American Journal of Alzheimer's Disease and Other Dementias, 29,* 150–158. doi:10.1177/1533317513506775

Kanazawa, S. (2006). Mind the gap . . . in intelligence: Reexamining the relationship between inequality and health. *British Journal of Health Psychology, 11,* 623–642.

Kandel, E. R. (2000). Nerve cells and behavior. In E. R. Kandel, J. H. Schwartz, & T. M. Jessell (Eds.), *Principles of neural science* (pp. 19–35). New York, NY: McGraw-Hill.

Kandel, E. R. (2001). The molecular biology of memory storage: A dialogue between genes and synapses. *Science, 294,* 1030–1038.

Kandel, E. R., Barres, B. A., & Hudspeth, A. J. (2013). Nerve cells, neural circuitry, and behavior. In E. R. Kandel, J. H. Schwartz, T. M. Jessell, S. A. Siegelbaum, & A. J. Hudspeth (Eds.), *Principles of neural science* (5th ed., pp. 21–38). New York, NY: McGraw-Hill.

Kandel, E. R., & Siegelbaum, S. A. (2013). Signaling at the nerve-muscle synapse: Directly gated transmission. In E. R. Kandel, J. H. Schwartz, T. M. Jessell, S. A. Siegelbaum, & A. J. Hudspeth (Eds.), *Principles of neural science* (5th ed.). New York, NY: McGraw-Hill.

Kane, J. M., Stroup, T. S., & Marder, S. R. (2009). Schizophrenia: Pharmacological treatment. In B. J. Sadock, V. A. Sadock, & P. Ruiz (Eds.), *Kaplan & Sadock's comprehensive textbook of psychiatry* (pp. 1547–1555). Philadelphia, PA: Lippincott Williams & Wilkins.

Kane, M. J., Brown, L. H., McVay, J. C., Silivia, P. J., Myin-Germeys, I., & Kwapil, T. R. (2007). For whom the mind wanders, and when: An experience-sampling study of working memory and executive control in daily life. *Psychological Science, 18,* 614–621.

Kang, D., Jo, H J., Jung, W. H., Kim, S. H., Jung, Y., Choi, C., . . . Kwon, J. S. (2013). The effect of mediation on brain structure: Cortical thickness mapping and diffusion tensor imaging. *Social Cognitive and Affective Neuroscience, 8,* 27–33. doi:10.1093/scan/nss056

Kanno, T., Iijima, K., Abe, Y., Koike, T., Shimada, N., Hoshi, T., . . . Shimosegawa, T. (2013). Peptic ulcers after the Great East Japan earthquake and tsunami: Possible existence of psychosocial stress ulcers in humans. *Journal of Gastroenterology, 48,* 483–490. doi:10.1007/s00535-012-0681-1

Kanwisher, N., & Yovel, G. (2009). Face perception. In G. G. Berntson & J. T. Cacioppo (Eds.), *Handbook of neuroscience for the behavioral sciences.* New York, NY: Wiley.

Kaplan, K. A., Itoi, A., & Dement, W. C. (2007). Awareness of sleepiness and ability to predict sleep onset: Can drivers avoid falling asleep at the wheel? *Sleep Medicine, 9*(1), 71–79. doi:10.1016/j.sleep.2007.02.001

Karasu, T. B. (2005). Psychoanalysis and psychoanalytic psychotherapy. In B. J. Sadock & V. A. Sadock (Eds.), *Kaplan and Sadock's comprehensive textbook of psychiatry.* Philadelphia, PA: Lippincott Williams & Wilkins.

Karpicke, J. D. (2012). Retrieval-based learning: Active retrieval promotes meaningful learning. *Current Directions in Psychological Science, 21,* 157–163. doi:10.1177/0963721412443552

Karpicke, J. D., & Blunt, J. R. (2011). Retrieval practice produces more learning than elaborate studying with concept mapping. *Science, 331,* 772–775. doi:10.1126/science.1199327

Kassam, K. S., Gilbert, D. T., Swencionis, J. K., & Wilson, T. D. (2009). Misconceptions of memory: The Scooter Libby effect. *Psychological Science, 20*(5), 551–552. doi:10.1111/j.1467-9280.2009.02334.x

Kasser, T., & Sharma, Y. S. (1999). Reproductive freedom, educational equality, and females' preference for resource-aquisition characteristics in mates. *Psychological Science, 10,* 374–377.

Katsikopoulos, K. V., & Gigerenzer, G. (2013). Modeling decision heuristics. In J. D. Lee, & A. Kirlik (Eds.), *Oxford handbook of cognitive engineering.* New York, NY: Oxford University Press.

Katz-Wise, S. L., & Hyde, J. S. (2014). Sexuality and gender: The interplay. In D. L. Tolman, L. M. Diamond, J. A. Bauermeister, W. H. George, J. G. Pfaus, & L. M. Ward (Eds.), *APA handbook of sexuality and psychology: Vol. 1. Person-based approaches.* Washington, DC: American Psychological Association.

Kaufman, A. S. (2000). Tests of intelligence. In R. J. Sternberg (Ed.), *Handbook of intelligence* (pp. 445–476). New York, NY: Cambridge University Press.

Kaufman, J. C., & Baer, J. (2004). Hawking's haiku, Madonna's math: Why it is hard to be creative in every room of the house. In R. J. Sternberg, E. L. Grigorenko, & J. L. Singer (Eds.), *Creativity: From potential to realization.* Washington, DC: American Psychological Association.

Kaufman, J. C., Kaufman, S. B., & Plucker, J. A. (2013). Contemporary theories of intelligence. In D. Reisberg (Ed.), *Oxford handbook of cognitive psychology*. New York, NY: Oxford University Press.

Kaufman, J. C., & Plucker, J. A. (2011). Intelligence and creativity. In R. J. Sternberg, & S. B. Kaufman (Eds.), *Cambridge handbook of intelligence*. New York, NY: Cambridge University Press.

Kaufman, L., Vassiliades, V., Noble, R., Alexander, R., Kaufman, J., & Edlund, S. (2007). Perceptual distance and the moon illusion. *Spatial Vision, 20,* 155–175. doi:10.1163/156856807779369698

Kauwe, J. S. K., Ridge, P. G., Foster, N. L., Cannon-Albright, L. A. (2013). Strong evidence for a genetic contribution to late-onset Alzheimer's disease mortality: A population-based study. *PLoS ONE, 8,* e77087.

Kazdin, A. (1994). Methodology, design, and evaluation in psychotherapy research. In A. E. Bergin & S. L. Garfield (Eds.), *Handbook of psychotherapy and behavior change* (4th ed.). New York, NY: Wiley.

Kazdin, A. (2001). *Behavior modification in applied settings.* Belmont: Wadsworth.

Kazdin, A., & Benjet, C. (2003). Spanking children: Evidence and issues. *Current Directions in Psychological Science, 12*(3), 99–103.

Kazdin, A. E., & Blase, S. L. (2011). Rebooting psychotherapy research and practice to reduce the burden of mental illness. *Perspectives on Psychological Science, 6*(1), 21–37. doi:10.1177/1745691610393527

Kazdin, A. E., & Rabbitt, S. M. (2013). Novel models for delivering mental health services and reducing the burdens of mental illness. *Clinical Psychological Science, 1*(2), 170–191. doi:10.1177/2167702612463566

Keefer, L., Taft, T. h., & Kiebles, J. L. (2013). Gastrointestinal diseases. In A. M. Nezu, C. M. Nezu, P. A. Geller, & I. B. Weiner (Eds.), *Handbook of psychology: Vol. 9. Health psychology* (2nd ed.). New York, NY: Wiley.

Keel, P. K., Brown, T. A., Holland, L. A., & Bodell, L. P. (2012). Empirical classification of eating disorders. *Annual Review Of Clinical Psychology, 8*381–404. doi:10.1146/annurev-clinpsy-032511-143111

Keel, P. K., Forney, K. J., Brown, T. A., & Heatherton, T. F. (2013). Influence of college peers on disordered eating in women and men at 10-year follow-up. *Journal of Abnormal Psychology, 122,* 105–110. doi:10.1037/a0030081

Keenan, S., & Hirshkowitz, M. (2011). Monitoring and staging human sleep. In M. H. Kryger, T. Roth, & W. C. Dement (Eds.), *Principles and practice of sleep medicine* (5th ed.). Saint Louis, MO: Elsevier Saunders.

Keller, M. B., Boland, R., Leon, A., Solomon, D., Endicott, J., & Li, C. (2013). Clinical course and outcome of unipolar major depression. In M. B. Keller, W. H. Coryell, J. Endicott, J. D. Maser, & P. J. Schettler (Eds.), *Clinical guide to depression and bipolar disorder: Findings from the Collaborative Depression Study.* Washington, DC: American Psychiatric Press.

Kelley, H. H. (1950). The warm-cold variable in first impressions of persons. *Journal of Personality, 18,* 431–439.

Kelley, H. H. (1967). Attributional theory in social psychology. *Nebraska Symposium on Motivation, 15,* 192–241.

Kellner, C. H., Greenberg, R. M., Murrough, J. W., Bryson, E. O., Briggs, M. C., & Pasculli, R. M. (2012). ECT in treatment-resistant depression. *The American Journal of Psychiatry, 169,* 1238–1244. doi:10.1176/appi.ajp.2012.12050648

Kelman, H. C. (1967). Human use of human subjects: The problem of deception in social psychological experiments. *Psychological Bulletin, 67,* 1–11.

Kelman, H. C. (1982). Ethical issues in different social science methods. In T. L. Beauchamp, R. R. Faden, R. J. Wallace, Jr., & L. Walters (Eds.), *Ethical issues in social science research.* Baltimore: Johns Hopkins University Press.

Keltner, D., & Horberg, E. J. (2015). Emotion-cognition interactions. In M. Mikulincer, P. R. Shaver, E. Borgida, & J. A. Bargh (Eds.), *APA handbook of personality and social psychology: Vol. 1. Attitudes and social cognition.* Washington, DC: American Psychological Association. doi:10.1037/14341-020

Kemeny, M. E. (2011). Psychoneuroimmunology. In H. S. Friedman (Ed.), *Oxford handbook of health psychology.* New York, NY: Oxford University Press.

Kempton, M. J., Salvador, Z., Munafò, M. R., Geddes, J. R., Simmons, A., Frangou, S., & Williams, S. R. (2011). Structural neuroimaging studies in major depressive disorder: Meta-analysis and comparison with bipolar disorder. *Archives of General Psychiatry, 68,* 675–690. doi:10.1001/archgenpsychiatry.2011.60

Kendzerska, T., Mollayeva, T., Gershon, A. S., Leung, R. S., Hawker, G., & Tomlinson, G. (2014). Untreated obstructive sleep apnea and the risk of serious long-term adverse outcomes: A systematic review. *Sleep Medicine Reviews, 18,* 49–59. doi:10.1016/j.smrv.2013.01.003

Kenfield, S. A., Stampfer, M. J., Rosner, B. A., & Colditz, G. A. (2008). Smoking and smoking cessation in relation to mortality in women. *JAMA, 299,* 2037–2047.

Kenrick, D. T., Griskevicius, V., Neuberg, S. L., & Schaller, M. (2010). Renovating the pyramid of needs: Contemporary extensions built upon ancient foundations. *Perspectives on Psychological Science, 5*(3), 292–314. doi:10.1177/1745691610369469

Kenrick, D. T., & Gutierres, S. E. (1980). Contrast effects and judgments of physical attractiveness: When beauty becomes a social problem. *Journal of Personality and Social Psychology, 38,* 131–140.

Kenrick, D. T., Neuberg, S. L., & White, A. E. (2013). Relationships from an evolutionary life history perspective. In J. A. Simpson & L. Campbell (Eds.), *Oxford handbook of close relationships.* New York, NY: Oxford University Press.

Kenrick, D. T., Trost, M. R., & Sundie, J. M. (2004). Sex roles as adaptations: An evolutionary perspective on gender differences and similarities. In A. H. Eagly, A. E. Beall, & R. J. Sternberg (Eds.), *The psychology of gender.* New York, NY: Guilford Press.

Kermer, D. A., Driver-Linn, E., Wilson, T. D., & Gilbert, D. T. (2006). Loss aversion is an affective forecasting error. *Psychological Science, 17,* 649–653.

Kern, M. L., Della Porta, S. S., & Friedman, H. S. (2014). Lifelong pathways to longevity: Personality, relationships, flourishing, and health. *Journal of Personality, 82,* 472–484. doi:10.1111/jopy.12062

Kesebir, S., Graham, J., & Oishi, S. (2010). A theory of human needs should be human-centered, not animal-centered: Commentary on Kenrick et al. (2010). *Perspectives on Psychological Science, 5*(3), 315–319. doi:10.1177/1745691610369470

Ketter, T. A., & Chang, K. D. (2014). Bipolar and related disorders. In R. E. Hales, S. C. Yudofsky, & L. W. Roberts (Eds.), *The American Psychiatric Publishing textbook of psychiatry* (6th ed.). Washington, DC: American Psychiatric Publishing.

Kiang, L., & Buchanan, C. M. (2014). Daily stress and emotional well-being among Asian American adolescents: Same-day, lagged, and chronic associations. *Developmental Psychology, 50,* 611–621. doi:10.1037/a0033645

Kiecolt-Glaser, J. K. (2009). Psychoneuroimmunology: Psychology's gateway to biomedical future. *Perspective on Psychological Science, 4,* 367-369. doi:10.1111/j.1745-6924.2009.01139.x

Kiecolt-Glaser, J. K., Garner, W., Speicher, C., Penn, G. M., Holliday, J., & Glaser, R. (1984). Psychosocial modifiers of immunocompetence in medical students. *Psychosomatic Medicine, 46*(1), 7–14.

Kihlstrom, J. F. (2004). An unbalanced balancing act: Blocked, recovered, and false memories in the laboratory and clinic. *Clinical Psychology: Science & Practice, 11*(1), 34–41.

Kihlstrom, J. F., & Cork, R. C. (2007). Consciousness and anesthesia. In M. Velmans & S. Schneider (Eds.), *The Blackwell companion to consciousness.* Malden, MA: Blackwell.

Killeen, P. R. (1981). Learning as causal inference. In M. L. Commons & J. A. Nevin (Eds.), *Quantitative analyses of behavior: Vol. 1. Discriminative properties of reinforcement schedules.* Cambridge, MA: Ballinger.

Killen, M., Hitti, A., & Mulvey, K. L. (2015). Social development and intergroup relations. In M. Mikulincer, P. R. Shaver, J. F. Dovidio, & J. A. Simpson (Eds.), *APA handbook of personality and social psychology: Vol. 2. Group processes* (pp. 177–201). doi.org/10.1037/14342-007

Killen, M., Richardson, C. B., & Kelly, M. C. (2010). Developmental perspectives. In J. F. Dovidio, M. Hewstone, P. Glick, & V. M. Esses (Eds.), *The Sage handbook of prejudice, stereotyping, and discrimination.* Los Angeles, CA: Sage.

Killingsworth, M. A., & Gilbert, D. T. (2010). A wandering mind is an unhappy mind. *Science, 330,* 932.

Kiluk, B. D., Sugarman, D. E., Nich, C., Gibbons, C. J., Martino, S., Rounsaville, B. J., & Carroll, K. M. (2011). A methodological analysis of randomized clinical trials of computer-assisted therapies for psychiatric disorders: Toward improved standards for an emerging field. *The American Journal of Psychiatry, 168,* 790–799. doi:10.1176/appi.ajp.2011.10101443

Kim, H., & Markus, H. R. (1999). Deviance or uniqueness, harmony or conformity? A cultural analysis. *Journal of Personality and Social Psychology, 77,* 785–800.

Kim, H. S., Sherman, D. K., & Taylor, S. E. (2008). Culture and social support. *American Psychologist, 63*(6), 518–526. doi:10.1037/0003-066X

Kim, K. H. (2005). Can only intelligent people be creative? *Journal of Secondary Gifted Education, 16,* 57–66.

Kim, S., Plumb, R., Gredig, Q., Rankin, L., & Taylor, B. (2008). Medium-term post-Katrina health sequelae among New Orleans residents: Predictors of poor mental and physical health. *Journal of Clinical Nursing, 17*(17), 2335–2342

Kimmel, A. J. (1996). *Ethical issues in behavioral research: A survey*. Cambridge, MA: Blackwell.

Kimura, D. (1973). The asymmetry of the human brain. *Scientific American, 228*, 70–78.

King, B. M. (2013). The modern obesity epidemic, ancestral hunter-gatherers, and the sensory/reward control of food intake. *American Psychologist, 68*(2), 88–96. doi:10.1037/a0030684

King, D. B., Woody, W. D., & Viney, W. (2013). *A history of psychology: Ideas and context*. New York, NY: Pearson.

Kinsey, A. C., Pomeroy, W. B., & Martin, C. E. (1948). *Sexual behavior in the human male*. Philadelphia, PA: Saunders.

Kinsey, A. C., Pomeroy, W. B., Martin, C. E., & Gebhard, P. H. (1953). *Sexual behavior in the human female*. Philadelphia, PA: Saunders.

Kirby, D. (2005). *Evidence of harm: Mercury in vaccines and the autism epidemic: A medical controversy*. New York, NY: St. Martin's Press.

Kirk, R. E. (2013). Experimental design. In J. A. Schinka, W. F. Velicer, & I. B. Weiner (Eds.), *Handbook of psychology: Vol. 2. Research methods in psychology* (2nd ed.). Hoboken, NJ: Wiley.

Kirk, S. A., Gomory, T., & Cohen, D. (2013). *Mad science: Psychiatric coercion, diagnosis, and drugs*. New Brunswick, NJ: Transaction Publishers.

Kirov, G., & Owen, M. J. (2009). Genetics of schizophrenia. In B. J. Sadock, V. A. Sadock, & P. Ruiz (Eds.), *Kaplan & Sadock's comprehensive textbook of psychiatry* (9th ed., Vol. 1, pp. 1462–1472). Philadelphia, PA: Lippincott Williams & Wilkins.

Kirsch, I. (2000). The response set theory of hypnosis. *American Journal of Clinical Hypnosis, 42*, 274–292.

Kirsch, I. (2010). *The emperor's new drugs: Exploding the antidepressant myth*. New York, NY: Basic Books.

Kirsch, I., Mazzoni, G., & Montgomery, G. H. (2007). Remembrance of hypnosis past. *American Journal of Clinical Hypnosis, 49*, 171–178.

Kissileff, H. R., Thornton, J. C., Torres, M. I., Pavlovich, K., Mayer, L. S., Kalari, V., . . . Rosenbaum, M. (2012). Leptin reverses declines in satiation in weight-reduced obese humans. *The American Journal of Clinical Nutrition, 95*, 309–317.

Klatzky, R. L., & Lederman, S. J. (2013). Touch. In A. F. Healy, R. W. Proctor, & I. B. Weiner (Eds.), *Handbook of psychology: Vol. 4.*

Experimental psychology (2nd ed.). New York, NY: Wiley.

Klein, D. N., & Allmann, A. E. (2014). Course of depression: Persistence and recurrence. In I. H. Gotlib & C. L. Hammen (Eds.), *Handbook of depression* (3rd ed.). New York, NY: Guilford Press.

Kleinke, C. L. (2007). What does it mean to cope? In A. Monat, R. S. Lazarus, & G. Reevy (Eds.), *The Praeger handbook on stress and coping*. Westport, CT: Praeger.

Kleinmuntz, B. (1980). *Essentials of abnormal psychology*. San Francisco, CA: Harper & Row.

Kleinmuntz, B., & Szucko, J. J. (1984). Lie detection in ancient and modern times: A call for contemporary scientific study. *American Psychologist, 39*(7), 766–776. doi:10.1037/0003-066X.39.7.766

Kleinspehn-Ammerlahn, A., Kotter-Grühn, D., & Smith, J. (2008). Self-perceptions of aging: Do subjective age and satisfaction with aging change during old age? *The Journals of Gerontology: Series B: Psychological Sciences and Social Sciences, 63B*(6), 377–385.

Klosch, G., & Kraft, U. (2005). Sweet dreams are made of this. *Scientific American Mind, 16*(2), 38–45.

Klump, K. L. (2013). Puberty as a critical risk period for eating disorders: A review of human and animal behaviors. *Hormones and Behavior, 64*, 399–410. doi:10.1016/j.yhbeh.2013.02.019

Knapp, C. M., & Kornetsky, C. (2009). Neural basis of pleasure and reward. In G. G. Berntson & J. T. Cacioppo (Eds.), *Handbook of neuroscience for the behavioral sciences* (Vol. 1, pp. 781–806). New York, NY: Wiley.

Knauss, W. (2005). Group psychotherapy. In G. O. Gabbard, J. S. Beck, & J. Holmes (Eds.), *Oxford textbook of psychotherapy*. New York, NY: Oxford University Press.

Knecht, S., Drager, B., Floel, A., Lohmann, H., Breitenstein, C., Henningsen, H., & Ringelstein, E. B. (2001). Behavioural relevance of atypical language lateralization in healthy subjects. *Brain, 124*, 1657–1665.

Knight, J. (2004). The truth about lying. *Nature, 428*, 692–694.

Knutson, K. L. (2012). Does inadequate sleep play a role in vulnerability to obesity? *American Journal of Human Biology, 24*, 361–371.

Knutson, K. L., & Van Cauter, E. (2008). Associations between sleep loss and increased risk of obesity and diabetes. In D. W. Pfaff, & B. L.

Kieffer (Eds.), *Annals of the New York Academy of Sciences. Molecular and biophysical mechanisms of arousal, alertness, and attention* (pp. 287–304). Malden, MA: Blackwell.

Kobrin, J. L., Patterson, B. F., Shaw, E. J., Mattern, K. D., & Barbuti, S. M. (2008). *Validity of the SAT for predicting first-year college grade point average* (College Board research report no. 2008-5). New York, NY: College Board.

Koehl, M., & Abrous, D. N. (2011). A new chapter in the field of memory: Adult hippocampal neurogenesis. *European Journal of Neuroscience, 33*, 1101–1114. doi:10.1111/j.1460-9568.2011.07609.x

Koenig, A. M., & Dean, K. K. (2011). Cross-cultural differences and similarities in attribution. In K. D. Keith (Ed.), *Cross-cultural psychology: Contemporary themes and perspectives*. Malden, MA: Wiley-Blackwell.

Kofink, D., Boks, M. M., Timmers, H. M., & Kas, M. J. (2013). Epigenetic dynamics in psychiatric disorders: Environmental programming of neurodevelopmental processes. *Neuroscience and Biobehavioral Reviews, 37*, 831–845. doi:10.1016/j.neubiorev.2013.03.020

Kohlberg, L. (1963). The development of children's orientations toward a moral order: I. Sequence in the development of moral thought. *Vita Humana, 6*, 11–33.

Kohlberg, L. (1969). Stage and sequence: The cognitive-developmental approach to socialization. In D. A. Goslin (Ed.), *Handbook of socialization theory and research*. Chicago, IL: Rand McNally.

Kohlberg, L. (1976). Moral stages and moralization: Cognitive-developmental approach. In T. Lickona (Ed.), *Moral development and behavior: Theory, research and social issues*. New York, NY: Holt, Rinehart & Winston.

Kohlberg, L. (1984). *Essays on moral development: Vol. 2. The psychology of moral development*. San Francisco, CA: Harper & Row.

Kohman, R. A., & Rhodes, J. S. (2013). Neurogenesis, inflammation and behavior. *Brain, Behavior, and Immunity, 27*, 22–32. doi:10.1016/j.bbi.2012.09.003

Koob, G. F. (2012). Neuroanatomy of addiction. In K. D. Brownell & M. S. Gold (Eds.), *Food and addiction: A comprehensive handbook*. New York, NY: Oxford University Press.

Koob, G. F., Everitt, B. J., & Robbins, T. W. (2008). Reward, motivation, and addiction. In L. Squire, D. Berg, F. Bloom, S. Du Lac, A. Ghosh, N. Spitzer (Eds.), *Fundamental neuroscience* (3rd ed., pp. 87–111). San Diego, CA: Elsevier.

Koob, G. F., & Le Moal, M. (2006). *Neurobiology of addiction*. San Diego, CA: Academic Press.

Koriat, A., & Bjork, R. A. (2005). Illusions of competence in monitoring one's knowledge during study. *Journal of Experimental Psychology: Learning, Memory, and Cognition, 31*(2), 187–194.

Koriat, A., Lichtenstein, S., & Fischhoff, B. (1980). Reasons for confidence. *Journal of Experimental Psychology, 6*, 107–118.

Korn, J. H. (1997). *Illusions of reality: A history of deception in social psychology*. Albany, NY: State University of New York Press.

Kornell, N., Castel, A. D., Eich, T. S., & Bjork, R. A. (2010). Spacing as the friend of both memory and induction in young and older adults. *Psychology and Aging, 25*(2), 498–503. doi:10.1037/a0017807

Kornell, N., Hays, M., & Bjork, R. A. (2009). Unsuccessful retrieval attempts enhance subsequent learning. *Journal of Experimental Psychology: Learning, Memory, and Cognition, 35*(4), 989–998. doi:10.1037/a0015729

Kornell, N., & Metcalfe, J. (2014). The effects of memory retrieval, errors and feedback on learning. In V. A. Benassi, C. E. Overson, & C. M. Hakala (Eds.), *Applying science of learning in education: Infusing psychological science into the curriculum*. Washington, DC: Society for the Teaching of Psychology.

Kosfeld, M., Heinrichs, M., Zak, P. J., Fischbacher, U., & Fehr, E. (2005). Oxytocin increases trust in humans. *Nature, 435*(7042), 673–676. doi:10.1038/nature03701

Kotovsky, K., Hayes, J. R., & Simon, H. A. (1985). Why are some problems hard? Evidence from Tower of Hanoi. *Cognitive Psychology, 17*, 248–294.

Kotulak, R. (1996). *Inside the brain: Revolutionary discoveries of how the mind works*. Kansas City, MO: Andrews McMeel.

Kouzma, N. M., & Kennedy, G. A. (2004). Self-reported sources of stress in senior high school students. *Psychological Reports, 94*, 314–316.

Kowalski, P., & Taylor, A. K. (2009). The effect of refuting misconceptions in the introductory psychology class. *Teaching of Psychology, 36*(3), 153–159. doi:10.1080/00986280902959986

Kozorovitskiy, Y., & Gould, E. (2007). Adult neurogenesis and regeneration in the brain. In Y. Sern (Ed.), *Cognitive reserve: Theory and applications*. Philadelphia, PA: Taylor and Francis.

Kozorovitskiy, Y., & Gould, E. (2008). Adult neurogenesis in the hippocampus. In C. A. Nelson, &

M. Luciana (Eds.), *Handbook of developmental cognitive neuroscience* (2nd ed., pp. 51–61). Cambridge, MA: MIT Press.

Kozulin, A. (2005). The concept of activity in Soviet psychology: Vygotsky, his disciples and critics. In H. Daniels (Ed.), *An introduction to Vygotsky.* New York, NY: Routledge.

Kracke, W. (1991). Myths in dreams, thought in images: An Amazonian contribution to the psychoanalytic theory of primary process. In B. Tedlock (Ed.), *Dreaming: Anthropological and psychological interpretations.* Santa Fe, NM: School of American Research Press.

Kraemer, H. C. (2008). DSM categories and dimensions in clinical and research contexts. In J. E. Helzer, H. C. Kraemer, R. F. Krueger, H.-U. Wittchen, P. J. Sirovatka, et al. (Eds.), *Dimensional approaches in diagnostic classification: Refining the research agenda for DSM-V* (pp. 5–17). Washington, DC: American Psychiatric Association.

Kraha, A., & Boals, A. (2014). Why so negative? Positive flashbulb memories for a personal event. *Memory, 22,* 442–449. doi:10.1080/09658211.2013.798121

Krahe, B. (2013). Violent video games and aggression. In K. E. Dill (Ed.), *Oxford handbook of media psychology.* New York, NY: Oxford University Press.

Krahe, B., Moller, I., Huesmann, L. R., Kirwil, L., Felber, J., & Berger, A. (2011). Desensitization to media violence: Links with habitual media violence exposure, aggressive cognitions, and aggressive behavior. *Journal of Personality and Social Psychology, 100,* 630–646. doi:10.1037/a0021711

Krakauer, D., & Dallenbach, K. M. (1937). Gustatory adaptation to sweet, sour, and bitter. *American Journal of Psychology, 49,* 469–475.

Krakauer, J. (1998). *Into thin air: A personal account of the Mount Everest disaster.* New York, NY: Villard.

Kramer, P. D. (2006). *Freud: Inventor of the modern mind.* New York, NY: HarperCollins.

Krebs, D. L., & Denton, K. (1997). Social illusions and self-deception: The evolution of biases in person perception. In J. A. Simpson & D. T. Kenrick (Eds.), *Evolutionary social psychology.* Mahwah, NJ: Erlbaum.

Krebs, D. L., & Denton, K. (2005). Toward a more pragmatic approach to morality: A critical evaluation of Kohlerg's model. *Psychological Review, 112,* 629–649.

Kreiner, D. S. (2011). Language and culture: Commonality, variation, and mistaken assumptions. In K. D. Keith (Ed.), *Cross-cultural psychology: Contemporary themes and perspectives.* Malden, MA: Wiley-Blackwell.

Kremen, W. S., Jacobsen, K. C., Xian, H., Eisen, S. A., Eaves, L. J., Tsuang, M. T., & Lyons, M. J. (2007). Genetics of verbal working memory processes: A twin study of middle-aged men. *Neuropsychology, 21*(5), 569–580. doi:10.1037/0894-4105.21.5.569

Kriegsfeld, L. J., & Nelson, R. J. (2009). Biological rhythms. In G. G. Berntson & J. T. Cacioppo (Eds.), *Handbook of neuroscience for the behavioral sciences* (Vol. 1, pp. 56–81). New York, NY: Wiley.

Kripke, D. F., Langer, R. D., & Kline, L. E. (2012). Hypnotics' association with mortality or cancer: A matched cohort study. *British Medical Journal Open, 2,* e000850. doi:10.1136/bjmopen-2012-000850

Kroger, J. (2003). Identity development during adolescence. In G. R. Adams & M. D. Berzonsky (Eds.), *Blackwell handbook of adolescence.* Malden, MA: Blackwell.

Kroger, J., & Marcia, J. E. (2011). The identify statuses: Origins, meanings, and interpretations. In S. J. Schwartz, K. Luyckx, & V. L. Vignoles (Eds.), *Handbook of identity theory and research* (Vol. 1 & 2). New York, NY: Springer Science + Business Media.

Krosnick, J. A. (1999). Survey research. *Annual Review Psychology, 50,* 537–567.

Krosnick, J. A., & Fabrigar, L. R. (1998). *Designing good questionnaires: Insights from psychology.* New York, NY: Oxford University Press.

Krosnick, J. A. Lavrakas, P. J., & Kim, N. (2014). Survey research. In H. T. Reis & C. M. Judd (Eds.), *Handbook of research methods in social and personality psychology* (2nd ed.). New York, NY: Cambridge University Press.

Kross, E., Verduyn, P., Demiralp, E., Park, J., Lee, D. S., Lin, N., . . . Ybarra, O. (2013). Facebook use predicts declines in subjective well-being in young adults. *PLoS ONE, 8,* e69841.

Krueger, J., Ham, J. J., & Linford, K. M. (1996). Perceptions of behavioral consistency: Are people aware of the actor-observer effect? *Psychological Science, 7,* 259–264.

Krueger, R. F., & Johnson, W. (2008). Behavioral genetics and personality: A new look at the integration of nature and nurture. In O. P. John, R. W. Robbins, & L. A. Pervin (Eds.), *Handbook of personality: Theory and research* (Vol. 3, pp. 287–310). New York, NY: Guilford Press.

Krueger, R. F., & Markon, K. E. (2014). The role of the DSM-5 personality trait model in moving toward a quantitative and empirically based approach to classifying personality and psychopathology. *Annual Review of Clinical Psychology, 10,* 477–501. doi:10.1146/annurev-clinpsy-032813-153732

Krug, S. E. (2013). Objective personality testing. In K. F. Geisinger, B. A. Bracken, J. F. Carlson, J. C. Hansen, N. R. Kuncel, S. P. Reise, & M. C. Rodriguez (Eds.), *APA handbook of testing and assessment in psychology: Vol. 1. Test theory and testing and assessment in industrial and organizational psychology.* Washington, DC: American Psychological Association. doi:10.1037/14047-019

Krull, D. S. (2001). On partitioning the fundamental attribution error: Dispositionalism and the correspondence bias. In G. B. Moskowitz (Ed.), *Cognitive social psychology: The Princeton Symposium on the legacy and future of social cognition.* Mahwah, NJ: Erlbaum.

Krull, D. S., & Erickson, D. J. (1995). Inferential hopscotch: How people draw social inferences from behavior. *Current Directions in Psychological Science, 4,* 35–38.

Kübler-Ross, E. (1969). *On death and dying.* New York, NY: Macmillan.

Kübler-Ross, E. (1970). The dying patient's point of view. In O. G. Brim, Jr., H. E. Freeman, S. Levine, & N. A. Scotch (Eds.), *The dying patient.* New York, NY: Sage.

Kucharczyk, E. R., Morgan, K., & Hall, A. P. (2012). The occupational impact of sleep quality and insomnia symptoms. *Sleep Medicine Reviews, 16,* 547–559. doi:10.1016/j.smrv.2012.01.005

Kulick, A. R., Pope, H. G., & Keck, P. E. (1990). Lycanthropy and self-identification. *Journal of Nervous & Mental Disease, 178*(2), 134–137.

Kuncel, N. R., & Hezlett, S. A. (2010). Fact and fiction in cognitive ability testing for admissions and hiring decisions. *Current Directions in Psychological Science, 19,* 339–345. doi:10.1177/0963721410389459

Kung, S., & Mrazek, D. A. (2005). Psychiatric emergency department visits on full-moon nights. *Psychiatric Services, 56,* 221–222.

Kunitoh, N. (2013). From hospital to the community: The influence of deinstitutionalization on discharged long-stay psychiatric patients. *Psychiatry and Clinical Neurosciences, 67,* 384–396. doi:10.1111/pcn.12071

Kupfer, D. J., Kuhl, E. A., & Regier, D. A. (2013). DSM-5: The future arrived. *JAMA, 309,* 1691–1692.

Kushlev, K., & Dunn, E. W. (2012). Affective forecasting: Knowing how we will feel in the future. In S. Vazire, & T. D. Wilson (Eds.), *Handbook of self-knowledge.* New York, NY: Guilford Press.

Kwan, V. S., & Herrmann, S. D. (2015). The interplay between culture and personality. In M. Mikulincer, P. R. Shaver, M. L. Cooper, & R. J. Larsen (Eds.), *APA handbook of personality and social psychology: Vol. 4. Personality processes and individual differences.* Washington, DC: American Psychological Association.

Kyaga, S., Landén, M., Boman, M., Hultman, C. M., Långström, N., & Lichtenstein, P. (2013). Mental illness, suicide and creativity: 40-year prospective total population study. *Journal of Psychiatric Research, 47*(1), 83–90. doi:10.1016/j.jpsychires.2012.09.010

Laborda, M. A., McConnell, B. L., & Miller, R. R. (2011). Behavioral techniques to reduce relapse after exposure therapy: Applications of studies of experimental extinction. In T. R. Schachtman, & S. Reilly (Eds.), *Associative learning and condition theory: Human and non-human applications.* New York, NY: Oxford University Press.

Lachman, S. J. (1996). Processes in perception: Psychological transformations of highly structured stimulus material. *Perceptual and Motor Skills, 83,* 411–418.

Lachter, J., Forster, K. I., & Ruthruff, E. (2004). Forty-five years after Broadbent (1958): Still no identification without attention. *Psychological Review, 111,* 880–913.

la Cour, L. T., Stone, B.W., Hopkins, W., Menzel, C., & Fragaszy, D. M. (2014). What limits tool use in nonhuman primates? Insights from tufted capuchin monkeys (Sapajus spp.) and chimpanzees (Pan troglodytes) aligning three-dimensional objects to a surface. *Animal Cognition, 17*(1), 113–125. doi:10.1007/s10071-013-0643-x

Lader, M. H. (2002). Managing dependence and withdrawal with newer hypnotic medications in the treatment of insomnia. *Journal of Clinical Psychiatry, 4*(suppl 1), 33–37.

Laeng, B., Sirois, S., & Gredeback, G. (2012). Pupillometry: A window to the preconscious? *Perspective on Psychological Science, 7*(1), 18–27. doi:10.1177/1745691611427305

Laird, J. D., & Lacasse, K. (2014). Bodily influences on emotional feelings: Accumulating evidence and extensions of William James's theory of emotion. *Emotion Review, 6*(1), 27–34. doi:10.1177/1754073913494899

Lakein, A. (1996). *How to get control of your time and your life.* New York, NY: New American Library.

Lakey, B. (2013). Perceived social support and happiness: The role of personality and relational processes. In S. A. David, I. Boniwell, & A. Conley Ayers (Eds.), *The Oxford handbook of happiness*. New York, NY: Oxford University Press.

Lamb, M. E., Ketterlinus, R. D., & Fracasso, M. P. (1992). Parent-child relationships. In M. H. Bornstein & M. E. Lamb (Eds.), *Developmental psychology: An advanced textbook* (3rd ed.). Hillsdale, NJ: Erlbaum.

Lamb, M. E., & Lewis, C. (2011). The role of parent-child relationships in child development. In M. H. Bornstein & M. E. Lamb (Eds.), *Developmental science: An advanced textbook* (pp. 469–518). New York, NY: Psychology Press.

Lambert, M. J. (2011). Psychotherapy research and its achievements. In J. C. Norcross, G. R. Vandenbos, & D. K. Freedheim (Eds.), *History of psychotherapy: Continuity and change* (2nd ed.). Washington, DC: American Psychological Association.

Lambert, M. J. (2013). The efficacy and effectiveness of psychotherapy. In M. J. Lambert (Ed.). *Bergin and Garfield's handbook of psychotherapy and behavior change* (6th ed.). New York, NY: Wiley.

Lambert, M. J., & Ogles, B. M. (2014). Common factors: Post hoc explanation or empirically based therapy approach? *Psychotherapy, 51,* 500–504. doi:10.1037/a0036580

Lamkin, J., Clifton, A., Campbell, W. K., & Miller, J. D. (2014). An examination of the perceptions of social network characteristics associated with grandiose and vulnerable narcissism. *Personality Disorders: Theory, Research, and Treatment, 5*(2), 137–145. doi:10.1037/per0000024

Lampinen, J. M., Neuschatz, J. S., & Payne, D. G. (1999). Source attributions and false memories: A test of the demand characteristics account. *Psychonomic Bulletin & Review, 6,* 130–135.

Lampl, M., & Johnson, M. L. (2011). Infant growth in length follows prolonged sleep and increased naps. *Sleep: Journal of Sleep and Sleep Disorders Research, 34,* 641–650.

Lampl, M., Veldhuis, J. D., & Johnson, M. L. (1992). Saltation and stasis: A model of human growth. *Science, 258,* 801–803.

Landau, M. J., & Sullivan, D. (2015). Terror management motivation at the core of personality. In M. Mikulincer, P. R. Shaver, M. L. Cooper, & R. J. Larsen (Eds.), *APA handbook of personality and social psychology: Vol. 4. Personality processes and individual differences*. Washington, DC: American Psychological Association.

Landau, S. M., Marks, S. M., Mormino, E. C., Rabinovici, G. D., Oh, H., O'Neil, J. P., . . . Jagust, W. J. (2012). Association of lifetime cognitive engagement and low β-amyloid deposition. *Archive of Neurology, 69,* 623–629. doi:10.1001/archneurol.2011.2748

Lane, A., Luminet, O., Rimé, B., Gross, J. J., de Timary, P., & Mikolajczak, M. (2013). Oxytocin increases willingness to socially share one's emotions. *International Journal of Psychology, 48,* 676–681. doi:10.1080/00207594.2012.677540

Laney, C. (2013). The sources of memory errors, In D. Reisberg (Ed.), *Oxford handbook of cognitive psychology*. New York, NY: Oxford University Press.

Laney, C., & Loftus, E. F. (2013). Recent advances in false memory research. *South African Journal of Psychology, 43,* 137–146. doi:10.1177/0081246313484236

Lange, C. (1885). One leuds beveegelser. In K. Dunlap (Ed.), *The emotions*. Baltimore, MD: Williams & Wilkins.

Langlois, J. H., Kalakanis, L., Rubenstein, A. J., Larson, A., Hallam, M., & Smoot, M. (2000). Maxims or myths of beauty? A meta-analytic and theoretical review. *Psychological Bulletin, 126,* 390–423.

Lango, A. H., Estrada, K., Lettre, G., Berndt, S. I., Weedon, M. N., & Rivadeneira, F., et al. (2010). Hundreds of variants clustered in genomic loci and biological pathways affect human height. *Nature, 467,* 832–838.

Large, M., Sharma, S., Compton, M. T., Slade, T., & Nielssen, O. (2011). Cannabis use and earlier onset of psychosis: A systematic meta-analysis. *Archives of General Psychiatry, 68,* 555–561. doi:10.1001/archgenpsychiatry.2011.5

Larsen, J. T., Berntson, G. G., Poehlmann, K. M., Ito, T. A., & Cacioppo, J. T. (2008). The psychophysiology of emotion. In M. Lewis, J. M. Haviland-Jones, & L. F. Barrett (Eds.), *Handbook of emotions* (3rd ed., pp. 180–195). New York, NY: Guilford Press.

Larsen, J. T., & McGraw, A. P. (2011). Further evidence for mixed emotions. *Journal of Personality and Social Psychology, 100,* 1095–1110. doi:10.1037/a0021846

Laska, K. M., Gurman, A. S., & Wampold, B. E. (2014). Expanding the lens of evidence-based practice in psychotherapy: A common factors perspective. *Psychotherapy, 51,* 467–481. doi:10.1037/a0034332

Laska, M., Seibt, A., & Weber, A. (2000). "Microsmatic" primates revisited: Olfactory sensitivity in the squirrel monkey. *Chemical Senses, 25,* 47–53. doi:10.1093/chemse/25.1.47

Latané, B. (1981). The psychology of social impact. *American Psychologist, 36,* 343–356.

Latané, B., & Nida, S. A. (1981). Ten years of research on group size and helping. *Psychological Bulletin, 89,* 308–324.

Latané, B., Williams, K., & Harkins, S. (1979). Many hands make light the work: The causes and consequences of social loafing. *Journal of Personality and Social Psychology, 37,* 822–832.

Lau, C., Wang, H., Hsu, J., & Liu, M. (2013). Does the dopamine hypothesis explain schizophrenia? *Reviews in the Neurosciences, 24,* 389–400. doi:10.1515/revneuro-2013-0011

Lau, J. Y., Lester, K. J., Hodgson, K., & Eley, T. C. (2014). The genetics of mood disorders. In I. H. Gotlib & C. L. Hammen (Eds.), *Handbook of depression* (3rd ed.). New York, NY: Guilford Press.

Laughlin, H. (1967). *The neuroses*. Washington, DC: Butterworth.

Laughlin, H. (1979). *The ego and its defenses*. New York, NY: Jason Aronson.

Laumann, E. O., Gagnon, J. H., Michael, R. T., & Michaels, S. (1994). *The social organization of sexuality: Sexual practices in the United States*. Chicago, IL: University of Chicago Press.

Lawrie, S. M., & Pantelis, C. (2011). Structural brain imaging in schizophrenia and related populations. In D. R. Weinberger & P. Harrison (Eds.), *Schizophrenia* (3rd ed.). Malden, MA: Wiley-Blackwell.

Lazarus, A. A. (1987). The need for technical eclecticism: Science, breadth, depth, and specificity. In J. K. Zeig (Ed.), *The evolution of psychotherapy*. New York, NY: Brunner/Mazel.

Lazarus, A. A. (2008). Technical eclecticism and multimodal therapy. In J. L. Lebow (Ed.), *Twenty-first century psychotherapies: Contemporary approaches to theory and practice*. New York, NY: Wiley.

Lazarus, R. S. (1993). Why we should think of stress as a subset of emotion. In L. Goldberger & S. Breznitz (Eds.), *Handbook of stress: Theoretical and clinical aspects* (2nd ed.). New York, NY: Free Press.

Lazarus, R. S. (2006). Emotions and interpersonal relationships: Toward a person-centered conceptualization of emotions and coping. *Journal of Personality, 71,* 9–46.

Lazarus, R. S., & Folkman, S. (1984). *Stress, appraisal, and coping*. New York, NY: Springer.

Leahey, T. H. (2013). Cognition and learning. In D. K. Freedheim, & I. B. Weiner (Eds.), *Handbook of psychology Vol. 1: History of psychology* (2nd ed., pp. 129–154). New York, NY: Wiley.

Leaper, C. (2013). Gender development during childhood. In P. D. Zelazo (Ed.), *Oxford handbook of developmental psychology: Vol. 2. Self and other*. New York, NY: Oxford University Press. doi:10.1093/oxfordhb/9789199958474.013.0014

Leavitt, F. (1995). *Drugs and behavior* (3rd ed.). Thousand Oaks, CA: Sage.

LeBoeuf, R. A., & Shafir, E. (2012). Decision making. In K. J. Holyoak, & R. G. Morrison (Eds.), *Oxford handbook of thinking and reasoning*. New York, NY: Oxford University Press.

Lebow, J. L. (2008). Couple and family therapy. In J. L Lebow (Ed.), *Twenty-first century psychotherapies: Contemporary approaches to theory and practice* (pp. 307–346). New York, NY: Wiley.

Lebow, J. L., & Stroud, C. B. (2013). Family therapy. In G. Stricker & T. A. Widiger (Eds.), *Handbook of psychology: Vol. 8. Clinical psychology* (2nd ed.). New York, NY: Wiley.

Lechner, S. C., Tennen, H., & Affleck, G. (2009). Benefit-finding and growth. In S. J. Lopez & C. R. Snyder (Eds.), *Oxford handbook of positive psychology* (2nd ed.). New York, NY: Oxford University Press.

LeDoux, J. E. (1994). Emotion, memory and the brain. *Scientific American, 270,* 50–57.

LeDoux, J. E. (1995). Emotion: Clues from the brain. *Annual Review of Psychology, 46,* 209–235.

LeDoux, J. E. (1996). *The emotional brain*. New York, NY: Simon & Schuster.

LeDoux, J. E. (2000). Emotion circuits in the brain. *Annual Review of Neuroscience, 23,* 155–184.

LeDoux, J. E., & Damasio, A. R. (2013). Emotions and feelings. In E. R. Kandel, J. H. Schwartz, T. M. Jessell, S. A. Siegelbaum, & A. J. Hudspeth (Eds.), *Principles of neural science* (5th ed., pp. 1079–1093). New York, NY: McGraw-Hill.

Lee, J. D., McNeely, J., & Gourevitch, M. N. (2011). Medical complications of drug use/dependence. In P. Ruiz, & E. C. Strain (Eds.), *Lowinson and Ruiz's substance abuse: A comprehensive textbook* (5th ed.). Philadelphia, PA: Wolters Kluwer Lippincott Williams & Wilkins.

Lee, J. E., Lee, C. H., Lee, S. J., Ryu, Y., Lee, W. H., Yoon, I. Y., . . . Kim, J. W. (2013). Mortality of patients with obstructive sleep apnea in Korea.

Journal of Clinical Sleep Medicine, 9, 997–1002.

Lee, K. A., & Rosen, L. A. (2012). Sleep and human development. In C. M. Morin, & C. A. Espie (Eds.), *Oxford handbook of sleep and sleep disorders.* New York, NY: Oxford University Press.

Lee, S. J., Grogan-Kaylor, A., & Berger, L. M. (2014). Parental spanking of 1-year old children and subsequent child protective services involvement. *Child Abuse & Neglect, 38,* 875–883. doi:10.1016 /j.chiabu.2014.01.018

Lee, S. Y., Gregg, A. P., & Park, S. H. (2013). The person in the purchase: Narcissistic consumers prefer products that positively distinguish them. *Journal of Personality and Social Psychology, 105,* 335–352. doi:10.1037 /a0032703

Lee, Y., & Styne, D. (2013). Influences on the onset and tempo of puberty in human beings and implications for adolescent psychological development. *Hormones and Behavior, 64,* 250–261. doi:10.1016/j.yhbeh.2013.03.014

Lee-Chiong, T., & Sateia, M. (2006). Pharmacologic therapy of insomnia. In T. Lee-Chiong (Ed.), *Sleep: A comprehensive handbook.* Hoboken, NJ: Wiley-Liss.

Leeper, R. W. (1935). A study of a neglected portion of the field of learning: The development of sensory organization. *Journal of Genetic Psychology, 46,* 41–75.

Lefcourt, H. M. (2001). The humor solution. In C. R. Snyder (Ed.), *Coping with stress: Effective people and processes* (pp. 68–92). New York, NY: Oxford University Press.

Lefcourt, H. M. (2005). Humor. In C. R. Snyder & S. J. Lopez (Eds.), *Handbook of positive psychology.* New York, NY: Oxford University Press.

Lefcourt, H. M., Davidson, K., Shepherd, R., Phillips, M., Prkachin, K., & Mills, D. (1995). Perspective-taking humor: Accounting for stress moderation. *Journal of Social and Clinical Psychology, 14,* 373–391.

Leff, J. (2006). Whose life is it anyway? Quality of life for long-stay patients discharged from psychiatric hospitals. In H. Katschnig, H. Freeman, & N. Sartorius (Eds.), *Quality of life in mental disorders.* New York, NY: Wiley.

Leff, J. P., & Vaughn, C. E. (1981). The role of maintenance therapy and relatives' expressed emotion in relapse of schizophrenia: A two-year follow-up. *The British Journal of Psychiatry, 139,* 102–104. doi:org/10.1192 /bjp.139.2.102

Leff, J. P., & Vaughn, C. E. (1985). *Expressed emotion in families.* New York, NY: Guilford Press.

Legault, E., & Laurence, J.-R. (2007). Recovered memories of childhood sexual abuse: Social worker, psychologist, and psychiatrist reports of beliefs, practices, and cases. *Australian Journal of Clinical & Experimental Hypnosis, 35,* 111–133.

Leighton, J. P., & Sternberg, R. J. (2003). Reasoning and problem solving. In A. F. Healy & R. W. Proctor (Eds.), *Handbook of psychology: Vol. 4. Experimental psychology.* New York, NY: Wiley.

Leon, D. A., Lawlor, D. A., Clark, H. H., Batty, G. D., & Macintyre, S. S. (2009). The association of childhood intelligence with mortality risk from adolescence to middle age: Findings from the Aberdeen Children of the 1950s cohort study. *Intelligence, 37*(6), 520–528. doi:10.1016/j.intell .2008.11.00

Lepine, R., Barrouillet, P., & Camos, V. (2005). What makes working memory spans so predictive of high-level cognition? *Psychonomic Bulletin & Review, 12*(1), 165–170.

Lerman, H. (1986). *A mote in Freud's eye: From psychoanalysis to the psychology of women.* New York, NY: Springer.

Lervag, A., & Aukrust, V. G. (2010). Vocabulary knowledge is a critical determinant of the difference in reading comprehension growth between first and second language learners. *Journal of Child Psychology and Psychiatry, 51,* 612–620. doi:10.1111/j.1469 -7610.2009.02185.x

Letra, L., Santana, I., & Seiça, R. (2014). Obesity as a risk factor for Alzheimer's disease: The role of adipocytokines. *Metabolic Brain Disease, 29,* 563–568. doi:10.1007/s11011 -014-9501-z

Leuner, B., & Gould, E. (2010). Structural plasticity and hippocampal function. *Annual Review of Psychology, 61,* 111–140. doi:10.1146/annurev .psych.093008.100359

Leuner, B., Gould, E., & Shors, T. J. (2006). Is there a link between adult neurogenesis and learning? *Hippocampus, 16,* 216–224.

Levenson, R. W. (2014). The autonomic nervous system and emotion. *Emotion Review, 6*(2), 100–112. doi:10.1177/1754073913512003

Levine, J. M., & Tindale, R. S. (2015). Social influence in groups. In M. Mikulincer, P. R. Shaver, J. F. Dovidio, & J. A. Simpson (Eds.), *APA handbook of personality and social psychology Vol. 2: Group processes.* Washington, DC: American Psychological Association.

Levine, M. P., & Harrison, K. (2004). Media's role in the perpetuation and prevention of negative body image and disordered eating. In J. K. Thompson (Ed.), *Handbook of eating disorders and obesity.* New York, NY: Wiley.

Levinthal, C. F. (2014). *Drugs, behavior, and modern society* (8th ed.). Boston, MA: Pearson.

Levis, D. J. (1989). The case for a return to a two-factor theory of avoidance: The failure of non-fear interpretations. In S. B. Klein & R. R. Bowrer (Eds.), *Contemporary learning theories: Pavlovian conditioning and the status of traditional learning theory.* Hillsdale NJ: Erlbaum.

Levitt, J. B. (2010). Receptive fields. In E. B. Goldstein (Ed.), *Encyclopedia of perception.* Thousand Oaks, CA: Sage.

Levy, G. D., Taylor, M. G., & Gelman, S. A. (1995). Traditional and evaluative aspects of flexibility in gender roles, social conventions, moral rules, and physical laws. *Child Development, 66,* 515–531.

Levy, J., Trevarthen, C., & Sperry, R. W. (1972). Perception of bilateral chimeric figures following hemispheric disconnection. *Brain, 95,* 61–78.

Levy, K. N. (2012). Subtypes, dimensions, levels, and mental states in narcissism and narcissistic personality disorder. *Journal of Clinical Psychology, 68,* 886–897. doi:10.1002/jclp .21893

Lewin, K. (1935). *A dynamic theory of personality.* New York, NY: McGraw-Hill.

Lewis, S. J., Zuccolo, L., Davey Smith, G., Macleod, J., Rodriguez, S., Draper, E. S., . . . Gray, R. (2012). Fetal alcohol exposure and IQ at age 8: Evidence from a population-based birth-cohort study. *PLoS One, 7,* e49407. doi:10.1371/journal.pone.0049407

Li, C., & Hoffstein, V. (2011). Snoring. In M. H. Kryger, T. Roth, & W. C. Dement (Eds.), *Principles and practice of sleep medicine* (5th ed.). Saint Louis, MO: Elsevier Saunders.

Li, N. P., Yong, J. C., Tov, W., Sng, O., Fletcher, G. O., Valentine, K. A., . . . Balliet, D. (2013). Mate preferences do predict attraction and choices in the early stages of mate selection. *Journal of Personality and Social Psychology, 105,* 757–776. doi:10.1037/a0033777

Libby, P., Tabas, I., Fredman, G., & Fisher, E. A. (2014). Inflammation and its resolution as determinants of acute coronary syndromes. *Circulation Research, 114,* 1867–1879. doi:10.1161 /CIRCRESAHA.114.302699

Lichstein, K. L., Taylor, D. J., McCrae, C. S., & Ruiter, M. E. (2011). Insomnia: Epidemiology and risk factors. In M. H. Kryger, T. Roth, & W. C. Dement (Eds.), *Principles and practice of sleep medicine* (5th ed.). Saint Louis, MO: Elsevier Saunders.

Liddle, P. F. (2009). Descriptive clinical features of schizophrenia. In M. C. Gelder, N. C. Andreasen, J. J. López-Ibor, Jr., & J. R. Geddes (Eds.). *New Oxford textbook of psychiatry* (2nd ed., Vol. 1). New York, NY: Oxford University Press.

Liefbroer, A. C., & Dourleijn, E. (2006). Unmarried cohabitation and union stability: Testing the role of diffusion using data from 16 European countries. *Demography, 43,* 203–221.

Lien, M.-C., Ruthruff, E., & Johnston, J. C. (2006). Attentional limitations in doing two tasks at once. *Current Directions in Psychological Science, 15,* 89–93.

Lilienfeld, S. O. (2007). Psychological treatments that cause harm. *Perspectives on Psychological Science, 2,* 53–70.

Lilienfeld, S. O., Ammirati, R., & Landfield, K. (2009). Giving debiasing away: Can psychological research on correcting cognitive errors promote human welfare? *Perspectives on Psychological Science, 4*(4), 390–398. doi:10.1111/j.1745 -6924.2009.01144.x

Lilienfeld, S. O., & Arkowitz, H. (2009, February/March). Lunacy and the full moon: Does a full moon really trigger strange behavior? *Scientific American Mind,* 64–65.

Lilienfeld, S., & Arkowitz, H. (2011, September/October). Can People Have Multiple Personalities? *Scientific American Mind,* 64–65.

Lilienfeld, S. O., & Landfield, K. (2008). Issues in diagnosis: Categorical vs. dimensional. In W. E. Craighead, D. J. Miklowitz, & L. W. Craighead (Eds.), *Psychopathology: History, diagnosis, and empirical foundations.* New York, NY: Wiley.

Lilienfeld, S. O., & Lynn, S. J. (2003). Dissociative identity disorder: Multiple personalities, multiple controversies. In S. O. Lilienfeld, S. J. Lynn, & J. M. Lohr (Eds.), *Science and pseudoscience in clinical psychology.* New York, NY: Guilford Press.

Lilienfeld, S. O., Lynn, S. J., Kirsch, I., Chaves, J. F., Sarbin, T. R., Ganaway, G. K., & Powell, R. A. (1999). Dissociative identity disorder and the sociocognitive model: Recalling the lessons of the past. *Psychological Bulletin, 125,* 507–523.

Lilienfeld, S. O., Lynn, S. J., Ruscio, J., & Beyerstein, B. L. (2010). *50 great myths of popular psychology: Shattering widespread misconceptions about human behavior.* Malden, MA: Wiley-Blackwell.

Lilienfeld, S. O., Ritschel, L. A., Lynn, S. J., Cautin, R. L., & Latzman, R. D. (2014). Why ineffective psychotherapies appear to work: A taxonomy of causes of spurious therapeutic effectiveness. *Perspectives on Psychological Science, 9,* 355–387. doi:10.1177/1745691614535216

Lilienfeld, S. O., Wood, J. M., & Garb, H. N. (2000). The scientific status of projective tests. *Psychological Science in the Public Interest, 1*(2), 27–66.

Lim, M. M., & Young, L. J. (2006). Neuropepridergic regulation of affiliative behavior and social bonding in animals. *Hormones and Behavior, 50*(4), 506–517.

Lin, H., Katsovich, L., Ghebremichael, M., Findley, D. B., Grantz, H., Lombroso, P. J., & . . . Leckman, J. F. (2007). Psychosocial stress predicts future symptom severities in children and adolescents with Tourette syndrome and/or obsessive-compulsive disorder. *Journal of Child Psychology and Psychiatry, 48*(2), 157–166. doi:10.1111/j.1469-7610.2006.01687.x

Lindau, S., & Gavrilova, N. (2010). Sex, health, and years of sexually active life gained due to good health: Evidence from two U.S. population based cross sectional surveys of ageing. *British Medical Journal, 340,* c810. doi:10.1136/bmj.c810

Lindgren, H. C. (1969). *The psychology of college success: A dynamic approach.* New York, NY: Wiley.

Lindquist, K. A., Wager, T. D., Kober, H., Bliss-Moreau, E., & Barrett, L. F. (2012). The brain basis of emotion: A meta-analytic review. *Behavioral and Brain Sciences, 35*(3), 121–143. doi:10.1017/S0140525X11000446

Lindsay, M., & Lester, D. (2004). *Suicide by cop: Committing suicide by provoking police to shoot you (death, value and meaning).* Amityville, NY: Baywood Publishing.

Lindsay, P. H., & Norman, D. A. (1977). *Human information processing.* New York, NY: Academic Press.

Lindsay, S. D., Allen, B. P., Chan, J. C. K., & Dahl, L. C. (2004). Eyewitness suggestibility and source similarity: Intrusions of details from one event into memory reports of another event. *Journal of Memory & Language, 50*(1), 96–111.

Lippa, R. A. (1994). *Introduction to social psychology.* Pacific Grove, CA: Brooks/Cole.

Lisberger, S. G., & Thach, W. T. (2013). The cerebellum. In E. R. Kandel, J. H. Schwartz, T. M. Jessell, S. A. Siegelbaum, & A. J. Hudspeth (Eds.), *Principles of neural science* (5th ed.). New York, NY: McGraw-Hill.

Lisdahl, K. M., Thayer, R., Squeglia, L. M., McQueeny, T. M., & Tapert, S. F. (2013). Recent binge drinking predicts smaller cerebellar volumes in adolescents. *Psychiatry Research:*
Neuroimaging, 211(1), 17–23. doi: 10.1016/j.pscychresns.2012.07.009

Lissek, S., Rabin, S., Heller, R. E., Lukenbaugh, D., Geraci, M., Pine, D. S., & Grillon, C. (2010). Overgeneralization of conditioned fear as a pathogenic marker of panic disorder. *American Journal of Psychiatry, 167*(1), 47–55. doi:10.1176/appi.ajp.2009.09030410

Little, A. C., Jones, B. C., & Burriss, R. P. (2007). Preferences for masculinity in male bodies change across the menstrual cycle. *Hormones and Behavior, 51,* 633–639.

Little, A. C., & Mannion, H. (2006). Viewing attractive or unattractive same-sex individuals changes self-rated attractiveness and face preferences in women. *Animal Behaviour, 72,* 981–987.

Liverant, G. I., Sloan, D. M., Pizzagalli, D. A., Harte, C. B., Kamholz, B.W., Rosebrock, L. E., . . . Kaplan, G. B. (2014). Associations among smoking, anhedonia, and reward learning in depression. *Behavior Therapy, 45*(5), 651–663. doi:10.1016/j.beth.2014.02.004.

Lockhart, R. S. (2000). Methods of memory research. In E. Tulving & F. I. M. Craik (Eds.), *The Oxford handbook of memory* (pp. 45–58). New York, NY: Oxford University Press.

Lockhart, R. S., & Craik, F. I. (1990). Levels of processing: A retrospective commentary on a framework for memory research. *Canadian Journal of Psychology, 44*(1), 87–112.

Loehlin, J. C. (1992). *Genes and environment in personality development.* Newbury Park, CA: Sage.

Loftus, E. F. (1979). *Eyewitness testimony.* Cambridge, MA: Harvard University Press.

Loftus, E. F. (1992). When a lie becomes memory's truth: Memory distortion after exposure to misinformation. *Current Directions in Psychological Science, 1,* 121–123.

Loftus, E. F. (2003). Make believe memories. *American Psychologist, 58,* 864–873.

Loftus, E. F. (2004). Memories of things unseen. *Current Directions in Psychological Science, 13*(4), 145–147.

Loftus, E. F. (2005). Planting misinformation in the human mind: A 30-year investigation of the malleability of memory. *Learning & Memory, 12,* 361–366.

Loftus, E. F. (2013). 25 years of eyewitness science . . . finally pays off. *Perspectives on Psychological Science, 8,* 556–557. doi:10.1177/1745691613500995

Loftus, E. F., & Cahill, L. (2007). Memory distortion: From misinformation to rich false memory. In
J. S. Nairne (Ed.), *The foundations of remembering: Essays in honor of Henry L. Roediger III.* New York, NY: Psychology Press.

Loftus, E. F., & Davis, D. (2006). Recovered memories. *Annual Review of Clinical Psychology, 2,* 469–498.

Loftus, E. F., & Palmer, J. C. (1974). Reconstruction of automobile destruction: An example of the interaction between language and memory. *Journal of Verbal Learning and Verbal Behavior, 13,* 585–589.

Logie, R. H. (2011). The functional organization and capacity limits of working memory. *Current Directions in Psychological Science, 20,* 240–245. doi:10.1177/0963721411415340

Logue, A. W. (1991). *The psychology of eating and drinking* (2nd ed.). New York, NY: W. H. Freeman.

Lohmann, R. I. (2007). Dreams and ethnography. In D. Barrett & P. McNamara (Eds.), *The new science of dreaming.* Westport, CT: Praeger.

Long, Z., Medlock, C., Dzemidzic, M., Shin, Y., Goddard, A. W., & Dydak, U. (2013). Decreased GABA levels in anterior cingulate cortex/medial prefrontal cortex in panic disorder. *Progress in Neuro-Psychopharmacology & Biological Psychiatry, 44,* 131–135. doi:10.1016/j.pnpbp.2013.01.020

Longman, D. G., & Atkinson, R. H. (2005). *College learning and study skills.* Belmont, CA: Wadsworth.

Lonner, W. J. (2009). A retrospective on the beginnings of JCCP and IACCP. *Journal of Cross-Cultural Psychology, 40*(2), 167–169. doi:10.1177/0022022109332406

Lopez, R., Jaussent, I., Scholz, S., Bayard, S., Montplaisir, J., & Dauvilliers, Y. (2013). Functional impact in adult sleepwalkers: A case-control study. *SLEEP, 36,* 345–351.

López, S. R., Barrio, C., Kopelowicz, A., & Vega, W. A. (2012). From documenting to eliminating disparities in mental health care for Latinos. *American Psychologist, 67,* 511–523. doi:10.1037/a0029737

Lopez-Caneda, E., Rodriguez Holguin, S., Corral, M., Doallo, S., & Cadaveira, F. (2014). Evolution of the binge drinking pattern in college students: Neurophysiological correlates. *Alcohol, 48,* 407-418. doi:10.1016/j.alcohol.2014.01.009

Lorenzo, G. L., Biesanz, J. C., & Human, L. J. (2010). What is beautiful is good and more accurately understood: Physical attractiveness and accuracy in first impressions of personality. *Psychological Science, 21*(12), 1777–1782. doi:10.1177/0956797610388048
Lothane, Z. (2006). Freud's legacy: Is it still with us? *Psychoanalytic Psychology, 23*(2), 285–301. doi:10.1037/0736-9735.23.2.285

Lourenco, O. (2012). Piaget and Vygotsky: Many resemblances, and a crucial difference. *New Ideas in Psychology, 30,* 281–295. doi:10.1016/j.newideapsych.2011.12.006

Lu, C. Y., Zhang, F., Lakoma, M. D., Madden, J. M., Rusinak, D., Penfold, R. B., . . . Soumerai, S. B. (2014). Changes in antidepressant use by young people and suicidal behavior after FDA warnings and media coverage: quasi-experimental study. *British Medical Journal, 348,* g3596. doi:10.1136/bmj.g3596

Lu, F. G., Lewis-Fernandez, R., Primm, A. B., Lim, R. F., & Aggarwal, N. K. (2014). Treatment of culturally diverse populations. In R. E. Hales, S. C. Yudofsky, & L. W. Roberts (Eds.), *The American Psychiatric Publishing textbook of psychiatry* (6th ed.). Washington, DC: American Psychiatric Publishing.

Luborsky, E. B., O'Reilly-Landry, M., & Arlow, J. A. (2011). Psychoanalysis. In R. J. Corsini & D. Wedding (Eds.), *Current psychotherapies* (9th ed.). Belmont, CA: Brooks/Cole.

Luborsky, L., & Barrett, M. S. (2006). The history and empirical status of key psychoanalytic concepts. *Annual Review Clinical Psychology, 2,* 1–19.

Luborsky, L., Singer, B., & Luborsky, L. (1975). Comparative studies of psychotherapies: Is it true that everyone has won and all must have prizes? *Archives of General Psychiatry, 32,* 995–1008.

Lucas, A. R., Beard, C. M., O'Fallon, W. M., & Kurland, L. T. (1991). 50-year trends in the incidence of anorexia nervosa in Rochester, Minn.: A population-based study. *American Journal of Psychiatry, 148,* 917–922.

Lucas, R. E. (2007). Adaptation and the set-point model of subjective well-being: Does happiness change after major life events? *Current Directions in Psychological Science, 16,* 75–79.

Lucas, R. E., Clark, A. E., Georgellis, Y., & Diener, E. (2004). Unemployment alters the set point for life satisfaction. *Psychological Science, 15*(1), 8–13.

Lucas, R. E., & Diener, E. (2015). Personality and subjective well-being: Current issues and controversies. In M. Mikulincer, P. R. Shaver, M. L. Cooper, & R. J. Larsen (Eds.), *APA handbook of personality and social psychology: Vol. 4. Personality processes and individual differences.* Washington, DC: American Psychological Association.

Luchins, A. S. (1942). Mechanization in problem solving. *Psychological Monographs, 54* (6, Whole No. 248).

Luders, E., Narr, K. L., Thompson, P. M., & Toga, A. W. (2009). Neuroanatomical correlates of intelligence. *Intelligence, 37*(2), 156–163. doi:10.1016/j.intell.2008.07.002

Luders, E., Thompson, P. M., Kurth, F., Hong, J., Phillips, O. R., Wang, Y., . . . Toga, A. W. (2013). Global and regional alterations of hippocampal anatomy in long-term meditation practitioners. *Human Brain Mapping, 34*, 3369–3375. doi:10.1002/hbm.22153

Ludwig, A. M. (1994). Mental illness and creative activity in female writers. *American Journal of Psychiatry, 151*, 1650–1656.

Ludwig, A. M. (1995). *The price of greatness: Resolving the creativity and madness controversy.* New York, NY: Guilford Press.

Luh, C. W. (1922). The conditions of retention. *Psychological Monographs, 31.*

Lukaszewski, A. W., & Roney, J. R. (2011). The origins of extraversion: Joint effects of facultative calibration and genetic polymorphism. *Personality and Social Psychology Bulletin, 37*, 409–421. doi:10.1177/0146167210397209

Luna, B., Paulsen, D. J., Padmanabhan, A., & Geier, C. (2013). The teenage brain: Cognitive control and motivation. *Current Directions in Psychological Science, 22*, 94–100. doi:10.1177/0963721413478416

Lundberg, U. (2007). Catecholamines. In G. Fink (Ed.), *Encyclopedia of stress.* San Diego, CA: Elsevier.

Lupien, S. J., & Maheu, F. S. (2007). Memory and stress. In G. Fink (Ed.), *Encyclopedia of stress.* San Diego, CA: Elsevier.

Luppi, P., Clément, O., & Fort, P. (2013). Paradoxical (REM) sleep genesis by the brainstem is under hypothalamic control. *Current Opinion in Neurobiology, 23*, 786–792. doi:10.1016/j.conb.2013.02.006

Lustig, C., Berman, M. G., Nee, D., Lewis, R. L., Sledge Moore, K., & Jonides, J. (2009). Psychological and neural mechanisms of short-term memory. In G. G. Berntson & J. T. Cacioppo (Eds.), *Handbook of neuroscience for the behavioral sciences* (Vol 1, pp. 567–585). Hoboken, NJ: Wiley.

Lynn, D. J., & Vaillant, G. E. (1998). Anonymity, neutrality, and confidentiality in the actual methods of Sigmund Freud: A review of 43 cases, 1907–1939. *American Journal of Psychiatry, 155*, 163–171.

Lynn, R. (2009). What has caused the Flynn effect? Secular increases in the development quotients of infants. *Intelligence, 37*(1), 16–24. doi:10.1016/j.intell.2008.07.00

Lynn, S. J., Kirsch, I., & Hallquist, M. N. (2008). Social cognitive theories of hypnosis. In M. R. Nash & A. J. Barnier (Eds.). *Oxford handbook of hypnosis: Theory, research and practice* (pp. 111–140). New York, NY: Oxford University Press.

Lynn, S. J., Kirsch, I., Knox, J., Fassler, O., & Lilienfeld, S. O. (2007). Hypnotic regulation of consciousness and the pain neuromatrix. In G. A. Jamieson (Ed.), *Hypnosis and conscious states: The cognitive neuroscience perspective.* New York, NY: Oxford University Press.

Lynn, S. J., Lilienfeld, S. O., Merckelbach, H., Giesbrecht, T., & van der Kloet, D. (2012). Dissociation and dissociative disorders: Challenging conventional wisdom. *Current Directions in Psychological Science, 21*(1), 48–53. doi:10.1177/0963721411429457

Lynne, S. D., Graber, J. A., Nichols, T. R., & Brooks-Gunn, J., & Botwin, G. J. (2007). Links between pubertal timing, peer influences, and externalizing behaviors among urban students followed through middle school. *Journal of Adolescent Health, 40*(2).

Lyubomirsky, S., Sheldon, K. M., & Schkade, D. (2005). Pursuing happiness: The architecture of sustainable change. *Review of General Psychology, 9*, 111–131.

Maas, J. B. (1998). *Power sleep.* New York, NY: Harper Perennial.

Maccoby, E. E. (2000). Parenting and its effects on children: On reading and misreading behavior genetics. *Annual Review of Psychology, 51*, 1–27.

MacCoun, R. J. (1998). Biases in the interpretation and use of research results. *Annual Review Psychology, 49*, 259–287.

MacGregor, J. N., Ormerod, T. C., & Chronicle, E. P. (2001). Information-processing and insight: A process model of performance on the nine-dot and related problems. *Journal of Experimental Psychology: Learning, Memory, and Cognition, 27*, 176–201.

Machado, S., Arias-Carrión, O., Castillo, A. O., Lattari, E., Silva, A. C., & Nardi, A. E. (2013). Hemispheric specialization and regulation of motor behavior on a perspective of cognitive neuroscience. *Salud Mental, 3*, 513–520.

Machado, V., Leonidas, C., Santos, M. A., & Souza, J. (2012). Psychiatric readmission: An integrative review of the literature. *International Nursing Review, 59*, 447–457. doi:10.1111/j.1466-7657.2012.01011.x

Mack, A. (2003). Inattentional blindness: Looking without seeing. *Current Directions in Psychological Science, 12*(5), 180–184.

MacKellar, D. A., Valleroy, L. A., Secura, G. M., Behel, S., Bingham, T., Celentano, . . . Young Men's Survey Study Group. (2005). Unrecognized HIV infection, risk behaviors, and perceptions of risk among young men who have sex with men: Opportunities for advancing HIV prevention in the third decade of HIV/AIDS. *Journal of Acquired Immune Deficiency Syndromes, 38*, 603–614.

MacKenzie, M. J., Nicklas, E., Waldfogel, J., & Brooks-Gunn, J. (2013). Spanking and child development across the first decade of life. *Pediatrics, 132*, e1118–e1125. doi:10.1542/peds.2013-1227.

Mackey, A. P., Whitaker, K. J., & Bunge, S. A. (2012). Experience-dependent plasticity in white matter microstructure: reasoning training alters structural connectivity. *Frontiers in Neuroanatomy, 6*(32). doi:10.3389/fnana.2012.00032

Mackinnon, S. P., Jordan, C. H., & Wilson, A. E. (2011). Birds of a feather sit together: Physical similarity predicts seating choice. *Personality and Social Psychology Bulletin, 37*, 879–892. doi:10.1177/0146167211402094

Mackintosh, N. J. (1998). *IQ and human intelligence.* Oxford: Oxford University Press.

Mackintosh, N. J. (2011). History of theories and measurement of intelligence. In R. J. Sternberg, & S. B. Kaufman (Eds.), *Cambridge handbook of intelligence.* New York, NY: Cambridge University Press.

MacLean, P. D. (1954). Studies on limbic system ("visceal brain") and their bearing on psychosomatic problems. In E. D. Wittkower & R. A. Cleghorn (Eds.), *Recent developments in psychosomatic medicine.* Philadelphia, PA: Lippincott.

MacLean, P. D. (1993). Cerebral evolution of emotion. In M. Lewis & J. M. Haviland (Eds.), *Handbook of emotions.* New York, NY: Guilford Press.

MacLeod, A. K. (2013). Suicide and attempted suicide. In M. Power (Ed.), *The Wiley-Blackwell handbook of mood disorders* (2nd ed.). Malden, MA: Wiley-Blackwell.

MacMillan, H. L., Fleming, J. E., Trocme, N., Boyle, M. H., Wong, M., Racine, . . . Offord, D. R. (1997). Prevalence of child physical and sexual abuse in the community: Results from the Ontario health supplement. *JAMA, 278*, 131–135.

MacNeil, L., Espostio-Smythers, C., Mahlenbeck, R., & Weismoore, J. (2012). The effects of avoidance coping and coping self-efficacy on eating disorder attitudes and behaviors: A stress-diathesis model. *Eating Behaviors, 13*, 293–296. doi:10.1016/j.eatbeh.2012.06.005

Macrae, C. N., & Quadflieg, S. (2010). Perceiving people. In S. T. Fiske, D. T. Gilbert, & G. Lindzey (Eds.), *Handbook of social psychology* (5th ed., Vol. 1, pp. 353–393). Hoboken, NJ: Wiley.

Macritchie, K., & Blackwood, D. (2013). Neurobiological theories of bipolar disorder. In M. Power (Ed.), *The Wiley-Blackwell handbook of mood disorders* (2nd ed.). Malden, MA: Wiley-Blackwell.

MacWhinney, B. (2001). Emergentist approaches to language. In J. Bybee & P. Hooper (Eds.), *Frequency and the emergence of linguistic structure.* Amsterdam: John Benjamins Publishing.

MacWhinney, B. (2004). A multiple process solution to the logical problem of language acquisition. *Journal of Child Language, 31*, 883–914.

Maddux, W. W., & Galinsky, A. D. (2009). Cultural borders and mental barriers: The relationship between living abroad and creativity. *Journal of Personality and Social Psychology, 96*(5), 1047–1061. doi:10.1037/a0014861

Madill, A. (2012). Interviews and interviewing techniques. In H. Cooper, P. M. Camic, D. L. Long, A. T. Panter, D. Rindskopf, & K. J. Sher (Eds.), *APA handbook of research methods in psychology: Vol. 1. Foundations, planning, measures, and psychometrics.* Washington, DC: American Psychological Association.

Magee, C. A., Holliday, E. G., Attia, J., Kritharides, L., & Banks, E. (2013). Investigation of the relationship between sleep duration, all-cause mortality, and preexisting disease. *Sleep Medicine, 14*, 591–596. doi:10.1016/j.sleep.2013.02.002

Magnavita, J. J. (2008). Psychoanalytic psychotherapy. In J. L. Lebow (Ed.), *Twenty-first century psychotherapies: Contemporary approaches to theory and practice.* New York, NY: Wiley.

Maguire, W., Weisstein, N., & Klymenko, V. (1990). From visual structure to perceptual function. In K. N. Leibovic (Ed.), *Science of vision.* New York, NY: Springer-Verlag.

Magun-Jackson, S., & Burgette, J. E. (2013). Moral development. In B. J. Irby, G. Brown, R. Lara-Alecio, & S. Jackson (Eds.), *The handbook of educational theories.* Charlotte, NC: IAP—Information Age Publishing.

Mahar, I., Bambico, F. R., Mechawar, N., & Nobrega, J. N. (2014). Stress, serotonin, and hippocampal neurogenesis in relation to depression and antidepressant effects. *Neuroscience and*

Biobehavioral Reviews, 38, 173–192. doi:10.1016/j.neubiorev.2013.11.009

Maher, B. A. (2001). Delusions. In P. B. Sutker & H. E. Adams (Eds.), *Comprehensive handbook of psychopathology* (3rd ed., pp. 309–370). New York, NY: Kluwer Academic/Plenum Publishers.

Mahn, H., & John-Steiner, V. (2013). Vygotsky and sociocultural approaches to teaching and learning. In W. M. Reynolds, G. E. Miller, & I. B. Weiner (Eds.), *Handbook of psychology: Vol. 7. Educational psychology* (2nd ed.). Hoboken, NJ: Wiley.

Mahowald, M. W., & Schenck, C. H. (2005). Insights from studying human sleep disorders. *Nature, 437,* 1279–1285.

Maier, N. R. F. (1931). Reasoning and learning. *Psychological Review, 38,* 332–346.

Maio, G. R., Olson, J. M., & Cheung, I. (2013). Attitudes in social behavior. In H. Tennen, J. Suls, & I. B. Weiner (Eds.), *Handbook of psychology: Vol. 5. Personality and social psychology* (2nd ed.). New York, NY: Wiley.

Maldonado, J. R., & Spiegel, D. (2008). Dissociative disorders. In R. E. Hales, S. C. Yudofsky, & G. O. Gabbard (Eds.), *The American Psychiatric Publishing textbook of psychiatry* (5th ed., pp. 665–710). Washington, DC: American Psychiatric Publishing.

Maldonado, J. R., & Spiegel, D. (2014). Dissociative disorders. In R. E. Hales, S. C. Yudofsky, & L. W. Roberts (Eds.), *The American Psychiatric Publishing textbook of psychiatry* (6th ed.). Washington, DC: American Psychiatric Publishing.

Malin, K., & Littlejohn, G. O. (2013). Stress modulates key psychological processes and characteristic symptoms in females with fibromyalgia. *Clinical Experimental Rheumatology, 31,* S64-S71.

Malinowski, J., & Horton, C. L. (2014). Evidence for the preferential incorporation of emotional waking-life experiences into dreams. *Dreaming, 24,* 18–31. doi:10.1037/a0036017

Mandelman, S. D., & Grigorenko, E. L. (2011). Intelligence: Genes, environments, and their interactions. In R. J. Sternberg, & S. B. Kaufman (Eds.), *Cambridge handbook of intelligence.* New York, NY: Cambridge University Press.

Mandler, G. (1984). *Mind and body.* New York, NY: Norton.

Mandler, G. (1993). Thought, memory, and learning: Effects of emotional stress. In L. Goldberger & S. Breznitz (Eds.), *Handbook of stress: Theoretical and clinical aspects* (2nd ed.). New York, NY: Free Press.

Mandler, G. (2002). Origins of the cognitive revolution. *Journal of the History of the Behavioral Sciences, 38,* 339–353.

Maner, J. K., & Ackerman, J. M. (2013). Love is a battlefield: Romantic attraction, intrasexual competition, and conflict between the sexes. In J. A. Simpson & L. Campbell (Eds.), *Oxford handbook of close relationships.* New York, NY: Oxford University Press.

Manna, A., Raffone, A., Perrucci, M., Nardo, D., Ferretti, A., Tartaro, A., et al. (2010). Neural correlates of focused attention and cognitive monitoring in meditation. *Brain Research Bulletin, 82*(1–2), 46–56. doi:10.1016/j.brainresbull.2010.03.001

Manning, W. D., Brown, S. L., & Payne, K. K. (2014). Two decades of stability and change in age at first union formation. *Journal of Marriage and Family, 76,* 247–260. doi:10.1111/jomf.12090

Manning, W. D., & Cohen, J. A. (2012). Premarital cohabitation and marital dissolution: An examination of recent marriages. *Journal of Marriage and Family, 74,* 377–387. doi:10.1111/j.1741-3737.2012.00960.x

Manuck, S. B., & McCaffery J. M. (2014). Gene-environment interaction. *Annual Review of Psychology, 65,* 41–70. doi:10.1146/annurev-psych-010213-115100.

Marchand, W. R. (2013). Mindfulness meditation practices as adjunctive treatments for psychiatric disorders. *Psychiatric Clinics of North America, 36*(1), 141–152. doi:10.1016/j.psc.2013.01.002

Marcia, J. E. (1966). Development and validation of ego identity status. *Journal of Personality and Social Psychology, 3,* 551–558.

Marcia, J. E. (1980). Identity in adolescence. In J. Adelson (Ed.), *Handbook of adolescent psychology.* New York, NY: Wiley.

Marcia, J. E. (1994). The empirical study of ego identity. In H. A. Bosma, T. L. G. Graafsma, H. D. Grotevant, & D. J. de Levita (Eds.), *Identity and development: An interdisciplinary approach.* Thousand Oaks, CA: Sage.

Marder, S. R., Hurford, I. M., & van Kammen, D. P. (2009). Second-generation antipsychotics. In B. J. Sadock, V. A. Sadock, & P. Ruiz (Eds.), *Kaplan & Sadock's comprehensive textbook of psychiatry* (pp. 3206–3240). Philadelphia, PA: Lippincott Williams & Wilkins.

Marewski, J. N., Gaissmaier, W., & Gigerenzer, G. (2010). Good judgments do not require complex cognition. *Cognitive Processing, 11*(2), 103–121. doi:10.1007/s10339-009-0337-0

Markus, H. R., & Hamedani, M. G. (2007). Sociocultural psychology: The dynamic interdependence among self systems and social systems. In S. Kitayama & D. Cohen (Eds.), *Handbook of cultural psychology.* New York, NY: Guilford Press.

Markus, H. R., & Kitayama, S. (1991). Culture and the self: Implications for cognition, emotion, and motivation. *Psychological Review, 98,* 224–253.

Markus, H. R., & Kitayama, S. (1994). The cultural construction of self and emotion: Implications for social behavior. In S. Kitayama & H. R. Markus (Eds.), *Emotions and culture: Empirical studies of mutual influence.* Washington, DC: American Psychological Association.

Markus, H. R., & Kitayama, S. (2003). Culture, self, and the reality of the social. *Psychological Inquiry, 14*(3–4), 277–283.

Marsh, E. J. (2007). Retelling is not the same as recalling: Implications for memory. *Current Directions in Psychological Science, 16*(1), 16–20.

Marsh, E. J., & Roediger, H. I. (2013). Episodic and autobiographical memory. In A. F. Healy, R. W. Proctor, & I. B. Weiner (Eds.), *Handbook of psychology: Vol. 4. Experimental psychology* (2nd ed.). New York, NY: Wiley.

Marsh, E. J., & Tversky, B. (2004). Spinning the stories of our lives. *Applied Cognitive Psychology, 18,* 491–503.

Marsh, J. M., & Butler, A. C. (2013). Memory in educational settings, In D. Reisberg (Ed.), *Oxford handbook of cognitive psychology.* New York, NY: Oxford University Press.

Marsh, L., & Margolis, R. L. (2009). Neuropsychiatric aspects of movement disorders. In B. J. Sadock, V. A. Sadock, & P. Ruiz, *Kaplan & Sadock's comprehensive textbook of psychiatry* (9th ed., pp. 481–493). Philadelphia, PA: Lippincott Williams & Wilkins.

Marsland, A. L., Bachen, E. A., & Cohen, S. (2012). Stress, immunity, and susceptibility to upper respiratory infectious disease. In A. Baum, T. A. Revenson, & J. Singer (Eds.), *Handbook of health psychology.* New York, NY: Psychology Press.

Marteau, T. M., & Weinman, J. (2004). Communicating about health threats and treatments. In S. Sutton, A. Baum, & M. Johnston (Ed), *The Sage handbook of health psychology.* Thousand Oaks, CA: Sage.

Martin, C. L., & Ruble, D. (2004). Children's search for gender cues: Cognitive perspectives on gender development. *Current Directions in Psychological Science, 13*(2), 67–70.

Martin, L. (1986). "Eskimo words for snow": A case study in the genesis and decay of an anthropological example. *American Psychologist, 88,* 418–423.

Martin, R., & Leventhal, H. (2004). Symptom perception and health care–seeking behavior. In J. M. Raczynski & L. C. Leviton (Eds.), *Handbook of clinical health psychology: Vol. 2. Disorders of behavior and health.* Washington, DC: American Psychological Association.

Martin, R. A. (2002). IS laughter the best medicine? Humor, laughter, and physical health. *Current Directions in Psychological Science, 11*(6), 216–220.

Martin, S. (2011). The behavioral scientist behind eHarmony said today's web technology offers rich possibilities for researchers. *Monitor on Psychology, 42,* 69.

Martinez, M., Marangell, L. B., & Martinez, J. M. (2008). Psychopharmacology. In R. E. Hales, S. C. Yudofsky, & G. O. Gabbard (Eds.), *The American Psychiatric Publishing textbook of psychiatry* (pp. 1053–1132). Washington, DC: American Psychiatric Publishing.

Martins, C. S., de Carvalho Tofoli, S. M., Von Werne Baes, C., & Juruena, M. (2011). Analysis of the occurrence of early life stress in adult psychiatric patients: A systematic review. *Psychology & Neuroscience, 4*(2), 219–227. doi:10.3922/j.psns.2011.2.007

Maslow, A. H. (1954). *Motivation and personality.* New York, NY: Harper & Row.

Maslow, A. H. (1968). *Toward a psychology of being.* New York, NY: Van Nostrand.

Maslow, A. H. (1970). *Motivation and personality.* New York, NY: Harper & Row.

Masters, W. H., & Johnson, V. E. (1966). *Human sexual response.* Boston, MA: Little, Brown.

Masters, W. H., & Johnson, V. E. (1970). *Human sexual inadequacy.* Boston, MA: Little, Brown.

Masuda, T. (2010). Cultural effects on visual perception. In E. B. Goldstein (Ed.), *Encyclopedia of perception.* Thousand Oaks, CA: Sage.

Masuda, T., & Nisbett, R. E. (2001). Attending holistically versus analytically: Comparing the context sensitivity of Japanese and Americans. *Journal of Personality and Social Psychology, 81,* 922–934.

Mathieu, C., & St-Jean, É. (2013). Entrepreneurial personality: The role of narcissism. *Personality and Individual Differences, 55,* 527–531. doi:10.1016/j.paid.2013.04.026

Matlin, M. W. (1989). *Cognition.* New York, NY: Holt, Rinehart & Winston.

Matlin, M. W. (2008). *The psychology of women.* Belmont, CA: Wadsworth.

Matsumoto, D. (2003). Cross-cultural research. In S. F. Davis (Ed.), *Handbook of research methods in experimental psychology.* Malden, MA: Blackwell.

Matsumoto, D., & Hwang, H. S. (2011). Culture, emotion, and expression. In K. D. Keith (Ed.), *Cross-cultural psychology: Contemporary themes and perspectives.* Malden, MA: Wiley-Blackwell.

Matsumoto, D., & Juang, L. (2008). *Culture and psychology.* Belmont, CA: Wadsworth.

Matsumoto, D., Nezlek, J. B., & Koopmann, B. (2007). Evidence for universality in phenomenological emotion response system coherence. *Emotion, 7,* 57–67.

Matsumoto, D., & Willingham, B. (2009). Spontaneous facial expressions of emotion of congenitally and non-congenitally blind individuals. *Journal of Personality and Social Psychology, 96*(1), 1–10. doi:10.1037/a0014037

Matsumoto, D., & Yoo, S. (2006). Toward a new generation of cross-cultural research. *Perspectives on Psychological Science, 1,* 234–250.

Matthey, S. (1998). P<.05—But is it clinically *significant?:* Practical examples for clinicians. *Behaviour Change, 15,* 140–146.

Maugh, T. H., II. (2008, December 9). Henry M. dies at 82: Victim of brain surgery accident offered doctors key insights into memory. *Los Angeles Times.* Retrieved from http://latimes.com

Mays, V. M., Rubin, J., Sabourin, M., & Walker, L. (1996). Moving toward a global psychology: Changing theories and practice to meet the needs of a changing world. *American Psychologist, 51,* 485–487.

Mazzetti, G., Schaufeli, W. B., & Guglielmi, D. (2014). Are workaholics born or made? Relations of workaholism with person characteristics and overwork climate. *International Journal of Stress Management, 21,* 227–254. doi:10.1037/a0035700

Mazzoni, G., Heap, M., & Scoboria, A. (2010). Hypnosis and memory: Theory, laboratory research, and applications. In S. Lynn, J. W. Rhue, & I. Kirsch (Eds.), *Handbook of clinical hypnosis* (2nd ed., pp. 709–741). Washington, DC: American Psychological Association.

Mazzoni, G., Laurence, J., & Heap, M. (2014). Hypnosis and memory: Two hundred years of adventures and still going!. *Psychology of Consciousness: Theory, Research, and Practice, 1,* 153–167. doi:10.1037/cns0000016

Mazzoni, G., Venneri, A., McGeown, W. J., & Kirsch, I. (2013). Neuroimaging resolution of the altered state hypothesis. *Cortex: A Journal Devoted to the Study of the Nervous System and Behavior, 49,* 400–410. doi:10.1016/j.cortex.2012.08.005

McAbee, S. T., & Oswald, F. L. (2013). The criterion-related validity of personality measures for predicting GPA: A meta-analytic validity competition. *Psychological Assessment, 25,* 532–544. doi:10.1037/a0031748

McBride-Chang, C., & Jacklin, C. N. (1993). Early play arousal, sex-typed play, and activity level as precursors to later rough-and-tumble play. *Early Education & Development, 4,* 99–108.

McCabe, J., Fairchild, E., Grauerholz, L., Pescosolido, B. A., & Tope, D. (2011). Gender in twentieth-century children's books: Patterns of disparity in titles and central character. *Gender & Society, 25,* 197–226. doi:10.1177/0891243211398358

McCabe, R. E., & Antony, M. M. (2008). Anxiety disorders: Social and specific phobias. In A. Tasman, J. Kay, J. A. Lieberman, M. B. First, & M. Maj (Eds.), *Psychiatry* (3rd ed.). New York, NY: Wiley-Blackwell.

McCaffrey, T. (2012). Innovation relies on the obscure: A key to overcoming the classic problem of functional fixedness. *Psychological Science, 23,* 215–218. doi:10.1177/0956797611429580

McCall, W. V., Reboussin, D., Prudic, J., Haskett, R. F., Isenberg, K., Olfson, M., . . . Sackeim, H. A. (2013). Poor health-related quality of life prior to ECT in depressed patients normalizes with sustained remission after ECT. *Journal of Affective Disorders, 147*(1-3), 107–111. doi:10.1016/j.jad.2012.10.018

McCarley, R. W. (1994). Dreams and the biology of sleep. In M. H. Kryger, T. Roth, & W. C. Dement (Eds.), *Principles and practice of sleep medicine* (2nd ed.). Philadelphia, PA: Saunders.

McCauley, M. E., Eskes, G., & Moscovitch, M. (1996). The effect of imagery on explicit and implicit tests of memory in young and old people: A double dissociation. *Canadian Journal of Experimental Psychology, 50,* 34–41.

McClelland, D. C. (1975). *Power: The inner experience.* New York, NY: Irvington.

McClelland, D. C. (1985). How motives, skills and values determine what people do. *American Psychologist, 40,* 812–825.

McClelland, D. C., Atkinson, J. W., Clark, R. A., & Lowell, E. L. (1953). *The achievement motive.* New York, NY: Appleton-Century-Crofts.

McClelland, D. C., & Koestner, R. (1992). The achievement motive. In C. P. Smith (Ed.), *Motivation and personality: Handbook of thematic content analysis.* New York, NY: Cambridge University Press.

McClure, M. J., & Lydon, J. E. (2014). Anxiety doesn't become you: How attachment anxiety compromises relational opportunities. *Journal of Personality and Social Psychology, 106,* 89–111. doi:10.1037/aa34532

McCormick, D. A. (2008). Membrane potential and action potential. In L. Squire, D. Berg, F. Bloom, S. Du Lac, A. Ghosh, & N. Spitzer (Eds.), *Fundamental neuroscience* (3rd ed., pp. 112–132). San Diego, CA: Elsevier.

McCrae, R. R. (1984). Situational determinants of coping responses: Loss, threat and challenge. *Journal of Personality and Social Psychology, 46,* 919–928.

McCrae, R. R., Chan, W., Jussim, L., De Fruyt, F., Löckenhoff, C. E., De Bolle, M., . . . Terracciano, A. (2013). The inaccuracy of national character stereotypes. *Journal of Research in Personality, 47,* 831–842. doi:10.1016/j.jrp.2013.08.006

McCrae, R. R., & Costa, P. T., Jr. (1985). Updating Norman's "adequate taxonomy": Intelligence and personality dimensions in natural language and in questionnaires. *Journal of Personality and Social Psychology, 49,* 710–721.

McCrae, R. R., & Costa, P. T., Jr. (1987). Validation of the five-factor model of personality across instruments and observers. *Journal of Personality and Social Psychology, 52,* 81–90.

McCrae, R. R., & Costa, P. T., Jr. (1990). *Personality in adulthood.* New York, NY: Guilford Press.

McCrae, R. R., & Costa, P. T., Jr. (1997). Personality trait structure as a human universal. *American Psychologist, 52,* 509–516.

McCrae, R. R., & Costa, P. T., Jr. (2007). Brief versions of the NEO-PI-3. *Journal of Individual Differences, 28,* 116–128.

McCrae, R. R., & Costa, P. T., Jr. (2008). The five-factor theory of personality. In O. P. John, R. W. Robbins, & L. A. Pervin (Eds.), *Handbook of personality: Theory and research* (Vol. 3, pp. 159–181). New York, NY: Guilford Press.

McCrae, R. R., & Costa, P. T., Jr. (2010). *Professional manual for the NEO Inventories.* Lutz, FL: Psychological Assessment Resources.

McCrae, R. R., Gaines, J. F., & Wellington, M. A. (2013).The five-factor model in fact and fiction. In H. Tennen, J. Suls, & I. B. Weiner (Eds.), *Handbook of psychology: Vol. 5. Personality and social psychology* (2nd ed.). New York, NY: Wiley.

McCrae, R. R., & Sutin, A. R. (2009). Openness to experience. In M. R. Leary & R. H. Hoyle (Eds.), *Handbook of individual differences in social behavior* (pp. 257–273). New York, NY: Guilford Press.

McCrae, R. R., & Terracciano, A. (2006). National character and personality. *Current Directions in Psychological Science, 15,* 156–161.

McCrae, R. R., & Terracciano, A., & Personality Profiles of Cultures Project. (2005). Personality profiles of cultures: Aggregate personality traits. *Journal of Personality and Social Psychology, 89,* 407–425.

McCrink, K., & Wynn, K. (2004). Large-number addition and subtraction by 9-month-old infants. *Psychological Science, 15,* 776–781.

McCullough, M. E. (2001). Forgiving. In C. R. Snyder (Ed.), *Coping with stress: Effective people and processes* (pp. 93–113). New York, NY: Oxford University Press.

McCullough, M. E., Kurzban, R., & Tabak, B. A. (2013). Cognitive systems for revenge and forgiveness. *Behavioral and Brain Science, 36,* 1–15. doi:10.1017/S0140525X11002160

McCullough, M. E., Pedersen, E. J., Tabak, B. A., & Carter, E. C. (2014). Conciliatory gestures promote forgiveness and reduce anger in humans. *PNAS Proceedings of the National Academy of Sciences of the United States of America, 111,* 11211–11216. doi:10.1073/pnas.1405072111

McCullough, M. E., & Witvliet, C. V. (2002). The psychology of forgiveness. In C. R. Synder & S. J. Lopez (Eds.), *Handbook of positive psychology.* New York, NY: Oxford University Press.

McDaniel, M. A., & Einstein, G. O. (1986). Bizarre imagery as an effective memory aid: The importance of distinctiveness. *Journal of Experimental Psychology: Learning, Memory & Cognition, 12,* 54–65.

McDaniel, M. A., Waddill, P. J., & Shakesby, P. S. (1996). Study strategies, interest, and learning from text: The application of material appropriate processing. In D. J. Herrmann, C. McEvoy, C. Hertzog, P. Hertel, & M. K. Johnson (Eds.), *Basic and applied memory research: Theory in context* (Vol. 1). Mahwah, NJ: Erlbaum.

McDermott, K. B. (2007). Inducing false memories through associated lists: A window onto everyday false memories? In J. S. Nairne (Ed.), *The foundations of remembering: Essays in honor of Henry L. Roediger III.* New York, NY: Psychology Press.

McDermott, K. B., Agarwal, P. K., D'Antonio, L., Roediger, H. I., & McDaniel, M. A. (2014). Both multiple-choice and short-answer quizzes enhance later exam performance in middle and high school classes. *Journal of Experimental Psychology: Applied, 20*(1), 3–21. doi:10.1037/xap0000004

McDevitt, M. A., & Williams, B. A. (2001). Effects of signaled versus unsignaled delay of reinforcement on choice. *Journal of the Experimental Analysis of Behavior, 75,* 165–182. doi:10.1901/jeab.2001.75-165

McDonald, C., & Murphy, K. C. (2003). The new genetics of schizophrenia. *Psychiatric Clinics of North America, 26*(1), 41–63.

McEvoy, J. P., Byerly, M., Hamer, R. M., Dominik, R., Swartz, M. S., Rosenheck, R. A., . . . Stroup, T. S. (2014). Effectiveness of paliperidone palmitate vs haloperidol decanoate for maintenance treatment of schizophrenia: A randomized clinical trial. *JAMA, 311,* 1978–1986. doi:10.1001/jama.2014.4310

McEwen, B. S. (2009). Stress and coping. In G. G. Berntson & J. T. Cacioppo (Eds.), *Handbook of neuroscience for the behavioral sciences* (Vol. 2, pp. 1220–1235). Hoboken, NJ: Wiley.

McGeoch, J. A., & McDonald, W. T. (1931). Meaningful relation and retroactive inhibition. *American Journal of Psychology, 43,* 579–588.

McGinty, D., & Szymusiak, R. (2011). Neural control of sleep in mammals. In M. H. Kryger, T. Roth, & W. C. Dement (Eds.), *Principles and practice of sleep medicine* (5th ed., pp. 76–91). St. Louis, MO: Elsevier Saunders.

McGinty, E. E., Webster, D. W., & Barry, C. L. (2013). Effects of news media messages about mass shootings on attitudes toward persons with serious mental illness and public support for gun control policies. *The American Journal of Psychiatry, 170,* 494–501. doi:10.1176/appi.ajp.2013.13010014

McGrath, J. J., & Murray, R. M. (2011). Environmental risk factors for schizophrenia. In D. R. Weinberger & P. Harrison (Eds.), *Schizophrenia* (3rd ed.). Malden, MA: Wiley-Blackwell.

McGue, M., Bouchard, T. J., Jr., Iacono, W. G., & Lykken, D. T. (1993). Behavioral genetics of cognitive ability: A life-span perspective. In R. Plomin & G. E. McClearn (Eds.), *Nature, nurture and psychology.* Washington, DC: American Psychological Association.

McGugin, R. W., Gatenby, J. C., Gore, J. C., & Gauthier, I. (2012). High-resolution imaging of expertise reveals reliable object selectivity in the fusiform face area related to

perceptual performance. *Proceedings of the National Academy of Sciences, 109*(42), 17063–17068. doi:10.1073/pnas.1116333109

McGuigan, F. J., & Lehrer, P. M. (2007). Progressive relaxation: Origins, principles, and clinical applications. In P. M. Lehrer, R. L. Woolfolk, & W. E. Sime (Eds.), *Principles and practice of stress management.* New York, NY: Guilford Press.

McInnis, M. G., Ribia, M., & Greden, J. F. (2014). Anxiety disorders. In R. E. Hales, S. C. Yudofsky, & L. W. Roberts (Eds.), *The American Psychiatric Publishing textbook of psychiatry* (6th ed.). Washington, DC: American Psychiatric Publishing.

McLanahan, S., Tach, L., & Schneider, D. (2013). The causal effects of father absence. *Annual Review of Sociology, 39,* 399–427.

McLay, R. N., Daylo, A. A., & Hammer, P. S. (2006). No effect of lunar cycle on psychiatric admissions or emergency evaluations. *Military Medicine, 171,* 1239–1242.

McLellan, A. T., Lewis, D. C., O'Brien, C. P., & Kleber, H. D. (2000). Drug dependence, a chronic mental illness: Implications for treatment, insurance, and outcome evaluation. *JAMA, 284,* 1689–1695.

McLoughlin, K., & Paquet, M. (2005, December 14). Gambling led Hogan to robbery, lawyer says. *Lehigh University's The Brown and White.* Retrieved from www.bw.lehigh.edu/story.asp?ID=19313.

McLoyd, V. C. (1998). Socioeconomic disadvantage and child development. *American Psychologist, 53,* 185–204.

McNally, R. J. (2009). Posttraumatic stress disorder. In P. H. Blaney & T. Millon (Eds.), *Oxford textbook of psychopathology* (2nd ed., pp. 176–197). New York, NY: Oxford University Press.

McNally, R. J. (2012). Searching for repressed memory. In R. F. Belli (Ed.), *True and false recovered memories: Toward a reconciliation of the debate.* New York, NY: Springer.

McNally, R. J., & Geraerts, E. (2009). A new solution to the recovered memory debate. *Perspectives on Psychological Science, 4*(2), 126–134. doi:10.1111/j.1745-6924.2009.01112.x

McNamara, T. P. (2013). Semantic memory and priming. In A. F. Healy, R. W. Proctor, & I. B. Weiner (Eds.), *Handbook of psychology: Vol. 4. Experimental psychology* (2nd ed.). New York, NY: Wiley.

McWhorter, K. T. (2007). *College reading & study skills.* New York, NY: Pearson Longman.

Mechanic, D. (1980). *Mental health and social policy.* Englewood Cliffs, NJ: Prentice-Hall.

Mednick, S. C., & Drummond, S. P. A. (2009). Napping. In R. Stickgold & M. P. Walker (Eds.), *The neuroscience of sleep* (pp. 254–262). San Diego, CA: Academic Press.

Meeus, W., van de Schoot, R., Keijsers, L., Schwartz, S. J., & Branje, S. (2010). On the progression and stability of adolescent identity formation: A five-wave longitudinal study in early-to-middle and middle-to-late adolescence. *Child Development, 81*(5), 1565–1581. doi:10.1111/j.1467-8624.2010.01492.x

Mehl, M. R., & Robbins, M. L. (2012). Naturalistic observation sampling: The Electronically Activated Recorder (EAR). In M. R. Mehl & T. S. Connor (Eds.), *Handbook of research methods for studying daily life.* New York, NY: Guilford Press.

Meillon, S., Thomas, A., Havermans, R., Pénicaud, L., & Brondel, L. (2013). Sensory-specific satiety for a food is unaffected by the ad libitum intake of other foods during a meal. Is SSS subject to dishabituation? *Appetite, 63,* 112–118. doi:10.1016/j.appet.2012.12.004

Meister, B. (2007). Neurotransmitters in key neurons of the hypothalamus that regulate feeding behavior and body weight. *Physiology & Behavior, 92,* 263–271.

Meister, M., & Tessier-Lavigne, M. (2013). Low-level visual processing: The retina. In E. R. Kandel, J. H. Schwartz, T. M. Jessell, S. A. Siegelbaum, & A. J. Hudspeth (Eds.), *Principles of neural science* (5th ed.). New York, NY: McGraw-Hill.

Meltzer, A. L., McNulty, J. K., Jackson, G. L., & Karney, B. R. (2014). Sex differences in the implications of partner physical attractiveness for the trajectory of marital satisfaction. *Journal of Personality and Social Psychology, 106,* 418–428. doi:10.1037/a0034424

Meltzer, H. Y., & Bobo, W. V. (2009). Antipsychotic and anticholinergic drugs. In M. C. Gelder, N. C. Andreasen, J. J. López-Ibor, Jr., & J. R. Geddes (Eds.), *New Oxford textbook of psychiatry* (2nd ed., Vol. 1). New York, NY: Oxford University Press.

Melzack, R., & Wall, P. D. (1965). Pain mechanisms: A new theory. *Science, 150,* 971–979.

Men, W., Falk, D., Sun, T., Chen, W., Li, J., Yin, D., . . . Fan, M. (2013). The corpus callosum of Albert Einstein's brain: Another clue to his high intelligence? *Brain, 24,* 1–8. doi:10.1093/brain/awt252

Mendelson, W. (2011). Hypnotic medications: Mechanisms of action

and pharmacologic effects. In M. H. Kryger, T. Roth, & W. C. Dement (Eds.), *Principles and practice of sleep medicine* (5th ed.). Saint Louis, MO: Elsevier Saunders.

Menninger, W. W. (2005). Role of the psychiatric hospital in the treatment of mental illness. In B. J. Sadock & V. A. Sadock (Eds.), *Kaplan & Sadock's comprehensive textbook of psychiatry.* Philadelphia, PA: Lippincott Williams & Wilkins.

Merolla, J. L., Burnett, G., Pyle, K. V., Ahmadi, S., & Zak, P. J. (2013). Oxytocin and the biological basis for interpersonal and political trust. *Political Behavior, 35,* 753–776. doi:10.1007/s11109-012-9219-8

Mesmer-Magnus, J., Glew, D. J., & Viswesvaran, C. (2012). A meta-analysis of positive humor in the work-place. *Journal of Managerial Psychology, 27,* 155–190. doi:10.1108/02683941211199554

Mesquita, B., & Leu, J. (2007). The cultural psychology of emotion. In S. Kitayama & D. Cohen (Eds.), *Handbook of cultural psychology.* New York, NY: Guilford Press.

Mesulam, M. (2013). Cholinergic circuitry of the human nucleus basalis and its fate in Alzheimer's disease. *The Journal of Comparative Neurology, 521,* 4124–4144. doi:10.1002/cne.23415

Meyer, G. J., Hsiao, W., Viglione, D. J., Mihura, J. L., & Abraham, L. M. (2013). Rorschach scores in applied clinical practice: A survey of perceived validity by experienced clinicians. *Journal of Personality Assessment, 95,* 351–365. doi:10.1080/00223891.2013.770399

Meyer, G. J., & Viglione, D. J. (2008). An introduction to Rorschach assessment. In R. P. Archer, & S. R. Smith (Eds.), *Personality assessment.* New York, NY: Routledge/Taylor & Francis Group.

Meyer, O., Zane, N., & Cho, Y. I. (2011). Understanding the psychological processes of the racial match effect in Asian Americans. *Journal of Counseling Psychology, 58*(3), 335–345. doi:10.1037/a0023605

Meyer, R. E. (1996). The disease called addiction: Emerging evidence in a 200-year debate. *The Lancet, 347,* 162–166.

Meyer, R. G. (1992). *Practical clinical hypnosis: Techniques and applications.* New York, NY: Lexington Books.

Meyerbröker, K., & Emmelkamp, P. G. (2010). Virtual reality exposure therapy in anxiety disorders: A systematic review of process-and-outcome studies. *Depression and Anxiety, 27*(10), 933–944. doi:10.1002/da.20734

Mezulis, A. H., Abramson, L. Y., Hyde, J. S., & Hankin, B. L. (2004). Is there a universal positivity bias in attributions? A meta-analytic review of individual, developmental and cultural differences in the self-serving attributional bias. *Psychological Bulletin, 130*, 711–747.

Michael, E. B., & Gollan, T. H. (2005). Being and becoming bilingual: Individual differences and consequences for language production. In J. F. Kroll & A. B. de Groot (Eds.), *Handbook of bilingualism: Psycholinguistic approaches* (pp. 389–407). New York, NY: Oxford University Press.

Michels, N., Sioen, I., Braet, C., Eiben, G., Hebestreit, A., Huybrechts, I., . . . De Henauw, S. (2012). Stress, emotional eating behaviour and dietary patterns in children. *Appetite, 59*, 762–769. doi:10.1016 /j.appet.2012.08.010

Miklowitz, D. J. (2014). Pharmacotherapy and psychosocial treatments. In I. H. Gotlib & C. L. Hammen, (Eds.), *Handbook of depression* (3rd ed). New York, NY: Guilford Press.

Mikulincer, M., & Shaver, P. R. (2013). The role of attachment security in adolescent and adult close relationships. In J. A. Simpson & L. Campbell (Eds.), *Oxford handbook of close relationships*. New York, NY: Oxford University Press.

Milad, M. R., & Quirk, G. J. (2012). Fear extinction as a model for translational neuroscience: Ten years of progress. *Annual Review of Psychology, 63*, 129–151. doi:10.1146/annurev. psych.121208.131631

Milar, K. S. (2000). The first generation of women psychologists and the psychology of women. *American Psychologist, 55*, 616–619.

Milgram, S. (1963). Behavioral study of obedience. *Journal of Abnormal and Social Psychology, 67*, 371–378.

Milgram, S. (1964). Issues in the study of obedience. *American Psychologist, 19*, 848–852.

Milgram, S. (1968). Reply to the critics. *International Journal of Psychiatry, 6*, 294–295.

Millecamps, M., Seminowicz, D. A., Bushnell, M. C., & Coderre, T. J. (2013). The biopsychology of pain. In R. J. Nelson, S. Y. Mizumori, & I. B. Weiner (Eds.), *Handbook of psychology: Vol. 3. Behavioral neuroscience* (2nd ed., pp. 240–271). New York, NY: Wiley.

Miller, A. G. (1986). *The obedience experiments: A case study of controversy in social science*. New York, NY: Praeger.

Miller, A. G. (2014). The explanatory value of Milgram's obedience experiments: A contemporary appraisal. *Journal of Social Issues, 70*, 558–573. doi:10.1111/josi.12078

Miller, B. J., Culpepper, N., Rapaport, M. H., & Buckley, P. (2013). Prenatal inflammation and neurodevelopment in schizophrenia: A review of human studies. *Progress in Neuro-Psychopharmacology & Biological Psychiatry, 42*, 92–100. doi:10.1016/j.pnpbp .2012.03.010

Miller, D. I., & Halpern, D. F. (2014). The new science of cognitive sex difference. *Trends in Cognitive Sciences, 18*, 37–45. doi:10.1016/j.tics.2013 .10.011

Miller, E., & Wallis, J. (2008). The prefrontal cortex and executive brain functions. In L. Squire, D. Berg, F. Bloom, S. Du Lac, A. Ghosh, & N. Spitzer (Eds.), *Fundamental neuroscience* (3rd ed., pp. 1199–1222). San Diego, CA: Elsevier.

Miller, G. (2009). The brain collector. *Science, 324*(5935), 1634–1636.

Miller, G., Tybur, J. M., & Jordan, B. D. (2007). Ovulatory cycle effects on tip earnings by lap dancers: Economic evidence for human estrus? *Evolution and Human Behavior, 28*, 375–381.

Miller, G. A. (1956). The magical number seven, plus or minus two: Some limits on our capacity for processing information. *Psychological Review, 63*, 81–97.

Miller, G. A. (2003). The cognitive revolution: A historical perspective. *Trends in Cognitive Sciences, 7*(3), 141–144.

Miller, I. J., & Reedy, F. E. Jr. (1990). Variations in human taste-bud density and taste intensity perception. *Physiological Behavior, 47*, 1213–1219.

Miller, J. D., Gentile, B., Wilson, L., & Campbell, W. K. (2013). Grandiose and vulnerable narcissism and the DSM-5 pathological personality trait model. *Journal of Personality Assessment, 95*(3), 284–290. doi:10.1080/00 223891.2012.685907

Miller, J. G. (2006). Insights into moral development from cultural psychology. In M. Killen & J. G. Smetana (Eds.), *Handbook of moral development*. Mahwah, NJ: Erlbaum.

Miller, J. M., & Peterson, D. A. M. (2004). Theoretical and empirical implications of attitude strength. *Journal of Politics, 66*, 847–867.

Miller, K. J., Dye, R. V., Kim, J., Jennings, J. L., O'Toole, E., Wong, J., & Siddarth, P. (2013). Effect of a computerized brain exercise program on cognitive performance in older adults. *The American Journal of Geriatric Psychiatry, 21*, 655–663. doi:10.1016/j.jagp.2013.01.077

Miller, N. E. (1944). Experimental studies of conflict. In J. M. Hunt (Ed.), *Personality and the behavior disorders* (Vol. 1). New York, NY: Ronald.

Miller, N. E. (1959). Liberalization of basic S-R concepts: Extension to conflict behavior, motivation, and social learning. In S. Koch (Ed.), *Psychology: A study of a science* (Vol. 2). New York, NY: McGraw-Hill.

Miller, N. E. (1985). The value of behavioral research on animals. *American Psychologist, 40*, 423–440.

Miller, R. R., & Grace, R. C. (2013). Conditioning and learning. In A. F. Healy, R. W. Proctor, & I. B. Weiner (Eds.), *Handbook of psychology: Vol. 4. Experimental psychology* (2nd ed.). New York, NY: Wiley.

Miller Burke, J., & Attridge, M. (2011a). Pathways to career and leadership success: Part 1—A psychosocial profile of $100k professionals. *Journal of Workplace Behavioral Health, 26*(3), 175-206. http://dx.doi.org/10.1 080/15555240.2011.589718

Miller Burke, J., & Attridge, M. (2011b). Pathways to career and leadership success: Part 2—Striking gender similarities among $100k professionals. *Journal of Workplace Behavioral Health, 26*(3), 207–239.http://dx.doi. org/10.1080/15555240.2011.589722

Milligan, E. D., & Watkins, L. R. (2009). Pathological and protective roles of glia in chronic pain. *Nature Reviews Neuroscience, 10*(1), 23–36. doi:10.1038/nrn2533

Mills, K. L., Goddings, A., Clasen, L. S., Giedd, J. N., & Blakemore, S. (2014). The developmental mismatch in structural brain maturation during adolescence. *Developmental Neuroscience, 36*, 147–160. doi:10.1159/000362328

Millstone, E. (1989). Methods and practices of animal experimentation. In G. Langley (Ed.), *Animal experimentation: The consensus changes*. New York, NY: Chapman & Hall.

Miltenberger, R. G. (2012). *Behavior modification: Principles and procedures*. Belmont, CA: Cengage Learning.

Mineka, S. (2013). Individual differences in the acquisition of fears. In D. Hermans, B. Rimé, & B. Mesquita (Eds.), *Changing emotions*. New York, NY: Psychology Press.

Mineka, S., & Öhman, A. (2002). Phobias and preparedness: The selective, automatic and encapsulated nature of fear. *Biological Psychiatry, 52*, 927–937.

Minkel, J. D., & Dinges, D. F. (2009). Circadian rhythms in sleepiness, alertness, and performance. In R. Stickgold & M. P. Walker (Eds.), *The neuroscience of sleep* (pp. 183–190). San Diego, CA: Academic Press.

Minzenberg, M. J., Yoon, J. H., & Carter, C. S. (2008). Schizophrenia. In R. E. Hales, S. C. Yudofsky, &

G. O. Gabbard (Eds.), *The American Psychiatric Publishing textbook of psychiatry* (5th ed., pp. 407–456). Washington, DC: American Psychiatric Publishing.

Miranda, J., Bernal, G., Lau, A., Kohn, L., Hwang, W., & LaFromboise, T. (2005). State of the science on psychosocial interventions for ethnic minorities. *Annual Review of Clinical Psychology, 1*, 113–42.

Mischel, W. (1968). *Personality and assessment*. New York, NY: Wiley.

Mischel, W. (1973). Toward a cognitive social learning conceptualization of personality. *Psychological Review, 80*, 252–283.

Mischel, W. (1984). Convergences and challenges in the search for consistency. *American Psychologist, 39*, 351–364.

Mitchell, J. E., & Wonderlich, S. A. (2014). Feeding and eating disorders. In R. E. Hales, S. C. Yudofsky, & L. W. Roberts (Eds.), *The American Psychiatric Publishing textbook of psychiatry* (6th ed.). Washington, DC: American Psychiatric Publishing.

Mitchell, T., O'Sullivan, P. B., Smith, A., Burnett, A. F., Straker, L., Thornton, J., & Rudd, C. J. (2009). Biopsychosocial factors are associated with low back pain in female nursing students: A cross-sectional study. *International Journal of Nursing Studies, 46*(5), 678–688. doi:10.1016 /j.ijnurstu.2008.11.004

Mitterauer, B. J. (2011). Possible role of glia in cognitive impairment in schizophrenia. *CNS Neuroscience & Therapeutics, 17*, 333–344. doi:10.1111/j.1755-5949.2009 .00113.x

Miyamoto, S., Merrill, D. B., Lieberman, J. A., Fleischacker, W. W., & Marder, S. R. (2008). Antipsychotic drugs. In A. Tasman, J. Kay, J. A. Lieberman, M. B. First, & M. Maj (Eds.), *Psychiatry* (3rd ed.). New York, NY: Wiley-Blackwell.

Modestin, J. (1992). Multiple personality disorder in Switzerland. *American Journal of Psychiatry, 149*, 88–92.

Moè, A., & De Beni, R. (2004). Studying passages with the loci method: Are subject-generated more effective than experimenter-supplied loci pathways? *Journal of Mental Imagery, 28*(3–4), 75–86.

Mojtabai, R., & Olfson, M. (2010). National trends in psychotropic medication polypharmacy in office-based psychiatry. *Archives of General Psychiatry, 67*(1), 26–36.

Molitor, A., & Hsu, H. (2011). Child development across cultures. In K. D. Keith (Ed.), *Cross-cultural psychology: Contemporary themes and perspectives*. Malden, MA: Wiley-Blackwell.

Moll, H., & Meltzoff, A. N. (2011). How does it look? Level 2 perspective-taking at 36 months of age. *Child Development,82*(2), 661–673. doi:org/10.1111/j.1467-8624.2010.01571.x

Moneta, G. B. (2011). Need for achievement, burnout, and intention to leave: Testing an occupational model in educational settings. *Personality and Individual Differences, 50,* 274–278. doi:10.1016/j.paid.2010.10.002

Monk, C., Georgieff, M. K., & Osterholm, E. A. (2013). Research review: Maternal prenatal distress and poor nutrition: Mutually influencing risk factors affecting infant neurocognitive development. *Journal of Child Psychology and Psychiatry, 54,* 115–130. doi:10.1111/jcpp.12000

Monk, T. H. (2000). Shift work. In M. H. Kryger, T. Roth, & W. C. Dement (Eds.), *Principles and practice of sleep medicine*. Philadelphia, PA: Saunders.

Monk, T. H. (2006). Jet lag. In T. Lee-Chiong (Ed.), *Sleep: A comprehensive handbook*. Hoboken, NJ: Wiley-Liss.

Monroe, S. M. (2008). Modern approaches to conceptualizing and measuring human life stress. *Annual Review of Clinical Psychology, 4,* 33–52.

Monroe, S. M., & Harkness, K. L. (2005). Life stress, the "kindling" hypothesis, and the recurrence of depression: Considerations from a life stress perspective. *Psychological Review, 112,* 417–445. doi:10.1037/0033-295X.112.2.417

Monroe, S. M., Slavich, G. M., & Georgiades, K. (2014). The social environment and depression: The roles of life stress. In I. H. Gotlib & C. L. Hammen (Eds.), *Handbook of depression* (3rd ed.). New York, NY: Guilford Press.

Montoya, R., & Horton, R. S. (2012). The reciprocity of liking effect. In M. A. Paludi (Ed.), *The psychology of love*. Santa Barbara, CA: Praeger/ABC-CLIO.

Moon, C., Lagercrantz, H., & Kuhl, P. K. (2012). Language experienced in utero affects vowel perception after birth: A two-country study. *Acta Paediatrica, 102,* 156–160. doi:10.1111/apa.12098

Moore, B. C. J. (2010). Audition. In E. B. Goldstein (Ed.), *Encyclopedia of perception*. Thousand Oaks, CA: Sage.

Moore, K. L., Persaud, T. V. N., & Torchia, M. G. (2013). *Before we are born: Essentials of embryology and birth defects* (8th ed.). Philadelphia, PA: Elsevier.

Moore, R. Y. (2006). Biological rythms and sleep. In T. Lee-Chiong (Ed.), *Sleep: A comprehensive handbook*. Hoboken, NJ: Wiley-Liss.

Moore, S. C., Patel, A. V., Matthews, C. E., Berrington de Gonzalez, A., Park, Y., Katki, H. A., . . . Lee, I. M. (2012). Leisure time physical activity of moderate to vigorous intensity and mortality: A large pooled cohort analysis. *PLoS Medicine, 9,* e1001335. doi:10.1371/journal.pmed.1001335

Moore, S. M., Thomas, A. C., Kalé, S., Spence, M., Zlatevska, N., Staiger, P. K., . . . Kyrios, M. (2013). Problem gambling among international and domestic university students in Australia: Who is at risk? *Journal of Gambling Studies, 29,* 217–230.

Moran, T. H., & Sakai R. R. (2013). Food and fluid intake. In R. J. Nelson, S. Y. Mizumori, & I. B. Weiner (Eds.), *Handbook of psychology: Vol. 3. Behavioral neuroscience* (2nd ed.). New York, NY: Wiley.

Moreno, S., Bialystok, E., Barac, R., Schellenberg, E. G., Cepeda, N. J., & Chau, T. (2011). Short-term music training enhances verbal intelligence and executive function. *Psychological Science, 22,* 1425–1433. doi:10.1177/0956797611416999

Morewedge, C. K., & Norton, M. I. (2009). When dreaming is believing: The (motivated) interpretation of dreams. *Journal of Personality and Social Psychology, 96*(2), 249–264. doi:10.1037/a0013264

Morgado, P., Freitas, D., Bessa, J. M., Sousa, N., & Cerqueira, J. J. (2013). Perceived stress in obsessive-compulsive disorder is related with obsessive but not compulsive symptoms. *Frontiers In Psychiatry, 4,* Article ID 21.

Morgan, K. (2012). The epidemiology of sleep. In C. M. Morin, & C. A. Espie (Eds.), *Oxford handbook of sleep and sleep disorders*. New York, NY: Oxford University Press.

Morgan, R. D., & Cohen, L. M. (2008). Clinical and counseling psychology: Can differences be gleaned from printed recruiting materials? *Training and Education in Professional Psychology, 2*(3), 156–164.

Morin, C. M. (2011). Psychological and behavioral treatments for insomnia I: Approaches and efficacy. In M. H. Kryger, T. Roth, & W. C. Dement (Eds.), *Principles and practice of sleep medicine* (5th ed.). Saint Louis, MO: Elsevier Saunders.

Morrison, A. R. (2003). The brain on night shift. *Cerebrum, 5*(3), 23–36.

Morry, M. M. (2009). Similarity principle of attraction. In H. T. Reis & S. Sprecher (Eds.), *Encyclopedia of human relationships* (pp. 1500–1504)., Los Angeles, CA: Sage.

Moskowitz, J. T., & Saslow, L. R. (2014). Health and psychology: The importance of positive affect. In M. M. Tugade, M. N. Shiota, &

L. D. Kirby (Eds.), *Handbook of positive emotions*. New York, NY: Guilford Press.

Moskowitz, J. T., Shmueli-Blumberg, D., Acree, M., & Folkman, S. (2012). Positive affect in the midst of distress: Implications for role functioning. *Journal of Community & Applied Social Psychology, 22,* 502–518. doi:10.1002/casp.1133

Most, S. B., Scholl, B. J., Clifford, E. R., & Simons, D. J. (2005). What you see is what you set: Sustained inattentional blindness and the capture of awareness. *Psychological Review, 112,* 217–242.

Most, S. B., Simons, D. J., Scholl, B. J., Jimenez, R., Clifford, E., & Chabris, C. F. (2001). How not to be seen: The contribution of similarity and selective ignoring to sustained inattentional blindness. *Psychological Science, 12*(1), 9–17.

Mostofsky, E., Penner, E. A., Mittleman, M. A. (2014). Outbursts of anger as trigger of acute cardiovascular events: A systematic review and meta-analysis. *European Heart Journal, 35,* 1404–1410. doi:10.1093/eurheartj/ehu033

Motivala, S. J., & Irwin, M. R. (2007). Sleep and immunity: Cytokine pathways linking sleep and health outcomes. *Current Directions in Psychological Science, 16,* 21–25.

Moullin, S., Waldfogel, J., & Washbrook, E. (2014). *Baby bonds: Parenting, attachment and a secure base for children*. London, UK: The Sutton Trust.

Mowrer, O. H. (1947). On the dual nature of learning: A reinterpretation of "conditioning" and "problem-solving." *Harvard Educational Review, 17,* 102–150.

Muchnik, C., Amir, N., Shabtai, E., & Kaplan-Neeman, R. (2012). Preferred listening levels of personal listening devices in young teenagers: Self reports and physical measurements. *International Journal of Audiology, 51*(4), 287–293. doi:10.3109/14992202 7.2011.631590

Mueser, K. T., Deavers, F., Penn, D. L., & Cassisi, J. E. (2013). Psychosocial treatments for schizophrenia. *Annual Review of Clinical Psychology, 9,* 465–497. doi:10.1146/annurev-clinpsy-050212-185620

Muller, K. W., Glaesmer, H., Brahler, E., Woelfling, K., & Beutel, M. E. (2014). Prevalence of Internet addiction in the general population: Results from a German population-based survey. *Behaviour & Information Technology, 33,* 757–766. doi:10.1080/0144929X.2013.810778

Mulligan, N. W., & Besken, M. (2013). Implicit memory, In D.

Reisberg (Ed.), *Oxford handbook of cognitive psychology*. New York, NY: Oxford University Press.

Munafò, M. R., & Flint, J. (2011). Dissecting the genetic architecture of human personality. *Trends in Cognitive Sciences, 15,* 395–400.

Munck, A. (2007). Corticosteroids and stress. In G. Fink (Ed.), *Encyclopedia of stress*. San Diego, CA: Elsevier.

Murdock, B. (2001). Analysis of the serial position curve. In H. L. Roediger III, J. S. Nairne, I. Neath, & A. M. Surprenant (Eds.), *The nature of remembering: Essays in honor of Robert G. Crowder* (pp. 151–170). Washington, DC: American Psychological Association.

Murphy, K. R. (2002). Can conflicting perspectives on the role of g in personnel selection be resolved? *Human Performance, 15,* 173–186.

Muscanell, N. L., Guadagno, R. E., & Murphy, S. (2014). Weapons of influence misused: A social influence analysis of why people fall pretty to Internet scams. *Social and Personality Psychology Compass, 8,* 388–396. doi:10.1111/spc3.12115

Musick, K., & Bumpass, L. (2012). Reexamining the case for marriage: Union formation and changes in well-being. *Journal of Marriage and Family, 74*(1), 1–18.

Mustanski, B. S., Chivers, M. L., & Bailey, J. M. (2002). A critical review of recent biological research on human sexual orientation. *Annual Review of Sex Research, 12,* 89–140.

Mustanski, B. S., Kuper, L., & Greene, G. J. (2014). Development of sexual orientation and identity. In D. L. Tolman, L. M. Diamond, J. A. Bauermeister, W. H. George, J. G. Pfaus, & L. M. Ward (Eds.), *APA handbook of sexuality and psychology: Vol. 1. Person-based approaches*. Washington, DC: American Psychological Association.

Mutz, D. C., & Goldman, S. K. (2010). Mass media. In J. F. Dovidio, M. Hewstone, P. Glick, & V. M. Esses (Eds.), *The Sage handbook of prejudice, stereotyping, and discrimination*. Los Angeles, CA: Sage.

Myers, D. (2010). *Social psychology* (10th ed.). New York, NY: McGraw-Hill.

Myers, D. G. (1992). *The pursuit of happiness: Who is happy—and why*. New York, NY: Morrow.

Myers, D. G. (2013). Religious engagement and well-being. In S. A. David, I. Boniwell, & A. Conley Ayers (Eds.), *The Oxford handbook of happiness*. New York, NY: Oxford University Press.

Myers, L. B., Burns, J. W., Derakshan, N., Elfant, E., Eysenck, M. W., &

Phipps, S. (2007). Current issues in repressive coping and health. In J. Denollet, I. Nyklicek, & A. Vingerhoets (Eds.), *Emotion regulation: Conceptual and clinical issues* (pp. 69–86). New York, NY: Springer.

Nadal, K. L., Wong, Y., Sriken, J., Griffin, K., & Fujii-Doe, W. (2014). Racial microaggressions and Asian Americans: An exploratory study on within-group differences and mental health. *Asian American Journal of Psychology*, np. doi:10.1037/a0038058

Nadelson, C. C., Notman, M. T., & McCarthy, M. K. (2005). Gender issues in psychotherapy. In G. O. Gabbard, J. S. Beck, & J. Holmes (Eds.), *Oxford textbook of psychotherapy*. New York, NY: Oxford University Press.

Nadkarni, A., & Hofmann, S. G. (2012). Why do people use Facebook? *Personality and Individual Differences*, 52, 243–249. doi:10.1016/j.paid.2011.11.007

Nairne, J. S. (2003). Sensory and working memory. In A. F. Healy & R. W. Proctor (Eds.), *Handbook of psychology: Vol. 4. Experimental psychology*. New York, NY: Wiley.

Nairne, J. S., & Neath, I. (2013). Sensory and working memory. In A. F. Healy, R. W. Proctor, & I. B. Weiner (Eds.), *Handbook of psychology: Vol. 4. Experimental psychology* (2nd ed.). New York, NY: Wiley.

Naish, P. L. N. (2006). Time to explain the nature of hypnosis? *Contemporary Hypnosis*, 23, 33–46.

Narr, K. L., Woods, R. P., Thompson, P. M., Szeszko, P., Robinson, D., Dimtcheva, T., . . . Bilder, R. M. (2007). Relationships between IQ and regional cortical gray matter thickness in healthy adults. *Cerebral Cortex*, 17(9), 2163–2171. doi:10.1093/cercor/bhl125

National Institute on Alcohol Abuse and Alcoholism. (2013). *Alcohol facts and statistics*. Retrieved from www.niaaa.nih.gov/alcohol-health/overview-alcohol-consumption/alcohol-facts-and-statistics

National Sleep Foundation. (2010). *Sleep in America poll: Summary of findings*. Retrieved from www.sleepfoundation.org/sites/default/files/nsaw/NSF%20Sleep%20in%20%20America%20Poll%20-%20Summary%20of%20Findings%20.pdf

Neal, T. M. S., Guadagno, R. E., Eno, C. A., & Brodsky, S. L. (2012). Warmth and competence on the witness stand: Implications for the credibility of male and female expert witnesses. *Journal of the American Academy of Psychiatry and the Law*, 40, 488–497.

Nedergaard, M., & Verkhratsky, A. (2012). Artifact versus reality: How astrocytes contribute to synaptic events. *Glia*, 60, 1013–1023. doi:10.1002/glia.22288

Neff, L. A., & Geers, A. L. (2013). Optimistic expectations in early marriage: A resource or vulnerability for adaptive relationship function? *Journal of Personality and Social Psychology*, 105, 38–60. doi:10.1037/a0032600

Neisser, U. (1967). *Cognitive psychology*. New York, NY: Appleton-Century-Crofts.

Nelson, N. L., & Russell, J. A. (2013). Universality revisited. *Emotion Review*, 5(1), 8–15. doi:10.1177/1754073912457227

Nemeroff, C. B., Kalali, A., Keller, M. B., Charney, D. S., Lenderts, S. E., Cascade, E. F., . . . Schatzberg, A. F. (2007). Impact of publicity concerning pediatric suicidality data on physician practice patterns in the United States. *Archives of General Psychiatry*, 64, 466–472.

Nestler, E. J. (2014). Epigenetic mechanisms of drug addiction. *Neuropharmacology*, 76(Part B), 259–268. doi:10.1016/j.neuropharm.2013.04.004

Nestler, S., Egloff, B., Küfner, A. P., & Back, M. D. (2012). An integrative lens model approach to bias and accuracy in human inferences: Hindsight effects and knowledge updating in personality judgments. *Journal of Personality and Social Psychology*, 103, 689–717. doi:10.1037/a0029461

Nettle, D. (2006). The evolution of personality variation in humans and other animals. *American Psychologist*, 61, 622–631.

Neuberg, S. L., Kenrick, D. T., & Schaller, M. (2010). Evolutionary social psychology. In S. T. Fiske, D. T. Gilbert, & G. Lindzey (Eds.), *Handbook of social psychology*, (5th ed., Vol. 2, pp. 761–796). Hoboken, NJ: Wiley.

Neuberg, S. L., & Schaller, M. (2015). Evolutionary social cognition. In M. Mikulincer, P. R. Shaver, E. Borgida, & J. A. Bargh (Eds.), *APA handbook of personality and social psychology Vol. 1: Attitudes and social cognition*. Washington, DC: American Psychological Association.

Neuschatz, J. S., Lampinen, J. M., Preston, E. L., Hawkins, E. R., & Toglia, M. P. (2002). The effect of memory schemata on memory and the phenomenological experience of naturalistic situations. *Applied Cognitive Psychology*, 16, 687–708.

Newell, B. R. (2013). Judgment under uncertainty. In D. Reisberg (Ed.), *Oxford handbook of cognitive psychology*. New York, NY: Oxford University Press.

Newman, M. G., & Llera, S. J. (2011). A novel theory of experiential avoidance in generalized anxiety disorder: A review and synthesis of research supporting a contrast avoidance model of worry. *Clinical Psychology Review*, 31, 371–382. doi:10.1016/j.cpr.2011.01.008

Newman, M. G., Llera, S. J., Erickson, T. M., Przeworski, A., Castonguay, L. G. (2013). Worry and generalized anxiety disorder: A review and theoretical synthesis of evidence on nature, etiology, mechanisms, and treatment. *Annual Review of Clinical Psychology*, 9, 275–297. doi:10.1146/annurev-cinpsy-050212-185544

Newschaffer, C. J., Croen, L. A., Daniels, J., Giarelli, E., Grether, J. K., Levy, S. E., . . . Windham, G. C. (2007). The epidemiology of autism spectrum disorders. *Annual Review of Public Health*, 28, 235–258.

Newton, N. J., & Stewart, A. J. (2012). Personality development in adulthood. In S. K. Whitbourne & M. J. Sliwinski (Eds.), *Wiley-Blackwell handbook of adulthood and aging*. Malden, MA: Wiley-Blackwell.

Nezu, A. M., Raggio, G., Evans, A. N., & Nezu, C. M. (2013). Diabetes mellitus. In A. M. Nezu, C. M. Nezu, P. A. Geller, & I. B. Weiner (Eds.), *Handbook of psychology: Vol. 9. Health psychology* (2nd ed.). New York, NY: Wiley.

Nguyen, N. D., Tucker, M. A., Stickgold, R., & Wamsley, E. J. (2013). Overnight sleep enhances hippocampus-dependent aspects of spatial memory. *Sleep: Journal of Sleep and Sleep Disorders Research*, 36, 1051–1057.

Nguyen, T. A., Heffner, J. L., Lin, S. W., & Anthenelli, R. M. (2011). Genetic factors in the risk for substance use disorders. In P. Ruiz, & E. C. Strain (Eds.), *Lowinson and Ruiz's substance abuse: A comprehensive textbook* (5th ed.). Philadelphia, PA: Lippincott Williams & Wilkins.

Niccols, A. (2007). Fetal alcohol syndrome and the developing socio-emotional brain. *Brain and Cognition*, 65, 135–142.

Nickerson, R. S., & Adams, M. J. (1979). Long-term memory for a common object. *Cognitive Psychology*, 11, 287–307.

Niebyl, J. R., & Simpson, J. L. (2012). Drug and environmental agents in pregnancy and lactation: Embryology, teratology, epidemiology. In S. G. Gabbe, J. R. Niebyl, J. L. Simpson, M. B. Landon, H. L. Galan, E. R. M. Jauniaux, & D. A. Driscoll (Eds.), *Obstetrics: Normal and problem pregnancies* (6th ed.). Philadelphia, PA: Elsevier.

Nied_wie_ska, A., & Barzykowski, K. (2012). The age prospective memory paradox within the same sample in time-based and event-based tasks. *Aging, Neuropsychology, and Cognition*, 19(1–2), 58–83. doi:10.1080/13825585.2011.628374

Nielsen, J. A., Zielinski, B. A., Ferguson, M. A., Lainhart, J. E., & Anderson, J. S. (2013). An evaluation of the left-brain vs. right-brain hypothesis with resting state functional connectivity magnetic resonance imaging. *PLoS One*, 8, e71275.

Nielsen, N. M., Hansen, A. V., Simonsen, J., & Hviid, A. (2010). Prenatal stress and risk of infectious diseases in offspring. *American Journal of Epidemiology*, 173, 990–997. doi:10.1093/aje/kwq492

Nielsen, R. E., Uggerby, A. S., Jensen, S. W., & McGrath, J. J. (2013). Increasing mortality gap for patients diagnosed with schizophrenia over the last three decades: A Danish nationwide study from 1980 to 2010. *Schizophrenia Research*, 146(1–3), 22–27. doi:10.1016/j.schres.2013.02.025

Nielsen, T. (2011). Ultradian, circadian, and sleep-dependent features of dreaming. In M. H. Kryger, T. Roth, & W. C. Dement (Eds.), *Principles and practice of sleep medicine* (5th ed.). Saint Louis, MO: Elsevier Saunders.

Nielsen, T. A., Zadra, A. L., Simard, V., Saucier, S., Stenstrom, P., Smith, C., & Kuiken, D. (2003). The typical dreams of Canadian university students. *Dreaming*, 13(4), 211–235.

Nikelly, A. G. (1994). Alcoholism: Social as well as psycho-medical problem: The missing "big picture." *Journal of Alcohol & Drug Education*, 39, 1–12.

Nir, Y., & Tononi, G. (2010). Dreaming and the brain: From phenomenology to neurophysiology. *Trends in Cognitive Sciences*, 14(2), 88–100. doi:10.1016/j.tics.2009.12.001

Nisbett, R. E. (Ed.). (1993). *Rules for reasoning*. Hillsdale, NJ: Erlbaum.

Nisbett, R. E. (2005). Heredity, environment, and race differences in IQ: A commentary on Rushton and Jensen. *Psychology, Public Policy, and the Law*, 11, 302–310.

Nisbett, R. E. (2009). *Intelligence and how to get it: Why schools and cultures count*. New York, NY: Norton.

Nisbett, R. E., Aronson, J., Blair, C., Dickens, W., Flynn, J., Halpern, D. F., & Turkheimer, E. (2012). Intelligence: New findings and theoretical developments. *American Psychologist*, 67, 130–159. doi:10.1037/a0026699

Nisbett, R. E., & Miyamoto, Y. (2005). The influence of culture: Holistic versus analytic perception. *Trends in Cognitive Sciences*, 9, 467–473.

Nisbett, R. E., Peng, K., Choi, I., & Norenzayan, A. (2001). Culture and systems of thought: Holistic versus analytic cognition. *Psychological Review, 108,* 291–310.

Nist, S. L., & Holschuh, J. L. (2000). Comprehension strategies at the college level. In R. F. Flippo & D. C. Caverly (Eds.), *Handbook of college reading and study strategy research.* Mahwah, NJ: Erlbaum.

Nithianantharajah, J., & Hannan, A. J. (2006). Enriched environments, experience–dependent plasticity and disorders of the nervous system. *Nature Reviews Neuroscience, 7,* 697–709.

Niu, W., & Brass, J. (2011). Intelligence in worldwide perspective. In R. J. Sternberg, & S. B. Kaufman (Eds.), *Cambridge handbook of intelligence.* New York, NY: Cambridge University Press.

Noble, K. G., McCandliss, B. D., & Farah, M. J. (2007). Socioeconomic gradients predict individual differences in neurocognitive abilities. *Developmental Science, 10,* 464–480.

Nobler, M. S., & Sackeim, H. A. (2006). Electroconvulsive therapy and transcranial magnetic stimulation. In D. J. Stein, D. J. Kupfer, & A. F. Schatzberg (Eds.), *Textbook of mood disorders.* Washington, DC: American Psychiatric Publishing.

Nock, M. K., Millner, A. J., Deming, C. A., & Glenn, C. R. (2014). Depression and suicide. In I. H. Gotlib & C. L. Hammen (Eds.), *Handbook of depression* (3rd ed.). New York, NY: Guilford Press.

Noftle, E. E., & Robins, R. W. (2007). Personality predictors of academic outcomes: Big Five correlates of GPA and SAT scores. *Journal of Personality and Social Psychology, 93,* 116–130.

Nolen-Hoeksema, S. (1991). Responses to depression and their effects on the duration of depressive episodes. *Journal of Abnormal Psychology, 100,* 569–582.

Nolen-Hoeksema, S. (2000). The role of rumination in depressive disorders and mixed anxiety/depressive symptoms. *Journal of Abnormal Psychology, 109,* 504–511.

Nolen-Hoeksema, S. (2001). Gender differences in depression. *Current Directions in Psychological Science, 10,* 173–176.

Nolen-Hoeksema, S., Wisco, B. E., & Lyubomirsky, S. (2008). Rethinking rumination. *Perspectives on Psychological Science, 3*(5), 400–424. doi:10.1111/j.1745-6924.2008 .00088.x

Nomaguchi, K. M., & Milkie, M. A. (2003). Costs and rewards of children: The effects of becoming a parent on adults' lives. *Journal of Marriage and the Family, 65,* 356–374.

Norenzayan, A., & Heine, S. J. (2005). Psychological universals: What are they and how can we know? *Psychological Bulletin, 131,* 763–784.

Norris, I. J., & Larsen, J. T. (2011). Wanting more than you have and its consequences for well-being. *Journal of Happiness Studies, 12,* 877–885. doi:10.1007/s10902-010-9232-8

North, C. S., Eyrich, K. M., Pollio, D. E., & Spitznagel, E. L. (2004). Are rates of psychiatric disorders in the homeless population changing? *American Journal of Public Health, 94*(1), 103–108.

Norton, C. (2005). Animal experiments: A cardinal sin? *The Psychologist, 18*(2), 69.

Nosek, B. A., Greenwald, A. G., & Banaji, M. R. (2007). The Implicit Association Test at age 7: A Methodological and conceptual review. In J. A. Bargh (Ed.), *Social psychology and the unconscious: The automaticity of higher mental processes* (pp. 265–292). New York, NY: Psychology Press.

Novakova, B., Harris, P. R., Ponnusamy, A., & Reuber, M. (2013). The role of stress as a trigger for epileptic seizures: A narrative review of evidence from human and animal studies. *Epilepsia, 54,* 1866–1876. doi:10.1111/epi.12377

Novella, E. J. (2010). Mental health care in the aftermath of deinstitutionalization: A retrospective and prospective view. *Health Care Analysis, 18*(3), 222–238. doi:10.1007/s10728-009 -0138-8

Novemsky, N., & Kahneman, D. (2005). The boundaries of loss aversion. *Journal of Marketing Research, 42,* 119–128.

Noyes, R., Clarkson, C., Crowe, R. R., Yates, W. R., & McChesney, C. M. (1987). A family study of generalized anxiety disorder. *American Journal of Psychiatry, 144,* 1019–1024.

Nyberg, L., Lovden, M., Riklund, K., Lindenberger, U., & Backman, L. (2012). Memory aging and brain maintenance. *Trends in Cognitive Science, 16,* 292–305. doi:10.1016/j. tics.2012.04.005

Oberauer, K, & Lewandowsky, S. (2014). Further evidence against decay in working memory. *Journal of Memory and Language, 73,* 15–30. doi:10.1016/j.jml.2014.02.003

Obulesu, M., & Jhansilakshmi, M. (2014). Neuroinflammation in Alzheimer's disease: An understanding of physiology and pathology. *International Journal of Neuroscience, 124,* 227–235. doi:10.3109/00207454.201 3.831852

O'Connor, D. B., & Conner, M. (2011). Effects of stress on eating behavior. In R. J. Contrada & A. Baum (Eds.), *The handbook of stress science: Biology, psychology, and health* (pp. 111–121). New York, NY: Springer.

Oechslin, M. S., Descloux, C., Croquelois, A., Chanal, J., Van De Ville, D., Lazeyras, F., & James, C. E. (2013). Hippocampal volume predicts fluid intelligence in musically trained people. *Hippocampus, 23*(7), 552–558. doi:10.1002/hipo.22120

Oehlberg, K., & Mineka, S. (2011). Fear conditioning and attention to threat: An integrative approach to understanding the etiology of anxiety disorders. In T. R. Schachtman, & S. Reilly (Eds.), *Associative learning and condition theory: Human and non-human applications.* New York, NY: Oxford University Press.

Ogden, C. L., Lamb, M. M., Kit, B. K., & Wright, J. D. (2012). Weight and diet among children and adolescents in the United States. In K. D. Brownell, & M. S. Gold (Eds.), *Food and addiction: A comprehensive handbook.* New York, NY: Oxford University Press.

Ogden, J. (2010). *The psychology of eating: From healthy to disordered behavior.* Malden, MA: Wiley-Blackwell.

Ogle, C. M., Rubin, D. C., Berntsen, D., & Siegler, I. C. (2013). The frequency and impact of exposure to potentially traumatic events over the life course. *Clinical Psychological Science, 1,* 426–434. doi:10.1177/2167702613485076

Ogles, B. M. (2013). Measuring change in psychotherapy research. In M. J. Lambert (Ed.). *Bergin and Garfield's handbook of psychotherapy and behavior change* (6th ed.). New York, NY: Wiley.

Ohayon, M. M., Carskadon, M. A., Guilleminault, C., & Vitiello, M. V. (2004). Meta-analysis of quantitative sleep parameters from childhood to old age in healthy individuals: Developing normative sleep values across the human lifespan. *Sleep: Journal of Sleep & Sleep Disorders Research, 27,* 1255–1273.

Ohayon, M. M., Mahowald, M. W., Dauvilliers, Y., Krystal, A. D., & Leger, D. (2012). Prevalence and comorbidity of nocturnal wandering in the US adult general population. *Neurology, 78,* 1583–1589.

Öhman, A., & Mineka, S. (2001). Fears, phobias, and preparedness: Toward an evolved module of fear and fear learning. *Psychological Review, 108,* 483–522.

Oken, B. S. (2008). Placebo effects: Clinical aspects and neurobiology. *Brain: A Journal of Neurology, 131*(11), 2812–2823. doi:10.1093 /brain/awn116.

Olabarria, M., Noristani, H. N., Verkhratsky, A., & Rodríguez, J. J. (2010). Concomitant astroglial atrophy and astrogliosis in a triple transgenic animal model of Alzheimer's disease. *Glia, 58,* 831–838.

O'Leary, K. D., Acevedo, B. P., Aron, A., Huddy, L., & Mashek, D. (2012). Is long-term love more than a rare phenomenon? If so, what are its correlates? *Social Psychological and Personality Science, 3,* 241–249. doi:10.1177/1948550611417015

O'Leary, K. D., Kent, R. N., & Kanowitz, J. (1975). Shaping data collection congruent with experimental hypotheses. *Journal of Applied Behavior Analysis, 8,* 43–51.

Olds, J. (1956). Pleasure centers in the brain. *Scientific American, 193,* 105–116.

Olds, J., & Milner, P. (1954). Positive reinforcement produced by electrical stimulation of the septal area and other regions of the rat brain. *Journal of Comparative and Physiological Psychology, 47,* 419–427.

Olds, M. E., & Fobe, J. L. (1981). The central basis of motivation: Intracranial self-stimulation studies. *Annual Review of Psychology, 32,* 523–574.

Olfson, M., Blanco, C., Liu, S.-M., Wang, S., & Correll, C. U. (2012). National trends in the office-based treatment of children, adolescents, and adults with antipsychotics. *JAMA Psychiatry, 69*(12), 1247–1256.

Olfson, M., Cherry, D. K., & Lewis-Fernández, R. (2009). Racial differences in visit duration of outpatient psychiatric visits. *Archives of General Psychiatry, 66*(2), 214–221.

Olfson, M., Kroenke, K., Wang, S., & Blanco, C. (2014). Trends in office-based mental health care provided by psychiatrists and primary care physicians. *Journal of Clinical Psychiatry, 75,* 247–253. doi:10.4088/ JCP.13m08834

Olfson, M., & Marcus, S. C. (2009). National patterns in antidepressant medication treatment. *Archives of General Psychiatry, 66*(8), 848–856.

Olfson, M., & Marcus, S. C. (2010). National trends in outpatient psychotherapy. *The American Journal of Psychiatry, 167*(12), 1456–1463. doi:10.1176/appi.ajp.2010.10040570

Olivola, C. Y., & Todorov, A. (2010). Elected in 100 milliseconds: Appearance-based trait inferences and voting. *Journal of Nonverbal Behavior, 34,* 83–110. doi:10.1007/s10919-009 -0082-1

Oller, K., & Pearson, B. Z. (2002). Assessing the effects of bilingualism.

In D. K. D. Oller & R. E. Eilers (Eds.), *Language and literacy in bilingual children*. Clevedon, UK: Multilingual Matters.

Olson, J. M., Roese, N. J., & Zanna, M. P. (1996). Expectancies. In E. T. Higgins & A. W. Kruglanski (Eds.), *Social psychology: Handbook of basic principles*. New York, NY: Guilford Press.

Ones, D. S., Viswesvaran, C., & Dilchert, S. (2005). Cognitive ability in selection decisions. In O. Wilhelm & R. W. Engle (Eds.), *Handbook of understanding and measuring intelligence*. Thousand Oaks, CA: Sage.

Ong, A. D. (2010). Pathways linking positive emotion and health in later life. *Current Directions in Psychological Science, 19*(6), 358–362. doi:10.1177/0963721410388805

Ong, A. D., Burrow, A. L., Fuller-Rowell, T. E., Ja, N. M., & Sue, D. W. (2013). Racial microaggressions and daily well-being among Asian Americans. *Journal of Counseling Psychology, 60*, 188–199. doi:10.1037/a0031736

Ono, K. (1987). Supersitious behavior in humans. *Journal of the Experimental Analysis of Behavior, 47*(3), 261–271. doi:10.1901/jeab.1987.47-261

Oppliger, P. A. (2007). Effects of gender stereotyping on socialization. In R. W. Preiss, B. M. Gayle, N. Burrell, M. Allen, & J. Bryant (Eds.), *Mass media effects research: Advances through meta-analysis* (pp. 192–214). Mahwah, NJ: Erlbaum.

Opriş, D., Pintea, S., García-Palacios, A., Botella, C., Szamosközi, Ş., & David, D. (2012). Virtual reality exposure therapy in anxiety disorders: A quantitative meta-analysis. *Depression and Anxiety, 29*(2), 85–93. doi:10.1002/da.20910

Orne, M. T. (1951). The mechanisms of hypnotic age regression: An experimental study. *Journal of Abnormal and Social Psychology, 46*, 213–225.

Orne, M. T., & Holland, C. C. (1968). On the ecological validity of laboratory deceptions. *International Journal of Psychiatry, 6*, 282–293.

Ortmann, A., & Hertwig, R. (1997). Is deception acceptable? *American Psychologist, 52*, 746–747.

Ost, J. (2013). Recovered memories and suggestibility for entire events. In A. M. Ridley, F. Gabbert, & D. J. La Rooy (Eds.), *Suggestibility in legal contexts: Psychological research and forensic implications*. Wiley-Blackwell.

Otero, T. L., Schatz, R. B., Merrill, A. C., & Bellini, S. (2015). Social skills training for youth with autism spectrum disorders: A follow-up.

Child and Adolescent Psychiatric Clinics of North America, 24(1), 99–115. doi:10.1016/j.chc.2014.09.002

Outtz, J. L. (2002). The role of cognitive ability tests in employment selection. *Human Performance, 15*, 161–171.

Ouweneel, E., Schaufeli, W. B., & Le Blanc, P. M. (2013). Believe, and you will achieve: Changes over time in self-efficacy, engagement, and performance. *Applied Psychology: Health and Well-Being, 5*(2), 225–247.

Overall, N. C., Girme, Y. U., Lemay, Jr., E. P., & Hammond, M. D. (2014). Attachment anxiety and reactions to relationship threat: The benefits and costs of inducing guilt in romantic partners. *Journal of Personality and Social Psychology, 106*, 235–256. doi:10.1037/a0034371

Overy, R. (2014). "Ordinary men," extraordinary circumstances: Historians, social psychology, and the Holocaust. *Journal of Social Issues, 70*, 515–530. doi:10.1111/josi.12075

Ozer, E. J., Best, S. R., Lipsey, T. L., & Weiss, D. S. (2003). Predictors of posttraumatic stress disorder and symptoms in adults: A meta-analysis. *Psychological Bulletin, 129*, 52–73.

Ozgen, E. (2004). Language, learning, and color perception. *Current Directions in Psychological Science, 13*(3), 95–98.

Pacchiarotti, I., Bond, D. J., Baldessarini, R. J., Nolen, W. A., Grunze, H., Licht, R. W., . . . Vieta, E. (2013). The International Society for Bipolar Disorders (ISBD) task force report on antidepressant use in bipolar disorders. *The American Journal of Psychiatry, 170*, 1249–1262. doi:10.1176/appi.ajp.2013.13020185

Pace-Schott, E. F. (2011). The neurobiology of dreaming. In M. H. Kryger, T. Roth, & W. C. Dement (Eds.), *Principles and practice of sleep medicine* (5th ed.). Saint Louis, MO: Elsevier Saunders.

Pace-Schott, E. F., Nave, G., Morgan, A., & Spencer, R. M. C. (2012). Sleep-dependent modulation of affectively guided decision-making. *Journal of Sleep Research, 21*, 30–39. doi:10.1111/j.1365-2869.2011.00921.x

Pachur, T., Todd, P. M., Gigerenzer, G., Schooler, L. J., & Goldstein, D. G. (2012). When is the recognition heuristic an adaptive tool? In P. M. Todd, & G. Gigerenzer (Eds.), *Ecological rationality: Intelligence in the world*. New York, NY: Oxford University Press. doi:10.1093/acprof:oso/9780195315448.003.0035

Packer, I. K. (2015). Legal insanity and mens rea defenses. In B. L. Cutler,

P. A. Zapf, B. L. Cutler, P. A. Zapf (Eds.), *APA handbook of forensic psychology: Vol. 1. Individual and situational influences in criminal and civil contexts*. Washington, DC: American Psychological Association. doi:10.1037/14461-004

Paczynski, R. P., & Gold, M. S. (2011). Cocaine and crack. In P. Ruiz, & E. C. Strain (Eds.), *Lowinson and Ruiz's substance abuse: A comprehensive textbook* (5th ed., pp. 191–213). Philadelphia, PA: Lippincott Williams & Wilkins.

Padalia, D. (2014). Conformity bias: A fact or an experimental artifact? *Psychological Studies, 59*, 223–230. doi:10.1007/s12646-014-0272-8

Paivio, A. (1986). *Mental representations: A dual coding approach*. New York, NY: Oxford University Press.

Paivio, A. (2007). *Mind and its evolution: A dual coding theoretical approach*. Mahwah, NJ: Erlbaum.

Paivio, A., Khan, M., & Begg, I. (2000). Concreteness of relational effects on recall of adjective-noun pairs. *Canadian Journal of Experimental Psychology, 54*(3), 149–160.

Paivio, A., Smythe, P. E., & Yuille, J. C. (1968). Imagery versus meaningfulness of nouns in paired-associate learning. *Canadian Journal of Psychology, 22*, 427–441.

Pan, B. A., & Uccelli, P. (2009). Semantic development: Learning the meaning of words. In J. B. Gleason & N. B. Ratner (Eds.), *The development of language*. Boston, MA: Pearson.

Panksepp, J. (1991). Affective neuroscience: A conceptual framework for the neurobiological study of emotions. In K. T. Strongman (Ed.), *International review of studies on emotion*. Chichester, England: Wiley.

Parakh, P., & Basu, D. (2013). Cannabis and psychosis: Have we found the missing links? *Asian Journal of Psychiatry, 6*, 281–287. doi:10.1016/j.ajp.2013.03.012

Parise, E., & Csibra, G. (2012). Electrophysiological evidence for the understanding of maternal speech by 9-month-old infants. *Psychological Science, 23*, 728–733. doi:10.1177/0956797612438734

Parish-Morris, J., Golinkoff, R. M., & Hirsh-Pasek, K. (2013). From coo to code: A brief story of language development. In P. D. Zelazo (Ed.), *Oxford handbook of developmental psychology: Vol. 1. Body and mind*. New York, NY: Oxford University Press.

Park, D. C., Lodi-Smith, J., Drew, L., Haber, S., Hebrank, A., Bischof, G. N., & Aamodt, W. (2014). The impact of sustained engagement of cognitive function in older adults: The synapse project.

Psychological Science, 25, 103–112. doi:10.1177/0956797613499592

Park, J., & Jang, S. (2013). Confused by too many choices? Choice overload in tourism. *Tourism Management, 35*, 1–12. doi:10.1016/j.tourman.2012.05.004

Park, J. H. (2012). Evolutionary perspectives on intergroup prejudice: Implications for promoting tolerance. In S. C. Roberts (Ed.), *Applied evolutionary psychology*. New York, NY: Oxford University Press.

Partinen, M., & Hublin, C. (2011). Epidemiology of sleep disorders. In M. H. Kryger, T. Roth, & W. C. Dement (Eds.), *Principles and practice of sleep medicine* (5th ed.). Saint Louis, MO: Elsevier Saunders.

Parwani, R., & Parwani, S. R. (2014). Does stress predispose to periodontal disease? *Dental Update, 41*, 260–264.

Pascual-Leone, A. (2009). Characterizing and modulating neuroplasticity of the adult human brain. In M. S. Gazzangia (Ed.), *The cognitive neurosciences* (4th ed., pp. 141–152). Cambridge, MA: MIT Press.

Pashler, H., & Harris, C. R. (2012). Is the replicability crisis overblown? Three arguments examined. *Perspectives on Psychological Science, 7*(6), 531–536. doi:10.1177/1745691612463401.

Pashler, H., Johnston, J. C., & Ruthruff, E. (2001). Attention and performance. *Annual Review of Psychology, 52*, 629–651.

Patel, S. R., Malhotra, A., Gottlieb, D. J., White, P., & Hu, F. B. (2006). Correlates of long sleep deprivation. *Sleep: Journal of Sleep and Sleep Disorders Research, 29*, 881–889.

Patel, S. R., Zhu, X., Storfer-Isser, A., Mehra, R., Jenny, N. S., Tracy, R., & Redline, S. (2009). Sleep duration and biomarkers of inflammation. *Sleep: Journal of Sleep and Sleep Disorders Research, 32*(2), 200–204.

Patihis, L., Ho, L. Y., Tingen, I. W., Lilienfeld, S. O., & Loftus, E. F. (2014). Are the "memory wars" over? A scientist-practitioner gap in beliefs about repressed memory. *Psychological Science, 25*, 519–530. doi:10.1177/0956797613510718

Patrick, S. W., Schumacher, R. E., Benneyworth, B. D., Krans, E. E., McAllister, J. M., & Davis, M. M. (2012). Neonatal abstinence syndrome and associated health care expenditures: United States, 2000–2009. *JAMA, 9*, 1934–1940. doi:10.1001/jama.2012.3951

Patston, L. M., Kirk, I. J., Rolfe, M. S., Corballis, M. C., & Tippett, L. J. (2007). The unusual symmetry of musicians: Musicians have equilateral interhemispheric transfer for visual information. *Neuropsychologia, 45*(9), 2059–2065. doi:10.1016/j.neuropsychologia.2007.02.001

Pattanashetty, R., Sathiamma, S., Talakkad, S., Nityananda, P., Trichur, R., & Kutty, B. M. (2010). Practitioners of vipassana meditation exhibit enhanced slow wave sleep and REM sleep states across different age groups. *Sleep and Biological Rhythms, 8*(1), 34–41. doi:10.1111/j.1479-8425.2009.00416.x

Paul, R. (2009). Parents ask: Am I risking autism if I vaccinate my children? *Journal of Autism and Developmental Disorders, 39*(6), 962–963.

Paulos, J. A. (1995). *A mathematician reads the newspaper.* New York, NY: Doubleday.

Paulson, G. W. (2012). *Closing the asylums: Causes and consequences of the deinstitutionalization movement.* Jefferson, NC: McFarland & Co.

Paunonen, S. V., & Hong, R. Y. (2015). On the properties of personality traits. In M. Mikulincer, P. R. Shaver, M. L. Cooper, & R. J. Larsen (Eds.), *APA handbook of personality and social psychology: Vol. 4. Personality processes and individual differences.* Washington, DC: American Psychological Association.

Paunonen, S. V., & LeBel, E. P. (2012). Socially desirable responding and its elusive effects on the validity of personality assessments. *Journal of Personality and Social Psychology, 103*(1), 158–175. doi:10.1037/a0028165

Pavlov, I. P. (1906). The scientific investigation of psychical faculties or processes in the higher animals. *Science, 24,* 613–619.

Pavlov, I. P. (1927). *Conditioned reflexes* (G. V. Anrep, Trans.). London: Oxford University Press.

Pavot, W, & Diener, E. (2013). Happiness experienced: The science of subjective well-being. In S. A. David, I. Boniwell, & A. Conley Ayers (Eds.), *The Oxford handbook of happiness.* New York, NY: Oxford University Press.

Payne, B. K. (2006). Weapon bias: Split-second decisions and unintended stereotyping. *Current Directions in Psychological Science, 15,* 287–291. doi:10.1111/j.1467-8721.2006.00454.x

Payne, D. G., & Blackwell, J. M. (1998). Truth in memory: Caveat emptor. In S. J. Lynn & K. M. McConkey (Eds.), *Truth in memory.* New York, NY: Guilford Press.

Payne, J. D., Tucker, M. A., Ellenbogen, J. M., Wamsley, E. J., Walker, M. P., Schacter, D. L., & Stickgold, R. (2012). Memory for semantically related and unrelated declarative information: The benefit of sleep, the cost of wake. *PLoS ONE, 7,* e33079. doi:10.1371/journal.pone.0033079

Pchelin, P., & Howell, R. T. (2014). The hidden cost of value-seeking: People do not accurately forecast the economic benefits of experiential purchases. *The Journal of Positive Psychology, 9,* 322–334. doi:10.1080/17439760.2014.898316

Pedersen, A. F., Bovbjerg, D. H., & Zachariae, R. (2011). Stress and susceptibility to infectious disease. In R. J. Contrada & A. Baum (Eds.), *The handbook of stress science: Biology, psychology, and health* (pp. 111–121). New York, NY: Springer.

Peele, S. (1989). *Diseasing of America: Addiction treatment out of control.* Lexington, MA: Lexington Books.

Peele, S. (2000). What addiction is and is not: The impact of mistaken notions of addiction. *Addiction Research, 8,* 599–607.

Peigneux, P., Urbain, C., & Schmitz, R. (2012). Sleep and the brain. In C. M. Morin, & C. A. Espie (Eds.), *Oxford handbook of sleep and sleep disorders.* New York, NY: Oxford University Press.

Peng, J. H., Tao, Z. Z., & Huang, Z. W. (2007). Risk of damage to hearing from personal listening devices in young adults. *Journal of Otolaryngology, 36*(3), 181–185. doi:10.2310/7070.2007.0032

Pennebaker, J. W., Colder, M., & Sharp, L. K. (1990). Accelerating the coping process. *Journal of Personality and Social Psychology, 58,* 528–537.

Peper, J. S., & Dahl, R. E. (2013). The teenage brain: Surging hormones—Brain-behavior interactions during puberty. *Current Directions in Psychological Science, 22,* 134–139. doi:10.1177/0963721412473755

Perez, G. K., Cruess, D. G., & Kalichman, S. C. (2010). Effects of stress on health in HIV/AIDS. In R. Contrada & A. Baum (Eds.), *Handbook of stress science: Biology, psychology, & health.* New York, NY: Springer.

Perilloux, C. (2014). (Mis)reading the signs: Men's perception of women's sexual interest. In V. A. Weekes-Shackelford & T. K. Shackelford (Eds.), *Evolutionary perspectives on human sexual psychology and behavior.* New York, NY: Spring Science + Business Media.

Perilloux, C., Easton, J. A., & Buss, D. M. (2012). The misperception of sexual interest. *Psychological Science, 23,* 146–151. doi:10.1177/0956797611424162

Perkins, D. O., Miller-Anderson, L., & Lieberman, J. A. (2006). Natural history and predictors of clinical course. In J. A. Lieberman, T. S. Stroup, & D. O. Perkins (Eds.), *Textbook of schizophrenia.* Washington, DC: American Psychiatric Publishing.

Perkins, K. A., Parzynski, C., Mercincavage, M., Conklin, C. A., & Fonte, C. A. (2012). Is self-efficacy for smoking abstinence a cause of, or a reflection on, smoking behavior change? *Experimental and Clinical Psychopharmacology, 20*(1), 56–62. doi:10.1037/a0025482

Perlis, R. H., Perlis, C. S., Wu, Y., Hwang, C., Joseph, M., & Nierenberg, A. A. (2005). Industry sponsorship and financial conflict of interest in the reporting of clinical trials in psychiatry. *American Journal of Psychiatry, 162,* 1957–1960.

Perone, M., Galizio, M., & Baron, A. (1988). The relevance of animal-based principles in the laboratory study of human operant conditioning. In G. Davey & C. Cullen (Eds.), *Human operant conditioning and behavior modification.* New York, NY: Wiley.

Perry, J. C., & Bond, M. (2012). Change in defense mechanisms during long-term dynamic psychotherapy and five-year outcome. *The American Journal of Psychiatry, 169,* 916–925.

Person, E. S. (1990). The influence of values in psychoanalysis: The case of female psychology. In C. Zanardi (Ed.), *Essential papers in psychoanalysis.* New York, NY: New York University Press.

Pert, C. B., & Snyder, S. H. (1973). Opiate receptor: Demonstration in the nervous tissue. *Science, 179,* 1011–1014.

Perugini, E. M., Kirsch, I., Allen, S. T., Coldwell, E., Meredith, J. M., Montgomery, G. H., & Sheehan, J. (1998). Surreptitious observation of response to hypnotically suggested hallucinations: A test of the compliance hypothesis. *International Journal of Clinical & Experimental Hypnosis, 46,* 191–203.

Pescosolido, B. A., Martin, J. K., Long, J., Medina, T. R., Phelan, J. C., & Link, B. G. (2010). "A disease like any other"? A decade of change in public reactions to schizophrenia, depression, and alcohol dependence. *American Journal of Psychiatry, 167*(11), 1321–1330. doi:10.1176/appi.ajp.2010.09121743

Peters, M. N., Moscona, J. C., Katz, M. J., Deandrade, K. B., Quevedo, H. C., Tiwari, S., . . . Irimpen, A. M. (2014). Natural disasters and myocardial infarction: The six years after Hurricane Katrina. *Mayo Clinic Proceedings, 89,* 472–477. doi:10.1016/j.mayocp.2013.12.013

Petersen, J. L., & Hyde, J. S. (2011). Gender differences in sexual attitudes and behaviors: A review of meta-analytic results and large datasets. *Journal of Sex Research, 48,* 149–165. doi:10.1080/00224499.2011.551851

Peterson, C., & Park, N. (2009). Positive psychology. In B. J. Sadock, V. A. Sadock, & P. Ruiz (Eds.), *Kaplan & Sadock's comprehensive textbook of psychiatry* (pp. 2939–2951). Philadelphia, PA: Lippincott Williams & Wilkins.

Peterson, C., Seligman, M. E. P., Yurko, K. H., Martin, L. R., & Friedman, H. S. (1998). Catastrophizing and untimely death. *Psychological Science, 9,* 127–130.

Peterson, L. R., & Peterson, M. J. (1959). Short-term retention of individual verbal items. *Journal of Experimental Psychology, 58,* 193–198.

Peterson, M. A., & Kimchi, R. (2013). Perceptual organization in vision. In D. Reisberg (Ed.), *The oxford handbook of cognitive psychology.* New York, NY: Oxford University Press.

Petrie, K. J., & Pennebaker, J. W. (2004). Health-related cognitions. In S. Sutton, A. Baum, & M. Johnston (Eds.), *The Sage handbook of health psychology.* Thousand Oaks, CA: Sage.

Petrill, S. A. (2005). Behavioral genetics and intelligence. In O. Wilhelm & R. W. Engle (Eds.), *Handbook of understanding and measuring intelligence.* Thousand Oaks, CA: Sage.

Petry, N. M. (2005). *Pathological gambling: Etiology, comorbidity, and treatment.* Washington, DC: American Psychological Association.

Pettit, J. W., Lewinsohn, P. M., Seeley, J. R., Roberts, R. E., & Yaroslavsky, I. (2010). Developmental relations between depressive symptoms, minor hassles, and major events from adolescence through age 30 years. *Journal of Abnormal Psychology, 119,* 811–824. doi:10.1037/a0020980

Petty, R. E., & Briñol, P. (2010). Attitude change. In R. F. Baumeister & E. J. Finkel (Eds.), *Advanced social psychology: The state of the science* (pp. 217–259). New York, NY: Oxford University Press.

Petty, R. E., & Briñol, P. (2012). The elaboration likelihood model. In P. A. M. Van Lange, A. W. Kruglanski, & E. T. Higgins (Eds.), *Handbook of theories of social psychology* (Vol. 1). CA: Sage.

Petty, R. E., & Briñol, P. (2015). Processes of social influence through attitude change. In M. Mikulincer, P. R. Shaver, E. Borgida, & J. A. Bargh (Eds.), *APA handbook of personality and social psychology Vol. 1: Attitudes and social cognition.* Washington, DC: American Psychological Association.

Petty, R. E., & Cacioppo, J. T. (1986). *Communication and persuasion: Central and peripheral routes to attitude change.* New York, NY: Springer-Verlag.

Petty, R. E., & Wegener, D. T. (1998). Attitude change: Multiple roles for persuasion variables. In D. T. Gilbert, S. T. Fiske, & G. Lindzey (Eds.), *The handbook of social psychology.* New York, NY: McGraw-Hill.

Petty, R. E., Wheeler, S. C., & Tormala, Z. L. (2013). Persuasion and attitude change. In H. Tennen, J. Suls, & I. B. Weiner (Eds.), *Handbook of psychology: Vol. 5. Personality and social psychology* (2nd ed.). New York, NY: Wiley.

Petty, S. C., Sachs-Ericsson, N., & Joiner, T. E., Jr. (2004). Interpersonal functioning deficits: Temporary or stable characteristics of depressed individuals. *Journal of Affective Disorders, 81,* 115–122.

Pfau, M., Kenski, H. C., Nitz, M., & Sorenson, J. (1990). Efficacy of inoculation strategies in promoting resistance to political attack messages: Application to direct mail. *Communication Monographs, 57,* 25–43.

Phelan, J. C., Link, B. G., & Tehranifar, P. (2010). Social conditions as fundamental causes of health inequalities: Theory, evidence, and policy implications. *Journal of Health and Social Behavior, 51,* S28–S40. doi:10.1177/0022146510383498

Phelps, E. A. (2005). The interaction of emotion and cognition: The relation between the human amygdala and cognitive awareness. In R. R. Hassin, J. S. Uleman, & J. A. Bargh (Eds.), *The new unconcious: Oxford series in social cognition and social neuroscience.* New York, NY: Oxford University Press.

Phelps, E. A. (2006). Emotion and cognition: Insights from studies of the human amygdala. *Annual Review of Psychology, 57,* 27–53.

Philip, P., Sagaspe, P., & Taillard, J. (2011). Drowsy driving. In M. H. Kryger, T. Roth & W. C. Dement (Eds.), *Principles and practice of sleep medicine* (5th ed.). Saint Louis, MO: Elsevier Saunders.

Phillips, B. A., & Kryger, M. H. (2011). Management of obstructive sleep apnea-hypopnea syndrome. In M. H. Kryger, T. Roth, & W. C. Dement (Eds.), *Principles and practice of sleep medicine* (5th ed.). Saint Louis, MO: Elsevier Saunders.

Phillips, W. L. (2011). Cross-cultural differences in visual perception of color, illusions, depth, and pictures. In K. D. Keith (Ed.), *Cross-cultural psychology: Contemporary themes and perspectives.* Malden, MA: Wiley-Blackwell.

Piaget, J. (1929). *The child's conception of world* (J. Tomlinson, Trans.).

New York, NY: Harcourt Brace. (Original work published in 1926.)

Piaget, J. (1952). *The origins of intelligence in children* (M. Cook, Trans.). New York, NY: International Universities Press. (Original work published in 1933.)

Piaget, J. (1983). Piaget's theory (G. Cellerier & J. Langer, Trans.). In P. H. Mussen (Series Ed.) & W. Kessen (Vol. Ed.), *Handbook of child psychology: History, theory, and methods* (4th ed., Vol. 1, pp. 103–126). New York, NY: Wiley. (Original work published in 1970.)

Pietromonaco, P. R., & Beck, L. A. (2015). Attachment processes in adult romantic relationships. In M. Mikulincer, P. R. Shaver, J. A. Simpson, & J. F. Dovidio (Eds.), *APA handbook of personality and social psychology Vol. 3: Interpersonal relations.* Washington, DC: American Psychological Association.

Pietschnig, J., Voracek, M., & Formann, A. K. (2010). Mozart effect–Shmozart effect: A meta-analysis. *Intelligence, 38*(3), 314–323. doi:10.1016/j.intell.2010.03.001

Piff, P. K. (2014). Wealth and the inflated self: Class, entitlement, and narcissism. *Personality and Social Psychology Bulletin, 40*(1), 34–43. doi:10.1177/0146167213501699

Pilling, M., & Davies, I. R. L. (2004). Linguistic relativism and colour cognition. *British Journal of Psychology, 95,* 429–455.

Pinel, J. P. J., Assanand, S., & Lehman, D. R. (2000). Hunger, eating, and ill health. *American Psychologist, 55,* 1105–1116.

Pink, D. H. (2005). *A whole new mind: Why right-brainers will rule the future.* New York, NY: Penguin.

Pintar, J. (2010). Il n'y a pas d'hypnotisme: A history of hypnosis in theory and practice. In S. J. Lynn, J. W. Rhue, & I. Kirsch (Eds.), *Handbook of Clinical Hypnosis* (2nd ed., pp. 19–46). Washington, DC: American Psychological Association.

Piper, W. E., & Hernandez, C. A. (2013). Group psychotherapies. In G. Stricker & T. A. Widiger (Eds.), *Handbook of psychology: Vol. 8. Clinical psychology* (2nd ed.). New York, NY: Wiley.

Pittman, F., III. (1994, January/February). A buyer's guide to psychotherapy. *Psychology Today,* 50–53, 74–81.

Plomin, R. (2013). Child development and molecular genetics: 14 years later. *Child Development, 84,* 104–120. doi:10.1111/j.1467-8624.2012.01757.x

Plomin, R., DeFries, J. C., Knopik, V. S., & Neiderhiser, J. M. (2013).

Behavioral genetics (6th ed.). New York, NY: Worth Publishers.

Plomin, R., DeFries, J. C., McClearn, G. E., & McGuffin, P. (2001). *Behavioral genetics.* New York, NY: Freeman.

Plomin, R., Haworth, C. A., Meaburn, E. L., Price, T. S., & Davis, O. P. (2013). Common DNA markers can account for more than half of the genetic influence on cognitive abilities. *Psychological Science, 24,* 562–568. doi:10.1177/0956797612457952

Plomin, R., & Spinath, F. M. (2004). Intelligence: Genetics, genes, and genomics. *Journal of Personality & Social Psychology, 86,* 112–129.

Plucker, J. A., & Makel, M. C. (2010). Assessment of creativity. In J. C. Kaufman & R. J. Sternberg (Eds.), *The Cambridge handbook of creativity* (pp. 48–73). New York, NY: Cambridge University Press.

Pluess, M., & Belsky, J. (2010). Differential susceptibility to parenting and quality child care. *Developmental Psychology, 46,* 379–390. doi:10.1037/a0015203

Plutchik, R. (1984). Emotions: A general psychoevolutionary theory. In K. R. Scherer & P. Ekman (Eds.), *Approaches to emotion.* Hillsdale, NJ: Erlbaum.

Plutchik, R. (1993). Emotions and their vicissitudes: Emotions and psychopathology. In M. Lewis & J. M. Haviland (Eds.), *Handbook of emotions.* New York, NY: Guilford Press.

Pogue-Geile, M. F., & Yokley, J. L. (2010). Current research on the genetic contributors to schizophrenia. *Current Directions in Psychological Science, 19*(4), 214–219. doi:10.1177/0963721410378490

Popenoe, D. (2009). *Families without fathers: Fathers, marriage, and children in American society.* Piscataway, NJ: Transaction.

Popkin, B. M. (2012). The changing face of global diet and nutrition. In K. D. Brownell, & M. S. Gold (Eds.), *Food and addiction: A comprehensive handbook.* New York, NY: Oxford University Press.

Porter, J., Craven, B., Khan, R. M., Chang, S., Kang, I., Judkewitz, B., Volpe, J., et al. (2007). Mechanisms of scent-tracking in humans. *Nature Neuroscience, 10*(1), 27–29. doi:10.1038/nn1819

Porter, S., & Porter, S. (2007). Psychopathy and Violent Crime. In H. Hervé, J. C. Yuille, H. Hervé, & J. C. Yuille (Eds.), *The Psychopath: Theory, Research, and Practice.* Mahwah, NJ: Lawrence Erlbaum Associates Publishers.

Porter, S., Yuille, J. C., & Lehman, D. R. (1999). The nature of real, implanted, and fabricated memories for emotional childhood events: Implications for the recovered memory debate. *Law and Human Behavior, 23,* 517–537.

Posada, G., Kaloustian, G., Richmond, K., & Moreno, A. J. (2007). Maternal secure base support and preschoolers' secure base behavior in natural environments. *Attachment & Human Development, 9,* 393–411.

Post, J. M. (2011). Crimes of obedience: "Groupthink" at Abu Ghraib. *International Journal of Group Psychotherapy, 61,* 49-66. doi:10.1521/ijgp.2011.61.1.48

Post, R. M., & Altshuler, L. L. (2009). Mood disorders: Treatment of bipolar disorders. In B. J. Sadock, V. A. Sadock, & P. Ruiz (Eds.), *Kaplan & Sadock's comprehensive textbook of psychiatry* (pp. 1743–1812). Philadelphia, PA: Lippincott Williams & Wilkins.

Postman, L. (1985). Human learning and memory. In G. A. Kimble & K. Schlesinger (Eds.), *Topics in the history of psychology.* Hillsdale, NJ: Erlbaum.

Powell, R. A., & Gee, T. L. (1999). The effects of hypnosis on dissociative identity disorder: A reexamination of the evidence. *Canadian Journal of Psychiatry, 44,* 914–916.

Powley, T. L. (2008). Central control of autonomic functions: Organization of the autonomic nervous system. In L. Squire, D. Berg, F. Bloom, S. Du Lac, A. Ghosh, & N. Spitzer (Eds.), *Fundamental neuroscience* (3rd ed., pp. 809–828). San Diego, CA: Elsevier.

Powley, T. L. (2009). Hunger. In G. G. Berntson & J. T. Cacioppo (Eds.), *Handbook of neuroscience for the behavioral sciences,* (Vol. 2, pp. 659–679). Hoboken, NJ: Wiley.

Prat-Sala, M., & Redford, P. (2010). The interplay between motivation, self-efficacy, and approaches to studying. *British Journal of Educational Psychology, 80*(2), 283–305. doi:10.1348/000709909X480563

Prescott, J. (2010). Taste: Supertasters. In E. B. Goldstein (Ed.), *Encyclopedia of perception.* Thousand Oaks, CA: Sage.

Pressman, S. D., & Cohen, S. (2012). Positive emotion word use and longevity in famous deceased psychologists. *Health Psychology, 31,* 297–305. doi:10.1037/a0025339

Price, R. A. (2012). Genetics and common human obesity. In J. J. Nurnberger, & W. H. Berrettini (Eds.), *Principles of psychiatric genetics.* New York, NY: Cambridge University Press. doi:10.1017/CBO9781139025997.022

Priester, J. R., & Petty, R. E. (2003). The influence of spokesperson trustworthiness on message elaboration, attitude strength, and advertising. *Journal of Consumer Psychology, 13,* 408–421.

Prince, M., Albanese, E., Guerchet, M., & Prina, M. (2014). *World Alzheimer report 2014 dementia and risk reduction: An analysis of protective and modifiable factors.* London, UK: Alzheimer's Disease International.

Prislin, R., & Crano, W. D. (2012). A history of social influence research. In A. W. Kruglanski & W. Stroebe (Eds.), *Handbook of the history of social psychology.* New York, NY: Psychology Press.

Prochaska, J. O., Velicer, W. F., Prochaska, J. M., & Johnson, J. L. (2004). Size, consistency, and stability of stage effects for smoking cessation. *Addictive Behaviors, 29,* 207–213.

Proffitt, D. R., & Caudek, C. (2013). Depth perception and the perception of events. In A. F. Healy, R. W. Proctor, & I. B. Weiner (Eds.), *Handbook of psychology: Vol. 4. Experimental psychology* (2nd ed.). New York, NY: Wiley.

Prolo, P., & Chiappelli, F. (2007). Immune suppression. In G. Fink (Ed.), *Encyclopedia of stress.* San Diego, CA: Elsevier.

Pronin, E., Berger, J., & Molouki, S. (2007). Alone in a crowd of sheep: Asymmetric perceptions of conformity and their roots in an introspection illusion. *Journal of Personality and Social Psychology, 92,* 585–595. doi:10.1037/0022-3514.92.4.585

Pronin, E., Wegner, D. M., McCarthy, K., & Rodriguez, S. (2006). Everyday magical powers: The role of apparent mental causation in the overestimation of personal influence. *Journal of Personality and Social Psychology, 91,* 218–231. doi:10.1037/0022-3514.91.2.218

Proulx, C. M., Helms, H. M., & Buehler, C. (2007). Marital quality and personal well-being: A meta-analysis. *Journal of Marriage and Family, 69*(3), 576–593. doi:10.1111/j.1741-3737.2007.00393

Prudic, J. (2009). Electroconvulsive therapy. In B. J. Sadock, V. A. Sadock, & P. Ruiz (Eds.), *Kaplan & Sadock's comprehensive textbook of psychiatry* (pp. 3285–3300). Philadelphia, PA: Lippincott Williams & Wilkins.

Pullum, G. K. (1991). *The great Eskimo vocabulary hoax.* Chicago, IL: University of Chicago Press.

Purves, D. (2009). Vision. In G. G. Berntson & J. T. Cacioppo (Eds.), *Handbook of neuroscience for the behavioral sciences.* New York, NY: Wiley.

Pyc, M. A., Agarwal, P. K., & Roediger, H. I. (2014). Test-enhanced learning. In V. A. Benassi, C. E. Overson, & C. M. Hakala (Eds.), *Applying science of learning in education: Infusing psychological science into the curriculum.* Washington, DC: Society for the Teaching of Psychology.

Pyszczynski, T., Solomon, S., & Greenberg, J. (2003). *In the wake of 9/11: The psychology of terror.* Washington, DC: American Psychological Association.

Pyszczynski, T., Sullivan, D., & Greenberg, J. (2015). Experimental existential psychology: Living in the shadow of the facts of life. In M. Mikulincer, P. R. Shaver, E. Borgida, & J. A. Bargh (Eds.), *APA handbook of personality and social psychology: Vol. 1. Attitudes and social cognition.* Washington, DC: American Psychological Association.

Qin, S., Young, C. B., Duan, X., Chen, T., Supekar, K., & Menon, V. (2014). Amygdala subregional structure and intrinsic functional connectivity predicts individual differences in anxiety during early childhood. *Biological Psychiatry, 75,* 892–900. doi:10.1016/j.biopsych.2013.10.006

Quinn, K. A., Macrae, C. N., & Bodenhausen, G. V. (2003). Stereotyping and impression formation: How categorical thinking shapes person perception. In M. A. Hogg & J. Cooper (Eds.), *The Sage handbook of social psychology.* Thousand Oaks, CA: Sage.

Rachman, S. J. (2009). Psychological treatment of anxiety: The evolution of behavior therapy and cognitive behavior therapy. *Annual Review of Clinical Psychology, 5,* 97–119.

Radak, Z., Hart, N., Sarga, L., Koltai, E., Atalay, M., Ohno, H., & Boldogh, I. (2010). Exercise plays a preventive role against Alzheimer's disease. *Journal of Alzheimer's Disease, 20*(3), 777–783.

Rains, G. D. (2002). *Principles of human neuropsychology.* New York, NY: McGraw-Hill.

Rama, A. N., Cho, S. C., & Kushida, C. A. (2006). Normal human sleep. In T. Lee-Chiong (Ed.), *Sleep: A comprehensive handbook.* Hoboken, NJ: Wiley-Liss.

Ramchandani, P. G., Domoney, J., Sethna, V., Psychogiou, L., Vlachos, H., & Murray, L. (2013). Do early father-infant interactions predict the onset of externalizing behaviours in young children? Findings from a longitudinal cohort study. *Journal of Child Psychology and Psychiatry, 54,* 56–64. doi:10.1111/j.1469-7610.2012.02583.x

Ramirez-Esparza, N., Mehl, M. R., Alvarez-Bermudez, J., & Pennebaker, J. W. (2009). Are Mexicans more or less sociable than Americans? Insights from a naturalistic observation study. *Journal of Research in Personality, 43*(1), 1–7. doi:doi:10.1016/j.jrp.2008.09.002

Ramsay, D. S., & Woods, S. C. (2012). Food intake and metabolism. In K. D. Brownell, & M. S. Gold (Eds.), *Food and addiction: A comprehensive handbook.* New York, NY: Oxford University Press.

Rapoport, J. L., Giedd, J. N., & Gogtay, N. (2012). Neurodevelopmental model of schizophrenia: Update 2012. *Molecular Psychiatry, 17,* 1228–1238. doi:10.1038/mp.2012.23

Rasinski, K. A., Lee, L., & Krishnamurty, P. (2012). Question order effects. In H. Cooper, P. M. Camic, D. L. Long, A. T. Panter, D. Rindskopf, & K. J. Sher (Eds.), *APA handbook of research methods in psychology: Vol. 1. Foundations, planning, measures, and psychometrics.* Washington, DC: American Psychological Association.

Raskin, N. J., Rogers, C. R., & Witty, M. C. (2011). Client-centered therapy. In R. J. Corsini & D. Wedding (Eds.), *Current psychotherapies* (9th ed.). Belmont, CA: Brooks/Cole.

Raskin, R. N., & Hall, C. S. (1979). A narcissistic personality inventory. *Psychological Reports, 45*(2), 590.

Raskin, R. N., & Hall, C. S. (1981). The Narcissistic Personality Inventory: Alternate form reliability and further evidence of construct validity. *Journal of Personality Assessment, 45*(2), 159–162. doi:10.1207/s15327752jpa4502_10

Raskin, R. N., & Terry, H. (1988). A principal-components analysis of the Narcissistic Personality Inventory and further evidence of its construct validity. *Journal of Personality and Social Psychology, 54*(5), 890–902. doi:10.1037/0022-3514.54.5.890

Raub, S., & Liao, H. (2012). Doing the right thing without being told: Joint effects of initiative climate and general self-efficacy on employee proactive customer service performance. *Journal of Applied Psychology, 97,* 651–667. doi:10.1037/a0026736

Rauscher, F. H., Shaw, G. L., & Ky, K. N. (1993). Music and spatial task performance. *Nature, 365,* 611.

Rauscher, F. H., Shaw, G. L., & Ky, K. N. (1995). Listening to Mozart enhances spatial-temporal reasoning: Towards a neurophysiological basis. *Neuroscience Letters, 185,* 44–47.

Ravizza, S. M., Hambrick, D. Z., & Fenn, K. M. (2014). Non-academic Internet use in the classroom is negatively related to classroom learning regardless of intellectual ability. *Computers & Education, 78,* 109–114. doi:10.1016/j.compedu.2014.05.007.

Raynor, J. O., & Entin, E. E. (1982). Future orientation and achievement motivation. In J. O. Raynor & E. E. Entin (Eds.), *Motivation, career striving, and aging.* New York, NY: Hemisphere.

Read, J., Cartwright, C., & Gibson, K. (2014). Adverse emotional and interpersonal effects reported by 1829 New Zealanders while taking antidepressants. *Psychiatry Research, 216*(1), 67–73. doi:10.1016/j.psychres.2014.01.042

Reber, R. (2004). Availability. In F. P. Rudiger (Ed.), *Cognitive illusions.* New York, NY: Psychology Press.

Rebok, G. W., Ball, K., Guey, L. T., Jones, R. N., Kim, H., King, J. W., . . . Willis, S. L. (2014). Ten-year effects of the advanced cognitive training for independent and vital elderly cognitive training trial on cognition and everyday functioning in older adults. *Journal of The American Geriatrics Society, 62*(1), 16–24. doi:10.1111/jgs.12607

Recht, L. D., Lew, R. A., & Schwartz, W. J. (1995). Baseball teams beaten by jet lag. *Nature, 377,* 583.

Redline, S. (2011). Genetics of obstructive sleep apnea. In M. H. Kryger, T. Roth, & W. C. Dement (Eds.), *Principles and practice of sleep medicine* (5th ed.). Saint Louis, MO: Elsevier Saunders.

Rees, C. J., & Metcalfe, B. (2003). The faking of personality questionnaire results: Who's kidding whom? *Journal of Managerial Psychology, 18*(2), 156–165.

Reeves, A. J. (2010). Visual light- and dark-adaptation. In E. B. Goldstein (Ed.), *Encyclopedia of perception.* Thousand Oaks, CA: Sage.

Refinetti, R. (2006). *Circadian physiology.* Boca Raton, FL: Taylor & Francis.

Regan, P. C. (2008). *The mating game: A primer on love, sex, and marriage* (2nd ed.). Thousand Oaks, CA: Sage.

Reger, G. M., Holloway, K. M., Candy, C., Rothbaum, B. O., Difede, J., Rizzo, A. A., & Gahm, G. A. (2011). Effectiveness of virtual reality exposure therapy for active duty soldiers in a military mental health clinic. *Journal of Traumatic Stress, 24*(1), 93–96. doi:10.1002/jts.20574

Regier, D. A., & Burke, J. D. (2000). Epidemiology. In B. J. Sadock & V. A. Sadock (Eds.), *Kaplan and Sadock's comprehensive textbook of psychiatry.* Philadelphia, PA: Lippincott Williams & Wilkins.

Reicher, S. D., & Haslam, S. A. (2006). Rethinking the psychology tyranny:

The BBC prison study. *British Journal of Social Psychology, 45,* 1–40.

Reicher, S. D., Haslam, S. A., & Miller, A. G. (2014). What makes a person a perpetrator? The intellectual, moral, and methodological arguments for revisiting Milgram's research on the influence of authority. *Journal of Social Issues, 70,* 393–408. doi:10.1111/josi.12067

Reicher, S. D., Haslam, A., & Smith, J. R. (2012). Working toward the experimenter: Reconceptualizing obedience within the Milgram paradigm as identification-based followership. *Perspectives on Psychological Science, 7,* 315–324. doi:10.1177/1745691612448482

Reichert, T. (2003). The prevalence of sexual imagery in ads targeted to young adults. *Journal of Consumer Affairs, 37,* 403–412.

Reichert, T., Heckler, S. E., & Jackson, S. (2001). The effects of sexual social marketing appeals on cognitive processing and persuasion. *Journal of Advertising, 30*(1), 13–27.

Reichert, T., & Lambiase, J. (2003). How to get "kissably close": Examining how advertisers appeal to consumers' sexual needs and desires. *Sexuality & Culture: An Interdisciplinary Quarterly, 7*(3), 120–136.

Reid, R. C., & Usrey, W. M. (2008). Vision. In L. Squire, D. Berg, F. Bloom, S. du Lac, A. Ghosh, & N. Spitzer (Eds.), *Fundamental neuroscience.* San Diego, CA: Elsevier.

Reilly, S., & Schachtman, T. R. (2009). *Conditioned taste aversion: Behavioral and neural processes.* New York, NY: Oxford University Press.

Reina, C. S., Zhang, Z., & Peterson, S. J. (2014). CEO grandiose narcissism and firm performance: The role of organizational identification. *The Leadership Quarterly, 25*(5), 958–971. doi:10.1016/j.leaqua.2014.06.004

Reinhold, S. (2010). Reassessing the link between premarital cohabitation and marital instability. *Demography, 47,* 719–733. doi:10.1353/dem.0.0122

Reis, H. T., & Aron, A. (2008). Love: What is it, why does it matter, and how does it operate? *Perspectives on Psychological Science, 3,* 80–86.

Reis, H. T., & Holmes, J. G. (2012). Perspectives on the situation. In K. Deaux, & M. Snyder (Eds.), *The Oxford handbook of personality and social psychology* (pp. 64–92). New York, NY: Oxford University Press.

Reisenzein, R., & Stephan, A. (2014). More on James and the physical basis of emotion. *Emotion Review, 6*(1), 35–46. doi:10.1177/1754073913501395

Reisner, A. D. (1998). Repressed memories: True and false. In

R. A. Baker (Ed.), *Child sexual abuse and false memory syndrome.* Amherst, NY: Prometheus Books.

Rescorla, R. A. (1978). Some implications of a cognitive perspective on Pavlovian conditioning. In S. H. Hulse, H. Fowler, & W. K. Honig (Eds.), *Cognitive processes in animal behavior.* Hillsdale, NJ: Erlbaum.

Rescorla, R. A. (1980). *Pavlovian second-order conditioning.* Hillsdale, NJ: Erlbaum.

Resick, P. A., Monson, C. M., & Rizvi, S. L. (2008). Posttraumatic stress disorder. In W. E. Craighead, D. J. Miklowitz, & L. W. Craighead (Eds.), *Psychopathology: History, diagnosis, and empirical foundations.* New York, NY: Wiley.

Rest, J. R. (1986). *Moral development: Advances in research and theory.* New York, NY: Praeger.

Reuter-Lorenz, P. A., & Miller, A. C. (1998). The cognitive neuroscience of human laterality: Lessons from the bisected brain. *Current Directions in Psychological Science, 7,* 15–20.

Reutskaja, E., & Hogarth, R. M. (2009). Satisfaction in choice as a function of the number of alternatives: When "goods satiate." *Psychology & Marketing, 26*(3), 197–203. doi:10.1002/mar.20268

Rhodes, G. (2013). Face recognition. In D. Reisberg (Ed.), *The oxford handbook of cognitive psychology.* New York, NY: Oxford University Press.

Rhodewalt, F., & Peterson, B. (2009). Narcissism. In M. R. Leary & R. H. Hoyle (Eds.), *Handbook of individual differences in social behavior* (pp. 547–560). New York, NY: Guilford Press.

Ribkoff, F. (2013). Unheeded posttraumatic unpredictability: Philip G. Zimbardo's Stanford Prison Experiment as absurdist performance. *Liminalities: A Journal of Performance Studies, 9,* np. Retrieved from http://liminalities.net/9-1/unheeded.pdf

Rice, W. R., Friberg, U., & Gavrilets, S. (2012). Homosexuality as a consequence of epigenetically canalized sexual development. *The Quarterly Review of Biology, 87,* 343–368.

Richards, S. S., & Sweet, R. A. (2009). Dementia. In B. J. Sadock, V. A. Sadock, & P. Ruiz (Eds.), *Kaplan & Sadock's comprehensive textbook of psychiatry* (9th ed., Vol. 1, pp. 1167–1197). Philadelphia, PA: Lippincott Williams & Wilkins.

Richardson, C. R., Kriska, A. M., Lantz, P. M., & Hayward, R. A. (2004). Physical activity and mortality across cardiovascular disease risk groups. *Medicine and Science in Sports and Exercise, 36,* 1923–1929.

Rieger, G., Linsenmeier, J. W., Gygax, L., & Bailey, J. (2008). Sexual orientation and childhood gender nonconformity: Evidence from home videos. *Developmental Psychology, 44*(1), 46–58. doi:10.1037/0012-1649.44.1.46

Riggio, H. R., & Halpern, D. F. (2006). Understanding human thought: Educating students as critical thinkers. In W. Buskist & S. F. Davis (Eds.), *Handbook of the teaching of psychology.* Malden, MA: Blackwell.

Riis, J., Loewenstein, G., Baron, J., Jepson, C., Fagerlin, A., & Ubel, P. A. (2005). Ignorance of hedonic adaptation to hemodialysis: A study using ecological momentary assessment. *Journal of Experimental Psychology: General, 134*(1), 3–9.

Rijsenbilt, A., & Commandeur, H. (2013). Narcissus enters the courtroom: CEO narcissism and fraud. *Journal of Business Ethics, 117,* 413–429. doi:10.1007/s10551-012-1528-7

Riley, B., & Kendler, K. S. (2011). Classical genetic studies of schizophrenia. In D. R. Weinberger & P. Harrison (Eds.), *Schizophrenia* (3rd ed.). Malden, MA: Wiley-Blackwell.

Risch, N., Hoffmann, T. J., Anderson, M., Croen, L. A., Grether, J. K., & Windham, G. C. (2014). Familial recurrence of autism spectrum disorder: Evaluating genetic and environmental contributions. *The American Journal of Psychiatry, 171,* 1206–1213. doi:10.1176/appi.ajp.2014.13101359

Risen, J. L., & Gilovich, T. (2008). Why people are reluctant to tempt fate. *Journal of Personality and Social Psychology, 95,* 293–307. doi:10.1037/0022-3514.95.2.293

Risen, J. L., Gilovich, T., & Dunning, D. (2007). One-shot illusory correlations and stereotype formation. *Personality and Social Psychology Bulletin, 33,* 1492–1502. doi:10.1177/0146167207305862

Riskind, J. H. (2005). Cognitive mechanisms in generalized anxiety disorder: A second generation of theoretical perspectives. *Cognitive Therapy & Research, 29*(1), 1–5.

Ritter, R. C. (2004). Gastrointestinal mechanisms of satiation for food. *Physiology & Behavior, 81,* 249–273.

Rizzolatti, G., & Craighero, L. (2004). The mirror-neuron system. *Annual Review of Neuroscience, 27,* 169–192.

Roberson, D., Davidoff, J., Davies, I. R. L., & Shapiro, L. R. (2005). Color categories: Evidence for the cultural relativity hypothesis. *Cognitive Psychology, 50,* 378–411.

Roberson, D., Davidoff, J., & Shapiro, L. (2002). Squaring the circle: The

cultural relativity of good shape. *Journal of Cognition & Culture, 2*(1), 29–51.

Roberson, D., Davies, I., & Davidoff, J. (2000). Color categories are not universal: Replications and new evidence from a stone-age culture. *Journal of Experimental Psychology: General, 129,* 369–398.

Roberts, B. W., Caspi, A., & Moffitt, T. (2003). Work experiences and personality development in young adulthood. *Journal of Personality and Social Psychology, 84,* 582–593.

Roberts, B. W., & DelVecchio, W. F. (2000). The rank-order consistency of personality traits from childhood to old age: A quantitative review of longitudinal studies. *Psychological Bulletin, 126,* 3–25.

Roberts, B. W., Donnellan, M. B., & Hill, P. L. (2013). Personality trait development in adulthood. In H. Tennen, J. Suls, & I. B. Weiner (Eds.), *Handbook of psychology: Vol. 5. Personality and social psychology* (2nd ed.). Hoboken, NJ: Wiley.

Roberts, B. W., Jackson, J. J., Fayard, J. V., Edmonds, G., & Meints, J. (2009). Conscientiousness. In M. R. Leary & R. H. Hoyle (Eds.), *Handbook of individual differences in social behavior* (pp. 257–273). New York, NY: Guilford Press.

Roberts, B. W., Kuncel, N. R., Shiner, R., Caspi, A., & Goldberg, L. R. (2007). The power of personality: The comparative validity of personality traits, socioeconomic status, and cognitive ability for predicting important life outcomes. *Perspectives on Psychological Science, 2,* 313–345.

Roberts, B. W., & Mroczek, D. (2008). Personality trait change in adulthood. *Current Directions in Psychological Science, 17,* 31–35.

Roberts, J. E., & Ciesla, J. A. (2007). Stress generation. In G. Fink (Ed.), *Encyclopedia of stress.* San Diego, CA: Elsevier.

Roberts, M. E., Tchanturia, K., & Treasure, J. L. (2010). Exploring the neurocognitive signature of poor set-shifting in anorexia and bulimia nervosa. *Journal of Psychiatric Research, 44,* 964–970. doi:10.1016/j.jpsychires.2010.03.001

Robertson, B. R., Prestia, D., Twamley, E. W., Patterson, T. L., Bowie, C. R., & Harvey, P. D. (2014). Social competence versus negative symptoms as predictors of real world social functioning in schizophrenia. *Schizophrenia Research, 160*(1-3), 136–141. doi:10.1016/j.schres.2014.10.037

Rockey, D. L., Jr., Beason, K. R., Howington, E. B., Rockey, C. M., & Gilbert, J. D. (2005). Gambling by Greek-affiliated college students: An association between affiliation and gambling. *Journal of College Student Development, 46,* 75–87.

Rodgers, J. E. (1982). The malleable memory of eyewitnesses. *Science Digest, 3,* 32–35.

Rodrigues, A. C., Loureiro, M. A., & Caramelli, P. (2010). Musical training, neuroplasticity and cognition. *Dementia & Neuropsychologia, 4,* 277–286.

Roediger, H. L., III. (1980). Memory metaphors in cognitive psychology. *Memory & Cognition, 8,* 231–246.

Roediger, H. L., III, Agarwal, P. K., Kang, S. K., & Marsh, E. J. (2010). Benefits of testing memory: Best practices and boundary conditions. In G. M. Davies & D. B. Wright, (Eds.), *Current issues in applied memory research* (pp. 13–49). New York, NY: Psychology Press.

Roediger, H. L., III, Gallo, D. A., & Geraci, L. (2002). Processing approaches to cognition: The impetus from the levels-of-processing framework. *Memory, 10,* 319–332.

Roediger, H. L., III, & McDermott, K. B. (1995). Creating false memories: Remembering words not presented in lists. *Journal of Experimental Psychology: Learning, Memory, and Cognition, 21,* 803–814.

Roediger, H. L., III, & McDermott, K. B. (2000). Tricks of memory. *Current Directions in Psychological Science, 9,* 123–127.

Roediger, H. I., III, Weinstein, Y., & Agarwal, P. K. (2010). Forgetting: Preliminary considerations. In S. Della Sala (Ed.), *Forgetting.* New York, NY: Psychology Press.

Roediger, H. I., III, Wixted, J. H., & DeSoto, K. A. (2012). The curious complexity between confidence and accuracy in reports from memory. In L. Nadel, & W. P. Sinnott-Armstrong (Eds.), *Memory and law.* New York, NY: Oxford University Press.

Roese, N. J., & Vohs, K. D. (2012). Hindsight bias. *Perspectives on Psychological Science, 7,* 411–426. doi:10.1177/1745691612454303

Rogers, C. R. (1951). *Client-centered therapy: Its current practice, implications, and theory.* Boston, MA: Houghton Mifflin.

Rogers, C. R. (1961). *On becoming a person: A therapist's view of psychotherapy.* Boston, MA: Houghton Mifflin.

Rogers, C. R. (1980). *A way of being.* Boston, MA: Houghton Mifflin.

Rogers, C. R. (1986). Client-centered therapy. In I. L. Kutash & A. Wolf (Eds.), *Psychotherapist's casebook.* San Francisco, CA: Jossey-Bass.

Rogoff, B. (2003). *The cultural nature of human development.* New York, NY: Oxford University Press.

Rohde, P., Lewinsohn, P. M., Klein, D. N., Seeley, J. R., & Gau, J. M. (2013). Key characteristics of major depressive disorder occurring in childhood, adolescence, emerging adulthood, and adulthood. *Clinical Psychological Science, 1*(1), 41–53. doi:10.1177/2167702612457599

Rollman, G. B. (2010). Pain: Cognitive and contextual influences. In E. B. Goldstein (Ed.), *Encyclopedia of perception.* Thousand Oaks, CA: Sage.

Rolls, B. J. (2012). The impact of portion size and energy density on eating. In K. D. Brownell, & M. S. Gold (Eds.), *Food and addiction: A comprehensive handbook.* New York, NY: Oxford University Press.

Ronksley, P. E., Brien, S. E., Turner, B. J., Mukamal, K. J., & Ghali, W. A. (2011). Association of alcohol consumption with selected cardiovascular disease outcomes: a systematic review and meta-analysis. *British Medical Journal, 342*(7795), 479.

Rönnlund, M., & Nilsson, L. (2009). Flynn effects on sub-factors of episodic and semantic memory: Parallel gains over time and the same set of determining factors. *Neuropsychologia, 47,* 2174–2180. doi:10.1016/j.neuropsychologia.2008.11.007

Roofeh, D., Tumuluru, D., Shilpakar, S., & Nimgaonkar, V. L. (2013). Genetics of schizophrenia. Where has the heritability gone? *International Journal of Mental Health, 42*(1), 5–22. doi:10.2753/IMH0020-7411420101

Rosario, M., & Schrimshaw, E. W. (2014). Theories and etiologies of sexual orientation. In D. L. Tolman, L. M. Diamond, J. A. Bauermeister, W. H. George, G. J. Pfaus, & L. M. Ward (Eds.), *APA handbook of sexuality and psychology: Vol. 1. Person-based approaches.* Washington, DC: American Psychological Association.

Rosch, E. H. (1973). Natural categories. *Cognitive Psychology, 4,* 328–350.

Rose, D., Wykes, T., Leese, M., Bindman, J., & Fleischmann, P. (2003). Patient's perspectives on electroconvulsive therapy: Systematic review. *British Medical Journal, 326,* 1363–1365.

Roseboom, T., de Rooij, S., & Painter, R. (2006). The Dutch famine and its long-term consequences for adult health. *Early Human Development, 82,* 485–491.

Rosemond, J. K. (2005). The diseasing of America's children: The politics of diagnosis. In R. H. Wright & N. A. Cummings (Eds.), *Destructive trends in mental health: The well-intentioned path to harm.* New York, NY: Routledge.

Rosenbaum, M., Kissileff, H. R., Mayer, L. S., Hirsch, J., & Leibel, R. L. (2010). Energy intake in weight-reduced humans. *Brain Research, 1350,* 95–102. doi:10.1016/j.brainres.2010.05.062

Rosenblum, K. (2009). Conditioned taste aversion and taste learning: Molecular mechanisms. In J. H. Byrne (Ed.), *Concise learning and memory: The editor's selection.* San Diego, CA: Elsevier.

Rosenkranz, M. A., Davidson, R. J., MacCoon, D. G., Sheridan, J. F., Kalin, N. H., & Lutz, A. (2013). A comparison of mindfulness-based stress reduction and an active control in modulation of neurogenic inflammation. *Brain, Behavior, and Immunity, 27,* 174–184. doi:10.1016/j.bbi.2012.10.013

Rosenthal, H. (1988). *Not with my life I don't: Preventing suicide and that of others.* Muncie, IN: Accelerated Development.

Rosenthal, R. (1976). *Experimenter effects in behavioral research.* New York, NY: Halsted.

Rosenthal, R. (1994). Interpersonal expectancy effects: A 30-year perspective. *Current Directions in Psychological Science, 3,* 176–179.

Rosenthal, R. (2002). Experimenter and clinical effects in scientific inquiry and clinical practice. *Prevention & Treatment, 5*(38).

Rosenthal, R., & Fode, K. L. (1963). Three experiments in experimenter bias. *Psychological Reports, 12,* 491–511.

Rosenzweig, M. R., & Bennet, E. L. (1996). Psychobiology of plasticity: Effects of training and experience on brain and behavior. *Behavioural Brain Research, 78*(5), 57–65.

Rosenzweig, M. R., Krech, D., & Bennett, E. L. (1961). Heredity, environment, brain biochemistry, and learning. In *Current trends in psychological theory.* Pittsburgh: University of Pittsburgh Press.

Rosenzweig, M. R., Krech, D., Bennett, E. L., & Diamond, M. (1962). Effects of environmental complexity and training on brain chemistry and anatomy: A replication and extension. *Journal of Comparative and Physiological Psychology, 55,* 429–437.

Ross, C. A., & Ness, L. (2010). Symptom patterns in dissociative identity disorder patients and the general population. *Journal of Trauma & Dissociation, 11,* 458–468. doi:10.1080/15299732.2010.495939

Ross, H., & Plug, C. (2002). *The mystery of the moon illusion: Exploring the size perception.* New York, NY: Oxford.

Ross, L., & Nisbett, R. E. (1991). *The person and the situation: Perspectives of social psychology.* New York, NY: McGraw-Hill.

Rosso, I. M., Weiner, M. R., Crowley, D. J., Silveri, M. M., Rauch, S. L., & Jensen, J. E. (2014). Insula and anterior cingulate GABA levels in posttraumatic stress disorder: Preliminary findings using magnetic resonance spectroscopy. *Depression and Anxiety, 31*(2), 115–123. doi:10.1002/da.22155

Rothberg, B., & Feinstein, R. E. (2014). Suicide. In J. L. Cutler (Ed.), *Psychiatry* (3rd ed.). New York, NY: Oxford University Press.

Routh, D. K. (2013). Clinical psychology. In D. K. Freedheim, & I. B. Weiner (Eds.), *Handbook of psychology Vol. 1: History of psychology* (2nd ed., pp. 377–387). New York, NY: Wiley.

Rowa, K., & Antony, M. M. (2008). Generalized anxiety disorders. In W. E. Craighead, D. J. Miklowitz, & L. W. Craighead (Eds.), *Psychopathology: History, diagnosis, and empirical foundations.* New York, NY: Wiley.

Rowe, M. L., Raudenbush, S. W., & Goldin-Meadow, S. (2012). The pace of vocabulary growth helps predict later vocabulary skill. *Child Development, 83,* 508–525.

Rowe, S. M., & Wertsch, J. V. (2002). Vygotsky's model of cognitive development. In U. Goswami (Ed.), *Blackwell handbook of childhood cognitive development.* Malden, MA: Blackwell.

Rowny, S., & Lisanby, S. H. (2008). Brain stimulation in psychiatry. In A. Tasman, J. Kay, J. A. Lieberman, M. B. First, & M. Maj (Eds.), *Psychiatry* (3rd ed.). New York, NY: Wiley-Blackwell.

Rozin, P. (2007). Food and eating. In S. Kitayama & D. Cohen (Eds.), *Handbook of cultural psychology.* New York, NY: Guilford Press.

Rubin, M., & Badea, C. (2012). They're all the same! . . . but for several different reasons: A review of the multicausal nature of perceived group variability. *Current Direction in Psychological Science, 21,* 367–372. doi:10.1177/0963721412457363

Ruble, D. N., & Martin, C. L. (1998). Gender development. In W. Damon (Ed.), *Handbook of child psychology (Vol. 3): Social, emotional, and personality development.* New York, NY: Wiley.

Ruiz, J. M., Prather, C. C., & Steffen, P. (2012). Socioeconomic status and health. In A. Baum, T. A. Revenson, & J. Singer (Eds.), *Handbook of health psychology* (2nd ed.). New York, NY: Psychology Press.

Ruiz, P., & Strain, E. C. (2011). *Lowinson and Ruiz's substance abuse: A comprehensive textbook* (5th ed.). Philadelphia, PA: Lippincott Williams & Wilkins.

Rummel, J., & Boywitt, C. D. (2014). Controlling the stream of thought: Working memory capacity predicts adjustment of mind-wandering to situational demands. *Psychonomic Bulletin & Review, 21*, 1309–1315. doi:10.3758/s13423-013-0580-3

Runco, M. A. (2010). Divergent thinking, creativity, and ideation. In J. C. Kaufman, & R. J. Sternberg (Eds.), *Cambridge handbook of creativity*. New York, NY: Cambridge University Press. doi:10.1017 /CBO9780511763205.026

Rundle, A., Hoepner, A., Hassoun, S., Oberfield, G., Freyer, D., Holmes, M., . . . Whyatt, R. (2012). Association of childhood obesity with maternal exposure to ambient air polycyclic aromatic hydrocarbons during pregnancy. *American Journal of Epidemiology, 175*, 1163–1172. doi:10.1093/aje /kwr455

Runyan, W. M. (2006). Psychobiography and the psychology of science: Understanding relations between the life and work of individual psychologists. *Review of General Psychology, 10*, 147–162.

Rüsch, N., Corrigan, P. W., Heekeren, K., Theodoridou, A., Dvorsky, D., Metzler, S., . . . Rössler, W. (2014). Well-being among persons at risk of psychosis: The role of self-labeling, shame, and stigma stress. *Psychiatric Services, 65*, 483–489. doi:10.1176 /appi.ps.201300169

Ruscio, J. (2006). *Clear thinking with psychology: Separating sense from nonsense*. Belmont, CA: Wadsworth.

Rushton, J. P. (2003). Race differences in g and the "Jensen effect." In H. Nyborg (Ed.), *The scientific study of general intelligence: Tribute to Arthur R. Jensen*. Oxford, UK: Pergamon.

Rushton, J. P., & Jensen, A. R. (2005). Thirty years of research on race differences in cognitive ability. *Psychology, Public Policy, and Law, 11*, 235–294.

Rushton, J. P., & Jensen, A. R. (2010). The rise and fall of the Flynn effect as a reason to expect a narrowing of the black-white IQ gap. *Intelligence, 38*(2), 213–219. doi:10.1016/j.intell.2009 .12.002

Russell, J. A. (1991). Culture and the categorization of emotions. *Psychological Bulletin, 110*, 426–450.

Russo, N. F., & Denmark, F. L. (1987). Contributions of women to

psychology. Annual Review of Psychology, 38, 279–298.

Rutherford, A. (2000). Radical behaviorism and psychology's public: B. F. Skinner in the popular press, 1934–1990. *History of Psychology, 3*, 371–395.

Rutherford, W. (1886). A new theory of hearing. *Journal of Anatomy and Physiology, 21*, 166–168.

Rutkowski, E. M., & Connelly, C. D. (2012). Self-efficacy and physical activity in adolescent and parent dyads. *Journal for Specialists in Pediatric Nursing, 17*, 51–60. doi:10.1111 /j.1744-6155.2011.00314.x

Rutter, M. (2012). Gene-environment interdependence. *European Journal of Developmental Psychology, 9*, 391–412. doi:10.1080/17405629 .2012.661174

Ruvio, A., Somer, E., & Rindfleisch, A. (2014). When bad gets worse: The amplifying effect of materialism on traumatic stress and maladaptive consumption. *Journal of the Academy of Marketing Science, 42*, 90–101. doi:10.1007/s11747-013-0345-6

Ryder, R. D. (2006). Speciesism in the laboratory. In P. Singer (Ed.), *In defense of animals: The second wave*. Malden, MA: Blackwell.

Sachdev, P. S. (2013). Is DSM-5 defensible? *Australian and New Zealand Journal of Psychiatry, 47*(1), 10–11. doi:10.1177/0004867412468164

Sackeim, H. A. (2014). Autobiographical memory and electroconvulsive therapy: Do not throw out the baby. *The Journal of ECT, 30*(3), 177–186. doi:10.1097/YCT.0000000000000117

Sackeim, H. A., Prudic, J., Fuller, R., Keilp, J., Lavori, P. W., & Olfson, M. (2007). The cognitive effects of electroconvulsive therapy in community settings. *Neuropsychopharmacology, 32*, 244–254.

Sacks, O. (1987). *The man who mistook his wife for a hat*. New York, NY: Harper & Row.

Sadler, J. Z. (2005). *Values and psychiatric diagnosis*. New York, NY: Oxford University Press.

Sadock, B. J., Sadock, V. A., & Ruiz, P. (2015). *Kaplan and Sadock's synopsis of psychiatry: Behavioral sciences/ clinical psychiatry* (11th ed.). Philadelphia, PA: Wolters Kluwer.

Sakurai, T. (2013). Orexin deficiency and narcolepsy. *Current Opinion in Neurobiology, 23*, 760–766. doi:10.1016/j.conb.2013.04.007

Salter, S. P., Mixon, F. G., Jr., & King, E. W. (2012). Broker beauty and boon: A study of physical attractiveness and its effect on real estate brokers' income and productivity. *Applied Financial

Economics, 22*, 811–825. doi:10.1080 /09603107.2011.627211

Salthouse, T. A. (1996). The processing-speed theory of adult age differences in cognition. *Psychological Review, 103*, 403–428.

Salthouse, T. A. (2000). Aging and measures of processing speed. *Biological Psychology, 54*, 35–54.

Salthouse, T. A. (2003). Memory aging from 18–80. *Alzheimer Disease & Associated Disorders, 17*(3), 162–167.

Salthouse, T. A. (2004). What and when of cognitive aging. *Current Directions in Psychological Science, 13*(4), 140–144.

Salthouse, T. A., & Mandell, A. R. (2013). Do age-related increases in tip-of-the-tongue experiences signify episodic memory impairments? *Psychological Science, 24*, 2489–2497. doi:10.1177/0956797613495881

Samberg, E., & Marcus, E. R. (2005). Process, resistance, and interpretation. In E. S. Person, A. M. Cooper, & G. O. Gabbard (Eds.), *Textbook of psychoanalysis*. Washington, DC: American Psychiatric Publishing.

Samnaliev, M., & Clark, R. E. (2008). The economics of schizophrenia. In K. T. Mueser & D. V. Jeste (Eds.), *Clinical handbook of schizophrenia* (pp. 25–34). New York, NY: Guilford Press.

Sana, F., Weston, T., & Cepeda, N. J. (2013). Laptop multitasking hinders classroom learning for both users and nearby peers. *Computers & Education, 62*, 24–31. doi:10.1016 /j.compedu.2012.10.003.

Sanbonmatsu, D. M., Strayer, D. L., Medeiros-Ward, N., & Watson, J. M. (2013). Who multi-tasks and why? Multi-tasking ability, perceived multi-tasking ability, impulsivity, and sensation seeking. *PloS One, 8*, e54402. doi:10.1371/journal. pone.0054402

Sanders, M. H., & Givelber, R. J. (2006). Overview of obstructive sleep apnea in adults. In T. Lee-Chiong (Ed.), *Sleep: A comprehensive handbook*. Hoboken, NJ: Wiley-Liss.

Sandoval, T. C., Gollan, T. H., Ferreira, V. S., & Salmon, D. P. (2010). What causes the bilingual disadvantage in verbal fluency? The dual-task analogy. *Bilingualism: Language and Cognition, 13*(2), 231–252. doi:10.1017/S1366728909990514

Sandstrom, G. M., & Dunn, E. W. (2014). Social interactions and well-being: The surprising power of weak ties. *Personality and Social Psychology Bulletin, 40*, 910–922. doi:10.1177/0146167214529799

Sanes, J. R., & Jessell, T. M. (2013). Formation and elimination of synapses. In E. R. Kandel, J. H. Schwartz, T. M. Jessell, S. A. Siegelbaum, & A. J. Hudspeth (Eds.), *Principles of neural science* (5th ed.). New York, NY: McGraw-Hill.

Sanjuan, P., & Magallares, A. (2014). Coping strategies as mediating variables between self-serving attributional bias and subjective well-being. *Journal of Happiness Studies, 15*, 443–453. doi:10.1007/s10902-013-9430-2

Saper, C. B. (2000). Brain stem, reflexive behavior, and the cranial nerves. In E. R. Kandel, J. H. Schwartz, & T. M. Jessell (Eds.), *Principles of neural science* (pp. 873–888). New York, NY: McGraw-Hill.

Saper, C. B. (2013). The central circadian timing system. *Current Opinion in Neurobiology, 23*, 747–751. doi:10.1016/j.conb.2013.04.004

Saphire-Bernstein, S., & Taylor, S. E. (2013). Close relationships and happiness. In S. A. David, I. Boniwell, & A. Conley Ayers (Eds.), *The Oxford handbook of happiness*. New York, NY: Oxford University Press.

Sapolsky, R. M. (2007). Stress, stress-related disease, and emotion regulation. In J. J. Gross (Ed.), *Handbook of emotion regulation*. New York, NY: Guilford Press.

Sassen, M., Kraus, L., & Bühringer, G. (2011). Differences in pathological gambling prevalence estimates: Facts or artefacts? *International Journal of Methods in Psychiatric Research, 20*(4), e83–e99. doi:10.1002/mpr.354

Satel, S., & Lilienfeld, S. O. (2013). *Brainwashed: The seductive appeal of mindless neuroscience*. New York, NY: Basic Books.

Saucier, G., & Srivastava S. (2015). What makes a good structural model of personality? Evaluating the big five and alternatives. In M. Mikulincer, P. R. Shaver, M. L. Cooper, & R. J. Larsen (Eds.), *APA handbook of personality and social psychology: Vol. 4. Personality processes and individual differences*. Washington, DC: American Psychological Association.

Saunders, J., Worth, R., & Fernandes, M. (2012). Repressive coping style and mnemic neglect. *Journal of Experimental Psychopathology, 3*, 346–367.

Savin-Williams, R. C. (2006). Who's gay? Does it matter? *Current Directions in Psychological Science, 15*, 40–44.

Schachter, R. (2011). Using the group in cognitive group therapy. *Group, 35*(2), 135-149.

Schachter, S. (1959). *The psychology of affiliation*. Stanford, CA: Stanford University Press.

Schachter, S. (1964). The interaction of cognitive and physiological determinants of emotional state. In L. Berkowitz (Ed.), *Advances in experimental social psychology* (Vol. 1). New York, NY: Academic Press.

Schachtman, T. R., & Reilly, S. (2011). Things you always wanted to know about conditioning but were too afraid to ask. In T. R. Schachtman, & S. Reilly (Eds.), *Associative learning and condition theory: Human and non-human applications*. New York, NY: Oxford University Press.

Schachtman, T. R., Walker, J., & Fowler, S. (2011). Effects of conditioning in advertising. In T. R. Schachtman, & S. Reilly (Eds.), *Associative learning and condition theory: Human and non-human applications*. New York, NY: Oxford University Press.

Schacter, D. L. (1996). *Searching for memory: The brain, the mind, and the past*. New York, NY: Basic Books.

Schacter, D. L. (1999). The seven sins of memory: Insights from psychology and cognitive neuroscience. *American Psychologist, 54*, 182–203.

Schacter, D. L. (2001). *The seven sins of memory: How the mind forgets and remembers*. Boston, MA: Houghton Mifflin.

Schacter, D. L., & Loftus, E. F. (2013). Memory and law: What can cognitive neuroscience contribute? *Nature Neuroscience, 16*, 119–123. doi:10.1038/nn.3294

Schaefer, A. (2005). Commuting takes its toll. *Scientific American Mind, 16*(3), 14–15.

Schaeffer, N. C. (2000). Asking questions about threatening topics: A selective overview. In A. A. Stone, J. S. Turkkan, C. A. Bachrach, J. B. Jobe, H. S. Kurtzman, & V. Cain (Eds.), *The science of self-report: Implications for research and practice*. Mahwah, NJ: Erlbaum.

Scheele, D., Striepens, N., Güntürkün, O., Deutschländer, S., Maier, W., Kendrick, K. M., & Hurlemann, R. (2012). Oxytocin modulates social distance between males and females. *The Journal of Neuroscience, 32*, 16074–16079. doi:10.1523/JNEUROSCI.2755-12.2012

Scheer, F. L., Morris, C. J., & Shea, S. A. (2013). The internal circadian clock increases hunger and appetite in the evening independent of food intake and other behaviors. *Obesity, 21*, 421–423. doi:10.1002/oby.20351

Scheier, M. F., Carver, C. S., & Armstrong, G. H. (2012). Behavioral self-regulation, health, and illness. In A. Baum, T. A. Revenson, & J. Singer (Eds.), *Handbook of health psychology* (2nd ed.). New York, NY: Psychology Press.

Schellenberg, E. G. (2006). Long-term positive associations between music lessons and IQ. *Journal of Educational Psychology, 98*(2), 457–468. doi:10.1037/0022-0663.98.2.457

Schellenberg, E. G. (2011). Examining the association between music lessons and intelligence. *British Journal of Psychology, 102*, 283–302. doi:10.1111/j.2044-8295.2010.02000.x

Schieber, F. (2006). Vision and aging. In J. E. Birren & K. W. Schaie (Eds.), *Handbook of the psychology of aging*. San Diego, CA: Academic Press.

Schiff, M., & Lewontin, R. (1986). *Education and class: The irrelevance of IQ genetic studies*. Oxford: Clarendon Press.

Schirillo, J. A. (2010). Gestalt approach. In E. B. Goldstein (Ed.), *Encyclopedia of perception*. Thousand Oaks, CA: Sage.

Schmaling, K. B. (2012). Asthma. In A. M. Nezu, C. M. Nezu, P. A. Geller, & I. B. Weiner (Eds.), *Handbook of psychology: Vol. 9. Health psychology* (2nd ed.). New York, NY: Wiley.

Schmid, P. C., Mast, M. S., Bombari, D., & Mast, F. W. (2011). Gender effects in information processing on a nonverbal decoding task. *Sex Roles, 65*, 102–107. doi:10.1007/s11199-011-9979-3

Schmidt, F. L. (2013). Meta-analysis. In J. A. Schinka, W. F. Velicer, & I. B. Weiner (Eds.), *Handbook of psychology: Vol. 2. Research methods in psychology* (2nd ed.). Hoboken, NJ: Wiley.

Schmidt, F. L., & Hunter, J. (2004). General mental ability in the world of work: Occupational attainment and job performance. *Journal of Personality and Social Psychology, 86*, 162–173.

Schmidt, H. D., Vassoler, F. M., & Pierce, R. C. (2011). Neurobiological factors of drug dependence and addiction. In P. Ruiz, & E. C. Strain (Eds.), *Lowinson and Ruiz's substance abuse: A comprehensive textbook* (5th ed., pp. 55–78). Philadelphia, PA: Lippincott Williams & Wilkins.

Schmitt, D. P. (2005). Fundamentals of human mating strategies. In D. M. Buss (Ed.), *The handbook of evolutionary psychology*. New York, NY: Wiley.

Schmitt, D. P. (2014). Evaluating evidence of mate preference adaptations: How do we really know what Homo sapiens sapiens really want? In V. A. Weekes-Shackelford, & T. K. Shackelford (Eds.), *Evolutionary perspectives on human sexual psychology and behavior*. New York, NY: Springer Science + Business Media. doi:10.1007/978-1-4939-0314-6_1

Schmitt, D. P., & International Sexuality Description Project. (2003). Universal sex differences in the desire for sexual variety: Tests from 52 nations, 6 continents, and 13 islands. *Journal of Personality and Social Psychology, 85*, 85–104.

Schmolck, H., Buffalo, E. A., & Squire, L. R. (2000). Memory distortions develop over time: Recollections of the O. J. Simpson trial verdict after 15 and 32 months. *Psychological Science, 11*, 39–45.

Schneider, K. J., & Längle, A. (2012). The renewal of humanism in psychotherapy: A roundtable discussion. *Psychotherapy, 49*, 427–429. doi:10.1037/a0027111.

Schneider, R. H., Grim, C. E., Rainforth, M. V., Kotchen, T., Nidich, S. I., Gaylord-King, C., ... Alexander, C. N. (2012). Stress reduction in the secondary prevention of cardiovascular disease: Randomized, controlled trial of transcendental meditation and health education in blacks. *Circulation: Cardiovascular Quality and Outcomes, 5*, 750–758. doi:10.1161/CIRCOUTCOMES.112.967406

Schneier, F. R., Vidair, H. B., Vogel, L. R., & Muskin, P. R. (2014). Anxiety, obsessive-compulsive, and stress disorders. In J. L. Cutler (Ed.), *Psychiatry* (3rd ed.). New York, NY: Oxford University Press.

Schnittker, J. (2008). An uncertain revolution: Why the rise of a genetic model of mental illness has not increased tolerance. *Social Science & Medicine, 67*(9), 1370–1381. doi:10.1016/j.socscimed.2008.07.007

Schooler, C. (2007). Use it—and keep it, longer, probably: A reply to Salthouse. *Perspectives on Psychological Science, 2*, 24–29.

Schramm, D. G., Marshall, J. P., Harris, V. W., & Lee, T. R. (2005). After "I do": The newlywed transition. *Marriage and Family Review, 38*, 45–67.

Schramm, S. H., Moebus, S., Lehmann, N., Galli, U., Obermann, M., Bock, E., ... Katsarava, Z. (2014). The association between stress and headache: A longitudinal population-based study. *Cephalalgia*. Advance online publication. doi:10.1177/0333102414563087

Schreiner, A. M., & Dunn, M. E. (2012). Residual effects of cannabis use on neurocognitive performance after prolonged abstinence: A meta-analysis. *Experimental and Clinical Psychopharmacology, 20*, 420–429. doi:10.1037/a0029117

Schultz, D. S., & Brabender, V. M. (2013). More challenges since Wikipedia: The effects of exposure to Internet information about the Rorschach on selected Comprehensive System variables. *Journal of Personality Assessment, 95*(2), 149–158. doi:10.1080/00223891.2012.725438

Schultz, J. H., & Luthe, W. (1959). *Autogenic training*. New York, NY: Grune & Stratton.

Schulz-Hardt, S., Frey, D., Luethgens, C., & Moscovici, S. (2000). Biased information search in group decision making. *Journal of Personality & Social Psychology, 78*, 655–669.

Schuman, H., & Kalton, G. (1985). Survey methods. In G. Lindzey & E. Aronson (Eds.), *Handbook of social psychology* (3rd ed.). New York, NY: Random House.

Schwabe, L., Nader, K., & Pruessner, J. C. (2014). Reconsolidation of human memory: Brain mechanisms and clinical relevance. *Biological Psychiatry, 76*, 274–280. doi:10.1016/j.biopsych.2014.03.008

Schwartz, B. (2004). *The paradox of choice: Why more is less*. New York, NY: Ecco.

Schwartz, B., & Sommers, R. (2013). Affective forecasting and well-being. In D. Reisberg (Ed.), *The Oxford handbook of cognitive psychology*. New York, NY: Oxford University Press. doi:10.1093/oxfordhb/9780195376746.013.0044

Schwartz, B. L., & Metcalfe, J. (2011). Tip-of-the-tongue (TOT) states: Retrieval, behavior, and experience. *Memory & Cognition, 39*, 737–749. doi:10.3758/s13421-010-0066-8

Schwartz, B. L., & Metcalfe, J. (2014). Tip-of-the-tongue (TOT) states: Mechanisms and metacognitive control. In B. L. Schwartz, & A. S. Brown (Eds.), *Tip-of-the-tongue states and related phenomena*. New York, NY: Cambridge University Press.

Schwartz, G. J. (2012). Peripheral regulation of hunger and satiety. In K. D. Brownell, & M. S. Gold (Eds.), *Food and addiction: A comprehensive handbook*. New York, NY: Oxford University Press.

Schwartz, J. H., & Javitch, J. A. (2013). Neurotransmitters. In E. R. Kandel, J. H. Schwartz, T. M. Jessell, S. A. Siegelbaum, & A. J. Hudspeth (Eds.), *Principles of neural science* (5th ed., pp. 289–305). New York, NY: McGraw-Hill.

Schwartz, S. J., Donnellan, M. B., Ravert, R. D., Luyckx, K., & Zamboanga, B. L. (2013). Identity development, personality, and well-being in adolescence and emerging adulthood: Theory, research, and recent advances. In R. M. Lerner, M. A. Easterbrooks, J. Mistry, & I. B. Weiner (Eds.), *Handbook of psychology: Vol. 6. Developmental psychology*. New York, NY: Wiley.

Schwarz, N., & Strack, F. (1999). Reports of subjective well-being:

Judgmental processes and their methodological implications. In D. Kahneman, E. Diener, & N. Schwarz (Eds.), *Well-being: The foundations of hedonic psychology*. New York, NY: Russell Sage Foundation.

Schwarz, T. L. (2008). Release of neurotransmitters. In L. Squire, D. Berg, F. Bloom, S. Du Lac, A. Ghosh, & N. Spitzer (Eds.), *Fundamental neuroscience* (3rd ed., pp. 157–180). San Diego, CA: Elsevier.

Schwarzer, R., & Luszczynska, A. (2013). Stressful life events. In A. M. Nezu, C. M. Nezu, P. A. Geller, & I. B. Weiner (Eds.), *Handbook of psychology: Vol. 9. Health psychology* (2nd ed.). New York, NY: Wiley.

Scott, B. A., & Judge, T. A. (2013). Beauty, personality, and affect as antecedents of counterproductive work behavior receipt. *Human Performance, 26,* 93–113. doi:10.1080/08959285. 2013.765876

Scott, K. (2008). Chemical senses: Taste and olfaction. In L. Squire, D. Berg, F. Bloom, S. du Lac, A. Ghosh, & N. Spitzer (Eds.), *Fundamental Neuroscience*. San Diego, CA: Elsevier.

Scott, V., McDade, D. M., & Luckman, S. M. (2007). Rapid changes in the sensitivity of arcuate nucleus neurons to central ghrelin in relation to feeding status. *Physiology & Behavior, 90,* 180–185.

Scoville, W. B., & Milner, B. (1957). Loss of recent memory after bilateral hippocampal lesions. *Journal of Neurology, Neurosurgery & Psychiatry, 20,* 11–21.

Scull, A. (1990). Deinstitutionalization: Cycles of despair. *The Journal of Mind and Behavior, 11*(3/4), 301–312.

Scully, J. A., Tosi, H., & Banning, K. (2000). Life event checklists: Revisiting the social readjustment rating scale after 30 years. *Educational & Psychological Measurement, 60,* 864–876.

Searleman, A., & Herrmann, D. (1994). *Memory from a broader perspective*. New York, NY: McGraw-Hill.

Seaton, S. E., King, S., Manktelow, B. N., Draper, E. S., & Field, D. J. (2013). Babies born at the threshold of viability: Changes in survival and workload over 20 years. *Archive of Disease of Childhood: Fetal and Neonatal Edition, 98,* F15–F20. doi:10.1136 /fetalneonatal-2011-301572

Sebastian, C., Burnett, S., & Blakemore, S. (2010). The neuroscience of social cognition in teenagers: Implications for inclusion in society. In C. L. Cooper, J. Field, U. Goswami, R. Jenkins, & B. J. Sahakian (Eds.), *Mental capital and wellbeing*. Hoboken, NJ: Wiley-Blackwell.

Sedikides, C., & Strube, M. J. (1997). Self-evaluation: To thine own self be good, to thine own self be sure, to thine own self be true, and to thine own self be better. In M. P. Zanna (Ed.), *Advances in experimental social psychology*. New York, NY: Academic Press.

Sedlmeier, P., Eberth, J., Schwarz, M., Zimmermann, D., Haarig, F., Jaeger, S., & Kunze, S. (2012). The psychological effects of meditation: A meta-analysis. *Psychological Bulletin, 138,* 1139–1171. doi:10.1037/a0028168

Seery, M. D. (2011). Resilience: A silver lining to experiencing adverse life events? *Current Directions in Psychological Science, 20,* 390–394. doi: 10.1177/0963721411424740

Seery, M. D., Leo, R. J., Lupien, S. P., Kondrak, C. L., & Almonte, J. L. (2013). An upside to adversity? Moderate cumulative lifetime adversity is associated with resilient responses in the face of controlled stressors. *Psychological Science, 24,* 1181–1189. doi:10.1177/0956797612469210

Segal-Caspi, L., Roccas, S., & Sagiv, L. (2012). Don't judge a book by its cover, revisited: Perceived and reported traits and values of attractive women. *Psychological Science, 23,* 1112–1116. doi:10.1177/0956797612446349

Segall, M. H., Campbell, D. T., Herskovits, M. J. (1966). *The influence of culture on visual perception*. Indianapolis: Bobbs-Merrill.

Segerstrom, S. C., & O'Connnor, D. B. (2012). Stress, health, and illness: Four challenges for the future. *Psychology and Health, 27,* 128–140. doi:10.1080 /08870446.2012.659516

Segerstrom, S. C., & Sephton, S. E. (2010). Optimistic expectancies and cell-mediated immunity: The role of positive affect. *Psychological Science, 21*(3), 448–455. doi:10.1177/0956797610362061

Seifer, R. (2001). Socioeconomic status, multiple risks, and development of intelligence. In R. J. Sternberg & E. L. Grigorenko (Eds.), *Environmental effects on cognitive abilities* (pp. 59–82). Mahwah, NJ: Erlbaum.

Seligman, M. E. P. (1971). Phobias and preparedness. *Behavior Therapy, 2,* 307–321.

Seligman, M. E. P. (1974). Depression and learned helplessness. In R. J. Friedman & M. M. Katz (Eds.), *The psychology of depression: Contemporary theory and research*. New York, NY: Wiley.

Seligman, M. E. P. (1990). *Learned optimism*. New York, NY: Pocket Books.

Seligman, M. E. P. (1992). *Helplessness: On depression, development, and death*. New York, NY: Freeman.

Seligman, M. E. P. (2003). The past and future of positive psychology. In C. L. M. Keyes & J. Haidt (Eds.), *Flourishing: Positive psychology and the life well-lived*. Washington, DC: American Psychological Association.

Seligman, M. E. P., & Hager, J. L. (1972, August). Biological boundaries of learning (the sauce béarnaise syndrome). *Psychology Today*, pp. 59–61, 84–87.

Selye, H. (1936). A syndrome produced by diverse nocuous agents. *Nature, 138,* 32.

Selye, H. (1956). *The stress of life*. New York, NY: McGraw-Hill.

Selye, H. (1973). The evolution of the stress concept. *American Scientist, 61*(6), 672–699.

Selye, H. (1974). *Stress without distress*. New York, NY: Lippincott.

Senders, A., Bourdette, D., Hanes, D., Yadav, V., & Shinto, L. (2014). Perceived stress in multiple sclerosis: The potential role of mindfulness in health and well-being. *Journal of Evidence-Based Complementary and Alternative Medicine, 19,* 104–111. doi:10.1177/2156587214523291

Senior, C., Thomson, K., Badger, J., & Butler, M. J. R. (2007). Interviewing strategies in the face of beauty: A psychophysiological investigation into the job negotiation process. *Annals of the New York Academy of Sciences, 1118,* 142–162.

Serper, M. R. (2011). Aggression in schizophrenia. *Schizophrenia Bulletin, 37*(Suppl 5), 897–898. doi:10.1093 /schbul/sbr090

Seta, J. J., Seta, C. E., & McElroy, T. (2002). Strategies for reducing the stress of negative life experiences: An average/summation analysis. *Personality and Social Psychology Bulletin, 28,* 1574–1585.

Shamay-Tsoory, S. G., Abu-Akel, A., Palgi, S., Sulieman, R., Fischer-Shofty, M., Levkovitz, Y., & Decety, J. (2013). Giving peace a chance: Oxytocin increases empathy to pain in the context of the Israeli–Palestinian conflict. *Psychoneuroendocrinology, 38,* 3139–3144. doi:10.1016 /j.psyneuen.2013.09.015

Shanahan, M. J., Hill, P. L., Roberts, B. W., Eccles, J., & Friedman, H. S. (2014). Conscientiousness, health, and aging: The life course of personality model. *Developmental Psychology, 50,* 1407–1425. doi:10.1037/a0031130

Sharpe, D., Adair, J. G., & Roese, N. J. (1992). Twenty years of deception research: A decline in subjects' trust? *Personality and Social Psychology Bulletin, 18,* 585–590.

Sharps, M. J., & Wertheimer, M. (2000). Gestalt perspectives on cognitive science and on experimental psychology. *Review of General Psychology, 4,* 315–336.

Shaw, J. S. I., McClure, K. A., & Dykstra, J. A. (2007). Eyewitness confidence from the witnessed event through trial. In M. P. Toglia, J. D. Read, D. F. Ross, & R. C. L. Lindsay (Eds.), *Handbook of eyewitness psychology: Vol. 1. Memory for events*. Mahwah, NJ: Erlbaum.

Shea, A. K., & Steiner, M. (2008). Cigarette smoking during pregnancy. *Nicotine & Tobacco Research, 10,* 267–278.

Shearer, B. (2004). Multiple intelligences theory after 20 years. *Teachers College Record, 106*(1), 2–16.

Shedler, J. (2010). The efficacy of psychodynamic psychotherapy. *American Psychologist, 65*(2), 98–109. doi:10.1037/a0018378

Sheehan, S. (1982). *Is there no place on earth for me?* Boston, MA: Houghton Mifflin.

Sheldon, K. M., Abad, N., & Hinsch, C. (2011). A two-process view of Facebook use and relatedness need-satisfaction: Disconnection drive use, and connection rewards it. *Journal of Personality and Social Psychology, 100,* 766–775. doi:10.1037/a0022407

Sheldon, K. M., & Kasser, T. (2001). Goals, congruence, and positive well-being: New empirical support for humanistic theories. *Journal of Humanistic Psychology, 41*(1), 30–50.

Shenton, M. E., & Kubicki, M. (2009). Structural brain imaging in schizophrenia. In B. J. Sadock, V. A. Sadock, & P. Ruiz (Eds.), *Kaplan & Sadock's comprehensive textbook of psychiatry* (9th ed., Vol. 1, pp. 1494–1506). Philadelphia, PA: Lippincott Williams & Wilkins.

Shepard, R. N. (1990). *Mind sights*. New York, NY: W. H. Freeman.

Shepherd, G. M. (2004). The human sense of smell: Are we better than we think? *PLoS Biology, 2*(5), 0572–0575. doi:10.1371/journal.pbio.0020146

Sher, K. J., Talley, A. E., Littlefield, A. K., & Martinez, J. A. (2011). Alcohol use and alcohol use disorders. In H. S. Friedman (Ed.), *Oxford handbook of health psychology*. New York, NY: Oxford University Press.

Sherif, M., Harvey, O., White, B., Hood, W., & Sherif, C. (1961). *Intergroup conflict and cooperation: The Robber's Cave experiment*. Norman: University of Oklahoma, Institute of Group Behavior.

Sherman, M., & Key, C. B. (1932). The intelligence of isolated mountain children. *Child Development, 3,* 279–290.

Shermer, M. (2004, March). None so blind. *Scientific American*, p. 42.

Shiue, Y., Chiu, C., & Chang, C. (2010). Exploring and mitigating social loafing in online communities. *Computers in Human Behavior, 26*(4), 768–777. doi:10.1016/j.chb.2010.01.014

Shlisky, J. D., Hartman, T. J., Kris-Etherton, P. M., Rogers, C. J., Sharkey, N. A., & Nickols-Richardson, S. M. (2012). Partial sleep deprivation and energy balance in adults: An emerging issue for consideration by dietetics practitioners. *Journal of the Academy of Nutrition and Dietetics, 112*, 1785–1797.

Shneidman, E. S., Farberow, N. L., & Litman, R. E. (1994). *The psychology of suicide: A clinician's guide to evaluation and treatment*. Northvale, NJ: Jason Aronson.

Shobe, K. K., & Schooler, J. W. (2001). Discovering fact and fiction: Case-based analyses of authentic and fabricated discovered memories of abuse. In G. M. Davies & T. Dalgleish (Eds.), *Recovered memories: Seeking the middle ground*. Chichester, UK: Wiley.

Shrager, Y., & Squire, L. R. (2009). Medial temporal lobe function and human memory. In M. S. Gazzaniga (Eds.), The cognitive neurosciences (4th ed., pp. 675–690). Cambridge, MA: MIT Press.

Shuman, V., Sander, D., & Scherer, K. R. (2013). Levels of valence. *Frontiers in Psychology, 4*. doi:10.3389/fpsyg.2013.00261

Siegel, J. M. (2011). REM sleep. In M. H. Kryger, T. Roth, & W. C. Dement (Eds.), *Principles and practice of sleep medicine* (5th ed.). Saint Louis, MO: Elsevier Saunders.

Siegelbaum, S. A., & Kandel, E. R. (2013). Overview of synaptic transmission. In E. R. Kandel, J. H. Schwartz, T. M. Jessell, S. A. Siegelbaum, & A. J. Hudspeth (Eds.), *Principles of neural science* (5th ed., pp. 177–188). New York, NY: McGraw-Hill.

Siegler, R. S. (1992). The other Alfred Binet. *Developmental Psychology, 28*, 179–190.

Signorielli, N. (2001). Television's gender role images and contribution to stereotyping: Past present future. In D. G. Singer & J. L. Singer (Eds.), *Handbook of children and the media*. Thousand Oaks, CA: Sage.

Silver, E., Cirincione, C., & Steadman, H. J. (1994). Demythologizing inaccurate perceptions of the insanity defense. *Law and Human Behavior, 18*(1), 63–70. doi:10.1007/BF01499144

Silverman, I., & Choi, J. (2005). Locating places. In D. M. Buss (Ed.), *The handbook of evolutionary psychology*. New York, NY: Wiley.

Silverman, I., Choi, J., & Peters, M. (2007). The hunter-gatherer theory of sex differences in spatial abilities: Data from 40 countries. *Archives of Sexual Behavior, 36*(2), 261–268. doi:10.1007/s10508-006-9168-6

Silverman, I., & Eals, M. (1992). Sex differences in spatial ability: Evolutionary theory and data. In J. Barkow, L. Cosmides, & J. Tooby (Eds.), *The adapted mind*. New York, NY: Oxford University Press.

Silverstein, L. B., & Auerbach, C. F. (1999). Deconstructing the essential father. *American Psychologist, 54*, 397–407.

Silvia, P. J., & Kaufman, J. C. (2010). Creativity and mental illness. In J. C. Kaufman & R. J. Sternberg (Eds.), *The Cambridge handbook of creativity* (pp. 381–394). New York, NY: Cambridge University Press.

Simeon, D., & Loewenstein, R. J. (2009). Dissociative disorders. In B. J. Sadock, V. A. Sadock, & P. Ruiz (Eds.), *Kaplan & Sadock's comprehensive textbook of psychiatry* (9th ed., pp. 1965–2026). Philadelphia, PA: Lippincott Williams & Wilkins.

Simon, H. A. (1957). *Models of man*. New York, NY: Wiley.

Simon, H. A. (1974). How big is a chunk? *Science, 183*, 482–488.

Simon, R. I., & Shuman, D. W. (2008). Psychiatry and the law. In R. E. Hales & S. C. Yudofsky (Eds.), *The American Psychiatric Publishing textbook of psychiatry* (5th ed.). Washington, DC: American Psychiatric Publishing.

Simon, R. I., & Shuman, D. W. (2014). Clinical issues in psychiatry and the law. In R. E. Hales, S. C. Yudofsky, & L. W. Roberts (Eds.), *The American Psychiatric Publishing textbook of psychiatry* (6th ed.). Washington, DC: American Psychiatric Publishing.

Simons, D. J. (2014). The value of direct replication. *Perspectives on Psychological Science, 9*(1), 76–80. doi:10.1177/1745691613511475

Simons, D. J., & Chabris, C. F. (1999). Gorillas in our midst: Sustained inattentional blindness for dynamic events. *Perception, 28*, 1059–1074.

Simons, D. J., & Chabris, C. F. (2011). What people believe about how memory works: A representative survey of the US population. *PLoS One, 6*(8), e22757. doi:10.1371/journal.pone.0022757

Simpson, J. L., & Jauniaux, E. (2012). Pregnancy loss. In S. G. Gabbe, J. R. Niebyl, J. L. Simpson, M. B. Landon, H. L. Galan, E. R. M. Jauniaux, & D. A. Driscoll (Eds.), *Obstetrics: Normal and problem pregnancies* (6th ed.). Philadelphia, PA: Elsevier.

Simpson, J. A., & Winterheld, H. A. (2012). Person-by-situation perspectives on close relationships. In K. Deaux & M. Snyder (Eds.), *Oxford handbook of personality and social psychology*. New York, NY: Oxford University Press.

Singer, W. (2007). Large-scale temporal coordination of cortical activity as a prerequisite for conscious experience. In M. Velmans & S. Schneider (Eds.), *The Blackwell companion to consciousness*. Malden, MA: Blackwell.

Singh, D., Dixson, B. J., Jessop, T. S., Morgan, B. B., & Dixson, A. F. (2010). Cross-cultural consensus for waist-hip ratio and women's attractiveness. *Evolution and Human Behavior, 31*, 176–181. doi:10.1016/j.evolhumbehav.2009.09.001

Sio, U. N., Monaghen, P., & Ormerod, T. (2013). Sleep on it, but only if it is difficult: Effects of sleep on problem solving. *Memory & Cognition, 41*, 159–166.

Sireci, S. G., & Sukin, T. (2013). Test validity. In K. F. Geisinger, B. A. Bracken, J. F. Carlson, J. C. Hansen, N. R. Kuncel, S. P. Reise, & M. C. Rodriguez (Eds.), *APA handbook of testing and assessment in psychology: Vol. 1. Test theory and testing and assessment in industrial and organizational psychology*. Washington, DC: American Psychological Association. doi:10.1037/14047-004

Sisti, D. A., Segal, A. G., & Emanuel, E. J. (2015). Improving long-term psychiatric care: Bring back the asylum. *JAMA, 313*(3), 243–244. doi:10.1001/jama.2014.16088

Sivertsen, B., Lallukka, T., Salo, P., Pallesen, S., Hysing, M., Krokstad, S., & Overland, S. (2014). Insomnia as a risk factor for ill health: Results from the large population-based prospective HUNT study in Norway. *Journal of Sleep Research, 23*, 124–132.

SJB. (2006, March 6). Overcoming problem gambling [Why?]. Message posted to www.gamcare.org.uk/forum/index.php?tid=7193.

Skinner, A. E. G. (2001). Recovered memories of abuse: Effects on the individual. In G. M. Davies, & T. Dalgleish (Eds.), *Recovered memories: Seeking the middle ground*. Chichester, England: Wiley & Sons.

Skinner, B. F. (1938). *The behavior of organisms*. New York, NY: Appleton-Century-Crofts.

Skinner, B. F. (1945, October). Baby in a box: The mechanical baby-tender. *Ladies' Home Journal*, pp. 30–31, 135–136, 138.

Skinner, B. F. (1948). Superstition in the pigeon. *Journal of Experimental Psychology, 38*, 168–172. doi:10.1037/0096-3445.121.3.273

Skinner, B. F. (1953). *Science and human behavior*. New York, NY: Macmillan.

Skinner, B. F. (1957). *Verbal behavior*. New York, NY: Appleton-Century-Crofts.

Skinner, B. F. (1969). *Contingencies of reinforcement*. New York, NY: Appleton-Century-Crofts.

Skinner, B. F. (1971). *Beyond freedom and dignity*. New York, NY: Knopf.

Skinner, B. F. (1984). Selection by consequences. *Behavioral and Brain Sciences, 7*(4), 477–510.

Skodol, A. E., Bender, D. S., & Morey, L. C. (2014). Narcissistic personality disorder in DSM-5. *Personality Disorders: Theory, Research, and Treatment, 5*, 422–427. doi:10.1037/per0000023

Skogen, J. C., & Overland, S. (2012). The fetal origins of adult disease: A narrative review of the epidemiological literature. *Journal of the Royal Society of Medicine, 3*, 59. doi:10.1258/shorts.2012.012048

Slamecka, N. J. (1985). Ebbinghaus: Some associations. *Journal of Experimental Psychology: Learning, Memory and Cognition, 11*, 414–435.

Slatcher, R. B., & Pennebaker, J. W. (2005). Emotional processing of traumatic events. In C. L. Cooper (Ed.), *Handbook of stress medicine and health*. Boca Raton, FL: CRC Press.

Slater, E., & Shields, J. (1969). Genetical aspects of anxiety. In M. H. Lader (Ed.), *Studies of anxiety*. Ashford, England: Headley Brothers.

Sletten, T. L., & Arendt, J. (2012). Circadian rhythm disorders III: Jet lag. In C. M. Morin, & C. A. Espie (Eds.), *Oxford handbook of sleep and sleep disorders*. New York, NY: Oxford University Press.

Slopen, N., Kontos, E. Z., Ryff, C. D., Ayanian, J. Z., Albert, M. A., & Williams, D. R. (2013). Psychosocial stress and cigarette smoking persistence, cessation, and relapse over 9–10 years: A prospective study of middle-aged adults in the United States. *Cancer Causes & Control, 24*, 1849–1863.

Slovic, P., & Fischhoff, B. (1977). On the psychology of experimental surprises. *Journal of Experimental Psychology: Human Perception and Performance, 3*, 544–551.

Slovic, P., Fischhoff, B., & Lichtenstein, S. (1982). Facts versus fears: Understanding perceived risk. In D. Kahneman, P. Slovic, &

A. Tversky (Eds.), *Judgment under uncertainty: Heuristics and biases*. Cambridge, England: Cambridge University Press.

Slutske, W. S., Cho, S. B., Piasecki, T. M., & Martin, N. G. (2013). Genetic overlap between personality and risk for disordered gambling: Evidence from a national community-based Australian twin study. *Journal of Abnormal Psychology, 122*, 250–255. doi:10.1037/a0029999.

Small, B. J., Rawson, K. S., Eisel, S., & McEvoy, C. L. (2012). Memory and aging. In S. K. Whitbourne & M. J. Sliwinski (Eds.), *Wiley-Blackwell handbook of adulthood and aging*. Malden, MA: Wiley-Blackwell.

Small, S. A., & Heeger, D. J. (2013). Functional imaging of cognition. In E. R. Kandel, J. H. Schwartz, T. M. Jessell, S. A. Siegelbaum, & A. J. Hudspeth (Eds.), *Principles of neural science* (5th ed.). New York, NY: McGraw-Hill.

Smedley, S. R., & Eisner, T. (1996). Sodium: A male moth's gift to its offspring. *Proceedings of the National Academy of Sciences, 93*, 809–813.

Smetana, J. G., Campione-Barr, N., & Metzger, A. (2006). Adolescent development in interpersonal and societal contexts. *Annual Review of Psychology, 57*, 255–284.

Smith, B. L. (2012). The case against spanking. *Monitor on Psychology, 43*, 60–63.

Smith, B. W., Epstein, E. M., Ortiz, J. A., Christopher, P. J., & Tooley, E. M. (2013). The foundations of resilience: What are the critical resources for bouncing back from stress? In S. Prince-Embury & D. H. Saklofske (Eds.), *Resilience in children, adolescents, and adults: Translating research into practice*. New York, NY: Spring Science + Business Media.

Smith, E. R. (2014). Research design. In H. T. Reis & C. M. Judd (Eds.), *Handbook of research methods in social and personality psychology* (2nd ed.). New York, NY: Cambridge University Press.

Smith, G. T., Spillane, N. S., & Annus, A. M. (2006). Implications of an emerging integration of universal and culturally specific psychologies. *Perspectives on Psychological Science, 1*, 211–233.

Smith, J. C. (2007). The psychology of relaxation. In P. M. Lehrer, R. L. Woolfolk, & W. E. Sime (Eds.), *Principles and practice of stress management*. New York, NY: Guilford Press.

Smith, J. C., Nielson, K. A., Antuono, P., Lyons, J., Hanson, R. J., Butts, A. M., . . . Verber, M. D. (2013). Semantic memory functional MRI and cognitive function after exercise intervention in mid cognitive impairment. *Journal of Alzheimer's Disease, 37*, 197–215. doi:10.3233/JAD-130467

Smith, M. R., Fogg, L. F., & Eastman, C. I. (2009). A compromise circadian phase position for permanent night work improves mood, fatigue, and performance. *Sleep: Journal of Sleep and Sleep Disorders Research, 32*(11), 1481–1489.

Smith, P. B. (2001). Cross-cultural studies of social influence. In D. Matsumoto (Ed.), *The handbook of culture and psychology*. New York, NY: Oxford University Press.

Smith, T. W. (2011). Measurement in health psychology research. In H. S. Friedman (Ed.), *Oxford handbook of health psychology*. New York, NY: Oxford University Press.

Smith, T. W., & Gallo, L. C. (2001). Personality traits as risk factors for physical illness. In A. Baum, T. A. Revenson, & J. E. Singer (Eds.), *Handbook of health psychology* (pp. 139–174). Mahwah, NJ: Erlbaum.

Smith, T. W., Gallo, L. C., Shivpuri, S., & Brewer, A. L. (2012). Personality and health: Current issues and emerging perspectives. In A. Baum, T. A. Revenson, & J. Singer (Eds.), *Handbook of health psychology* (2nd ed.). New York, NY: Psychology Press.

Smith, T. W., Williams, P. G., Segerstrom, S. C. (2015). Personality and physical health. In M. Mikulincer, P. R. Shaver, M. L. Cooper, & R. J. Larsen (Eds.), *APA handbook of personality and social psychology: Vol. 4. Personality processes and individual differences*. Washington, DC: American Psychological Association.

Smolak, L., & Murnen, S. K. (2001). Gender and eating problems. In R. H. Striegel-Moore & L. Smolak (Eds.), *Eating disorders: Innovative directions in research and practice* (pp. 91–110). Washington, DC: American Psychological Association.

Smrt, D. L., & Karau, S. J. (2011). Protestant work ethic moderates social loafing. *Group Dynamics: Theory, Research, and Practice, 15*, 267–274. doi:10.1037/a0024484

Smyth, J. M., Pennebaker, J. W., & Arigo, D. (2012). What are the health effects of disclosure? In A. Baum, T. A. Revenson, & J. Singer (Eds.), *Handbook of health psychology* (2nd ed.). New York, NY: Psychology Press.

Snedecor, S. M., Pomerleau, C. S., Mehringer, A. M., Ninowski, R., & Pomerleau, O. F. (2006). Differences in smoking-related variables based on phenylthiocarbamide "taster" status. *Addictive Behaviors, 31*, 2309–2312.

Snow, C. E. (1998). Bilingualism and second language acquisition. In J. B. Gleason & N. B. Ratner (Eds.), *Psycholinguistics*. Fort Worth, TX: Harcourt College Publishers.

Snowden, L. R. (2012). Health and mental health policies' role in better understanding and closing African American–White American disparities in treatment access and quality of care. *American Psychologist, 67*, 524–531. doi:10.1037/a0030054

Snowden, L. R., & Hu, T. W. (1996). Outpatient service use in minority-serving mental health programs. *Administration and Policy in Mental Health, 24*, 149–159.

Snowden, L. R., & Yamada, A. (2005). Cultural differences in access to care. *Annual Review of Clinical Psychology, 1*, 143–166.

Soldatos, C. R., Allaert, F. A., Ohta, T., & Dikeos, D. G. (2005). How do individuals sleep around the world? Results from a single-day survey in ten countries. *Sleep Medicine, 6*, 5–13.

Solomon, S., Greenberg, J., & Pyszczynski, T. (1991). A terror management theory of social behavior: The psychological functions of self-esteem and cultural worldviews. In M. Zanna (Ed.), *Advances in experimental social psychology* (Vol. 24). Orlando, FL: Academic Press.

Solomon, S., Greenberg, J., & Pyszczynski, T. (2004). The cultural animal: Twenty years of terror management. In J. Greenberg, S. L. Koole, & T. Pyszczynski (Eds.), *Handbook of experimental existential psychology*. New York, NY: Guilford Press.

Solowij, N., Stephens, R. S., Roffman, R. A., Babor, T., Kadden, R., Miller, M., . . . Vendetti, J. (2002). Cognitive functioning of long-term heavy cannabis users seeking treatment. *JAMA, 287*, 1123–1131.

Solso, R. L. (1994). *Cognition and the visual arts*. Cambridge, MA: MIT Press.

Somerville, L. H. (2013). The teenage brain: Sensitivity to social evaluation. *Current Directions in Psychological Science, 22*, 121–127. doi:10.1177/0963721413476512

Soto, C. J., John, O.P., Gosling, S. D., & Potter, J. (2011). Age differences in personality traits from 10 to 65: Big five domains and facets in a large cross-sectional sample. *Journal of Personality and Social Psychology, 100*, 330–348. doi:10.1037/a0021717

South, S. C., Reichborn-Kjennerud, T., Eaton, N. R., & Krueger, R. F. (2013). Genetics of personality. In H. Tennen, J. Suls, & I. B. Weiner (Eds.), *Handbook of psychology: Vol. 5. Personality and social psychology* (2nd ed.). New York, NY: Wiley.

South, S. C., Reichborn-Kjennerud, T., Eaton, N. R., & Krueger, R. F. (2015). Genetics of personality. In M. Mikulincer, P. R. Shaver, M. L. Cooper, & R. J. Larsen (Eds.), *APA handbook of personality and social psychology: Vol. 4. Personality processes and individual differences*. Washington, DC: American Psychological Association.

Spangler, W. D. (1992). Validity of questionnaire and TAT measures of need for achievement: Two meta-analyses. *Psychological Bulletin, 112*, 140–154.

Spanos, N. P. (1991). A sociocognitive approach to hypnosis. In S. J. Lynn & J. W. Rhue (Eds.), *Theories of hypnosis: Current models and perspectives* (pp. 324–361). New York, NY: Guilford Press.

Sparks, J. A., Duncan, B. L., & Miller, S. D. (2008). Common factors in psychotherapy. In J. L. Lebow (Ed.), *Twenty-first century psychotherapies: Contemporary approaches to theory and practice*. New York, NY: Wiley.

Spear, J. H. (2007). Prominent schools or other active specialties? A fresh look at some trends in psychology. *Review of General Psychology, 11*(4), 363–380. doi:10.1037/1089-2680.11.4.363.

Speed, A., & Gangestad, S. W. (1997). Romantic popularity and mate preferences: A peer-nomination study. *Personality and Social Psychology Bulletin, 23*, 928–936.

Spelke, E. S., & Kinzler, K. D. (2007). Core knowledge. *Developmental Science, 10*(1), 89–96.

Spelke, E. S., & Newport, E. L. (1998). Nativism, empiricism, and the development of knowledge. In W. Damon (Ed.), *Handbook of child psychology (Vol. 1): Theoretical models of human development*. New York, NY: Wiley.

Spence, I., Wong, P., Rusan, M., & Rastegar, N. (2006). How color enhances visual memory for natural scenes. *Psychological Science, 14*(1), 1–6.

Sperling, G. (1960). The information available in brief visual presentations. *Psychological Monographs, 74*(11, Whole No. 498).

Sperry, R. W. (1982). Some effects of disconnecting the cerebral hemispheres. *Science, 217*, 1223–1226, 1250.

Spiegel, D. (2003a). Hypnosis and traumatic dissociation: Therapeutic opportunities. *Journal of Trauma & Dissociation, 4*(3), 73–90.

Spiegel, D. (2003b). Negative and positive visual hypnotic hallucinations: Attending inside and out. *International Journal of Clinical & Experimental Hypnosis, 51*(2), 130–146.

Spiegel, D., Cutcomb, S., Ren, C., & Pribram, K. (1985). Hypnotic hallucination alters evoked potentials. *Journal of Abnormal Psychology, 94,* 249–255.

Spiegler, M. D. (2016). *Contemporary behavior therapy* (6th ed.). Belmont, CA: Wadsworth.

Spielman, L. J., Little, J. P., & Klegeris, A. (2014). Inflammation and insulin/igf-1 resistance as the possible link between obesity and neurodegeneration. *Journal of Neuroimmunology, 273*(1–2), 8–21. doi:10.1016/j.jneuroim.2014.06.004

Spielmans, G. I., & Kirsch, I. (2014). Drug approval and drug effectiveness. *Annual Review of Clinical Psychology, 10,* 741–766. doi:10.1146/annurev-clinpsy-050212-185533

Spitz, H. I. (2009). Group psychotherapy. In B. J. Sadock, V. A. Sadock, & P. Ruiz (Eds.), *Kaplan & Sadock's comprehensive textbook of psychiatry* (pp. 2832–2856). Philadelphia, PA: Lippincott Williams & Wilkins.

Sprecher, S. (2014). Effects of actual (manipulated) and perceived similarity on liking in get-acquainted interactions: The role of communication. *Communication Monographs, 81,* 4–27. doi:10.1080/03637751.2013.839884

Sprecher, S., & Duck, S. (1994). Sweet talk: The importance of perceived communication for romantic and friendship attraction experienced during a get-acquainted date. *Personality and Social Psychology Bulletin, 20,* 391–400.

Sprecher, S., Felmlee, D., Metts, S., & Cupach, W. (2015). Relationship initiation and development. In M. Mikulincer, P. R. Shaver, J. A. Simpson, & J. F. Dovidio (Eds.), *APA handbook of personality and social psychology Vol. 3: Interpersonal relations.* Washington, DC: American Psychological Association.

Sprenger, C., Eippert, F., Finsterbusch, J., Bingel, U., Rose, M., & Buchel, C. (2012). Attention modulates spinal cord responses to pain. *Current Biology, 22*(11), 1019–1022. doi:10.1016/j.cub.2012.04.006

Springer, S. P., & Deutsch, G. (1998). *Left brain, right brain.* New York, NY: W. H. Freeman.

Sproesser, G., Schupp, H. T., & Renner, B. (2014). The bright side of stress-induced eating: Eating more when stressed but less when pleased. *Psychological Science, 25*(1), 58–65. doi:10.1177/0956797613494849

Squire, L. R. (2004). Memory systems of the brain: A brief history and current perspective. *Neurobiology of Learning & Memory, 82*(3), 171–177.

Squire, L. R. (2009). Memory and brain systems: 1969–2009. *The Journal of Neuroscience, 29*(41), 12711–12716. doi:10.1523/JNEUROSCI.3575-09.2009

Squire, L. R., Knowlton, B., & Musen, G. (1993). The structure and organization of memory. *Annual Review of Psychology, 44,* 453–495.

Staats, A. W., & Staats, C. K. (1963). *Complex human behavior.* New York, NY: Holt, Rinehart & Winston.

Staddon, J. E. R., & Simmelhag, V. L. (1971). The "superstition" experiment: A reexamination of its implications for the principles of adaptive behavior. *Psychological Review, 78,* 3–43. doi:10.1037/h0030305

Stahre, M., Roeber, J., Kanny, D., Brewer, R. D., & Zhang, X. (2014). Contribution of excessive alcohol consumption to deaths and years of potential life lost in the United States. *Preventing Chronic Disease, 11,* 130293. doi:10.5888/pcd11.130293

Staley, J. K., & Krystal, J. H. (2009). Radiotracer imaging and positron emission topography and single photon emission computer topography. In B. J. Sadock, V. A. Sadock, & P. Ruiz (Eds.), *Kaplan & Sadock's comprehensive textbook of psychiatry* (9th ed., Vol. 1, pp. 42–64). Philadelphia, PA: Lippincott Williams & Wilkins.

Stanley, M. A., & Beidel, D. C. (2009). Behavior therapy. In B. J. Sadock, V. A. Sadock, & P. Ruiz (Eds.), *Kaplan & Sadock's comprehensive textbook of psychiatry* (pp. 2781–2803). Philadelphia, PA: Lippincott Williams & Wilkins.

Stanovich, K. E. (2004). *How to think straight about psychology.* Boston, MA: Allyn & Bacon.

Stanovich, K. E. (2012). On the distinction between rationality and intelligence: Implications for understanding individual differences in reasoning. In K. J. Holyoak, & R. G. Morrison (Eds.), *Oxford handbook of thinking and reasoning.* New York, NY: Oxford University Press.

Stanton, A. L., Lobel, M., Sears, S., & DeLuca, R. S. (2002). Psychosocial aspects of selected issues in women's reproductive health: Current status and future directions. *Journal of Consulting & Clinical Psychology, 70,* 751–770.

Starcevic, V. (2013). Is Internet addiction a useful concept? *Australian and New Zealand Journal of Psychiatry, 47,* 16–19. doi:10.1177/0004867412461693

Staub, E. (2014). Obeying, joining, following, resisting and other processes in Milgram's studies, and in the Holocaust and other genocides: Situations, personality, and bystanders.

Journal of Social Issues, 70, 501–514. doi:10.1111/josi.12074

Steblay, N. K., Wells, G. L., & Douglass, A. B. (2014). The eyewitness post identification feedback effect 15 years later: Theoretical and policy implications. *Psychology, Public Policy, and Law, 20*(1), 1–18. doi:10.1037/law0000001

Steele, K. M. (2003). Do rats show a Mozart effect? *Music Perception, 21,* 251–265.

Steiger, H., Bruce, K. R., & Israël, M. (2013). Eating disorders: Anorexia nervosa, bulimia nervosa, and binge eating disorder. In G. Stricker, T. A. Widiger, & I. B. Weiner (Eds.), *Handbook of psychology: Vol. 8. Clinical psychology* (2nd ed.). New York, NY: Wiley.

Stein, B. E., Wallace, M. T., & Stanford, T. R. (2000). Brain mechanisms for synthesizing information from different sensory modalities. In E. B. Goldstein (Ed.), *Blackwell handbook of perception.* Malden, MA: Blackwell.

Stein, D. J., Craske, M. A., Friedman, M. J., & Phillips, K. A. (2014). Anxiety disorders, obsessive-compulsive and related disorders, trauma- and stressor-related disorders, and dissociative disorders in DSM-5. *The American Journal of Psychiatry, 171,* 611–613. doi:10.1176/appi.ajp.2014.14010003

Steinberg, L. (2008). A social neuroscience perspective on adolescent risk-taking. *Developmental Review, 28*(1), 78–106. doi:10.1016/j.dr.2007.08.002

Steinberg, L., & Morris, A. S. (2001). Adolescent development. *Annual Review of Psychology, 52,* 83–110.

Stellar, E. (1954). The physiology of motivation. *Psychological Review, 61,* 5–22.

Steptoe, A., Shankar, A., Demakakos, P., & Wardle, J. (2013). Social isolation, loneliness, and all-cause mortality in older men and women. *PNAS Proceedings of the National Academy of Sciences of the United States of America, 110,* 5797–5801.

Sternberg, R. J. (1985). *Beyond IQ: A triarchic theory of human intelligence.* New York, NY: Cambridge University Press.

Sternberg, R. J. (1986). *Intelligence applied: Understanding and increasing your intellectual skills.* New York, NY: Harcourt Brace Jovanovich.

Sternberg, R. J. (1991). Theory-based testing of intellectual abilities: Rationale for the triarchic abilities test. In H. A. H. Rowe (Ed.), *Intelligence: Reconceptualization and measurement.* Hillsdale, NJ: Erlbaum.

Sternberg, R. J. (1999). The theory of successful intelligence. *Review of General Psychology, 3,* 292–316.

Sternberg, R. J. (2003a). Construct validity of the theory of successful intelligence. In R. J. Sternberg, J. Lautrey, & T. I. Lubart (Eds.), *Models of intelligence: International perspectives.* Washington, DC: American Psychological Association.

Sternberg, R. J. (2003b). My house is a very, very, very fine house—But it is not the only house. In H. Nyborg (Ed.), *The scientific study of general intelligence: Tribute to Arthur R. Jensen.* Oxford, UK: Pergamon.

Sternberg, R. J. (2004). Culture and Intelligence. *American Psychologist, 59,* 325–338.

Sternberg, R. J. (2005a). There are no public policy implications: A reply to Rushton and Jensen. *Psychology, Public Policy, and the Law, 11,* 295–301.

Sternberg, R. J. (2005b). The triarchic theory of successful intelligence. In D. P. Flanagan & P. L. Harrison (Eds.), *Contemporary intellectual assessment: Theories, tests and issues* (pp. 103–119). New York, NY: Guilford Press.

Sternberg, R. J. (2007). Intelligence and culture. In S. Kitayama & D. Cohen (Eds.), *Handbook of cultural psychology* (pp. 547–568). New York, NY: Guilford Press.

Sternberg, R. J. (2011). The theory of successful intelligence. In R. J. Sternberg, & S. B. Kaufman (Eds.), *Cambridge handbook of intelligence.* New York, NY: Cambridge University Press.

Sternberg, R. J. (2012). The triarchic theory of successful intelligence. In D. P. Flanagan, & P. L. Harrison (Eds.), *Contemporary intellectual assessment: Theories, tests, and issues* (3rd ed.). New York, NY: Guilford Press.

Sternberg, R. J., Conway, B. E., Ketron, J. L., & Bernstein, M. (1981). People's conceptions of intelligence. *Journal of Personality and Social Psychology, 41,* 37–55.

Sternberg, R. J., Grigorenko, E. L., & Kidd, K. K. (2005). Intelligence, race, and genetics. *American Psychologist, 60,* 45–69.

Stevenson, S. (2014). *Sleep smarter: 21 proven tips to sleep your way to a better body, better health and bigger success.* Florissant, MO: Model House Publishing.

Stewart, J. A., Russakoff, M., & Stewart, J. W. (2014). Pharmacotherapy, ECT, and TMS. In J. L. Cutler, (Ed.), *Psychiatry* (3rd ed). New York, NY: Oxford University Press.

Stewart, W. H., Jr., & Roth, P. L. (2007). A meta-analysis of achievement motivation differences between entrepreneurs and managers. *Journal of Small Business Management, 45,* 401–421.

Stickgold, R. (2013). Parsing the role of sleep in memory processing. *Current Opinion in Neurobiology, 23,* 847–853. doi:10.1016/j.conb.2013.04.002

Stickgold, R., & Walker, M. P. (2004). To sleep, perchance to gain creative insight. *Trends in Cognitive Sciences, 8*(5), 191–192.

Stickgold, R., & Walker, M. P. (2013). Sleep-dependent memory triage: Evolving generalization through selective processing. *Nature Neuroscience, 16,* 139–145. doi:10.1038/nn.3303

Stickgold, R., & Wamsley, E. J. (2011). Why we dream. In M. H. Kryger, T. Roth, & W. C. Dement (Eds.), *Principles and practice of sleep medicine* (5th ed.). Saint Louis, MO: Elsevier Saunders.

St. Jacques, P. L., & Schacter, D. L. (2013). Modifying memory: Selectively enhancing and updating personal memories for a museum tour by reactivating them. *Psychological Science, 24,* 537–543. doi:10.1177/0956797612457377

Stockman, A. (2010). Color mixing. In E. B. Goldstein (Ed.), *Encyclopedia of perception.* Thousand Oaks, CA: Sage.

Stoddard, F. J., Simon, N. M., & Pitman, R. K. (2014). Trauma- and stressor-related disorders. In R. E. Hales, S. C. Yudofsky, & L. W. Roberts (Eds.), *The American Psychiatric Publishing textbook of psychiatry* (6th ed.). Washington, DC: American Psychiatric Publishing.

Stoddard, G. (1943). *The meaning of intelligence.* New York, NY: Macmillan.

Stoet, G., & Geary, D. C. (2013). Sex differences in mathematics and reading achievement are inversely related: Within- and across-nation assessment of 10 years of PISA data. *PLoS ONE, 8,* e57988. doi:10.1371/journal.pone.0057988

Stone, L. (1977). *The family, sex and marriage in England 1500–1800.* New York, NY: Harper & Row.

Stone, W. N. (2008). Group psychotherapy. In A. Tasman, J. Kay, J. A. Lieberman, M. B. First, & M. Maj (Eds.), *Psychiatry* (3rd ed.). New York, NY: Wiley-Blackwell.

Stoner, J. A. F. (1961). *A comparison of individual and group decisions involving risk.* Unpublished master's thesis, Massachusetts Institute of Technology.

Stoner, R., Chow, M. L., Boyle, M. P., Sunkin, S. M., Mouton, P. R., Roy, S., . . . Courchesne, E. (2014). Patches of disorganization in the neocortex of children with autism. *The New England Journal of Medicine, 370,* 1209–1219. doi:10.1056/NEJMoa1307491

Storandt, M. (2008). Cognitive deficits in the early stages of Alzheimer's disease. *Current Directions in Psychological Science, 17*(3), 198–202. doi:10.1111/j.1467-8721.2008.00574.x

Storm, B. C. (2011). The benefit of forgetting in thinking and remembering. *Current Directions in Psychological Science, 20,* 291–295. doi:10.1177/0963721411418469

Stowell, J. R., Robles, T. F., & Kane, H. S. (2013). Psychoneuroimmunology: Mechanisms, individuals differences, and interventions. In A. M. Nezu, C. M. Nezu, P. A. Geller, & I. B. Weiner (Eds.), *Handbook of psychology: Vol. 9. Health psychology* (2nd ed.). New York, NY: Wiley.

Strahan, E. J., Lafrance, A., Wilson, A. E., Ethier, N., Spencer, S. J., & Zanna, M. P. (2008). Victoria's dirty secret: How sociocultural norms influence adolescent girls and women. *Personality and Social Psychology Bulletin, 34*(2), 288–301.

Strange, D., Clifasefi, S., & Garry, M. (2007). False memories. In M. Garry & H. Hayne (Eds.), *Do justice and let the sky fall: Elizabeth F. Loftus and her contributions to science, law, and academic freedom.* Mahwah, NJ: Erlbaum.

Stranges, S., Tigbe, W., Gomez-Olive, F. X., Thorogood, M., & Kandala, N. (2012). Sleep problems: An emerging global epidemic? Findings from the INDEPTH WHO-SAGE study among more than 40,000 older adults from 8 countries across Africa and Asia. *SLEEP, 35,* 1173–1181.

Straus, M. A., Douglas, E. M., & Medeiros, R. A. (2014). *The primordial violence: Spanking children, psychological development, violence, and crime.* New York, NY: Routledge/Taylor & Francis Group.

Strayer, D. L., Drews, F. A., & Crouch, D. J. (2006). A comparison of the cell phone driver and the drunk driver. *Human Factors, 48,* 381–391.

Streissguth, A. (2007). Offspring effects of prenatal alcohol exposure from birth to 25 years: The Seattle prospective longitudinal study. *Journal of Clinical Psychology in Medical Settings, 14,* 81–101.

Strenze, T. (2007). Intelligence and socioeconomic success: A meta-analytic review of longitudinal research. *Intelligence, 35,* 401–426.

Strick, M., van Baaren, R. B., Holland, R. W., & van Knippenberg, A. (2009). Humor in advertisements enhances product liking by mere association. *Journal of Experimental Psychology: Applied, 15,* 35–45.

Striegel-Moore, R. H., & Bulik, C. M. (2007). Risk factors for eating disorders. *American Psychologist, 62,* 181–198.

Stroebe, W., van Koningsbruggen, G. M., Papies, E. K., & Aarts, H. (2013). Why most dieters fail but some succeed: A goal conflict model of eating behavior. *Psychological Review, 120*(1), 110–138. doi:10.1037/a0030849

Stroup, T. S., Lawrence, R. E., Abbas, A. I., Miller, B. R., Perkins, D. O., & Lieberman, J. A. (2014). Schizophrenia spectrum and other psychotic disorders. In R. E. Hales, S. C. Yudofsky, & L. W. Roberts (Eds.), *The American Psychiatric Publishing textbook of psychiatry* (6th ed., pp. 273–310). Washington, DC: American Psychiatric Publishing.

Stubbe, J. H., Posthuma, D., Boomsma, D. I., & de Geus, E. J. C. (2005). Heritability of life satisfaction in adults: A twin study. *Psychological Medicine, 35,* 1581–1588.

Stunkard, A. J., Harris, J. R., Pederson, N. L., & McClearn, G. E. (1990). The body-mass index of twins who have been reared apart. *New England Journal of Medicine, 322,* 1483–1487.

Sturgis, P. (2006). Surveys and sampling. In G. M. Breakwell, S. Hammond, C. Fife-Schaw, & J. A. Smith (Eds.), *Research methods in psychology* (3rd ed.). London, UK: Sage.

Subotnik, K. L., Nuechterlein, K. H., Ventura, J., Gitlin, M. J., Marder, S., Mintz, J., . . . Singh, I. R. (2011). Risperidone nonadherence and return of positive symptoms in the early course of schizophrenia. *American Journal of Psychiatry, 168*(3), 286–292.

Sue, D. W. (2010). Microaggressions, marginality, and oppression: An introduction. In D. W. Sue (Ed.), *Microaggressions and marginality: Manifestation, dynamics, and impact.* Hoboken, NJ: Wiley.

Sue, D. W., & Sue, D. (1999). *Counseling the culturally different: Theory and practice.* New York, NY: Wiley.

Sue, S. (2003). In defense of cultural competency in psychotherapy and treatment. *American Psychologist, 58,* 964–970.

Sue, S., Cheng, J. Y., Saad, C. S., & Chu, J. P. (2012). Asian American mental health: A call to action. *American Psychologist, 67,* 532–544. doi:10.1037/a0028900

Sue, S., Zane, N., & Young, K. (1994). Research on psychotherapy with culturally diverse populations. In A. E. Bergin & S. L. Garfield (Eds.), *Handbook of psychotherapy and behavior change* (4th ed.). New York, NY: Wiley.

Sufka, K. J., & Price, D. D. (2002). Gate control theory reconsidered. *Brain & Mind, 3,* 277–290.

Sugita, Y. (2009). Innate face processing. *Current Opinion in Neurobiology, 19*(1), 39–44. doi:10.1016/j.conb.2009.03.001

Sugiyama, L. S. (2005). Physical attractiveness in adaptionist perspective. In D. M. Buss (Ed.), *The handbook of evolutionary psychology.* New York, NY: Wiley.

Suglia, S. F., Kara, S., & Robinson, W. R. (2014). Sleep duration and obesity among adolescents transitioning to adulthood: Do results differ by sex? *The Journal of Pediatrics, 165,* 750–754. doi:10.1016/j.jpeds.2014.06.052

Sullivan, P. F., Magnusson, C., Reichenberg, A., Boman, M., Dalman, C., Davidson, M., . . . Lichtenstein, P. (2012). Family history of schizophrenia and bipolar disorder as risk factors for autism. *JAMA Psychiatry, 69,* 1099–1103.

Suls, J. M., Luger, T., & Martin, R. (2010). The biopsychosocial model and the use of theory in health psychology. In J. M. Suls, K. W. Davidson, & R. M. Kaplan (Eds.), *Handbook of health psychology and behavioral medicine* (pp. 15–27). New York, NY: Guilford Press.

Sundie, J. M., Kenrick, D. T., Griskevicius, V., Tybur, J. M., Vohs, K. D., & Beal, D. J. (2011). Peacocks, Porsches, and Thorstein Veblen: Conspicuous consumption as a sexual signaling system. *Journal of Personality and Social Psychology, 100,* 664–680. doi:10.1037/a0021669

Super, C. M. (1976). Environmental effects on motor development: A case of African infant precocity. *Developmental Medicine and Child Neurology, 18,* 561–567.

Surtees, P., & Wainwright, N. (2007). Life events and health. In G. Fink (Ed.), *Encyclopedia of stress.* San Diego, CA: Elsevier.

Surtees, P., Wainwright, N., Luben, R., Wareham, N., Bingham, S., & Khaw, K. (2008). Depression and ischemic heart disease mortality: Evidence from the EPIC-Norfolk United Kingdom Prospective Cohort Study. *American Journal of Psychiatry, 165*(4), 515–523.

Susman, E. J., & Dorn, L. D. (2013). Puberty: Its role in development. In R. M. Lerner, M. A. Easterbrooks, J. Mistry, & I. B. Weiner (Eds.), *Handbook of psychology: Vol. 6. Developmental psychology.* New York, NY: Wiley.

Susman, E. J., Dorn, L. D., & Schiefelbein, V. L. (2003). Puberty, sexuality, and health. In R. M. Lerner, M. A. Easterbrooks, & J. Mistry (Eds.), *Handbook of psychology: Vol. 6. Developmental psychology.* New York, NY: Wiley.

Susser, E. B., Neugebauer, R., Hoek, H. W., Brown, A. S., Lin, S., Labovitz, D., & Gorman, J. M. (1996). Schizophrenia after prenatal famine: Further evidence. *Archives of General Psychiatry, 53,* 25–31.

Sussman, A. B., Petkova, K., & Todorov, A. (2013). Competence ratings in U.S. predict presidential election outcomes in Bulgaria. *Journal of Experimental Social Psychology, 49,* 771–775. doi:10.1016/j.jesp.2013 .02.003

Sussman, N. (2009). Selective serotonin reuptake inhibitors. In B. J. Sadock, V. A. Sadock, & P. Ruiz (Eds.), *Kaplan & Sadock's comprehensive textbook of psychiatry* (pp. 3190–3205). Philadelphia, PA: Lippincott Williams & Wilkins.

Sutker, P. B., & Allain, A. J. (2001). Antisocial personality disorder. In P. B. Sutker, H. E. Adams, P. B. Sutker, & H. E. Adams (Eds.), *Comprehensive handbook of psychopathology* (3rd ed.). New York, NY: Kluwer Academic/Plenum.

Suzuki, L. A., Short, E. L., & Lee, C. S. (2011). Racial and ethnic group differences in intelligence in the United States. In R. J. Sternberg, & S. B. Kaufman (Eds.), *Cambridge handbook of intelligence.* New York, NY: Cambridge University Press.

Swan, G. E., Hudmon, K. S., & Khroyan, T. V. (2003). Tobacco dependence. In A. M. Nezu, C. M. Nezu, & P. A. Geller (Eds.), *Handbook of psychology: Vol. 9. Health Psychology.* New York, NY: Wiley.

Swanson, J. W., McGinty, E. M., Fazel, S., & Mays, V. M. (2014). Mental illness and reduction of gun violence and suicide: Bringing epidemiologic research to policy. *Annals of Epidemiology, 30,* 1–11. doi:10.1016 /j.annepidem.2014.03.004

Swanson, S. A., Crow, S. J., Le Grange, D., Swendsen, J., & Merikangas, K. R. (2011). Prevalence and correlates of eating disorders in adolescents: Results from the national comorbidity survey replication adolescent supplement. *Archives of General Psychiatry, 68,* 714–723.

Sweldens, S., Corneille, O., & Yzerbyt, V. (2014). The role of awareness in attitude formation through evaluative conditioning. *Personality and Social Psychology Review, 18,* 187–209. doi:10.1177/1088868314527832

Swibel, M. (2006, July 3). Bad girl interrupted. *Forbes.* Retrieved from www.forbes.com/forbes/2006 /0703/118.html

Swim, J. K., & Sanna, L. J. (1996). He's skilled, she's lucky: A meta-analysis of observers' attributions for women's and men's successes and failures. *Personality and Social Psychology Bulletin, 22,* 507–519.

Szasz, T. (1974). *The myth of mental illness.* New York, NY: Harper & Row.

Szasz, T. (1990). Law and psychiatry: The problems that will not go away. *The Journal of Mind and Behavior, 11*(3/4), 557–564.

Szczytkowski, J. L., & Lysle, D. T. (2011). Conditioned immunomodulation. In T. R. Schachtman, & S. Reilly (Eds.), *Associative learning and condition theory: Human and non-human applications.* New York, NY: Oxford University Press.

Szigethy, E. M., & Friedman, E. S. (2009). Combined psychotherapy and pharmacology. In B. J. Sadock, V. A. Sadock, & P. Ruiz (Eds.), *Kaplan & Sadock's comprehensive textbook of psychiatry* (pp. 2923–2931). Philadelphia, PA: Lippincott Williams & Wilkins.

Szpunar, K. K., & McDermott, K. B. (2009). Episodic memory: An evolving concept. In J. H. Byrne (Ed.), *Concise learning and memory: The editor's selection.* San Diego, CA: Elsevier.

Szymusiak, R. (2009). Thermoregulation during sleep and sleep deprivation. In R. Stickgold & M. P. Walker (Eds.), *The neuroscience of sleep* (pp. 218–222). San Diego, CA: Academic Press.

Tach, L., & Halpern-Meekin, S. (2009). How does premarital cohabitation affect trajectories of marital quality? *Journal of Marriage and Family, 71*(2), 298–317. doi:10.1111 /j.1741-3737.2009.00600.x

Tadmor, C. T., Galinsky, A. D., & Maddux, W. W. (2012). Getting the most out of living abroad: Biculturalism and integrative complexity as key drivers of creative and professional success. *Journal of Personality and Social Psychology, 103,* 520–542. doi:10.1037/a0029360

Tait, D. M., & Carroll, J. (2010). Color deficiency. In E. B. Goldstein (Ed.), *Encyclopedia of perception.* Thousand Oaks, CA: Sage.

Taki, Y., Hashizume, H., Sassa, Y., Takeuchi, H., Asano, M., Asano, K., . . . Kawashima, R. (2012). Correlation among body height, intelligence, and brain gray matter volume in healthy children. *Neuroimage, 59,* 1023–1027. doi:10.1016/j.neuroimage.2011.08 .092

Talarico, J. M., & Rubin, D. C. (2003). Confidence, not consistency, characterizes flashbulb memories. *Psychological Science, 14,* 455–461.

Talarico, J. M., & Rubin, D. C. (2007). Flashbulb memories are special after all; in phenomenology, not accuracy. *Applied Cognitive Psychology, 21,* 557–578.

Talarico, J. M., & Rubin, D. C. (2009). Flashbulb memories result from ordinary memory processes and extraordinary event characteristics. In O. Luminet & A. Curci (Eds.), *Flashbulb memories: New issues and new perspectives* (pp. 79–97). New York, NY: Psychology Press.

Talati, A., Bao, Y., Kaufman, J., Shen, L., Schaefer, C. A., & Brown, A. S. (2013). Maternal smoking during pregnancy and bipolar disorder in offspring. *American Journal of Psychiatry, 170,* 1178–1185.

Talbott, J. A. (2004). Deinstitutionalization: Avoiding the disasters of the past. *Psychiatric Services, 55,* 1112–1115.

Talma, H., Schonbeck, Y., van Dommelen, P., Bakker, B., van Buuren, S., & Hirasang, R. A. (2013). Trends in menarcheal age between 1955 and 2009 in the Netherlands. *PLoS ONE, 8,* e60056. doi:10.1371/journal.pone .0060056

Talwar, S.K., Xu, S., Hawley, E. S., Weiss, S. A., Moxon, K. A., & Chapin, J. K. (2002). Behavioural neuroscience: Rat navigation guided by remote control. *Nature, 417,* 37–38.

Tamakoshi, A., Ohno, Y., & JACC Study Group. (2004). Self-reported sleep duration as a predictor of all-cause mortality: Results from JACC study, Japan. *Sleep: A Journal of Sleep and Sleep Disorders Research, 27,* 51–54.

Tamis-LeMonda, C. S., Kuchirko, Y., & Song, L. (2014). Why is infant language learning facilitated by parental responsiveness? *Current Directions in Psychological Science, 23,* 121–126. doi:10.1177/0963721414522813

Tanaka, J., Weiskopf, D., & Williams, P. (2001). The role of color in high-level vision. *Trends in Cognitive Sciences, 5,* 211–215.

Tang, J., Yu, Y., Du, Y., Ma, Y., Zhang, D., & Wang, J. (2014). Prevalence of Internet addiction and its association with stressful life events and psychological symptoms among adolescent Internet users. *Addictive Behaviors, 39,* 744–747. doi:10.1016/j.add-beh.2013.12.010

Taormina, R. J., & Gao, J. H. (2013). Maslow and the motivation hierarchy: Measuring satisfaction of the needs. *The American Journal of Psychology, 126*(2), 155–177. doi:10.5406/ amerjpsyc.126.2.0155

Tarabulsy, G. M., Pearson, J., Vaillancourt-Morel, M., Bussieres, E., Madigan, S., Lemelin, J., . . . Royer, F. (2014). Meta-analytic findings of the relation between maternal prenatal stress and anxiety and child cognitive outcome. *Journal of Developmental and Behavioral Pediatrics, 35,* 38–43.

Tart, C. T. (1988). From spontaneous event to lucidity: A review of attempts to consciously control nocturnal dreaming. In J. Gackenbach & S. LaBerge (Eds.), *Conscious mind, sleeping brain: Perspectives on lucid dreaming.* New York, NY: Plenum.

Tavris, C. (1998, September 13). Peer pressure (Review of *The Nurture Assumption*). *The New York Times Book Review, 103,* p. 14.

Taylor, E. (2001). Positive psychology and humanistic psychology: A reply to Seligman. *Journal of Humanistic Psychology, 41*(1), 13–29.

Taylor, L. S., Fiore, A. T., Mendelsohn, G. A., & Cheshire, C. (2011). "Out of my league": A real-world test of the matching hypothesis. *Personality and Social Psychology Bulletin, 37,* 942–954. doi:10.1177/0146167211409947

Taylor, S. E. (2011). Positive illusions: How ordinary people become extraordinary. In M. Gernsbacher, R. W. Pew, L. M. Hough, & J. R. Pomerantz (Eds.), *Psychology and the real world: Essays illustrating fundamental contributions to society.* New York, NY: Worth Publishers.

Taylor, S. E. (2015). Social cognition and health. In M. Mikulincer, P. R. Shaver, E. Borgida, & J. A. Bargh (Eds.), *APA handbook of personality and social psychology: Vol. 1. Attitudes and social cognition.* Washington, DC: American Psychological Association.

Taylor, S. E., & Brown, J. D. (1994). Positive illusions and well-being revisited: Separating fact from fiction. *Psychological Bulletin, 116,* 21–27.

Taylor, S. E., Welch, W. T., Kim, H. S., & Sherman, D. K. (2007). Cultural differences in the impact of social support on psychological and biological stress responses. *Psychological Science, 18*(9), 831–837. doi:10.1111/j.1467 -9280.2007.01987.x

Teachman, J. (2003). Premarital sex, premarital cohabitation and the risk of subsequent marital dissolution among women. *Journal of Marriage and Family, 65*(2), 444–455. doi:10.1111 /j.1741-3737.2003.00444.x

Tedlock, L. B. (1992). Zuni and Quiche dream sharing and interpreting. In B. Tedlock (Ed.), *Dreaming: Anthropoligical and psychological interpretations.* Santa Fe, NM: School of American Research Press.

Temoshok, L. (2011). HIV/AIDS. In H. S. Friedman (Ed.), *Oxford handbook of health psychology.* New York, NY: Oxford University Press.

Temple, J. L., Giacomelli, A. M., Roemmich, J. N., & Epstein, L. H. (2008). Dietary variety impairs habituation in children. *Health Psychology, 27,* S10–S19.

Terman, L. (1916). *The measurement of intelligence: An explanation of and a complete guide for the use of the Stanford revision and extension of the Binet-Simon Intelligence Scale.* Boston, MA: Houghton Mifflin.

Terr, L. (1994). *Unchained memories.* New York, NY: Basic Books.

Terracciano, A., Abdel-Khalak, A. M., Adam, N., Adamovova, L., Ahn, C. K., Ahn, H. N., . . . McCrae, R. R. (2005). National character does not reflect mean personality trait levels in 49 cultures. *Science, 310,* 96–100.

Teuber, M. (1974). Sources of ambiguity in the prints of Maurits C. Escher. *Scientific American, 231,* 90–104.

Thames, A. D., Arbid, N., & Sayegh, P. (2014). Cannabis use and neurocognitive functioning in a non-clinical sample of users. *Addictive Behaviors, 39,* 994–999. doi:10.1016/j.addbeh.2014.01.019

Thase, M. E. (2009). Selective serotonin-norepinephrine reuptake inhibitors. In B. J. Sadock, V. A. Sadock, & P. Ruiz (Eds.), *Kaplan & Sadock's comprehensive textbook of psychiatry* (pp. 3184–3189). Philadelphia, PA: Lippincott Williams & Wilkins.

Thase, M. E. (2012). Social skills training for depression and comparative efficacy research: A 30-year retrospective. *Behavior Modification, 36,* 545–557. doi:10.1177/0145445512445610

Thase, M. E., Hahn, C., & Berton, O. (2014). Neurobiological aspects of depression. In I. H. Gotlib & C. L. Hammen (Eds.), *Handbook of depression* (3rd ed.). New York, NY: Guilford Press.

Thayer, A., & Lynn, S. J. (2006). Guided imagery and recovered memory therapy: Considerations and cautions. *Journal of Forensic Psychology Practice, 6,* 63–73.

Thelen, E. (1995). Motor development: A new synthesis. *American Psychologist, 50,* 79–95.

Thies, W., & Bleiler, L. (2013). 2013 Alzheimer's disease facts and figures. *Alzheimer's and Dementia, 9,* 208–245. doi:10.1016/j.jalz.2013.02.003

Thomas, D. R. (1992). Discrimination and generalization. In L. R. Squire (Ed.), *Encyclopedia of learning and memory.* New York, NY: Macmillan.

Thompson, J. K., & Stice, E. (2001). Thin-ideal internalization: Mounting evidence for a new risk factor for body-image disturbance and eating pathology. *Current Directions in Psychological Science, 10*(5), 181–183.

Thompson, M. A., Aberg, J. A., Hoy, J. F., Telenti, A., Benson, C., Cahn, P., . . . Volberding, P. A. (2012). Antiretroviral treatment of adult HIV infection: 2012 recommendations of the International Antiviral Society: USA Panel. *JAMA, 308,* 387–402.

Thompson, R. A. (2008). Measure twice, cut once: Attachment theory and the NICHD Study of Early Child Care and Youth Development. *Attachment & Human Development, 10,* 287–297. doi:10.1080/14616730802113604

Thompson, R. A. (2013). Attachment theory and research: Precis and prospect. In P. D. Zelazo (Ed.), *Oxford handbook of developmental psychology: Vol. 2. Self and other.* New York, NY: Oxford University Press.

Thompson, R. A., & Nelson, C. A. (2001). Developmental science and the media: Early brain development. *American Psychologist, 56,* 5–15.

Thompson, R. F. (1992). Memory. *Current Opinion in Neurobiology, 2,* 203–208.

Thompson, R. F. (2005). In search of memory traces. *Annual Review of Psychology, 56,* 1–23.

Thompson, R. F. (2013). An essential memory trace found. *Behavioral Neuroscience, 127,* 669–675. doi:10.1037/a0033978

Thornhill, R. (1976). Sexual selection and nuptial feeding behavior in *Bittacus apicalis* (Insecta: Mecoptera). *American Naturalist, 110,* 529–548.

Thornton, B., & Maurice, J. K. (1999). Physical attractiveness contrast effect and the moderating influence of self-consciousness. *Sex Roles, 40,* 379–392.

Thorson, J. A., & Powell, F. C. (2000). Death anxiety in younger and older adults. In A. Tomer (Ed.), *Death attitudes and the older adult: Theories, concepts, and applications.* Philadelphia, PA: Brunner-Routledge.

Thun, M. J., Apicella, L. F., & Henley, S. J. (2000). Smoking vs. other risk factors as the cause of smoking-attributable deaths: Confounding in the courtroom. *JAMA, 284,* 706–712.

Thun, M. J., Carter, B. D., Freskanich, D., Freedman, N. D., Prentice, R., Lopez, A. D., . . . Gapstur, S. M. (2013). 50-year trends in smoking-related mortality in the United States. *The New England Journal of Medicine, 368,* 351–364. doi:10.1056/NEJMsa1211127

Till, B. D., & Priluck, R. L. (2000). Stimulus generalization in classical conditioning: An initial investigation and extension. *Psychology and Marketing, 17,* 55–72.

Tims, M., Bakker, A. B., & Derks, D. (2014). Daily job crafting and the self-efficacy: Performance relationship. *Journal of Managerial Psychology, 29,* 490–507. doi:10.1108/JMP-05-2012-0148

Tinti, C., Schmidt, S., Testa, S., & Levine, L. J. (2014). Distinct processes shape flashbulb and event memories. *Memory & Cognition, 42,* 539–551. doi:10.3758/s13421-013-0383-9

Titsworth, B. S., & Kiewra, K. A. (2004). Spoken organizational lecture cues and student notetaking as facilitators of student learning. *Contemporary Educational Psychology, 29,* 447–461.

Todd, J. T., & Morris, E. K. (1992). Case histories in the great power of steady misrepresentation. *American Psychologist, 47,* 1441–1453.

Tolman, E. C. (1932). *Purposive behavior in animals and men.* New York, NY: Appleton-Century-Crofts.

Tolman, E. C. (1938). The determiners of behavior at a choice point. *Psychological Reviews, 45,* 1-41.

Tolman, E. C. (1948). Cognitive maps in rats and men. *Psychological Review, 55,* 189–208.

Tolman, E. C., & Honzik, C. H. (1930). Introduction and removal of reward, and maze performance in rats. *University of California Publications in Psychology, 4,* 257–275.

Tolstrup, J. S., Stephens, R., & Gronbaek, M. (2014). Does the severity of hangovers decline with age? Survey of the incidence of hangover in different age groups. *Alcoholism: Clinical and Experimental Research, 38*(2), 466–470. doi:10.1111/acer.12238

Tomassy, G. S., Berger, D. R., Chen, H., Kasthuri, N., Hayworth, K. J., Vercelli, A., . . . Arlotta, P. (2014). Distinct profiles of myelin distribution along single axons of pyramidal neurons in the neocortex. *Science, 344,* 319–324. doi:10.1126/science.1249766

Tomkins, S. S. (1980). Affect as amplification: Some modifications in theory. In R. Plutchik & H. Kellerman (Eds.), *Emotion: Theory, research and experience* (Vol. 1). New York, NY: Academic Press.

Tomkins, S. S. (1991). *Affect, imagery, consciousness: Volume III. Anger and fear.* New York, NY: Springer-Verlag.

Tomko, R. L., Trull, T. J., Wood, P. K., & Sher, K. J. (2014). Characteristics of borderline personality disorder in a community sample: Comorbidity, treatment utilization, and general functioning. *Journal of Personality Disorders, 28,* 734–750. doi:10.1521/pedi_2012_26_093

Torgersen, S. (1979). The nature and origin of common phobic fears. *British Journal of Psychiatry, 119,* 343–351.

Torgersen, S. (1983). Genetic factors in anxiety disorders. *Archives of General Psychiatry, 40,* 1085–1089.

Torgersen, S. (2012). Epidemiology. In T. A. Widiger (Ed.), *The Oxford handbook of personality disorders.* New York, NY: Oxford University Press.

Tormala, Z. L., & Petty, R. E. (2002). What doesn't kill me makes me stronger: The effects of resisting persuasion on attitude certainty. *Journal of Personality and Social Psychology, 83,* 1298–1313.

Tormala, Z. L., & Petty, R. E. (2004). Resistance to persuasion and attitude certainty: The moderating role of elaboration. *Personality and Social Psychology Bulletin, 30,* 1446–1457.

Torrey, E. F. (1992). *Freudian fraud: The malignant effect of Freud's theory on American thought and culture.* New York, NY: Harper Perennial.

Torrey, E. F. (2014). *American psychosis: How the federal government destroyed the mental illness treatment system.* New York, NY: Oxford University Press.

Tourangeau, R. (2004). Survey research and societal change. *Annual Review of Psychology, 55,* 775–801.

Tourangeau, R., & Yan, T. (2007). Sensitive questions in surveys. *Psychological Bulletin, 133,* 859–883.

Tov, W., & Diener, E. (2007). Culture and subjective well-being. In S. Kitayama & D. Cohen (Eds.), *Handbook of cultural psychology.* New York, NY: Guilford Press.

Toyota, H., & Kikuchi, Y. (2004). Self-generated elaboration and spacing effects on incidental memory. *Perceptual and Motor Skills, 99,* 1193–1200.

Toyota, H., & Kikuchi, Y. (2005). Encoding richness of self-generated elaboration and spacing effects on incidental memory. *Perceptual and Motor Skills, 101,* 621–627.

Trace, S. E., Baker, J. H., Peñas-Lledó, E., & Bulik, C. M. (2013). The genetics of eating disorders. *Annual review of clinical psychology, 9,* 589–620. doi:10.1146/annurev-clinpsy-050212-185546

Treadway, M. T., Waskom, M. L., Dillon, D. G., Holmes, A. J., Park, M. M., Chakravarty, M. M., . . . Pizzagalli, D. A. (2015). Illness progression, recent stress, and morphometry of hippocampal subfields and medial prefrontal cortex in major depression. *Biological Psychiatry, 77*(3), 285–294. doi:10.1016/j.biopsych.2014.06.018

Triandis, H. C. (1989). Self and social behavior in differing cultural contexts. *Psychological Review, 96*, 269–289.

Triandis, H. C. (1994). *Culture and social behavior*. New York, NY: McGraw-Hill.

Triandis, H. C. (2001). Individualism and collectivism: Past, present, and future. In D. Matsumoto (Ed.), *The handbook of culture and psychology*. New York, NY: Oxford University Press.

Triandis, H. C. (2007). Culture and psychology: A history of the study of their relationship. In S. Kitayama & D. Cohen (Eds.), *Handbook of cultural psychology*. New York, NY: Guilford Press.

Triandis, H. C., & Gelfand, M. J. (2012). A theory of individualism and collectivism. In P. A. M. Van Lange, A. W. Kruglanski, & E. T. Higgins (Eds.), *Handbook of theories of social psychology* (Vol. 2). Thousand Oaks, CA: Sage.

Trivers, R. L. (1972). Parental investment and sexual selection. In B. Campbell (Ed.), *Sexual selection and the descent of man*. Chicago, IL: Aldine.

Trull, T. J., Carpenter, R. W., & Widiger, T. A. (2013). Personality disorders. In T. A. Widiger, G. Stricker, I. B. Weiner, G. Stricker, T. A. Widiger, & I. B. Weiner (Eds.), *Handbook of psychology: Vol. 8. Clinical psychology* (2nd ed.). New York, NY: Wiley.

Trull, T. J., Jahng, S., Tomko, R. L., Wood, P. K., & Sher, K. J. (2010). Revised NESARC personality disorder diagnoses: Gender, prevalence, and comorbidity with substance dependence disorders. *Journal of Personality Disorders, 24*, 412–426. doi:10.1521/pedi.2010.24.4.412

Tsankova, N., Renthal, W., Kumar, A., & Nestler, E. J. (2007). Epigenetic regulation in psychiatric disorders. *Nature Reviews Neuroscience, 8*(5), 355–367.

Tschernegg, M., Crone, J. S., Eigenberger, T., Schwartenbeck, P., Fauth-Bühler, M., Lemènager, T., . . . Kronbichler, M. (2013). Abnormalities of functional brain networks in pathological gambling: A graph-theoretical approach. *Frontiers in Human Neuroscience, 7*. doi:10.3389/fnhum.2013.00625.

Tse, P. U., & Palmer, S. E. (2013). Visual object processing. In A. F. Healy, R. W. Proctor, & I. B. Weiner (Eds.), *Handbook of psychology: Vol. 4. Experimental psychology* (2nd ed.). New York, NY: Wiley.

Tucker, A. M., Dinges, D. F., & Van Dongen, H. P. A. (2007). Trait interindividual differences in the sleep physiology of healthy young adults. *Journal of Sleep Research, 16*, 170–180.

Tucker-Drob, E. M., Briley, D. A., & Harden, K. P. (2013). Genetic and environmental influences on cognition across development and context. *Current Directions in Psychological Science, 22*, 349–355. doi:10.1177/0963721413485087

Tucker-Drob, E. M., Rhemtulla, M., Harden, K. P., Turkheimer, E., & Fask, D. (2011). Emergence of a gene × socioeconomic status interaction on infant mental ability between 10 months and 2 years. *Psychological Science, 22*(1), 125–133. doi:10.1177/0956797610392926

Tuckey, M. R., & Brewer, N. (2003). The influence of schemas, stimulus ambiguity, and interview schedule on eyewitness memory over time. *Journal of Experimental Psychology: Applied, 9*, 101–118.

Tugade, M. M., Devlin, H. C., & Fredrickson, B. L. (2014). Infusing positive emotions into life: The broaden-and-build theory and dual-process model of resilience. In M. M. Tugade, M. N. Shiota, & L. D. Kirby (Eds.), *Handbook of positive emotions*. New York, NY: Guilford Press.

Tugade, M. M., & Fredrickson, B. L. (2004). Resilient individuals use positive emotions to bounce back from negative emotional experiences. *Journal of Personality and Social Psychology, 86*, 320–333.

Tulving, E. (1993). What is episodic memory? *Current Directions in Psychological Science, 2*(3), 67–70.

Tulving, E. (2001). Origin of autonoesis in episodic memory. In H. L. Roediger III, J. S. Nairne, I. Neath, & A. M. Surprenant (Eds.), *The nature of remembering: Essays in honor of Robert G. Crowder* (pp. 17–34). Washington, DC: American Psychological Association.

Tulving, E. (2002). Episodic memory: From mind to brain. *Annual Review of Psychology, 53*, 1–25.

Tulving, E., & Thomson, D. M. (1973). Encoding specificity and retrieval processes in episodic memory. *Psychological Review, 80*, 352–373.

Turk, D. C., & Okifuji, A. (2003). Pain management. In A. M. Nezu, C. M. Nezu, & P. A. Geller (Eds.), *Handbook of psychology: Vol. 9. Health psychology*. New York, NY: Wiley.

Turk-Browne, N. B. (2013). Functional interactions as big data in the human brain. *Science, 342*, 580–584. doi:10.1126/science.1238409

Turkle, S. (2011). *Alone together: Why we expect more from technology and less from each other*. New York, NY: Basic Books.

Turner, E. H., Matthews, A. M., Linardos, E., Tell, R. A., & Rosenthal, R. (2008). Selective publication of antidepressant trials and its influence on apparent efficacy. *New England Journal of Medicine, 358*, 252–260.

Turner, J. C. (2006). Tyranny, freedom and social structure: Escaping our theoretical prisons. *British Journal of Social Psychology, 25*, 41–46.

Turner, J. R., & Wheaton, B. (1995). Checklist measurement of stressful life events. In S. Cohen, R. C. Kessler, & L. U. Gordon (Eds.), *Measuring stress: A guide for health and social scientists*. New York, NY: Oxford University Press.

Tversky, A., & Kahneman, D. (1973). Availability: A heuristic for judging frequency and probability. *Cognitive Psychology, 5*, 207–232.

Tversky, A., & Kahneman, D. (1974). Judgments under uncertainty: Heuristics and biases. *Science, 185*, 1124–1131.

Tversky, A., & Kahneman, D. (1982). Judgment under uncertainty: Heuristics and biases. In D. Kahneman, P. Slovic, & A. Tversky (Eds.), *Judgment under uncertainty: Heuristics and biases*. New York, NY: Cambridge University Press.

Tversky, A., & Kahneman, D. (1983). Extensional versus intuitive reasoning: The conjunction fallacy in probability judgment. *Psychological Review, 90*, 283–315.

Tversky, A., & Kahneman, D. (1988). Rational choice and the framing of decisions. In D. E. Bell, H. Raiffa, & A. Tversky (Eds.), *Decision making: Descriptive, normative, and prescriptive interactions*. New York, NY: Cambridge University Press.

Tversky, A., & Kahneman, D. (1991). Loss aversion in riskless choice: A reference-dependent model. *Quarterly Journal of Economics, 106*, 1039–1061.

Twenge, J. M. (2015). Time period and birth cohort differences in depressive symptoms in the U.S., 1982–2013. *Social Indicators Research, 121*, 437–454. doi:10.1007/s11205-014-0647-1

Twenge, J. M., & Campbell, W. (2009). *The narcissism epidemic: Living in the age of enlightenment*. New York, NY: Free Press.

Twenge, J. M., & Kasser, T. (2013). Generational changes in materialism and work centrality, 1976–2007: Associations with temporal changes in societal insecurity and materialistic role modeling. *Personality and Social Psychology Bulletin, 39*, 883–897. doi:10.1177/0146167213484586

Twenge, J. M., Campbell, W. K., & Foster, C. A. (2003). Parenthood and marital satisfaction: A meta-analytic review. *Journal of Marriage and the Family, 65*, 574–583.

Twenge, J. M., Gentile, B., & Campbell, W. K. (2015). Birth cohort differences in personality. In M. Mikulincer, P. R. Shaver, M. L. Cooper, & R. J. Larsen (Eds.), *APA handbook of personality and social psychology: Vol. 4. Personality processes and individual differences*. Washington, DC: American Psychological Association.

Twenge, J. M., Konrath, S., Foster, J. D., Campbell, W., & Bushman, B. J. (2008). Egos inflating over time: A cross-temporal meta-analysis of the Narcissistic Personality Inventory. *Journal of Personality, 76*(4), 875–902. doi:10.1111/j.1467-6494.2008.00507.x

Uchino, B. N., & Birmingham, W. (2011). Stress and support processes. In R. J. Contrada & A. Baum (Eds.), *The handbook of stress science: Biology, psychology, and health* (pp. 111–121). New York, NY: Springer Publishing.

Uleman, J. S., & Sairbay, S. A. (2012). Initial impressions of others. In K. Deaux & M. Snyder (Eds.), *Oxford handbook of personality and social psychology*. New York, NY: Oxford University Press.

Umbel, V. M., Pearson, B. Z., Fernandez, S. C., & Oller, D. K. (1992). Measuring bilingual children's receptive vocabularies. *Child Development, 63*, 1012–1020.

Underwood, B. J. (1961). Ten years of massed practice on distributed practice. *Psychological Review, 68*, 229–247.

Unsworth, N., Fukuda, K., Awh, E., & Vogel, E. K. (2014). Working memory and fluid intelligence: Capacity, attention control, and secondary memory retrieval. *Cognitive Psychology, 71*, 1–26. doi:10.1016/j.cogpsych.2014.01.003

Unsworth, N., Heitz, R. P., Schrock, J. C., & Engle, R. W. (2005). An automated version of the operation span task. *Behavior Research Methods, 37*(3), 498–505. doi:10.3758/BF03192720

Urbina, S. (2011). Tests of intelligence. In R. J. Sternberg, & S. B. Kaufman (Eds.), *Cambridge handbook of intelligence*. New York, NY: Cambridge University Press.

Urcelay, G. P., & Miller, R. R. (2014). The functions of contexts in associative learning. *Behavioural Processes, 104*, 2–12. doi:10.1016/j.beproc.2014.02.008

Ursano, A. M., Kartheiser, P. H., & Barnhill, L. J. (2008). Disorders usually first diagnosed in infancy, childhood, or adolescence. In R. E. Hales, S. C. Yudofsky, & G. O. Gabbard (Eds.), *The American Psychiatric Publishing textbook of psychiatry*

(5th ed., pp. 861–920). Washington, DC: American Psychiatric Publishing.

Ursano, R. J., & Carr, R. B. (2014). Psychodynamic psychotherapy. In R. E. Hales, S. C. Yudofsky, & L. W. Roberts (Eds.), *The American Psychiatric Publishing textbook of psychiatry* (6th ed.). Washington, DC: American Psychiatric Publishing.

U.S. Centers for Disease Control and Prevention. (2009). The power of prevention: Chronic disease . . . the public health challenge of the 21st century. Retrieved from www.cdc.gov /chronicdisease/pdf/2009-Power-of -Prevention.pdf

U.S. Centers for Disease Control and Prevention. (2011). Diagnoses of HIV infection and AIDS in the United States and dependent areas, 2009. *HIV Surveillance Report, 21*. Retrieved from www.cdc.gov/hiv/surveillance /resources/reports/2009report/

Väänänen, A. (2010). Psychosocial work environment and risk of ischaemic heart disease in women. *Occupational & Environmental Medicine, 67*(5), 291–292.

Vaillant, G. E. (1994). Ego mechanisms of defense and personality psychopathology. *Journal of Abnormal Psychology, 103*, 44–50.

Valentine, J. C. (2012). Meta-analysis. In H. Cooper, P. M. Camic, D. L. Long, A. T. Panter, D. Rindskopf, & K. J. Sher (Eds.), *APA handbook of research methods in psychology: Vol. 3. Data analysis and research publication.* Washington, DC: American Psychological Association.

Valli, K., & Revonsuo, A. (2009). Sleep: Dreaming data and theories. In W. P. Banks (Ed.), *Encyclopedia of Consciousness* (pp. 341–356). San Diego, CA: Academic Press.

Valsiner, J. (2012). Introduction: Culture in psychology: A renewed encounter of inquisitive minds. In Valsiner, J. (Ed.). *Oxford handbook of culture and psychology.* New York, NY: Oxford University Press.

Van Blerkom, D. L. (2012). *College study skills: Becoming a strategic learner.* Belmont, CA: Wadsworth.

Van de Castle, R. L. (1994). *Our dreaming mind.* New York, NY: Ballantine Books.

Vandenbroucke, J. P., & Psaty, B. M. (2008). Benefits and risks of drug treatments: How to combine the best evidence on benefits with the best data about adverse effects. *JAMA, 300*(20), 2417–2419.

Van den Heuvel, M. P., & Sporns, O. (2013). Network hubs in the human brain. *Trends in Cognitive Sciences, 17*, 683–696. doi:10.1016/j.tics.2013 .09.012

van der Hart, O., & Nijenhuis, E. R. S. (2009). Dissociative disorders. In P. H. Blaney & T. Millon (Eds.), *Oxford textbook of psychopathology* (2nd ed., pp. 452–481). New York, NY: Oxford University Press.

van der Kloet, D., Merckelbach, H., Giesbrecht, T., & Lynn, S. J. (2012). Fragmented sleep, fragmented mind: The role of sleep in dissociative symptoms. *Perspectives on Psychological Science, 7*(2), 159–175. doi:10.1177/1745691612437597

van Eck, M., Nicolson, N. A., & Berkhof, J. (1998). Effects of stressful daily events on mood states: Relationship to global perceived stress. *Journal of Personality and Social Psychology, 75*, 1572–1585.

van Herpen, E., Pieters, R., & Zeelenberg, M. (2014). When less sells more or less: The scarcity principle in wine choice. *Food Quality and Preference, 36*, 153–160. doi:10.1016 /j.foodqual.2014.04.004

van IJzendoorn, M. H., & Bakermans-Kranenburg, M. J. (2004). Maternal sensitivity and infant temperament in the formation of attachment. In G. Bremner & A. Slater (Eds.), *Theories of infant development*. Malden, MA: Blackwell.

van IJzendoorn, M. H., & Juffer, F. (2005). Adoption is a successful natural intervention enhancing adopted children's IQ and school performance. *Current Directions in Psychological Science, 14*, 326–330.

van IJzendoorn, M. H., & Kroonenberg, P. M. (1988). Cross-cultural patterns of attachment: A meta-analysis of the strange situation. *Child Development, 59*, 147–156.

van IJzendoorn, M. H., & Sagi-Schwartz, A. (2008). Cross-cultural patterns of attachment: Universal and contextual dimensions. In J. Cassidy & P. R. Shaver (Eds.), *Handbook of attachment: Theory, research, and clinical applications* (2nd ed., pp. 3–22). New York, NY: Guilford Press.

van Kammen, D. P., Hurford, I., & Marder, S. R. (2009). First-generation antipsychotics. In B. J. Sadock, V. A. Sadock, & P. Ruiz (Eds.), *Kaplan & Sadock's comprehensive textbook of psychiatry* (pp. 3105–3126). Philadelphia, PA: Lippincott Williams & Wilkins.

van Steenburgh, J. J., Fleck, J. I., Beeman, M., & Kounios, J. (2012). Insight. In K. J. Holyoak & R. G. Morrison (Eds.), *Oxford handbook of thinking and reasoning.* New York, NY: Oxford University Press.

Van Swol, L. M. (2009). Extreme members and group polarization. *Social Influence, 4*(3), 185–199. doi:10.1080/15534510802584368

van Winkel, R., & Kuepper, R. (2014). Epidemiological, neurobiological, and genetic clues to the mechanisms linking cannabis use to risk for nonaffective psychosis. *Annual Review of Clinical Psychology, 107*, 67–791. doi:10.1146/annurev-clinpsy-032813 -153631

Varnum, M. W., Grossmann, I., Kitayama, S., & Nisbett, R. E. (2010). The origin of cultural differences in cognition: The social orientation hypothesis. *Current Directions in Psychological Science, 19*(1), 9–13. doi:10.1177/0963721409359301

Vermeer, H. J., & Bakermans-Kranenburg, M. J. (2008). Attachment to mother and nonmaternal care: Bridging the gap. *Attachment & Human Development, 10*, 263–273. doi:10.1080/14616730802113588

Vernon, P. A., Wickett, J. C., Bazana, G. P., & Stelmack, R. M. (2000). The neuropsychology and psychophysiology of human intelligence. In R. J. Sternberg (Ed.), *Handbook of intelligence.* Cambridge, UK: Cambridge University Press.

Veru, F., Laplante, D. P., Luhesi, G., & King, S. (2014). Prenatal maternal stress exposure and immune function in the offspring. *Stress: The International Journal on the Biology of Stress, 17*, 133–148. doi:10.3109/10253890. 2013.876404

Victoroff, J. (2005). Central nervous system changes with normal aging. In B. J. Sadock & V. A. Sadock (Eds.), *Kaplan & Sadock's comprehensive textbook of psychiatry.* Philadelphia, PA: Lippincott Williams & Wilkins.

Vigod, S. N., Kurdyak, P. A., Seitz, D., Herrmann, N., Fung, K., Lin, E., . . . Gruneir, A. (2015). READMIT: A clinical risk index to predict 30-day readmission after discharge from acute psychiatric units. *Journal of Psychiatric Research, 61*, 205–213. doi:10.1016/j.jpsychires.2014.12.003

Vineis, P. (2005). Environmental tobacco smoke and risk of respiratory cancer and chronic obstructive pulmonary disease in former smokers and never smokers in the EPIC prospective study. *BMJ: British Medical Journal, 330*(7486), 277–280.

Viron, M., Bello, I., Freudenreich, O., & Shtasel, D. (2014). Characteristics of homeless adults with serious mental illness served by a state mental health transitional shelter. *Community Mental Health Journal, 50*, 560–565. doi:10.1007/s10597-013-9607-5

Visser, B. A., Ashton, M. C., & Vernon, P. A. (2006). Beyond g: Putting multiple intelligences theory to the test. *Intelligence, 34*, 487–502. doi:10.1016/j.intell.2006.02.004

Vogel, I., Brug, J., Hosli, E. J., van der Ploeg, C. P. B., & Raat, H. (2008).

MP3 players and hearing loss: Adolescents' perceptions of loud music and hearing conservation. *Journal of Pediatrics, 152*(3), 400–404. doi:10.1016 /j.jpeds.2007.07.009

Volkmar, F. R., Klin, A., Schultz, R. T., & State, M. W. (2009). Pervasive developmental disorders. In B. J. Sadock, V. A. Sadock, & P. Ruiz (Eds.), *Kaplan & Sadock's comprehensive textbook of psychiatry* (9th ed., pp. 3540–3559). Philadelphia, PA: Lippincott Williams & Wilkins.

Volkow, N. D., Baler, R. D., Compton, W. M., & Weiss, S. R. B. (2014). Adverse health effects of marijuana use. *New England Journal of Medicine, 370*, 2219–2227. doi:10.1056 /NEJMra1402309

Vondracek, F. W., & Crouter, A. C. (2013). Health and human development. In R. M. Lerner, M. A. Easterbrooks, J. Mistry, & I. B. Weiner (Eds.), *Handbook of psychology: Vol. 6. Developmental psychology.* New York, NY: Wiley.

Voyer, D., Nolan, C., & Voyer, S. (2000). The relation between experience and spatial performance in men and women. *Sex Roles, 43*, 891–915.

Vyas, M. V., Garg, A. X., Iansavichus, A. V., Costella, J., Donner, A., Laugsand, L. E., . . . Hackam, D. G. (2012). Shift work and vascular events: Systematic review and meta-analysis. *British Medical Journal, 345*, e4800. doi:10.1136/bmj.e4800

Vyse, S. A. (1997). *Believing in magic: The psychology of superstition.* New York, NY: Oxford University Press.

Waage, S., Moen, B., Pallesen, S., Eriksen, H. R., Ursin, H., Åkerstedt, T., & Bjorvatn, B. (2009). Shift work disorder among oil rig workers in the North Sea. *Sleep: Journal of Sleep and Sleep Disorders Research, 32*(4), 558–565.

Wager, T. D., Scott, D. J., & Zubieta, J. (2007). Placebo effects on human μ-opioid activity during pain. *PNAS Proceedings of the National Academy of Sciences of the United States of America, 104*(26), 11056–11061. doi:10.1073/pnas.0702413104.

Wagner, L., & Hoff, E. (2013). Language development. In R. M. Lerner, M. A. Easterbrooks, J. Mistry, & I. B. Weiner (Eds.), *Handbook of psychology: Vol. 6. Developmental psychology.* New York, NY: Wiley.

Wagstaff, G. F., David, D., Kirsch, I., & Lynn, S. J. (2010). The cognitive-behavioral model of hypnotherapy. In S. J. Lynn, J. W. Rhue, & I. Kirsch (Eds.), *Handbook of clinical hypnosis* (2nd ed., pp. 179–208). Washington, DC: American Psychological Association.

Wai, J., Putallaz, M., & Makel, M. C. (2012). Studying intellectual outliers:

Are there sex differences, and are the smart getting smarter? *Current Direction in Psychological Science, 21*, 382–390. doi:10.1177/0963721412455052

Wakeel, F., Wisk, L. E., Gee, R., Chao, S. M., & Witt, W. P. (2013). The balance between stress and personal capital during pregnancy and the relationship with adverse obstetric outcomes: Findings from the 2007 Los Angeles Mommy and Baby (LAMB) study. *Archives of Women's Mental Health, 16*, 435–451. doi:10.1007/s00737-013-0367-6

Walder, D. J., Laplante, D. P., Sousa-Pires, A., Veru, F., Brunet, A., & King, S. (2014). Prenatal maternal stress predicts autism traits in 6 1/2 year-old children: Project ice storm. *Psychiatry Research, 219*, 353–360. doi:10.1016/j.psychres.2014.04.034

Wales, W. J., Patel, P. C., & Lumpkin, G. T. (2013). In pursuit of greatness: CEO narcissism, entrepreneurial orientation, and firm performance variance. *Journal of Management Studies, 50*, 1041–1069. doi:10.1111/joms.12034

Walker, E., Mittal, V., & Tessner, K. (2008). Stress and the hypothalamic pituitary adrenal axis in the developmental course of schizophrenia. *Annual Review of Clinical Psychology, 4*, 189–216.

Walker, E., & Tessner, K. (2008). Schizophrenia. *Perspectives on Psychological Science, 3*, 30–37.

Walker, L. J. (1989). A longitudinal study of moral reasoning. *Child Development, 60*, 157–166.

Walker, L. J. (2007). Progress and prospects in the psychology of moral development. In G. W. Ladd (Ed.), *Appraising the human developmental sciences: Essays in honor of Merrill-Palmer Quarterly*. Detroit: Wayne State University Press.

Walker, M. P. (2012). The role of sleep in neurocognitive functioning. In C. M. Morin, & C. A. Espie (Eds.), *Oxford handbook of sleep and sleep disorders*. New York, NY: Oxford University Press.

Walker, M. P., Brakefield, T., Morgan, A., Hobson, J. A., & Stickgold, R. (2002). Practice with sleep makes perfect: Sleep dependent motor skill learning. *Neuron, 35*, 205–211.

Wallace, D. S., Paulson, R. M., Lord, C. G., & Bond, C. F. Jr. (2005). Which behaviors do attitudes predict? Meta-analyzing the effects of social pressure and perceived difficulty. *Review of General Psychology, 9*, 214–227.

Wallner, B., & Machatschke, I. H. (2009). The evolution of violence in men: The function of central cholesterol and serotonin. *Progress in Neuro-Psychopharmacology &*

Biological Psychiatry, 33(3), 391–397. doi:10.1016/j.pnpbp.2009.02.006

Walsh, B. T., Seidman, S. N., Sysko, R., & Gould, M. (2002). Placebo response studies of major depression: Variable, substantial and growing. *JAMA, 287*, 1840–1847.

Walsh, J. K., Dement, W. C., & Dinges, D. F. (2011). Sleep medicine, public policy, and public health. In M. H. Kryger, T. Roth, & W. C. Dement (Eds.), *Principles and practice of sleep medicine* (5th ed.). Saint Louis, MO: Elsevier Saunders.

Walsh, J. K., & Roth, T. (2011). Pharmacological treatment of insomnia: Benzodiazepine receptor agonists. In M. H. Kryger, T. Roth, & W. C. Dement (Eds.), *Principles and practice of sleep medicine* (5th ed.). Saint Louis, MO: Elsevier Saunders.

Walsh, R., & Shapiro, S. L. (2006). The meeting of meditative disciplines and Western psychology: A mutually enriching dialogue. *American Psychologist, 61*, 227–239.

Walter, C. A. (2000). The psychological meaning of menopause: Women's experiences. *Journal of Women and Aging, 12*(3–4), 117–131.

Walther, E., & Grigoriadis, S. (2003). Why sad people like shoes better: The influence of mood on the evaluative conditioning of consumer attitudes. *Psychology & Marketing, 10*, 755–775.

Walther, E., & Langer, T. (2008). Attitude formation and change through association: An evaluative conditioning account. In W. D. Crano, & R. Prislin (Eds.), *Attitudes and attitude change* (pp. 61–84). New York, NY: Psychology Press.

Walther, E., Nagengast, B., & Trasselli, C. (2005). Evaluative conditioning in social psychology: Facts and speculations. *Cognition and Emotion, 19*(2), 175–196.

Walther, E., Weil, R., & Dusing, J. (2011). The role of evaluative conditioning in attitude formation. *Current Directions in Psychological Science, 20*, 192–196. doi:10.1177/0963721411408771

Wampold, B. E. (2001). *The great psychotherapy debate*. Mahwah, NJ: Erlbaum.

Wampold, B. E. (2013). The good, the bad, and the ugly: A 50-year perspective on the outcome problem. *Psychotherapy, 50*(1), 16–24. doi:10.1037/a0030570

Wampold, B. E., Imel, Z. E., & Minami, T. (2007). The story of placebo effects in medicine: Evidence in context. *Journal of Clinical Psychology, 63*(4), 379–390. doi:10.1002/jclp.20354

Wampold, B. E., Minami, T., Tierney, S. C., Baskin, T. W., & Bhati, K. S. (2005). The placebo is powerful: Estimating placebo effects in medicine and psychotherapy from randomized clinical trials. *Journal of Clinical Psychology, 61*(7), 835–854. doi:10.1002/jclp.20129

Wamsley, E. J., & Stickgold, R. (2009). Incorporation of waking events into dreams. In R. Stickgold & M. P. Walker (Eds.), *The neuroscience of sleep* (pp. 330–337). San Diego, CA: Academic Press.

Wang, P. S., Berglund, P., Olfson, M., Pincus, H. A., Wells, K. B., & Kessler, R. C. (2005). Failure and delay in initial treatment contact after first onset of mental disorders in the National Comorbidity Survey Replication. *Archives of General Psychiatry, 62*, 603–613.

Wangensteen, O. H., & Carlson, A. J. (1931). Hunger sensation after total gastrectomy. *Proceedings of the Society for Experimental Biology, 28*, 545–547.

Wansink, B. (2012). Specific environmental drivers of eating. In K. D. Brownell, & M. S. Gold (Eds.), *Food and addiction: A comprehensive handbook*. New York, NY: Oxford University Press.

Wansink, B., & Chandon, P. (2014). Slim by design: Redirecting the accidental drivers of mindless overeating. *Journal of Consumer Psychology, 24*, 413–431. doi:10.1016/j.jcps.2014.03.006

Wansink, B., & Kim, J. (2005). Bad popcorn in big buckets: Portion size can influence intake as much as taste. *Journal of Nutrition Education and Behavior, 37*(5), 242–245. doi:10.1016/S1499-4046(06)60278-9

Wansink, B., & van Ittersum, K. (2013). Portion size me: Plate-size induced consumption norms and win-win solutions for reducing food intake and waste. *Journal of Experimental Psychology: Applied, 19*(4), 320–332. doi:10.1037/a0035053.

Wansink, B., van Ittersum, K., & Payne, C. R. (2014). Larger bowl size increases the amount of cereal children request, consume, and waste. *The Journal of Pediatrics, 164*, 323–326. doi:10.1016/j.jpeds.2013.09.036

Warburton, W. (2014). Apples, oranges, and the burden of proof—Putting media violence findings into context: A comment on Elson and Ferguson (2013). *European Psychologist, 19*, 60-67. doi:10.1027/1016-9040/a000166

Ward, B. W., Schiller, J. S., & Goodman, R. A. (2014). Multiple chronic conditions among U.S. adults: A 2012 update. *Preventing Chronic*

Disease, 11, 130389. doi:10.5888/pcd11.130389

Wäschle, K., Allgaier, A., Lachner, A., Fink, S., & Nückles, M. (2014). Procrastination and self-efficacy: Tracing vicious and virtuous circles in self-regulated learning. *Learning and Instruction, 29*, 103–114. doi:10.1016/j.learninstruc.2013.09.005

Washburn, M. F. (1908). *The animal mind*. New York, NY: MacMillan.

Waterhouse, L. (2006). Multiple intelligences, the Mozart effect, and emotional intelligence: A critical review. *Educational Psychologist, 41*, 207–225.

Watson, D., Klohen, E. C., Casillas, A., Nus Simms, E., Haig, J., & Berry, D. S. (2004). Match makers and deal breakers: Analyses of assortative mating in newlywed couples. *Journal of Personality, 72*, 1029–1068.

Watson, D. L., & Tharp, R. G. (2014). *Self-directed behavior: Self-modification for personal adjustment*. Belmont, CA: Cengage Learning.

Watson, J. B. (1913). Psychology as the behaviorist views it. *Psychological Review, 20*, 158–177.

Watson, J. B. (1919). *Psychology from the standpoint of a behaviorist*. Philadelphia, PA: Lippincott.

Watson, J. B. (1924). *Behaviorism*. New York, NY: Norton.

Watson, J. B., & Rayner, R. (1920). Conditioned emotional reactions. *Journal of Experimental Psychology, 3*, 1–14.

Watts, A. L., Lilienfeld, S. O., Smith, S. F., Miller, J. D., Campbell, W. K., Waldman, I. D., . . . Faschingbauer, T. J. (2013). The double-edged sword of grandiose narcissism: Implications for successful and unsuccessful leadership among U.S. Presidents. *Psychological Science, 24*, 2379–2389. doi:10.1177/0956797613491970

Waugh, N. C., & Norman, D. A. (1965). Primary memory. *Psychological Review, 72*, 89–104.

Waxman, S. (2002). Early word-learning and conceptual development: Everything had a name and each name gave birth to a new thought. In U. Goswami (Ed.), *Blackwell handbook of childhood cognitive development* (pp. 102–126). Malden, MA: Blackwell.

Weaver, T. E., & George, C. F. P. (2011). Cognition and performance in patients with obstructive sleep apnea. In M. H. Kryger, T. Roth, & W. C. Dement (Eds.), *Principles and practice of sleep medicine* (5th ed.). Saint Louis, MO: Elsevier Saunders.

Webb, W. B., & Dinges, D. F. (1989). Cultural perspectives on napping and the siesta. In D. F. Dinges &

R. J. Broughton (Eds.), *Sleep and alertness: Chronobiological, behavioral, and medical aspects of napping*. New York, NY: Raven.

Webster, G. D. (2009). Parental investment theory. In H. T. Reis & S. Sprecher (Eds.), *Encyclopedia of human relationships* (Vol. 3, pp. 1194–1197)., Los Angeles, CA: Sage.

Webster, M. (2010). Color perception. In E. B. Goldstein (Ed.), *Encyclopedia of perception*. Thousand Oaks, CA: Sage.

Wechsler, D. (1939). *The measurement of adult intelligence*. Baltimore: Williams & Wilkins.

Wechsler, H., Lee, J. E., Kuo, M, Seibring, M., Nelson, T. F., & Lee, H. (2002). Trends in college binge drinking during a period of increased prevention efforts: Findings from 4 Harvard School of Public Health College Alcohol Study surveys: 1993–2001. *Journal of American College Health, 50,* 203–217.

Wegner, D. M., & Wheatley, T. (1999). Apparent mental causation: Sources of the experience of will. *American Psychologist, 54,* 480–492. doi:10.1037/0003-066X.54.7.480

Wehby, G. L., Prater, K., McCarthy, A. M., Castilla, E. E., & Murray, J. C. (2011). The impact of maternal smoking during pregnancy on early child neurodevelopment. *Journal of Human Capital, 5,* 207–254.

Weich, S., Pearce, H. L., Croft, P., Singh, S., Crome, I., Bashford, J., & Fisher, M. (2014). Effect of anxiolytic and hypnotic drug prescriptions on mortality hazards: Retrospective cohort study. *British Medical Journal, 348,* g1996. doi:10.1136/bmj.g1996

Weinberg, R. A. (1989). Intelligence and IQ: Landmark issues and great debates. *American Psychologist, 44,* 98–104.

Weinberger, J. (1995). Common factors aren't so common: The common factors dilemma. *Clinical Psychology: Science and Practice, 2*(1), 45–69. doi:10.1111/j.1468-2850.1995.tb00024.x

Weiner, B. (1980). *Human motivation*. New York, NY: Holt, Rinehart & Winston.

Weiner, B. (1994). Integrating social and personal theories of achievement striving. *Review of Educational Research, 64,* 557–573.

Weiner, B. (2006). *Social motivation, justice, and the moral emotions*. Mahwah, NJ: Lawrence Erlbaum.

Weiner, B. (2012). An attribution theory of motivation. In P. A. M. Van Lange, A. W. Kruglanski, & E. T. Higgins (Eds.), *Handbook of theories of social psychology: Vol. 1.*, Los Angeles, CA: Sage.

Weiner, B., Osborne, D., & Rudolph, U. (2011). An attributional analysis of reactions to poverty: The political ideology of the giver and the perceived morality of the receiver. *Personality and Social Psychology Review, 15,* 199–213. doi:10.1177/1088868310387615

Weiner, I. B. (2013a). Applying Rorschach assessment. In G. P. Koocher, J. C. Norcross, & B. A. Greene (Eds.), *Psychologists' desk reference* (3rd ed.). New York, NY: Oxford University Press.

Weiner, I. B. (2013b). Assessment psychology. In D. K. Freedheim, & I. B. Weiner (Eds.), *Handbook of psychology: Vol. 1. History of psychology* (2nd ed.). New York, NY: Wiley.

Weiner, I. B., & Meyer, G. J. (2009). Personality assessment with the Rorschach Inkblot Method. In J. N. Butcher (Ed.), *Oxford handbook of personality assessment*. New York, NY: Oxford University Press. doi:10.1093/oxfordhb/9780195366877.013.0015

Weiner, M. F. (2014). Neurocognitive disorders. In R. E. Hales, S. C. Yudofsky, & L. W. Roberts (Eds.), *The American Psychiatric Publishing textbook of psychiatry* (6th ed., pp. 815–850). Washington, DC: American Psychiatric Publishing.

Weinfeld, N. S., Sroufe, L. A., Egeland, B., & Carlson, E. (2008). Individual differences in infant-caregiver attachment: Conceptual and empirical aspects of security. In J. Cassidy & P. R. Shaver (Eds.), *Handbook of attachment: Theory, research, and clinical applications* (2nd ed., pp. 78–101). New York, NY: Guilford Press.

Weinstein, N., Ryan, W. S., DeHaan, C. R., Przybylski, A. K., Legate, N., & Ryan, R. M. (2012). Parental autonomy support and discrepancies between implicit and explicit sexual identities: Dynamics of self-acceptance and defense. *Journal of Personality and Social Psychology, 102,* 815–832. doi:10.1037/a0026854

Weinsten, A., Curtiss, F., Rosenberg, K. P., & Dannon, P. (2014). Internet addiction disorder: Overview and controversies. In K. P. Rosenberg & L. Curtiss Feder (Eds.), *Behavioral addictions: Criteria, evidence, and treatment*. San Diego, CA: Elsevier Academic Press. doi:10.1016/B978-0-12-407724-9.00005-7

Weintraub, K. (2011). Autism counts. *Nature, 479*(7371), 22–24. doi:10.1038/479022a

Weisberg, R. W. (1986). *Creativity: Genius and other myths*. New York, NY: W. H. Freeman.

Weisberg, R. W. (1999). Creativity and knowledge: A challenge to theories. In R. J. Sternberg (Ed.), *Handbook of creativity*. New York, NY: Cambridge University Press.

Weisberg, R. W. (2006). *Creativity: Understanding innovation in problem solving, science, invention, and the arts*. New York, NY: Wiley.

Weisleder, A., & Fernald, A. (2013). Talking to children matters: Early language experience strengthens processing and builds vocabulary. *Psychological Science, 24,* 2143–2152. doi:10.1177/0956797613488145

Weisman, O., Zagoory-Sharon, O., & Feldman, R. (2014). Oxytocin administration, salivary testosterone, and father-infant social behavior. *Progress in Neuro-Psychopharmacology & Biological Psychiatry, 49,* 47–52. doi:10.1016/j.pnpbp.2013.11.006

Weiten, W. (1988). Pressure as a form of stress and its relationship to psychological symptomatology. *Journal of Social and Clinical Psychology, 6*(1) 127–139.

Weiten, W. (1998). Pressure, major life events, and psychological symptoms. *Journal of Social Behavior and Personality, 13,* 51–68.

Weiten, W., & Diamond, S. S. (1979). A critical review of the jury-simulation paradigm: The case of defendant characteristics. *Law and Human Behavior, 3,* 71–93.

Weiten, W., Guadagno, R. E., & Beck, C. A. (1996). Students' perceptions of textbook pedagogical aids. *Teaching of Psychology, 23,* 105–107.

Weiten, W., & Houska, J. A. (2015). Introductory psychology: Unique challenges and opportunities. In D. S. Dunn (Ed.), *The Oxford handbook of psychology education* (pp. 289–321). New York, NY: Oxford University Press.

Weiten, W., & Wight, R. D. (1992). Portraits of a discipline: An examination of introductory psychology textbooks in America. In A. E. Puente, J. R. Matthews, & C. L. Brewer (Eds.), *Teaching psychology in America: A history*. Washington, DC: American Psychological Association. doi:10.1037/10120-020.

Wells, G. L., & Bradfield, A. L. (1998). "Good, you identified the suspect": Feedback to eyewitnesses disorts their reports of the witnessing experience. *Journal of Applied Psychology, 83,* 360–376.

Wells, G. L., & Loftus, E. F. (2013). Eyewitness memory for people and events. In R. K. Otto & I. B. Weiner (Eds.). *Handbook of psychology: Vol. 11. Forensic psychology* (2nd ed., pp. 617-629). Hoboken, NJ: Wiley.

Wener, R. E., & Evans, G. W. (2011). Comparing stress of car and train commuters. *Transportation Research Part F: Traffic Psychology and Behavior, 14,* 111–116. doi:10.1016/j.trf.2010.11.008

Wertheimer, M. [Max]. (1912). Experimentelle studien über das sehen von bewegung. *Zeitschrift für Psychologie, 60,* 312–378.

Wertheimer, M. [Michael]. (2012). *A brief history of psychology*. New York, NY: Psychology Press.

Wertz, A. E., & Wynn, K. (2014). Selective social learning of plant edibility in 6- and 18-month-old infants. *Psychological Science, 25,* 874–882. doi:10.1177/0956797613516145

Westen, D. Gabbard, G. O., & Ortigo, K. M. (2008). Psychoanalytic approaches to personality. In O. P. John, R. W. Robins, & L. A. Pervin (Eds.), *Handbook of personality psychology: Theory and research*. New York, NY: Guilford Press.

Wetherby, A. M., & Prizant, B. M. (2005). Enhancing language and communication development in autism spectrum disorders: Assessment and intervention guidelines. In D. Zager (Ed.), *Autism spectrum disorders: Identification, education, and treatment* (3rd ed., pp. 327–365). Hillside, NJ: Lawrence Erlbaum Associates.

Whitaker, R. (2002). *Mad in America: Bad science, bad medicine, and the enduring mistreatment of the mentally ill*. New York, NY: Perseus Publishing.

Whitaker, R. (2009). Deinstitutionalization and neuroleptics: The myth and reality. In Y. O. Alanen, M. González de Chávez, A. S. Silver, & B. Martindale (Eds.), *Psychotherapeutic approaches to schizophrenic psychoses: Past, present and future*. New York, NY: Routledge/Taylor & Francis Group.

Whitbourne, S. K., Zuschlag, M. K., Elliot, L. B., & Waterman, A. S. (1992). Psychosocial development in adulthood: A 22-year sequential study. *Journal of Personality and Social Psychology, 63,* 260–271.

Whitchurch, E. R., Wilson, T. D., & Gilbert, D. T. (2011). "He loves me, he loves me not . . .": Uncertainty can increase romantic attraction. *Psychological Science, 22,* 172–175. doi:10.1177/0956797610393745

White, C. M., & Hoffrage, U. (2009). Testing the tyranny of too much choice against the allure of more choice. *Psychology & Marketing, 26*(3), 280–298. doi:10.1002/mar.20273

White, J. (2006). Multiple Invalidities. In J. A. Schaler (Ed.), *Howard Gardner under fire: The rebel psychologist faces his critics*. Chicago, IL: Open Court.

White, T., Ehrlich, S., Ho, B., Manoach, D. S., Caprihan, A., Schulz, S. C., . . . Magnotta, V. A. (2013). Spatial characteristics of white matter abnormalties in schizophrenia. *Schizophrenia Bulletin, 39,* 1077–1086. doi:10.1093/schbul/sbs106

Whorf, B. L. (1956). Science and linguistics. In J. B. Carroll (Ed.), *Language, thought and reality: Selected writings of Benjamin Lee Whorf.* Cambridge, MA: MIT Press.

Widiger, T. A. (2009). Neuroticism. In M. R. Leary & R. H. Hoyle (Eds.), *Handbook of individual differences in social behavior* (pp. 129–146). New York, NY: Guilford Press.

Widiger, T. A., & Crego, C. (2013). Diagnosis and classification. In T. A. Widiger, G. Stricker, I. B. Weiner, G. Stricker, T. A. Widiger, & I. B. Weiner (Eds.), *Handbook of psychology: Vol. 8. Clinical psychology* (2nd ed.). New York, NY: Wiley.

Widiger, T. A., Livesley, W., & Clark, L. (2009). An integrative dimensional classification of personality disorder. *Psychological Assessment, 21*(3), 243–255. doi:10.1037/a0016606

Widiger, T. A., & Sankis, L. M. (2000). Adult psychopathology: Issues and controversies. *Annual Review of Psychology, 51,* 377–404.

Widom, C. S., Czaja, S. J., & Paris, J. (2009). A prospective investigation of borderline personality disorder in abused and neglected children followed up into adulthood. *Journal of Personality Disorders, 23*(5), 433–446. doi:10.1521/pedi.2009.23.5.433

Wiese, A. M., & Garcia, E. E. (2006). Educational policy in the United States regarding bilinguals in early childhood education. In B. Spodek & O. N. Saracho (Eds.), *Handbook of research on the education of young children.* Mahwah, NJ: Erlbaum.

Wilde, E. A., Kim, H. F., Schulz, P. E., & Yudofsky, S. C. (2014). Neurocognitive disorders. In R. E. Hales, S. C. Yudofsky, & L. W. Roberts (Eds.), *The American Psychiatric Publishing textbook of psychiatry* (6th ed.). Washington, DC: American Psychiatric Publishing.

Wilding, J., & Valentine, E. (1996). Memory expertise. In D. J. Herrmann, C. McEvoy, C. Hertzog, P. Hertel, & M. K. Johnson (Eds.), *Basic and applied memory research: Theory in context* (Vol. 1). Mahwah, NJ: Erlbaum.

Wiley, J., & Jarosz, A. F. (2012). Working memory capacity, attentional focus, and problem solving. *Current Directions in Psychological Science, 21,* 258–262. doi:10.1177/0963721412447622

Wilke, A., Scheibehenne, B., Gaissmaier, W., McCanney, P., & Barrett, H. C. (2014). Illusionary pattern detection in habitual gamblers. *Evolution and Human Behavior, 35,* 291–297. doi:10.1016/j.evolhumbehav.2014.02.010

Williams, B. A. (1988). Reinforcement, choice, and response strength. In R. C. Atkinson, R. J. Herrnstein, G. Lindzey, & R. D. Luce (Eds.), *Stevens' handbook of experimental psychology.* New York, NY: Wiley.

Williams, J. E., Paton, C. C., Siegler, I. C., Eigenbrodt, M. L., Neito, F. J., & Tyroler, H. A. (2000). Anger proneness predicts coronary heart disease risk. *Circulation, 101,* 2034–2039.

Williams, P. (2005). What is psychoanalysis? What is a psychoanalyst? In E. S. Person, A. M. Cooper, & G. O. Gabbard (Eds.), *Textbook of psychoanalysis.* Washington, DC: American Psychiatric Publishing.

Williams, R. E., Kaliani, L., DiBenedetti, D. B., Zhou, X., Fehnel, S. E., & Clark, R. V. (2007). Healthcare seeking and treatment for menopausal symptoms in the United States. *Maturitas, 58,* 348–358.

Williams, R. L. (2013). Overview of the Flynn effect. *Intelligence, 41,* 753–764. doi:10.1016/j.intell.2013.04.010

Williams, W. M. (1998). Are we raising smarter children today? School-and-home-related infuences on IQ. In U. Neisser (Ed.), *The rising curve: Long-term gains in IQ and related measures.* Washington, DC: American Psychological Association.

Williams, W. M., & Ceci, S. J. (1997). Are Americans becoming more or less alike?: Trends in race, class, and ability differences in intelligence. *American Psychologist, 52,* 1226–1235.

Williamson, D. A., Zucker, N. L., Martin, C. K., & Smeets, M. A. M. (2001). Etiology and management of eating disorders. In P. B. Sutker & H. E. Adams (Eds.), *Comprehensive handbook of psychopathology.* New York, NY: Kluwer Academic/Plenum.

Willis, B. L., Gao, A., Leonard, D., Defina, L. F., & Berry, J. D. (2012). Midlife fitness and the development of chronic conditions in later life. *Archives of Internal Medicine, 172,* 1333–1340. doi:10.1001/archinternmed.2012.3400

Wilson, D. K., Zarrett, N., & Kitzman-Ulrich, H. (2011). Physical activity and health: Current research trends and critical issues. In H. S. Friedman (Ed.), *Oxford handbook of health psychology.* New York, NY: Oxford University Press.

Wilson, G. T. (2011). Behavior therapy. In R. J. Corsini & D. Wedding (Eds.), *Current psychotherapies* (9th ed.). Belmont, CA: Brooks/Cole.

Wilson, R. E., Gosling, S. D., & Graham, L. T. (2012). A review of Facebook research in the social sciences. *Perspectives on Psychological Science, 7,* 203–220. doi:10.1177/1745691612442904

Wilson, T. D., & Gilbert, D. T. (2003). Affective forecasting. In M. P. Zanna (Eds.), *Advances in experimental social psychology* (Vol. 35, pp. 345–411). San Diego, CA: Academic Press. doi:10.1016/S0065-2601(03)01006-2

Wilson, T. D., & Gilbert, D. T. (2005). Affective forecasting: Knowing what to want. *Current Directions in Psychological Science, 14,* 131–134.

Wilson, T. D., & Gilbert, D. T. (2013). The impact bias is alive and well. *Journal of Personality and Social Psychology, 105,* 740–748. doi:10.1037/a0032662

Wilt, J., & Revelle, W. (2009). Extraversion. In M. R. Leary & R. H. Hoyle (Eds.), *Handbook of individual differences in social behavior* (pp. 257–273). New York, NY: Guilford Press.

Wing, L., & Potter, D. (2009). The epidemiology of autism spectrum disorders: Is the prevalence rising? In S. Goldstein, J. A. Naglieri, & S. Ozonoff (Eds.), *Assessment of autism spectrum disorders* (pp. 18–54). New York, NY: Guilford Press.

Wingfield, A., Tun, P. A., & McCoy, S. L. (2005). Hearing loss in older adulthood: What it is and how it interacts with cognitive performance. *Current Directions in Psychological Science, 14,* 144–148.

Winn, P. (1995). The lateral hypothalmus and motivated behavior: An old syndrome reassessed and a new perspective gained. *Current Directions in Psychological Science, 4,* 182–187.

Winter, D. G. (2010). Why achievement motivation predicts success in business but failure in politics: The importance of personal control. *Journal of Personality, 78*(6), 1637–1667. doi:10.1111/j.1467-6494.2010.00665.x

Winton-Brown, T. T., Fusar-Poli, P., Ungless, M. A., & Howes, O. D. (2014). Dopaminergic basis of salience dysregulation in psychosis. *Trends in Neurosciences, 37*(2), 85–94. doi:10.1016/j.tins.2013.11.003

Wirth, M. M., & Gaffey, A. E. (2013). Hormones and emotion: Stress and beyond. In M. D. Robinson, E. Watkins, & E. Harmon-Jones (Eds.), *Handbook of cognition and emotion.* New York, NY: Guilford Press.

Wise, R. A. (2013). Dual roles of dopamine in food and drug seeking: The drive-reward paradox. *Biological Psychiatry, 73,* 819–826. doi:10.1016/j.biopsych.2012.09.001

Wittkower, E. D., & Warnes, H. (1984). Cultural aspects of psychotherapy. In J. E. Mezzich & C. E. Berganza (Eds.), *Culture and psychopathology.* New York, NY: Columbia University Press.

Wolfe, J. M., Kluender, K. R., Levi, D. M., Bartoshuk, L. M., Herz, R. S., Klatzky, R. L., & Lederman, S. J. (2006). *Sensation and perception.* Sunderland, MA: Sinauer Associates.

Wolford, G., Miller, M. B., & Gazzaniga, M. S. (2004). Split decisions. In M. S. Gazzaniga (Ed.), *The cognitive neurosciences.* Cambridge, MA: MIT Press.

Wolitzky, D. L. (2006). Psychodynamic theories. In J. C. Thomas, & D. L. Segal (Eds.), *Comprehensive handbook of personality and psychopathology.* New York, NY: Wiley.

Wollmer, M. A., de Boer, C., Kalak, N., Beck, J., Götz, T., Schmidt, T., . . . Kruger, T. H. (2012). Facing depression with botulinum toxin: A randomized controlled trial. *Journal of Psychiatric Research, 46,* 574–581. doi:10.1016/j.jpsychires.2012.01.027

Wollmer, M. A., Kalak, N., Jung, S., de Boer, C., Magid, M., Reichenberg, J. S., . . . Kruger, T. C. (2014). Agitation predicts response of depression to botulinum toxin treatment in a randomized controlled trial. *Frontiers in Psychiatry, 5,* 36. doi:10.3389/fpsyt.2014.00036

Wolpe, J. (1958). *Psychotherapy by reciprocal inhibition.* Stanford, CA: Stanford University Press.

Wonderlich, S. A. (2002). Personality and eating disorders. In C. G. Fairburn & K. D. Brownell (Eds.), *Eating disorders and obesity: A comprehensive handbook.* New York, NY: Guilford Press.

Wong, L. A. (2006). *Essential study skills.* Boston, MA: Houghton Mifflin.

Wood, J. M., Lilienfeld, S. O., Nezworski, M. T., Garb, H. N., Allen, K. H., & Wildermuth, J. L. (2010). Validity of Rorschach Inkblot scores for discriminating psychopaths from nonpsychopaths in forensic populations: A meta-analysis. *Psychological Assessment, 22,* 336–349. doi:10.1037/a0018998

Wood, J. N., & Spelke, E. S. (2005). Chronometric studies of numerical cognition in five-month-old infants. *Cognition, 97,* 23–39.

Woods, S. C., & Stricker, E. M. (2008). Food intake and metabolism. In L. Squire, D. Berg, F. Bloom, S. du Lac, A. Ghosh, & N. Spitzer, *Fundamental neuroscience* (3rd ed.). San Diego, CA: Academic Press.

Woody, E. Z., & Sadler, P. (2008). Dissociation theories of hypnosis. In M. R. Nash & A. J. Barnier (Eds.), *The Oxford handbook of hypnosis: Theory, research, and practice* (pp. 81–110). New York, NY: Oxford University Press.

Woolfolk, R. L., & Richardson, F. C. (1978). *Stress, sanity and survival.* New York, NY: Sovereign/Monarch.

Woollett, K., & Maguire, E. A. (2011). Acquiring "the knowledge" of London's layout drives structural brain changes. *Current Biology, 21,* 2109–2114. doi:10.1016/j.cub.2001.11.018

Worchel, S., Rothgerber, H., & Day, E. A. (2011). Social loafing and group development: When "I" comes last. *Current Research in Social Psychology, 17,* Article 4.

Worthen, J. B., & Wade, C. E. (1999). Direction of travel and visiting team athletic performance: Support for a circadian dysrhythmia hypothesis. *Journal of Sport Behavior, 22,* 279–287.

Worthington, E. L., Jr., & Scherer, M. (2004). Forgiveness is an emotion-focused coping strategy that can reduce health risks and promote health resilience: Theory, review, and hypotheses. *Psychology and Health, 19,* 385-405.

Worthington, R. L., Soth-McNett, A. M., & Moreno, M. V. (2007). Multicultural counseling competencies research: A 20-year content analysis. *Journal of Counseling Psychology, 54,* 351–361.

Wortman, C. B., Wolff, K., & Bonanno, G. A. (2004). Loss of an intimate partner through death. In D. J. Mashek & A. Aron (Eds.), *Handbook of closeness and intimacy.* Mahwah, NJ: Erlbaum.

Wright, J. H., Thase, M. E., & Beck, A. T. (2014). Cognitive-behavior therapy. In R. E. Hales, S. C. Yudofsky, & L. W. Roberts (Eds.), *The American Psychiatric Publishing textbook of psychiatry* (6th ed.). Washington, DC: American Psychiatric Publishing.

Wrosch, C. B. (2011). Self-regulation of unattainable goals and pathways to quality of life. In S. Folkman (Ed.), *Oxford handbook of stress, health, and coping.* New York, NY: Oxford University Press.

Wrosch, C. B., Miller, G. E., Scheier, M. F., & de Pontet, S. B. (2007). Giving up on unattainable goals: Benefits for health? *Personality and Social Psychology Bulletin, 33,* 251–265.

Wrosch, C. B., Scheier, M. F., Miller, G. E., & Carver, C. S. (2012). When meaning is threatened: The importance of goal adjustment for psychological and physical health. In P. T. P. Wong (Ed.), *Human quest for meaning: Theories, research, and applications* (2nd ed.). New York, NY: Routledge/Taylor & Francis Group.

Wrulich, M., Brunner, M., Stadler, G., Schalke, D., Keller, U., Chmiel, M., & Martin, R. (2013). Childhood intelligence and adult health: The mediating roles of education and socioeconomic

status. *Intelligence, 41,* 490–500. doi:10.1016/j.intell.2013.06.015

Wrulich, M., Brunner, M., Stadler, G., Schalke, D., Keller, U., & Martin, R. (2014). Forty years on: Childhood intelligence predicts health in middle adulthood. *Health Psychology, 33,* 292–296. doi:10.1037/a0030727

Wundt, W. (1874/1904). *Principles of physiological psychology.* Leipzig, Germany: Engelmann.

Wynn, K. (1992). Addition and subtraction by human infants. *Nature, 358,* 749–750.

Wynn, K. (1996). Infants' individuation and enumeration of sequential actions. *Psychological Science, 7,* 164–169.

Wynn, K. (1998). An evolved capacity for number. In D. D. Cummins & C. Allen (Eds.), *The evolution of mind.* New York, NY: Oxford University Press.

Yates, F. A. (1966). *The art of memory.* London: Routledge & Kegan Paul.

Yehuda, R., Flory, J. D., Pratchett, L. C., Buxbaum, J., Ising, M., & Holsboer, F. (2010). Putative biological mechanisms for the association between early life adversity and the subsequent development of PTSD. *Psychopharmacologia, 212,* 405–417. doi:10.1007/s00213-010-1969-6

Yeomans, M. R., Tepper, B. J., Rietzschel, J., & Prescott, J. (2007). Human hedonic responses to sweetness: Role of taste genetics and anatomy. *Physiology & Behavior, 91,* 264–273.

Yerkes, R. M., & Morgulis, S. (1909). The method of Pavlov in animal psychology. *Psychological Bulletin, 6,* 257–273.

Yoshikawa, H., Aber, J. L., & Beardslee, W. R. (2012). The effects of poverty on the mental, emotional, and behavioral health of children and youth: Implications for prevention. *American Psychologist, 67,* 272–284. doi:10.1037/a0028015

Yost, W. A. (2000). *Fundamentals of hearing: An introduction.* San Diego, CA: Academic Press.

Yost, W. A. (2010). Audition: Pitch perception. In E. B. Goldstein (Ed.), *Encyclopedia of perception.* Thousand Oaks, CA: Sage.

Yost, W. A. (2013). Audition. In A. F. Healy, R. W. Proctor, & I. B. Weiner (Eds.), *Handbook of psychology: Vol. 4. Experimental psychology* (2nd ed.). New York, NY: Wiley.

You, T., Arsenis, N. C., Disanzo, B. L., & LaMonte, M. J. (2013). Effects of exercising training on chronic inflammation in obesity: Current evidence and potential mechanisms. *Sports*

Medicine, 43, 243–256. doi:10.1007/s40279-13-0023-3

Young, A. M., & Havens, J. R. (2012). Transition from first illicit drug use to first injection drug use among rural Appalachian drug users: A cross-sectional comparison and retrospective survival analysis. *Addiction, 107,* 587–596.

Young, K. S. (2009). Internet addiction: Diagnosis and treatment considerations. *Journal of Contemporary Psychotherapy, 39*(4), 241–246. doi:10.1007/s10879-009-9120-x

Young, K. S. (2013). Treatment outcomes using CBT-IA with Internet-addicted patients. *Journal of Behavioral Addictions, 2,* 209-215. doi:10.1556/JBA.2.2013.4.3

Youngstrom, E., & Algorta, G. P. (2014). Features and course of bipolar disorder. In I. H. Gotlib & C. L. Hammen (Eds.), *Handbook of depression* (3rd ed.). New York, NY: Guilford Press.

Yu, C. K. (2014). Toward 100% dream retrieval by rapid-eye movement sleep awakening: A high-density electroencephalographic study. *Dreaming, 24,* 1–17. doi:10.1037/a0035792

Zadra, A., & Domhoff, G. W. (2011). Dream content: Quantitative findings. In M. H. Kryger, T. Roth, & W. C. Dement (Eds.), *Principles and practice of sleep medicine* (5th ed.). Saint Louis, MO: Elsevier Saunders.

Zadra, A., & Pilon, M. (2012). Parasomnias II: Sleep terrors and somnambulism. In C. M. Morin, & C. A. Espie (Eds.), *Oxford handbook of sleep and sleep disorders.* New York, NY: Oxford University Press.

Zahorodny, W., Shenouda, J., Howell, S., Rosato, N. S., Peng, B., & Mehta, U. (2014). Increasing autism prevalence in metropolitan New Jersey. *Autism, 18*(2), 117–126. doi:10.1177/1362361312463977

Zajonc, R. B. (1968). Attitudinal effects of mere exposure. *Journal of Personality and Social Psychology, 9,* 1–29.

Zane, N., Hall, G. C. N., Sue, S., Young, K., & Nunez, J. (2004). Research on psychotherapy with culturally diverse populations. In M. J. Lambert (Ed.), *Bergin and Garfield's handbook of psychotherapy and behavior change.* New York, NY: Wiley.

Zaragoza, M. S., Belli, R. F., & Payment, K. E. (2007). Misinformation effects and the suggestibility of eyewitness memory. In M. Garry & H. Hayne (Eds.), *Do justice and let the sky fall: Elizabeth F. Lotus and her contributions to science, law, and academic freedom.* Mahwah, NJ: Erlbaum.

Zautra, A. J., & Reich, J. W. (2011). Resilience: The meanings, methods, and measures of fundamental characteristics of human adaptation. In S. Folkman (Ed.), *Oxford handbook of stress, health, and coping.* New York, NY: Oxford University Press.

Zebrowitz, L. A., & Montepare, J. M. (2015). Face and first impressions. In M. Mikulincer, P. R. Shaver, E. Borgida, & J. A. Bargh (Eds.), *APA handbook of personality and social psychology Vol. 1: Attitudes and social cognition.* Washington, DC: American Psychological Association.

Zechmeister, E. B., & Nyberg, S. E. (1982). *Human memory: An introduction to research and theory.* Pacific Grove, CA: Brooks/Cole.

Zeidan, F., Gordon, N. S., Merchant, J., & Goolkasian, P. (2010). The effects of brief mindfulness meditation training on experimentally induced pain. *The Journal of Pain, 11*(3), 199–209. doi:10.1016/j.jpain.2009.07.015

Zeiler, M. (1977). Schedules of reinforcement: The controlling variables. In W. K. Honig & J. E. R. Staddon (Eds.), *Handbook of operant behavior.* Englewood Cliffs, NJ: Prentice-Hall.

Zeng, L., Proctor, R. W., & Salvendy, G. (2011). Can traditional divergent thinking tests be trusted in measuring and predicting real-world creativity? *Creativity Research Journal, 23*(1), 24–37. doi:10.1080/10400419.2011.545713

Zentner, M., & Mitura, K. (2012). Stepping out of the caveman's shadow: Nations' gender gap predicts degree of sex differentiation in mate preferences. *Psychological Science, 23,* 1176–1185. doi:10.1177/0956797612441004

Zhang, J. W., & Howell, R. T. (2011). Do time perspectives predict unique variance in life satisfaction beyond personality traits? *Personality and Individual Differences, 50,* 1261–1266. doi:10.1016/j.paid.2011.02.021

Zhang, J. W., Howell, R. T., & Howell, C. J. (2014). Living in wealthy neighborhoods increases material desires and maladaptive consumption. *Journal of Consumer Culture, 0,* 1–20. doi:10.1177/1469540514521085

Zhu, D. H. (2013). Group polarization on corporate boards: Theory and evidence on board decisions about acquisition premiums. *Strategic Management Journal, 34,* 800–822. doi:10.1002/smj.2039

Zhu, D. H. (2014). Group polarization in board decisions about CEO compensation. *Organization Science, 25,* 552–571. doi:10.1287/orsc.2013.0848

Zillmer, E. A., Spiers, M. V., & Culbertson, W. C. (2008). *Principles of neuropsychology.* Belmont, CA: Wadsworth.

Zimbardo, P. G. (2004, May 9). Power turns good soldiers into "bad apples." *Boston Globe*. Retrieved from www .boston.com/news/globe/editorial _opinion/oped/articles/2004/05/09.

Zimbardo, P. G., Haney, C., & Banks, W. C. (1973, April 8). The mind is a formidable jailer: A Pirandellian prison. *New York Times Magazine*, Section 6, p. 36.

Zimmerman, M., & Strouse, D. (2002). *Choosing a psychotherapist: A guide to navigating the mental health maze*. Lincoln, NE: Writers Club Press.

Zinbarg, R. E., & Griffith, J. W. (2008). Behavior Therapy. In J. L. Lebow (Ed.), *Twenty-first century psychotherapies: Contemporary approaches to theory and practice*. New York, NY: Wiley.

Zohar, J., Fostick, L., & Juven-Wetzler, E. (2009). Obsessive-compulsive disorder. In M. C. Gelder, N. C. Andreasen, J. J. López-Ibor, Jr., & J. R. Geddes (Eds.). *New Oxford textbook of psychiatry* (2nd ed., Vol. 1). New York, NY: Oxford University Press.

Zola, S. M., & Squire, L. R. (2000). The medial temporal lobe and the hippocampus. In E. Tulving & F. I. M. Craik (Eds.), *The Oxford handbook of memory* (pp. 485–500). New York, NY: Oxford University Press.

Zorumski, C. F., Isenberg, K. E., & Mennerick, S. (2009). Cellular and synaptic electrophysiology. In B. J. Sadock, V. A. Sadock, & P. Ruiz (Eds.), *Kaplan & Sadock's comprehensive textbook of psychiatry* (9th ed., Vol. 1, pp. 129–146). Philadelphia, PA: Lippincott Williams & Wilkins.

Zschucke, E., Renneberg, B., Dimeo, F., Wustenberg, T., & Strohle, A. (2015). The stress-buffering effect of acute exercise: Evidence for HPA axis negative feedback. *Psychoneuroendocrinology, 51*, 414–425. doi:10.1016 /j.psyneuen.2014.10.019

Zuckerman, M. (2013). Biological bases of personality. In H. Tennen, J. Suls, & I. B. Weiner (Eds.), *Handbook of psychology: Vol. 5. Personality and social psychology* (2nd ed.). New York, NY: Wiley.

Zurbriggen, E. L., & Sturman, T. S. (2002). Linking motives and emotions: A test of McClelland's hypothesis. *Personality & Social Psychology Bulletin, 28*, 521–535.

Long, Z., 73
Longman, D. G., 25
Lonner, W. J., 14
Lopez-Caneda, E., 171
Lopez, S. J., 161, 475
López, S. R., 553
Lorenzo, G. L., 420
Lothane, Z., 7
Loureiro, M. A., 103
Lowe Vandell, D., 347
Lu, C. Y., 550
Lu, F. G., 553
Luborsky, E. B., 7, 537
Luborsky, L., 539
Lucas, J. A., 246
Lucas, R. E., 331, 332, 333
Lucchina, L. A., 132
Luchins, A., 268
Luders, E., 169, 292
Ludwig, A., 297
Luger, T., 457
Luh, C. W., 239
Lukaszewski, A. W., 401
Lumpkin, G. T., 406
Luna, B., 360
Lundberg, U., 466
Lupien, S. J., 464
Luppi, P., 73
Lustig, C., 229
Luszczynska, A., 473
Luthe, W., 485
Lutz, C. K., 46
Lydon, J. E., 429
Lynn, D. J., 390
Lynn, R., 287
Lynn, S. J., 165–167, 243, 502
Lynne, S. D., 359
Lysle, D. T., 187
Lyubomirsky, S., 333, 507

M

Maas, J. B., 176
MacCoun, R. J., 51
MacGregor, J. N., 268, 271
Machado, V., 89, 559
Machatschke, I. H., 72
Mack, A., 119
MacKay, A., 103
MacKellar, D. A., 479
MacKenzie, M. S., 205
Mackey, A. P., 85
Mackinnon, A. J., 293
Mackinnon, S. P., 427
Mackintosh, N. J., 282, 284
MacLean, P., 81
MacLean, P. D., 323
MacLeod, A. K., 506
MacMillan, H. L., 243
MacNeil, L., 469
Macrae, C. N., 420, 422
Macritchie, K., 506
MacWhinney, B., 263
Maddux, W. W., 297
Madill, A., 51
Madsen, L., 323
Magallares, A., 425
Magee, C. A., 485
Magnavita, J. J., 539
Maguire, E. A., 85
Maguire, W., 114
Magun-Jackson, S., 356
Mahar, I., 466
Maher, B. A., 507, 509

Maheu, F. S., 464
Mahn, H., 355
Mahowald, M. W., 160–161
Maier, M., 33, 267
Maio, G. R., 433
Maj, M., 472
Makarius, E. E., 412
Makel, M. C., 296, 370
Maldonado, J. R., 502
Malin, K., 472
Malinowski, J., 162
Mallory, G. L., 303
Malthus, T., 96
Mancini, A. D., 476
Mandell, A. R., 235
Mandelman, S. D., 286
Mandler, G., 12, 464
Maner, J. K., 431
Mangum, G. R., 372
Manna, A., 168
Manning, W. D., 364
Mannion, H., 143
Mantarkov, M. Y., 514
Manuck, S. B., 22, 94–95
Marangell, L. B., 548
Marchand, W. R., 168
Marcia, J. E., 361
Marcovitch, H., 518
Marcus, E. R., 539
Marcus, S. C., 534, 535, 550
Marder, S. R., 548, 549
Mardon, S., 176
Marewski, J. N., 277
Margolis, R. L., 72, 80
Margrett, J. A., 393
Markon, K. E., 495
Markus, H. R., 21, 408, 409, 443
Marler, P. L., 51
Marlow, C., 430
Marsh, E. J., 237, 241
Marsh, J. M., 24–25, 253–254
Marsh, L., 72, 80
Marsland, A. L., 473
Marston, W., 322
Marteau, T. M., 187, 480
Martin, C. L., 373
Martin, L., 264
Martin, R., 457, 480
Martin, R. A., 483
Martin, S., 430
Martinez, J. M., 548
Martinez, M., 548
Martins, C. S., 524
Maslow, A. H., 10–11, 394, 396–398, 410
Mason, S. N., 412
Mast, M. S., 371
Masters, W., 312
Masuda, T., 126, 271
Masumi, I., 474
Mathieu, C., 403
Matlin, M. W., 372
Matsumoto, D., 14, 21, 325, 326
Matthey, S., 486
Maugh, T. H., 246
Maurice, J. K., 143
Mays, V. M., 13
Mazzetti, G., 319
Mazzoni, G., 166–167, 236
McAbee, S. T., 381
McBride-Chang, C., 373
McBurney, D. H., 74
McCabe, J., 373

McCabe, R. E., 497, 500
McCaffery, J. M., 22, 94–95
McCaffrey, T., 267
McCall, M., 481
McCall, W. V., 552
McCandliss, B. D., 290
McCarley, R. W., 153, 164
McCarthy, M. K., 562
McCartney, P., 510
McCauley, M. E., 227
McClelland, D. C., 120, 304, 318, 319
McClure, K. A., 257
McClure, M. J., 429
McConkey, K. M., 166
McConnell, B. L., 190
McCormick, D. A., 68
McCoy, S. L., 366
McCrae, R. R., 362, 381, 408, 411, 483
McCrink, K., 356
McCullough, M. E., 484
McDaniel, M. A., 254
McDermott, J. M., 287
McDermott, K., 244, 250, 253
McDevitt, M. A., 198
McDonald, C., 95
McDonald, W. T., 241
McElroy, T., 458
McEvoy, J. P., 549
McEwen, B. S., 466
McGeoch, J. A., 241
McGhee, D. E., 433
McGinty, D., 72, 80
McGrath, J. J., 514
McGraw, A. P., 321
McGue, M., 94, 284
McGugin, R. W., 115
McGuigan, F. J., 484
McInnis, M. G., 504
McKenna, K. Y. A., 429
McLanahan, S., 375
McLellan, A. T., 178
McLeod, P., 268
McLoughlin, D., 552
McLoughlin, K., 1
McLoyd, V. C., 375
McNally, R. J., 243–244, 499
McNamara, T. P., 250
McNeely, J., 174
McNeill, D., 235
McWhorter, K. T., 25
Mechanic, D., 558
Medeiros, R. A., 204
Mednick, S. C., 176
Meeus, W., 361
Mehl, M. R., 45
Meillon, S., 307
Meinz, E. J., 231
Meister, B., 306
Meister, M., 111
Meltzer, A. L., 431
Meltzer, H. Y., 549
Meltzoff, A. N., 354
Melzack, R., 135
Men, W., 89
Mendelson, W., 160
Mennerick, S., 66
Menninger, W. W., 558
Merolla, J. L., 90
Mertz, J. E., 373
Mesmer-Magnus, J., 483
Mesmer, F. A., 165
Mesquita, B., 326

Mesulam, M., 72
Metcalfe, B., 412
Metcalfe, J., 235, 253
Metzger, A., 366
Meyer, G. J., 413
Meyer, O., 556
Meyer, R. E., 178, 236
Meyerbröker, K., 546
Meyers, E., 115
Mezulis, A. H., 425, 426
Michael, E. B., 263
Michels, N., 307
Mickelson, K. D., 365
Miklowitz, D. J., 550
Mikulincer, M., 429
Milad, M. R., 189
Milgram, S., 440–444, 448
Milkie, M. A., 365
Millecamps, M., 73, 138
Miller Burke, J., 381
Miller-Anderson, L., 509
Miller, A. C., 101
Miller, A. G., 442, 443
Miller, B. J., 514
Miller, D. I., 373
Miller, E., 84
Miller, G., 246, 431
Miller, G. A., 12, 229
Miller, G. E., 473
Miller, I. J., 132
Miller, I. W., 551
Miller, J. D., 406
Miller, J. G., 358
Miller, J. L., 339
Miller, J. M., 436
Miller, K. J., 368
Miller, M. B., 86
Miller, N., 56
Miller, N. E., 459, 460
Miller, R. R., 188, 190, 199
Miller, S. D., 544
Milligan, E. D., 138
Mills, J., 438
Mills, K. L., 360
Millstone, E., 56
Milner, B., 245
Milner, P., 81
Miltenberger, R. G., 215
Mineka, S., 187, 207, 500
Minkel, J. D., 149
Minzenberg, M. J., 510
Miranda, J., 553, 556
Mischel, W., 391, 393, 394
Mitchell, J. E., 521
Mittal, V., 514
Mitterauer, B. J., 67
Mittleman, M. A., 472
Mitura, K., 315
Mixon, F. G., 420
Miyamoto, S., 548
Miyamoto, Y., 272
Modestin, J., 502
Moè, A., 255
Moffitt, T., 381
Mogil, J. S., 135
Mojtabai, R., 551
Molitor, A., 348, 355
Moll, H., 354
Molouki, S., 439
Monaghan, P., 158
Moneta, G. B., 319
Monk, C., 343
Monk, T. H., 151

person perception and, 422
REM/slow-wave sleep and, 157, 180
retrieval, 224, 235–237
sensory memory, 228–229
storage, 224
tip-of-the-tongue phenomenon, 223, 224, 235, 241, 258
See also forgetting; long-term memory; short-term memory
memory encoding
attention's role in, 223–225, 231, 240
defined, 223–224
dual-coding theory, 226–227
elaboration process, 226
encoding specificity principle, 242
enrichment of, 226–227
forgetting and, 238
levels of processing theory, 225–226
motivation to remember factor, 227
multitasking and, 224–225
phonemic encoding, 225, 226, 240
semantic encoding, 225, 226
structural encoding, 225–226
visual imagery factor, 226–227
memory retention
coding and, 240
defined, 239
distributed practice and, 253–254
forgetting curve graphing of, 238
method of loci and, 255
nonsense syllables and, 238–239
organized information and, 254
recall measure of, 239
recognition measure of, 239
rehearsal and, 252–253
relearning measure of, 239–240
retroactive/proactive interference, 241
for skills, 249
visual imagery and, 227
memory retrieval
context cues, 235–236
defined, 224
memory reconstruction, 236–237
misinformation effect, 236–237
retrieval cues, 235
source monitoring, 237
memory storage
Atkins/Shiffrin model, 228
categories, conceptual hierarchies, 233
defined, 224
schemas, 233–234, 236
semantic networks, 234–235, 257
sensory memory, 228–229, 257
See also long-term memory; short-term memory
memory systems
declarative vs. nondeclarative, 248–249
prospective vs. retrospective, 250–251
semantic vs. episodic, 249–250
menarche (menstruation), 358–359
menopause, 366, 377
mental hospitals, 32, 562
behavioral principles in, 9
disenchantment with, 558–559, 567

group therapy in, 541
insanity acquittees in, 526, 531
mental illness. *See* psychological disorders
mental set, problem-solving barrier, 266, 268, 270, 300
mercury poisoning, 518
mescaline, 169, 170, 181
message factors, in persuasion, 435–436
meta-analysis of research, 48–49
method of loci method, of memory improvement, 254–255
Mexican Americans, mental health services and, 556
midbrain, 73, 75, 78, 79, 80
middle ear, 128–129, 145
mindfulness meditation, 168
miscarriages, 318, 341, 343
misinformation effect, in memory retrieval, 236–237
missing heritability problem, 94
MMPI (Minnesota Multiphasic Personality Inventory), 411
mnemonic devices, for memory improvement, 252
mode, A-22–A-23
monoamine neurotransmitters. *See* dopamine; norepinephrine; serotonin
monocular cues, to depth perception, 122–124
mood disorders
antipsychotic drug treatments, 548–549
cognitive-behavioral treatments, 546–547
cognitive factors, 507–508, 546
concordance rates for, 500, 501, 517
creativity and, 297
electroconvulsive therapy for, 552
episodic, 503
genetic vulnerability to, 517
homelessness and, 559
hormonal factors, 507
interpersonal roots of, 508
neurochemical, neuroanatomical factors, 506–507
precipitating stress, 508–509
psychiatric treatment for, 536
stress-vulnerability models for, 525
suicide and, 506
moon illusion, 124
moral reasoning development, 356–358
morphine
endorphins and, 73, 138
mechanism of action, 74
uses/effects of, 169
mortality salience, 407, 417
motivated forgetting, 242
motivation
academic performance and, 21, 282
achievement and, 303
drive theories of, 304
drug use and, 170
educational psychology's focus in, 17
emotions and, 303

evolutionary theories of, 304–305
incentive theories of, 304
learning, cognition, and, 207–208
limbic system role in, 104
observational learning and, 210, 221
perception and, 118–119
psychoanalytic theory on, 6
sexual, and behavior, 312–318
for taking IQ tests, 281
motivation to remember (MTR), in encoding memories, 226–227, 258
motor development
cultural variations in, 345–346, 376
defined, 344
developmental norms, 345
prenatal alcohol consumption and, 343
prenatal stress and, 343
MRI (magnetic resonance imaging) scans, 78, 99
Müller-Lyer illusion, 124, 125
multiple personality disorder. *See* dissociative identity disorder
multitasking, 224
musical intelligence, 294
musical training, cognitive development and, 103
myelin sheath, 66–67
myths related to psychology, 2

N

narcissism, 402–403, 405, 417
narcissistic personality disorder, 519, 520, 531
Narcissistic Personality Inventory (NPI), 403
narcolepsy, 160, 169, 180
Native Americans, IQ scores, 289
nativist theories of language acquisition, 262–263
naturalistic observation, 33, 42, 45–46, 48, 54
naturalist intelligence, 294
natural selection
basic premise, 10, 14, 97
gender and, 27
mating preferences and, 32
nature vs. nurture debate, 7, 22, 91, 214, 262, 284, 371
nearsightedness, 110
negative correlation, 42, 43, 281, A-25–A-26, A-27
negatively skewed distribution, A-22, A-23
NEO Personality Inventory, 411
nervous system
central, 73, 74, 77
communication system, 65–74
endocrine system meshing with, 90
glia cells, 66–67, 138
organization of, 74–77
peripheral, 75–76
physiological psychology study of, 17
somatic, 75
See also neurons
neural circuits, emotions and, 323–324

neural development
in adolescence, 360, 377
key findings, 102
language acquisition and, 263
neural impulse, 67–70, 99
neural networks, 67, 70–71, 102
neurochemical factors
in anxiety disorders, 499, 517
in bipolar disorder, 506–507, 516
in depressive disorders, 506–507, 516
in pain and pleasure, 74
in schizophrenic disorders, 73, 512–513
neurons
action potential of, 68–70
axons of, 66–70, 75, 77, 85
defined, 66
dendrites of, 66–67
glia cells modulation role, 66–67
neural development research, 102–103
resting potential of, 68
signaling via synapses, 69–71
soma of, 66
synaptic cleft between, 69–70
terminal buttons in, 66–67, 69–70
neuroscience perspective, 12
neuroses, 185, 537, 566
neuroticism
assessment of, 411
characteristics of, 381
depression, smoking, and, 44, 62
illness and, 480
national character and, 408
personality stability and, 363
physical appearance and, 420
serotonin and, 400
stress and, 473, 488
twin study findings, 400
vulnerable narcissism and, 406
neurotransmitters
behavior and, 71–74
characteristics of, 71
defined, 70
mechanisms of secretion, 67, 69
See also specific neurotransmitters
nightmares, 161, 498
nonbenzodiazepine sedatives, 160
nonconformity, 297
nondeclarative memory system, 248–249, 259
non-REM (NREM) sleep, 153, 154, 155, 157, 180
nonsense syllables, 238
nontasters, 132
norepinephrine (NE), 71, 72, 73, 172, 506, 517
normal distribution, 279–280, 301, A-23, A-24–A25
null hypothesis, A-28

O

obedience
cultural variations in, 443
defined, 440
Milgram's studies of, 440–443, 455
operant conditioning and, 205
obesity
Alzheimer's disease and, 310
evaluative conditioning and, 187
evolutionary theory and, 97

exercise and, 311, 336
genetic vulnerability to, 311
heritability of, 310–311
prenatal development and, 344
roots of, 309–312
set-point concept, 311–312, 336
sleep deprivation and, 158, 311
snoring and, 176
twin studies, 310–311
object perception, 107, 108–110, 114–115, 118–120, 122–123
object permanence, 352
observational learning, 209–214
of attitudes, 437, 453
basic processes, 210, 212–213, 221
defined, 210, 392–393
eating habits and, 308, 336
gender differences and, 372–373, 377
media violence controversy and, 210–211, 214
motivation and, 210, 221
personality and, 392–393
of prejudice, 450
response tendencies and, 414
obsessive-compulsive disorder (OCD)
biological factors of, 499, 517
compulsive handwashing, 491, 498
described, 497–498, 516, 530
Freud's treatment of, 537
gender/population data, 498
interventions for, 546, 547, 557
serotonin and, 71, 72
occupational stereotypes, 421
odor perception, 134
Oedipal complex, 387–388, 390, 415, 416, 539
olfactory cilia, 133, 137, 145
olfactory system (smell), 85, 133–134, 136–137, 145
openness to experience, 381
operant conditioning, 193–205
acquisition in, 195, 196–197, 198, 220
animal research, 193–195
anxiety disorders and, 499–500
of attitudes, 435
escape learning in, 202, 221
extinction in, 195–198, 200–202, 220
gambling and, 213, 220
gender differences and, 372–373
prejudice and, 450–451
punishment in, 203–204, 372
renewal effect in, 196–197
shaping in, 195, 196, 197, 220
Skinner box use in research, 9, 193, 194, 195, 196, 201, 302
stimulus discrimination in, 192, 197, 198, 220
stimulus generalization in, 197, 198, 220
terminology and procedures, 193–194
See also reinforcement in operant conditioning
opponent process theory of color vision, 116–117
optic chiasm, 113, 114
optic disc, 109, 111, 112, 144
optic nerve, 109, 111, 112, 113, 114
optimism
in adjusting to marriage, 364, 377
in bipolar disorder, 504, 505

conscientiousness and, 475, 488
defined, 475
in emerging adulthood, 361
oral stage, 387
orgasm phase, in sexual response, 312–313
The Origin of Species (Darwin), 98
outgroup, 422, 451, 454, 455
outpatient psychotherapy data, 535
ovaries, 90, 342, 358, 359
overdosing on drugs, 160, 172, 173, 179, 181
overextension in using words, 348–349
overextrapolation, 102–103
overregularization, in combining words, 262, 349
oxycodone, 169
oxytocin, 90, 105

P

pain
animal studies, 55, 63
chronic pain, 67, 134–135, 138, 145, 159, 166
endorphins and, 71, 74, 104, 138
gate-control theory of, 135, 138
glia cells and, 67, 138
meditation and, 168–169
midbrain and, 80
placebo effects and, 49
skin receptors for, 135
panic disorder
characteristics of, 497, 516, 530
exposure therapy for, 546
Freud's treatment of, 537
stimulus generalization and, 191–192
stress and, 500
paranoid schizophrenia, 510
parasympathetic division, autonomic nervous system, 75–77, 104, 322
parathyroid glands, 90
parental favoritism in Eastern bluebirds study, 45
parental investment theory, 313–315, 336
parenthood, adjusting to, 365–366
Parkinsonism, 71
passionate love, 428, 429, 454
pathological gambling, 1–2, 495
patterns, visual perception of, 119, 123
Pavlovian conditioning, 184, 187, 218, 219
peer review process, 36
penis, 358, 359
penis envy, 387, 390–391
percentile scores, 280, 363, 381, A-24, A-25
perceptual asymmetries, 88, 100
perceptual constancies in vision, 124
perceptual processes (visual system), 118–126
constancies in vision, 124
depth/distance perception, 122–124
forms, perception of, 118–121, 122, 123
Gestalt principles of, 120–121
misleading cues/visual illusions, 124–126
objects, 107, 108–110, 114–115, 118–120, 122–123

patterns, 119, 123
visual illusions, 123, 124–126, 144
peripheral nervous system, 75–76, 80, 90
personal distress criteria, of abnormal behavior, 493, 494, 540
personality
academic motivation and, 282
achievement behavior and, 319
Bandura's social cognitive theory, 392–393
behavioral genetics and, 95, 399–401
behavioral perspectives, 391–393, 391–394
biological perspectives, 399–403
cerebral specialization and, 101
consistency tendency, 380
contemporary empirical approaches, 402–403, 406–407
creativity and, 297
culture and, 408–409
defined, 380
distinctiveness tendency, 380
drug influences on, 171
eating disorders and, 523
five-factor model of, 381, 399, 400, 408, 415, 417, 420, 474
Freud on structure of, 382–383
genetics and, 98, 332–333
grand theories of, 379
happiness and, 332
heritability of, 98, 379, 399–402, 417
hindsight and, 414–415
humanist perspectives, 394–398
Mischel/person-situation controversy, 393
narcissism and, 402–403, 405, 417
nature of, 380–381
observational learning and, 392–393
pain perception and, 135
psychoanalytic theory and, 6, 10
psychodynamic perspectives, 382–391
psychometrics study of, 17
self-efficacy and, 393, 416
self-report inventories, 50
terror management theory and, 406–407, 417
test design for studying, 34
twin studies, 93–94, 399–400
Type A, 471, 488
Type B, 471
Watson's theory on, 22
personality development
in childhood, 349–351
Erikson's stage theory, 350–351
Freud's stages of, 386–388
Skinner's ideas on, 391–392
personality disorders
antisocial personality disorder, 519, 520, 531
borderline personality disorder, 519, 520, 531
characteristics, 518
etiology of, 520
narcissistic personality disorder, 519, 520, 531
twin studies of, 520

personality structure
Eysenck's view of, 399, 403, 417
Freud's view of, 382–383, 384, 403, 416
Roger's view of, 394–395, 403
Skinner's view of, 391, 403
See also five-factor ("Big Five") model of personality
personality tests, 400, 411
See also MMPI; NEO Personality Inventory; projective personality tests
personality traits, 215, 339
assessment tools, 411–412
biological view of, 404
defined, 380
development over time, 349–351, 363
dimensions/dispositions, 380
evolution and, 96–97, 401
Eysenck's theory of, 399
heritability of, 11, 22, 93, 94–95, 105, 284, 333
individual uniqueness of, 380
Maslow's identification of, 397–398
MMPI measure of, 411
positive, 14
testing/data collection, 34
person-centered theory (Rogers), 394–396
person perception
defined, 420
effects of physical appearance, 420–421
evolutionary perspective on bias in, 422–423
illusory correlation in, 422
ingroups, 422, 446, 451, 454, 455
outgroups, 422, 451, 454, 455
stereotypes, 421–422
subjectivity in, 422
person-situation controversy, 393
persuasion
central route to, 438, 439
credibility and, 433–434, 438, 439, 455
elaboration likelihood model of, 438–439, 455
media's manipulation efforts, 219
message factors, 435–436, 455
peripheral route to, 438, 439
process overview, 435
receiver factors, 434, 435, 436, 455
source factors, 435, 455
PET (positive emission tomography) scans, 78
phallic stage, 387–388
phobias
avoidance learning and, 202
classical conditioning and, 185–187, 189–190, 218, 226
defined, 183
Freud's treatment of, 537
operant conditioning for preparedness and, 207, 221
treatments for, 32
phonemic encoding, 225–226, 240
physical appearance
attraction and, 430–432
effects of, 420–421
gender, self-esteem, and, 48–49

physical appearance bias, 420
physical attractiveness
  extraverted behavior and, 401
  extreme comparators and, 143
  gender, mate preferences, and,
    314–315, 431, 454
  intelligence and, 332
  matching hypothesis of, 427
  person perception and,
    420–421, 422
  similarity principle in, 427
physical punishment, 204, 205,
  221443
physiological psychology, 17, 19, 29,
  304, 336
physiological vulnerability, relaxing
  and minimizing, 484–485
physiology/physiological processes
  in aging adults, 366–367
  autonomic nervous system
    and, 76
  behavior-related studies, 99
  circadian rhythms, 149–151
  classical conditioning and,
    187, 220
  data collection techniques, 34
  of emotion, 322–324
  in hunger, 305–307
  meditation and, 168
  of memory, 245–248
  observational learning and, 211
  operant conditioning and, 198
  placebo effect and, 50
  in puberty, 358–360
  research origins, 3–4, 10, 12–13
  of stress, 465–466
pineal gland, 90, 150
pinna, of the ear, 128–129,
  137, 145
pituitary gland, 79, 89, 90, 105, 466,
  488, 3539
placebo effect, 50, 53, 57, 63, 135,
  138, 168, 171
placenta, 340
place theory, of hearing, 129–130,
  145
plateau phase, of sexual response,
  312
pleasure principle, 382, 384, 416
pointillism, 141
politics, classical conditioning
  in, 219
polygenic traits, 91, 94
polygraph (lie detector), 322–323
Ponzo illusion, 124
positive correlations, 42–44,
  281–282, 301, 331–333, 474,
  A-25, A-27
positively skewed distribution,
  A-22, A-23
positive psychology movement,
  14, 28
posthypnotic suggestions and
  amnesia, 166
postsynaptic potentials (PSPs),
  70, 73
posttraumatic stress disorder
  (PTSD), 498–499, 500, 546
practical intelligence, 282,
  293, 301
preconscious awareness, 383,
  384, 405
prefrontal cortex, 80, 83–84, 173,
  247, 360

prejudice
  defined, 449
  discrimination and, 449, 450
  ethnic/racial, 52
  forming and preserving, 450–451
  implicit attitudes and, 433–434
  Nazi propaganda method, 219
  observational learning of, 450
  operant conditioning and,
    450–451
  social class, 295
  social psychology's study of, 17, 433
  stereotyping and, 449–450
  terror management theory and,
    407–408, 417
prenatal development, 339–344
  drug/alcohol use and, 343
  embryonic stage, 67, 341, 376
  environmental toxins and, 344
  fetal origins of disease in adults,
    344–345
  fetal stage, 340, 341–342, 344, 376
  germinal stage, 340, 376
  homosexuality and, 317–318, 336
  maternal illness and, 343
  maternal nutrition and, 48, 53,
    342–343, 344
  socioeconomic influences, 291
  stress, emotions, and, 343
  threshold of viability, 341
prenatal malnutrition, 344
preoperational period, 352–353
pressure-related stress, 461–462
primary auditory cortex, 83, 137
primary colors, 116
primary motor cortex, 83, 84
primary-process thinking, 382
primary sensory cortex (parietal
  lobe), 82
primary sex characteristics, 358
primary visual cortex, 82, 83,
  113–114, 117, 119
Principles of Psychology (James), 5
probabilities
  in achievement behavior,
    319–320
  bystander effect and, 446–447
  in decision making, 274–277, 298
  in health statistic evaluations,
    486–487
  in medical adherence, 481
  in problem solving, 26, 29
  in sexual behavior, 479
  in thinking about mental illness,
    528–529
problems of arrangement, 266
problems of inducing structure, 266
problems of transformation, 266
problem solving, 265–272
  advances in, 12
  bilingualism's benefits for, 264
  cerebral specialization and, 86
  cognitive psychology's study
    of, 17
  culture, cognitive style, and, 272
  defined, 266
  dreaming and, 164
  EEG/states of consciousness
    and, 149
  gaming's benefits for, 214
  insight in, 268
  sleep's benefits for, 158
  standard problems use in
    studies, 267

See also problem-solving
  approaches; problem-solving
  barriers
problem-solving approaches
  changing the representation,
    270–271
  forming subgoals, 269
  incubation/taking a break, 271
  searching for analogies, 269
  trial and error heuristics, 269
problem-solving barriers
  functional fixedness, 267–268,
    300
  irrelevant information, 266–267,
    300
  mental set, 266, 268, 270, 300
  unnecessary constraints, 268, 300
professional specialties in psychology, 17–19
projection, as defense mechanism,
  385
projective personality tests, 411,
  412–413
prolonged stress, 465
PROP (propylthiouracil), 132
prospective memory, 250–251, 259
pseudoforgetting, 240
psilocybin, 169, 170
psychiatric nurses, 536, 567
psychiatric social workers, 536, 567
psychiatrists
  biomedical therapies of, 534
  dissociative identity disorder
    and, 502
  drug treatments given by,
    548–551
  ECT treatment given by, 551–552
  education background of, 18, 536
  ethnic group treatment data, 556
  as expert witnesses, 526
  methods of locating, 562
  recovered memory beliefs of, 243
  treating role of, 17–18
psychic reflexes (conditioned reflex),
  49, 184–185, 247–248
psychoactive drugs
  defined, 169
  direct negative effects, 173–174
  drug dependence, 173
  factors influencing effects, 170
  indirect negative effects, 175
  mechanisms of action, 172–173
  medical uses/effects, 169–170
  See also individual drugs
psychoanalysis
  behaviorism comparison, 8
  client-centered therapy compari-
    son, 541
  description, 537
  dream analysis in, 389, 538, 555
  free association in, 537–538, 555
  humanism comparison, 9–10
  humanism revolt against, 28
  insight therapy comparison, 534
  neuroses and, 185, 537, 566
  offspring of, 534
  patient resistance to, 539
  probing the unconscious with,
    537–539
  psychiatrists' use of, 536
  results of, 383
  transference in, 537, 539–540, 555
psychoanalytic theory (of Freud),
  13, 28

anal stage, 387
anxiety and defense mechanisms,
  384–386
conflict/tyranny of sex and
  aggression, 383–384
criticism of, 9
description, 6, 10
growing influence of, 7
humanism vs., 9–10
latency and genital stages, 388
levels of awareness in, 383
oral stage, 387
phallic stage, 387–388
principal contributors, 10
structure of personality in,
  382–383
psychodynamic perspective
  of Adler, 389–391
  of Freud, 382–388
  of Jung, 389
psychodynamic treatments,
  539–540, 542, 557, 563
psychological disorders
  abnormal behavior, criteria of,
    482–484
  abnormal behavior, medical
    model, 481–482
  adolescents, stress, and, 359
  adult disorders, role of early-life
    stress, 524
  case studies investigations, 47, 55
  creativity and, 297
  epigenetic changes in, 95
  Freud on origins of, 386, 388
  genetic overlap in, 524–525
  genetics/experience components,
    22
  legal issues related to, 526–527
  MMPI assessment of, 411
  probabilities in thinking about,
    528–529
  professional treatment specialties,
    17–18
  recovered memories and, 243
  See also individual disorders
psychologists
  helping goals of, 2
  professional specialties, 17–18
  setting-related employment, 16
  See also therapists
psychology
  common myths about, 2
  cultural diversity interests, 13–14
  defined, 15, 29
  early history of, 3–11, 28
  empiricism in, 19, 29, 31
  modern history of, 11–14, 28
  nature vs. nurture debate, 7, 22,
    91, 214, 262, 284, 371
  practicality of, 2
  professionalization of, 11–12
  professional specialties, 17–19
  psychiatry comparison, 18
  questions asked by, 1–2
  reasons for studying, 2
  research areas, 16
  sociohistorical context for,
    20, 29
  structuralism vs. functionalism,
    3–5
  theoretical diversity in, 19–20, 29
psychometrics research, 17
psychotherapy treatment process
  blending approaches to, 557

sensorimotor period, 351–352
sensory distortions, under hypnosis, 166
sensory memory, 228–229, 257
separation anxiety, 346, 347
serial-position effect, 253, 259
series completion problem, in problem-solving studies, 267
serotonin, 71, 72, 104, 172, 400, 499, 506
set-point for weight, 311–312, 336
sex characteristics, 358
sexist bias, 390
sexual arousal, 187
sexuality. *See* bisexuality; hetero-sexuality; homosexuality
sexual motivation, 312–319
    evolutionary analysis of, 313
    genetic differences, 314–315
    human sexual response, 312–313
    parental investment theory, 313–315, 336
    See also homosexuality
sexual orientation, 315–318
sexual response in humans, 312–313
shaping
    of behavior, 21–22, 29
    in classical conditioning, 185–186
    in operant conditioning, 195, 196, 197, 220
shared family environment, 400
short-term memory (STM)
    Atkins/Shiffrin model, 228
    capacity of storage, 229–230
    circadian rhythms and, 149
    defined, 229
    durability of storage, 229
    long-term memory interaction with, 230
    psychoactive drugs and, 169, 174
    as "working memory," 230–231
signal relations, 208
similarity
    adoption studies, 94, 285, 287
    analogies, problem solving, and, 269
    culture and, 265
    family studies, 92
    stimulus generalization and, 191
    trait similarity, 95
    twin studies, 92, 284–285
    visual perception and, 121
similarity effects, 427, 430, 454
skin, sensory systems in (touch), 134–135, 136, 138
Skinner box, 9, 193, 194, 195, 196, 201, 302
sleep
    age trends, 154, 155
    biological rhythms and, 149–151, 159, 180
    common questions about, 176–177
    cultural variations, 154, 156
    external awareness during, 148
    meditation and, 168
    nightmares, 161
    non-REM stage, 153, 154, 155, 157, 180
    personal thoughts about, 31
    serotonin and, 72
    snoring and, 161, 176
    stages of, 152–153

See also dreams (dreaming); insomnia; REM (rapid eye movement) sleep
sleep apnea, 160–161, 176, 180
sleep deprivation
    health consequences of, 158, 180
    memory issues from, 251
    obesity and, 158, 311
    partial, 156–157
    REM sleep and, 157–158
    slow-wave sleep and, 157
    somnambulism and, 161
sleep disorders
    insomnia, 154, 159–160, 176, 180
    narcolepsy, 160, 169, 180
    REM sleep behavior disorder, 151, 161, 180
    sleep apnea, 160–161, 176, 180
    somnambulism, 161, 180
slow-wave sleep, 152–153
    age and, 154, 155
    memory consolidation during, 157, 180
    napping and, 176
    sleepwalking during, 161
smell (olfactory system), 85, 133–134, 136–137, 145
smoking
    Alzheimer's disease and, 367
    depression and, 44, 62
    heart disease and, 470, 473, 475
    intelligence and, 293
    oral stage relation to, 387
    prenatal development and, 343
    quitting, challenges, 477
    quitting, strategies, 215, 217
    self-efficacy and, 393
    social class and, 475
    stress and, 468
    supertasters and, 132
snoring, 161, 176
    See also sleep apnea
social behavior
    attribution processes and, 423–426
    conformity and, 439–440
    cultural differences in, 139
    depression and, 45
    gender differences in, 370–371
    group behavior, 444–448
    interpersonal attraction and, 427–432
    obedience and, 441–444
    oxytocin's influence on, 90, 105
    person perception and, 420–422
    social judgments and, 432–438
social cognition bias, 426
social cognitive theory (Bandura), 392–393
social desirability bias, 50–51, 55, 412, 425, 455
social influence strategies, 4520453
social intelligence, 282
social motives, 305, 336
social psychology, 16, 17, 33, 53, 419, 448
Social Readjustment Rating Scale (SRRS), 460, 461
social roles, 444
social skills training, 546, 555, 557, 566
social workers, 536, 562
sociocultural theory (Vygotsky), 355

sociohistorical context of psychology, 20
soma, of neurons, 66
somatic nervous system, 75, 77
somatosensory cortex (brain), 82–83, 104, 134–135, 137
somnambulism (sleepwalking), 161, 180
sound
    physical properties of, 127
    processing in the ear, 128–129
    purity of, 127, 128, 137, 145
    See also auditory system
sound waves, 107, 127, 128–130, 136–137, 145
source factors, in persuasion, 435
source monitoring, in memory retrieval, 237
sour taste, 132
spatial intelligence, 294
specific phobia disorder, 496–497, 530
speech (language). *See* language/language acquisition
spermarche (first ejaculation), 359
spinal cord, 75, 77, 79, 80, 104, 110, 135, 513
split-brain research, 86–88
split-brain surgery, 86
spontaneous recovery, in classical conditioning, 189–190, 220
stage theory
    of Erikson, 350–351
    of Freud, 386
    of Kohlberg, 356–357, 358
stage theory of Piaget
    concrete operational period, 353
    evaluation of, 354–355
    formal operational period, 353–354
    preoperational period, 352–353
    sensorimotor period, 351–352
standard deviation (SD), 279–280, 368, A-23, A-24–A-25, A-28
Stanford-Binet Intelligence Scale, 278–279
Stanford Prison Simulation, 443–444
statistical methods, A-21–A-28
    central tendency measures, A-22–A-23
    correlation and prediction, A-26–A-27
    correlation measures, A-25–A-26
    empiricism and statics, A-28
    graphing data, A-21–A-22
    hypothesis testing, A-27–A-28
    measures of central tendency, A-22–A-23
    normal distribution, A-24–A-25
    statistical significance, A-28
    variability measures, A-23
statistical significance, 486, 487, 489, A-28
statistics
    defined, A-21
    descriptive, A-22
    health-related, 486
    inferential, A-27
stereotypes/stereotyping
    aging-related, 367
    cultural, 408
    defined, 421–422
    ethnic, 421

gender, 370–371, 373, 377, 421
    occupational, 421
    prejudice and, 219, 407
stillbirth, 343
stimulant drugs, 169
stimulus contiguity, 188
stimulus discrimination
    in classical conditioning, 192
    in operant conditioning, 197, 198, 220
stimulus generalization
    in classical conditioning, 190–192, 197, 198, 220
    in operant conditioning, 197, 198, 220
    in panic disorder, 191–192
stream of consciousness, 5, 148
stress
    aggressive response to, 467–468
    aging-related, 366
    anxiety disorders and, 500
    behavioral responses to, 466–470
    boredom, wandering mind, and, 148
    brain-body pathways of, 465–466
    caregiving-related, 367
    catecholamines and, 466, 488
    change-related, 460–461
    cognitive development and, 343
    cognitive reactions to, 463–464
    conscientiousness and, 475
    constructive coping with, 470–471
    corticosteroids and, 466, 488
    as a daily event, 457–458
    deceptive studies of, 53, 63
    defensive coping with, 469
    diseases of adaptation, 465
    divorce-related, 375
    dreaming and, 164, 178
    drug use, illness, and, 473, 482
    emotional arousal and, 323, 329, 337, 464–465, 498
    emotions and, 343, 346–347
    endocrine regulation of, 105
    endorphins and, 71, 74
    environmental causes, 457
    fear response and, 458, 462
    food consumption, and, 307, 336
    frustration-related, 459
    general adaptation syndrome to, 465
    hormonal fluctuations from, 322
    hypothalamus and, 90
    illness and, 473
    immune functioning and, 472–473
    internal-conflict related, 459–460
    learned helplessness response, 466–467, 507
    life event-related, 460–461
    marriage-related, 365
    meditation and, 168
    Milgram's experiments and, 442
    mindsets related to, 474–476
    moderating factors, 473–476
    optimism and, 475
    panic disorder and, 500
    physical health and, 470–476
    physiological responses to, 465–466
    positive effects of, 476
    prejudice-related, 449
    prenatal, 343

EVOLUTIONARY PSYCHOLOGY

CULTURAL FACTORS

(continues on following page)

GENDER ISSUES

NEUROSCIENCE (in addition to material in Chapter 3)